C000181607

STREET ATLAS
North Yorkshire

www.philips-maps.co.uk

First published in 2002 by

Philip's, a division of
Octopus Publishing Group Ltd
www.octopusbooks.co.uk
2-4 Heron Quays, London E14 4JP
An Hachette Livre UK Company

Second edition 2005
Second impression with revisions 2007
NYOBB

ISBN-10   0-540-08764-5 (spiral)
ISBN-13   978-0-540-08764-8 (spiral)

© Philip's 2007

OS Ordnance Survey®

This product includes mapping data licensed
from Ordnance Survey® with the permission of
the Controller of Her Majesty's Stationery Office.
© Crown copyright 2007. All rights reserved.
Licence number 100011710.

Printed by Toppan, China

Contents

III **Key to map symbols**

IV **Key to map pages**

VI **Route planning**

X **Administrative and Postcode boundaries**

1 **Street maps** at 1¾ inches to 1 mile

208 **Street maps** at 3½ inches to 1 mile

233 **Street map of York city centre**
at 7 inches to 1 mile

234 **Index** of towns and villages

238 **Index** of streets, hospitals, industrial estates, railway
stations, schools, shopping centres, universities
and places of interest

Digital Data

The exceptionally high-quality mapping found in this atlas is available as digital data in TIFF format, which is easily convertible to other bit mapped (raster) image formats.

The index is also available in digital form as a standard database table. It contains all the details found in the printed index together with the National Grid reference for the map square in which each entry is named.

For further information and to discuss your requirements, please contact james.mann@philips-maps.co.uk

22a	**Motorway** with junction number
	Primary route – dual/single carriageway
	A road – dual/single carriageway
	B road – dual/single carriageway
	Minor road – dual/single carriageway
	Other minor road – dual/single carriageway
	Road under construction
	Tunnel, covered road
	Rural track, private road or narrow road in urban area
	Gate or obstruction to traffic (restrictions may not apply at all times or to all vehicles)
	Path, bridleway, byway open to all traffic, road used as a public path
	Pedestrianised area
DY7	**Postcode boundaries**
	County and unitary authority boundaries
	Railway, tunnel, railway under construction
	Tramway, tramway under construction
	Miniature railway
Walsall	**Railway station**
	Private railway station
South Shields	**Metro station**
	Tram stop, tram stop under construction
	Bus, coach station

◆	**Ambulance station**
◆	**Coastguard station**
◆	**Fire station**
◆	**Police station**
✚	**Accident and Emergency entrance to hospital**
H	**Hospital**
+	**Place of worship**
i	**Information Centre** (open all year)
	Shopping Centre
P P&R	**Parking, Park and Ride**
PO	**Post Office**
Ⓧ 🚐	**Camping site, caravan site**
▶	**Golf course**
✕	**Picnic site**
Prim Sch	**Important buildings, schools, colleges, universities and hospitals**
	Built up area
	Woods
River Ouse	**Tidal water, water name**
	Non-tidal water – lake, river, canal or stream
	Lock, weir, tunnel
Church	**Non-Roman antiquity**
ROMAN FORT	**Roman antiquity**
87 / 246	**Adjoining page indicators and overlap bands** The colour of the arrow and the band indicates the scale of the adjoining or overlapping page (see scales below)

Acad	**Academy**	Inst	**Institute**	Recn Gd	**Recreation Ground**
Allot Gdns	**Allotments**	Ct	**Law Court**		
Cemy	**Cemetery**	L Ctr	**Leisure Centre**	Resr	**Reservoir**
C Ctr	**Civic Centre**	LC	**Level Crossing**	Ret Pk	**Retail Park**
CH	**Club House**	Liby	**Library**	Sch	**School**
Coll	**College**	Mkt	**Market**	Sh Ctr	**Shopping Centre**
Crem	**Crematorium**	Meml	**Memorial**	TH	**Town Hall/House**
Ent	**Enterprise**	Mon	**Monument**	Trad Est	**Trading Estate**
Ex H	**Exhibition Hall**	Mus	**Museum**	Univ	**University**
Ind Est	**Industrial Estate**	Obsy	**Observatory**	W Twr	**Water Tower**
IRB Sta	**Inshore Rescue Boat Station**	Pal	**Royal Palace**	Wks	**Works**
		PH	**Public House**	YH	**Youth Hostel**

Enlarged mapping only

	Railway or bus station building
	Place of interest
	Parkland

■ The small numbers around the edges of the maps identify the 1 kilometre National Grid lines
■ The dark grey border on the inside edge of some pages indicates that the mapping does not continue onto the adjacent page

The scale of the maps on the pages numbered in blue is 5.52 cm to 1 km • 3½ inches to 1 mile • 1: 18103

0	¼	½	¾	1 mile
0	250 m	500 m	750 m	1 kilometre

The scale of the maps on pages numbered in green is 2.76 cm to 1 km • 1¾ inches to 1 mile • 1: 36206

0	¼	½	¾	1 mile
0	250m	500m	750m	1 kilometre

The scale of the maps on pages numbered in red is 11.04 cm to 1 km • 7 inches to 1 mile • 1: 9051

0	220 yards	440 yards	660 yards	½ mile
0	125 m	250 m	375 m	½ kilometre

IV

Key to map pages

233	Map pages at 7 inches to 1 mile
215	Map pages at 3½ inches to 1 mile
186	Map pages at 1¾ inches to 1 mile

Spennymoor

Bishop Auckland

Newton Aycliffe

County Durham and Teeside STREET ATLAS

Gainford Piercebridge **Darlington**
Barnard Castle **1** Manfield **2** **3** Low Dinsdale
Eppleby **Hurworth-on-Tees** **4**

Kirkby Stephen

Croft-on-Tees

Cumbria STREET ATLAS

14	15	16	17	18	19	20	21	22	23

Ravenseat Whaw Langthwaite Washfold Melsonby North Cowton
Newsham Moulton

34	35	36	37	38	39	40	41	42	43

Keld Healaugh Reeth **Richmond** Danby Wiske
Muker Marrick 209 **Catterick** **Brompton**
Catterick Garrison 210

Kendal Sedbergh

Garsdale Head **Askrigg** Redmire **Leyburn** Hunton **Northallerton**

55	56	57	58	59	60	61	62	63	64

Hawes West Witton Middleham **Bedale** Leeming Newby Wiske
Thoralby

Kirkby Lonsdale

Stone House Stalling Busk Newbiggin Ellingstring Thornton Watlass

77	78	79	80	81	82	83	84	85	86	87	88

Carlton Snape
Cray Fearby **Masham** Baldersby

Cowan Bridge Buckden Grewelthorpe

102	103	104	105	106	107	108	109	110	111	112	113	114

Ingleton Horton in Ribblesdale Arncliffe Kettlewell Swetton **Ripon**
Burton in Lonsdale 214

High Bentham Austwick Kilnsey

128	129	130	131	132	133	134	135	136	137	138	139	140

Wray Langcliffe Malham **Grassington** **Pateley Bridge** Summerbridge Bishop Monkton
Settle

Cracoe Darley Head

152	153	154	155	156	157	158	159	160	161	162

Long Preston Airton Burnsall **Knaresborough**
Tosside **Gargrave** Embsay Blubberhouses 219 220 221
222 223 **Harrogate**

Spofforth

Lancashire STREET ATLAS

171	172	173	174	175	176	177	178	179

Skipton 216 217 Addingham Stainburn North Rigton
Barnoldswick Cononley **Earby** Silsden 218 **Burley in Wharfedale**
Ilkley

Chatburn Glusburn Otley Menston

186	187

Clitheroe Keighley **Guiseley** Yeadon
Trawden

Longridge **Bradford** **Leeds**
Barton Ribchester

West Yorkshire STREET ATLAS

Preston Burnley Queensbury

Blackburn Halifax

Leyland Dewsbury Wakefield
Chorley Rawtenstall Mirfield

Coppull Rochdale **Huddersfield**

Wigan Horwich Slaithwaite

Bury Heywood Meltham

Bolton **Greater Manchester STREET ATLAS** Oldham Holmfirth **Barnsley**

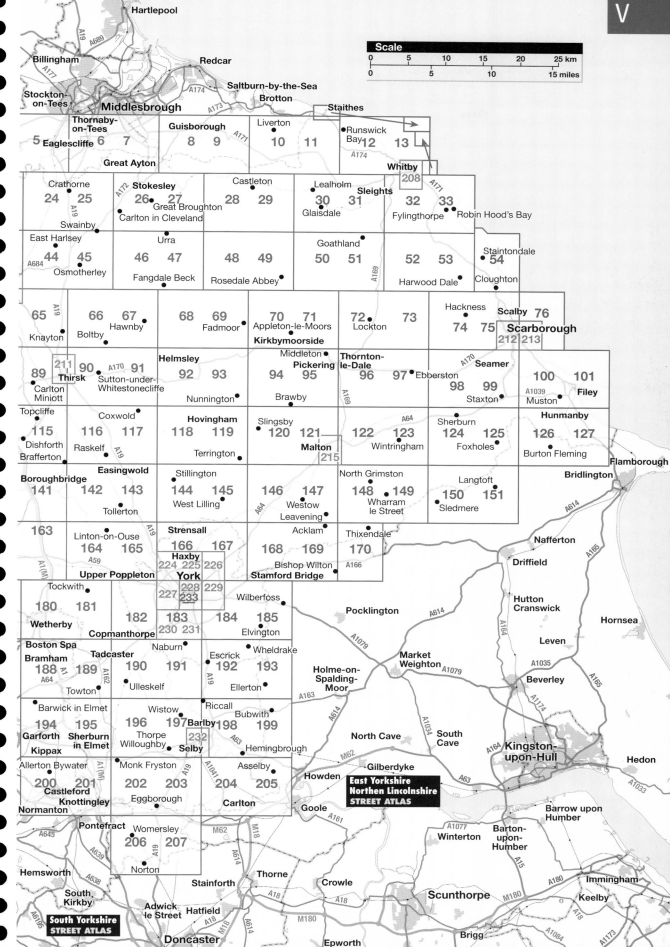

Scale

0 5 10 15 20 25 km

0 5 10 15 miles

Hartlepool

Billingham

Redcar

Stockton-on-Tees

Middlesbrough

Saltburn-by-the-Sea

Brotton

Staithes

Thornaby-on-Tees

Guisborough

Liverton

Runswick Bay **12** **13**

5 Eaglescliffe **6** **7** **8** **9** **10** **11**

Whitby

Great Ayton

208

Crathorne **24** **25** Stokesley **26** **27** Castleton **28** **29** Lealholm **30** **31** Sleights **32** **33**

Great Broughton

Swainby

Carlton in Cleveland

Glaisdale

Fylingthorpe

Robin Hood's Bay

East Harsley **44** **45** Urra **46** **47** **48** **49** Goathland **50** **51** **52** **53** Staintondale **54**

Osmotherley

Fangdale Beck

Rosedale Abbey

Harwood Dale

Cloughton

65 **66** **67** **68** **69** **70** **71** **72** **73** Hackness **74** **75** Scalby **76**

Knayton

Boltby

Hawnby

Fadmoor

Appleton-le-Moors

Lockton

Scarborough

Kirkbymoorside

212 **213**

89 **211** **90** **91** Helmsley **92** **93** Middleton **94** **95** Thornton-le-Dale **96** **97** Ebberston Seamer **98** **99** **100** **101**

Thirsk

Sutton-under-Whitestonecliffe

Pickering

Filey

Carlton Miniott

Nunnington

Brawby

Staxton

Muston

Topcliffe Coxwold Hovingham **118** **119** Slingsby **120** **121** **122** **123** Sherburn **124** **125** Hunmanby **126** **127**

115 **116** **117**

Dishforth

Raskelf

Malton

Wintringham

Foxholes

Burton Fleming

Brafferton

Terrington

215

Flamborough

Boroughbridge Easingwold **143** Stillington **144** **145** **146** **147** North Grimston **148** **149** Langtoft **150** **151** Bridlington

141 **142**

Tollerton

West Lilling

Westow

Wharram le Street

Sledmere

Leavening

Nafferton

163 Linton-on-Ouse Strensall Acklam Thixendale **170** Driffield

164 **165** **166** **167** **168** **169**

Haxby

224 **225** **226**

Upper Poppleton

York

Bishop Wilton

Stamford Bridge

Hutton Cranswick

Tockwith **227** **228** **229** Wilberfoss Pocklington Hornsea

233

180 **181** **182** **183** **184** **185** Leven

Wetherby

Copmanthorpe

230 **231**

Elvington

Market Weighton

Beverley

Boston Spa Naburn Escrick Wheldrake Holme-on-Spalding-Moor

Bramham Tadcaster **190** **191** **192** **193**

188 **189** Ulleskelf Ellerton North Cave South Cave

Towton

Barwick in Elmet Wistow Riccall Bubwith Kingston-upon-Hull

194 **195** **196** **197** Barlby **198** **199** Hedon

Garforth Sherburn Thorpe Selby Hemingbrough

Kippax in Elmet Willoughby **232**

Allerton Bywater Monk Fryston Asselby Howden **East Yorkshire Northen Lincolnshire STREET ATLAS** Barrow upon Humber

200 **201** **202** **203** **204** **205** Gilberdyke Barton-upon-Humber

Castleford Goole Winterton

Knottingley Eggborough Carlton

Normanton Pontefract Womersley **206** **207** Thorne Crowle Scunthorpe Immingham

Hemsworth Stainforth Keelby

South Kirkby Norton Adwick le Street Hatfield

South Yorkshire STREET ATLAS Doncaster Epworth Brigg

Route Planning

Scale

0	5	10	15 km
0		5	10 miles

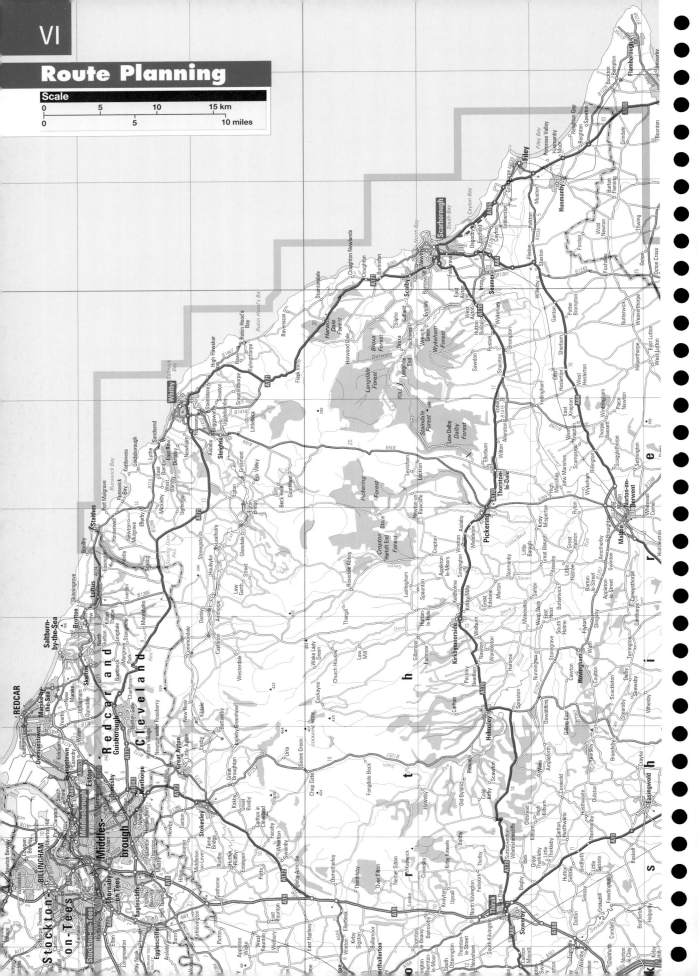

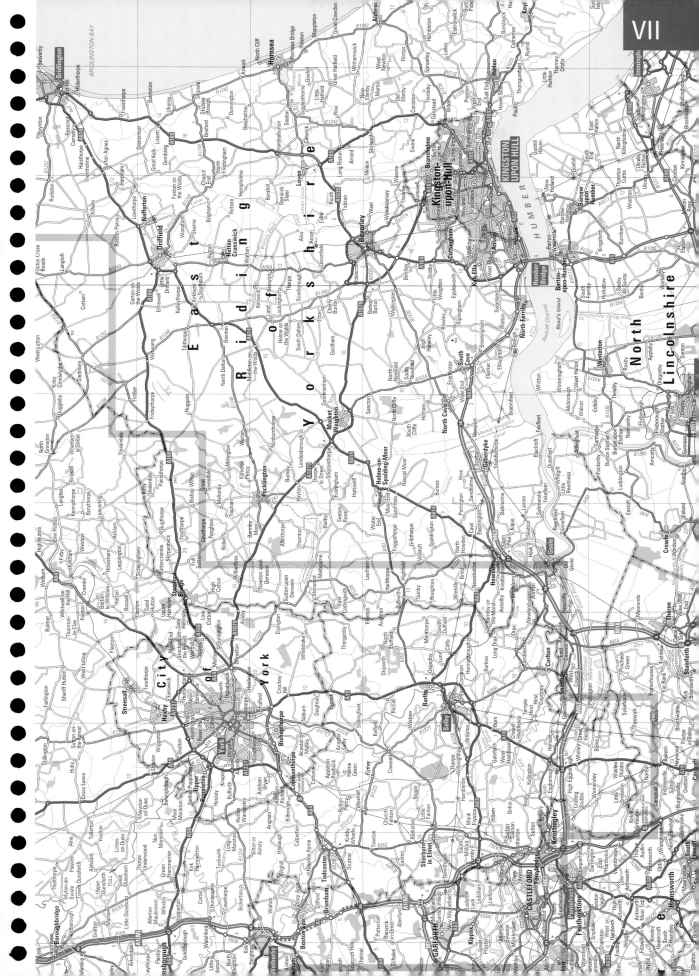

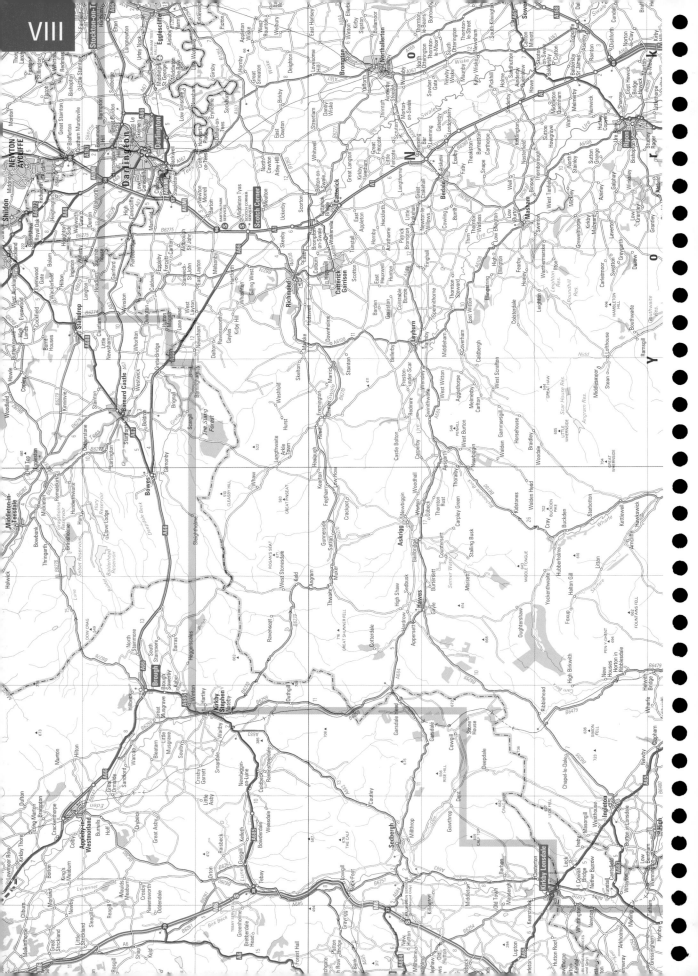

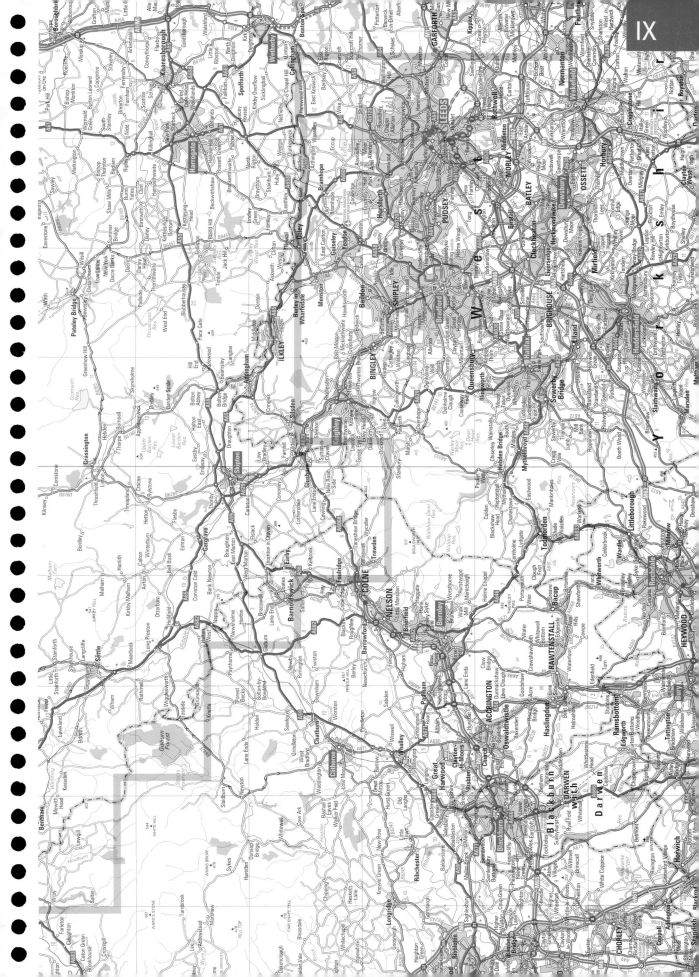

Administrative and Postcode boundaries

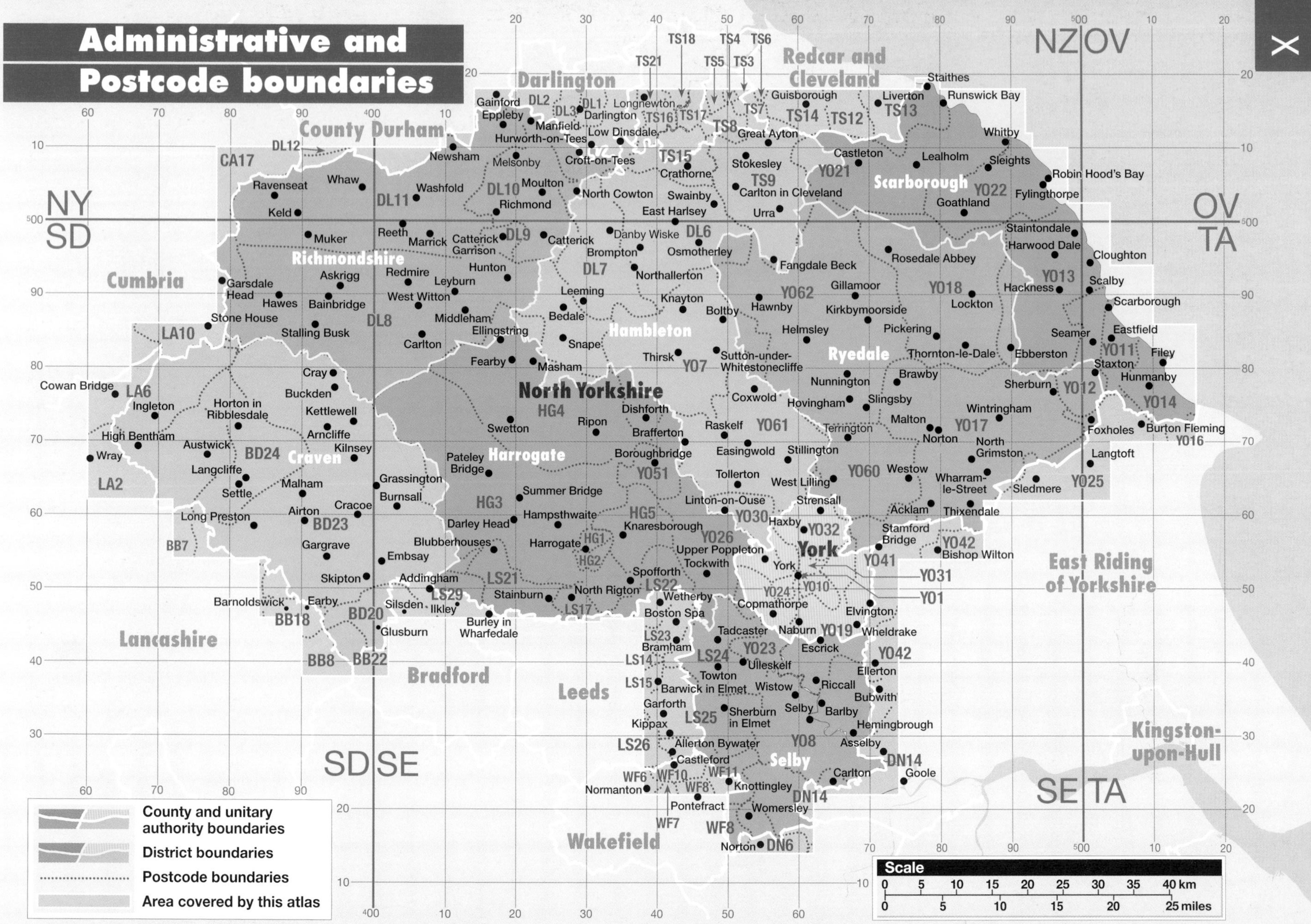

Scale

0 5 10 15 20 25 40 km
0 5 10 15 20 25 miles

County and unitary authority boundaries

District boundaries

Postcode boundaries

Area covered by this atlas

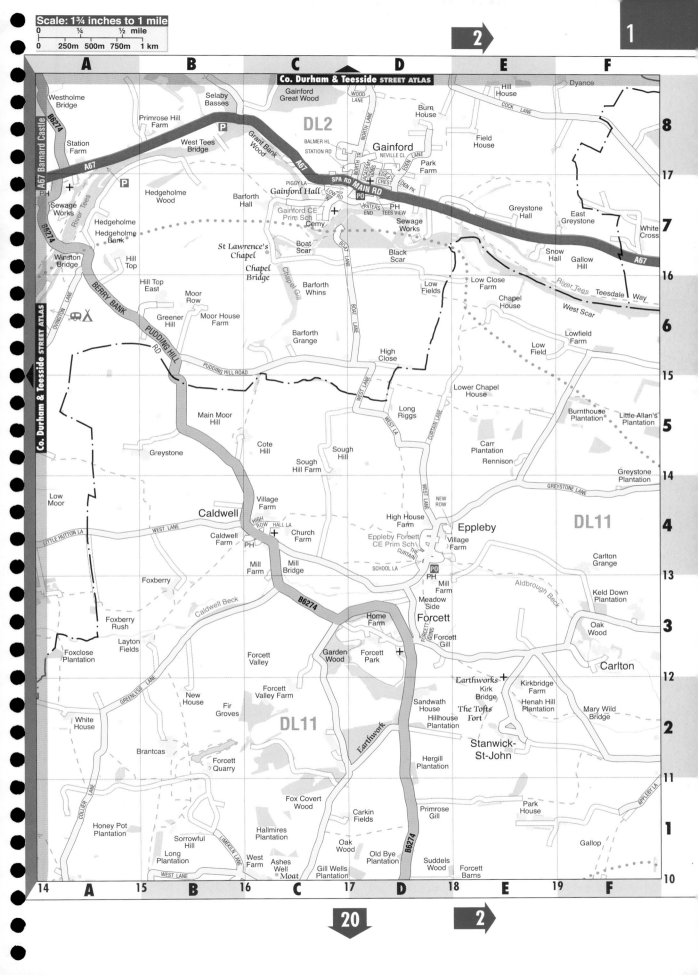

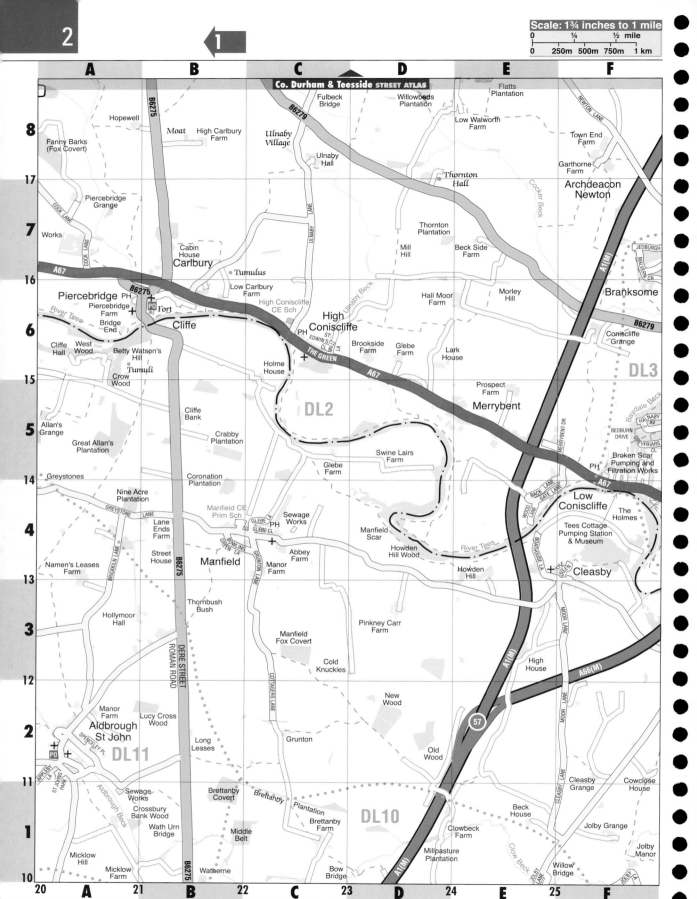

Co. Durham & Teesside STREET ATLAS

A   B   C   D   E   F

8

Hopewell

Fanny Barks
(Fox Covert)

Moat

High Carlbury
Farm

Fulbeck
Bridge

Willowbeds
Plantation

Flatts
Plantation

Town End
Farm

Garthorne
Farm

Ulnaby
Village

Low Walworth
Farm

17

Piercebridge
Grange

Ulnaby
Hall

Thornton
Hall

Archdeacon
Newton

7

Works

Cabin
House

Carlbury

Thornton
Plantation

Mill
Hill

Thornton
Plantation

Beck Side
Farm

Morley
Hill

JEDBURGH

MALVERN
CR

16

A67

Piercebridge

Piercebridge
Farm

Bridge
End

Cliffe

Low Carlbury
Farm

High Coniscliffe
CE Sch

High
Coniscliffe

Hall Moor
Farm

Branksome

B6279

Coniscliffe
Grange

6

PH
PO Fort

Cliffe
Hall

West
Wood

Betty Watson's
Hill

Holme
House

PH
THE GREEN

A67

Brookside
Farm

Glebe
Farm

Lark
House

DL3

15

River Tees

Crow
Wood

Tumuli

DL2

Prospect
Farm

Merrybent

Baydale Beck

HALNABY
AV

BEDBURN
DRIVE

GREYFRIARS
CL

5

Allan's
Grange

Great Allan's
Plantation

Cliffe
Bank

Crabby
Plantation

Glebe
Farm

Swine Lairs
Farm

MERRYBENT DR

Broken Scar
Pumping and
Filtration Works

14

Greystones

Nine Acre
Plantation

Coronation
Plantation

PH
A67

Low
Coniscliffe

The
Holmes

4

Namen's Leases
Farm

GREYSTONE
LANE

BRICKKILN LANE

Lane
Ends
Farm

Street
House

Manfield CE
Prim Sch

GLEBE LA
GLEBE CL

BOWLING LA
GREEN LA

Manfield

Sewage
Works

PH

Manor
Farm

Abbey
Farm

Manfield
Scar

Howden
Hill Wood

River Tees

WOOD LANE

BACK LANE
GATE LANE

BOATHOUSE LA

Tees Cottage
Pumping Station
& Museum

THE GREEN

Cleasby

13

Hollymoor
Hall

B6275

Thornbush
Bush

COTTAGENS LANE

Manor
Farm

Howden
Hill

3

Manor
Farm

Lucy Cross
Wood

DERE STREET ROMAN ROAD

Manfield
Fox Covert

Pinkney Carr
Farm

A1(M)

High
House

A66(M)

MOOR LANE

12

Aldbrough
St John

SPENCELEY PL

DL11

Long
Leases

Cold
Knuckles

New
Wood

57

Old
Wood

CLEASBY LANE

Cleasby
Grange

Cowclose
House

2

APPLEBY LA
ST JOHNS PARK

PO

Grunton

11

Aldbrough Beck

Sewage
Works

Brettanby
Covert

Brettanby
Plantation

DL10

Beck
House

Jolby Grange

1

Micklow
Hill

Micklow
Farm

Crossbury
Bank Wood

Wath Urn
Bridge

Middle
Belt

Brettanby
Farm

Bow
Bridge

Millpasture
Plantation

Clowbeck
Farm

Clow Beck

JOLBY LANE

Willow
Bridge

Jolby
Manor

JOLBY LA

10

B6275

B6279

Watherne

Cock Lane

Cocker Beck

Ulnaby Beck

Ulnaby Beck

ST EDWIN'S
CL MILL LA

ULNABY LANE

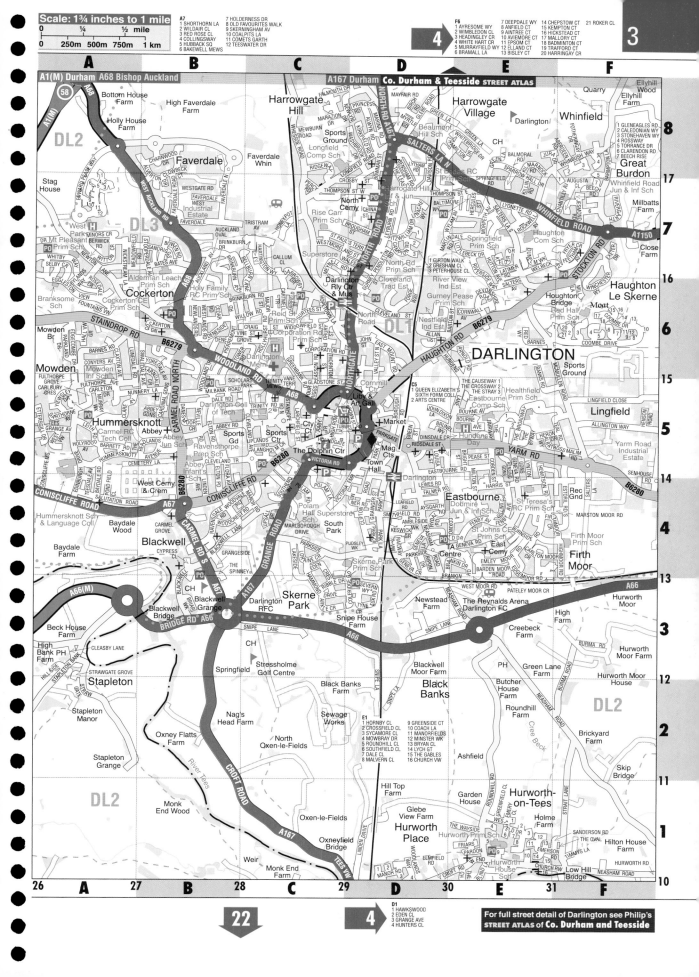

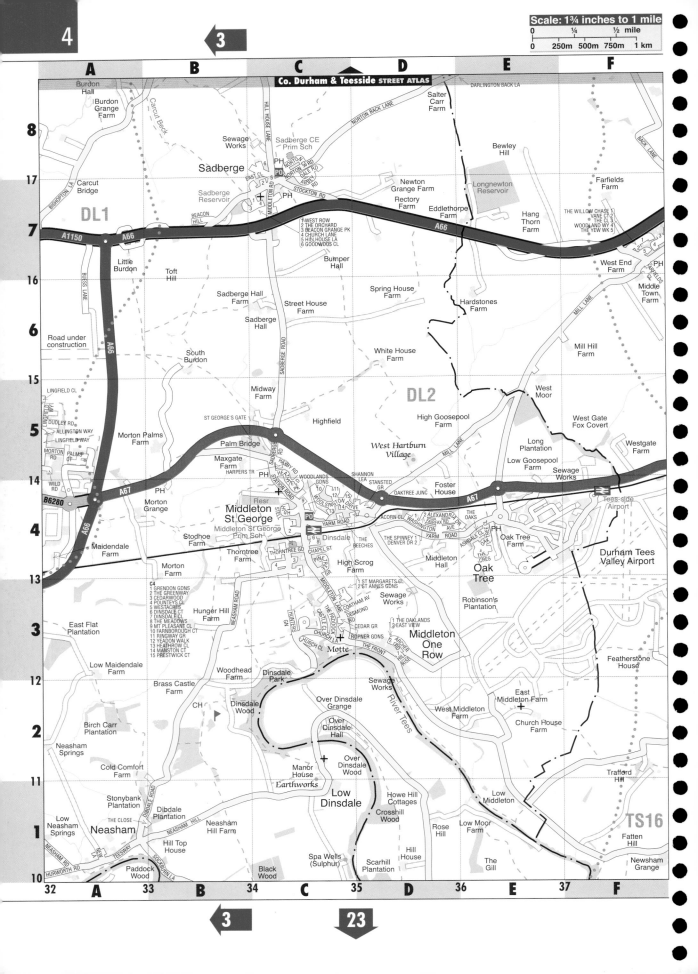

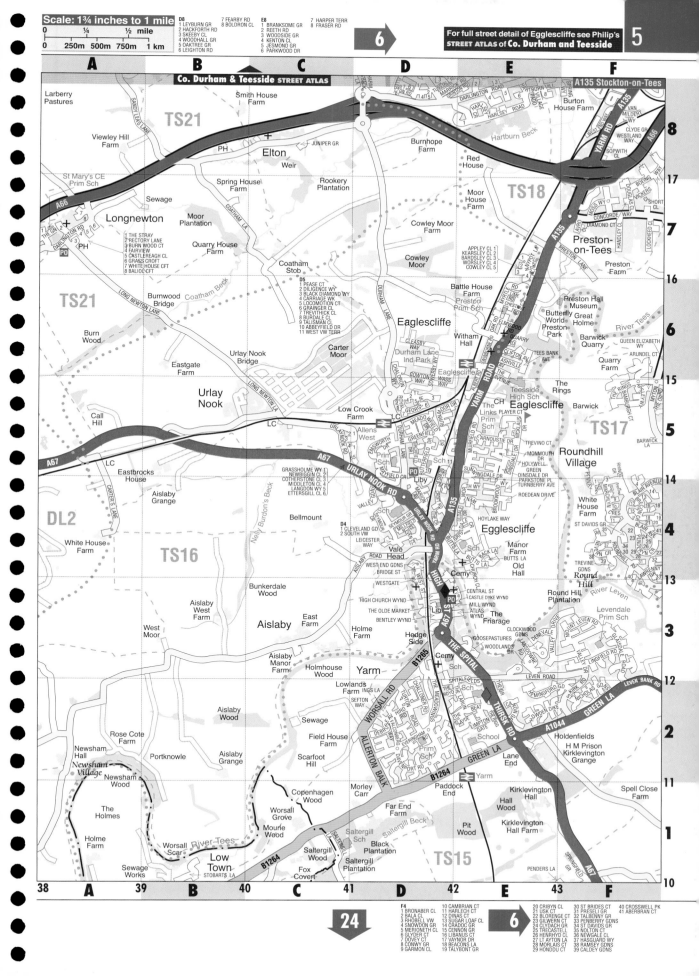

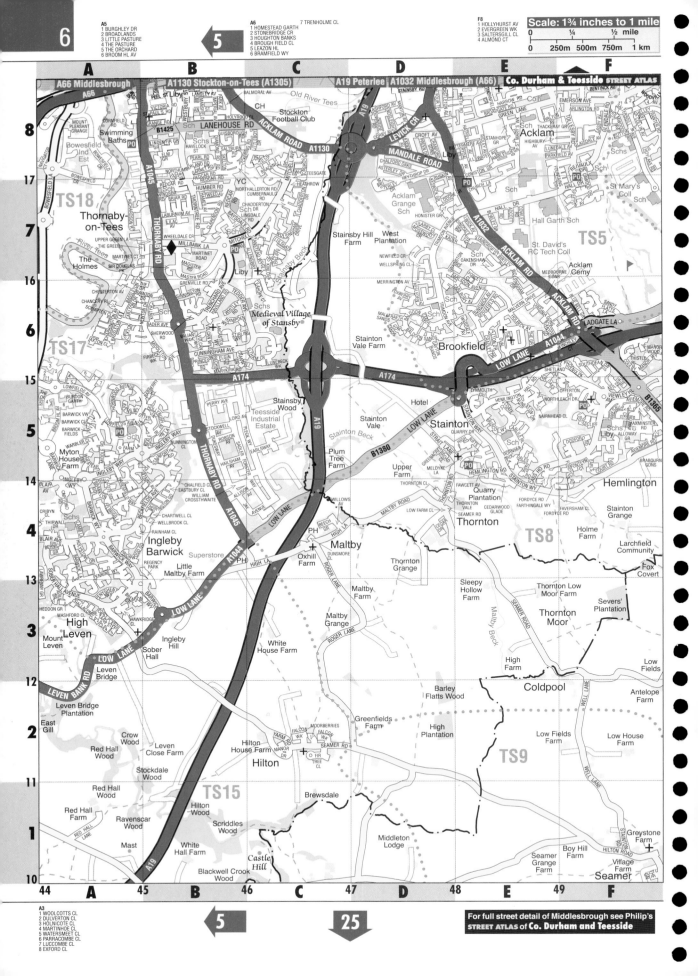

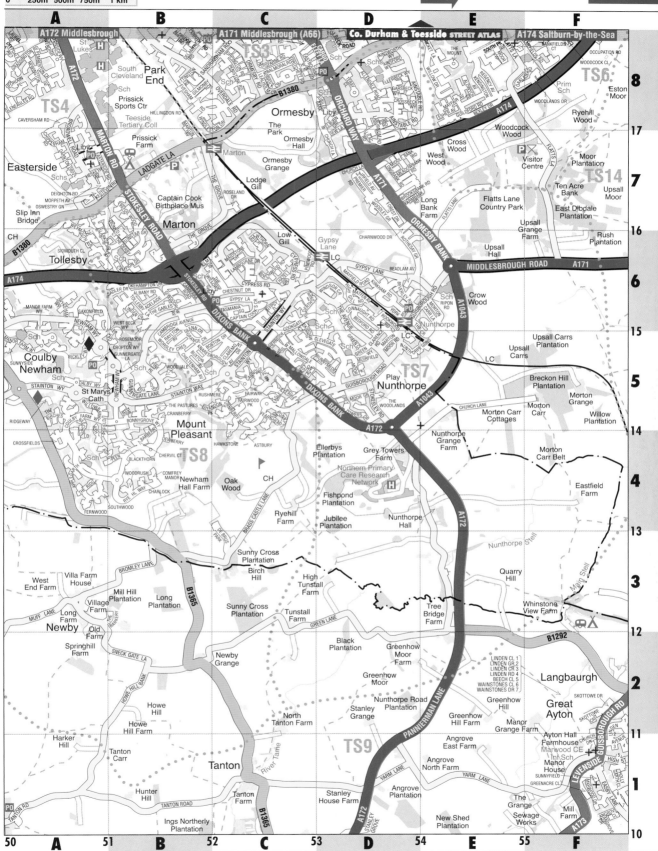

Scale: 1¾ inches to 1 mile

0   ¼   ½   mile
0 250m 500m 750m 1 km

8 ▶

B6
1 THE WICKETS
2 MEMORIAL DR
3 CLEVELAND DR

7

A172 Middlesbrough   A171 Middlesbrough (A66)   Co. Durham & Teesside STREET ATLAS   A174 Saltburn-by-the-Sea

St Lukes
H
H
South Cleveland
Park End
TS3
PO
TS6
Sch
Occupation Rd
Woodcock Cl

Prissick Sports Ctr
Sch
Schs
Eston Moor
8

TS4
Sch
The Mount
SOUTH PK
Woodcock Wood

Caversham Rd
Teeside Tertiary Coll
Ormesby
The Park
Liby
Marton
Woodlands Dr
Ryehill Wood
17

Easterside
Prissick Farm
Ormesby Hall
Cross Wood
Woodcock Wood
P
Visitor Centre
Moor Plantation
TS14

Schs
Ladgate La
P
Ormesby Grange
West Wood
Ten Acre Bank
Upsall Moor
7

Slip Inn Bridge
Captain Cook Birthplace Mus
Roseland Dr
Long Bank Farm
Flatts Lane Country Park
East Dibdale Plantation

CH
B1380
Marton
Lodge Gill
A171
Upsall Hall
Upsall Grange Farm
Rush Plantation
16

Tollesby
A174
Low Gill
Gypsy Lane
Charnwood Dr
Ormesby Bank
MIDDLESBROUGH ROAD   A171
6

Liby
PO
Gypsy La
Gypsy Lane
LC
Beadlam Av
Sch
Crow Wood
15

Dixons Bank
The Gables
Sch
Nunthorpe
A1043
Upsall Carrs Plantation

Coulby Newham
PO
Sch
St Marys Cath
Guisborough Road
Sch RIPON RD
LC
Upsall Carrs
Breckon Hill Plantation
5

Ridgeway
The Birches
Bonnygrove Wy
The Pastures
Cranberry
TS7
Nunthorpe
LC
Morton Carr
Morton Grange

Crossfields
Mount Pleasant
Hawkstone
Astbury
Play Sch
The Woodlands
Morton Carr Cottages
Willow Plantation
14

TS8
Chervil Ct
Ellerbys Plantation
Grey Towers Farm
Dixons Bank
A1043
Church Lane
Nunthorpe Grange Farm
Morton Carr Belt

Newham Hall Farm
Oak Wood
CH
Northern Primary Care Research Network
H
Eastfield Farm
4

Comfrey Manor
Woodrush
Fishpond Plantation
Jubilee Plantation
Nunthorpe Hall
A172
13

Fernwood
Southwood
Ryehill Farm
Nunthorpe Stell

West End Farm
Villa Farm House
Bromley Lane
Sunny Cross Plantation
Birch Hill
High Tunstall Farm
Quarry Hill
Main Stell
Whinstone View Farm
3

Muff Lane
Mill Hill Plantation
Long Plantation
B1365
Sunny Cross Plantation
Tunstall Farm
Tree Bridge Farm
B1292
12

Newby
Old Farm
Village Farm
Green Lane
Black Plantation
Greenhow Moor Farm
Langbaurgh
2

Springhill Farm
Sneck Gate La
Newby Grange
Greenhow Moor
LINDEN CL 1
LINDEN GR 2
LINDEN CR 3
LINDEN RD 4
BEECH CL 5
WAINSTONES CL 6
WAINSTONES DR 7
Greenhow Hill
SKOTTOWE DR
Great Ayton

Harker Hill
Howe Hill
Howe Hill Farm
North Tanton Farm
Stanley Grange
Nunthorpe Road Plantation
Pannierman Lane
Greenhow Hill Farm
Manor Grange Farm
Ayton Hall Farmhouse
Marwood CE Jun Sch
Manor House
11

Tanton Carr
TS9
Angrove East Farm
Yarm Lane
Sunnyfield
Greenacre Cl
Levenside
Guisborough Rd

Hunter Hill
Tanton Farm
Tanton
River Tame
Yarm Lane
Angrove North Farm
A172
The Grange
Mill Farm
A173

PO
Tanton Road
Tanton Farm
B1365
Stanley House Farm
Stanley Grove
Angrove Plantation
New Shed Plantation
Sewage Works
10

Ings Northerly Plantation

50   A   51   B   52   C   53   D   54   E   55   F

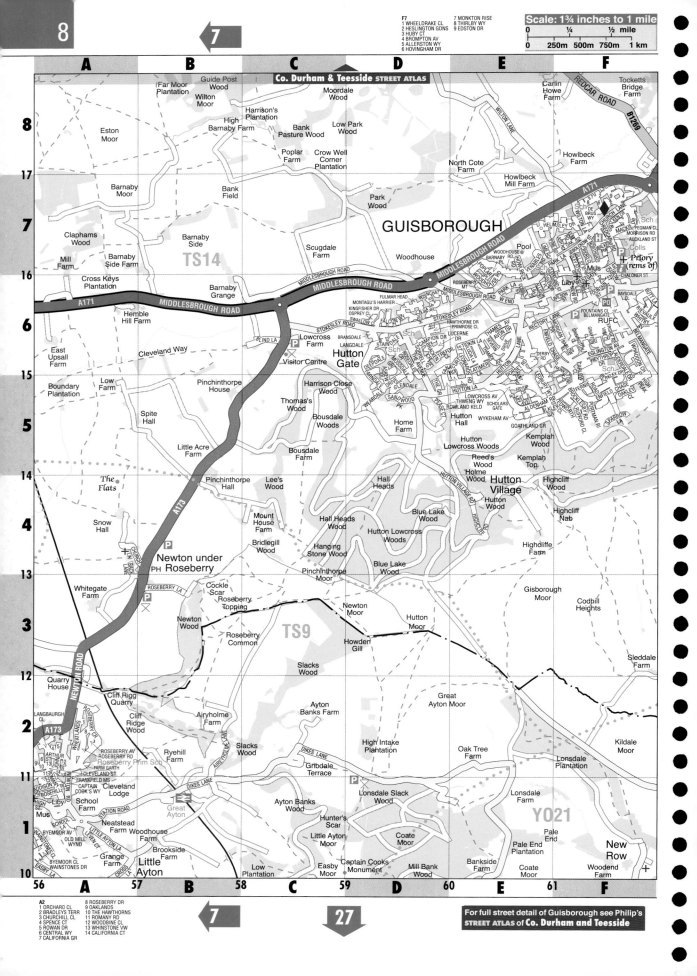

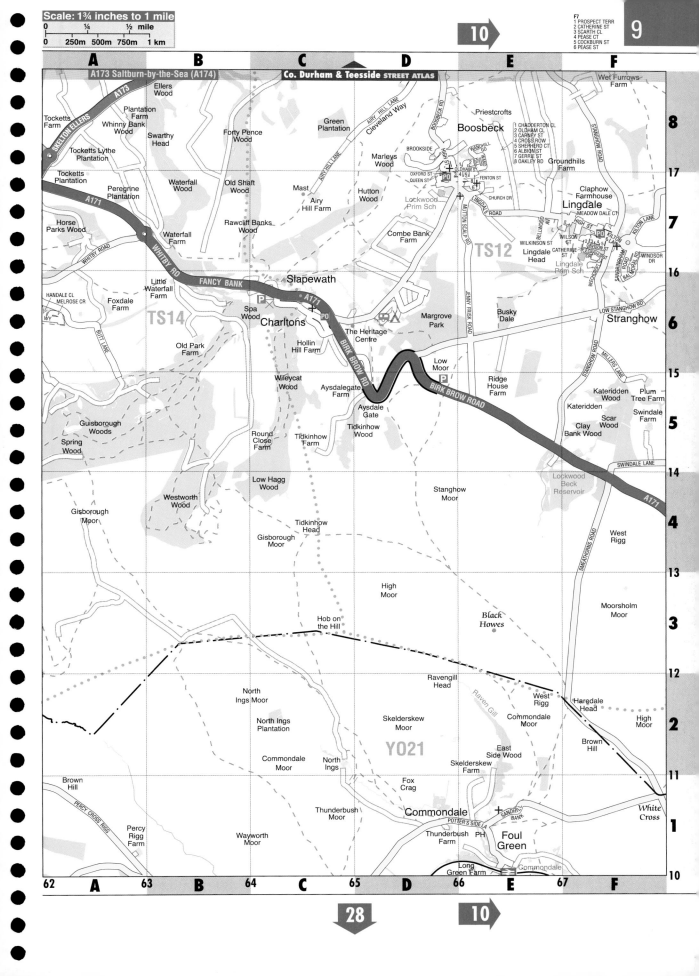

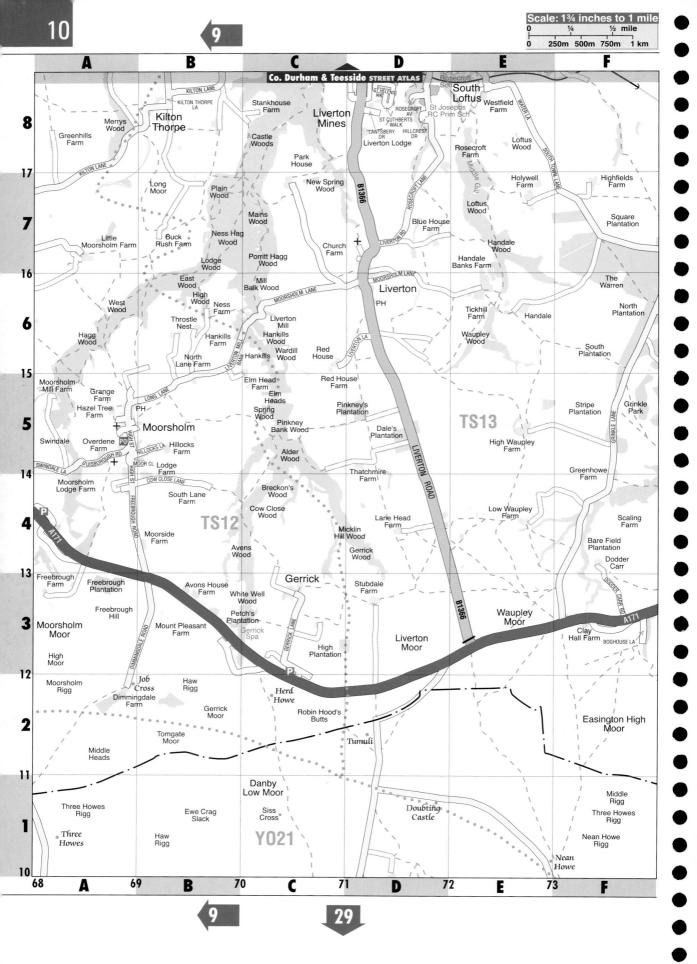

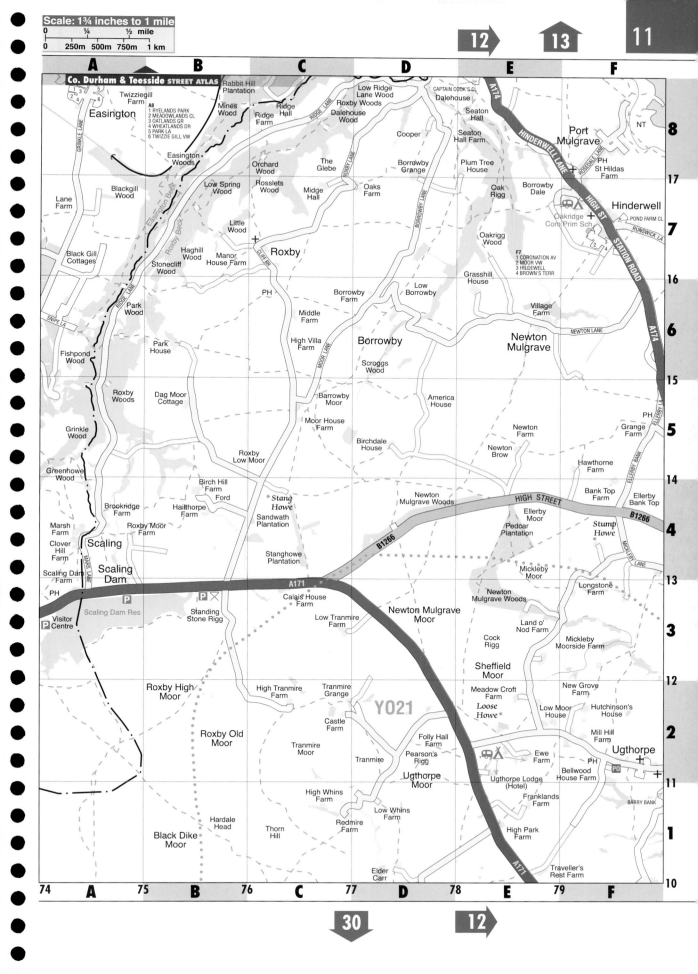

A B C D E F

Co. Durham & Teesside STREET ATLAS

Rabbit Hill Plantation

Twizziegill Farm

Mines Wood

Ridge Hall

Ridge Farm

Ridge Lane

Low Ridge Lane Wood

Roxby Woods

Dalehouse Wood

Dalehouse

CAPTAIN COOK'S CL

Seaton Hall

NT

Port Mulgrave

8

Easington

A8
1 RYELANDS PARK
2 MEADOWLANDS CL
3 OATLANDS GR
4 WHEATLANDS DR
5 PARK LA
6 TWIZZIE GILL VW

Easington Woods

Orchard Wood

The Glebe

Cooper

Borrowby Grange

Seaton Hall Farm

Plum Tree House

17

Lane Farm

Blackgill Wood

Low Spring Wood

Rosslets Wood

Midge Hall

Oaks Farm

Borrowby Lane

Oak Rigg

Borrowby Dale

Hinderwell

HIGH ST

St Hildas Farm

PH

ROSEDALE LANE

Black Gill Cottages

Little Wood

Roxby

Haghill Wood

Manor House Farm

CLIFF BR

Oakrigg Wood

Oakridge Com Prim Sch

Pond Farm Cl

RUNSWICK LA

7

Stonecliff Wood

PH

Borrowby Farm

Low Borrowby

Grasshill House

F7
1 CORONATION AV
2 MOOR VW
3 HILDEWELL
4 BROWN'S TERR

16

Park Wood

RIDGE LANE

SNIPE LA

Middle Farm

High Villa Farm

Borrowby

Village Farm

NEWTON LANE

A174

6

Fishpond Wood

Park House

MOOR LANE

Scroggs Wood

Newton Mulgrave

15

Roxby Woods

Dag Moor Cottage

Barrowby Moor

America House

PH

ELLERBY RY

Grange Farm

5

Grinkle Wood

Roxby Low Moor

Moor House Farm

Birchdale House

Newton Farm

Newton Brow

Hawthorne Farm

ELLERBY BANK

14

Greenhowe Wood

Birch Hill Farm

Ford

Stang Howe

Newton Mulgrave Woods

HIGH STREET

Bank Top Farm

Ellerby Bank Top

B1266

Brookridge Farm

Hailthorpe Farm

Sandwath Plantation

B1266

Ellerby Moor

Pedcar Plantation

Stump Howe

4

Marsh Farm

Roxby Moor Farm

Scaling

Stanghowe Plantation

Mickleby Moor

MICKLEBY LANE

Longstone Farm

13

Clover Hill Farm

Scaling Dam

A171

Calais House Farm

Newton Mulgrave Woods

Scaling Dam Farm

PH

Scaling Dam Res

P ✕

Standing Stone Rigg

Low Tranmire Farm

Newton Mulgrave Moor

Land o' Nod Farm

Mickleby Moorside Farm

3

P Visitor Centre

MARS LANE

Cock Rigg

Sheffield Moor

New Grove Farm

12

Roxby High Moor

High Tranmire Farm

Tranmire Grange

YO21

Meadow Croft Farm

Low Moor House

Hutchinson's House

Roxby Old Moor

Castle Farm

Tranmire Moor

Loose Howe

Mill Hill Farm

Ugthorpe

2

Tranmire

Folly Hall Farm

Pearson's Rigg

Ugthorpe Moor

Ewe Farm

PH

PO

Bellwood House Farm

11

High Whins Farm

Low Whins Farm

Ugthorpe Lodge (Hotel)

Franklands Farm

BARRY BANK

Hardale Head

Thorn Hill

Redmire Farm

High Park Farm

1

Black Dike Moor

A171

Traveller's Rest Farm

Elder Carr

10

74 **A** 75 **B** 76 **C** 77 **D** 78 **E** 79 **F**

Scale: 1¾ inches to 1 mile

0   ¼   ½ mile

0   250m   500m   750m   1 km

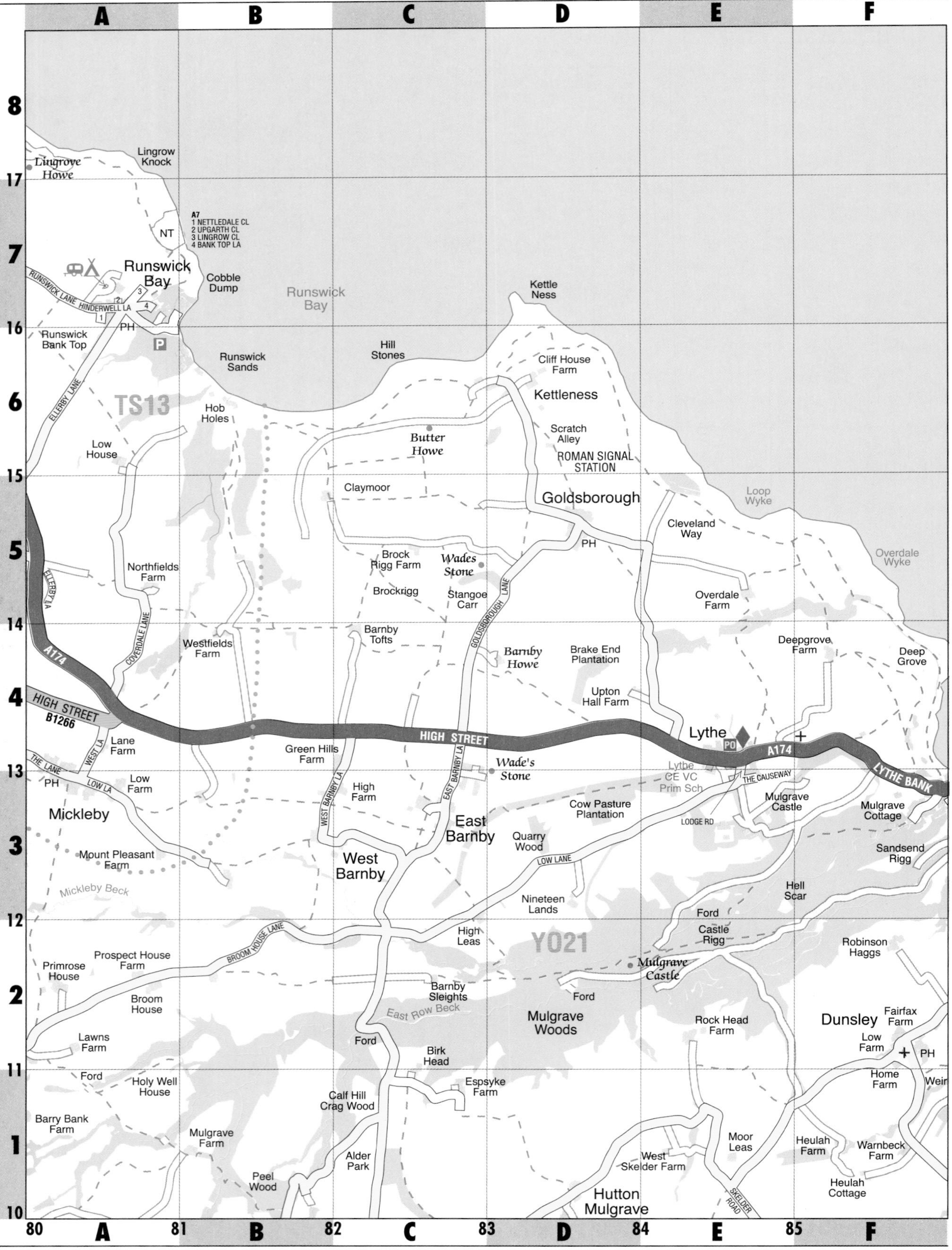

A   B   C   D   E   F

8

17

Lingrow Knock

Lingrove Howe

A7
1 NETTLEDALE CL
2 UPGARTH CL
3 LINGROW CL
4 BANK TOP LA

NT

7

Runswick Bay

Cobble Dump

Runswick Bay

Kettle Ness

16

Runswick Bank Top

PH

P

Runswick Sands

Hill Stones

Cliff House Farm

6

TS13

Hob Holes

Kettleness

Scratch Alley

ROMAN SIGNAL STATION

Low House

Butter Howe

15

Claymoor

Goldsborough

Loop Wyke

5

Northfields Farm

Brock Rigg Farm

Wades Stone

PH

Cleveland Way

Overdale Wyke

14

Westfields Farm

Brockrigg

Stangoe Carr

Barnby Tofts

Barnby Howe

Brake End Plantation

Overdale Farm

Deepgrove Farm

Deep Grove

A174

4

HIGH STREET

B1266

Lane Farm

Green Hills Farm

HIGH STREET

Upton Hall Farm

Lythe

A174

LYTHE BANK

13

THE LANE

LOW LA

WEST LA

Low Farm

High Farm

Wade's Stone

EAST BARNBY LA

Lythe CE VC Prim Sch

PO

THE CAUSEWAY

Mulgrave Castle

Mulgrave Cottage

PH

Mickleby

East Barnby

Cow Pasture Plantation

LODGE RD

Sandsend Rigg

3

Mount Pleasant Farm

WEST BARNBY LA

West Barnby

Quarry Wood

LOW LANE

Hell Scar

Mickleby Beck

Nineteen Lands

YO21

Castle Rigg

Robinson Haggs

12

Primrose House

Prospect House Farm

BROOM HOUSE LANE

High Leas

Mulgrave Castle

Ford

Fairfax Farm

2

Broom House

Barnby Sleights

Ford

Mulgrave Woods

Rock Head Farm

Dunsley

Low Farm

PH

Lawns Farm

East Row Beck

Ford

Birk Head

Home Farm

Weir

11

Ford

Holy Well House

Calf Hill Crag Wood

Espsyke Farm

Moor Leas

Heulah Farm

Warnbeck Farm

Barry Bank Farm

Mulgrave Farm

Alder Park

West Skelder Farm

SKELDER ROAD

Heulah Cottage

10

Peel Wood

Hutton Mulgrave

80   A   81   B   82   C   83   D   84   E   85   F

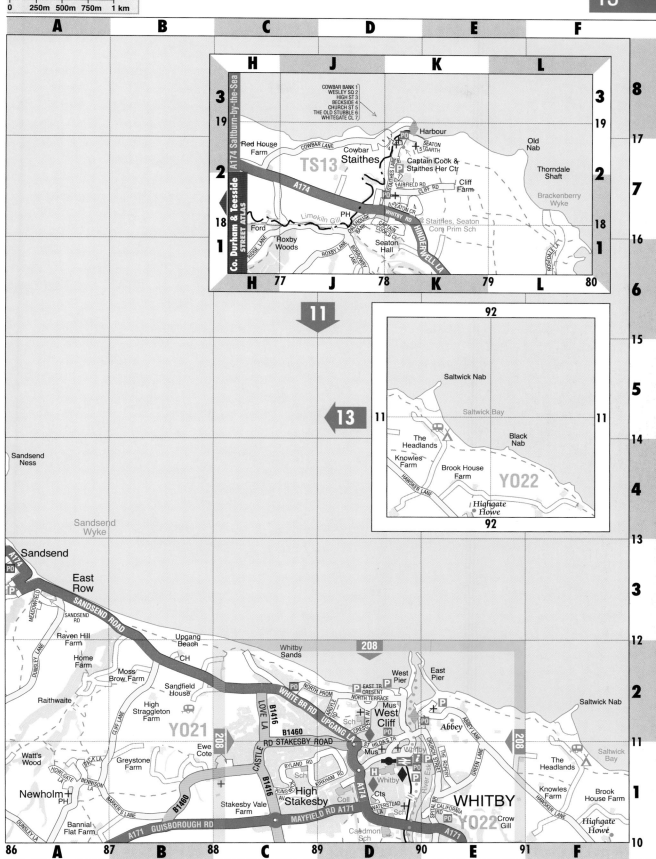

Scale: 1¾ inches to 1 mile

0   ¼   ½ mile
0   250m   500m   750m   1 km

A   B   C   D   E   F

Inset 1 (top):

H   J   K   L

COWBAR BANK 1
WESLEY SQ 2
HIGH ST 3
BECKSIDE 4
CHURCH ST 5
THE OLD STUBBLE 6
WHITEGATE CL 7

3   19

Co. Durham & Teesside STREET ATLAS

A174 Saltburn-by-the-Sea

Red House Farm
COWBAR LANE
Cowbar
Harbour
SEATON GARTH
TS13
Cowbar Staithes
Captain Cook & Staithes Her Ctr
Old Nab

2

A174
FAIRFIELD RD
CLIFF RD
Cliff Farm
Thorndale Shaft
Brackenberry Wyke

18

Ford
Limekiln Gill
PH
RIDGE LANE
Roxby Woods
DALEHOUSE BANK
ROXBY LANE
BOROWBY LANE
SEATON CR
Staithes, Seaton Com Prim Sch
HINDERWELL LA
CAPTAIN COOKS CL
Seaton Hall

1   18

ROSEDALE LA

H   77   J   78   K   79   L   80

Inset 2 (middle):

92

Saltwick Nab

11   Saltwick Bay   11

The Headlands
Black Nab

Knowles Farm
Brook House Farm
YO22

HAWSKER LANE

Highgate Howe

92

Main map:

8
17
7
16
6
15
5
14
4
13
3
12
2
11
1
10

Sandsend Ness

Sandsend Wyke

A174
Sandsend
PO
East Row
P

SANDSEND ROAD
SANDSEND RD
MEADOWFIELD
Raven Hill Farm
Home Farm
DUNSLEY LANE
Moss Brow Farm
Sandfield House
CH
Upgang Beach
Whitby Sands
208
West Pier
East Pier

Raithwaite
High Straggleton Farm
YO21
CLIFF LANE
B1416
208
Ewe Cote
LOVE LA
WHITE BR RD
B1460
UPGANG LA
RD STAKESBY ROAD
PO
NORTH PROM
NORTH TERRACE
EAST TR CRESENT
ARGYLE
CRESCENT AV
Sch
West Cliff
Mus
P
Abbey
P
208
Saltwick Nab

Watt's Wood
HOWGATE LA
BLACK LA
BENNISON LA
Greystone Farm
BARKER'S LANE
CASTLE
B1460
BYLAND RD
KIRKHAM RD
Sch
RUNS WK
ST HILDAS TR
Mus
Whitby
CHURCH ST
THE ROPERY
GREEN LANE
ABBEY LANE
The Headlands
Saltwick Bay

Newholm
PH
DUNSLEY LA
Bannial Flat Farm
A171 GUISBOROUGH RD
B1416
Stakesby Vale Farm
High Stakesby
BYLAND
Coll
A174
Cts
Whitby
WATERSTEAD
Caedmon Sch
H
MAYFIELD RD A171
CALIFORNIA
River Esk
WHITBY
YO22
PO
A171
Crow Gill
HAWSKER LANE
Knowles Farm
Brook House Farm
Highgate Howe

86   A   87   B   88   C   89   D   90   E   91   F

11

13

32

For full street detail of the highlighted area see page 208.

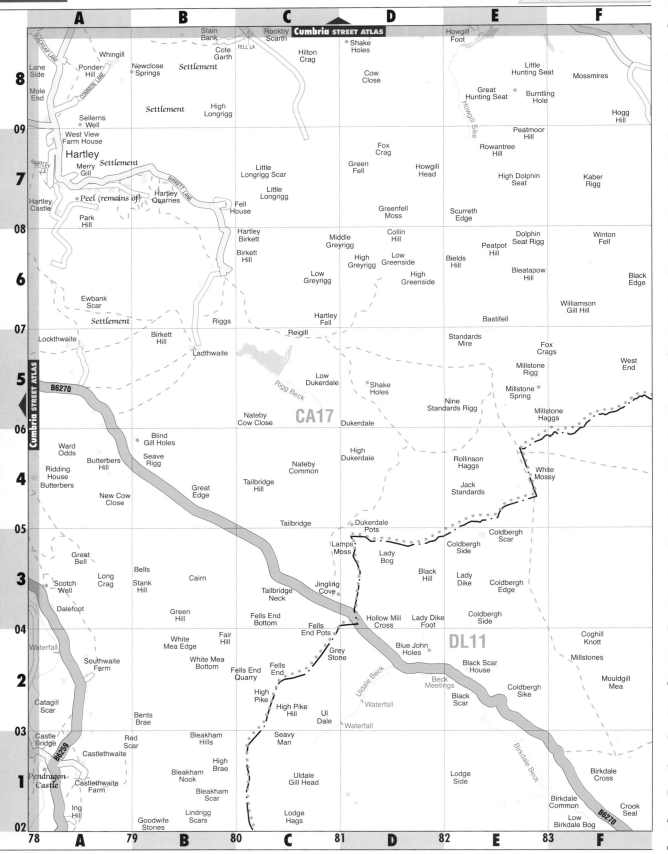

Stain Bank
Rookby Scarth
Cote Garth
Hilton Crag
Shake Holes
Howgill Foot
Whingill
Newclose Springs
Settlement
Cow Close
Little Hunting Seat
Mossmires
Lane Side
Ponder Hill
Mole End
Great Hunting Seat
Burntling Hole
Settlement
High Longrigg
Hogg Hill
Sellerns Well
Settlement
Peatmoor Hill
West View Farm House
Fox Crag
Rowantree Hill
Hartley
Little Longrigg Scar
Green Fell
Howgill Head
High Dolphin Seat
Kaber Rigg
Merry Gill
Settlement
Little Longrigg
Hartley Quarries
Fell House
Greenfell Moss
Scurreth Edge
Peel (remains of)
Hartley Castle
Hartley Birkett
Middle Greyrigg
Collin Hill
Peatpot Hill
Dolphin Seat Rigg
Winton Fell
Park Hill
Birkett Hill
High Greyrigg
Low Greenside
Bields Hill
Bleatapow Hill
Black Edge
Low Greyrigg
High Greenside
Ewbank Scar
Williamson Gill Hill
Settlement
Riggs
Hartley Fell
Bastifell
Lockthwaite
Birkett Hill
Reigill
Standards Mire
Fox Crags
Ladthwaite
Low Dukerdale
Millstone Rigg
West End
Rigg Beck
Shake Holes
Millstone Spring
Millstone Haggs
CA17
Nateby Cow Close
Dukerdale
Nine Standards Rigg
Ward Odds
Blind Gill Holes
High Dukerdale
Rollinson Haggs
Ridding House Butterbers
Butterbers Hill
Seave Rigg
Nateby Common
White Mossy
New Cow Close
Great Edge
Tailbridge Hill
Jack Standards
Great Bell
Tailbridge
Dukerdale Pots
Coldbergh Scar
Lamps Moss
Coldbergh Side
Bells
Long Crag
Stank Hill
Cairn
Lady Bog
Black Hill
Lady Dike
Coldbergh Edge
Scotch Well
Tailbridge Neck
Jingling Cove
Dalefoot
Green Hill
Fells End Bottom
Hollow Mill Cross
Lady Dike Foot
Coldbergh Side
Fells End Pots
Blue John Holes
DL11
Coghill Knott
White Mea Edge
Fair Hill
Grey Stone
Millstones
Southwaite Farm
White Mea Bottom
Fells End Quarry
Fells End
Black Scar House
Mouldgill Mea
Catagill Scar
High Pike
High Pike Hill
Ul Dale
Beck Meetings
Black Scar
Coldbergh Sike
Bents Brae
Waterfall
Waterfall
Castle Bridge
Red Scar
Bleakham Hills
Seavy Man
Castlethwaite
High Brae
Uldale Gill Head
Lodge Side
Birkdale Cross
Pendragon Castle
Castlethwaite Farm
Bleakham Nook
Bleakham Scar
Birkdale Common
Crook Seal
Ing Hill
Goodwife Stones
Lindrigg Scars
Lodge Hags
Low Birkdale Bog

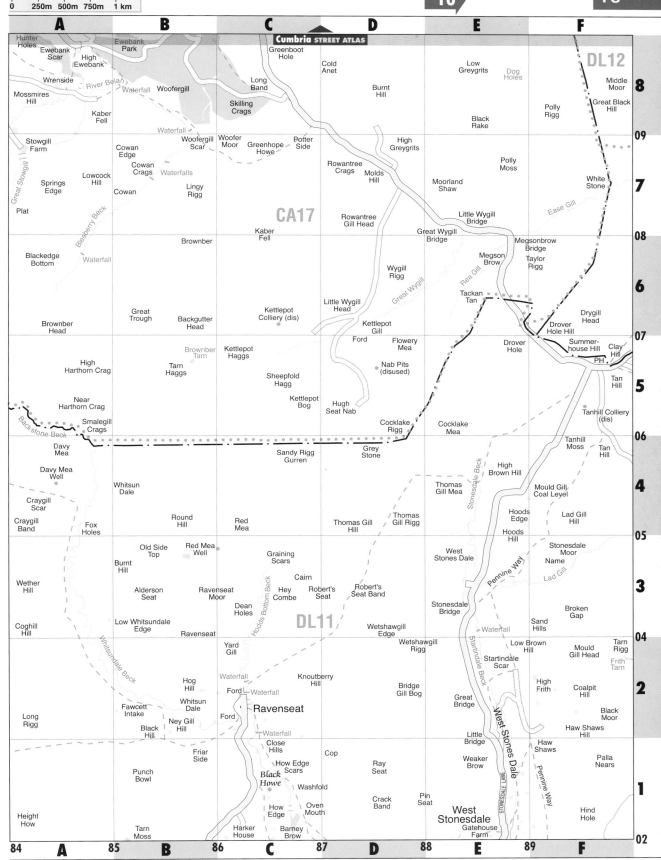

Cumbria STREET ATLAS

DL12

Row 8
Hunter Holes
Ewebank Scar
High Ewebank
Ewebank Park
Greenboot Hole
Cold Anet
Burnt Hill
Low Greygrits
Dog Holes
Middle Moor
Wrenside
River Belah
Long Band
Great Black Hill
Mossmires Hill
Woofergill
Skilling Crags
Black Rake
Polly Rigg
Kaber Fell
Waterfall

Row 09
Stowgill Farm
Cowan Edge
Woofergill Scar
Woofer Moor
Greenhope Howe
Potter Side
High Greygrits
White Stone
Lowcock Hill
Cowan Crags
Polly Moss
Waterfalls

Row 7
Springs Edge
Cowan
Lingy Rigg
Rowantree Crags
Molds Hill
Moorland Shaw
Ease Gill
Plat
Great Stowgill
Kaber Fell
CA17
Rowantree Gill Head
Little Wygill Bridge

Row 08
Bleaberry Beck
Brownber
Great Wygill Bridge
Megsonbrow Bridge
Blackedge Bottom
Waterfall
Wygill Rigg
Megson Brow
Taylor Rigg
Great Wygill

Row 6
Brownber Head
Great Trough
Backgutter Head
Kettlepot Colliery (dis)
Little Wygill Head
Rea Gill
Tackan Tan
Drygill Head
Drover Hole Hill

Row 07
Brownber Tarn
Kettlepot Haggs
Kettlepot Gill
Ford
Flowery Mea
Drover Hole
Summerhouse Hill
Clay Hill
PH
High Harthorn Crag
Tarn Haggs
Sheepfold Hagg
Nab Pits (disused)
Tan Hill

Row 5
Near Harthorn Crag
Smalegill Crags
Kettlepot Bog
Hugh Seat Nab
Cocklake Rigg
Cocklake Mea
Tanhill Colliery (dis)
Backstone Beck
Davy Mea
Sandy Rigg Gurren
Grey Stone
Tanhill Moss
Tan Hill

Row 06 / 4
Davy Mea Well
Whitsun Dale
High Brown Hill
Craygill Scar
Thomas Gill Mea
Stonesdale Beck
Mould Gill Coal Level
Craygill Band
Fox Holes
Round Hill
Red Mea
Thomas Gill Rigg
Thomas Gill Hill
Hoods Edge
Lad Gill Hill
Hoods Hill

Row 05 / 3
Old Side Top
Red Mea Well
Graining Scars
West Stones Dale
Stonesdale Moor Name
Wether Hill
Burnt Hill
Cairn
Lad Gill
Alderson Seat
Ravenseat Moor
Hey Combe
Robert's Seat
Robert's Seat Band
Pennine Way
Sand Hills
Broken Gap
Coghill Hill
Dean Holes
Low Whitsundale Edge
Ravenseat
Wetshawgill Edge
Stonesdale Bridge
DL11

Row 04 / 2
Whitsundale Beck
Yard Gill
Wetshawgill Rigg
Low Brown Hill
Mould Gill Head
Tarn Rigg
Hodds Bottom Beck
Startindale Beck
Startindale Scar
Frith Tarn
Long Rigg
Hog Hill
Knoutberry Hill
Bridge Gill Bog
High Frith
Coalpit Hill
Fawcett Intake
Whitsun Dale
Waterfall
Ford
Great Bridge
West Stones Dale
Black Moor
Ney Gill Hill
Black Hill
Ravenseat
Haw Shaws Hill

Row 1 / 02
Friar Side
Ford
Close Hills
Cop
Little Bridge
Haw Shaws
Palla Nears
Punch Bowl
How Edge Scars
Ray Seat
Weaker Brow
Pennine Way
Black Howe
Washfold
Crack Band
Pin Seat
Height How
How Edge
Oven Mouth
West Stonesdale
Hind Hole
Tarn Moss
Harker House
Barney Brow
Gatehouse Farm
Stonesdale Lane

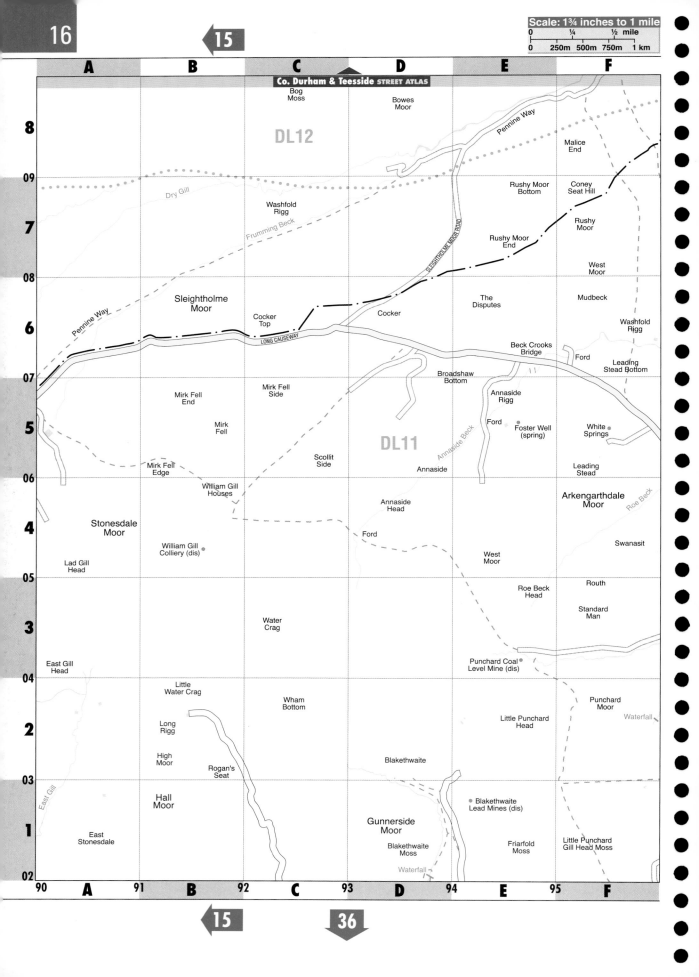

Scale: 1¾ inches to 1 mile

0   ¼   ½ mile
0   250m 500m 750m 1 km

A   B   C   D   E   F

Co. Durham & Teesside STREET ATLAS

Bog
Moss

Bowes
Moor

8

DL12

Pennine Way

Malice
End

09

Dry Gill

Washfold
Rigg

Rushy Moor
Bottom

Coney
Seat Hill

7

Frumming Beck

Rushy Moor
End

Rushy
Moor

08

West
Moor

Pennine Way

Sleightholme
Moor

The
Disputes

Mudbeck

6

Cocker
Top

Cocker

SLEIGHTHOLME MOOR ROAD

Washfold
Rigg

LONG CAUSEWAY

Beck Crooks
Bridge

Ford

Leading
Stead Bottom

07

Pennine Way

Mirk Fell
Side

Broadshaw
Bottom

Annaside
Rigg

Mirk Fell
End

Annaside
Beck

Ford

Foster Well
(spring)

White
Springs

5

Mirk
Fell

DL11

Scollit
Side

Annaside

Leading
Stead

06

Mirk Fell
Edge

William Gill
Houses

Annaside
Head

Arkengarthdale
Moor

Roe Beck

4

Stonesdale
Moor

Ford

Swanasit

William Gill
Colliery (dis)

West
Moor

Lad Gill
Head

05

Roe Beck
Head

Routh

3

Water
Crag

Standard
Man

East Gill
Head

04

Punchard Coal
Level Mine (dis)

Little
Water Crag

Punchard
Moor

2

Wham
Bottom

Little Punchard
Head

Waterfall

Long
Rigg

High
Moor

Rogan's
Seat

03

East Gill

Blakethwaite

Hall
Moor

Blakethwaite
Lead Mines (dis)

1

Gunnerside
Moor

Friarfold
Moss

Little Punchard
Gill Head Moss

East
Stonesdale

Blakethwaite
Moss

Waterfall

02

90   A   91   B   92   C   93   D   94   E   95   F

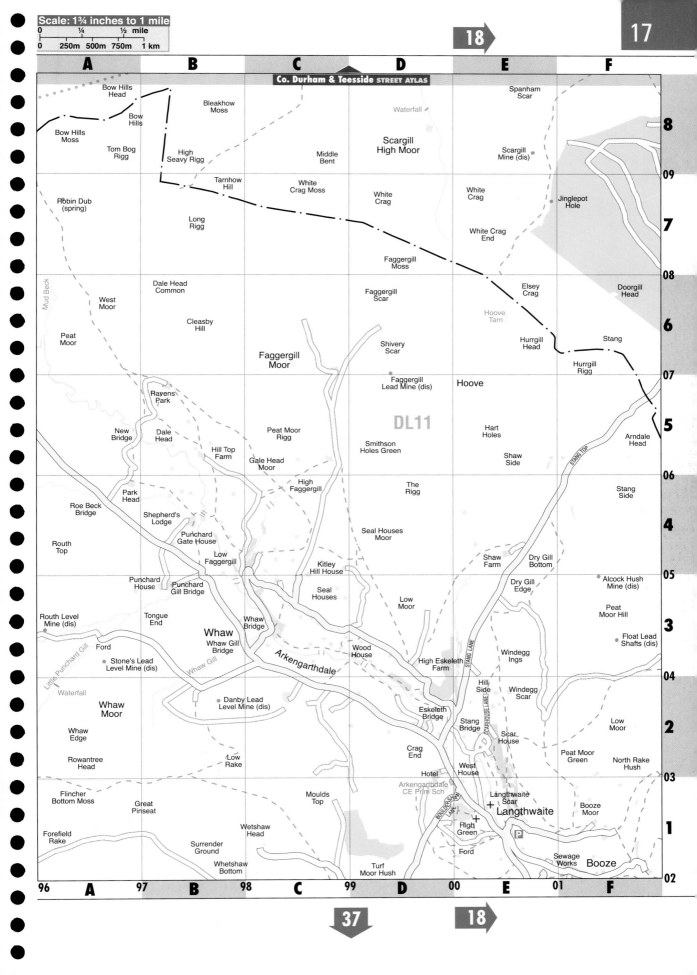

A   B   C   D   E   F

Co. Durham & Teesside STREET ATLAS

Bow Hills
Head

Bleakhow
Moss

Spanham
Scar

Waterfall

8

Bow
Hills

Scargill
High Moor

Scargill
Mine (dis)

Bow Hills
Moss

Tom Bog
Rigg

High
Seavy Rigg

Tarnhow
Hill

09

Robin Dub
(spring)

Long
Rigg

White
Crag Moss

White
Crag

White
Crag

Jinglepot
Hole

7

White Crag
End

08

Mud Beck

West
Moor

Dale Head
Common

Faggergill
Scar

Elsey
Crag

Doorgill
Head

Cleasby
Hill

Faggergill
Moss

Hoove
Tarn

Hurrgill
Head

6

Peat
Moor

Shivery
Scar

Stang

Faggergill
Moor

Hurrgill
Rigg

07

Ravens
Park

Faggergill
Lead Mine (dis)

Hoove

New
Bridge

Dale
Head

Peat Moor
Rigg

DL11

Hart
Holes

Arndale
Head

5

Park
Head

Hill Top
Farm

Smithson
Holes Green

Shaw
Side

Roe Beck
Bridge

Shepherd's
Lodge

Gale Head
Moor

High
Faggergill

The
Rigg

Stang
Side

06

Routh
Top

Punchard
Gate House

Seal Houses
Moor

Shaw
Farm

Dry Gill
Bottom

4

Punchard
House

Punchard
Gill Bridge

Low
Faggergill

Kitley
Hill House

Dry Gill
Edge

Alcock Hush
Mine (dis)

05

Routh Level
Mine (dis)

Tongue
End

Seal
Houses

Low
Moor

Peat
Moor Hill

Ford

Whaw
Bridge

Float Lead
Shafts (dis)

3

Stone's Lead
Level Mine (dis)

Whaw

Wood
House

Windegg
Ings

Whaw Gill
Bridge

High Eskeleth
Farm

04

Arkengarthdale

Whaw Gill

Hill
Side

Windegg
Scar

Low
Moor

Whaw
Moor

Danby Lead
Level Mine (dis)

Eskeleth
Bridge

Stang
Bridge

Scar
House

Peat Moor
Green

2

Whaw
Edge

Crag
End

West
House

North Rake
Hush

Rowantree
Head

Low
Rake

Hotel

Langthwaite
Scar

Booze
Moor

03

Flincher
Bottom Moss

Great
Pinseat

Moulds
Top

Arkengarthdale
CE Prim Sch

Langthwaite

Forefield
Rake

Wetshaw
Head

High
Green

P

Booze

1

Surrender
Ground

Ford

Sewage
Works

Whetshaw
Bottom

Turf
Moor Hush

02

96   A   97   B   98   C   99   D   00   E   01   F

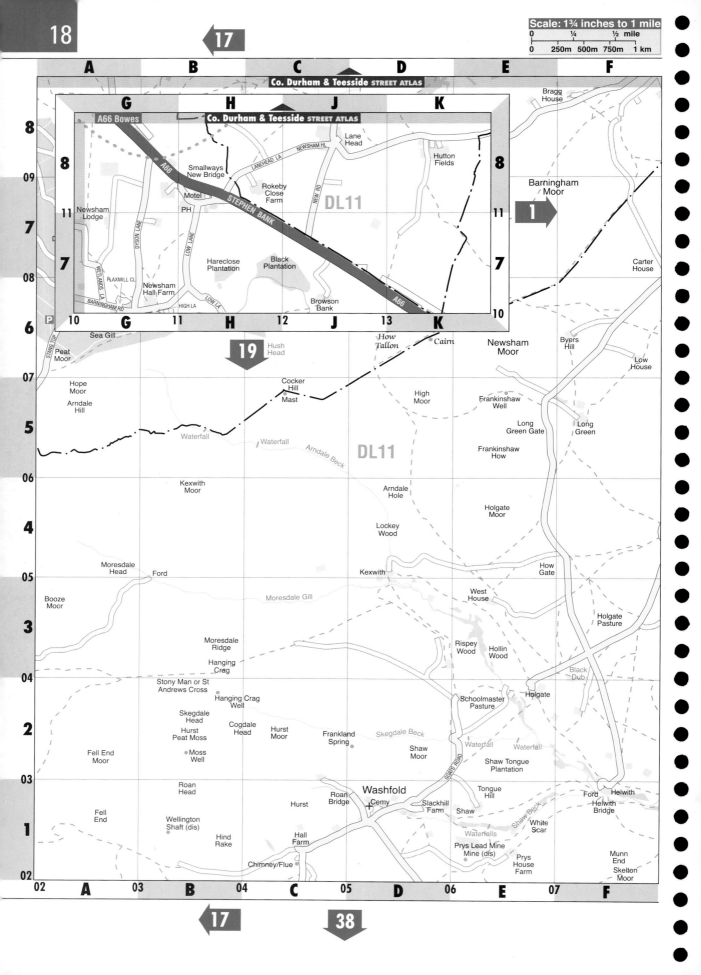

A   B   C   D   E   F

Inset map:

G   H   J   K

Co. Durham & Teesside STREET ATLAS

A66 Bowes

Bragg House

Lane Head

Newsham HL

Lanehead La

Smallways New Bridge

A66

Rokeby Close Farm

New Rd

Hutton Fields

DL11

Barningham Moor

1

Newsham Lodge

Motel

PH

Stephen Bank

Dyson Lane

Low Lane

Hareclose Plantation

Black Plantation

Carter House

Plaxmill Cl

Wetlands La

Newsham Hall Farm

Low La

Browson Bank

A66

Barningham Rd

High La

Sea Gill

19

Hush Head

How Tallon

Cairn

Newsham Moor

Byers Hill

Stang Top

Peat Moor

P

Cocker Hill

Mast

High Moor

Frankinshaw Well

Long Green Gate

Long Green

Low House

Hope Moor

Arndale Hill

Waterfall

Waterfall

Arndale Beck

DL11

Frankinshaw How

Kexwith Moor

Arndale Hole

Holgate Moor

Lockey Wood

Moresdale Head

Ford

Moresdale Gill

Kexwith

West House

How Gate

Holgate Pasture

Booze Moor

Black Dub

Moresdale Ridge

Hanging Crag

Rispey Wood

Hollin Wood

Holgate

Stony Man or St Andrews Cross

Hanging Crag Well

Schoolmaster Pasture

Skegdale Head

Cogdale Head

Hurst Moor

Frankland Spring

Skegdale Beck

Shaw Moor

Waterfall

Waterfall

Hurst Peat Moss

Fell End Moor

Moss Well

Shaw Tongue Plantation

Goats Road

Roan Head

Hurst

Roan Bridge

Washfold
Cemy

Slackhill Farm

Shaw

Tongue Hill

Ford

Helwith

Helwith Bridge

Fell End

Wellington Shaft (dis)

Hind Rake

Hall Farm

White Scar

Shaw Beck

Waterfalls

Prys Lead Mine
Mine (dis)

Munn End

Chimney/Flue

Prys House Farm

Skelton Moor

02   03   04   05   06   07

A   B   C   D   E   F

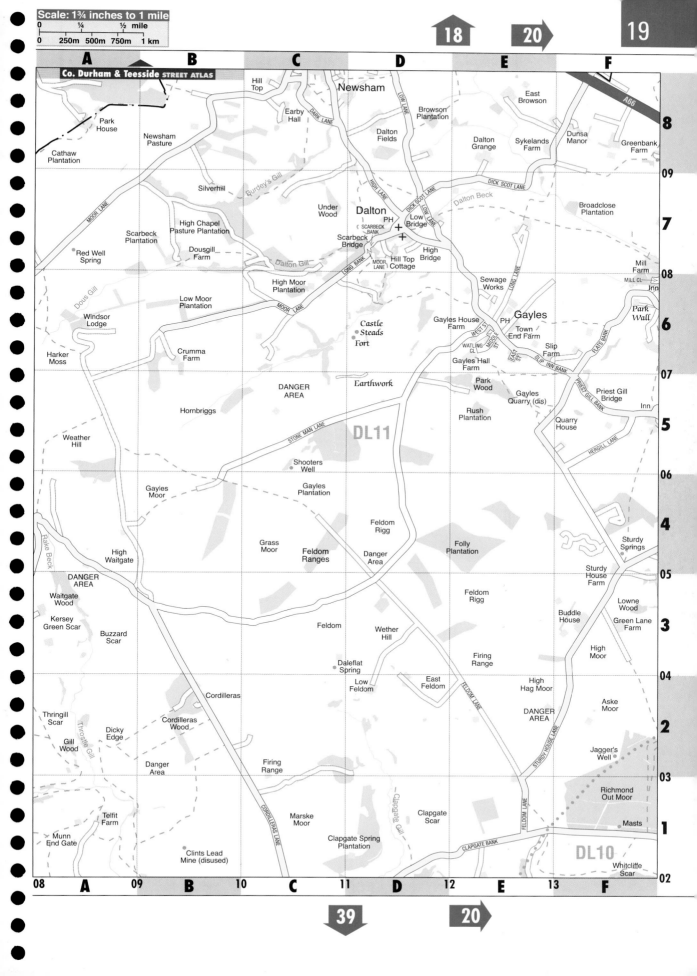

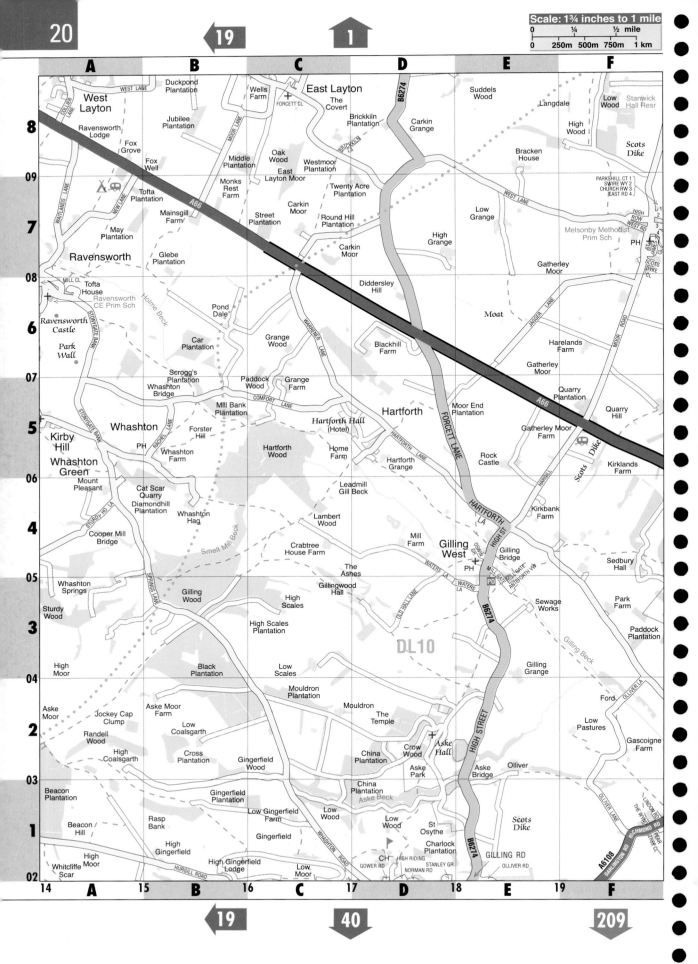

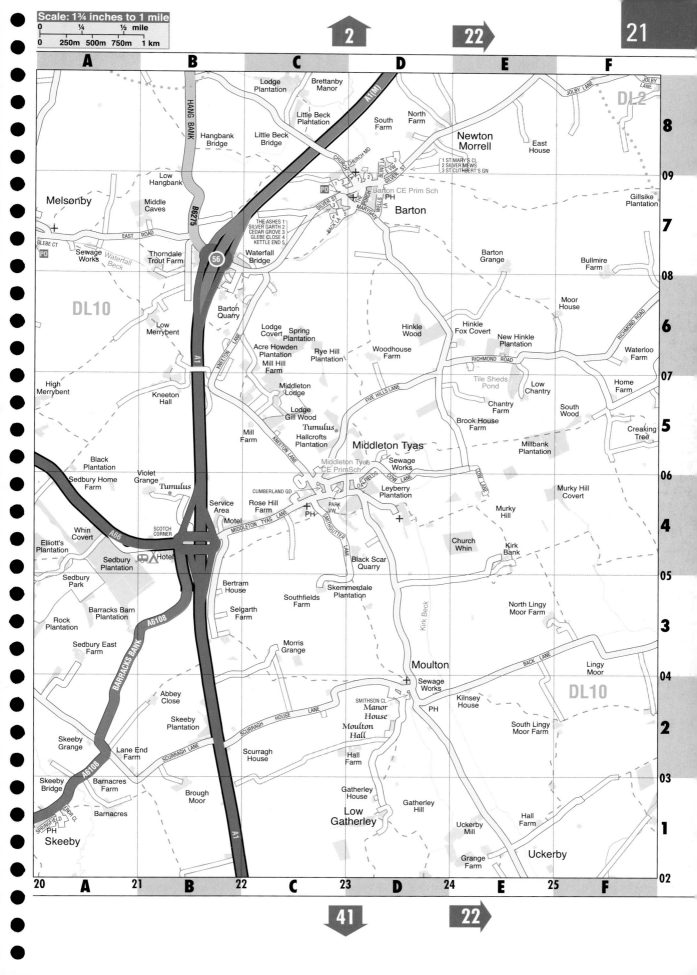

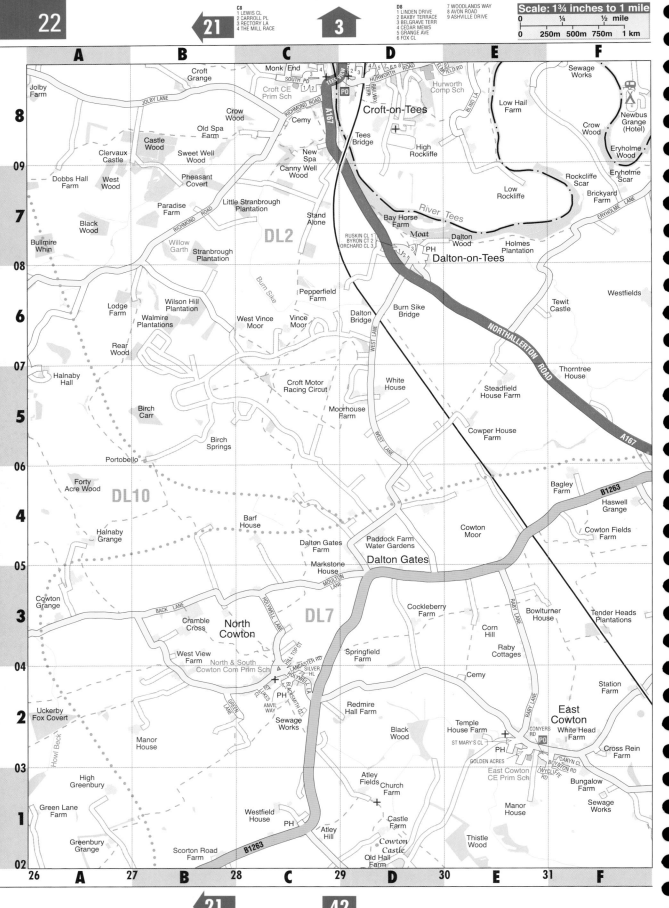

21

3

C8
1 LEWIS CL
2 CARROLL PL
3 RECTORY LA
4 THE MILL RACE

D8
1 LINDEN DRIVE
2 BAXBY TERRACE
3 BELGRAVE TERR
4 CEDAR MEWS
5 GRANGE AVE
6 FOX CL

7 WOODLANDS WAY
8 AVON ROAD
9 ASHVILLE DRIVE

Scale: 1¾ inches to 1 mile

0   ¼   ½   mile

0   250m   500m   750m   1 km

21

42

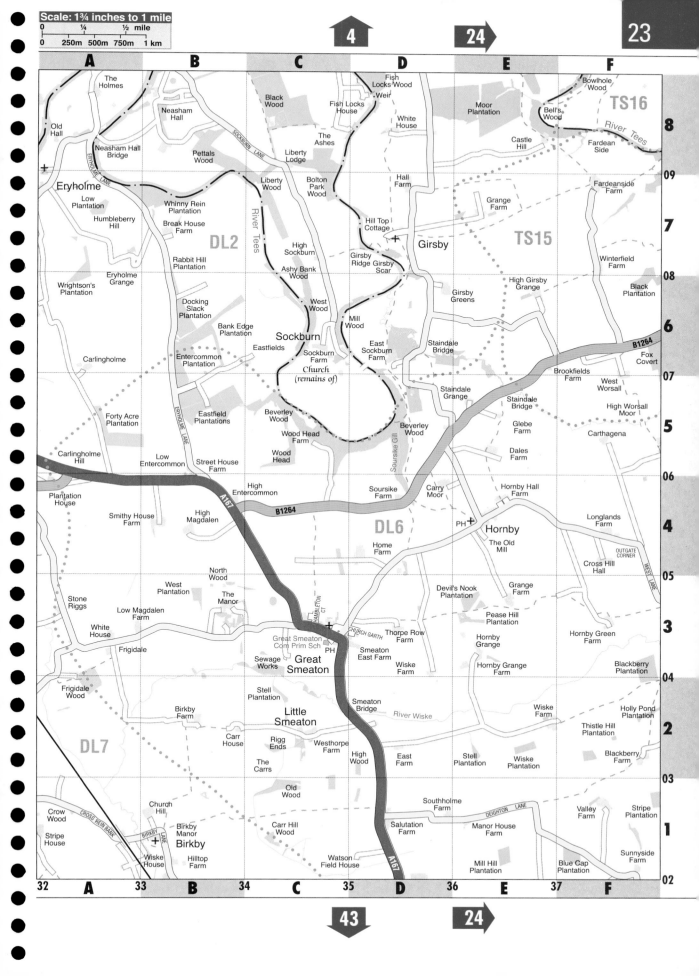

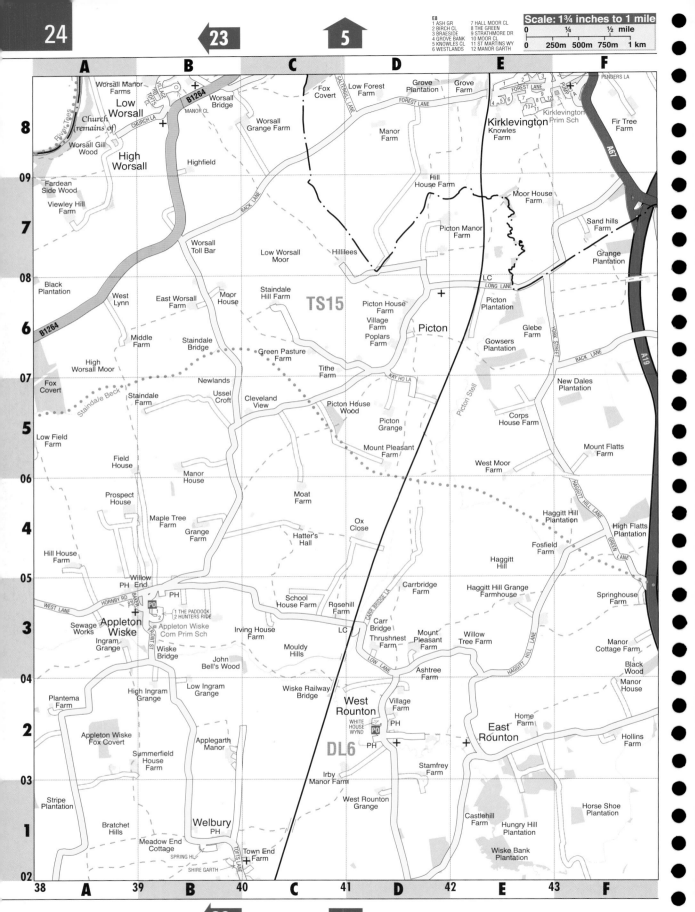

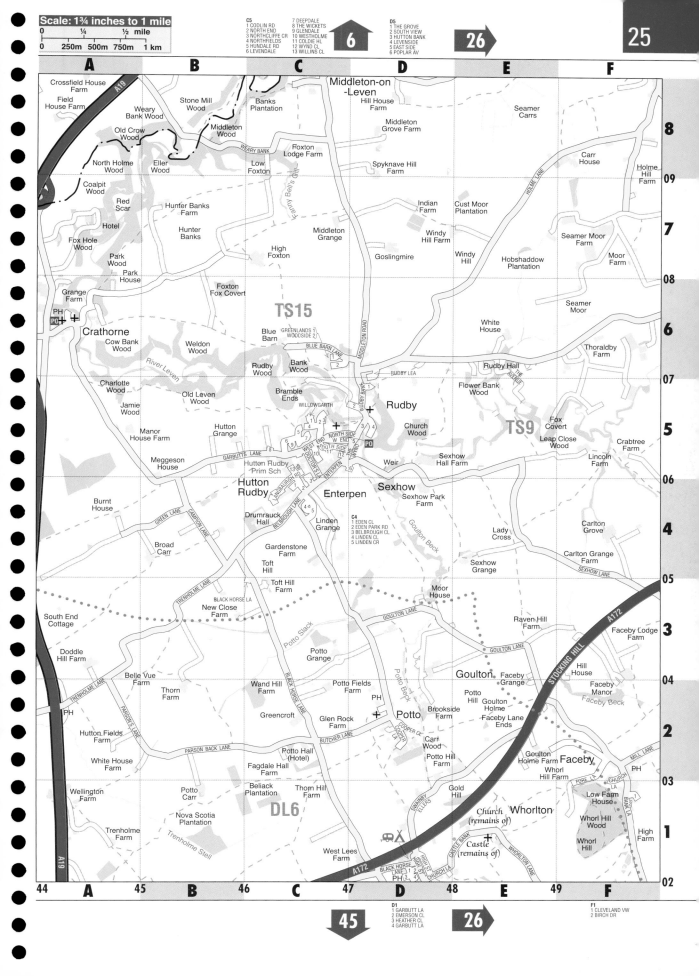

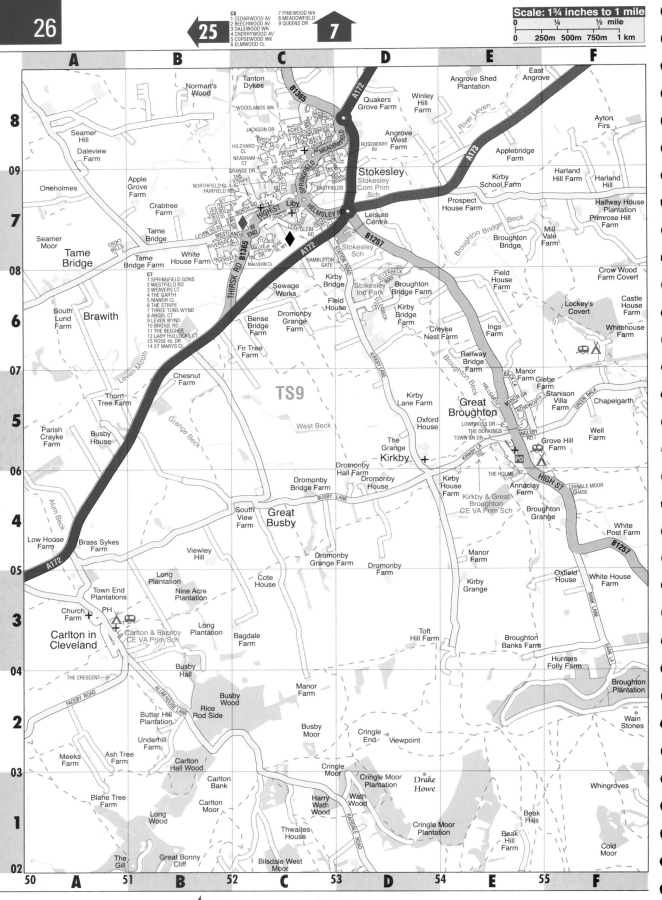

C8
1 CEDARWOOD AV
2 BEECHWOOD AV
3 DALEWOOD WK
4 CHERRYWOOD AV
5 COPSEWOOD WK
6 ELMWOOD CL
7 PINEWOOD WK
8 MEADOWFIELD
9 QUEENS DR

Scale: 1¾ inches to 1 mile

0   ¼   ½   mile
0 250m 500m 750m 1 km

C7
1 SPRINGFIELD GDNS
2 WESTFIELD RD
3 WEAVERS CT
4 THE GARTH
5 MANOR CL
6 THE STRIPE
7 THREE TUNS WYND
8 ANGEL CT
9 LEVEN WYND
10 BRIDGE RD
11 THE BEECHES
12 LADY HULLOCKS CT
13 ROSE HL DR
14 ST MARYS CL

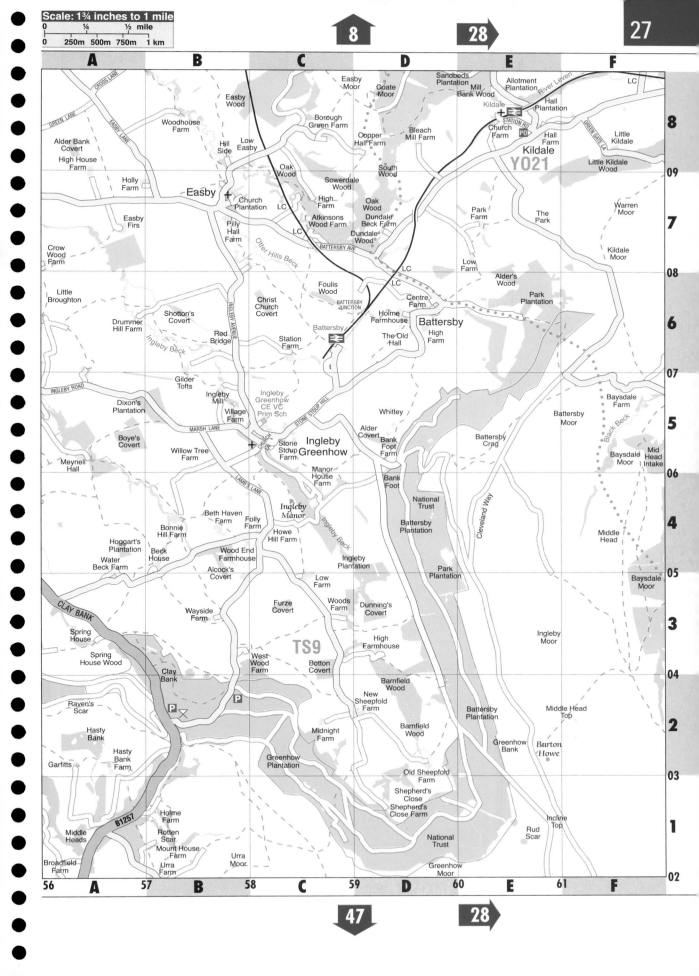

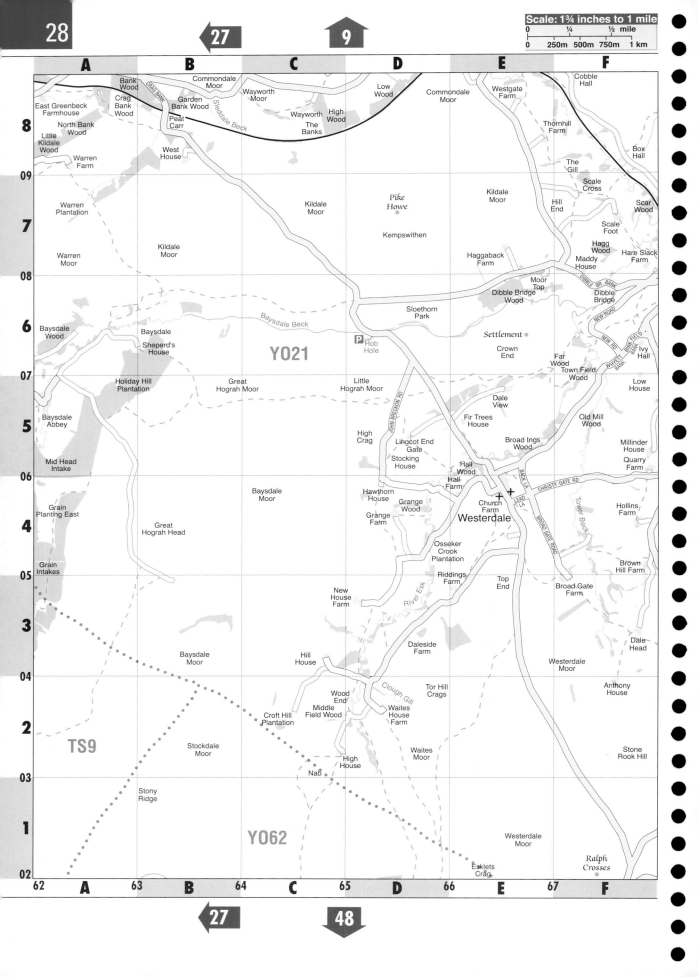

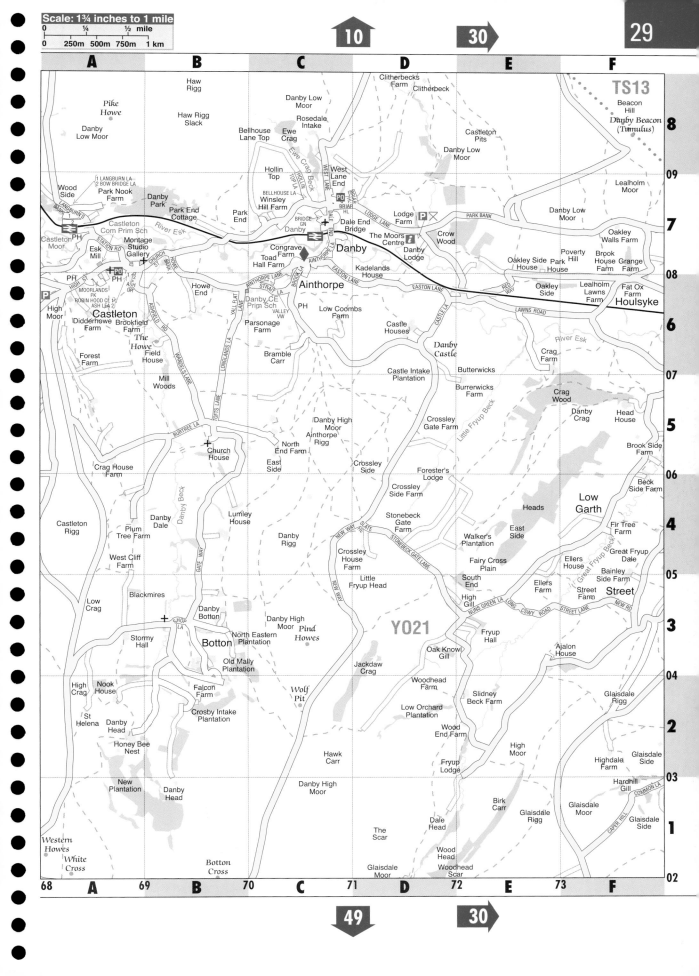

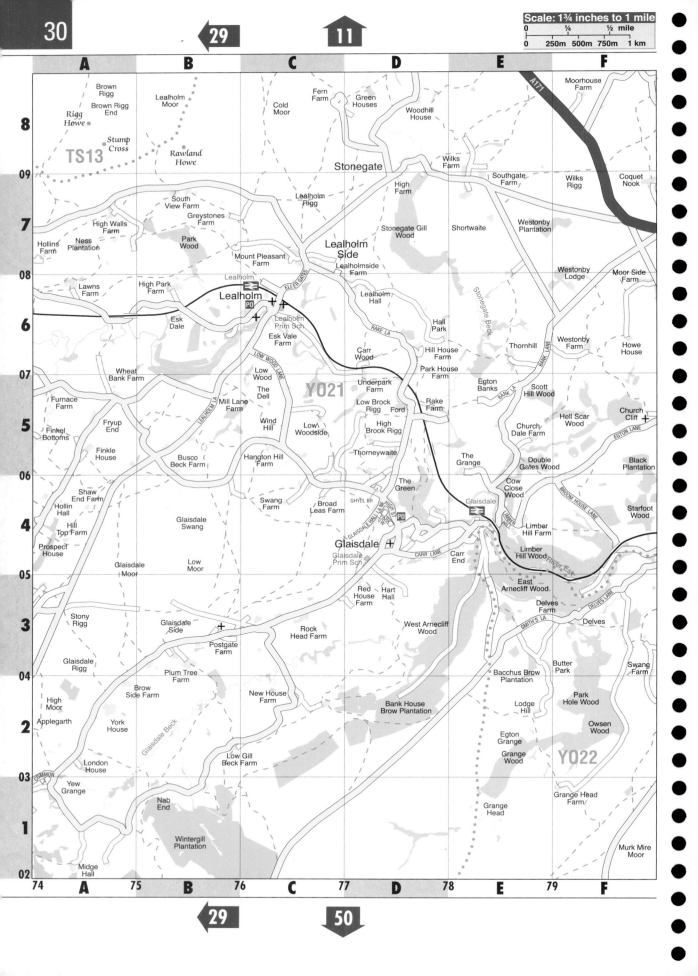

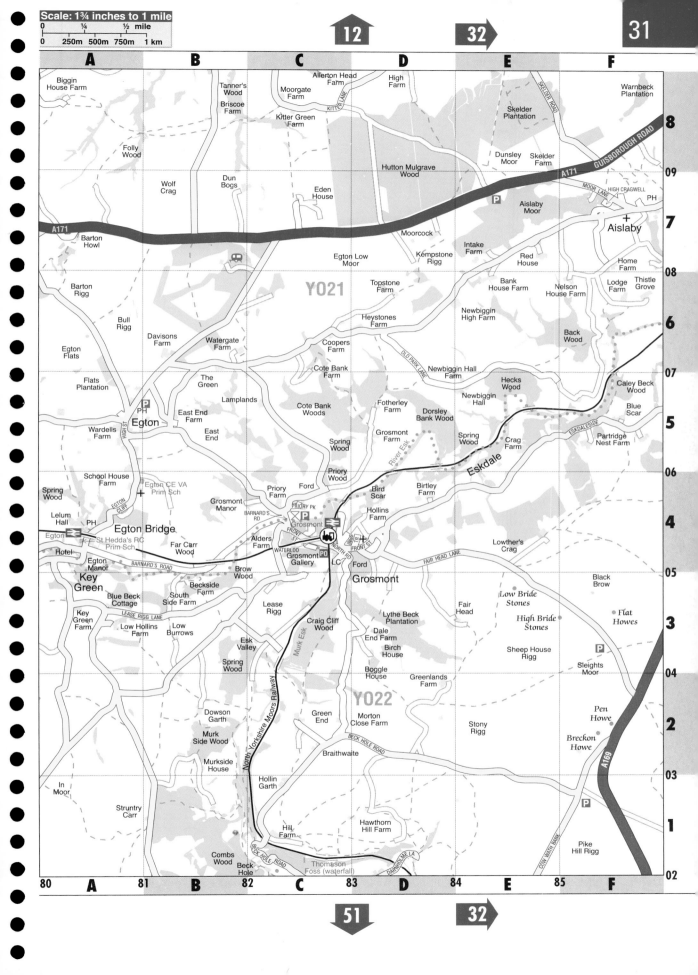

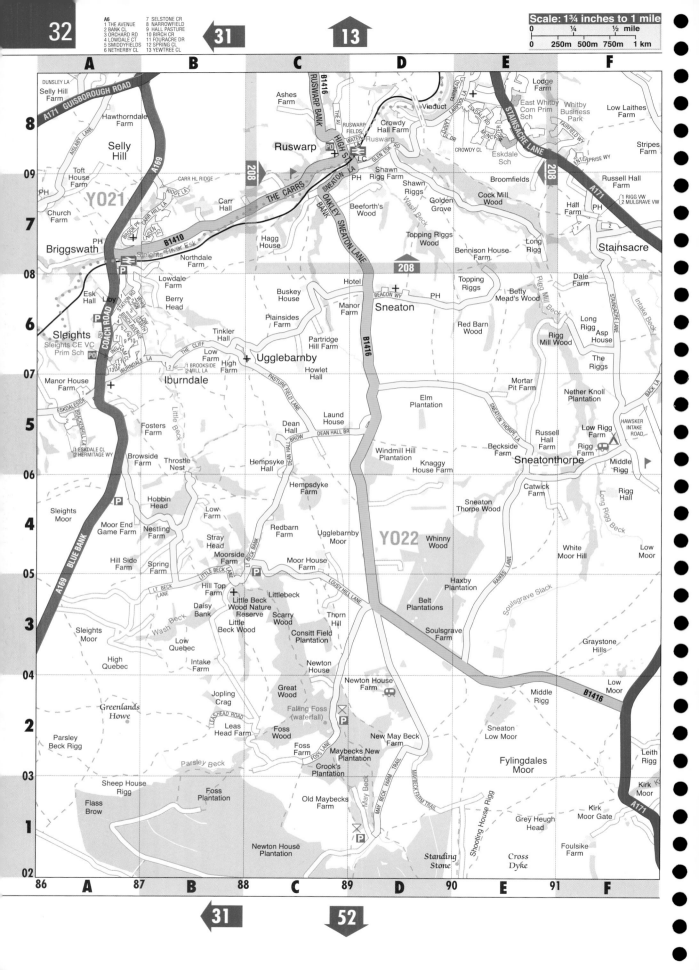

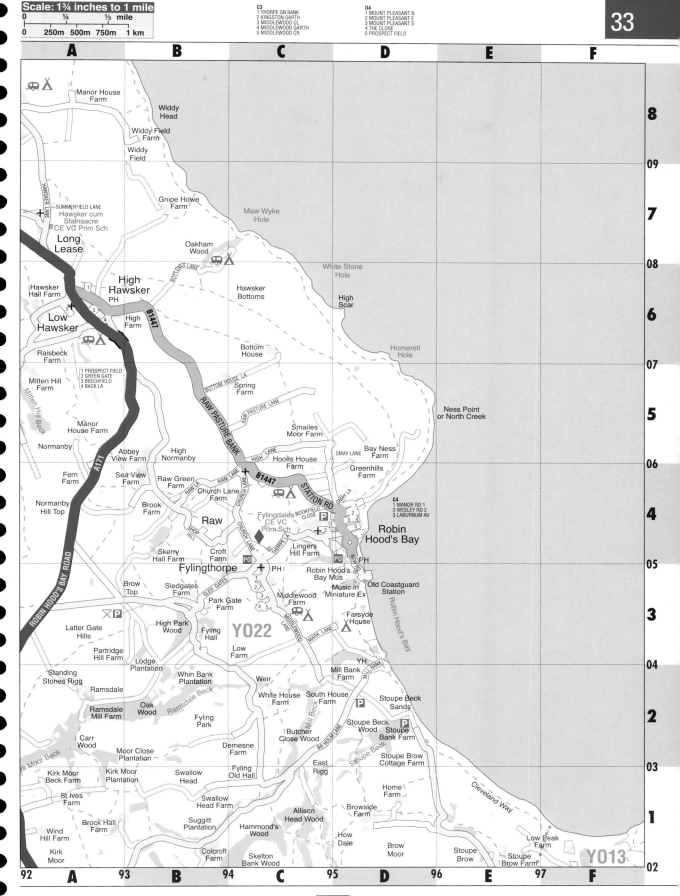

Scale: 1¾ inches to 1 mile

0   ¼   ½ mile
0   250m 500m 750m 1 km

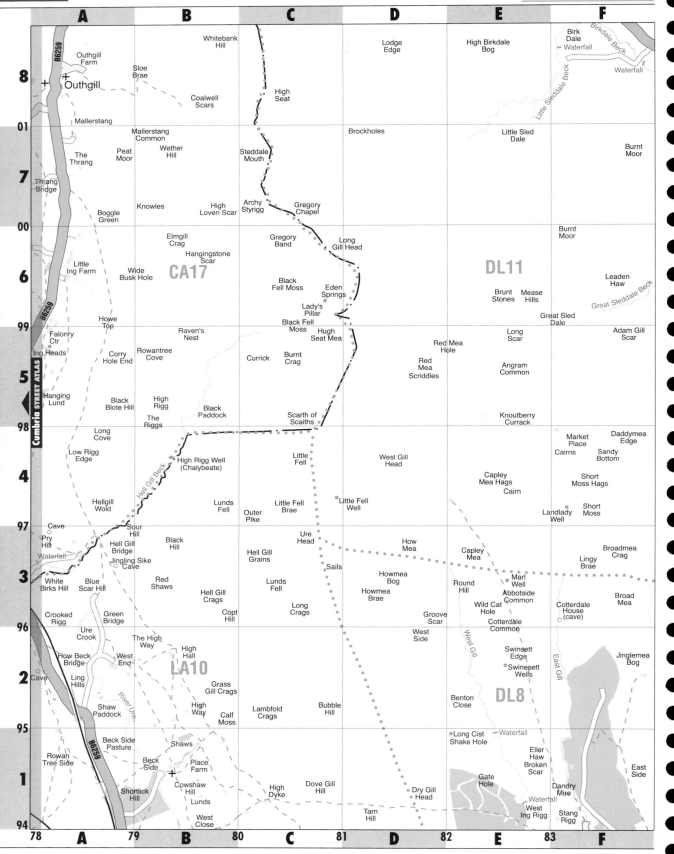

A · **B** · **C** · **D** · **E** · **F**

Birk
Dale
Waterfall

Birkdale Beck

Whitebank
Hill

Lodge
Edge

High Birkdale
Bog

B6259

Outhgill
Farm

Sloe
Brae

8

+ Outhgill

Coalwell
Scars

High
Seat

Waterfall

Little Sleddale Beck

01

Mallerstang

Mallerstang
Common

Wether
Hill

Brockholes

Little Sled
Dale

Burnt
Moor

Peat
Moor

Steddale
Mouth

7

The
Thrang

Thrang
Bridge

Knowles

High
Loven Scar

Archy
Styrigg

Gregory
Chapel

00

Boggle
Green

Elmgill
Crag

Gregory
Band

Long
Gill Head

Burnt
Moor

Little
Ing Farm

Hangingstone
Scar

CA17

DL11

6

Wide
Busk Hole

Black
Fell Moss

Eden
Springs

Brunt
Stones

Mease
Hills

Leaden
Haw

B6259

Howe
Top

Lady's
Pillar

Great Sleddale Beck

99

Falonry
Ctr

Raven's
Nest

Black Fell
Moss

Hugh
Seat Mea

Great Sled
Dale

Adam Gill
Scar

Ing Heads

Corry
Hole End

Rowantree
Cove

Currick

Burnt
Crag

Red Mea
Hole

Long
Scar

5

Hanging
Lund

Black
Blote Hill

High
Rigg

Black
Paddock

Red
Mea
Scriddles

Angram
Common

98

The
Riggs

Scarth of
Scaiths

Knoutberry
Currack

Long
Cove

High Rigg Well
(Chalybeate)

Little
Fell

West Gill
Head

Market
Place
Cairns

Daddymea
Edge

Sandy
Bottom

Low Rigg
Edge

4

Hellgill
Wold

Lunds
Fell

Little Fell
Brae

Little Fell
Well

Capley
Mea Hags

Cairn

Short
Moss Hags

Hell Gill Beck

Outer
Pike

Landlady
Well

Short
Moss

97

Cave

Pry
Hill

Sour
Hill

Black
Hill

Ure
Head

How
Mea

Capley
Mea

Lingy
Brae

Broadmea
Crag

Waterfall

Hell Gill
Bridge

Hell Gill
Grains

Sails

3

White
Birks Hill

Blue
Scar Hill

Jingling Sike
Cave

Red
Shaws

Lunds
Fell

Howmea
Bog

Round
Hill

Marl
Well

Abbotside
Common

Cotterdale
House
(cave)

Broad
Mea

Howmea
Brae

Wild Cat
Hole

Crooked
Rigg

Green
Bridge

Hell Gill
Crags

Long
Crags

Groove
Scar

Cotterdale
Common

East Gill

96

Ure
Crook

Copt
Hill

West
Side

West Gill

The High
Way

High
Hall

Swinsett
Edge

Jinglemea
Bog

How Beck
Bridge

West
End

LA10

Grass
Gill Crags

DL8

Swinsett
Wells

2

Cave

Ling
Hills

River Ure

High
Way

Calf
Moss

Lambfold
Crags

Bubble
Hill

Benton
Close

Shaw
Paddock

95

Beck Side
Pasture

Shaws

Long Cist
Shake Hole

Waterfall

Eller
Haw
Broken
Scar

Rowan
Tree Side

Beck
Side

Place
Farm

B6259

1

+

Cowshaw
Hill

High
Dyke

Dove Gill
Hill

Dry Gill
Head

Gate
Hole

Dandry
Mire

East
Side

Shortlick
Hill

Lunds

Tarn
Hill

Waterfall

West
Ing Rigg

Stang
Rigg

94

West
Close

78 · **A** · 79 · **B** · 80 · **C** · 81 · **D** · 82 · **E** · 83 · **F**

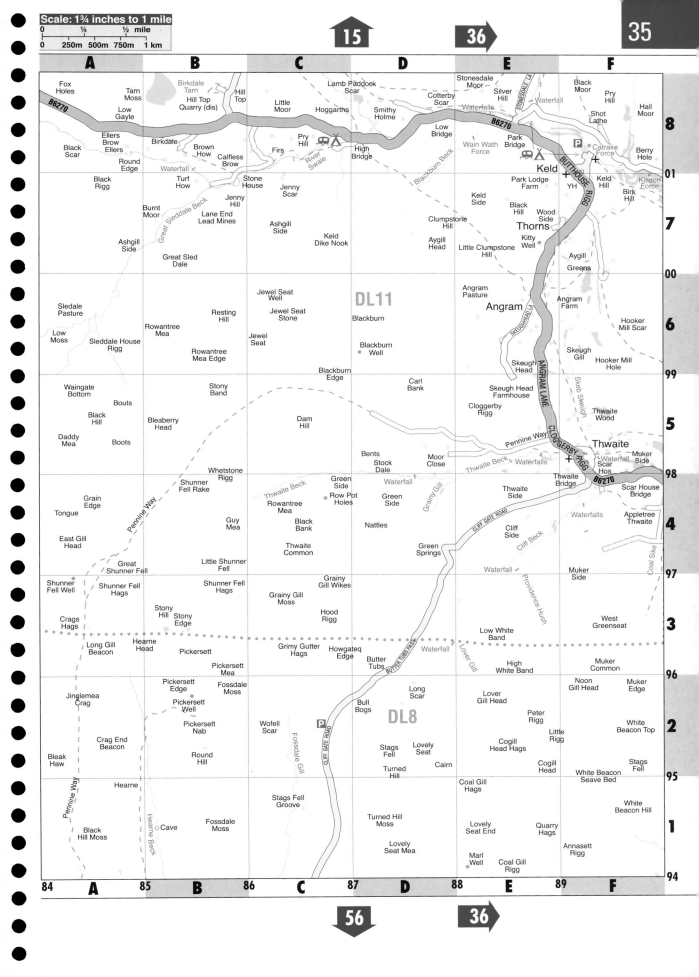

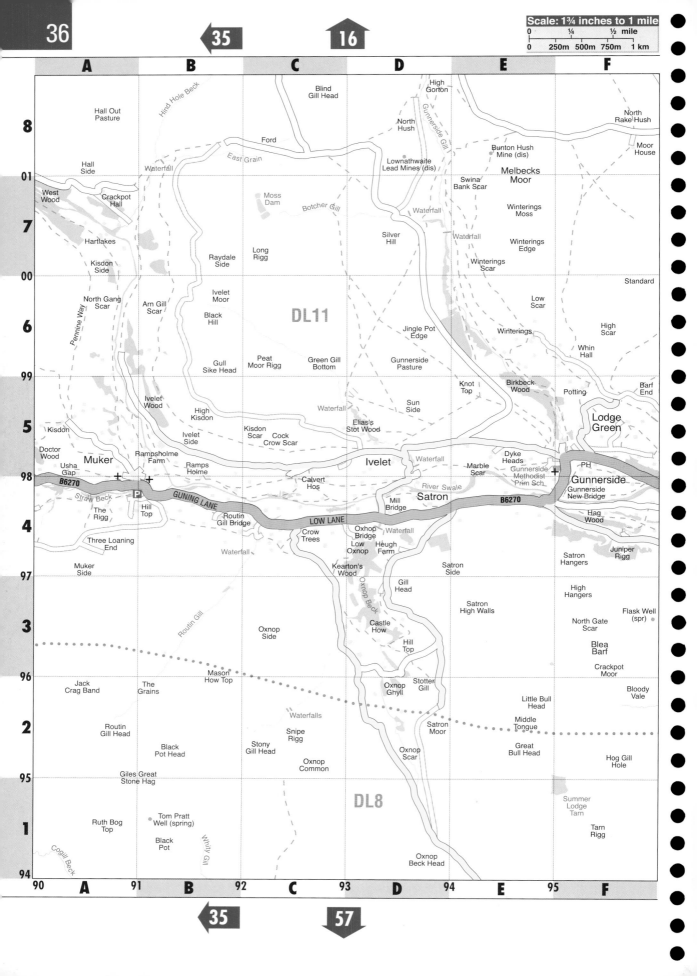

A   B   C   D   E   F

8

01

7

00

6

99

5

98

4

97

3

96

2

95

1

94

Hall Out
Pasture

Hind Hole Beck

Blind
Gill Head

High
Gorton

North
Rake Hush

Ford

North
Hush

Lownathwaite
Lead Mines (dis)

Bunton Hush
Mine (dis)

Moor
House

Hall
Side

East Grain

Waterfall

Melbecks
Moor

West
Wood

Crackpot
Hall

Moss
Dam

Botcher Gill

Swina
Bank Scar

Winterings
Moss

Hartlakes

Silver
Hill

Waterfall

Winterings
Edge

Waterfall

Kisdon
Side

Raydale
Side

Long
Rigg

Winterings
Scar

North Gang
Scar

Arn Gill
Scar

Ivelet
Moor

DL11

Jingle Pot
Edge

Low
Scar

Standard

Pennine Way

Black
Hill

Winterings

High
Scar

Whin
Hall

Gull
Sike Head

Peat
Moor Rigg

Green Gill
Bottom

Gunnerside
Pasture

Knot
Top

Birkbeck
Wood

Potting

Barf
End

Ivelet
Wood

High
Kisdon

Kisdon
Scar

Cock
Crow Scar

Sun
Side

Elias's
Stot Wood

Waterfall

Lodge
Green

Kisdon

Ivelet
Side

Doctor
Wood

Muker

Rampsholme
Farm

Ramps
Holme

Ivelet

Waterfall

Marble
Scar

Dyke
Heads

Gunnerside
Methodist
Prim Sch

PH

Gunnerside

Usha
Gap

B6270

Calvert
Hos

River Swale

Satron

B6270

Gunnerside
New Bridge

Straw Beck

GUNING LANE

Mill
Bridge

Hag
Wood

The
Rigg

Hill
Top

Routin
Gill Bridge

LOW LANE

Crow
Trees

Oxhop
Bridge

Waterfall

Satron
Hangers

Juniper
Rigg

Three Loaning
End

Low
Oxnop

Heugh
Farm

Muker
Side

Waterfall

Kearton's
Wood

Gill
Head

Satron
Side

High
Hangers

Gill
Head

Satron
High Walls

North Gate
Scar

Flask Well
(spr)

Routin Gill

Oxnop
Side

Castle
How

Hill
Top

Blea
Barf

Mason
How Top

Crackpot
Moor

Jack
Crag Band

The
Grains

Stotter
Gill

Oxnop
Ghyll

Little Bull
Head

Bloody
Vale

Waterfalls

Middle
Tongue

Routin
Gill Head

Snipe
Rigg

Stony
Gill Head

Satron
Moor

Great
Bull Head

Hog Gill
Hole

Black
Pot Head

Oxnop
Common

Oxnop
Scar

Giles Great
Stone Hag

DL8

Summer
Lodge
Tarn

Ruth Bog
Top

Tom Pratt
Well (spring)

Tarn
Rigg

Black
Pot

Whitly Gill

Cogill Beck

Oxnop
Beck Head

A   B   C   D   E   F

90   91   92   93   94   95

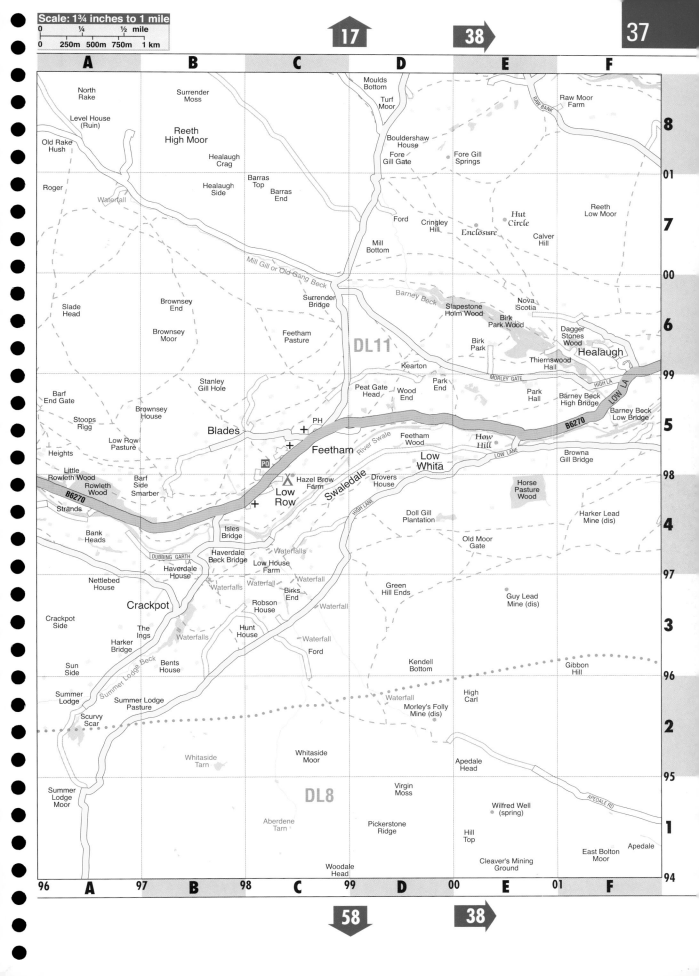

A   B   C   D   E   F

North Rake

Surrender Moss

Level House (Ruin)

Reeth High Moor

8

Old Rake Hush

Healaugh Crag

Bouldershaw House

Raw Moor Farm

RAW BANK

Roger

Healaugh Side

Barras Top

Barras End

Fore Gill Gate

Fore Gill Springs

01

Waterfall

Ford

Cringley Hill

Enclosure

Hut Circle

Reeth Low Moor

7

Slade Head

Brownsey End

Mill Bottom

Calver Hill

Mill Gill or Old-Gang Beck

00

Surrender Bridge

Barney Beck

Slapestone Holm Wood

Nova Scotia

Brownsey Moor

Feetham Pasture

Birk Park Wood

Dagger Stones Wood

6

DL11

Birk Park

Thiernswood Hall

Healaugh

Kearton

MORLEY GATE

Stanley Gill Hole

Peat Gate Head

Wood End

Park End

HIGH LA

LOW LA

99

Barf End Gate

Brownsey House

Park Hall

Barney Beck High Bridge

Stoops Rigg

Blades

PH

Low Row Pasture

Feetham

River Swale

Feetham Wood

How Hill

B6270

Barney Beck Low Bridge

5

Heights

LOW LANE

Browna Gill Bridge

Little Rowleth Wood

PO

Low Whita

98

B6270

Rowleth Wood

Barf Side

Smarber

Hazel Brow Farm

Swaledale

Drovers House

Horse Pasture Wood

Strands

Low Row

Bank Heads

Isles Bridge

HIGH LANE

Doll Gill Plantation

Harker Lead Mine (dis)

4

DUBBING GARTH LA

Haverdale Beck Bridge

Low House Farm

Old Moor Gate

Nettlebed House

Haverdale House

Waterfalls

97

Waterfall

Waterfall

Crackpot

Birks End

Green Hill Ends

Guy Lead Mine (dis)

3

Crackpot Side

The Ings

Robson House

Hunt House

Waterfall

Kendell Bottom

Gibbon Hill

Harker Bridge

Waterfalls

Ford

96

Sun Side

Bents House

Summer Lodge Beck

Waterfall

High Carl

2

Summer Lodge

Summer Lodge Pasture

Morley's Folly Mine (dis)

Scurvy Scar

Apedale Head

APEDALE RD

95

Summer Lodge Moor

Whitaside Tarn

Whitaside Moor

Virgin Moss

Wilfred Well (spring)

DL8

Hill Top

1

Aberdene Tarn

Pickerstone Ridge

Cleaver's Mining Ground

East Bolton Moor

Apedale

Woodale Head

94

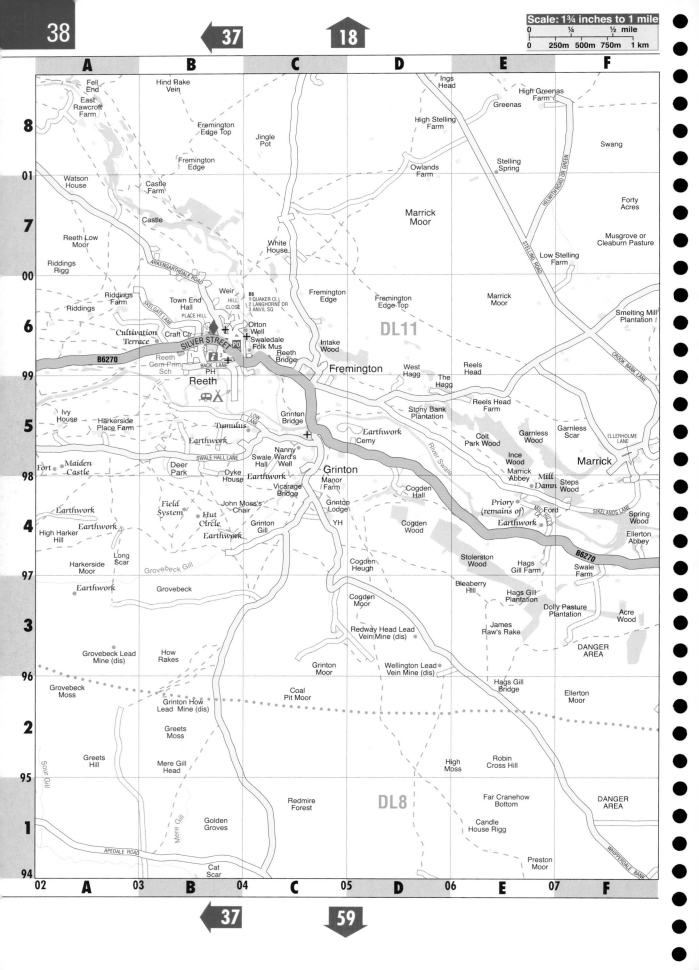

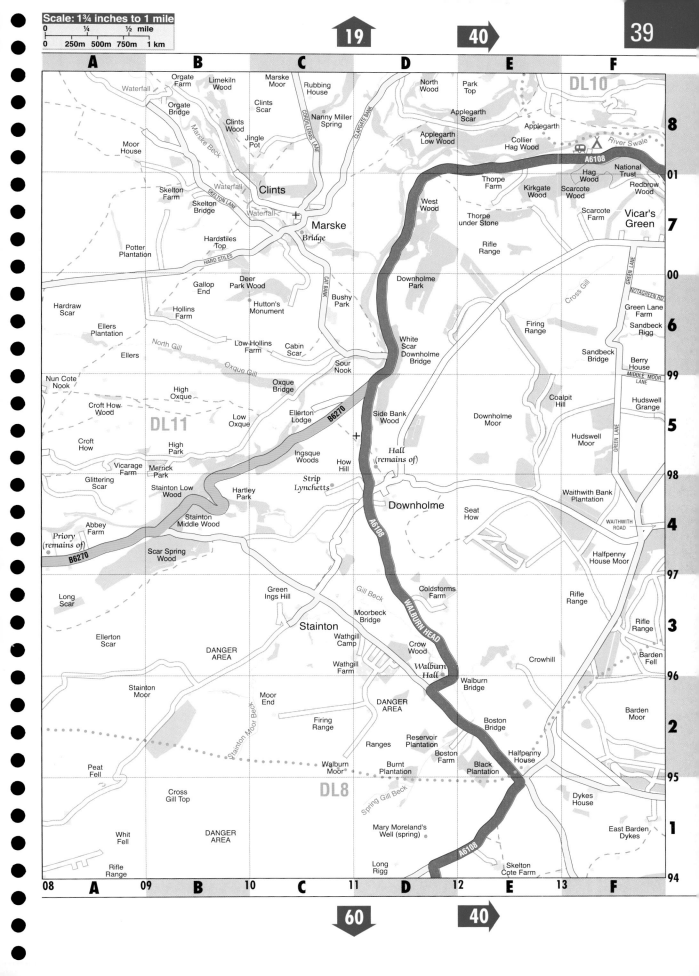

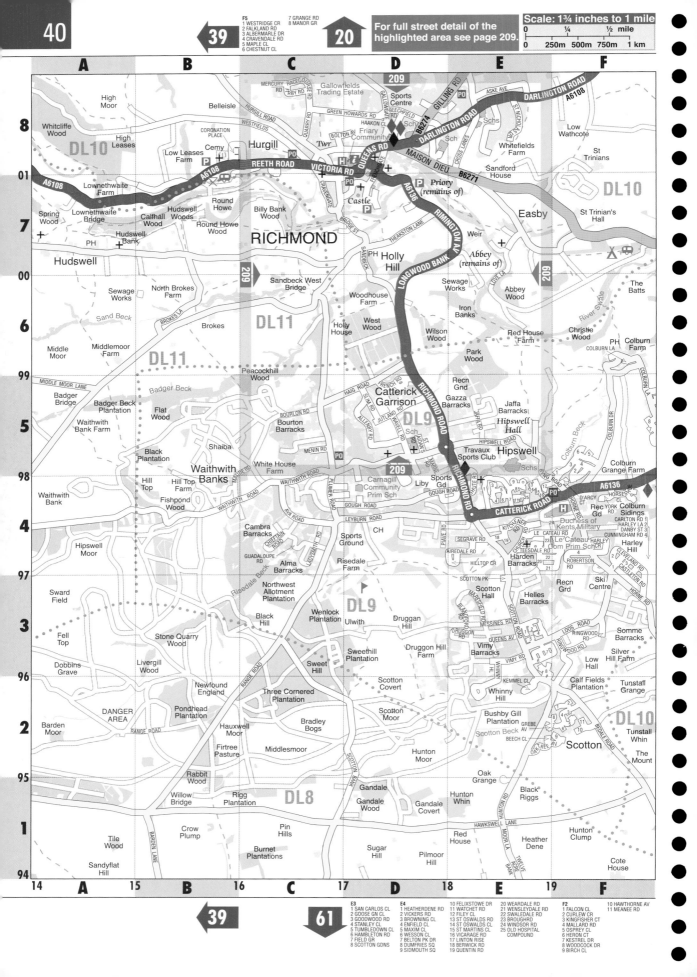

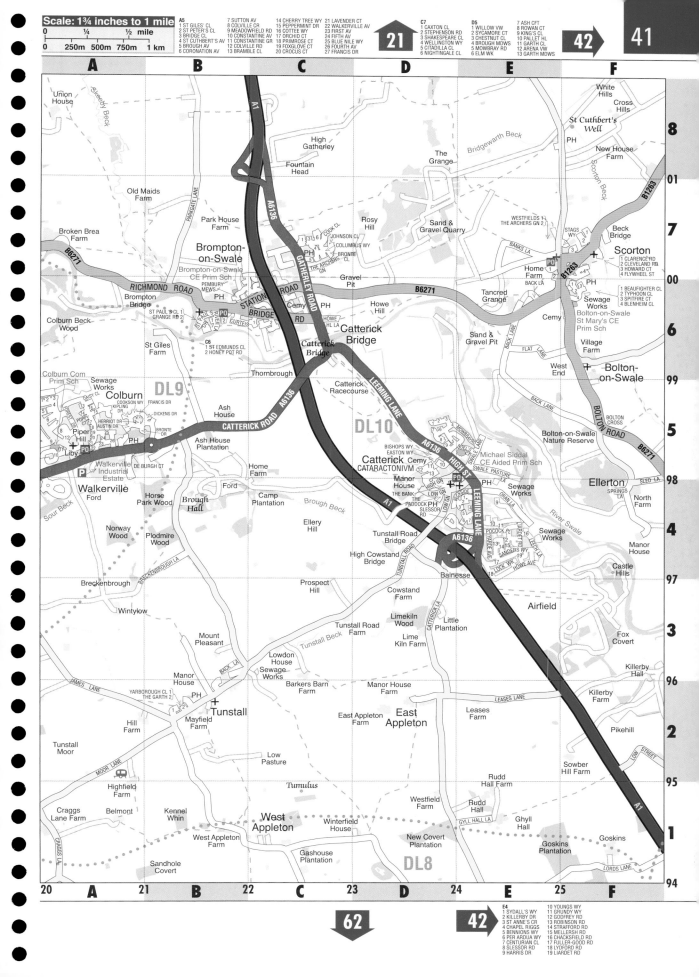

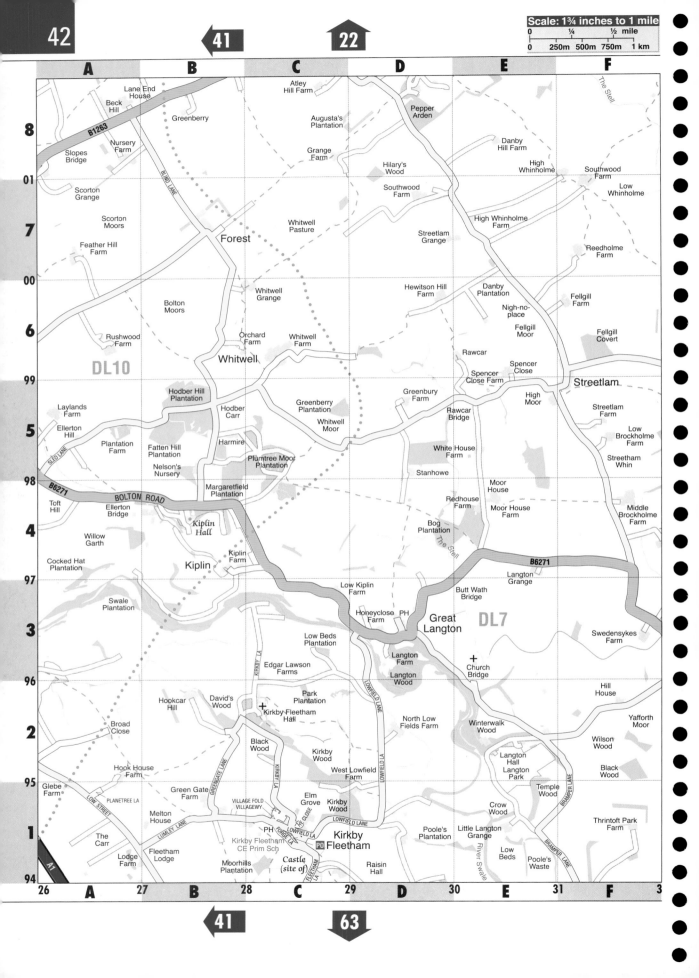

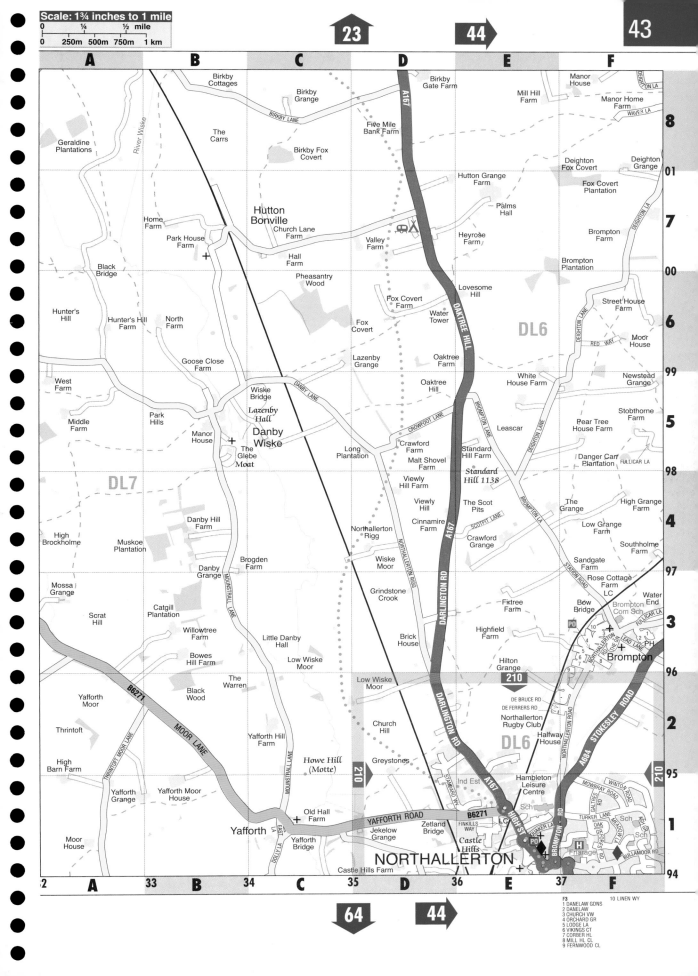

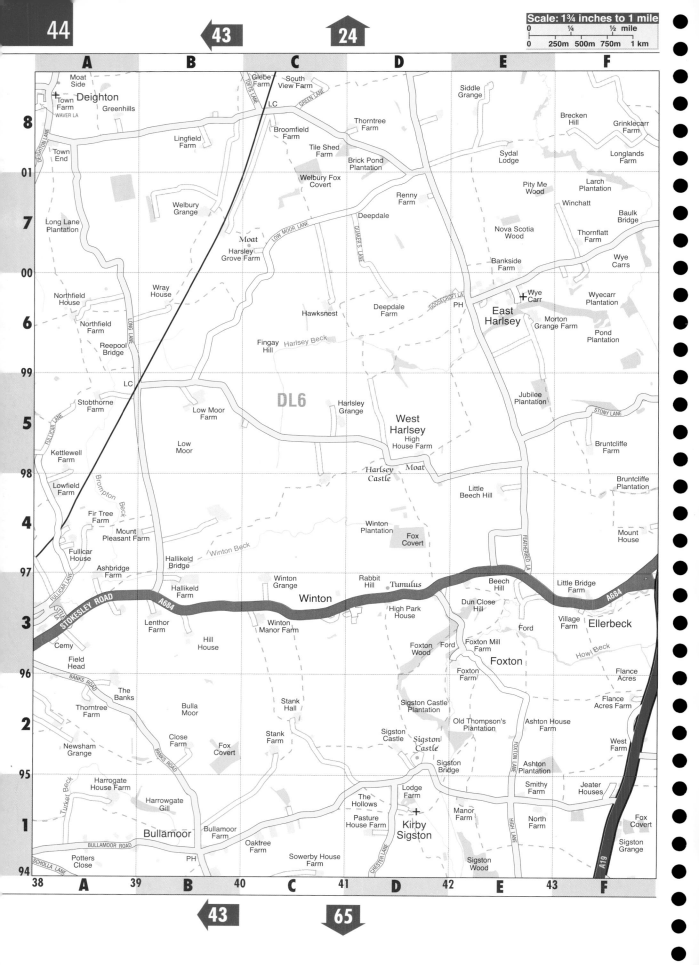

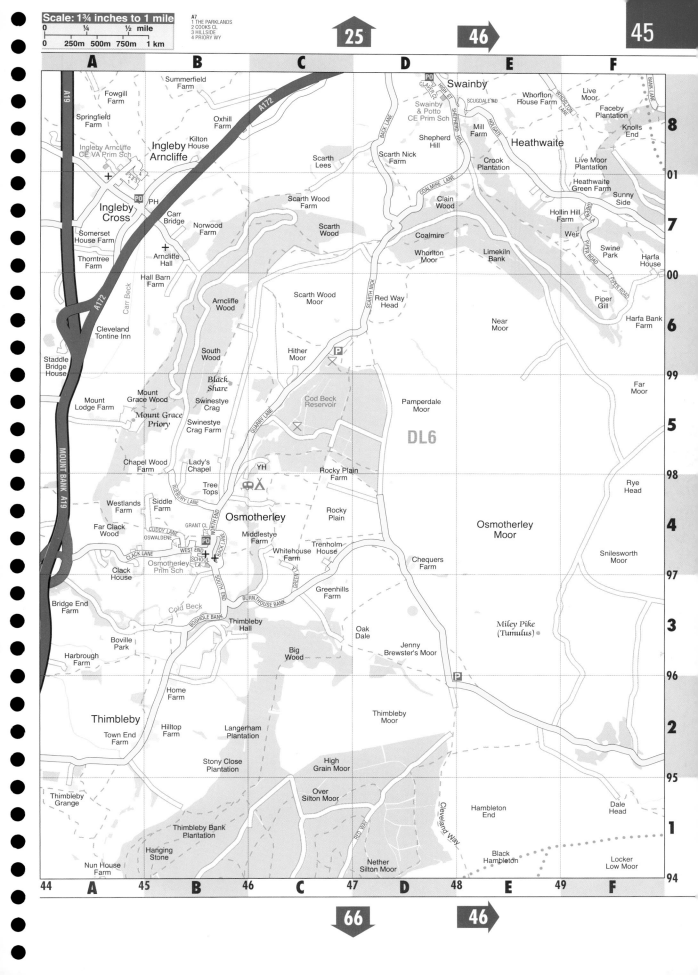

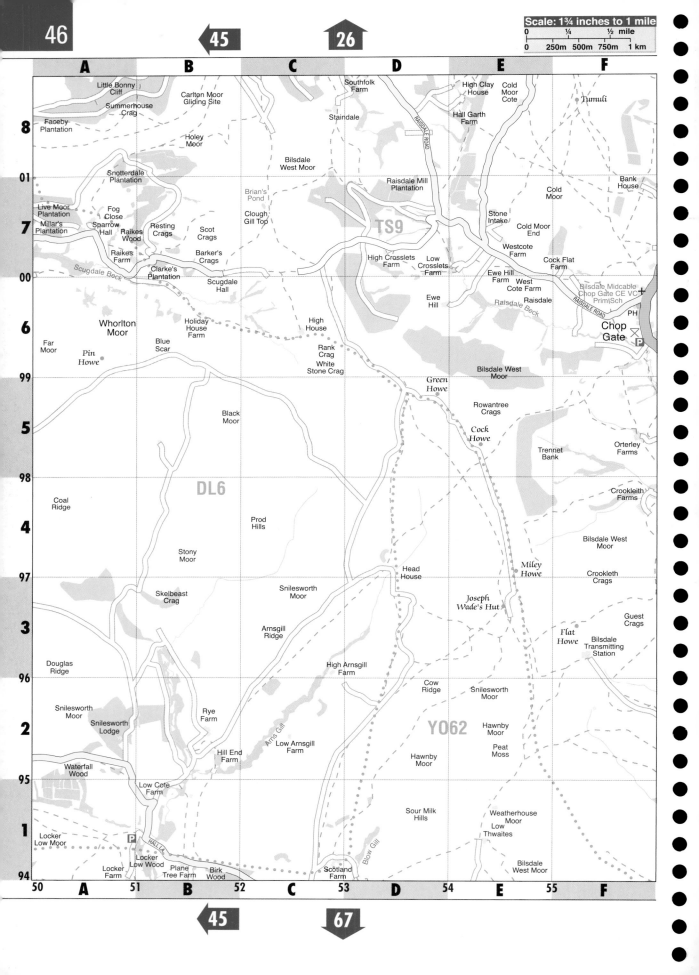

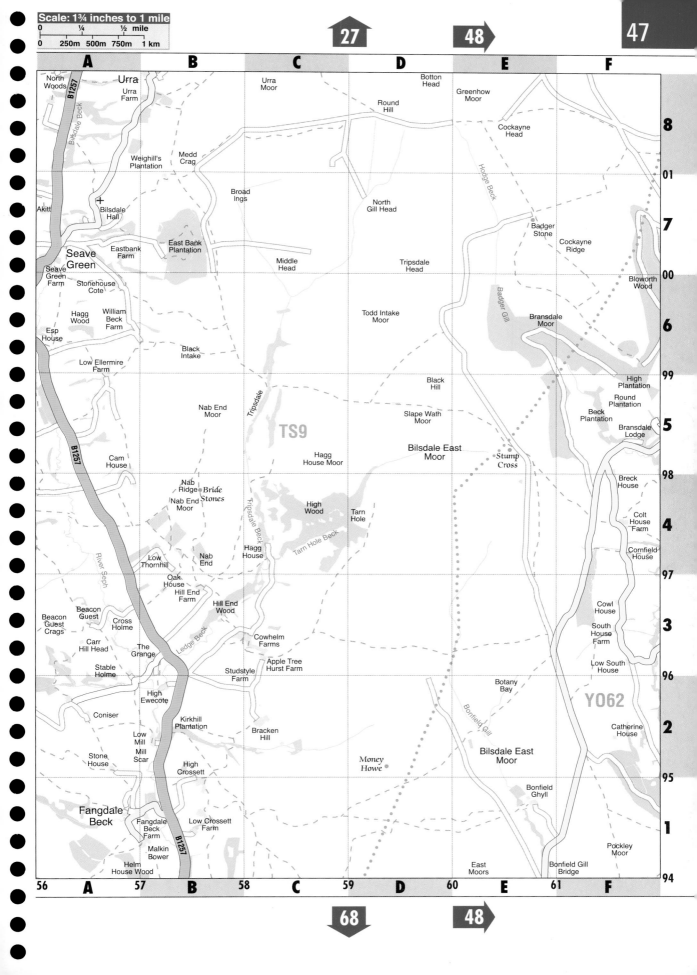

Scale: 1¾ inches to 1 mile

0   ¼   ½   mile
0   250m 500m 750m 1 km

North Woods
Urra
Urra Farm
B1257
Bilsdale Beck

Urra Moor

Botton Head

Greenhow Moor

8

Weighill's Plantation
Medd Crag

Round Hill

Cockayne Head

01

Akitt
Bilsdale Hall
Broad Ings

North Gill Head

Badger Stone
Cockayne Ridge

7

Seave Green
Eastbank Farm
East Bank Plantation

Middle Head

Tripsdale Head

Bloworth Wood

00

Seave Green Farm
Stonehouse Cote
Hagg Wood
William Beck Farm

Todd Intake Moor

Badger Gill
Bransdale Moor

6

Esp House
Black Intake

Low Ellermire Farm

Black Hill

High Plantation

99

Nab End Moor
Tripsdale
TS9
Slape Wath Moor

Round Plantation
Beck Plantation

5

Cam House
Hagg House Moor

Bilsdale East Moor
Stump Cross

Bransdale Lodge

98

Nab Ridge
Bride Stones
Nab End Moor
Tripsdale Beck
High Wood
Tarn Hole

Breck House

Colt House Farm
Cornfield House

4

River Seph
Low Thornhill
Nab End
Hagg House
Tarn Hole Beck

97

Oak House
Hill End Farm
Hill End Wood

Cowl House

Beacon Guest Crags
Beacon Guest
Cross Holme
Ledge Beck
Cowhelm Farms

South House Farm

3

Carr Hill Head
The Grange
Apple Tree Hurst Farm

Low South House

96

Stable Holme
Studstyle Farm

Botany Bay
YO62

High Ewecote
Coniser
Kirkhill Plantation
Bracken Hill

Catherine House

2

Low Mill
Mill Scar
Stone House
High Crossett

Money Howe

Bilsdale East Moor

95

Fangdale Beck
Fangdale Beck Farm
Low Crossett Farm

Bonfield Ghyll

Bonfield Gill

1

Malkin Bower
B1257

East Moors
Bonfield Gill Bridge

Pockley Moor

Helm House Wood

94

56   A   57   B   58   C   59   D   60   E   61   F

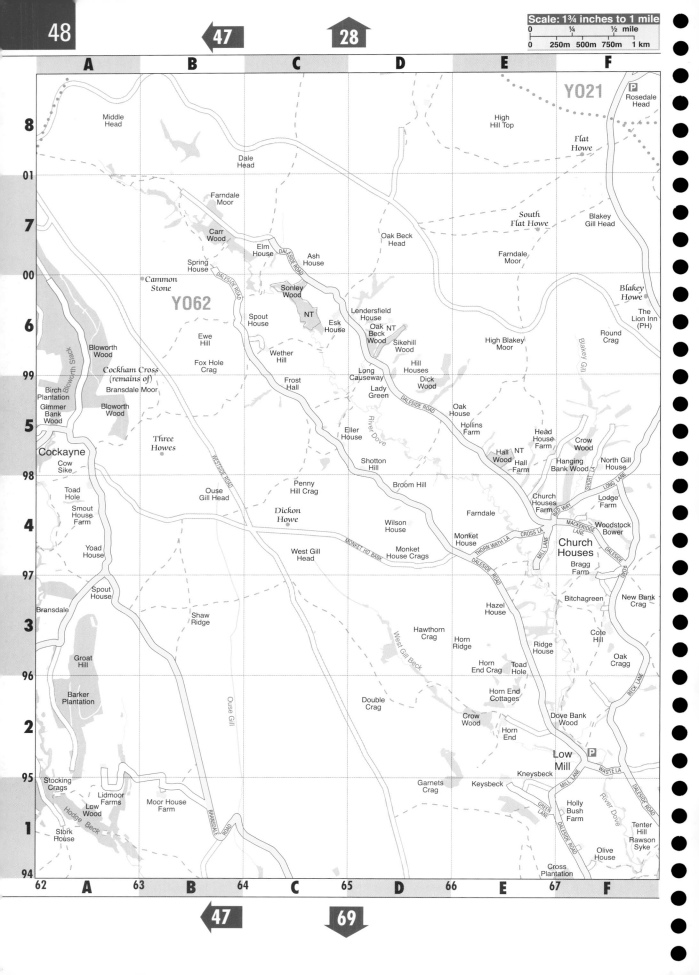

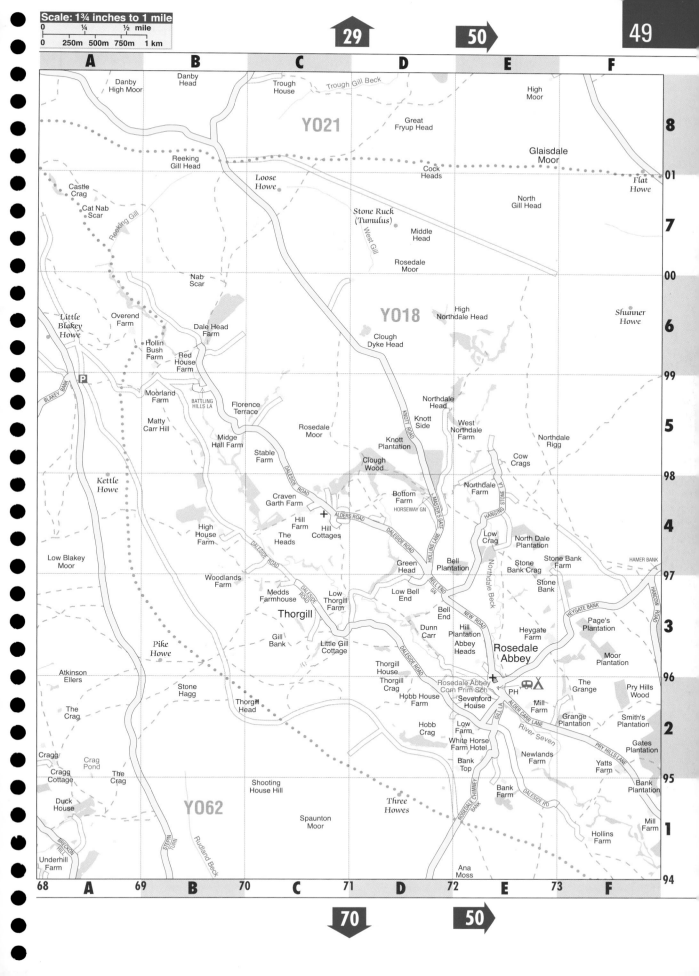

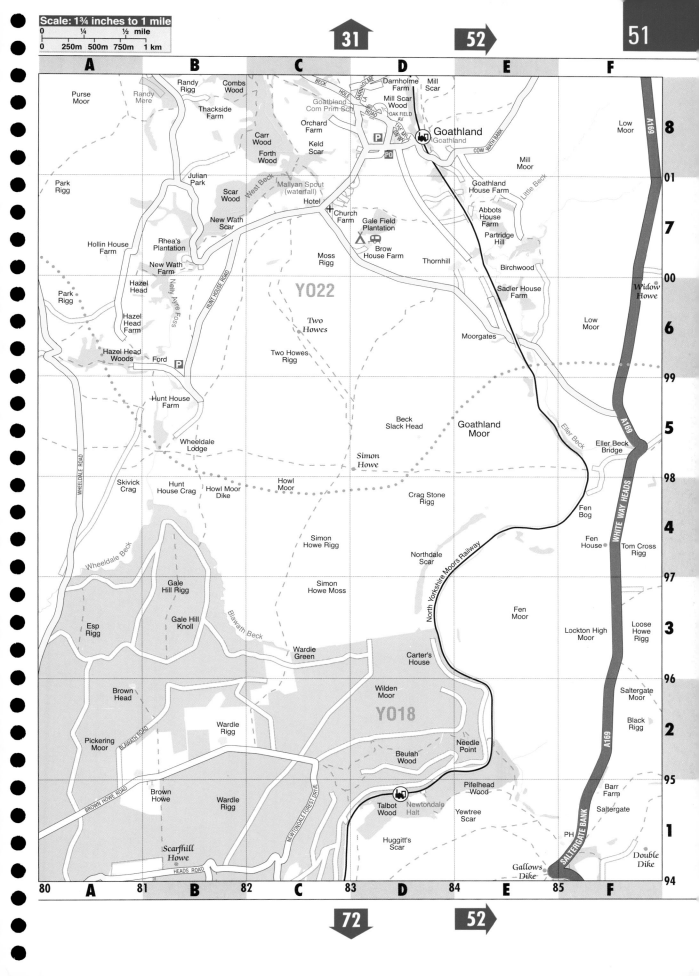

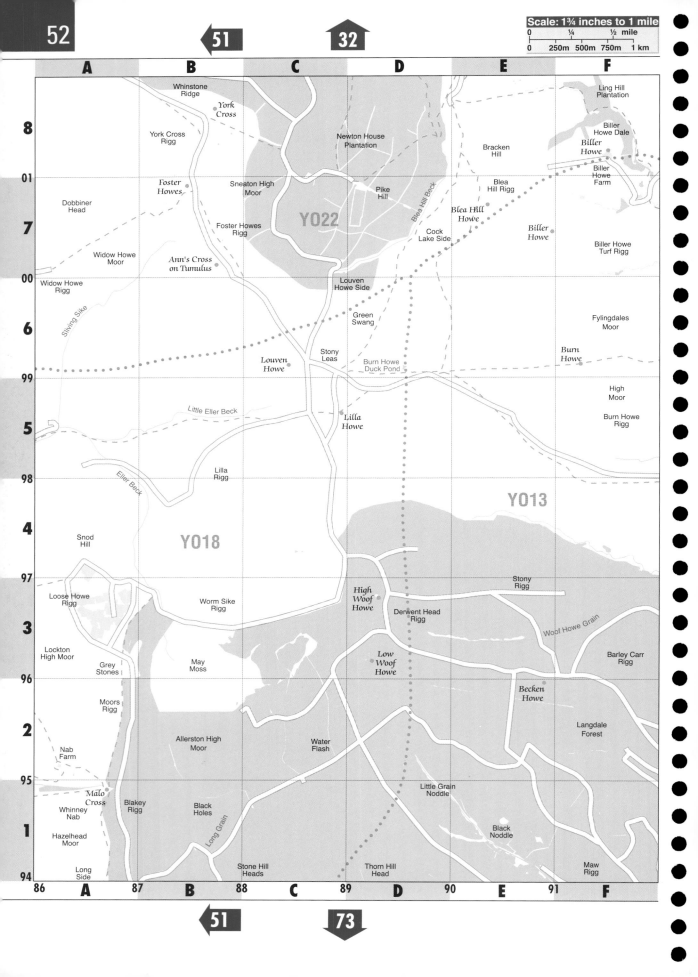

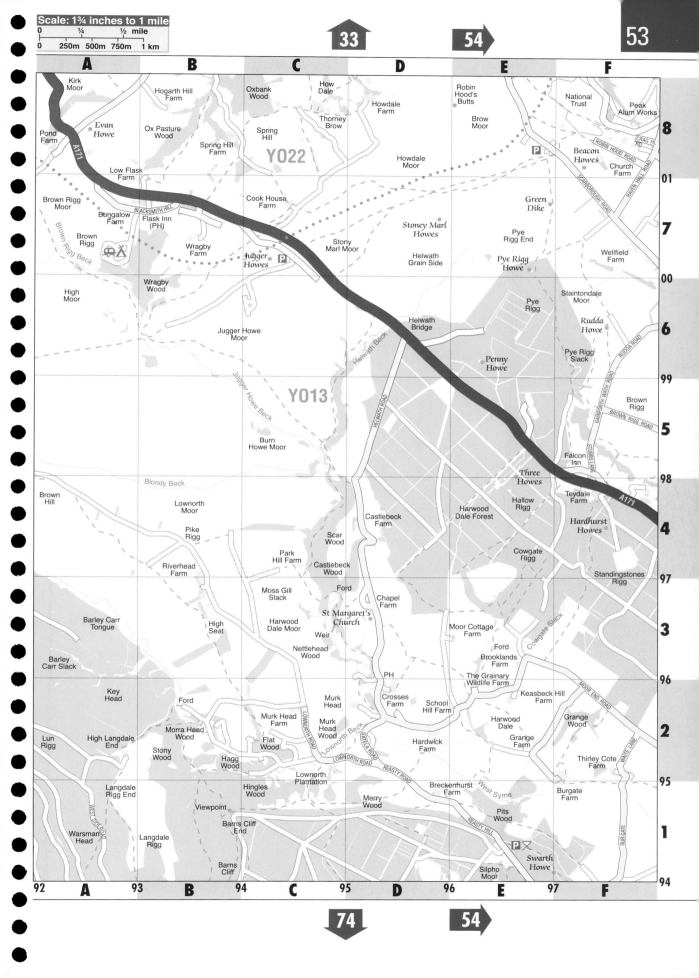

Scale: 1¾ inches to 1 mile
0   ¼   ½ mile
0 250m 500m 750m 1 km

A B C D E F

Old Peak or South Cheek

02

Ravenscar

Blea Wyke Point

8

THE AVG
HAMMOND RD
MARINE ESP
THE CRES
STATION ROAD
CLIFF RD
STATION RD
LORING RD
CHURCH ROAD
Church Rd Farm

01

Common Cliff

Bent Rigg Farm

7

Bent Rigg

BENT RIGG LANE

Danesdale Farm

WAR DIKE LANE

00

Bell Hill Farm

Grange Farm

BLOODY HILL

6

Rudda

RUDDA RD

Sandybed Wood

Prospect House Farm

Meeting House Farm

99

Church Farm

Wellington Lodge Llamas

Bees Nest Farm

Petard Point

TOFTA ROAD
PRIOR WATH ROAD

White Hall Farm

Plane Tree Farm

Cleveland Way

Tofta Farm

Rigg Hall

5

BROWN RIGG RD
PRIOR WATH RD

Staintondale Shire Horse Farm

Staintondale

Rigg Hall Farm

Island Farm

PH

PRIOR WATH RD

Shirehorse Centre

98

Crowdon

Quarry Farm

North Bridge End

White House Farm

Bridge Farm

DOWNDALE ROAD

Thorny Beck

Wyke Lodge

Whitestone Farm

Redhouse Farm

4

Hunter Howe

Cloughton Moor House

Hayburn Beck Farm

Hayburn Wyke

A171

HODGSON HILL

Nab End

Hayburn Wyke Hotel

97

Standingstones Rigg

RINGING KELD HILL

Cloughton Moor

NT

Hodgson Moor Plantation

YO13

CRAVEN'S HILL

3

Linglands Farm

Cloughton Woods

Rockwood Farm

The Hulleys

Newlands Farm

Caywood Plantation

Rodger Trod

96

Tongue Field Plantation

Gowland Farm

Cloughton Newlands

Sycarham Wood

Cloughton Plantations

Stone Dale Plantation

PH

MOOR END RD

GOWLAND LANE

TRATTLES HILL

HOOD LANE

2

Spring House Farm

Cloughton Woods

Little Moor Road

Greystone Farm

Sycarham Farm

Middle Part Farm

SALT PANS ROAD

Cloughton Wyke

95

Ellis Close Farm

HARWOOD DALE ROAD

Ripley's Farm

Little Moor

Moorside Farm

Court Green Farm

NEWLANDS LA

Hundale Point

Thirley Beck Farm

East Syme

HOLM HL WHITE WY WEST LA

Cloughton

1 COURT GREEN CL
2 LOCKWOOD CHASE

Cleveland Way

1

RIPLEY'S RD

Green Farming

PO

PH

Cloughton Fields Farm

Long Nab

Surgate Brow Plantation

RIPLEY'S ROAD

LITTLE MOOR CL 1
MOOR LA 2
BECK LA 3

A171

STATION LA

LINTON CL

94

98 A 99 B 00 C 01 D 02 E 03 F

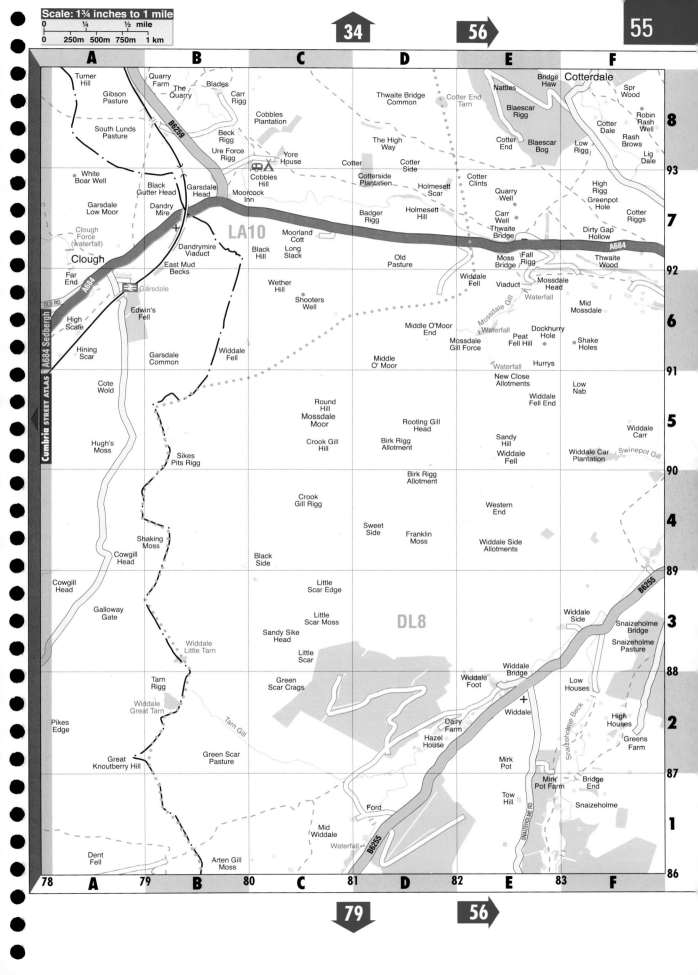

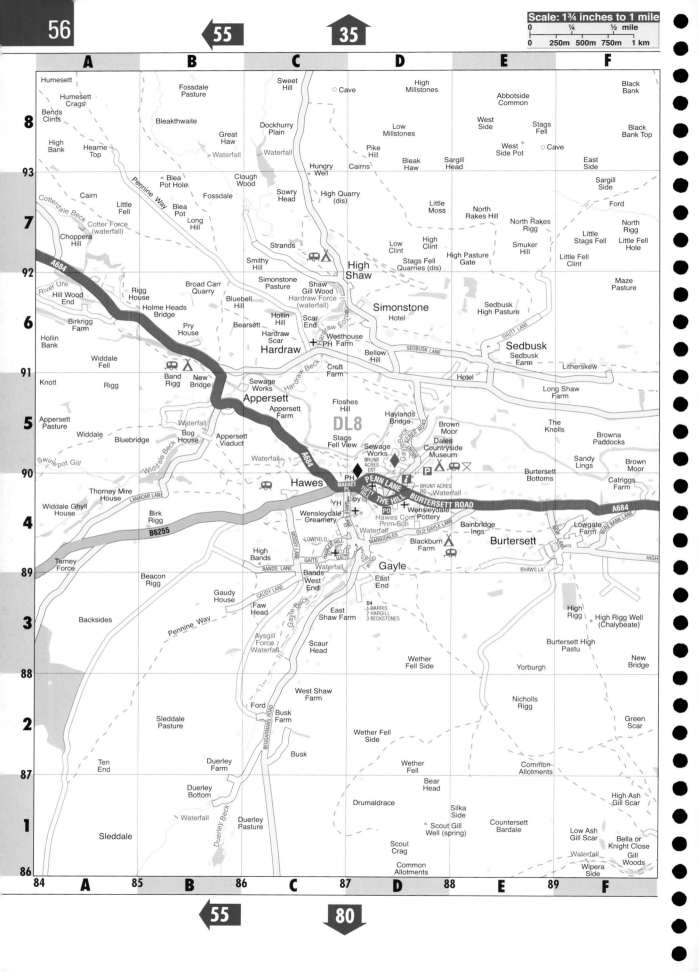

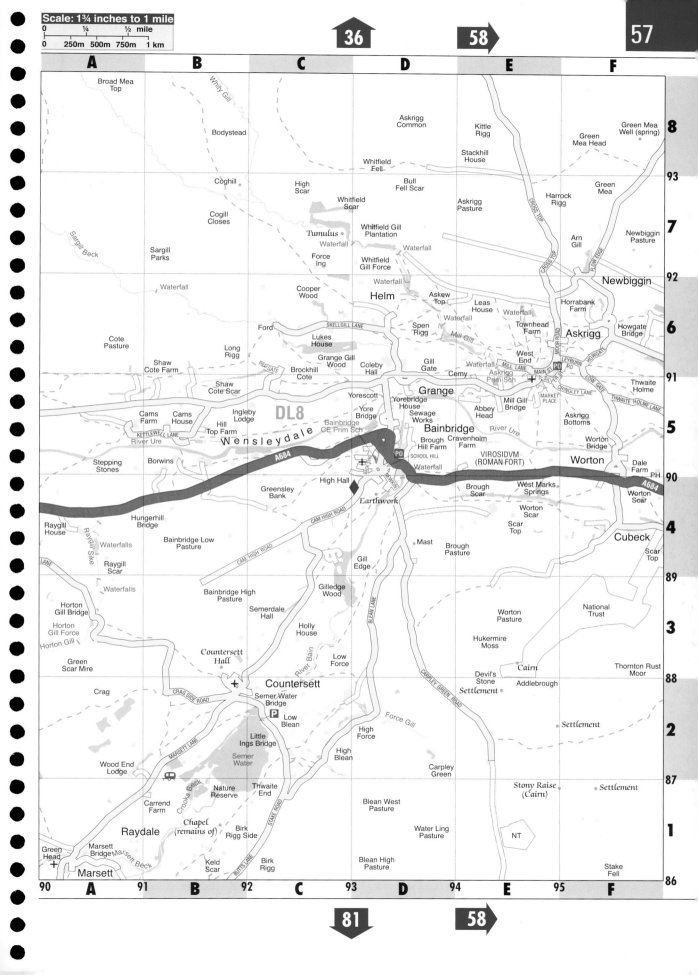

A   B   C   D   E   F

Broad Mea Top

Whitty Gill

Bodystead

Askrigg Common

Kittle Rigg

Green Mea Well (spring)   **8**

Green Mea Head

Whitfield Fell

Stackhill House

Coghill

High Scar

Whitfield Scar

Bull Fell Scar

Askrigg Pasture

Harrock Rigg

Green Mea   **93**

Cogill Closes

Tumulus

Whitfield Gill Plantation

Arn Gill

Newbiggin Pasture   **7**

Sargill Beck

Sargill Parks

Force Ing

Waterfall

Whitfield Gill Force

Waterfall

CROSS TOP

FLOW EDGE

Newbiggin   **92**

Waterfall

Cooper Wood

Helm

Waterfall

Askew Top

Leas House

Waterfall

Townhead Farm

Horrabank Farm

Askrigg

Howgate Bridge   **6**

Cote Pasture

Ford

SKELLGILL LANE

Lukes House

Spen Rigg

Mill Gill

West End

MOOR ROAD

Shaw Cote Farm

REDGATE

Long Rigg

Grange Gill Wood

Coleby Hall

Gill Gate

Cemy

Waterfall

MILL LANE

Askrigg Prim Sch

Main St

PO

LEYBURN RD

Thwaite Holme   **91**

Shaw Cote Scar

Brockhill Cote

Yorescott

Grange

SILVE...

CRINGLEY LANE

LOW GATE

THWAITE HOLME LANE

DL8

Ingleby Lodge

Hill Top Farm

Yore Bridge

Yorebridge House

Bainbridge CE Prim Sch

Sewage Works

Abbey Head

Mill Gill Bridge

MARKET PLACE

Askrigg Bottoms

Worton Bridge   **5**

Cams House

Cams Farm

Wensleydale

Brough Hill Farm

Bainbridge

Cravenholm Farm

River Ure

Worton

Dale Farm

KETTLEWELL LANE

River Ure

PO

SCHOOL HILL

VIROSIDVM (ROMAN FORT)

PH

Stepping Stones

Borwins

A684

School Hill

BENNIM...

Waterfall

Brough Scar

West Marks Springs

A684   **90**

Raygill House

Hungerhill Bridge

Greensley Bank

High Hall

Earthwork

Worton Scar

Worton Scar

Cubeck

Worton Scar   **4**

Raygill Sike

LANE

Waterfalls

CAM HIGH ROAD

CAM HIGH ROAD

Gill Edge

Mast

Brough Pasture

Scar Top

Scar Top

Raygill Scar

Bainbridge Low Pasture

Waterfalls

Bainbridge High Pasture

Semerdale Hall

Gilledge Wood

BLEAN LANE

Worton Pasture

National Trust   **89**

Horton Gill Bridge

Holly House

Hukermire Moss   **3**

Horton Gill Force

Green Scar Mire

Countersett Hall

River Bain

Low Force

CARPLEY GREEN ROAD

Devil's Stone

Cairn

Addlebrough

Settlement

Thornton Rust Moor

Horton Gill

Crag

CRAG SIDE ROAD

Countersett

Semer Water Bridge

P

Low Blean

High Force

Force Gill

Settlement   **88**

Settlement   **2**

Wood End Lodge

MARSETT LANE

Crooks Beck

Little Ings Bridge

Semer Water

High Blean

Carpley Green

Stony Raise (Cairn)

Settlement   **87**

Carrend Farm

Nature Reserve

Thwaite End

STAKE ROAD

Blean West Pasture

Water Ling Pasture

NT   **1**

Raydale

Chapel (remains of)

Birk Rigg Side

BUTTS LANE

Keld Scar

Birk Rigg

Blean High Pasture

Stake Fell

Green Head

Marsett Bridge

Marsett Beck

Marsett   **86**

90   A   91   B   92   C   93   D   94   E   95   F

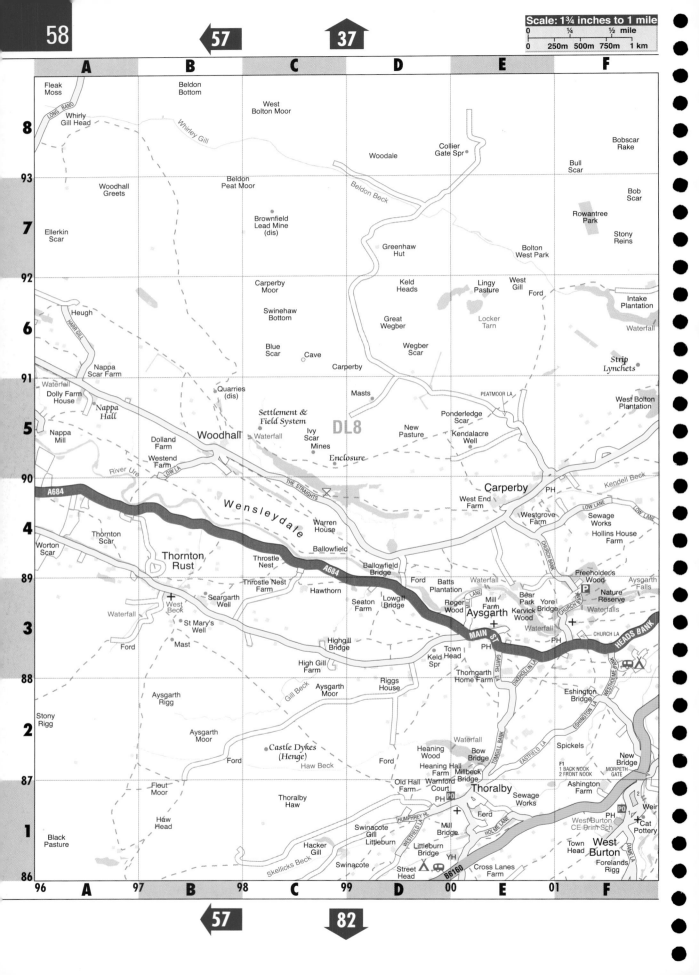

Scale: 1¾ inches to 1 mile

0   ¼   ½   mile
0   250m   500m   750m   1 km

Column A

Fleak Moss
Whirly Gill Head
LONG BAND
Whirley Gill
Woodhall Greets
Ellerkin Scar
Heugh
HARR GILL
Nappa Scar Farm
Waterfall
Dolly Farm House
Nappa Hall
Nappa Mill
Worton Scar
Black Pasture

Column B

Beldon Bottom
Beldon Peat Moor
Brownfield Lead Mine (dis)
Carperby Moor
Swinehaw Bottom
Blue Scar
Cave
Quarries (dis)
Settlement & Field System
Woodhall
Waterfall
Dolland Farm
Westend Farm
LOW LA
Thornton Scar
River Ure
Thornton Rust
Throstle Nest
Throstle Nest Farm
West Beck
Seargarth Well
St Mary's Well
Waterfall
Mast
Ford
Highgill Bridge
High Gill Farm
Aysgarth Rigg
Aysgarth Moor
Stony Rigg
Aysgarth Moor
Ford
Castle Dykes (Henge)
Haw Beck
Fleut Moor
Thoralby Haw
Haw Head
Hacker Gill
Skellicks Beck
Swinacote

Column C

West Bolton Moor
Woodale
Beldon Beck
Ivy Scar Mines
Enclosure
Hawthorn
Ballowfield
Ballowfield Bridge
Seaton Farm
Gill Beck
Riggs House
Ford
Swinacote Gill Littleburn
Littleburn Bridge
Street Head
YH

Column D

Collier Gate Spr
Greenhaw Hut
Keld Heads
Great Wegber
Carperby
Masts
New Pasture
DL8
Wensleydale
THE STRAIGHTS
Warren House
Lowgill Bridge
Ford
Batts Plantation
Roger Wood
Keld Spr
Town Head
Thorngarth Home Farm
Heaning Wood
Bow Bridge
Heaning Hall Farm
Millbeck
Warnford Court
Old Hall Farm
Mill Bridge
PH
Cross Lanes Farm
B6160

Column E

Lingy Pasture
West Gill Ford
Locker Tarn
Wegber Scar
PEATMOOR LA
Ponderledge Scar
Kendalacre Well
Carperby
West End Farm
Westgrove Farm
PH
Waterfall
Bear Park
Mill Farm
Kervick Wood
Aysgarth
Yore Bridge
Waterfall
PH
MAIN ST
GARTHS LA
DINHOLLIN LA
CHURCH LA
Waterfall
Waterfall
Thoralby
Sewage Works
Ferd
HOLME LANE
TONGILL BANK
EASTFIELD LA
Spickels
WESTHOLME BANK
ESHINGTON LA

Column F

Bobscar Rake
Bull Scar
Bob Scar
Rowantree Park
Stony Reins
Intake Plantation
Waterfall
Strip Lynchets
West Bolton Plantation
Kendell Beck
Low Lane
Low Lane
Sewage Works
Hollins House Farm
Freeholder's Wood
Aysgarth Falls
Nature Reserve
Waterfalls
HEADS BANK
CHURCH LA
PH
Eshington Bridge
New Bridge
MORPETH GATE
F1
1 BACK NOOK
2 FRONT NOOK
Ashington Farm
Weir
West Burton CE Prim Sch
PH
PO
Cat Pottery
Town Head
West Burton
Forelands Rigg
DALE LA

A684

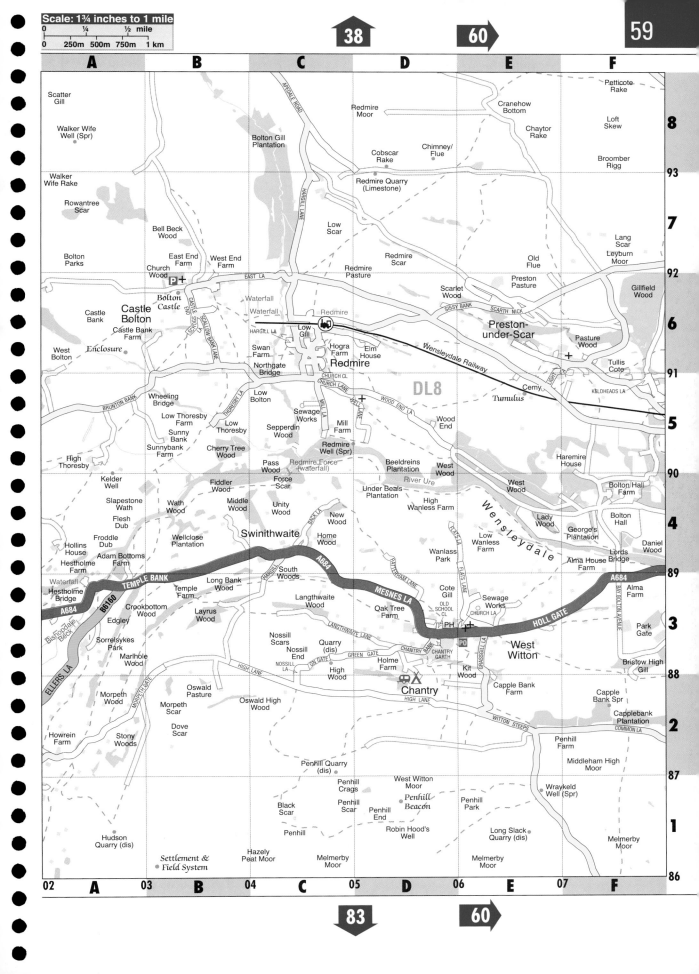

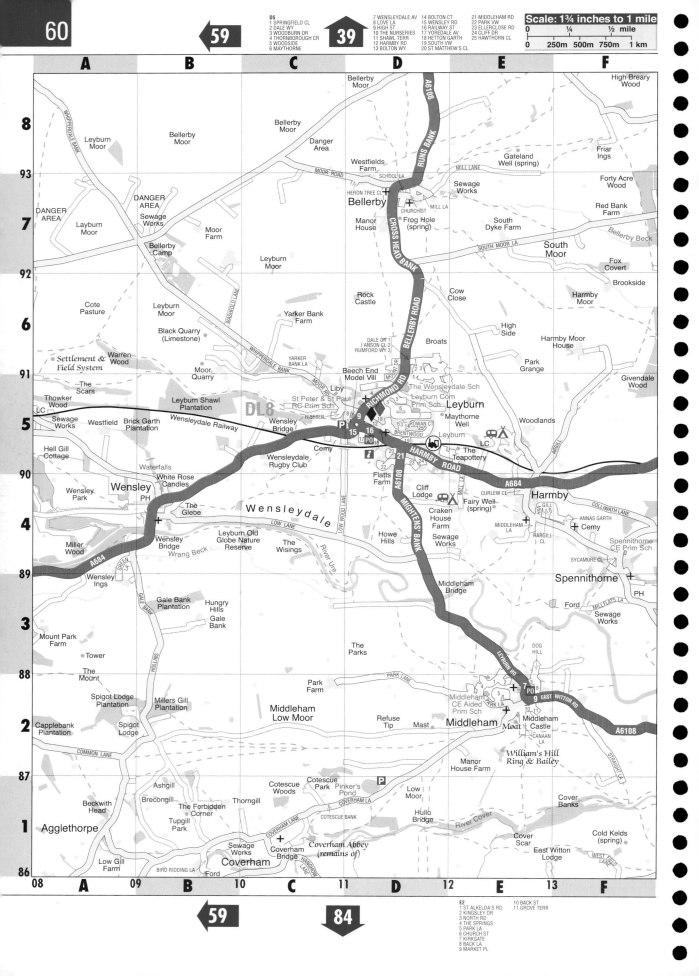

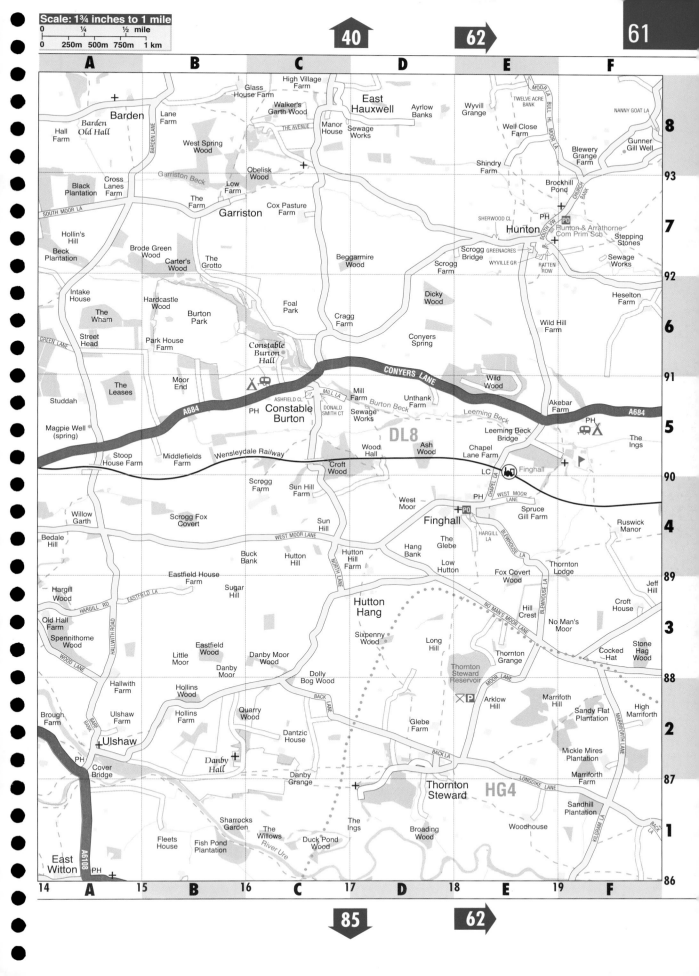

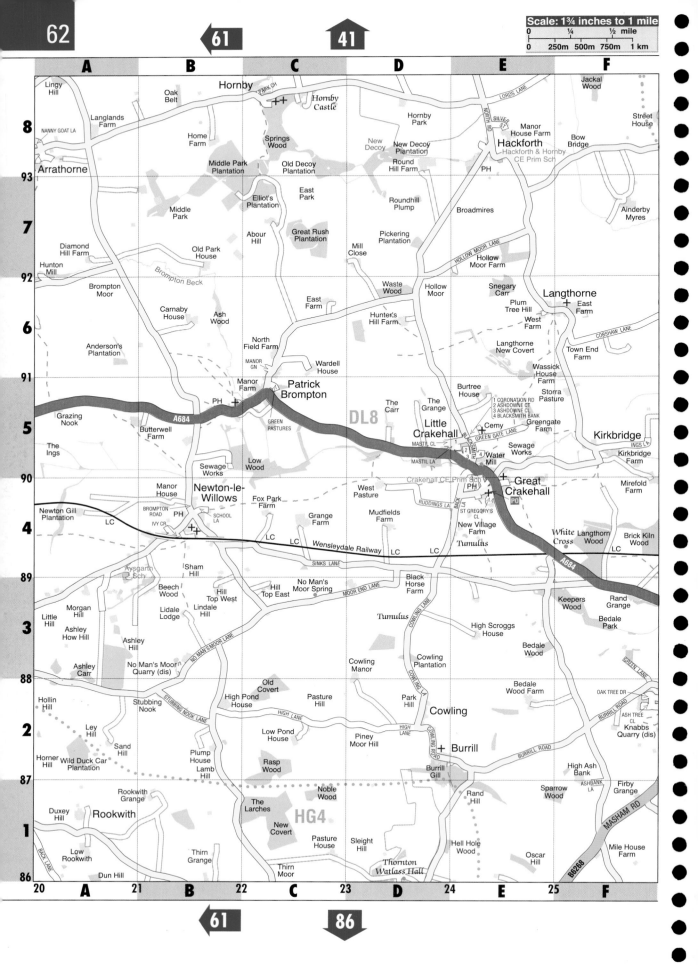

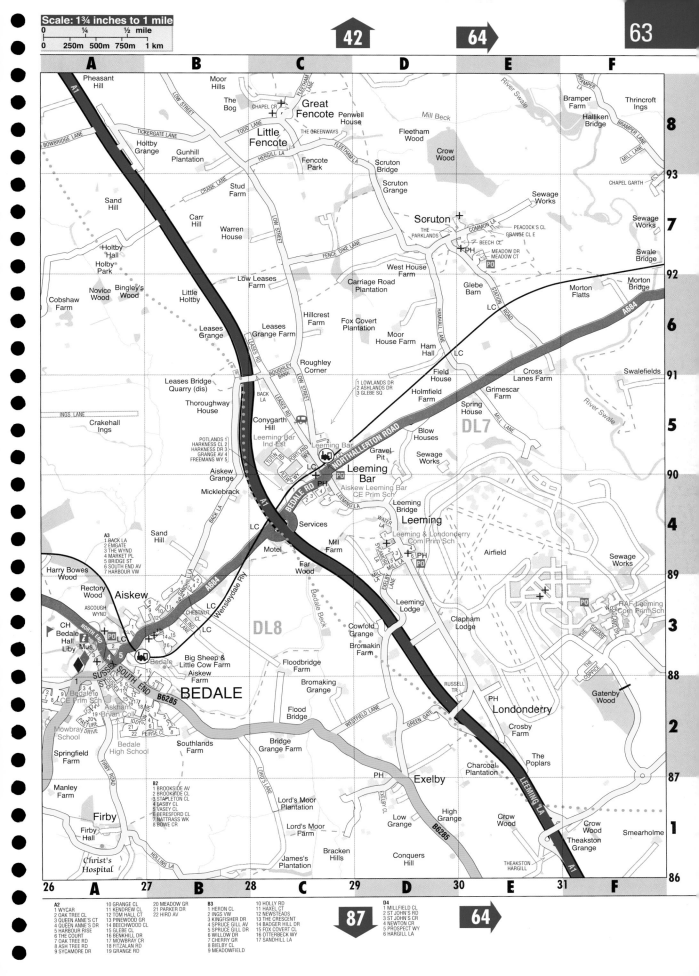

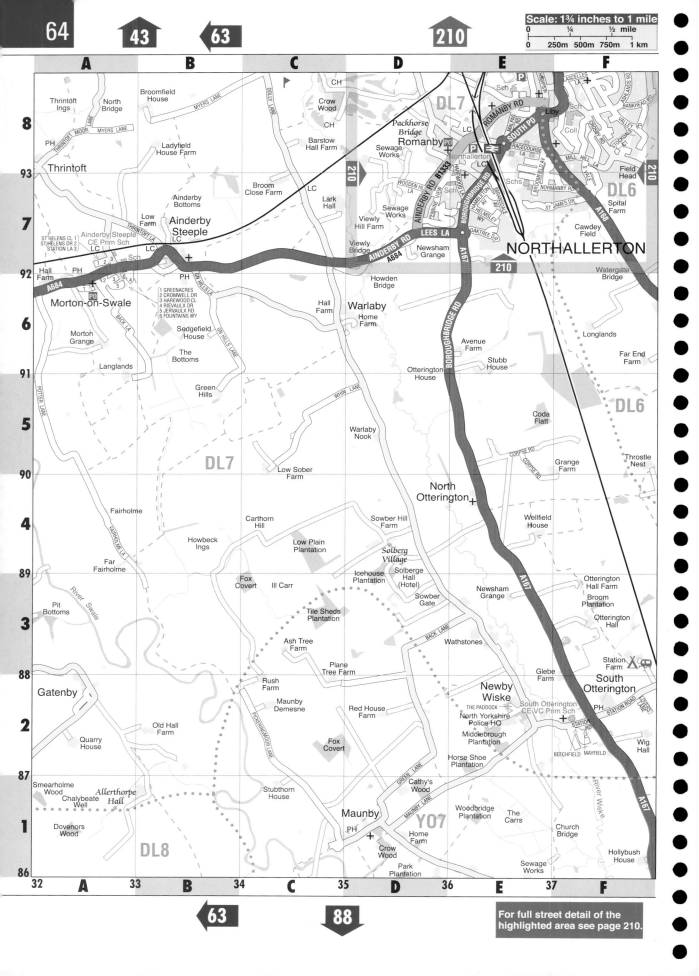

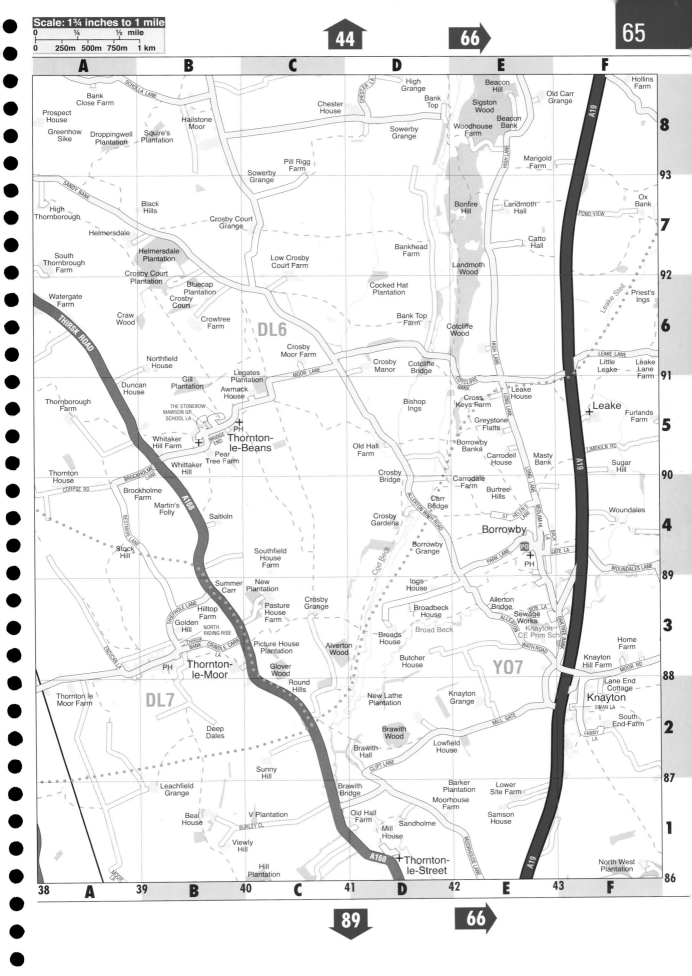

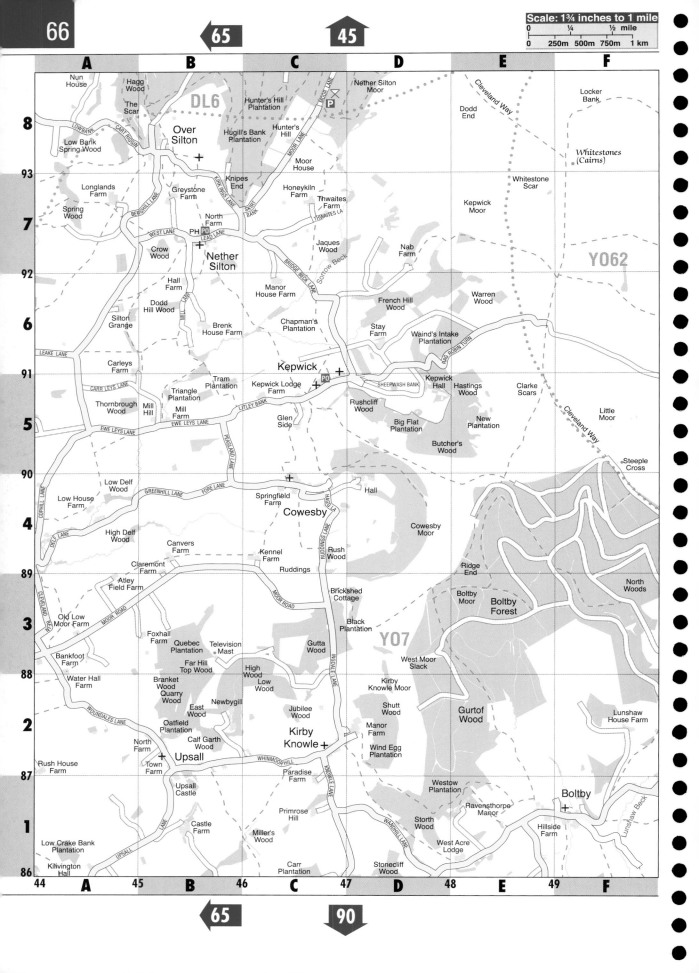

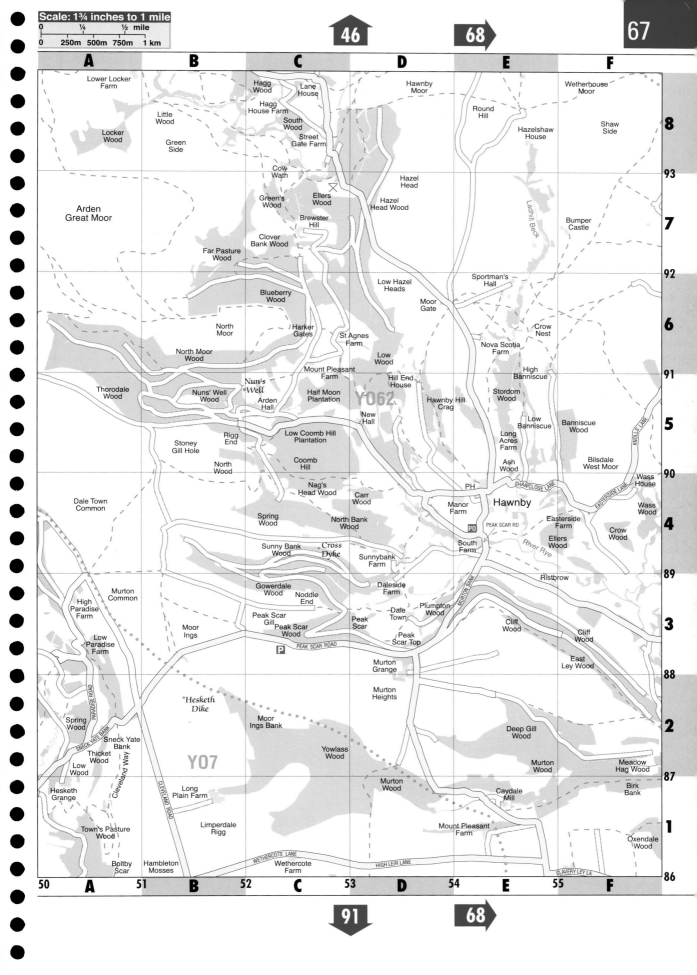

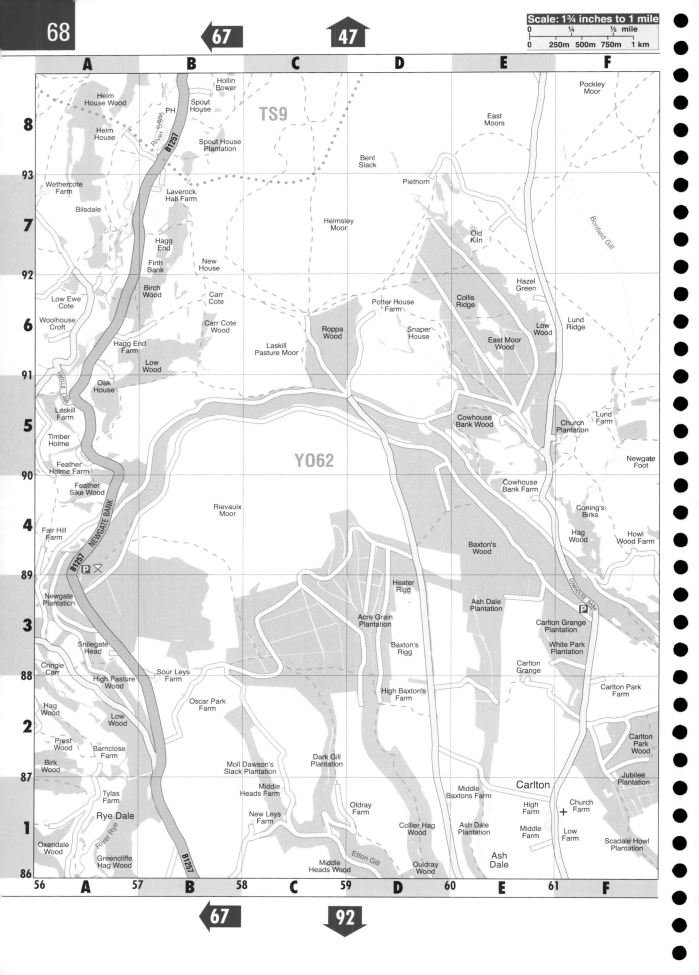

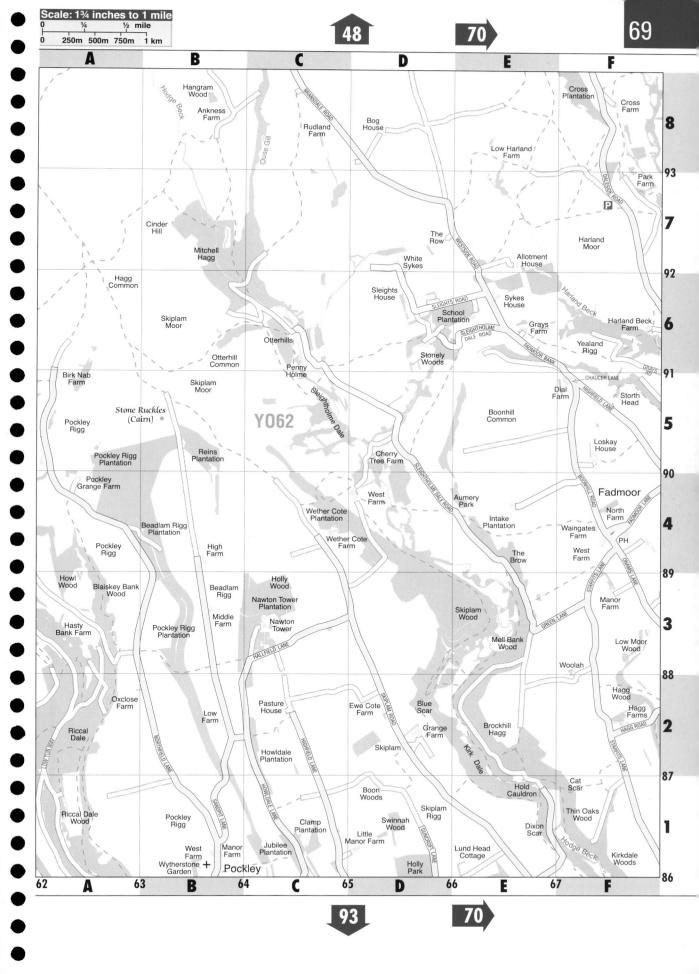

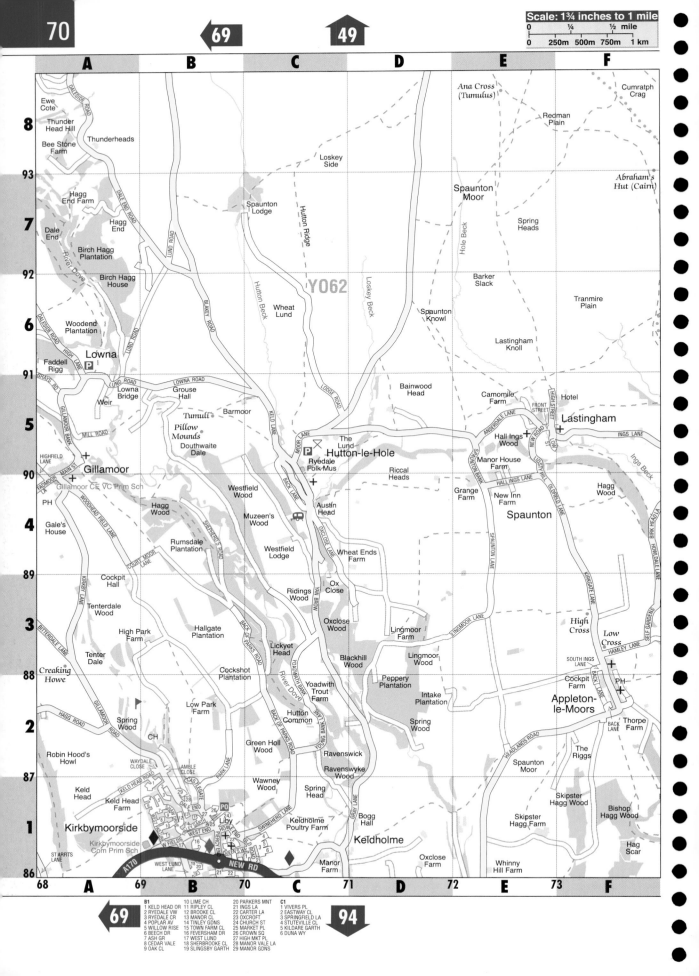

A   B   C   D   E   F

8
93
7
92
6
91
5
90
4
89
3
88
2
87
1
86

Ewe Cote
Thunder Head Hill
Bee Stone Farm
Thunderheads
DALE SIDE ROAD
Hagg End Farm
Dale End
Hagg End
River Dove
Birch Hagg Plantation
Birch Hagg House
DALESIDE ROAD
HIGH LANE
Woodend Plantation
DALE END ROAD
LUND ROAD
Faddell Rigg
Lowna
P
BRAYS RD
GILLAMOOR BANK
LUND ROAD
Weir
Lowna Bridge
MILL ROAD
Grouse Hall
Barmoor
LOWNA ROAD
Tumuli
Pillow Mounds
Douthwaite Dale
HIGHFIELD LANE
FADMOOR LA
Gillamoor
Gillamoor CE VC Prim Sch
MAIN ST
PH
WOODHEAD FIELD LANE
Hagg Wood
KIRKBY LANE
Gale's House
SHEPHERD'S ROAD
Rumsdale Plantation
Muzeen's Wood
Westfield Wood
BLAKEY ROAD
Hutton Beck
KELD LANE
MOOR LANE
BACK LANE
Wheat Lund
Spaunton Lodge
Hutton Ridge

Loskey Side
YO62
Loskey Beck
Hole Beck

Ana Cross (Tumulus)
Redman Plain
Cumratph Crag
Spaunton Moor
Abraham's Hut (Cairn)
Spring Heads
Barker Slack
Tranmire Plain
Spaunton Knowl
Lastingham Knoll

Bainwood Head
LODGE ROAD
The Lund
P
Hutton-le-Hole
Ryedale Folk Mus
Riccal Heads
Camomile Farm
ANSERDALE LANE
Hall Ings Wood
Manor House Farm
FRONT STREET
HIGH STREET
NEW ROAD
LIDSHY HILL
Hotel
Lastingham
INGS LANE
Ings Beck
OLD FIELD LANE
HALL INGS LANE
Grange Farm
New Inn Farm
SPAUNTON BANK
Spaunton
Hagg Wood
SPAUNTON LANE

Westfield Wood
Westfield Lodge
OXCLOSE LANE
YAN BROW
Austin Head
Wheat Ends Farm
Ridings Wood
Ox Close
Oxclose Wood
Lingmoor Farm
LINGMOOR LANE
Lingmoor Wood
High Cross
Low Cross
KIRKGATE LANE
HAMLEY LANE
SELF GARDENS
BIRK HEAD LA
HOWLDALE LANE

Cockpit Hall
Tenterdale Wood
High Park Farm
Hallgate Plantation
COURT MOOR LANE
BACK OF PARKS ROAD
Lickyet Head
Blackhill Wood
Peppery Plantation
Intake Plantation
SOUTH INGS LANE
High Cross
Low Cross
Cockpit Farm
PH
BACK LANE
Appleton-le-Moors

Tenter Dale
BITTERDALE LANE
Creaking Howe
HAGG ROAD
GILLAMOOR ROAD
Spring Wood
CH
Low Park Farm
Cockshot Plantation
River Dove
YOADWITH BANK
Yoadwith Trout Farm
Hutton Common
YORK BANK TOP
Spring Wood
Thorpe Farm
BACK LANE
The Riggs
Spaunton Moor

Robin Hood's Howl
WAYDALE CLOSE
AMBLE CLOSE
CAS LEGATE
PARK LANE
Green Holl Wood
Ravenswick
Ravenswyke Wood
GRAY LANE
HEADLANDS ROAD
Skipster Hagg Wood
Bishop Hagg Wood

Keld Head
Keld Head Farm
KELD HEAD ROAD
DALE END
PO
Kirkbymoorside
Kirkbymoorside Com Prim Sch
ST ARFITS LANE
SWINEHERD LANE
WEST END
QUEEN'S WY
Liby
Wawney Wood
Spring Head
Keldholme Poultry Farm
Bogg Hall
Keldholme
Skipster Hagg Farm
Hag Scar

A170
WEST LUND LANE
NEW RD
Manor Farm
Oxclose Farm
Whinny Hill Farm

68   A   69   B   70   C   71   D   72   E   73   F

B1
1 KELD HEAD OR
2 RYEDALE VW
3 RYEDALE CR
4 POPLAR AV
5 WILLOW RISE
6 BEECH DR
7 ASH GR
8 CEDAR VALE
9 OAK CL
10 LIME CH
11 RIPLEY CL
12 BROOKE CL
13 MANOR CL
14 TINLEY GDNS
15 TOWN FARM CL
16 FEVERSHAM DR
17 WEST LUND
18 SHERBROOKE CL
19 SLINGSBY GARTH
20 PARKERS MNT
21 INGS LA
22 CARTER LA
23 OXCROFT
24 CHURCH ST
25 MARKET PL
26 CROWN SQ
27 HIGH MKT PL
28 MANOR VALE LA
29 MANOR GDNS
C1
1 VIVERS PL
2 EASTWAY CL
3 SPRINGFIELD LA
4 STUTEVILLE CL
5 KILDARE GARTH
6 DUNA WY

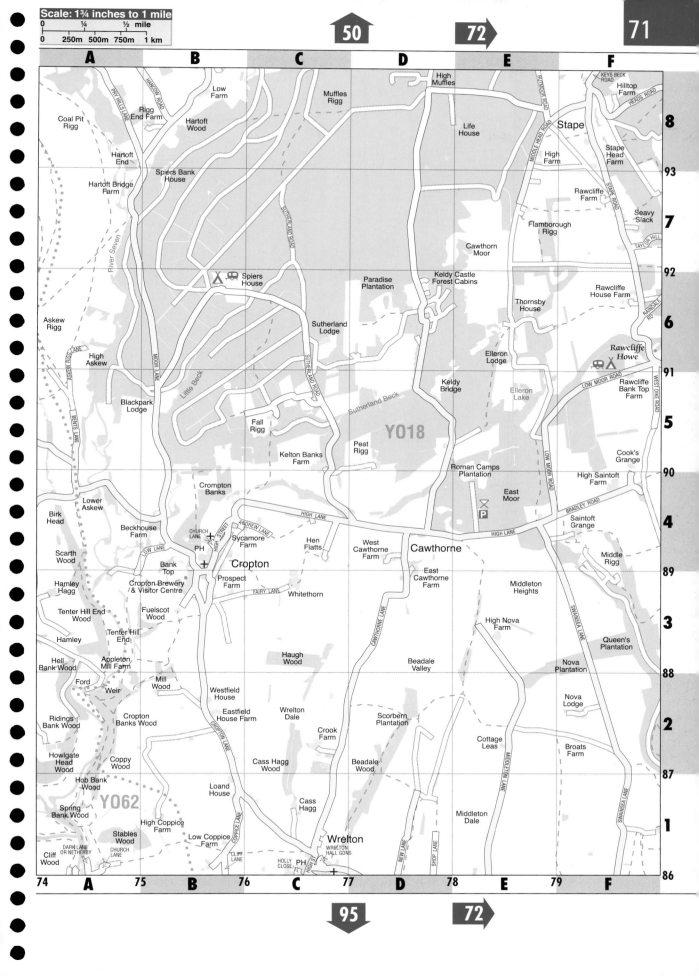

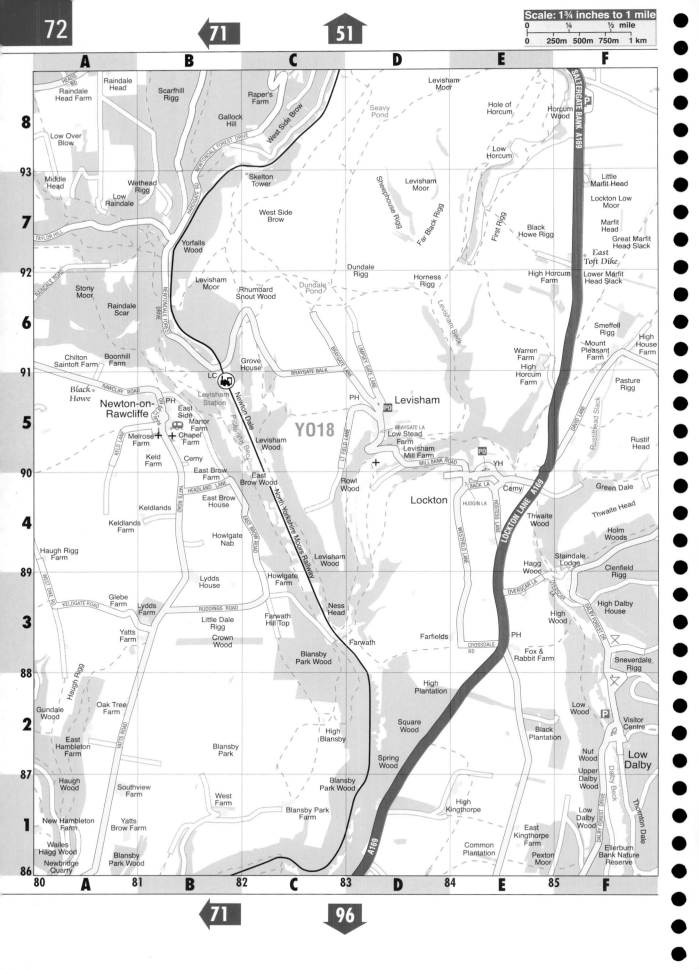

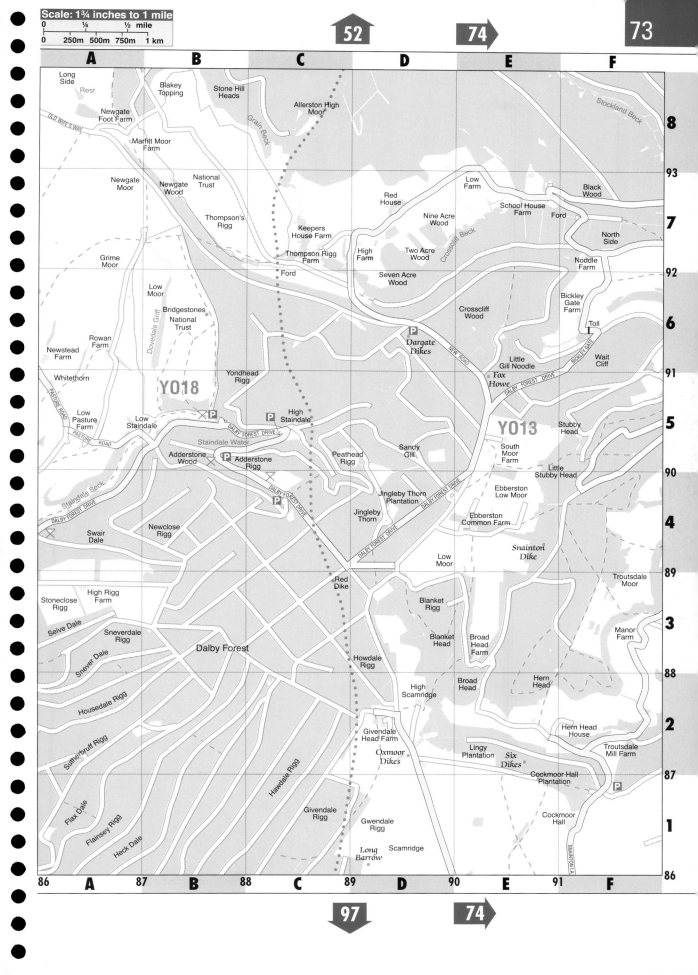

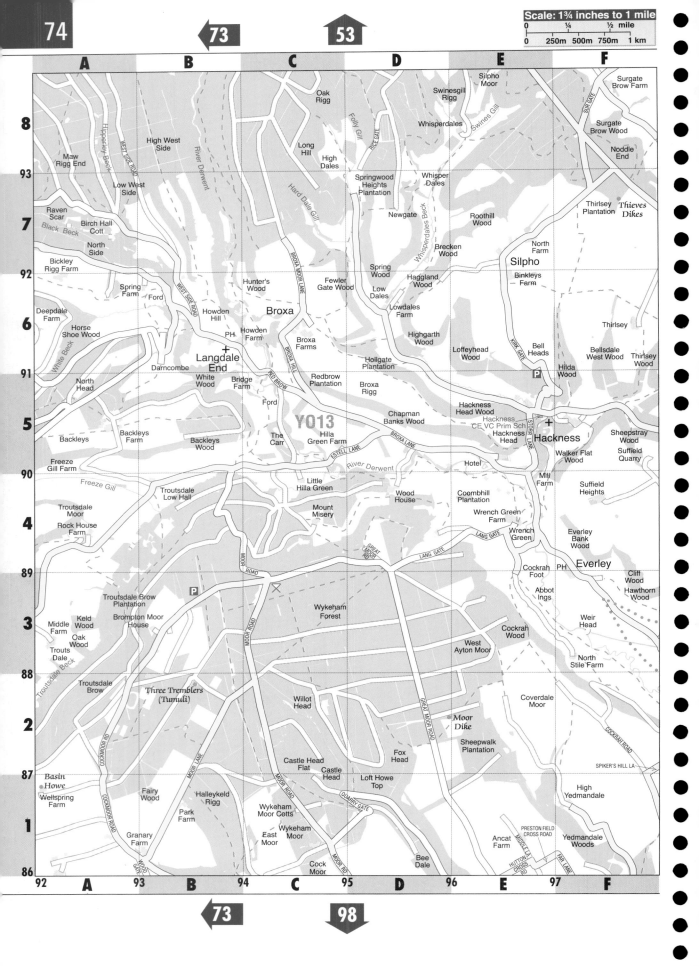

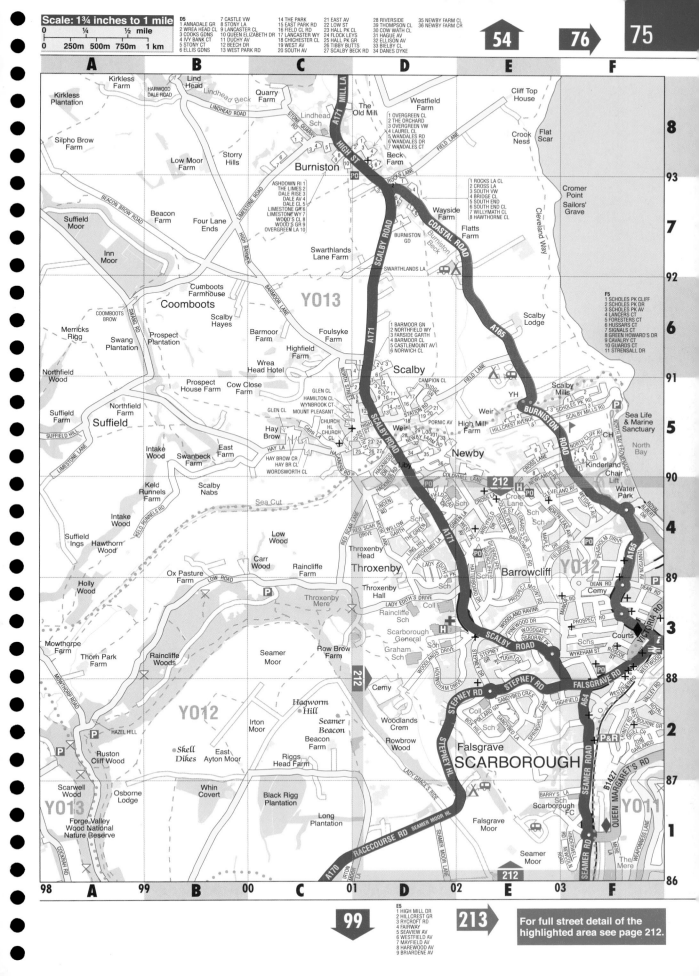

	A	B	C	D	E	F

8

93

7

92

6

91

5

90

213

North
Bay
YO12

4

Castle
Cliff

Castle

ROYAL ALBERT DRIVE

MARINE DRIVE

P

CASTLE RD

89

PO

LONGWESTGATE

YO11

P

C

QUEEN ST

ST THOMAS S

Sch

SANDSIDE

PO

FORESHORE RD

3

VERNON RD

Mus

SCARBOROUGH

213

Art
Gall

South
Sands

88

RAMSHILL RD

ALBION RD

WEST ST

The Spa
Complex

213

2

South
Bay

ESPLANADE

VICTORIA

FILEY RD

PO

Sch

87

TOLBECK RD

HOLBECK HILL

P

Black
Rocks

Sports
Ctr

A165

WEARDINNES RD

Schs

White
Nab

1

DEEPDALE AVE

COLLEGE LA

FILEY RD

YO11

Raven
Scar

Cornelian
Bay

CH

Univ

KNOX LA

86

213

04	A	05	B	06	C	07	D	08	E	09	F

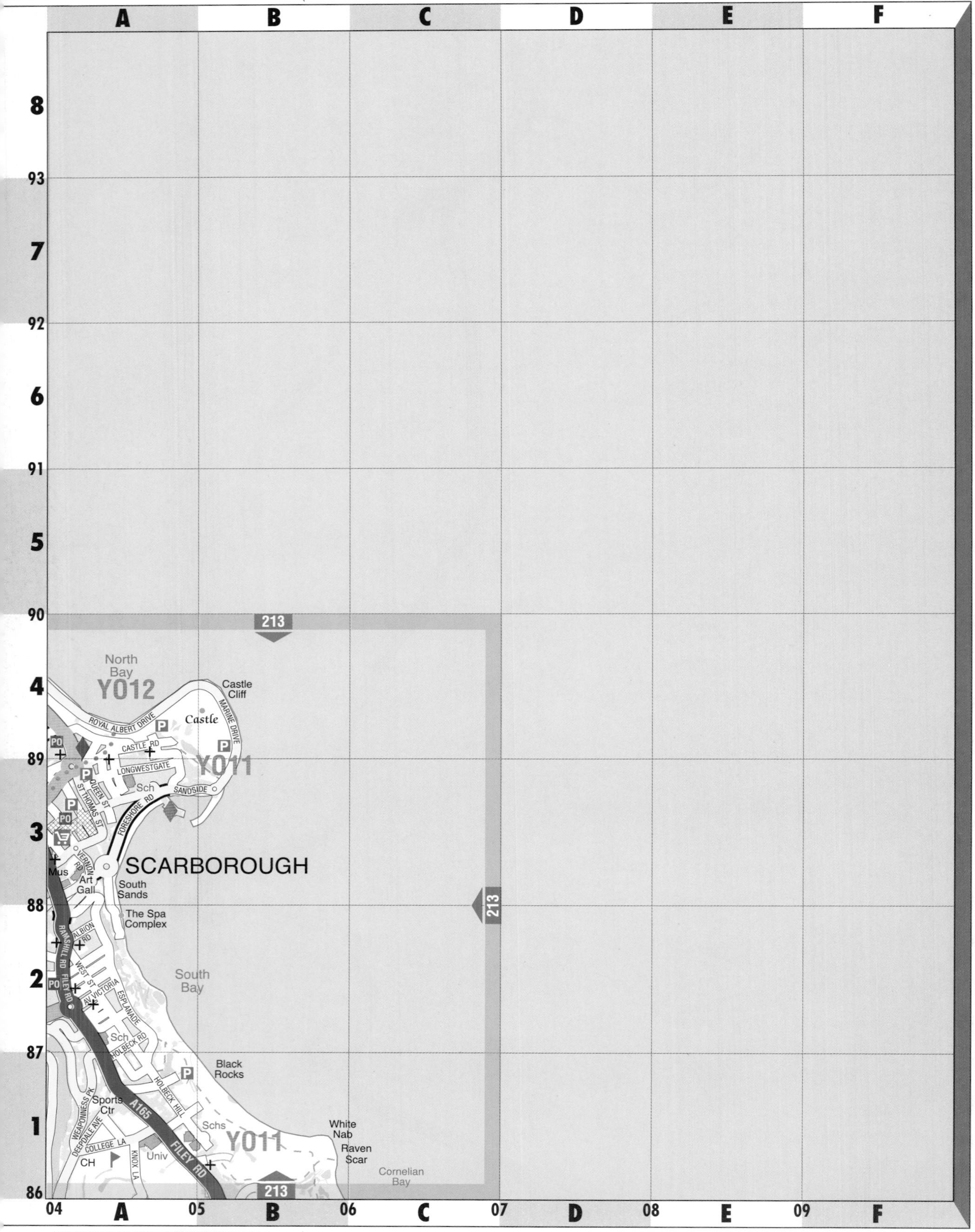

For full street detail of the
highlighted area see page 213.

212

100

A   B   C   D   E   F

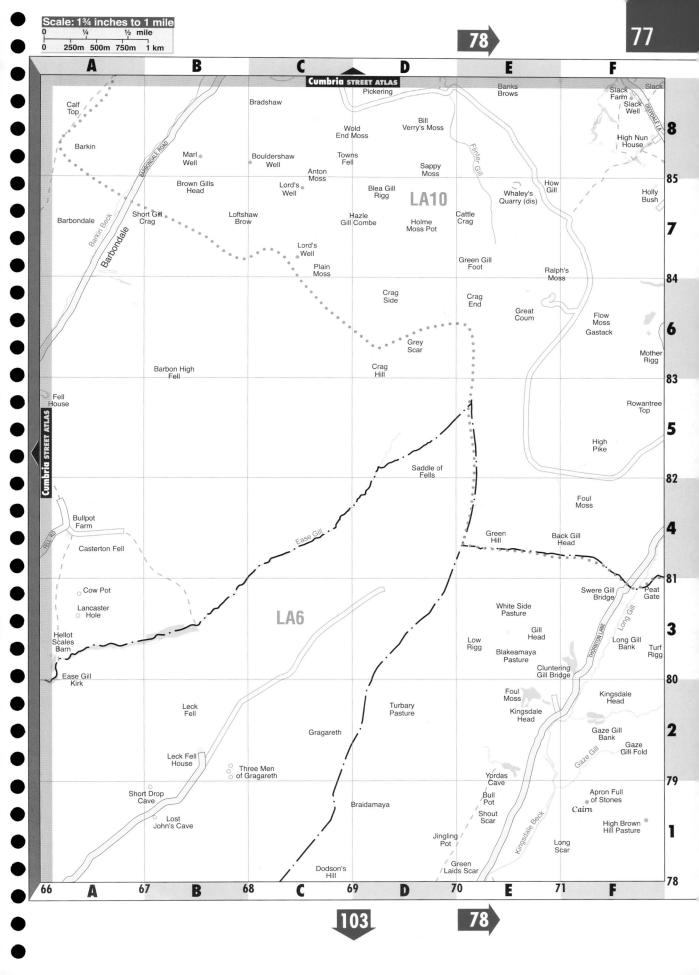

Cumbria STREET ATLAS

Pickering

Banks
Brows

Slack
Farm
Slack
Well

Slack

8

Calf
Top

Bradshaw

Bill
Verry's Moss

High Nun
House

Barkin

Marl
Well

Bouldershaw
Well

Wold
End Moss

Towns
Fell

Sappy
Moss

Whaley's
Quarry (dis)

How
Gill

Holly
Bush

85

Brown Gills
Head

Anton
Moss

Lord's
Well

Blea Gill
Rigg

LA10

Barbondale

Short Gill
Crag

Loftshaw
Brow

Hazle
Gill Combe

Holme
Moss Pot

Cattle
Crag

7

Lord's
Well

Green Gill
Foot

Ralph's
Moss

84

Plain
Moss

Crag
Side

Crag
End

Great
Coum

Flow
Moss
Gastack

6

Barbon High
Fell

Grey
Scar

Mother
Rigg

Crag
Hill

83

Fell
House

Rowantree
Top

5

Saddle of
Fells

High
Pike

82

Bullpot
Farm

Foul
Moss

4

Casterton Fell

Ease Gill

Green
Hill

Back Gill
Head

Swere Gill
Bridge

Peat
Gate

81

Cow Pot

LA6

White Side
Pasture

Long Gill

3

Lancaster
Hole

Gill
Head

Long Gill
Bank

Turf
Rigg

Hellot
Scales
Barn

Low
Rigg

Blakeamaya
Pasture

Cluntering
Gill Bridge

Kingsdale
Head

80

Ease Gill
Kirk

Leck
Fell

Turbary
Pasture

Foul
Moss

Kingsdale
Head

Gaze Gill
Bank

2

Gragareth

Kingsdale
Head

Gaze
Gill Fold

Leck Fell
House

Three Men
of Gragareth

Yordas
Cave

79

Short Drop
Cave

Braidamaya

Bull
Pot

Shout
Scar

Apron Full
of Stones

Cairn

Lost
John's Cave

High Brown
Hill Pasture

1

Jingling
Pot

Long
Scar

Dodson's
Hill

Green
Laids Scar

78

77

Scale: 1¾ inches to 1 mile
0 ¼ ½ mile
0 250m 500m 750m 1 km

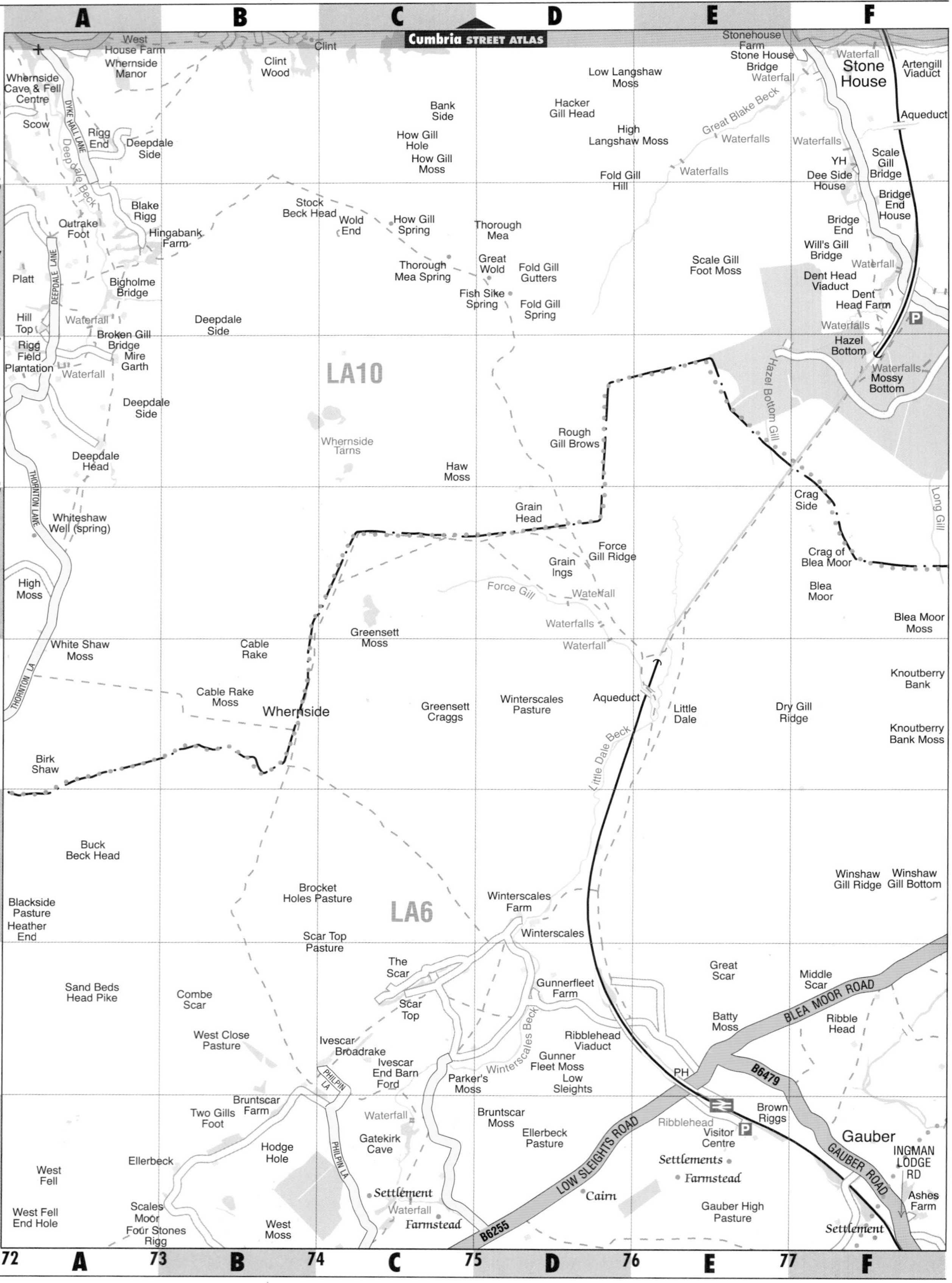
Cumbria STREET ATLAS
A B C D E F
72 73 74 75 76 77
8 85 7 84 6 83 5 82 4 81 3 80 2 79 1 78
West House Farm
Whernside Manor
Clint
Clint Wood
Whernside Cave & Fell Centre
DYKE HALL LANE
Scow
Rigg End
Deepdale Side
Deepdale Beck
Blake Rigg
Outrake Foot
Hingabank Farm
Platt
DEEPDALE LANE
Bigholme Bridge
Hill Top
Waterfall
Broken Gill Bridge
Rigg Field Plantation
Mire Garth
Deepdale Side
Deepdale Head
THORNTON LANE
Whiteshaw Well (spring)
High Moss
White Shaw Moss
THORNTON LA
Birk Shaw
Buck Beck Head
Blackside Pasture
Heather End
Sand Beds Head Pike
Combe Scar
West Close Pasture
Two Gills Foot
Bruntscar Farm
Ellerbeck
West Fell
West Fell End Hole
Scales Moor
Four Stones Rigg
West Moss
Hodge Hole
Bank Side
How Gill Hole
How Gill Moss
Stock Beck Head
Wold End
How Gill Spring
Thorough Mea Spring
Thorough Mea
Great Wold
Fish Sike Spring
Fold Gill Gutters
Fold Gill Spring
LA10
Whernside Tarns
Haw Moss
Cable Rake
Cable Rake Moss
Whernside
Greensett Moss
Greensett Craggs
Winterscales Pasture
Brocket Holes Pasture
LA6
Scar Top Pasture
The Scar
Scar Top
Ivescar
Broadrake
Ivescar End Barn Ford
PHILPIN LA
Waterfall
Gatekirk Cave
Settlement
Farmstead
B6255
Low Langshaw Moss
Hacker Gill Head
High Langshaw Moss
Fold Gill Hill
Great Blake Beck
Waterfalls
Rough Gill Brows
Grain Head
Force Gill Ridge
Grain Ings
Force Gill
Waterfall
Waterfalls
Aqueduct
Little Dale
Little Dale Beck
Winterscales Farm
Winterscales
Gunnerfleet Farm
Winterscales Beck
Parker's Moss
Ribblehead Viaduct
Gunner Fleet Moss
Low Sleights
Bruntscar Moss
Ellerbeck Pasture
PH
LOW SLEIGHTS ROAD
Ribblehead
Visitor Centre
Settlements
Farmstead
Cairn
Stonehouse Farm
Stone House Bridge
Stone House
Artengill Viaduct
Aqueduct
Waterfalls
YH
Scale Gill Bridge
Dee Side House
Bridge End House
Bridge End
Will's Gill Bridge
Scale Gill Foot Moss
Dent Head Viaduct
Dent Head Farm
Hazel Bottom
Hazel Bottom Gill
Mossy Bottom
Crag Side
Long Gill
Crag of Blea Moor
Blea Moor
Blea Moor Moss
Knoutberry Bank
Knoutberry Bank Moss
Dry Gill Ridge
Winshaw Gill Ridge
Winshaw Gill Bottom
Great Scar
Middle Scar
BLEA MOOR ROAD
Batty Moss
Ribble Head
B6479
Brown Riggs
Gauber
GAUBER ROAD
INGMAN LODGE RD
Ashes Farm
Gauber High Pasture
Settlement

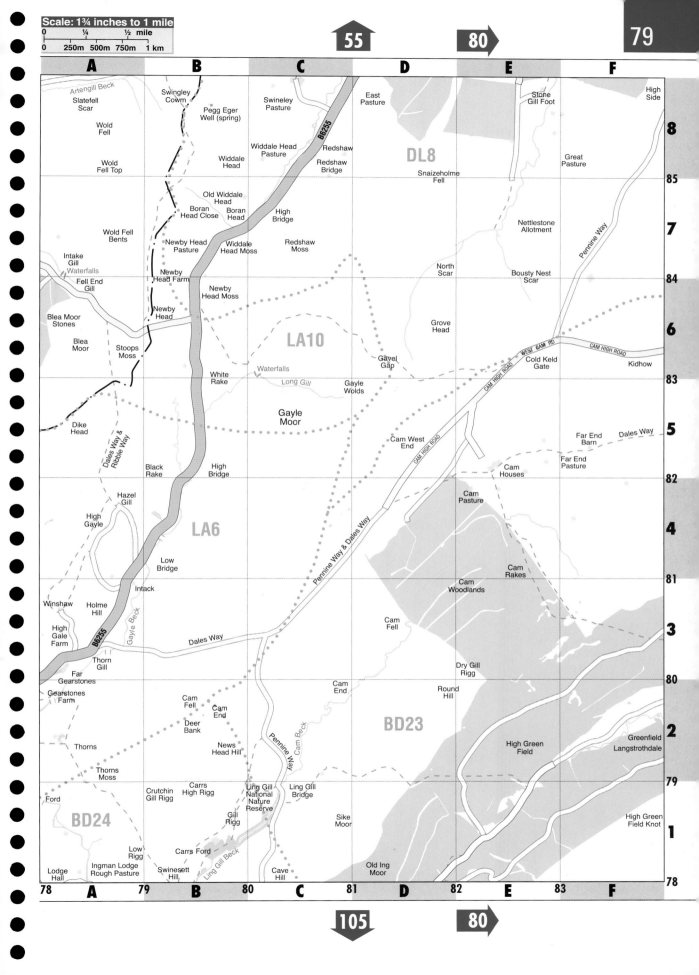

Scale: 1¾ inches to 1 mile

0   ¼   ½   mile
0 250m 500m 750m 1 km

A **B** **C** **D** **E** **F**

Artengill Beck

Slatefell Scar

Wold Fell

Wold Fell Top

Wold Fell Bents

Swingley Cowm

Pegg Eger Well (spring)

Old Widdale Head

Boran Head Close

Boran Head

Newby Head Pasture

Newby Head Farm

Newby Head Moss

Newby Head

Swineley Pasture

Widdale Head Pasture

Widdale Head

Widdale Head Moss

B6255

Redshaw

Redshaw Bridge

High Bridge

Redshaw Moss

East Pasture

Snaizeholme Fell

DL8

Stone Gill Foot

High Side

Great Pasture

Nettlestone Allotment

Pennine Way

North Scar

Bousty Nest Scar

Intake Gill Waterfalls

Fell End Gill

Blea Moor Stones

Blea Moor

Stoops Moss

LA10

Grove Head

Gavel Gap

Cold Keld Gate

WEST CAM RD

CAM HIGH ROAD

CAM HIGH ROAD

Kidhow

White Rake

Waterfalls

Long Gill

Gayle Wolds

Dike Head

Dales Way & Ribble Way

Black Rake

High Bridge

Gayle Moor

Cam West End

CAM HIGH ROAD

Far End Barn

Dales Way

Far End Pasture

Hazel Gill

High Gayle

LA6

Low Bridge

Cam Houses

Cam Pasture

Intack

Gayle Beck

Pennine Way & Dales Way

Cam Woodlands

Cam Rakes

Winshaw

Holme Hill

High Gale Farm

B6255

Thorn Gill

Dales Way

Cam Fell

Cam Fell

Dry Gill Rigg

Far Gearstones

Gearstones Farm

Cam End

Cam End

Round Hill

BD23

High Green Field

Greenfield Langstrothdale

Thorns

Cam Fell

Deer Bank

Cam End

News Head Hill

Pennine Way

Cam Beck

Thorns Moss

Ford

BD24

Crutchin Gill Rigg

Carrs High Rigg

Gill Rigg

Ling Gill National Nature Reserve

Ling Gill Bridge

Ling Gill

Sike Moor

High Green Field Knot

Low Rigg

Carrs Ford

Ling Gill Beck

Cave Hill

Old Ing Moor

Lodge Hall

Ingman Lodge Rough Pasture

Swinesett Hill

8
85
7
84
6
83
5
82
4
81
3
80
2
79
1
78

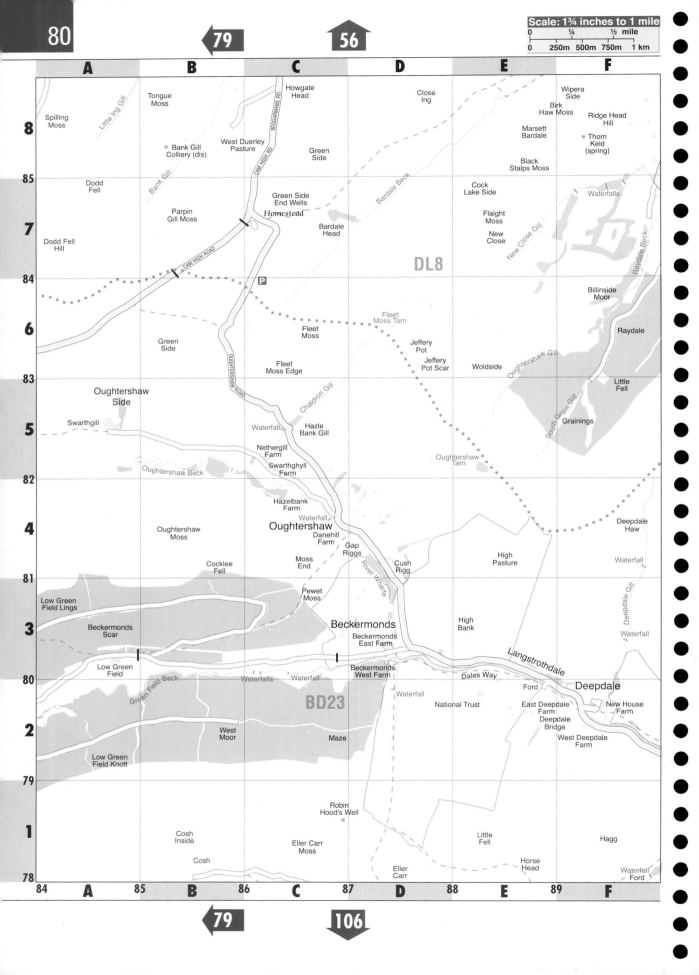

Scale: 1¾ inches to 1 mile

0   ¼   ½   mile

0   250m 500m 750m 1 km

Spilling Moss

Little Ing Gill

Tongue Moss

Howgate Head

Close Ing

Wipera Side

Birk Haw Moss

Ridge Head Hill

Bank Gill Colliery (dis)

West Duerley Pasture

Marsett Bardale

Thorn Keld (spring)

Dodd Fell

Bank Gill

Green Side

Black Stalps Moss

Dodd Fell Hill

Parpin Gill Moss

CAM HIGH ROAD

BEGGARMANS RD

Green Side End Wells

Homestead

Bardale Head

Bardale Beck

Cock Lake Side

Flaight Moss

New Close

Waterfalls

DL8

CAM HIGH ROAD

P

Billinside Moor

Raydale Beck

New Close Gill

Green Side

Fleet Moss Tarn

Fleet Moss

Jeffery Pot

Raydale

OUGHTERSHAW ROAD

Fleet Moss Edge

Jeffery Pot Scar

Woldside

Oughtershaw Gill

Oughtershaw Side

Chaldron Gill

Little Fell

Swarthgill

Waterfall

Hazle Bank Gill

South Grain Gill

Grainings

Nethergill Farm

Swarthghyll Farm

Oughtershaw Beck

Oughtershaw Tarn

Hazelbank Farm

Oughtershaw Moss

Waterfall

Oughtershaw

Deepdale Haw

Waterfall

Danehill Farm

Gap Riggs

High Pasture

Cocklee Fell

Moss End

Cush Rigg

River Wharfe

Deepdale Gill

Pewet Moss

Low Green Field Lings

Beckermonds Scar

Beckermonds

High Bank

Langstrothdale

Waterfall

Low Green Field

Beckermonds East Farm

Deepdale

Green Field Beck

Waterfalls

Waterfall

Beckermonds West Farm

Dales Way

Ford

New House Farm

West Moor

BD23

Maze

Waterfall

National Trust

East Deepdale Farm

Deepdale Bridge

West Deepdale Farm

Low Green Field Knott

Robin Hood's Well

Cosh Inside

Eller Carr Moss

Little Fell

Hagg

Cosh

Eller Carr

Horse Head

Waterfall Ford

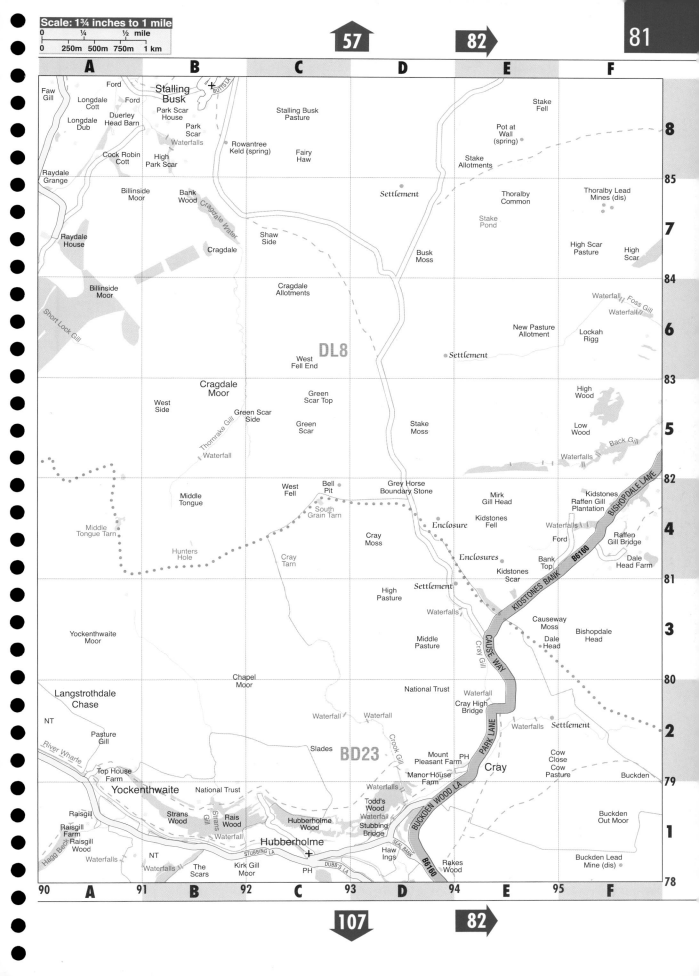

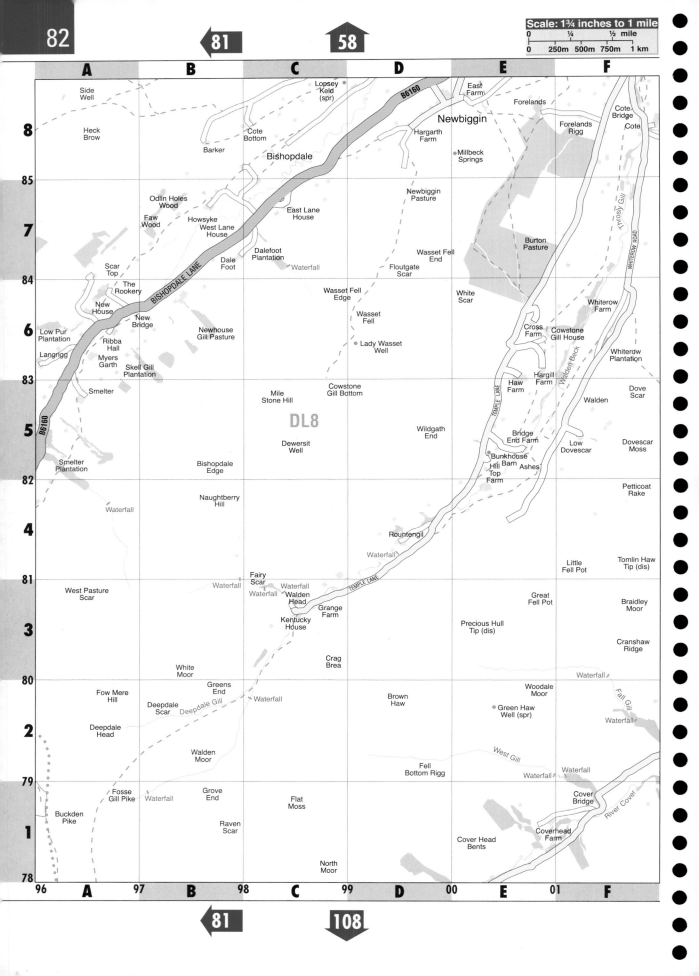

Scale: 1¾ inches to 1 mile

0   ¼   ½ mile
0   250m 500m 750m 1 km

A **B** **C** **D** **E** **F**

Side Well

Heck Brow

Lopsey Keld (spr)

B6160

East Farm

Newbiggin

Forelands

Cote Bridge

Cote

8

Cote Bottom

Barker

Bishopdale

Hargarth Farm

Millbeck Springs

Forelands Rigg

85

Odlin Holes Wood

East Lane House

Newbiggin Pasture

7

Faw Wood

Howsyke West Lane House

Burton Pasture

Whiterow Farm

Dalefoot Plantation

Wasset Fell End

Whiterow Road

84

Scar Top

Dale Foot

Waterfall

Floutgate Scar

The Rookery

Wasset Fell Edge

White Scar

Whiterow Plantation

6

New House

New Bridge

Newhouse Gill Pasture

Wasset Fell

Cross Farm

Cowstone Gill House

Low Pur Plantation

Ribba Hall

Lady Wasset Well

Walden Beck

Langrigg

Myers Garth

Skell Gill Plantation

Hargill Farm

Whiterow Plantation

83

Smelter

Mile Stone Hill

Cowstone Gill Bottom

Haw Farm

Dove Scar

Walden

DL8

5

B6160

Dewersit Well

Wildgath End

Bridge End Farm

Low Dovescar

Dovescar Moss

Smelter Plantation

Temple Lane

Bunkhouse Barn

Ashes

82

Bishopdale Edge

Hill Top Farm

Petticoat Rake

Naughtberry Hill

4

Waterfall

Rountengil

Waterfall

Little Fell Pot

Tomlin Haw Tip (dis)

81

Fairy Scar

Waterfall

Walden Head

Temple Lane

Great Fell Pot

Braidley Moor

West Pasture Scar

Waterfall

Grange Farm

Precious Hull Tip (dis)

3

Kentucky House

Cranshaw Ridge

Crag Brea

White Moor

Greens End

Waterfall

Brown Haw

Woodale Moor

80

Fow Mere Hill

Deepdale Scar

Deepdale Gill

Waterfall

Green Haw Well (spr)

Fall Gill

Waterfall

2

Deepdale Head

Walden Moor

West Gill

Waterfall

Waterfall

79

Fosse Gill Pike

Waterfall

Grove End

Flat Moss

Cover Bridge

River Cover

Buckden Pike

Raven Scar

1

Cover Head Bents

Coverhead Farm

North Moor

78

96 **A** 97 **B** 98 **C** 99 **D** 00 **E** 01 **F**

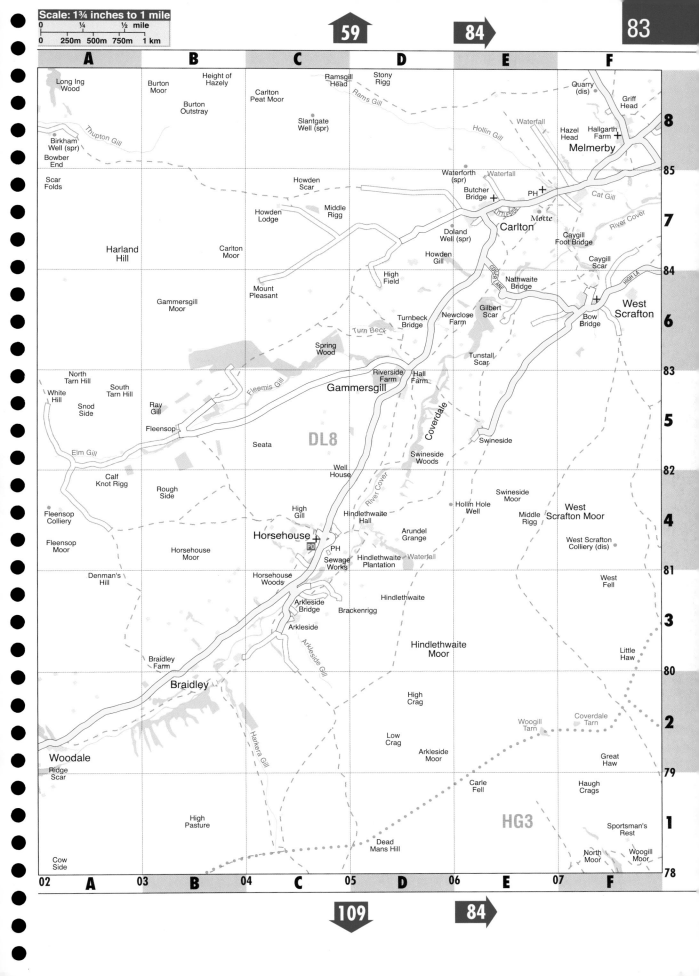

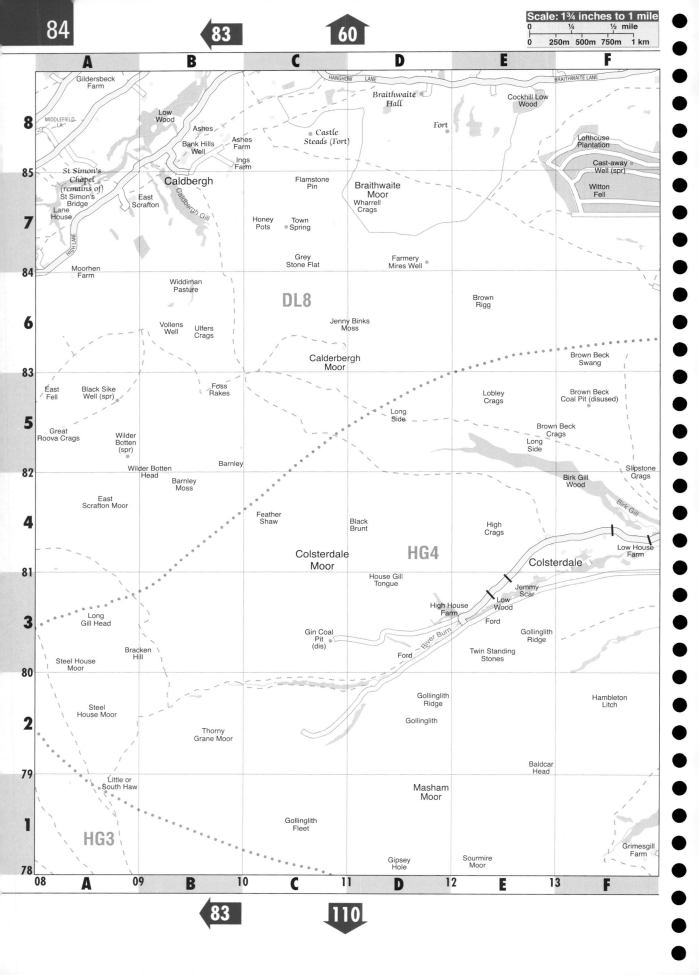

Scale: 1¾ inches to 1 mile
0   ¼   ½ mile
0   250m   500m   750m   1 km

A   B   C   D   E   F

HANGHOW LANE
BRAITHWAITE LANE

Gildersbeck Farm

MIDDLEFIELD LA

Braithwaite Hall

Cockhill Low Wood

8

Low Wood

Ashes

Castle Steads (Fort)

Fort

Lofthouse Plantation

Bank Hills Well

Ashes Farm

85

St Simon's Chapel (remains of)

Caldbergh

Ings Farm

Flamstone Pin

Braithwaite Moor

Cast-away Well (spr)

St Simon's Bridge

East Scrafton

Wharrell Crags

Witton Fell

Lane House

7

HIGH LANE

Caldbergh Gill

Honey Pots

Town Spring

Moorhen Farm

Grey Stone Flat

Farmery Mires Well

84

Widdiman Pasture

DL8

Brown Rigg

6

Vollens Well

Ulfers Crags

Jenny Binks Moss

83

Calderbergh Moor

Brown Beck Swang

East Fell

Black Sike Well (spr)

Foss Rakes

Lobley Crags

Brown Beck Coal Pit (disused)

5

Great Roova Crags

Wilder Botten (spr)

Long Side

Brown Beck Crags

Long Side

82

Wilder Botten Head

Barnley

Barnley Moss

Birk Gill Wood

Slipstone Crags

East Scrafton Moor

Feather Shaw

Black Brunt

High Crags

Birk Gill

4

Colsterdale Moor

HG4

Colsterdale

Low House Farm

81

House Gill Tongue

Long Gill Head

3

High House Farm

Low Wood

Jemmy Scar

Steel House Moor

Bracken Hill

Gin Coal Pit (dis)

Ford

Gollinglith Ridge

River Burn

Ford

Twin Standing Stones

80

Steel House Moor

Gollinglith Ridge

Hambleton Litch

2

Thorny Grane Moor

Gollinglith

79

Little or South Haw

Baldcar Head

Masham Moor

1

Gollinglith Fleet

HG3

Grimesgill Farm

Gipsey Hole

Sourmire Moor

78

08   A   09   B   10   C   11   D   12   E   13   F

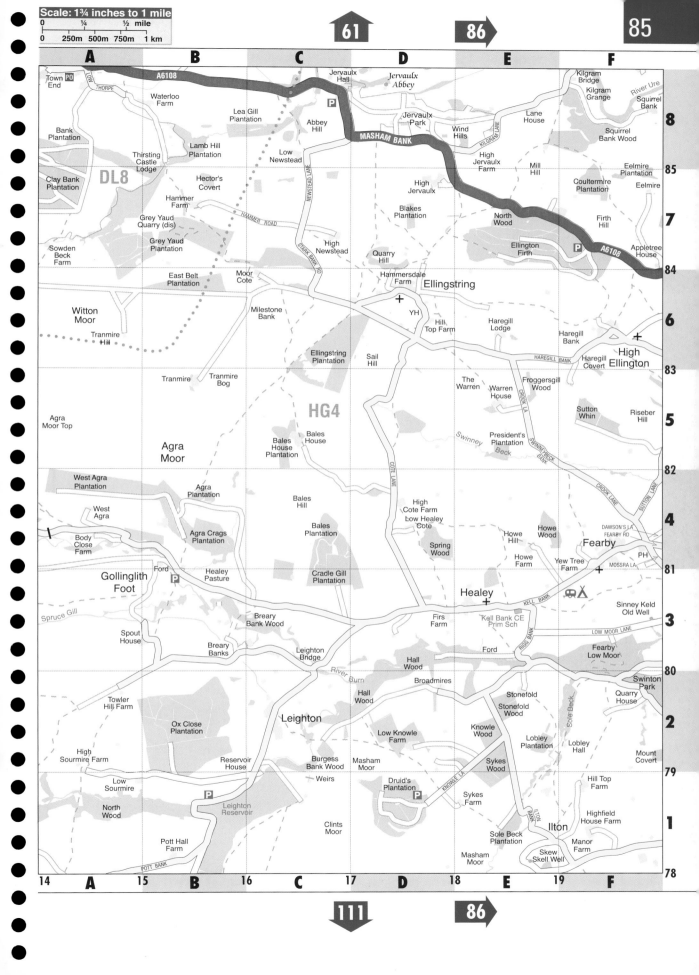

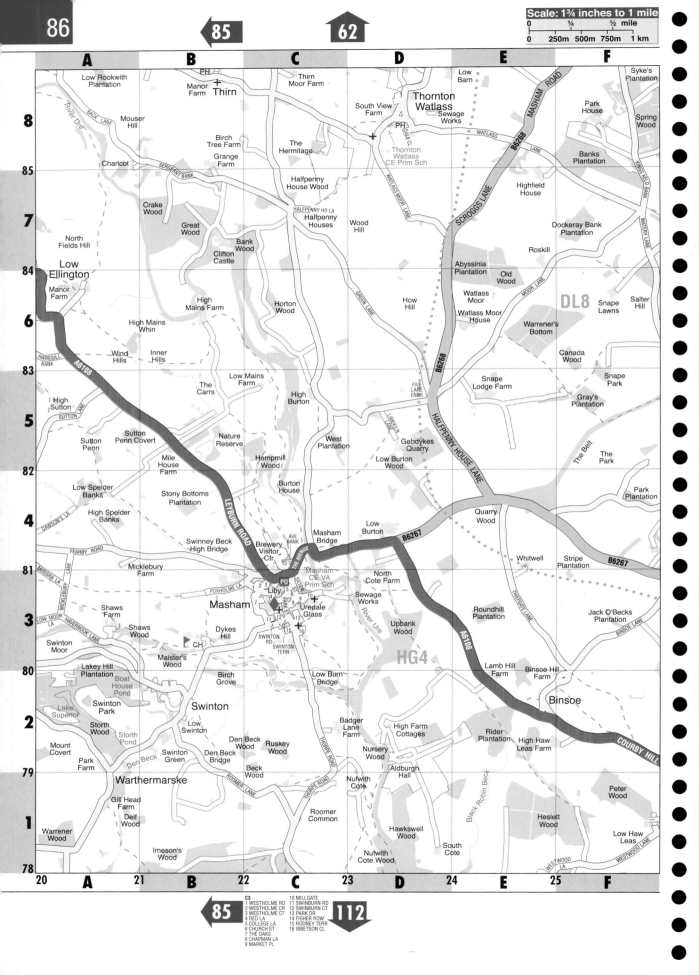

Scale: 1¾ inches to 1 mile
0   ¼   ½ mile
0   250m   500m   750m   1 km

A   B   C   D   E   F

Low Rookwith Plantation
Manor Farm
Thirn
PH
Thirn Moor Farm
Low Barn
Thornton Watlass
Syke's Plantation
MASHAM ROAD
Park House
Spring Wood
Mouser Hill
Birch Tree Farm
South View Farm
PH
Sewage Works
WATLASS
B6268 LANE
Banks Plantation
KINGS KELD BANK
Charlcot
Grange Farm
The Hermitage
Thornton Watlass CE Prim Sch
SERGEANT BANK
Halfpenny House Wood
Highfield House
WATERY LANE
Crake Wood
Great Wood
Bank Wood
HALFPENNY HO LA
Halfpenny Houses
Wood Hill
SCROGGS LANE
Dockeray Bank Plantation
North Fields Hill
Clifton Castle
Roskill
MOOR LANE
Low Ellington
Manor Farm
High Mains Farm
Horton Wood
GREEN LANE
How Hill
Abyssinia Plantation
Old Wood
DL8
Snape Lawns
Salter Hill
High Mains Whin
Watlass Moor
Watlass Moor House
Warrener's Bottom
Canada Wood
HAREGILL BANK
A6108
Wind Hills
Inner Hills
The Carrs
Low Mains Farm
High Burton
FIVE LANE ENDS
B6268
Snape Lodge Farm
Snape Park
Gray's Plantation
Snape Park
High Sutton
SUTTON LANE
Sutton Penn Covert
Nature Reserve
West Plantation
LIMEKILN LANE
Gebdykes Quarry
HALFPENNY HOUSE LANE
The Belt
The Park
Sutton Penn
Mile House Farm
Hempmill Wood
Low Burton Wood
Low Spelder Banks
Stony Bottoms Plantation
Burton House
Quarry Wood
Park Plantation
High Spelder Banks
DAWSON'S LA
LEYBURN ROAD
Swinney Beck High Bridge
AVE BANK
Masham Bridge
Low Burton
B6267
Whitwell
Stripe Plantation
B6267
FEARBY ROAD
Micklebury Farm
Brewery Visitor Ctr.
THE AVENUE
Masham CE VA Prim Sch
North Cote Farm
Roundhill Plantation
THIRGATE LANE
Jack O'Becks Plantation
MOSSRA LA
MICKLEBURY LANE
FOXHOLME LA
Liby
PO
SILVER ST
Sewage Works
River Ure
Upbank Wood
A6108
BINSOE LANE
Shaws Farm
Masham
Uredale Glass
LOW MOOR LA
HAVERNOOK LANE
Shaws Wood
CH
Dykes Hill
SWINTON RD
SWINTON TERR
HG4
Lamb Hill Farm
Binsoe Hill Farm
Swinton Moor
Maister's Wood
Birch Grove
Low Burn Bridge
Binsoe
Lakey Hill Plantation
Boat House Pond
Swinton Park
Low Swinton
Storth Wood
Storth Pond
Swinton Green
Den Beck Wood
Ruskey Wood
Badger Lane Farm
High Farm Cottages
Nursery Wood
Rider Plantation
High Haw Leas Farm
COURBY HILL
Lake Superior
Mount Covert
Park Farm
Swinton
Den Beck Bridge
Beck Wood
THORPE ROAD
Den Beck
Warthermarske
ROOMER LANE
Aldburgh Hall
Black Robin Beck
Heslett Wood
Peter Wood
Gill Head Farm
Delf Wood
Imeson's Wood
Roomer Common
Nufwith Cote
Hawkswell Wood
South Cote
WESTWOOD LA
Low Haw Leas
WESTWOOD LANE
Warrener Wood
Nutwith Cote Wood

8 85 7 84 6 83 5 82 4 81 3 80 2 79 1 78

20   A   21   B   22   C   23   D   24   E   25   F

C3
1 WESTHOLME RD
2 WESTHOLME CR
3 WESTHOLME CT
4 RED LA
5 COLLEGE LA
6 CHURCH ST
7 THE OAKS
8 CHAPMAN LA
9 MARKET PL
10 MILLGATE
11 SWINBURN RD
12 SWINBURN CT
13 PARK DR
14 FISHER ROW
15 RODNEY TERR
16 IBBETSON CL

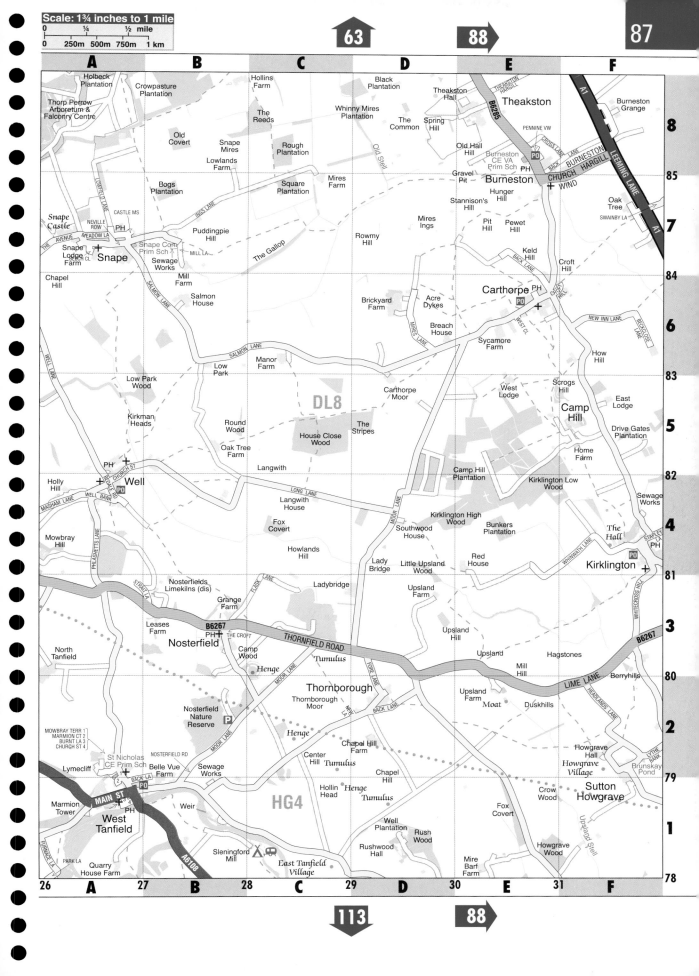

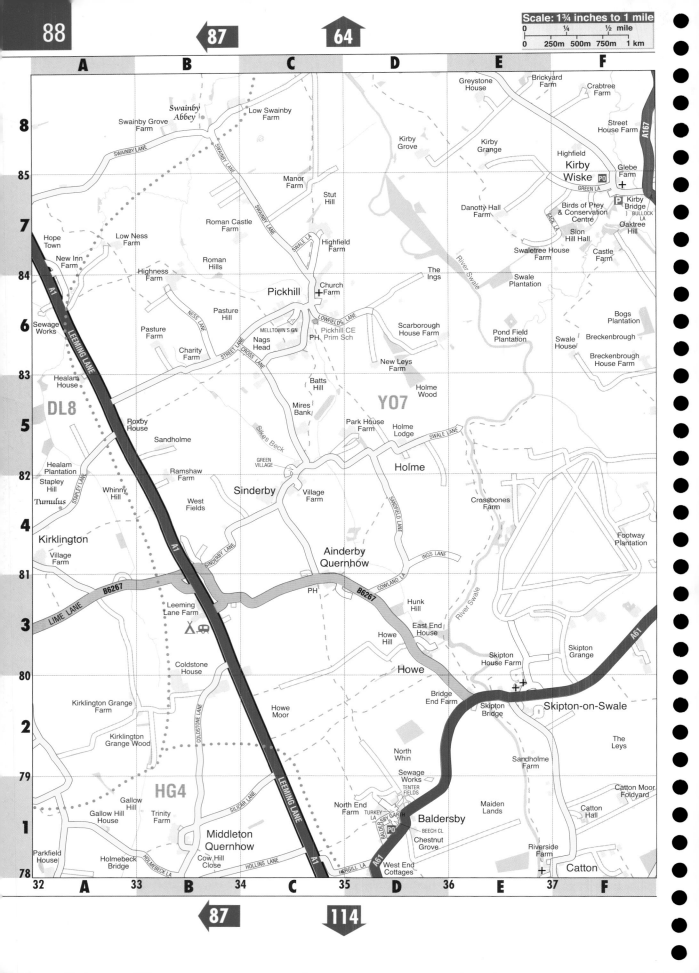

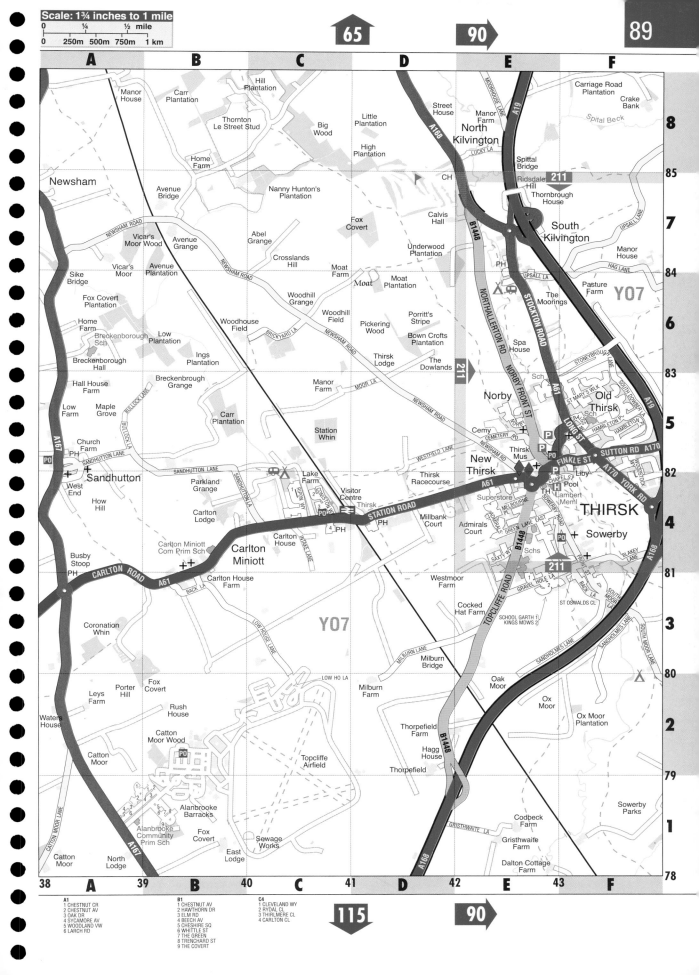

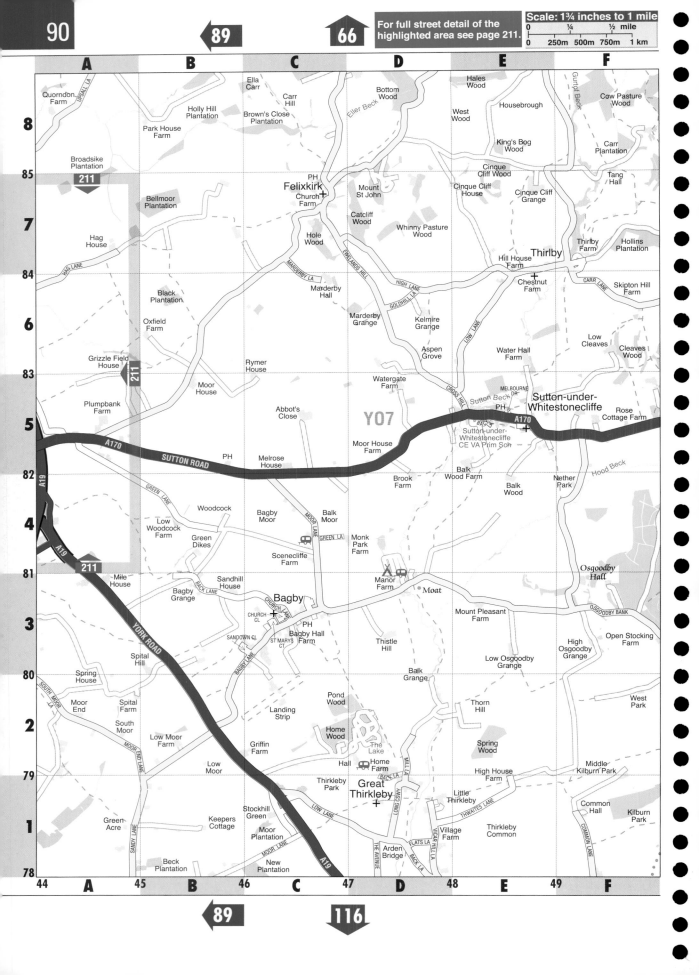

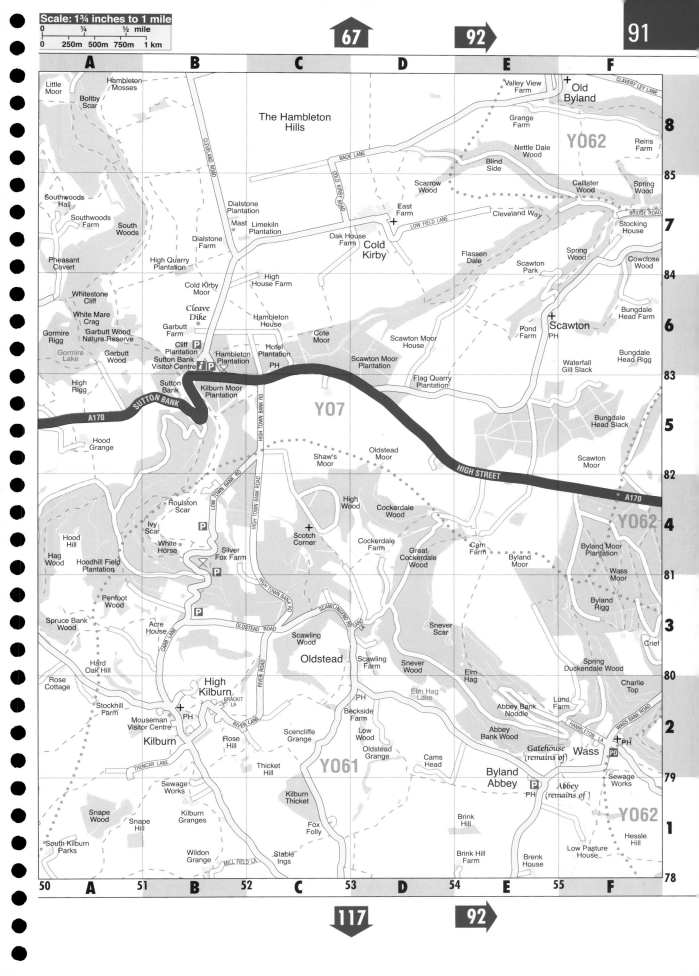

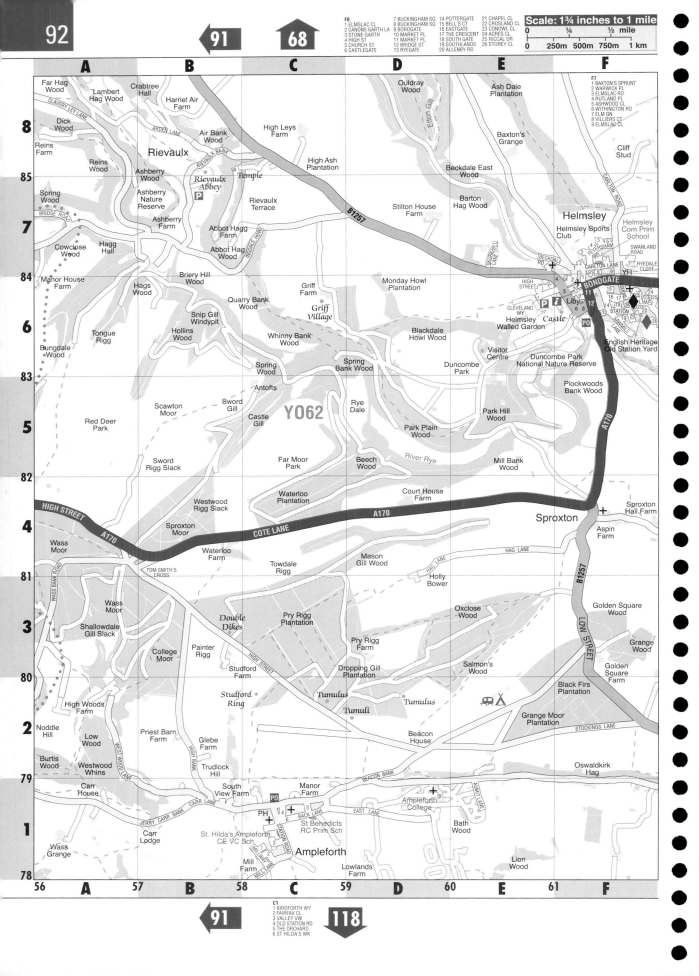

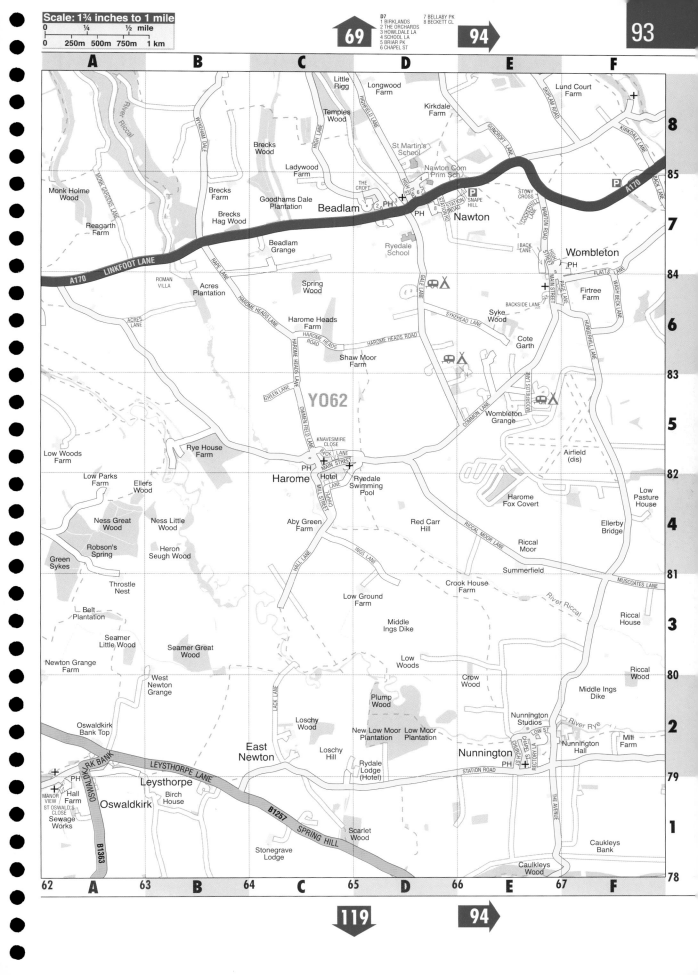

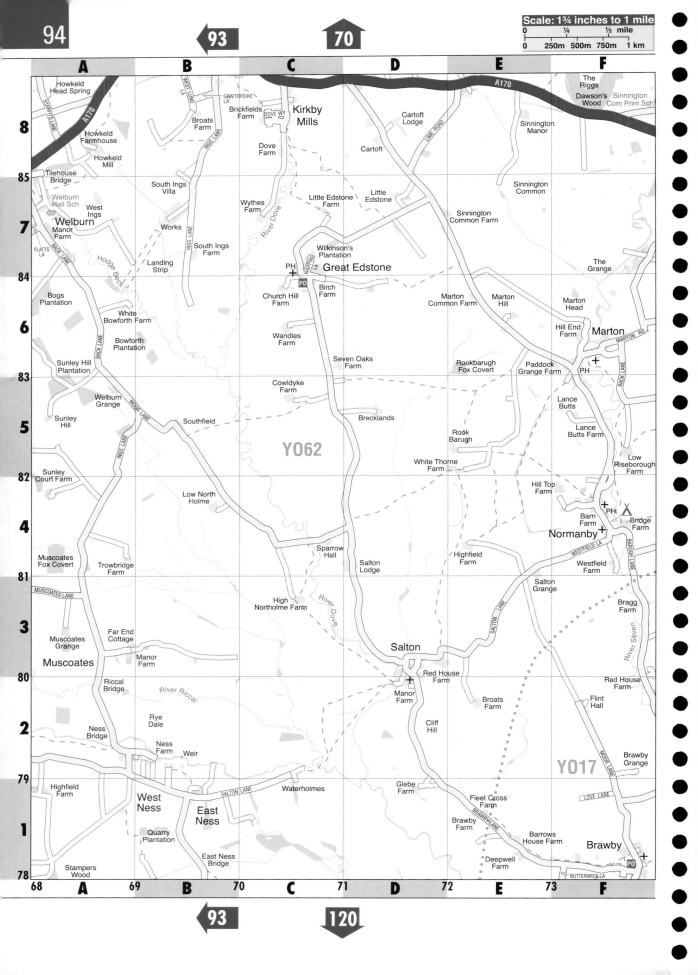

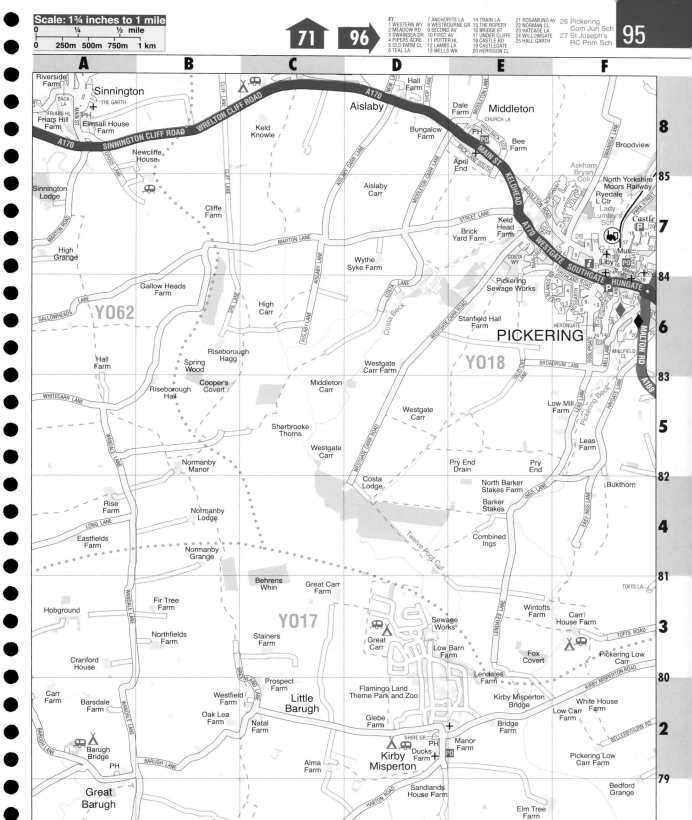

F7
1 WESTERN WY
2 MEADOW RD
3 SWAINSEA DR
4 PIPERS ACRE
5 OLD FARM CL
6 TEAL LA
7 ANCHORITE LA
8 WESTBOURNE GR
9 SECOND AV
10 FIRST AV
11 POTTER HL
12 LAMBS LA
13 WELLS WK
14 TRAIN LA
15 THE ROPERY
16 BRIDGE ST
17 UNDER CLIFFE
18 CASTLE RD
19 CASTLEGATE
20 HERISSON CL
21 ROSAMUND AV
22 NORMAN CL
23 HATCAGE LA
24 WILLOWGATE
25 HALL GARTH
26 Pickering
Com Jun Sch
27 St Joseph's
RC Prim Sch

74 A 75 B 76 C 77 D 78 E 79 F

121 96

F6
1 FIELD DR
2 PADDOCK CL
3 GARDEN WY
4 WESTERDALE
5 BRUCE WY
6 INGS CL
7 WEST PASTURE
8 PIKE RD
9 GOSLIPGATE
10 FISHERS GARTH
11 TROUTBECK CL
12 MALLARD CL
13 OTTER DR
14 KINGFISHER DR
15 MOLE END
16 WILLOW CT
17 RECREATION RD
18 KEEPERS GATE
19 SMIDDY HL
20 POOL CT
21 OUTGANG RD
22 CROSSGATE LA
23 GREBE WAY
24 DUNCOMBE DR

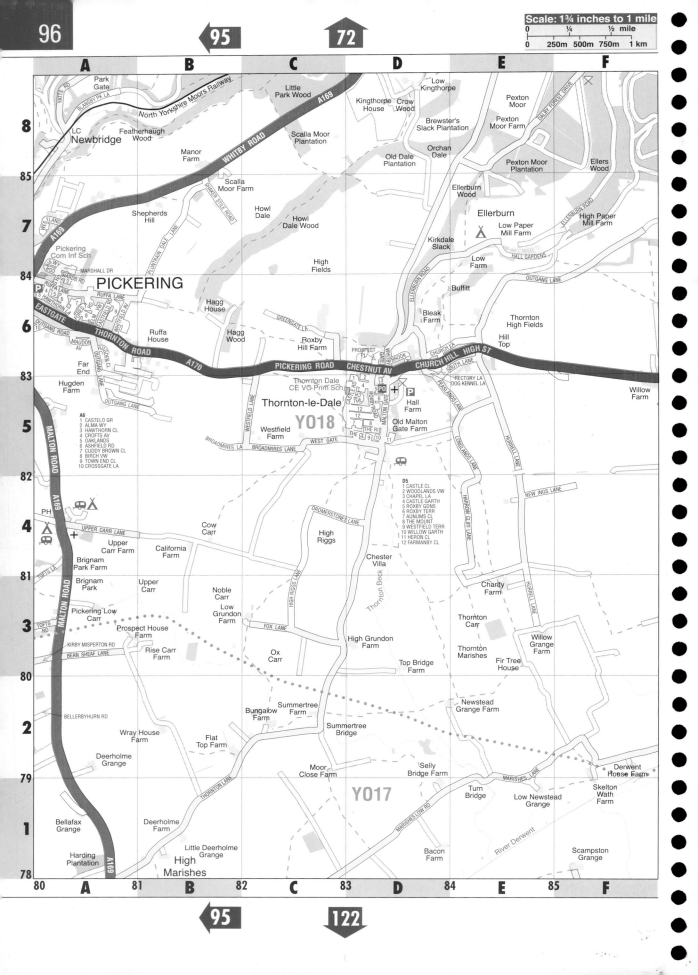

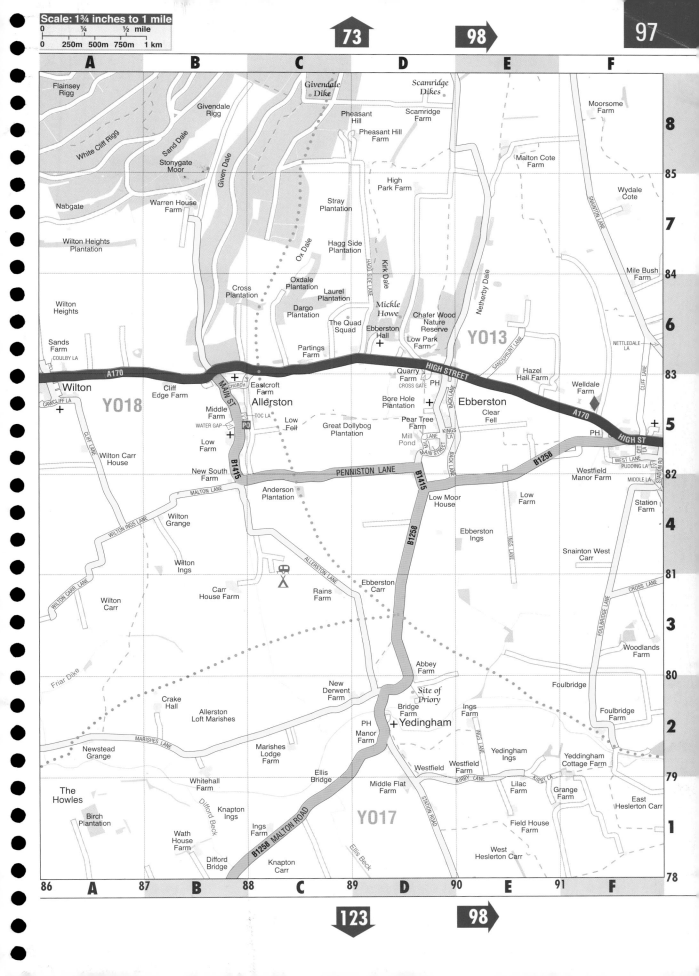

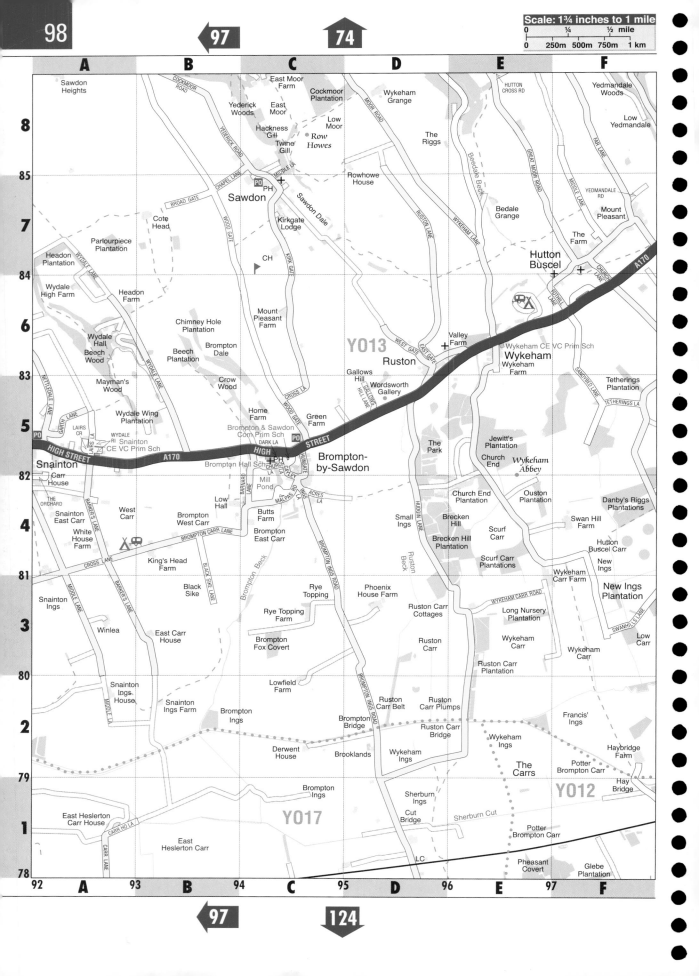

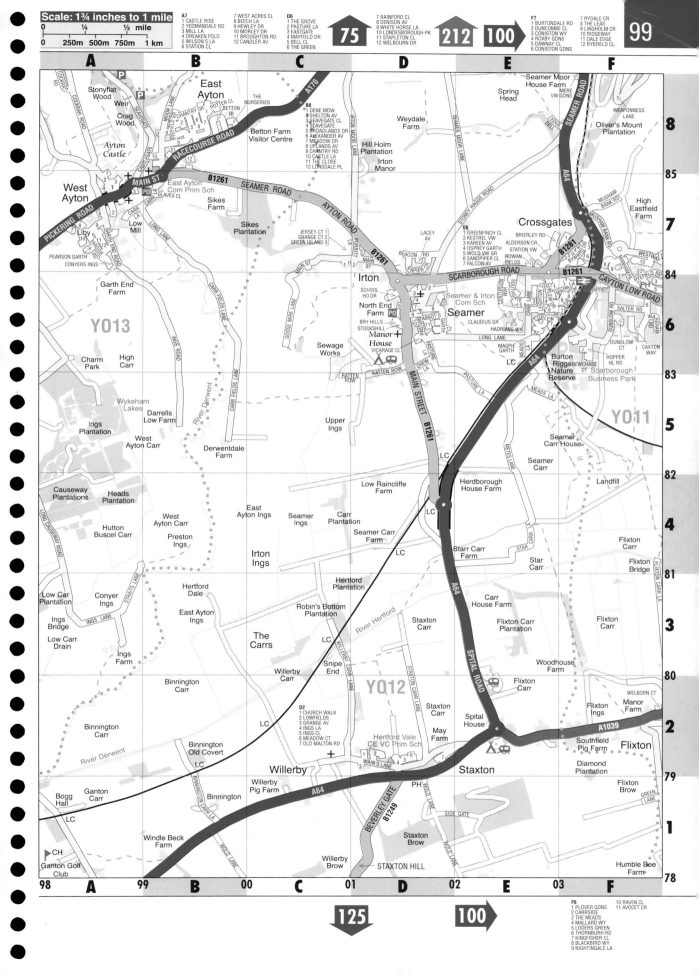

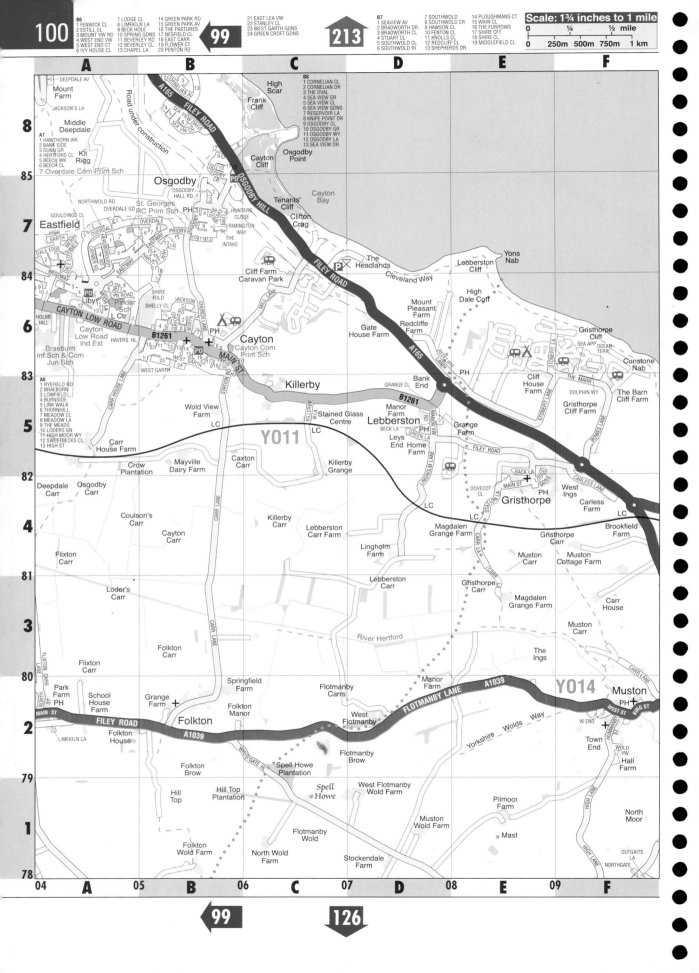

Scale: 1¾ inches to 1 mile

0 ¼ ½ mile
0 250m 500m 750m 1 km

A B C D E F

8 85 7 84 6 83 5 82 4 81 3 80 2 79 1 78

The Wyke

Cloakhouse End

Newbiggin

Newbiggin Farm West Moat

Crayke House Farm

Y014

Filey Dams Nature Reserve

Beacon Hill

Swimming Pool

Allison Field Farm

Mill Farm

Muston Grange

Lowfield Farm

North Moor

North Moor Farm

The Dams

King Hill

MOUNT VW

Centenary Way

MOOR ROAD

A165

SCARBOROUGH ROAD A1039

MUSTON ROAD

MILL LA

MOOR RD

Club Point

North Cliff

Cleveland Way

Filey Field

Filey Spa

North Cliff Ctry Park

Filey Brigg Nature Reserve

Filey Sands

Filey Folk Mus

Filey Jun Sch

FILEY

Evron Centre

Sun Lounge Theatre

Filey Bay

Muston Sands

Muston

CH

Filey Golf Club

South Cliff Dr

Hunmanby Sands

Primrose Valley

LAKESIDE

PH

Cherry Tree Dr

PINEWOOD AV

PLANE TREE WY

LC

A4
1 COPSE HL
2 HAZEL RD
3 ROWAN AV
4 WIDGEON CL
5 SNIPE CL
6 HERON CT
7 CYGNET CL
8 MALLARD CL
9 SHELDRAKE CL

B3
1 THE CROFT
2 ASHLEY CT
3 QUEEN'S TERR
4 LAUNDRY RD
5 CHURCH ST
6 ST OSWALDS CT
7 RAVINE TOP
8 BIRCH CL
9 CARLTON RD
10 VICTORIA AV
11 NORMAN CR
12 WEST RD
13 PROVIDENCE PL
14 QUEEN ST
15 REYNOLDS ST
16 MARINER'S TERR
17 WHITKIRK PL
18 WHISTON DR
19 LINTON CL
20 STATION AV
21 GRANVILLE RD
22 CROMWELLAV
23 CLAREMONT
24 MITFORD ST
25 CLIFFORD'S TERR
26 THE AVENUE
27 CHAPEL ST
28 UNION ST
29 RAINCLIFFE AV
30 HOPE ST
31 MURRAY ST
32 CARGATE HL
33 BELLE VUE CR
34 BELLE VUE ST
35 JOHN ST
36 WELFORD RD
37 WEST VALE
38 RUTLAND ST
39 HINDLE DR
40 FLOWER GARTH
41 HALLAM CL
42 ST JOHN'S AV
43 BROOKLANDS
44 BROOKLANDS CL
45 DORAN CL
46 PADBURY CL
47 CLARENCE AV
48 SOUTHDENE
49 COOPER RD
50 PADBURY AV
51 SOUTH CR CL
52 MELVILLE TERR
53 CRESCENT HL
54 SOUTH CR AV
55 BRIGG RD

B4
1 BACK SEA VW
2 THE CLOSE
3 HAWTHORN WY

A3
1 SANDPIPER CL
2 TEAL CL
3 CURLEW DR
4 HAREWOOD DR
5 SILVERWOOD AV
6 BURNSALL CL
7 LANGSETT AV
8 LEYBURN PL
9 BARDEN PL
10 RIVELIN WY
11 FEWSTON CL
12 COLLINGHAM WY
13 WASHBURN CL
14 WHARNCLIFFE PL
15 MIDHOPE WY
16 EWDEN CL

B4
1 LARCH GR
2 WILLOW CL
3 CEDAR GR
4 GROVE HILL RD
5 HORNDALE RD
6 THORN TREE AV
7 ALMOND CL
8 ARNDALE WY
9 CHURCH CLIFF DR
10 ELM CL
11 ALMOND GR
12 ASH GR
13 ASH RD
14 GROVE RD
15 THE GARDENS
16 THE CROFT
17 RAVINE HL
18 CHURCH CL

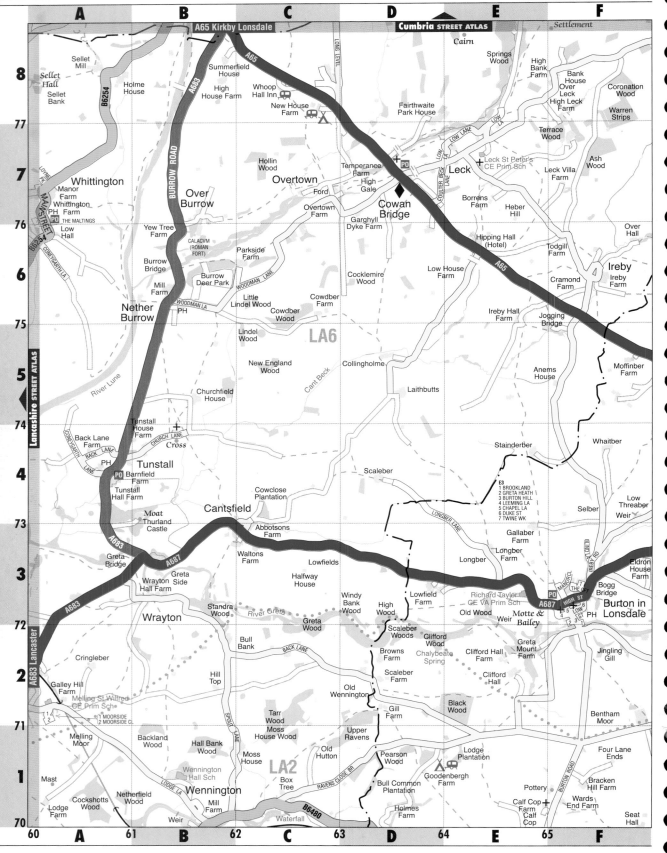

Scale: 1¾ inches to 1 mile

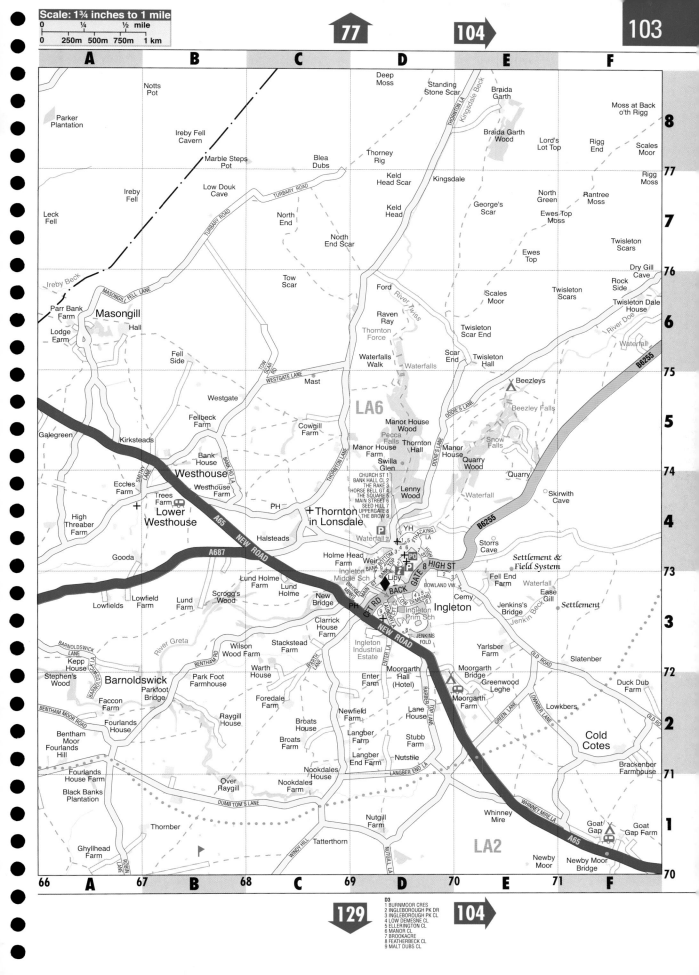

A **B** **C** **D** **E** **F**

8
77
7
76
6
75
5
74
4
73
3
72
2
71
1
70

Parker
Plantation

Notts
Pot

Deep
Moss

Standing
Stone Scar

Braida
Garth

Moss at Back
o'th Rigg

Ireby Fell
Cavern

Braida Garth
Wood

Lord's
Lot Top

Rigg
End

Scales
Moor

Marble Steps
Pot

Blea
Dubs

Thorney
Rig

Rigg
Moss

Low Douk
Cave

Turbary Road

Keld
Head Scar

Kingsdale

North
Green

Rantree
Moss

Leck
Fell

Ireby
Fell

North
End

Keld
Head

George's
Scar

Ewes Top
Moss

Twisleton
Scars

North
End Scar

Ewes
Top

Ireby Beck

Masongill Fell Lane

Tow
Scar

Ford

River Twiss

Scales
Moor

Twisleton
Scars

Rock
Side

Dry Gill
Cave

Twisleton Dale
House

River Doe

Parr Bank
Farm

Masongill

Raven
Ray

Thornton
Force

Twisleton
Scar End

Waterfall

B6255

Lodge
Farm

Hall

Waterfalls
Walk

Waterfalls

Scar
End

Twisleton
Hall

Fell
Side

Westgate Lane

Mast

LA6

Manor House
Wood

Beezleys

Beezley Falls

Westgate

Fellbeck
Farm

Cowgill
Farm

Pecca
Falls

Thornton
Hall

Manor
House

Snow
Falls

Galegreen

Kirksteads

Bank
House

Manor House
Farm

Swilla
Glen

Quarry
Wood

Skirwith
Cave

Eccles
Farm

Trees
Farm

Westhouse
Farm

Thornton Lane

CHURCH ST 1
BANK HALL CL 2
THE RAKE 3
HORSE BELL GT 4
THE SQUARE 5
MAIN STREET 6
SEED HILL 7
UPPERGATE 8
THE BROW 9

Lenny
Wood

Quarry

Westhouse

Lower
Westhouse

PH

Thornton
in Lonsdale

Waterfall

B6255

Storrs
Cave

Settlement &
Field System

High
Threaber
Farm

A65

NEW ROAD

Halsteads

YH

Waterfall

Gooda

A687

Lund Holme
Farm

Lund
Holme

New
Bridge

Holme Head
Farm

Weir

Ingleton
Middle Sch

8 HIGH ST

Fell End
Farm

Ingleton

Waterfall

Ease
Gill

Lowfields

Lowfield
Farm

Lund
Farm

Scrogg's
Wood

PH

Libry

BACK GATE

Cemy

Ingleton

Jenkins's
Bridge

Jenkin Beck

Settlement

Barnoldswick
Lane

River Greta

Wilson
Wood Farm

Stackstead
Farm

BENTHAM RD

Clarrick House
Farm

Ingleton
Prim Sch

Jenkins
Fold

Yarlsber
Farm

OLD ROAD

Slatenber

Kepp
House

Park Foot
Farmhouse

Warth
House

Ingleton
Industrial
Estate

Moorgarth
Hall
(Hotel)

Moorgarth
Bridge

Greenwood
Leghe

Lowkbers

Duck Dub
Farm

Stephen's
Wood

Barnoldswick

Faccon
Farm

Parkfoot
Bridge

Foredale
Farm

Enter
Farm

Moorgarth
Farm

GREEN LANE

LOWBER LANE

Cold
Cotes

Bentham Moor Road

Fourlands
House

Raygill
House

Broats
House

Newfield
Farm

Langber
Farm

Lane
House

Stubb
Farm

Brackenber
Farmhouse

Bentham
Moor
Fourlands
Hill

Broats
Farm

Langber
End Farm

Nutstile

WHINNEY MIRE LA

A65

Fourlands
House Farm

Over
Raygill

Nookdales
House

Nookdales
Farm

DUMB TOM'S LANE

LANGBER END LA

Whinney
Mire

Goat
Gap

Goat
Gap Farm

Black Banks
Plantation

Thornber

Nutgill
Farm

LA2

Newby
Moor

Newby Moor
Bridge

Ghyllhead
Farm

ROBIN LANE

Tatterthorn

WINDY HILL

NUTGILL LA

A65

A **B** **C** **D** **E** **F**

66   67   68   69   70   71

D3
1 BURNMOOR CRES
2 INGLEBOROUGH PK DR
3 INGLEBOROUGH PK CL
4 LOW DEMESNE CL
5 ELLERINGTON CL
6 MANOR CL
7 BROOKACRE
8 FEATHERBECK CL
9 MALT DUBS CL

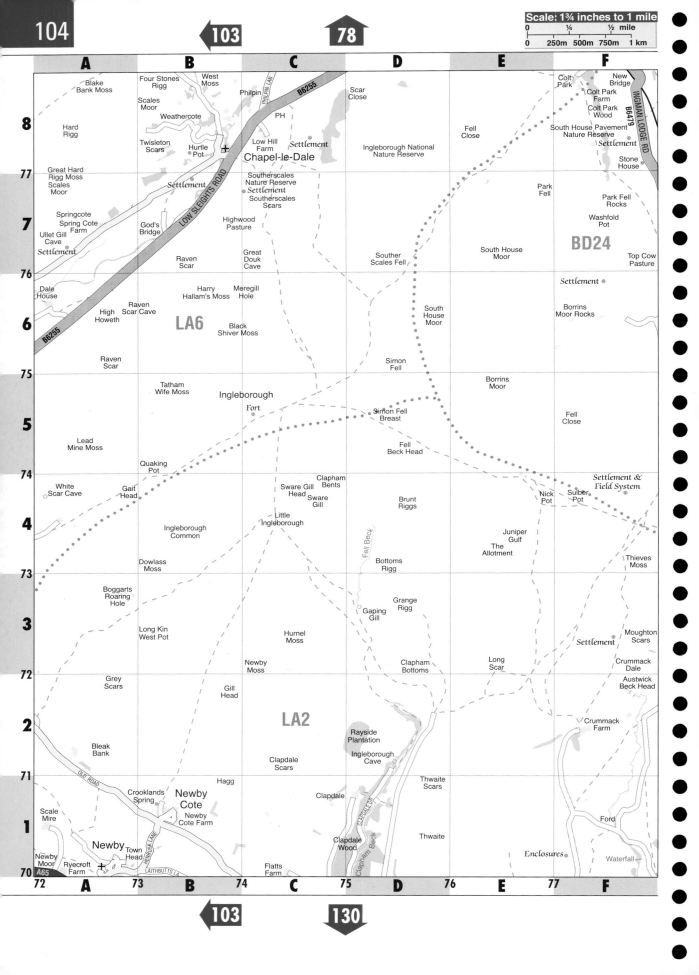

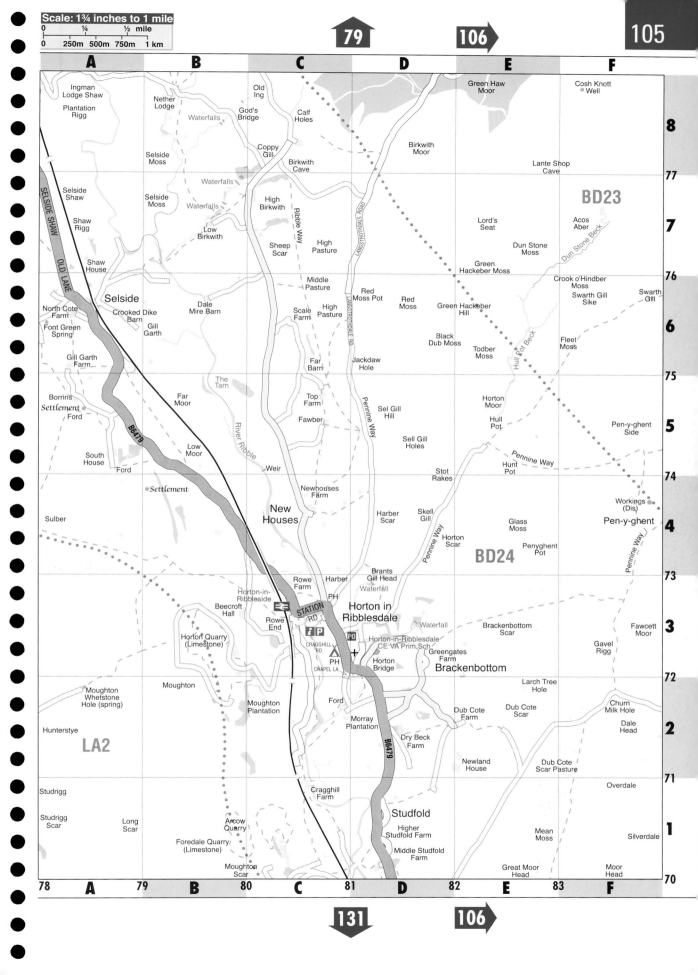

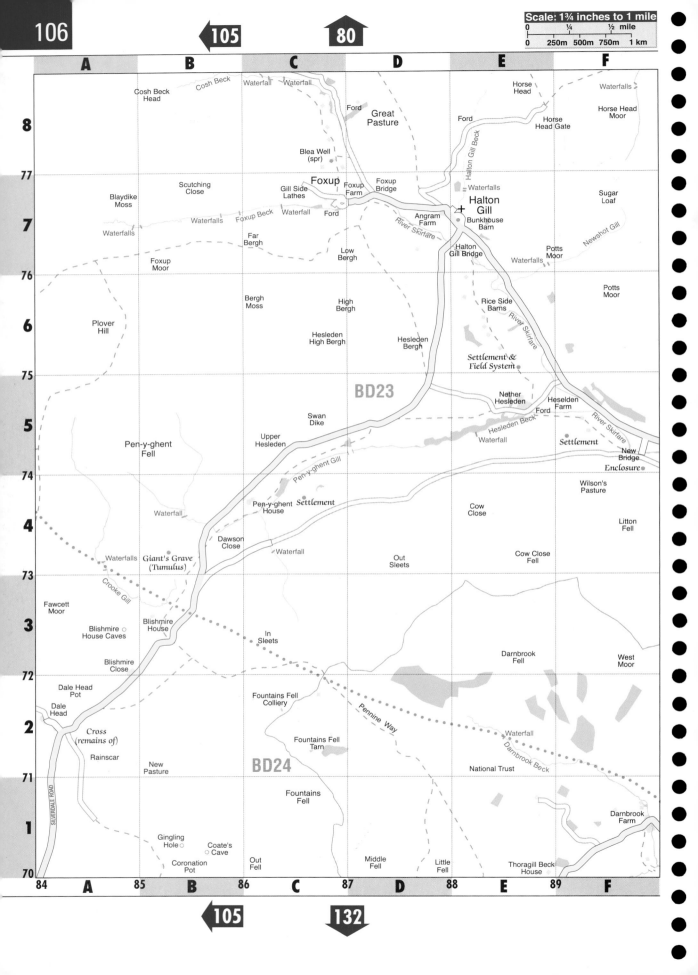

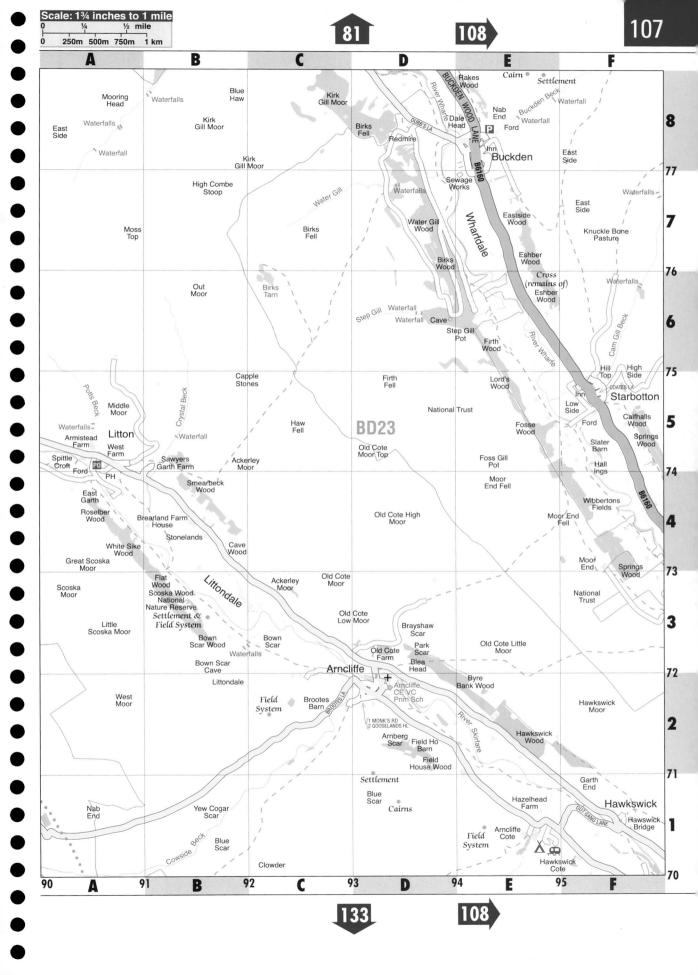

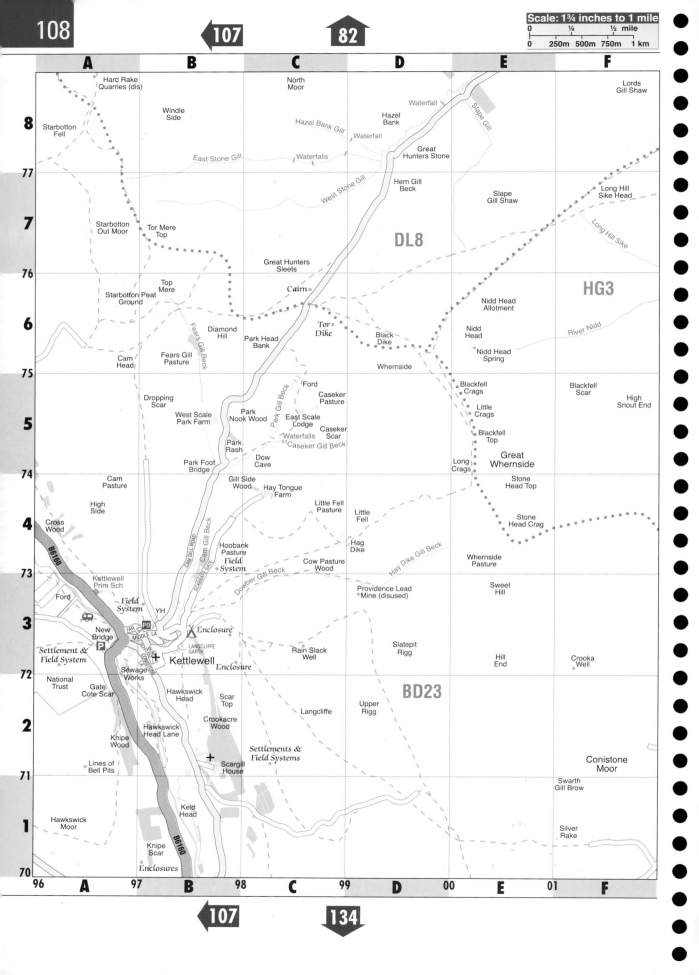

107
82

Scale: 1¾ inches to 1 mile

0   ¼   ½   mile
0   250m   500m   750m   1 km

A **B** **C** **D** **E** **F**

Hard Rake
Quarries (dis)

North
Moor

Lords
Gill Shaw

Windle
Side

Waterfall

Starbotton
Fell

Hazel Bank Gill

Hazel
Bank

Slape Gill

8

Waterfall

Great
Hunters Stone

East Stone Gill

Waterfalls

Long Hill
Sike Head

77

West Stone Gill

Hem Gill
Beck

Slape
Gill Shaw

Long Hill Sike

7

Starbotton
Out Moor

Tor Mere
Top

DL8

Long Hill Sike

Great Hunters
Sleets

76

Top
Mere

Cairn

HG3

Starbotton Peat
Ground

Nidd Head
Allotment

River Nidd

6

Diamond
Hill

Park Head
Bank

Tor
Dike

Nidd
Head

Fears Gill Beck

Fears Gill
Pasture

Black
Dike

Nidd Head
Spring

Cam
Head

Whernside

75

Ford

Blackfell
Crags

Blackfell
Scar

High
Snout End

Dropping
Scar

Caseker
Pasture

Little
Crags

Park Gill Beck

5

West Scale
Park Farm

Park
Nook Wood

East Scale
Lodge

Caseker
Scar

Blackfell
Top

Waterfalls

Park
Rash

Caseker Gill Beck

Dow
Cave

Long
Crags

Great
Whernside

Park Foot
Bridge

Stone
Head Top

74

Cam
Pasture

Gill Side
Wood

Hay Tongue
Farm

Stone
Head Crag

High
Side

Little Fell
Pasture

Little
Fell

4

Cross
Wood

B6160

Cam Gill Beck

Hoobank
Pasture
*Field
System*

Hag
Dike

Hay Dike Gill Beck

Whernside
Pasture

73

SCARGATE GATE

Kettlewell
Prim Sch

Cow Pasture
Wood

Providence Lead
Mine (disused)

Sweet
Hill

Dowber Gill Beck

Ford

*Field
System*

YH

3

New
Bridge

PO

Enclosure

Rain Slack
Well

Slatepit
Rigg

Hill
End

Crooka
Well

FAR
MIDDLE LA

△

LANGCLIFFE
GARTH

CONISTONE

*Settlement &
Field System*

Kettlewell

Enclosure

BD23

72

National
Trust

Sewage
Works

Hawkswick
Head

Scar
Top

Langcliffe

Upper
Rigg

Gate
Cote Scar

2

Knipe
Wood

Hawkswick
Head Lane

Crookacre
Wood

Conistone
Moor

Lines of
Bell Pits

*Settlements &
Field Systems*

Scargill
House

71

Swarth
Gill Brow

B6160

Hawkswick
Moor

Keld
Head

1

Knipe
Scar

Silver
Rake

Enclosures

70

96 **A** 97 **B** 98 **C** 99 **D** 00 **E** 01 **F**

107
134

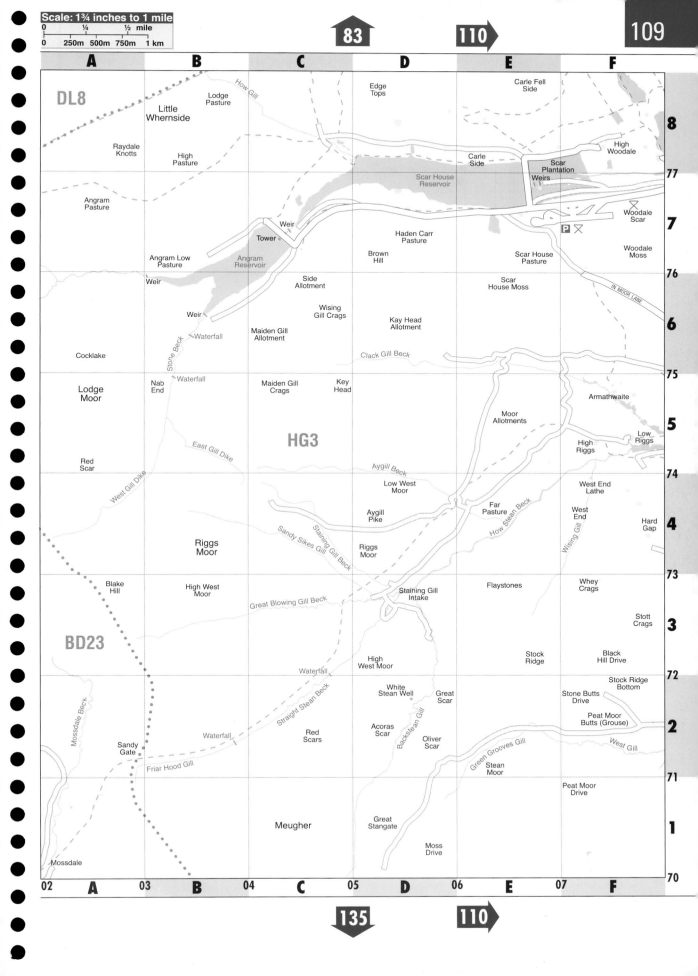

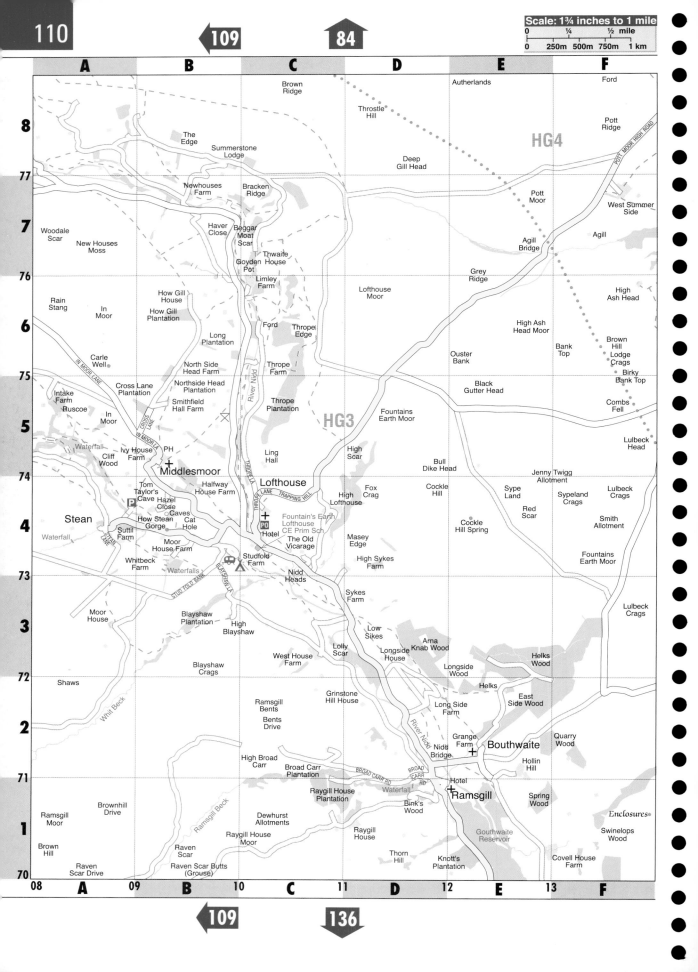

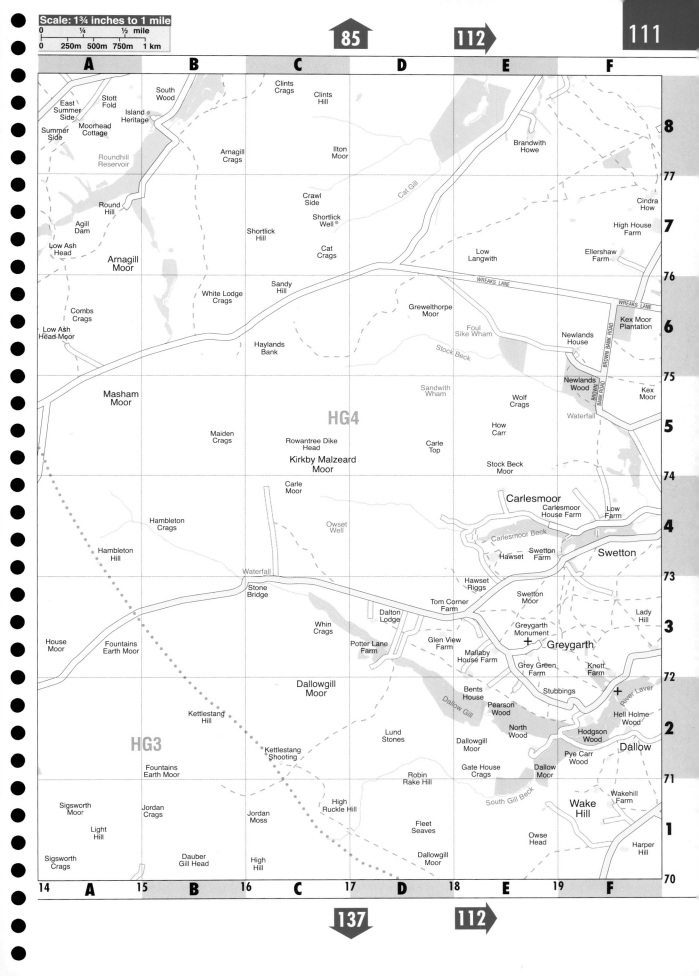

A   B   C   D   E   F

8

East Summer Side
Stott Fold
South Wood
Island Heritage
Summer Side
Moorhead Cottage
Clints Crags
Clints Hill

77

Roundhill Reservoir
Arnagill Crags
Ilton Moor
Brandwith Howe

7

Round Hill
Agill Dam
Crawl Side
Shortlick Well
Shortlick Hill
Cat Crags
Cindra How
High House Farm
Ellershaw Farm

Low Ash Head
Arnagill Moor
Sandy Hill
White Lodge Crags
Grewelthorpe Moor
Low Langwith
WREAKS LANE
WREAKS LANE

76

Combs Crags
Foul Sike Wham
Newlands House
Kex Moor Plantation

6

Low Ash Head Moor
Haylands Bank
Stock Beck
Newlands Wood
Waterfall
Kex Moor

75

Masham Moor
Sandwith Wham
Wolf Crags
How Carr

HG4

5

Maiden Crags
Rowantree Dike Head
Carle Top
Stock Beck Moor

Kirkby Malzeard Moor

74

Carle Moor
Carlesmoor
Carlesmoor House Farm
Low Farm

4

Hambleton Crags
Owset Well
Carlesmoor Beck
Hawset
Swetton Farm
Swetton

Hambleton Hill
Waterfall
Hawset Riggs

73

House Moor
Fountains Earth Moor
Stone Bridge
Whin Crags
Dalton Lodge
Tom Corner Farm
Swetton Moor
Lady Hill

3

Potter Lane Farm
Glen View Farm
Greygarth Monument
Greygarth

Mallaby House Farm
Grey Green Farm
Knott Farm

72

Kettlestang Hill
Dallowgill Moor
Bents House
Pearson Wood
Stubbings
Hell Holme Wood

HG3

2

Fountains Earth Moor
Kettlestang Shooting
Lund Stones
Dallowgill Moor
North Wood
Hodgson Wood
Pye Carr Wood
Dallow

Robin Rake Hill
Gate House Crags
Dallow Moor

71

Sigsworth Moor
Jordan Crags
Jordan Moss
High Ruckle Hill
South Gill Beck
Wake Hill
Wakehill Farm

1

Light Hill
Fleet Seaves
Owse Head
Harper Hill

Sigsworth Crags
Dauber Gill Head
High Hill
Dallowgill Moor

70

14   A   15   B   16   C   17   D   18   E   19   F

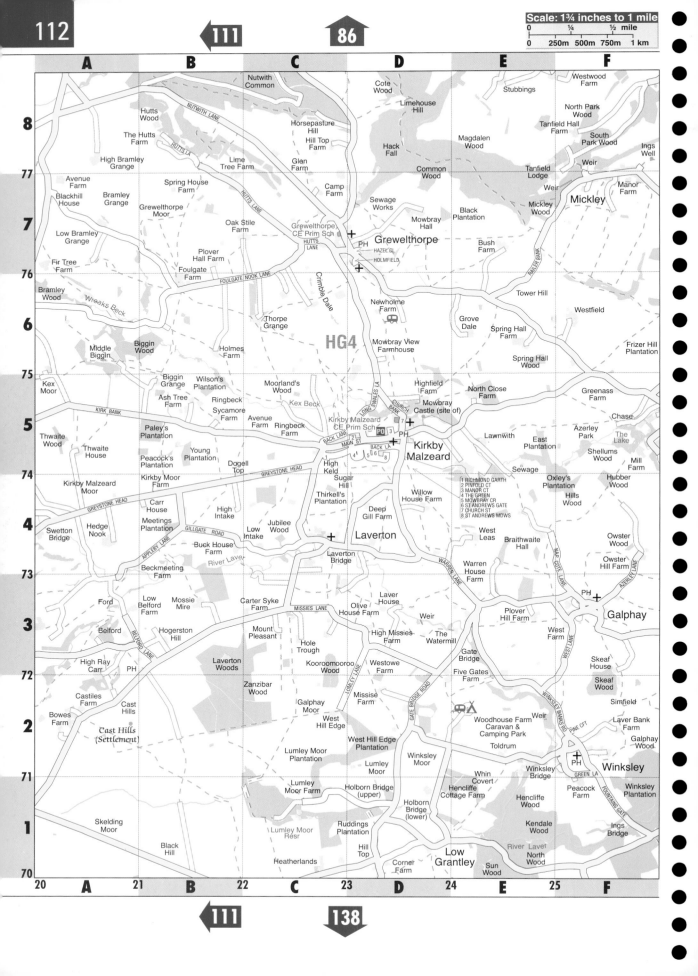

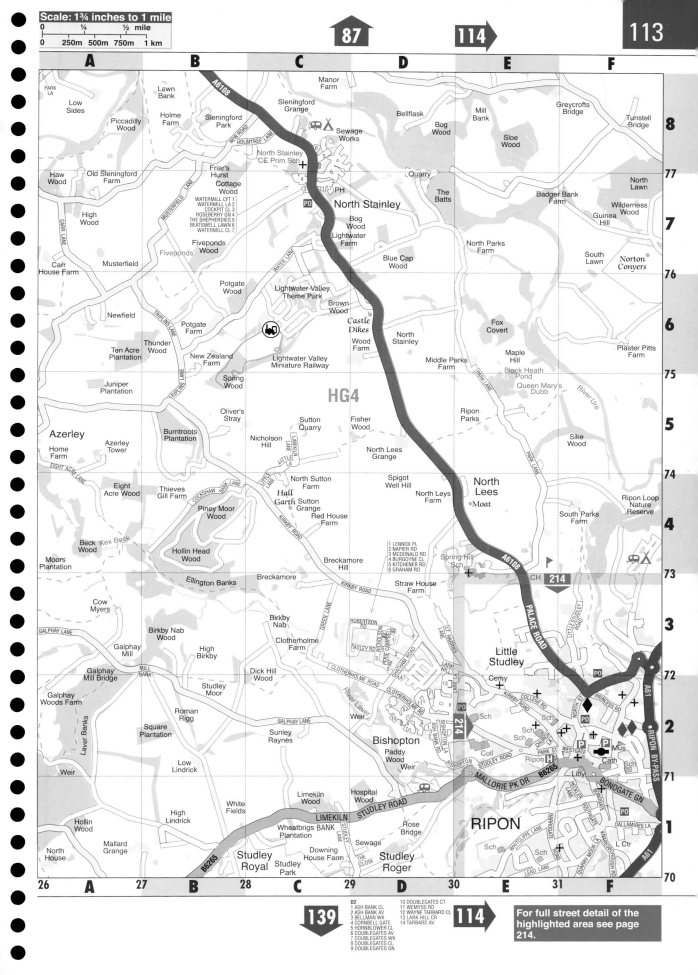

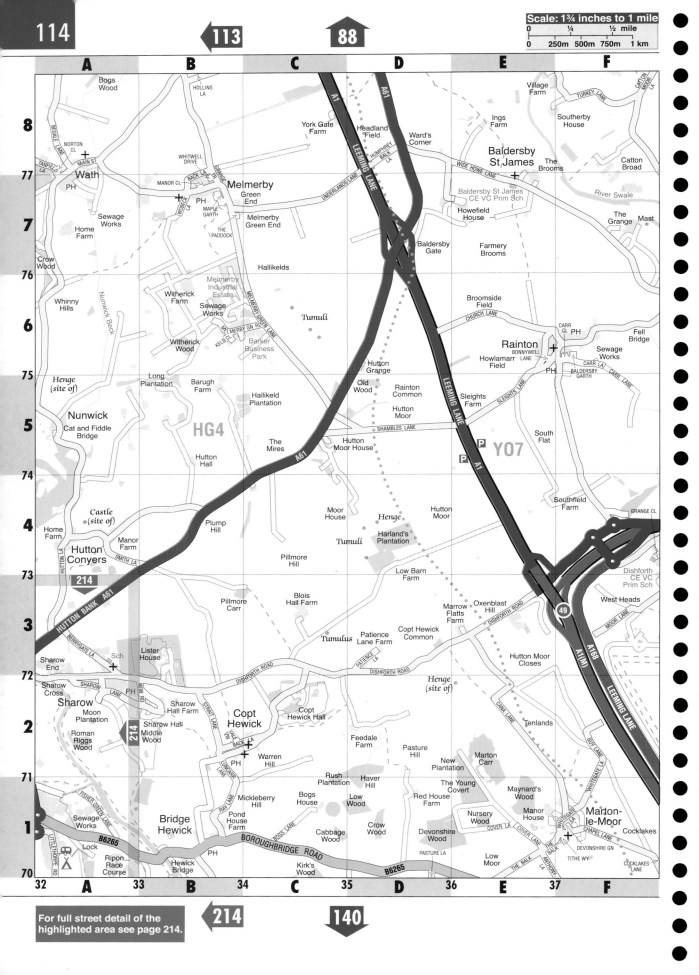

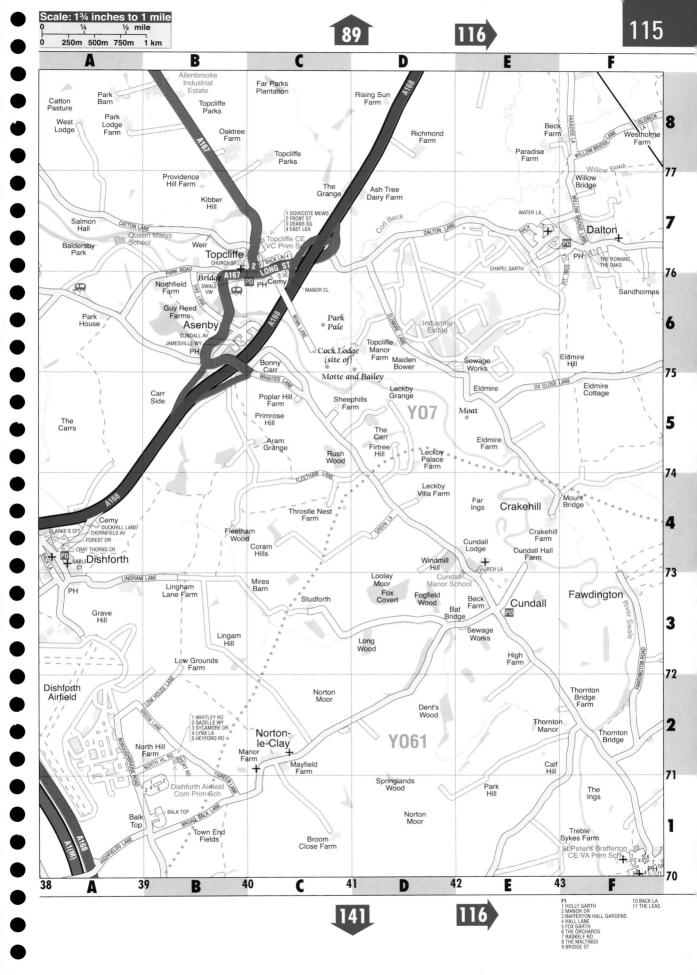

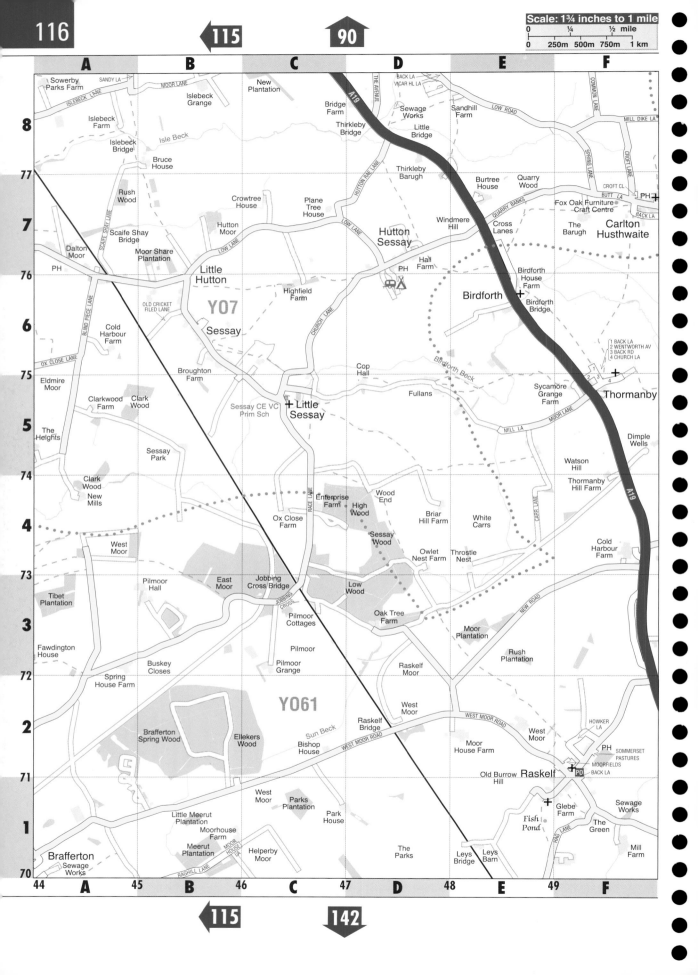

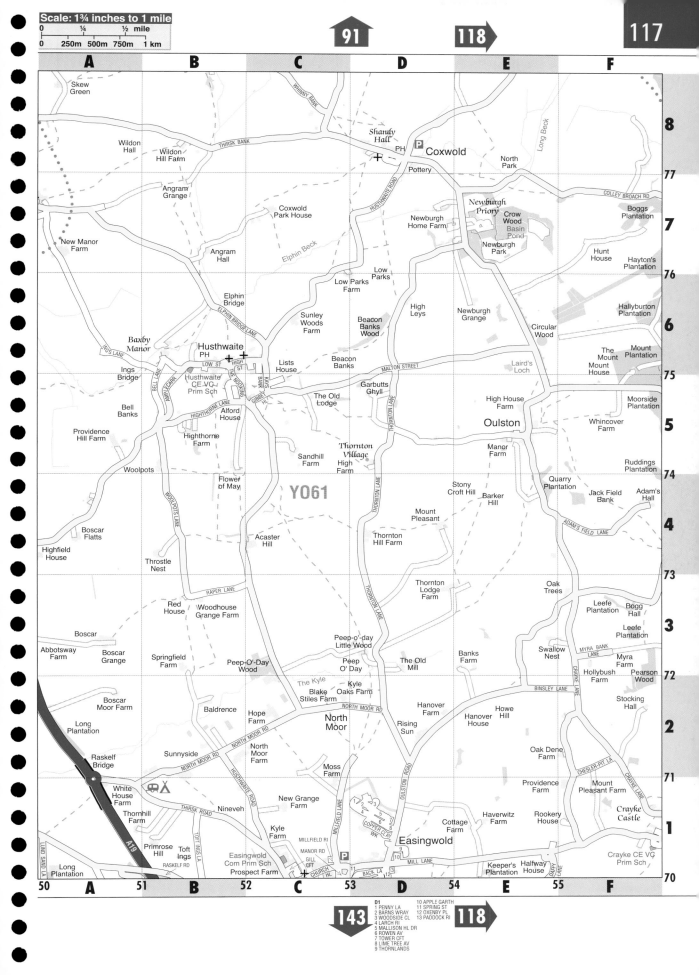

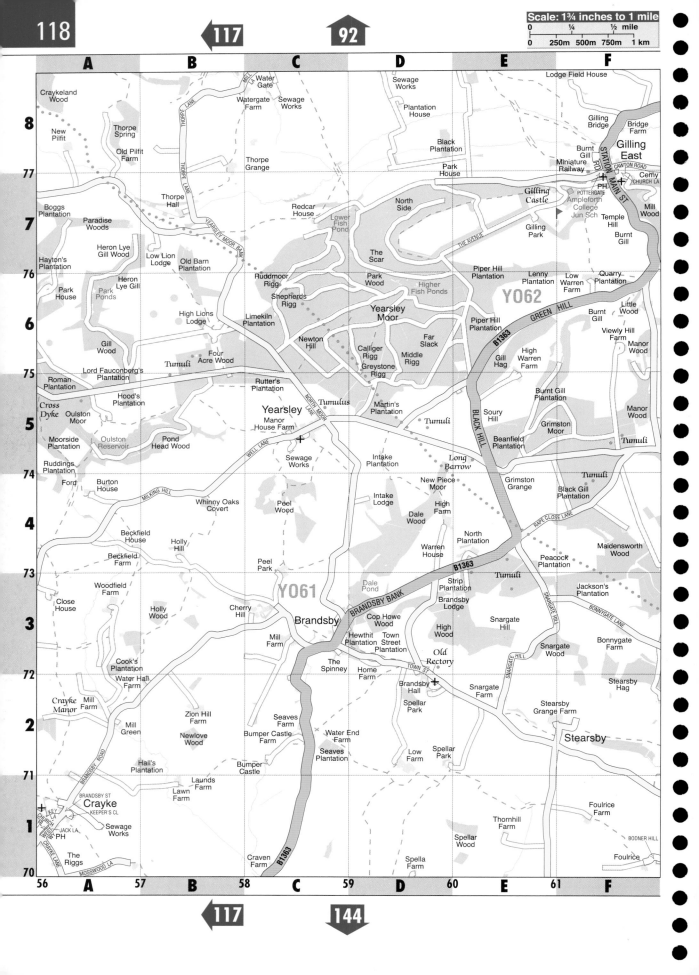

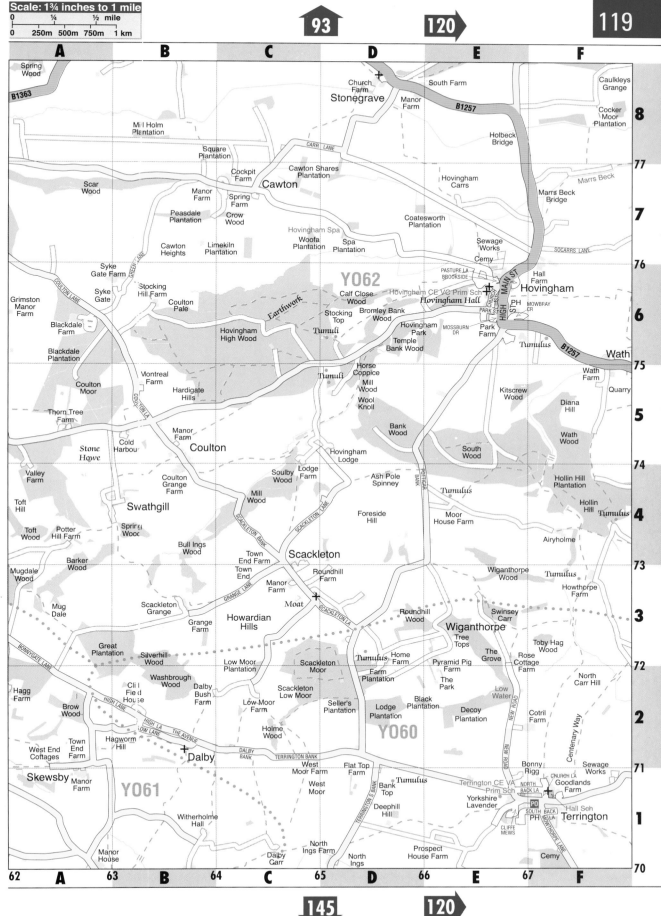

Scale: 1¾ inches to 1 mile

0   ¼   ½   mile
0   250m 500m 750m   1 km

A   B   C   D   E   F

Spring Wood

B1363

Mill Holm Plantation

Square Plantation

Scar Wood

Manor Farm

Peasdale Plantation

Crow Wood

Cockpit Farm

CARR LANE

Cawton Shares Plantation

Cawton

Church Farm

Stonegrave

Manor Farm

South Farm

B1257

Caulkleys Grange

Cocker Moor Plantation

Holbeck Bridge

Marrs Beck

8

77

Cawton Heights

Spring Farm

Limekiln Plantation

GREEN LANE

Hovingham Spa

Woofa Plantation

Spa Plantation

Hovingham Carrs

Coatesworth Plantation

Marrs Beck Bridge

SOCARRS LANE

7

Syke Gate Farm

Syke Gate

Stocking Hill Farm

Coulton Pale

COULTON LANE

Earthwork

Calf Close Wood

Stocking Top

Bromley Bank Wood

YO62

PASTURE LA
BROOKSIDE

Hovingham CE VC Prim Sch

Sewage Works

Cemy

Hall Farm

HIGH MAIN ST

Hovingham

PH

MOWBRAY CR

76

Grimston Manor Farm

Blackdale Farm

Blackdale Plantation

Coulton Moor

Montreal Farm

COULTON LA

Hovingham High Wood

Tumuli

Hardigate Hills

Temple Bank Wood

Hovingham Park

Hovingham Hall

MOSSBURN DR

Park Farm

PARK ST

Park Farm

Tumulus

B1257

Wath

6

Thorn Tree Farm

Cold Harbour

Manor Farm

Tumuli

Horse Coppice

Mill Wood

Wool Knoll

Bank Wood

Kitscrew Wood

Diana Hill

Wath Farm

Quarry

Wath Wood

75

Valley Farm

Toft Hill

Stone Howe

Coulton

Coulton Grange Farm

Mill Wood

Soulby Wood

Lodge Farm

Hovingham Lodge

Ash Pole Spinney

POTTICA BANK

Tumulus

South Wood

Hollin Hill Plantation

74

Toft Wood

Potter Hill Farm

Swathgill

Spring Wood

Bull Ings Wood

SCACKLETON BANK

SCACKLETON LANE

Foreside Hill

Moor House Farm

Hollin Hill

Tumulus

5

4

Mugdale Wood

Barker Wood

Town End Farm

Town End

Scackleton

Manor Farm

Roundhill Farm

GRANGE LANE

Moat

SCACKLETON LA

Roundhill Wood

Wiganthorpe Wood

Tumulus

Howthorpe Farm

Swinsey Carr

73

Mug Dale

BONNYGATE LANE

Scackleton Grange

Grange Farm

Great Plantation

Silverhill Wood

Howardian Hills

Low Moor Plantation

Scackleton Moor

Tumulus

Home Farm

Farm Plantation

Wiganthorpe

Tree Tops

Pyramid Pig Farm

The Park

The Grove

Toby Hag Wood

Rose Cottage Farm

Low Water

North Carr Hill

72

3

Hagg Farm

Brow Wood

HIGH LANE

Cliff Field House

Washbrough Wood

Dalby Bush Farm

Low Moor Farm

THE AVENUE

Seller's Plantation

Lodge Plantation

Black Plantation

YO60

Decoy Plantation

NEW ROAD

Cotril Farm

Centenary Way

2

West End Cottages

Town End Farm

Hagworm Hill

HIGH LA

LOW LANE

Dalby

DALBY BANK

Holme Wood

TERRINGTON BANK

Flat Top Farm

West Moor Farm

Tumulus

Bank Top

Terrington CE VA Prim Sch

NORTH BACK LA

Bonny Rigg

CHURCH LA

Goodlands Farm

Sewage Works

71

Skewsby

Manor Farm

YO61

Witherholme Hall

Manor House

Dalby Carr

West Moor

TERRINGTON S BANK

Deephill Hill

North Ings Farm

North Ings

Prospect House Farm

Yorkshire Lavender

SOUTH BACK LA

PO

PH

CLIFFE MEWS

Hall Sch

Terrington

TERRINGTON LANE

Cemy

1

70

62   A   63   B   64   C   65   D   66   E   67   F

119
94

Scale: 1¾ inches to 1 mile

0   ¼   ½   mile
0   250m 500m 750m 1 km

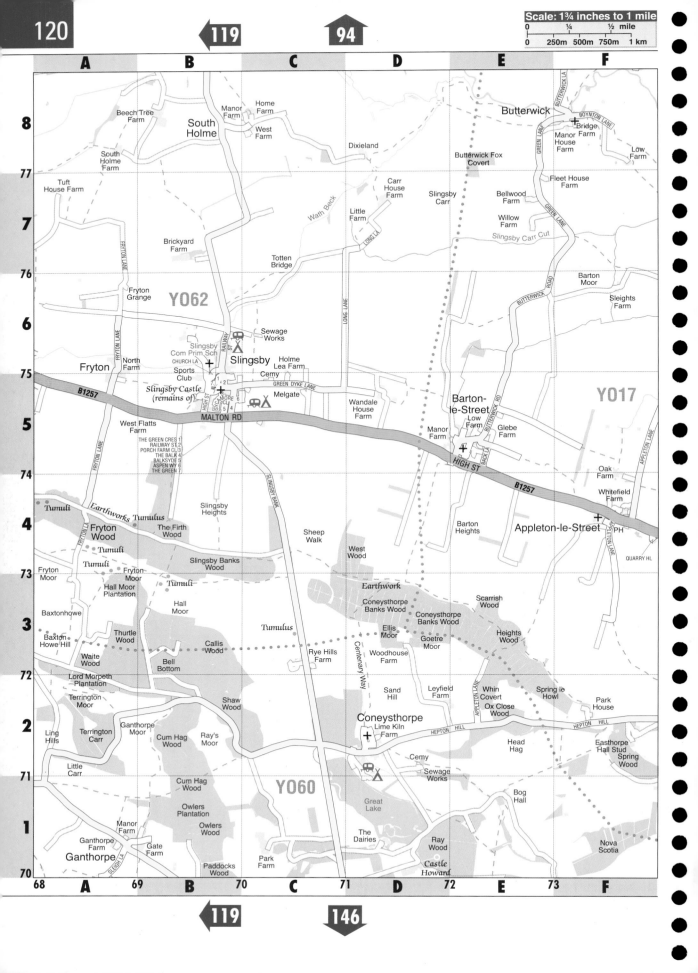

A   B   C   D   E   F

8

Beech Tree Farm

Manor Farm

Home Farm

Butterwick

BUTTERWICK LA

BOYNTON LANE

South Holme

West Farm

Bridge Farm

GREEN LANE

Manor House Farm

Low Farm

77

South Holme Farm

Dixieland

Butterwick Fox Covert

Fleet House Farm

Tuft House Farm

Carr House Farm

Slingsby Carr

Bellwood Farm

GREEN LANE

7

Wath Beck

Little Farm

Slingsby Carr Cut

Willow Farm

Brickyard Farm

LONG LA

Barton Moor

76

Totten Bridge

BUTTERWICK ROAD

Sleights Farm

Fryton Grange

YO62

FRYTON LANE

LONG LANE

6

Sewage Works

Slingsby Com Prim Sch

RAILWAY ST

YO17

Fryton

North Farm

CHURCH LA

Slingsby

Holme Lea Farm

BUTTERWICK RD

75

Sports Club

Cemy

Barton-le-Street

B1257

Slingsby Castle (remains of)

HIGH ST

SYCAMORE LE

GREEN DYKE LANE

Melgate

Wandale House Farm

Manor Farm

Low Farm

Glebe Farm

5

West Flatts Farm

MALTON RD

THE GREEN CRES 1
RAILWAY ST 2
PORCH FARM CL 3
THE BALK 4
BALKSYDE 5
ASPEN WY 6
THE GREEN 7

HIGH ST

BACK LA

APPLETON LANE

74

SLINGSBY BANK

Slingsby Heights

B1257

Oak Farm

Whitefield Farm

Tumuli

Earthworks Tumulus

4

Fryton Wood

FRYTON LA

The Firth Wood

Slingsby Heights

Sheep Walk

West Wood

Barton Heights

Appleton-le-Street

APPLETON LANE

PH

Tumuli

Slingsby Banks Wood

QUARRY HL

73

Fryton Moor

Tumuli

Fryton Moor

Tumuli

Earthwork

Scarrish Wood

Baxtonhowe

Hall Moor Plantation

Tumuli

Hall Moor

Tumulus

Coneysthorpe Banks Wood

Coneysthorpe Banks Wood

Heights Wood

3

Baxton Howe Hill

Thurtle Wood

Callis Wood

Ellis Moor

Goetre Moor

Rye Hills Farm

Woodhouse Farm

Waite Wood

Bell Bottom

CENTENARY WAY

72

Lord Morpeth Plantation

Sand Hill

Leyfield Farm

Whin Covert

Spring le Howl

Park House

Terrington Moor

Shaw Wood

APPLETON LANE

Ox Close Wood

HEPTON HILL

HEPTON HILL

2

Ling Hills

Terrington Carr

Ganthorpe Moor

Cum Hag Wood

Ray's Moor

Coneysthorpe

Lime Kiln Farm

Head Hag

Easthorpe Hall Stud

Spring Wood

Little Carr

Cemy

71

Cum Hag Wood

YO60

Sewage Works

Bog Hall

1

Manor Farm

Owlers Plantation

Owlers Wood

Great Lake

Ray Wood

Nova Scotia

Ganthorpe Farm

Gate Farm

SLEGRA LA

The Dairies

Castle Howard

Ganthorpe

Paddocks Wood

Park Farm

70

68   A   69   B   70   C   71   D   72   E   73   F

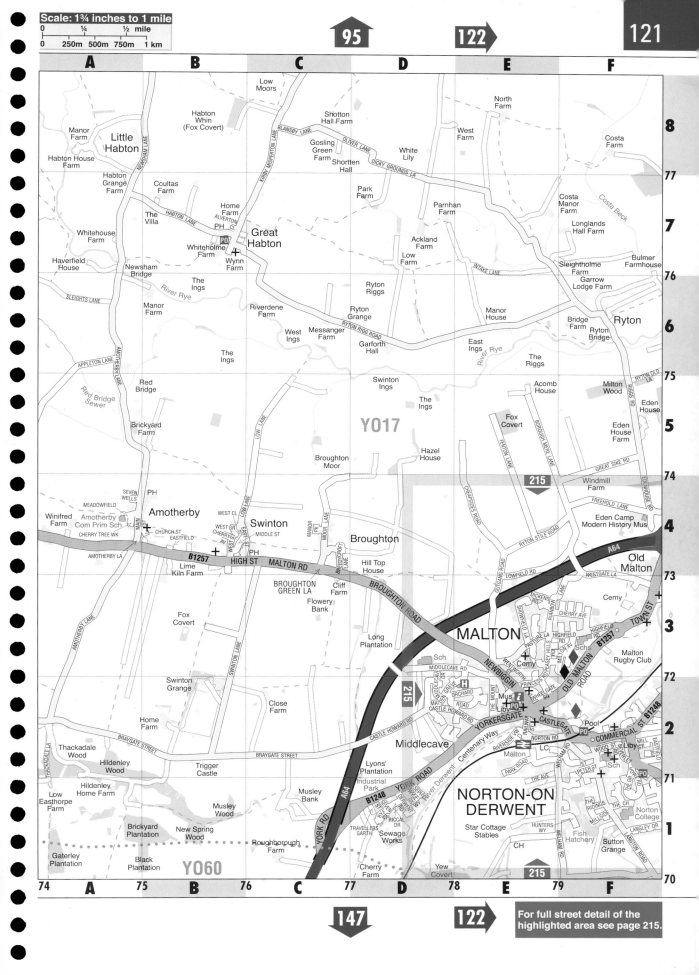

A   B   C   D   E   F

8

Low Bellafax Grange

White House Farm

The Riggs

Holme Farm

The Firs   High Carr

Redcarr Plantation

Golden Square

Sheepfoot Grange

Riggs Farm

The Howles

Viaduct Farm

River Derwent

High Carr Plantation

MARISHES LOW ROAD

Low Marishes

Wath Farm

77

Marishes

Low Moor Farm

Middle Farm

Middle Plantation

BACK LANE

Wath Hall

7

Middle Farm

Rillington Low Moor

Elm Farm

OUTGANG ROAD

Grove House Farm

North Ings

Newstead Farm

Sleights Farm

Abbey Farm

Lambert's Plantation

Howe Bridge Farm

Howe Bridge

76

Abbotts Farm

Ryton Ings

River Rye

South Ings

Low Moor S LA

Lilac Farm

LC

American Plantation

West Wykeham Ings

Castle Ings

Breckney Farm

The Breckneys

Ivy Lea Farm

LC

6

Howe Farm

Wykeham

Rye Mouth

Fox Covert

Manor Farm

The Howes

LOW MOOR LANE

LC

Plains Farm

Wykeham Farm

East Wykeham Ings

Villa Farm

Edge Plantation

Willow Farm

BRECKNEY LA

75

Old Malton Moor

HOWE ROAD

West Moor

Hawk Plantation

LC

Rillington Manor

RYTON OLD ROAD

Edenhouse Plantation

WYKEHAM ROAD

Long Ings

The Carrs

Sewage Works

Park Farm

Rillington

PH

SANDS LA

SCARBOROUGH RD

5

Black Wood

Espersykes

Y017

Ruston Plantation

MANOR VW 1
SLEDGATE GARTH 2
SOUTHLEA 3
MEADOW CT 4
SAXON DR 5
WOODLANDS AV 6
WOODLANDS GR 7

Rillington Cem Prim Sch

A169

Old Malton Moor

RABBIT LANE

River Derwent

Scagglethorpe Ings

West Field

MALTON ROAD

WESTGATE

PO

COLLINSONS LA

74

215

LC

Scagglethorpe Lane

Scagglethorpe Grange

Acuba Farm

Five Beeches

A64

THE OUTGANG

EDENHOUSE RD

WISE HOUSE LANE

Wyse House

Scagglethorpe Moor

Laurel Farm

Bassett House

Beech Tree Farm

Church Farm

4

Rixt Woods

Marr House

Willow Farm

Under Brow Farm

A64

Settrington Ings

Marr Whin

Manor Farm

Thorpe Bassett Wold

Spring Farm

73

Barr Farm

LASCELLES LANE

Abbey Ings

Beck House

PH

Brow Farm

Scagglethorpe Brow

Fish Ponds

Norton Parks

Scagglethorpe Bridge

Beech Tree Farm

Thorpe Bassett Wold

Villa Farm

3

SCARBOROUGH ROAD

Scagglethorpe

SOUTHFIELD

B1248

Whinflower Hall

Brambling Fields

Brow Farm

Ebor House

72

215

BULL PIECE LA

Crosscliffe Farm

Priorpot Bridge

Norton Grove Stud

HIGHFIELD LA

HIGHFIELD LA

Mast

Many Thorns Farm

2

HUGGIN WAY

The Moor

BRAMBLING FIELDS LA

Settrington Beck

The Holms

FORGERS LANE

Settrington All Saints CE VC Prim Sch

Settrington Cliffs

Cinquefoil Hill

THORPE BASSETT LANE

HIGH STREET

71

B1248

Centenary Way

MIDDLETON CL

Settrington Cliffs

Shepherdess Plantation

Town Wold

RYEDALE CL

TOWN ST

CHAPEL RD

Cemy

Settrington

HORSE COURSE LANE

Wold House

1

MOOR LA

Town Green Farm

BACK LANE

NEW RD

Wardale

Westfield Farm

SCARLET BALK LANE

CHURCH LA

Shepherdess Plantation

Settrington Plantation

Scarlet Balk Plantation

Rectory Farm

Settrington House

70

215

BEVERLEY ROAD

Gallops

LANGTON LA

80   A   81   B   82   C   83   D   84   E   85   F

For full street detail of the highlighted area see page 215.

215

148

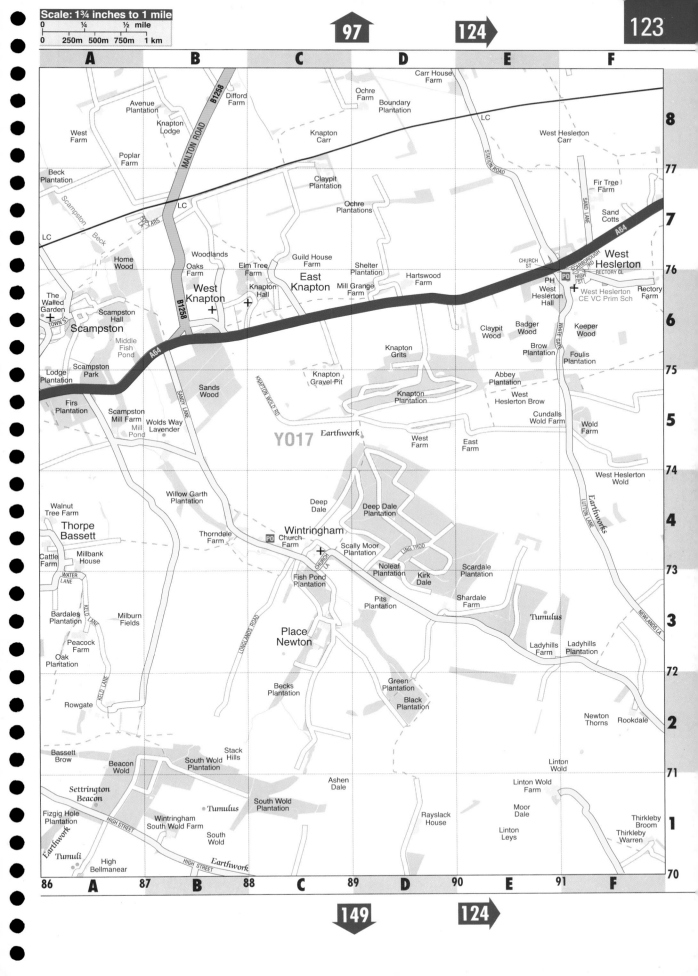

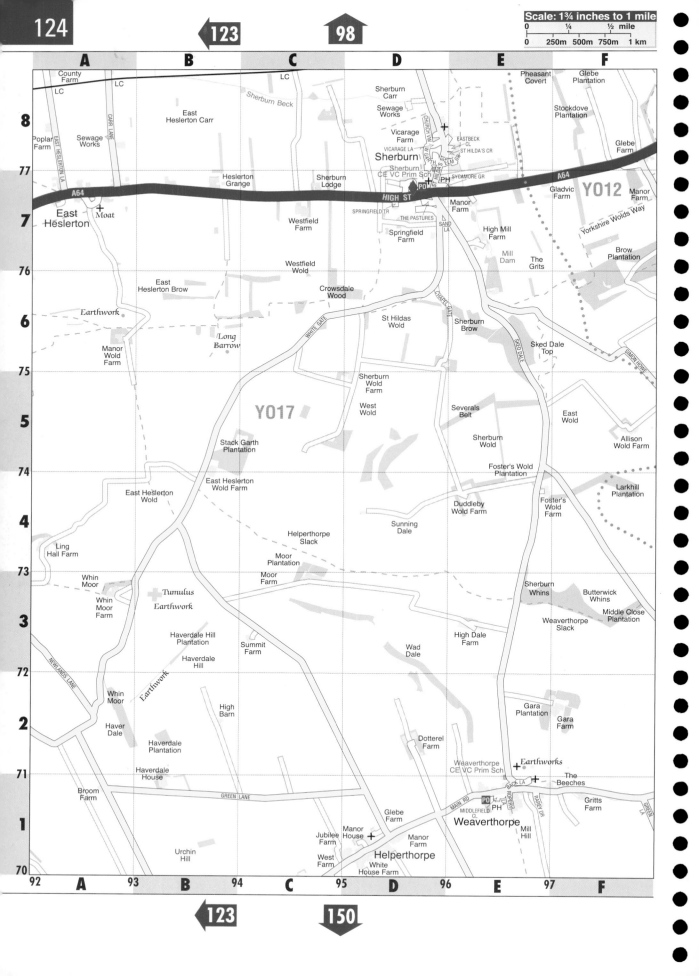

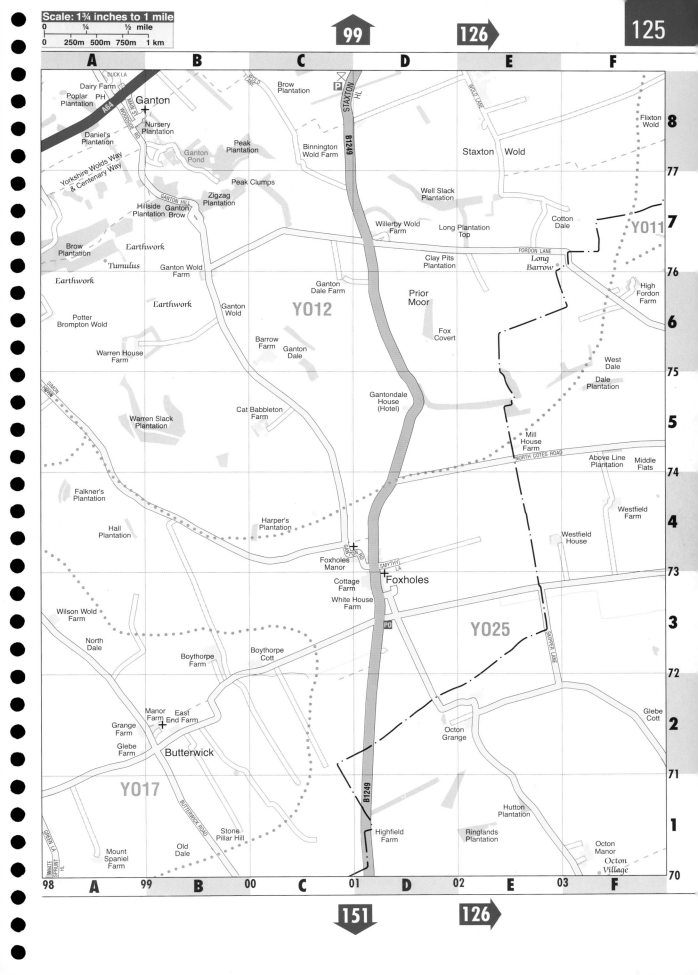

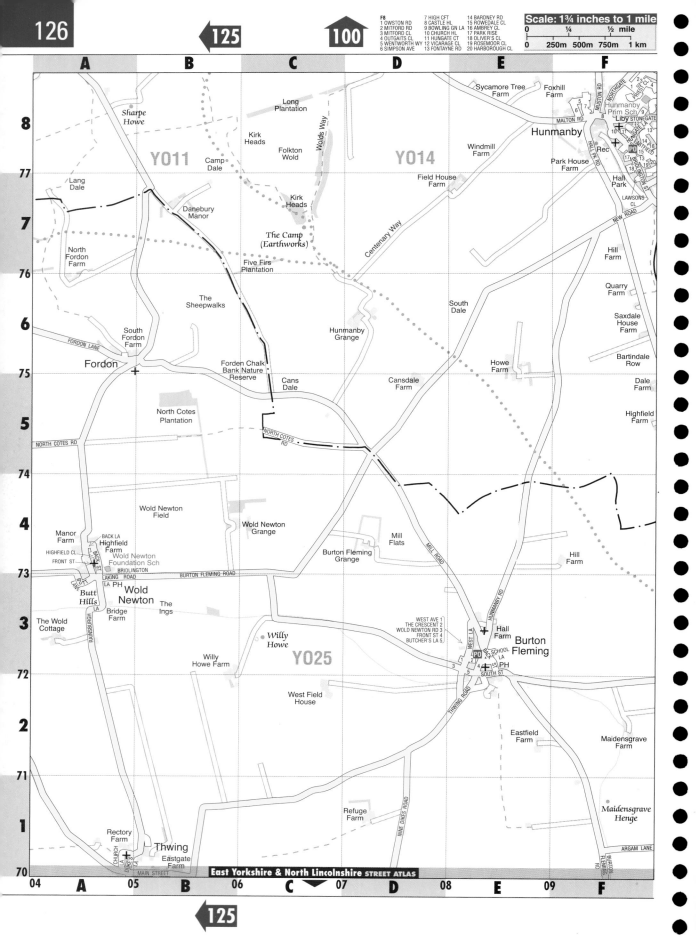

F8
1 OWSTON RD
2 MITFORD RD
3 MITFORD CL
4 OUTGAITS CL
5 WENTWORTH WY
6 SIMPSON AVE

7 HIGH CFT
8 CASTLE HL
9 BOWLING GN LA
10 CHURCH HL
11 HUNGATE CT
12 VICARAGE CL
13 FONTAYNE RD

14 BARDNEY RD
15 ROWEDALE CL
16 AMBREY CL
17 PARK RISE
18 OLIVER'S CL
19 ROSEMOOR CL
20 HARBOROUGH CL

Scale: 1¾ inches to 1 mile

YO11

YO14

YO25

Hunmanby

Fordon

Wold Newton

Burton Fleming

Thwing

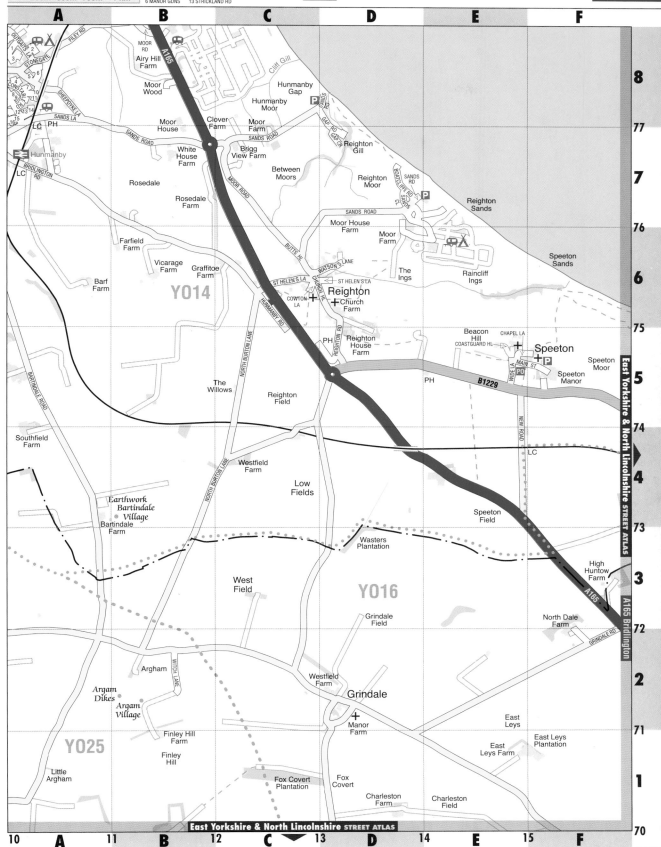

Scale: 1¾ inches to 1 mile
0   ¼   ½   mile
0   250m 500m 750m   1 km

A8
1 WRANGHAM DR
2 LENNOX CL
3 BURLYN RD
4 CHERRY RD
5 HAWKE GARTH
6 MANOR GDNS
7 CECIL RD
8 HOWES RD
9 WATSON CL
10 HAMERTON RD
11 HAMERTON CL
12 GRIMSTON RD
13 STRICKLAND RD
14 PERCY RD
15 HAVERCROFT RD
16 COWLINGS CL

101

East Yorkshire & North Lincolnshire STREET ATLAS

East Yorkshire & North Lincolnshire STREET ATLAS

E8
1 CROWTREES
2 DOCTOR'S HL

F8
1 YEWTREE DR
2 HILLSIDE RD
3 HARLEY CL

Scale: 1¾ inches to 1 mile

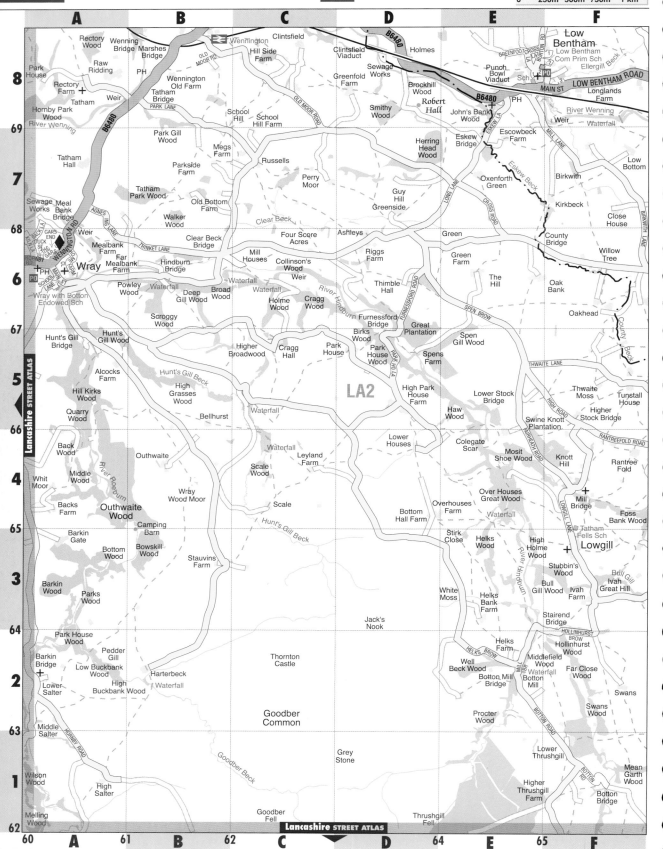

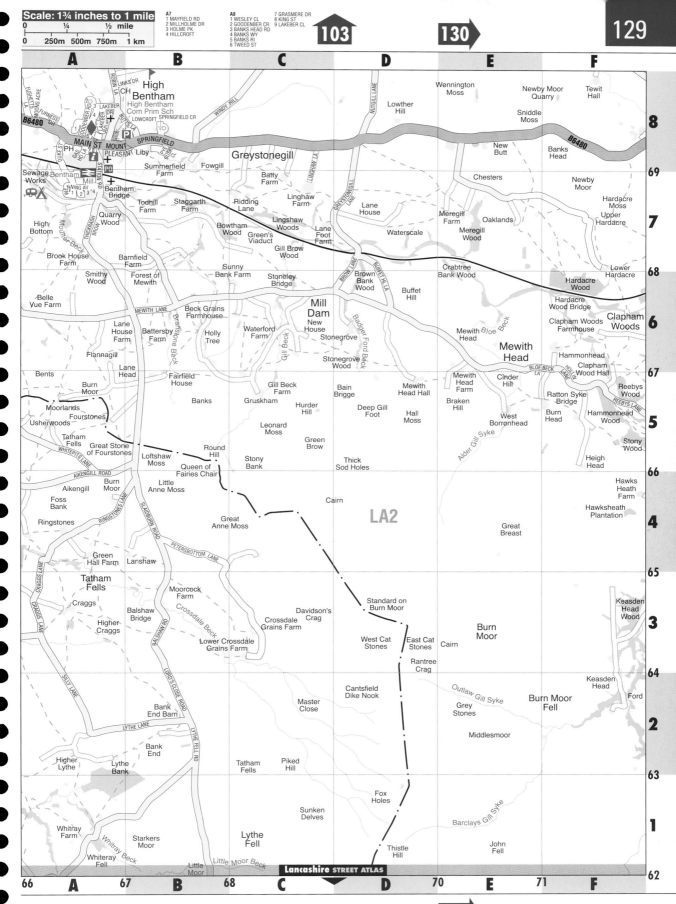

Scale: 1¾ inches to 1 mile

A7
1 MAYFIELD RD
2 MILLHOLME DR
3 HOLME PK
4 HILLCROFT

A8
1 WESLEY CL
2 GOODENBER CR
3 BANKS HEAD RD
4 BANKS WY
5 BANKS RI
6 TWEED ST

7 GRASMERE DR
8 KING ST
9 LAKEBER CL

103   130

High Bentham
High Bentham
Com Prim Sch
LOWCROFT
SPRINGFIELD CR
LINKS DR
CH
ROBIN LA
LAKEBER DR
GOODENBER RD
BUTTS LA
LAKEBER DR
FURNESS RD
FUSSELLS RD
MOORS ACRE
B6480
MAIN ST
MOUNT PLEASANT
Liby
SPRINGFIELD
DUKE ST
HOLME LA
PH
i
PO
Bentham
WING AV
Mill
Summerfield Farm
Fowgill
Sewage Works

Windy Hill
Greystonegill
Lowther Hill
Wennington Moss
Newby Moor Quarry
Tewit Hall
Sniddle Moss
New Butt
Banks Head
B6480

Batty Farm
Chesters
Newby Moor
Linghaw Farm
Lingshaw Woods
Lane House
Meregill Farm
Oaklands
Hardacre Moss
Upper Hardacre
Todhill Farm
Staggarth Farm
Ridding Lane
Green's Viaduct
Gill Brow Wood
Lane Foot Farm
Waterscale
Meregill Wood
Bowtham Wood

High Bottom
Mounter Beck
Quarry Wood
Sunny Bank Farm
Stoneley Bridge
Brown Bank Wood
Crabtree Bank Wood
Lower Hardacre
Hardacre Wood
Brook House Farm
Smithy Wood
Barnfield Farm
Forest of Mewith
Mewith Head
Mewith Head
Bloe Beck
Hardacre Wood Bridge

Belle Vue Farm
Mewith Lane
Beck Grains Farmhouse
Mill Dam
New House
Buffet Hill
Buffet Hill La
Bloe Beck
Clapham Woods Farmhouse
Clapham Woods
Brandstone Beck
Lane House Farm
Battersby Farm
Holly Tree
Waterford Farm
Stonegrove
Badger Ford Beck
Mewith Head
Hammonhead
Clapham Wood Hall
Flannagill
Stonegrove Wood
Mewith Head Hall
Cinder Hill
Ratton Syke Bridge
Reebys Wood

Bents
Burn Moor
Fairfield House
Banks
Gill Beck Farm
Bain Brigge
Mewith Head Hall
Mewith Head Farm
Braken Hill
Burn Head
Hammonhead Wood
Reebys Lane
Moorlands
Fourstones
Usherwoods
Lane Head
Gruskham
Hurder Hill
Deep Gill Foot
Hall Moss
West Borronhead
Stony Wood
Tatham Fells
Whitepits Lane
Leonard Moss
Green Brow
Alder Gill Syke
Heigh Head

Great Stone of Fourstones
Aikengill Road
Loftshaw Moss
Round Hill
Stony Bank
Thick Sod Holes
Hawks Heath Farm
Aikengill
Burn Moor
Queen of Fairies Chair
Cairn
Hawksheath Plantation
Foss Bank
Little Anne Moss
Ringstones
Ringstones Lane
Great Anne Moss
LA2
Great Breast

Green Hall Farm
Petersbottom Lane
Lanshaw
Craggs Lane
Tatham Fells
Craggs
Moorcock Farm
Crossdale Beck
Davidson's Crag
Standard on Burn Moor
Keasden Head Wood
Balshaw Bridge
Crossdale Grains Farm
West Cat Stones
East Cat Stones
Cairn
Burn Moor
Higher Craggs
Balshaw Rd
Lord's Close Road
Lower Crossdale Grains Farm
Rantree Crag
Keasden Head
Ford
Silly Lane
Bank End Barn
Cantsfield Dike Nook
Outlaw Gill Syke
Burn Moor Fell
Lythe Lane
Master Close
Grey Stones
Lythe Fell Rd
Higher Lythe
Bank End
Middlesmoor
Lythe Bank
Tatham Fells
Piked Hill
Fox Holes
Barclays Gill Syke
Whitray Farm
Whitray Beck
Starkers Moor
Sunken Delves
John Fell
Whiteray Fell
Little Moor Beck
Little Moor
Lythe Fell
Thistle Hill

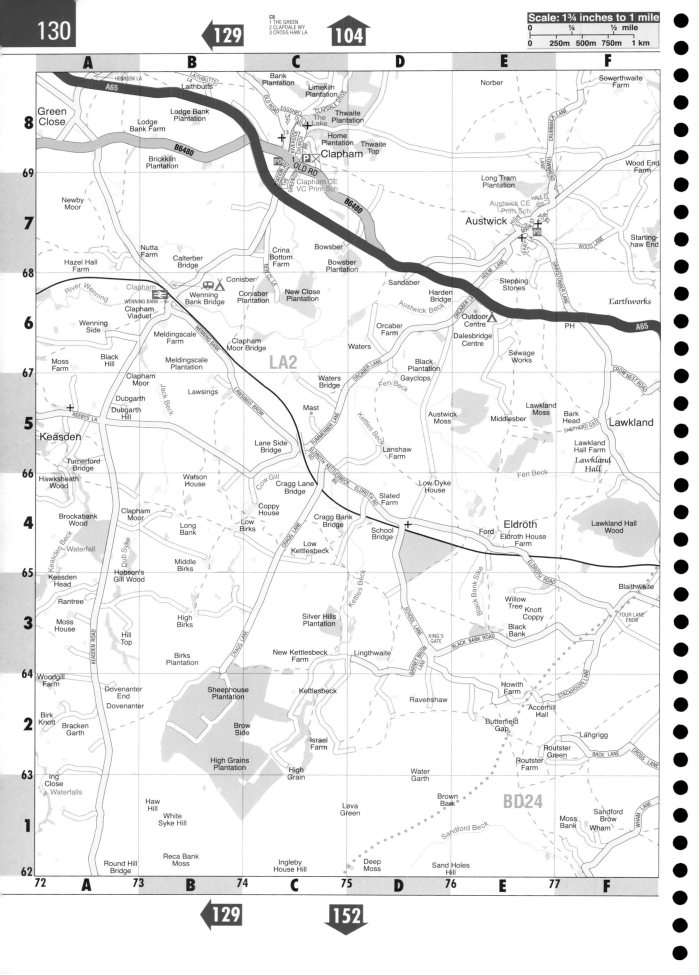

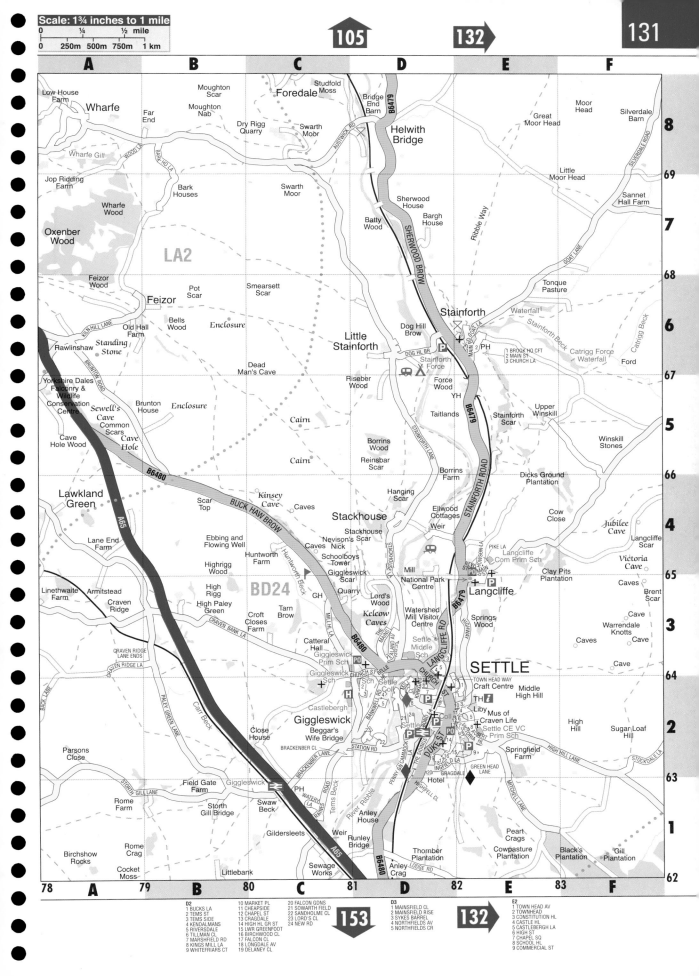

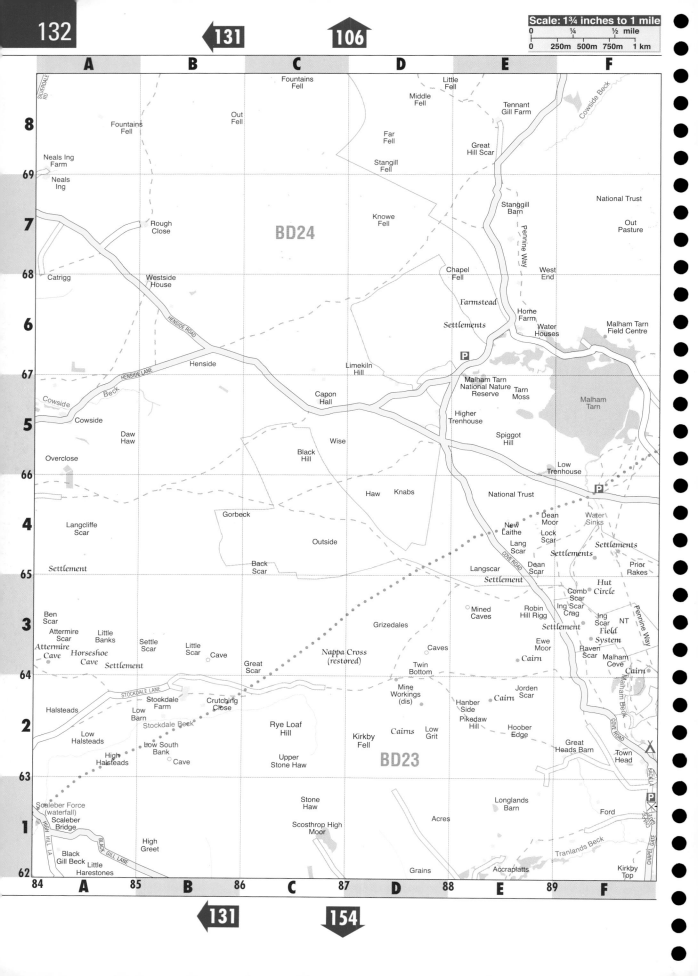

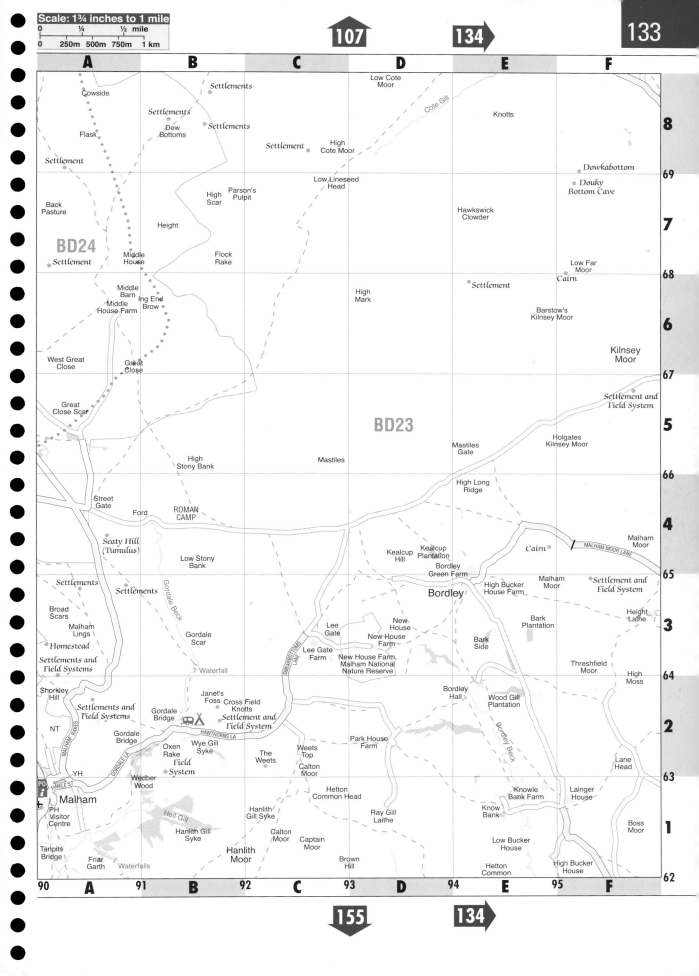

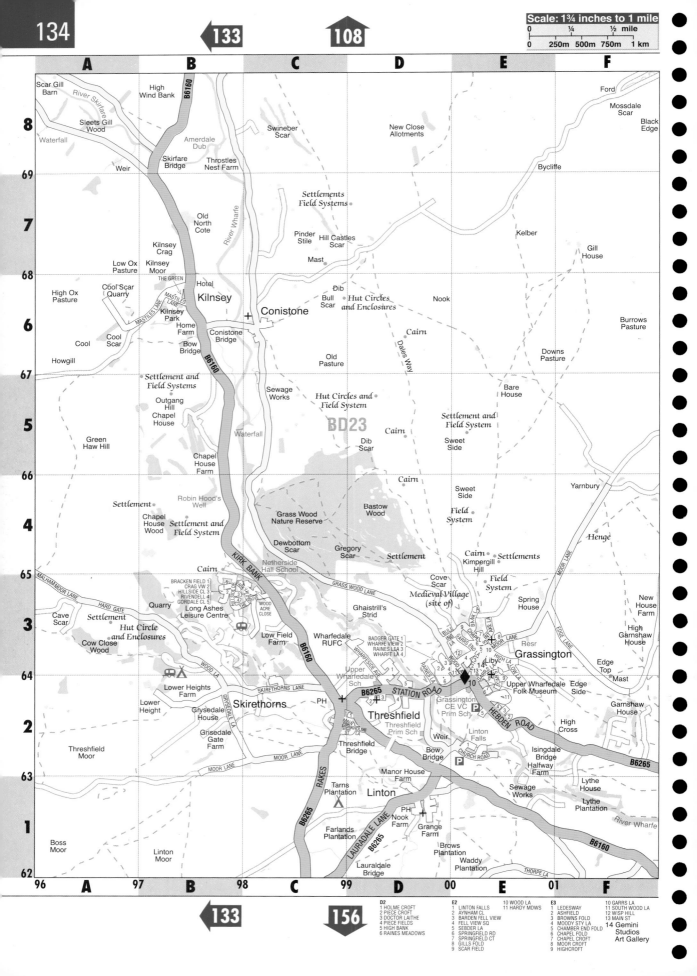

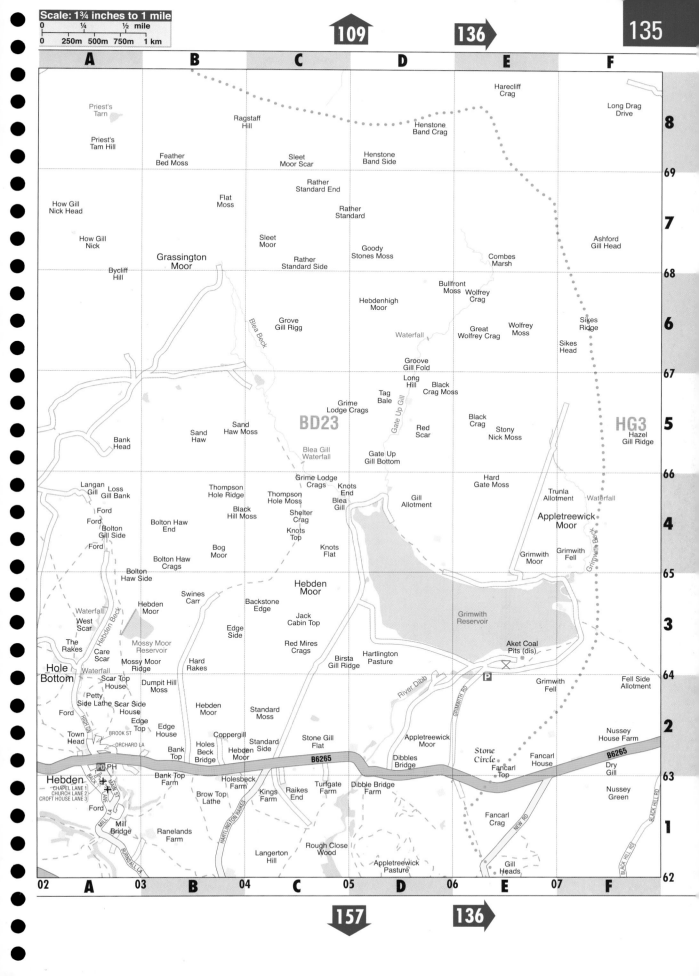

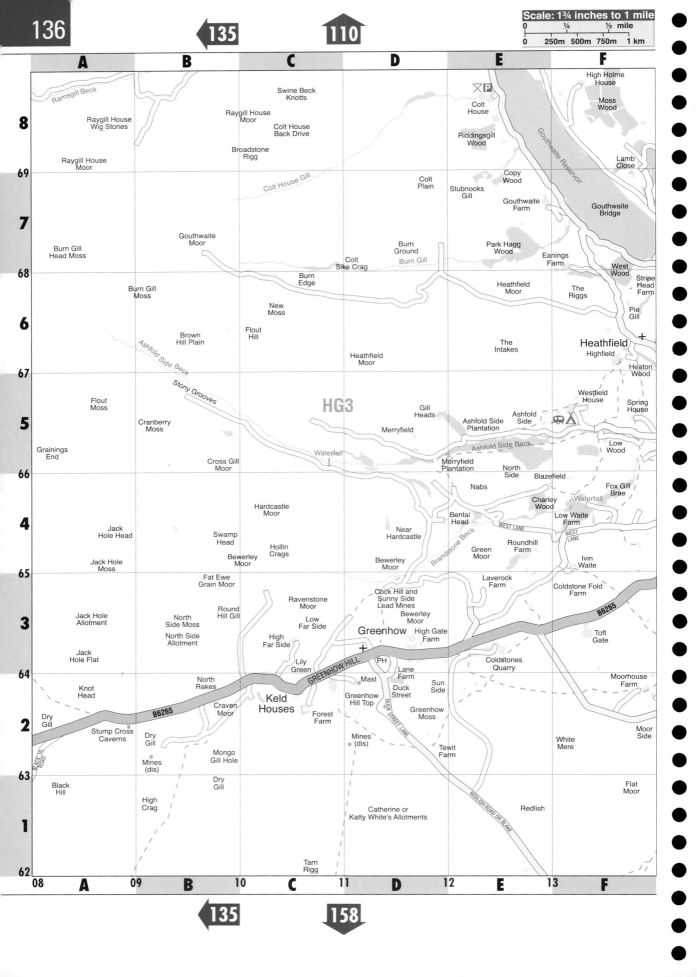

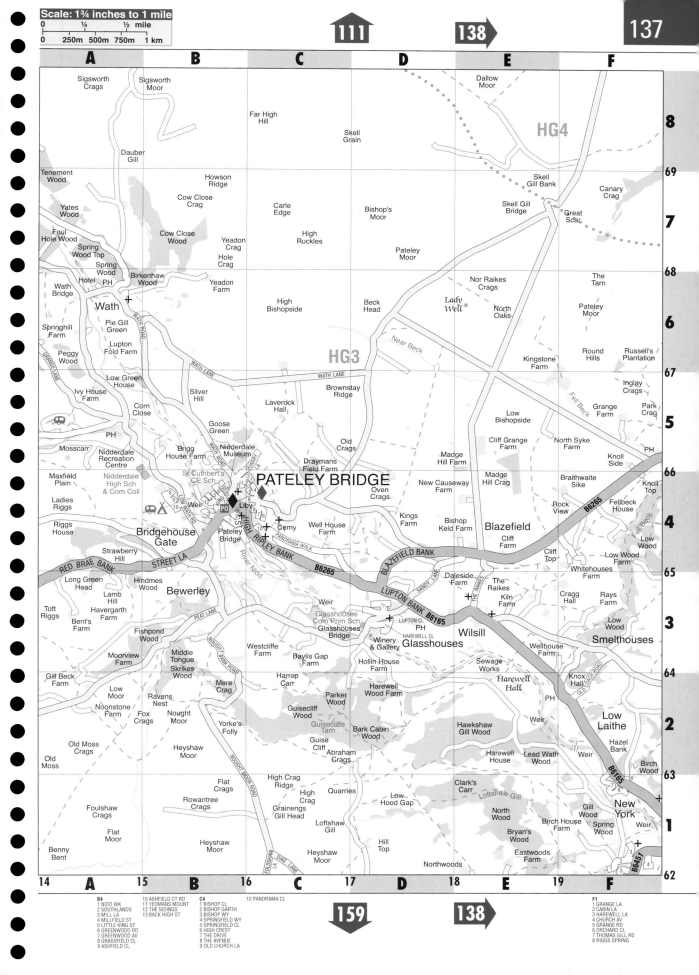

Scale: 1¾ inches to 1 mile

0   ¼   ½   mile
0   250m   500m   750m   1 km

111
138

A · **B** · **C** · **D** · **E** · **F**

Sigsworth Crags
Sigsworth Moor
Dauber Gill
Far High Hill
Skell Grain
Dallow Moor
HG4

Tenement Wood
Howson Ridge
Carle Edge
Bishop's Moor
Skell Gill Bank
Canary Crag

Yates Wood
Cow Close Crag
Skell Gill Bridge
Great Scar

Foul Hole Wood
Cow Close Wood
Yeadon Crag
High Ruckles
Pateley Moor

Spring Wood Top
Hole Crag
Nor Raikes Crags
The Tarn

Spring Wood
Birkenhaw Wood
Yeadon Farm
North Oaks
Pateley Moor

Wath Bridge
Hotel PH
High Bishopside
Beck Head
Lady Well

Wath

Springhill Farm
Pie Gill Green
Near Beck
Low Bishopside
Kingstone Farm
Round Hills
Russell's Plantation

Peggy Wood
Lupton Fold Farm
HG3
Inglay Crags

Ivy House Farm
Low Green House
WATH LANE
Cliff Grange Farm
North Syke Farm
Grange Farm
Park Crag

Mosscarr
Corn Close
Silver Hill
Brownstay Ridge
Madge Hill Farm
Knoll Side
PH

Maxfield Plain
Nidderdale Recreation Centre
Goose Green
Laverock Hall
Old Crags
Madge Hill Crag
Rock View
Braithwaite Sike
Knoll Top

Ladies Riggs
Nidderdale High Sch & Com Coll
St Cuthbert's CE Sch
Nidderdale Museum
Draymans Field Farm
New Causeway Farm
B6265
Fellbeck House

Riggs House
PATELEY BRIDGE
Oven Crags
Bishop Keld Farm
Blazefield
Low Wood Farm

Bridgehouse Gate
Weir
Liby
Cemy
Well House Farm
Kings Farm
Cliff Farm
Low Wood

Strawberry Hill
Pateley Bridge
Panorama Walk
BLAZEFIELD BANK
Cliff Top
Whitehouses Farm

RED BRAE BANK
STREET LA
River Nidd
B6265
Daleside Farm
The Raikes
Cragg Hall
Rays Farm

Long Green Head
Hindmes Wood
Bewerley
LUPTON BANK
SANDY LANE
Kiln Farm
Low Wood

Toft Riggs
Lamb Hill
Havergarth Farm
Weir
B6165
Glasshouses Com Prim Sch
LUPTON CL
PH
Wilsill
Smelthouses

Bent's Farm
Fishpond Wood
PEAT LANE
Glasshouses Bridge
HAREWELL CL
Glasshouses
Wellhouse Farm

Gill Beck Farm
Moorview Farm
Middle Tongue Skrikes Wood
Westcliffe Farm
Baylis Gap Farm
Winery & Gallery
Sewage Works

Low Moor
Mere Crag
Harrop Carr
Hollin House Farm
Harewell Hall
PH
Knox Hall

Noonstone Farm
Ravens Nest
Nought Moor
Parker Wood
Harewell Wood Farm
Weir
Low Laithe

Old Moss Crags
Fox Crags
Yorke's Folly
Guisecliff Wood
Bark Cabin Wood
Hawkshaw Gill Wood
Hazel Bank

Old Moss
Heyshaw Moor
Guisecliff Tarn
Harewell House
Lead Wath Wood
Weir
Birch Wood

Flat Crags
Guise Cliff
Abraham Crags
B6165

Benny Bent
Rowantree Crags
High Crag Ridge
Quarries
Clark's Carr
Loftshaw Gill
Gill Wood
New York
Weir

Foulshaw Crags
Graineng Gill Head
High Crag
Low Hood Gap
North Wood
Birch House Farm
Spring Wood

Flat Moor
Heyshaw Moor
Loftshaw Gill
Hill Top
Bryan's Wood
B6451

FOLDSHAW LA
DIKE LANE
Heyshaw Moor
Northwoods
Eastwoods Farm

B4
1 NIDD WK
2 SOUTHLANDS
3 MILL LA
4 MILLFIELD ST
5 LITTLE KING ST
6 GREENWOOD RD
7 GREENWOOD AV
8 GRASSFIELD CL
9 ASHFIELD CL
10 ASHFIELD CT RD
11 YEOMANS MOUNT
12 THE SIDINGS
13 BACK HIGH ST

C4
1 BISHOP CL
2 BISHOP GARTH
3 BISHOP WY
4 SPRINGFIELD WY
5 SPRINGFIELD CL
6 HIGH CREST
7 THE DRIVE
8 THE AVENUE
9 OLD CHURCH LA
10 PANORAMA CL

F1
1 GRANGE LA
2 CABIN LA
3 HAREWELL LA
4 CHURCH AV
5 GRANGE RD
6 ORCHARD CL
7 THOMAS GILL RD
8 RIGGS SPRING

159
138

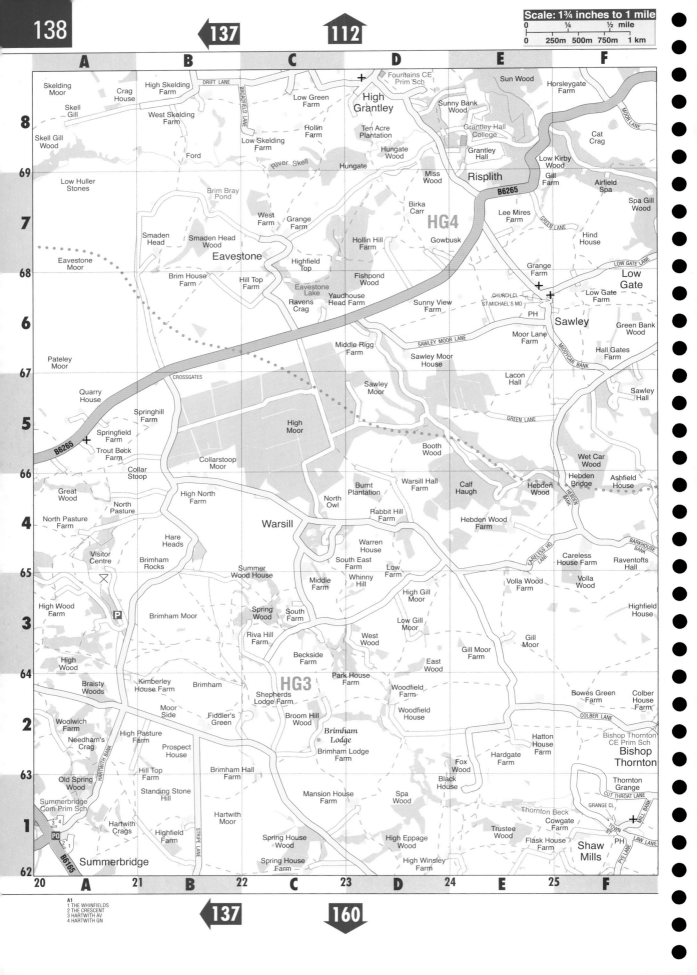

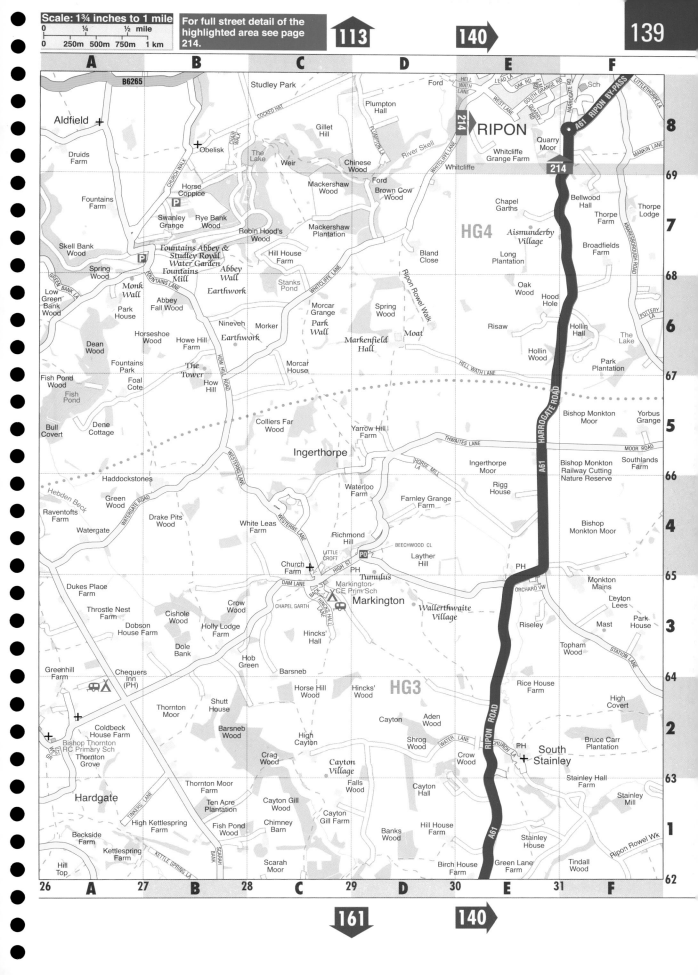

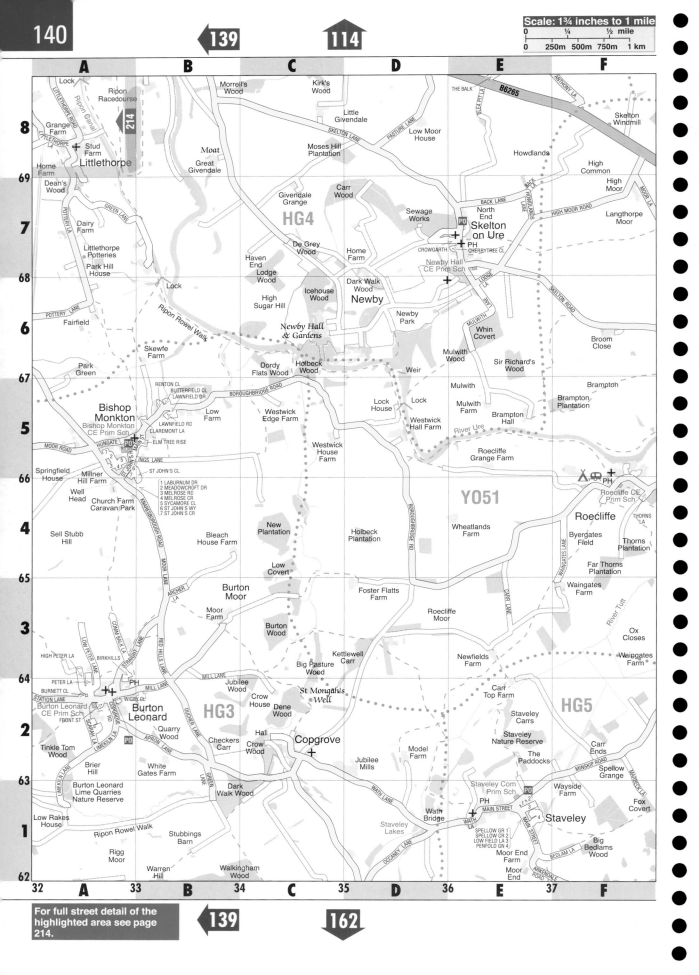

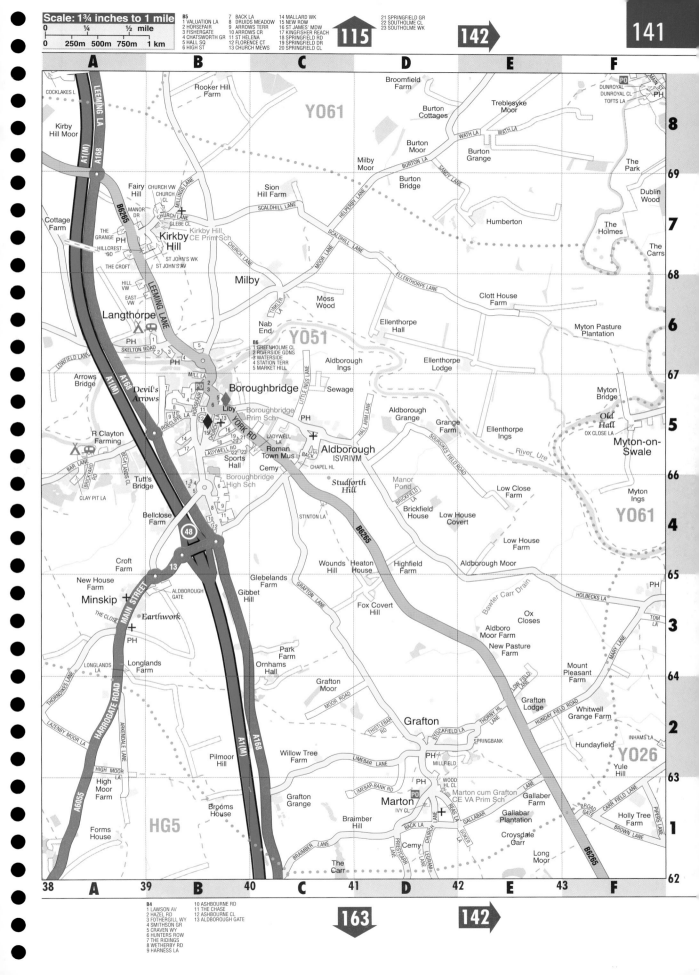

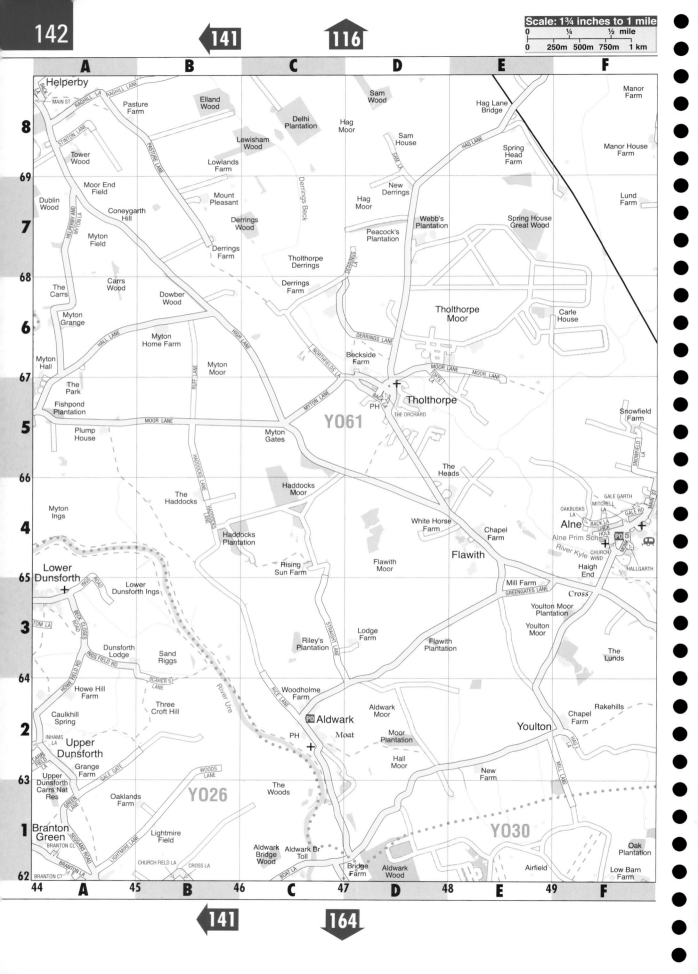

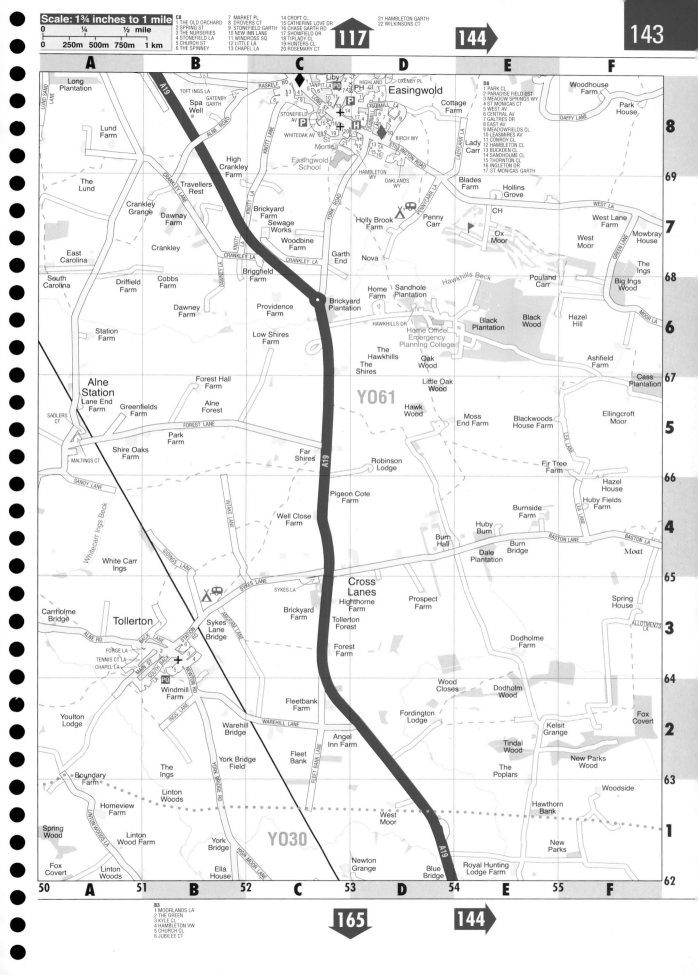

Scale: 1¾ inches to 1 mile
0   ¼   ½   mile
0   250m 500m 750m 1 km

A   B   C   D   E   F

Foss Walk
B1363
Abbey Farm
Marton Park
Marton Bridge
Marton Abbey (Priory)
South Farm
Moat
Deepley Farm
Novay Farm

New Grange Farm
Outfit Plantation
JACK LANE
HARRYFIELD LANE
Marton Grange
THE GAOL
Foulrice Farm
Kay's Wood

Stillington Grange
Stonecote Farm
Marton-in-the-Forest
Church Farm
Greenlands Farm

The Ings
WEST LANE
VICAR'S LA 1
SOUTH BACK LA 2
NORTH BACK LA 3
HILL VW 4
Wits End
Stillington Prim Sch
Home Farm
Mill Bridge
Marton Priory
Farlington
PH

INGS LANE
Roseberry Farm
WANDELL BALK
HIGH ST
MAIN ST
PO
PH
Mill Farm
Raisbeck
Whitestone Farm
Blackcollar Farm

Cottage Farm
Stillington
CARR LA
PARKFIELD
Sewage Works
Skeugh Farm
MOOR LANE
WANDELL BALK
Carr Plantation
ROSEBERRY LANE
St John's Well
SKEUGH LANE
The Skeugh

SAND LANE
Woodland Farm
Pennyflats Farm
YO61
Moxby Hall Farm
Johnson's Wood

Cass Plantation
Fox Covert
North Carrs
Middle Field
Ravensdale
Moxby Priory
Moat
Moxby
Woodside
Lower Towthorpe

Folly Wood
SAND LA
Barfs Hill
MAPLE CFT
HORNER AV
Diana Field
SPARRINGTON LA
Moxby Moor Farm
Moxby Moor
Wandmire Farm

West Field
WHITE ROSE CL
HORNER CL
SHAW CR
Barley Carr
OXCLOSE LA
MOXBY LANE
Foss Bridge
River Foss

STILLINGTON ROAD
1 TALLY HILL
2 MAPLE LA
3 CHAPEL CT
4 WALTON CL
Mile End Bungalow
Low Inhams
Plantation Farm
Brown Moor Farm

PH
PO
ROBIN LA
Huby
GRACIOUS ST
CHURN ROAD
Kirkmoor Farm
North Field
B1363
High Inhams
GREEN LA
Brown Moor

Huby CE VC Prim Sch
PH
BELTVILLA
Kirk Moor
Lund House Farm
St John's Well Plantation
St John's Well

BASTON LANE
SCHOOL CL
SKATES LA
SKATES LANE
Cemy
COOMBES CL
Sutton-on-the-Forest CE VC Prim Sch
STERNE WY
Thorpe Hill
Brown Moor
Whitecarr Beck

LINDGREEN LA
Brown Moor Lane Farm
HUBY RD
GREY CL
PH
MAIN ST
Manor House Farm
Thrush House

Hollin Hill Farm
WEST END
NEWTON HO CT
Sutton Park
GOWANS
HARLAND CL
Sutton-on-the-Forest
The Common
East Moor
White Carr Farm

ALLOTMENTS LA
Alcar Farm
BROWNMOOR LANE
Westfield
Sutton Grange
Home Farm
Brotherton Cottage Farm
Woodside Farm
High Carr Wood
Whitecarr Ings
YO32

Woodhouse
YORK ROAD
Nickynack Wood
Goose Farm
GOOSE LANE
CARR LA
High Carr
High Bohemia
Bohemia
BROWNMOOR LA
Goose Wood
Birch Wood
Forest Hill Farm

B1363
Sewage Works
Low Carr
Low Carr Wood
Low Carr Farm
Hundred Acre Farm

56 57 58 59 60 61

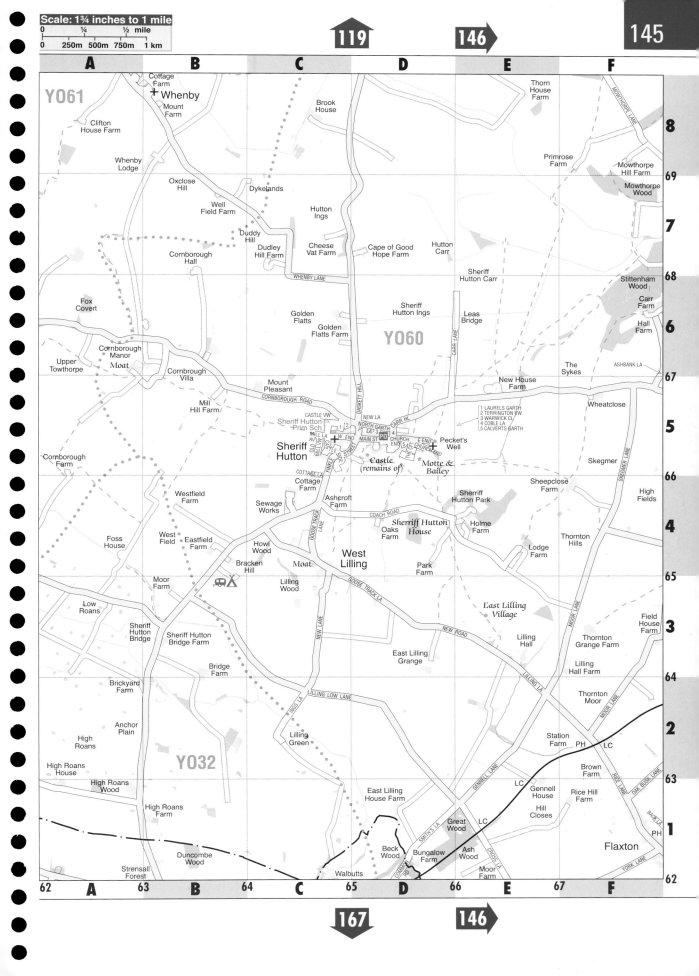

A · B · C · D · E · F

8
Rough Hills Farm · Mowthorpe Dale · Mowthorpe Dale Wood · Sata Wood · Kew at Castle Howard · Bracken Hill Plantation · Brick Kiln Wood · Gate House · Swiss Cottage · Castle Howard Gardens · South Lake · The Temple · Mount Sion Wood · Mausoleum · Low Gaterley · Etty Little Wood · Ready Wood · High Gaterley

69
Mowthorpe · Dale Wood · Brandrith Farm · Lands End · Boyes Wood · New River (pond) · Lowdy Hill Wood · Pretty Wood · Tumulus · The Pyramid · Greystone Wood

7
Mowthorpe Bridge · Centenary Way · Ox Pasture Wood · Northfield Farm · Brandrith Wood · Carmire Gate · Tumulus · Sewage Works · The Pyramid · Four Faces · Hutton Little Wood · Todd Wood · Hutton Hill

Stittenham Wood · Welburn · Primrose Hill

68
Ashbank Lane · Bulmer Beck · Hunger Hill · West End · Welburn Corn Prim Sch · PH · Water La · Church La · Chanting Hl · Chestnut Ave · Gillylees Wood · Chanting Hill · Spring Wood · A64

6
Cross Field Farm · Bulmer Bridge · Bulmer · The Rigg · Stittenham Hill · Bulmer Hill · Wandales Lane · East Fields · Monument Plantation · Bulmer Hag · Bank Wood · Greets Farm · Holmes Cr · Crambeck · Ox Carr · Crambeck Bridge

Conduit Head · Scugdale · Monument Farm · Whitwell Road · Jamie's Cragg · Park Wood

67
Mill House · The Old Glebe Farm · Old Beck Wood · High Moor · Whitwell Grange · Mount Pleasant Farm · Ox Carr Wood · Ben Wood

5
West Mill House · Low Fields · East Ings · Hathwoods · YO60 · Bellmire Hill · Belmire Farm · Kirkham Park Wood · The Park · The Hall · Manor Farm · PH

Stittenham Ings · Thornton Carr · Whitwell-on-the-Hill · Shepherdfields Lane · Kirkham Bridge

66
Gower Hall Farm · Foston Grange · Park House · Springwood Wood Farm · Spring Farm · Beech Cr · Onhams La · Kirkham Priory (remains of) · LC · Manor Farm · Kirkham Valley

4
High Street Farm · Gravel Pit Farm · Fox Covert · Foston Lodge · Shoulder of Mutton Plantation · Cliffe House Farm · Cliff Lane · Oak Cliff Wood · Kirkham Valley

Village Farm · Thornton-le-Clay · High St · Foston · Sewage Works · Whitwell Cliff · Crambe

65
PH · Low St · Foston CE VC Prim Sch · Foston Rectory · Village Farm · Foston Hall · Foston Bridge · Sweet Hill · Manor Farm · Beck Farm

3
Rectory Farm · Demming Hill · Spital Bridge · Barton Hill · Pasture House · Crambe Bank · Hillside Farm · LC · Riders Lane

Foston Gates · LC · LC · Plain Moor

64
Cuddy House · Foston Lane · Barton Hill House · Barton Hill · Barton Bridge · LC · Howsham Gates · River Derwent

Barton Moor Plantation · Barton Moor House · Barton Moor · Willow End · Green Farm · Spital Beck · Rider Lane Farm · Crambe Grange

2
Oak Busk La · The Grange · Kirk Hills · Red House · Steelmoor Lane · Manor Farm · Butts La · Lodge Farm · Howsham Hall · Howsham Hall Prep Sch

Cherry Tree Farm · Barton-le-Willows · Howsham · Old Church Farm

63
Back La · Barney La · Malton Lane · Stugdale House · PH · Golden Hill · Bosendale Wood · Weir · Braithwaites Wood · Howsham Bridge

1
The Crofts · A64 · Field House · Elm Tree House Farm · Graves Plantation · Willowbridge Wood · Braithwaite Bridge · Bridge Wood · Howsham Bridge

62
Beech Tree Farm · Carr Plantation

68 · A · 69 · B · 70 · C · 71 · D · 72 · E · 73 · F

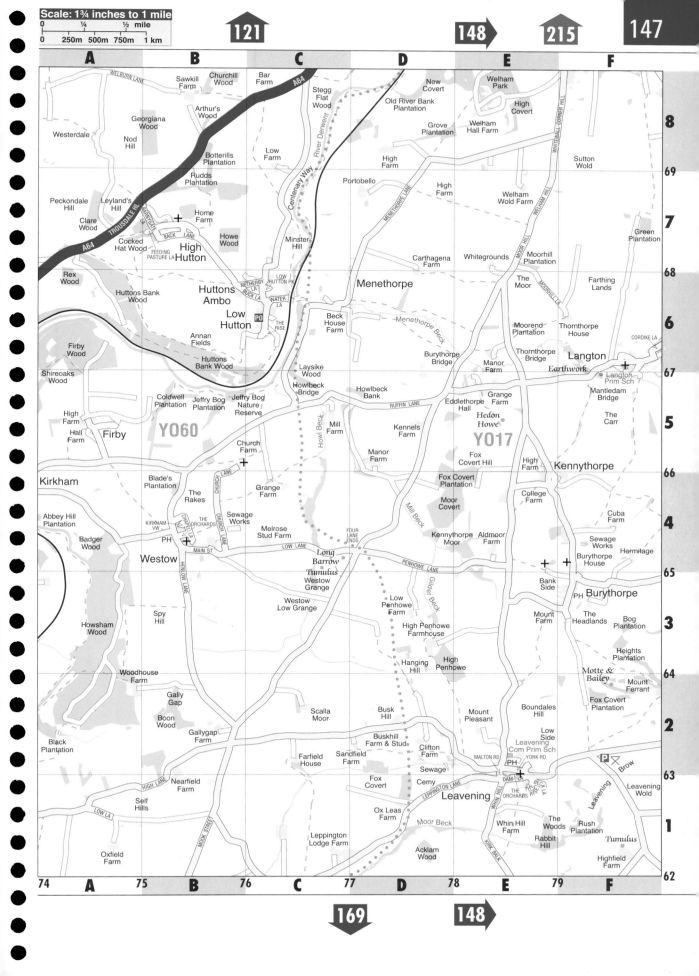

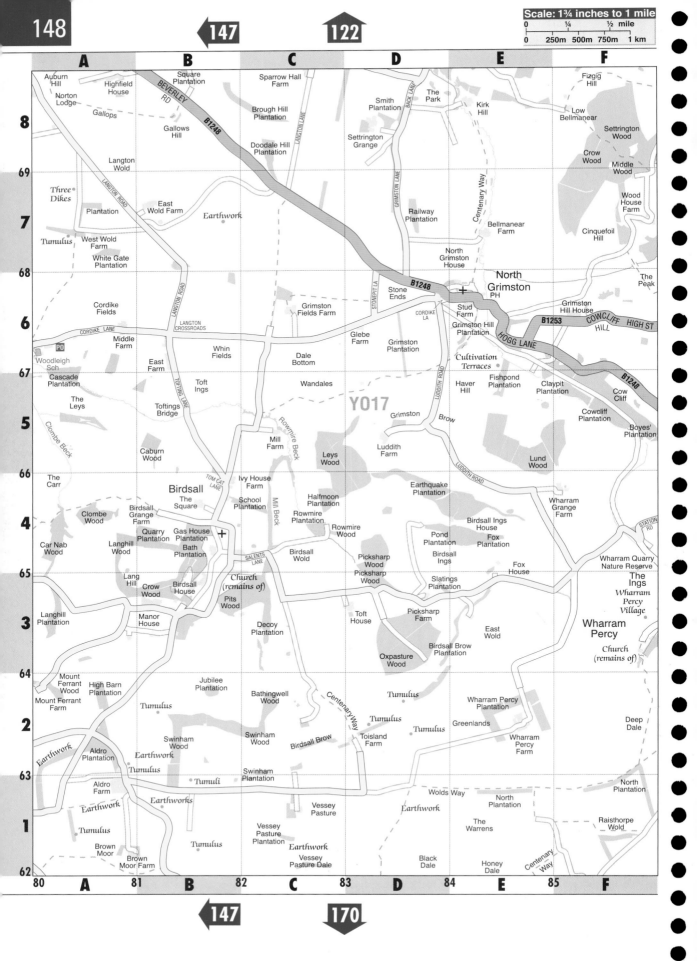

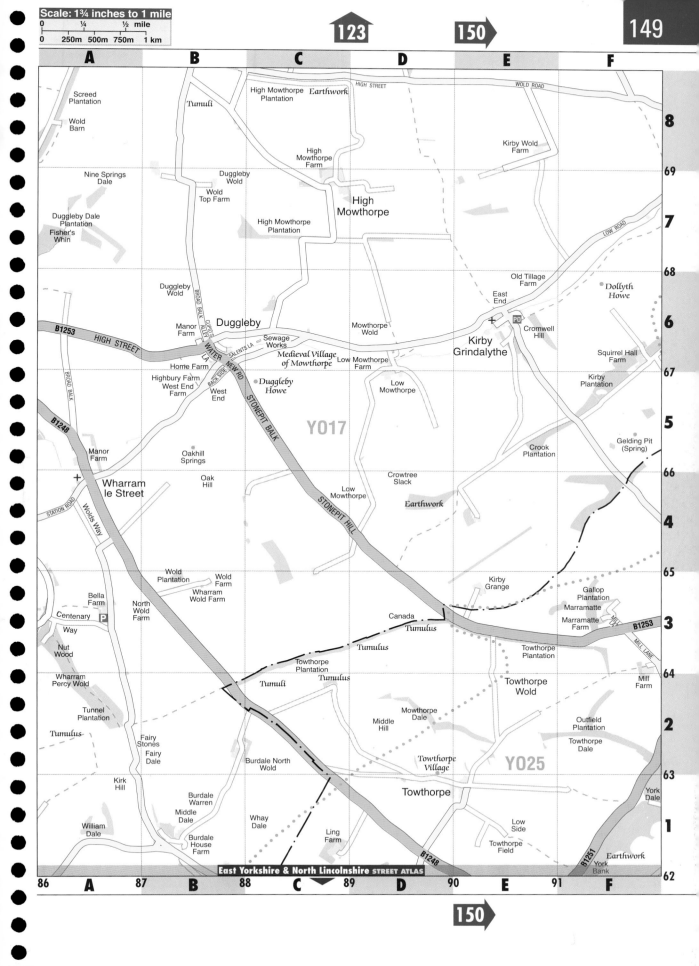

A   B   C   D   E   F

Screed Plantation

Wold Barn

Tumuli

High Mowthorpe Plantation   Earthwork   HIGH STREET   WOLD ROAD

Kirby Wold Farm

8

Nine Springs Dale

Duggleby Wold

High Mowthorpe Farm

69

Wold Top Farm

Duggleby Dale Plantation

Fisher's Whin

High Mowthorpe Plantation

High Mowthorpe

7

Duggleby Wold

Old Tillage Farm

Dollyth Howe

68

East End

BROAD BALK   CUPID'S ALLEY

Manor Farm

Duggleby

Kirby Grindalythe

PO   Cromwell Hill

B1253   HIGH STREET   WATER LA   NEW RD

Home Farm

Sewage Works

Mowthorpe Wold

6

SALENTS LA

Medieval Village of Mowthorpe   Low Mowthorpe Farm

Squirrel Hall Farm

Highbury Farm   West End Farm   BACK SIDE

West End

Duggleby Howe

Low Mowthorpe

Kirby Plantation

67

BROAD BALK   STONEPIT BALK

YO17

Low Mowthorpe

B1248

Manor Farm

Oakhill Springs

Oak Hill

Crowtree Slack

Crook Plantation

Gelding Pit (Spring)

5

+

Wharram le Street

STONEPIT HILL

Earthwork

66

STATION ROAD   Wolds Way

Low Mowthorpe

4

Wold Plantation

Wold Farm

Kirby Grange

Gallop Plantation   Marramatte

65

Wharram Wold Farm

Bella Farm

North Wold Farm

Canada   Tumulus

Towthorpe Plantation

Marramatte Farm   MILL   B1253

3

Centenary   P Way

Tumulus

Nut Wood

Tumulus

Towthorpe Wold

MILL LANE

Mill Farm

64

Wharram Percy Wold

Towthorpe Plantation

Tumuli   Tumulus

2

Tunnel Plantation

Fairy Stones   Fairy Dale

Middle Hill

Mowthorpe Dale

Outfield Plantation

Towthorpe Dale

Tumulus

Burdale North Wold

Towthorpe Village

YO25

York Dale

63

Kirk Hill

Burdale Warren

Towthorpe

William Dale

Middle Dale

Whay Dale

Ling Farm

Low Side

Towthorpe Field

1

Burdale House Farm

B1248

B1251

York Bank

Earthwork

62

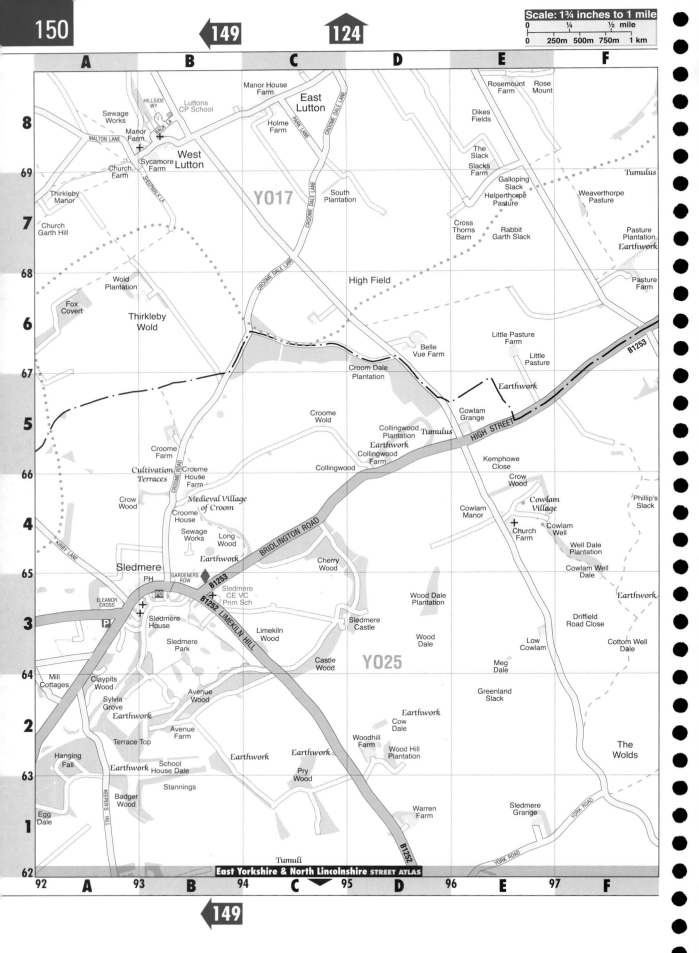

150

149

124

Scale: 1¾ inches to 1 mile

0   ¼   ½   mile
0   250m 500m 750m 1 km

A   B   C   D   E   F

8

Manor House Farm

East Lutton

Rosemount Farm   Rose Mount

Sewage Works

HILLSIDE WY

Luttons CP School

Holme Farm

Dikes Fields

Manor Farm

BACK LA

MALTON LANE

PARK LANE

CROOME DALE LANE

The Slack

Slacks Farm

69

West Lutton

Sycamore Farm

Church Farm

SHEEPWALK LA

YO17

South Plantation

Galloping Slack

Helperthorpe Pasture

Weaverthorpe Pasture

Thirkleby Manor

CROOME DALE LANE

7

Church Garth Hill

Cross Thorns Barn

Rabbit Garth Slack

Pasture Plantation

Earthwork

Tumulus

68

Wold Plantation

High Field

Pasture Farm

Fox Covert

6

Thirkleby Wold

Belle Vue Farm

Little Pasture Farm

Little Pasture

B1253

67

Croom Dale Plantation

Earthwork

Cowlam Grange

Croome Wold

Collingwood Plantation

Tumulus

HIGH STREET

5

Croome Farm

CROOME ROAD

Collingwood Farm

Earthwork

Kemphowe Close

Cultivation Terraces

Croome House Farm

Collingwood

Crow Wood

66

Crow Wood

Medieval Village of Croom

Cowlam Manor

Cowlam Village

Phillip's Slack

Croome House

Church Farm

Cowlam Well

4

Sewage Works

Long Wood

Earthwork

BRIDLINGTON ROAD

Cherry Wood

Well Dale Plantation

65

Sledmere

PH

GARDENERS ROW

B1253

Sledmere CE VC Prim Sch

Wood Dale Plantation

Cowlam Well Dale

Earthwork

ELEANOR CROSS

PO

B1252

LIMEKILN HILL

Limekiln Wood

Sledmere Castle

Driffield Road Close

3

P

Sledmere House

Sledmere Park

Wood Dale

Low Cowlam

Cottom Well Dale

KIRBY LANE

Mill Cottages

YO25

Meg Dale

64

Claypits Wood

Avenue Wood

Castle Wood

Greenland Slack

Sylvia Grove

Earthwork

Earthwork

Cow Dale

2

Terrace Top

Avenue Farm

Earthwork

Earthwork

Woodhill Farm

Wood Hill Plantation

The Wolds

Hanging Fall

School House Dale

Pry Wood

63

Earthwork

Stannings

KEEPER'S HILL

Badger Wood

Warren Farm

Sledmere Grange

YORK ROAD

1

Egg Dale

B1252

YORK ROAD

62

Tumuli

East Yorkshire & North Lincolnshire STREET ATLAS

92   A   93   B   94   C   95   D   96   E   97   F

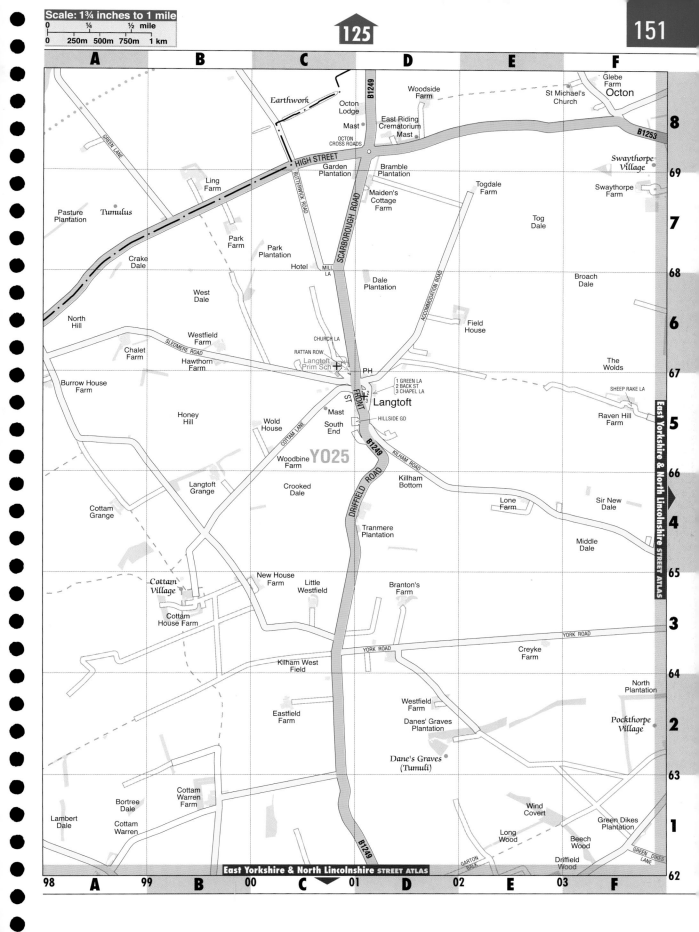

A   B   C   D   E   F

Green Lane

Earthwork

Octon Lodge

B1249

Woodside Farm

St Michael's Church

Glebe Farm

Octon

8

Mast

East Riding Crematorium Mast

B1253

OCTON CROSS ROADS

Swaythorpe Village

69

HIGH STREET

Garden Plantation

Bramble Plantation

Swaythorpe Farm

Ling Farm

BUTTERWICK ROAD

Maiden's Cottage Farm

Togdale Farm

Pasture Plantation

Tumulus

Park Farm

SCARBOROUGH ROAD

Tog Dale

7

Crake Dale

Park Plantation

Hotel

MILL LA

Dale Plantation

ACCOMMODATION ROAD

Broach Dale

68

West Dale

Field House

North Hill

SLEDMERE ROAD

Westfield Farm

CHURCH LA

The Wolds

6

Chalet Farm

Hawthorn Farm

RATTAN ROW

Langtoft Prim Sch

PH

SHEEP RAKE LA

Burrow House Farm

Langtoft

1 GREEN LA
2 BACK ST
3 CHAPEL LA

Raven Hill Farm

67

Honey Hill

COTTAM LANE

Mast

FRONT ST

South End

HILLSIDE GD

5

Wold House

Woodbine Farm

YO25

B1249

KILHAM ROAD

Killham Bottom

66

Langtoft Grange

Crooked Dale

Lone Farm

Sir New Dale

4

Cottam Grange

DRIFFIELD ROAD

Tranmere Plantation

Middle Dale

65

Cottam Village

New House Farm

Little Westfield

Branton's Farm

3

Cottam House Farm

York Road

Creyke Farm

YORK ROAD

64

Kilham West Field

North Plantation

Eastfield Farm

Westfield Farm

Danes' Graves Plantation

Pockthorpe Village

2

Bortree Dale

Cottam Warren Farm

Dane's Graves (Tumuli)

63

Lambert Dale

Cottam Warren

Wind Covert

Green Dikes Plantation

1

Long Wood

Beech Wood

GREEN DIKES LANE

B1249

GARTON BALK

Driffield Wood

62

98   A   99   B   00   C   01   D   02   E   03   F

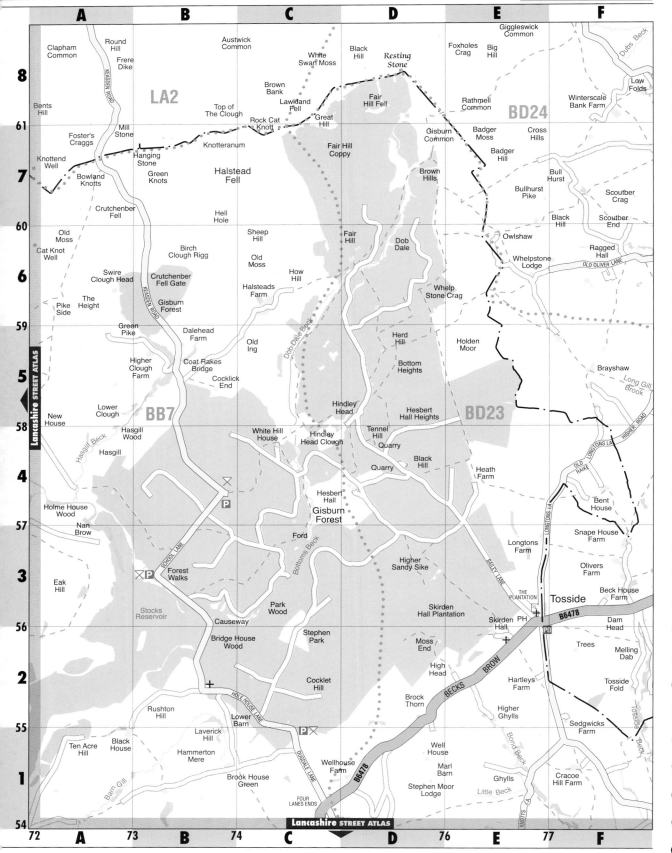

Scale: 1¾ inches to 1 mile

0 ¼ ½ mile
0 250m 500m 750m 1 km

A B C D E F

8

Clapham Common
Round Hill
Frere Dike
Austwick Common
White Swan Moss
Black Hill
Resting Stone
Foxholes Crag
Big Hill
Giggleswick Common
Low Folds
Winterscale Bank Farm

LA2
Brown Bank
Lawkland Fell
Fair Hill Fell
Rathmell Common
BD24

61
Bents Hill
Foster's Craggs
Mill Stone
Top of The Clough
Rock Cat Knott
Great Hill
Gisburn Common
Badger Moss
Cross Hills
Knotteranum
Badger Hill
Bull Hurst

7
Knottend Well
Bowland Knots
Hanging Stone
Green Knots
Halstead Fell
Fair Hill Coppy
Brown Hills
Bullhurst Pike
Black Hill
Scoutber Crag
Scoutber End

Crutchenber Fell
Hell Hole

60
Old Moss
Sheep Hill
Fair Hill
Dob Dale
Owlshaw
Ragged Hall

Cat Knot Well
Birch Clough Rigg
Old Moss
OLD OLIVER LANE

6
Swire Clough Head
Crutchenber Fell Gate
How Hill
Whelpstone Lodge

Pike Side
The Height
Gisburn Forest
Halsteads Farm
Whelp Stone Crag

59
Green Pike
Dalehead Farm
Old Ing
Herd Hill
Holden Moor
Brayshaw

Long Gill Brook

5
Higher Clough Farm
Coat Rakes Bridge
Cocklick End
Bottom Heights

New House
Lower Clough
BB7
Hindley Head
Hesbert Hall Heights
BD23

58
Hasgill Wood
White Hill House
Hindley Head Clough
Tennel Hill
Quarry

Hasgill
Quarry
Black Hill
Heath Farm

4
Holme House Wood
Hesbert Hall
Bent House

57
Nan Brow
Gisburn Forest
Longtons Farm
Snape House Farm

Ford
Higher Sandy Sike
Olivers Farm
Beck House Farm

3
Eak Hill
Forest Walks
THE PLANTATION
Tosside
B6478

Stocks Reservoir
Park Wood
Skirden Hall Plantation
Skirden Hall
PH
Dam Head

56
Causeway
Stephen Park
Moss End
Trees
Melling Dab

2
Bridge House Wood
Cocklet Hill
High Head
Hartleys Farm
Tosside Fold

Rushton Hill
Lower Barn
Brock Thorn
Higher Ghylls
Sedgwicks Farm

55
Laverick Hill
Wellhouse Farm
Well House
Ghylls
Cracoe Hill Farm

Ten Acre Hill
Black House
Hammerton Mere
Marl Barn

1
Brook House Green
Stephen Moor Lodge
Little Beck

FOUR LANES ENDS

54

72 A 73 B 74 C 76 D E 77 F

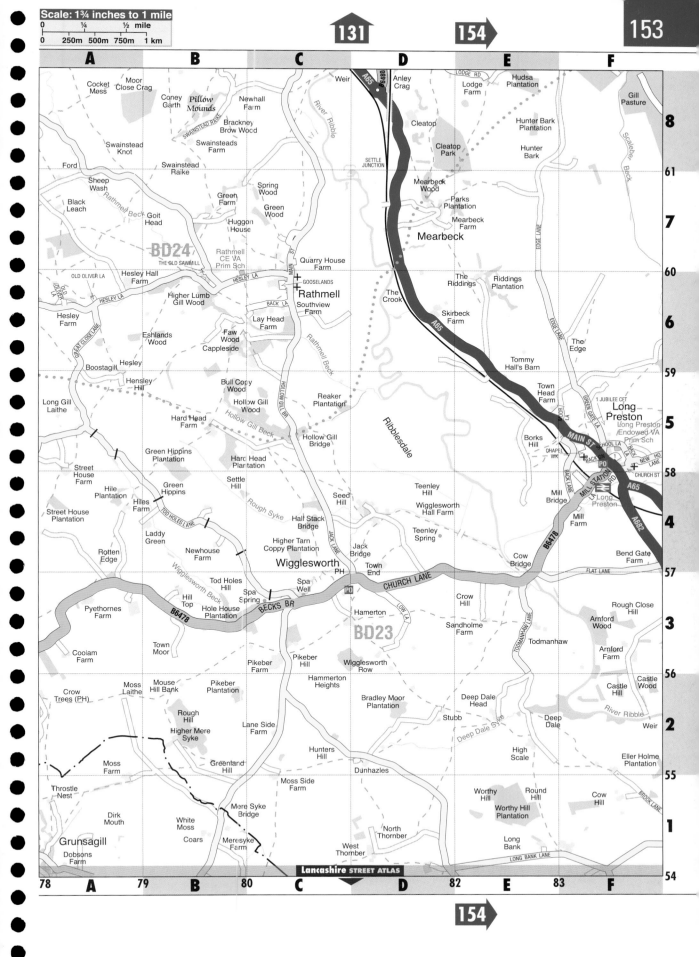

A   B   C   D   E   F

Cocket Moss
Moor Close Crag
Coney Garth
Pillow Mounds
Newhall Farm
Weir
River Ribble
Anley Crag
LODGE RD
Lodge Farm
Hudsa Plantation
Gill Pasture
8

Swainstead Raike
Brackney Brow Wood
Cleatop
Cleatop Park
Hunter Bark Plantation
Hunter Bark

Swainstead Knot
Swainsteads Farm
SETTLE JUNCTION
Mearbeck Wood
61

Ford
Sheep Wash
Swainstead Raike
Spring Wood
Green Farm
Green Wood
Parks Plantation
Mearbeck Farm
Mearbeck
7

Black Leach
Goit Head
Huggon House
BD24
THE OLD SAWMILL
Rathmell CE VA Prim Sch
Quarry House Farm
Gooselands
60

Old Oliver La
Hesley Hall Farm
HESLEY LA
MAIN ST
Rathmell
Southview Farm
The Crook
The Riddings
Riddings Plantation
EDGE LANE
6

Hesley Farm
GREAT CLOSE LANE
Higher Lumb Gill Wood
BACK LANE
Lay Head Farm
A65
Skirbeck Farm
The Edge

Eshlands Wood
Faw Wood
Cappleside
Rathmell Beck
Tommy Hall's Barn
59

Boostagill
Hensley Hill
Bull Copy Wood
HOLLOW GILL BR
Reaker Plantation
Ribblesdale
Town Head Farm
1 JUBILEE CFT
Long Preston
5

Long Gill Laithe
Hard Head Farm
Hollow Gill Wood
Hollow Gill Bridge
Hollow Gill Beck
Long Preston Endowed VA Prim Sch
MAIN ST
GREEN GATE LA
Borks Hill
CHAPEL WK
PO
SCHOOL LA
BACK LA

Street House Farm
Hile Plantation
Green Hippins Plantation
Hard Head Plantation
Settle Hill
Rough Syke
Seed Hill
Teenley Hill
Wigglesworth Hall Farm
Mill Bridge
MILL STATION
Long Preston
A65
CHURCH ST
58

Street House Plantation
Hiles Farm
Green Hippins
Hall Stack Bridge
Jack Bridge
Teenley Spring
Mill Farm
BACK LANE
A682
4

Rotten Edge
Laddy Green
Newhouse Farm
TOD HOLES LANE
Higher Tarn Coppy Plantation
JACK LANE
Town End
CHURCH LANE
Cow Bridge
B6478
Bend Gate Farm
57

Pyethornes Farm
Wigglesworth Beck
Tod Holes Hill
Spa Spring
Hole House Plantation
BECKS BR
Spa Well
PO
Hamerton
LOW LA
Crow Hill
FLAT LANE
Rough Close Hill
3

Coolam Farm
B6478
Town Moor
Pikeber Plantation
Pikeber Hill
Wigglesworth Row
Sandholme Farm
TODMANHAW LANE
Todmanhaw
Arnford Wood
Arnford Farm
BD23

Crow Trees (PH)
Moss Laithe
Mouse Hill Bank
Pikeber Farm
Hammerton Heights
Bradley Moor Plantation
Deep Dale Head
Castle Hill
Castle Wood
56

Rough Hill
Higher Mere Syke
Lane Side Farm
Stubb
Deep Dale Syke
Deep Dale
River Ribble
Weir
2

Moss Farm
Greenland Hill
Hunters Hill
High Scale
Eller Holme Plantation

Throstle Nest
Dirk Mouth
White Moss Coars
Mere Syke Bridge
Moss Side Farm
Dunhazles
Worthy Hill
Round Hill
Cow Hill
BROOK LANE
55

Grunsagill
Dobsons Farm
Meresyke Farm
West Thornber
North Thornber
Worthy Hill Plantation
High Scale
Long Bank
LONG BANK LANE

78   A   79   B   80   C   82   D   E   83   F   **54**

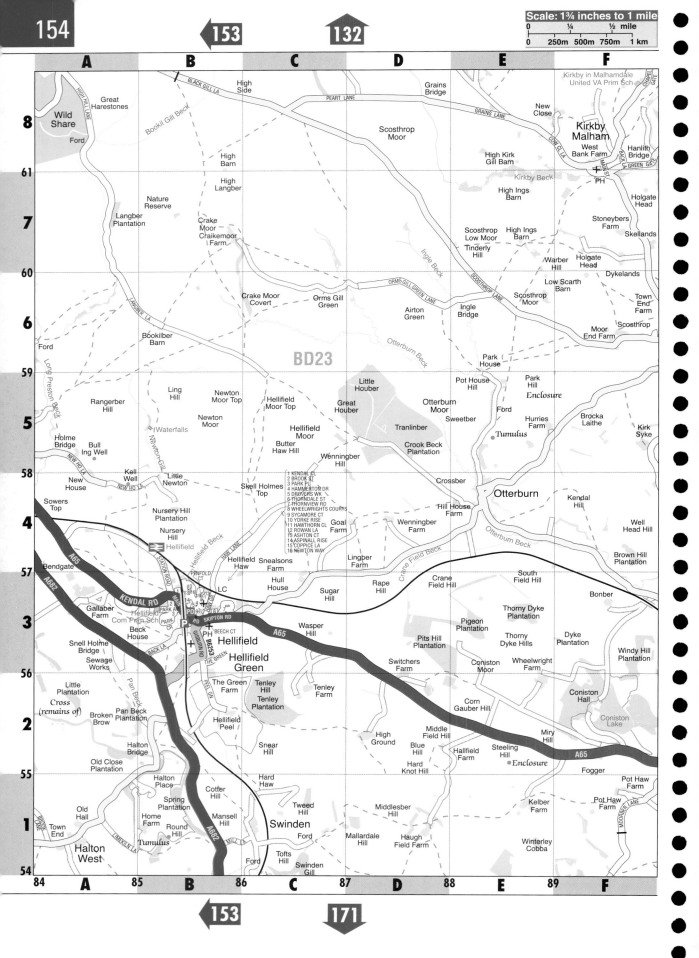

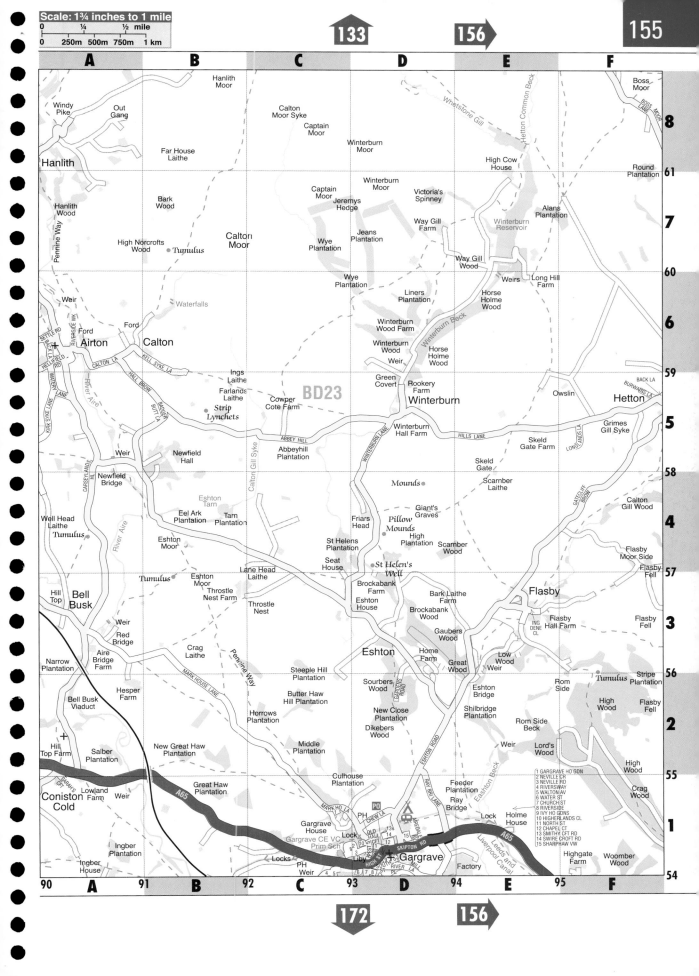

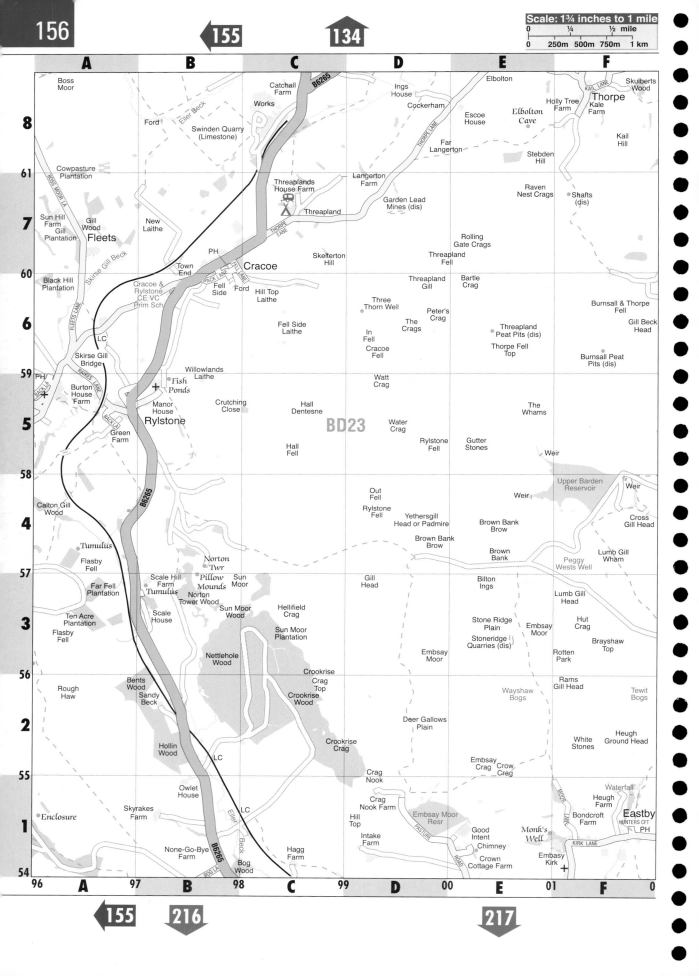

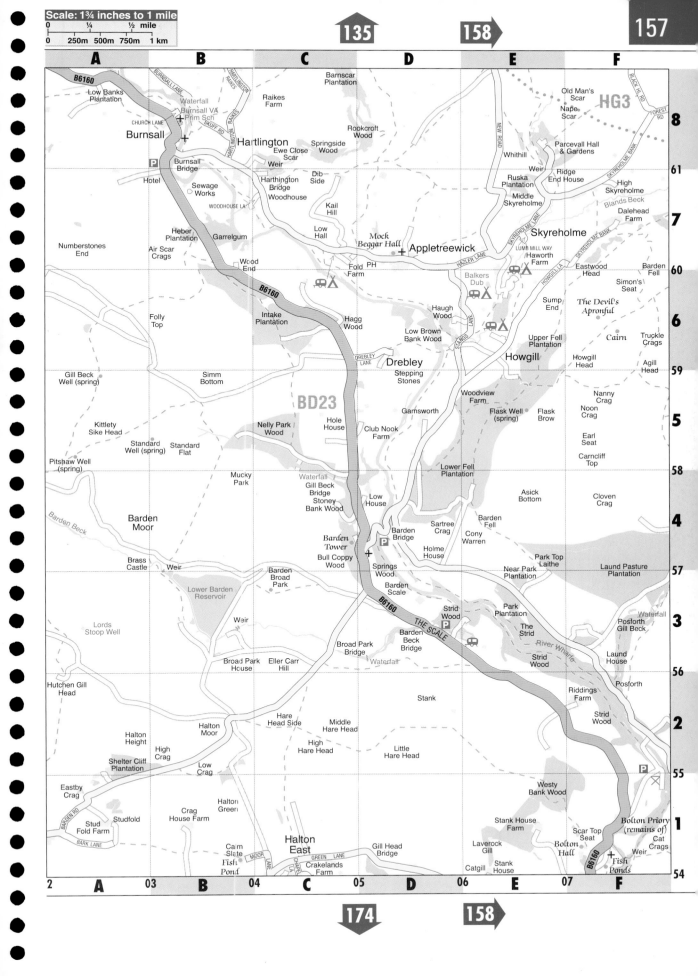

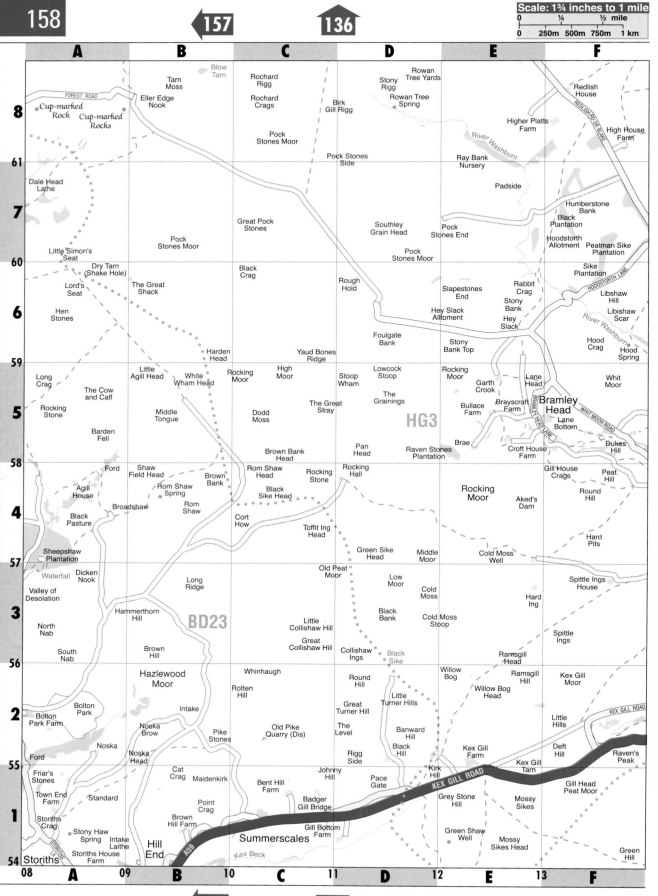

157
136

A   **B**   **C**   **D**   **E**   **F**

Blow Tarn

8 Cup-marked Rock   Cup-marked Rocks   Tarn Moss   Rochard Rigg   Stony Rigg   Rowan Tree Yards   Redlish House

FOREST ROAD   Eller Edge Nook   Rochard Crags   Birk Gill Rigg   Rowan Tree Spring   Higher Platts Farm   High House Farm

Pock Stones Moor   River Washburn

61   Pock Stones Side   Ray Bank Nursery

Dale Head Lathe   Padside   Humberstone Bank

7   Great Pock Stones   Southley Grain Head   Pock Stones End   Black Plantation   Hoodstorth Allotment   Peatman Sike Plantation

Pock Stones Moor   Pock Stones Moor   Sike Plantation

60   Little Simon's Seat   Dry Tarn (Shake Hole)   Black Crag   Rough Hold   Slapestones End   Rabbit Crag   Libshaw Hill

Lord's Seat   The Great Shack   Hey Slack Allotment   Stony Bank   Hey Slack   Libishaw Scar

6   Hen Stones   River Washburn

Foulgate Bank   Stony Bank Top   Hood Crag   Hood Spring

Harden Head   Yaud Bones Ridge

59   Long Crag   Little Agill Head   White Wham Head   Rocking Moor   High Moor   Stoop Wham   Lowcock Stoop   Rocking Moor   Lane Head   Whit Moor

The Cow and Calf   Garth Crook   Brayscroft Farm   **Bramley Head**

5   Rocking Stone   Middle Tongue   Dodd Moss   The Great Stray   The Grainings   Bullace Farm   Lane Bottom

Barden Fell   HG3   Brae   Croft House Farm   Dukes Hill

Brown Bank Head   Pan Head   Raven Stones Plantation

58   Ford   Shaw Field Head   Rom Shaw Head   Rocking Stone   Rocking Hall   Gill House Crags   Peat Hill

Agill House   Rom Shaw Spring   Brown Bank   Black Sike Head   Round Hill

4   Black Pasture   Broadshaw   Rom Shaw   Cort How   Rocking Moor   Aked's Dam   Hard Pits

Toffit Ing Head

57   Sheepshaw Plantation   Green Sike Head   Middle Moor   Cold Moss Well   Spittle Ings House

Waterfall   Dicken Nook   Old Peat Moor

3   Valley of Desolation   Long Ridge   Low Moor   Cold Moss   Hard Ing   Spittle Ings

North Nab   Hammerthorn Hill   BD23   Little Collishaw Hill   Black Bank   Cold Moss Stoop

South Nab   Great Collishaw Hill   Collishaw Ings   Black Sike   Ramsgill Head

56   Whinhaugh   Round Hill   Willow Bog   Ramsgill Hill   Kex Gill Moor

Hazlewood Moor   Rotten Hill   Willow Bog Head

2   Bolton Park   Intake   Great Turner Hill   Little Turner Hills   Little Hills   KEX GILL ROAD

Bolton Park Farm   Noska Brow   Pike Stones   Old Pike Quarry (Dis)   The Level   Banward Hill   Kex Gill Farm   Deft Hill   Raven's Peak

Noska   Rigg Side   Black Hill   Kirk Hill   Kex Gill Tarn

Ford   Noska Head   Johnny Hill   Pace Gate   KEX GILL ROAD   Gill Head Peat Moor

55   Friar's Stones   Cat Crag   Maidenkirk   Bent Hill Farm   Grey Stone Hill   Mossy Sikes

Town End Farm   Standard   Point Crag   Badger Gill Bridge   Green Shaw Well   Mossy Sikes Head   Green Hill

1   Storiths Crag   Brown Hill Farm   Gill Bottom Farm

Stony Haw Spring   Intake Laithe   **Summerscales**

54   Storiths   Storiths House Farm   Hill End   A59   Kex Beck

08   **A**   **09**   **B**   **10**   **C**   **11**   **D**   **12**   **E**   **13**   **F**

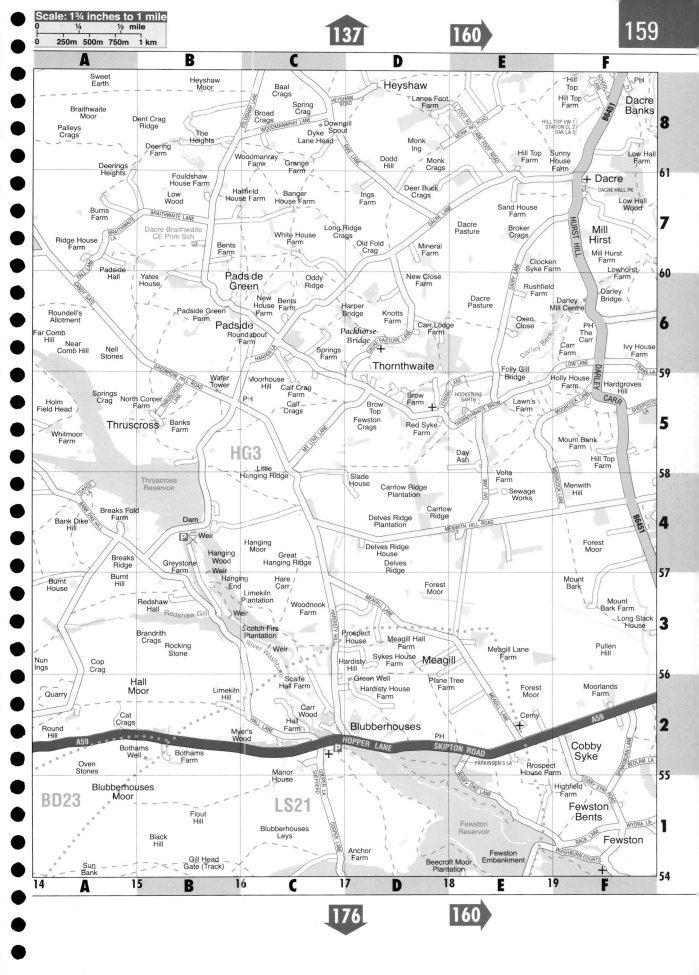

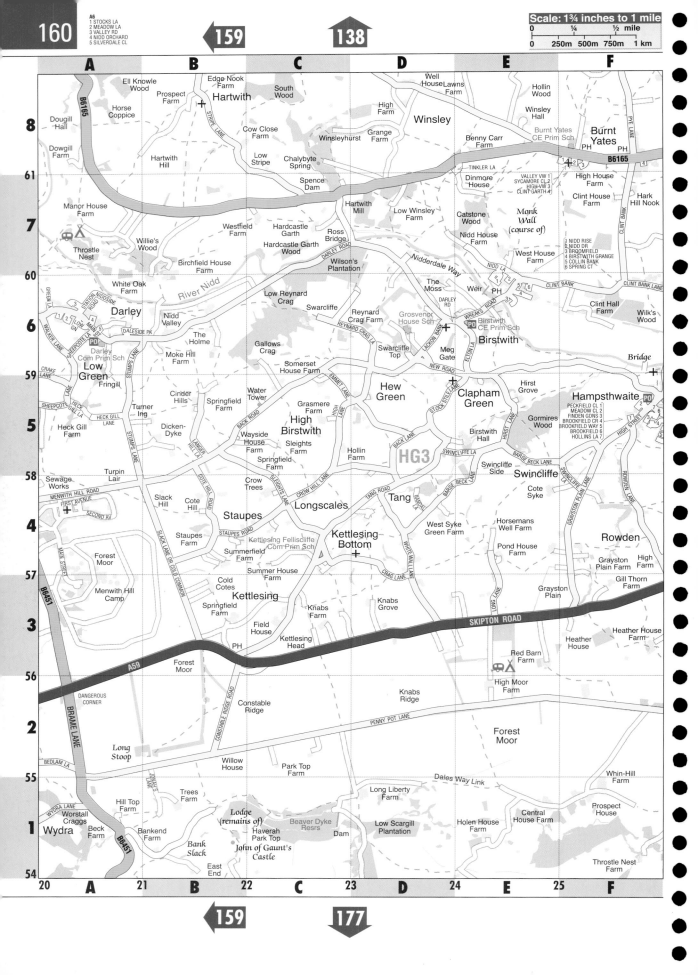

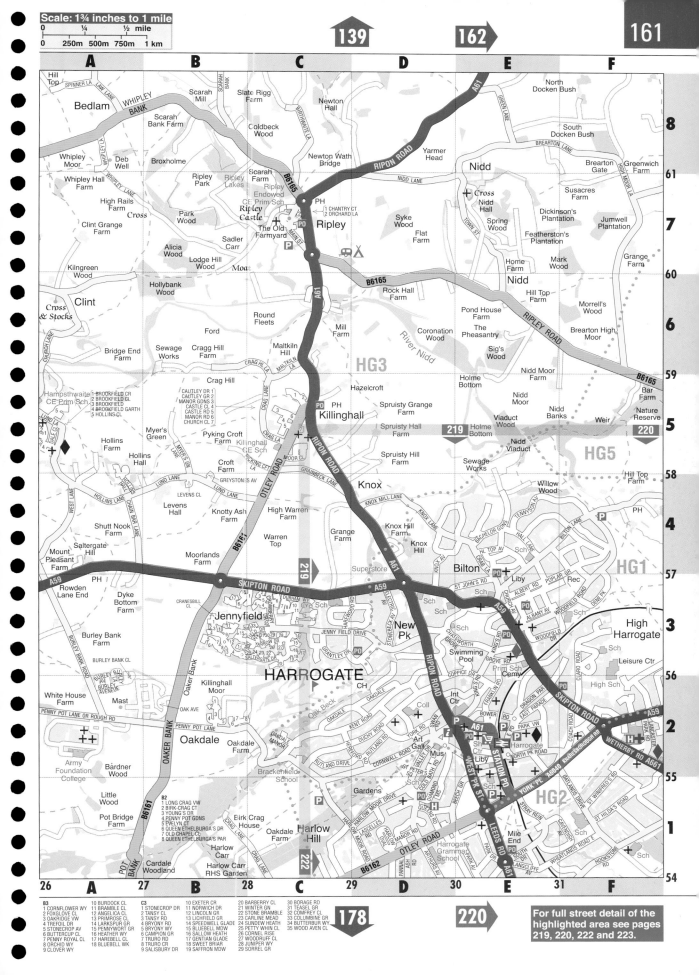

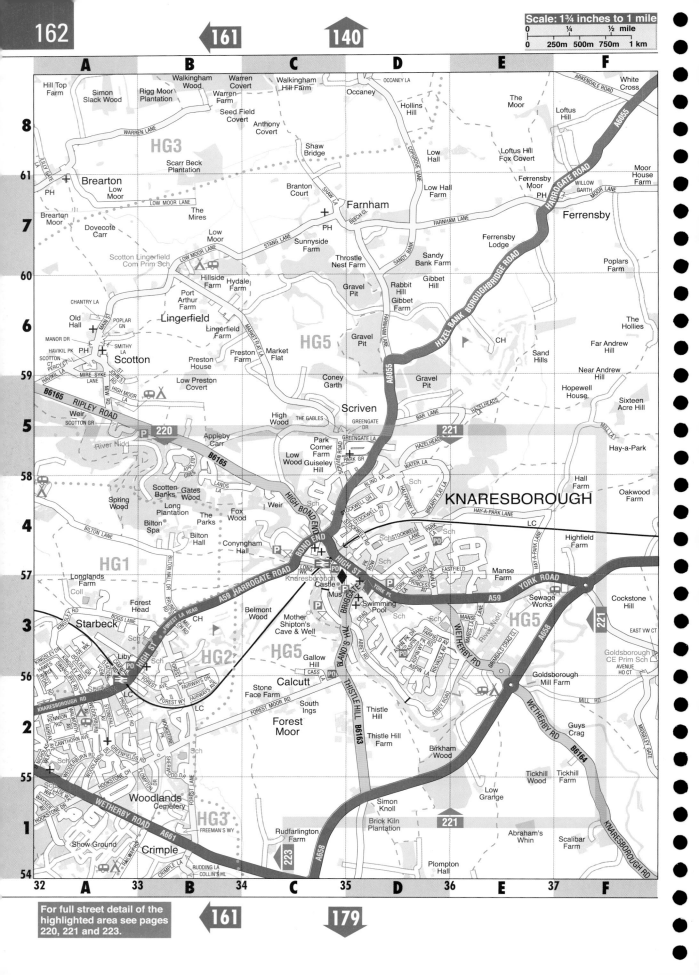

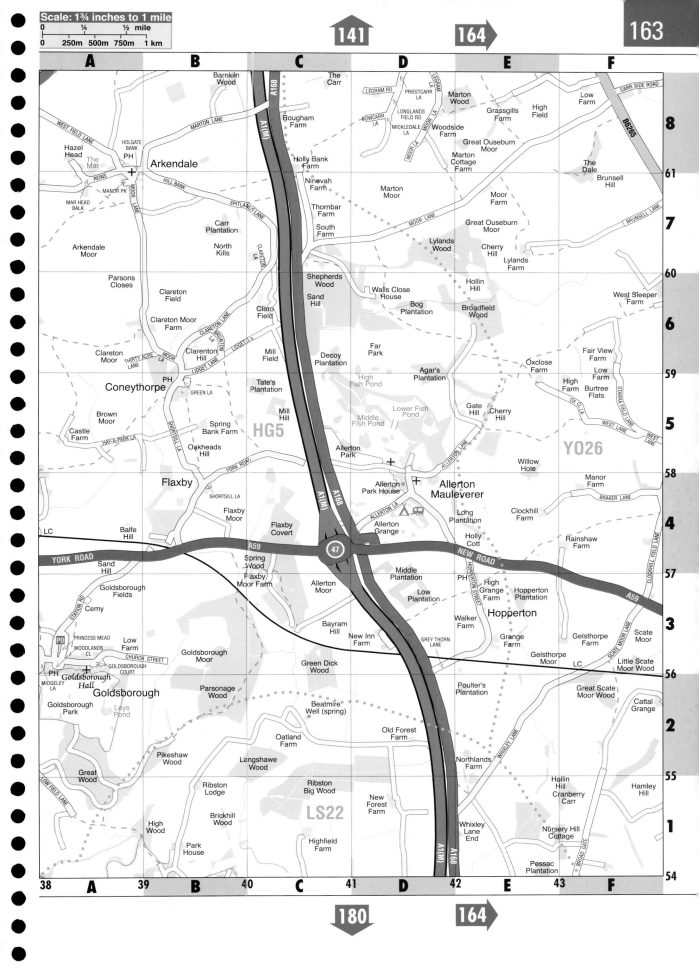

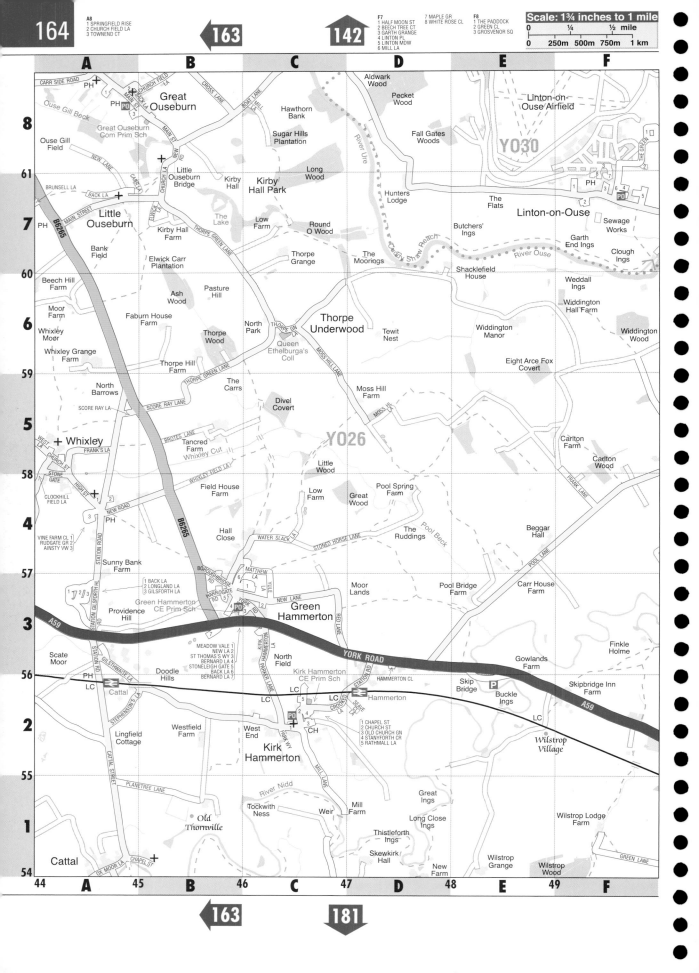

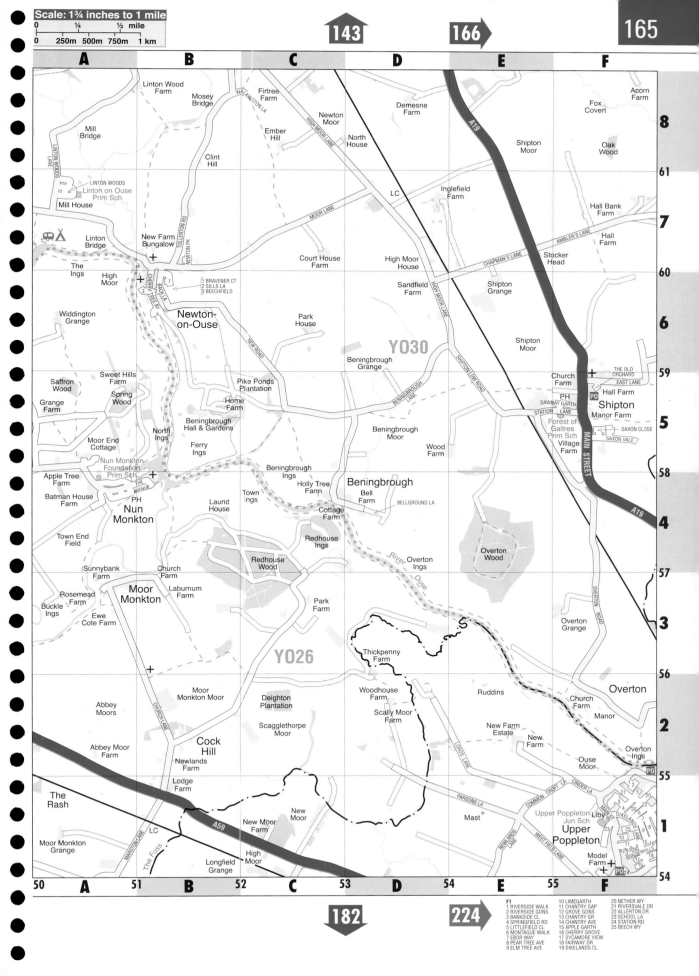

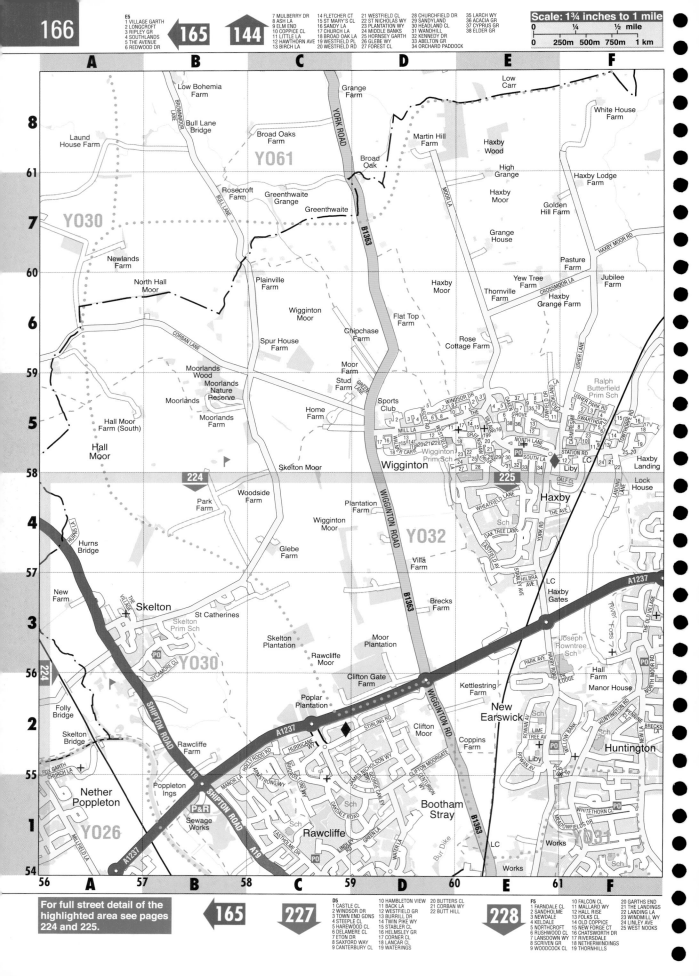

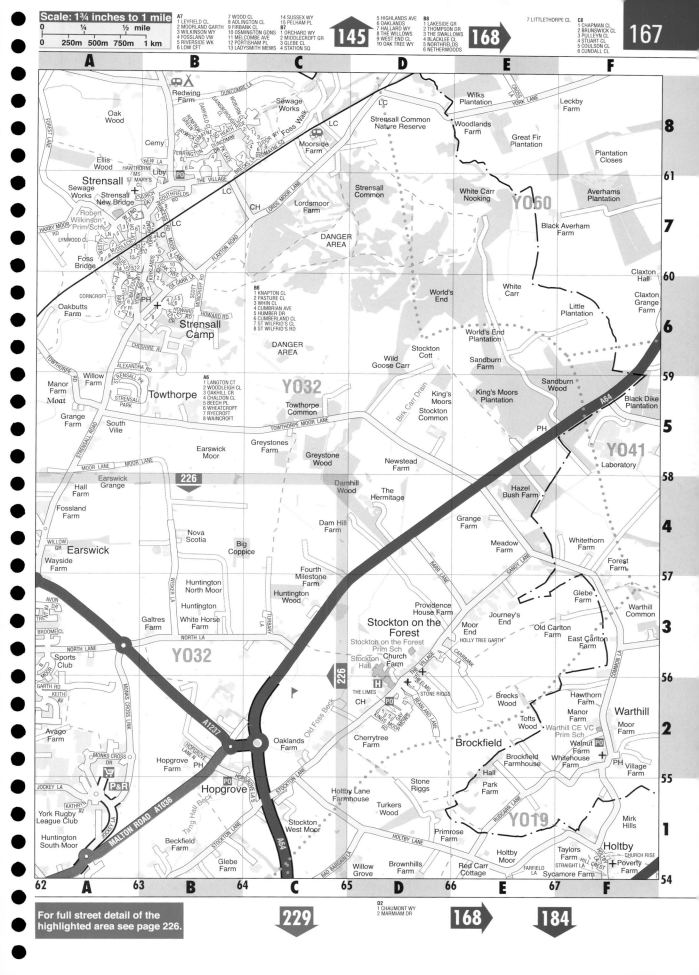

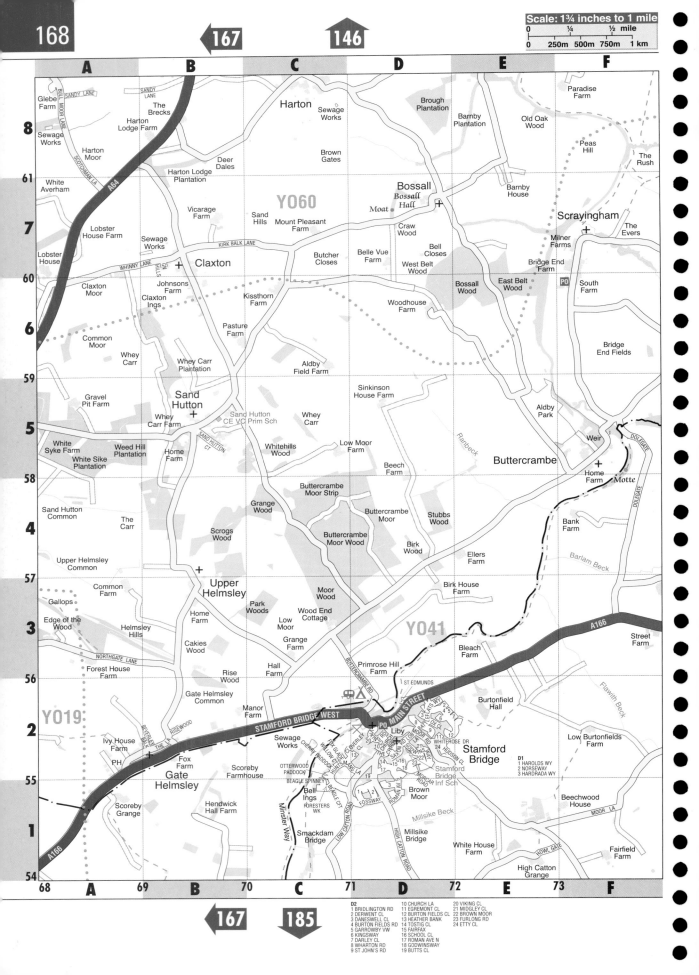

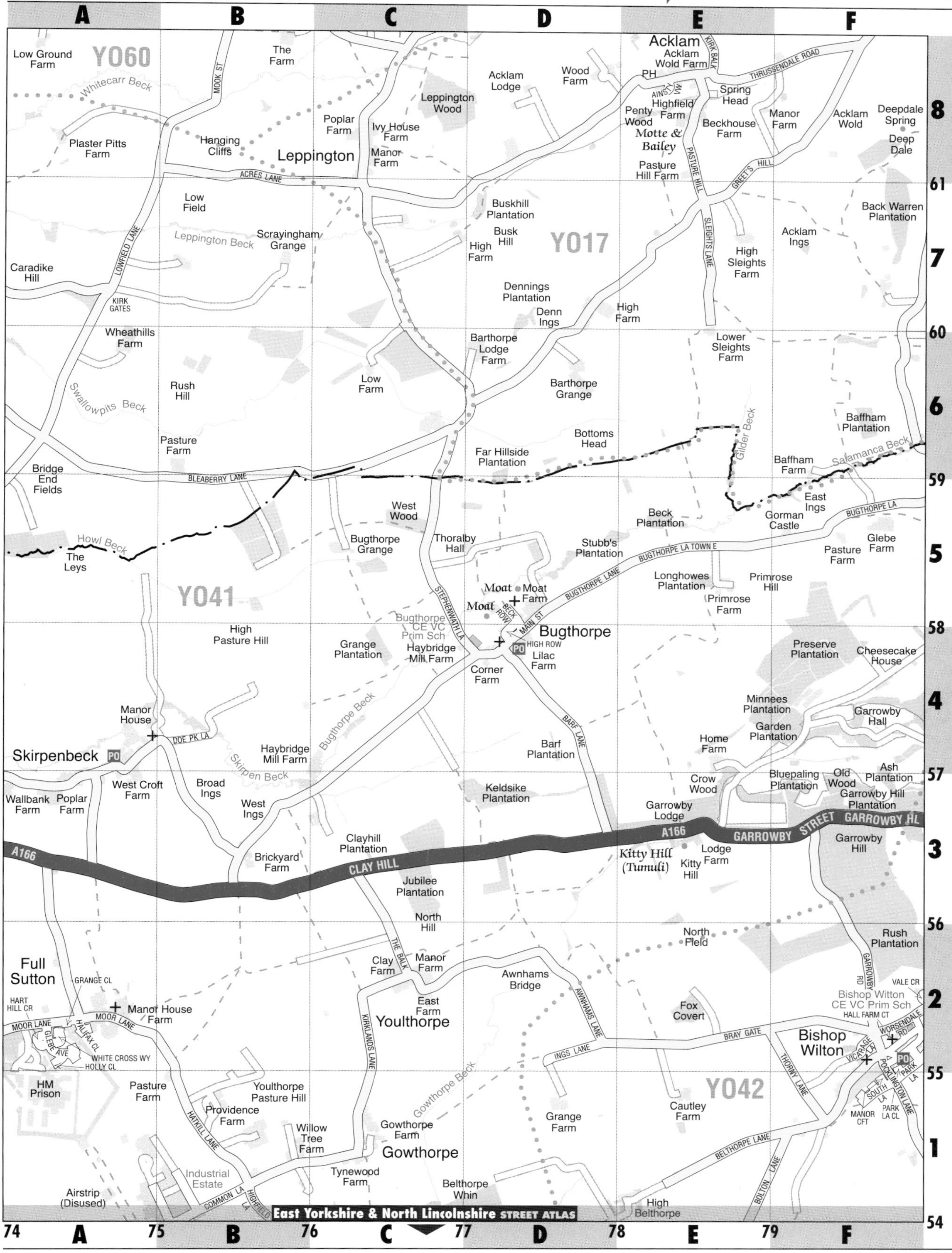
A
B
C
D
E
F
Low Ground Farm
YO60
Whitecarr Beck
The Farm
MOOK ST
Acklam
Acklam Wold Farm
KIRK BALK
THRUSSENDALE ROAD
Acklam Lodge
Wood Farm
PH
Leppington Wood
AINSTY
Highfield Farm
Spring Head
Penty Wood
Motte & Bailey
Beckhouse Farm
Manor Farm
Acklam Wold
Deepdale Spring
Deep Dale
Plaster Pitts Farm
Hanging Cliffs
Poplar Farm
Ivy House Farm
Leppington
Manor Farm
Pasture Hill Farm
PASTURE HILL
GREET'S HILL
ACRES LANE
Low Field
Buskhill Plantation
Back Warren Plantation
Leppington Beck
Scrayingham Grange
Busk Hill
High Farm
YO17
SLEIGHTS LANE
Acklam Ings
High Sleights Farm
Caradike Hill
LOWFIELD LANE
KIRK GATES
Dennings Plantation
Denn Ings
High Farm
Wheathills Farm
Barthorpe Lodge Farm
Lower Sleights Farm
Rush Hill
Low Farm
Barthorpe Grange
Swallowpits Beck
Gilder Beck
Baffham Plantation
Pasture Farm
Bottoms Head
Far Hillside Plantation
Baffham Farm
Salamanca Beck
Bridge End Fields
BLEABERRY LANE
East Ings
West Wood
Beck Plantation
Gorman Castle
BUGTHORPE LA
Howl Beck
The Leys
Bugthorpe Grange
Thoralby Hall
Stubb's Plantation
BUGTHORPE LA TOWN E
Glebe Farm
Pasture Farm
YO41
Moat
Moat Farm
Longhowes Plantation
Primrose Hill
Moat
BUGTHORPE LANE
Primrose Farm
STEPHENWATH LA
BECK ROW
MAIN ST
Bugthorpe
Bugthorpe CE VC Prim Sch
High Pasture Hill
Grange Plantation
Haybridge Mill Farm
PO
HIGH ROW
Lilac Farm
Preserve Plantation
Cheesecake House
Corner Farm
Minnees Plantation
Bugthorpe Beck
Garrowby Hall
Manor House
BARF LANE
Garden Plantation
DOE PK LA
Home Farm
Skirpenbeck
PO
Haybridge Mill Farm
Barf Plantation
Ash Plantation
Skirpen Beck
Crow Wood
Bluepaling Plantation
Old Wood
Garrowby Hill Plantation
Wallbank Farm
Poplar Farm
West Croft Farm
Broad Ings
West Ings
Keldsike Plantation
Garrowby Lodge
A166
GARROWBY STREET
GARROWBY HL
Clayhill Plantation
Kitty Hill (Tumuli)
Kitty Hill
Lodge Farm
Garrowby Hill
A166
Brickyard Farm
CLAY HILL
Jubilee Plantation
North Hill
North Field
Rush Plantation
Full Sutton
GRANGE CL
Clay Farm
THE BALK
Manor Farm
GARROWBY RD
Awnhams Bridge
VALE CR
HART HILL CR
Manor House Farm
East Farm
Youlthorpe
Fox Covert
Bishop Wilton CE VC Prim Sch
HALL FARM CT
MOOR LANE
GLEBE AVE
HALIFAX CL
MOOR LANE
KIRKLANDS LANE
AWNHAMS LANE
BRAY GATE
Bishop Wilton
WORSENDALE RD
WHITE CROSS WY
HOLLY CL
INGS LANE
VICARAGE LA
PO
HM Prison
Pasture Farm
Youlthorpe Pasture Hill
Gowthorpe Beck
YO42
THORNY LANE
SOUTH LA
PARK LA
POCKLINGTON LANE
Providence Farm
Cautley Farm
HATKILL LANE
Willow Tree Farm
Gowthorpe Farm
Grange Farm
MANOR CFT
PARK LA CL
Gowthorpe
BELTHORPE LANE
Industrial Estate
Tynewood Farm
Belthorpe Whin
BOLTON LANE
Airstrip (Disused)
COMMON LA
HIGHFIELD LA
High Belthorpe
8
61
7
60
6
59
5
58
4
57
3
56
2
55
1
54
74
75
76
77
78
79

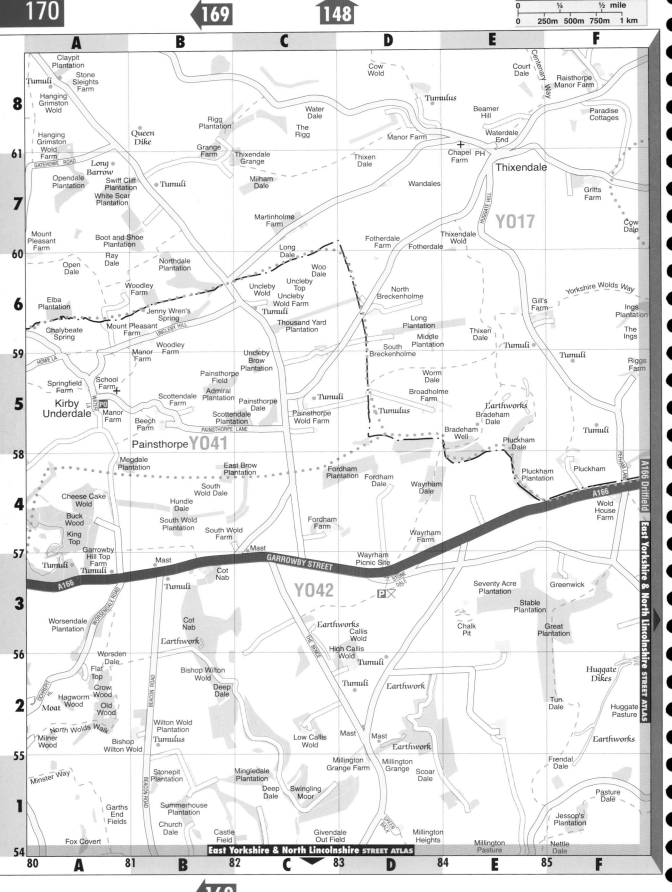

Scale: 1¾ inches to 1 mile
0   ¼   ½   mile
0   250m 500m 750m 1 km

A **B** **C** **D** **E** **F**

Claypit Plantation
Tumuli
Stone Sleights Farm
Cow Wold
Tumulus
Court Dale
Centenary Way
Raisthorpe Manor Farm

8

Hanging Grimston Wold
Water Dale
Beamer Hill
Paradise Cottages

Hanging Grimston Wold Farm
GATEHOWE ROAD
Rigg Plantation
The Rigg
Manor Farm
Waterdale End

61

Long Barrow
Queen Dike
Grange Farm
Thixendale Grange
Thixen Dale
Chapel Farm
PH
Thixendale
YO17
Gritts Farm

Opendale Plantation
Swiff Cliff Plantation
Tumuli
Milham Dale
Wandales

7

White Scar Plantation
Martinholme Farm
Huggate Hill
Cow Dale

Mount Pleasant Farm
Boot and Shoe Plantation
Long Dale
Fotherdale Farm
Thixendale Wold

60

Open Dale
Ray Dale
Northdale Plantation
Woo Dale
Fotherdale
Fotherdale

Elba Plantation
Woodley Farm
Uncleby Wold
Uncleby Top
North Breckenholme
Gill's Farm
Yorkshire Wolds Way
Ings Plantation

6

Chalybeate Spring
Jenny Wren's Spring
Uncleby Wold Farm
Tumuli
Long Plantation
The Ings

Mount Pleasant Farm
UNCLEBY HILL
Thousand Yard Plantation
Middle Plantation
Thixen Dale
Tumuli
Tumuli

59

HOWE LA
Woodley Farm
Manor Farm
Uncleby Brow Plantation
South Breckenholme
Worm Dale
Riggs Farm

Springfield Farm
School Farm
Painsthorpe Field
Tumuli
Broadholme Farm
Earthworks

5

Kirby Underdale
WATER LA
PO
Manor Farm
Admiral Plantation
Painsthorpe Dale
Tumuli
Tumulus
Bradeham Dale
Tumuli

Scottendale Farm
Beech Farm
Scottendale Plantation
PAINSTHORPE LANE
Painsthorpe Wold Farm
Bradeham Well
Pluckham Dale

58

Painsthorpe YO41
East Brow Plantation
Fordham Plantation
Pluckham Plantation
Pluckham

Megdale Plantation
South Wold Dale
Fordham Dale
Wayrham Dale
PERHAM LANE

4

Cheese Cake Wold
Hundle Dale
Fordham Farm
A166
Wold House Farm

Buck Wood
South Wold Plantation
Fordham Farm
Wayrham Farm
A166 Driffield

King Top
South Wold Farm
Mast
Wayrham Picnic Site

57

Garrowby Hill Top Farm
Mast
GARROWBY STREET
STONE DALE
Seventy Acre Plantation
Greenwick

Tumuli
Tumuli
Cot Nab
YO42
P
Stable Plantation
Great Plantation

3

Worsendale Plantation
WORSENDALE ROAD
Tumuli
Cot Nab
Earthworks
Callis Wold
Chalk Pit

Earthwork
High Callis Wold
Huggate Dikes

56

Worsden Dale
Bishop Wilton Wold
Tumuli
Earthwork

Flat Top
Crow Wood
Deep Dale
Tumuli
Tun Dale
Huggate Pasture

2

Moat
Hagworm Wood
Old Wood
BEACON ROAD
Earthwork

Milner Wood
North Wolds Walk
Wilton Wold Plantation
Tumulus
Mast
Mast
Earthworks

55

Bishop Wilton Wold
Mingledale Plantation
Millington Grange Farm
Millington Grange
Earthwork
Scoar Dale
Frendal Dale

Minster Way
Stonepit Plantation
Deep Dale
Swingling Moor
Pasture Dale

1

OCKREPT HL
Garths End Fields
Summerhouse Plantation
Church Dale
Castle Field
GREEN BALK
Givendale Out Field
Millington Heights
Jessop's Plantation

Fox Covert
Millington Pasture
Nettle Dale

54

A166 Drffield | East Yorkshire & North Lincolnshire STREET ATLAS

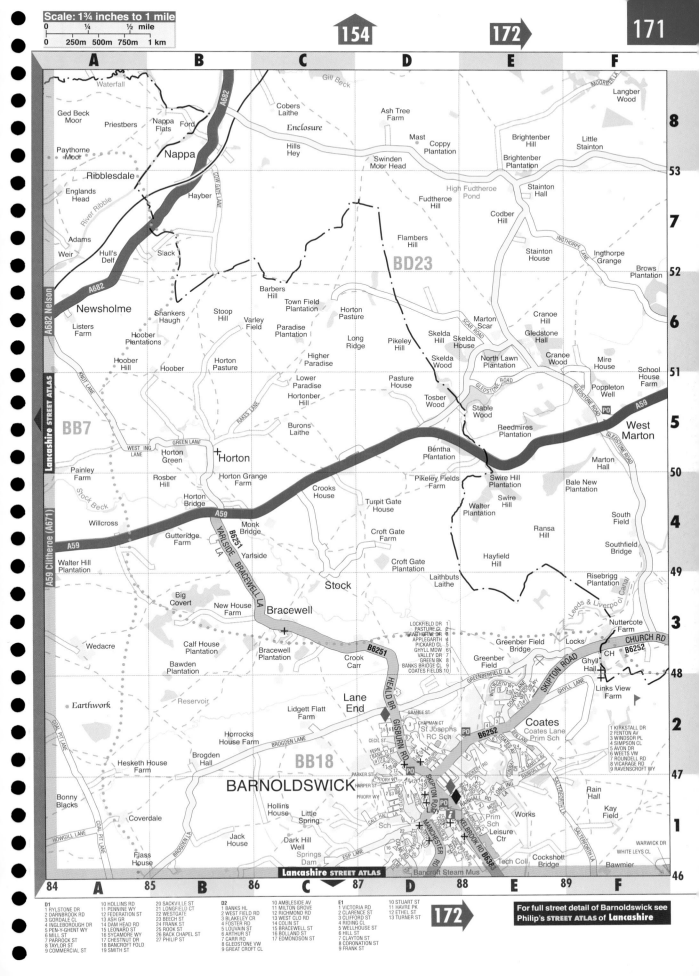

A B C D E F

8
53
7
52
6
51
5
50
4
49
3
48
2
47
1
46

90 91 92 93 94 95

Viaduct
Weir
Weir
MARTON ROAD
WALTON CL
MOSBER LA
CHURCH-CFT
Moat
Gargrave
PH
CHURCH LA
Weir
Gargrave
River Aire
Woomber Wood
Highgate Bridge (swing)
Sulber Laithe
A65
Leeds and Liverpool Canal

Aqueduct
Priest Holme Bridge
Mosber La Bridge
Lobby Bridge
Kelber Hill Farm
Kirk Sink Farm
Sewage Works
Robin Wood
Thorlby Bridge (swing)

Newton Hall
Locks Parkers Farm
Bank Newton
Scaleber
Butter Haw Farm
Broughton Quarry
Smellows Quarry
Copy Hill Plantation
Small House
Copy Hill

Lock
Pennine Way
Moorber Hill
Church Street
River Aire

Newton Bridge
Newton Grange Farm
Pasture House
Oxen Close
Oxenclose Farm
Hall Close Wood
Broughton Copy Farm

Brows Plantation
Greenbank Farm
Turnbers Hill Plantation
Acliffe Hill Plantation
Clints Delf (dis)
Skinnerground Wood
Broughton

Green Bank
Langber Plantation
Trenet Laithe
Corringer Hill
BD23
Skinner Ground Farm
Deer Haw Plantation
Gargrave Road
OLD LA
A59
Heslaker Bridge

Tempest Farm
Williamson Bridge
Deer Haw
PH
Weir
Dancliff Plantation
HEBER DR
A59
Church Farm Barn
PH
CHURCH LA
East Marton
Mickethorne Farm
Mill Wood
Broughton Hall
The Grove Hall

Sewage Works
Crickle Farm
Broughton Fields Farm
Primrose Hill
Home Farm
Denbers Plantation

Pennine Way
EDMONDSON'S LANE
A56
BROUGHTON RD
Low Ground Farm
Pasture House Farm

Langber
Gubbs Hill Farm
COLNE AND BROUGHTON RD
PH Elslack Bridge
Church Lane
Eller Gill Lane
Croft Wood
Yellison House

Far Fence End Farm
Johnsons Gate Farm
ELSLACK LA
BURWEN CASTLE RD
White House Farm
Yellison Wood
Lower Scarcliffe Farm
Scarcliffe Farm

Old Cote Farm
Fence End
Merlinwood
Elslack Hall
BURWEN CASTLE FARM (ROMAN FORT)
Higher Scarcliff
Lane Head Quarry

CAM LA
BREARLANDS
A56
Earby Beck
Brown House Bridge
Thompson House Farm
Smearber Farm
Mitton House
Redfirth Gill Cote
Baxter House

Thornton in Craven Com Prim Sch
OLD ROAD
Brown House
Park House Farm
Mill Fold
Stories House Farm
Standrise Plantation
Baxter House Farm

Thornton-in-Craven
Rectory Farm
PO
1 THE FOLD
2 QUEENS GARTH
Wood House
MOOR LANE
Gawthorpe House

CHURCH RD
B6252
Hotel
BROUGHTON LANE
Elslack Resr
Frozen Well

SUMMERFIELD
THORNTON KIRK
Pennine Way
CLOGGER LANE
Ransable Well
Clarke Moss Hill
Carleton Moor

SKIPTON RD
Booth Bridge Farm
Little Moor
Elslack Moor
Broughton Hill

Pendle Way
PH
Batty House
Oak Slack Farm
P
Thornton Moor
Pinhaw Moor
Pinhaw
Kirk Sykes Farm

Grange Farm
Mine Mus
SCHOOL FIELDS
Sewage Works
Cowgarth Farm
YH
Marl Field Farm
B81
Hewitts Farm

PO
Wentcliff Brook
GAYLANDS LANE
MILL BR RD
BIRCH HALL LA
Mill Bridge
DARK LA
Sunny Side

HILLTOP LA
A56
RED LION ST
STONEY BANK RD
Raike Bank Farm
Windle Field Farm
DODGSON LA
Out Laithe Farm
Calf Edge Farm
Knott Farm

COLNE RD
NEW RD
BARNWOOD CR
Earby Springfield Prim Sch
Highbank Farm
STANDRIDGE CLOUGH LA
Lower Verjuice Farm
Dodgsons Farm
MITTON LA
Hill Top
Harrow Ings Farm
WHITE HL LA
The Fold

SALTERFORTH RD
EARBY
Bleara Moor
Mitton House
WINTER GAP LANE
CALF WOOD LANE
LTT WD
Pennine Way

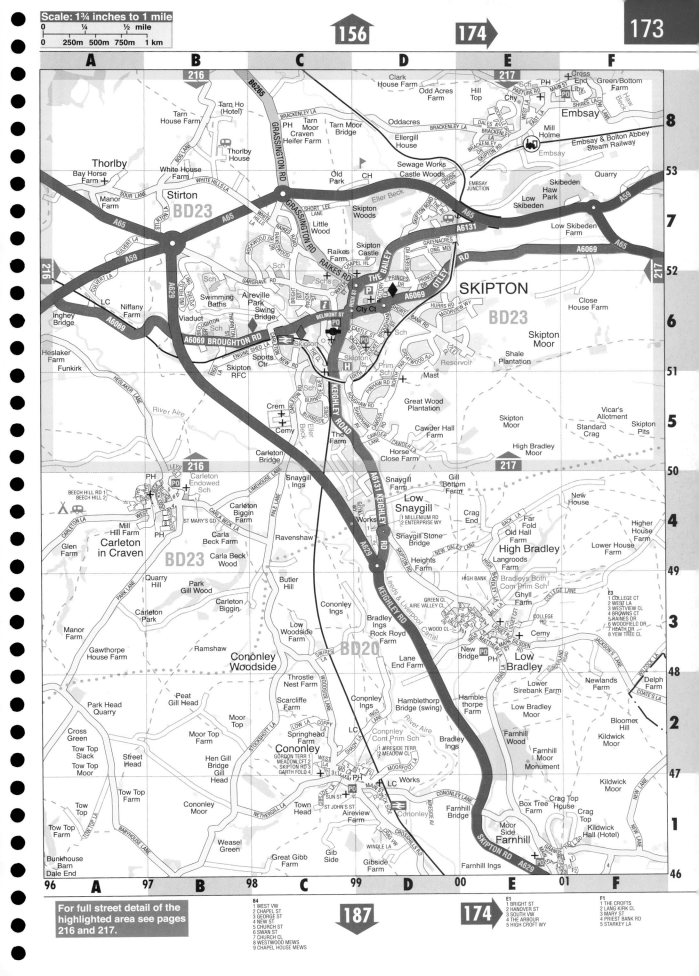

Scale: 1¾ inches to 1 mile

0   ¼   ½ mile
0   250m 500m 750m 1 km

156

174

For full street detail of the highlighted area see pages 216 and 217.

187

174

B4
1 WEST VW
2 CHAPEL ST
3 GEORGE ST
4 NEW ST
5 CHURCH ST
6 SWAN ST
7 CHURCH CL
8 WESTWOOD MEWS
9 CHAPEL HOUSE MEWS

E1
1 BRIGHT ST
2 HANOVER ST
3 SOUTH VW
4 THE ARBOUR
5 HIGH CROFT WY

F1
1 THE CROFTS
2 LANG KIRK CL
3 MARY ST
4 PRIEST BANK RD
5 STARKEY LA

E3
1 COLLEGE CT
2 WEST LA
3 WESTVIEW CL
4 BROWNS CT
5 RAINES DR
6 WOODFIELD DR
7 HEATH DR
8 YEW TREE CL

E4
1 PARSON'S LA
2 MOOR PK CL
3 MOOR PK CR
4 TURNER LA
5 BIG MD DR
6 GILL CL
7 STAMP HL CL
8 THE STREET
9 BROADFIELD WY
10 LIME CL
11 HAWTHORN CL

Scale: 1¾ inches to 1 mile

0   ¼   ½   mile
0   250m   500m   750m   1 km

Grid	Label

Fish Pond

Halton East

Chapel La   Gaw La

Waterfall   Halton Gill Wood

Hesketh House

Bolton Abbey

Bank Wood   Struff Wood

Low Lane   Holme Lane   Newbridge La

Embsay & Bolton Abbey Steam Rly   Holywell Halt

LONG CAUSEWAY

Hambleton

Bolton Abbey

A59

Dales Way   B6160

Hotel   Bolton Bridge

The Boyle & Petyt Prim Sch

Holywell Bridge

Prior's La

Huffa Bridge

High Skibeden Farm

Hayneholme

Waterfall

Harry Wall Gill

Beamsley

Beamsley Lane   Lowfield

Meadowcroft   Low La

Field House Farm

Banks Wood

BD23

Hawpike Farm

Home Farm

River Wharfe   BOLTON ROAD

Draughton

THE CROFT   SPRING RI

A65

Wheelam Rock   THE SPINNEY   WEST VW

Lane End Farm

Berwick

Haw Pike

Lob Wood

Wind Pumps

Eller Carr Wood

Farfield Hall

B6160

Ellenber Farm

Draughton Heights Farm

Draughton Height

Berwick Intake Farm

Banks Gill

Mines

Chelker Reservoir

Hag Head Laithe

Syke House Farm

Back Plantation

Chelker House Farm

Highfield Farm

Highfield House

Farfield Farm

Nor Hill Well

Draughton Moor

The Bogs

Upper White Well

High Sanfitt Farm

High Cross Bank Farm

Cross Bank

ADDINGHAM WHARFEDALE ROAD

CH

Riddings Farm

SPRINGFIELD MOUNT   HARCOURT DR

Addingham Prim Sch

BACK BECK

Skipton Moor

Snow Hill Farm

Snow Hill Plantation   Haygill Farm

Height Lane   Haworth Moor

Bank End Farm

Addingham Low Moor

HEATHNESS RD   SKIPTON RD   LONG RIDDINGS

HODGSON FOLD

SCHOOL GREEN LA

Addingham

High Bradley Moor

High Edge

Middlesbrough Farm

Counter Hill

Round Dikes   Earthwork

Tumulus

High Cross Bank Farm

MOOR LA

SILSDEN RD   LIBY

MAIN ST   PO

Low Edge Farm

High Edge Farm

Carr Bog Farm

Cowburn Beck Farm

Woofa Bank Farm

Tumulus

Lower Turner Lane Farm

A65   SILSDEN RD

Addingham

ADDINGHAM WHARFEDALE ROAD

Moor Gate Farm   Moorgate Jenkin

Great Gill

RIDGE LANE   WALKER'S LANE   BANK LANE   JOWETT'S LA   CRINGLES LANE

Silsden Moor

Walton Hole

Marchup Plantation

Lower Marchup Farm

LS29

Coppy Hill

Nudge Hill Farm

Little Round Wood

Street Farm

High Bracken Hill Farm

Marlpit Plantation

Middle Marchup Farm

Marchup Height

Gildersber

KILN HILL LA   GREEN

Lane House Farm

Silsden Moor

Foster Cliffe Farm North

Far Cringles Farm

Old Tower

BOLTON RD

Addingham Middle Moor

Deif Hill

COCKING LA   COCKING LA

High Brockabank

Small Banks

Smoulden Farm

Heights Farm

KITT LANE   LOW LANE

Silsden Moor

Foster Cliffe Farm South

Great Gill

Cringles

Brook's Hill

Sea Moor Hill

LIPPERSLEY LANE

Brocka Bank Moor

School Wood

Horne House

Brook's Crag

Sea Moor Farm

Nudge Hill

TURNER LA   STRAIGHT LA

Hodson's Farm

HEIGHTS LANE   HORN LANE

Dales Bank Farm

Silsden Reservoir

Hay Hills Farms

Horn Crag

Asker Hill

Crag House

Hang Goose Farm

Slade Farm

Addingham Moorside

COATE'S LANE

Stakehill Plantation

Lower Heights Farm

HAYHILLS LA

BD20

FISHBECK LA

Well House Farm

LEFT BANK LANE

Nab End

Bloomer Hill Farm

Bridge House

Hole Farm

Raikes Head Farm

Beck Wood

Brown Bank Lane

Brown Bank

Light Bank

Windgate Nick

Addingham High Moor

NEW DENNIS LA   HOLE LANE

Low Bracken Hill Farm

WEST DENE   BREAKMOOR AV   NAB DR

BROWCLIFF   THORNER GR

SILSDEN

Town Head

SWARTHA

White Crag

White Crag Plantation

Tar Topping

BURNSALL MEWS   KILNSEY FOLD

BRADLEY ROAD   BRACKENLEY

A6034

BANKLANDS AV   HAWBER COTE DR

Swartha

North End Farm

White Crag

Cup and Ring Marked Rocks

High Cross Moor Farm

HIGH GREEN DR   SKIPTON RD

SILSDEN HOUSE GARDENS   SKIPTON ROAD

KIRKGATE   Liby   Theatre   PO

Brunthwaite

Brunthwaite Crag

White Crag Moor

JERRY LA

Kildwick Grange

SVW TERR   ELLIOTT STREET   Sch   Coll

PICKARD LA   CRAVEN CT   MIDDLEWAY

JACQUES GR

Black Pots Farm

Airedale House Farm

GLOUCESTER AVE

02   A   03   B   04   C   D   06   E   07   F

F4
1 MOOR PK WY
2 MOOR PK GR
3 CRAVEN CR
4 BURNS HILL
5 COCKSHOTT PL
6 WHARFEDALE VW
7 HIGH BANK CL
8 CHAPEL ST
9 SUGAR HILL
10 AYNHOLME CL
11 KILNERS CFT
12 TOWNHEAD FOLD
13 BECKSIDE CL
14 RIDLEYS FOLD
15 GEORGE ST
16 DRUGGIST LA
17 JONATHAN GARTH
18 HILLSIDE CL
19 WEST CFT
20 OLD STATION WY
21 ACRE FOLD
22 SOUTHFIELD TERR
23 SOUTHFIELD LA
24 BROWNSFIELD RD
25 ST JOHNS AV
26 MOUNT PLEASANT
27 ST CHRISTOPHERS DR
28 SOUTHFIELD WY
29 ST MICHAELS WY
30 ST LEONARDS CL
31 ST PETERS CT
32 ST IANS CFT

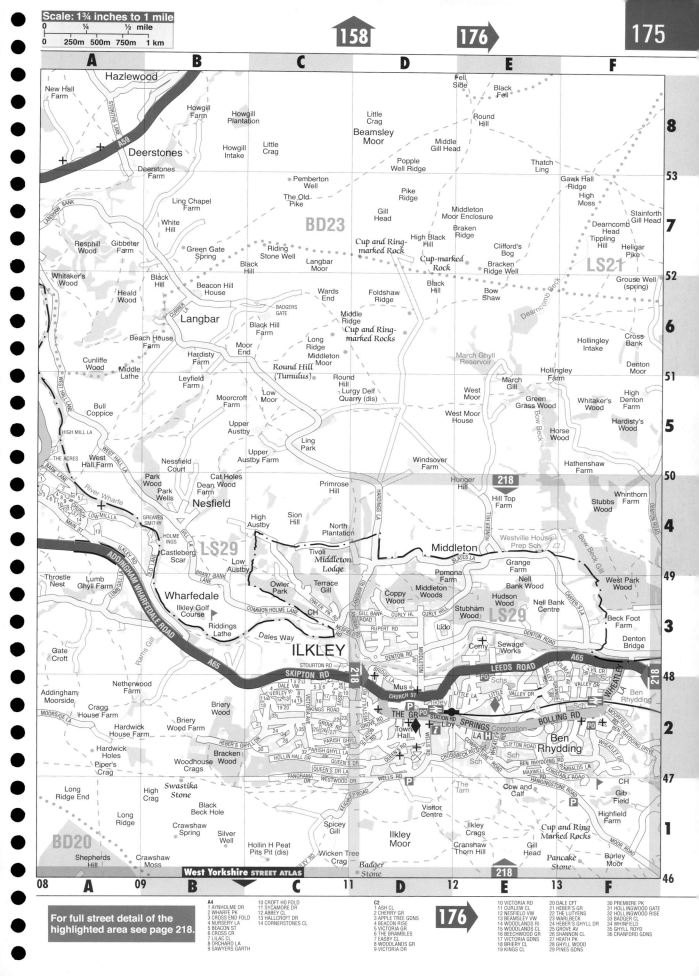

A   B   C   D   E   F

New Hall Farm
Hazlewood
Howgill Farm
Howgill Plantation
Howgill Intake
Little Crag
Fell Side
Black Fell
Round Hill
8

STORITHS LANE
A59
Deerstones
Deerstones Farm
Little Crag
Beamsley Moor
Middle Gill Head
Thatch Ling
53

LANSHAW BANK
Resphill Wood
Gibbeter Farm
Ling Chapel Farm
White Hill
Green Gate Spring
Riding Stone Well
Black Hill
The Old Pike
Langbar Moor
Pemberton Well
Pike Ridge
Gill Head
Middleton Moor Enclosure
Braken Ridge
Popple Well Ridge
High Black Hill
Cup and Ring-marked Rock
Cup-marked Rock
Clifford's Bog
Bracken Ridge Well
Gawk Hall Ridge
High Moss
Stainforth Gill Head
Dearncomb Head
Tippling Hill
Heligar Pike
LS21
BD23
7

Whitaker's Wood
Heald Wood
Black Hill
Beacon Hill House
CURREY LA
BADGERS GATE
Wards End
Foldshaw Ridge
Middle Ridge
Black Hill
Bow Shaw
Grouse Well (spring)
52

WEST HALL LANE
Cunliffe Wood
Middle Lathe
Langbar
Black Hill Farm
Hardisty Farm
Moor End
Long Ridge
Cup and Ring-marked Rocks
Round Hill (Tumulus)
Round Hill
March Ghyll Reservoir
Hollingley Intake
Cross Bank
Denton Moor
6

Beach House Farm
Leyfield Farm
Middleton Moor
Low Moor
Lurgy Delf Quarry (dis)
West Moor
March Gill
Hollingley
Green Grass Wood
Whitaker's Wood
High Denton Farm
Hardisty's Wood
51

HIGH MILL LA
Bull Coppice
Moorcroft Farm
Ling Park
West Moor House
Bow Beck
Horse Wood
Hathenshaw Farm
5

THE ACRES
PARK LANE
West Hall Farm
West Hall LA
Park Wood
Nessfield Court
Upper Austby
Upper Austby Farm
Cat Holes
Dean Wood Farm
Hunger Hill
Hill Top Farm
218
Whinthorn Farm
Stubbs Wood
50

River Wharfe
LOW MILL LA
CHURCH ST
MAIN ST
GREAVES SMITHY
HOLME INGS
GILL LA
Park Wells
Nesfield
Dean Hill
Primrose Hill
HARDINGS LA
Westville House Prep Sch
Bow Beck Gill
DENTON ROAD
4

ADDINGHAM WHARFEDALE ROAD
LS29
OLD LANE
BRANT BANK LANE
High Austby
Sion Hill
North Plantation
Middleton
Pomona Farm
Grange Farm
SLATES LA
Nell Bank Wood
West Park Wood
49

Throstle Nest
Lumb Ghyll Farm
YATTING
Castleberg Scar
Low Austby
Tivoli
Middleton Lodge
Terrace Gill
Coppy Wood
Middleton Woods
Stubham Wood
Hudson Wood
Nell Bank Centre
LS29
CARTER S LA
Beck Foot Farm
Denton Bridge
3

Gate Croft
Wharfedale
Ilkley Golf Course
COMMON HOLME LANE
OWLER PK RD
Owler Park
CH
NESFIELD RD
GILL BANK RD
CURLY HL
CURLY HILL
Rupert Rd
Lido
Cemy
Sewage Works
A65
2

Rams Gill
MOORS/DE LA
Addingham Moorside
Cragg House Farm
Netherwood Farm
Briery Wood
Riddings Lathe
Dales Way
A65
SKIPTON RD
218
STOURTON RD
DALE VW
BRIDGE LA
Mus
DENTON RD
Ilkley
Schs
LEEDS ROAD
Ben Rhydding
218
WHEATLEY
48

BD20
Hardwick House Farm
Hardwick Holes
Piper's Crag
Briery Wood Farm
Woodhouse Crags
Bracken Wood
HEBER'S GHYLL DR
HOLLIN HALL DR
PANORAMA DR
WESTWOOD DR
KINGS ROAD
GROVE RD
PARISH GHYLL LA
QUEEN'S DR
Queen's Dr
WELLS RD
VICTORIA RD
CHURCH ST
THE GR
Town Hall
Liby
PO
SPRINGS
Coronation
LA
H
CLIFTON AV
Sch
BOLLING RD
Ben Rhydding
BEN RHYDDING DRIVE
MOORFIELD
COMBALDS LA
CH
47

Long Ridge End
High Crag
Swastika Stone
Black Beck Hole
Crawshaw Spring
Silver Well
Hollin H Peat Pits Pit (dis)
Wicken Tree Crag
KEIGHLEY ROAD
Spicey Gill
Ilkley Moor
Badger Stone
Visitor Centre
The Tarn
Ilkley Crags
Cranshaw Thorn Hill
Gill Head
218
Cow and Calf
HANGINGSTONE ROAD
Cup and Ring Marked Rocks
Pancake Stone
MOOR ROAD
Burley Moor
Gib Field
Highfield Farm
1

West Yorkshire STREET ATLAS

08   A   09   B   10   C   11   D   12   E   13   F   46

For full street detail of the highlighted area see page 218.

A4
1 AYNHOLME DR
2 WHARFE PK
3 CROSS END FOLD
4 NURSERY LA
5 BEACON ST
6 CROSS CR
7 LILAC CL
8 ORCHARD LA
9 SAWYERS GARTH
10 CROFT HO FOLD
11 SYCAMORE DR
12 ABBEY CL
13 HALLCROFT DR
14 CORNERSTONES CL

C2
1 ASH CL
2 CHERRY GR
3 APPLE TREE GDNS
4 BEACON RISE
5 VICTORIA GR
6 THE BRAMBLES
7 EASBY CL
8 WOODLANDS GR
9 VICTORIA DR
10 VICTORIA RD
11 CURLEW CL
12 NESFIELD VW
13 BEAMSLEY VW
14 WOODLANDS RI
15 WOODLANDS CL
16 BEECHWOOD GR
17 VICTORIA GDNS
18 BRIERY CL
19 KINGS CL
20 DALE CFT
21 HEBER'S GR
22 THE LUTYENS
23 WARLBECK
24 HEBER'S GHYLL DR
25 GROVE AV
26 SHANNON CL
27 HEATH PK
28 GHYLL WOOD
29 PINES GDNS
30 PREMIERE PK
31 HOLLINGWOOD GATE
32 HOLLINGWOOD RISE
33 BADGER CL
34 WHINFIELD
35 GHYLL ROYD
36 CRANFORD GDNS

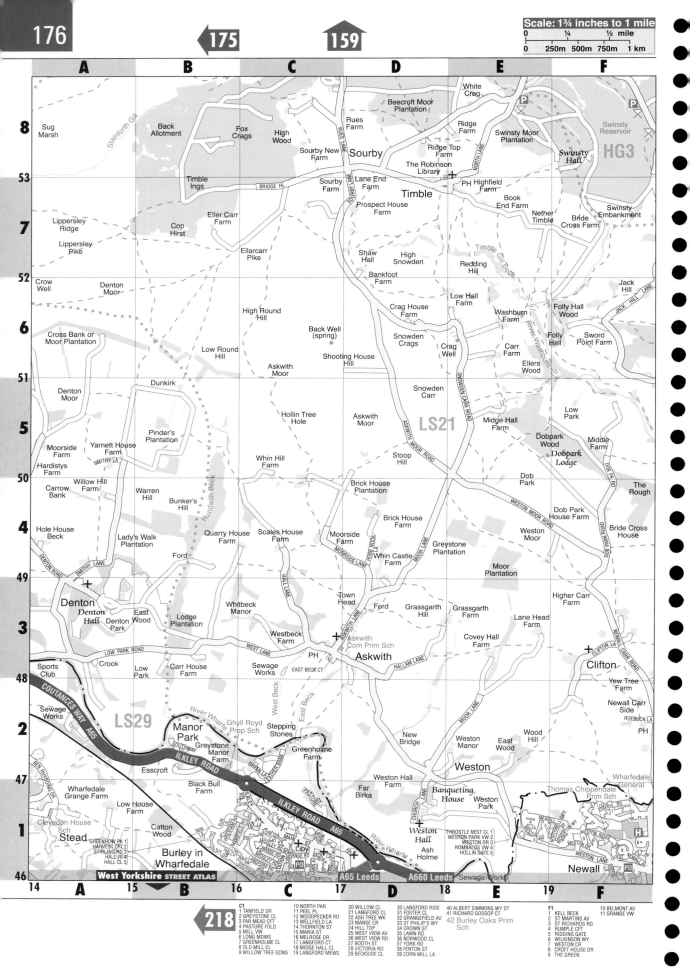

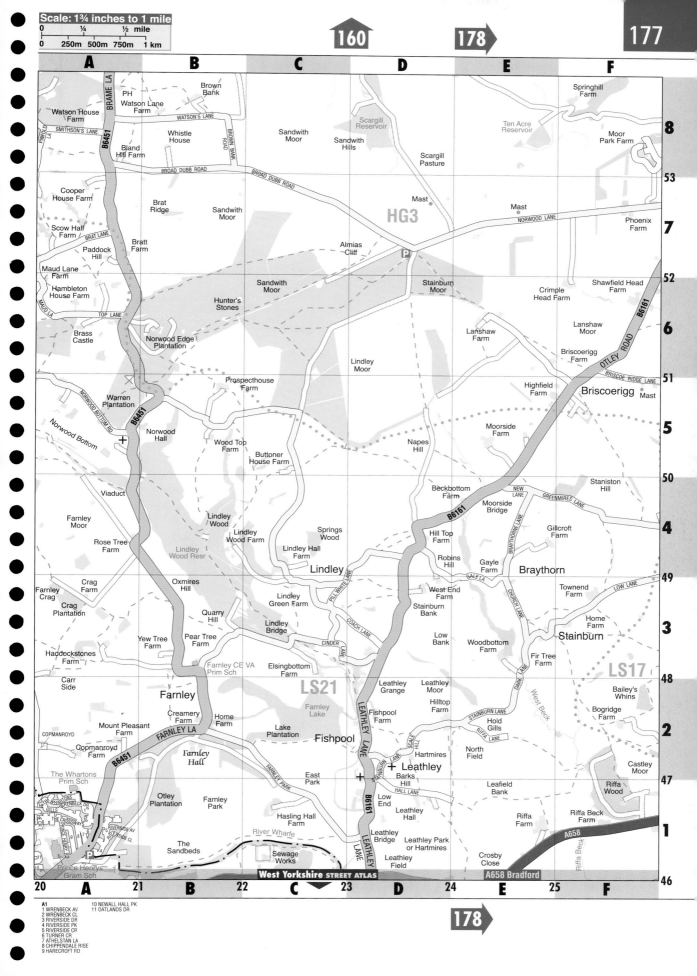

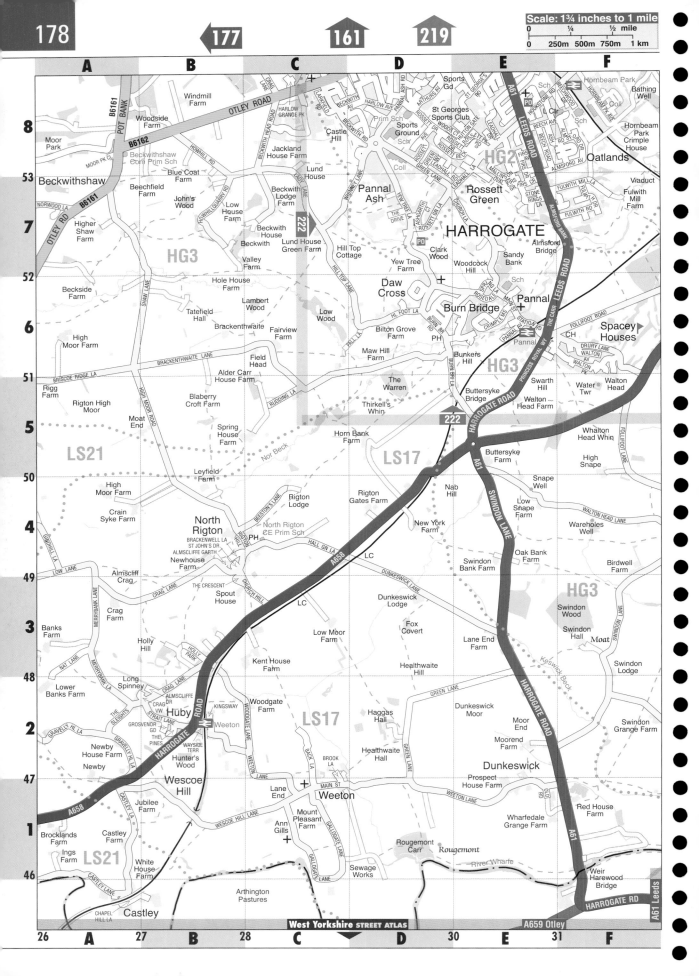

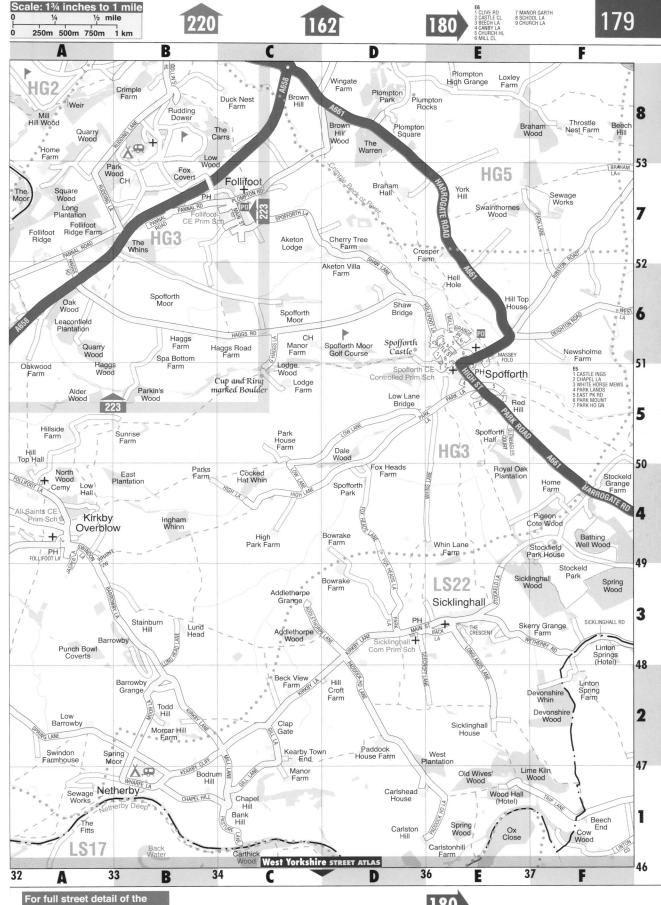

E6
1 CLIVE RD
2 CASTLE CL
3 BEECH LA
4 CANBY LA
5 CHURCH HL
6 MILL CL
7 MANOR GARTH
8 SCHOOL LA
9 CHURCH LA

For full street detail of the
highlighted area see pages
222 and 223.

180

West Yorkshire STREET ATLAS

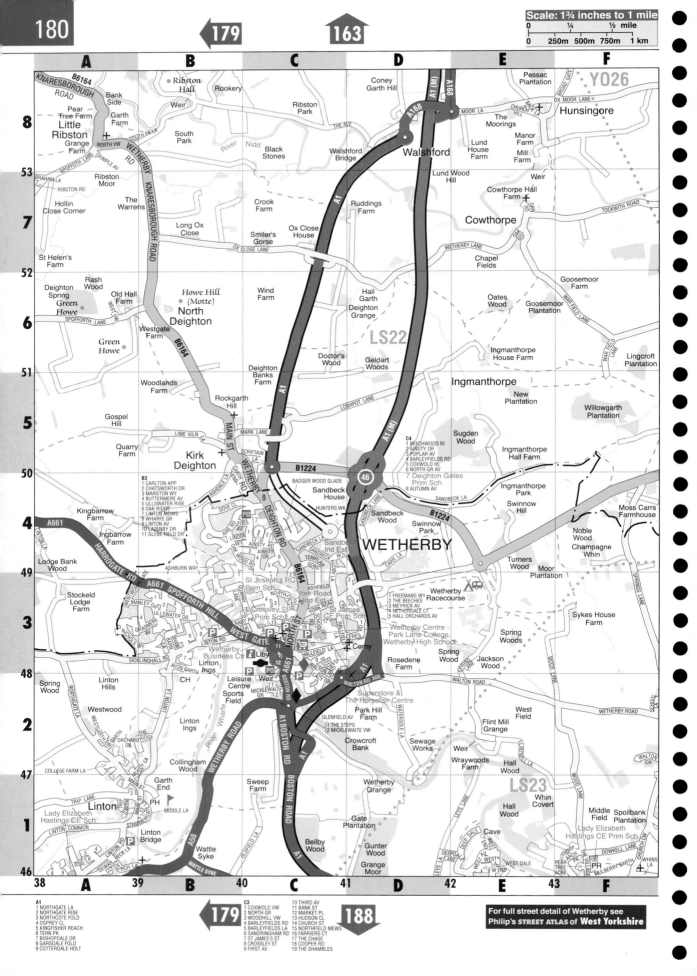

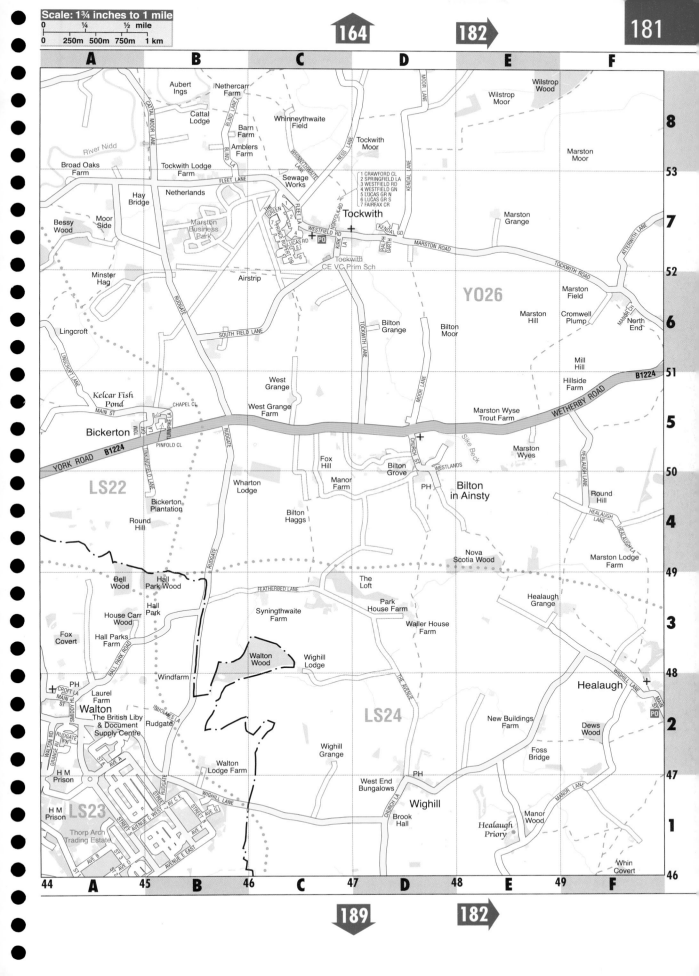

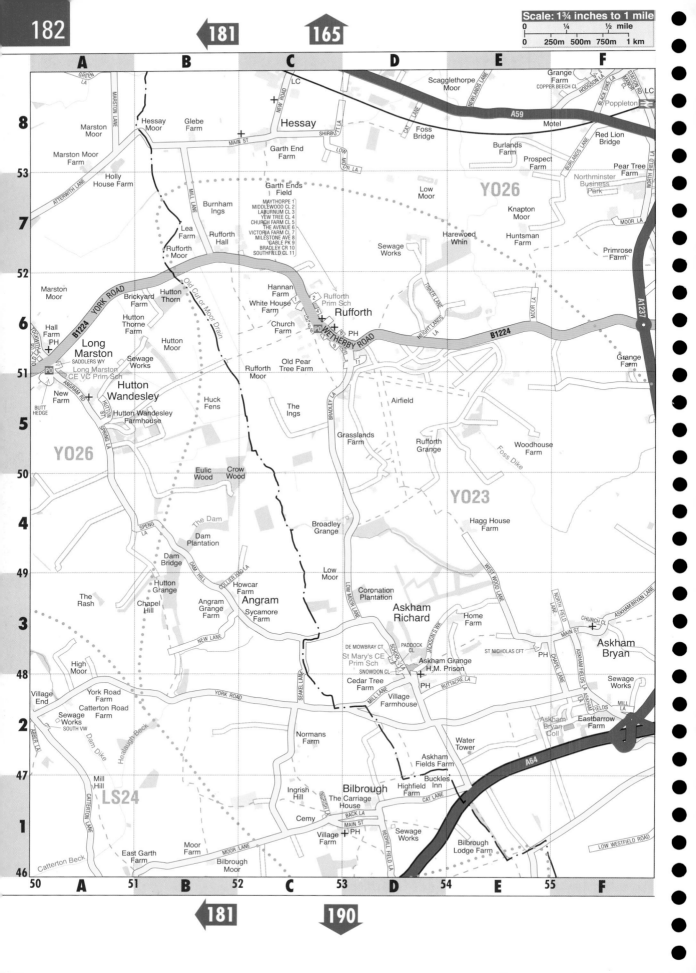

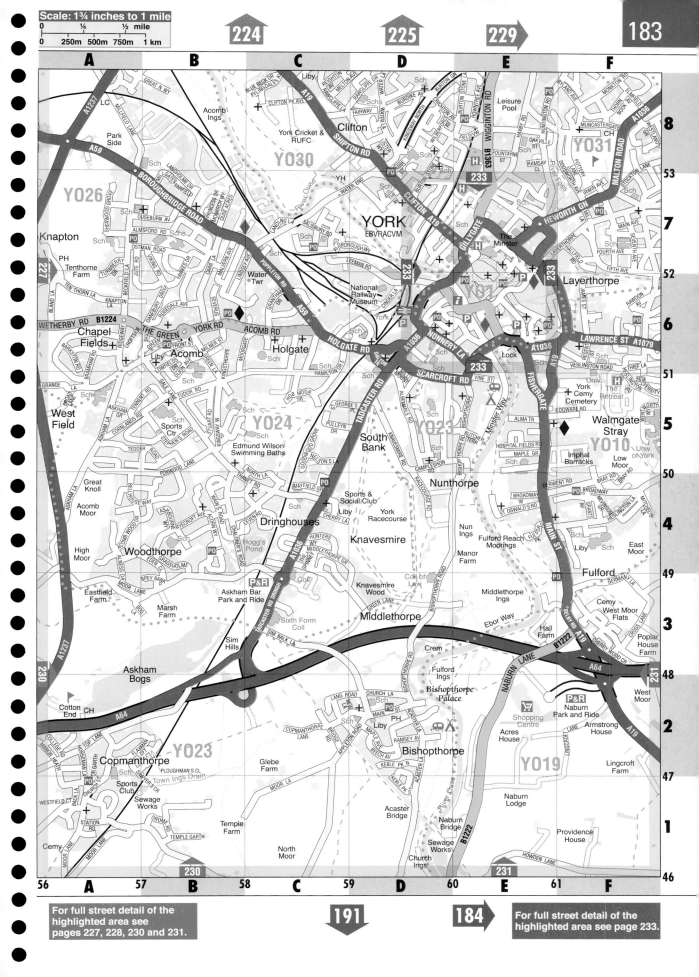

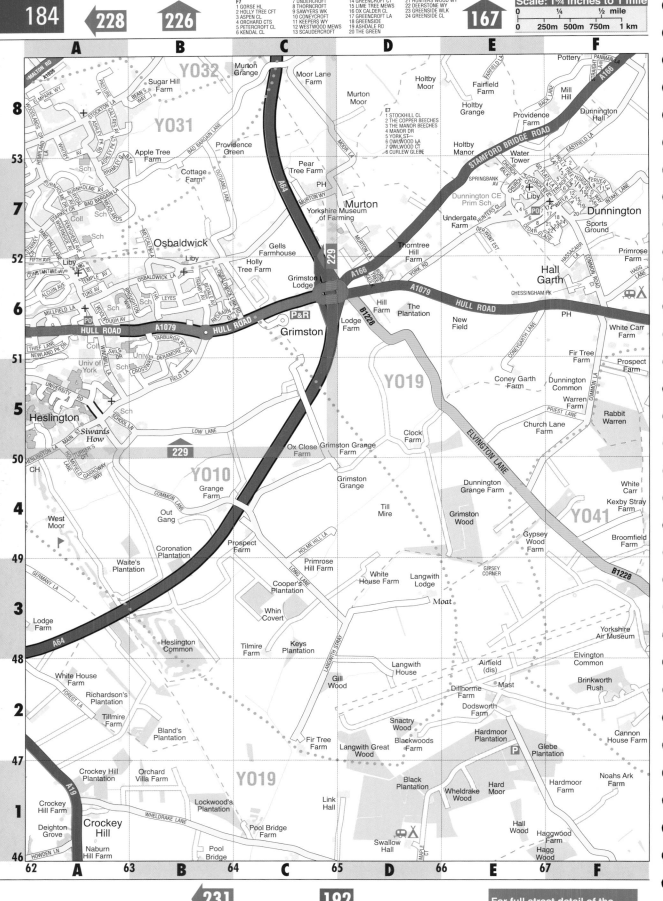

0   ¼   ½ mile
0   250m 500m 750m 1 km

A B C D E F

Wilson's Plantation

Corner Farm

LOW CATTON RD
CHURCH LANE

HIGH CATTON RD
MITCHELL LA
HOWL GATE

Burton Gates Farm

Black Wood

Low Catton

High Catton

Lodge Farm

COMMON LANE

Black Plantation

8

Limefield Farm

West Farm

River Derwent

Town End Farm

Town End Farm

Town End Farm

Common Farm

Field House Farm

53

Bull Ings

Scoreby Manor House

WATH LA

BROAD LA

LOFTHOUSE LA

SMEATON ROAD

Mast

Primrose Hill

Catton Park Farm

7

Hagg Wood

Cowslip Hill

Londesborough Lodge

Scoreby Wood

Throwmires Beck

Primrose Hill Farm

Common Park

Whinberry Hill

LING LANE

The Haggs

South Farm

Minster Way

Throwmires

Catton Park

Foss Beck

52

Cottage Plantation

Millfield Wood

LONG LANE

Kexby House

Mill
Mound

Mill House

Kexby House

Mast

Moorfield Farm

Moorfield Farm

WINDMILL MDWS 1
MOORFIELD DR 2
MILLFIELD CL 3
HAWTHORN DR 4
PEAR TREE CL 5
ORCHARD CL 6

Mill Farm

St Oswald's Cl

Wilberfoss CE VC Prim Sch

STORKING LA

BIRKER LANE

1 THE CLOISTERS
2 BECKSIDE
3 PRIORY CL

6

Lodge Farm

Cherry Tree Farm

Scoreby Lodge

A1079

White Carr

Kexby

Kexby Bridge

Arnull Bridge

Cuckoo Nest Farm

Moat

Wilberfoss

WOLDVIEW RD

A1079 Beverley (A1035)

51

Ivy House

Far Farm

OLD HALL LA
THE CRESCENT

Hotel
Manor Farm

Low Grange Farm

Hill Farm

West Moor

MAIN ST
THE PADDOCK

5 26 7

WILLOW PK RD

PH

A1079

5

White Carr

White Carr

Carr Wood

The Ings

Y041

BACK LA 1
STONE BR DR 2
FOSS GARTH 3

Cobb Flatts Farm

White Carr Farm

Seamour Wood

Newton Lodge

Mast

Holly Farm

50

KEXBY STRAY

DAUBY LANE

Kitching Plantation

MASK LANE

BIRKER LANE

Derwent Farm

Hall Farm

JACKSON LA

CARR LANE

Carr Farm

Wood Farm

Dodsworth Wood

Old Hall Farm

Thackmire Ings

Moats

St Lois Farm

Manor House Farm

PH

Newton upon Derwent

BULL BALK

4

Broad Oak Farm

Village Farm

BACK O'NEWTON

49

WHITLEY RD

Elvington Industrial Estate

Laveracks Industrial Estate

DAUBY LA

DERWENT CL

Sutton Wood

Moat

Penrose Farm

HIGH LANE

Gale Farm

Sutty Moor

Carrhold Ings

3

HALIFAX WY

Brinkworth Hall

ELVINGTON PK

Elvington CE Prim Sch

Works

Northland Ings

Hoppet Moor

Grange Farm

Crow Wood

48

Elvington Grange Farm

Sewage Works

B1228

PH

Roxby Farm

MAIN ST

Elvington

North Ings

Sutton Bridge

WOLDCROFT

Lock

Hotel

DEEPFURROWS LANE

Glebe Farm

SANDHILL LANE

Sandhill Bridge

Woodhouse Farm

2

The Grange

Manor Farm House

PH

Manor Farm

Sutton upon Derwent CE VC Prim Sch

The Park

PH

DERWENT CT

JARVIC CT

Blackfoss Beck

Woodhouse Grange

47

WHEELWRIGHT CL

CARLTON RD

WYNAM LA

Haxby Plantation

Grange Farm

Elvington Wood

Hagghill Leas Ings

MAIN ST

Sutton upon Derwent

Cockshaw Plantation

Mickfield Plantation

1

Westhouse Farm

GREENGALES LA

Y019

Gravelpit Farm

B1228

Wynam Bottoms

46

68   A   69   B   70   C   71   D   72   E   73   F

East Yorkshire & North Lincolnshire STREET ATLAS

B2
1 WHITE HOUSE GR
2 BEECH CL
3 LORRAINE AVE
4 HILLGARTH CT
5 DOVECOTE GARTH
6 BECK CL
7 BECKSIDE
8 BELVOIR AVE
9 ALVIN WK

C2
1 RIVERSIDE CL
2 RIVERSIDE GDNS
3 CHURCH GN
4 CHURCH LA

A   B   C   D   E   F

KENILWORTH DR
COOLHAM LA
Reservoir
STANDRIDGE CLOUGH
LANE
DODGSON LA
MITTON LA
Lothersdale
Comy Prim Sch
ROOK ST
Lower Spen
House

Bleara
Moor
Bent
Hall
Raygill
SIDEGATE LANE
Woodhead
Farm

8
SOUGH LA
Bleara
Moor
Bleara
Lowe
Salt Pye
Farm
BD20
Hawshaw
Moor
WINTER GAP LANE
RAYGILL LANE
Town
Edge

Kelbrook
Tunstead
Farm
BB18
Broom House
Farm
Springs
Farm
Hawshaw
Cottage

45
HEADS LANE
COLNE ROAD
HARDEN RD
Paris Farm
Copy
House
BLEARA ROAD
BLEARA ROAD
Hawshaw
Side
Hawshaw
Side
Oliver
Farm
COWLING HILL LANE
Haws

7
A56 Colne
DOTCLIFFE ROAD
Harden Old
House
Harden Beck
Brown
Hill
Hawshaw
Lodge
HAWSHAW ROAD

Kelbrook
Prim Sch
Thick
Bank
Harden New
Hall
Kitchen
East Hainslack
Farm
Westfield

44
Moor
Gate
Hard
Clough
OLD LA
COB LANE
Kelbrook
Wood
Dukes
Hainslack
CENTRE ROAD
TOM LANE
Stone Head
Brow
Stone Head
Farm

6
Hague
House
The
Hill
Kelbrook
Wood
PH
Copy
House
WARLEY WISE LANE
Warley
Wise
Hazelgrove
Lodge
STONE HEAD LANE
Hardfield

Oxenards
Hague
Laycock
Piked
Edge
Gruntland
Hall
HILL END LANE
Bawsedge

43
Ambwell
Earl
Hall
Great
Edge
Shaw
Head Farm
Pasture
SANDYFORTH LANE
Sandyforth
MOSS END LANE
PARK LANE

Nonya
Hill
Nonya
End
Great
Edge
Flass
Bent
Knarrs Hill
Farm
Bowes
Edge
A6068
REEDSHAW LANE
Park
PARK LANE

5
White House
Farm
Bent
Laithe
Knarr
Side
Knarrs
Laneshaw
Resr
Reedshaw
Moss
Fleet

42
Moss
Houses
Near
Salter
Syke
Far Salter
Syke
SKIPTON OLD ROAD
Shaw
Gate
Shawhead Beck
Earl
Hall
Pad
Cote

4
Lower
Clough
COCKHILL LANE
CH
Wicken
Syke
LONG LANE
Flass
Barnside
Monkroyd
PH
Monkroyd
Farm
KEIGHLEY RD
Corn
Close
Reedshaw
Moss

White
Syke
Blue
Bell
HILL LANE
Flass
Laneshaw
Bridge
Corn Close Bent
Moor
Coppy
Hill

41
CASTLE ROAD
Hedroyd
Christ Church
CE Prim Sch
ALMA RD
LADY
HARTLEY CT
EMMOTT LA
SCHOOL LANE
KEIGHLEY ROAD
Upper
Emmott
Robert
Laith

3
A6068 Nelson
SKIPTON OLD RD
DENT LANE
VERNON RD
KINGSLEY RD
SHERIDAN RD
BB8
Lower
Emmott
Emmott
Moor

P
A6068
STANDROYD
Colne Water
Mill
Weir
Hill Top
Farm
KEIGHLEY RD
WYCOLLER BECK

40
Cotton
Tree
COTTON TREE
B6250
STANDROYD DR
ROSLEY ST
WINEWALL LANE
TOP
LANE
Slack
Oak House
Farm
Lowlands
Farm
P
Herder's
Common

BANKFIELD ST
SKIPTON ROAD
Winewall
Rec
Grd
BECKSIDE
BANNISTER CL
CARRIER'S ROW
Wycoller
Country
Park
Visitor
Centre

2
MIRE RIDGE
LEYLAND CL
LACHAN
HALL
MDWS
RIVER ST
B6250
Higher
Stunstead
Bracken
Hill
Wycoller
PH
Combe
Hill

39
GOOSE GN LA
CLIFTON ST
FOULDS ROAD
DEAN LA
STANSTEAD
RD
Slackhead
Onion
Bank

Prospect
Farm
COLNE RD
WEAVERS CT
BRIGHT
TR
GREEN
END
WHITE LEE RD
PO
TRAWDEN
Near
Wanless
Copy
House
Dean
House

1
BURLEY RD
FOULDS ROAD
CHURCH
ST
LEE
HOUSE LANE
Germany
Farm
Sheepfold
Cross
Bent

38
Beardshaw Beck
BOULSWORTH
DRIVE

90   A   91   B   92   C   93   D   94   E   95   F

A3
1 KEIGHLEY RD
2 CLARENCE ST
3 CRAVEN ST
4 BOULSWORTH GR
5 MONMOUTH ST
6 ACRESFIELD
7 LONG MEADOW
8 LAMBETH ST
9 HOLLINGTON ST

10 CLARENDON ST
11 WINEWALL RD
12 HOLME ST
13 HARTINGTON ST
14 DUKE ST
15 BRIGHT ST
16 ING DENE AV

B1
1 CLARENCE ST
2 LAMBERT ST
3 EAST VIEW

4 Trawden Forest
Prim Sch

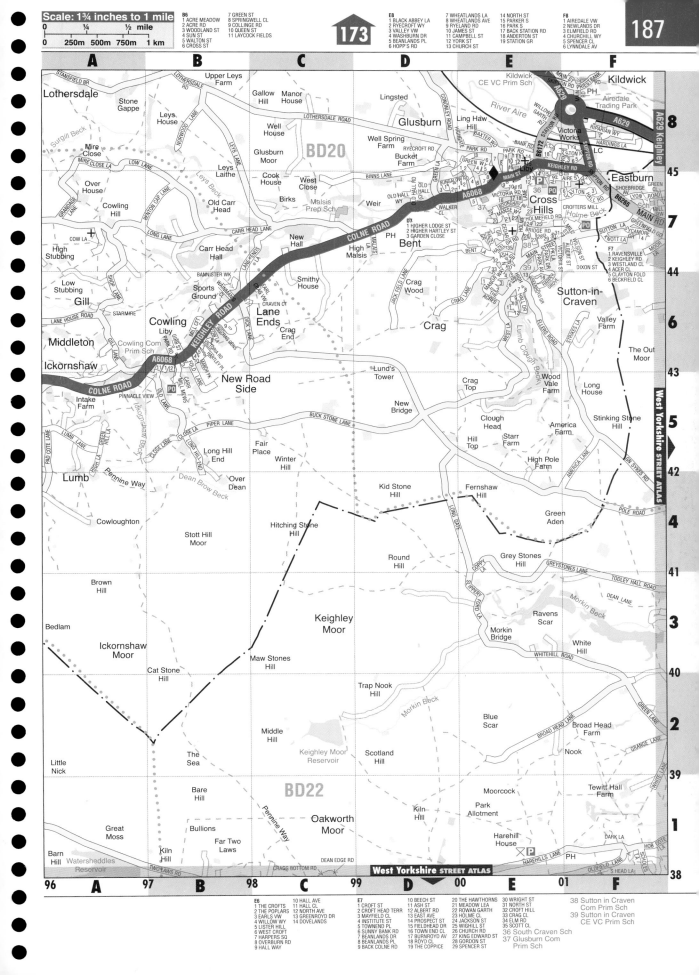

A8
1 BISHOPDALE DR
2 COVERDALE GARTH
3 LANGWITH AV
4 GREEN LA
5 THE CROFT
6 THE CLOSE
7 MILLGARTH CT
8 THE GARTH
9 LOWCROFT
10 THE VALE

E8
1 SPRINGFIELD
2 CHESTNUT AV
3 St Edwards Com Prim Sch
4 West Oaks Sch

5 Primrose Lane Prim Sch
6 St Mary's CE Prim Sch
7 St Johns Catholic Sch for the Deaf

Scale: 1¾ inches to 1 mile
0   ¼   ½ mile
0   250m   500m   750m   1 km

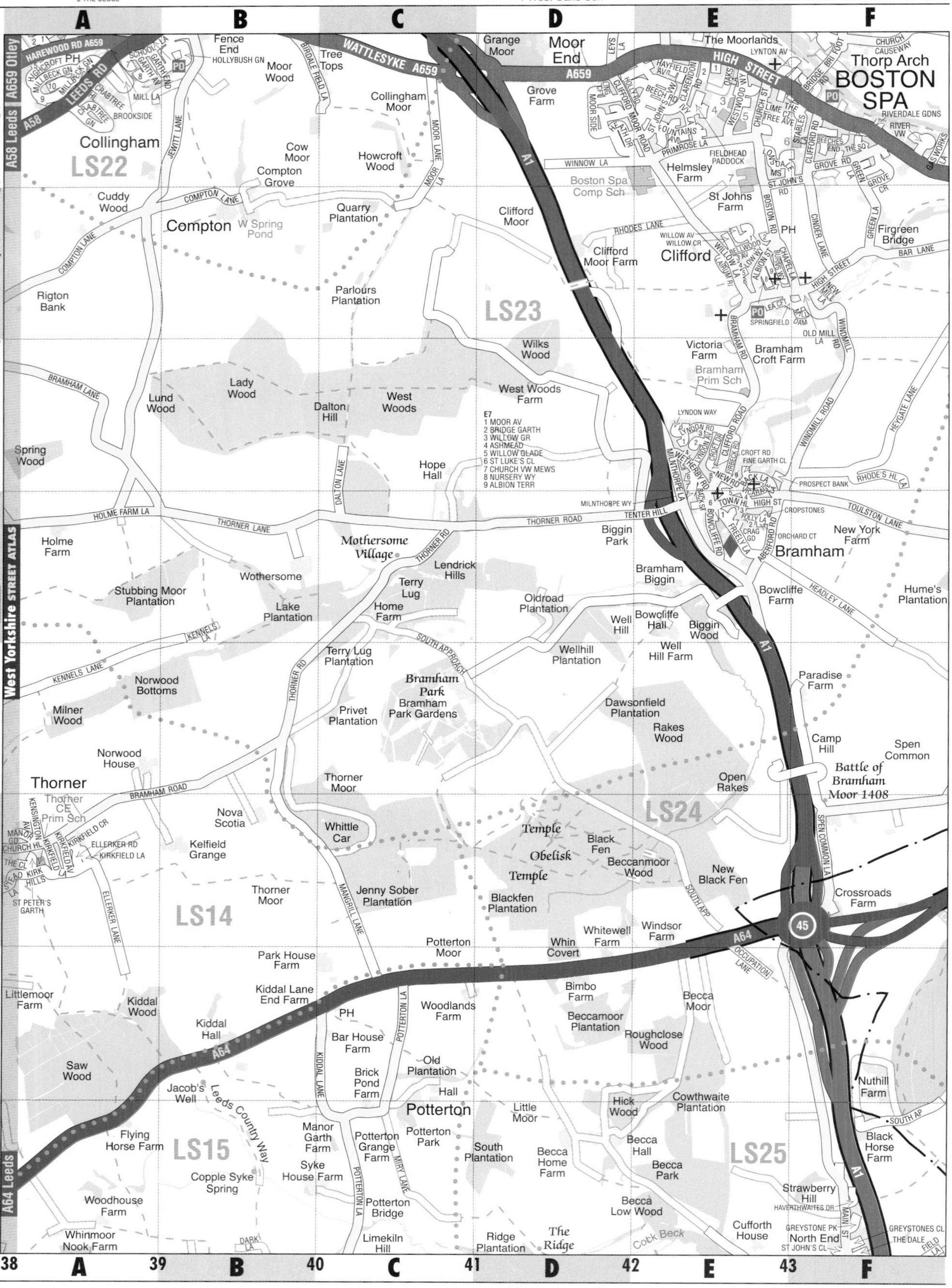

E7
1 MOOR AV
2 BRIDGE GARTH
3 WILLOW GR
4 ASHMEAD
5 WILLOW GLADE
6 St LUKE'S CL
7 CHURCH VW MEWS
8 NURSERY WY
9 ALBION TERR

West Yorkshire STREET ATLAS

LS22
LS23
LS24
LS14
LS15
LS25

Collingham
Compton
Moor End
BOSTON SPA
Thorp Arch
Clifford
Bramham
Thorner
Potterton
Battle of Bramham Moor 1408

E5
1 ALMSHOUSE HL
2 FOLLY VW
3 THE CRAG
4 CHURCH HL
5 LOW WY
6 FRONT ST
7 FREELY FIELDS

E6
1 LYNDON CL
2 LYNDON SQ
3 THE KNOLL
4 LYNDON CR
5 MILNTHORPE GDNS
6 MILNTHORPE CL
7 MILNTHORPE GARTH
8 BRADFORDS CL
9 CHURCH MDWS

For full street detail of Boston Spa see Philip's STREET ATLAS of West Yorkshire

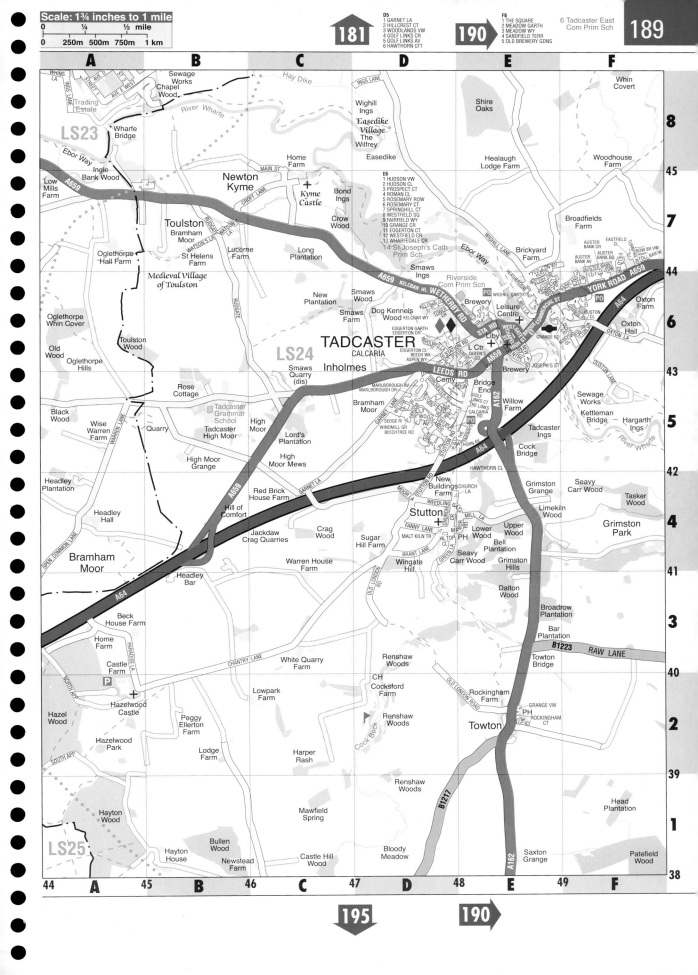

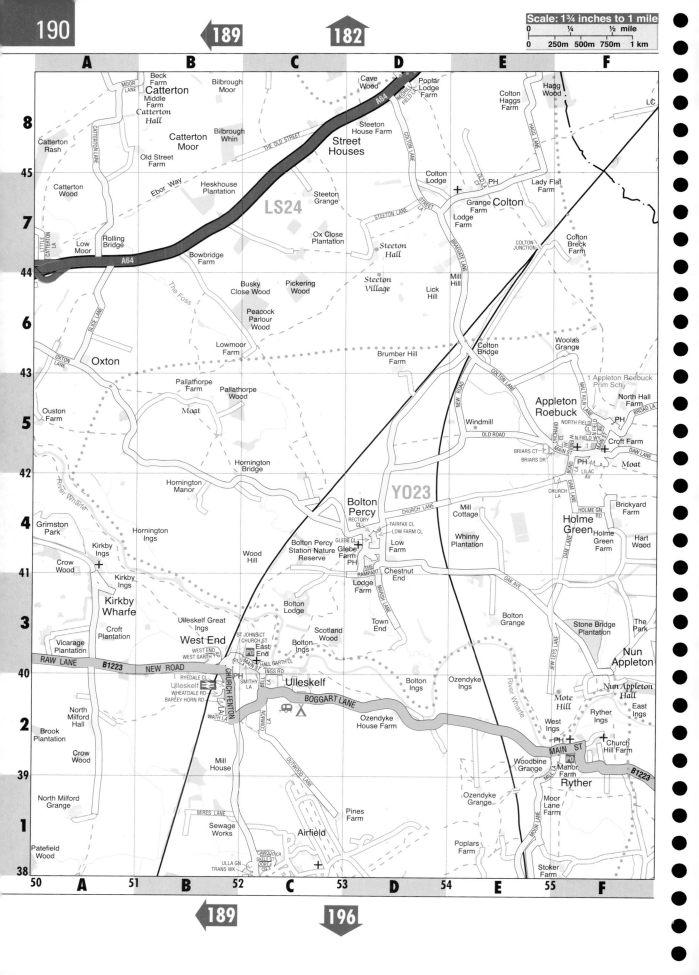

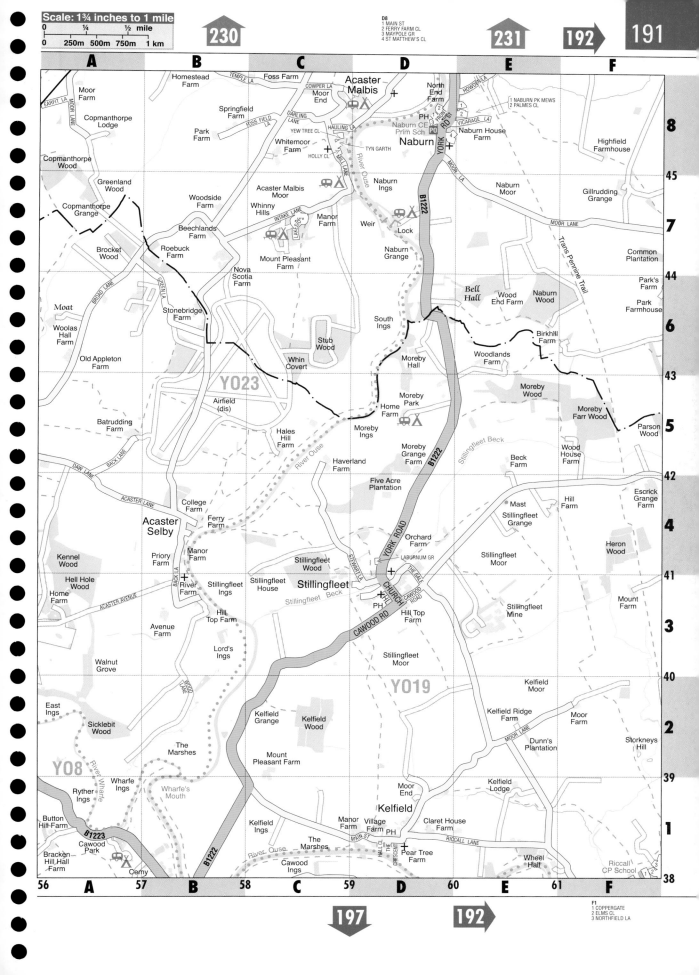

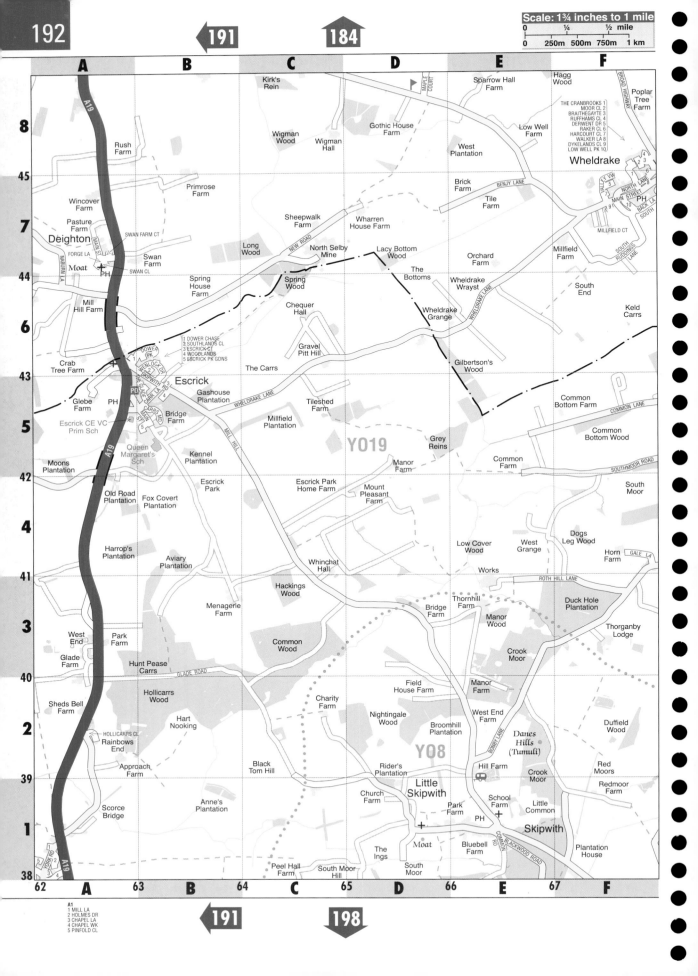

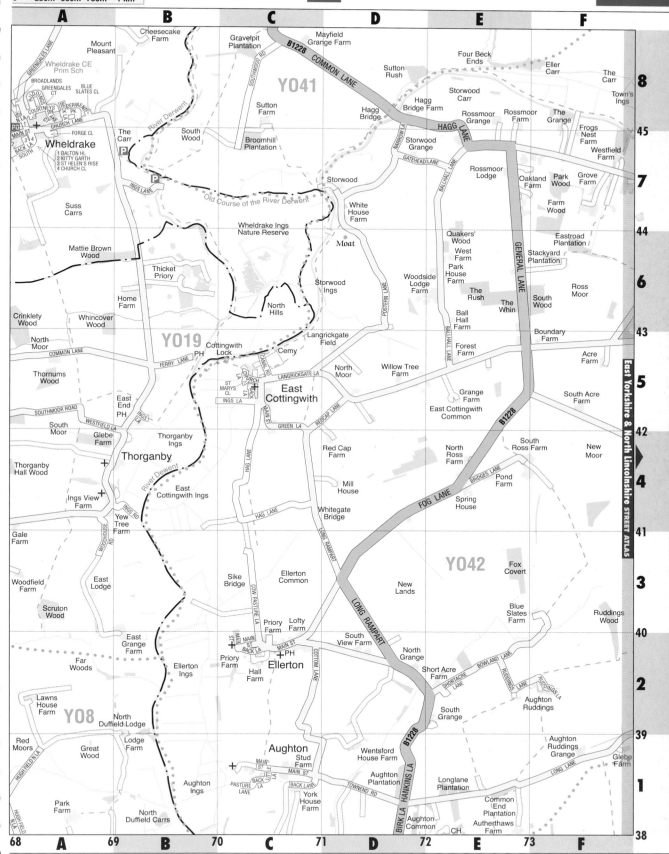

East Yorkshire & North Lincolnshire STREET ATLAS

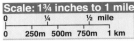

Scale: 1¾ inches to 1 mile

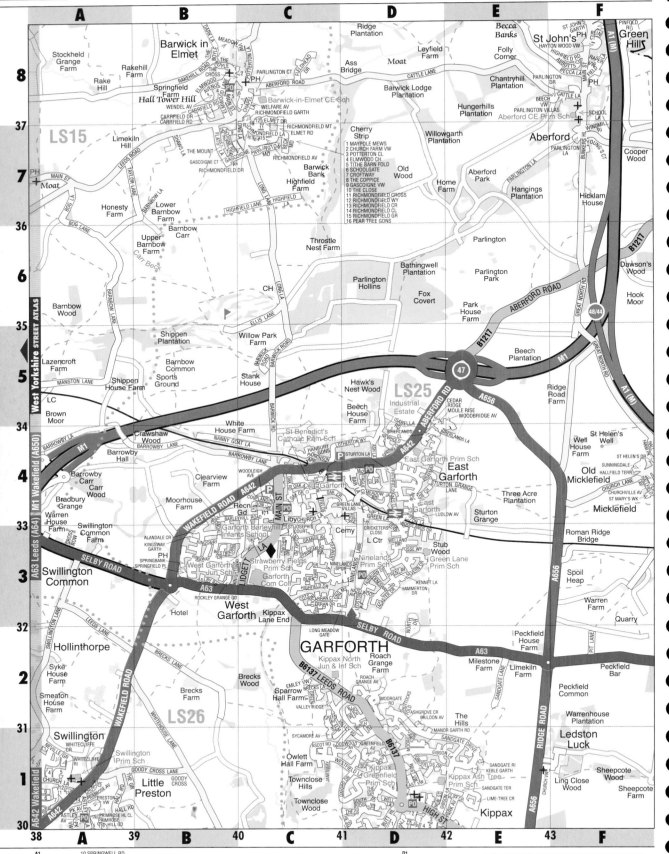

A1
1 WHITECLIFFE DR
2 LOWTHER DR
3 LOWTHER CR
4 CHURCH CL
5 SMEATON GR
6 THE PLEASANCE
7 SPRINGWELL AV
8 WOODLAND CR
9 THE CREST
10 SPRINGWELL RD
11 SPRINGWELL AV
12 THE DRIVE
13 SCOTT CL
14 ST MARY'S AV
15 PRIMROSE HL DR
16 PRIMROSE HL GR

D1
1 TATEFIELD PL
2 HANOVER PL
3 THE INTAKE
4 APPLE TREE LA
5 APPLE TREE MS
6 CHURCHFIELD LA
7 APPLE TREE WALK

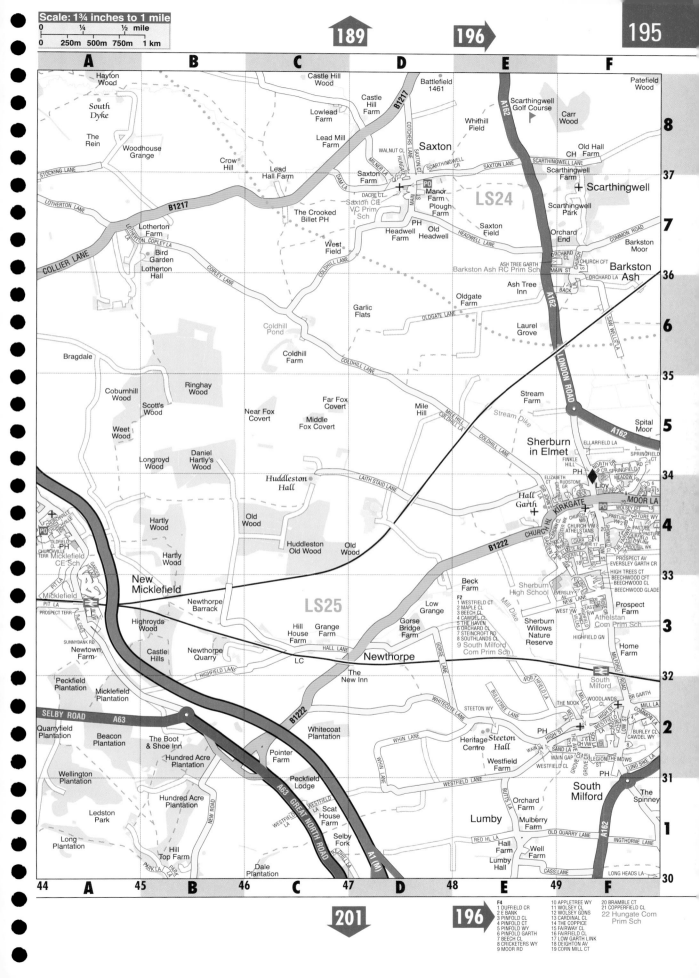

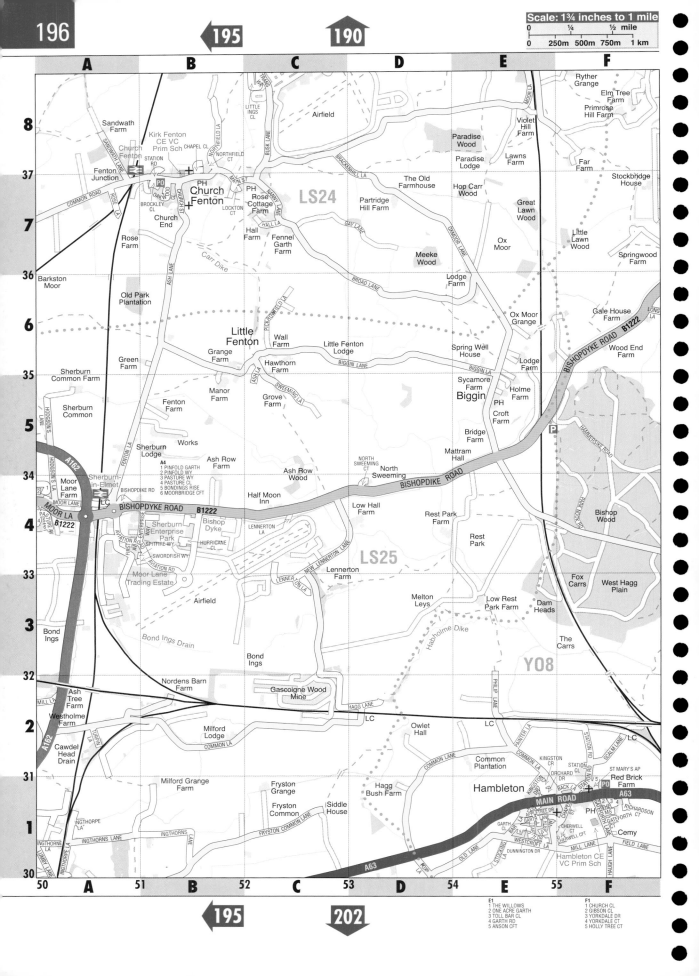

Scale: 1¾ inches to 1 mile

0   ¼   ½ mile
0   250m 500m 750m 1 km

E1
1 THE WILLOWS
2 ONE ACRE GARTH
3 TOLL BAR CL
4 GARTH RD
5 ANSON CFT

F1
1 CHURCH CL
2 GIBSON CL
3 YORKDALE DR
4 YORKDALE CT
5 HOLLY TREE CT

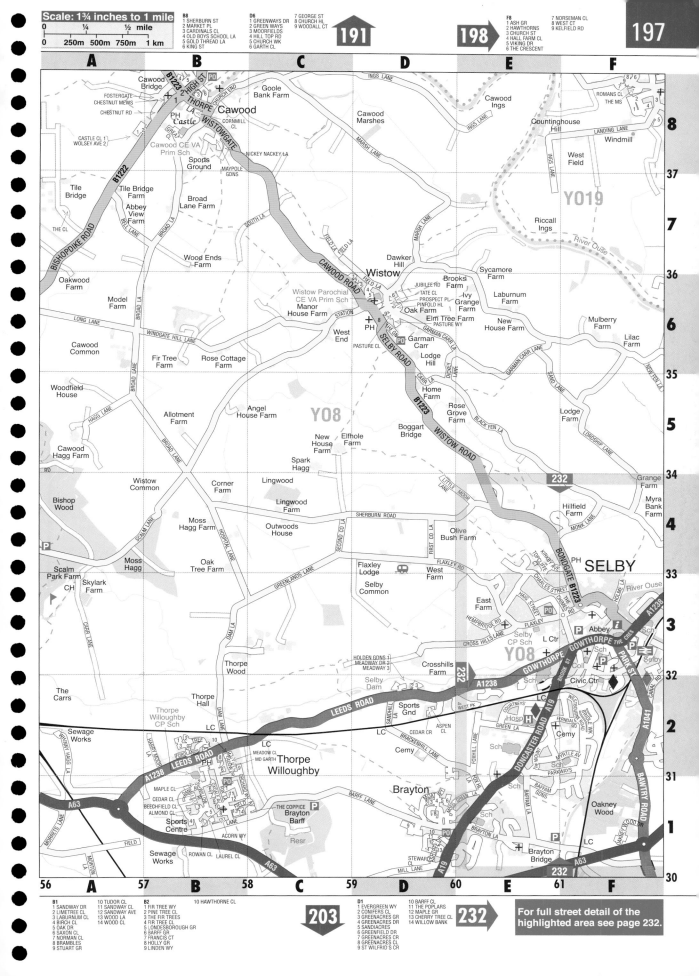

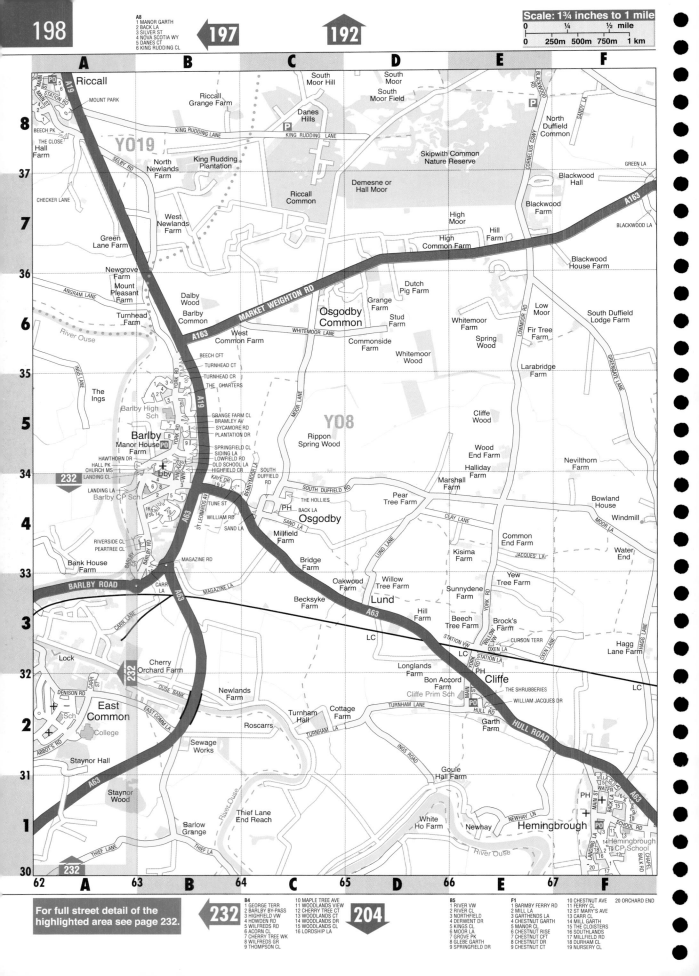

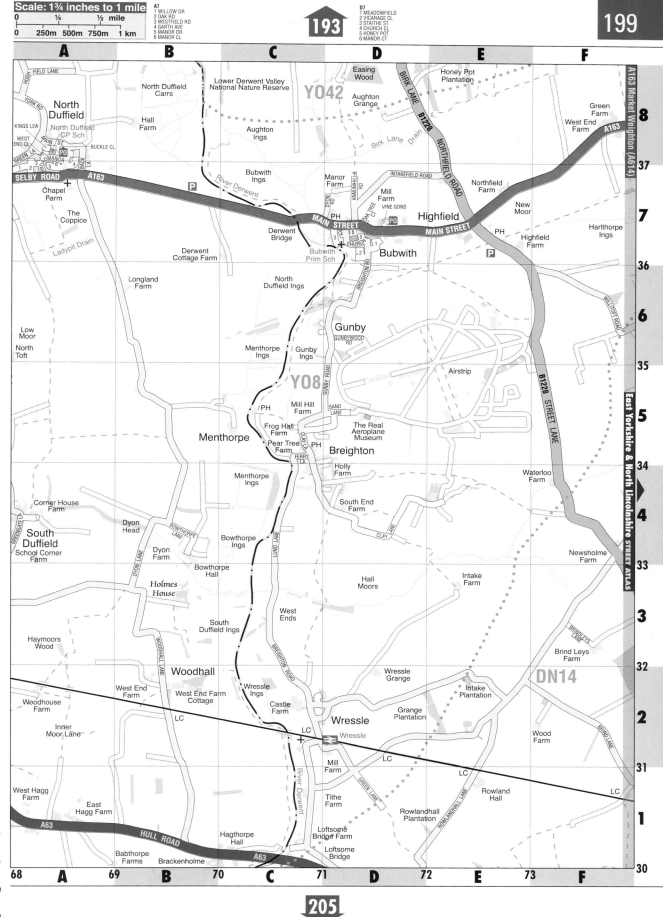

Scale: 1¾ inches to 1 mile
0   ¼   ½ mile
0   250m 500m 750m 1 km

A7
1 WILLOW DR
2 OAK RD
3 WESTFIELD RD
4 GARTH AVE
5 MANOR DR
6 MANOR CL

D7
1 MEADOWFIELD
2 VICARAGE CL
3 STAITHE ST
4 CHURCH CL
5 HONEY POT
6 MANOR CT

A163 Market Weighton (A614)

East Yorkshire & North Lincolnshire STREET ATLAS

North Duffield
Lower Derwent Valley National Nature Reserve
YO42
Easing Wood
Honey Pot Plantation
Green Farm
West End Farm
North Duffield Carrs
Hall Farm
Aughton Grange
Aughton Ings
Manor Farm
Northfield Farm
New Moor
Harlthorpe Ings
Highfield Farm
Highfield
Bubwith
Main Street
Chapel Farm
The Coppice
Derwent Cottage Farm
Derwent Bridge
North Duffield Ings
Longland Farm
Gunby
Gunby Ings
Menthorpe Ings
Menthorpe
Frog Hall Farm
Pear Tree Farm
Breighton
Mill Hill Farm
The Real Aeroplane Museum
Airstrip
Waterloo Farm
Low Moor North Toft
Holly Farm
South End Farm
Corner House Farm
Dyon Head
Bowthorpe Ings
Bowthorpe Hall
Hall Moors
Intake Farm
Newsholme Farm
South Duffield
School Corner Farm
Dyon Farm
Holmes House
Haymoors Wood
South Duffield Ings
West Ends
Brind Leys Farm
DN14
Woodhouse Farm
Woodhall
West End Farm
West End Farm Cottage
Wressle Ings
Wressle Grange
Intake Plantation
Wood Farm
Inner Moor Lane
Castle Farm
Wressle
Grange Plantation
Rowland Hall
West Hagg Farm
East Hagg Farm
Mill Farm
Tithe Farm
Rowlandhall Plantation
A63
Hull Road
Babthorpe Farms
Brackenholme
Hagthorpe Hall
Loftsome Bridge Farm
Loftsome Bridge
River Derwent

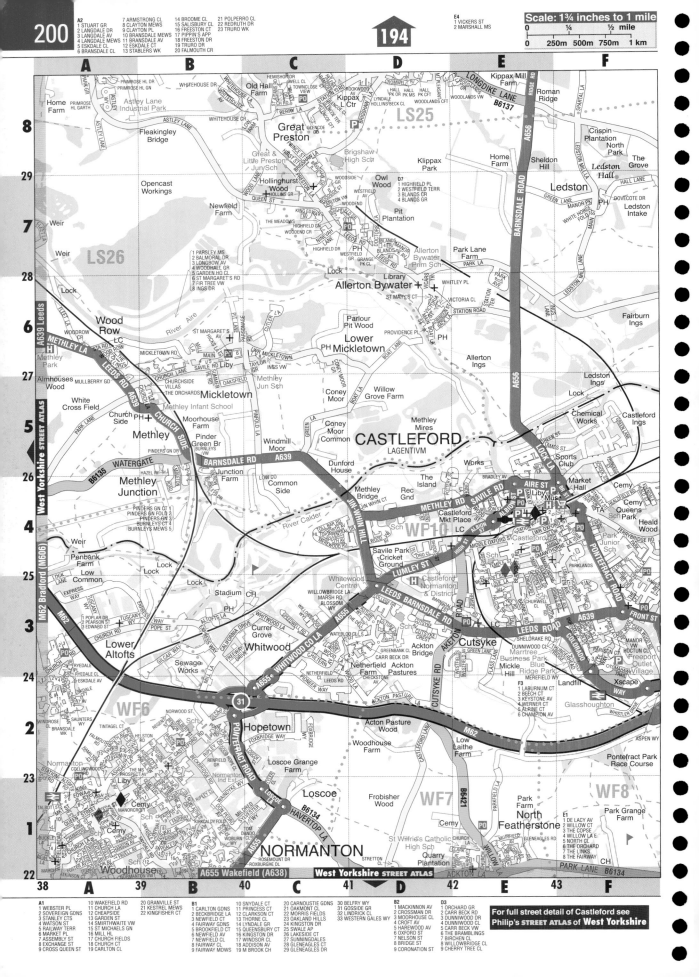

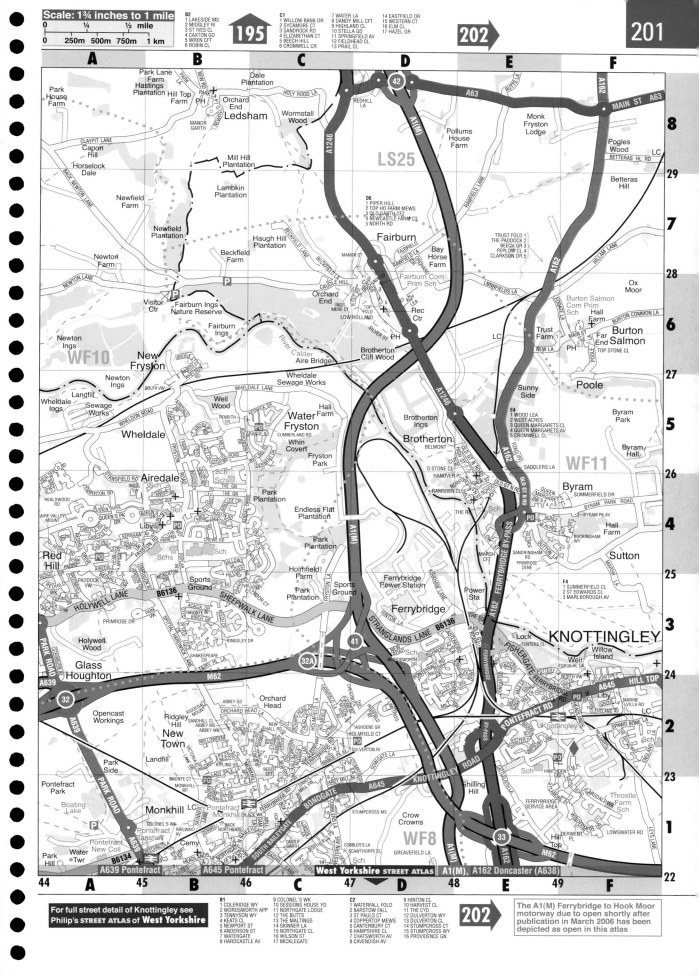

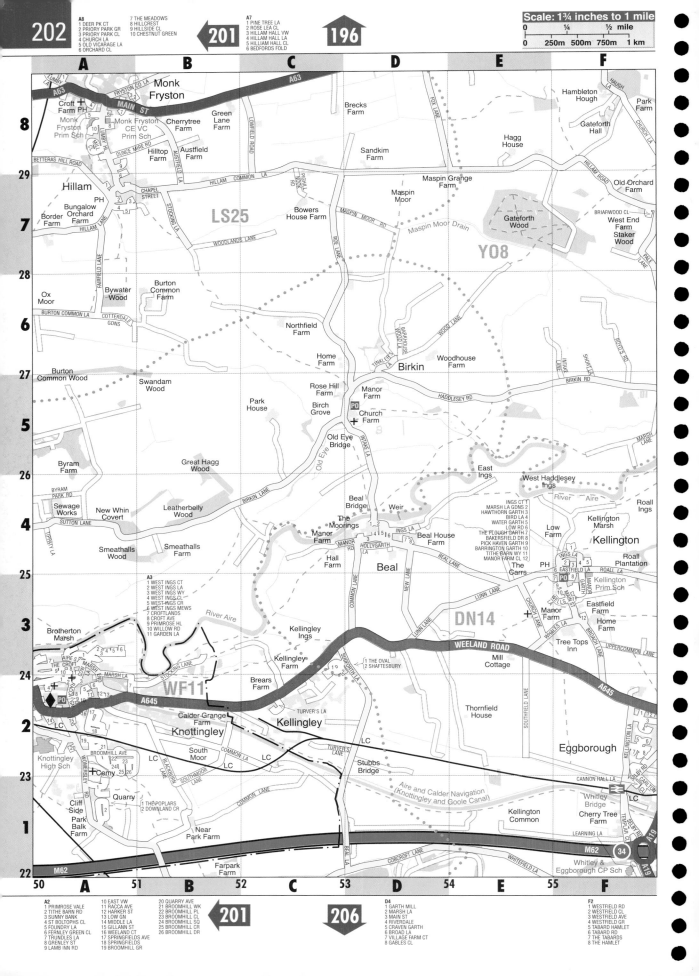

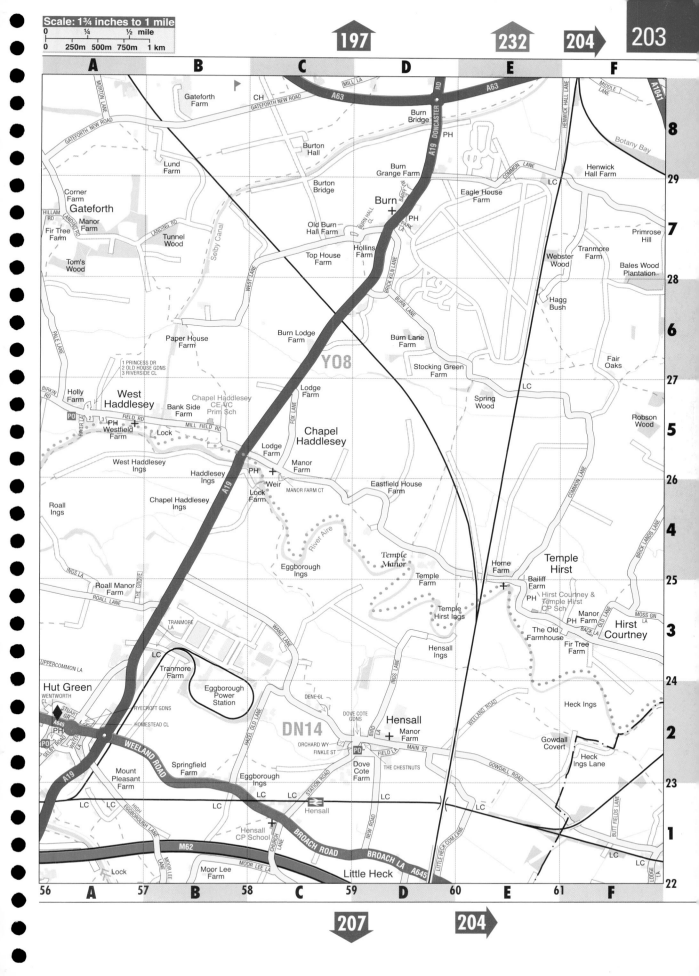

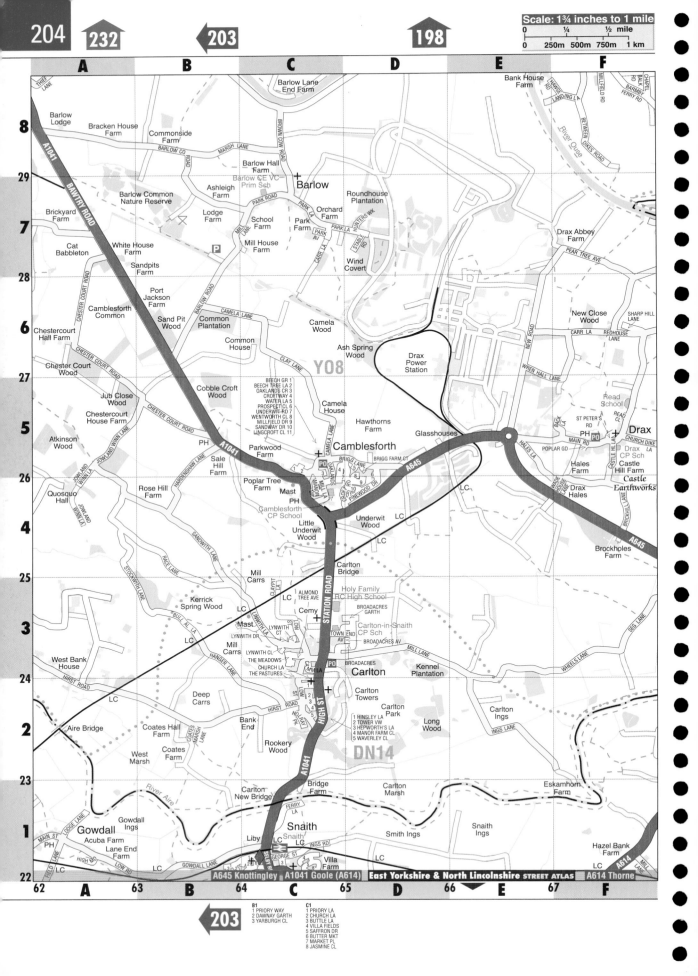

Scale: 1¾ inches to 1 mile

| 0 | ¼ | ½ | mile |

| 0 | 250m | 500m | 750m | 1 km |

Hemingbrough Grange

YO8

Babthorpe Hall Farm

BRIDGE CR

River Derwent

Sewage Works

Old Derwent

Newsholme

Newsholme Farm

Beech Tree Farm

GREEN LANE

A63

Warp Farm

Parks Farm

Newsholme Parks

8

Small Ings

Barmby Marsh

DN14

Barn Hill

Barnhill Hall

29

P

Corner Farm

HIGH ST

FLEET LA

NORTH ST

SOUTH ST

PH

Barmby on the Marsh

Barmby on the Marsh Prim Sch

Fairfield Farm

STATION LANE

West End Farm

MARSH LANE

MAIN ST

Asselby

Old Hall

Manor Farm

Elmer Wood

BARNHILL LANE

B1228

BOOTH FERRY ROAD

Home Farm

A63 Kingston upon Hull (M62)

7

28

Long Drax

Nellifield Farm

GREEN LA

BARMBY FERRY RD

BANKFIELD LANE

REDHOUSE LANE

GATELAND FIELD LANE

Seave Carr Bottoms

Seave Carr

BACK LA

Back Lane Farm

PH

LANDING LANE

The Craggs

Knedlington

PINFOLD LANE

PINFOLD RD

HOWDENSHIRE WY

B1228

A614 Market Weighton

6

Mole End

Rusholme Hall

Trans Pennine Trail

Rusholme Grange

River Ouse

YO8

Asselby Island

Boothferry

Villa Farm

A614

Ouse Carr

PH

27

5

Scurff Hall

RUSHOLME LANE

CHURCH DIKE LA

Halfway Houses

NEW LANE

BRIER LANE

Fort Hill

Little Airmyn

Ferry Farm

Oaklands Small Sch

BRIDGE RD

BEECH AV

FERRY LA

PH

B1228

Boothferry Bridge

M62 Kingston upon Hull

HOOK LANE

26

4

NEW LA

MILL LANE

Manor Farm

Newland

Downe's Ground

DN14

River Aire

Court House Farm

Airmyn Wood

North Airmyn Grange

AIRMYN ROAD

HIGH STREET

PO

PARK RD

Airmyn Park Prim Sch

Airmyn

PH

WOOD VW

Airmyn New Wood

Sch

Woodfield Rd

WESTERN RD

ILKESTON AV

LETON GR

AIRMYN RD

West Park

SHAFTE

SALBURY AV

Sch

LANSDOWN AV

BOOTHFERRY RD

Coll

Sch

MARCUS ST

KENT RD

DUNHILL RD

A161

A161 Goole

East Yorkshire & North Lincolnshire STREET ATLAS

25

3

24

White House Farm

Brickhill Farm

A645

A614

RAWCLIFFE ROAD

White Gate Farm

Sutton Lodge Farm

Airmyn Grange

A614

RAWCLIFFE RD

36

RAWCLIFFE RD

A614

NEW POTTER GRANGE RD

LODGE ROAD

Mast

A W Nielson Rd

LARSEN RD

SEAVY GRANGE RD

GRANGE RD

NEWLAND

2

BANK SIDE

RAWCLIFFE LANE

HIGH ST

SMITH RD

RIVERSIDE

BELL LA

W END

PO

Liby

1 RIVERSIDE CT
2 FIELD LA
3 POST OFFICE ROW
4 CREYKE VW
5 CHAPEL LA
6 BOYNTON LA
7 ST JAMES CT
8 CHAPEL CL
9 CHARTER AVE
10 WESTFIELD AVE
11 WESTFIELD RD
12 RIDDING LA
13 RIDDING CR
14 DOBELLA AVE
15 HALL GDNS
16 MANOR FIELDS

Bramley Wood

Rawcliffe Pastures

Percy Lodge

Potter Grange

M62 Trading Estate

BRITANNIA RD

BRITANNIA WY

ANDERSEN RD

23

Rawcliffe

Rawcliffe In Snaith Prim Sch

Rawcliffe Prim Sch

STATION RD

Rawcliffe Pastures

Rawcliffe Pastures

Aire and Calder Navigation

The Waterways Museum & Adventure Centre

HOOK PASTURE LANE

1

Field House Farm

Soiling Farm

DOBELLA LANE

M62

Dobeller Wood

Rawcliffe Pastures

South Airmyn Grange

22

| 68 | A | 69 | B | 70 | C | 71 | D | 72 | E | 73 | F |

E4
1 BEECH GR
2 CHESTNUT AVE
3 BEECH AVE
4 PERCY DR
5 HALL CL
6 PARK CL
7 COURTS CL
8 WOODLAND WY
9 ST DAVID'S VW
10 PARSONS CL
11 PARSON'S WK
12 CHURCH VW
13 THE CROSSINGS
14 THE PADDOCK

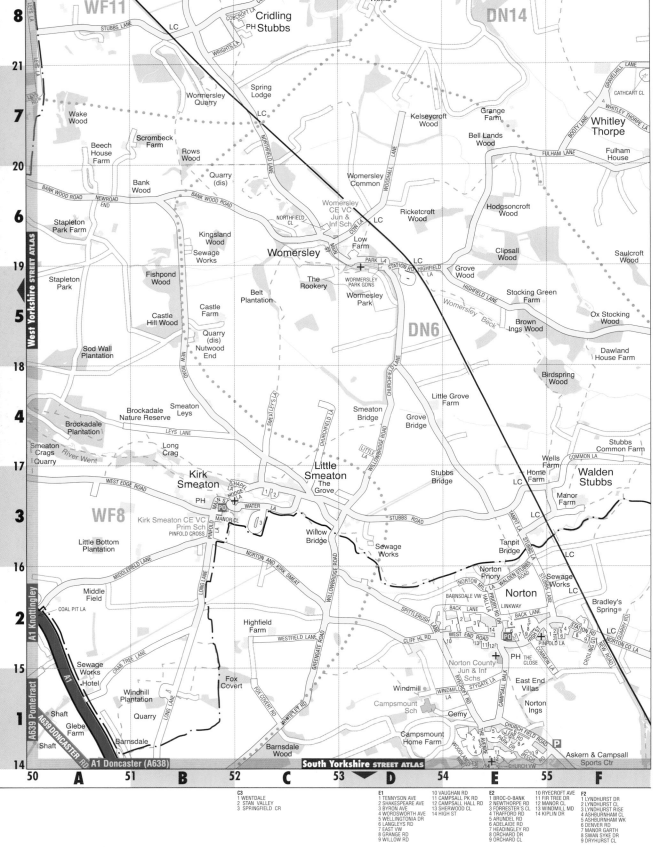

Scale: 1⅜ inches to 1 mile

0   ¼   ½   mile
0   250m   500m   750m   1 km

West Yorkshire STREET ATLAS

A1 Knottingley
A639 Pontefract
A639 DONCASTER
A1
A1 Doncaster (A638)

WF11

WF8

DN14

DN6

Whitley Thorpe

Cridling Stubbs

Womersley

Kirk Smeaton

Little Smeaton

Norton

Walden Stubbs

Askern & Campsall Sports Ctr

A   B   C   D   E   F

Whitley Farm
Copper Beech Dr
Hill Top
MOOR LEE LA
Mill Farm
MOOR LEE LA
MILL BALK
LONG LA
BROACH RD
East Farm
GOWDALL BROACH
M62
A645
Lodge Farm
NEWBY LA

Hollins Farm
INTAKE LANE
PH
Heck Bridge
MAIN ST
LONG GREEN LA
Bridge Farm
Works
Heck Hall Farm
GREEN LA
Gowdall Broach Farm
FIELD LANE
A645 Snaith M62 Goole

PH
COLLEGE FARM CL
Poplar Farm
Whitley
Watkin's Lower Plantation
HECK LANE
Shaw Wood
Bridge End
Great Heck
HIGHFIELD
SNAITH RD
8
21

A19
YEW TREE PK
Woodview Cl
Whitley Farm
LEE VIEW
LEE CT
Quarryside Farm
Depot
HECK AND POLLINGTON LANE
GOWDALL LANE
7

SHEEP WASH LA
SILVER STREET
BALNE MOOR CROSS ROAD
BALNE MOOR ROAD
Balne Moor
Moor Farm
BALNE MOOR ROAD
Works
Balne Moor
PROSPECT CL
ORCHARD END
Orchard End
WEST END
Works
Pollington
BALK LANE
20

BUTCHER LANE
Butcher Lane Farm
HAIGH LANE
Haigh End
HAZING LANE
WESTEND LANE
Grange Farm
Yew Tree Farm
Balne Moor Drain
PH
THORNTREE LANE
Sunnyside Farm
LC
High Gate Farm
CROSSHILL LANE
CANAL GARTH
GREENFIELDS
PO
MAIN ST
6

Blowell Bridge
Wood View Farm
West End
JENNY LANE
PARK LANE
Ash Tree Farm
Parkshaw Wood
Chapel Hill
LITTLE COMMON LA
Balne
HIGHGATE
Highgate
High Gate
DN14
CAT LANE
Cross Hill
Fir Tree Farm
Sheepwash Bridge
Pollington Bridge
PH
BRIDGE LA
LOCK CL
WATER WY
GARTH
Pollington-Balne CE Prim Sch
Pollington Lock
Swing Bridge
19
5

SELBY ROAD
Works
Lake Bridge
Lake Drain
Blowell Drain
GORE LANE
TOADHAM LANE
NEVILLE PITS LANE
Barn Fall Wood
South End
SOUTH END LA
Lockgate Farm
LC
LOCKGATE ROAD
LOWGATE
Cherry Tree Farm
Lowgate Farm
Lowgate
Balne Hall
BALNE HALL RD
18
4

BADGER LANE
COMMON LANE
BADGER LA
Fox Covert
River Went
River Went
Fleet Drain
17

Stubbs Grange
COMMON LA
Went Bridge
Stubbs Common
Went Farm
LC
Gate Farm
Fenwick
PH
Orchard End
LAWN LANE
Riddings Farm
Fenwick Hall
Bungalow Farm
WEST LA
3

Norton Common Farm
Went Lows
Moat Hill Farm
FENWICK LANE
Shoemaker's Hill
SHAW LA
FENWICK COMMON LANE
HAGGS LANE
West End
FLASHLEY CARR LANE
16
2

A19
Toll Bar
Rose Grove
Norton Common
NORTON COMMON RD
NORTON COMMON ROAD
CLOUGH LANE
Ladythorpe Farm
Moat Hill
DN6
Fenwick Common
Cemy
Jett Hall
CONDON LANE
MOSS HAVEN
Wood Grove
Parkgate Farm
Moss Farm
Moseley Grange
Flashley Carr
MOSS ROAD
Fenwick Grange
Flashley Carr Drain
15
1

LC
A19 Doncaster
FENWICK LANE
WILLOW GARTH LANE
Elmfield Farm
MOSS ROAD
LC
Manor Farm
PH
PINFOLD LA
TRUMFLEET LA
MOSS RD
Moss
14

East Yorkshire & North Lincolnshire STREET ATLAS

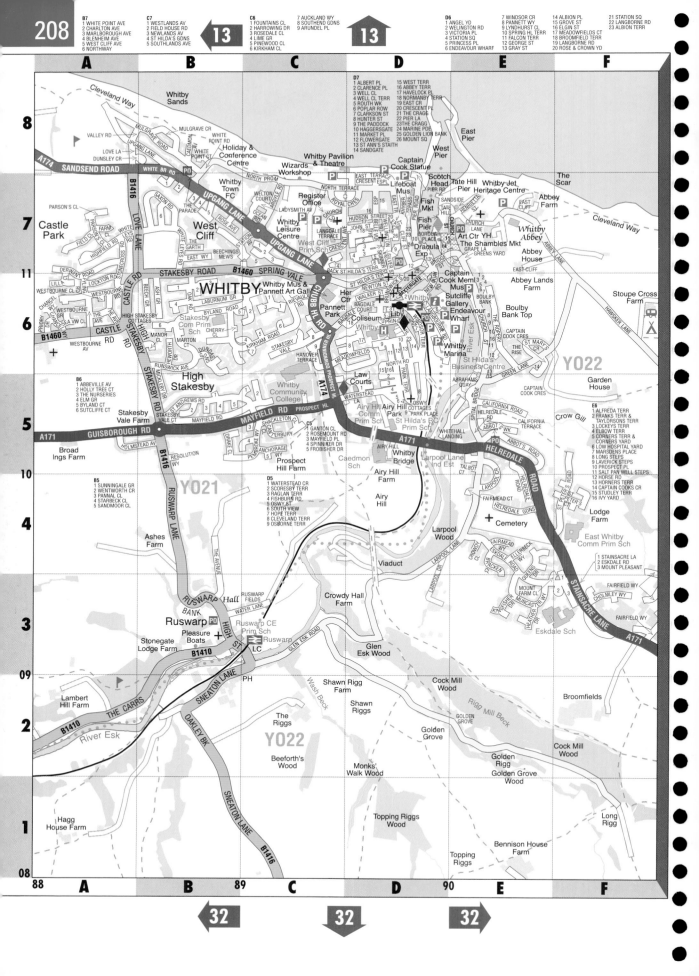

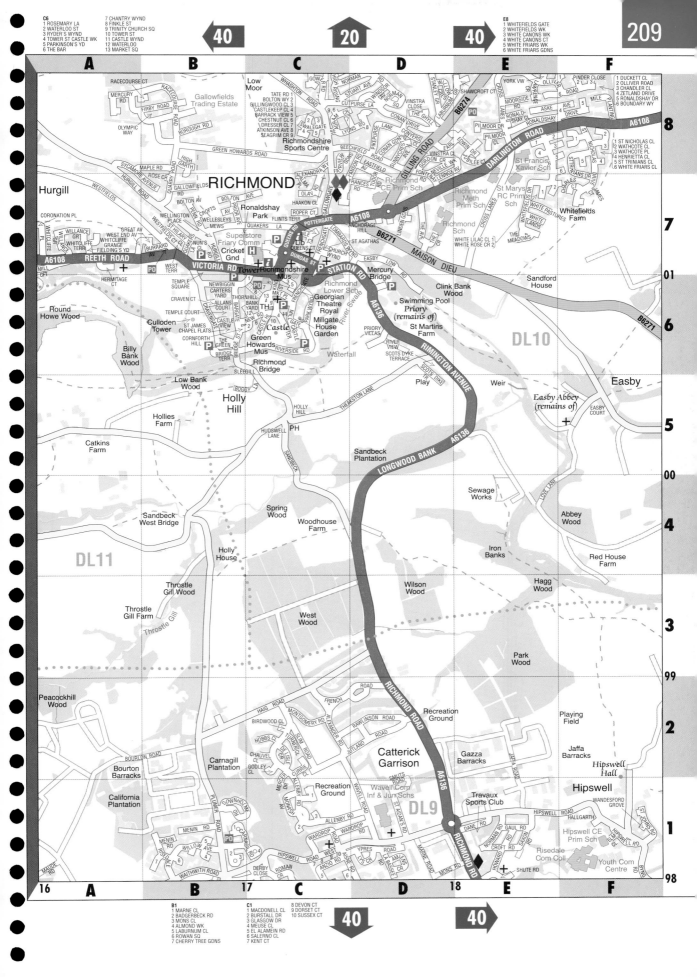

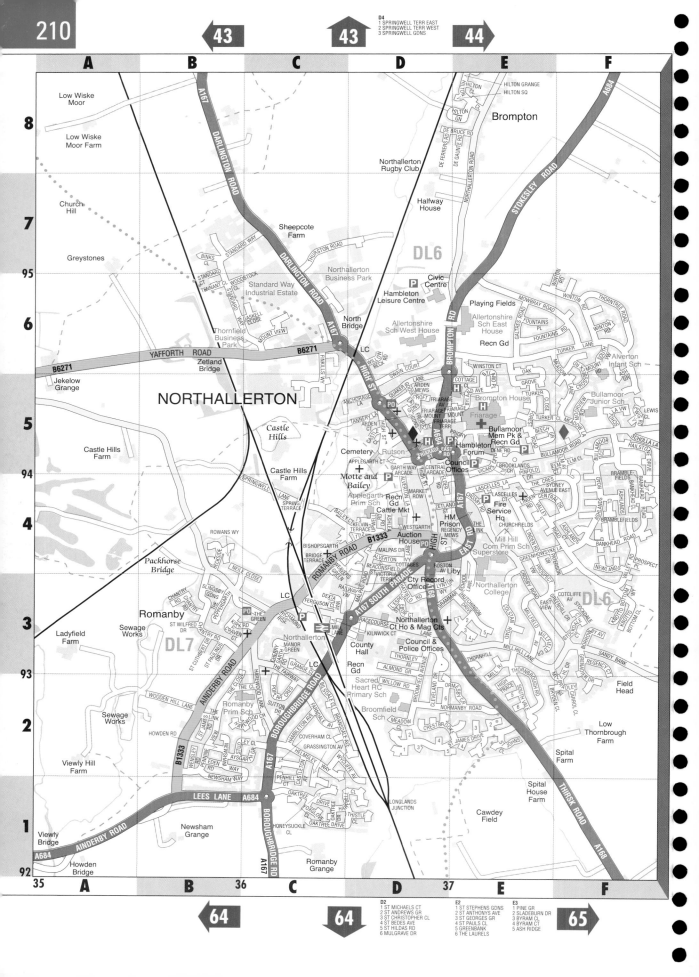

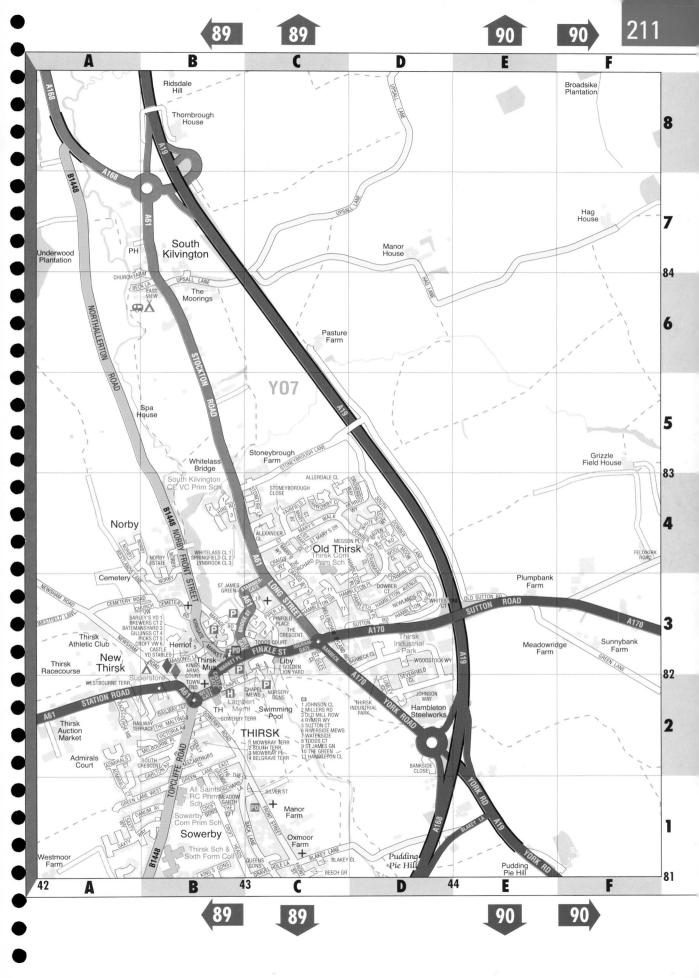

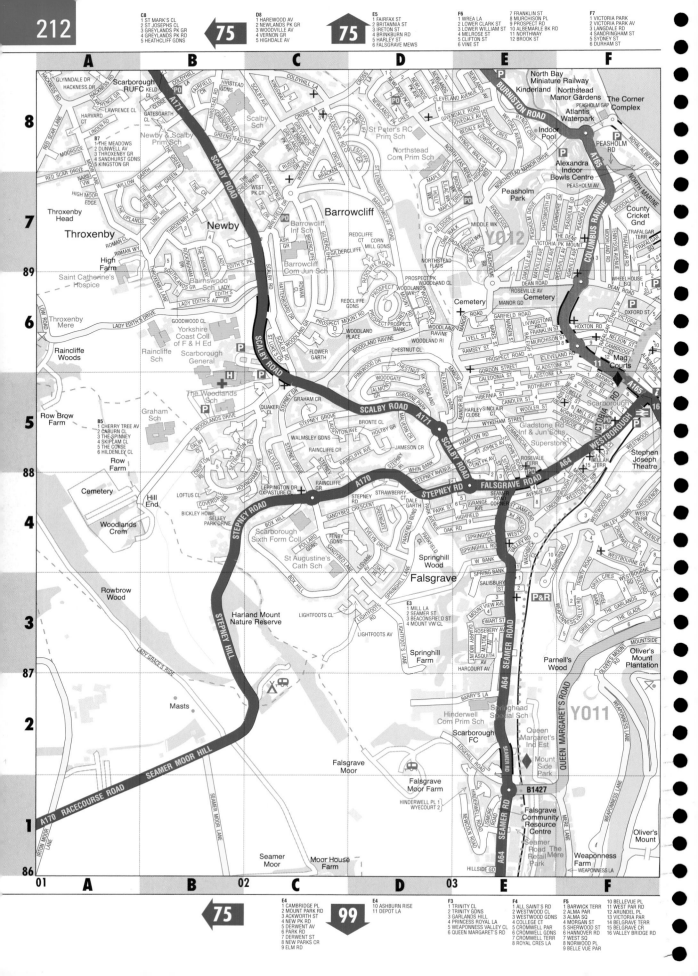

North Bay

SCARBOROUGH

South Sands

South Bay

A7
1 ALBERT RD
2 CLARENCE RD
3 HOWARD ST
4 STANLEY ST
5 DURHAM PL
6 DURHAM ST
7 CLARK ST
8 ALBERT ST
9 VINCENT ST
10 NEW QUEEN ST
11 MARLBOROUGH ST
12 BLENHEIM ST
13 LOWER CLARK ST

B6
1 GARIBALDI ST
2 CHURCH ST
3 CHURCH SR ST
4 SPRINGFIELD
5 COOK'S ROW
6 ST MARY'S ST
7 ST SEPULCHRE ST
8 LEADING POST ST
9 GLOBE ST
10 MERCHANT'S ROW
11 PRINCESS SQ
12 PRINCESS LA
13 TUTHILL
14 EAST SANDGATE
15 BURR BANK
16 CASTLE TERR
17 PRINCESS TERR
18 WHITEHEAD HILL
19 WEST SANDGATE TERR

A5
1 WESTBOROUGH
2 VERNON RD
3 VERNON PL
4 HARCOURT PL
5 ST NICHOLAS CLIFF
6 CLIFF BR PL
7 CLIFF BR TERR
8 CRESCENT BACK RD
9 BELVOIR TERR
10 FALCONERS SQ
11 PAVILION SQ
12 PAVILION TERR

A4
1 CAMBRIDGE TERR
2 GROSVENOR CR
3 ALBION CR
4 OLIVER ST
5 ST MARTIN'S SQ
6 CARLTON TERR
7 SOUTH ST
8 GREENFIELD RD
9 ST MARTIN'S RD
10 ST MARTIN'S PL
11 WESTBOURNE GR
12 ROYAL CR

A3
1 PRINCESS ROYAL PK
2 BACK AVENUE VICTORIA
3 GRANVILLE SQ

A6
1 REGENT ST
2 JAMES PL
3 GEORGE ST
4 NORTH TERR
5 AUBOROUGH ST
6 LANCASTER ST
7 CLARENCE PL
8 SILVER ST
9 MARIAS CT
10 FRIAR'S GDNS
11 FRIARS WY
12 UNION ST
13 BEDFORD ST
14 SUSSEX ST
15 PROVIDENCE PL
16 ABERDEEN WK
17 ABERDEEN ST
18 ALBEMARLE CR
19 ABERDEEN LA
20 ABERDEEN PL
21 ABERDEEN TERR
22 NORTH ST LA
23 CHAPEL RD
24 MARKET ST
25 MARKET WY
26 ST HELEN'S SQ
27 BLAND'S CLIFF
28 PROSPECT PL
29 WATERHOUSE LA

76 76 100 76

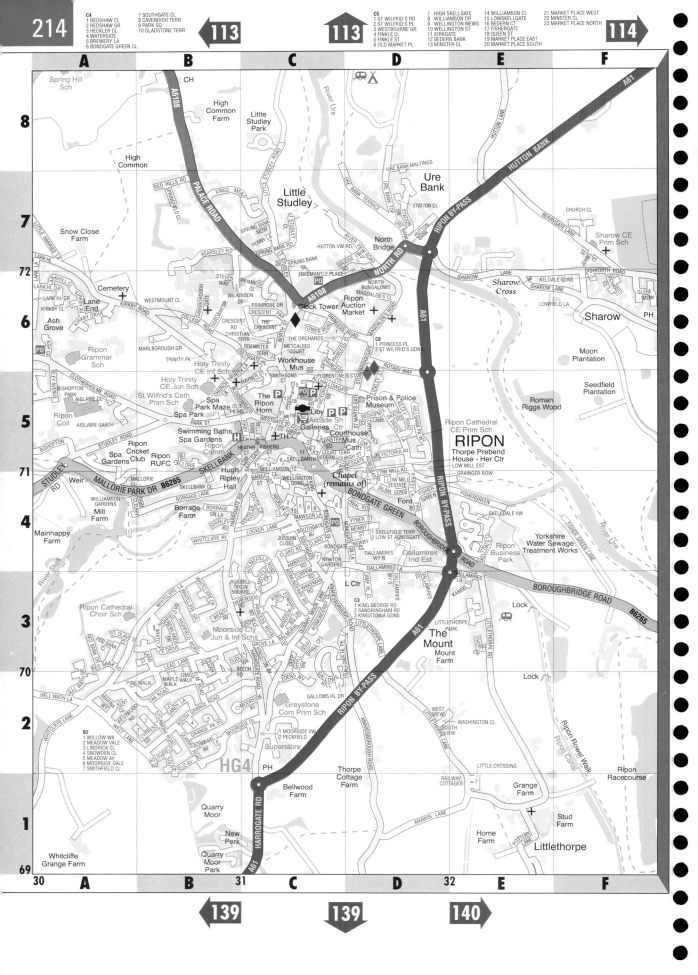

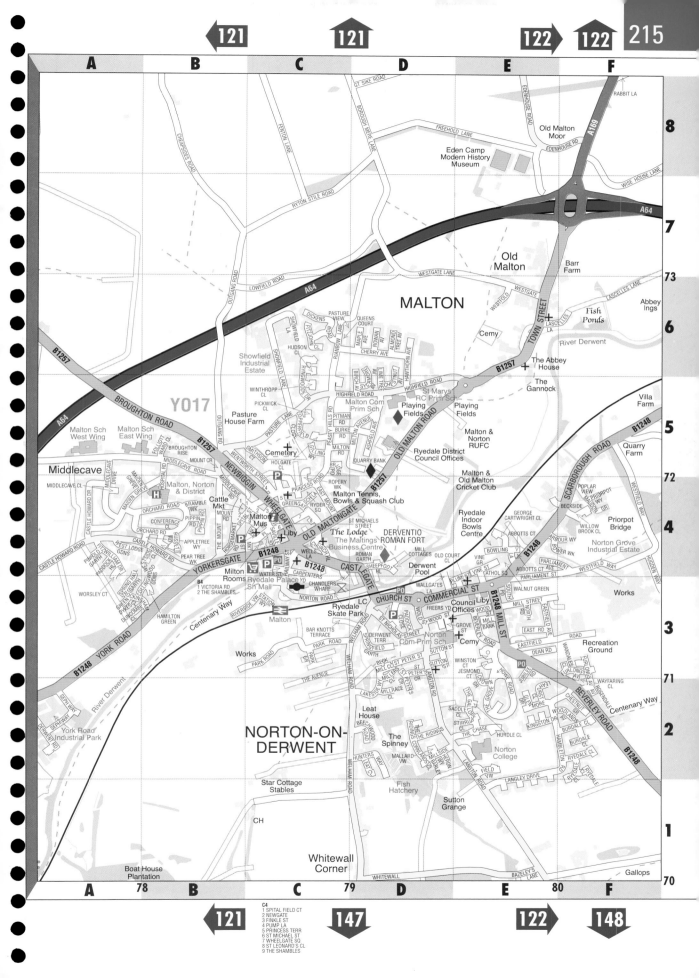

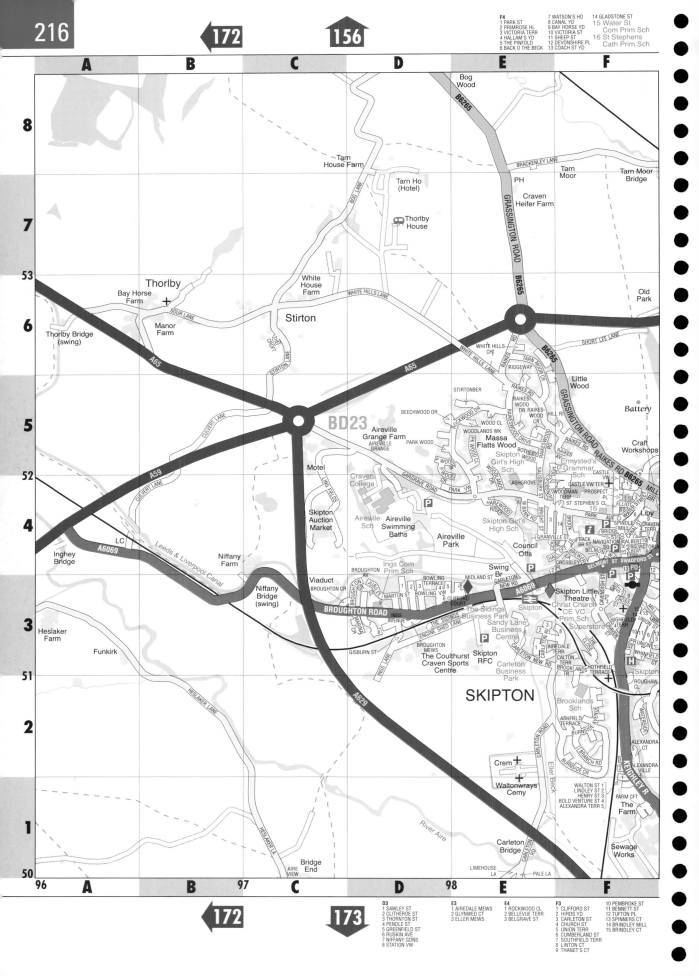

F4
1 PARK ST
2 PRIMROSE HL
3 VICTORIA TERR
4 HALLAM'S YD
5 THE PINFOLD
6 BACK O THE BECK

7 WATSON'S HO
8 CANAL ST
9 BAY HORSE YD
10 VICTORIA ST
11 SHEEP ST
12 DEVONSHIRE PL
13 COACH ST YD

14 GLADSTONE ST
15 Water St
   Com Prim Sch
16 St Stephens
   Cath Prim Sch

D3
1 SAWLEY ST
2 CLITHEROE ST
3 THORNTON ST
4 PENDLE ST
5 GREENFIELD ST
6 RUSKIN AVE
7 NIFFANY GDNS
8 STATION VW

E3
1 AIREDALE MEWS
2 GLYNWED CT
3 ELLER MEWS

E4
1 ROCKWOOD CL
2 BELLEVUE TERR
3 BELGRAVE ST

F3
1 CLIFFORD ST
2 HIRDS YD
3 CARLETON ST
4 CHURCH ST
5 UNION TERR
6 CUMBERLAND ST
7 SOUTHFIELD TERR
8 LINTON CT
9 THANET S CT

10 PEMBROKE ST
11 BENNETT ST
12 TUFTON PL
13 SPINNERS CT
14 BRINDLEY MILL
15 BRINDLEY CT

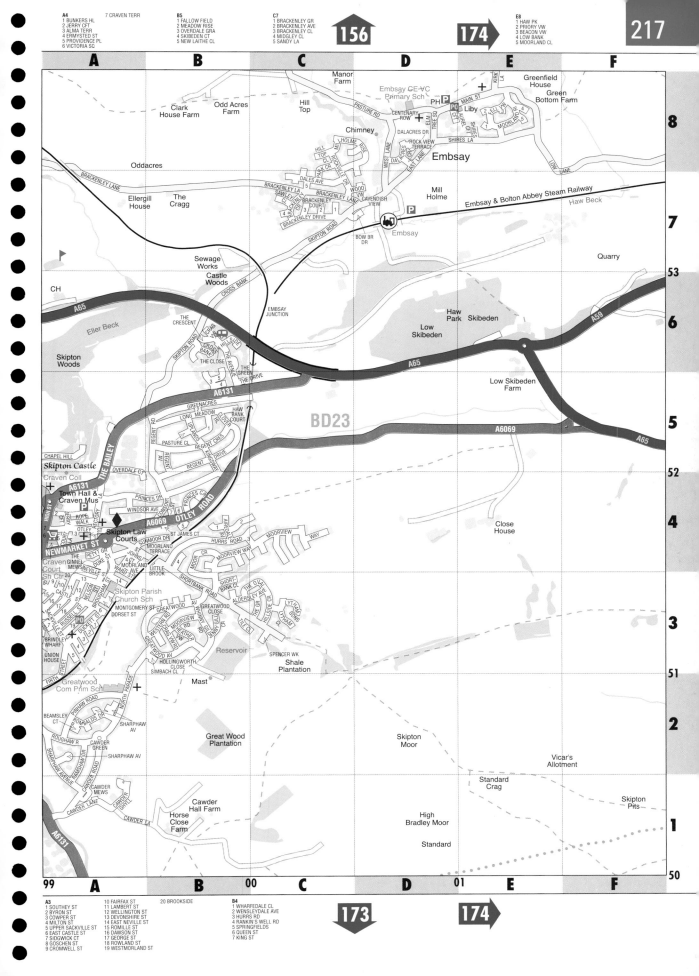

156
174

173
174

A4
1 BUNKERS HL
2 JERRY CFT
3 ALMA TERR
4 ERMYSTED ST
5 PROVIDENCE PL
6 VICTORIA SQ

7 CRAVEN TERR

B5
1 FALLOW FIELD
2 MEADOW RISE
3 OVERDALE GRA
4 SKIBEDEN CT
5 NEW LAITHE CL

C7
1 BRACKENLEY GR
2 BRACKENLEY AVE
3 BRACKENLEY CL
4 MIDGLEY CL
5 SANDY LA

E8
1 HAW PK
2 PRIORY VW
3 BEACON VW
4 LOW BANK
5 MOORLAND CL

A3
1 SOUTHEY ST
2 BYRON ST
3 COWPER ST
4 MILTON ST
5 UPPER SACKVILLE ST
6 EAST CASTLE ST
7 SIDGWICK CT
8 GOSCHEN ST
9 CROMWELL ST

10 FAIRFAX ST
11 LAMBERT ST
12 WELLINGTON ST
13 DEVONSHIRE ST
14 EAST NEVILLE ST
15 ROMILLE ST
16 DAWSON ST
17 GEORGE ST
18 ROWLAND ST
19 WESTMORLAND ST

20 BROOKSIDE

B4
1 WHARFEDALE CL
2 WENSLEYDALE AVE
3 HURRS RD
4 RANKIN'S WELL RD
5 SPRINGFIELDS
6 QUEEN ST
7 KING ST

Manor Farm
Embsay CE VC Primary Sch
Greenfield House
Green Bottom Farm
KIRK LA
MAIN ST
Liby
PASTURE RD
CENTENARY ROW
ELM TREE SQ
LAUREL CT
ELL VW
MOORLAND RI
SHIRES
Clark House Farm
Odd Acres Farm
Hill Top
Chimney
DALACRES DR
ROCK VIEW TERRACE
Embsay
SHIRES LA
HILL TOP
HOLME RISE
ROCKVILLE DR
WEST LANE
DALACRES
EAST LANE
LONG LANE
Oddacres
BRACKENLEY LANE
Ellergill House
The Cragg
BRACKENLEY LA
SAWLEY LA
BRACKENLEY LANE
BRACKENLEY CT
BRACKENLEY LANE
DALES AVE
CAVENDISH VIEW
WOOD VW
Mill Holme
Embsay & Bolton Abbey Steam Railway
Haw Beck
BRACKENLEY DRIVE
SKIPTON ROAD
BOW BR DR
Embsay
Sewage Works
Castle Woods
CROSS BANK
Quarry
CH
THE CRESCENT
CROSS BANK
HILLSIDE
THE CLOSE
THE GREEN
Haw Park
Skibeden
53
A65
Eller Beck
SKIPTON ROAD
THE AVENUE
THE DRIVE
EMBSAY JUNCTION
A65
Low Skibeden
A59
6
Skipton Woods
A6131
Low Skibeden Farm
BD23
GREENACRES
HAW BANK COURT
LONG MEADOW
UPLANDS
CLOVER
A6069
A65
5
REGENT RD
PASTURE CL
REGENT CRES
KINGSWAY
REGENT DRIVE
REGENT
52
Chapel Hill
CHAPEL HILL
Skipton Castle
Craven Coll
OVERDALE CT
THE BAILEY
PRINCES DR
WINDSOR AVE
PRINCES CR
Close House
A6131
Town Hall & Craven Mus
ROPE WALK
RECTORY LA
OTLEY ST
A6069
OTLEY ROAD
ST JAMES CT
AIREDALE
HURRS ROAD
MOORVIEW
WAY
4
HIGH ST
JERRY
Skipton Law Courts
NEWMARKET ST
SUNMOOR DR
MOORLAND TERRACE
MOOR CR
MOORVIEW WAY
PETTY GH
JOHNS
DUKE ST
MOORLAND AVE
Craven Court Sh Ctr
GINNEL MEWS
NEVILLE
WARD ST
LITTLE BROOK
SHORTBANK ROAD
SHORT-BANK CL
ALDERSLEY AVE
THE GREAVES
HILLSIDE CR
LYTHAM GDNS
LYTHAM
CASTLE
RUSSELL ST
NELSON
BROUGHAM
Skipton Parish Church Sch
MONTGOMERY ST
DORSET ST
GREATWOOD
WHINNY GILL RD
GREATWOOD CLOSE
TILE CL
THE OVAL
BRINDLEY WHARF
PO
DUCKETT ST
SACKVILLE ST
WESTON RD
MOORVIEW RD
HEATHER
GREATWOOD DR
Reservoir
SPENCER WK
UNION HOUSE
FIRTH STREET
HOLLINGWORTH CLOSE
SIMBACH CL
Shale Plantation
3
Greatwood Com Prim Sch
GREATWOOD AV
Mast
51
Beamsley Ct
PINHAW ROAD
ROMBALDS DR
NORTH PARADE
SHARPHAW AV
Great Wood Plantation
Skipton Moor
Vicar's Allotment
2
ROUGHAW R
CAWDER GREEN
SHARPHAW AV
Standard Crag
Skipton Pits
SHARPHAW AVENUE
RANSHAW DR
CAWDER ROAD
CAWDER MEWS
Cawder Hall Farm
High Bradley Moor
CAWDER LANE
CAWDER GHYLL
Horse Close Farm
Standard
1
A6131
99
A
00
B
C
01
D
E
F
50

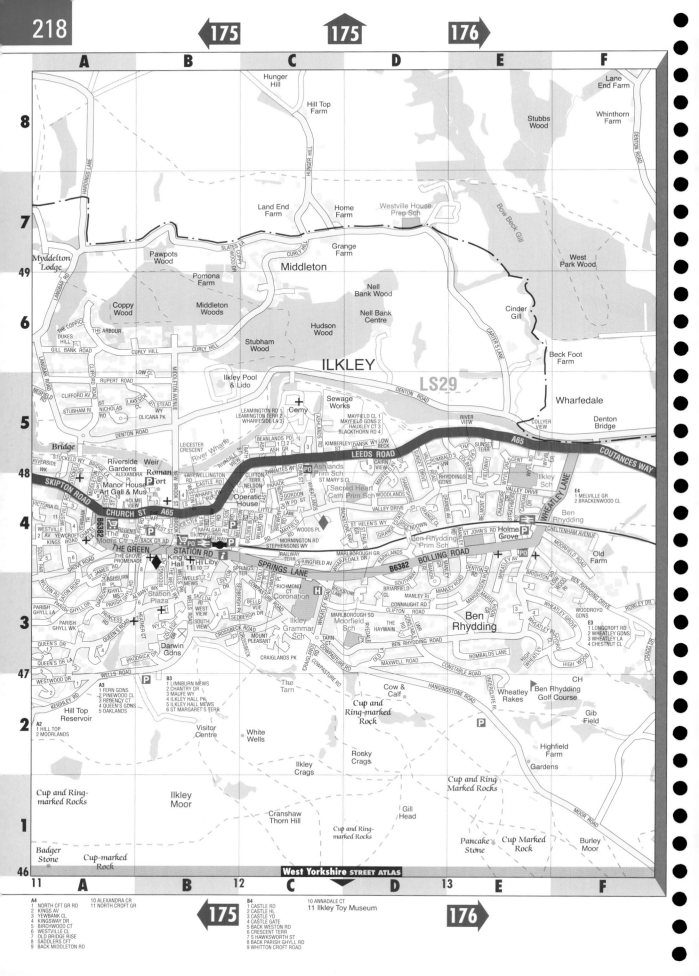

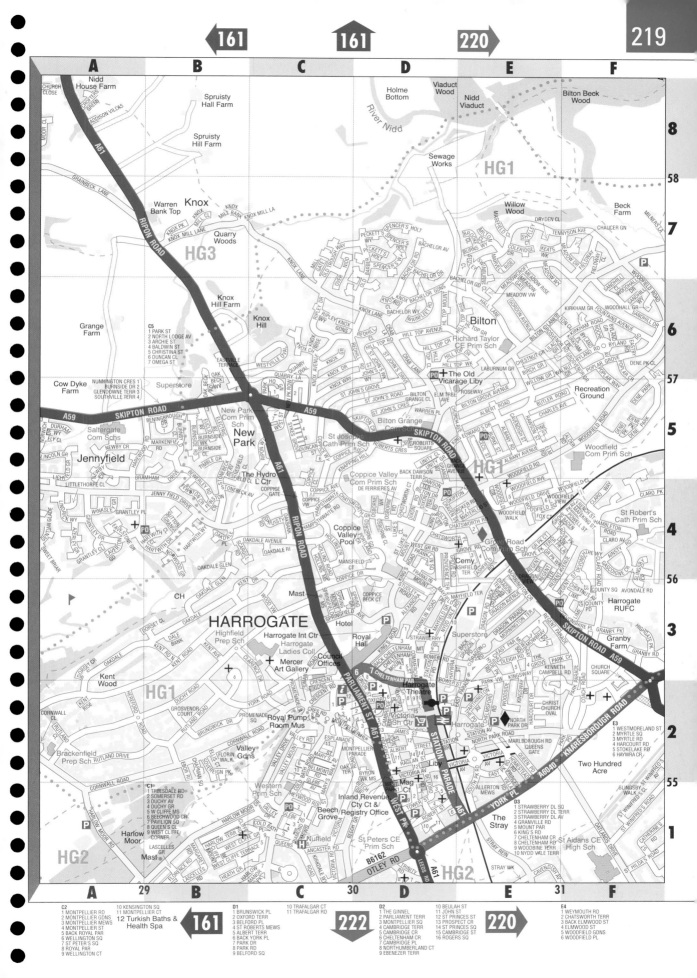

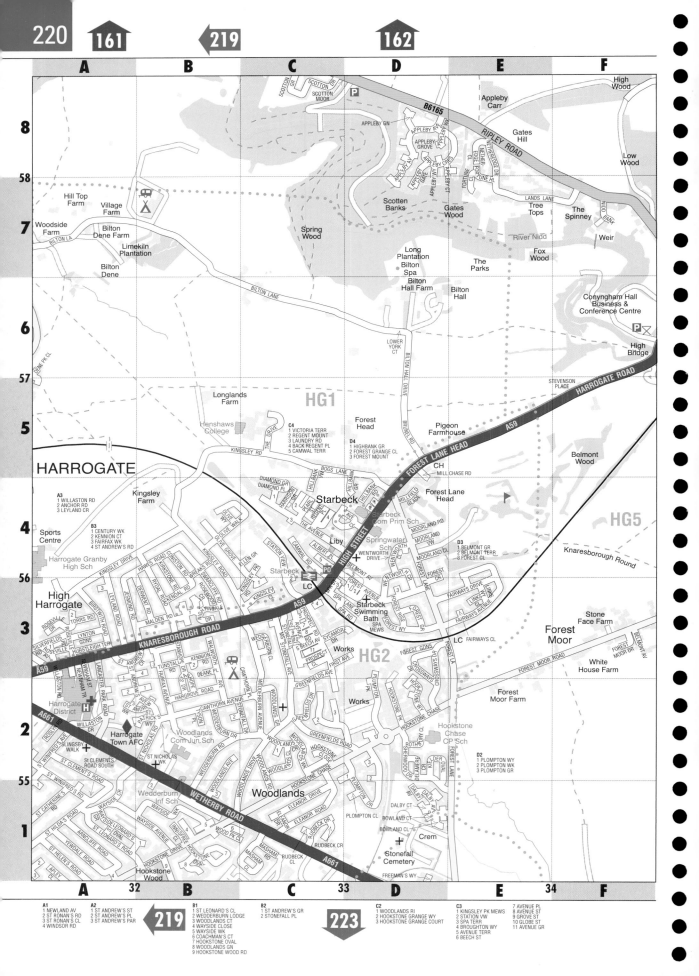

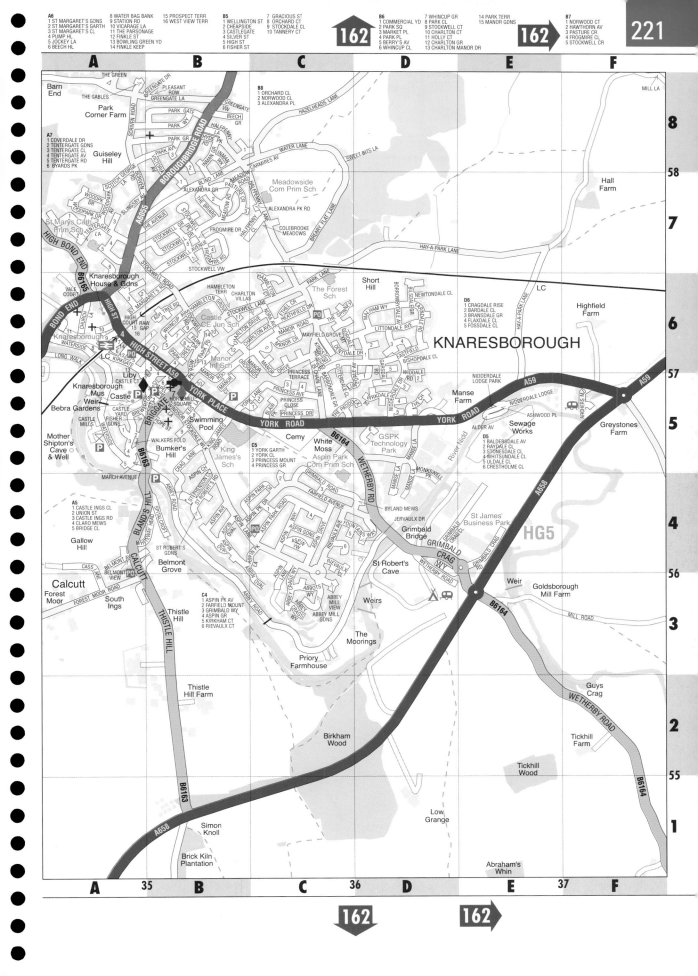

A6
1 ST MARGARET'S GDNS
2 ST MARGARET'S GARTH
3 ST MARGARET'S CL
4 PUMP HL
5 JOCKEY LA
6 BEECH HL

8 WATER BAG BANK
9 STATION RD
10 VICARAGE LA
11 THE PARSONAGE
12 FINKLE ST
13 BOWLING GREEN YD
14 FINKLE KEEP

15 PROSPECT TERR
16 WEST VIEW TERR

A7
1 COVERDALE DR
2 TENTERGATE GDNS
3 TENTERGATE CL
4 TENTERGATE AV
5 TENTERGATE RD
6 BYARDS PK

B5
1 WELLINGTON ST
2 CHEAPSIDE
3 CASTLEGATE
4 SILVER ST
5 HIGH ST
6 FISHER ST

B8
1 ORCHARD CL
2 NORWOOD CL
3 ALEXANDRA PL

7 GRACIOUS ST
8 ORCHARD CT
9 STOCKDALE CL
10 TANNERY CT

B6
1 COMMERCIAL YD
2 PARK SQ
3 MARKET PL
4 PARK PL
5 BERRY'S AV
6 WHINCUP CL

7 WHINCUP GR
8 PARK CL
9 STOCKWELL CT
10 CHARLTON CT
11 HOLLY CT
12 CHARLTON GR
13 CHARLTON MANOR DR

14 PARK TERR
15 MANOR GDNS

B7
1 NORWOOD CT
2 HAWTHORN AV
3 PASTURE CR
4 FROGMIRE CL
5 STOCKWELL CR

KNARESBOROUGH

HG5

D6
1 CRAGDALE RISE
2 BARDALE CL
3 BRANSDALE GR
4 FLAXDALE CL
5 FOSSDALE CL

D5
1 BALDERSDALE AV
2 RAYDALE CL
3 STONESDALE CL
4 WHITSUNDALE CL
5 ULDALE CL
6 CRESTHOLME CL

A5
1 CASTLE INGS CL
2 UNION ST
3 CASTLE INGS RD
4 CLARO MEWS
5 BRIDGE CL

C5
1 YORK GARTH
2 YORK CL
3 PRINCESS MOUNT
4 PRINCESS GR

C4
1 ASPIN PK AV
2 FARFIELD MOUNT
3 GRIMBALD WY
4 ASPIN GR
5 KIRKHAM CT
6 RIEVAULX CT

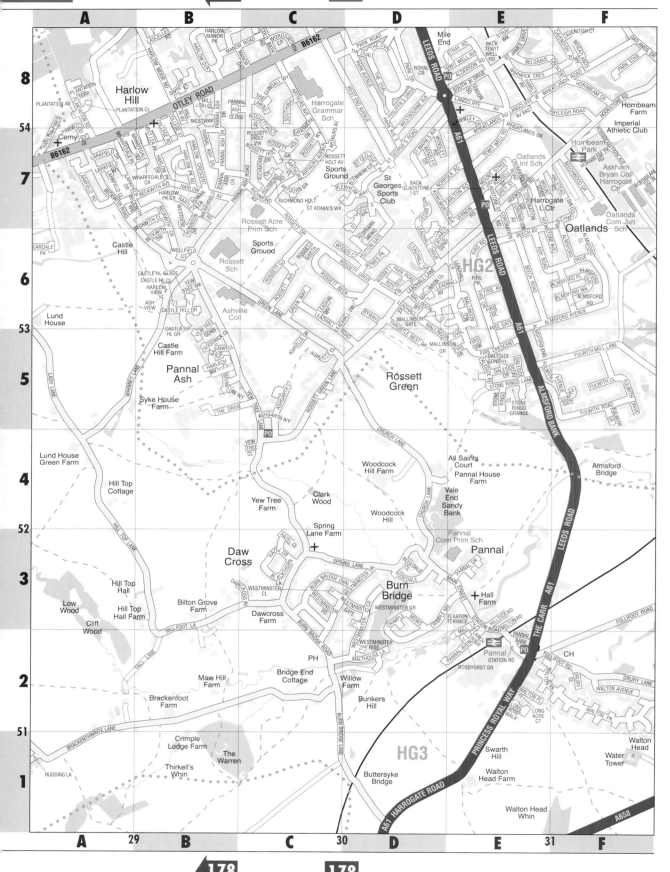

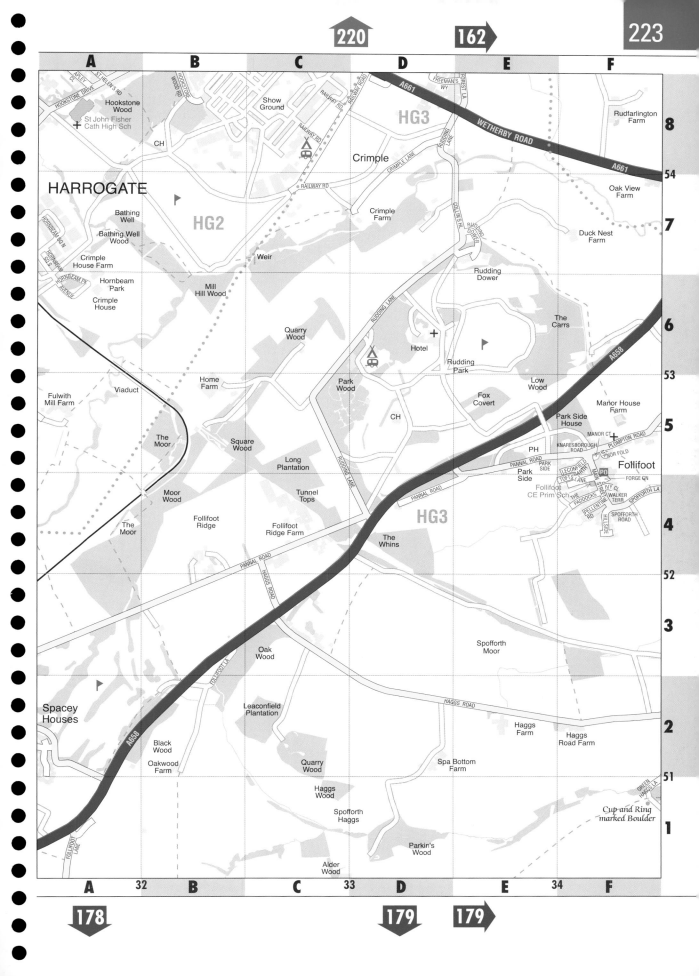

A   B   C   D   E   F

8
54
7
6
53
5
52
3
2
51
1

32   33   34

HARROGATE

HOOKSTONE DRIVE
APLEY CL
ST HELEN'S RD
HOOKSTONE WOOD RD
St John Fisher Cath High Sch
Hookstone Wood
CH
Show Ground
RAILWAY RD
RAILWAY RD
RAILWAY RD

HG3
A661
WETHERBY ROAD
A661
Rudfarlington Farm

Crimple
CRIMPLE LANE
Oak View Farm

HG2
Bathing Well
Bathing Well Wood
Crimple House Farm
HORNBEAM SQ N
HORNBEAM SQ S
HORNBEAM PK
HORNBEAM AVENUE
Hornbeam Park
Crimple House
Mill Hill Wood
Weir
Crimple Farm

COLLINS HILL
RUDDING LANE
RUDDING DOWER
Rudding Dower
Duck Nest Farm

Quarry Wood
Home Farm
Park Wood
Hotel
Rudding Park
The Carrs
A658

Fulwith Mill Farm
Viaduct
The Moor
Square Wood
Long Plantation
CH
Fox Covert
Low Wood
Manor House Farm

Park Side House
Park Side
PH
KNARESBOROUGH ROAD
MANOR CT
PLOMPTON ROAD
NOR FOLD
Follifoot

Moor Wood
The Moor
Follifoot Ridge
Tunnel Tops
Follifoot Ridge Farm
RUDDING LANE
PANNAL ROAD
Pannal Road
PARK SIDE
LECONFIELD GARTH
TOFTS LANE
THE PADDOCKS
PELLENTINE RD
FORGE GN
IVY CL
WALKER TERR
SPOFFORTH LA
HILLSIDE
Follifoot CE Prim Sch
PO

HG3

The Whins

HAGGS ROAD
PANNAL ROAD
PANNAL ROAD
HAGGS ROAD
Spofforth Moor
SPOFFORTH ROAD

Oak Wood

Spacey Houses
A658
FOLLIFOOT LA
Black Wood
Oakwood Farm
Leaconfield Plantation
Quarry Wood
Haggs Wood
Spofforth Haggs
Spa Bottom Farm
Haggs Farm
Haggs Road Farm
GREEN HAGGS LA

Parkin's Wood
Cup and Ring marked Boulder

Alder Wood
FOLLIFOOT LANE

165
166

A B C D E F

8 7 57 6 56 5 56 4 3 55 2 1 54

Hall Moor

Wide Open Farm
Woodside Farm
CH
SKELTON LANE
Park Farm
YO32
MOOR LANE
Wigginton Moor

A19
HURNS LA
Hurns Bridge

Glebe Farm

Nova Scotia Plantation

Skelton Moor

New Farm

Hall
ST GILES ROAD
THE VILLAGE
CHURCH LANE
Skelton
MOORLANDS LANE
THE VILLAGE
St Catherines
Skelton Moor

Skelton Plantation

YO30

Skelton Prim Sch
BRECKSFIELD

B5
1 THE GREEN
2 THE MEADOWS
3 ORCHARD VIEW
4 THE WHEELHOUSE
5 THE DELL
6 ARTHUR PLACE

PH
STRIPE LANE
GRANGE CL
ST GILES
PASTURE CL
PASTURE LA
PO
SYCAMORE CL
1 RATCLIFFE CT
2 GREGORY CL
3 ST CATHERINES CL

Rawcliffe Moor

CH
FAIRFIELDS GR
BURTREE AV
1 THE ROWMANS
2 THE BEECHES
Tees, East & North Yorkshire Ambulance Service HQ
PARK CL
Rawcliffe Moor Farm

Hotel

E2
1 CONINGHAM AVE
2 MANOR PK GR
3 ELMA GR
4 BARTON CL
5 RAWCLIFFE CL
6 CHESHIRE CL
7 DEANHEAD GR

1 LANGSETT GR
2 RINGSTONE RD
3 BLAKELEY GR
4 ROSEBERRY GR

Poplar Plantation

A1237
Clifton Moor Sh Ctr
STIRLING RD
Clifton Moor Retail Park

E3
1 CAITHNESS CL
2 CONWAY CL
3 HATFIELD CL
4 OSBOURNE DR
5 GRENWICH CL
6 SOMERSET CL
7 HIGHGROVE CL
8 LONGWOOD LINK
9 WINSCAR GR

BLENHEIM CT

River Ouse

Overton Ings
Moat
Skelton Bridge
CHURCH LANE

Rawcliffe Farm
Rawcliffe Landing
Tom Cobleighs Riverside Farm
MARLBOROUGH CL

Rawcliffe Village
HURRICANE WAY
RAWCLIFFE VILLAGE
Clifton Without
ST JAMES
HOLLYWOOD AVE
MITCHELL
LINDLEYWOOD
DEER HL GR
LONGWOOD RD
GILLINGWOOD RD
OLD DYKE LA
AMY JOHNSON WY
AVIATOR CL

Folly Bridge

POPPLETON HALL GD
CHURCH LANE
Manor Farm
HILLCREST AV
FOX GARTH

Nether Poppleton

MANOR LANE
ST CUTHAM
MANOR LANE
ST JAMES CT
VILLAGE STREET
BROADSTONE WY
MITTON WY
RIVELIN WAY
SOUTHWAITH CL
BOOTHWOOD RD
MOREHALL CL
WHARNSCLIFFE DR 2
RYBURN CL 3

HAREWOOD CL 1
KENSINGTON RD 2
A1237
A19
SHIPTON ROAD
P&R
ECCLES CL
MANOR LA
FLORENCE GR
RAWCLIFFE CFT
HOWARD RD
ST MARK'S CL
ST THOUSBALE
MANOR PK WAY
RAWCLIFFE LINK
ROUND HL LINK
BILSDALE CL
DALE DIKE GR
STAINDALE CL
Lakeside Prim Sch
RUSSWORTH
ELDWICK CL
LANGHAM GFT

YO26
NURSERY ROAD
MILL FIELD
LONG RIDGE LANE
EASTHORPE DR
MIDWAY AVE
ALLERTON DRIVE
LONG RIDGE

Sewage Works

Rawcliffe Ings

INGS VIEW
HOWARD DRIVE
FURNESS CL
BOWNESS DR
BUTTERMERE DR
EASTHOLME DR
PATTERDALE DR
WESTHOLME DR
Manor
Rawcliffe Inf Sch
HAVERAH COURT
BEAVERDYKE

Rawcliffe

A1237
Hotel
WESTMINSTER PLACE
INGS LA
WHITE ROSE CLOSE
WHITE ROSE WAY
Poppleton Ings
ORCHARD RD

A19
SHIPTON ROAD
ALWYNE DRIVE
ALWYNE GR
NORTHOLME GR
SHELLEY GR
KENTMERE DR
GRISEDALE RD
BORROWDALE DR
CHYKELL CL
CHYLEA CL
RAWCLIFFE LA
PO

56 57 58

165
227

E1
1 CONISTON CL
2 WASDALE CL
3 GARBURN GR
4 SCAFELL CL
5 LOWESWATER RD
6 FYLINGDALES AVE

F1
1 EMBLETON DR
2 COLEDALE CL
3 LEIGHTON CFT
4 BARMBY CL
5 GRASMERE GR
6 BARDEN CT
7 SOUTHOLME DR
8 MILTON CARR
9 FEWSTON DR

10 REIGHTON DR

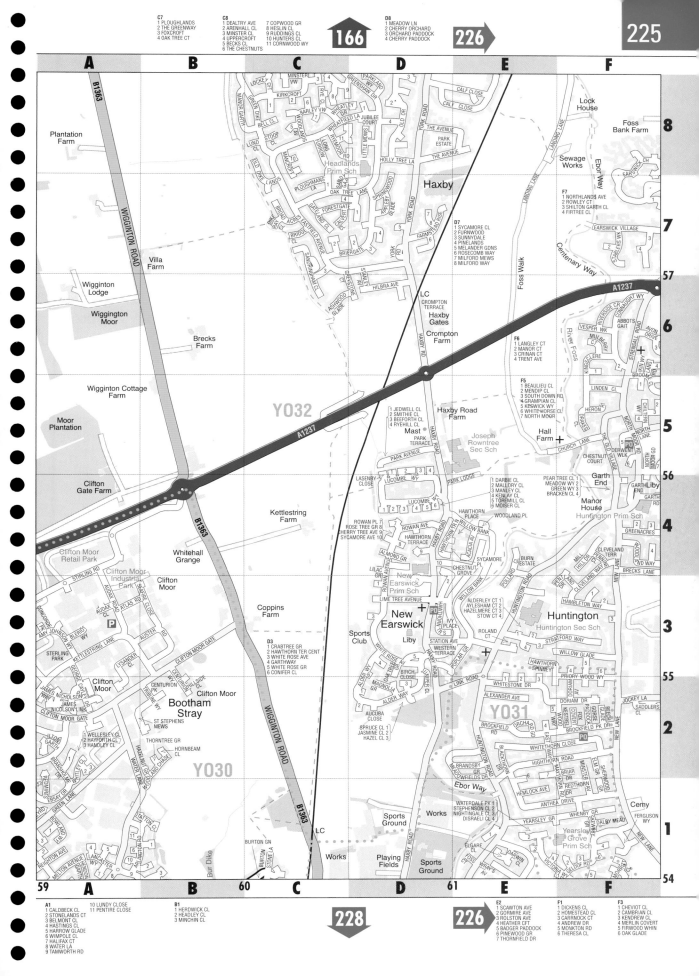

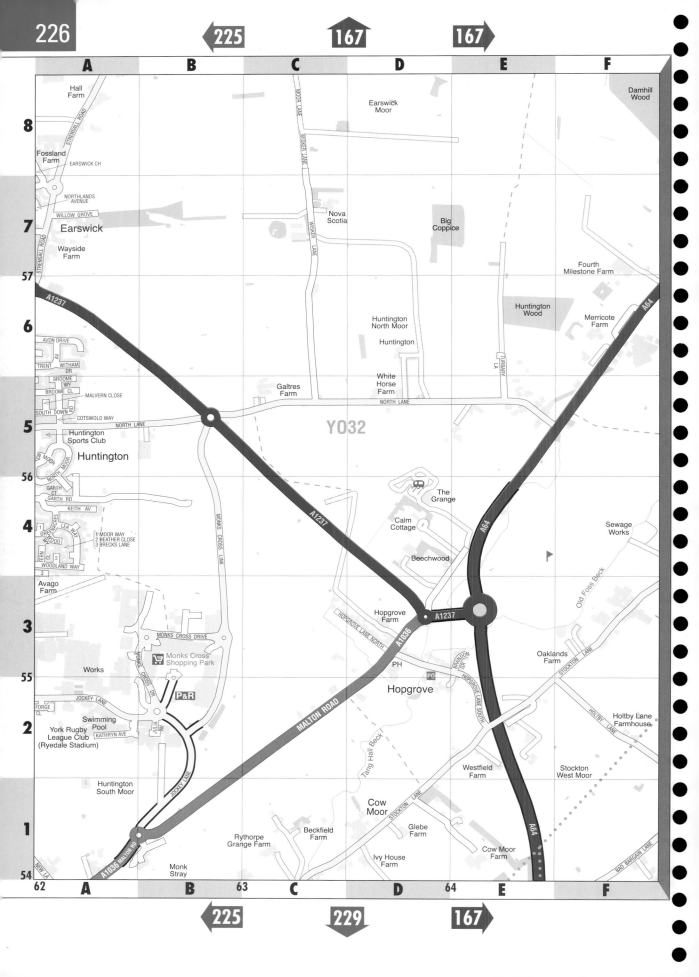

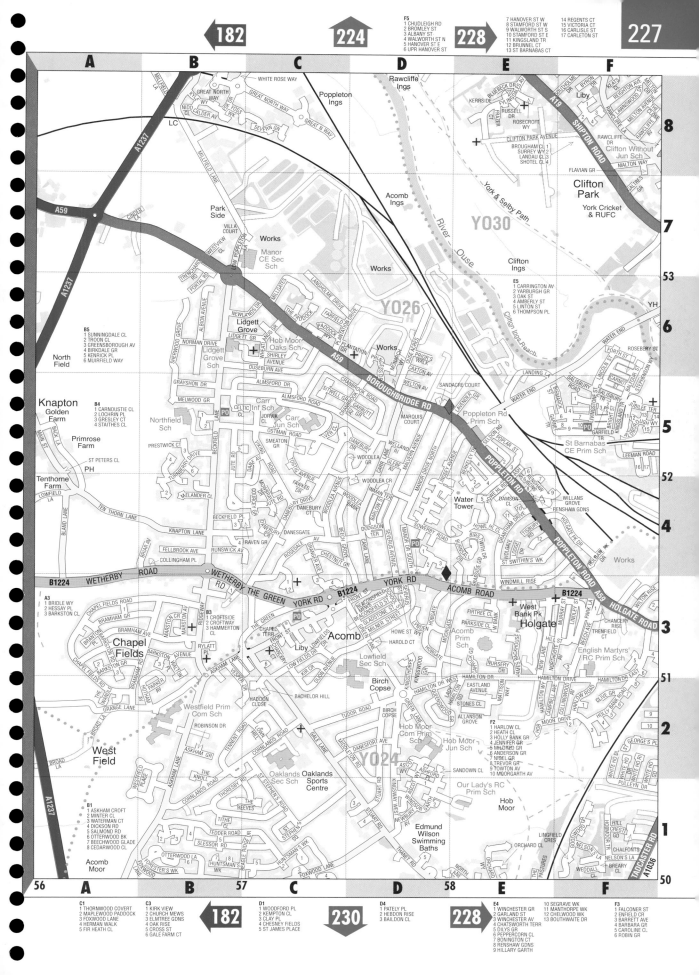

F5
1 CHUDLEIGH RD
2 BROMLEY ST
3 ALBANY ST
4 WALWORTH ST N
5 HANOVER ST N
6 UPR HANOVER ST

7 HANOVER ST W
8 STAMFORD ST W
9 WALWORTH ST S
10 STAMFORD ST E
11 KINGSLAND TR
12 BRUNNEL ST
13 ST BARNABAS CT

14 REGENTS CT
15 VICTORIA CT
16 CARLISLE ST
17 CARLETON ST

C1
1 THORNWOOD COVERT
2 MAPLEWOOD PADDOCK
3 FOXWOOD LANE
4 HERMAN WALK
5 FIR HEATH CL

C3
1 KIRK VIEW
2 CHURCH MEWS
3 ELMTREE GDNS
4 OAK RISE
5 CROSS ST
6 GALE FARM CT

D1
1 WOODFORD PL
2 KEMPTON CL
3 CLAY PL
4 CHESNEY FIELDS
5 ST JAMES PLACE

D4
1 PATELY PL
2 HEBDON RISE
3 BAILDON CL

E4
1 WINCHESTER GR
2 GARLAND ST
3 WINCHESTER AV
4 CHATSWORTH TERR
5 DILYS GR
6 PEPPERCORN CL
7 BONINGTON CT
8 RENSHAW GDNS
9 HILLARY GARTH

10 SEGRAVE WK
11 MANTHORPE WK
12 CHELWOOD WK
13 BOUTHWAITE DR

F3
1 FALCONER ST
2 ENFIELD CR
3 BARRETT AVE
4 BARBARA GR
5 CAROLINE CL
6 ROBIN GR

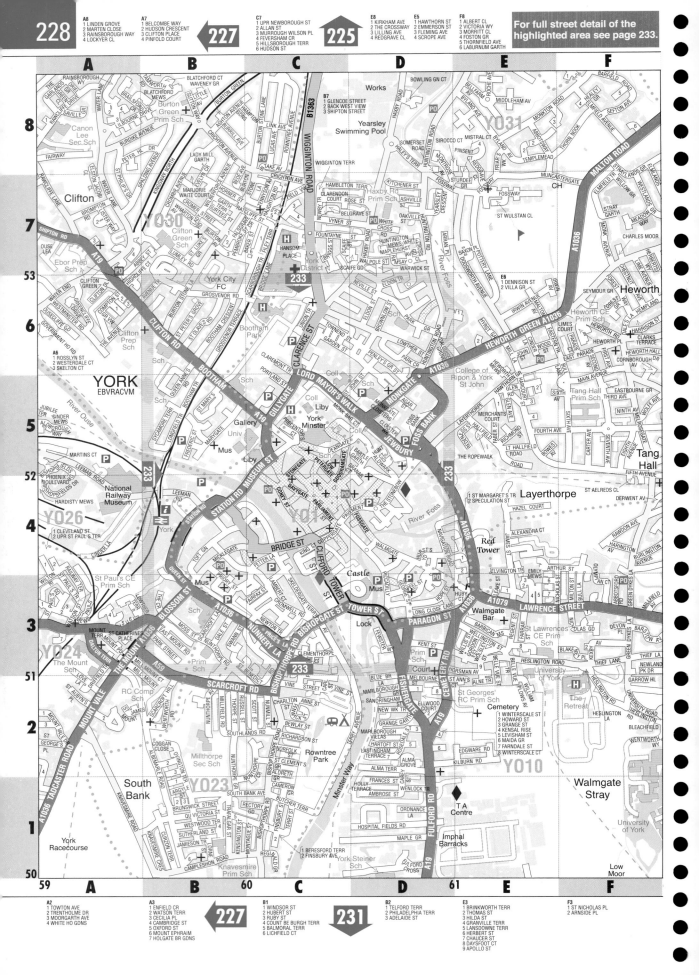

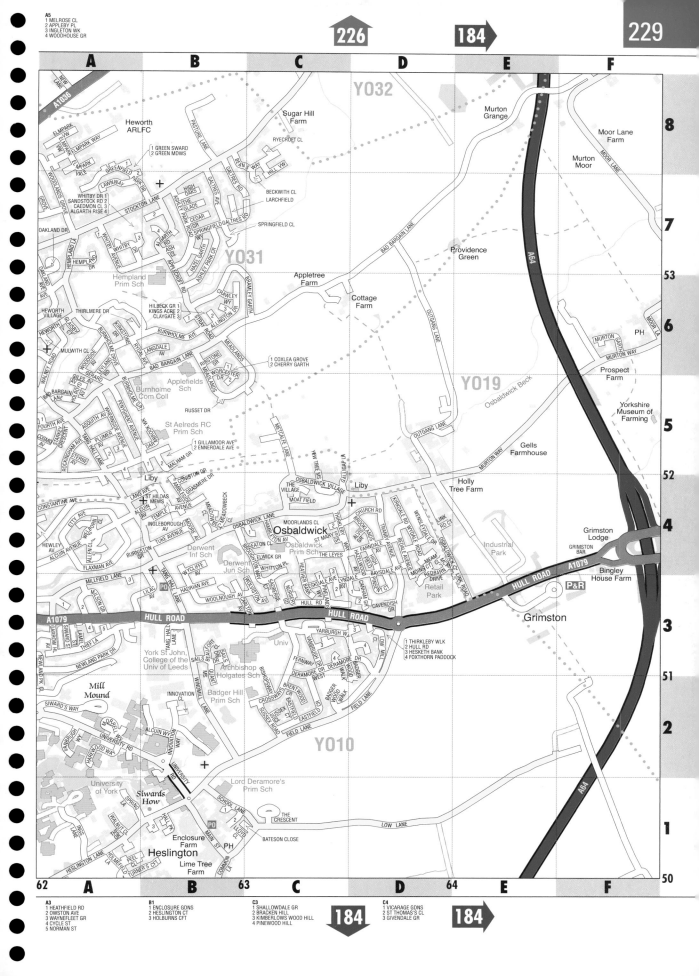

A B C D E F

8
7
53
6
5
52
4
3
51
2
1
50

A1036
YO32
Heworth
ARLFC
Sugar Hill
Farm
Murton
Grange
Moor Lane
Farm
Murton
Moor
ELMPARK VW
ELMPARK WAY
GREENFIELD PARK DR
PASTURE LANE
RYECROFT CL
1 GREEN SWARD
2 GREEN MDWS
BEAN'S WAY
HILL VW
WOODLANDS GROVE
LAWNWAY
HIGH
OAKS
GALTRES RD
GALTRES AVE
BECKWITH CL
LARCHFIELD
BAD BARGAIN LANE
WHITBY DR 1
SANDSTOCK RD 2
CAEDMON CL 3
ALGARTH RISE 4
STOCKTON LANE
ASHLEY PARK ROAD
THE GLADE
CEDAR
ASH
SPRINGFIELD
GALTRES RD
SPRINGFIELD CL
Providence
Green
A64
OAKLAND DR
WHITBY AVENUE
WHITBY DR
ALGARTH RD
HAZEL GARTH
ASHLEY PARK CR
Appletree
Farm
OUTGANG LANE
YO31
HEMPLAND LA
HEMPLAND DR
Hempland
Prim Sch
BRAMLEY GARTH
ALLINGTON DR
CRAWLEY WY
Cottage
Farm
YO19
MURTON
MURTON GARTH
PH
OAKLAND AVE
HEWORTH
VILLAGE
THIRLMERE DR
HEWORTH RD
WOODSIDE
KIRKSTONE DRIVE
RYDAL AVE
BURNHOLME AVE
LANGDALE AV
BAD BARGAIN LANE
1 HILBECK GR
2 KINGS ACRE
3 CLAYGATE
RIBSTONE GR
MEADLANDS
WORCESTER DR
1 COXLEA GROVE
2 CHERRY GARTH
Osbaldwick Beck
Murton Way
MURTON
GARTH WAY
Prospect
Farm
Yorkshire
Museum of
Farming
MULWITH CL
WALNEY ROAD
GILES AV
GERARD
BEVERLEY RD
BURNHOLME DR
Applefields
Sch
Burnholme
Com Coll
RUSSET DR
St Aelreds RC
Prim Sch
METCALFE LANE
Gells
Farmhouse
BAD BARGAIN
LANE
FOURTH AVE
STARCEY
CRESCENT
ASQUITH AV
LLOYD
PLUMER AV
MALHAM GR
1 GILLAMOOR AVE
2 ENNERDALE AVE
YEW TREE MS
Osbaldwick
Village
Liby
Holly
Tree Farm
COSMO AVE
ROCKINGHAM AVE
STERNE
WEIRSIDE AVENUE
HALL LANE
CONISTON DR
Liby
St HILDAS
MEWS
ALCUIN AV
GRASMERE DR
THE
VILLAGE
MOAT FIELD
CHURCH RD
Industrial
Park
Grimston
Lodge
CONSTANTINE AVE
CITY AVE
HEWLEY
AV
ALCUIN AVENUE
WELFORN RD
ALLEN CL
TEMPLE
INGLEBOROUGH
AV
MEADOWBECK
TUKE AVENUE
OSBALDWICK LANE
MOORLANDS CL
Osbaldwick
ST MARY'S
THIRKLEBY WY
Osbaldwick
Prim Sch
BROOKLANDS
KINKDALE RD
WENSLEYDALE RD
REDAL AVENUE
OSBALDWICK LN LINK ROAD
LINK
RD CT
GRIMSTON
BAR
Bingley
House Farm
Grimston
FLAXMAN LANE
MILLFIELD LANE
BURNSTON GR
BEATON CL
WYCLIFFE
Derwent
Inf Sch
DERWENT
JUN SCH
ELWICK GR
WHITTON PL
THE LEYES
HEATHER BANK
BEESKDALE AVE
FARNDALE
HAZELWOOD
HIGH
OSBALDWICK LN
MOINS CT
REDBARN
DRIVE
Retail
Park
HULL ROAD
A1079
HULL ROAD
P&R
LILAC AV
TANG HALL LANE
HADRIAN AVE
WOOLNOUGH AVE
WOOLSTON
DALTON
NURSERY
HULL RD
CAVENDISH
GR
Grimston
PO
HULL ROAD
A1079
HULL ROAD

GARROW HL
SIWARD ST
THIEF LA
LANE
NEWLAND PARK DR
TANG HALL LANE
SAILS DR
Univ
YARBURGH WY
LOW MILL
1 THIRKLEBY WLK
2 HULL RD
3 HESKETH BANK
4 FOXTHORN PADDOCK
NEWLAND PK
York St John,
College of the
Univ of Leeds
Archbishop
Holgates Sch
FERNWAY
DERAMORE DR
DERAMORE DR WEST
BADGER
WOOD
WALK
BADGER
WOOD
DRIVE
Mill
Mound
INNOVATION
CL
WINDMILL LANE
QUANT
Badger Hill
Prim Sch
BISHOPDALE
BRENTWOOD CR
EASTFIELD
CROSSWAYS
SUSSEX CL
SUSSEX RD
EASTFIELD
BARBER
WOOD
WALK
FIELD LANE
YO10
Siward's Way
MORRELL
SIWARD'S WAY
ALCUIN WYATON
INNOVATION WAY
Lord Deramore's
Prim Sch
YARBURGH
HAREWOOD WA
UNIVERSITY RD
University
of York
Siwards
How
UNIVERSITY RD
SPRING LA
SCHOOL LANE
THE CRESCENT
LOW LANE
A64
WALNUT CL
HALF PK
MAIN ST
LLOYD CL
PO
PH
Enclosure
Farm
Heslington
Lime Tree
Farm
HESLINGTON LANE
HOLMEFIELD
PEEL CL
TURNER'S CFT
COMMON
BATESON CLOSE

62 A B 63 C D 64 E F 50

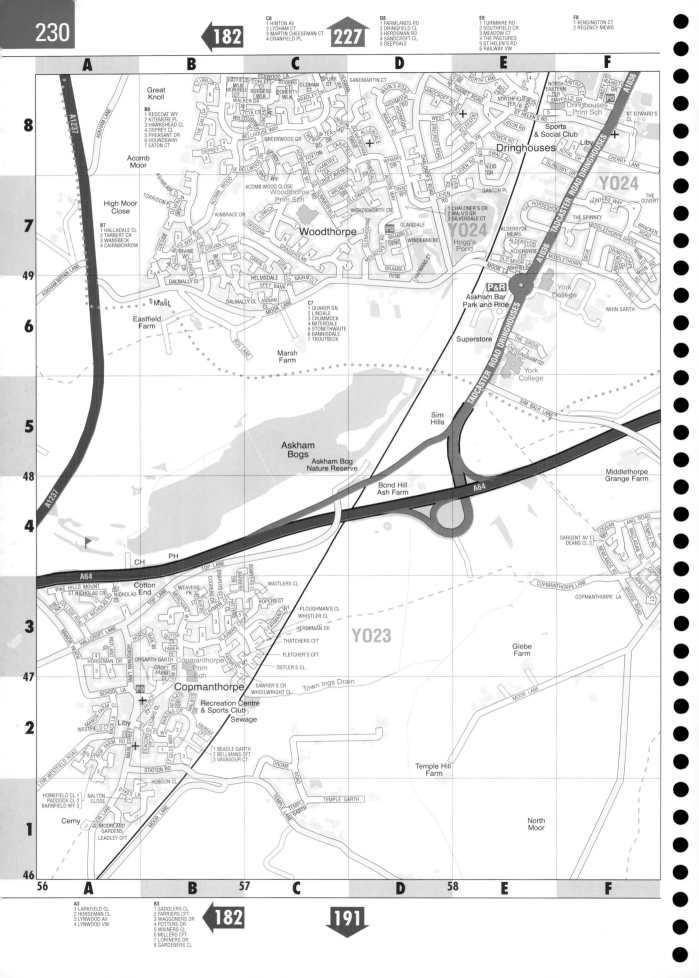

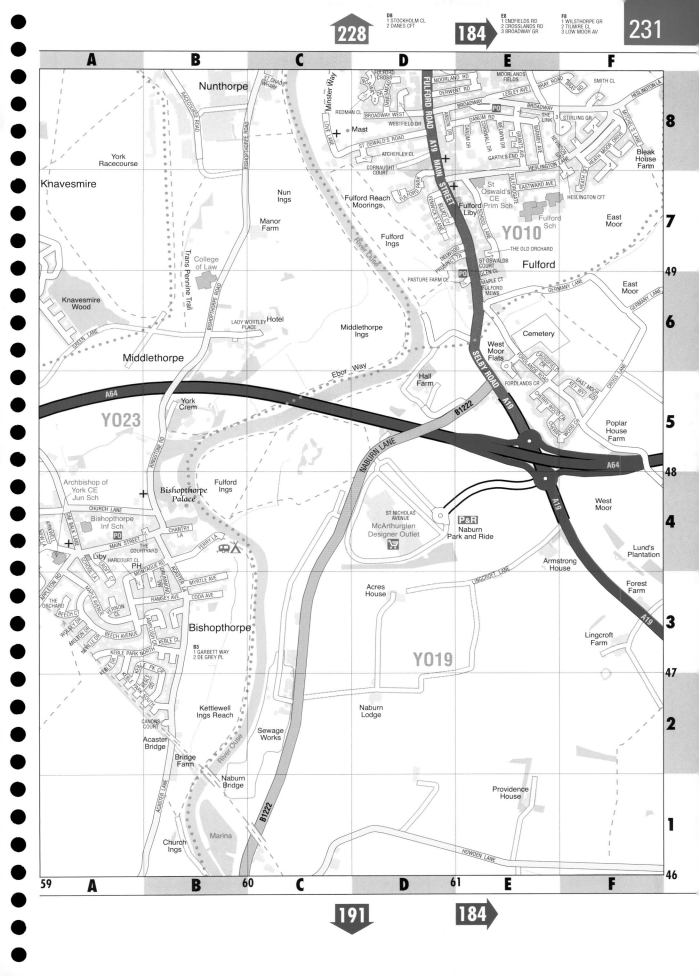

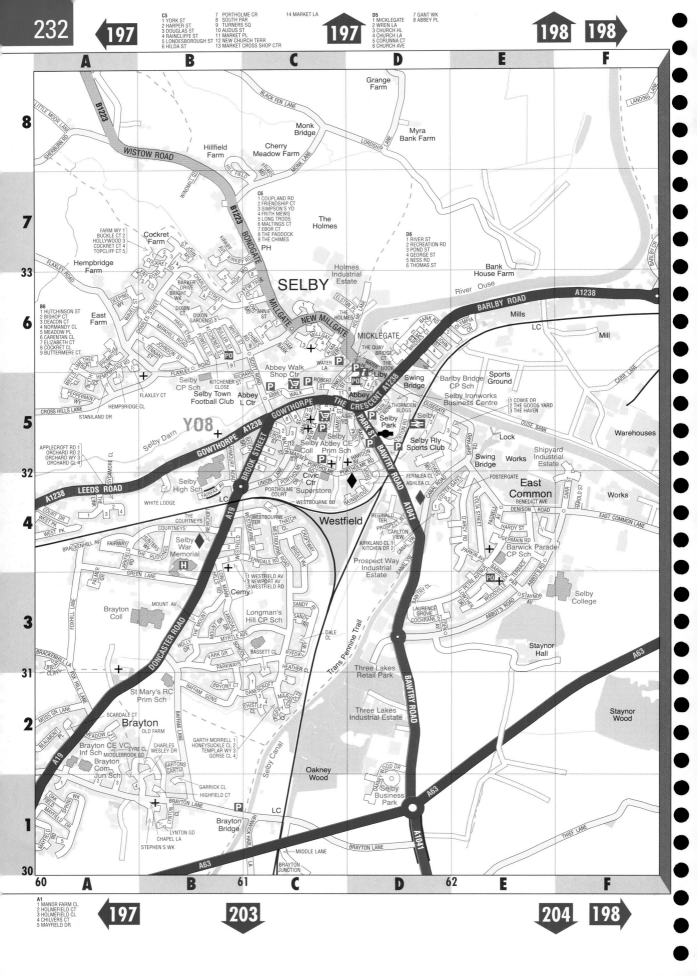

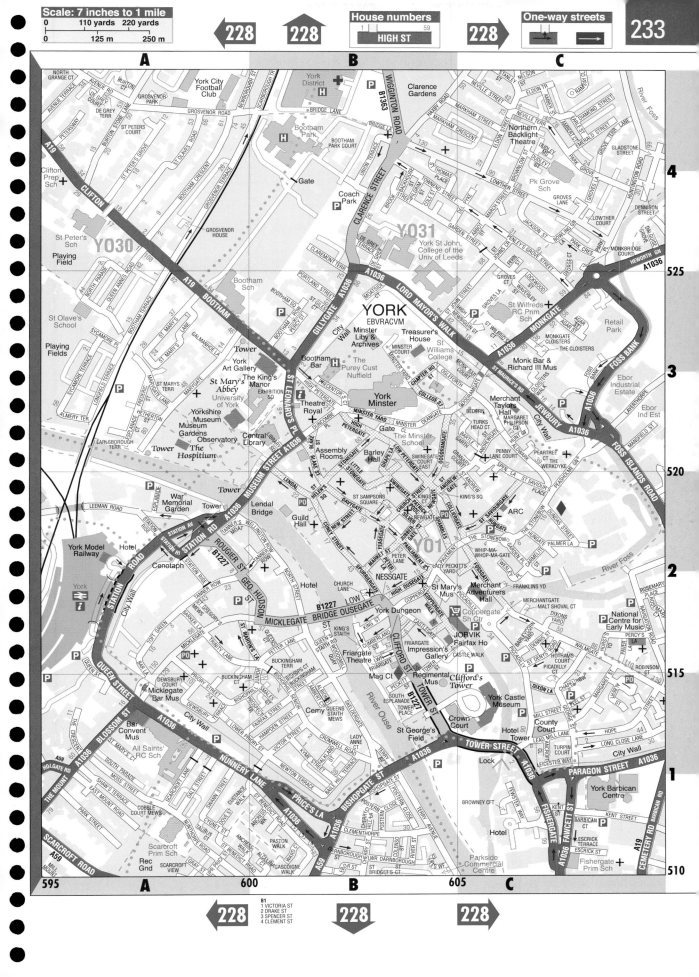

Index

Place name May be abbreviated on the map

Church Rd 6 Beckenham BR2..........53 C6

Location number Present when a number indicates the place's position in a crowded area of mapping

Locality, town or village Shown when more than one place has the same name

Postcode district District for the indexed place

Page and grid square Page number and grid reference for the standard mapping

Public and commercial buildings are highlighted in magenta **Places of interest** are highlighted in blue with a star*

Abbreviations used in the index

Acad	Academy	Comm	Common	Gd	Ground	L	Leisure	Prom	Promenade
App	Approach	Cott	Cottage	Gdn	Garden	La	Lane	Rd	Road
Arc	Arcade	Cres	Crescent	Gn	Green	Liby	Library	Recn	Recreation
Ave	Avenue	Cswy	Causeway	Gr	Grove	Mdw	Meadow	Ret	Retail
Bglw	Bungalow	Ct	Court	H	Hall	Meml	Memorial	Sh	Shopping
Bldg	Building	Ctr	Centre	Ho	House	Mkt	Market	Sq	Square
Bsns, Bus	Business	Ctry	Country	Hospl	Hospital	Mus	Museum	St	Street
Bvd	Boulevard	Cty	County	HQ	Headquarters	Orch	Orchard	Sta	Station
Cath	Cathedral	Dr	Drive	Hts	Heights	Pal	Palace	Terr	Terrace
Cir	Circus	Dro	Drove	Ind	Industrial	Par	Parade	TH	Town Hall
Cl	Close	Ed	Education	Inst	Institute	Pas	Passage	Univ	University
Cnr	Corner	Emb	Embankment	Int	International	Pk	Park	Wk, Wlk	Walk
Coll	College	Est	Estate	Intc	Interchange	Pl	Place	Wr	Water
Com	Community	Ex	Exhibition	Junc	Junction	Prec	Precinct	Yd	Yard

Index of localities, towns and villages

A

Aberford 194 F7
Acaster Malbis 191 D8
Acaster Selby 191 B4
Acklam
  Middlesbrough........... 6 E8
  Stamford Bridge 169 E8
Acomb 227 C3
Addingham 174 F5
Agglethorpe 60 A1
Ainderby Quernhow..... 88 C4
Ainderby Steeple 64 B7
Ainthorpe 29 C6
Airedale 201 B4
Aire View.............. 173 D1
Airmyn 205 E4
Airton 155 A6
Airy Hill 208 D4
Aiskew 63 A3
Aislaby
  Egglescliffe 5 C3
  Pickering 95 D8
  Whitby 31 F7
Aldborough............. 141 C5
Aldbrough St John 2 A2
Aldfield 139 A8
Aldwark 142 C2
Allerston 97 C5
Allerton Bywater....... 200 D6
Allerton Mauleverer.... 163 E4
Alne................... 142 F4
Alne Station 143 A5
Amotherby 121 B4
Ampleforth 92 C1
Angram
  Keld 35 E6
  York................. 182 C3
Appersett.............. 56 C5
Appleton-le-Moors 70 F2
Appleton-le-Street 120 F4
Appleton Roebuck 190 F5
Appleton Wiske 24 B3
Appletreewick 157 D7
Archdeacon Newton......2 F7
Arkendale 163 B8
Arncliffe 107 D2
Arrathorne 62 A8
Asenby 115 B6
Askham Bryan 182 F3
Askham Richard 182 D3
Askrigg 57 F6
Askwith 176 D3
Asselby 205 D7
Aughton 193 C1
Austwick 130 E7

Aysgarth............... 58 E3
Azerley 113 A5

B

Bagby 90 C3
Bainbridge 57 D5
Baldersby 88 D1
Baldersby St James ... 114 E8
Balne.................. 207 C5
Bank Newton 172 B8
Barden 61 A8
Barkston Ash 195 F7
Barlby 198 B5
Barlow 204 C7
Barmby on the Marsh .. 205 B7
Barnoldswick
  Earby 171 D1
  Ingleton 103 A2
Barrowcliff 212 D7
Barton 21 D7
Barton Hill............ 146 D3
Barton-le-Street...... 120 E5
Barton-le-Willows 146 D1
Barwick in Elmet...... 194 B8
Battersby 27 D6
Beadlam 93 C7
Beal 202 D4
Beamsley 174 F7
Beckermonds........... 80 D3
Beckwithshaw 178 A7
Bedale 63 B2
Bedlam 161 A8
Bell Busk 155 A3
Bellerby 60 D7
Beningbrough 165 D4
Ben Rhydding 218 E3
Bent.................. 187 D7
Bewerley 137 B3
Bickerton............. 181 A5
Biggin 196 E5
Bilbrough 182 D1
Bilton 219 E6
Bilton in Ainsty 181 E4
Binsoe 86 F2
Birdforth 116 E6
Birdsall 148 B4
Birkby 23 B1
Birkin 202 D6
Birstwith 160 E6
Bishop Monkton 140 A5
Bishop Thornton 138 F2
Bishopthorpe 231 B3
Bishopton 113 D2
Bishop Wilton 169 F2
Black Banks 3 D2

Blackwell..............3 B4
Blades................. 37 B5
Blazefield 137 E4
Blubberhouses......... 159 D2
Boltby 66 F1
Bolton Abbey 174 E8
Bolton Bridge......... 174 F8
Bolton-on-Swale 41 F6
Bolton Percy.......... 190 D4
Boosbeck..............9 E8
Bootham Stray........ 225 F3
Boothferry............ 205 F5
Booze 17 F1
Bordley............... 133 D3
Boroughbridge 141 C5
Borrowby
  Northallerton......... 65 E4
  Whitby.............. 11 D6
Bossall 168 D7
Boston Spa 188 F8
Botton................ 29 B3
Bouthwaite 110 E2
Bracewell 171 C3
Brackenbottom 105 E3
Brafferton 116 A1
Braidley 83 B2
Bramham 188 F5
Brandsby 118 C3
Bransome 2 F6
Branton Green 142 A1
Brawby 94 F1
Brawith 26 A6
Braythorn 177 E4
Brayton 232 A2
Brearton 162 A7
Breighton 199 D5
Bridge Hewick 114 B1
Bridgehouse Gate..... 137 B4
Briggswath 32 B7
Briscoerigg........... 177 F5
Brockfield 167 E2
Brompton 43 F3
Brompton-by-Sawdon .. 98 C5
Brompton-on-Swale ... 41 B7
Brookfield 6 E6
Brotherton 201 D5
Broughton
  Malton 121 D4
  Skipton............. 172 E6
Broxa 74 C6
Brunthwaite 174 D1
Bubwith 199 D7
Buckden 107 E8
Bugthorpe 169 D4
Bullamoor 44 B1
Bulmer 146 B6
Burley in Wharfedale.. 176 B1

Burn 203 D7
Burn Bridge 222 D3
Burneston 87 E7
Burniston 75 C8
Burnsall 157 B8
Burnt Yates 160 F8
Burrill 62 E2
Burtersett 56 E4
Burton Fleming 126 E3
Burton in Lonsdale ... 102 F3
Burton Leonard 140 B2
Burton Salmon 201 F6
Burythorpe 147 F3
Buttercrambe 168 E5
Butterwick
  Brawby 120 E8
  Foxholes 125 B2
Byland Abbey 91 E1
Byram 201 F4

C

Calcutt 221 A3
Caldbergh 84 B7
Caldwell...............1 B4
Calton 155 B6
Cambleforth 204 D5
Camp Hill 87 F5
Cantsfield 102 B4
Carlbury..............2 B7
Carlesmoor 111 E4
Carleton in Craven ... 173 A4
Carlton
  Cambleforth......... 204 D3
  Darlington 1 D3
  Helmsley 68 E1
  West Witton......... 83 E7
Carlton Husthwaite ... 116 F7
Carlton in Cleveland .. 26 A3
Carlton Miniott 89 C4
Carperby 58 E4
Carthorpe 87 E6
Castle Bolton 59 A6
Castleford 200 E4
Castleton 29 A6
Castley 178 A1
Cattal 164 A1
Catterick 41 D5
Catterick Bridge 41 D6
Catterick Garrison ... 209 D2
Catterton 190 B8
Catton................ 88 F1
Cawood 197 B8
Cawthorne 71 D4
Cawton 119 C7
Cayton 100 C6

Chantry 59 D2
Chapel Fields 227 A3
Chapel Haddlesey 203 C5
Chapel-le-Dale 104 C8
Charltons 9 C6
Chop Gate 46 F6
Church Fenton 196 B7
Church Houses 48 F4
Clapham 130 C8
Clapham Green 160 E5
Claxton 168 B7
Cleasby................2 F4
Cliffe
  Darlington 2 B6
  Selby............... 198 E2
Clifford 188 E7
Clifton
  Ilkley 176 F3
  York................ 228 A7
Clifton Park 227 F7
Clint 161 A6
Clints 39 C7
Clough 55 A7
Cloughton 54 C1
Cloughton
  Newlands............ 54 C2
Coates 171 E2
Cobby Syke 159 F2
Cockayne 48 A5
Cockerton 3 B6
Cock Hill 165 B2
Colburn 41 A5
Cold Cotes 103 F2
Cold Kirby 91 D7
Collingham 188 A8
Colsterdale 84 E4
Colton 190 E7
Commondale 9 D1
Coneysthorpe 120 D2
Coneythorpe.......... 163 A5
Coniston Cold 155 A1
Conistone 134 C6
Cononley 173 C2
Cononley Woodside ... 173 C3
Constable Burton 61 C5
Coomboots 75 B6
Copgrove 140 C2
Copmanthorpe........ 230 B2
Copt Hewick 114 C2
Cotterdale............ 55 F8
Cotton Tree 186 A2
Coulby Newham 7 A5
Coulton 119 B5
Countersett 57 C2
Coverham 60 C1
Cowan Bridge......... 102 D7
Cowesby 66 C4

Cowling
Bedale 62 D2
Glusburn 187 B6
Cowthorpe 180 E7
Coxwold 117 D8
Crackpot 37 B3
Cracoe 156 C7
Crag 187 D6
Crakehill 115 E4
Crambe 146 F3
Crambeck 146 F6
Crathorne 25 A6
Cray 81 E2
Crayke 118 A1
Cridling Stubbs 206 C8
Crimple 223 D8
Cringles 174 C3
Crockey Hill 184 A1
Croft-on-Tees 22 D8
Cropton 71 B4
Crosby Court 65 B6
Crossgates 99 E7
Cross Hills 187 E7
Cross Lanes 143 D3
Crowdon 54 A4
Cubeck 57 F4
Cundall 115 E3
Cutsyke 200 E3

D

Dacre 159 F7
Dacre Banks 159 F8
Dalby 119 B2
Dalesbridge Centre 130 E6
Dallow 111 F2
Dalton
Newsham 19 D7
Topcliffe 115 F7
Dalton Gates 22 D4
Dalton-on-Tees 22 E6
Danby 29 C7
Danby Wiske 43 C5
Darley 160 A6
Darlington 3 E6
Daw Cross 222 B3
Deepdale 80 F2
Deerstones 175 B8
Deighton
Brompton 44 A8
Escrick 192 A7
Denton 176 A3
Dishforth 115 A4
Downholme 39 D4
Draughton 174 B7
Drax 204 F5
Drebley 157 D6
Dringhouses 230 E8
Duggleby 149 B6
Dunkeswick 178 E2
Dunnington 184 F7
Dunsley 12 F2

E

Eaglescliffe 5 E5
Earby 172 B1
Earswick 226 A7
Easby
Richmond 209 F5
Stokesley 27 B7
Easington 11 A8
Easingwold 143 D8
East Appleton 41 D2
East Ayton 99 B8
East Barnby 12 C3
Eastbourne 3 E4
Eastburn 187 F7
Eastby 156 F1
East Common 232 E4
East Cottingwith 193 C5
East Cowton 22 F2
Easterside 7 A7
Eastfield 100 A7
East Garforth 194 E4
East Harlsey 44 E6
East Hauxwell 61 D8
East Heslerton 124 A7
East Knapton 123 C6
East Layton 20 C8
East Lutton 150 C8
East Marton 172 B6
East Ness 94 B1
East Newton 93 C2
East Rounton 24 E2
East Row 13 A3
East Witton 61 C4
Eavestone 138 B7
Ebberston 97 E5
Eggborough 202 F2
Egglescliffe 5 E4
Egton 31 B5
Egton Bridge 31 A4
Eldroth 130 E4
Ellerbeck 44 F3
Ellerburn 96 E7
Ellerton
Catterick 41 F4
Wheldrake 193 C2
Ellingstring 85 D6
Elton 5 C8

Elvington 185 B2
Embsay 217 D8
Enterpen 25 C4
Eppleby 1 E4
Eryholme 23 A7
Escrick 192 B5
Eshton 155 D3
Everley 74 F4
Exelby 63 D1

F

Faceby 25 F2
Fadmoor 69 F4
Fairburn 201 D7
Falsgrave 212 D3
Fangdale Beck 47 A1
Farlington 144 F6
Farnham 162 D7
Farnhill 173 E1
Farnley 177 B2
Faverdale 3 B8
Fawdington 115 F3
Fearby 85 F4
Feetham 37 C5
Feizor 131 B6
Felixkirk 90 C7
Fenwick 207 D3
Ferrensby 162 F7
Ferrybridge 201 D3
Fewston 159 F1
Fewston Bents 159 F1
Filey 101 C3
Finghall 61 D4
Firby
Bedale 63 A1
Westow 147 A5
Firth Moor 3 F4
Fishpool 177 C2
Flasby 155 E3
Flawith 142 E4
Flaxby 163 B4
Flaxton 145 F1
Fleets 156 A7
Flixton 99 F2
Folkton 100 B2
Follifoot 223 F5
Forcett 1 D3
Fordon 126 A6
Foredale 131 C8
Forest 42 B7
Forest Moor 220 F3
Foston 146 B4
Foul Green 9 E1
Foxholes 125 D3
Foxton 44 E3
Foxup 106 C7
Fremington 38 D6
Fryton 120 A6
Fulford 231 E7
Full Sutton 169 A2
Fylingthorpe 33 B3

G

Gainford 1 D8
Galphay 112 F3
Gammersgill 83 C5
Ganthorpe 120 A1
Ganton 125 B8
Gargrave 155 D1
Garriston 61 B7
Gateforth 203 D3
Gate Helmsley 168 B2
Gatenby 64 A2
Gauber 78 F1
Gayle 56 D4
Gayles 19 E6
Gerrick 10 C3
Giggleswick 131 C2
Gill 187 A6
Gillamoor 70 A5
Gilling East 118 F8
Gilling West 20 E4
Girsby 23 D7
Glaisdale 30 D4
Glass Houghton 201 A3
Glasshouses 137 D4
Glusburn 187 D8
Goathland 51 E8
Goldsborough
Knaresborough 163 A2
Whitby 12 D5
Gollinglith Foot 85 B3
Goulton 25 E3
Gowdall 204 A1
Gowthorpe 169 C1
Grafton 141 D8
Grange 57 D5
Grassington 134 D1
Great Ayton 7 F2
Great Barugh 95 A1
Great Broughton 26 E5
Great Burdon 3 F8
Great Busby 26 C4
Great Crakehall 62 E4
Great Edstone 94 C7
Great Fencote 63 C8
Great Habton 121 C7
Great Heck 207 D7

Great Langton 42 D3
Great Ouseburn 164 B8
Great Preston 200 D5
Great Smeaton 23 C3
Great Thirkleby 90 D1
Green Close 130 A8
Green Hammerton 164 C3
Green Hill 194 F8
Greenhow 136 D3
Grewelthorpe 112 D7
Greygarth 111 F3
Greystonegill 129 C8
Grimston 229 E3
Grindale 127 D2
Grinton 38 C5
Gristhorpe 100 E4
Grosmont 31 D3
Grunsagill 153 A1
Guisborough 8 D7
Gunby 199 D6
Gunnerside 36 F4

H

Hackforth 62 E8
Hackness 74 F5
Hall Garth 184 F6
Halton East 174 C8
Halton Gill 106 E7
Halton West 154 A1
Hambleton
Selby 196 F1
Skipton 174 D8
Hampsthwaite 160 F5
Hanlith 155 A8
Hardgate 139 A1
Hardraw 56 C6
Harlow Hill 222 A8
Harmby 60 E4
Harome 93 C4
Harrogate 219 D1
Harrowgate Hill 3 C8
Harrowgate Village 3 E8
Hartforth 20 D5
Hartley 14 A7
Hartlington 157 C8
Harton 168 C8
Hartwith 160 B8
Haughton Le Skerne 3 F6
Hawes 56 D4
Hawkswick 107 F1
Hawnby 67 E4
Haxby 225 D2
Hazlewood 175 A8
Healaugh 37 F6
Healey 85 E3
Heathfield 136 F6
Heathwaite 45 E8
Hebden 135 A1
Hellifield 154 B3
Hellifield Green 154 B3
Helm 57 D6
Helmsley 92 F7
Helperby 142 A4
Helperthorpe 124 D1
Helwith Bridge 131 D8
Hemingbrough 198 F1
Hemlington 6 F4
Hensall 203 D2
Heslington 229 B1
Hessay 182 C8
Hetton 155 F5
Hew Green 160 D5
Heworth 228 F6
Heyshaw 159 D5
High Bentham 129 B8
High Birstwith 160 D5
High Bradley 173 E4
High Catton 185 D8
High Coniscliffe 2 C5
High Ellington 85 F6
Highfield 199 E7
High Grantley 138 D8
High Harrogate 220 A3
High Hawsker 33 B6
High Hutton 147 B7
High Kilburn 91 B2
High Leven 6 A3
High Marishes 96 B1
High Mowthorpe 149 D7
High Shaw 56 D7
High Stakesby 208 B5
High Worsall 24 A5
Hillam 202 A7
Hilton 6 C2
Hinderwell 11 F7
Hipswell 209 F1
Hirst Courtney 203 F3
Hole Bottom 135 A3
Holgate 227 D3
Hollinthorpe 194 A2
Holly Hill 209 B5
Holme 88 D5
Holme Green 190 F4
Holtby 167 F1
Hopetown 200 C2
Hopgrove 226 D2
Hopperton 163 E3
Hornby
Bedale 62 B8
Croft-on-Tees 23 A4
Horsehouse 83 C4

Horton 171 B5
Horton in Ribblesdale . . 105 C3
Houlsyke 29 F6
Hovingham 119 F6
Howe 88 E3
Howgill 157 E6
Howsham 146 F1
Hubberholme 81 C1
Huby
Harrogate 178 B2
Stillington 144 A4
Hudswell 40 A7
Hummersknott 3 A5
Hunmanby 126 F8
Hunsingore 180 F8
Huntington 225 E3
Hunton 61 E7
Hurgill 209 A7
Hurworth-on-Tees 3 E1
Hurworth Place 3 D1
Hut Green 203 A2
Hutton Bonville 43 C7
Hutton Buscel 98 C7
Hutton Conyers 114 A4
Hutton Gate 8 D6
Hutton Hang 61 D3
Hutton-le-Hole 70 C5
Hutton Mulgrave 12 D1
Hutton Rudby 25 C5
Huttons Ambo 147 B6
Hutton Sessay 116 D7
Hutton Village 8 E4
Hutton Wandesley 182 A5

I

Ickornshaw 187 A6
Ilkley 218 B4
Ilton 85 E1
Ingerthorpe 139 C5
Ingleby Arncliffe 45 B8
Ingleby Barwick 6 B4
Ingleby Cross 45 A7
Ingleby Greenhow 27 C8
Ingleton 103 D3
Ingmanthorpe 180 E5
Inholmes 189 C6
Ireby 102 F6
Irton 99 D6
Ivelet 36 D5

J

Jennyfield 219 A5
Junction 187 F8

K

Keasden 130 A5
Kelbrook 186 A8
Keld 35 E8
Keldholme 70 D1
Keld Houses 136 C2
Kelfield 191 D1
Kellingley 202 C2
Kellington 202 F4
Kennythorpe 147 F5
Kepwick 66 C5
Kettleness 12 D6
Kettlesing 160 C3
Kettlesing Bottom 160 D4
Kettlewell 108 B3
Kexby 185 C6
Key Green 31 A3
Kilburn 91 B2
Kildale 27 E8
Kildwick 187 E8
Killerby 100 C5
Killinghall 161 C5
Kilnsey 134 B6
Kilton Thorpe 10 B8
Kiplin 42 B4
Kippax 194 E1
Kirby Grindalythe 149 E6
Kirby Hill 20 A5
Kirby Knowle 66 C2
Kirby Misperton 95 D2
Kirby Sigston 44 D1
Kirby Underdale 170 A5
Kirby Wiske 88 F3
Kirkbridge 62 F5
Kirkby 26 D5
Kirkby Fleetham 42 D1
Kirkby Hill 141 B7
Kirkby Malham 154 F8
Kirkby Malzeard 112 D5
Kirkby Mills 94 C8
Kirkbymoorside 70 B1
Kirkby Overblow 179 A4
Kirkby Wharfe 190 A3
Kirk Deighton 180 B5
Kirkham 147 A4
Kirk Hammerton 164 C2
Kirklevington 24 F8
Kirklington 88 A4
Kirk Smeaton 206 B3
Knapton 227 A5
Knaresborough 221 A6
Knavesmire 231 A7
Knayton 65 F2

Knedlington 205 E6
Knottingley 201 F3
Knox 219 B7

L

Lane End 171 C2
Lane Ends 187 C6
Laneshaw Bridge 186 C4
Langbar 175 B6
Langbaurgh 7 C5
Langcliffe 131 E3
Langthorne 62 F6
Langthorpe 141 A6
Langthwaite 17 E1
Langtoft 151 D5
Langton 147 F6
Lastingham 70 F5
Laverton 112 D4
Lawkland 130 F5
Lawkland Green 131 A4
Layerthorpe 228 E4
Leake 65 F5
Lealholm 30 B6
Lealholm Side 30 D7
Leathley 177 D2
Leavening 147 E1
Lebberston 100 D5
Leck 102 E7
Ledsham 201 B8
Ledston 200 F7
Ledston Luck 194 F1
Leeming 63 D4
Leeming Bar 63 C5
Leighton 85 C2
Leppington 169 C8
Levisham 72 D5
Leyburn 60 D5
Leysthorpe 93 B1
Lindley 177 C4
Lingdale 9 F7
Lingerfield 162 B6
Lingfield 3 F5
Linton
Grassington 134 D1
Wetherby 180 A1
Linton-on-Ouse 164 E7
Little Airmyn 205 E4
Little Ayton 8 B1
Little Barugh 95 C2
Little Crakehall 62 D5
Little Fencote 63 C8
Little Fenton 196 B6
Little Habton 121 A8
Little Heck 203 D1
Little Hutton 116 B7
Little Ouseburn 164 A7
Little Preston 194 B1
Little Ribston 180 A8
Little Sessay 116 C5
Little Skipwith 192 D1
Little Smeaton
North Cowton 23 C2
Norton 206 C3
Little Stainforth 131 D6
Little Studley 214 C7
Littlethorpe 214 F1
Litton 107 A5
Liverton 10 D6
Liverton Mines 10 C8
Lockton 72 D4
Lodge Green 36 F5
Lofthouse 110 C4
Londonderry 63 E2
Long Drax 205 A6
Long Lease 33 A7
Long Marston 182 A6
Longnewton 5 A7
Long Preston 153 F5
Longscales 160 C4
Loscoe 200 C1
Lothersdale 187 A8
Low Bentham 128 F8
Low Bradley 173 E3
Low Catton 185 C8
Low Coniscliffe 2 F1
Low Dalby 72 F2
Low Dinsdale 4 C1
Low Ellington 86 A6
Lower Altofts 200 A3
Lower Dunsforth 142 A4
Lower Mickletown 200 D6
Lower Westhouse 103 B4
Low Garth 29 F4
Low Gate 138 F6
Low Gatherley 21 D1
Lowgill 128 F3
Low Grantley 112 E1
Low Green 160 A6
Low Hawsker 33 A6
Low Hutton 147 C6
Low Laithe 137 F2
Low Marishes 122 C8
Low Mill 48 E2
Lowna 70 A6
Low Row 37 C4
Low Snaygill 173 D4
Low Town 5 B1
Low Whita 37 D5
Low Worsall 24 A8
Lumb 187 A4
Lumby 195 E1

Lund 198 D3
Lythe 12 E4

M

Malham 133 A1
Maltby 6 C4
Malton 215 C4
Manfield 2 B4
Manor Park 176 B2
Margrove Park 9 D6
Markington 139 D3
Marrick 38 F5
Marsett 57 A1
Marske 39 C7
Marton
  Boroughbridge 141 D1
  Middlesbrough 7 B7
  Pickering 94 F6
Marton-in-the-Forest . . 144 E7
Marton-le-Moor 114 F1
Masham 86 B3
Masongill 103 A6
Maunby 64 D1
Meagill 159 D3
Mearbeck 153 D7
Melmerby
  Carlton 83 F8
  Ripon 114 C7
Melsonby 21 A7
Menethorpe 147 D6
Menthorpe 199 C5
Merrybent 2 E5
Methley 200 B5
Methley Junction 200 A4
Mewith Head 129 E6
Mickleby 12 A4
Micklefield 194 F4
Mickletown 200 B5
Mickley 112 F7
Middlecave 215 A5
Middleham 60 E2
Middlesmoor 110 B5
Middlethorpe 231 B6
Middleton
  Glusburn 187 A6
  Ilkley 218 C7
  Pickering 95 E8
Middleton One Row 4 D3
Middleton-on-Leven 25 D8
Middleton Quernhow . . . 88 B1
Middleton St George 4 B4
Middleton Tyas 21 D5
Milby 141 B6
Mill Dam 129 C6
Mill Hirst 159 F7
Minskip 141 A3
Monk Fryston 202 B8
Monkhill 201 B1
Monkroyd 186 D4
Moor End 188 D8
Moor Monkton 165 A3
Moorsholm 10 B5
Morton-on-Swale 64 A4
Moss 207 D1
Moulton 21 D3
Mount Pleasant 7 B5
Mowden 3 A6
Moxby 144 D5
Muker 36 A5
Murton 184 D7
Muscoates 94 A3
Muston 100 F2
Myton-on-Swale 141 F5

N

Naburn 191 D8
Nappa 171 B8
Nawton 93 E7
Neasham 4 A1
Nesfield 175 B4
Nether Burrow 102 B6
Nether Poppleton 224 A2
Nether Silton 66 B7
Newall 176 F1
Newbiggin
  Askrigg 57 F6
  Filey 101 F5
  Thoralby 82 D8
Newbridge 96 A8
Newby
  Ingleton 104 A1
  Middlesbrough 7 A3
  Ripon 140 D6
  Scarborough 75 E5
Newby Cote 104 B1
Newby Wiske 64 E2
New Earswick 225 D3
New Fryston 201 B6
Newholm 13 A1
New Houses 105 C4
Newland 205 B3
New Micklefield 195 A3
New Park 219 B5
New Road Side 187 B5
New Row 8 F1
Newsham
  Barnard Castle 19 D8
  Thirsk 89 A8

Newsholme
  Asselby 205 E8
  Barnoldswick 171 A6
New Thirsk 211 A3
Newthorpe 195 D3
Newton Kyme 189 B7
Newton-le-Willows 62 B4
Newton Morrell 21 E8
Newton Mulgrave 11 E6
Newton-on-Ouse 165 B6
Newton-on-Rawcliffe . . 72 A5
Newton under Roseberry . .8 B4
Newton upon Derwent . 185 E4
New Town 201 B2
New York 137 F1
Nidd 161 E6
Norby 211 A4
Normanby 94 F4
Normanton 200 C1
Northallerton 210 C5
North Cowton 22 C3
North Deighton 180 B6
North Duffield 199 A8
North Featherstone . . . 200 E1
North Grimston 148 E6
North Ings 119 D1
North Kilvington 89 E8
North Lees 113 E4
North Otterington 64 D4
North Rigton 178 B5
North Stainley 113 D7
Norton 206 E2
Norton-le-Clay 115 C2
Norton-on-Derwent . . . 215 D3
Nosterfield 87 B3
Nun Appleton 190 F3
Nun Monkton 165 A4
Nunnington 93 E2
Nunthorpe
  Middlesbrough 7 D5
  York 231 B8
Nunwick 114 A5

O

Oakdale 161 B2
Oak Tree 4 E4
Oatlands 222 F6
Octon 151 F8
Old Byland 91 F8
Old Malton 215 E7
Old Micklefield 194 F4
Oldstead 91 C3
Old Thirsk 211 C4
Ormesby 7 C8
Osbaldwick 229 C4
Osgodby
  Seamer 100 B7
  Selby 198 C4
Osgodby Common 198 C6
Osmotherley 45 C4
Oswaldkirk 93 A1
Otterburn 154 E4
Oughtershaw 80 C4
Oulston 117 E5
Outhgill 34 A8
Over Burrow 102 B7
Over Silton 66 B8
Overton 165 F2
Overtown 102 C7
Oxton 190 A6

P

Padside 159 B6
Padside Green 159 C6
Painsthorpe 170 B5
Pannal 222 E3
Pannal Ash 222 B5
Park 186 F5
Park End 7 B8
Parlington 194 E6
Pateley Bridge 137 D4
Patrick Brompton 62 C5
Pickering 95 E6
Pickhill 88 C6
Picton 24 D6
Piercebridge 2 A6
Place Newton 123 C3
Pockley 69 B1
Pollington 207 F6
Poole 201 F5
Port Mulgrave 11 F8
Potterton 188 C1
Potto 25 D2
Preston-on-Tees 5 F7
Preston-under-
  Scar 59 E6
Primrose Valley 101 C1

R

Rainton 114 E6
Ramsgill 110 E1
Raskelf 116 E2
Rathmell 153 C6
Ravenscar 54 A8
Ravenseat 15 C2
Ravensworth 20 A7
Raw 33 B4

Rawcliffe
  Carlton 205 A1
  York 224 E2
Raydale 57 A1
Raygill 186 E8
Red Hill 201 A4
Redmire 59 C6
Reeth 38 B6
Reighton 127 D6
Riccall 198 A8
Richmond 209 C7
Rievaulx 92 B8
Rillington 122 F5
Ripley 161 C7
Ripon 214 E5
Risplith 138 E7
Robin Hood's Bay 33 D4
Roecliffe 140 F4
Romanby 210 B3
Rookwith 62 A1
Rosedale Abbey 49 E3
Rossett Green 222 D5
Roundhill Village 5 F5
Rowden 160 F4
Roxby 11 C7
Rudby 25 D5
Rufforth 182 C6
Runswick Bay 12 A7
Rushton 98 D6
Ruswarp 208 B3
Rylstone 156 B5
Ryther 190 F1
Ryton 121 F6

S

Sadberge 4 B8
St John's 194 F8
Salton 94 D3
Sandhutton 89 A4
Sand Hutton 168 B5
Sandsend 13 A3
Satron 36 D4
Sawdon 98 C7
Sawley 138 F6
Saxton 195 D8
Scackleton 119 C4
Scagglethorpe 122 D3
Scalby 75 D6
Scaling 11 A4
Scaling Dam 11 A4
Scampston 123 A6
Scarborough 213 B5
Scarthingwell 195 F7
Scawton 91 E6
Scorton 41 F7
Scotton
  Harrogate 162 A6
  Richmond 40 F2
Scrayingham 168 F7
Scriven 162 D5
Scruton 63 D7
Seamer
  Middlesbrough 6 F1
  Scarborough 99 E6
Seave Green 47 A7
Sedbusk 56 E6
Selby 232 C6
Selly Hill 32 A8
Selside 105 A6
Sessay 116 B6
Settle 131 E3
Settrington 122 D1
Sexhow 25 D4
Sharow 214 F6
Shaw Mills 138 F1
Sherburn 124 D8
Sherburn in Elmet 195 E5
Sheriff Hutton 145 C5
Shipton 165 F5
Sicklinghall 179 E3
Silpho 74 E7
Silsden 174 C2
Simonstone 56 D6
Sinderby 88 C4
Sinnington 95 A8
Skeeby 21 A1
Skelton 224 C6
Skelton on Ure 140 E7
Skerne Park 3 C3
Skewsby 119 A1
Skipton 216 F4
Skipton-on-Swale 88 E2
Skipwith 192 E1
Skirethorns 134 C2
Skirpenbeck 169 A4
Skyreholme 157 E7
Slapewath 9 C6
Sledmere 150 A4
Sleights 32 A6
Slingsby 120 C6
Small Banks 174 F3
Smelthouses 137 F3
Snainton 98 A5
Snaith 204 C1
Snape 87 A7
Sneaton 32 D6
Sneatonthorpe 32 F5
Sockburn 23 C6
Sourby 176 D8
South Bank 228 B1
South Duffield 199 A4

South Holme 120 B8
South Kilvington 211 B7
South Loftus 10 E8
South Milford 195 F1
South Otterington 64 F2
South Stainley 139 E2
Sowerby 211 B1
Spacey Houses 223 A2
Spaunton 70 E4
Speeton 127 F5
Spennithorne 60 F3
Spofforth 179 E5
Sproxton 92 F4
Stackhouse 131 D4
Stainburn 177 F3
Stainforth 131 E6
Stainsacre 32 F7
Stainton
  Marrick 39 C3
  Middlesbrough 6 D5
Staintondale 54 B5
Stalling Busk 81 B8
Stamford Bridge 168 E2
Stanwick-St-John 1 E2
Stape 3 A2
Stapleton 71 F8
Starbeck 220 C4
Starbotton 107 F5
Staupes 160 C4
Staveley 140 F1
Staxton 99 E2
Stead 176 A1
Stean 110 A4
Stearsby 118 F2
Stillingfleet 191 C3
Stillington 144 C6
Stirton 216 C6
Stock 171 C3
Stockton on the Forest . 167 D3
Stokesley 26 D7
Stonegate 30 D8
Stonegrave 119 D8
Stone House 78 F8
Stranghow 9 F6
Street 29 F3
Street Houses 190 C8
Streetlam 42 F5
Strensall 167 A7
Strensall Camp 167 B6
Studfold 105 D1
Studley Roger 113 D1
Studley Royal 113 C1
Stutton 189 D4
Suffield 75 A5
Summerbridge 138 A1
Summerscales 158 C1
Sutton 201 F4
Sutton Howgrave 87 F1
Sutton-in-Craven 187 F6
Sutton-on-the-Forest . . 144 C3
Sutton-under-
  Whitestonecliffe 90 E5
Sutton upon Derwent . . 185 C4
Swainby 45 B8
Swaledale 37 C4
Swartha 174 D1
Swathgill 119 B4
Swetton 111 F4
Swillington 194 A1
Swillington Common . . 194 A3
Swincliffe 160 E4
Swinden 154 C1
Swinithwaite 59 C4
Swinton
  Malton 121 C4
  Masham 86 B2

T

Tadcaster 189 D6
Tame Bridge 26 A7
Tang 160 D4
Tang Hall 228 F5
Tanton 7 C1
Temple Hirst 203 E4
Terrington 119 F1
Theakston 87 E8
The Mount 214 D3
The Spa 213 B4
Thimbleby 45 A2
Thirlby 90 E7
Thirn 86 B8
Thirsk 211 C2
Thixendale 170 E7
Tholthorpe 142 D5
Thoralby 58 E1
Thorganby 193 B4
Thorgill 49 C3
Thorlby 216 B6
Thormanby 116 F5
Thornaby-on-Tees 6 A7
Thornborough 87 C2
Thorns 35 E7
Thornthwaite 159 D6
Thornton 6 E4
Thornton-in-Craven . . . 172 A3
Thornton in Lonsdale . . 103 C4
Thornton-le-Beans 65 B5
Thornton-le-Clay 146 A4
Thornton-le-Dale 96 D5
Thornton-le-Moor 65 B3
Thornton-le-Street 65 D1

Thornton Rust 58 B4
Thornton Steward 61 D1
Thornton Watlass 86 D8
Thorp Arch 188 F8
Thorpe 156 F8
Thorpe Bassett 123 A4
Thorpe Underwood . . . 164 C6
Thorpe Willoughby 197 C2
Threshfield 134 C2
Thrintoft 64 A8
Throxenby 212 A2
Thruscross 159 A5
Thwaite 35 F5
Thwing 126 B1
Timble 176 D7
Tockwith 181 D7
Tollerton 143 A3
Tollesby 7 A6
Topcliffe 115 B7
Tosside 152 F3
Toulston 189 B7
Town Head 174 C1
Towthorpe
  Sledmere 149 D1
  York 167 B5
Towton 189 E2
Trawden 186 B1
Tunstall
  Catterick 41 B2
  Cowan Bridge 102 B4

U

Uckerby 21 E1
Ugglebarnby 32 C6
Ugthorpe 11 F2
Ulleskelf 190 C2
Ulshaw 61 A2
Upper Dunsforth 142 A2
Upper Helmsley 168 B3
Upper Poppleton 165 F1
Upsall 66 B2
Ure Bank 214 D7
Urlay Nook 5 B5
Urra 47 A8

V

Vicar's Green 39 F7

W

Waithwith Banks 40 B5
Wake Hill 111 F1
Walden Stubbs 206 F3
Walkerville 41 A4
Walmgate Stray 228 F1
Walshford 180 D8
Walton 181 A2
Warlaby 64 D6
Warsill 138 C4
Warthermarske 86 A1
Warthill 167 F2
Washfold 18 D1
Wass 91 F2
Water Fryston 201 C5
Wath
  Hovingham 119 F6
  Pateley Bridge 137 A6
  Ripon 114 A7
Weaverthorpe 124 E1
Weeton 178 C1
Welburn
  Pickering 94 A7
  Westow 146 B7
Welbury 24 B1
Well 87 A4
Wennington 102 B1
Wensley 60 A4
Wensleydale 57 A5
Wescoe Hill 178 B1
West Appleton 41 C1
West Ayton 99 A7
West Barnby 12 C3
West Burton 58 F1
West Cliff 208 B7
Westerdale 28 E4
Westfield 232 C4
West Field 227 A2
West Garforth 194 B3
West Haddlesey 203 A5
West Harlsey 44 D5
West Heslerton 123 F7
Westhouse 103 C4
West Knapton 123 B6
West Layton 20 A8
West Lilling 145 C4
West Lutton 150 B8
West Marton 171 F5
West Ness 94 B1
Weston 176 E2
Westow 147 B4
West Rounton 24 D2
West Scrafton 83 F6
West Stonesdale 15 E1
West Tanfield 87 A1
West Witton 59 E3
Wetherby 180 D4
Wharfe 131 A8
Wharram le Street 149 A4

Whashton 20 A5
Whashton Green 20 A5
Whaw 17 B3
Wheldale 201 B5
Wheldrake 192 F8
Whenby 145 B8
Whinfield 3 F8
Whitby 208 C6
Whitewall Corner 215 C1
Whitley 207 A7
Whitley Thorpe 206 F7
Whittington 102 A7
Whitwell 42 B6

Whitwell-on-the-Hill .. 146 E4
Whitwood 200 C3
Whixley 164 A5
Whorlton 25 E1
Wiganthorpe 119 E3
Wigginton 166 D5
Wigglesworth 153 C4
Wighill 181 D1
Wilberfoss 185 F6
Willerby 99 C2
Wilsill 137 E3
Wilton 97 A5
Winewall 186 B2

Winksley 112 F2
Winsley 160 D8
Winterburn 155 D5
Winton 44 C3
Wintringham 123 C4
Wistow 197 D6
Wold Newton 126 A3
Wombleton 93 F7
Womersley 206 C6
Woodale 83 A2
Woodhall Selby 199 B2
  Thoralby 58 B5
Woodhouse 200 A1

Woodlands 220 C1
Wood Row 200 A6
Woodthorpe 230 C7
Worton 57 F5
Wray 128 A6
Wrayton 102 B3
Wrelton 71 C1
Wressle 199 D2
Wycoller 186 C2
Wydra 160 A1
Wykeham
  Malton 122 B6
  Seamer 98 E6

Y

Yafforth 43 C1
Yarm 5 D3
Yearsley 118 C5
Yedingham 97 D2
Yockenthwaite 81 A1
York 233 B3
Youlthorpe 169 C2
Youlton 142 E2

A

Abber La LS24 . . . . .182 A2
Abbeville Ave **1** YO21 . .208 B6
Abbey Cl **12** LS29 . . . . . .175 A4
Abbey Crags Way
　HG5 . . . . .221 C3
Abbey Gdns WF8 . . . . . .201 B2
Abbey Hill BD23 . . . . . . .155 C5
Abbey Inf Sch DL3 . . . . . . .3 B5
Abbey Jun Sch DL3 . . . . . . .3 B5
Abbey La YO22 . . . . . . .208 A7
Abbey Leisure Ctr
　YO8 . . . . .232 C5
Abbey Mews WF8 . . . . . .201 B2
Abbey Mill Gdns HG5 . . .221 C3
Abbey Mill View HG5 . . .221 C3
Abbey Pl **9** YO8 . . . . . . .232 D5
Abbey Rd Darlington DL3 . .3 B5
　Knaresborough HG5 . . . .221 B3
　Sadberge DL2 . . . . .4 C7
Abbey St YO30 . . . . . . .228 A7
Abbey Terr **16** YO21 . . . .208 D7
Abbey Wlk
　Pontefract WF8 . . . . . . .201 B2
　Selby YO8 . . . . .232 C5
Abbey Wlk Sh Ctr
　YO8 . . . . .232 C6
Abbey Yd YO8 . . . . .232 C5
Abbeyfield Dr **10** TS16 . . . .5 D5
Abbot St YO31 . . . . .233 C4
Abbot's Garth YO12 . . . . .99 D6
Abbot's Rd Selby YO8 . . .232 E3
　Whitby YO22 . . . . .208 A5
Abbot's Wlk YO22 . . . . . .208 E5
Abbots Gait YO32 . . . . . .225 F6
Abbots Way HG5 . . . . . . .221 C3
Abbotsford Rd YO10 . . . .228 E3
Abbotsway YO31 . . . . . . .228 E8
Abbotts Cl LS25 . . . . . . .194 F8
Abbotts Ct YO17 . . . . . . .215 E4
Abelton Gr **33** YO12 . . . .166 E5
Aberbran Ct **41** TS17 . . . . .5 F4
Aberdeen La **19** YO11 . . .213 A6
Aberdeen Pl **20** YO11 . . .213 A6
Aberdeen Rd DL1 . . . . .3 E8
Aberdeen St **17** YO11 . . .213 A6
Aberdeen Terr **21** YO11 . .213 A6
Aberdeen Wlk **16** YO11 . .213 A6
Aberford CE Prim Sch
　LS25 . . . . .194 F8
Aberford Rd
　Barwick in Elmet & Scholes
　LS15 . . . . .194 C8
　Bramham cum Oglethorpe
　LS23 . . . . .188 E5
　Garforth LS25 . . . . .194 D4
Abrahams Quay YO22 . . .208 E5
Abram's View YO11 . . . . .213 B2
Acacia Ave YO32 . . . . . . .225 E4
Acacia Dr WF10 . . . . . . .201 B4
Academy Gdns DL2 . . . . . . .1 D8
Acaster Ave YO23 . . . . . .191 A4
Acaster Dr LS25 . . . . . . .194 D3
Acaster La
　Acaster Malbis YO23 . . . .231 B1
　Acaster Selby YO23 . . . . .191 A4
Accommodation Rd
　YO25 . . . . .151 D6
Acer Cl **4** BD20 . . . . . . .187 F7
Acklam Grange Sch TS5 . .6 D7
Acklam Rd TS17 . . . . .6 C8
Acklam Whin Prim Sch
　TS5 . . . . .6 D6
Ackton La WF7 . . . . .200 D1
Ackton Pasture La
　WF7 . . . . .200 D3
Ackton Pastures Prim Sch
　WF10 . . . . .200 D3
Ackworth St **3** YO12 . . .212 E4
Acomb Prim Sch
　YO24 . . . . .227 E3
Acomb Rd YO24 . . . . . . .227 E3
Acomb Wood Cl YO24 . . .230 C7
Acomb Wood Dr YO24 . . .230 B7
Acorn Cl **6** Barlby YO8 . .198 B4
　Middleton St George DL2 . . .4 D4
Acorn Way
　Gateforth YO8 . . . . .197 B1
　York YO24 . . . . .230 D7
Acre Fold **21** LS29 . . . . .174 F4
Acre Mdw **1** BD22 . . . . .187 B6
Acre Rd **2** BD22 . . . . . .187 B6
Acres Cl **24** YO62 . . . . . .92 F6
Acres La Brompton YO13 . .98 C4
　Helmsley YO62 . . . . .93 B4
　Scrayingham YO41 . . . . .169 B8
Acres The
　Addingham LS29 . . . . . . .175 A5
　Glusburn BD20 . . . . . . .187 E6
　Stokesley TS9 . . . . .26 C6
Acresfield **6** BB8 . . . . . .186 A3
Adam's Field La YO61 . . .117 C4
Adcott Rd TS5 . . . . .6 E7
Addingham Prim Sch
　LS29 . . . . .174 F5
Addingham Wharfedale Rd
　LS29 . . . . .174 E4
Addison Ave **18** WF6 . . .200 B1
Addison Rd TS9 . . . . .8 A1
Addison Villas HG3 . . . . .219 A8
Addlethorpe La LS22 . . . .179 C5

Adelaide Rd
　Middlesbrough TS7 . . . . . .7 B6
　6 Norton DN6 . . . . . . .206 E2
Adelaide St **3** YO23 . . . .228 B2
Adlington Cl **8** YO32 . . .167 A7
Admirals Ct YO7 . . . . . . .211 A2
Admirals' Ct YO7 . . . . . .211 A2
Agar St YO31 . . . . .233 C3
Agnes Ing La LA2 . . . . . .128 A7
Agnesgate HG4 . . . . .214 D5
Aikengill Rd LA2 . . . . . . .129 A4
Ailcey Rd HG4 . . . . .214 D5
Ainderby Rd DL7 . . . . . . .210 B2
Ainderby Steeple CE Prim Sch
　DL7 . . . . .64 A7
Ainsford Way TS7 . . . . . . .7 D8
Ainstable Rd TS7 . . . . . . .7 D8
Ainsty Ave YO24 . . . . . . .230 F8
Ainsty Dr **2** LS22 . . . . . .180 C4
Ainsty Gr YO24 . . . . .230 F8
Ainsty Rd
　Harrogate HG1 . . . . .219 F4
　Wetherby LS22 . . . . . . .180 C4
Ainsty View
　Acklam YO17 . . . . .169 E8
　Whixley YO26 . . . . .164 A4
Ainsworth Way TS7 . . . . . .7 D8
Ainthorpe La YO21 . . . . . .29 C7
Aintree Ct
　9 Darlington DL1 . . . . . . .3 F6
　York YO24 . . . . .230 F8
Aire Cres BD20 . . . . .187 E7
Aire Rd LS22 . . . . .180 B4
Aire St Castleford WF10 . .200 E4
　Glusburn BD20 . . . . . . .187 F7
　Knottingley WF11 . . . . . .202 A3
Aire Valley Cl BD20 . . . . .173 D3
Aire Valley Dr BD20 . . . . .173 D3
Aire Valley Mount
　WF10 . . . . .201 A4
Aire View BD23 . . . . .216 C1
Aire View Inf Sch
　BD20 . . . . .174 C1
Airedale Ave
　Gargrave BD23 . . . . . . .155 D1
　Skipton BD23 . . . . .217 B4
Airedale Dr WF10 . . . . . .201 B5
Airedale High Sch
　WF10 . . . . .201 B4
Airedale Inf Sch WF10 . . .201 B4
Airedale Mews **1** BD23 . .216 E3
Airedale Rd
　Castleford WF10 . . . . . .201 A4
　Scotton DL9 . . . . .40 D4
Airedale Terr BD23 . . . . .216 E3
Airedale Trading Pk
　BD20 . . . . .187 F8
Airedale View **1** BD20 . .187 F8
Aireside Ave BD20 . . . . . .173 D1
Aireside Terr BD20 . . . . . .173 D2
Aireville Dr BD20 . . . . . . .174 C1
Aireville Grange BD23 . . .216 D5
Aireville Sch BD23 . . . . . .216 D4
Aireville Swimming Baths
　BD23 . . . . .216 D4
Aireyholme La TS9 . . . . . .8 B2
Airmyn Pk Prim Sch
　DN14 . . . . .205 E4
Airmyn Rd DN14 . . . . . . .205 D3
Airy Hill YO21 . . . . .208 D5
Airy Hill Com Prim Sch
　YO21 . . . . .208 D5
Airy Hill La TS12 . . . . . . .9 D8
Aiskew Leeming Bar CE Prim Sch
　DL7 . . . . .63 C4
Aislabie Cl HG4 . . . . .214 A5
Aislabie Garth HG4 . . . . .214 A5
Aislaby Carr La YO18 . . . .95 C7
Aislaby La Aislaby YO21 . .32 A8
　Aislaby YO18 . . . . .95 C6
Aislaby Rd TS16 . . . . .5 D4
Aismunderby Cl HG4 . . . .214 C3
Aismunderby Rd HG4 . . . .214 C4
Aisne Rd DL9 . . . . .209 C1
Aketon Rd WF10 . . . . . . .200 D1
Alanbrooke Com Prim Sch
　YO7 . . . . .89 A1
Alanbrooke Ind Est
　YO7 . . . . .115 B8
Alandale Cres LS25 . . . . .194 B3
Alandale Rd LS25 . . . . . .194 B4
Albany Ave HG1 . . . . . . .219 E5
Albany Rd
　Harrogate HG1 . . . . .219 E5
　Middlesbrough TS7 . . . . . .7 B6
Albany St **3** YO30 . . . . .227 F5
Albany Wlk LS29 . . . . . . .218 A3
Albatross Way DL1 . . . . . .3 E5
Albemarle Back Rd **10**
　YO11 . . . . .212 F6
Albemarle Cres **18**
　YO11 . . . . .213 A6
Albemarle Rd YO23 . . . . .228 B2
Albemarle Dr **3** DL9 . . . .40 F5
Albert Cl **1** YO32 . . . . . .228 F8
Albert Hill BD24 . . . . . . .131 E2
Albert Pl
　Harrogate HG1 . . . . .220 C4
　1 Whitby YO21 . . . . . .208 D7
Albert Rd
　Eaglescliffe TS16 . . . . . . .5 E5
　12 Glusburn BD20 . . . .187 E7
　Harrogate HG1 . . . . .219 E5
　1 Scarborough YO12 . . .213 A7
Albert Simmons Way St **40**
　LS29 . . . . .176 C1
Albert Sq BD23 . . . . .216 F4
Albert St **33** Earby BB18 . .172 A1

Albert St continued
　Glusburn BD20 . . . . . . .187 F7
　Harrogate HG1 . . . . .219 D2
　Normanton South WF6 . . .200 B2
　8 Scarborough YO12 . . .213 A7
　York YO10 . . . . .233 C1
Albert Terr
　5 Harrogate HG1 . . . . .219 D1
　Skipton BD23 . . . . .216 F4
Albion Ave YO26 . . . . . . .227 B6
Albion Cres **3** YO11 . . . .213 A4
Albion Pl **14** YO21 . . . . .208 D6
Albion Rd **25** Earby BB18 .172 A1
　Scarborough YO11 . . . . .213 A4
Albion St Boosbeck TS12 . . .9 E7
　Boston Spa LS23 . . . . . .188 E7
　Castleford WF10 . . . . . .200 E4
　28 Earby BB18 . . . . . . .172 A1
　York YO1 . . . . .233 B1
Albion Terr
　9 Boston Spa LS23 . . . .188 E7
　23 Whitby YO21 . . . . . .208 D6
Alcelina Ct YO23 . . . . . . .233 B1
Alcuin Ave YO10 . . . . . . .229 A4
Alcuin Way YO10 . . . . . . .229 A4
　York YO32 . . . . .225 D4
Almond Tree Ave
　Carlton DN14 . . . . .204 C3
　Malton YO17 . . . . .215 D6
Aldborough Gate **13**
　YO51 . . . . .141 B4
Aldborough Way YO26 . . .227 F5
Aldbrough & Boroughbridge
　Com Prim Sch YO51 . . . .141 B4
Aldenham Rd TS14 . . . . . .8 E5
Alder Ave HG5 . . . . .221 C6
Alder Carr La YO18 . . . . . .49 E2
Alder Hill St **1** BB18 . . . .172 B1
Alder Rd HG1 . . . . .219 F5
Alder Way YO32 . . . . . . .225 D2
Alderley Ct YO32 . . . . . . .225 E3
Alderman Leach Prim Sch
　DL3 . . . . .3 B6
Alders Rd YO18 . . . . .49 C4
Aldersley Ave BD23 . . . . .217 B3
Alderson Cres YO12 . . . . .99 E7
Alderson Rd HG2 . . . . . . .222 E8
Alderson Sq HG2 . . . . . . .222 E8
Aldersyde YO24 . . . . .230 E7
Aldersyde Ct YO24 . . . . . .230 E7
Aldersyde Mews YO24 . . .230 E7
Aldreth Gr YO23 . . . . . . .228 C2
Aldridge Rd TS3 . . . . .7 B8
Aldwark YO1 . . . . .233 C3
Aldwych Cl TS6 . . . . .7 E8
Alexander Ave
　6 East Ayton/West Ayton
　YO13 . . . . .99 B8
　York YO31 . . . . .225 E2
Alexander Cl YO7 . . . . . . .211 C4
Alexander Rd DL9 . . . . . .209 C2
Alexandra Cres **10** LS29 .218 A4
Alexandra Ct
　Skipton BD23 . . . . .216 F2
　York YO10 . . . . .228 E4
Alexandra Gr HG4 . . . . . .221 B7
Alexandra Pk YO12 . . . . .212 D5
Alexandra Pk Rd HG5 . . .221 C7
Alexandra Pl
　Ilkley LS29 . . . . .218 A4
　3 Knaresborough HG5 . .221 B8
Alexandra Rd
　Harrogate HG1 . . . . .219 D3
　Strensall YO32 . . . . .167 A6
Alexandra Terr BD23 . . . .216 F2
Alexandra Ville BD23 . . . .216 F2
Alexandra Way DL10 . . . .209 C2
Alexandria Dr DL2 . . . . . .4 D4
Alfreda Terr **1** YO22 . . . .208 E6
Alga Terr YO11 . . . . .213 A4
Algarth Rd YO31 . . . . . . .229 B7
Algarth Rise YO31 . . . . . .229 B7
All Saint's Rd **1** YO12 . .212 F4
All Saints CE Jun & Inf Sch
　WF7 . . . . .200 D1
All Saints CE Prim Sch
　HG3 . . . . .179 A4
All Saints RC Prim Sch
　YO7 . . . . .211 B2
All Saints' RC Sch
　YO24 . . . . .233 A1
Allan St Darlington DL1 . . .3 D6
　2 York YO30 . . . . .228 C7
Allans Ct DL10 . . . . .209 D6
Allanson Gr YO24 . . . . . .227 E2
Allen Cl YO10 . . . . .229 A4
Allen Gr TS9 . . . . .26 B7
Allenby Rd
　20 Helmsley YO62 . . . . .92 F6
　Hipswell DL9 . . . . .209 C1
Allendale YO24 . . . . .230 D8
Allendale Rd TS7 . . . . .7 D8
Allens W Sta TS16 . . . . . .5 D5
Allensway TS17 . . . . .6 C7
Allerdale Cl YO7 . . . . . . .211 C4
Allerston La YO18 . . . . . . .97 C4
Allerston Way **5** TS14 . . .8 F7
Allerton Balk TS15 . . . . . .5 D2
Allerton Bywater Prim Sch
　WF10 . . . . .200 D7
Allerton Dr **2** YO26 . . . .165 F1
Allerton La HG5 . . . . .163 D4
Allerton Mews HG1 . . . . .219 E1
Allerton Pk House★
　HG5 . . . . .163 D4
Allerton Sch E House
　DL6 . . . . .210 E6
Allerton Wath Rd DL6 . . . .65 D4
Allertonshire W House Sch
　DL6 . . . . .210 D6
Allhallowgate HG4 . . . . . .214 C5
Allington Dr YO31 . . . . . .229 B6

Allington Way
　Darlington DL1 . . . . .3 F5
　Great Burdon DL1 . . . . . .4 A5
Allison Ave TS17 . . . . . . .101 B4
Allison St TS14 . . . . .8 E6
Allotments La YO61 . . . . .143 F3
Alloway Gr TS8 . . . . .6 F5
Alma Gdns HG4 . . . . .214 D4
Alma Gr YO10 . . . . .228 D2
Alma Par **2** YO11 . . . . .212 F5
Alma Pl DL7 . . . . .209 C2
Alma Rd BB8 . . . . .186 B3
Alma Sq **3** YO11 . . . . . .212 F5
Alma Terr Selby YO8 . . . .232 C6
　York YO10 . . . . .228 D2
Alma Way **2** YO18 . . . . .96 A6
Almery Terr YO30 . . . . . . .233 A3
Hambleton YO8 . . . . . . .197 B1
Almond Cl **7** Filey YO14 .101 B4
Almond Ct **4** TS4 . . . . . . .6 F8
Almond Gr **11** Filey YO14 .101 B4
　Northallerton DL7 . . . . . .210 D3
　Scarborough YO12 . . . . .212 D5
　York YO32 . . . . .225 D4
Almond Tree Ave
　Carlton DN14 . . . . .204 C3
　Malton YO17 . . . . .215 D6
Almond Wlk **6** YO11 . . . .213 A1
Almscliffe Dr LS17 . . . . . .178 B2
Almscliffe Garth LS17 . . . .178 B2
Almsford Ave HG2 . . . . . .222 E6
Almsford Bank HG2 . . . . .222 E5
Almsford Cl HG2 . . . . . . .222 F6
Almsford Dr
　Harrogate HG2 . . . . .222 F6
　York YO26 . . . . .227 C5
Almsford End HG2 . . . . . .222 E6
Almsford Oval HG2 . . . . . .222 F6
Almsford Pl HG2 . . . . . . .222 F6
Almsford Rd
　Harrogate HG2 . . . . .222 F6
　York YO26 . . . . .227 C5
Almsford Wlk HG2 . . . . . .222 F6
Almshouse Hill **1** LS23 . .188 E5
Alne Prim Sch YO61 . . . . .142 F4
Alne Rd
　Easingwold YO61 . . . . . .143 B8
　Tollerton YO61 . . . . .143 A3
Alne Terr YO10 . . . . .228 E2
Alness Dr YO30 . . . . .230 B7
Alpine Ct **5** WF10 . . . . . .200 B3
Altofts La WF10 . . . . .200 B3
Altofts Rd WF6 . . . . .200 A1
Alum House La TS9 . . . . . .26 B2
Alverton Cl YO17 . . . . . . .121 B7
Alverton Dr DL3 . . . . .3 B8
Alverton Inf Sch DL6 . . . .210 D4
Alverton La DL7 . . . . .210 D4
Alvin Wlk **9** YO41 . . . . . .185 B2
Alvis Gr YO10 . . . . .229 D4
Alwyn Rd DL3 . . . . .3 D8
Alwyne Dr YO30 . . . . . . .224 E1
Alwyne Gr YO30 . . . . . . .224 E1
Amber Ct YO31 . . . . .233 C4
Amber St YO31 . . . . .233 C4
Amberly St **4** YO26 . . . .227 E5
Amble Cl YO62 . . . . .70 B2
Ambler St WF10 . . . . .200 E4
Ambler's La YO30 . . . . . .165 F7
Ambleside Ave
　10 Barnoldswick BB18 . .171 D2
　York YO10 . . . . .229 B4
Ambleside Gr TS5 . . . . . . .6 E8
Ambleside Wlk DL1 . . . . . .3 D4
Ambrey Cl **16** YO14 . . . .126 F8
Ambrose Rd HG4 . . . . . . .214 C4
Ambrose St YO10 . . . . . . .228 D1
America La BD20 . . . . . . .187 D1
Amesbury Cres TS8 . . . . . .6 F5
Amiens Cres DL9 . . . . . . .209 D1
Amotherby Com Prim Sch
　YO17 . . . . .121 A4
Amotherby La YO17 . . . . .121 A6
Amplecarr YO61 . . . . .117 B5
Ampleforth Coll YO62 . . . .92 F4
Ampleforth Coll Jun Sch
　YO62 . . . . .118 F7
Ampleforth St Benedicts RC
　Prim Sch YO62 . . . . .92 C4
Amy Johnson Way
　YO30 . . . . .225 A3
Anchor Rd **2** HG1 . . . . . .220 A3
Anchorage Hill DL10 . . . .209 D7
Anchorage La DL7 . . . . . .210 C5
Anchorage Way YO21 . . . .208 C5
Anchorite **4** YO18 . . . . . .95 F7
Ancress Wlk YO23 . . . . . .233 A1
Ancroft Cl YO1 . . . . .233 C1
Anderson Gr **6** YO24 . . . .227 F2
Anderson St **6** WF8 . . . .201 B1
Anderton St **18** BD20 . . .187 E8
Andrew Dr **4** YO32 . . . . .225 F1
Andrew La YO18 . . . . .71 B4
Anfield Ct **8** DL1 . . . . . . .3 F6
Angel Ct **8** TS9 . . . . .26 C7
Angel Yd **1** YO21 . . . . . .208 D6
Angelica Ct **12** HG3 . . . .161 B3
Angram Cl YO30 . . . . . . .224 F1
Angram La
　Barlby with Osgodby
　YO19 . . . . .198 A6
　Muker DL11 . . . . .35 E6
　Tollerton YO61 . . . . .143 B3
Angram Rd YO26 . . . . . . .182 A5
Angrove Cl TS9 . . . . .7 F1
Angrove Dr TS9 . . . . .7 F1
Annan Cl YO24 . . . . .230 C6

Annandale Ct **10** LS29 . .218 B4
Annandale Gr **1** YO13 . . .75 D5
Annas Garth DL8 . . . . . . .60 F4
Anne St YO23 . . . . .228 C2
Annie St YO8 . . . . .232 C6
Annumhills Rd YO8 . . . . .199 D7
Anserdale La YO62 . . . . . .70 E5
Anson Croft **5** YO8 . . . . .196 E1
Anson Dr YO10 . . . . .231 D8
Anthea Dr YO31 . . . . .225 E1
Anthony La HG4 . . . . .114 E1
Anvil Sq **3** DL11 . . . . . . .38 B6
Anvil Way DL7 . . . . .22 C2
Anzio Rd DL9 . . . . .209 C1
Apedale Rd
　Castle Bolton with East &
　West Bolton DL8 . . . . . . .37 F1
　Redmire DL8 . . . . .59 C8
Apley Cl HG2 . . . . .220 A1
Apollo St **9** YO10 . . . . . .228 E3
Apple Garth
　10 Easingwold YO61 . . .117 D1
　15 Poppleton YO26 . . . .165 F1
Apple Tree Gdns **2**
　LS29 . . . . .175 C2
Apple Tree La **4** LS25 . . .194 D1
Apple Tree Mews **5**
　LS25 . . . . .194 D1
Apple Tree Wlk **7** LS25 . .194 D1
Appleby Ave HG5 . . . . . . .220 D8
Appleby Cres HG5 . . . . . .220 D8
Appleby Ct HG5 . . . . .220 D8
Appleby Gate HG5 . . . . . .220 D7
Appleby Glade YO32 . . . .225 D7
Appleby Gn HG5 . . . . . . .220 D8
Appleby Glade YO32 . . . .225 D7
Appleby La
　Aldbrough DL11 . . . . .1 F1
　Kirkby Malzeard HG4 . . . .112 A4
Appleby Pl **2** YO31 . . . . .229 A5
Appleby Way HG5 . . . . . .220 D7
Appleby Wlk HG5 . . . . . . .220 D8
Applecroft Rd
　Selby YO8 . . . . .232 A4
　York YO31 . . . . .229 B7
Applefields Sch YO31 . . . .229 B5
Applegarth
　Barnoldswick BB18 . . . . .171 E2
　Coulby Newham TS8 . . . . .7 A4
Applegarth Ct DL7 . . . . . .210 D5
Applegarth Prim Sch
　DL7 . . . . .210 D4
Applegarth St **18** BB18 . .172 A1
Appleton Ct YO23 . . . . . .230 F3
Appleton La
　Appleton-le-Street with
　Easthorpe YO17 . . . . . . .120 F4
　Coneysthorpe YO60 . . . . .120 E2
Appleton Rd YO23 . . . . . .231 A3
Appleton Roebuck Prim Sch
　1 YO23 . . . . .190 F5
Appleton Wiske Com Prim
　Sch DL6 . . . . .24 B3
Appletree Dr YO8 . . . . . . .196 E1
Appletree Way
　Malton YO17 . . . . .215 B4
　10 Sherburn in Elmet LS25 195 F4
Appletreewick Stone Circ★
　BD23 . . . . .135 E2
Appley Cl TS16 . . . . .5 E7
Apron La HG3 . . . . .140 B2
Apsley Way TS17 . . . . .5 F5
Arbour The
　4 Glusburn BD20 . . . . .173 E1
　Ilkley LS29 . . . . .218 A6
Arbour Way YO17 . . . . . .215 E4
ARC★ YO1 . . . . .233 C2
Arc The LS29 . . . . .218 B4
Arcade Sh Ctr★ HG1 . . . .214 C5
Archbishop Holgate's Sch
　YO10 . . . . .229 B3
Archbishop of York CE Jun
　Sch YO23 . . . . .231 A4
Archer La HG3 . . . . .140 B3
Archer Rd DL2 . . . . .4 D3
Archers Gn The DL10 . . . .41 C7
Archers Mdw HG5 . . . . . .221 F5
Archie St **3** HG1 . . . . . . .219 C5
Arden Ct DL7 . . . . .210 D5
Arden La YO62 . . . . .92 B8
Arden Mews DL7 . . . . . . .210 D5
Arena View **12** DL10 . . . .41 D5
Arenhall Cl **2** YO32 . . . .225 C8
Argam Dikes★ YO25 . . . .127 B2
Argam La YO25 . . . . .126 F1
Argill DL8 . . . . .60 F5
Argyle Rd YO21 . . . . .208 C2
Argyle St YO23 . . . . .228 B1
Arkendale La HG5 . . . . . .141 A2
Arkendale Rd HG5 . . . . . .162 F8
Arkengarthdale CE Prim Sch
　DL11 . . . . .17 D1
Arkengarthdale Rd
　DL11 . . . . .38 B7
Arkle Cres DL1 . . . . .3 C3
Arlington Rd
　Middlesbrough TS5 . . . . . .6 F8
　York YO30 . . . . .225 A1
Armoury Rd YO8 . . . . . . .232 B5
Armstrong Cl **7** WF6 . . .200 A2
Armstrong Way YO32 . . . .226 E3
Army Foundation Coll
　HG3 . . . . .161 A2
Arncliffe CE VC Prim Sch
　BD23 . . . . .107 C2
Arncliffe Dr WF11 . . . . . .201 D2
Arncliffe Rd HG2 . . . . . . .220 A1

Arndale Way 8 YO14 . . .101 B4
Arnold Rd DL1 . . . . .3 E6
Arnside Cres WF10 . . . .201 B4
Arnside Pl 2 YO10 . . . . .228 F3
Arran Ct LS25 . . . . .194 C3
Arran Dr LS25 . . . . .194 C3
Arran Pl YO31 . . . . .228 D7
Arrows Cres 10 YO51 . . .141 B5
Arrows Terr 9 YO51 . . . .141 B5
Art Ctr The★ YO22 . . . .208 E7
Arthington Ave HG1 . . .219 E2
Arthur Pl 6 YO30 . . . . . .224 B5
Arthur St
6 Barnoldswick BB18 . . .171 D2
Earby BB18 . . . . .186 A8
Great Ayton TS9 . . . . .8 A2
York YO10 . . . . .228 E4
Arthurs Ave HG2 . . . . . .222 C7
Arthurs Cl HG2 . . . . . . .222 C7
Arthurs Gr HG2 . . . . . . .222 C7
Arundel Ct TS17 . . . . .5 F6
Arundel Gr YO24 . . . . . .230 C7
Arundel Pl
12 Scarborough YO11 . . . .212 F5
9 Whitby YO21 . . . . .208 C6
Arundel Rd 5 DN6 . . . . .206 E2
Ascot Rd LS25 . . . . .194 C1
Ascot Way YO24 . . . . . .227 D1
Ascough Wynd DL8 . . . . .63 D3
Ash Bank Ave 2 HG4 . . . .113 D2
Ash Bank Cl 1 HG4 . . . .113 D2
Ash Bank Rd HG4 . . . . . .113 D2
Ash Cl 1 Ilkley LS29 . . . .175 C2
Newton on Derwent
YO41 . . . . .185 E4
York YO31 . . . . .229 B7
Ash Croft 7 DL10 . . . . . . .41 D5
Ash Gn TS8 . . . . .7 A4
Ash Gr
18 Barnoldswick BB18 . . .171 D1
Danby YO21 . . . . .29 A6
12 Filey YO14 . . . . .101 B4
Glusburn BD20 . . . . .187 E7
Ilkley LS29 . . . . .218 C5
7 Kirkbymoorside YO62 . . . .70 B1
1 Kirklevington TS15 . . . . .24 E8
Northallerton DL6 . . . . . . .210 F5
1 Riccall YO19 . . . . .197 F8
Ripon HG4 . . . . .214 A6
Scarborough YO12 . . . . . .212 C7
Whitby YO21 . . . . .208 B6
Ash Hill TS8 . . . . .7 B5
Ash La
Church Fenton LS24 . . . . .196 B6
Garforth LS25 . . . . .194 D4
8 Haxby YO32 . . . . .166 E5
Little Fenton LS25 . . . . . . .196 C5
Ash Lea Danby YO21 . . . . .29 A6
Fairburn WF11 . . . . .201 D6
Ash Rd 13 Filey YO14 . . . .101 B4
Guisborough TS14 . . . . .8 F7
Harrogate HG2 . . . . .222 E6
Ash Ridge 5 DL6 . . . . . .210 E3
Ash St 11 Glusburn BD20 . .187 E7
Ilkley LS29 . . . . .218 C5
Trawden BB8 . . . . .186 B1
York YO26 . . . . .227 E4
Ash Tree Cl DL8 . . . . .62 F2
Ash Tree Garth LS24 . . . .195 E7
Ash Tree Rd
8 Bedale DL8 . . . . .63 A2
Knaresborough HG5 . . . . .221 B6
Ash Tree Wlk 22 LS29 . . .176 C1
Ash View HG2 . . . . .222 B6
Ashbank La Firby DL8 . . . .62 F1
Sheriff Hutton YO60 . . . . .145 F6
Ashberry Nature Reserve★
YO62 . . . . .92 B7
Ashbourne Cl 12 YO51 . . .141 B4
Ashbourne Rd 10 YO51 . . .141 B4
Ashbourne Way YO24 . . .230 C8
Ashburn Pl LS29 . . . . . . .218 A3
Ashburn Rise 10 YO11 . . .212 E4
Ashburn Way LS22 . . . . .180 B4
Ashburnham Cl 4 DN6 . .206 F2
Ashburnham Wlk 5
DN6 . . . . .206 F2
Ashdale Cl DL2 . . . . .4 E4
Ashdale La LS22 . . . . . .180 B4
Ashdale Rd
19 Dunnington YO19 . . . . .184 F7
Helmsley YO62 . . . . .92 F6
Ashdene Gr WF8 . . . . . .201 D2
Ashdown Rise YO13 . . . . .75 C8
Ashdowne Cl DL8 . . . . . . .62 E5
Ashdowne Ct DL8 . . . . . . .62 E5
Ashes The DL10 . . . . .21 C7
Ashfield
2 Grassington BD23 . . . .134 E3
Wetherby LS22 . . . . .180 C3
Ashfield Ave YO17 . . . . .215 D5
Ashfield Cl
9 Constable Burton DL8 . . .61 C5
9 Pateley Bridge HG3 . . . .137 B4
Ashfield Ct YO24 . . . . . .230 E7
Ashfield Ct Rd 10 HG3 . . .137 B4
Ashfield Rd Danby YO21 . . .29 B6
Harrogate HG1 . . . . .219 E4
6 Pickering YO18 . . . . .96 A6
Ashfield St WF6 . . . . . . .200 A2
Ashfield Terr
Harrogate HG1 . . . . .219 E4
Skipton BD23 . . . . .216 F2
Ashford Ave TS5 . . . . .6 D8
Ashford Pl YO24 . . . . . .227 D2
Ashgap La WF6 . . . . . . .200 A2
Ashgarth Ct HG2 . . . . . .222 C5
Ashgarth Way HG2 . . . .222 C5
Ashgrove BD23 . . . . .216 E4
Ashgrove Cres LS25 . . . .194 D2
Ashlands Cl DL6 . . . . . . .210 F4
Ashlands Ct DL6 . . . . . . .210 F4
Ashlands Dr DL7 . . . . . . .63 C5
Ashlands Prim Sch
LS29 . . . . .218 C5
Ashlands Rd
Ilkley LS29 . . . . .218 C5
Northallerton DL6 . . . . . .210 F4
Ashlea Cl YO8 . . . . .232 D4
Ashlea Rd DL7 . . . . .210 D4
Ashley Ct 2 YO14 . . . . . .101 B3
Ashley Pk Cres YO31 . . .229 B6
Ashley Pk Rd YO31 . . . .229 B7
Ashmead 4 LS23 . . . . . .188 E7
Ashmeade Cl YO24 . . . .230 B8
Ashton Ave YO30 . . . . . .228 B8
Ashton Ct BD23 . . . . . . .154 B3
Ashton Rd WF10 . . . . . .200 E3
Ashtree Dr YO8 . . . . . . .197 D1
Ashville Ave
Eaglescliffe TS16 . . . . .5 E6
Scarborough YO12 . . . . . .212 F6
Ashville Cl HG2 . . . . . . .222 C5
Ashville Coll HG2 . . . . .222 B6
Ashville Dr 9 DL2 . . . . . . .22 E8
Ashville Gr HG2 . . . . . . .222 C5
Ashville St YO31 . . . . . .228 D7
Ashwood Cl 5 YO62 . . . . .92 F7
Ashwood Dr TS9 . . . . .26 C8
Ashwood Glade YO32 . . .225 C6
Ashwood Pl HG5 . . . . . .221 E5
Ashworth Rd WF8 . . . . .201 C2
Askam Ave WF8 . . . . . . .201 C2
Aske Ave DL10 . . . . .209 E8
Aske Hall★ DL10 . . . . . . .20 D2
Askern & Campsall Sports Ctr
DN6 . . . . .206 F1
Askew Dale TS14 . . . . .8 E8
Askew Rigg La YO18 . . . .71 A5
Askham Bog Nature
Reserve★ TO23 . . . . . .230 C5
Askham Bryan Coll
Askham Bryan YO23 . . . . .182 F2
Bedale DL8 . . . . .63 A2
Pickering YO18 . . . . .95 F8
Askham Bryan Coll Harrogate
Ctr HG2 . . . . .223 A7
Askham Bryan La
YO23 . . . . .230 A6
Askham Croft 1 YO24 . . .227 B1
Askham Fields La
YO23 . . . . .182 F2
Askham Gr YO24 . . . . . .227 B2
Askham La
Askham Bryan YO24 . . . . .230 A8
York YO24 . . . . .227 B1
Askrigg Prim Sch DL8 . . .57 E5
Askwith Com Prim Sch
LS21 . . . . .176 D3
Askwith La LS21 . . . . . .176 D3
Askwith Moor Rd
LS21 . . . . .176 D5
Aspen Cl
3 Dunnington YO19 . . . . .184 F7
Pickering YO18 . . . . .95 F7
Selby YO8 . . . . .197 D2
Aspen La BB18 . . . . . . .172 A1
Aspen Way
Slingsby YO62 . . . . .120 B5
Tadcaster LS24 . . . . .189 D6
Aspin Ave HG5 . . . . . . .221 B4
Aspin Chase HG5 . . . . . .221 B4
Aspin Dr HG5 . . . . .221 C4
Aspin Gdns HG5 . . . . . .221 C4
Aspin Gr 4 HG5 . . . . . . .221 C4
Aspin La HG5 . . . . .221 C3
Aspin Oval HG5 . . . . . . .221 B4
Aspin Pk Ave 1 HG5 . . . .221 C4
Aspin Pk Com Prim Sch
HG5 . . . . .221 C5
Aspin Pk Cres HG5 . . . .221 B4
Aspin Pk Dr HG5 . . . . . .221 B4
Aspin Pk La HG5 . . . . . .221 C4
Aspin Pk Rd HG5 . . . . . .221 C4
Aspin View HG5 . . . . . .221 C4
Aspin Way HG5 . . . . . . .221 C4
Aspinall Rise 18 BD23 . . .154 B3
Asquith Ave
Scarborough YO12 . . . . . .212 E3
York YO31 . . . . .229 A5
Assembly St 7 WF6 . . . .200 A1
Astbury TS8 . . . . .7 C4
Asterley Dr TS5 . . . . .6 D8
Astley Ave LS26 . . . . . .194 A1
Astley La
Great & Little Preston
LS26 . . . . .200 B8
Swillington LS26 . . . . . . .194 A1
Astley La Ind Pk LS26 . . .200 B8
Astley Way LS26 . . . . . .200 A8
Atcherley Cl YO10 . . . . .231 D8
Athelstan Com Prim Sch
LS25 . . . . .195 F3
Athelstan La 7 LS21 . . . .177 A1
Athelstans Ct LS25 . . . . .195 F4
Athol Sq YO17 . . . . .215 E4
Atkinson Ave DL10 . . . . .209 D8
Atkinson Ct WF6 . . . . . .200 A1
Atkinson La WF8 . . . . . .201 C1
Atlantis Wr Pk★ YO12 . .212 F8
Atlas Rd YO30 . . . . .225 A3
Atlas Wynd TS16 . . . . .5 E3
Attermire Cave★
BD24 . . . . .132 A3
Atterwith La YO26 . . . . .182 A7
Auborough St 5 YO11 . . .213 A6
Auckland Ave DL3 . . . . . . .3 B6
Auckland Oval DL3 . . . . . .3 B7
Auckland St TS14 . . . . .8 F7
Auckland Way 7 YO21 . .208 C6
Aucuba Cl YO32 . . . . . .225 D2
Audax Cl YO30 . . . . . . .225 A3
Audax Rd YO30 . . . . . . .225 A3
Audby La LS22 . . . . . . .180 C4
Audus St 10 YO8 . . . . . .232 C5
Augusta Cl DL1 . . . . .3 F7
Aumit La YO62 . . . . .92 E1
Aunums Cl 7 YO18 . . . . .96 D5
Auster Bank Ave LS24 . .189 F7
Auster Bank Cres
LS24 . . . . .189 F7
Auster Bank Rd LS24 . .189 F7
Auster Bank View
LS24 . . . . .189 F7
Auster Rd YO30 . . . . . . .225 B3
Austfield La LS25 . . . . . .202 B8
Austin Dr DL9 . . . . .41 A5
Austin Rd WF10 . . . . . . .201 B4
Austwick CE Prim Sch
LA2 . . . . .130 E7
Austwick Rd BD24 . . . . .131 C8
Autumn Ave 8 LS22 . . . . . .8 C4
Ava Rd DL9 . . . . .40 C4
Avalon Ct TS8 . . . . .6 F5
Avens Way TS17 . . . . .6 A5
Avenue A LS23 . . . . .181 A2
Avenue B LS23 . . . . .181 A1
Avenue Bank HG4 . . . . . .86 C4
Avenue C E LS23 . . . . . .181 B1
Avenue C W LS23 . . . . . .181 A1
Avenue Cl HG2 . . . . . . .220 D4
Avenue D LS23 . . . . .181 A1
Avenue E E LS23 . . . . . .181 B1
Avenue E W LS23 . . . . . .189 A8
Avenue F LS23 . . . . .181 B1
Avenue G LS23 . . . . .181 B1
Avenue Gr 11 HG2 . . . . .220 C3
Avenue House Ct HG5 . .162 F3
Avenue Pl 7 HG2 . . . . . .220 C3
Avenue Prim Sch The
TS7 . . . . .7 D6
Avenue Rd
Harrogate HG2 . . . . .220 C3
Scarborough YO12 . . . . . .212 E4
York YO30 . . . . .233 A4
Avenue St 8 HG2 . . . . . .220 C3
Avenue Terr
5 Harrogate HG2 . . . . . . .220 C3
York YO30 . . . . .233 A4
Avenue The
Campsall DN6 . . . . .206 E1
Collingham LS22 . . . . . . .180 A1
Dalby-cum-Skewsby
YO60 . . . . .119 B2
Eaglescliffe TS16 . . . . .5 E6
26 Filey YO14 . . . . .101 B3
Gilling East YO62 . . . . . . .118 E7
Great Ribston with Walshford
LS22 . . . . .180 C8
Guisborough TS14 . . . . .8 D6
Harrogate HG1 . . . . .220 C4
5 Haxby YO32 . . . . .166 E5
Knaresborough HG5 . . . . .221 A7
Masham HG4 . . . . .86 C3
Middlesbrough TS5 . . . . .6 F8
Norton YO17 . . . . .215 C2
Nun Monkton YO26 . . . . . .165 A4
Nunnington YO62 . . . . .93 E1
8 Pateley Bridge HG3 . . . .137 C4
Richmond DL10 . . . . .209 D7
Rufforth YO23 . . . . .182 C6
Skipton BD23 . . . . .217 B6
Skutterskelfe TS15 . . . . . . .25 E6
1 Sleights YO22 . . . . .32 A6
Snape with Thorp DL8 . . . . .87 A7
South Milford LS25 . . . . . .195 F2
Stainton Dale YO13 . . . . . . .54 A8
Stokesley TS9 . . . . .26 C7
Thirkleby High & Low
with Osgodby YO7 . . . . .116 D8
West Hauxwell DL8 . . . . . . .61 C8
Whitby YO21 . . . . .208 B4
Wighill LS24 . . . . .181 D2
York YO30 . . . . .228 A6
Avenue Victoria YO11 . .213 A3
Aviation Rd LS25 . . . . . .196 A4
Aviator Ct YO30 . . . . . .224 F3
Aviemore Ct 10 DL1 . . . . . .3 F6
Aviemore Rd TS8 . . . . .6 F5
Avocet Cres 11 YO12 . . . . .99 F6
Avon Dr
Barnoldswick BB18 . . . . .171 E2
Guisborough TS14 . . . . .8 E6
York YO32 . . . . .225 F6
Avon Garth LS22 . . . . . .180 B3
Avon Rd 8 DL2 . . . . .22 D8
Avondale Rd HG1 . . . . .219 F4
Avro Cl TS18 . . . . .5 F7
Awnhams La YO42 . . . . .169 D2
Axminster Rd TS8 . . . . . . .6 F5
Axton Cl TS17 . . . . .6 A6
Aylesham Ct YO32 . . . . .225 E3
Aylton Dr TS5 . . . . .6 E6
Aynham Cl 2 BD23 . . . . .134 E2
Aynholme Cl 10 LS29 . . .174 F4
Aynholme Dr 1 LS29 . . .175 A4
Ayresome Way 1 DL1 . . . .3 F6
Aysgarth Falls★ DL8 . . . .58 F3
Aysgarth Gr DL7 . . . . . .210 B2
Aysgarth Rd DL1 . . . . .3 D4
Aysgarth Sch DL8 . . . . . .62 A4
Ayton Castle★ YO13 . . . .99 A8
Ayton Rd YO12 . . . . .99 C7
Azerley Gr HG3 . . . . . . .219 A4
Azerley La HG4 . . . . . . .112 F3

B

Babyhouse La BD20 . . .173 A1
Bachelor Ave HG1 . . . . .219 D7
Bachelor Dr HG1 . . . . . .219 D7
Bachelor Gdns HG1 . . .219 D6
Bachelor Hill YO24 . . . .227 C2
Bachelor Rd HG1 . . . . .219 D6
Bachelor Way HG1 . . . .219 D6
Back Ave Victoria 2
YO11 . . . . .213 A3
Back Beck La LS29 . . . .174 F4
Back Bridge St BD23 . . .216 F4
Back Cheltenham Mount
HG1 . . . . .219 D3
Back Colne Rd 9 BD20 .187 E7
Back Dawson Terr
HG1 . . . . .219 D5
Back Dragon Par HG1 .219 E3
Back Dragon Rd HG1 . .219 E3
Back Elmwood St 3
HG1 . . . . .219 E4
Back Gate LA6 . . . . .103 D3
Back Gladstone St
HG2 . . . . .222 D7
Back Gn BD23 . . . . .153 F5
Back Gr Rd LS29 . . . . . .218 B4
Back Grange Ave HG1 .219 D5
Back High St 13 HG3 . . .137 B4
Back La
Acaster Selby YO23 . . . . .191 B3
Airton BD23 . . . . .155 A6
Aiskew DL7 . . . . .63 C5
Alne YO61 . . . . .142 F4
Ampleforth YO62 . . . . .92 C1
Appleton Roebuck YO23 . .191 A5
Appleton-le-Moors YO62 . . .70 F2
Asselby DN14 . . . . .205 D6
Bagby YO7 . . . . .90 B3
Barkston Ash LS24 . . . . . .195 F6
Barlby with Osgodby
YO8 . . . . .198 C4
Barton DL10 . . . . .21 C7
Barton-le-Street YO17 . . . .120 E5
1 Bedale DL8 . . . . .63 A3
Bilbrough YO23 . . . . .182 D1
Birstwith HG3 . . . . .160 D5
Bolton-on-Swale DL10 . . . . .41 E5
7 Boroughbridge YO51 . . .141 B5
Borrowby YO7 . . . . .65 E4
Bradleys Both BD20 . . . . .173 E4
10 Brafferton YO61 . . . . . .115 F1
Bramham LS23 . . . . .188 E6
Burley in Warfedale
LS29 . . . . .176 C1
Carlton Miniott YO7 . . . . . .89 B3
Carthorpe DL8 . . . . .87 E7
Cold Kirby YO7 . . . . .91 C8
Copmanthorpe YO23 . . . . .230 A2
Copt Hewick HG4 . . . . . . .114 B2
Cottingwith YO42 . . . . . . .193 C5
Crakehall DL8 . . . . .62 E4
Crathorne TS15 . . . . .24 F6
Dalton YO7 . . . . .115 E7
Dishforth YO7 . . . . .115 A4
Drax YO8 . . . . .204 F5
Eaglescliffe TS16 . . . . .5 E4
Easingwold YO61 . . . . . . .117 D1
East Tanfield DL8 . . . . .87 D2
Ebberston & Yedingham
YO13 . . . . .97 D5
Ellerton YO42 . . . . .193 C1
Fewston HG3 . . . . .159 F1
Flaxton YO60 . . . . .145 F1
Giggleswick BD24 . . . . . .130 F2
Great & Little Broughton
TS9 . . . . .26 E5
Great Ouseburn YO26 . . . .164 A8
Great Preston WF10 . . . . .200 D6
Gristlthorp YO14 . . . . .100 E5
Guisborough TS9 . . . . .8 A4
Hambleton YO8 . . . . .196 F1
Harome YO62 . . . . .93 C5
Hawksker-cum-Stainsacre
YO22 . . . . .32 F5
11 Haxby YO32 . . . . .166 D5
Hebden BD23 . . . . .135 A2
Hellifield BD23 . . . . .154 B3
Hemingbrough YO8 . . . . . .198 F1
Hetton BD23 . . . . .155 F5
Hirst Courtney YO8 . . . . . .203 F3
Holtby YO19 . . . . .184 E8
Hunsingore LS22 . . . . .180 E8
Hutton-le-Hole YO62 . . . . . .70 C4
Huttons Ambo YO60 . . . . . .147 B7
Kirby Wiske YO7 . . . . .88 E7
Kirkby Malham BD23 . . . . .154 F8
Kirkby Malzeard HG4 . . . . .112 C5
Lockton YO18 . . . . .72 E4
Long Preston BD23 . . . . . .153 F5
Longnewton TS21 . . . . .4 F8
Low Coniscliffe & Merrybent
DL2 . . . . .2 E4
Low Worsall TS15 . . . . .24 C7
Luttons YO17 . . . . .150 B8
Malham BD23 . . . . .132 F2
Markington with Wallerthwaite
HG3 . . . . .139 C3
Marton YO62 . . . . .94 F5
Marton cum Grafton
YO51 . . . . .141 D1
Melmerby HG4 . . . . .114 B7
8 Middleham DL8 . . . . .60 E2
Morton-on-Swale DL7 . . . . .64 A6
Moulton DL10 . . . . .21 E3
Back La continued
Newby Wiske DL7 . . . . .64 D3
Newholm-cum-Dunsley
YO21 . . . . .13 A1
Newton-on-Ouse YO30 . . .165 B6
North Cowton DL7 . . . . .22 B3
North Duffield YO8 . . . . . .199 A7
Norton DN6 . . . . .206 E2
Osmotherley DL6 . . . . .45 B4
Raskelf YO61 . . . . .116 F2
Rathmell BD24 . . . . .153 C6
Reeth, Fremington & Healaugh
DL11 . . . . .38 B6
2 Riccall YO19 . . . . .198 A8
Rookwith HG4 . . . . .86 A8
Scorton DL10 . . . . .41 E6
Settrington YO17 . . . . . . .148 D8
Sicklinghall LS22 . . . . .179 E3
Sinnington YO62 . . . . .95 A8
Skelton HG4 . . . . .140 E7
Sutton-under-Whitestonecliffe
YO7 . . . . .90 E5
Thirkleby High & Low
with Osgodby YO7 . . . . .116 D8
Thirsk YO7 . . . . .211 B1
Tholthorpe YO61 . . . . .142 D5
Thormanby YO61 . . . . .116 F6
Thornton Steward DL8 . . . . .61 C2
Topcliffe YO7 . . . . .115 C7
Trawden BB8 . . . . .186 A1
Tunstall DL10 . . . . .41 B3
Tunstall LA6 . . . . .102 A4
Weaverthorpe YO17 . . . . . .124 E1
Weeton LS17 . . . . .178 C2
Wennington LA2 . . . . .102 C2
West Tanfield HG4 . . . . .87 A1
West Witton DL8 . . . . .59 C4
Westerdale YO21 . . . . .28 E5
Whixley YO26 . . . . .164 A3
Whorlton DL6 . . . . .45 D8
Wilberfoss YO41 . . . . .185 F5
Wold Newton YO25 . . . . . .126 A4
Wombleton YO62 . . . . .93 E7
Wray-with-Botton LA2 . . . .128 A6
York YO26 . . . . .227 A5
Back La S
Middleton YO18 . . . . .95 E8
Wheldrake YO19 . . . . .192 F7
Back Middleton Rd 9
LS29 . . . . .218 A4
Back Newton La
WF10 . . . . .201 A7
Back Nook 1 DL8 . . . . . . .58 F1
Back Northgate WF8 . . .201 B1
Back O' Newton YO41 . .185 E3
Back of Parks Rd YO62 . .70 C2
Back of the Beck 6
BD23 . . . . .216 F4
Back Parish Ghyll Rd 8
LS29 . . . . .218 B4
Back Pk St YO8 . . . . . . .232 D5
Back Rd Birstwith HG3 . . .160 B5
Thormanby YO61 . . . . . . .116 F5
Back Regent Pl 4 HG1 . .220 C4
Back Royal Par 5 HG1 . .219 C2
Back Sea View YO14 . . .101 C1
Back Side YO17 . . . . . . .149 B5
Back St
Boroughbridge YO51 . . . . .141 C5
Bramham LS23 . . . . .188 E6
Burton Fleming YO25 . . . .126 E3
Langtoft YO25 . . . . .151 D5
10 Middleham DL8 . . . . .60 E2
Wold Newton YO25 . . . . . .126 A4
Back St Hilda's Terr
YO21 . . . . .208 D7
Back Sta Rd 17 BD20 . . . .187 E8
Back Syke DL8 . . . . .57 D5
Back Tewit Well Rd
HG2 . . . . .222 E8
Back W View 2 YO30 . . .228 B7
Back Weston Rd 5
LS29 . . . . .218 B4
Back York Pl 6 HG1 . . . .219 D1
Backhouse St YO31 . . . .233 B4
Backside La YO62 . . . . . .93 E6
Backstone La LS29 . . . .218 C3
Backstone Way LS29 . . .218 C4
Bacon Ave WF6 . . . . . . .200 B2
Bad Bargain La YO31 . .229 A5
Baden St HG1 . . . . .219 F4
Bader Ave TS17 . . . . .6 B6
Bader Prim Sch TS17 . . . .6 B6
Badger Butt La BD23 . . .155 B5
Badger Cl 33 LS29 . . . . .175 C2
Badger Gate BD23 . . . . .134 D3
Badger Hill Dr 14 DL8 . . .63 B3
Badger Hill Prim Sch
YO10 . . . . .229 B2
Badger La DN6 . . . . .207 A3
Badger Paddock 5
YO31 . . . . .225 E2
Badger Wood Glade
LS22 . . . . .180 C4
Badger Wood Wlk
YO10 . . . . .229 D3
Badgerbeck Rd 2 DL9 . .209 B1
Badgers Gate LS29 . . . .175 C6
Badminton Ct 18 DL1 . . . . .3 F6
Baek Chapel St 26 BB18 171 D1
Baffam Gdns YO8 . . . . .232 B2
Baffam La YO8 . . . . .232 B2
Bagby La YO7 . . . . .90 B2
Bagdale YO21 . . . . .208 C6
Bagdale Ct YO21 . . . . . .208 D6

Baghill La WF8 ....201 C1
Baildon Ave LS25 ....194 D2
Baildon Cl 3 YO26 ....227 C4
Baile Hill Terr YO1 ...233 B1
Bailey Ct DL7 ....210 C4
Bailey La BD23 ....152 E3
Bailey St BB18 ....172 A1
Bailey The BD23 ....217 A4
Bainbridge CE Prim Sch
   DL8 ....57 D5
Bainbridge Dr YO8 ....232 C4
Bairnswood Sch YO12 .212 B6
Baker St
   Appleton Wiske DL6 ...24 A3
   York YO30 ....228 C7
Bakersfield Dr DN14 ..202 F3
Bakewell Mews 6 DL3 ..3 A7
Bala Cl 2 TS17 ....5 A4
Baldersby Garth
   Baldersby YO7 ....88 D1
   Rainton YO7 ....114 F6
Baldersby St James CE VC
   Prim Sch YO7 ....114 E7
Baldersdale Ave 1
   HG5 ....221 D5
Baldoon Sands TS5 .....6 C4
Baldwin St 4 HG1 .....219 C5
Balfour St YO26 ....227 F5
Balfour Terr TS5 ......6 C8
Balfour Way YO32 .....167 A6
Baliol Croft TS21 .....5 A7
Balk La DN14 ....207 F7
Balk The
   Bishop Wilton YO41 ...169 C2
   Marton-le-Moor HG4 ..114 E1
   Slingsby YO62 ....120 B5
Balk Top YO7 ....115 B1
Balksyde YO62 ....120 B5
Ball Gr Dr BB8 ....186 A3
Ballhall La YO42 ......193 E6
Balmer Hill DL2 ....1 C8
Balmoral Ave TS17 .....6 C8
Balmoral Dr LS26 .....200 B6
Balmoral Rd
   Barmpton DL1 ....3 E8
   Lingdale TS12 ....9 F6
   Middlesbrough TS3 .....7 C8
   Ripon HG4 ....214 C3
Balmoral Terr 5 YO23 .228 B1
Balne Hall Rd DN14 ...207 F5
Balne Moor Rd DN14 ..207 B6
Balshaw Rd LA2 ......129 B3
Baltimore Way DL1 .....3 D7
Bamburgh Ct TS17 .....5 F5
Banbury Rd WF8 ......201 C2
Bancroft Fold 18 BB18 171 D1
Bancroft Steam Mus★
   BB18 ....171 D1
Bands La DL8 ....56 C4
Bank Bottom LA6 .....103 D3
Bank Cl 2 YO22 ......32 A6
Bank Dike Hill HG3 ...159 A4
Bank Hall Cl LA6 .....103 D4
Bank House La LA6 ...103 B5
Bank La Egton YO21 ...30 C5
   Faceby TS9 ....25 F1
   Grassington BD23 ....134 E3
   Great & Little Broughton
   TS9 ....26 B4
   Silsden BD20 ....174 C4
Bank Rd Glusburn BD20 187 B8
   Selby YO8 ....232 D6
Bank Side
   2 Eastfield YO11 .....100 A7
   Rawcliffe DN14 ......205 A2
Bank St
   Barnoldswick BB18 ...171 D1
   Castleford WF10 .....200 E4
   11 Wetherby LS22 ...180 C3
Bank The DL10 ....41 D6
Bank Top La 4 TS13 ...12 A7
Bank Wood Rd WF8 ..206 A6
Bank Yd DL10 ....209 C6
Bankfield La DN14 ....205 A7
Bankfield St BB18 .....186 A2
Bankhead Cl DL6 .....210 F4
Bankhead Rd DL6 ....210 F4
Banklands Ave BD20 ..174 C1
Banklands La BD20 ...174 C1
Banks Bridge Cl BB18 171 E2
Banks Hill 1 BB18 ...171 D1
Banks La DL10 ....41 E2
Banks Rd Brompton DL6 44 A2
   Darlington DL1 ....3 E6
Banksfields Ct TS6 .....7 F8
Bankside Cl
   3 Poppleton YO26 ...165 F1
   Thirsk YO7 ....211 D2
Bankwell Rd BD20 ....131 D2
Bannisdale 6 YO24 ...230 C7
Bannister Cl BB8 .....186 B2
Bannister Wlk BD22 ..187 B6
Banqueting House★
   LS21 ....176 D1
Bar Convent Mus★
   YO24 ....233 A1
Bar Knotts Terr YO17 .215 C3
Bar La
   Bramham cum Oglethorpe
   LS23 ....188 F1
   Garforth LS25 ....194 D4
   Hambleton YO8 ......196 E1
   Knaresborough HG5 ..162 D5
   Roecliffe YO51 ......141 A5

Bar La continued
   York YO1 ....233 A2
Bar Pl HG1 ....219 D5
Bar St YO11 ....213 A6
Bar The 6 DL10 ......209 C6
Barbara Gr 4 YO24 ...227 F3
Barbeck YO7 ....211 C3
Barbeck Cl YO7 ......211 D3
Barberry 15 ....7 B4
Barberry Cl Ingleby TS17 ..6 B5
   20 Killinghall HG3 ....161 B3
Barbers Dr YO23 .....230 B4
Barbican Ct YO10 ....233 C1
Barbican Mews YO10 .228 C1
Barbican Rd YO10 ....233 C1
Barbondale Gr HG5 ..221 C5
Barbondale Rd LA10 ...77 A7
Bardale Cl 2 HG5 ....221 D6
Barden Cl 6 YO30 ...224 F1
Barden Fell View 3
   BD23 ....134 E2
Barden La DL8 ....40 B1
Barden Moor Rd DL1 ...3 E4
Barden Pl 9 YO14 ....101 A3
Barden Rd BD23 ......157 A1
Bardney Rd 14 YO14 .126 F8
Bardsley Cl TS16 ......5 E7
Barefoot St YO8 ......214 C4
Barf Bank DL8 ....61 A2
Barf La YO41 ....169 D4
Barff Cl 10 YO8 ......197 D1
Barff Gr 6 YO8 ......197 B2
Barff La YO8 ....197 C1
Barff View YO8 ......203 D7
Barfield Rd YO31 ....228 F8
Bargate DL10 ....209 B6
Bark House La LA2 ...131 B8
Bark La
   Addingham LS29 ....175 A5
   Embsay with Eastby
   BD23 ....157 A1
Barker Bsns Pk HG4 .114 C6
Barker Dr YO8 ....232 B6
Barker La YO1 ....233 A2
Barker's La
   Newholm-cum-Dunsley
   YO21 ....13 A1
   Snainton YO13 ....98 A4
Barkery The TS8 ....7 B3
Barkhouse Bank HG3 .138 F4
Barkhouse Wood La
   WF11 ....202 D6
Barkston Ash Cath Prim Sch
   LS24 ....195 E7
Barkston Ave YO26 ...227 B3
Barkston Cl 3 YO26 ..227 A3
Barkston Gr YO26 ....227 A3
Barkston Rd YO26 ....227 A3
Barlby Bridge CP Sch
   YO8 ....232 D5
Barlby By-pass 2 YO8 198 B4
Barlby CP Sch YO8 ...198 B4
Barlby Cres YO8 .....232 F7
Barlby High Sch YO8 .198 B5
Barlby Rd YO8 ....232 E6
Barley Cl YO17 ......215 D2
Barley Hall★ YO1 ....233 B3
Barley Horn Rd LS24 .190 B2
Barley Rise YO32 ....167 A6
Barley View YO32 ....225 C8
Barleycorn Yd YO1 ...233 C2
Barleycroft YO11 ....213 C1
Barleyfields La 5 LS22 180 C3
Barleyfields Rd 4 LS22 180 C3
Barleyhill Rd LS25 ...194 B4
Barley's Yd YO7 .....211 B3
Barlow CE VC Prim Sch
   YO8 ....204 C7
Barlow Cl TS14 ....8 F6
Barlow Comm Nature
   Reserve★ YO8 .....204 B7
Barlow Comm Rd YO8 204 B8
Barlow Rd YO8 ......204 B6
Barlow St YO26 ......227 D4
Barmby Ave YO10 ...231 E8
Barmby Cl 4 YO30 ..224 F1
Barmby Ferry Rd 1
   YO8 ....198 F1
Barmby on the Marsh Prim
   Sch DN14 ....205 B7
Barmoor Cl YO13 .....75 D6
Barmoor Gn YO13 ....75 D6
Barmoor La YO13 .....75 C6
Barmpton La DL1 ......3 F7
Barn Field Cl BB8 ....186 A3
Barnaby Pl TS14 ......8 E7
Barnard La YO13 ......98 C4
Barnard's Rd YO21 ...31 A4
Barnbow La LS15 ....194 A6
Barnes Rd
   Castleford WF10 .....200 E3
   Darlington DL3 ....3 A6
Barney La YO60 ......146 A1
Barnfield Way YO23 ..230 A2
Barnhill La DN14 ....205 F7
Barningham Rd DL11 .18 G7
Barnoldswick CE Prim Sch
   BB18 ....171 D1
Barnoldswick La LA6 .103 A2
Barns Wray 2 YO61 ..117 D1
Barnsdale Est WF11 ..200 D3
Barnsdale Rd
   Ledston WF10 ....200 E7
   Mickletown LS26 ....200 B5
Barnsdale View DN6 ..206 E2
Barnwell Cres HG2 ...222 B5
Barnwood Cres BB18 .172 B1

Barnwood Rd BB18 ...172 A1
Barnygate La YO60 ...147 A2
Barons Cres YO23 ....230 B2
Barr La YO32 ....167 D4
Barrack View YO11 ...213 A6
Barracks Bank DL10 ...21 A2
Barret St 13 BB18 ....172 A1
Barrett Ave 3 YO24 ..227 F3
Barrett Rd DL3 ....3 A5
Barrington Garth
   DN14 ....202 F3
Barrowby La
   Austhorpe LS15 .....194 A4
   Kirkby Overblow HG3 .179 A3
Barrowcliff Com Jun Sch
   YO12 ....212 C7
Barrowcliff Cty Jun Sch
   YO12 ....212 C7
Barrowcliff Inf Sch
   YO12 ....212 C7
Barrowcliff Rd YO12 .212 D7
Barry Bank YO21 ......11 F1
Barry's La YO12 .....212 E2
Barse Beck La HG3 ..160 D5
Barstow Ave YO10 ...228 F3
Barstow Fall 2 WF8 .201 C2
Bartindale Rd YO14 ..127 A5
Bartle Garth YO1 ....233 C3
Barton CE Prim Sch
   DL10 ....21 D7
Barton Cl 4 YO31 ....225 E3
Barton St DL1 ....3 E6
Bartons Garth YO8 ..232 B2
Barugh La
   Barugh (Great & Little)
   YO17 ....95 B2
   Normanby YO62 ......94 F4
Barwic Par YO8 ......232 E4
Barwick Fields TS7 ....6 A5
Barwick La Ingleby TS17 ..6 A4
   Ingleby Barwick TS17 ..5 F5
Barwick Par CP Sch
   YO8 ....232 E4
Barwick Rd LS25 ....194 C5
Barwick St YO12 ....212 F5
Barwick Terr 1 YO12 212 F5
Barwick View TS17 ....6 A4
Barwick Way TS17 ....6 A4
Barwick-in-Elmet CE Sch
   LS15 ....194 C8
Bassett Cl YO8 ......232 C3
Bassleton La TS17 ....6 A6
Baston La YO61 .....143 E4
Batemans Yd YO7 ...211 B3
Bates Ave DL3 ....3 B7
Bateson Cl YO10 ....229 C1
Bath St LS29 ....218 C5
Battersby Ave TS9 ...27 C7
Battersby Sta TS9 ...27 C6
Battle of Bramham Moor
   (site of)★ LS24 ....188 F4
Battle of Marston Moor (site
   of)★ YO26 ....181 E7
Battle of Standard Hill (site
   of)★ DL6 ....43 E4
Battle of Towton (site of)★
   LS24 ....195 D6
Battleflats Way YO41 168 D2
Battling Hills La YO18 .49 B5
Bawhead Rd 23 BB18 .172 A1
Bawtry Cl YO8 ....232 D3
Bawtry Rd YO8 ......232 D3
Baxby Manor★ YO61 .117 B6
Baxby Terr 2 DL2 .....22 D8
Baxter Wood BD20 ..187 E8
Baxtergate YO10 ....206 D6
Baxton's Sprunt 1 YO62 .92 F7
Bay Cres YO14 ......101 B2
Bay Bolton Ave DL8 ..59 F3
Bay Horse Yd 8 BD23 216 F4
Baydale Rd DL3 ....3 A4
Baysdale Ave YO10 ..229 D3
Baysdale Cl TS14 .....8 F6
Baysdale Rd TS17 ....6 B7
Bazeley's La YO17 ...215 E1
Beach Rd The YO14 .101 B3
Beach The YO14 ....101 B3
Beacon Bank YO62 ...92 D1
Beacon Brow Rd YO13 .75 A7
Beacon Grange Pk DL2 ..4 C7
Beacon Hill DL2 .....4 B7
Beacon Rise 4 LS29 .175 C2
Beacon St LS29 .....175 A4
Beacon View 3 BD23 217 E8
Beacon Way YO22 ....32 D6
Beacons La 18 TS17 ...5 F4
Beaconsfield Mews
   YO24 ....227 D3
Beaconsfield St
   Northallerton DL7 ...210 D4
   3 Scarborough YO12 212 E3
   York YO24 ....227 D3
Beadlam Ave TS7 .....7 D6
Beadle Garth YO23 ..230 B2
Beagle Croft YO41 ..168 C1
Beagle Ridge Dr YO24 227 C1
Beagle Spinney YO41 168 C1
Beal La Beal DN14 ...202 D4
   Cridling Stubbs WF11 .202 C1
Beale Cl TS17 ....6 B5
Beamsley Ct BD23 ...217 A2
Beamsley La BD23 ...174 F7
Beamsley View 13 LS29 175 C2
Bean Sheaf La YO17 ..96 A3
Beancroft Rd WF10 .200 E3

Beancroft St WF10 ..200 E3
Beanland La YO32 ...167 D2
Beanlands Dr 7 BD20 187 E7
Beanlands Par LS29 .218 C5
Beanlands Pl 8 BD20 187 E7
Bean's Way YO31 ....229 B8
Beatswell Lawn HG4 .113 C8
Beaufighter Cl DL10 ..41 F6
Beaufort Cl YO30 ....229 B3
Beaulieu Cl 1 YO32 .225 F5
Beaumont Hill Sch DL1 ..3 D8
Beaumont Pl YO8 ...232 B4
Beaverdyke YO30 ....224 F1
Becca La LS25 ......194 F8
Beck Cl 6 YO41 .....185 B2
Beck Closes Rd YO32 142 A3
Beck Hole 9 YO11 ...100 B6
Beck Hole Rd YO22 ..31 C1
Beck Isle Mus of Rural Life★
   YO18 ....95 F7
Beck La Cloughton YO13 .54 C1
   Collingham LS22 ....180 A1
   Farndale East YO62 ..48 A5
   Leavening YO17 .....147 E1
   Lebberston YO11 ....100 D5
   South Kilvington YO7 211 B6
   Wheldrake YO19 ....193 A8
Beck Mdw LS15 .....194 C7
Beck Mill Cl YO17 ...215 D3
Beck Row YO41 .....169 D5
Beck Side BD23 .....173 B4
Beck Side Cl BD20 ..173 C1
Beckbridge La 2 WF6 200 B1
Beckbridge Rd WF6 .200 B1
Beckbridge Way WF6 200 B1
Beckclose La DL8 ....87 C6
Beckdale Rd YO62 ....92 E7
Beckett Cl 8 YO62 ...93 D7
Beckfield Cl 6 BD20 .187 E7
Beckfield La
   Fairburn WF11 ......201 C7
   York YO26 ....227 B5
Beckfield Pl YO26 ...227 B4
Beckfields Ave TS17 ..6 A4
Becklands Cl YO51 ..141 A5
Becklands La YO51 ..141 A5
Becks Brow BD23 ...153 C3
Becks Cl 5 YO32 ....225 C8
Beckside Catterick DL10 ..41 A4
   7 Elvington YO41 ...185 B2
   Malton YO17 ....215 F4
   Northallerton DL7 ...210 B4
   4 Staithes TS13 .....13 K2
   Trawden Forest BB8 .186 B2
   Wilberfoss YO41 ....185 F6
Beckside Cl
   16 Addingham LS29 174 F4
   29 Burley in Wharfedale
   LS29 ....176 C1
Beckwith Ave HG2 ...222 B7
Beckwith Cl
   Harrogate HG2 .....222 A6
   Heworth YO31 ......229 C7
Beckwith Cres HG2 .222 B7
Beckwith Dr HG2 ....222 B6
Beckwith Head Rd
   HG3 ....178 C8
Beckwith Rd HG2 ...222 A7
Beckwith Wlk HG2 ..222 A7
Beckwithshaw Com Prim Sch
   HG3 ....178 A8
Bedale Ave
   Scarborough YO12 ..212 B8
   York YO26 ....229 D4
Bedale CE Prim Sch
   DL8 ....63 A2
Bedale High Sch DL8 .63 A2
Bedale La HG4 ......114 A8
Bedale Mus★ DL8 ...63 A3
Bedale Rd Aiskew DL7 .63 A2
   Scotton DL9 ....40 F2
   Well DL8 ....87 A4
Bedale Sta DL8 ......63 A3
Bedburn Dr DL3 ......2 F5
Bede Ave YO30 .....228 B7
Bedern YO1 ....233 C3
Bedern Bank 13 HG4 214 C5
Bedern Ct 16 HG4 ..214 C5
Bedford Rd TS7 ....7 D6
Bedford St 13 YO11 .213 A6
Bedfords Fold 6 LS25 202 A7
Bedlam Hill YO7 ......65 E4
Bedlam La
   Fewston HG3 ....159 F2
   Staveley HG5 ....140 E1
Bedstile Rd 3 DL10 ...3 A6
Beech Ave
   3 Airmyn DN14 ....205 E4
   Bishopthorpe YO23 .231 A3
   1 Earby BB18 ......172 A1
   Harrogate HG2 .....222 E6
   4 Topcliffe YO7 .....89 B1
   York YO24 ....227 F3
Beech Cl Baldersby YO7 88 D1
   6 Eastfield YO11 ...100 A7
   2 Elvington YO41 ..185 B2
   Farnham HG5 ....162 D7
   Great Ayton TS9 .....7 F1
   Hunton DL9 ....40 E2
   7 Sherburn in Elmet LS25 195 F4
   Snape with Thorp DL8 .87 A7
   3 South Milford LS25 195 F2
   Tadcaster LS24 .....189 F6
Beech Cres
   Castleford WF10 ....201 B3
   Whitwell-on-the-Hill
   YO60 ....146 E4

Beech Croft
   Barlby with Osgodby
   YO8 ....198 B6
   Pontefract WF8 .....201 C2
Beech Ct
   Bishopthorpe YO23 .231 A3
   2 Castleford WF10 .200 F3
   Hellifield BD23 .....154 B3
Beech Dr
   6 Kirkbymoorside YO62 ..70 B1
   12 Scalby YO13 .....75 C5
   South Milford LS25 .195 F2
Beech End Model Village★
   DL8 ....60 D7
Beech Glade YO31 ..225 F2
Beech Gr
   1 Airmyn DN14 ....205 E4
   Burton Salmon LS25 201 F6
   Camblesforth YO8 ..204 C5
   Harrogate HG2 .....219 C1
   Knaresborough HG5 .221 B8
   Maltby TS8 ....6 C4
   Northallerton DL6 ..210 E5
   Selby YO8 ....232 C5
   Sherburn in Elmet LS25 195 F4
   Sowerby YO7 ....211 C1
   Whitby YO21 ....208 B6
   York YO26 ....227 C4
Beech Hill
   Carleton BD23 ......173 A4
   6 Knaresborough HG5 221 A6
   5 Pontefract WF8 ..201 C1
Beech Hill Rd BD23 .173 A4
Beech La
   8 East Ayton/West Ayton
   YO13 ....99 A7
   3 Spofforth HG3 ....179 E6
Beech Pk YO19 .....198 A8
Beech Pl 5 YO32 ....167 A6
Beech Rd
   Boston Spa LS23 ...188 E8
   Campsall DN6 ......206 E1
   Darlington DL1 ....3 F7
   Harrogate HG2 .....222 E6
   Ripon HG4 ....214 B3
Beech Rise DL1 ....3 F7
Beech St
   28 Barnoldswick BB18 171 D1
   10 Glusburn BD20 .187 E7
   6 Harrogate HG2 ..220 C3
Beech Tree Ct 2 YO10 164 F7
Beech Tree La 7 YO8 204 C5
Beech View LS25 ....194 E8
Beech Way 23 YO26 .165 F1
Beech Wlk
   5 Eastfield YO11 ...100 A7
   Tadcaster LS24 .....189 D6
Beechcroft Cl TS12 ...9 F6
Beeches End LS23 ..188 F8
Beeches The
   Middleton St George DL2 ..4 D4
   Skelton YO30 ....224 C4
   11 Stokesley TS9 ...26 C7
   Wetherby LS22 .....180 D4
Beechfield
   Coulby Newham TS8 ..7 A5
   Hawsker-cum-Stainsacre
   YO22 ....33 A6
   Newby Wiske DL7 ...64 F2
   Newton-on-Ouse YO30 165 B6
Beechfield Cl YO8 ...197 B1
Beechfield Rd DL10 .209 C8
Beechings Mews
   YO21 ....208 B7
Beechnut La WF8 ...201 B1
Beechtree Rd LS24 .189 D5
Beechville Ave YO12 212 F6
Beechwood Ave 2 TS9 .26 C8
Beechwood Cl
   14 Bedale DL8 ......63 A2
   Markington with Wallerthwaite
   HG3 ....139 D4
   Sherburn in Elmet LS25 195 F3
Beechwood Cres 6
   HG2 ....219 C1
Beechwood Croft
   LS25 ....195 F3
Beechwood Dr BD23 .216 D5
Beechwood Glade
   Sherburn in Elmet LS25 195 F3
   7 York YO24 ....227 B1
Beechwood Gr
   Harrogate HG2 .....222 F7
   16 Ilkley LS29 .....175 C2
Beechwood Rd YO17 215 D2
Beechwood Rise 1
   LS22 ....180 C4
Beeforth Cl YO32 ...225 D5
Beeston's La LS17 ..178 C4
Beggarmans Rd DL8 ..80 C8
Belbrough Cl 3 TS15 .25 C4
Belbrough La TS15 ...25 C4
Belcombe Way 1 YO30 228 A7
Belford La HG4 .....112 A3
Belford Pl 8 HG1 ...219 D1
Belford Rd HG1 .....219 D1
Belford Sq 9 HG1 ..219 D1
Belfry Way 30 WF6 .200 B1
Belgrave Cres
   Harrogate HG2 .....222 E8
   15 Scarborough YO12 212 F5
Belgrave St
   3 Skipton BD23 ....216 E4
   York YO31 ....228 C7
Belgrave Terr
   3 Hurworth-on-Tees DL2 ..22 D8
   14 Scarborough YO11 212 F5
   Thirsk YO7 ....211 B2

Bell Cl Haxby YO32 ....225 C8
5 Seamer YO12 ....99 D6
Bell End Gn YO18 ....49 D3
Bell Hall★ YO19 ....191 E6
Bell La Cawood YO8 ......197 A4
Huby YO61 ....144 A4
Husthwaite YO61 ....117 B5
Rawcliffe DN14 ....205 A2
Ulleskelf LS24 ....190 C2
Bellaby Pk **7** YO62 ....93 D7
Bellburn La DL3 ....3 B7
Belle Hill BD24 ....131 B3
Belle Vue LS29 ....218 C3
Belle Vue Cres **33** YO14 ..101 B3
Belle Vue Par **9** YO11 ...212 F5
Belle Vue Pl **10** YO11 ....212 F5
Belle Vue St
34 Filey YO14 ....101 B3
Scarborough YO12 ......212 F5
York YO10 ....228 E3
Belle Vue Terr
Whitby YO21 ....208 D7
York YO10 ....228 E3
Bellerby Camp DL8 ....60 B7
Bellerby Rd DL8 ....60 D6
Bellerbyhurn Rd YO17 ..95 F2
Bellevue Terr
Ripon HG4 ....214 C5
2 Skipton BD23 ....216 E4
Bellfarm Ave YO31 ......228 E8
Bellground La YO30 .....165 D4
Bellhouse La YO21 ....29 C3
Bellhouse Way YO24 ....230 B4
Bellingham Cl YO7 ......211 C3
Bellman Wlk **3** HG4 .....113 D2
Bellmans Croft YO23 ....230 B2
Bell's Ct **15** YO62 ....92 F6
Bellwood Ave
Boston Spa LS23 ....188 E7
Lockwood TS12 ....9 E7
Bellwood Dr YO24 ......230 B8
Belmangate TS14 ....8 F6
Belmont WF11 ....201 D5
Belmont Ave
Harrogate HG2 ....220 D4
10 Otley LS21 ....176 F1
Belmont Cl **3** YO30 .....225 A1
Belmont Gr **1** HG2 .....220 D4
Belmont Prim Sch TS14 ..8 F6
Belmont Rd
Harrogate HG2 ....219 C2
Ilkley LS29 ....218 E4
Scarborough YO11 ......213 A4
Belmont St BD23 ....216 F4
Belmont Terr **2** HG2 ....220 D4
Belmont View HG2 ......221 A4
Belmont Wharf BD23 ....216 F4
Belthorpe La YO41 ......169 E1
Belton Pk Dr **7** DL9 .....40 E4
Belvedere Hospl YO11 ..213 A3
Belvedere Pl YO11 ......213 A3
Belvedere Rd YO11 .....213 A3
Belvedere Terr YO11 ....213 A3
Belvoir Ave **8** YO41 .....185 B2
Belvoir Dr WF11 ....201 F2
Belvoir Terr **9** YO11 ....213 A3
Ben La BB18 ....171 E2
Ben Rhydding Dr LS29 ..218 F3
Ben Rhydding Prim Sch
LS29 ....218 E4
Ben Rhydding Rd
LS29 ....218 D3
Ben Rhydding Sta
LS29 ....218 F4
Bence The YO42 ....170 C3
Benedict Ave YO8 ......232 E4
Beningbrough Hall &
Gdns★ YO30 ....165 B5
Beningbrough Dr HG3 ..219 B5
Beningbrough La
YO30 ....165 D5
Benjamin Thomas
Woodwork★ BD24 ....131 E2
Benjy La YO19 ....192 E7
Benkhill Dr **16** DL8 ......63 A2
Bennett St **11** BD23 ....216 F3
Bennions Way **5** DL10 ..41 E4
Bennison La YO21 ....13 A1
Bennymoor La YO8 .....198 C4
Bensham Rd DL1 ....3 D1
Benson La WF6 ....200 B2
Bent La Colne BB8 ......186 A3
Sutton BD20 ....187 E7
Bent Rigg La YO13 ......54 B7
Bentham Moor Rd
LA6 ....103 A2
Bentham Rd LA6 ....103 B3
Bentham Sta LA2 ....129 A7
Bentinck Ave TS5 ....6 F8
Bentley Wynd TS16 ......5 D3
Benton Cap La BD22 ...187 B7
Bents La YO18 ....71 A5
Beresford Cl **8** DL8 .....63 B2
Beresford Terr YO23 ....228 C1
Berghill La YO7 ....66 A7
Berkeley Terr YO26 .....227 E6
Berkley Dr TS14 ....8 F5
Bernard La YO7 ....164 B3
Bernica Gr TS17 ....6 A4
Berry Bank DL11 ....1 A6
Berry La LS26 ....200 C8
Berrygate La HG4 ......214 E2
Berry's Ave **5** HG5 .....221 B6
Berwick Rd
Archdeacon Newton DL3 ..3 A4
18 Scotton DL9 ....40 E4
Bestmire La YO8 ....65 A4
Betteras Hill Rd LS25 ..202 A8

Betton Farm Visitor Ctr★
YO13 ....99 C8
Betton Rise YO13 ....99 B8
Between Dikes Rd
YO8 ....204 F8
Beulah St **10** HG1 ......219 D3
Beulah Terr YO11 ....212 F5
Beverley Balk YO41 ....168 A3
Beverley Cl **12** YO11 ...100 B6
Beverley Gate YO12 .....99 D1
Beverley Rd
11 Eastfield YO11 ......100 B6
Middlesbrough TS7 ....7 D6
Norton YO17 ....215 E3
Beverley Rise LS29 .....175 C2
Beverley Sch TS4 ....6 F8
Bewerley Rd HG1 ....219 B5
Bewlay St YO23 ....228 C2
Bewley Gr TS5 ....6 F8
Bexhill Rd WF8 ....201 C1
Bexley Dr TS6 ....7 A8
Bickerton Way LS21 ....176 F1
Bickley Gate YO13 ......73 F6
Bickley Howe YO12 ....212 B4
Bickley Way TS8 ....7 A5
Bielby Cl **8** Bedale DL8 ..63 B3
33 Scalby YO12 ....75 D5
Big Mdw Dr **5** LS29 ....174 E4
Big Sheep & Little Cow
Farm★ DL8 ....63 B3
Biggin La LS25 ....196 C6
Bilsdale Cl
Northallerton DL7 ......210 C2
York YO10 ....224 E2
Bilsdale Gr HG5 ....221 D6
Bilsdale Midcable Chop Gate
CE VC Prim Sch 46 F6
Bilton Cl HG1 ....219 E6
Bilton Dr HG1 ....219 D4
Bilton Gr Ave HG1 .....219 E5
Bilton Grange Cl HG1 ..219 D5
Bilton Grange Com Prim Sch
........................219 D5
Bilton Hall Dr HG1 .....220 D6
Bilton La HG1 ....219 E6
Binks Cl DL6 ....210 B7
Binnington Carr La
YO12 ....99 B1
Binns La BD20 ....187 D7
Binsley La YO61 ....117 E2
Binsoe La HG4 ....86 F3
Birch Ave Malton YO17 ..15 B8
Sleights YO22 ....32 A6
Birch Cl **8** Filey YO14 ..101 B3
9 Hunton DL9 ....40 F2
2 Kirklevington TS15 ...24 E8
4 Thorpe Willoughby YO8 197 B1
York YO32 ....225 D3
Birch Copse YO24 ......227 D3
Birch Cres **10** YO12 ....32 A6
Birch Dr **2** Faceby TS9 ..25 E1
Kippax LS25 ....194 D2
Birch Gr
Castleford WF10 ....201 B3
Harrogate HG1 ....219 E6
Kippax LS25 ....194 D1
Birch Hall La BB18 .....172 B1
Birch La BD23 ....174 D8
Birch Rd DL1 ....3 D8
Birch View **8** YO18 ......96 A6
Birch Way YO61 ....143 D8
Birchen Cl **7** YO30 .....200 D3
Birches The TS8 ....7 A5
Birchfield Dr TS16 ......5 D5
Birchwood Cl **16** BD24 ..131 B3
Birchwood Ct **5** LS29 ..218 A4
Birchwood Mews HG2 ..222 F7
Birchwood Rd TS7 ......7 C6
Bird Gdn★ LS25 ....195 B7
Bird La Hensall DN14 ...203 D2
Kellington DN14 ....202 F4
Bird Ridding La DL8 ....60 B1
Birdale Field La LS22 ..188 B8
Birdforth Way **1** YO62 ..92 C1
Birds of Prey & Conservation
Area★ YO7 ....88 F7
Birdwood Cl DL9 ....209 C2
Birk Brow Rd TS12 ......9 D5
Birk Field Bank YO21 ....28 F6
Birk Head La YO62 ......70 F4
Birk La YO42 ....199 D8
Birkby La DL7 ....23 B1
Birkdale Ave HG5 ......221 D5
Birkdale Gr **4** YO26 ....227 B5
Birker La
Newton on Derwent
YO41 ....185 D4
Wilberfoss YO41 ....185 F6
Birkett La CA17 ....14 B7
Birkhills HG3 ....140 A3
Birkin Rd YO8 ....202 F5
Birklands **1** YO62 ......93 D7
Birkwith La LA2 ....128 F7
Birmham Rocks★
HG3 ....138 B4
Birstwith CE Prim Sch
HG3 ....160 E6
Birstwith Dr YO26 .....227 E4
Birstwith Grange HG3 ..160 E6
Birstwith Rd HG3 ......160 E6
Birthwaite La HG3 .....161 C8
Birtley Ave YO12 ....6 F2
Bishop Cl **1** HG3 ......137 C4
Bishop Ct **2** YO8 ......232 B6
Bishop Garth **2** HG3 ..137 C4

Bishop Monkton CE Prim Sch
HG3 ....140 A5
Bishop Monkton Rly Cutting
Nature Reserve★
HG3 ....139 F5
Bishop Thornton CE Prim Sch
HG3 ....139 F2
Bishop Thornton RC Prim
Sch HG3 ....139 A2
Bishop Way **3** HG3 ....137 C4
Bishop Wilton CE VC Prim
Sch YO42 ....169 F2
Bishopdale Cl HG5 .....221 D6
Bishopdale Dr **7** LS22 ..180 A1
Bishopdike Rd
Cawood YO8 ....197 A6
Sherburn in Elmet LS25 ..196 A4
Bishopgate St YO23 ....233 B1
Bishophill Jun YO1 .....233 A1
Bishophill Senior YO1 ..233 B1
Bishops Ct YO1 ....233 B1
Bishops Way DL10 ......41 D5
Bishopsfields Dr YO26 .228 A5
Bishopsgarth DL7 ......210 C4
Bishopsway YO10 ......229 C3
Bishopthorpe Inf Sch
YO23 ....231 A4
Bishopthorpe Pal★
YO23 ....231 B4
Bishopthorpe Rd
YO23 ....231 B5
Bishopton HG4 ....214 A5
Bishopton La
Great Burdon DL1 ....4 A7
Ripon HG4 ....113 D2
Bishopton Pk YO26 ....214 A5
Bisley Ct **13** DL1 ....3 F6
Bismarck St YO26 ......227 E5
Bitterdale La YO62 ......70 A3
Black Abbey La **1** BD20 187 E8
Black Bank Rd LA2 .....130 E3
Black Diamond Way **3**
TS16 ....5 D5
Black Dike La YO26 ....182 B3
Black Fen La YO8 ......232 C8
Black Gill La
Airton BD23 ....154 B8
Settle BD23 ....132 A1
Black Hill YO13 ....118 E5
Black Hill Rd HG3 .....157 F5
Black Horse La TS15 ....25 C3
Black Sike La YO13 ......98 B4
Black Wlk WF8 ....201 B1
Blackbird Way **8** YO12 ..99 F6
Blackburn La WF11 ....202 B2
Blacklee Cl **4** YO32 ....167 B8
Blacksmith Bank DL8 ...62 E5
Blacksmith Ct DL7 .....22 C2
Blacksmith Hill YO62 ..53 A7
Blackthorn TS8 ....7 B4
Blackthorn Dr YO31 ....225 E2
Blackthorn La HG3 .....222 C3
Blackthorn Rd LS29 ....218 D5
Blackwell DL3 ....3 B3
Blackwell La DL3 ....3 B4
Blackwood La YO8 .....198 D7
Blackwood Rd YO8 ....198 E8
Blair Ave TS17 ....5 F4
Blair Pk HG5 ....221 C5
Blake Ct YO19 ....193 A8
Blake Gate HG3 ....136 E1
Blake St YO1 ....233 B3
Blakeley Cres **3** BB18 ..171 D2
Blakeley Gr YO30 ......224 F3
Blakeney Pl YO10 ......228 F3
Blakey Bank YO62 ......49 A5
Blakey Cl YO7 ....211 C1
Blakey La YO7 ....211 C1
Blakey Rd YO62 ....70 B6
Bland La YO26 ....227 A4
Bland's Cliff **27** YO11 ..213 A6
Bland's Hill HG5 ....221 A4
Blandford Rd **3** DL8 ....40 E3
Blands Ave WF10 ......200 D7
Blands Cres **3** WF10 ..200 D7
Blands Gr **4** WF10 ....200 D7
Blands Terr WF10 ......200 D7
Blansby La YO17 ......121 C8
Blansby Pk La YO18 .....96 A8
Blatchford **2**
YO30 ....228 B8
Blawath Rd YO18 ....51 A2
Blayshaw La HG3 ......110 B4
Blazefield Bank HG3 ...137 D3
Blea Moor Rd LA6 ......78 E2
Blea Pit La HG4 ....140 E8
Bleaberry La YO41 .....169 B5
Bleachfield YO10 ......228 F2
Blean La DL8 ....57 D3
Bleara Rd BB18 ....186 B8
Blenheim Ave **4** YO11 ..208 B7
Blenheim Cl DL10 ......41 F6
Blenheim Ct
Harrogate HG2 ....222 D7
Rawcliffe YO30 ....224 D3
Blenheim St **12** YO12 ..213 A7
Blenheim Terr YO12 ....213 A7
Blenheim Way HG2 ....222 C7
Bleriot Way YO30 ......225 A3
Blewhouse La DL8 ......61 E3
Blind La Aiskew DL8 ....63 B3
Barton DL10 ....21 D7
Burton in Lonsdale LA6 ..102 F3
Guisborough TS14 ....8 C6
Hurworth DL2 ....22 E8
Knaresborough HG5 ....221 B7
Scorton DL10 ....42 B8

Blind La continued
Tockwith YO26 ....181 B8
Blind Piece La YO7 .....116 A6
Bloe Beck La LA2 ......129 E6
Bloody Beck Hill YO13 ..54 A7
Blorenge Ct **22** TS17 ....5 F4
Blossom St YO24 ......233 A1
Blossom Way WF10 ....200 D3
Blossomgate HG4 ......214 B5
Blue Bank YO22 ....32 A4
Blue Barn La TS15 ......25 C6
Blue Bell Gr TS15 ......25 C6
Blue Bridge La YO10 ..228 D2
Blue Nile Way **25** DL9 ..41 A1
Blue Ridge Pk WF10 ...200 E3
Blue Slates Cl YO19 ...193 A8
Bluebell Mdw **4** HG1 ..161 B3
Bluebell Wlk **18** HG3 ..161 B3
Blyth Cl YO8 ....232 A6
Boar La TS17 ....5 B5
Boat La Barforth DL11 ....1 C7
Great Ouseburn YO26 ..164 C8
Kirby Hall YO26 ....142 C1
Micklesown LS26 ......200 D5
Boatcliffe Rd YO14 ....127 D7
Boathouse La DL2 ......2 E4
Bob La YO7 ....65 E3
Bodmin Dr WF6 ....200 A2
Bodner Hill YO61 ......118 F1
Boeing Way TS18 ......5 F7
Bog Hall YO21 ....208 D5
Bog La
Askham Bryan YO24 ....230 B6
Barwick in Elmet & Scholes
LS15 ....194 A7
Stirton with Thorlby
BD23 ....216 D7
Wetherby LS22 ....180 C2
Boggart La LS24 ......190 C2
Boggy La DL10 ....209 B5
Boghole Bank HG4 .....45 B3
Boghouse La TS13 .....10 F3
Bogs La
Bridge Hewick HG4 .....114 C1
Harrogate HG1 ....220 C5
Bolckow St TS14 ....8 F7
Bold Venture St BD23 ..216 F2
Boldron Cl **8** TS18 ......5 D8
Bolland St **16** BB18 ....171 D2
Bolling Rd LS29 ....218 D4
Boltby Rd YO30 ....224 F2
Bolton Abbey Sta
BD23 ....174 D8
Bolton Ave DL10 ......209 B7
Bolton Castle★ DL8 ....59 B6
Bolton Cross DL10 .....41 F5
Bolton Ct **14** DL8 ......60 D5
Bolton Hall★ BD23 ....157 F1
Bolton La YO42 ....169 E1
Bolton on Swale St Mary's CE
Prim Sch DL10 ....41 F6
Bolton Percy Sta Nature
Reserve★ YO23 ......190 C4
Bolton Priory (rems of)★
BD23 ....157 F1
Bolton Rd
Draughton BD23 ....174 F7
Ellerton DL10 ....41 F5
Silsden BD20 ....174 D3
Bolton St HG1 ....219 D4
Bolton Way
13 Leyburn DL8 ....60 D5
Richmond DL10 ....209 C8
Bolton-on-Swale Nature
Reserve★ DL10 ....41 F5
Bonby La YO8 ....192 E2
Bond End HG5 ....221 A6
Bond La
Appleton Roebuck YO23 ..190 F5
Settle BD24 ....131 D2
Bond St WF8 ....201 C1
Bondgate Helmsley YO62 ..92 F6
Pontefract WF8 ....201 C1
Ripon HG4 ....214 C4
Selby YO8 ....232 B7
Bondgate Ct HG4 ......214 C4
Bondgate Gn HG4 .....214 C4
Bondgate Gn Cl **6** HG4 214 C4
Bondgate Gn La HG4 ..214 C4
Bondings Rise **5** LS25 ..196 A4
Bonington Ct **7** YO26 ..227 E4
Bonny Gr TS8 ....7 C5
Bonnygate YO61 ....118 F3
Bonnygrove Way TS8 ....7 B5
Bonnywell La YO7 .....114 E6
Boonhill Rd YO62 ......69 F4
Boosbeck Rd TS12 ......9 D8
Boot St **26** BB18 ......172 A1
Booth Bridge La BD23 ..172 A3
Booth Ferry Rd DN14 ..205 F6
Booth St **27** LS29 .....176 C1
Bootham YO30 ....233 A3
Bootham Bar★ YO31 ...233 B3
Bootham Cres YO30 ...233 A4
Bootham Pk Ct YO31 ..233 B4
Bootham Pk Hospl
YO31 ....233 B4
Bootham Row YO31 ...233 B3
Bootham Sch YO31 ....233 A3
Bootham Sq YO31 .....233 B3
Bootham Terr YO30 ....233 A3
Boothwood Rd YO30 ..224 E2
Booty La DN14 ....206 F7
Borage Rd **30** HG1 .....219 D1
Bore Tree Baulk YO19 ..184 D6
Borogate **9** YO62 ......92 F6
Borough Mere La
YO17 ....215 D8

Borough Rd
Darlington DL1 ....3 D5
Richmond DL10 ....208 D7
Boroughbridge High Sch
YO51 ....141 B5
Boroughbridge Prim Sch
YO51 ....141 B5
Boroughbridge Rd
Bishop Monkton HG3 ..140 B5
Bridge Hewick HG4 ....114 B1
Dishforth YO7 ....115 A2
Knaresborough HG5 ...221 B7
North Otterington DL7 ..64 E6
Northallerton DL7 .....210 C1
Ripon HG4 ....214 E3
Scriven HG5 ....162 E6
Westwick YO51 ....140 D4
Whixley YO26 ....164 B4
York YO26 ....227 D5
Borrage Gn La HG4 ....214 B4
Borrage La HG4 ....214 B4
Borrowby Ave DL6 ....210 F3
Borrowby La
Borrowby TS13 ....11 D7
Staithes TS13 ....13 J1
Borrowbydale Ave
HG5 ....221 D6
Borrowdale Dr
Castleford WF10 ....201 B5
York YO30 ....224 F1
Boss Moor La BD23 ...155 F8
Boston Ave DL6 ....210 D4
Boston Dr TS7 ....7 C8
Boston Rd Clifford LS23 188 E7
Wetherby LS22 ....180 C2
Boston Spa Comp Sch
LS23 ....188 D8
Botheby Wood BD23 ..216 E5
Bottom House La YO22 ..33 B5
Bottoms La YO22 ....33 B6
Botton Rd LA2 ....128 E2
Boulby Bank YO22 .....208 E6
Bouldershaw La DL11 ..17 D1
Boulsworth Dr BB8 ....186 B1
Boulsworth Gr **4** BB8 ..186 A3
Boundary Ave BD20 ...187 E7
Boundary Way DL10 ..209 F8
Bourlon Rd DL9 ....209 A2
Bourn Ave DL1 ....3 E5
Bournemouth Rd TS3 ...7 C8
Bouthwaite Dr **15** YO26 227 E4
Bow Bridge Dr BD23 ..217 D7
Bow Bridge La YO21 ...29 A7
Bow Bridge View
LS24 ....189 F7
Bow St TS14 ....8 F7
Bowbridge La DL7 ......63 A8
Bowcarr La YO26 ......163 D8
Bowcliffe Rd LS23 .....188 E5
Bowe Cres **8** DL8 ......63 B2
Bowen Rd DL3 ....3 B7
Bower St HG1 ....219 D2
Bower Wlk YO17 ......215 E4
Bowes Ave YO31 ......228 E5
Bowes La YO14 ....100 F5
Bowes Pk HG2 ....222 D6
Bowesfield Cres TS18 ...6 A8
Bowesfield Ind Est TS18 ..6 A8
Bowesfield La TS18 .....6 A7
Bowland Cl HG2 ....220 D1
Bowland Ct HG2 ......220 D1
Bowland La YO42 .....193 E2
Bowland View LA6 ....103 E3
Bowland Way HG2 ....225 A1
Bowling Gn Ct YO31 ..228 D8
Bowling Gn La
9 Hunmanby YO14 ....126 F8
Manfield DL2 ....2 B4
York YO31 ....233 C4
Bowling Gn Yd **13** HG5 221 A6
Bowling La YO17 ......215 E4
Bowling Terr BD23 ....216 D3
Bowling View BD23 ...216 D3
Bowman St DL3 ....3 D7
Bowness Dr YO30 .....224 E1
Bowthorpe La YO8 ....199 B4
Bowyers Cl YO23 .....230 C4
Box Hill YO12 ....212 C3
Box La WF8 ....201 C1
Boyle & Petyt Sch The
BD23 ....174 F8
Boyle The LS15 ....194 B8
Boynton La
Barton-le-Street YO17 ..120 F8
Rawcliffe DN14 ....205 A1
Boynton Rd DL7 ....22 E2
Brabourn Gdns TS8 .....6 F5
Bracewell La BD23 .....171 B4
Bracewell St **15** BB18 ..171 D2
Bracken Cl
Whitby YO22 ....208 A4
York YO32 ....225 F4
Bracken Cres TS14 ......8 E6
Bracken Field BD23 ...134 B3
Bracken Hill
Scarborough YO12 .....212 C7
2 York YO10 ....229 C3
Bracken Rd YO24 .....230 F7
Brackenber Cl BD24 ...131 C2
Brackenber La BD24 ...131 C1
Brackenfield Prep Sch
HG1 ....219 A2
Brackenhill Ave YO8 ..232 A4

Brackenhill La
Brayton YO8 . . . .**232** A3
Church Fenton LS24 . . . . . .**196** C6
Sleights YO22 . . . .**32** A5
Brackenhills YO26 . . . . .**165** F1
Brackenhoe Sch TS4 . . . .**7** B4
Brackenley Ave 2
BD23 . . . .**217** C7
Brackenley Cl 3 BD23 . .**217** C7
Brackenley Cres BD23 . .**217** C7
Brackenley Ct BD23 . . . .**217** C7
Brackenley Dr BD23 . . . .**217** C7
Brackenley Gr 1 BD23 . .**217** C7
Brackenley La BD23 . . . .**217** C7
Brackenthwaite La
HG3 . . . .**222** A1
Brackenwell La LS17 . . .**178** B4
Brackenwood Cl 2
LS29 . . . .**218** E4
Brackit La YO61 . . . .**91** B2
Bracknell Rd TS17 . . . .**6** C8
Bradfords Cl 8 LS23 . . .**188** E6
Bradley Ave
Castleford WF10 . . . .**200** E4
Northallerton DL6 . . . .**210** F2
Bradley Cres YO23 . . . . .**182** D6
Bradley Dr YO24 . . . .**230** D4
Bradley Gr BD20 . . . .**174** B1
Bradley Gr YO23 . . . .**182** C5
Bradley Rd
Pickering YO18 . . . .**71** F4
Silsden BD20 . . . .**174** B1
Bradley Rise BD20 . . . . .**174** B1
Bradleys Both Com Prim Sch
BD20 . . . .**173** E3
Bradleys Terr 2 TS9 . . . . .**8** A7
Bradworth Cl 3 YO11 . . .**100** B7
Bradworth Dr 2 YO11 . . .**100** B7
Braeburn Inf Sch & Com Jun
Sch YO11 . . . .**100** A6
Braegate La LS24 . . . . . .**190** E7
Braemar Dr LS25 . . . . . .**194** D4
Braeside 3 TS15 . . . .**24** E8
Braeside Gdns YO24 . . .**227** E3
Brafferton Hall Gdn 3
YO61 . . . .**115** F1
Braham La HG5 . . . .**179** F7
Brailsford Cres YO30 . . .**228** A8
Braimber La YO51 . . . . . .**141** C1
Braithegayte YO19 . . . . .**192** F4
Braithwaite Hall ★ DL8 .**84** D8
Braithwaite La
Dacre HG3 . . . .**159** A4
East Witton Town DL8 . . . .**84** E8
Braker La YO26 . . . .**163** F4
Bramall La 6 DL1 . . . .**3** F6
Bramble Cl
18 Colburn DL9 . . . .**41** A5
11 Killinghall HG3 . . . .**161** B3
Bramble Ct 20 LS25 . . . .**195** A4
Bramble Dene YO24 . . . .**230** D7
Bramble Wlk YO17 . . . . .**215** B4
Bramblefields DL6 . . . . .**210** F4
Brambles 8 YO8 . . . .**197** B1
Brambles The 6 LS29 . . .**175** C2
Brambling Fields La
YO17 . . . .**122** C2
Bramblings The 6
WF10 . . . .**200** D3
Bramcote Prep Sch for Boys
YO11 . . . .**213** A3
Brame La HG3 . . . .**177** A8
Bramfield Way 6 TS17 . . .**6** D6
Bramham Ave YO26 . . . . .**227** A3
Bramham Dr HG3 . . . . . .**219** A4
Bramham Gr YO26 . . . . . .**227** A3
Bramham La LS23 . . . . . .**188** A6
Bramham Pk ★ LS23 . . .**188** C4
Bramham Pk Gdns ★
LS23 . . . .**188** C4
Bramham Prim Sch
LS23 . . . .**188** E6
Bramham Rd
Boston Spa LS23 . . . .**188** E7
Thorner LS14 . . . .**188** A3
York YO26 . . . .**227** A2
Bramley Ave YO8 . . . . . .**198** B5
Bramley Garth YO31 . . . .**229** B6
Bramley Head La HG3 . . .**158** F5
Bramper La DL7 . . . .**42** E1
Branch Rd BD23 . . . .**216** F2
Brandon Gr YO32 . . . . . .**226** E3
Brandsby Bank YO61 . . . .**118** D3
Brandsby Gr YO31 . . . . .**225** E2
Brandsby Rd YO61 . . . . .**118** A1
Brandsby St YO61 . . . . . .**118** A1
Brankin Dr DL1 . . . .**3** E4
Brankin Rd DL1 . . . .**3** D3
Branklyn Gdns TS17 . . . . .**6** A4
Branksome Gr 1 TS18 . . .**5** E8
Branksome Sch DL3 . . . . .**3** A6
Bransdale TS14 . . . .**8** D6
Bransdale Ave
Northallerton DL7 . . . .**210** C2
11 Pontefract WF6 . . . . . .**200** A2
Bransdale Cl 6 WF6 . . . .**200** A2
Bransdale Gr 3 HG5 . . . .**221** C6
Bransdale Mews 10
WF6 . . . .**200** A2
Bransdale Rd YO62 . . . . .**48** B1
Bransdale Wlk WF6 . . . .**200** A2
Bransholme Dr YO30 . . . .**225** A2
Brant Bank La LS29 . . . .**175** B3
Brant La LS24 . . . .**189** C4
Branton Cl YO26 . . . .**142** A1

Branton Ct YO26 . . . .**142** A1
Branton La YO26 . . . .**142** A1
Branton Pl YO26 . . . .**227** A1
Brass Castle La TS8 . . . .**7** C3
Brat La LS21 . . . .**177** A7
Bravener Ct YO30 . . . . . .**165** B6
Brawby La YO62 . . . .**94** E1
Bray Gate YO42 . . . .**169** E2
Bray Rd YO10 . . . .**231** F8
Braygate Balk YO18 . . . . .**72** C5
Braygate La YO18 . . . .**72** D5
Braygate St YO17 . . . . . .**121** C4
Braythorne La LS21 . . . .**177** E4
Brayton CE VC Sch
YO8 . . . .**232** A2
Brayton Coll YO8 . . . . . .**232** A3
Brayton Com Jun Sch
YO8 . . . .**232** A2
Brayton Junc YO8 . . . . . .**232** C1
Brayton La YO8 . . . .**232** B1
Breakmoor Ave BD20 . . .**174** C2
Brearlands BD23 . . . .**172** A3
Brearton La HG3 . . . .**161** E8
Breary Cl YO24 . . . .**227** F1
Breary Flat La HG5 . . . . .**221** C7
Brechin Dr TS17 . . . .**6** B6
Breckenbrough La
DL10 . . . .**41** A3
Breckenbrough Sch
YO7 . . . .**89** A6
Breckney La YO17 . . . . . .**122** D5
Breckon Hill YO62 . . . . . .**49** A1
Brecks La Kippax LS25 . . .**194** C2
Pockley YO62 . . . .**93** B8
Strensall YO32 . . . .**167** B7
Swillington LS26 . . . .**194** B2
York YO32 . . . .**225** F4
Brecksfield YO30 . . . . . .**224** C5
Brecon Cres TS17 . . . .**5** F4
Breedycroft La YO17 . . . .**121** C4
Breighton Rd
Bubwith YO8 . . . .**199** D6
Wressle YO8 . . . .**199** C3
Brendon Gr TS17 . . . .**6** A3
Brentwood DL8 . . . .**60** D5
Brentwood Cres YO10 . . .**229** C2
Brewers Ct YO7 . . . .**211** B3
Brewerton St HG5 . . . . . .**221** A5
Brewery La
5 Ripon HG4 . . . .**214** C4
Skipton BD23 . . . .**216** F4
Brewery Rd LS29 . . . . . .**218** C4
Brewery Visitor Ctr ★
HG4 . . . .**86** C4
Brewster Terr HG4 . . . . .**214** C6
Briar Ave YO26 . . . .**227** B4
Briar Cliffe YO8 . . . .**232** A3
Briar Dr YO31 . . . .**225** F2
Briar Pk 5 YO62 . . . .**93** C1
Briar Rd TS17 . . . .**6** B7
Briar Wlk YO8 . . . .**3** B3
Briardene Ave 9 YO12 . . .**75** E5
Briarfield Cl LS29 . . . . . .**218** D3
Briars Ct YO23 . . . .**190** E5
Briars Dr YO23 . . . .**190** E5
Briars The HG5 . . . .**221** B7
Briarwood Cl YO8 . . . . . .**202** F7
Brick Kiln La YO8 . . . . . .**203** D6
Brick Lands La YO8 . . . .**203** F4
Brickfield La YO51 . . . . .**141** D4
Brickhill La YO8 . . . .**204** F4
Brickkiln La
Aldbrough DL11 . . . .**2** A3
Forcett & Carkin DL11 . . . .**20** C8
Brickyard La YO7 . . . .**89** C6
Brickyard Rd YO51 . . . . .**141** A4
Bridge Beck La YO7 . . . . .**66** C7
Bridge Cl
Burniston YO13 . . . .**75** D7
3 Colburn DL9 . . . .**41** A5
Haxby YO32 . . . .**225** C7
5 Knaresborough HG5 . . .**221** A5
Bridge Cres DN14 . . . . . .**205** C4
Bridge Ct YO8 . . . .**232** D6
Bridge End DL6 . . . .**65** B5
Bridge Foot LS23 . . . . . .**188** F8
Bridge Garth
2 Boston Spa LS23 . . . . .**188** E7
South Milford LS25 . . . . . .**195** F2
Bridge Gn YO21 . . . .**29** C2
Bridge Hill LS21 . . . .**176** C7
Bridge Holm La YO22 . . . .**33** C2
Bridge La Ilkley LS29 . . . .**218** A5
Pollington DN14 . . . .**207** F6
York YO30 . . . .**233** A4
Bridge Mews LA6 . . . . . .**103** C4
Bridge Rd
Bishopthorpe YO23 . . . . . .**230** F3
Boston Spa LS23 . . . .**188** F8
Brompton-on-Swale DL10 . .**41** B6
Glusburn BD20 . . . .**187** E7
Hurworth DL2 . . . .**3** B3
Malton YO17 . . . .**215** C5
Old Byland & Scawton
YO7 . . . .**91** F7
10 Stokesley TS9 . . . .**26** C7
Bridge St 5 Bedale DL8 . .**63** A3
9 Brafferton YO61 . . . . . .**115** F1
Castleford WF10 . . . .**200** F4
Egglescliffe TS16 . . . .**5** D4
12 Helmsley YO62 . . . .**92** F6
8 Normanton South WF6 .**200** B2
16 Pickering YO18 . . . .**95** F7
Richmond DL10 . . . .**209** B6
Skipton BD23 . . . .**216** F4
Tadcaster LS24 . . . .**189** E6
Thirsk YO7 . . . .**211** B3
Whitby YO22 . . . .**208** D7

Bridge St *continued*
York YO1 . . . .**233** B2
Bridge Terr
Northallerton DL7 . . . .**210** C4
Richmond DL10 . . . .**209** B6
Bridge View Rd HG4 . . . .**214** C5
Bridges Ct YO8 . . . .**232** D6
Bridges La YO42 . . . .**193** E4
Bridgestones ★ YO18 . . .**73** B6
Bridle Way 1 YO26 . . . . .**227** A3
Bridle Wlk YO8 . . . .**232** C4
Bridlington Rd
Hunmanby YO14 . . . .**127** A7
Sledmere YO25 . . . .**150** C4
1 Stamford Bridge YO41 . .**168** D2
Wold Newton YO25 . . . . . .**126** A4
Bridlington St YO14 . . . .**126** F8
Brier Hill YO21 . . . .**29** C7
Brier La YO8 . . . .**205** A4
Briercliffe YO12 . . . .**212** C7
Briergate YO32 . . . .**225** C7
Brierley Cl LS25 . . . .**194** D4
Brierlands La LS25 . . . . .**194** E4
Brierley Rd YO12 . . . .**99** E7
Brier Cl 18 LS25 . . . .**175** C2
Darlington DL1 . . . .**3** E5
1 Glusburn BD20 . . . .**173** E1
Skipton BD23 . . . .**216** E4
15 Trawden BB8 . . . .**186** A3
York YO26 . . . .**227** F5
Brigg Farm Ct YO8 . . . . .**204** D5
Brigg La YO8 . . . .**204** D5
Brigg Rd 55 YO14 . . . . . .**101** B3
Brigg's Ave WF10 . . . . . .**200** E3
Briggate HG5 . . . .**221** B5
Briggs St YO31 . . . .**228** C7
Bright St 18 Colne BB8 . .**186** A3
Darlington DL1 . . . .**3** E5
1 Glusburn BD20 . . . .**173** E1
Skipton BD23 . . . .**216** E4
15 Trawden BB8 . . . .**186** A3
York YO26 . . . .**227** F5
Bright Terr BB8 . . . .**186** A1
Bright Wlk YO8 . . . .**232** B6
Brighton Rd LS29 . . . . . .**218** E3
Brigshaw Dr WF10 . . . . .**200** C8
Brigshaw High Sch
WF10 . . . .**200** C8
Brigshaw La WF10 . . . . .**200** C8
Brimham Rocks ★
HG3 . . . .**138** B4
Brind La YO8 . . . .**199** F2
Brindle Pk Dr WF10 . . . .**201** A3
Brindley Ct 15 BD23 . . . .**216** F3
Brindley Mill BD23 . . . . .**216** F3
Brindley Wharf BD23 . . .**217** A3
Brindleys La DN14 . . . . .**199** F3
Brinkburn Ave DL3 . . . . . .**3** B7
Brinkburn Dr DL3 . . . .**3** B6
Brinkburn Rd
Darlington DL3 . . . .**3** B6
4 Scarborough YO12 . . . .**212** C5
Brinklow Way HG2 . . . . .**222** B5
Brinkworth Terr 1
YO10 . . . .**228** E3
Briscoe Ridge La HG3 . . .**177** F6
Briscoe Way TS8 . . . .**6** E5
Britannia St 2 YO12 . . . .**212** E5
Broach La Heck DN14 . . .**203** D1
Kellington DN14 . . . .**202** F3
Broach Rd Heck DN14 . . .**207** D8
Hensall DN14 . . . .**203** C1
Broad Acres YO32 . . . . .**225** C7
Broad Balk YO17 . . . .**149** A5
Broad Balk La YO7 . . . . .**115** B1
Broad Carr Rd HG3 . . . . .**110** D2
Broad Cl TS8 . . . .**6** D5
Broad Dubb Rd HG3 . . . .**177** C8
Broad Gate
Brompton YO13 . . . .**98** B7
Hunsingore YO26 . . . .**180** F8
Marton cum Grafton
YO26 . . . .**141** F1
Broad Gate Rd YO21 . . . . .**28** E4
Broad Head La BD22 . . . .**187** E2
Broad Highway YO19 . . . .**192** F8
Broad La
Appleton Roebuck YO23 . . .**191** A6
6 Beal DN14 . . . .**202** D4
Catton YO41 . . . .**185** C7
Cawood YO8 . . . .**197** A6
Church Fenton LS24 . . . . .**196** D6
Rufforth YO23 . . . .**227** A2
Wistow YO8 . . . .**197** A5
Broad Oak YO61 . . . .**166** D8
Broad Oak La 8 YO32 . . .**166** E5
Broadacres DN14 . . . . . .**204** D3
Broadacres Ave DN14 . . .**204** D3
Broadacres Garth
DN14 . . . .**204** D3
Broadfield La DN14 . . . . .**138** B8
Broadfield Way 9 LS29 . .**174** E4
Broadgate Rd TS5 . . . .**6** E8
Broadlands
2 Roundhill Village TS17 . .**6** A5
Wheldrake YO19 . . . .**193** A8
Broadlands Dr 5 YO13 . . .**99** B8
Broadmanor YO8 . . . .**199** A7
Broadmires La YO18 . . . .**96** C5
Broadrum La YO18 . . . . . .**95** E6
Broadstone Way YO30 . . .**224** E3
Broadway
Scarborough YO12 . . . . . .**212** D7
York YO10 . . . .**231** E8
Broadway Gr 3 YO10 . . . .**231** E8
Broadway The DL1 . . . .**3** E5
Broadway W YO10 . . . . . .**231** D8
Broadwell Rd TS4 . . . .**7** A8
Brockadale Nature Reserve ★
WF8 . . . .**206** B4
Brockfield Pk Dr YO31 . . .**225** F2
Brockfield Rd YO31 . . . . .**225** E2
Brockholme La DL6 . . . . .**65** A4

Brocklesby Rd TS14 . . . . .**8** F5
Brockley Cl LS24 . . . .**196** B7
Broc-o-bank 1 DN6 . . . .**206** E2
Brodrick Dr LS29 . . . . . .**218** A3
Brogden La BB18 . . . . . .**171** B1
Brokes La DL11 . . . .**40** B6
Bromley La TS8 . . . .**7** C2
Bromley St 2 YO26 . . . . .**227** F5
Brompton & Sawdon Com
Prim Sch YO13 . . . .**98** C5
Brompton Ave TS14 . . . . .**8** F7
Brompton Carr La
YO13 . . . .**98** B4
Brompton Com Prim Sch
DL6 . . . .**43** F3
Brompton Hall Sch
YO13 . . . .**98** C5
Brompton House Day Hospl
DL6 . . . .**210** E5
Brompton Ings Rd
YO13 . . . .**98** D3
Brompton La DL6 . . . .**43** E4
Brompton Rd
Newton-le-Willows DL8 . . . .**62** B4
Northallerton DL6 . . . .**210** D5
York YO30 . . . .**228** A7
Brompton-on-Swale CE Prim
Sch DL10 . . . .**41** B4
Bronaber Cl 1 TS17 . . . . .**5** F4
Bronte Cl
Brompton on Swale DL10 . .**41** C7
Scarborough YO12 . . . . . .**212** C6
Bronte Ct WF8 . . . .**201** B1
Bronte Dr DL9 . . . .**41** A5
Bronte Rise WF10 . . . . . .**201** B3
Brook House Croft
BD24 . . . .**131** E6
Brook La Danby YO21 . . . .**29** F6
Halton West BD23 . . . .**153** F1
Thornton Dale YO18 . . . . . .**96** D6
Weeton LS17 . . . .**178** C2
Brook Pk YO21 . . . .**32** A7
Brook St
Castleford WF10 . . . .**201** B6
18 Earby BB18 . . . .**172** A1
Hebden BD23 . . . .**135** A2
Hellifield BD23 . . . .**154** B3
Ilkley LS29 . . . .**218** B4
12 Scarborough YO12 . . .**212** F6
Selby YO8 . . . .**232** C4
York YO31 . . . .**233** B4
Brook View BD23 . . . . . .**173** B4
Brookacre 7 LA6 . . . .**103** D3
Brooke Cl
Harrogate HG1 . . . .**219** E7
12 Kirkbymoorside YO62 . .**70** B1
Brookfield HG3 . . . .**160** F5
Brookfield Cl HG3 . . . . . .**161** A5
Brookfield Cres HG3 . . . .**161** A5
Brookfield Ct 5 WF6 . . . .**200** B1
Brookfield Garth HG3 . . .**161** A5
Brookfield Way
7 Earby BB18 . . . .**172** A1
Hampsthwaite HG3 . . . . . .**160** F5
Brookland 1 LA6 . . . .**102** F2
Brooklands
43 Filey YO14 . . . .**101** B3
York YO10 . . . .**229** D4
Brooklands Cl 44 YO14 . .**101** B3
Brooklands Cres DL6 . . .**210** E5
Brooklands Sch BD23 . . .**216** F2
Brooklands Terr BD23 . . .**216** F3
Brooksbank Rd TS7 . . . . . .**7** D7
Brookside
Collingham LS22 . . . .**188** A8
Hovingham YO62 . . . .**119** E6
Skelton & Brotton TS12 . . . .**9** D8
Skipton BD23 . . . .**217** A3
Sleights YO22 . . . .**32** A5
Brookside Ave 1 DL8 . . . .**63** B2
Brookside Cl 2 DL8 . . . . .**63** B2
Brookwood Way TS16 . . . .**5** E4
Broom Hill Ave 6 TS17 . . .**6** D5
Broom House La
Egton YO21 . . . .**30** F4
Ugthorpe YO21 . . . .**12** B2
Broom Rd LS24 . . . .**189** D5
Broom Wlk YO12 . . . .**212** F4
Broome Cl
14 Pontefract WF6 . . . . .**200** A2
York YO32 . . . .**225** F5
Broome Way YO32 . . . . .**226** A5
Broomfield HG3 . . . .**160** E6
Broomfield Ave DL7 . . . .**210** D2
Broomfield Com Prim Sch
DL7 . . . .**210** D2
Broomfield Terr 18
YO21 . . . .**208** D6
Broomhill WF10 . . . .**201** A3
Broomhill Cl 23 WF11 . . .**202** A2
Broomhill Cres 25
WF11 . . . .**202** A2
Broomhill Dr 26 WF11 . . .**202** A2
Broomhill Gr 19 WF11 . . .**202** A2
Broomhill Pl 22 WF11 . . .**202** A2
Broomhill Sq 24 WF11 . . .**202** A2
Broomhill Wlk 21 WF11 . .**202** A2
Brootes La BD23 . . . .**107** C2
Brotes La YO26 . . . .**164** B5
Brotherton & Byram Com
Prim Sch WF11 . . . .**201** E4
Brough Ave 5 DL9 . . . . . .**41** A5
Brough Field Cl 4 TS17 . . .**6** D6
Brough Hall ★ DL10 . . . .**41** B4
Brough Mdws DL10 . . . . .**41** A5
Brough Rd 28 DL9 . . . . . .**40** E4
Brougham Cl YO30 . . . . .**227** F8

Brougham St
Darlington DL3 . . . .**3** C7
Skipton BD23 . . . .**217** A3
Broughton Ave BD23 . . . .**216** D3
Broughton Cres BD23 . . .**216** C4
Broughton Gn La
YO17 . . . .**121** C9
Broughton Gr BD23 . . . . .**216** D3
Broughton Mews
BD23 . . . .**216** D3
Broughton Rd
Broughton YO17 . . . .**121** C9
11 East Ayton/West Ayton
YO13 . . . .**99** A1
Malton YO17 . . . .**215** A5
Skipton BD23 . . . .**216** C3
Broughton Rise YO17 . . .**215** B5
Broughton Way
4 Harrogate HG2 . . . . . .**220** C3
York YO10 . . . .**229** A4
Brow La LA2 . . . .**129** D6
Browcliff BD20 . . . .**174** C2
Brown Bank La BD20 . . . .**174** D2
Brown Bank Rd
Kirkby Malzeard HG4 . . . . .**111** F5
Norwood HG3 . . . .**177** B8
Brown Cow Rd YO8 . . . . .**204** C8
Brown Howe Rd YO18 . . . .**51** A1
Brown La YO26 . . . .**141** F1
Brown Moor 22 YO41 . . . .**168** D2
Brown Rigg Rd YO13 . . . .**53** F5
Brown's Terr 4 TS13 . . . .**11** F7
Browney Croft YO10 . . . .**233** C1
Browning Cl 3 DL9 . . . . . .**40** E4
Brownlow St YO31 . . . . . .**233** C4
Brownmoor La
Huby YO61 . . . .**144** A2
Sutton-on-the-Forest
YO61 . . . .**166** B8
Brownroyd 14 BB18 . . . .**172** B1
Browns Ct 4 BD20 . . . . .**173** E3
Browns Fold 3 BD23 . . . .**134** E3
Browsfield Rd 24 LS29 . .**174** F4
Broxa Hill YO13 . . . .**74** C6
Broxa La YO13 . . . .**74** D5
Broxa Moor La YO13 . . . . .**74** C7
Bruce Way 5 YO18 . . . . . .**95** F6
Brunel Ct 12 YO26 . . . . .**227** F5
Brunel Rd HG1 . . . .**220** D5
Brunel Way DL1 . . . .**3** D5
Brunsell La YO26 . . . .**163** F7
Brunswick Cl 2 YO32 . . .**167** C8
Brunswick Dr HG1 . . . . .**219** B2
Brunswick Pl 1 HG1 . . . .**219** D1
Brunswick Sh Ctr
YO11 . . . .**213** A5
Brunswick St
Whitby YO21 . . . .**208** D6
York YO23 . . . .**228** B1
Brunt Acres Est DL8 . . . . .**56** D5
Brunt Acres Rd DL8 . . . . .**56** D4
Brunthwaite La BD20 . . .**174** C1
Brunton Bank DL8 . . . . . .**59** A5
Brunton La HG5 . . . .**163** B6
Brunton Rd LA2 . . . .**131** A6
Bry Hills YO12 . . . .**99** D6
Bryan Cl 18 DL2 . . . .**3** E1
Bryden Cl DL6 . . . .**210** E2
Bryony Ct YO8 . . . .**232** B2
Bryony Rd 4 HG3 . . . . . .**161** B3
Bryony Way 5 HG3 . . . . .**161** B3
Bubwith Prim Sch
YO8 . . . .**199** D7
Buck Haw Brow BD24 . . .**131** B4
Buck La YO60 . . . .**147** B6
Buck Stone La BD20 . . . .**187** C5
Buckden Cl 13 YO61 . . . .**143** D8
Buckden Wood La
BD23 . . . .**107** D8
Buckingham Ct YO1 . . . .**233** A1
Buckingham Sq 7 YO62 . .**92** F6
Buckingham St YO1 . . . .**233** B1
Buckingham Terr YO1 . . .**233** B2
Buckingham Way
WF11 . . . .**201** F4
Buckle Cl YO8 . . . .**199** A8
Buckle Ct YO8 . . . .**232** B2
Buckle La WF6 . . . .**200** A1
Bucks La 1 BD24 . . . . . .**131** D2
Buess La DL1 . . . .**4** A7
Buffet Hill La LA2 . . . . . .**129** D7
Bugthorpe La YO41 . . . . .**169** D5
Bugthorpe La Town E
YO41 . . . .**169** E5
Bull Alley La DN14 . . . . .**204** B3
Bull Balk YO41 . . . .**185** E4
Bull Hill DL8 . . . .**61** E8
Bull Ing La BD23 . . . .**134** D3
Bull La Huby YO61 . . . . . .**166** B7
York YO10 . . . .**228** F3
Bull Moor La YO60 . . . . .**168** A8
Bull Piece La YO17 . . . . .**122** D3
Bullamoor Cl DL6 . . . . . .**210** F5
Bullamoor Jun Sch
DL6 . . . .**210** F6
Bullamoor Rd DL6 . . . . .**210** E5
Buller St YO8 . . . .**232** B6
Bullock La
Newsham YO7 . . . .**88** F8
Newsham with Breckenbrough
YO7 . . . .**89** A5
Bullytree La LS25 . . . . . .**195** E2
Bulmer Hill YO60 . . . . . .**146** B6
Bungalow Rd BD20 . . . . .**187** D7
Bunkers Hill
Aberford LS25 . . . .**194** F7
1 Skipton BD23 . . . .**217** A4

Burdale Cl
8 Eaglescliffe TS16 ....5 D5
Norton YO17 ....215 F2
Burdike Ave YO30 ....228 A8
Burdock Cl 10 HG3 ....161 D5
Burdon Garth TS17 ......6 D5
Burgate YO18 ....95 F7
Burgess Wlk YO24 ....230 C8
Burghley Dr 1 TS17 .....6 A5
Burgoyne Cl HG4 .....113 D3
Burke Rd YO17 ....215 C5
Burke St HG1 ....219 E5
Burlands La YO26 .....182 F7
Burley Ave HG3 ......161 A2
Burley Bank Cl HG3 ..161 A3
Burley Bank Rd HG3 ..161 A3
Burley Cl
  South Milford LS25 ...195 F2
  Thornton-le-Street YO7 ..65 B1
Burley La HG3 ....161 A3
Burley Oaks Prim Sch 42
  LS29 ....176 C1
Burlyn Rd 3 YO14 ....127 A8
Burma Rd DL2 ....3 F2
Burn Bridge La HG3 ..222 C2
Burn Bridge Oval HG3 .222 C3
Burn Bridge Rd HG3 ..222 C3
Burn Est YO32 ....225 D4
Burn Hall Cl YO8 .....203 D7
Burn La YO8 ....203 D6
Burn Wood Ct TS21 .....5 A7
Burnby Cl HG3 ....219 B5
Burneston CE VA Prim Sch
  DL8 ....87 E8
Burneston Hargill DL8 ..87 F8
Burnett Cl HG3 ......140 A2
Burnham Rd LS25 ....194 C3
Burnholme Ave YO31 ..229 B6
Burnholme Com Coll
  YO31 ....229 A5
Burnholme Dr YO31 ...229 A6
Burnholme Gr YO31 ...229 A5
Burniston Gdns YO13 ..75 D7
Burniston Rd YO12 ...212 E8
Burniston Gr YO10 ...229 A4
Burnley Rd BB8 ......186 A1
Burnleys Ct LS26 ....200 B4
Burnleys Dr LS26 ....200 B4
Burnleys Mews LS26 ..200 B4
Burnleys View LS26 ..200 B5
Burnmoor Cres LA6 ..103 D3
Burnmoor Dr TS16 .....5 D5
Burnroyd Ave 17 BD20 187 E7
Burns Ct YO24 ......230 B7
Burns Hill 4 LS29 ...174 F4
Burns Way
  Boston Spa LS23 ....188 E7
  Harrogate HG1 .....219 F2
Burnsall Cl 6 YO14 ..101 A3
Burnsall Dr YO26 ....227 E4
Burnsall La BD23 ....135 A1
Burnsall Mews BD20 ..174 B2
Burnsall VA Prim Sch
  BD23 ....157 B8
Burnside Ave BD23 ...216 F2
Burnside Cl HG1 .....219 B5
Burnside Cres BD23 ..216 F2
Burnside Dr HG1 .....219 B5
Burnside Rd
  Darlington DL1 ....3 E4
  Harrogate HG1 .....219 B5
Burnside Wlk HG1 ...219 B5
Burnt La HG4 ....87 A1
Burnt Yates CE Prim Sch
  HG3 ....160 F8
Burnthouse Bank DL6 ..45 B3
Burr Bank 15 YO11 ...213 B6
Burrard Ave DL10 ....209 B7
Burrill Ave YO30 ....228 B8
Burrill Dr 13 YO32 ...166 D5
Burrill Rd DL8 ....62 F2
Burrow Rd LA6 ......102 B7
Burstall Dr 2 DL9 ...209 C1
Burtersett Rd DL8 ....56 D4
Burton Ave YO30 ....228 B7
Burton Comm La
  LS25 ....202 A6
Burton Ct YO30 .....233 A4
Burton Fields Cl 12
  YO41 ....168 D2
Burton Fields Rd 4
  YO41 ....168 D2
Burton Fleming Rd
  YO25 ....126 B3
Burton Gn YO30 .....228 B8
Burton Gn Prim Sch
  YO30 ....228 B8
Burton Hill 3 LA6 ...102 F3
Burton La YO61 .....141 D8
Burton Leanard Lime
  Quarries Nature Reserve★
  HG3 ....140 A1
Burton Leonard CE Prim Sch
  HG3 ....140 A2
Burton Rd LA2 ......128 E8
Burton Riggs Nature
  Reserve★ YO11 .....99 F6
Burton Salmon Com Prim
  Sch LS25 ....201 F6
Burton Stone La YO30 .233 A4
Burtondale Rd 1 YO12 .99 F7
Burtree Ave YO30 ...224 B4
Burtree La YO21 .....29 B5
Burwains La BD23 ...155 F5

Burwen Castle (Roman
  Fort)★ BD23 ....172 C4
Burwen Castle Rd
  BD23 ....172 C4
Busby La TS9 ....26 C4
Busk La LS24 ....196 C8
Busky Dike La LS21 ..159 E2
Butcher La Potto DL6 ..25 C2
  Whitley DN14 ....207 A6
Butcher Terr YO23 ...228 C1
Butcher's La YO25 ...126 E3
Butler Rd HG1 ....219 E5
Butt Fields La DN14 ..203 F1
Butt Hedge YO26 ....182 A5
Butt Hill 22 Haxby YO32 166 D5
  Kippax LS25 ....194 D1
Butt Hills★ YO25 ...126 A3
Butt La
  Carlton Husthwaite YO7 116 F7
  Guisborough TS14 .....9 A4
  Wold Newton YO25 ..126 A3
Buttacre La YO23 ....182 D2
Butter Mkt 8 DN14 ..204 C1
Butterbur Way 34 HG3 161 B3
Buttercrambe Rd
  YO41 ....168 C3
Buttercup Cl 6 HG3 ..161 B3
Butterfield Cl HG3 ...140 B5
Butterfield Dr TS16 ....5 D5
Buttermere Ave
  Middlesbrough TS5 ....6 E8
  4 Wetherby LS22 ...180 B3
Buttermere Ct 9 YO8 232 B6
Buttermere Dr YO30 .224 E1
Butters Cl 20 YO32 ..166 D5
Butterwick La YO17 ..120 F8
Butterwick Rd
  Barton-le-Street YO17 ..120 E5
  Foxholes YO25 ......125 B1
  Langtoft YO25 ......151 C7
Butthouse Rigg DL11 ..35 F8
Buttle La 3 DN14 ...204 C1
Butts YO25 ....171 D1
Butts Cl 19 YO41 ....168 D2
Butts Hill YO14 .....127 C6
Butts La Bainbridge DL8 .81 B8
  Barton-le-Willows YO60 146 D2
  Bentham LA2 ....129 A8
  Eaglescliffe TS16 .....5 D4
  Monk Fryston LS25 ...201 E8
  South Milford LS25 ..195 E1
Butts The 12 NYE8 ..201 B1
Buxton Ave TS7 ......7 B5
Byards Pk 6 HG5 ....221 A4
Byefield Gr YO13 .....99 B8
Byemoor Ave TS9 .....8 A1
Byemoor Cl TS9 ......8 A1
Byland Abbey (rems of)★
  YO61 ....91 E1
Byland Ave
  Northallerton DL6 ...210 E5
  Thirsk YO7 ....211 C3
  York YO31 ....228 E8
Byland Ct 5 YO21 ...208 B6
Byland Gr HG1 ......219 F6
Byland Mews HG5 ...221 D4
Byland Pl
  Harrogate HG1 .....219 F6
  Northallerton DL6 ..210 E5
Byland Rd
  Harrogate HG1 .....219 F6
  Whitby YO21 ....208 B6
Bylands Way DL3 ......3 A6
Byng Rd DL9 ....209 F1
Byram Cl 3 DL6 .....210 E3
Byram Ct 4 DL6 ....210 E3
Byram Pk Ave WF11 ..201 F4
Byram Pk Rd WF11 ..202 A4
Byron Ave DN6 ......206 E1
Byron Ct 22 D7
Byron Dr YO30 .....227 F8
Byron St 2 BD23 ....217 A3
Byron Wlk Mews HG2 219 D2
Byward Dr YO12 .....99 F7
Byway The DL1 ....3 E5
Byways HG2 ....222 D6

C

Cabin La 2 HG3 .....137 F1
Caburn Cl 2 YO12 ...212 B5
Caedmon Ave YO21 ..208 B8
Caedmon Cl YO31 ...229 A7
Caedmon Sch YO21 ..208 B8
Cairn View LS29 ....218 D5
Cairnborrow 4 YO24 .230 B7
Caithness Cl 1 YO30 224 E3
Calcaria Cres LS24 ..189 D5
Calcaria Rd LS24 ....189 E5
Calcutt HG5 ....221 A4
Caldbeck Cl 1 YO30 .225 A1
Calder Ave YO26 ....227 B8
Calder Cres DN14 ...207 F6
Caldey Gdns 39 TS17 ..5 F4
Caledonia St YO12 ..212 E5
Caledonian Way DL1 ..3 F8
Calf Cl YO32 ....225 D8
Calf Hall La BB18 ...171 D1
Calf Wood La BD20 ..172 E1
California Ct 14 TS9 ...8 D2
California Dr YO11 ...200 B3
California Gr 7 TS9 ....8 D2
California Rd YO22 ..208 E5
California Terr YO22 .208 E5
Callum Cl DL3 ....3 C7
Calton La BD23 .....155 A6

Calton Terr BD23 ...216 F3
Calvert Cl YO32 ....225 C7
Calvert Hos DL11 ....36 C4
Calverts Garth YO60 145 D5
Cam Gill Rd BD23 ...108 B4
Cam High Rd BD23 ...79 D5
Cam La BD23 ....172 A3
Camblesforth CP Sch
  YO8 ....204 C4
Cambrain Ct 10 TS17 ..5 F4
Cambrian Cl 2 YO32 225 F3
Cambridge Ave TS7 ..7 B5
Cambridge Cres 5
  HG1 ....219 D2
Cambridge Pl
  7 Harrogate HG1 ...219 D2
  1 Scarborough YO12 212 E4
Cambridge Rd
  Harrogate HG1 .....219 D2
  Middlesbrough TS5 ....6 E8
Cambridge St
  15 Harrogate HG1 ..219 D2
  Normanton South WF6 200 A1
  Scarborough YO12 ...212 F6
  4 York YO24 ....228 A3
Cambridge Terr
  7 Harrogate HG1 ...219 D2
  1 Scarborough YO11 213 A4
Camden Rd WF10 ...201 B4
Camela La YO8 .....204 B6
Cameron Gr YO23 ...228 C1
Camm La DN14 ....204 C3
Cammock La BD24 ..131 D2
Camp Hill Cl HG4 ...214 D3
Camp the (Earthworks)★
  YO11 ....126 C7
Campbell Ave
  Ripon HG4 ....113 D3
  York YO24 ....227 E2
Campbell St 11 BD20 187 E8
Campion Cl YO13 ....75 D5
Campion Dr TS14 .....8 D6
Campion Gr
  Coulby Newham TS7 ..7 B6
  6 Harrogate HG3 ..161 B3
Campion La LS15 ....25 B4
Campion Rd DL1 ......3 D7
Campleshon Rd YO23 228 B1
Campsall Balk DN6 ..206 A1
Campsall Hall Rd 12
  DN6 ....206 A1
Campsall Pk Rd 11 DN6 206 E1
Campsmount Sch
  DN6 ....206 D1
Camwal Rd HG1 ....220 C4
Camwal Terr 5 HG1 .220 C4
Cana La HG4 ....114 E2
Canaan St LS24 .....60 E2
Canal Garth DN14 ..207 F6
Canal Rd
  Cottingwith YO42 ...193 C5
  Ripon HG4 ....214 D4
  Selby YO8 ....232 D4
Canal St BD23 ......216 F4
Canal View YO8 ....232 D3
Canal Yd 8 BD23 ...216 F4
Canberra Rd TS7 .....7 B6
Canby La 4 HG3 ....179 E6
Candler Ave 12 YO13 ..99 A7
Candler St YO12 ....212 E5
Canham Gr YO10 ...229 D3
Cannon Hall La DN14 202 F1
Cannon St WF10 ....200 F3
Canon Gr YO15 ......5 E2
Canon Lee Sec Sch
  YO30 ....228 A8
Canons Cl YO23 ....231 B2
Canons Garth La 2 YO62 92 F6
Canterbury Cl
  9 Haxby YO32 .....166 D5
  Whitby YO21 ......208 C5
Canterbury Ct 5 WF8 201 C2
Canton Gdns TS5 .....6 E6
Caper Hill YO21 ......29 C1
Captain Cook & Staithes
  Heritage Ctr★ TS13 ..13 K2
Captain Cook Birthplace
  Mus★ TS7 ....7 B7
Captain Cook Cres
  YO22 ....208 E6
Captain Cook Meml Mus★
  YO22 ....208 E7
Captain Cook Prim Sch
  TS7 ....7 B6
Captain Cook's Cl
  Hinderwell TS13 .....11 D8
  Staithes TS13 ....13 K1
Captain Cook's Cres 7 TS6 .7 C6
Captain Cook's Mon★
  TS9 ....8 D1
Captain Cook's Schoolroom
  Mus★ YO22 ....208 E6
Captain Cook's Way TS9 .8 A1
Captain Cooks Cres 14
  YO22 ....208 E6
Cardale Pk HG3 ....222 A6
Cardan Dr LS29 ....218 E4
Cardinal Cl 18 LS25 ..195 F4
Cardinal Gdns DL3 ...3 B5
Cardinals Cl 3 YO8 .197 B8
Careless House La
  HG3 ....138 C4
Carentan Cl 6 YO8 ..232 B6
Carey St YO10 .....228 D1
Cargate Hill 32 YO14 .101 B3
Cargo Fleet La TS3 ...7 C8
Carl St YO23 ....228 C2
Carla Beck La BD23 ..173 B4

Carlbury Ave TS5 .....6 D6
Carlbury Cres DL3 ....3 A5
Carless La YO14 ....100 F4
Carleton Ave BD23 ..216 E3
Carleton Bsns Pk 216 E3
Carleton Dr DL3 ......3 A5
Carleton Endowed Sch
  BD23 ....173 B4
Carleton La BD23 ...173 A4
Carleton New Rd BD23 216 E3
Carleton Rd BD23 ...216 E1
Carleton St
  3 Skipton BD23 ....216 F3
  17 York YO26 ......227 F5
Carlile Hill TS8 ......6 E5
Carline Mead 23 HG3 161 B3
Carlisle St 16 YO26 ..227 F5
Carlow Cl TS14 ....8 F6
Carlton & Faceby CE VA Prim
  Sch TS9 ....26 A3
Carlton App 1 LS22 .180 B3
Carlton Ave Thirsk YO7 211 B1
  York YO10 ....229 D3
Carlton Cl
  4 Carlton Miniott YO7 89 C4
  Eggborough DN14 ...202 F1
  19 Normanton South WF6 200 A1
Carlton Dr TS17 ......6 A6
Carlton Gdns WF6 ..200 B1
Carlton La YO62 .....92 F7
Carlton Lanes Sh Ctr
  WF10 ....200 F4
Carlton Miniott Com Prim
  Sch YO7 ....89 B4
Carlton Moor Cres DL1 .3 E4
Carlton Rd
  Carlton Miniott YO7 ..89 A3
  Catterick Garrison DL9 40 F4
  9 Filey YO14 ......101 B3
  Harrogate HG2 .....222 D7
  Helmsley YO62 ......92 F7
  Sutton upon Derwent
  YO41 ....185 C1
Carlton St 6 YO11 ..213 A4
Carlton Terr 6 YO11 213 A4
Carlton Twrs★ DN14 204 D2
Carlton View
  Great Preston WF10 200 C7
  Selby YO8 ....232 D4
Carlton-in-Snaith CP Sch
  DN14 ....204 C3
Carlyle Cres WF10 ..201 A4
Carlyle Rd WF10 ....201 A4
Carmel Gr DL3 ......3 B4
Carmel RC Tech Coll
  DL3 ....3 A5
Carmel Rd N DL3 ....3 B5
Carmel Rd S DL3 ....3 A4
Carmelite St YO1 ...233 C2
Carmires Ave
  Haxby YO32 ....166 F5
  Knaresborough HG5 ..221 C8
Carnagil Rd DL9 ....209 B1
Carnagill Com Prim Sch
  DL9 ....40 D4
Carney St TS12 ......9 D7
Carnot St YO26 .....227 F5
Carnoustie Cl 1 YO26 227 E4
Carnoustie Dr TS16 ..5 E5
Carnoustie Gdns 20
  WF6 ....200 B1
Carnoustie Way TS8 ..7 A5
Caroline Cl 5 YO26 ..227 F3
Carousel Wlk LS25 ..195 F4
Carpenters Yd YO17 215 C4
Carpley Gn Rd DL8 ..57 D3
Carr Ave LS25 ......195 F4
Carr Beck Cl YO26 ..200 D3
Carr Beck Rd 2 WF10 200 D3
Carr Beck View 5
  WF10 ....200 D3
Carr Bridge La DL6 ..24 C7
Carr Cl
  13 Hemingbrough YO8 198 F1
  Rainton with Newby YO7 114 F6
  Ripon HG4 ....214 B3
Carr Field La YO26 ..141 F1
Carr Fields La YO12 ..99 B5
Carr Head La BD20 ..187 B7
Carr Hill YO60 .....145 D5
Carr Hill La YO21 ....32 B7
Carr Hill Ridge YO21 .32 B7
Carr House La
  Cayton YO11 ......100 A5
  Heslerton YO17 .....98 A1
Carr Inf Sch YO26 ..227 E5
Carr Jun Sch YO26 .227 E5
Carr La Ampleforth YO62 92 B1
  Azerley HG4 ....113 A7
  Barlby with Osgodby
  YO8 ....232 F5
  Barlow YO8 ....204 C4
  Castleford WF10 ....200 F3
  Cawton YO62 ......119 C8
  Cayton YO11 ......100 B4
  East Ayton YO13 ....99 B7
  Escrick YO19 ......192 B5
  Glaisdale YO21 .....30 D4
  Gristhorpe YO11 ...100 E4
  Heslerton YO17 ....124 A8
  Kilburn High & Low YO61 .91 B3
  Little Ouseburn YO26 164 A7
  Long Drax YO8 ....204 F6
  Muston YO14 ......100 F3
  Newby & Scalby YO13 .75 C5
  Newton on Derwent
  YO41 ....185 F4
  Rainton with Newby YO7 114 F6

Carr La continued
  Roecliffe YO51 .....140 E3
  Sheriff Hutton YO60 .145 E6
  Stillington YO61 ....144 C6
  Sutton-on-the-Forest
  YO61 ....144 D2
  Thirlby YO7 ....90 F6
  Thormanby YO61 ...116 E4
  Wetherby LS22 ....180 D4
  Wistow YO8 ....197 A3
  York YO17 ....227 D5
Carr Leys La YO7 ....66 A5
Carr Mill Mews BD22 187 B5
Carr Rd 7 BB18 ....171 D2
Carr Side Rd YO26 ..163 F8
Carr St YO8 ....232 F4
Carr The HG3 ......222 E2
Carr Wood Rd WF10 200 F3
Carrbank La YO32 ..167 E3
Carrfield YO24 .....230 C8
Carrfield Dr LS15 ...194 B8
Carrfield Rd LS15 ..194 B8
Carriage Wlk 4 TS16 ..5 D5
Carrick Gdns YO24 .227 E3
Carrier's Row BB8 ..186 B2
Carrington Ave 1 YO26 227 E5
Carrnock Ct 3 YO32 225 F1
Carrol Cl DL6 ......210 F2
Carroll Pl 2 DL2 ....22 C8
Carron Cres YO24 ..230 B7
Carrs Mdw YO19 ...192 B5
Carrs The YO21 ....208 A2
Carrside 2 YO11 .....99 F6
Carseylands Hill BD23 155 A4
Cart Riggin YO7 .....66 A8
Carter Ave YO31 ...228 F5
Carter La 2 YO62 ...70 B1
Carter's La Ilkley LS29 218 E6
  Longnewton TS16 .....5 A4
Carters Yd DL10 ...209 B6
Cartmell Terr DL3 ....3 C6
Cass House Rd TS8 ...6 E4
Cass La
  Knaresborough HG5 .221 A4
  South Milford LS25 ..195 E1
Castelo Gr 1 YO11 ...96 A6
Castle Bank DL6 ....25 C1
Castle CE Jun Sch
  HG5 ....221 B6
Castle Cl Cawood YO8 197 A8
  1 Haxby YO32 .....166 D5
  Killinghall HG3 ....161 C5
  Middleton St George DL2 .4 C3
  2 Spofforth HG3 ...179 E6
  1 Thornton Dale YO18 96 D5
Castle Cres YO11 ...213 B7
Castle Ct HG5 .....221 A5
Castle Dyke Wynd TS16 .5 E3
Castle Earthworks★
  YO8 ....204 F4
Castle End DL8 ......59 B6
Castle Garth
  Pontefract WF8 ....201 C1
  4 Thornton Dale YO18 96 D5
Castle Gate 4 LS29 .218 B4
Castle Gdns YO11 ..213 B6
Castle Hill
  8 Hunmanby YO14 126 F8
  2 Ilkley LS29 ....218 B4
  Richmond DL10 ....209 C6
  4 Settle BD24 .....131 E2
Castle Hill Cl HG2 ..222 B6
Castle Hill Dr HG2 ..222 B6
Castle Hill Glade HG2 222 B6
Castle Hill Gr HG2 ..222 B6
Castle Hill La YO8 ..204 F5
Castle Howard★
  YO60 ....120 D1
Castle Howard Dr
  YO17 ....215 A4
Castle Howard Rd
  YO17 ....215 A4
Castle Ings 1 HG3 ..179 E6
Castle Ings Cl 1 HG5 221 A5
Castle Ings Rd 3 HG5 221 A5
Castle La Danby YO21 .29 D6
  10 East Ayton/West Ayton
  YO13 ....99 B8
Castle Mdws DL8 ....87 A7
Castle Mills HG5 ...221 A5
Castle Rd Colne BB8 186 A4
  1 Ilkley LS29 ......218 B4
  Killinghall HG3 ....161 C5
  18 Pickering YO18 ...95 F7
  Scarborough YO11 .213 A6
  Thornton Dale YO18 ..96 D5
  Whitby YO21 ......208 A6
Castle Rise 1 YO13 ..99 A7
Castle Side YO60 ...145 D5
Castle St Skipton BD23 217 A3
  Spofforth HG3 .....179 E6
Castle Steads (Fort)★
  DL8 ....84 C8
Castle Steads★ DL11 .19 D6
Castle Terr
  Richmond DL10 ....209 C6
  16 Scarborough YO11 213 B6
Castle View
  7 Newby & Scalby YO13 .75 D5
  Richmond DL10 ....209 B6
  Sheriff Hutton YO60 .145 C5
Castle View Terr BD23 216 F4
Castle Wlk YO1 ....233 C2
Castle Wynd 11 DL10 209 C6

Castle Yd 🖪 Ilkley LS29 ..**218** B4
  Knaresborough HG5 ....**221** A5
Castle Yd Stables YO7 ..**211** B3
Castlebergh Hospl
  BD24 ....**131** C2
Castlebergh La 🖪 BD24 **131** E2
Castleford High Sch Tech
  Coll WF10 ....**200** F4
Castleford La
  Featherstone WF7 ......**200** D2
  Knottingley WF11 ......**201** D3
Castleford Mkt Pl★
  WF10 ....**200** D4
Castleford Mus Rm★
  WF10 ....**200** E4
Castleford Normanton &
  District Hospl WF10 .**200** D3
Castleford Rd WF6 ....**200** B2
Castleford Redhill Jun Sch
  WF10 ....**201** B4
Castleford Sta WF10 ..**200** C4
Castleford Three La Ends
  Prim Sch WF10 ....**200** D4
Castlegate
  East Ayton/West Ayton
  YO13 ....**99** A7
  🖪 Helmsley YO62 ......**92** F6
  Kirkbymoorside YO62 ....**70** B1
  🖪 Knaresborough HG5 ..**221** B5
  Malton YO17 ....**215** C4
  🟫 Pickering YO18 ......**95** F7
  Scarborough YO11 .....**213** B7
  Thirsk YO7 ....**211** B2
  York YO1 ....**233** B2
Castlekeep Cl DL10 ....**209** C8
Castlemount Ave YO13 ..**75** D6
Castlereagh Cl TS21 ....**5** A7
Castleton Ave
  Middlesbrough TS5 ......**6** D8
  Northallerton DL7 .....**210** C1
Castleton Com Prim Sch
  YO21 ....**29** A7
Castleton Moor Sta
  YO21 ....**29** A7
Castleton Rd DL9 ......**40** F4
Castley La LS21 ....**178** A1
Cat Bank DL11 ....**39** C6
Cat La Balne DN14 ....**207** E5
  Bilbrough YO23 ....**182** D1
Cat Pottery★ DL8 ......**58** F1
Cathcart Cl DN14 .....**206** F7
Cathedral Cl HG4 .....**214** D5
Catherine Love Dr 🟫
  YO61 ....**143** C8
Catherine St 🖪 TS12 ....**9** F7
Cattal Moor La YO26 ..**181** B8
Cattal St YO26 ....**164** A2
Cattal Sta YO26 ......**164** A2
Catterick Bridge★
  DL10 ....**41** C6
Catterick La DL10 ......**41** D3
Catterick Racecourse
  DL10 ....**41** C5
Catterick Rd DL9 ......**40** F4
Catterton La
  Catterton LS24 ....**190** A8
  Healaugh LS24 ....**182** A1
Cattle La LS25 ....**194** F8
Catton La YO7 ....**115** A7
Catton Moor La YO7 ..**114** F8
Caudle Hill WF11 .....**201** C6
Causeway BD23 ....**81** E3
Causeway The DL1 ......**3** E5
Cautley Dr HG3 ....**161** C5
Cautley Gr HG3 ....**161** C5
Cavalry Ct 🟫 YO12 ....**75** F5
Cavendish Ave
  Harrogate HG2 ....**219** E1
  🖪 Pontefract WF8 .....**201** C2
Cavendish Ct HG2 .....**222** F8
Cavendish Gr YO10 ....**229** D3
Cavendish Rd TS4 ......**7** A8
Cavendish St
  Barnoldswick BB18 ....**171** D1
  Harrogate HG1 ....**219** E5
  Skipton BD23 ....**216** F3
Cavendish Terr 🖪 HG4 ..**214** C5
Cavendish View BD23 ..**217** D7
Caversham Rd TS4 ......**7** A8
Cawcliff La YO18 ......**97** A5
Cawdel Cl 🖪 LS25 .....**195** F2
Cawdel Way LS25 .....**195** F2
Cawder Ghyll BD23 ...**217** A1
Cawder Gn BD23 ......**217** A2
Cawder La BD23 ......**217** A1
Cawder Mews BD23 ...**217** A1
Cawder Rd BD23 ......**217** A1
Cawood CE VA Prim Sch
  YO8 ....**197** B8
Cawood Cres LS24 ....**190** C1
Cawood Dr TS5 ....**6** F7
Cawood Rd
  Stillingfleet YO19 .....**191** D3
  Wistow YO8 ....**197** C7
Cawthorn Rd HG2 .....**220** B2
Cawthorn Pl HG2 .....**220** B3
Cawthorne Cres YO11 ..**101** A3
Cawthorne La YO18 ....**71** D3
Cawton Rd YO62 ......**118** F8
Caxton Ave YO26 .....**227** D6
Caxton Cl 🖪 DL10 .....**41** C7
Caxton Gdns 🖪 WF8 ..**201** B2
Caxton Way YO11 .....**99** F6
Cayley Cl YO30 ....**224** F1

Cayley La YO13 ....**98** C5
Caymer Rd YO11 .....**100** A7
Cayton Com Prim Sch
  YO11 ....**100** B6
Cayton Low Rd YO11 ...**99** F1
Cayton Low Rd Ind Est
  YO11 ....**100** A6
Cecil Rd 🖪 YO14 .....**127** A8
Cecil St
  Barnoldswick BB18 ....**171** D2
  Harrogate HG1 ....**219** E5
Cecilia Pl 🖪 YO24 ....**228** A3
Cedar Cl
  Hambleton YO8 ....**197** B1
  Ripon HG4 ....**214** B3
Cedar Cres YO8 ......**197** D2
Cedar Dr
  Coulby Newham TS8 .....**6** D4
  Tadcaster LS24 ....**189** D6
Cedar Glade YO19 ....**184** E7
Cedar Gr Barton DL10 ..**21** C7
  🖪 Filey YO14 ....**101** B4
  Middleton One Row DL2 ..**4** D3
  Sutton BD20 ....**187** E7
  York YO31 ....**229** B3
Cedar Grange YO22 ...**222** D7
Cedar Mews 🖪 DL2 ....**22** D8
Cedar Rd DL3 ....**3** B6
Cedar Ridge LS25 ....**194** E5
Cedar Vale 🖪 YO62 ....**70** B1
Cedarhurst Dr TS12 ....**9** F7
Cedarwood 🖪 DL2 ......**4** C4
Cedarwood Ave 🖪 TS9 ..**26** C8
Cedarwood Cl 🖪 YO24 ..**227** B1
Cedarwood Glade TS8 ...**6** C4
Celtic Cl YO26 ....**227** B5
Cemetery La DL3 ....**3** A5
Cemetery Rd
  🟫 Earby BB18 ....**172** A1
  Normanton South WF6 ..**200** B1
  Thirsk YO7 ....**211** A3
  York YO10 ....**233** C1
Cennon Gr 🟫 TS17 ......**5** F4
Centenary Row BD23 ..**217** D8
Central Arc DL6 ......**210** D5
Central Av 🖪 YO61 ....**143** D8
Central Dr
  Castleford WF10 ......**200** C4
  Northallerton DL6 ....**210** E4
Central St TS16 ....**5** E3
Central Way 🖪 TS9 .....**8** A2
Centre La LS24 ....**189** E6
Centre Rd BD20 ......**186** D7
Centurion Cl 🟫 DL10 ...**41** E4
Centurion Pk YO30 ...**225** B2
Centurion Way
  Clifton YO30 ....**225** B3
  Crossgates YO12 ....**99** E4
Century Wlk 🟦 HG2 ...**220** B3
Ceres Rd LS22 ....**180** C3
Chacksfield Rd 🟫 DL10 ..**41** E4
Chadderton Cl TS12 .....**9** E8
Chadderton Dr TS17 .....**6** C7
Chafer Wood Nature
  Reserve★ YO13 ....**97** D6
Chain Bar La HG3 .....**161** A4
Chain La HG5 ....**221** A6
Chair Wlk HG4 ....**139** B8
Chaldon Cl 🟦 YO32 ...**167** A6
Chaldron Way TS16 .....**5** D6
Chalfield Cl TS17 ....**6** B4
Chalfonts YO24 ......**227** F1
Chalford Oaks TS5 .....**6** D8
Challacombe Cres TS17 ..**6** A3
Challoner Rd TS15 .....**5** D2
Chaloner St TS14 ....**8** F6
Chaloner's Cres YO24 ..**230** D7
Chaloner's Rd YO24 ...**230** D8
Chamber End Fold 🟦
  BD23 ....**134** E3
Champion Ave 🟫 WF10 ..**200** F3
Chancel Way YO11 ....**208** A6
Chancery Ct YO24 ....**227** C3
Chancery Rise
  Stockton-on-Tees TS18 ...**6** A6
  York YO24 ....**227** F2
Chandler Cl DL10 ....**209** F8
Chandlers Ct YO11 ...**213** B2
Chandlers Ridge Prim Sch
  TS7 ....**7** D5
Chandlers Wharf
  YO17 ....**215** C3
Chantilly Ave DL3 ......**3** F7
Chanting Hill Cl YO60 ..**146** B6
Chantry Ave 🟦 YO26 ..**165** F1
Chantry Bank DL8 .....**59** D3
Chantry Cl YO24 .....**230** C8
Chantry Ct HG3 ......**161** C7
Chantry Dr
  East Ayton/West Ayton
  YO13 ....**99** B8
  🖪 Ilkley LS29 ....**218** B3
Chantry Gap 🟦 YO26 ..**165** F1
Chantry Garth DL8 .....**59** D3
Chantry Gr 🟦 YO26 ...**165** F1
Chantry La
  Bishopthorpe YO23 ....**231** B4
  Scotton HG5 ....**162** A6
  Stutton with Hazlewood
  LS24 ....**189** B3
Chantry Rd
  🟫 East Ayton/West Ayton
  YO13 ....**99** B8
  Northallerton DL7 ....**210** B3
Chantry Wynd 🟫 DL10 .**209** C6
Chapel Balk Rd YO8 ...**198** F1
Chapel Bridge★ DL11 ...**1** C7

Chapel Cl
  Bilton-in-Ainsty with Bickerton
  LS22 ....**181** B5
  Church Fenton LS24 ...**196** B8
  🟫 Helmsley YO62 .....**92** F6
  Rawcliffe DN14 ....**205** A1
Chapel Cres DL7 ......**63** C8
Chapel Croft 🟫 BD23 ..**134** E3
Chapel Ct
  Gargrave BD23 ....**155** D1
  Huby YO61 ....**144** A4
Chapel Fields Rd
  YO26 ....**227** A3
Chapel Fold 🟫 BD23 ..**134** E3
Chapel Garth
  Dalton YO7 ....**115** E7
  Markington with Wallerthwaite
  HG3 ....**139** C3
  Thrintoft DL7 ....**63** F7
Chapel Gate
  Kirkby Malham BD23 ..**154** F8
  Malham BD23 ....**132** F1
  Sherburn YO17 ....**124** D6
Chapel Haddlesey CE VC
  Prim Sch YO8 ....**203** B5
Chapel Hill
  Boroughbridge YO51 ..**141** C5
  Kearby with Netherby
  LS22 ....**179** B1
  Skipton BD23 ....**217** A5
Chapel Hill La LS24 ...**178** A1
Chapel House Mews 🟫
  BD23 ....**173** B4
Chapel La
  Askham Bryan YO23 ...**182** F3
  Barwick in Elmet LS15 .**194** C8
  Boston Spa LS23 .....**188** E7
  Brayton YO8 ....**232** B1
  Brompton YO13 ....**98** B7
  🟪 Burton in Lonsdale LA6 **102** F3
  🟫 Easingwold YO61 ..**143** C5
  🟫 Eastfield YO11 ....**100** B6
  Finghall DL8 ....**61** E4
  Halton East BD23 ....**174** C8
  Harome YO62 ....**93** C4
  Hebden BD23 ....**135** A2
  Horton in Ribblesdale
  BD24 ....**105** C3
  Ilkley LS29 ....**218** A4
  Langtoft YO25 ....**151** D5
  Little Smeaton WF8 ...**206** B3
  Marton-le-Moor HG4 ..**114** F1
  Rawcliffe DN14 ....**205** A2
  Reighton YO14 ....**127** E5
  🖪 Riccall YO19 ......**192** A1
  🖪 Spofforth HG3 .....**179** E5
  🖪 Thornton Dale YO18 ..**96** D5
  Tollerton YO61 ....**143** A3
  Westow YO60 ....**147** B4
Chapel Mews YO7 ....**211** C2
Chapel of Our Lady★
  YO11 ....**213** C7
Chapel Rd
  🟫 Scarborough YO11 .**213** A6
  Settrington YO17 .....**122** D1
Chapel Riggs 🟦 DL10 ...**41** E4
Chapel Row YO11 .....**233** C1
Chapel Sq 🟫 BD24 ....**131** E2
Chapel St
  🟦 Addingham LS29 ...**174** F4
  🟫 Beadlam YO62 .....**93** D7
  Carleton BD23 ....**173** B4
  Cattal YO26 ....**164** A1
  🟫 Earby BB18 ....**172** A1
  🟫 Filey YO14 ....**101** B3
  Grassington BD23 ....**134** E3
  Hambleton YO8 ....**196** F1
  Hillam LS25 ....**202** B7
  Kirk Hammerton YO26 .**164** C2
  Knaresborough HG5 ...**221** B5
  Middleton St George DL2 ..**4** C4
  Nunnington YO62 ......**93** E2
  🟫 Settle BD23 ....**131** D2
  Tadcaster LS24 ......**189** E6
  Thirsk YO7 ....**211** B2
Chapel Terr YO24 ....**227** C3
Chapel Wlk
  Long Preston BD23 ...**153** F5
  🟫 Riccall YO19 ......**192** A1
Chapman Cl 🟦 YO32 ..**167** C8
Chapman Ct BB18 ....**171** D2
Chapman La 🟫 HG4 ....**86** C3
Chapman Sq HG1 .....**219** B2
Chapman's La YO30 ..**165** E7
Chapmans Ct YO24 ...**230** D6
Chapter House St YO1 .**233** B3
Charles Ave HG1 .....**219** E5
Charles Ct DL10 .....**209** F7
Charles Moor YO31 ...**228** F7
Charles St YO8 ......**232** B6
Charles Wesley Dr
  YO8 ....**232** B2
Charlock TS8 ....**7** B4
Charlton Ave
  Knaresborough HG5 ...**221** B6
  🟫 Whitby YO21 ......**208** B7
Charlton Ct 🟪 HG5 ...**221** B6
Charlton Dr HG5 .....**221** B6
Charlton Gr 🟦 HG5 ...**221** B6
Charlton Manor Dr 🟫
  HG5 ....**221** B6
Charlton St YO23 ....**228** C2
Charlton Villas HG5 ..**221** B6
Charnwood Dr TS7 .....**7** D6
Charrington Ave TS17 ...**6** A6
Charter Ave DN14 ....**205** A1
Charters The YO8 ....**198** B5
Chartwell Cl TS17 .....**6** B4

Chase Garth Rd 🟫
  YO61 ....**143** C8
Chase Side Ct YO24 ..**230** E8
Chase The
  🟦 Boroughbridge YO51 **141** B4
  Garforth LS25 ....**194** D4
  Hurworth-on-Tees DL2 ..**3** E1
  Knaresborough HG5 ...**221** D5
  Norton YO17 ....**215** E2
  🟫 Wetherby LS22 ....**180** C3
Chastworth Ct HG1 ...**219** D4
Chatham Rd HG4 .....**113** D2
Chatsworth Ave 🟫 WF8 **201** C2
Chatsworth Dr
  🟫 Haxby YO32 ......**166** F5
  🟦 Wetherby LS22 ....**180** B3
Chatsworth Gdns
  YO12 ....**212** E7
Chatsworth Gr
  🟦 Boroughbridge YO51 **141** B5
  Harrogate HG1 ....**219** C4
Chatsworth Rd HG1 ...**219** D4
Chatsworth Terr
  🟦 Harrogate HG1 ....**219** E4
  🟦 York YO26 ....**227** E4
Chaucer Gn HG1 .....**219** F7
Chaucer La YO62 ......**69** F5
Chaucer St 🟫 YO10 ..**228** C2
Chaumont Way 🟦 YO32 **167** D2
Chauvel Cl DL9 ......**209** C2
Cheapside
  🟦 Knaresborough HG5 .**221** B5
  🟫 Normanton South WF6 **200** A1
  🟦 Settle BD23 ....**131** D2
Cheapsides Rd YO17 ..**215** B8
Checker La YO19 .....**198** A7
Checkstone Ave
  WF10 ....**200** D2
Chelkar Way YO30 ....**224** F1
Chelmsford Rd HG1 ...**219** E2
Cheltenham Ave
  Ilkley LS29 ....**218** E4
  Middlesbrough TS7 ......**7** B5
Cheltenham Cres 🟫
  HG1 ....**219** D2
Cheltenham Mount
  HG1 ....**219** D3
Cheltenham Par HG1 ..**219** D3
Cheltenham Rd 🟫 HG1 **219** D3
Chelwood Wlk 🟫 YO24 **227** E4
Chepstow Ct 🟦 DL1 .....**3** F6
Cherry Ave
  Malton YO17 ....**215** D6
  Swinton YO17 ....**121** B4
Cherry Cl YO21 ......**208** B3
Cherry Garth YO31 ...**229** B5
Cherry Garth Rd DL7 .**210** C3
Cherry Gr 🟫 Bedale DL8 **63** B3
  🟦 Ilkley LS29 ....**175** C2
  🟫 Poppleton YO26 ...**165** F1
Cherry Hill La YO23 ...**233** B1
Cherry La YO24 ......**230** E6
Cherry Orch 🟫 YO32 ..**225** D8
Cherry Paddock
  🟫 Haxby YO32 ......**225** D8
  Kexby YO41 ....**168** C2
Cherry Rd 🟫 YO14 ...**127** A8
Cherry St YO23 ......**233** B1
Cherry Tree Ave
  Newton-on-Ouse YO30 .**165** B6
  🟦 Scarborough YO12 .**212** B5
  York YO32 ....**225** D4
Cherry Tree Cl
  🟫 Brayton YO8 ......**197** D1
  🟫 Castleford WF10 ..**200** D4
Cherry Tree Ct 🟫 YO8 .**198** B4
Cherry Tree Dr YO14 ..**101** A4
Cherry Tree Gdns 🟫
  DL9 ....**209** B1
Cherry Tree Way 🟫 DL9 ..**41** A5
Cherry Tree Wlk
  Amotherby YO17 .....**121** A4
  🟫 Barlby YO8 ....**198** B4
Cherry Wood Cres
  YO19 ....**231** B5
Cherrytree Cl HG4 ...**140** E7
Cherrywood Ave 🟫 TS9 ..**26** C8
Chervil Ct TS8 ....**7** B4
Cherwell Croft YO8 ...**196** F1
Cherwell Ct YO8 .....**196** F1
Cheshire Ave YO32 ...**167** A6
Cheshire Cl 🟦 YO32 ..**226** E4
Cheshire Sq 🟦 YO7 ...**89** B1
Chesler-pit La YO61 ..**117** F2
Chesney Fields 🟫 YO24 **227** D1
Chessingham Gdns
  YO24 ....**230** E6
Chessingham Pk YO19 **184** F6
Chester Ct YO8 ......**204** A6
Chester La DL6 ....**65** D8
Chesterton Ave TS17 ...**6** A6
Chestnut Ave
  🟫 Airmyn DN14 .....**205** A4
  Harrogate HG1 ....**219** F3
  🟫 Hemingbrough YO8 **198** F1
  Malton YO17 ....**215** D6
  🟫 Topcliffe YO7 .....**89** A1
  Welburn YO60 ....**146** A6
  York YO31 ....**228** F6
Chestnut Bank YO12 ..**212** D6
Chestnut Cl Bedale DL8 ..**63** B3
  🟫 Catterick DL10 ....**41** D5
  🟫 Ilkley LS29 ....**218** E4
  Richmond DL10 ......**209** C8
  Scarborough YO12 ...**212** D6

Chestnut Cres
  🟫 Catterick Garrison DL9 ..**40** F5
  🟦 Catton YO7 ....**89** A1
Chestnut Croft 🟫 YO8 ..**198** F1
Chestnut Ct
  🟫 Hemingbrough YO8 **198** F1
  York YO32 ....**225** F5
Chestnut Dr
  🟫 Barnoldswick BB18 **171** D1
  🟫 Hemingbrough YO8 **198** F1
  Middlesbrough TS7 .....**7** C6
Chestnut Garth 🟫 YO8 **198** F1
Chestnut Gn 🟫 LS25 ..**202** A8
Chestnut Gr
  Acomb YO26 ....**227** C4
  Harrogate HG1 ....**219** E6
  Huntington YO32 .....**225** E4
  Norton YO17 ....**215** E4
Chestnut Mews YO8 ..**197** A8
Chestnut Rd
  Cawood YO8 ....**197** A8
  Eaglescliffe TS16 ......**5** E6
Chestnut Rise 🟫 YO8 ..**198** F1
Chestnuts The
  🟫 Haxby YO32 ......**225** C8
  Hensall DN14 ....**203** D2
  Pontefract WF8 ......**201** C2
  Scarborough YO12 ...**212** B7
Chevin Dr YO14 ......**101** A3
Cheviot Cl 🟫 YO32 ...**225** F3
Chew St
  Gargrave BD23 ....**155** D1
  Seamer YO12 ....**99** D6
Chichester Cl 🟫 YO13 ..**75** D5
Chieftain Rd DL9 ......**40** C4
Chiltern Ave WF10 ...**200** C3
Chiltern Way YO32 ...**225** F5
Chilvers Ct 🟦 YO8 ...**232** A1
Chimes Rd YO8 ......**232** C6
Chimes The 🟫 YO8 ...**232** C6
China St DL3 ....**3** D7
Chippendale Rise 🟫
  LS21 ....**177** A1
Chippenham Rd TS4 .....**7** A7
Cholmley Way YO22 ..**208** F3
Christ Church CE Prim Sch
  BB8 ....**186** A3
Christ Church CE VC Prim
  Sch BD23 ....**216** F3
Christ Church Oval
  HG1 ....**219** E6
Christina St 🟦 HG1 ...**219** C5
Christ's Hospl DL8 ....**63** A1
Christy Gate Rd YO21 ..**28** C3
Chubb Hill Rd YO21 ..**208** C6
Chudleigh Rd
  Harrogate HG1 ....**219** E3
  🟫 York YO26 ....**227** C4
Church Ave
  Clapham LA2 ....**130** C8
  🟫 Dacre HG3 ....**137** F1
  Harrogate HG1 ....**219** D5
  🟫 Selby YO8 ....**232** C4
Church Balk YO19 ....**184** E7
Church Bank
  Aysgarth DL8 ....**58** F3
  Hunton DL8 ....**61** F7
  Kirkby Malzeard HG4 ..**112** D5
Church Cl
  Askham Bryan YO23 ...**182** F3
  Bagby YO7 ....**90** C3
  🟫 Bubwith YO8 .....**199** D7
  Carleton BD23 ....**173** B4
  🟫 Filey YO14 ....**101** B4
  🟦 Hambleton YO8 ...**196** F1
  Killinghall HG3 ......**219** A8
  Kirby Hill YO51 ......**141** B7
  Middleton St George DL2 ..**4** C3
  Newby & Scalby YO13 ..**75** C5
  Redmire DL8 ....**59** C5
  Sawley HG4 ....**138** E6
  Sharow HG4 ....**214** F7
  🟫 Swillington LS26 ..**194** A1
  🟫 Tollerton YO61 ...**143** B3
  Wheldrake YO19 .....**193** A4
Church Cliff Dr 🟫 YO14 **101** B4
Church Cres
  Stutton with Hazlewood
  LS24 ....**189** D4
  Swillington LS26 .....**194** A1
Church Croft
  Barkston Ash LS24 ...**195** F7
  Gargrave BD23 ....**172** C8
Church Cswy LS23 ....**188** F8
Church Ct 🟫 WF6 ....**200** A1
Church Dike La YO8 ..**204** B6
Church Dr
  Great Ayton TS9 ....**7** F1
  Lockwood TS12 ....**9** E7
Church End
  Cawood YO8 ....**197** B8
  Sheriff Hutton YO60 ..**145** D5
Church Farm YO7 ....**211** A6
Church Farm Cl YO23 .**182** C6
Church Farm View
  LS15 ....**194** C8
Church Fenton La
  LS24 ....**190** B3
Church Fenton Sta
  LS24 ....**196** A8
Church Field La 🟦
  YO26 ....**164** A8
Church Field Rd DN6 .**206** E1
Church Fields 🟫 WF6 .**200** C4
Church Garth DL6 .....**23** C3
Church Gdns LS25 ....**194** C3
Church Gn 🟫 YO41 ...**185** C2

Church Hill
4 Bramham LS23 ....188 E5
Crayke YO61 ....118 A1
Easingwold YO61 ......117 C1
10 Hunmanby YO14 ......126 F8
Hunsingore LS22 ....180 E8
Malton YO17 ....215 C4
Newby & Scalby YO13 ....75 C5
North Rigton LS17 ......178 B3
Reighton YO14 ....127 C6
3 Selby YO8 ....232 E5
Sherburn in Elmet LS25 ..195 E4
5 Spofforth HG3 ....179 E6
Stillingfleet YO19 .....191 A8
Thorner LS14 ....188 A3
Thornton Dale YO18 .....96 D6
8 Wistow YO8 ....197 D6
Church La
Allerston YO18 ....97 B5
Appleton Roebuck YO23 ..190 F4
Aysgarth DL8 ....58 A1
Bagby YO7 ....90 C3
Barton DL10 ....21 C8
Bishopthorpe YO23 ....231 A4
Bolton Percy YO23 .....190 D4
Boroughbridge YO51 ...141 B5
Brompton YO13 ....98 C5
Burnsall BD23 ....157 A8
Carlton DN14 ....204 C3
Catton YO41 ....185 D8
Cayton YO11 ....100 B6
Collingham LS22 ......180 A1
Cropton YO18 ....71 B4
Cundall with Leckby
YO61 ....115 E3
Dunnington YO19 .....184 E7
Elslack BD23 ....172 D4
4 Elvington YO41 .....185 C2
Faceby TS9 ....25 F1
Fylingdales YO22 ......33 C4
Garforth LS25 ....194 C4
Gargrave BD23 ....172 D8
Gateforth YO8 ....202 F8
Gilling East YO62 .....118 F7
Guisborough TS7 ....7 C5
Hampsthwaite HG3 ....161 A6
17 Haxby YO32 ....166 E5
Hebden BD23 ....135 A1
Hensall DN14 ....203 C1
Hutton Buscel YO13 ....98 F7
Ingleby Greenhow TS9 ...27 B5
Kelbrook & Sough BB18 .186 A4
Kellington DN14 ......202 E3
Kirby Hall YO26 ......164 B7
Kirby Hill YO51 ......141 B7
Knaresborough HG5 ...221 A6
Langtoft YO25 ....151 C1
Low Worsall TS15 .....24 A8
Marton cum Grafton
YO51 ....141 D1
Martons Both BD23 ....172 A5
Micklefield LS25 ......194 F4
Mickletown LS26 .....200 B5
Middlesbrough TS5 ......6 E7
Middleton YO18 ....95 E8
Middleton St George DL2 ..4 C3
Milby YO51 ....141 B7
4 Monk Fryston LS25 ..202 A8
Moor Monkton YO26 ...165 B2
Nether Poppleton YO26 .224 B3
New Earswick YO32 ...225 F5
11 Normanton South WF6 .200 A1
North Featherstone
WF7 ....200 E1
Pannal HG3 ....222 D4
Poppleton YO26 ......224 A3
Rainton YO7 ....114 E6
Redmire DL8 ....59 C5
Ripon HG4 ....214 B5
Sadberge DL2 ....4 C7
Scarborough YO11 .....213 B7
4 Selby YO8 ....232 D5
Sessay YO7 ....116 C6
Settrington YO17 .....122 D1
Sinnington YO62 ......71 A1
Skelton YO30 ....224 B5
Slingsby YO62 ....120 B6
2 Snaith DN14 ....204 C1
South Stainley with Cayton
HG3 ....139 E2
9 Spofforth HG3 .....179 E6
Stainburn LS21 ......177 E3
Stainforth BD24 ......131 E3
10 Stamford Bridge YO41 .168 D2
Strensall YO32 ....167 A7
Stutton with Hazlewood
LS24 ....189 E4
Swillington LS26 .....194 A1
Terrington YO60 ......119 F1
Thormanby YO61 .....116 F5
Thornton Dale YO18 ....96 D6
Thwing YO25 ....126 A1
Tunstall LA6 ....102 B4
Welburn YO60 ....146 E6
Weston LS21 ....176 D1
Westow YO60 ....147 B4
Wheldrake YO19 .....193 A7
Whitby YO22 ....208 E7
Whorlton DL6 ....25 D1
Wigglesworth BD23 ...153 D3
Wighill LS24 ....181 D1
Wintringham YO17 ....123 C4
York YO1 ....233 B2
Church Mdw DL10 ....21 D8
Church Mdws 9 LS23 .188 E6
Church Mews
Barlby YO8 ....198 A5
13 Boroughbridge YO51 .141 B5

Church Mews *continued*
Sherburn in Elmet LS25 .195 F4
2 York YO26 ....227 C3
Church Rd
26 Glusburn BD20 .....187 E5
Great Preston LS26 ...200 C8
Linton BD23 ....134 E2
Pontefract WF6 ......200 A3
Scotton DL9 ....40 E4
Stainton Dale YO13 ....54 A7
Stamford Bridge YO41 .168 D2
Thornton in Craven
BD23 ....171 F3
York YO10 ....229 D4
Church Rise YO19 ....167 F1
Church Row
Hurworth-on-Tees DL2 ...3 E1
Melsonby DL10 ....20 F7
Church Side LS26 ...200 B5
Church Sq
Harrogate HG1 ....219 F3
Whitby YO21 ....208 C7
Church St
Addingham LS29 .....175 A4
Amotherby YO17 .....121 D1
Asenby YO7 ....115 B7
Barkston Ash LS24 ...195 F7
Bellerby DL8 ....60 D7
Bilton-in-Ainsty with Bickerton
YO26 ....181 D5
Boston Spa LS23 .....188 E8
Broughton BD23 .....172 D7
Bubwith YO8 ....199 D7
Carleton BD23 ....173 B4
Church Fenton LS24 ..196 B7
Copmanthorpe YO23 ..230 B2
Danby YO21 ....29 B7
Dunnington YO19 ....184 E7
5 Easingwold YO61 ..143 C8
5 Filey YO14 ....101 B3
Gargrave BD23 ......155 D1
13 Glusburn BD20 ...187 E8
Goldsborough HG5 ...163 A3
Guisborough TS14 ....8 F7
5 Helmsley YO62 .....92 F6
Heslerton YO17 .....123 E7
Hovingham YO62 ....119 E6
Ilkley LS29 ....218 A4
Ingleton LA6 ....103 D4
Kirk Hammerton YO26 .164 C2
Kirkby Malzeard HG4 .112 D5
24 Kirkbymoorside YO62 .70 B1
Knottingley WF11 ....201 E4
Long Preston BD23 ...153 F4
6 Masham HG4 ....86 C3
6 Middleham DL8 .....60 E2
Norton YO17 ....215 D3
Nunnington YO62 ....93 E2
2 Scarborough YO11 .213 B6
Settle BD24 ....131 D3
4 Skipton BD23 ......216 F3
5 Staithes TS13 ....13 K2
Trawden BB8 ....186 B1
Ulleskelf LS24 ......190 C3
Well DL8 ....87 A4
West Tanfield HG4 ....87 A1
14 Wetherby LS22 ....180 C3
Whitby YO22 ....208 E6
Whixley YO26 ......164 A5
York YO1 ....233 B2
Church Strs St 3 YO11 .213 B6
Church View
12 Airmyn DN14 .....205 E4
3 Brompton DL6 .....43 F3
16 Hurworth DL2 ......3 E1
Kirby Hill YO51 ......141 B7
Ledston LS25 ....194 E1
Norton DN6 ....206 E1
Sherburn YO17 .....124 D8
Sherburn in Elmet LS25 .195 F4
South Milford LS25 ...195 F2
Thirsk YO7 ....211 A3
Church View Mews 7
LS23 ....188 E7
Church Wind
Alne YO61 ....142 F4
Burneston DL8 ....87 E7

Church Wlk
Lindrick with Studley
Royal & Fountains HG4 .139 B7
1 Willerby YO12 .....99 D2
5 Wistow YO8 ......197 D6
Church Wynd DL10 ..209 C7
Churchfield Dr 28 YO32 .166 E5
Churchfield La
Castleford WF10 .....200 F3
6 Kippax LS25 ......194 D1
Little Smeaton DN6 ..206 C4
Churchfields DL6 ...210 E4
Churchill Cl 3 TS9 ...8 A2
Churchill Way 4 BD20 .187 F8
Churchside Villas
LS26 ....200 B5
Churchville LS25 ....195 A4
Churchville Ave LS25 .194 F4
Churchville Dr LS25 ..195 A4
Churchville Terr LS25 .195 A4
Churwell Cl WF10 ...200 E3
Cinder La
Castleford WF10 .....200 E4
6 Clifford LS23 ......188 F7
Lindley LS21 ....177 C3
Upper Poppleton YO26 .227 A4
York YO1 ....228 A4
Cinder Mews YO26 ..228 A5
Citadilla Cl 6 DL10 ..41 C7
Clack La 45 A4
Clapdale Dr LA2 ....130 C8

Clapdale Way 2 LA2 .130 C8
Clapham CE VC Prim Sch
LA2 ....130 C7
Clapham Sta LA2 ...130 C8
Clare Ave DL3 ......3 C5
Claremont 23 YO14 .101 B3
Claremont Dr TS7 ...7 C5
Claremont La YO14 .140 B5
Claremont St BB8 ..186 A3
Claremont Terr YO31 .233 B4
Clarence Ave 47 YO14 .101 B3
Clarence Dr Filey YO14 .101 B3
Harrogate HG1 ......219 B3
Clarence Pl
7 Scarborough YO11 .213 A6
2 Whitby YO21 .....208 D7
Clarence Rd
Middlesbrough TS7 ....7 D5
2 Scarborough YO12 .213 A7
Scorton DL10 ....41 F7
Clarence St
2 Barnoldswick BB18 .171 E1
2 Colne BB8 ....186 A3
1 Trawden Forest BB8 .186 B1
York YO31 ....233 B4
Clarendon Ct YO31 ..228 C7
Clarendon Rd
Boston Spa LS23 ....188 E8
Great Burdon DL1 .....3 F7
Thornaby TS17 ....6 B8
Clarendon St 10 BB8 .186 A3
Clareton La HG5 ....163 B6
Clark Ct WF7 ......200 E1
Clark St 7 YO12 ...213 A7
Clarke's Croft YO7 ..115 A4
Clarks Terr YO31 ...228 F6
Clarkson Cl 12 YO14 .100 B1
Clarkson Dr LS25 ..201 F6
Clarkson St 7 YO21 .208 D7
Claro Ave HG1 ......219 A4
Claro Mews 4 HG5 .221 A5
Claro Pk HG1 ......219 F4
Claro Rd
Harrogate HG1 ......219 F3
Ripon HG4 ....214 C4
Claro Way HG1 .....219 F4
Claude Ave TS5 .....6 E8
Claudius Gr YO12 ...99 E6
Claver Cl DL6 ......45 D8
Clavery Ley La YO62 ..67 E1
Claxton Ave DL3 .....3 A6
Clay Bank TS9 ......27 A3
Clay Hill YO41 .....169 C3
Clay La Bubwith YO8 .199 C5
Camblesforth YO8 ...204 C6
Cliffe YO8 ....198 D4
Clay Pit La YO51 ...141 A4
Clay Pl 3 YO24 ....227 D1
Claygate YO31 .....229 B6
Claypit La
Carlton DN14 ....204 C3
Ledston WF10 ......201 A8
Claypit La
Carlton DN14 ....204 C3
Clayton Fold 5 BD20 .187 F7
Clayton Hall Rd BD20 .187 F7
Clayton Mews 8 WF6 .200 A2
Clayton Pl 9 WF6 ...200 A2
Clayton St 7 BB18 ..171 E1
Cleasby La YO7 ....115 C7
Cleasby Way TS16 ...5 D6
Clement St 4 YO21 .233 B1
Clementhorpe YO23 .233 B1
Clevedon House Sch
LS29 ....176 A1
Clevegate YO7 ....7 C5
Cleveland Ave
Darlington DL3 ......3 C5
Knottingley WF11 ...201 F2
Scalby YO12 ....212 D8
Stokesley TS9 ....26 C8
Cleveland Coll of Art &
Design TS5 ....6 E8
Cleveland Dr
Middlesbrough TS7 ...7 B6
Northallerton DL7 ...210 D2
Cleveland Ind Est DL3 .3 D6
Cleveland Rd Boltby YO7 .91 B8
Catterick Garrison DL9 ..40 F4
Scarborough YO12 ...212 E6
Scorton DL10 ....41 F7
Cleveland Rein YO7 ..66 A3
Cleveland St
Darlington DL1 ....3 D6
Great Ayton TS9 ......8 A2
Guisborough TS14 ....8 E6
York YO24 ....228 A4
Cleveland Terr
Darlington DL3 ....3 B5
8 Whitby YO21 .....208 D5
York YO32 ....225 F4
Cleveland Trad Est DL1 .3 C5
Cleveland View 1 TS9 .25 F1
Cleveland Way
1 Carlton Miniott YO7 ..89 C4
Helmsley YO62 ......92 E6
York YO32 ....225 F3
Cliff Bridge Pl 6 YO11 .213 A5
Cliff Bridge Terr 7
YO11 ....213 A5
Cliff Brow TS13 .....11 C7
Cliff Cres LS25 .....194 E4
Cliff Dr 2 DL8 ......60 D5
Cliff Gate Rd LA2 ....35 E4
Cliff Hill Rd DN6 ...206 D2
Cliff La
Newholm-cum-Dunsley
YO21 ....13 B2

Cliff La *continued*
Snainton YO13 ......97 F5
Whitwell-on-the-Hill
YO60 ....146 A4
Wilton YO18 ....97 A5
Wrelton YO18 ....95 B8
Cliff Rd
Stainton Dale YO13 ...54 A8
Staithes TS13 ....13 K2
Cliff St YO21 ......208 D7
Cliff The YO22 .....32 B6
Cliffe Mews YO60 ..119 E1
Cliffe Rd HG2 .....219 B1
Cliffe VC Prim Sch
YO8 ....198 E2
Clifford Ave LS23 ..218 A5
Clifford Ct BD23 ...216 D3
Clifford Moor Rd
LS23 ....188 D8
Clifford Rd
Boston Spa LS23 ....188 F8
Ilkley LS29 ....218 A6
Clifford St
3 Barnoldswick BB18 .171 E1
1 Skipton BD23 ....216 F3
York YO1 ....233 B2
Clifford's Terr 25 YO14 .101 B3
Clifford's Twr ★ YO1 .233 B1
Clifton YO30 ....233 A4
Clifton Ave TS18 ....5 E6
Clifton Dale YO30 ..228 A6
Clifton Gn YO30 ...228 A6
Clifton Gn Jun Sch
YO30 ....228 B7
Clifton Gn Sch YO30 .228 B7
Clifton La LS21 ....176 F3
Clifton Moor Gate
YO30 ....225 A2
Clifton Moor Ind Pk ★
YO30 ....225 A4
Clifton Moor Ret Pk
YO30 ....224 E3
Clifton Moor Sh Ctr
YO30 ....224 F3
Clifton Moorgate
YO30 ....225 B3
Clifton Pk Ave YO30 .227 E8
Clifton Pl 3 YO30 ..228 A7
Clifton Prep Sch
YO30 ....233 A4
Clifton Rd Darlington DL1 .3 D4
Ilkley LS29 ....218 A3
Clifton St Earby BB18 .186 A8
5 Scarborough YO12 .212 F6
Trawden Forest BB8 .186 A1
Clifton Terr LS29 ..218 C4
Clifton Without Jun Sch
YO30 ....227 F8
Clint Bank HG3 ....160 E6
Clint Bank La HG3 ..160 F6
Clint Garth HG3 ...160 F8
Clipt La YO7 ....65 D2
Clitheroe St 2 BD23 .216 D2
Clive Gr YO24 .....227 F2
Clive Rd 1 HG3 ...179 E6
Clock Twr ★ HG4 ..214 C6
Clockhill Field La
YO26 ....163 F3
Clockwood Gdns TS16 .5 K8
Clogger La BD23 ...172 D3
Cloggerby Rigg DL11 .35 E5
Cloisters The
15 Hemingbrough YO8 .198 F1
Wilberfoss YO41 ...185 F6
York YO31 ....233 C3
Cloisters Wlk YO31 .233 C3
Close La BD22 .....187 B5
Close Rd WF10 ....200 F4
Close The
Barwick in Elmet LS15 .194 B7
Boroughbridge YO51 .141 A3
Boston Spa LS23 ....188 E8
Cawood YO8 ....197 A7
6 Collingham LS22 .188 A7
11 East Ayton/West Ayton
YO13 ....99 B8
4 Fylingdales YO22 ...33 C4
Hunmanby Sands YO14 .101 C1
Kirkby Fleetham DL7 ..42 C1
Longnewton TS21 ....4 F7
Neasham DL2 ....4 A1
Northallerton DL7 ...210 B4
Norton DN6 ....206 E2
Riccall YO19 ....198 A8
Scalby YO12 ....212 D8
Studley Roger HG4 ..113 D1
Thirsk YO7 ....211 C1
Thorner LS14 ......188 A3
Thornton Dale YO18 ..96 D5
Towton LS24 ....189 E4
York YO30 ....227 F8
Clotherholme Rd HG4 .214 A5
Clough La DN6 ....207 B2
Clover Hill BD23 ...217 B5
Clover Way 9 HG3 .161 B3
Cloverley Cl YO12 ..168 C2
Clowbeck Ct DL3 ....3 B8
Clydach Gr 24 TS17 ..5 F8
Clyde Gr TS18 .....5 F8
Coach La
10 Hurworth-on-Tees DL2 .3 E1
Lindley LS21 ....177 D3
Coach Rd
Harrogate HG1 .....219 F2
Sheriff Hutton YO60 .145 D4
Sleights YO22 ....32 A6
Coach St BD23 ....216 F4

Coach St Yd 13 BD23 .216 F4
Coachman's Ct 6 HG2 .220 B1
Coal Pit La
Kirk Smeaton WF8 ..206 A2
Rimington BB7 .....171 A1
Coalmire La DL6 ....45 D7
Coalpits La 10 DL3 ...3 A7
Coarse La HG3 .....159 A4
Coastal Rd YO13 ....75 D7
Coastguard Hill YO14 .127 E5
Coate Cl TS8 ....6 E5
Coate's La BD20 ...173 F2
Coates Ave BB18 ...171 E2
Coates Fields BB18 .171 E2
Coates La
Barnoldswick BB18 ..171 E2
Kettlewell with Starbotton
BD23 ....107 F5
Coates La Prim Sch
BB18 ....171 E2
Coates Marsh La
DN14 ....204 B2
Coatham Ave DL2 ....4 D3
Coatham La TS21 ....5 B7
Cob Castle ★ DL8 ...63 B1
Cob La BB18 ....186 A6
Cobble Carr TS14 ....8 A7
Cobble Ct Mews YO24 .233 A1
Cobbler's La WF8 ..201 C1
Cobblers La WF8 ...201 C1
Cobblers La Inf Sch
WF8 ....201 D1
Cobby Syke Rd HG3 .159 F1
Cobcroft La WF11 ..206 B8
Cobden St
Barnoldswick BB18 ..171 D1
Darlington DL1 ......3 E5
Thornaby TS17 ......6 B8
Cobham Way YO32 .226 E3
Coble La YO60 .....145 D5
Cobshaw La DL8 ....62 F6
Cochrane St YO8 ...232 D3
Cock Garth YO17 ..122 D1
Cock La Gainford DL2 .1 E8
Piercebridge DL2 .....2 A7
Cock Lodge (site of) ★
YO7 ....115 C6
Cockburn St 5 TS12 ..9 F7
Cocked Hat HG4 ..139 C8
Cockerhill La YO62 ..93 E7
Cockerton CE Prim Sch
DL3 ....3 A6
Cockerton Gn DL3 ...3 B6
Cockhill La BB8 ....186 A4
Cocking La LS29 ...174 E3
Cocklakes La YO7 ..114 F1
Cockmoor Rd YO13 ..74 A1
Cockpit Cl HG4 ....113 C7
Cockrah Rd YO13 ...74 F2
Cockret Cl 8 YO8 ..232 B6
Cockret Ct YO8 ....232 B7
Cockret Rd YO8 ...232 B7
Cockshaw Bank La
HG4 ....113 B4
Cockshott Pl 5 LS29 .174 F4
Coda Ave YO23 ....231 B3
Codlin Rd 1 TS15 ...25 C5
Coeside YO24 ......230 B7
Coggan Cl YO23 ...228 B2
Coggan Way YO23 .230 F4
Colber La HG3 .....138 F2
Colbert Ave LS29 ..218 E5
Colburn Com Prim Sch
DL9 ....41 A5
Colburn Dr DL9 ....40 F5
Colburn La DL9 ....40 F6
Colburn Sidings DL9 ..40 F4
Cold Bath Pl HG2 ..219 C1
Cold Bath Rd HG2 .222 C8
Cold Cotes Rd HG3 .160 B4
Cold Kirby Rd YO7 ..91 C8
Coldhill La LS25 ...195 C4
Coldie Hill 11 TS15 ..25 C5
Coldstone La YO7 ...88 B2
Coldyhill La YO12 ..212 B8
Cole St YO31 ......233 B4
Colebrooke Mdws
HG5 ....221 C7
Coledale Cl 2 YO30 .224 F1
Colenso St YO23 ...233 B1
Coleridge Dr HG1 ..219 E7
Coleridge Gdns DL1 ..3 D3
Coleridge Way 1 WF8 .201 B1
Colescliffe Cres YO12 .212 C8
Colescliffe Rd YO12 .212 C8
Colin St 14 BB18 ..171 D2
Coliseum ★ YO31 ..228 E6
Coll of Ripon & York St John
YO31 ....228 E6
College Ave YO11 ..213 A2
College Ct
1 Low Bradley BD20 .173 E3
2 Scarborough YO11 .212 F4
College Dr LS29 ...218 B3
College Farm Cl DN14 .207 A8
College Farm La LS22 .180 A2
College Gr WF10 ..200 D3
College La
Bradleys Both BD20 .173 E3
5 Masham HG4 ......86 C3
Scarborough YO11 ..213 A1
College of Law YO23 .231 B7
College of Ripon & York St
John HG4 ....214 B6

College Rd
Bradleys Both BD20 ......**173** E3
Copmanthorpe YO23 ....**230** A3
Harrogate HG2 ....**222** B8
Ripon HG4 ....**214** B6
College St
Harrogate HG2 ....**222** B8
York YO1 ....**233** B3
Colley Broach Rd
YO61 ....**117** F7
Collier Hag La YO23 ..**182** B3
Collier La
Lotherton cum Aberford
LS25 ....**195** A6
West Layton DL11 ....**20** A8
Colliergate YO1 ....**233** B2
Collin Ave TS4 ....**6** F8
Collin Bank HG3 ....**160** B2
Collinge Rd 9 BD22 ...**187** B6
Collingham Way 12
YO14 ....**101** A3
Collingsway 4 DL3 .....**3** A7
Collingwood Ave
YO24 ....**227** F2
Collingwood Gdns
YO17 ....**215** A3
Collingwood Rd WF6 ..**200** A2
Collin's Hill HG3 ....**223** D7
Collinsons La YO17 ...**122** F1
Colliwath La DL8 ....**60** F4
Collyer View LS29 .....**218** E5
Colne & Broughton Rd
BD23 ....**172** C4
Colne Rd
Barnoldswick BB18 .....**171** D1
Cowling BD22 ....**187** A1
Earby BB18 ....**172** A1
Kelbrook & Sough BB18 ..**186** A8
Sutton BD20 ....**187** C7
Trawden Forest BB8 ....**186** A1
Colonel's Wlk 9 WF8 ..**201** B1
Colorado Way WF10 ...**200** F2
Colstan Rd DL6 ....**210** E3
Colton La YO23 ....**190** E6
Coltsgate Hill HG4 .....**214** B6
Columbine Gr 33 HG3 ..**161** B3
Columbus Ravine
YO12 ....**212** F7
Columbus Way DL10 ...**41** C7
Colville Cres 8 DL9 ....**41** A5
Colville Rd 12 DL9 .....**41** A5
Comercial St
9 Barnoldswick BB18 ..**171** D1
Harrogate HG1 ....**219** D3
Norton YO17 ....**215** D3
Scarborough YO12 .....**212** E5
Tadcaster LS24 ....**189** E6
Comercial Yd 1 HG5 ...**221** B6
Comets Garth 11 DL3 ..**3** A7
Comfort La DL10 ....**20** C5
Comfrey Cl 32 HG3 .....**161** B3
Comfrey Manor TS8 ....**7** B4
Commercial St 9 BD24 **131** B3
Common Croft La
YO26 ....**165** E1
Common La Beal DN14 **202** D3
Burn YO8 ....**203** E7
Catton YO41 ....**185** E8
Dunnington YO19 ......**184** F5
Fangfoss YO41 ....**169** B1
Knottingley WF11 ......**202** B1
Norton DN6 ....**206** E2
Sutton upon Derwent
YO41 ....**193** C8
Temple Hirst YO8 ......**203** F4
Thorganby YO19 ....**192** F5
Walden Stubbs DN6 ....**206** F4
Warthill YO19 ....**167** F2
York YO10 ....**229** B1
Common Rd
Dunnington YO19 ......**184** F7
Skipwith YO8 ....**192** E1
Comon Balk La HG3 ...**140** A3
Comon Holme La
LS29 ....**175** C3
Comon La
Carlton Husthwaite YO7 ..**116** F8
Coverham with Agglethorpe
DL8 ....**60** A2
Glaisdale YO21 ....**29** F1
Hambleton YO8 ....**196** D6
Harome YO62 ....**93** E5
Hartley CA17 ....**14** A8
Scruton DL7 ....**63** E7
South Milford LS25 .....**195** F2
Ulleskelf LS24 ....**190** C2
West Witton DL8 ....**59** F2
Comon Rd
Barkston Ash LS24 .....**195** F7
Church Fenton LS24 ....**196** A7
Strensall YO60 ....**145** D1
Comondale Sta YO21 ..**9** E1
Compton Cl LS23 ......**188** A7
Compton St YO30 .....**228** A6
Conan Dr DL10 ....**209** D8
Conan Gdns DL10 .....**209** D8
Concorde Pk YO30 ....**225** A3
Concorde Way TS18 ...**5** F7
Coney Moor Gr LS26 ..**200** C6
Coney St YO1 ....**233** B2
Coneycroft 10 YO19 ...**184** F7
Coneygarth La
Dunnington YO19 ......**184** E5
Tunstall LA6 ....**102** A4
Conference Cl YO17 ...**215** B4

Conifer Cl 6 YO32 .....**225** D3
Conifers Cl 2 YO8 .....**197** D1
Coningham Ave 1
YO30 ....**224** E2
Coniscliffe Mews DL3 ..**3** A4
Coniscliffe Rd DL3 .....**3** A4
Coniston Ave BB18 ....**171** D1
Coniston Cl 1 YO30 ...**224** E1
Coniston Dr
Castleford WF10 ....**201** C4
York YO1 ....**229** B4
Coniston Gdns 6 YO12 **99** F7
Coniston Gr TS5 ....**6** C1
Coniston Rd HG1 ......**220** B4
Coniston Way
3 Eastfield YO12 ......**99** F7
Thirsk YO7 ....**89** C4
Conistone La BD23 ....**108** B3
Connaught Rd
Ilkley LS29 ....**218** D3
Middlesbrough TS7 ....**7** D6
Connaught Way YO32 .**225** F6
Conoley Ave YO32 ....**166** B6
Conoley Cl 2 YO8 .....**197** D1
Conoley La YO32 .....**224** E2
Consort St BD23 ......**217** B6
Constable Burton Hall★
DL8 ....**61** C6
Constable Rd
Hunmanby YO14 ....**127** A8
Ilkley LS29 ....**218** D3
Constable Ridge Rd
HG3 ....**160** B2
Constantine Ave
10 Colburn DL9 ....**41** A5
York YO10 ....**229** A4
Constantine Gr 11 DL9 **41** A5
Constitution Hill 3
BD24 ....**131** E2
Conway Cl 2 YO30 ....**224** E3
Conway Cres BB18 ....**171** E1
Conway Gr 8 TS17 ....**5** F4
Conyers Ave DL3 .....**3** A6
Conyers Cl YO13 .....**99** A7
Conyers Ings YO13 ...**99** A7
Conyers La DL8 ....**61** D6
Conyers Rd DL7 ......**22** E2
Conyers Sch TS15 ....**5** E2
Conyngham Hall HG5 .**220** F6
Cook Cl DL10 ....**41** C7
Cook's Row 5 YO11 ..**213** B6
Cookgate TS7 ....**7** C5
Cooks Cl 2 DL6 ....**45** A7
Cooks Gdns 3 YO13 ..**75** D5
Cookson Way 4 DL9 ..**41** A5
Coolham La BB18 .....**186** B8
Coombe Dr DL1 ......**3** F6
Coombes Cl YO61 ....**144** C3
Coomboots Brow YO13 **75** A6
Cooper Cl DL6 ....**25** D2
Cooper La
Blubberhouses LS21 ...**159** C1
Potto DL6 ....**25** D2
Cooper La Shepherd
LS21 ....**159** C2
Cooper Rd 49 Filey YO14 **101** B3
18 Wetherby LS22 ......**180** C3
Coopers Dr YO23 .....**230** B3
Copgrove La HG5 ....**162** D8
Copgrove Rd HG3 ....**140** A2
Cophill La YO7 ....**66** A4
Copley La LS25 ....**195** B7
Copmanroyd LS21 ....**177** A4
Copmanthorpe La
YO23 ....**230** E3
Copmanthorpe Prim Sch
YO23 ....**230** B3
Copmanthorpe Sports Club
YO23 ....**230** B2
Copper beech Cl
YO26 ....**182** F8
Copper Beech Dr
DN14 ....**207** A8
Copper Beeches The 2
YO19 ....**184** E7
Copperclay Wlk YO61 .**117** D1
Copperfield Cl
Malton YO17 ....**215** C5
21 Sherburn in Elmet LS25 **195** F4
Coppergate
1 Riccall YO19 ....**191** F1
York YO1 ....**233** B2
Coppergate Sh Ctr
YO1 ....**233** B2
Coppergate Wlk YO1 ..**233** B2
Coppertop Mews 4
WF8 ....**201** C2
Coppice Ave YO61 ....**219** C4
Coppice Beck Ct HG1 .**219** D3
Coppice Cl
Harrogate HG1 ....**219** C4
10 Haxby YO32 ....**166** E5
Coppice Dr YO61 .....**219** C3
Coppice Gate HG1 ....**219** C4
Coppice La
14 Hellifield BD23 .....**154** B3
Wrelton YO18 ....**71** B1
Coppice Rise HG1 ....**219** C5
Coppice The
Barwick in Elmet LS15 ..**194** B7
Bishopthorpe YO23 ...**230** F4
Brayton YO8 ....**197** C1
Ilkley LS29 ....**218** A6
Leeming DL7 ....**63** F3

Coppice The continued
14 Sherburn in Elmet LS25 **195** F4
19 Sutton BD20 ......**187** E7
Coppice Valley Com Prim
Sch HG1 ....**219** C5
Coppice Valley Pool
HG1 ....**219** D4
Coppice View HG1 ....**219** C4
Coppice Way HG1 ....**219** C5
Coppy La
Cononley BD20 ....**173** C2
Sutton BD22 ....**187** A6
Coppy Rd LS29 ....**174** F4
Coppy Wood Dr LS29 .**218** B2
Copse Hill 1 YO14 ....**101** A4
Copse The
3 North Featherstone
WF7 ....**200** E1
5 Scarborough YO12 ..**212** B5
Copwood Gr 7 YO32 ..**225** C8
Corban La YO32 ......**166** B6
Corban Way 21 YO32 .**166** C5
Corber Hill 7 DL6 .....**43** F3
Corbie Way YO18 .....**96** A7
Corby La TS5 ....**6** D8
Cordike La
Birdsall YO17 ....**148** D6
Langton YO17 ....**147** F6
Cordilleras La DL11 ...**39** C8
Corlett Ct YO24 ......**230** C8
Corn Mill Ct 19 LS25 ..**195** F4
Corn Mill Gdns YO12 .**212** D7
Corn Mill La 39 LS29 ..**176** D1
Cornaught Ct YO10 ...**231** D8
Cornbell Gate 4 HG4 .**113** D7
Cornborough Av YO31 **228** F6
Cornborough Rd
YO60 ....**145** C5
Cornel Rise 26 HG3 ...**161** B3
Cornelian Ave YO11 ..**100** B8
Cornelian Cl YO11 ....**213** C1
Cornelian Dr YO11 ....**213** C1
Cornelius Cswy YO8 ..**198** E8
Corner Cl 17 YO32 ....**166** C5
Corner Complex The★
YO12 ....**212** F8
Corners Terr 5 YO22 ..**208** E6
Corners Yd 5 YO22 ...**208** E6
Cornerstones Cl LS29 .**175** A4
Cornfield Rd TS17 ....**6** A8
Cornforth Hill DL10 ...**209** B6
Cornlands YO17 ......**215** D2
Cornlands Rd YO24 ...**227** B1
Cornmill Cl YO8 ....**197** B8
Cornmill Sh Ctr DL1 ..**3** C5
Cornwall Ave
Darlington DL1 ....**3** E6
Silsden BD20 ....**174** B1
Cornwall Cl HG1 ......**219** A2
Cornwall Dr YO10 ....**231** E8
Cornwall Rd HG1 .....**219** B2
Cornwood Way 11 YO32 **225** C8
Coronation Ave
6 Colburn DL9 ....**41** A5
Harrogate HG2 ....**222** E7
1 Hinderwell TS13 ....**11** F7
Coronation Gr HG2 ...**222** E7
Coronation Hospl
LS29 ....**218** C3
Coronation Pl DL10 ...**209** C7
Coronation Rd
Crakehall DL8 ....**62** E4
Harrogate HG2 ....**222** E7
Coronation St
8 Barnoldswick BB18 .**171** E1
Castleford WF6 ....**200** B2
Corporation Rd DL3 ...**3** C6
Corporation Rd Jun & Inf Sch
DL3 ....**3** C6
Corporation Rd Prim Sch
DL3 ....**3** C6
Corpse Rd
North Otterington DL7 ..**64** C5
Thornton-le-Moor DL6 ..**65** A4
Corrunna Ct YO8 .....**232** D5
Cosmo Ave YO31 .....**229** A5
Costa La YO18 ....**95** D6
Costa Way YO18 .....**95** E7
Cotchers La LS24 ....**195** D8
Cotcliffe Ave DL6 ....**210** F3
Cotcliffe Bank DL6 ...**65** E5
Cote Hill Rd HG3 .....**160** B4
Cote La Healey HG4 ..**85** D5
Sproxton YO62 ....**92** C4
Cotescue Bank DL8 ..**60** C1
Cotherstone Cl TS16 .**5** C5
Cotswold Dr LS25 ....**194** C6
Cotswold Way YO32 ..**226** A5
Cottage Cl DL6 ....**210** E5
Cottage La WF6 ......**200** C4
Cottagers La DL2 ....**2** C3
Cottam La YO25 ......**151** C5
Cottee Way 16 DL9 ...**41** A5
Cotterdale Cl HG5 ....**221** C6
Cotterdale Gdns LS25 **202** A6
Cotterdale Holt 9 LS22 **180** A1
Cottom La YO42 ......**193** C2
Cotton Tree La BB8 ..**186** A3
Coulby Farm Way TS8 **7** A5
Coulby La YO18 ......**97** A6
Coulby Manor Way TS8 **6** F6
Coulby Newham Sch
TS8 ....**7** A5
Coulson Cl 5 YO32 ...**167** C8
Coulter Beck La LA6 ..**102** D7

Coulthurst Craven Sports Ctr
The BD23 ....**216** F3
Coulton La YO62 .....**119** A6
Count De Burgh Terr 4
YO23 ....**228** B1
County Par HG1 ......**219** F3
County Sq HG1 ....**219** F3
Coupland Rd
Garforth LS25 ....**194** C4
1 Selby YO8 ....**232** C6
Courby Hill YO4 ......**86** F2
Courcey Gr YO26 ....**227** C4
Court Dr YO8 ....**232** A4
Court Gn Cl YO13 ....**54** D1
Court La BD23 ....**217** A4
Court Moor La YO62 .**70** A4
Court Terr HG4 ......**214** C5
Court The 6 DL8 .....**63** A2
Courthouse Mus★
HG4 ....**214** C5
Courtneys Selby YO8 .**232** B4
Wheldrake YO19 ......**193** A8
Courtneys The YO8 ..**232** B4
Courts Cl 7 DN14 ....**205** E4
Courtyard The
Bishopthorpe YO23 ...**231** B4
11 Pontefract WF8 ....**201** C2
Coutances Way LS29 .**218** F5
Cove Rd BD23 ....**132** F2
Cover La
Carlton Town DL8 .....**83** C7
Marton-le-Moor HG4 ..**114** E1
Coverdale Dr
1 Knaresborough HG5 ..**221** A7
Scarborough YO12 ....**212** B4
Coverdale Garth 2
LS22 ....**188** A8
Coverdale La TS13 ...**12** A4
Coverham Abbey (rems of)★
DL8 ....**60** C1
Coverham Cl DL7 .....**210** C2
Coverham La DL8 ....**60** C1
Covert The
9 Topcliffe YO7 ......**89** B1
York YO24 ....**230** F7
Cow & Calf Rocks★
LS29 ....**218** D2
Cow Cl La
Kirkby Malham BD23 ...**154** E8
Lockwood TS12 ....**10** A4
Cow Gate La BD23 ...**171** B7
Cow La Cowling BD22 .**187** B6
Knottingley WF11 .....**202** A2
Lothersdale BD20 .....**172** F1
Middleton Tyas DL10 ..**21** C5
Womersley DN6 ......**206** C6
Cow Pasture La YO42 **193** C3
Cow Wath Bank YO22 **51** A3
Cow Wath Cl 1 TS13 .**13** K2
Cowbar Bank 1 TS13 .**13** K2
Cowbar La TS13 .....**13** J2
Cowcliff Hill YO17 ....**148** F6
Cowgarth La 15 BB18 .**172** B1
Cowgill St 8 BB18 ....**172** A1
Cowhouse Bank YO62 **68** D3
Cowie Dr YO8 ....**232** D5
Cowland La YO7 ......**88** D3
Cowley Cl TS16 ......**5** E7
Cowley Rd TS5 ....**6** E1
Cowling Com Prim Sch
BD22 ....**187** A6
Cowling Hill La BD22 .**186** F7
Cowling La DL8 ......**62** D3
Cowling Rd DL8 ......**62** D2
Cowlings Cl 16 YO14 .**127** A8
Cowpasture Rd LS29 .**218** C3
Cowper La YO23 .....**191** C8
Cowper St 3 BD23 ...**217** A3
Cowton La YO14 .....**127** C6
Cowton Way TS16 ...**5** D6
Coxlea Gr YO31 ......**229** B6
Coxwold Dr DL1 .....**3** D4
Coxwold Hill 5 LS22 ..**180** C4
Coxwold Pottery★
YO61 ....**117** D7
Coxwold View 1 LS22 **180** C3
Crab La Harrogate HG1 **219** D6
Seamer YO12 ....**99** E6
Crab Tree La WF8 ...**206** A1
Crabmill La YO61 ....**143** D6
Crabtree Gn LS22 ....**188** A8
Crabtree Gr 1 YO32 ..**225** D3
Crabtree Hill LS22 ...**188** A8
Cracoe & Rylstone VC CE
Prim Sch BD23 ....**156** B6
Cradley Dr TS5 ......**6** E6
Cradoc Gr 14 TS17 ..**5** F4
Craft Ctr★ DL11 .....**38** B6
Crag Bank YO21 .....**28** B8
Crag Cl 33 BD20 .....**187** C6
Crag Gdns LS23 .....**188** E5
Crag Hill La HG3 .....**161** B6
Crag Hill Rd YO13 ...**53** F8
Crag La
Bradleys Both BD20 ...**173** E2
Fellscliffe HG3 ....**160** D4
Huby HG3 ....**178** B2
Killinghall HG3 ....**161** B1
Knaresborough HG5 ..**221** B5
North Rigton LS17 ....**178** B3
Pannal HG3 ....**178** C8
Sutton BD20 ....**187** D6
Crag Side Rd DL8 ....**57** B2
Crag The 3 LS23 ....**188** E5
Crag View
Cononley BD20 ....**173** D1

Crag View continued
Skipton BD23 ....**217** B6
Threshfield BD23 .....**134** B3
Weeton LS17 ....**178** B2
Crag View Rd BD23 ..**217** B3
Cragdale 13 BD24 ...**131** D2
Cragdale Rise 1 HG5 **221** D6
Cragg Bottom Rd
BD22 ....**187** C1
Cragg Dr LS29 ....**218** F3
Cragg Hill Rd BD24 ..**105** C3
Cragg La LA2 ....**130** C2
Cragg The 21 YO21 ..**208** D7
Craggs La
Arrathorne DL10 ......**41** A1
Tatham LA2 ....**129** A3
Craig St DL3 ....**3** C6
Craiglands Pk LS29 ..**218** C3
Craiglands Rd LS29 ..**218** C3
Craigmore Dr LS29 ..**218** E4
Craigs Way YO7 .....**211** C4
Crake La HG3 ....**159** F6
Crakehall CE Prim Sch
DL8 ....**62** E4
Cranberry TS8 ....**7** B5
Cranbrook Ave YO26 .**227** C5
Cranbrook Rd YO26 ..**227** C5
Cranbrooks The YO19 **192** F8
Cranesbill Cl HG3 ....**161** B3
Cranfield Pl 4 YO24 ..**230** C8
Cranford Gdns TS5 ..**6** D8
Crank La DL7 ....**63** B7
Crankley La YO61 ...**143** B7
Cranwell Gr TS17 ...**6** B6
Craven Bank La BD24 **131** B3
Craven Coll
Settle BD24 ....**131** D2
Skipton BD23 ....**217** A4
Craven Cres 3 LS29 .**174** F4
Craven Ct
Cowling BD22 ....**187** C6
Northallerton DL7 ....**210** B3
Richmond DL10 ......**209** B6
Silsden BD20 ....**174** C1
Skipton BD23 ....**217** A4
Craven Ct Sh Ctr
BD23 ....**217** A4
Craven Dr BD20 .....**174** C1
Craven Garth 5 DN14 **202** D7
Craven Mus★ BD23 ..**217** A4
Craven Ridge La BD24 **131** B3
Craven Ridge La Ends
BD24 ....**131** B3
Craven St 3 Colne BB8 **186** A3
Harrogate HG1 ....**219** D4
Scarborough YO11 ...**213** A4
Skipton BD23 ....**216** F3
Craven Terr BD23 ....**216** F4
Craven Way
5 Boroughbridge YO51 **141** B3
Dent LA10 ....**78** B8
Cravendale Rd 4 DL9 **40** F5
Cravengate DL10 ....**209** B6
Craven's Hill YO13 ...**54** C3
Crawford Cl YO26 ...**181** C7
Crawley Way YO31 ..**229** B6
Cray Thorns Cres YO7 **115** C4
Crayke Castle★ YO61 **117** F1
Crayke CE VC Prim Sch
YO61 ....**117** F1
Crayke La YO61 .....**117** F2
Crayke Manor★ YO61 **118** A2
Crescent Arts★ YO11 **213** A6
Crescent Ave YO21 ..**208** C7
Crescent Back Rd 8
YO11 ....**213** A5
Crescent Ct LS29 ....**218** B4
Crescent Gdns HG1 ..**219** C2
Crescent Hill 53 YO14 **101** B3
Crescent Par HG4 ...**214** C6
Crescent Pl 20 YO21 .**208** D7
Crescent Rd
Harrogate HG1 ....**219** C2
Ripon HG4 ....**214** B6
Crescent Terr 6 LS29 **218** B4
Crescent The
13 Bedale DL8 ....**63** B3
Burton Fleming YO25 .**126** E3
Carlton TS9 ....**26** A2
Eaglescliffe TS16 ....**5** D4
Filey YO14 ....**101** B3
Garforth LS25 ....**194** D4
17 Helmsley YO62 ...**92** F6
Ilkley LS29 ....**218** E5
Kelfield YO19 ....**191** D1
Kexby YO41 ....**185** D1
Kippax LS25 ....**194** D1
Micklefield LS25 .....**195** A3
Middlesbrough TS7 ..**7** D6
Middleton St George DL2 **4** E4
North Rigton LS17 ...**178** B3
Northallerton DL6 ....**210** E4
Otley LS21 ....**177** A3
6 Riccall YO19 ....**197** F8
Richmond DL10 ......**209** D7
Ripon HG4 ....**214** B6
Scalby YO12 ....**212** B4
Scarborough YO11 ..**213** A5
Sicklinghall LS22 ....**179** E3
Skipton BD23 ....**217** B6
Stainton Dale YO13 ..**54** A8
Stamford Bridge YO41 **168** D2
2 Summerbridge HG3 **138** A1
Thirsk YO7 ....**211** D2
Thornaby TS17 ......**6** B8
Thornton Dale YO18 .**96** D5
York YO24 ....**233** A1
Crest The LS26 .....**194** A1

Crestbrooke DL7 . . . . . .210 D2
Crestholme Cl 6 HG5 .221 D5
Crewe Rd WF10 . . . . . .201 B4
Creyke View DN14 . . . .205 A1
Cribyn Cl 20 TS17 . . . . . . .5 F4
Crichton Ave YO30 . . . .228 B8
Cricket La TS6 . . . . .7 E8
Cricketers Cl LS25 . . . .194 D3
Cricketers Way 8 LS25 .195 F4
Cridling Gdns DN6 . . . .206 F2
Crimple Ave LS22 . . . . .180 A8
Crimple La HG3 . . . . . .223 D7
Crimple Mdws HG3 . . . .222 D3
Crinan Ct
  Pontefract WF6 . . . . . .200 A2
  3 York YO32 . . . . . . .225 F6
Crindle Carr La DL7 . . .65 B3
Cringle Moor Chase
  TS9 . . . . .26 F4
Cringles La BD20 . . . . .174 C4
Cringley La DL8 . . . . . . .57 E5
Crocus Ct 20 DL9 . . . . . .41 A5
Croft Ave
  8 Knottingley WF11 . . .202 A3
  Middlesbrough TS5 . . . . .6 D8
  4 Normanton South WF6 .200 B2
  Otley LS21 . . . . .176 F1
Croft CE Prim Sch DL2 .22 C8
Croft Cl
  Carlton Husthwaite YO7 .116 F7
  14 Easingwold YO61 . . .143 C8
  Ingleton LA6 . . . . .103 D3
Croft Ct YO23 . . . . . . .231 A4
Croft Dr LS23 . . . . .188 E6
Croft Farm Cl YO23 . . .230 B3
Croft Gdns YO7 . . . . . .211 B3
Croft Head Terr 2
  BD20 . . . . .187 E7
Croft Heads YO7 . . . . .211 B1
Croft Hill Carthorpe DL8 .87 E6
  32 Glusburn BD20 . . . .187 E7
Croft Hills TS9 . . . . .26 A7
Croft House Dr 8 LS21 .176 F1
Croft House Fold 10
  LS29 . . . . .175 A4
Croft House La BD23 . .135 A1
Croft La
  Carlton Husthwaite YO7 .116 F8
  Newton Kyme cum Toulston
  LS24 . . . . .189 B7
  Snainton YO13 . . . . . . .97 F5
  Walton LS23 . . . . .181 A2
Croft Motor Racing Circut★
  DL2 . . . . .22 C5
Croft Rd
  Bramham cum Oglethorpe
  LS23 . . . . .188 A3
  Catterick Garrison DL9 .209 C1
  Eaglescliffe TS16 . . . . . .5 D4
  Hurworth DL2 . . . . .3 B2
  Ingleton LA6 . . . . .103 D3
Croft St 12 Earby BB18 .172 B1
  1 Glusburn BD20 . . . . .187 E7
Croft The Beadlam YO62 .93 D7
  Burton in Lonsdale LA6 .102 F3
  Castleford WF10 . . . . .200 F3
  5 Collingham LS22 . . . .188 A8
  Draughton BD23 . . . . .174 B7
  1 Filey YO14 . . . . .101 B3
  Knottingley WF11 . . . . .202 A3
  Langthorpe YO51 . . . . .141 A7
  Scalby YO12 . . . . .212 B7
  Sheriff Hutton YO60 . . .145 D3
  Stirton with Thorlby
  BD23 . . . . .216 C6
  Thirsk YO7 . . . . .211 B1
  West Tanfield DL8 . . . . .87 B3
Croft View YO7 . . . . . .211 B3
Crofters Gn HG3 . . . . .219 A8
Crofters Mill BD20 . . . .187 B7
Croftlands 7 WF11 . . . .202 A3
Crofts Ave
  4 Pickering YO18 . . . . .96 A6
  Richmond DL10 . . . . . .209 B7
Crofts The
  1 Glusburn BD20 . . . . .173 F1
  3 Sutton BD20 . . . . . . .187 E6
Croftside 1 YO26 . . . . .227 B3
Croftway
  Barwick in Elmet LS15 .194 C8
  Camblesforth YO8 . . . .204 C5
  Selby YO8 . . . . .232 C4
  Sherburn in Elmet LS25 .195 F4
  2 York YO26 . . . . .227 B3
Crombie Ave YO30 . . . .228 B7
Cromer St YO30 . . . . . .228 B7
Crompton Terr YO32 . . .225 D6
Cromwell Ave 22 YO14 .101 B3
Cromwell Cl 5 WF11 . . .201 E4
Cromwell Cres 6 WF8 .201 C1
Cromwell Dr 64 A6
Cromwell Gdns 6 YO11 .212 F4
Cromwell Par 5 YO11 .212 F4
Cromwell Rd
  Harrogate HG2 . . . . . .222 E7
  Scarborough YO11 . . . .212 F4
  York YO1 . . . . .233 B1
Cromwell Rise LS25 . . .200 D8
Cromwell St 9 BD23 . . .217 A3
Cromwell Terr 7 YO11 .212 F4
Crook Bank La DL11 . . .38 F6
Crook La HG4 . . . . .85 E5
Crooked La YO26 . . . . .164 C2
Crookland La YO32 . . . .166 F5
Croom Medieval Village★
  YO25 . . . . .150 B4
Croome Dale La YO17 .150 C6

Croome Rd YO25 . . . . .150 B4
Cropstones LS23 . . . . .188 F5
Cropton Brewery & Visitor
  Ctr★ YO18 . . . . .71 B3
Cropton La YO18 . . . . . .71 B2
Cropton Rise YO12 . . . .212 B4
Cropton Way TS8 . . . . . .7 B5
Crosby DL6 . . . . .210 E4
Crosby St DL3 . . . . .3 C7
Crosland Cl 22 YO62 . . .92 F6
Cross Bank BD23 . . . . .217 B6
Cross End Fold 3 LS29 .175 A4
Cross Gate YO13 . . . . . .97 D5
Cross Haw La 3 LA2 . . .130 C8
Cross Head Bank DL8 . .60 D1
Cross Hill
  Fairburn WF11 . . . . . . .201 D6
  Sutton-under-Whitestonecliffe
  YO7 . . . . .90 D5
Cross Hills La YO8 . . . .232 A5
Cross La Bentham LA2 . .128 C8
  Brompton YO13 . . . . . . .98 C5
  Burneston DL8 . . . . . . .87 F4
  Burniston YO13 . . . . . . .75 D7
  Farndale East YO62 . . . .48 A4
  Flaxton YO60 . . . . .167 E8
  Fulford YO19 . . . . .231 E5
  Giggleswick BD24 . . . . .130 F2
  Great Ouseburn YO26 . .164 B8
  Little Ayton TS9 . . . . . . .27 A8
  Pickhill with Roxby YO7 . .88 C6
  Scalby YO12 . . . . .212 C8
  Sinnington YO62 . . . . . .95 A8
  Snainton YO13 . . . . . . .97 F3
  Stonebeck Up HG3 . . . .110 B5
Cross La Hospl YO12 . .212 B4
Cross Lanes DL10 . . . .209 E7
Cross Queen St 9 WF6 .200 A1
Cross Rd LA2 . . . . .128 E7
Cross Rein Bank DL7 . . .23 A1
Cross Row Boosbeck TS12 .9 E7
  Swillington LS15 . . . . . .194 A3
Cross St 6 Cowling BD22 .187 B6
  14 Earby BB18 . . . . . . .172 A1
  Scarborough YO11 . . . .213 A6
  Skipton BD23 . . . . .216 F3
  5 York YO24 . . . . .227 C3
Cross The TS15 . . . . . .194 B8
Cross Top DL8 . . . . .57 F7
Crossbeck Cl LS29 . . . .218 B3
Crossbeck Rd
  Ilkley LS29 . . . . .218 B3
  Northallerton DL6 . . . . .210 F5
Crossbeck Way TS7 . . . .7 D6
Crosscliff TS8 . . . . .6 F5
Crossdale Rd YO18 . . . .72 C3
Crossfield Cl 2 DL2 . . . . .3 E1
Crossfield Cres YO19 . .231 E6
Crossfields 7 A4
Crossgate La 22 YO18 . .95 C5
Crossgates HG3 . . . . . .138 B5
Crosshill La DN14 . . . .207 E6
Crosshills Rd BD20 . . . .173 D1
Crossings The 13 DN14 .205 E4
Crosslands Rd 2 YO10 .231 E8
Crossley Pl BD23 . . . . .216 F4
Crossley St 8 LS22 . . . .180 C3
Crossley St Prim Sch
  LS22 . . . . .180 C3
Crossman Dr 2 WF6 . . .200 B2
Crossmoor La YO60 . . .166 E6
Crossway The
  Darlington DL1 . . . . .3 E5
  2 York YO31 . . . . .228 E8
Crossways YO10 . . . . . .229 C2
Crossways Cres HG2 . .220 D3
Crossways Dr HG2 . . . .220 D2
Crossways The LS21 . . .177 A1
Crosswell Pk 40 TS17 . . .5 F4
Crow Hill La HG3 . . . . .160 C4
Crow Nest Rd LA2 . . . .130 F6
Crowberry Dr HG3 . . . .161 B3
Crowdy Cl YO22 . . . . . .208 E2
Crowfoot La DL6 . . . . . .43 D5
Crowgarth HG4 . . . . . .140 D7
Crown Cres YO11 . . . . .213 A4
Crown Gr YO17 . . . . . .215 E3
Crown Sq 26 YO62 . . . . .70 B1
Crown St
  34 Burley in Warfedale
  LS29 . . . . .176 C1
  Darlington DL1 . . . . .3 C5
Crown Terr YO11 . . . . .213 A4
Crowood Ave TS9 . . . . .26 C8
Crowtrees LA2 . . . . . . .128 E8
Crummack La LA2 . . . .130 E8
Crummock 3 YO24 . . . .230 C7
Cswy The YO7 . . . . .12 E3
Cuddy Brown Cl 7 YO18 .96 A6
Culloden Twr (Heritage)★
  DL10 . . . . .209 B6
Culvert La BD23 . . . . . .216 A4
Cumberland Gdns
  DL10 . . . . .21 C4
Cumberland Rd WF10 . .201 C6
Cumberland St
  6 Skipton BD23 . . . . . .216 F3
  York YO1 . . . . .233 B1
Cumbernauld Rd TS17 . .6 F7
Cumbrian Ave 4 YO32 .167 A6
Cundall Ave YO7 . . . . .115 B6
Cundall Cl 6 YO32 . . . .167 C8
Cundall Manor Sch
  YO61 . . . . .115 E3
Cundall Way HG2 . . . . .222 C8
Cunliffe Rd LS29 . . . . .218 B3

Cunningham Ave TS17 . . .6 B6
Cunningham Rd DL9 . . .40 F4
Cupid's Alley YO17 . . . .149 B6
Curfew Rd HG4 . . . . . .214 C3
Curlew Cl 11 Ilkley LS29 .175 C2
  Leyburn DL8 . . . . .60 E4
Curlew Cres 2 DL9 . . . .40 F2
Curlew Dr
  Crossgates YO12 . . . . . .99 E6
  3 Filey YO14 . . . . .101 A3
Curlew Glebe 8 YO19 .184 E7
Curly Hill LS29 . . . . . . .218 C4
Currer La LS29 . . . . . . .175 B6
Currie Cl DL9 . . . . .209 C2
Curson Terr YO8 . . . . . .198 E3
Curtain La DL11 . . . . .1 D1
Curtain The DL11 . . . . . .1 D4
Curteis Dr DL10 . . . . . . .41 B6
Curzon Terr YO23 . . . . .228 B1
Custance Wlk YO23 . . .233 A1
Cut Rd WF11 . . . . .201 D6
Cut Throat La HG3 . . . .138 F1
Cutler La LS26 . . . . . . .200 C5
Cutpurse La DL10 . . . . .209 C8
Cutsyke Ave WF10 . . . .200 D3
Cutsyke Crest WF10 . . .200 D2
Cutsyke Rd WF10 . . . . .200 D2
Cycle St 1 YO10 . . . . . .229 A3
Cygnet Cl 7 YO14 . . . . .101 A4
Cygnet St 9 YO23 . . . . .233 A1
Cyndor Ct WF10 . . . . . .201 C3
Cypress Cl DL3 . . . . .3 B4
Cypress Gdns HG4 . . . .214 B2
Cypress Rd TS7 . . . . .7 C6

D

Dacre Braithwaite CE Prim
  Sch HG3 . . . . .159 B7
Dacre Ct LS24 . . . . . . .195 D7
Dacre Hall Pk HG3 . . . .159 F7
Dacre La HG3 . . . . .159 D7
Dacre Pasture La
  HG3 . . . . .159 D6
Daffy La YO61 . . . . .117 E1
Dairy La HG3 . . . . .159 E6
Daisy Cl HG3 . . . . .41 A5
Daisy Hill BD20 . . . . . .174 C1
Dakyn Cl DL7 . . . . .22 F2
Dalacres Cres BD23 . . .217 D8
Dalacres Dr BD23 . . . . .217 D8
Dalby Ave HG2 . . . . . . .220 D1
Dalby Bank YO60 . . . . .119 C2
Dalby Cl YO12 . . . . . . .212 B5
Dalby Cl HG2 . . . . .220 D1
Dalby Forest Dr YO18 . .96 E8
Dalby Mead YO32 . . . . .225 F1
Dalby Way TS8 . . . . .7 A5
Dale Ave YO13 . . . . .75 C8
Dale Bank HG1 . . . . . . .219 B3
Dale Cl Burniston YO13 . .75 C8
  Hampsthwaite HG3 . . . .161 A5
  7 Hurworth-on-Tees DL2 . .3 E1
  Selby YO8 . . . . .232 C4
  Thornton Watlass HG4 . . .86 D8
Dale Cres BD23 . . . . . .173 A4
Dale Croft 20 LS29 . . . .175 C2
Dale Dike Gr YO30 . . . .224 F2
Dale Edge 11 YO11 . . . .99 F7
Dale End Danby YO21 . . .29 C7
  Kirkbymoorside YO62 . . .70 B1
Dale End Rd YO62 . . . . .70 A7
Dale Garth YO12 . . . . .212 D4
Dale Gr DL8 . . . . .60 D6
Dale Rd Carleton BD23 .173 A4
  Darlington DL3 . . . . .3 B5
  Sadberge DL2 . . . . .4 C7
Dale Rise YO13 . . . . . . .75 C8
Dale St Earby BB18 . . . .172 B1
  York YO23 . . . . .233 A1
Dale Stone Cl WF11 . . .201 D5
Dale The LS25 . . . . . . .188 F1
Dale View 6 Earby BB18 .172 A1
  Ilkley LS29 . . . . .175 C2
Dale Way 2 DL8 . . . . . . .60 D5
Dalefield Ave WF6 . . . .200 A1
Dalefield Rd WF6 . . . . .200 A1
Dalehouse Bank TS13 . .13 J1
Dales Ave BD23 . . . . . .217 C7
Dales Countryside Mus★
  DL8 . . . . .56 D5
Dales Pk Rd TS8 . . . . . . .6 E5
Dales Sch DL7 . . . . .64 A7
Dalesbridge Outdoor Ctr★
  LA2 . . . . .130 E6
Daleside Ave HG2 . . . . .222 E5
Daleside Dr HG2 . . . . . .222 E5
Daleside Gdns HG2 . . . .222 E5
Daleside Pk HG3 . . . . . .160 A6
Daleside Rd
  Farndale East YO62 . . . .48 C7
  Farndale West YO62 . . . .48 B6
  Harrogate HG2 . . . . . . .222 E5
  Rosedale East Side YO18 .49 C5
  Rosedale West Side YO18 .49 C3
Dalewood Wlk 3 TS9 . . .26 C8
Dalguise Gr YO31 . . . . .233 C4
Dallamires Cl HG4 . . . .214 D3
Dallamires Ind Est
  HG4 . . . . .214 D4
Dallamires La HG4 . . . .214 E3
Dallamires Way N
  HG4 . . . . .214 D4
Dallamires Way S
  HG4 . . . . .214 D3
Dalmally Cl YO24 . . . . .230 B6

Dalton Hill YO19 . . . . . .193 A8
Dalton La Dalton YO7 . .115 D7
  Wothersome LS23 . . . . .188 C5
Dalton Terr YO24 . . . . .228 A3
Dam Bank YO8 . . . . . . .232 C6
Dam Head Rd 14 BB18 . .171 D1
Dam Hill YO23 . . . . . . .182 B1
Dame La DL8 . . . . .58 F1
Damson Cl YO26 . . . . . .227 B4
Danby Castle★ YO21 . . .29 D6
Danby CE VC Prim Sch
  YO21 . . . . .29 B6
Danby La DL7 . . . . .43 C5
Danby St DL9 . . . . .40 F4
Danby Sta YO21 . . . . . . .29 C7
Dandy Mill Ave WF8 . . .201 C1
Dandy Mill Croft 8
  WF8 . . . . .201 C1
Dandy Mill View WF8 . .201 C1
Dane Ave
  Thorpe Willoughby YO8 .197 B1
  York YO26 . . . . .227 C5
Dane Rd DL9 . . . . .209 E1
Dane's Graves (Tumuli)★
  YO25 . . . . .151 D2
Danebury Cres YO26 . .227 C4
Danebury Ct YO26 . . . .227 C4
Danebury Dr YO26 . . . .227 C4
Danelaw Gdns 1 DL6 . .43 F3
Danelaw Rd 2 DL6 . . . .43 F3
Danes Croft 2 YO10 . . .231 D8
Danes Cl 5 YO19 . . . . .198 A8
Danes Dyke 34 YO12 . . .75 D5
Danes Hills (Tumuli)★
  YO8 . . . . .192 E2
Danescroft YO8 . . . . . .232 C2
Danesfort Ave YO24 . . .227 D2
Danesgate YO26 . . . . . .227 C4
Danesmead YO10 . . . . .231 D8
Danesmoor Cres DL3 . . .3 B5
Daneswell Cl 3 YO41 . .168 D2
Dangerous Cnr HG3 . . .160 A2
Dansk Way LS29 . . . . . .218 D5
Danum Ave YO7 . . . . . .211 A1
Danum Dr YO10 . . . . . .231 E8
Danum Rd YO10 . . . . . .231 E8
Darbie Cl YO32 . . . . . . .225 D4
D'arcy Ct DL9 . . . . .40 F4
D'arcy Rd YO8 . . . . . . .232 E4
Darfield Cl 3 YO32 . . . .167 B8
Dark La
  Barwick in Elmet & Scholes
  LS15 . . . . .194 B8
  Brompton YO13 . . . . . . .98 C5
  Earby BB18 . . . . .172 B1
  Newsham DL11 . . . . . . .19 C8
  Sinnington YO62 . . . . . .71 A1
  Spofforth with Stockeld
  HG5 . . . . .179 F7
  Stainburn LS21 . . . . . .177 E2
  Sutton BD20 . . . . .187 F1
Darkfield La WF8 . . . . .201 C2
Darley Carr HG3 . . . . . .159 F6
Darley Cl 7 YO41 . . . . .168 D2
Darley Com Prim Sch
  HG3 . . . . .160 A6
Darley Mill Ctr★ HG3 . .159 F6
Darley Rd HG3 . . . . . . .160 D6
Darling La YO23 . . . . . .191 C8
Darlington (Bank Top) Sta
  DL1 . . . . .3 D4
Darlington Arts Ctr★ 2
  DL3 . . . . .3 C5
Darlington Back La DL2 . .4 E8
Darlington Coll of Tech
  DL3 . . . . .3 B5
Darlington Meml Hospl
  DL3 . . . . .3 C6
Darlington Rd
  Easby DL10 . . . . .20 F1
  Longnewton TS21 . . . . . .5 A7
  Northallerton DL6 . . . . .210 C7
  Richmond DL10 . . . . . .209 E8
  Stockton-on-Tees TS18 . . .5 E8
Darlington Rly Ctr & Mus
  DL3 . . . . .3 C6
Darnborough Gate
  HG4 . . . . .214 B6
Darnborough St YO23 . .233 B1
Darnbrook Rd 2 BB18 .171 D1
Darnbrook Wlk HG3 . . .229 B5
Darnholme La YO22 . . . .51 D8
Darnton Dr TS4 . . . . .7 A7
Darrowby Ct YO7 . . . . .211 C4
Darrowby Dr DL3 . . . . . .3 C6
Darwin Cl YO31 . . . . . .225 E1
Daskett Hill YO60 . . . . .145 D5
Dauby La YO41 . . . . . . .185 B3
Davenport Rd TS15 . . . . .5 D2
David La YO18 . . . . .72 F5
Davis Ave WF10 . . . . . .201 B3
Davison Rd DL1 . . . . .3 D7
Davison St TS12 . . . . . . .9 F7
Davygate YO1 . . . . .233 B2
Daw La YO23 . . . . .191 A5
Dawcross Rise HG3 . . . .222 B3
Dawes Ave WF10 . . . . .201 A3
Dawnay 5 YO12 . . . . . . .99 F7
Dawnay Garth
  Shipton YO30 . . . . .165 E5
  2 Snaith DN14 . . . . . . .204 B1

Dawney La YO61 . . . . .143 B6
Dawson St 16 BD23 . . .217 A3
Dawson Terr HG1 . . . . .219 D4
Dawson's La HG4 . . . . . .85 F4
Dawtrie St WF10 . . . . . .201 B4
Day La HG3 . . . . .159 F4
Daysfoot Ct 8 YO10 . . .228 E3
De Bruce Rd DL6 . . . . .210 D8
De Brus Pk TS8 . . . . .7 C4
De Brus Way TS14 . . . . . .8 F7
De Burgh Cl DL9 . . . . . .41 A5
De Ferrers Rd DL6 . . . .210 D8
De Ferrieres Ave HG1 . .219 C2
De Gaunte Rd DL6 . . . .210 E8
De Grey Ct YO30 . . . . .233 A4
De Grey Pl 2 YO23 . . . .231 B3
De Grey St YO31 . . . . . .233 B4
De Grey Terr YO30 . . . .233 A4
De Lacy Ave 1 WF7 . . .200 E1
De Lisle Cres DL7 . . . . .209 C2
De Mowbray Ct YO23 . .182 D3
Deacon Ct 3 YO8 . . . . .232 B6
Deacons Ct YO23 . . . . .230 B2
Dealtry Ave 1 YO32 . . .225 C8
Dean Edge Rd BD22 . . .187 C1
Dean Hall Brow YO22 . . .32 C5
Dean La BD22 . . . . .187 F3
Dean Rd Norton YO17 . .215 E3
  Scarborough YO12 . . . .212 E6
Dean St Ilkley LS29 . . . .218 C5
  Trawden Forest BB8 . . .186 A1
Deane Pl HG2 . . . . .220 B3
Deangate YO1 . . . . .233 B3
Deanhead Gr 7 YO30 . .224 F2
Deans Ct YO23 . . . . . . .230 A4
Deans Sq YO7 . . . . .115 C7
Debruse Ave TS15 . . . . . .5 D2
Dee Cl YO24 . . . . .230 B7
Deep Dale LS23 . . . . . .188 E1
Deep Ghyll Croft HG4 . .214 C3
Deep Ghyll Wlk HG4 . . .214 C3
Deepdale
  Guisborough TS14 . . . . . .8 D6
  7 Hutton Rudby TS15 . . .25 C5
  5 York YO24 . . . . .230 D8
Deepdale Ave
  Eastfield YO11 . . . . . . .100 A8
  Middlesbrough TS4 . . . . . .7 A8
  Scarborough YO11 . . . .213 A1
Deepdale Cl
  Boston Spa LS23 . . . . .180 D1
  Dent LA10 . . . . .77 F8
Deepdale Way 7 DL1 . . .3 F6
Deepfurrows La YO41 . .185 D3
Deeping Way YO8 . . . . .232 A6
Deer Hill Gr YO30 . . . . .224 F3
Deer Pk Ct 1 LS25 . . . .202 A8
Deerstone Way 22 YO19 .184 F7
Deighton La 18 LS25 . .195 F4
Deighton La
  Brompton DL6 . . . . .43 E5
  Little Smeaton DL6 . . . .23 E1
Deighton Rd
  Coulby Newham TS4 . . . .7 A7
  Spofforth with Stockeld
  HG3 . . . . .179 F6
  Wetherby LS22 . . . . . . .180 C4
Deigton Gates Prim Sch 7
  LS22 . . . . .180 C4
Del Pyke YO31 . . . . . . .233 C4
Delamere Cl 6 YO32 . . .166 D5
Delamere Cres HG2 . . .220 D1
Delamere Rd TS3 . . . . . .7 B8
Delaney Cl 19 BD24 . . .131 D2
Delf La YO7 . . . . .66 A4
Dell The 5 YO30 . . . . . .224 F3
Delves La YO22 . . . . . . .30 F3
Delwood YO10 . . . . . . .231 D7
Dene Cl DN14 . . . . .203 C2
Dene Gr DL3 . . . . .3 C6
Dene Mdw 1 YO13 . . . .99 B8
Dene Pk HG1 . . . . .219 F5
Dene Pk Cl HG1 . . . . . .219 F6
Dene Rd DL6 . . . . .210 E5
Dene The YO12 . . . . . . .212 E4
Deneside Rd DL3 . . . . . .3 B6
Denesway LS25 . . . . . .194 D3
Denevale TS15 . . . . . . .194 B8
Denison Ave 8 YO12 . . .99 D6
Denison Rd YO8 . . . . . .232 E4
Dennis La BD20 . . . . . .174 A2
Dennis St YO1 . . . . .233 C2
Dennison St YO31 . . . . .233 C4
Dentdale Dr HG5 . . . . . .221 C6
Denton Hall LS29 . . . . .218 A5
Denton Terr WF10 . . . . .200 F4
Denver Dr DL2 . . . . .4 D4
Denver Rd 6 DN6 . . . . .206 F2
Denwell Terr WF8 . . . . .201 B1
Depot La 11 YO12 . . . . .212 F4
Deramore Dr YO10 . . . .229 C3
Deramore Dr W YO10 . .229 C3
Derby Cl DL9 . . . . .209 C1
Derby Rd TS14 . . . . .8 E6
Derby The TS7 . . . . .7 B6
Dere St Roman Rd★
  DL11 . . . . .2 B2
Derrings La YO61 . . . . .142 D6
Derventio Roman Fort★
  YO17 . . . . .215 D4
Derwent Ave
  Garforth LS25 . . . . .194 C3
  5 Scarborough YO12 . . .212 E4
  York YO31 . . . . .228 F4

Derwent Cl
Elvington YO41 ....185 B3
2 Stamford Bridge YO41 ..168 D2
Derwent Ct YO41 ......185 D2
Derwent Dr
4 Barlby YO8 ....198 B5
Castleford WF10 ....201 C5
Wheldrake YO19 ....192 F7
Derwent Est YO19 .....184 E4
Derwent Inf Sch YO10 ..229 B4
YO10 ....229 B4
Derwent Pk YO19 .....193 B8
Derwent Pl WF11 .....201 F1
Derwent Pool YO17 ...215 D4
Derwent Rd
Harrogate HG1 ....220 B3
Huttons Ambo YO17 ...215 A2
Whitby YO21 ....208 A7
York YO10 ....231 D8
Derwent St 7 YO12 ...212 E4
Derwent Swimming Pool &
Fitness Ctr YO17 ....215 D4
Derwent Terr YO17 ...215 D4
Derwent Wlk YO32 ...225 F5
Desmond Rd DL2 ......4 C3
Deveron Way YO24 ...230 E7
Devil's Arrows Standing
Stones* YO51 ......141 B5
Devon Ct 8 DL9 .....209 C1
Devon Pl YO10 ....228 F3
Devonshire Dr YO12 ..212 E7
Devonshire Gn HG4 ...114 F1
Devonshire Pl
Harrogate HG1 ....219 E3
12 Skipton BD23 ......216 F4
Devonshire Rd DL1 .....3 E6
Devonshire St 13 BD23 217 A4
Devonshire Way HG1 ..219 F4
Dew La TS7 ....7 D7
Dewberry TS1 ....7 B4
Dewsbury Ct YO1 ....233 A1
Dewsbury Terr YO1 ...233 A1
Dexta Way DL7 ......210 C3
Diamond Ct TS18 .....5 F7
Diamond Gr HG4 .....220 C4
Diamond Mews HG2 ...219 C1
Diamond Pl HG1 .....220 C4
Diamond Rd TS17 .....6 B8
Diamond St YO31 ....233 C4
Dibble Bridge Bank
YO21 ....28 F6
Dibdale Rd DL2 ....4 A1
Dick La BD22 ....187 B6
Dick Scot La DL11 ....19 D7
Dickens Cl 1 YO32 ...225 F1
Dickens Dr DL9 ......41 B5
Dickens Rd YO17 ....215 C6
Dickey La YO8 ....197 D5
Dickson Rd 4 YO24 ..227 B1
Dicky Grounds La
YO17 ....121 D8
Dijon Ave YO24 .....227 C2
Dike La HG3 ....159 C4
Dike Ray Cl YO32 ...225 C7
Dikehollin La DL8 ....58 E2
Dikelands Cl 19 YO26 165 F1
Dikelands La YO26 ...165 F1
Dikes La TS9 ....8 C2
Diligence Way 2 TS16 ..5 D5
Dilys Gr 5 YO26 ....227 E4
Dimmingdale Rd TS12 ..10 A3
Dinas Ct 12 TS17 .....5 F4
Dinsdale Ave TS5 .....6 E7
Dinsdale Cl 7 DL2 ....4 C4
Dinsdale Cres DL1 ....3 D5
Dinsdale Ct 6 DL2 ....4 C4
Dinsdale Dr TS16 .....5 E5
Dinsdale Sta DL2 ......4 C4
Diomed Ct TS7 ....7 B7
Dishforth Airfield
YO7 ....115 A2
Dishforth Airfield Com Prim
Sch YO7 ....115 B2
Dishforth CE VC Prim Sch
YO7 ....114 F4
Dishforth Rd
Copt Hewick HG4 .....114 B2
Sharow HG4 ....214 F6
Disraeli Cl YO32 .....225 E1
Dixon Cl YO8 ....232 B6
Dixon Gdns YO8 .....232 B6
Dixon La YO1 ....233 C1
Dixon Rd HG1 ....219 D4
Dixon St BD20 ......187 F7
Dixon Terr HG1 .....219 D4
Dixons Bank TS8 .....7 C5
Dixons Yd YO1 .....233 C2
Dob Pk Rd LS21 .....176 F4
Dobella Ave DN14 ...205 A1
Doctor Laithe 3 BD23 134 C2
Doctor's Hill LA2 ....128 E8
Doctors La TS15 .....25 C5
Doctors La WF10 ....200 D2
Dodder Carr Rd TS13 ..10 F3
Dodford Rd TS8 ....6 F5
Dodgson La
Lothersdale BD20 ....186 D8
Thornton in Craven
BB18 ....172 C1
Dodgson Terr YO26 ..227 D4
Dodmire Jun & Inf Sch
DL1 ....3 E4
Dodsworth Ave YO31 .228 E7
Doe Pk YO30 ....224 F2

Doe Pk La YO41 ......169 B4
Dog Hill DL8 ....60 E3
Dog Hill Brow BD24 ..131 D6
Dog Kennel La YO18 ...96 E5
Doherty Wlk YO24 ...230 C8
Doldhin Ctr The DL1 ...3 C5
Dolegate YO41 ......168 F4
Dolly La DL7 ....64 C8
Dollyth Howe* YO17 .149 F6
Dolphin Ctr The DL3 ...3 C5
Dolphin Way YO14 ...100 F5
Don Ave YO24 ......230 E8
Don Pedro Ave WF6 ..200 B1
Don Pedro Cl WF6 ..200 B1
Donald Smith Ct DL8 ..61 C5
Doncaster Rd
Brayton YO8 ....232 B3
Knottingley WF11 ....201 E2
North Elmsall WF8 ...206 A1
Doran La 45 YO14 ...101 B3
Dorchester Rd LS24 ..189 D5
Doriam Ave YO31 ...225 F2
Doriam Dr YO31 ....225 F2
Dorkings The TS9 ....26 E5
Dorset Cl HG1 ......219 A3
Dorset Cres HG1 ....219 A3
Dorset Ct 9 DL9 ....209 C1
Dorset Rd TS14 ......8 E5
Dorset St BD7 ......217 A3
Dorts Cres LS24 ....190 C1
Dotcliffe Rd BB18 ...186 A7
Doublegates Ave 6
HG4 ....113 D2
Doublegates Cl 8 HG4 113 D2
Doublegates Ct 10 HG4 113 D2
Doublegates Gn 9 HG4 113 D2
Doublegates Wlk 7
HG4 ....113 D2
Doubting Castle*
YO21 ....10 D1
Douglas Cl TS18 ......5 F7
Douglas St 3 YO8 ...232 C5
Douky Bottom Cave*
BD23 ....133 F7
Dove Cl LS22 ....180 B4
Dove Cote Gdns DN14 203 D2
Dove St YO23 ....233 A1
Dove Way YO62 .....94 C8
Dovecot Cl YO14 ...100 E4
Dovecote Dr WF10 ..200 F7
Dovecote Garth 5
YO41 ....185 B2
Dovecote Mews YO1 .115 C7
Dovedale Ave YO12 .212 D8
Dovelands 14 BD20 ..187 E6
Dovey Ct 7 TS17 .....5 F4
Dower Ct YO7 ......211 D3
Dower Way YO7 ....211 D3
Dower Chase YO19 ..192 A6
Dower Pk YO19 ....192 B6
Dowkell La LS23 ....180 F1
Downdale Rd YO13 ...54 B4
Downdinner Hill YO21 208 C6
Downholme Rd DL9 ..209 B1
Downland Cres WF11 202 A1
Downside Rd TS5 .....6 D8
Dracula Experience*
YO21 ....208 D7
Dragon Ave HG1 ....219 E3
Dragon Par HG1 ....219 E3
Dragon Rd HG1 ....219 E3
Dragon Terr HG1 ...219 E3
Dragon View HG1 ..219 E4
Drake Cl YO21 .....208 B5
Drake St 2 YO23 ...233 B1
Drakes Cl YO32 ....225 F5
Drapers Croft YO23 .230 B4
Drax CP Sch YO8 ..204 F5
Dreaken Fold 4 YO13 .99 A7
Drebley La BD23 ...157 D6
Dresser Cl DL10 ...209 C8
Driffield Rd YO25 ..151 C4
Driffield Terr YO24 .228 A2
Drift La HG4 ....138 B8
Dringfield Cl 2 YO24 230 D8
Dringhouses Prim Sch
YO24 ....230 F8
Dringhouses Sports Club
YO24 ....230 F8
Dringthorpe Rd YO24 230 F7
Drive The
Harrogate HG1 ....220 C5
7 High & Low Bishopside
HG3 ....137 C4
Kippax LS25 ....194 D1
Middlesbrough TS17 ...6 A6
Skipton BD23 ....217 B5
12 Swillington LS26 ..194 A1
Threshfield BD23 ...134 B3
Drome Rd YO23 ....230 C2
Drovers Ct 8 YO61 .143 C8
Drovers Way YO7 ..211 D4
Drovers Wlk BD23 ..154 B3
Druggist La 16 YO61 174 F4
Druggon Rd DL9 ....40 E3
Druids Mdw 8 YO51 141 B5
Drummond View
YO23 ....231 B4
Drury Cl HG3 ......222 F2
Drury La HG3 ......222 F2
Drury St DL3 ....3 C6
Dryden Cl HG1 ....219 D7
Dryhurst Cl 9 DN6 ..206 F1
Dubbing Garth La DL11 37 B4
Dubb's La BD23 ....81 C1
Duchess of Kents Military
Hospl DL9 ....40 F4

Duchy Ave
3 Harrogate HG2 ....219 C1
11 Scalby YO13 ......75 D5
Duchy Gr 4 HG2 ...219 C1
Duchy Rd HG1 .....219 B2
Duck Hill HG4 .....214 C5
Duck La YO12 .....125 A8
Duck St LA2 ....128 A6
Duck St La HG3 ...136 D2
Duckett Cl DL10 ...209 F8
Duckett St BD23 ..217 A3
Duckhill La YO7 ...115 A4
Dudley Mews YO31 ..233 C4
Dudley St YO31 ...233 C4
Dudley Wlk HG4 ..214 B3
Duffield Cres 1 LS25 .195 F4
Dugdale La BB7 ...152 C1
Duggleby Howe*
YO17 ....149 C5
Duke St
6 Burton in Lonsdale LA6 102 F3
High Bentham LA2 ..129 A8
Settle BD23 ....131 D2
Skipton BD23 ....217 A4
14 Trawden Forest BB8 .186 A3
Duke's La YO25 ...126 A1
Dukes Hill LS29 ...218 A6
Dukes Wharf YO23 .233 B1
Dukesway TS17 .....6 B5
Dulverton Cl
2 High Leven TS17 ...6 A3
13 Pontefract WF8 ..201 C2
Dulverton Rise WF8 .201 C2
Dulverton Way 7 WF8 201 C2
Dumb Tom's La LA6 ..103 B1
Dumfries Sq 8 DL9 ..40 E4
Duna Way 6 YO62 ..70 C1
Duncan Cl 6 HG1 ..219 C5
Duncan St YO31 ...219 C5
Dunce Mire Rd LS25 202 A8
Duncombe Cl
2 Eastfield YO12 ....99 F7
Malton YO17 ....215 A3
Duncombe Dr
24 Pickering YO18 ...95 F7
Strensall YO32 .....167 B8
Duncombe La YO32 ..167 B8
Duncombe Pk* YO62 ..92 E6
Duncombe Pl YO1 ..233 B3
Dundas Gdns YO21 .208 B6
Dundas St
Richmond DL10 ....209 C7
York YO1 ....233 C2
Dunderdale Cres
WF10 ....201 B5
Dunelm Wlk DL1 ....3 C7
Dunkeswick La LS17 178 D4
Dunn Gr 3 YO11 ...100 A7
Dunnington CE Prim Sch
YO19 ....184 E7
Dunnington Dr YO8 ..196 F1
Dunniwood Cl 4 WF10 200 D3
Dunniwood Dr 3 WF10 200 D3
Dunroyal YO61 .....141 F8
Dunroyal Cl YO61 ..141 F8
Dunsley Cres YO21 .208 A8
Dunsley La YO21 ...32 A8
Dunslow Ct YO11 ....99 F6
Dunslow Rd YO11 ...99 F6
Dunsmore Ct TS8 ....6 C4
Dunwell Ave 2 YO12 212 B7
Durham Cl 18 YO8 ..198 F1
Durham La TS16 .....5 D5
Durham La Ind Pk TS16 .5 D6
Durham La Prim Sch
TS16 ....5 D5
Durham Pl 5 YO12 ..213 A7
Durham St
Castleford WF10 ...200 F3
6 Scarborough YO12 212 F7
Durham Tees Valley Airport
DL2 ....4 F4
Durham Way HG3 ..219 A5
Durlston Dr YO32 ..167 A7
Duxbury St 11 BB18 172 B1
Dyke Hall La LA10 ...78 A8
Dykelands Cl YO19 .192 F7
Dykes La YO23 ....230 A1
Dyon La YO8 ......199 B3
Dyon Rd YO8 .....199 D7
Dyson la DL11 ......18 G7

E

Eagle Pk TS8 ....7 C5
Eaglescliffe Sta TS16 ..5 E6
Earby Springfield Prim Sch
BB18 ....172 B1
Earfit La YO23 .....191 A8
Earl Crag View BD22 187 C6
Earl Edwin Dr DL10 209 D8
Earle St YO31 .....233 C4
Earlham St 10 BB18 172 B1
Earls Ct Rd TS8 .....6 F5
Earls View BD20 ...187 E6
Earlsborough Terr
YO30 ....233 A3
Earlsdon Ave TS5 ...6 D7
Earlsway TS17 .....6 C5
Earswick Chase YO32 225 F7
Earswick Village YO32 225 F7
Easby Abbey (rems of)*
DL10 ....209 E5
Easby Ave TS5 ......7 C5
Easby Cl 4 Bedale DL8 .63 B2
7 Ilkley LS29 ....175 C2

Easby Ct DL10 .....209 F5
Easby Dr LS29 ....175 C2
Easby La Easby TS9 ..27 A8
Great Ayton TS9 ......7 F1
Easby Low Rd DL10 209 D7
Easingwold Com Prim Sch
YO61 ....117 C1
Easingwold Sch YO61 143 C8
Eason Rd YO24 ....230 E8
Eason View YO24 ..230 E8
Easson Rd DL3 ....3 C5
East Acres WF11 ...201 F4
East Ave
8 Easingwold YO61 .143 D8
13 Glusburn BD20 ..187 E7
21 Scalby YO13 .....75 D5
East Ayton Com Prim Sch
YO13 ....99 A8
East Bank 2 LS25 ..195 F4
East Barnby La YO21 .12 C3
East Beck Ct LS21 ..176 C3
East Brow Rd YO18 ..72 C4
East Carr 18 YO11 ..100 B6
East Castle St 6 BD23 217 A3
East Cl DL2 ....4 C7
East Cliff YO22 ....208 E7
East Comm La YO8 .232 F4
East Cowton CE Prim Sch
DL7 ....22 E1
East Cres 19 YO21 ..208 D7
East Down WF10 ..201 A4
East End YO60 ....145 D5
East Garforth Prim Sch
LS25 ....194 D4
East Garforth Sta
LS25 ....194 D3
East Gate YO13 .....98 D6
East Heslerton La
YO17 ....124 A8
East Ings La YO18 ...95 F4
East La Ampleforth YO62 92 D1
Castle Bolton with East &
West Bolton DL8 ...59 B6
Embsay BD23 ......217 D7
Yafforth DL7 ....43 C1
East Lea YO7 ......115 C7
East Lea View 21 YO11 100 B6
East Moor Gdns YO19 231 F5
East Mount YO17 ..215 C4
East Mount Rd
Darlington DL1 ......3 D6
York YO24 ....233 A1
East Neville St 14 BD23 217 A3
East Parade
Harrogate HG1 .....219 E2
Ilkley LS29 ....218 C4
York YO31 ....228 E4
East Pk Rd
Harrogate HG1 .....219 E2
15 Scalby YO13 .....75 D5
5 Spofforth HG3 ...179 E5
East Rd Melsonby DL10 ..21 F7
Northallerton DL6 ..210 E4
Norton YO17 ......215 E3
East Sandgate 14 YO11 213 B6
East Side 5 TS15 ...25 D5
East St Gargrave BD23 155 D1
Gayles DL11 ....19 E6
Swinton YO17 .....121 B4
East Terr YO21 ....208 D7
East Terr Cresent
YO21 ....208 D7
East View Barton DL10 .21 D8
7 Campsall DN6 ....206 E1
10 Knottingley WF11 202 A2
Langthorpe YO51 ..141 A6
Middleton St George DL2 ..4 D3
Northallerton DL6 ..210 E3
Sherburn in Elmet LS25 195 F3
South Kilvington YO7 211 B6
3 Trawden BB8 ....186 B1
East View Ct HG5 ..162 F3
East Way Whitby YO21 208 B7
York YO31 ....225 C2
East Whitton Com Prim Sch
YO22 ....208 A4
East Witton Rd DL8 ..60 E2
Eastbeck Cl YO17 ..124 E8
Eastborough YO11 .213 B6
Eastbourne Comp Sch
DL1 ....3 E5
Eastbourne Gdns TS3 ..7 C8
Eastbourne Gr YO31 228 E5
Eastbourne Rd DL3 ..3 D5
Eastburn Jun & Inf Sch
BD20 ....187 F7
Eastbury Cl TS17 ....6 B4
Eastby Rd HG1 ....219 F6
Eastern Terr YO31 ..228 E6
Easterside La YO62 ..67 F4
Easterside Prim Sch
TS4 ....7 A7
Easterside Rd TS4 ...7 A7
Eastfield
Amotherby YO17 ...121 B4
Hunmanby YO14 ...126 F8
Knaresborough HG5 221 D6
Eastfield Ave
Haxby YO32 ....225 C7
Norton YO17 ......215 E3
Richmond DL10 ...209 D8
Eastfield Cl LS24 ..189 F7
Eastfield Cres YO10 229 C2
Eastfield Ct YO10 ..229 C2
Eastfield Dr 14 WF8 201 C1
Eastfield Gr WF6 ..200 B2

Eastfield La
Dunnington YO19 ..184 F8
Kellington DN14 ...202 F4
Spennithorne DL8 ..61 A3
Thoralby DL8 ......58 E2
Eastfield Rd
Norton YO17 ......215 E3
Pickering YO18 .....96 A6
Eastfields TS9 .....26 C7
Eastgate 16 Helmsley YO62 92 F6
Pickering YO18 .....96 A6
3 Seamer YO12 .....99 D6
Eastholme Dr YO30 .224 E1
Easthorpe Dr YO26 .224 A1
Eastland Ave YO24 .227 E2
Easton La YO21 .....29 D6
Easton Way 4 DL8 ...41 B5
Eastville Terr HG1 ..219 B6
Eastward Ave YO10 231 E7
Eastway YO11 .....100 A7
Eastway Cl 2 YO62 ..70 C1
Eaton Ct 7 YO24 ..230 B8
Eaton Rd LS29 ....218 A3
Eavestone Gr HG3 .219 A1
Ebberston Hall* YO13 ..97 D6
Ebenezer Terr 9 HG1 219 D2
Ebor Cl DL10 ....21 A1
Ebor Ct
Northallerton DL7 ..210 D3
7 Selby YO8 ....232 C6
Ebor Ind Est YO31 .233 C3
Ebor Mount LS25 ..194 D1
Ebor Prep Sch YO30 228 A2
Ebor Rise YO31 ...219 B2
Ebor St Selby YO8 .232 C5
York YO23 ....233 B1
Ebor Way YO26 ...224 A2
Ebsay Dr YO30 ....225 A1
Eccles Cl YO30 ....224 D2
Edale Ave YO31 ...225 A1
Eden Camp Modern History
Mus* YO17 ....215 E8
Eden Cl
2 Hurworth-on-Tees DL2 ..3 D1
1 Hutton Rudby TS15 .25 C4
York YO24 ....230 C7
Eden Cres DL1 ......3 C4
Eden Crest DL2 .....1 D7
Eden La DL2 ....1 D8
Eden Pk DL2 ....1 D7
Eden Pk Rd 2 TS15 ..25 C4
Eden Rd DL7 ......210 B2
Edendale WF10 ....200 F4
Edenhouse Rd YO17 215 E8
Edens Way HG4 ...214 C2
Edge Dell YO11 .....99 E8
Edge La
Grassington BD23 ..134 F3
Long Preston BD23 153 E6
Edgecombe Dr DL3 ..3 A6
Edgehill Rd YO12 ..212 E2
Edgemoor Rd DL1 ...3 A4
Edgerton Cl LS24 ..189 D6
Edgerton Ct 11 LS24 189 D6
Edgerton Dr LS24 ..189 D6
Edgerton Garth LS24 189 D6
Edgware Rd YO10 .228 E2
Edinburgh Dr DL3 ...3 A4
Edmondson St 17 BB18 171 D2
Edmondson's La BD23 172 C5
Edmund Wilson Swimming
Baths YO24 ....227 D1
Edston Dr 9 TS14 ...8 F7
Edward Pease Way DL3 3 A7
Edward St
27 Earby BB18 ....172 A1
Pontefract WF6 ...200 A1
Egglescliffe CE VC Sch
TS16 ....5 E4
Egglescliffe Sch TS16 ..5 D4
Eggleston View DL3 ..3 A6
Eggshell La LA2 ...130 C8
Eglington Ave TS14 ..8 F6
Egremont Cl 17 YO41 168 D2
Egton Ave TS7 .....7 C5
Egton CE VA Prim Sch
YO21 ....31 B5
Egton Cliff YO21 ....31 A4
Egton La YO21 ......30 F5
Egton Sta YO21 .....31 A4
Eight Acre La HG4 .113 A5
Eighth Ave YO31 ..228 F5
El Alamein Rd 5 DL9 209 C1
Elbolton Cave* BD23 156 E8
Elbow Terr 4 YO22 .208 E6
Elder Rd DL6 ......210 D4
Elder's St YO11 ....213 A6
Eldmire La YO7 ....115 C6
Eldon St YO31 ....233 C4
Eldon Terr YO31 ..233 C4
Eldroth Rd LA2 ...130 C5
Eldwick Cl YO30 ..224 F2
Eleanor Dr HG2 ...220 C1
Eleanor Rd HG2 ...220 C1
Electric Ave HG1 ..219 B5
Elgar Cl YO31 ....225 E1
Elgin Rd TS17 ......6 B6
Elgin St 16 YO21 ..208 D6
Elizabeth Ct
7 Selby YO8 ....232 B6
Sherburn in Elmet LS25 195 E4
Elizabeth Dr WF10 201 B4
Elizabethan Ct 4 WF8 201 C1
Elland Ct 12 DL1 ....3 F6
Ellarfield La LS25 ..195 F5
Ellen Gr HG1 ......220 C4
Ellenthorpe La YO51 141 D6
Eller Gates YO21 ...30 C6

Eller Gill La BD23 ...172 D4
Eller Mews 3 BD23 ...216 E3
Ellerbeck Ct TS9 ...26 D6
Ellerbeck Way
  Great & Little Broughton
  TS9 ...26 D6
  Middlesbrough TS7 ...7 D8
  Whitby YO22 ...208 E4
Ellerburn Rd YO18 ...96 F7
Ellerby Bank TS13 ...11 F4
Ellerby La TS13 ...11 F5
Ellerclose Rd 28 DL8 ...60 D5
Ellerholme La DL11 ...38 F5
Ellerington Cl 5 LA6 ...103 D3
Ellerker La LS28 ...188 A3
Ellerker Rd LS14 ...188 A3
Ellers La DL8 ...59 A2
Ellers Rd BD20 ...187 E6
Ellerton Bank Nature
  Reserve★ YO8 ...72 F1
Ellerton Priory (rems of)★
  DL11 ...39 A4
Ellerton Rd TS18 ...5 D8
Elliot Cl YO10 ...231 D7
Elliot St BD23 ...216 F4
Elliott St BD20 ...174 B1
Ellis Ct HG1 ...219 B2
Ellis Gdns 6 YO13 ...75 D5
Ellis La LS25 ...194 C5
Ellison Ave 32 YO12 ...75 D5
Ellwood Cotts BD24 ...131 D4
Ellwood Ct YO10 ...228 D2
Elm Ave Kippax LS25 ...194 C2
  Northallerton DL6 ...210 F5
Elm Cl
  Barnoldswick BB18 ...171 D1
  10 Filey YO14 ...101 B4
  Hipswell DL9 ...209 F1
  Northallerton DL6 ...210 F5
Elm Ct DL6 ...210 E5
Elm Dr TS7 ...7 B6
Elm End 9 YO32 ...166 E5
Elm Gn 7 YO62 ...92 F7
Elm Gr Sherburn YO17 ...124 D8
  Thornaby TS17 ...6 B8
  4 Whitby YO21 ...208 B6
  York YO31 ...225 D4
Elm Pl WF11 ...201 F2
Elm Rd 34 Glusburn BD20 ...187 E7
  Guisborough TS14 ...8 F7
  Harrogate HG1 ...219 E5
  Ripon HG4 ...214 B2
  3 Scarborough YO12 ...212 E4
  3 Topcliffe YO7 ...89 B1
Elm St YO8 ...232 D6
Elm Tree Ave
  Harrogate HG1 ...219 D5
  9 Poppleton YO26 ...165 F1
Elm Tree Rise HG3 ...140 B5
Elm Tree Sq BD23 ...217 D8
Elm View YO18 ...96 A6
Elm Wlk 6 DL10 ...41 D5
Elma Gr 3 YO30 ...224 E2
Elmet Dr TS15 ...194 C8
Elmet Rd LS15 ...194 C7
Elmete Ave LS25 ...195 F4
Elmete Rd WF10 ...201 B4
Elmfield Ave YO31 ...228 F8
Elmfield Rd
  3 Glusburn BD20 ...187 F8
  Hurworth DL2 ...3 D1
  Hurworth-on-Tees DL2 ...22 D8
Elmfield Terr YO31 ...228 F7
Elmlands Gr YO31 ...228 E8
Elmpark Vale YO31 ...229 A8
Elmpark View YO31 ...229 A8
Elmpark Way YO31 ...229 A8
Elms Cl 2 YO19 ...167 F1
Elms The YO32 ...167 D2
Elmslac Cl 1 YO62 ...92 F6
Elmslac Rd 3 YO62 ...92 F7
Elmtree Gdns YO26 ...227 C3
Elmville Ave YO12 ...212 E4
Elmwood Ave LS15 ...194 B8
Elmwood Chase LS15 ...194 B8
Elmwood Cl 6 TS9 ...26 C8
Elmwood La LS15 ...194 B8
Elmwood Rd TS16 ...5 E6
Elmwood St 4 HG1 ...219 E4
Elphin Bridge La
  YO61 ...117 B6
Elslack La BD23 ...172 C4
Elston Cl YO30 ...228 A8
Elston Pl YO8 ...232 C6
Eltham Cres TS17 ...6 C6
Elton La HG3 ...160 E6
Elton Par DL3 ...3 B5
Elton Rd DL3 ...3 B5
Elvington CE Prim Sch
  YO41 ...185 B3
Elvington Ind Est
  YO41 ...185 A3
Elvington La YO19 ...184 E6
Elvington Pk YO41 ...185 A3
Elvington Terr YO10 ...228 E4
Elwick Ave TS5 ...6 E7
Elwick Gr YO10 ...229 C4
Elwick Rd YO26 ...164 B7
Ely Cl HG3 ...219 A5
Embleton Dr 1 YO30 ...224 F1
Embleton Rd LS26 ...200 B4
Embsay CE VC Prim Sch
  BD23 ...217 D8
Embsay Sta BD23 ...217 D7
Embsay Steam Rly★
  BD23 ...217 D7
Emerald St YO31 ...233 C4
Emerson Ave TS5 ...6 F8

Emerson Cl 2 DL6 ...25 D1
Emerson Rd DL2 ...3 E1
Emery Cl DL2 ...3 E1
Emgate 2 DL8 ...63 A3
Emily Mews YO10 ...228 E4
Emley Moor Rd DL1 ...3 F6
Emley View LS25 ...194 C2
Emmerson St 2 YO31 ...228 E5
Emmet La HG3 ...160 C5
Emmott Ct BB8 ...186 A3
Emmott La BB8 ...186 B4
Emsworth Dr TS16 ...5 D5
Enclosure Gdns 1
  YO10 ...229 B1
Endcliff Cres YO12 ...212 D8
Endeavour Wharf 6
  YO21 ...208 D6
Endfields Rd 1 YO10 ...231 E8
Endican La DL7 ...65 D3
Endsleigh Dr TS5 ...6 D8
Enfield Chase TS14 ...8 F5
Enfield Cl 4 DL9 ...40 E4
Enfield Cres 1 YO24 ...228 A3
Engine Shed La BD23 ...216 D3
England La WF11 ...201 F2
English Martyrs' RC Prim Sch
  YO24 ...227 D1
Ennerdale Ave YO31 ...229 B5
Enter La LA6 ...103 D3
Enterpen TS15 ...25 C4
Enterprise Way
  Bradleys Both BD20 ...173 D4
  Sherburn in Elmet LS25 ...196 B4
  Whitby YO22 ...32 A5
Eppleby Forcett CE Prim Sch
  DL11 ...1 D4
Epsom Cl 11 DL1 ...3 F6
Eridge Rd DL1 ...8 F6
Ermysted St 4 BD23 ...217 A4
Ermysted's Gram Sch
  BD23 ...216 F4
Eryholme La DL2 ...22 F7
Escrick CE VC Prim Sch
  YO19 ...192 A5
Escrick Ct YO19 ...192 A5
Escrick Pk Gdns YO19 ...192 B5
Escrick St YO10 ...233 C1
Escrick Terr YO10 ...233 C1
Esher Ave TS6 ...7 E8
Eshington La DL8 ...58 F7
Eshton Rd BD23 ...155 D2
Esk Dr YO26 ...227 B8
Esk Rd DL1 ...3 D3
Eskdale Sch YO22 ...208 E3
Eskdale Ave
  Normanton WF6 ...200 A2
  York YO31 ...229 C3
Eskdale Cl
  5 Pontefract WF6 ...200 A2
  Sleights YO22 ...32 A5
Eskdale Croft WF6 ...200 A2
Eskdale Ct 12 WF6 ...200 A2
Eskdale Rd YO22 ...208 F3
Eskdaleside YO22 ...31 F5
Eskew La LA2 ...128 C4
Eskitt Hill YO12 ...212 D4
Esp La BB18 ...171 C1
Esplanade
  Harrogate HG2 ...219 C2
  Scarborough YO11 ...213 A4
  Whitby YO21 ...208 D7
  York YO26 ...233 A2
Esplanade Cres YO11 ...213 B2
Esplanade Gdns YO11 ...213 A4
Esplanade Rd YO11 ...213 A3
Estell La YO13 ...74 C5
Estill Cl 2 YO11 ...100 B6
Estoril Rd S DL1 ...3 F4
Ethel Cres HG5 ...221 C6
Ethel St 12 BB18 ...171 E1
Etive Pl YO24 ...230 B7
Eton Dr 7 YO32 ...166 E5
Eton Rd TS5 ...6 E8
Ettersgill Cl TS16 ...5 D5
Ettersgill Dr DL3 ...3 A5
Ettington Ave TS3 ...7 B8
Etty Ave YO10 ...229 A4
Etty Cl 24 YO41 ...168 D2
Euclid Ave HG1 ...219 B5
Eva Ave YO30 ...224 D2
Evelyn Cres YO30 ...228 B7
Evelyn Ct 5 HG3 ...161 B2
Evelyn Dr YO12 ...212 D4
Evergreen Way 1 YO8 ...197 D1
Evergreen Wlk 2 TS4 ...6 F8
Everingham Rd TS15 ...5 D2
Eversley Ave LS25 ...195 F3
Eversley Ct LS25 ...195 F4
Eversley Garth Cres
  LS25 ...195 F4
Eversley Mount LS25 ...195 F3
Evesham Rd TS3 ...7 A8
Evron Ctr YO14 ...101 B3
Ewart St YO12 ...212 E3
Ewden Cl 16 YO14 ...101 A3
Ewe Leys La YO7 ...66 A5
Ewelands Hill YO7 ...90 C7
Exchange St 8 WF6 ...200 A1
Exelby Cl 8 DL8 ...63 D1
Exelby La DL7 ...63 D2
Exeter Cres 10 HG3 ...161 B3
Exeter Dr DL1 ...3 F7
Exford Cl 8 DL7 ...63 A3
Exhibition Sq YO1 ...233 B3
Express Way WF6 ...200 A3
Eyre Cl YO8 ...232 A4

F

Faber Cl YO23 ...230 B3
Faber St YO31 ...228 E5
Faceby Rd TS9 ...26 A2
Fadmoor Bank YO62 ...69 E6
Fadmoor La YO62 ...69 E6
Fair Head La YO22 ...31 D4
Fairburn Dr LS25 ...194 D3
Fairburn Prim Sch
  WF11 ...201 D6
Fairburn Sports & Recn Ctr
  WF11 ...201 D6
Fairfax YO41 ...168 D2
Fairfax Ave
  Harrogate HG2 ...220 B2
  North Featherstone
  WF7 ...200 E1
  Selby YO8 ...232 B4
Fairfax Cl
  2 Ampleforth YO62 ...92 C1
  Bolton Percy YO23 ...190 D4
Fairfax Cres YO26 ...181 C7
Fairfax Croft YO23 ...230 B2
Fairfax House★ YO1 ...233 C2
Fairfax Rd DL2 ...4 D4
Fairfax St
  1 Scarborough YO12 ...212 E5
  10 Skipton BD23 ...217 A3
  York YO1 ...233 B1
Fairfax Wlk 3 HG2 ...220 B3
Fairfield
  Fairburn WF11 ...201 D7
  Thirsk YO7 ...211 C4
Fairfield Ave TS7 ...7 D7
Fairfield Cl 16 LS25 ...195 F4
Fairfield Cres YO12 ...212 B8
Fairfield La LS25 ...202 A6
Fairfield Link LS25 ...195 F4
Fairfield Rd
  Staithes TS13 ...13 K2
  Stokesley TS9 ...26 B7
  Tadcaster LS24 ...189 E6
Fairfield St DL3 ...3 C6
Fairfield Way
  9 Tadcaster LS24 ...189 E6
  Whitby YO22 ...208 F3
Fairfields Dr YO30 ...224 B5
Fairheath Rd LA2 ...128 E5
Fairholme La DL7 ...64 A4
Fairmead Ct YO22 ...208 E4
Fairmead Way YO22 ...208 E4
Fairview TS21 ...5 A7
Fairview Gdns DL10 ...209 C8
Fairway
  Normanton South WF6 ...200 B1
  4 Scalby YO12 ...75 D5
  Selby YO8 ...232 A4
  York YO30 ...228 A8
Fairway App WF6 ...200 B1
Fairway Ave WF6 ...200 B1
Fairway Cl
  8 Normanton South WF6 ...200 B1
  15 Sherburn in Elmet LS25 ...195 F4
Fairway Dr
  Normanton South WF6 ...200 B1
  18 Poppleton YO26 ...165 F1
Fairway Gdns 4 WF6 ...200 B1
Fairway Mdws 9 WF6 ...200 B1
Fairway The
  Darlington DL1 ...3 E5
  Middlesbrough TS8 ...7 C5
  8 North Featherstone
  WF7 ...200 E1
  Northallerton DL7 ...210 C3
  Sherburn in Elmet LS25 ...195 F4
Fairways Ave HG2 ...220 E3
Fairways Cl HG2 ...220 E3
Fairways Dr HG2 ...220 D3
Fairways The LS24 ...189 E5
Fairwood Pk TS5 ...7 C5
Fairy Hill La WF8 ...201 B3
Fairy La YO18 ...71 C3
Falcon Ave 7 YO12 ...99 E6
Falcon Cl 10 Haxby YO32 ...166 F5
  1 Scotton DL9 ...40 F2
  17 Settle BD24 ...131 D2
Falcon Dr WF10 ...200 E3
Falcon Gdns 20 BD24 ...131 D2
Falcon Terr 11 YO21 ...208 D6
Falcon Way TS14 ...8 D6
Falcon Wlk TS15 ...6 C2
Falconberg Way TS15 ...5 D2
Falconer St 1 YO24 ...227 F3
Falconers Rd YO11 ...213 A5
Falconers Sq 10 YO11 ...213 A5
Falkland Rd 2 DL9 ...40 F5
Falkland St YO1 ...233 B1
Fall La Pannal HG3 ...222 B2
  Thornthwaite with Padside
  HG3 ...159 A6
Falling Foss (Waterfall)★
  YO22 ...32 C2
Fallow Field 1 BD23 ...217 B5
Falmer Rd DL1 ...3 F6
Falmouth Ave WF6 ...200 A2
Falmouth Cres 20 WF6 ...200 A2
Falmouth Dr DL3 ...3 C8
Falmouth Rd WF6 ...200 A2
Falsgrave Com Resource
  Ctr★ YO12 ...212 E1
Falsgrave Cres YO30 ...228 B7
Falsgrave Mews 6
  YO12 ...212 E5
Falsgrave Rd YO12 ...212 F5
Fanacurt Rd TS14 ...8 D6
Fancy Bank TS14 ...9 B6

Fanny La Knayton YO7 ...65 F2
  Stutton with Hazlewood
  LS24 ...189 D4
Far La
  Hutton Buscel YO13 ...98 F8
  Kettlewell with Starbotton
  BD23 ...108 A3
Far Mead Croft 3 LS29 ...176 C1
Farfield YO26 ...227 C6
Farfield Ave YO19 ...184 E8
Farfield lane YO19 ...167 E1
Farfield Mount 4 HG5 ...221 C4
Farfields Cl TS21 ...4 F6
Farm Cl YO21 ...208 A7
Farm Croft BD23 ...216 F1
Farm Garth TS9 ...8 A2
Farm La TS7 ...6 A5
Farm Way YO8 ...232 B7
Farmanby Cl 12 YO18 ...96 D5
Farmbank Rd TS7 ...7 E7
Farmers Way YO23 ...230 B3
Farmlands Rd 1 YO24 ...230 D8
Farmstead Rise YO32 ...225 D7
Farnborough Ct 10 DL2 ...4 C4
Farndale Ave
  Northallerton DL7 ...210 D3
  York YO10 ...229 D4
Farndale Cl 1 YO32 ...166 F5
Farndale Cres DL3 ...3 B6
Farndale Dr TS14 ...8 D6
Farndale Rd HG5 ...221 D6
Farndale St YO10 ...228 D2
Farnham La HG5 ...162 D7
Farnley CE VA Prim Sch
  LS21 ...177 B3
Farnley Hall★ LS21 ...177 B2
Farnley La LS21 ...177 B2
Farnley Pk LS21 ...177 C2
Farrar St YO10 ...228 D2
Farriers Croft 2 YO23 ...230 B3
Farriers Ct 16 LS22 ...180 C3
Farside Garth YO13 ...75 D6
Farside Rd YO13 ...99 A7
Farthingale Way TS8 ...6 E4
Favell Ave WF6 ...200 A1
Faven Field Rd YO7 ...211 D4
Faverdale DL3 ...3 B7
Faverdale N DL3 ...3 B7
Faverdale Rd DL3 ...3 B7
Faverdale W DL3 ...3 B7
Faversham Cl TS8 ...6 F4
Favordale Rd BB8 ...186 A3
Fawcett Ave TS8 ...6 E4
Fawcett St YO10 ...233 C1
Fawdington Rd YO61 ...115 F2
Fawkes Dr YO26 ...227 C4
Fearby Rd Fearby HG4 ...85 F4
  Masham HG4 ...86 A4
  7 Stockton-on-Tees TS18 ...5 D8
Fearnhead TS8 ...7 C5
Feasegate YO1 ...233 B2
Featherbeck Cl 8 LA6 ...103 D3
Featherbed La
  Bilton-in-Ainsty with Bickerton
  LS24 ...181 C3
  Ellerbeck DL6 ...44 E4
Federation St 12 BB18 ...171 D1
Feeding Pasture La
  YO60 ...147 B7
Feetham Ave DL1 ...3 F7
Feethams Sports Gd
  DL1 ...3 C5
Felbrigg La TS17 ...6 A4
Feldom La DL11 ...19 E1
Felixkirk Rd YO7 ...211 F4
Felixstowe Dr 10 DL9 ...40 E4
Fell La Cracoe BD23 ...156 B7
  Winton CA17 ...14 C8
Fell Rd LA6 ...77 A4
Fell View BD23 ...217 E8
Fell View Sq 4 BD23 ...134 E2
Fellbrook Ave YO26 ...227 B4
Fenby Ave DL1 ...3 F4
Fenby Gdns YO12 ...212 C4
Fence Dike La DL7 ...63 C7
Fenton Ave BB18 ...171 E2
Fenton Cl 10 YO11 ...100 B7
Fenton La Malton YO17 ...122 A4
  Sherburn in Elmet LS25 ...196 A5
Fenton St Boosbeck TS12 ...9 D7
  38 Burley in Warfedale
  LS29 ...176 C1
Fenwick Cl 1 YO11 ...100 B6
Fenwick Comm La
  DN6 ...207 D2
Fenwick La DN6 ...207 B1
Fenwick St YO23 ...228 C2
Fenwick's La YO10 ...231 D7
Ferguson Cl DL7 ...210 C3
Ferguson Way YO32 ...225 F1
Fern Bank Ave BB18 ...171 D2
Fern Cl YO32 ...226 A4
Fern Gdns 1 LS29 ...218 A3
Fern St YO31 ...233 C4
Ferndale Rd YO8 ...232 C4
Fernie Rd TS14 ...8 F5
Fernlea Cl YO8 ...232 B4
Fernley Gn Cl 6 WF11 ...202 A2
Fernway YO10 ...229 C3
Fernwood TS8 ...7 C5
Fernwood Cl 9 DL6 ...43 D6
Ferry Cl 11 YO8 ...198 F1
Ferry Farm Cl 2 YO19 ...191 D8
Ferry La
  Bishopthorpe YO23 ...231 B4
  Bubwith YO8 ...199 C5
  Snaith & Cowick DN14 ...204 C1

Ell - Fir 249

Ferry La continued
  Thorganby YO19 ...193 B5
Ferrybridge By-pass
  WF11 ...201 E3
Ferrybridge Inf Sch
  WF11 ...201 E3
Ferrybridge Rd
  Castleford WF10 ...200 F4
  Pontefract WF8 ...201 C1
Fetter La YO1 ...233 B2
Feversham Cres 4
  YO31 ...228 C7
Feversham Dr 16 YO62 ...70 B1
Feversham Rd YO62 ...92 F7
Fewster Way YO1 ...233 C1
Fewston Cl 11 YO14 ...101 A3
Fewston Cres YO14 ...219 B4
Fewston Dr 9 YO30 ...224 F1
Field Ave YO8 ...197 B1
Field Cl YO21 ...208 A7
Field Cl Rd 16 YO13 ...75 D5
Field Dr 1 Pickering YO18 ...95 F6
  Tadcaster LS24 ...189 F7
Field Gr 7 DL9 ...40 E3
Field Head YO41 ...185 F6
Field House Rd 2 YO21 ...208 C7
Field La Aberford LS25 ...194 F8
  Burniston YO13 ...75 D8
  Gowdall DN14 ...207 F8
  Hambleton YO8 ...196 F1
  Hensall DN14 ...203 D2
  Heslington YO10 ...229 C2
  Newby & Scalby YO13 ...75 E5
  Rawcliffe DN14 ...205 A1
  Wistow YO8 ...197 C7
Field La Sports Ctr
  YO8 ...197 B1
Field Rd YO8 ...203 C4
Field View
  Norton YO17 ...215 E2
  York YO31 ...228 C7
Fieldhead Cl 12 WF8 ...201 C1
Fieldhead Dr
  Barwick in Elmet LS15 ...194 C8
  15 Glusburn BD20 ...187 E7
Fieldhead Paddock
  LS23 ...188 E8
Fielding's Yd DL10 ...209 A7
Fieldside YO12 ...212 D7
Fieldstead Cres YO12 ...212 B8
Fieldway
  Harrogate HG1 ...219 F7
  Ilkley LS29 ...218 E4
Fieldway Cl HG1 ...219 F7
Fifth Ave 24 Colburn DL9 ...41 A5
  York YO31 ...228 F4
Filey Ave HG4 ...214 A6
Filey Brigg Nature Reserve★
  YO14 ...101 D4
Filey CE VC Inf Sch
  YO14 ...101 B3
Filey Cl 12 DL9 ...40 E4
Filey Dams Nature Reserve★
  YO14 ...101 B3
Filey Jun Sch YO14 ...101 A3
Filey Mus★ YO14 ...101 B3
Filey Rd Folkton YO11 ...100 A2
  Hunmanby YO14 ...127 A8
  Scarborough YO11 ...213 A2
Filey Sch YO14 ...101 A3
Filey Sta YO14 ...101 B3
Filey Terr YO30 ...228 C2
Finchley Ct TS5 ...6 E6
Finden Gdns HG3 ...160 F5
Fine Garth Cl LS23 ...188 E6
Finghall Sta DL8 ...61 E5
Finkills Way DL7 ...210 C6
Finkle Cl 4 HG4 ...214 C5
Finkle Hill LS25 ...195 F5
Finkle Keep 14 HG5 ...221 A6
Finkle St Hensall DN14 ...203 D2
  12 Knaresborough HG5 ...221 A6
  Malham BD23 ...133 A1
  3 Malton YO17 ...215 C4
  8 Richmond DL10 ...209 C6
  5 Ripon HG4 ...214 C5
  Selby YO8 ...232 C5
  Sheriff Hutton YO60 ...145 C5
  Thirsk YO7 ...211 C3
Finsbury Ave YO23 ...228 C1
Finsbury St YO23 ...228 C1
Fir Gr TS17 ...6 B8
Fir Heath Cl 5 YO24 ...227 C1
Fir Tree Cl Hilton TS15 ...6 C2
  Thorpe Willoughby YO8 ...197 B2
Fir Tree Dr Filey YO14 ...101 B4
  11 Norton DN6 ...206 E2
Fir Tree La YO8 ...197 B2
Fir Tree View LS26 ...200 C6
Fir Tree Way YO8 ...197 B2
Fir Trees The YO8 ...197 B2
Firbank Cl 9 YO32 ...167 A7
Firbeck Rd LS23 ...188 E6
Firbeck Wlk TS17 ...5 B6
Firby La HG4 ...214 B5
Firby Rd Bedale DL8 ...63 A2
  Richmond DL10 ...209 B8
Firs Ave Harrogate HG2 ...222 E6
  Ripon HG4 ...214 D4
Firs Cl HG2 ...222 E6
Firs Cres HG2 ...222 E5
Firs Dr HG2 ...222 E6
Firs Gate HG2 ...222 E5
Firs Gr HG2 ...222 E5
Firs Pk HG2 ...222 E6

Firs Rd HG2 ....222 E6
Firs View HG2 ....222 E5
First Ave 23 Colburn DL9 ..41 A5
  Harrogate HG2 ....220 C3
  Menwith with Darley
  HG3 ....160 A4
  10 Pickering YO18 ......95 F7
  Sherburn in Elmet LS25 ..196 A4
  9 Wetherby LS22 ......180 A5
  York YO31 ....228 F6
First Comm La YO8 ....197 D4
Firth St BD23 ....217 A2
Firthfields LS25 ......194 D4
Firthland Rd YO18 .....95 F7
Firthmoor Cres DL1 ....3 E4
Firthmoor Prim Sch DL1 .3 F4
Firtree Ave TS6 ....7 E8
Firtree Cl
  4 Earswick YO32 ......225 F7
  York YO24 ....227 E3
Firtree Cres LS24 .....189 D5
Firville Ave WF6 ......200 A1
Firwood Whin 5 YO32 ..225 F3
Fishbeck Rd BD20 .....174 D2
Fishburn Rd 4 YO21 ...208 D5
Fisher Gdns HG4 ......221 A5
Fisher Gn La HG4 .....214 F4
Fisher Row 14 HG4 .....86 C3
Fisher St 6 HG5 ......221 B5
Fishergate
  3 Boroughbridge YO51 .141 B5
  Knottingley WF11 ......201 E3
  17 Ripon HG4 ....214 C5
  York YO10 ....233 C1
Fishergate Prim Sch
  YO10 ....233 C1
Fishergreen HG4 ......214 D4
Fishers Ct HG4 ....214 C5
Fishers Garth 10 HG4 ...95 F6
Fitzalan Rd 18 DL8 .....63 A2
Fitzjohn Ct YO17 .....215 C4
Fitzwilliam Dr
  Darlington DL1 ....3 D7
  Malton YO17 ....215 A4
Five Hills La DL10 ....21 D5
Five La Ends HG4 ......86 D5
Flake La TS13 ....12 A3
Flamingo Land Theme Pk &
  Zoo★ YO17 ....95 D2
Flashley Carr La DN6 ..207 F1
Flask La DL8 ....87 C3
Flass La WF10 ....200 E3
Flat Cliffs YO14 .....101 C4
Flat La
  Bolton-on-Swale DL10 ..41 E6
  Hellifield BD23 ....153 F3
Flats Bank DL11 ......19 F6
Flats La
  Barwick in Elmet LS15 ..194 B7
  Thirkleby High & Low
  with Osgodby YO7 .....90 D1
  West Witton DL8 ....59 D4
Flatts La
  Eston & South Bank TS6 ..7 F7
  Welburn YO62 ....94 A7
  Wombleton YO62 ....93 F6
Flavian Gr YO30 ......227 E4
Flaxdale Cl 4 HG5 ....221 D6
Flaxley Ct YO8 ....232 B5
Flaxley Rd YO8 ....232 A7
Flaxman Ave YO10 .....229 A4
Flaxman Croft YO23 ...230 B3
Flaxmill Cl DL11 .....18 G7
Flaxton Rd YO32 ......167 B7
Flaxton Terr HG3 .....222 E3
Fleck Way TS17 ....6 B5
Fleet Bank La YO61 ...143 C1
Fleet La
  Barmby on the Marsh
  DN14 ....205 A7
  Mickletown LS26 ......200 A6
  Tockwith YO26 ....181 D7
Fleetham La
  Cundall with Leckby YO7 ..115 C4
  Kirkby Fleetham with Fencote
  DL7 ....63 C4
Fleets La BD23 ....156 A6
Fleming Ave 3 YO31 ...228 E5
Fletcher Ct 14 YO32 ...166 E5
Fletcher's Croft YO23 .230 C3
Flintmill La LS23 .....180 E2
Flints Terr DL1 ......209 C7
Flixton Carr La YO11 ..99 F4
Flock Leys 24 YO13 ...75 D5
Flora Ave DL3 ....3 B5
Florence Ct 12 YO51 ..141 B5
Florence Gr YO30 .....224 D2
Florence Rd HG2 ......219 B1
Florentine's Ct HG4 ..214 C5
Florin Wlk HG1 ....219 B2
Flotmanby La YO14 ....100 D2
Flow Edge DL8 ....57 F7
Flower Ct 19 YO11 ....100 B6
Flower Garth
  40 Filey YO14 ....101 B3
  Scarborough YO12 .....212 C6
Flowergate 12 YO21 ...208 D7
Flywheel St DL10 .....41 F7
Fog La YO42 ....193 E4
Fold La BD23 ....187 B6
Fold The Filey YO14 ...101 B1
  Thornton in Craven
  BD23 ....172 A3
Foldshaw La HG3 .....159 C8
Folks Cl 13 YO32 .....166 F5

Follifoot CE Prim Sch
  HG3 ....223 F4
Follifoot La HG3 .....223 B2
Folliott Rd HG3 ......222 F3
Folliott Ward Cl YO17 .215 B5
Folly View LS23 ......188 E5
Folly View 2 LS23 ....188 E5
Fontenay Rd DL10 .....209 D8
Fonteyn Ct TS8 ....6 F5
Forbidden Cnr The★
  DL8 ....60 B1
Forcett Cl
  East Layton DL11 .....20 C8
  Middlesbrough TS5 ....6 E7
Forcett Gdns DL11 ....1 D3
Forcett La DL10 ......20 D5
Forden Chalk Bank Nature
  Reserve★ YO25 ....126 C4
Fordlands YO8 ....197 B2
Fordlands Cres YO19 ..231 E5
Fordlands Rd YO19 ....231 E6
Fordon La
  Willerby YO12 ....125 E7
  Wold Newton YO25 .....126 A6
Fordon Pl TS4 ....7 A8
Fordyce Rd TS8 ......6 E4
Fore La Cowesby YO7 ..66 B4
  West Tanfield DL8 .....87 D3
  Whorlton DL6 ....25 F1
Foreshore Rd YO11 ...213 A5
Forest Cl
  3 Harrogate HG2 ......220 D3
  27 Haxby YO32 ....166 E5
Forest Cres HG2 .....220 D4
Forest Dr Colburn DL9 .41 A5
  Dishforth YO7 ....115 A4
  Middlesbrough TS7 ....7 D7
Forest Gdns HG2 .....220 D3
Forest Gr
  Harrogate HG2 ....220 D3
  York YO31 ....228 F6
Forest Grange Cl 2
  HG2 ....220 D4
Forest La Alne YO61 ..143 B5
  Fulford YO19 ....184 A2
  Harrogate HG2 ....220 D3
  Kirklevington TS15 ....24 D8
  Strensall YO32 ....167 A8
Forest La Head HG2 ...220 D5
Forest Moor Dr HG5 ...220 F3
Forest Moor Rd HG5 ...220 D4
Forest Mount HG5 ....220 D4
Forest of Galtres Prim Sch
  YO30 ....165 F5
Forest Rd
  Appletreewick HG3 ....157 F8
  Northallerton DL6 .....210 E5
  Pickering YO18 ....96 A6
Forest Rise HG2 .....220 D3
Forest Sch The HG5 ..221 C6
Forest Way
  Harrogate HG2 ....220 D3
  York YO31 ....228 F6
Forester's Wlk YO24 ..227 B1
Foresters Ct 5 YO12 ..75 F5
Foresters Wlk YO41 ...168 C1
Forestgate YO32 .....225 C7
Forge Cl
  Huntington YO32 .....226 A2
  Wheldrake YO19 ......193 A7
Forge Gn HG3 ....223 F4
Forge Hill WF11 .....201 F3
Forge La
  Deighton YO19 ....192 A7
  Kirkby Fleetham with Fencote
  DL7 ....42 C1
  Tollerton YO61 ....143 A3
Forge Valley Wood National
  Nature Reserve★
  YO12 ....75 A1
Forkers La YO17 .....122 D2
Forrester's Cl 3 DN6 .206 E2
Forth St YO26 ....227 F6
Fortune Cl HG5 ......220 E7
Fortune Hill HG5 ....220 E8
Foss Ave LS22 ....180 B4
Foss Bank YO31 ......233 C3
Foss Ct YO31 ....225 E1
Foss Field La YO23 ...191 B8
Foss Garth YO41 .....185 F5
Foss Islands Rd YO31 .233 C3
Foss La YO22 ....32 C2
Foss Wlk YO26 ....227 B8
Fossdale Cl 5 HG5 ...221 D6
Fosse Way LS25 ......194 D3
Fossgate YO1 ....233 C2
Fossland View 4 YO32 .167 A7
Fossway
  Stamford Bridge YO41 .168 D1
  York YO31 ....228 D7
Foster Ave
  Normanton South WF6 .200 A1
  Silsden BD20 ....174 B1
Foster Cl 31 LS29 ....176 C1
Foster Gate YO8 .....232 D4
Foster Rd 4 BB18 ....171 D2
Foster Wlk LS25 .....195 F4
Fostergate YO8 ......197 A8
Foston CE VC Prim Sch
  YO60 ....146 A3
Foston Gr 4 YO31 ....228 E8
Foston Gr YO60 ......146 B2
Fother Ingay Dr DL1 ..3 F8
Fothergill Way 3 YO51 .141 B4
Fothill La YO13 ......98 E6
Foulbridge La YO13 ...97 F3

Foulds Rd BB8 ....186 A1
Foulgate Nook La
  HG4 ....112 B6
Foundry La 5 WF11 ...202 A2
Fountain St TS14 .....8 F6
Fountains Abbey & Studley
  Royal Wr Gdn★ HG4 ..139 B7
Fountains Ave
  Boston Spa LS23 ......188 E3
  Harrogate HG1 ....219 F6
  Ingleby LS17 ....6 B5
Fountains CE Prim Sch
  HG4 ....138 D7
Fountains Cl
  Guisborough TS14 .....8 F6
  1 Whitby YO21 ....208 C6
Fountains Dr TS5 ....6 D8
Fountains Earth Lofthouse CE
  Endowed Prim Sch
  HG3 ....110 A3
Fountains Gate HG4 ..112 F1
Fountains Mill★ HG4 ..139 B7
Fountains Pl DL6 ....210 E6
Fountains Rd DL6 ....210 E6
Fountains View DL3 ...3 A6
Fountains Way
  Knaresborough HG5 ...221 C4
  Morton-on-Swale DL7 ..64 A7
Fountayne Rd 13 YO14 .126 F8
Fountayne St YO31 ...228 C7
Four La Ends
  Burythorpe YO17 .....147 D4
  Lawkland BD24 ....130 A3
Four Lanes Ends BB7 .152 C1
Four Riggs DL3 ......3 C5
Fouracre Dr 11 YO22 .32 A6
Fourth Ave
  26 Colburn DL9 ......41 A5
  York YO31 ....228 F6
Fox Cl 6 DL2 ....22 D8
Fox Covert YO31 .....225 F2
Fox Covert Cl 15 DL8 .63 B3
Fox Covert Rd WF8 ...206 C1
Fox Ct HG1 ....219 E4
Fox Garth
  5 Brafferton YO61 ....115 F1
  Poppleton YO26 ......224 A3
Fox Glade YO41 ......168 C2
Fox Heads La LS22 ...179 D4
Fox Hill La YO8 .....232 A3
Fox La
  Chapel Haddlesey YO8 .203 C5
  Hambleton LS25 ......196 D1
  Thornton-le-Dale YO18 .96 C3
  Thorpe Willoughby YO8 .197 B1
Fox Oak Furniture Craft Ctr★
  YO7 ....116 F7
Fox Terr WF8 ....201 C1
Foxberry Ave TS5 ....6 D6
Foxbridge Way WF6 ..200 C2
Foxcliff WF11 ....201 E5
Foxcroft 3 YO32 .....225 C4
Foxdale Ave YO8 .....197 B1
Foxglove Cl
  2 Killinghall HG3 .....161 B3
  Northallerton DL7 .....210 C1
Foxglove Ct 19 DL9 ...41 A5
Foxhill La YO8 ....232 A4
Foxholme La HG4 .....86 B3
Foxthorn Paddock
  YO10 ....229 D3
Foxton Cl YO24 ......230 C8
Foxton La DL6 ....44 E2
Foxwood La 3 YO24 ..227 C1
Foxwood Sch BD24 ...105 C4
Frances Rd DL10 .....209 C7
Frances St YO10 .....228 D1
Francis Ct 7 YO8 ....197 B2
Francis Dr 27 DL9 ....41 A5
Frank La YO26 ....164 F4
Frank St 9 BB18 .....171 E1
Frank's La YO26 .....164 A5
Frankfield Mews TS9 ..8 D1
Franklin Mount HG1 ..219 D3
Franklin Rd HG1 .....219 D3
Franklin Sq HG1 .....219 D3
Franklin St 7 YO12 ...212 F6
Franks Terr 8 YO22 ..208 E6
Fraser Rd 8 TS18 ....5 E8
Frazer Ct YO30 ......227 E8
Frederic St YO30 ....233 A3
Freebrough Rd TS12 ..10 A4
Freehold Ct YO17 ....215 D8
Freely Fields 7 LS23 .188 E5
Freely La LS23 ......188 E5
Freeman's Way HG3 ..223 D8
Freemans Way
  Leeming DL7 ....63 C4
  Wetherby LS22 ....180 D3
Freemantle Pl HG4 ...214 C6
Freeport Outlet Village★
  WF10 ....200 F3
Freers Yd YO17 .....215 D3
Freeston Ct 16 WF6 ..200 A2
Freeston Dr 18 WF6 ..200 A2
Freeway Dr WF10 ....200 B3
French Rd DL9 ......209 C2
French St HG1 ....219 F4
Frenchgate DL10 ....209 C6
Friarage Ave DL6 ....210 D5
Friarage Com Prim Sch
  YO11 ....213 B6
Friarage Gdns DL6 ...210 E5
Friarage Hospl DL6 ..210 E5
Friarage Mount DL6 ..210 D5
Friarage St DL6 .....210 D5
Friarage Terr DL6 ...210 D5

Friar's Gdns 10 YO11 .213 A6
Friar's Way 11 YO11 ..213 A6
Friar's Wlk YO31 ....228 E8
Friargate
  Scarborough YO11 ....213 A6
  York YO1 ....233 B2
Friargate Theatre★
  YO1 ....233 B2
Friars Cl YO19 ......184 D7
Friars Hill YO62 ....95 A8
Friars Mdw YO8 .....232 C8
Friars Pardon DL2 ...3 E1
Friary Com Hospl
  DL10 ....209 B7
Friendship Ct 7 YO8 .232 C6
  1 Whitby YO21 ....208 C6
Frith Mews 4 YO8 ....232 C6
Frobisher Dr 5 YO21 .208 C6
Frogmire Cl 4 HG5 ...221 B7
Frogmire Dr 5 HG5 ...221 B7
Frogmire Rd HG5 ....221 B7
Front Nook 2 DL8 ....58 F1
Front St
  Appleton Wiske DL6 ..24 B3
  6 Bramham LS23 .....188 E5
  Burton Fleming YO25 .126 E3
  Burton Leonard HG3 ..140 A2
  Castleford WF10 .....200 F3
  Grosmont YO22 ......31 C4
  Langtoft YO25 ....151 C5
  Lastingham YO62 ....70 E5
  Naburn YO19 ....191 D8
  Thirsk YO7 ....211 C1
  Topcliffe YO7 ....115 C7
  Wold Newton YO25 ...126 A4
  York YO24 ....227 C3
Front The DL2 ....4 D3
Fryer Cres DL1 ......3 F7
Fryston Comm La
  LS25 ....202 A8
Fryston La WF11 .....201 C4
Fryston Rd WF10 ....201 B5
Fryton La YO62 ......120 A7
Fryup Cres TS14 .....8 E5
Fulbeck Rd TS5 .....7 D8
Fulford Cross YO10 ..228 D1
Fulford Mews YO10 ..231 E6
Fulford Pk YO10 ....231 D7
Fulford Rd
  Scarborough YO11 ...212 F3
  York YO10 ....231 D8
Fulford Sch YO10 ...231 E7
Fulfordgate YO10 ...231 E7
Fulham La YO14 .....206 E2
Fuller-Good Rd 17 DL10 .41 E4
Fullicar La DL6 .....43 F3
Fulmar Head TS14 ...8 D6
Fulthorpe Ave DL3 ...3 A5
Fulthorpe Gr DL3 ...3 A5
Fulwith Ave HG2 ....222 E5
Fulwith Cl HG2 .....222 F5
Fulwith Dr HG2 .....222 F5
Fulwith Gate HG2 ...222 F5
Fulwith Gr HG2 .....222 F5
Fulwith Mill La HG2 .222 F5
Fulwith Rd HG2 .....222 F5
Fummerber La LA2 ...130 C5
Furlong Rd 28 YO41 .168 D2
Furlongs Ave YO17 ..215 F3
Furnace La HG4 .....87 A1
Furness Dr
  Bentham LA2 ....129 A8
  York YO30 ....224 E1
Furnessford Rd LA2 .128 D6
Furnwood 2 YO32 ...225 D7
Furrows The 16 YO11 .100 B7
Fushetts La LA2 ....129 A8
Futurist Theatre★
  YO11 ....213 A6
Fyling Rd YO11 .....208 A6
Fylingdales Ave 6
  YO30 ....224 E1
Fylingdales CE VC Prim Sch
  YO22 ....33 C4

G

Gable Ct YO7 ....115 A4
Gable Pk YO23 ......182 C6
Gables Cl 8 DN14 ...202 D4
Gables The
  15 Hurworth-on-Tees DL2 .3 E1
  Knaresborough HG5 ...221 A4
  Middlesbrough TS7 ...7 B6
  Scriven HG5 ....162 C5
Gainford CE Prim Sch
  DL2 ....1 C7
Gainforth Wath Rd
  YO13 ....53 F5
Gainsborough Cl
  YO32 ....167 B8
Gainsborough Ct
  BD23 ....216 E4
Gaits DL8 ....56 C4
Gale Bank DL8 ......60 B3
Gale Farm Ct 6 YO24 .227 C2
Gale Garth YO61 ....142 F4
Gale Gate YO26 .....142 A1
Gale La Beadlam YO62 .93 D6
  Stainburn LS21 ......177 C3
  Thorganby YO19 .....192 F4
  York YO24 ....227 C2
Gale Rd YO61 ....142 F4
Gale The YO19 ......191 D4
Gallabar La YO51 ....141 E1
Galley Hill Prim Sch
  TS14 ....8 D6
Galligap La YO10 ...229 C4

Gallogate La LS17 ...178 C1
Gallops The
  Norton YO17 ....215 E2
  York YO24 ....230 B8
Gallowfields Rd DL10 .209 B7
Gallowfields Trad Est
  DL10 ....209 B8
Gallowgate DL10 ....209 B7
Gallowheads La YO62 .95 A6
Gallows Hill
  Castleford WF10 ....201 B4
  Ripon HG4 ....214 C2
Gallows Hill Dr HG4 .214 C2
Gallows Hill La YO13 .98 D5
Gallows Hill Pk HG4 .214 D2
Galmanhoe La YO30 .233 A3
Galphay La HG4 .....113 A3
Galtres Ave YO31 ...229 B7
Galtres Dr 7 YO61 ..143 D8
Galtres Gr YO30 ....227 F7
Galtres Rd
  Northallerton DL6 ...210 E6
  York YO31 ....229 B7
Gant Wlk 7 YO30 ....232 D5
Ganton Cl 1 YO21 ...208 C5
Ganton Hill YO12 ...125 B7
Ganton Pl YO24 ....230 E7
Ganton Rd YO25 ....125 C4
Gaol The YO61 ......144 E7
Gap Cres YO14 .....127 D8
Gap Rd YO14 ....127 D8
Garbett Way 1 YO23 .231 B3
Garburn Gr 3 YO30 .224 E1
Garbutt Gr YO26 ....227 D5
Garbutt La 1 DL6 ...25 D1
Garbutt Wood Nature
  Reserve★ YO7 ......91 A6
Garbutts La TS15 ...25 B5
Garden Cl
  3 Glusburn BD20 ....187 D5
  Sherburn in Elmet LS25 .195 E4
Garden Flats La YO19 .184 E7
Garden House Cl LS26 .200 B6
Garden La
  11 Knottingley WF11 .202 A3
  Sherburn in Elmet LS25 .195 E4
Garden Pl YO1 ......233 C2
Garden St
  Castleford WF10 ....200 E3
  13 Normanton South WF6 .200 A1
  York YO31 ....233 B4
Garden Village LS25 .195 A3
Garden Way 3 YO18 ..95 F6
Gardeners Cl 8 YO23 .230 B3
Gardeners Row YO13 .150 B3
Gardens Rd BD23 ...155 D2
Gardens The 15 YO14 .101 B4
Garfield Rd YO12 ...212 E6
Garfield Terr YO26 ..227 F5
Garforth Barleyhill Infants
  Sch LS25 ....194 C3
Garforth Com Coll
  LS25 ....194 C3
Garforth Gn La Prim Sch
  LS25 ....194 D3
Garforth Leisure Ctr
  LS25 ....194 D3
Garforth Sta LS25 ...194 C4
Gargrave CE VC Prim Sch
  BD23 ....155 C1
Gargrave House Gdn
  BD23 ....155 C1
Gargrave Rd
  Broughton BD23 .....172 D6
  Skipton BD23 ....216 D4
Gargrave Sta BD23 ..172 C8
Garibaldi St 1 YO11 .213 B6
Garland St 2 YO26 ..227 F5
Garlands Hill 3 YO11 .212 F3
Garlands The
  Scarborough YO11 ...212 F3
  York YO30 ....228 A8
Garman Carr La YO8 .197 D6
Garnet Brow La LA2 .130 D2
Garnet La 1 LS24 ...189 D5
Garnet Rd TS17 ....6 B8
Garnet Terr YO26 ...227 E5
Garrick Cl YO8 .....232 B1
Garrow Hill YO10 ...228 F2
Garrow Hill Ave YO10 .229 A3
Garroway Way YO10 .184 A4
Garrowby Hill YO41 .169 F3
Garrowby Rd YO42 ..169 E3
Garrowby St YO41 ...169 E3
Garrowby View 5 YO41 .168 D2
Garrs End La BD23 ..134 C3
Garrs La 10 BD23 ...134 E3
Gars End LA2 ....128 A6
Gars The LA2 ....128 A6
Garsbeck Way TS7 ..7 D8
Garsdale Fold 8 LS22 .180 A1
Garsdale Rd HG5 ...221 D6
Garsdale Sta LA10 ..55 A6
Garth Ave
  Collingham LS22 ....188 A8
  4 Nth Duffield YO8 ..199 A7
Garth Cl 11 Catterick DL10 .41 D5
  Hambleton YO8 ......196 E1
  6 Wistow YO8 ....197 D6
Garth Ct YO32 ......226 A4
Garth Dr YO8 ....196 E1
Garth End
  Collingham LS22 ....188 A8
  Kirk Deighton LS22 ..180 B5
  York YO32 ....225 F4
Garth End Rd YO13 ..99 A7

Garth Fold BD20 173 C1
Garth Glebe 8 YO8 198 B5
Garth Grange 3 YO30 164 F7
Garth La
Hambleton YO8 196 E1
Snainton YO13 98 A5
Garth Mdws 13 DL10 41 D5
Garth Mill 1 DN14 202 D4
Garth Morrell YO8 232 C2
Garth Rd
4 Hambleton YO8 196 E1
York YO32 225 F4
Garth Terr YO30 228 B7
Garth The
8 Collingham LS22 188 A8
Sinnington YO62 95 A8
4 Stokesley TS9 26 C7
Tunstall DL10 41 B2
Whitby YO21 208 B7
Garth View YO8 196 E1
Garth Way Arc DL7 210 D5
Garth's End YO10 231 E8
Garthends La 3 YO8 198 F1
Garthorne Ave DL3 3 A5
Garths End 20 YO32 166 F5
Garths La DL8 58 E3
Garthway 4 YO32 225 D3
Gas House La LA2 129 A8
Gas St BD23 216 F3
Gas Works La LS23 188 F8
Gascoigne Ave LS15 194 B7
Gascoigne Cres HG1 219 F4
Gascoigne Ct LS15 194 B7
Gascoigne Rd LS15 194 B7
Gascoigne View LS15 194 B7
Gascoigne Wlk YO23 233 B1
Gascoigne Wood Mine LS25 196 C2
Gaskell Cl DL7 210 C6
Gate Bridge Rd HG4 112 D2
Gate La Borrowby YO7 65 E4
Low Coniscliffe & Merrybent DL2 2 E4
Gate Way YO21 29 B4
Gatecliff Brow BD23 155 F4
Gateforth Ct YO8 196 F1
Gateforth La YO8 196 F1
Gateforth New Rd YO8 203 A8
Gatehead La YO42 193 D7
Gatehowe Rd YO17 170 A7
Gatela Rd YO13 53 D2
Gateland Cl YO32 225 C7
Gateland Field La DN14 205 B6
Gatenby Garth YO61 143 B8
Gatesgarth Cl YO12 212 B8
Gatherley Rd DL10 41 C7
Gauber Rd LA6 78 F1
Gaudy La DL8 56 C3
Gauk St WF11 201 D6
Gaul Rd DL9 209 E1
Gaw La BD23 174 C8
Gawtersike La YO62 94 B8
Gay La LS24 196 C7
Gay Mdws YO32 167 D2
Gaylands La BB18 172 B1
Gayle La DL8 56 C4
Gayton Sands TS5 6 D6
Gazelle Way YO7 115 B1
Geecroft La LS22 179 D3
Geldof Rd YO32 225 F1
Gemini Studios Art Gall★ BD23 134 E3
General La YO42 193 E6
Geneva Cres DL1 3 D4
Geneva La DL1 3 D4
Geneva Rd DL1 3 E5
Gennell La YO60 145 E1
Gentian Glade HG3 219 A4
George Cartwright Cl YO17 215 E4
George Cayley Dr YO30 225 A3
George Ct YO31 233 C3
George Hudson St YO1 233 B2
George St
15 Addingham LS29 174 F4
Carleton BD23 173 B4
19 Earby BB18 172 A1
3 Scarborough YO12 213 A6
4 Selby YO8 232 D6
17 Skipton BD23 217 A3
Snaith DN14 204 C1
12 Whitby YO21 208 D6
7 Wistow YO8 197 D6
York YO1 233 C1
George Terr 1 YO8 198 B4
Georgian Theatre Royal & Mus★ DL10 209 C6
Gerard Ave YO31 229 A5
Germain Rd YO8 232 E4
Germany La YO19 231 E6
Gerrick La TS12 10 C3
Gerrie St TS12 9 D7
Ghyll Brow YO21 30 D4
Ghyll La BB18 171 E2
Ghyll Mdws BB18 171 E2
Ghyll Mews LS29 218 A3
Ghyll Royd Prep Sch LS29 176 B2
Ghyll The DL10 209 D8
Ghyll Way BD23 173 D4
Ghyll Wood 28 LS29 175 C2
Gibb St BD22 187 B6
Gibbet Hill YO61 117 C5
Gibside La BD20 173 C1
Gibson Cl 2 YO8 196 F1
Gibson La LS25 194 D1
Giggleswick Prim Sch BD24 131 D3
Giggleswick Sch BD24 131 C2
Giggleswick Sta BD24 131 C1
Gilcar St WF6 200 B2
Gilcar Way WF6 200 B3
Gildercliffe YO12 212 C7
Giles Ave YO31 229 A5
Gill Bank Rd LS29 218 A6
Gill Cl 6 LS29 174 E4
Gill Croft YO61 117 C1
Gill La Cowling BD22 187 A6
Kearby with Netherby LS22 179 C1
Nesfield with Langbar LS29 175 B4
Rosedale West Side YO18 49 E2
Gillamoor Ave YO31 229 B5
Gillamoor Bank YO62 70 A5
Gillamoor CE VC Prim Sch YO62 70 A4
Gillamoor Rd YO62 70 A2
Gillann St 15 WF11 202 A2
Gillgate Rd HG4 112 B4
Gilling Castle★ YO62 118 E7
Gilling Cres DL1 3 E4
Gilling Rd Aske DL10 20 E1
Richmond DL10 209 D7
Gilling Way YO17 215 C5
Gillings Ct YO7 211 B3
Gillingwood Cl DL10 209 C8
Gillingwood Rd YO30 224 F3
Gills Fold 8 BD23 134 E2
Gills The LS21 177 A1
Gillylees YO12 212 C5
Gilmonby Rd TS3 7 B8
Gilsforth Hill YO26 164 A3
Gilsforth La YO26 164 A3
Gilstead Way LS29 218 B5
Gilsthwaite La YO26 164 A3
Gilwern Ct 23 TS17 5 F4
Gindhill La LS21 178 A4
Ginnel Mews The BD23 217 A4
Ginnel The 1 HG1 219 D2
Gipsey Cnr YO19 184 E3
Girls High Sch BD23 216 E4
Girton Wlk DL1 3 D7
Girvan Cl YO24 230 B7
Gisburn Rd
Barnoldswick BB18 171 D2
Hellifield BD23 154 B3
Gisburn Rd Com Prim Sch BB18 171 D1
Gisburn St
Barnoldswick BB18 171 D2
Skipton BD23 216 D3
Givendale Gr 3 YO10 229 C4
Givendale Rd YO12 212 D8
Glade Rd YO19 192 B2
Glade The
Escrick YO19 192 A6
Scarborough YO11 212 F3
York YO31 229 B7
Gladstone La YO12 212 E5
Gladstone Rd YO12 212 E5
Gladstone Rd Inf Sch YO12 212 E5
Gladstone Rd Jun Sch YO12 212 E5
Gladstone St
Darlington DL3 3 C5
Harrogate HG2 222 E7
Normanton South WF6 200 B2
Scarborough YO12 212 E6
14 Skipton BD23 216 F4
York YO31 233 C4
Gladstone Terr 10 HG4 214 C4
Glaisby Ct YO31 229 A6
Glaisdale YO24 230 D7
Glaisdale Ave TS5 6 F8
Glaisdale Hall La YO21 30 C4
Glaisdale Prim Sch YO21 30 D4
Glaisdale Rd TS15 5 F3
Glaisdale Sta YO21 30 E4
Glasgow Dr 3 DL9 209 C1
Glasshoughton Sta WF10 200 F2
Glasshouses Com Prim Sch HG3 137 D3
Glaves Cl YO13 99 B7
Glebe Ave
Full Sutton YO41 169 A2
Harrogate HG2 219 C2
York YO26 227 D5
Glebe Cl Barton DL10 21 C7
15 Bedale DL8 63 A2
Bolton Percy YO23 190 D4
Kirby Hill YO51 141 B7
Manfield DL2 2 C4
3 Strensall YO32 167 B7
Glebe Ct DL10 21 A7
Glebe Field Dr 11 LS22 180 B3
Glebe Gdns TS13 11 A8
Glebe La DL2 2 C4
Glebe Mdw HG4 214 F6
Glebe Rd Campsall DN6 206 E1
Darlington DL1 3 D8
Harrogate HG2 219 C1
Stokesley TS9 26 C7
Glebe Sq DL7 63 C5
Glebe St WF10 200 E4
Glebe Way 26 YO32 166 E5
Gledstone Rd BD23 171 E5
Gledstone View 8 BB18 171 D2
Glen Ave YO31 228 E5
Glen Cl
Newby & Scalby YO13 75 C5
York YO10 231 E6
Glen Esk Rd YO22 208 C3
Glen Rd YO31 228 E5
Glencoe Cl LS25 200 C8
Glencoe Croft LS25 200 C8
Glencoe Gdns LS25 200 C8
Glencoe St 1 YO30 228 B7
Glencoe Terr LS25 200 C8
Glendale
Guisborough TS14 8 D5
9 Hutton Rudby TS15 25 C5
Glendale Rd TS5 6 F8
Glendowne Terr HG1 219 B5
Gleneagles Ct
28 Castleford WF6 200 B1
Spofforth HG3 179 E5
Gleneagles Dr 29 WF6 200 B1
Gleneagles Rd
Darlington DL1 3 F8
Middlesbrough TS4 7 A8
North Featherstone WF7 200 E1
Glenfield Ave LS22 180 C2
Glenmore Dr YO17 215 E2
Glenn Cres TS7 7 B5
Glenridding YO24 230 D7
Glenside YO12 212 E7
Globe St
10 Harrogate HG2 220 C3
9 Scarborough YO11 213 B6
Gloucester Ave BD20 174 B1
Glusburn Com Prim Sch 37 BD20 187 E7
Glyder Ct 6 TS17 5 F4
Glynndale Dr YO12 212 A8
Glynwed Ct 2 BD23 216 E3
Goat La BD24 131 F7
Goathland Com Prim Sch YO22 51 C8
Goathland Gr TS14 8 E5
Goathland Sta YO22 51 D8
Goats Rd DL11 18 D2
Godfrey Rd 12 DL10 41 E4
Godley Cl DL9 209 C2
Godwinsway 18 YO41 168 D2
Goker La YO51 141 E1
Gold Thread La 5 YO8 197 B8
Golden Acres DL7 22 E2
Golden Butts Rd LS29 218 C4
Golden Gr YO22 208 E2
Golden Lion Bank 25 YO21 208 D7
Golden Lion Yd YO7 211 C3
Goldhill La YO7 90 D6
Goldsborough CE Prim Sch HG5 162 F3
Goldsborough Ct HG5 163 A3
Goldsborough La YO21 12 C4
Golf Links Ave 5 LS24 189 D5
Golf Links Cres 4 LS24 189 D5
Golf Links Ct LS24 189 E5
Good Hope Cl WF6 200 B2
Goodall Cl 31 BB18 172 A1
Goodenber Rd LA2 129 A8
Goodramgate YO1 233 B2
Goodrick Cl HG2 222 B5
Goods Yd The YO8 232 D5
Goodwood Ave LS25 194 C1
Goodwood Cl
Sadberge DL2 4 B8
Scalby YO12 212 B6
Goodwood Gr YO24 227 F1
Goodwood Rd 3 DL9 40 E3
Goody Cross LS26 194 B1
Goody Cross La LS26 194 A1
Goose Gn Cl 2 DL9 40 E3
Goose Gn la BB8 186 A1
Goose La YO61 144 C1
Goose Mire La YO12 99 C6
Goose Tk La YO60 145 C3
Goosecroft Gdns DL6 210 D5
Goosecroft La
East Harlsey DL6 44 D6
Northallerton DL6 210 D5
Gooselands BD24 153 C6
Gooselands Hill BD23 107 D2
Goosepastures TS16 5 E3
Gordale Cl
3 Barnoldswick BB18 171 D1
Skirethorns BD23 134 B3
Gordale La BD23 133 A2
Gordale Mount HG5 221 C6
Gordon Ave HG1 219 E6
Gordon Cres DL10 209 D8
Gordon St
28 Glusburn BD20 187 E7
Ilkley LS29 218 C4
Scarborough YO12 212 E5
York YO10 228 E3
Gordon Terr BD20 173 C1
Gore La DN14 207 B5
Gore Sands TS5 6 D6
Gorman Cl 9 TS17 5 F4
Gormire Ave 2 YO31 225 E2
Gormire Cl YO7 211 D3
Gorse Cl YO8 232 C2
Gorse Hill 1 YO19 184 F7
Gorse La LS25 195 D3
Gorse Paddock YO32 225 F2
Goschen St 8 BD23 217 A3
Goslipgate 9 YO18 95 F6
Gosside Gr 31 WF6 200 B1
Gough Rd DL9 40 D4
Gouldings Cl YO11 100 A7
Goulton La TS9 25 E3
Gouthwaith Cl YO30 224 F2
Government House Rd YO30 228 A6
Gowans The YO61 144 C3
Gowdall Broach DN14 207 E8
Gowdall La
Pollington DN14 207 F7
Snaith & Cowick DN14 204 B1
Gowdall Rd DN14 203 E2
Gower Rd Aske DL10 20 D1
Richmond DL10 209 C8
York YO24 230 E8
Gowland La YO13 54 B2
Gowthorpe YO8 232 C5
Gr Prom The LS29 218 A4
Gracious St Huby YO61 144 A4
7 Knaresborough HG5 221 B5
Grafton Cl TS14 8 F6
Grafton La YO51 141 C3
Grafton St WF10 200 F3
Graham Cl YO11 213 B7
Graham Cres YO12 212 C5
Graham Dr WF10 201 A4
Graham Rd HG4 113 D3
Graham Sch YO12 212 B5
Grainary Wildlife Farm The★ YO13 53 E3
Grainbeck La HG3 219 A7
Grainger Cl 6 TS16 5 D5
Grainger Row HG4 214 D5
Grainger St DL1 3 D4
Grains La BD23 154 E8
Grammar Sch La DL6 210 D3
Grampian Cl 4 YO32 225 F5
Granary Ct YO1 233 B3
Granby Pk HG1 219 F3
Granby Rd HG1 219 F3
Grandage La BD22 187 A7
Grange Ave Aiskew DL7 63 C4
Filey YO14 101 B3
Garforth LS25 194 C3
Harrogate HG1 219 D5
3 Hurworth-on-Tees DL2 3 D1
Ilkley LS29 218 D4
Scarborough YO12 212 E4
Spofforth HG3 179 E6
Tadcaster LS24 189 F6
Thorp Arch LS23 181 A2
3 Willerby YO12 99 D2
Grange Cl 10 Bedale DL8 63 A2
Bishop Thornton HG3 138 F1
Dishforth YO7 114 F4
Full Sutton YO41 169 A2
Ilkley LS29 218 D4
Lebberston YO11 100 D5
Northallerton DL7 210 C3
Skelton YO30 224 B5
Grange Cl E DL7 63 E7
Grange Cres
Middlesbrough TS7 7 B5
10 Tadcaster LS24 189 E6
Grange Ct YO12 99 D7
Grange Dr TS9 26 C7
Grange Est LS29 218 D4
Grange Farm Cl YO8 198 B5
Grange Garth YO10 228 D2
Grange La 1 Dacre HG3 137 F1
Rufforth YO26 227 A2
Scackleton YO62 119 C3
Stonebeck Down HG3 137 A6
Sutton BD22 187 F2
Grange Pk Cl WF10 200 D7
Grange Pk Rd HG4 214 B2
Grange Rd 19 Bedale DL8 63 A2
Brompton-on-Swale DL10 41 B6
Burley in Warfedale LS29 176 C1
8 Campsall DN6 206 E1
Castleford WF10 201 B5
Colburn DL9 40 F5
5 Dacre HG3 137 F1
Darlington DL1 3 C4
Farnhill BD20 173 E1
Tadcaster LS24 189 E6
Thornaby TS17 6 B8
Grange St YO10 228 D2
Grange Terr HG4 114 B8
Grange The
Kirby Hill YO51 141 A7
Thirsk YO7 211 B2
Grange View
11 Otley LS21 176 F1
Towton LS24 189 E2
Grangefield Ave 32 LS29 176 C1
Granger Ave YO26 227 C4
Grangeside DL3 3 B4
Grant Cl DL6 45 B4
Grantham Dr YO26 227 E4
Grantley Cl HG3 219 A4
Grantley Dr HG3 219 A4
Grantley Hall Coll HG4 138 E8
Grantley Pl HG3 219 A4
Grants Ave YO10 231 E8
Granville Rd
21 Filey YO14 101 B3
4 Harrogate HG1 219 D3
Scarborough YO11 213 A3
Granville Sq 3 YO11 213 A3
Granville St
20 Normanton South WF6 200 A1
Skipton BD23 216 E4
Granville Terr 4 YO10 228 E3
Grape La Whitby YO22 208 E7
York YO1 233 B3
Grasmere Ave LS22 180 A3
Grasmere Cres HG2 222 C7
Grasmere Dr YO10 229 B4
Grasmere Gr 5 YO30 224 F1
Grass Croft TS21 5 A7
Grass Wood La BD23 134 C3
Grass Wood Nature Reserve★ BD23 134 C4
Grassfield Cl 8 HG3 137 B4
Grassgill La DL8 59 E3
Grassholme YO24 230 C7
Grassholme Way TS16 5 D5
Grassington Ave DL7 210 C2
Grassington CE Prim Sch BD23 134 E2
Grassington Rd
Middlesbrough TS4 7 A8
Skipton BD23 216 F5
Gravel Hole La
Sowerby YO7 89 E3
Thirsk YO7 211 C1
Gravelhill La DN14 206 F7
Gravelly Hill La LS17 178 A2
Gray La YO62 70 D1
Gray St 13 Whitby YO21 208 D6
York YO23 233 A1
Grays Rd YO62 69 F6
Grayshon Dr YO26 227 B5
Grayston Plain La HG3 160 F4
Graystonber La LA2 130 E7
Great & Little Preston Jun Sch LS26 200 C8
Great Auk TS14 8 D6
Great Ave DL10 209 A7
Great Ayton Sta TS9 8 B1
Great Cl YO8 197 B8
Great Cl La BD24 153 A6
Great Croft Cl 9 BB18 171 D2
Great Moor Rd YO13 74 D2
Great N Rd
Ledsham LS25 195 C1
Micklefield LS25 194 F5
Great N Way YO26 227 B8
Great Ouseburn Com Prim Sch YO26 164 B8
Great Pasture LS29 176 C1
Great Sike Rd YO17 215 D8
Great Smeaton Com Prim Sch DL6 23 C3
Greatwood Ave BD23 217 A3
Greatwood Cl BD23 217 B3
Greatwood Com Prim Sch BD23 217 A2
Greavefield La WF8 201 D1
Greaves Smithy LS29 175 B4
Grebe Ave DL9 40 E2
Grebe Way YO18 95 F7
Green Ave LS25 194 C2
Green Balk
Great & Little Broughton TS9 26 F5
Millington YO42 170 D1
Green Bank BB18 171 E2
Green Bank La HG4 139 A6
Green Cl
Bradleys Both BD20 173 D3
2 Linton-on-Ouse YO30 164 F8
Middlesbrough TS7 7 D5
Steeton with Eastburn BD20 187 F7
York YO30 228 A8
Green Cres The YO62 120 B5
Green Croft Gdns 24 YO11 100 B6
Green Dike YO32 225 C8
Green Dikes La YO25 151 F1
Green Dyke La YO62 120 C5
Green Dykes YO17 215 A3
Green Dykes La YO10 228 F3
Green End Ave 35 BB18 172 A1
Green End Rd 34 BB18 172 A1
Green Gate
Exelby, Leeming & Newton DL8 63 D2
Hawsker-cum-Stainsacre YO22 33 A6
Kirkby Malham BD23 154 F8
West Witton DL8 59 C3
Green Gate La
Crakehall DL8 62 E5
Kildale YO21 27 F8
Long Preston BD23 153 F5
Green Haggs La HG3 223 F1
Green Hammerton CE Prim Sch YO26 164 B3
Green Head La BD24 131 E2
Green Hill YO62 118 E6
Green Hill La BD22 187 A5
Green Hills YO60 168 B7
Green Hills La DL7 64 B6
Green Howard's Dr 8 YO12 75 F5
Green Howards Mus★ DL10 209 C6
Green Howards Rd
Pickering YO18 96 A6
Richmond DL10 209 B8
Green Island YO12 99 D7
Green La Acomb YO24 227 D2
Addingham LS29 174 F4
Appleton Roebuck YO23 191 B6
Barmby on the Marsh DN14 205 A6
Barton-le-Street YO17 120 E8

Green La *continued*
Bedale DL8 . . . . .62 F3
Bishopthorpe YO24 . . . . .231 A6
Boston Spa LS23 . . . . . . .188 F7
Bradleys Both BD20 . . . .174 A3
Burton Leonard HG3 . . . .140 B2
Burton-on-Yore HG4 . . . . .86 D6
Castleford WF10 . . . . . . .200 E3
Cawton YO62 . . . . .119 B6
Collingham LS22 . . . . . . .188 A8
Coneythorpe & Clareton
  HG5 . . . . .163 B5
Constable Burton DL8 . . . .61 A6
Cottingwith YO42 . . . . . .193 C5
Cundall with Leckby
  YO61 . . . . .115 D4
Darlington DL1 . . . . .3 D8
Dishforth YO7 . . . . .115 A3
East Rounton TS15 . . . . . .24 F4
Fadmoor YO62 . . . . .69 C3
Farndale West YO62 . . . . .48 E1
Folkton YO12 . . . . .99 F1
Garforth LS25 . . . . .194 D4
Glusburn BD20 . . . . .187 D7
Great Ouseburn YO26 . . .142 A1
Halton East BD23 . . . . . .157 C1
Harome YO62 . . . . .93 C5
Harrogate HG2 . . . . .222 C6
Heck DN14 . . . . .207 D8
Horton BD23 . . . . .171 B5
Hudswell DL11 . . . . .39 F5
Hutton Rudby TS15 . . . . . .25 B4
Ilkley LS29 . . . . .176 C2
Ingleton LA6 . . . . .103 C2
Kippax LS25 . . . . .194 C2
Kirby Wiske YO7 . . . . .88 F7
Kirkby Overblow LS17 . . .178 D2
Kirklevington TS15 . . . . . . .5 E2
Langtoft YO25 . . . . .151 D5
Lebberston YO11 . . . . . . .100 H1
Ledston WF10 . . . . .200 E7
Little Ayton TS9 . . . . .27 A8
Littlethorpe HG4 . . . . . . .140 A7
Marrick DL11 . . . . .38 E7
Maunby YO7 . . . . .64 D1
Menwith with Darley
  HG3 . . . . .160 A6
Mickletown LS26 . . . . . . .200 C5
Middlesbrough TS5 . . . . . . .6 E8
Moor Monkton YO26 . . . .164 F1
Newby TS7 . . . . .7 C3
North Cowton DL7 . . . . . . .22 B2
North Duffield YO8 . . . . . .198 F8
Otley LS21 . . . . .176 F1
Rawcliffe YO30 . . . . .225 A1
Ripon HG4 . . . . .113 C3
Sawley HG4 . . . . .138 E7
Scalby YO12 . . . . .212 C6
Selby YO8 . . . . .232 A3
South Stainley with Cayton
  HG3 . . . . .161 E8
Stutton with Hazlewood
  LS24 . . . . .189 D4
Sutton BD22 . . . . .187 F2
Sutton-on-the-Forest
  YO61 . . . . .144 E4
Thirsk YO7 . . . . .211 F3
Weaverthorpe YO17 . . . . .124 F1
Welbury DL6 . . . . .44 C8
Wensley DL8 . . . . .60 A4
Whitby YO22 . . . . .208 H1
Whorlton DL6 . . . . .45 F7
Wigginton YO32 . . . . . . .166 D5
Winksley HG4 . . . . .112 F2
Wressle DN14 . . . . .205 D8
Green La E YO7 . . . . . .211 B1
Green La Prim Sch TS5 . . .6 E8
Green La Villas LS25 . .194 D4
Green La W YO7 . . . . .211 A1
Green Mdw BB8 . . . . . .186 A1
Green Mdws YO31 . . . .229 A7
Green Pastures DL8 . . . .62 C5
Green Pk Ave 15 YO11 .100 B6
Green Pk Rd 14 YO11 . .100 B6
Green Row LS26 . . . . . .200 B5
Green St
  Castleford WF10 . . . . . .200 E5
  7 Cowling BD22 . . . . . .187 B6
  Darlington DL1 . . . . .3 D5
Green Sward YO31 . . . .229 A8
Green Sykes Rd BD20 . .187 F4
Green The Brompton DL6 .43 F3
  1 Clapham LA2 . . . . . . .130 C8
  Cleasby DL2 . . . . .2 F4
  Conistone with Kilnsey
    BD23 . . . . .134 B6
  20 Dunnington YO19 . . .184 F7
  Garforth LS25 . . . . .194 D3
  Hellifield BD23 . . . . . . .154 B3
  High Coniscliffe DL2 . . . . .2 C6
  Kettlewell with Starbotton
    BD23 . . . . .108 B3
  Kirkby Malzeard HG4 . . .112 D5
  8 Kirklevington TS15 . . .24 E8
  Knaresborough HG5 . . . .221 A8
  Linton-on-Ouse YO30 . . .164 F8
  Longnewton TS21 . . . . . . .5 A7
  Middlesbrough TS17 . . . . .6 D7
  Northallerton DL7 . . . . . .210 C3
  9 Otley LS21 . . . . .176 F1
  Rawcliffe DN14 . . . . . . .205 A1
  Richmond DL10 . . . . . . .209 B6
  Scalby YO12 . . . . .212 B7
  Seamer TS9 . . . . .6 F1

Green The *continued*
  6 Seamer YO12 . . . . .99 D6
  1 Skelton YO30 . . . . . . .224 B6
  Skipton BD23 . . . . .217 B6
  Slingsby YO62 . . . . .120 B5
  10 Thirsk YO7 . . . . .211 C3
  Tockwith YO26 . . . . .181 C7
  2 Tollerton YO61 . . . . . .143 B3
  7 Topcliffe YO7 . . . . .89 B1
  Wistow YO8 . . . . .197 D6
  York YO26 . . . . .227 C3
Green Village YO7 . . . . .88 C5
Green Way
  Glusburn BD20 . . . . .187 E8
  Harrogate HG2 . . . . .222 C6
  Middlesbrough TS7 . . . . . . .7 D5
  York YO32 . . . . .225 F4
Green Ways 2 YO8 . . .197 D6
Green Wlk 5 BB18 . . . .172 A1
Greenacre Cl TS9 . . . . . . .7 F1
Greenacres Hunton DL8 . .61 F4
  Morton-on-Swale DL7 . . . .64 A6
  Skipton BD23 . . . . .217 B5
  Stainton & Thornton TS8 . . .6 D5
  York YO32 . . . . .225 F4
Greenacres Cl 8 YO8 . .197 D1
Greenacres Cres 7
  YO8 . . . . .197 D1
Greenacres Dr 4 YO8 . .197 D1
Greenacres Gr 3 YO8 . .197 D1
Greenbank 5 DL6 . . . . .210 E2
Greenbank Cl WF10 . . .200 D3
Greenbank Pl DL3 . . . . . .3 C6
Greenberfield La
  BB18 . . . . .171 E2
Greencliffe Dr YO30 . . .228 A6
Greencroft Ct 14 YO19 .184 F7
Greencroft La 17 YO19 .184 F7
Greendown Cl LS29 . . .218 A4
Greenfield Ave LS25 . . .194 D1
Greenfield Cl DL2 . . . . . . .3 E1
Greenfield Dr
  6 Brayton YO8 . . . . . . .197 D1
  Eaglescliffe TS16 . . . . .5 D5
Greenfield Gdns BD20 . .187 F7
Greenfield Pk Dr
  YO31 . . . . .229 A7
Greenfield Rd 8 YO11 . .213 A4
Greenfield St 5 BD23 . .216 D3
Greenfields DN14 . . . . .207 F6
Greenfields Ave HG2 . . .220 C2
Greenfields Dr HG2 . . . .220 C2
Greenfields Rd HG2 . . . .220 C2
Greenfinch Cl 1 YO12 . . .99 E6
Greenfoot La LA2 . . . . . .128 E8
Greengales Ct YO19 . . . .193 A8
Greengales La YO19 . . . .193 A8
Greengate
  Malton YO17 . . . . .215 C4
  Scarborough YO12 . . . . .212 D4
Greengate Dr HG5 . . . . .221 B8
Greengate La
  Cliffe YO8 . . . . .198 F6
  Kirkby Fleetham with Fencote
    DL7 . . . . .42 B1
  Knaresborough HG5 . . . .221 B8
  Thornton-le-Dale YO18 . . .96 C6
Greengate Rd WF8 . . . .206 C1
Greengate View HG5 . . .221 B8
Greengates La YO61 . . .142 E3
Greenhill Cres DL6 . . . .210 E3
Greenhill La YO7 . . . . . . .66 B4
Greenholme Cl
  1 Boroughbridge YO51 . .141 B6
  7 Burley in Wharfedale
    LS29 . . . . .176 C1
Greenhow Hill HG3 . . . .136 C2
Greenhow Hill Rd
  HG3 . . . . .159 B6
Greenhow Pk LS29 . . . .176 B1
Greenhowsyke La DL6 . .210 E4
Greenland La YO17 . . . . .95 B3
Greenlands TS15 . . . . . . .25 C6
Greenlands La LS29 . . . .176 C1
Greenlands Rd YO18 . . . .95 F6
Greenless La DL11 . . . . . .1 A2
Greenmires La LS21 . . .177 E4
Greenroyd Gr 13 BD20 .187 E6
Greens Yd YO22 . . . . . .208 E7
Greensborough Ave 3
  YO26 . . . . .227 B5
Greenshaw Dr YO32 . . .225 D6
Greenside 18 YO19 . . . .184 F7
Greenside Cl 24 YO19 . .184 F7
Greenside Ct 9 DL2 . . . . .3 E1
Greenside Wlk 23 YO19 .184 F7
Greenstead Rd YO12 . . .212 B8
Greenway The
  2 Haxby YO32 . . . . . . .225 C7
  2 Middleton St George DL2 .4 C4
Greenways Dr 1 YO8 . . .197 D6
Greenways The DL2 . . . . .63 C8
Greenwood Ave 7 HG3 .137 B4
Greenwood Dr YO24 . . .230 C8
Greenwood Rd 6 HG3 . .137 B4
Greet's Hill YO17 . . . . . .169 E7
Gregory Cl YO30 . . . . . .224 C5
Grenadier Dr DL6 . . . . . .210 F3
Grendon Gdns 1 DL2 . . . .4 C4
Grenley St 8 WF11 . . . .202 A2
Grenville Rd TS17 . . . . . . .6 B6
Grenwich Cl 5 YO30 . . .224 C3
Gresham Cl DL1 . . . . .3 D7
Gresley Ct 3 YO26 . . . .227 B4
Greta Ave DL10 . . . . . . .209 D7
Greta Heath 2 LA6 . . . .102 F7
Grewelthorpe CE Prim Sch
  HG4 . . . . .112 C7

Grey Cl YO61 . . . . .144 C3
Grey St HG2 . . . . .222 E7
Grey Thorn La HG5 . . . .163 D3
Grey Twrs Dr TS7 . . . . . . .7 D5
Greyfriars Cl DL3 . . . . . . .2 F5
Greylands Pk Ave
  YO12 . . . . .212 C8
Greylands Pk Dr YO12 . .212 C8
Greylands Pk Gr 3
  YO12 . . . . .212 C8
Greylands Pk Rd
  YO12 . . . . .212 C8
Greystoke Rd YO30 . . . .224 C1
Greystone Cl 2 LS29 . . .176 C1
Greystone Com Prim Sch
  HG4 . . . . .214 C2
Greystone Ct YO32 . . . .225 C7
Greystone Head HG4 . . .112 A4
Greystone La
  Aldbrough DL2 . . . . .2 A4
  Stanwick St John DL11 . . . .1 E4
Greystonegill La LA2 . . .129 D7
Greystones Ave HG3 . . .161 B4
Greystones Cl LS25 . . . .188 F1
Greystones La BD22 . . . .187 E4
Grimbald Crag Cl
  HG5 . . . . .221 D4
Grimbald Crag Rd
  HG5 . . . . .221 E4
Grimbald Crag Way
  HG5 . . . . .221 D4
Grimbald Way 3 HG5 . .221 C4
Grimston Bar YO19 . . . .229 F4
Grimston La YO17 . . . . .148 D7
Grimston Rd 12 YO14 . .127 A8
Grimwith Garth YO30 . .224 C2
Grimwith Rd BD23 . . . . .135 E2
Grindale Rd YO16 . . . . .127 F2
Grinkle La TS13 . . . . .10 F5
Grinton Rd TS18 . . . . .5 D8
Grisedale Cres TS16 . . . . .5 E4
Gristhwaite La YO7 . . . . .89 D1
Grosvenor Cres 2
  YO11 . . . . .213 A4
Grosvenor Ct HG1 . . . . .219 B2
Grosvenor Gdns LS17 . .178 B2
Grosvenor Gr HG1 . . . . .219 F6
Grosvenor House
  YO30 . . . . .233 A4
Grosvenor House Sch
  HG3 . . . . .160 D6
Grosvenor Pk YO30 . . . .233 A4
Grosvenor Pl TS14 . . . . . .8 E6
Grosvenor Rd
  Harrogate HG1 . . . . .219 E6
  Scarborough YO11 . . . . .212 F4
  York YO30 . . . . .233 A4
Grosvenor Sq 3 YO30 . .164 F8
Grosvenor Terr YO30 . . .233 A4
Grove Ave LS25 . . . . . . .175 C2
Grove Bank 4 TS15 . . . .24 E8
Grove Cl HG4 . . . . .214 C3
Grove Cres
  Boston Spa LS23 . . . . . .188 F8
  South Milford LS25 . . . . .195 F2
Grove Gdns 12 YO26 . . .165 F1
Grove Hill Rd 4 YO14 . .101 B4
Grove La
  Knottingley WF11 . . . . . .201 F2
  Ripon HG4 . . . . .214 C3
Grove Pk 7 YO8 . . . . . .198 B5
Grove Pk Ave HG1 . . . . .219 E4
Grove Pk Ct HG1 . . . . . .219 E4
Grove Pk La HG1 . . . . . .219 E4
Grove Pk Terr HG1 . . . . .219 E4
Grove Pk View HG1 . . . .219 E4
Grove Pk Wlk HG1 . . . . .219 E4
Grove Rd
  Boston Spa LS23 . . . . . .188 F8
  14 Filey YO14 . . . . .101 B4
  Harrogate HG1 . . . . .219 D4
  Ilkley LS29 . . . . .218 A3
Grove Rd Com Prim Sch
  HG1 . . . . .219 E4
Grove St 38 Earby BB18 .172 A1
  9 Harrogate HG2 . . . . . .220 C3
  Norton YO17 . . . . .215 E3
  15 Whitby YO21 . . . . . .208 D6
Grove Terr 11 DL8 . . . . .60 E2
Grove Terr La YO31 . . . .233 C4
Grove The
  Eaglescliffe TS15 . . . . .5 E2
  Guisborough TS14 . . . . . . .8 D5
  Harrogate HG1 . . . . .219 D4
  1 Hutton Rudby TS15 . . .25 D5
  Ilkley LS29 . . . . .218 A4
  Kellington DN14 . . . . . . .203 A3
  Kippax LS25 . . . . .194 D1
  Middlesbrough TS5 . . . . . . .6 E8
  Normanton South WF6 . .200 A1
  Norton YO17 . . . . .215 E2
  1 Seamer YO12 . . . . . . .99 D6
  Skipton BD23 . . . . .217 C3
  Swillington LS26 . . . . . . .194 A1
  York YO24 . . . . .230 E6
Grove View YO30 . . . . . .228 A6
Groves Cl YO31 . . . . . . .233 C3
Groves La YO31 . . . . . . .233 C3
Grundy Way 11 DL10 . . . .41 E4
Grunton Cl DL2 . . . . .2 C4
Grysedale La BD23 . . . . .134 B2
GSPK Tech Pk HG5 . . . .221 D5
Guadaloupe Rd DL9 . . . . .40 C4
Guards Ct 10 YO12 . . . . .75 F5

Guildford Rd TS6 . . . . . . .7 E8
Guisborough Mus★
  TS14 . . . . .8 F7
Guisborough Priory★
  TS14 . . . . .8 F7
Guisborough Rd
  Aislaby YO21 . . . . .31 F8
  Great Ayton TS9 . . . . .7 F1
  Lockwood TS12 . . . . .10 A5
  Middlesbrough TS7 . . . . . . .7 D5
  Thornaby TS17 . . . . .6 B8
  Whitby YO21 . . . . .208 A5
Guisborough Swimming Pool
  TS14 . . . . .8 E7
Gunby Rd YO8 . . . . .199 D5
Gunbywood Rd YO8 . . . .199 D6
Guncroft La YO62 . . . . . .69 C1
Guning La DL11 . . . . .36 B4
Gunnergate La TS8 . . . . . .7 B5
Gunnerside Methodist Prim
  Sch DL11 . . . . .36 E5
Gurney Pease Prim Sch
  DL1 . . . . .3 D6
Gurney St DL1 . . . . .3 D6
Guy La YO7 . . . . .114 F2
Gyll Hall La DL10 . . . . . . .41 E1
Gypsy La
  Castleford WF10 . . . . . . .201 B3
  Middlesbrough TS7 . . . . . . .7 C6
Gypsy La Sta TS7 . . . . . . .7 D6

H

Haakon Cl DL10 . . . . . .209 C7
Habton La YO17 . . . . . . .121 B7
Habton Rd 8 YO17 . . . . .95 D1
Hackforth & Hornby CE Prim
  Sch DL8 . . . . .62 E8
Hackforth Rd 2 TS18 . . . .5 D8
Hackness CE VC Prim Sch
  YO13 . . . . .74 E5
Hackness Dr YO12 . . . . .212 A8
Hackness Rd YO12 . . . . .212 A8
Haddlesey Rd WF11 . . . .202 D5
Haddocks La YO61 . . . . .142 B4
Haddon Cl YO24 . . . . . . .227 C2
Hadrian Ave YO10 . . . . .229 B3
Hadrians Wlk 1 YO12 . . .99 E6
Hag La
  Cottingwith YO42 . . . . . .193 C4
  Raskelf YO61 . . . . .142 E8
  South Kilvington YO7 . . . .211 D6
  Sproxton YO62 . . . . .92 D4
  Youlton YO61 . . . . .142 F2
Hagg La Colton LS24 . . .190 E8
  Cottingwith YO42 . . . . . .193 E8
  Cowesby YO7 . . . . .66 C4
  Dunnington YO19 . . . . . .184 F6
  Hemingbrough YO8 . . . . .198 F3
  South Milford LS25 . . . . .196 C2
Hagg Rd YO62 . . . . .69 F2
Hagg Side La YO13 . . . . .97 D6
Haggersgate 10 YO21 . .208 D7
Haggitt Hill La DL6 . . . . .24 F3
Haggs La DN6 . . . . .207 D2
Haggs Rd HG3 . . . . .223 C4
Hague Ave 3 YO12 . . . . .75 D5
Haig Rd DL10 . . . . .209 C2
Haig St YO8 . . . . .232 B6
Haigh La DN14 . . . . .207 A6
Hailsham Ave TS17 . . . . . .6 B5
Hailstone Dr DL6 . . . . . .210 F5
Hales La YO8 . . . . .204 E5
Haley's Terr YO31 . . . . . .228 D8
Half Moon St 1 YO30 . . .164 F7
Halfpenny Cl HG5 . . . . . .221 B7
Halfpenny La HG5 . . . . . .221 B7
Halifax Cl YO41 . . . . . . .169 A2
Halifax Ct 7 YO30 . . . . .225 A1
Halifax Way YO41 . . . . . .185 A3
Hall Arm La YO51 . . . . . .141 D5
Hall Ave 10 BD20 . . . . . .187 E6
Hall Brow BD23 . . . . . . .155 A5
Hall Cl 5 Airmyn DN14 . .205 E4
  Austwick LA2 . . . . .130 E7
  Burley in Wharfedale
    LS29 . . . . .176 B1
  Cawood YO8 . . . . .191 D1
  11 Glusburn BD20 . . . . .187 E6
Hall Croft BD23 . . . . . . .216 E4
Hall Ct WF11 . . . . .201 E4
Hall Dr
  Burley in Wharfedale
    LS29 . . . . .176 B1
  Glusburn BD20 . . . . .187 E6
  Middlesbrough TS5 . . . . . . .6 F7
Hall Farm Cl 4 YO19 . . .197 F8
Hall Farm Ct YO42 . . . . .169 F2
Hall Farm Pk LS25 . . . . .194 F4
Hall Garth 25 YO19 . . . . .95 F7
Hall Garth Cl LS24 . . . . .190 C4
Hall Garth Sch TS5 . . . . . .6 F7
Hall Garths★ LS25 . . . . .195 B8
Hall Gdns Ellerburn YO18 .96 E7
  Farnhill BD20 . . . . .173 F1
  Rawcliffe DN14 . . . . . . .205 B2
Hall Gn La LS17 . . . . . . .178 C4
Hall Ings La YO62 . . . . . .70 E4
Hall La Askwith LS21 . . . .176 F4
  Blubberhouses LS21 . . . .159 C2
  4 Brafferton YO61 . . . . .115 F1
  Caldwell DL11 . . . . .1 C4
  Church Fenton LS24 . . . .196 C7
  Harome YO62 . . . . .93 C4
  Harrogate HG1 . . . . .219 E6
  Hawnby DL6 . . . . .46 B1

Hall La *continued*
  Huddleston with Newthorpe
    LS25 . . . . .195 C3
  Leathley LS21 . . . . .177 C1
  Ledston WF10 . . . . .200 F7
  Myton-on-Swale YO61 . . .142 A6
Hall Mdws BB8 . . . . . . .186 A2
Hall Moor Cl 7 TS15 . . . .24 E8
Hall Orchards Ave
  LS22 . . . . .180 D3
Hall Pasture 9 YO22 . . . .32 A6
Hall Pk Wistow YO8 . . . .198 A5
  York YO10 . . . . .229 B1
Hall Pk Cl 23 YO13 . . . . .75 D5
Hall Pk Croft LS25 . . . . .200 D8
Hall Pk Gr 24 YO13 . . . . .75 D5
Hall Pk Mdws LS25 . . . .200 D8
Hall Pk Orch LS25 . . . . .200 D8
Hall Pk Rd
  Hunmanby YO14 . . . . . .126 F8
  Walton LS23 . . . . .181 A2
Hall Rd
  Swillington LS26 . . . . . . .194 A1
  Trawden Forest BB8 . . . .186 A2
Hall Rise
  Burley in Warfedale
    LS29 . . . . .176 B1
  12 Haxby YO32 . . . . . . .166 F5
Hall Sq 5 YO51 . . . . . . .141 B5
Hall Twr Hill★ LS15 . . . .194 B8
Hall View Dr DL3 . . . . .3 A6
Hall Way 9 BD20 . . . . . .187 E6
Halladale Cl 1 YO24 . . . .230 B7
Hallam Cl 41 YO14 . . . . .101 B3
Hallam La LS21 . . . . . . .176 D3
Hallam's Yd 4 BD23 . . . .216 F4
Hallard Way 7 YO32 . . . .167 B7
Hallcroft Dr 18 LS29 . . .175 A4
Hallcroft La YO23 . . . . . .230 A3
Hallfield Ave LS25 . . . . .194 F4
Hallfield La
  Nawton YO62 . . . . .69 C3
  Wetherby LS22 . . . . .180 C3
Hallfield Rd YO31 . . . . . .228 E6
Hallfield Terr LS25 . . . . .194 F4
Hallgarth Alne YO61 . . . .142 F4
  Great & Little Broughton
    TS9 . . . . .26 C5
  Hipswell DL9 . . . . .209 F1
Hallwith Rd DL8 . . . . . . .61 A3
Halnaby Ave DL3 . . . . .2 F5
Halstead Rd HG2 . . . . . .222 E7
Hambleton Ave
  Northallerton DL7 . . . . . .210 C2
  Thirsk YO7 . . . . .211 D3
  York YO10 . . . . .229 C4
Hambleton CE VC Prim Sch
  YO8 . . . . .196 F1
Hambleton Cl
  12 Easingwold YO61 . . .143 D8
  11 Thirsk YO7 . . . . .211 C3
Hambleton Ct
  Great Smeaton DL6 . . . . .23 C3
  Knaresborough HG5 . . . .221 C6
Hambleton Dr YO7 . . . . .211 C3
Hambleton Forum★
  DL6 . . . . .210 E5
Hambleton Garth 21
  YO61 . . . . .143 C8
Hambleton Gate TS9 . . . .26 C7
Hambleton Gr HG5 . . . . .221 B6
Hambleton La YO61 . . . . .91 F2
Hambleton Leisure Ctr
  DL6 . . . . .210 D6
Hambleton Pl YO7 . . . . .211 C3
Hambleton Rd
  6 Catterick Garrison DL9 . .40 E3
  Harrogate HG5 . . . . .219 F4
  Norton YO17 . . . . .215 E2
Hambleton Terr
  Knaresborough HG5 . . . .221 B6
  York YO31 . . . . .228 C7
Hambleton View
  10 Haxby YO32 . . . . . . .166 F5
  Thirsk YO7 . . . . .211 D3
  4 Tollerton YO61 . . . . . .143 B3
Hambleton Way
  Easingwold YO61 . . . . . .143 D8
  York YO32 . . . . .225 F2
Hamer Bank YO18 . . . . .49 F4
Hamerton Cl 11 YO14 . . .127 A8
Hamerton Rd 10 YO14 . .127 A8
Hamhall La DL7 . . . . .63 D6
Hamilton Ave HG2 . . . . .222 E8
Hamilton Cl YO13 . . . . . . .75 C5
Hamilton Ct WF6 . . . . . .200 A2
Hamilton Dr
  Darlington DL1 . . . . .3 D8
  York YO24 . . . . .227 E2
Hamilton Dr E YO24 . . . .227 E2
Hamilton Dr W YO24 . . .227 D2
Hamilton Gn YO17 . . . . .215 B3
Hamilton Way YO24 . . . .227 E2
Hamlet The 8 DN14 . . . .202 F2
Hamley La YO62 . . . . . . .70 F3
Hammer Rd HG4 . . . . . . .85 B7
Hammersike Rd
  Cawood YO8 . . . . .196 F5
  Wistow YO8 . . . . .197 A4
Hammerton Cl
  Green Hammerton YO26 .164 C3
  3 York YO26 . . . . .227 B3
Hammerton Dr
  Garforth LS25 . . . . .194 D3
  Hellifield BD23 . . . . .154 B3
Hammerton Sta YO26 . . .164 D2
Hammond Dr DL1 . . . . . . .3 C4
Hammond Rd YO13 . . . . .54 A8

Hampden St YO1 . . . . .233 B1
Hampden Way TS17 . . . .6 B6
Hampshire Cl
  Ilkley LS29 . . . . .218 D4
  6 Pontefract WF8 . . . .201 C2
Hampson Gdns YO30 . .228 B8
Hampsthwaite CE Prim Sch
  HG3 . . . . .161 A5
Hampsthwaite Rd
  HG1 . . . . .219 C4
Hampton Gdns YO30 . .228 C8
Hampton Rd YO12 . . . .212 E5
Hanbury Gdns LS25 . . .194 C4
Hancow Rd
  Hartoft YO18 . . . . .50 A1
  Rosedale East Side YO18 . .49 F3
Handale Cl TS14 . . . . . . .9 A6
Handley Cl
  Stockton-on-Tees TS18 . . . .5 F7
  York YO30 . . . . .225 A2
Hang Bank DL10 . . . . . . .21 B8
Hanger La DN14 . . . . . .204 B3
Hanghow La DL8 . . . . . .84 C8
Hanging Stone La YO18 . .49 E4
Hangingstone Rd
  LS29 . . . . .218 D2
Hankins La YO42 . . . . . .193 D1
Hanover Pl
  2 Kippax LS25 . . . . . . .194 D1
  Knottingley WF11 . . . . . .201 D4
Hanover Rd 6 YO11 . . .212 F5
Hanover St 2 BD20 . . .173 E1
Hanover St E 5 YO26 . .227 F5
Hanover St W 7 YO26 . .227 F5
Hanover Terr YO21 . . . .208 C6
Hansom Pl YO31 . . . . . .228 C7
Hanson Ave WF6 . . . . . .200 A1
Harborough Cl 20 YO14 .126 F8
Harbour Rise 5 DL8 . . . .63 A2
Harbour View 7 DL8 . . . .63 A3
Harcourt Ave YO12 . . . .212 E3
Harcourt Dr
  Bishopthorpe YO23 . . . . .231 A4
  Wheldrake YO19 . . . . . .192 F7
Harcourt Dr
  Addingham LS29 . . . . . . .174 F5
  Harrogate HG3 . . . . . . .219 E2
Harcourt Pl 4 YO11 . . .213 A5
Harcourt Rd 4 HG1 . . .219 E3
Harcourt St YO31 . . . . .228 E5
Hard Gate BD23 . . . . . .134 A3
Hard Stiles DL11 . . . . . . .39 B7
Hardcastle Ave 8 WF8 .201 B1
Harden Cl YO30 . . . . . . .224 F2
Harden Rd BB18 . . . . . . .186 A7
Hardenshaw La YO8 . . .204 B4
Hardigate Rd YO18 . . . . .72 B7
Hardings La
  Glusburn BD20 . . . . .187 F8
  Middleton LS29 . . . . . . .218 A8
Hardisty Hill HG3 . . . . .159 C3
Hardisty Mews YO26 . . .228 A4
Hardrada Way 3 YO41 .168 D1
Hardy Mdws 11 BD23 . .134 E2
Hardy St YO8 . . . . .232 E4
Harebell Cl
  17 Harrogate HG3 . . . . .161 B3
  Northallerton DL7 . . . . . .210 C1
Harecroft Rd 9 LS21 . . .177 A1
Harehills La BD22 . . . . .187 E1
Haresfield Way TS17 . . . . .6 A5
Harewell Cl HG3 . . . . . .137 D3
Harewell La 3 HG3 . . . .137 F3
Harewood Ave
  5 Normanton South WF6 .200 B2
  1 Scalby YO12 . . . . . . .212 D8
Harewood Chase DL7 . .210 B2
Harewood Cl
  Morton-on-Swale DL7 . . . . .64 A6
  Rawcliffe YO30 . . . . . . .224 D2
  5 Wigginton YO32 . . . . .166 D5
Harewood Dr 4 YO14 . .101 A3
Harewood La DL7 . . . . .210 C3
Harewood Rd
  Collingham LS22 . . . . . . .188 A8
  Harrogate HG3 . . . . . . .219 A5
  Ripon HG4 . . . . .214 B3
  Skipton BD23 . . . . .216 E4
Harewood Way YO10 . . .229 A2
Harford Rd YO11 . . . . . .100 B6
Hargill
  Gilling with Hartforth & Sedbury
    DL10 . . . . .20 E4
  Harmby DL8 . . . . .60 E4
  West Witton DL8 . . . . . . .59 C3
Hargill Cl DL8 . . . . .60 E4
Hargill La Finghall DL8 . .61 E4
  6 Leeming DL7 . . . . . . .63 D4
  Redmire DL8 . . . . .59 C7
Hargill Rd DL8 . . . . .61 A3
Hargrove Rd HG2 . . . . .220 D2
Harington Ave YO10 . . .228 F4
Harker Hill DL8 . . . . .56 C4
Harker St 12 WF11 . . . .202 A2
Harkness Cl DL7 . . . . . . .63 C4
Harkness Dr DL7 . . . . . . .63 C4
Harland Cl YO61 . . . . . .144 C3
Harland Mount Nature
  Reserve ★ YO12 . . . . .212 B3
Harlech Ct 11 TS17 . . . . .5 F4
Harlech Way HG2 . . . . .222 B5
Harley Cl YO12 . . . . . . .212 E5
Harley Cres DL9 . . . . . . .40 F4
Harley La DL9 . . . . .40 F4
Harley St 5 YO12 . . . . .212 E5
Harlow Ave HG2 . . . . . .222 B5

Harlow Carr RHS Gdn ★
  HG3 . . . . .161 B1
Harlow Cl 1 YO24 . . . .227 F2
Harlow Cres YO24 . . . .222 B7
Harlow Grange Pk
  HG3 . . . . .178 C8
Harlow Manor Pk
  HG2 . . . . .222 B8
Harlow Moor Dr HG2 . .219 B1
Harlow Moor Rd HG2 . .219 A1
Harlow Oval HG2 . . . . .222 B8
Harlow Pines HG2 . . . .222 A7
Harlow Pk Cres HG2 . . .222 B7
Harlow Pk Dr HG2 . . . .222 B7
Harlow Pk Rd HG2 . . . .222 B7
Harlow Rd YO24 . . . . . .227 F2
Harlow Terr HG2 . . . . . .219 B1
Harlow View HG2 . . . . .222 B6
Harlsey Castle ★ DL6 . . .44 D5
Harlsey Cres TS18 . . . . . .5 E8
Harlsey Rd TS18 . . . . . . .5 E8
Harmby Rd 12 DL8 . . . . .60 D5
Harness La 9 YO51 . . . .141 B4
Harold Ct YO24 . . . . . . .227 D3
Harold St YO8 . . . . .232 F4
Harolds Way 1 YO41 . . .168 D1
Harome Heads La YO62 . .93 B6
Harome Heads Rd
  YO62 . . . . .93 C6
Harper Gr BD20 . . . . . .187 F8
Harper La HG3 . . . . . . .159 C6
Harper St
  Barnoldswick BB18 . . . . .171 C1
  2 Selby YO8 . . . . .232 C5
Harper Terr 7 TS18 . . . . .5 E8
Harpers Sq 7 BD20 . . . .187 E6
Harpers Terr DL2 . . . . . . .4 B5
Harr Gill DL8 . . . . .58 A6
Harringax Cres 20 DL1 . . .3 F6
Harris Dr 9 DL10 . . . . . .41 E4
Harris St DL1 . . . . .3 E4
Harrison Gr HG1 . . . . . .220 C4
Harrison St
  Barnoldswick BB18 . . . . .171 C1
  York YO31 . . . . .228 F6
Harrogate Coll HG1 . . . .219 D2
Harrogate Ctr The ★
  HG1 . . . . .219 D3
Harrogate District Hospl
  HG2 . . . . .220 B1
Harrogate Gram Sch
  HG2 . . . . .222 C8
Harrogate Granby High Sch
  HG1 . . . . .220 A4
Harrogate Hill Inf & Jun Sch
  DL3 . . . . .3 D7
Harrogate Ladies Coll
  HG1 . . . . .219 C3
Harrogate Leisure Ctr
  HG2 . . . . .222 E7
Harrogate Rd
  Bishop Monkton HG3 . . . .139 C5
  Boroughbridge HG5 . . . .141 A2
  Ferrensby HG5 . . . . .162 E7
  Green Hammerton YO26 . .164 B3
  Kirkby Overblow HG3 . . . .222 D1
  Knaresborough HG5 . . . . .220 F5
  Littlethorpe HG4 . . . . . .214 C1
  Spofforth with Stockeld
    LS22 . . . . .180 A4
  Weeton LS17 . . . . .178 B2
Harrogate Sta HG1 . . . .219 D2
Harrogate Theatre ★
  HG1 . . . . .219 D2
Harrow Cliff La YO18 . . . .96 E4
Harrow Glade 5 YO30 . .225 A1
Harrow Rd TS5 . . . . .6 E8
Harrowing Dr 2 YO21 . .208 C6
Harry Moor La YO8 . . . .197 B2
Harryfield La YO61 . . . .144 C7
Hart Hill Cres YO41 . . . .169 A2
Hart Rhydding La
  LS29 . . . . .174 F4
Hartburn Village TS18 . . .5 E8
Hartoft St YO10 . . . . . . .228 D2
Hartwith Ave 3 HG3 . . .138 A1
Hartwith Bank HG3 . . . .138 A1
Hartwith Cl HG3 . . . . . .219 A4
Hartwith Dr HG3 . . . . . .219 B4
Hartwith Gn 4 HG3 . . . .138 A1
Hartwith Way HG1 . . . .219 B4
Harvard Ct YO12 . . . . . .212 A8
Harvest Cl 10 WF8 . . . .201 C2
Harvest Croft LS29 . . . .176 B1
Harvest Way YO11 . . . . .100 B7
Harwood Dale Rd YO13 . .54 A1
Hasguard Way 37 TS17 . . .5 F4
Hassacarr La YO19 . . . .184 F6
Hastings Cl 4 YO30 . . . .225 A1
Hastings Cres WF10 . . .201 A4
Hatcase La 28 YO18 . . . .95 F7
Hatfield Ave TS5 . . . . . . .6 E8
Hatfield Cl 3 YO30 . . . .224 E3
Hatfield Rd DL7 . . . . . .210 D3
Hatfield Wlk YO24 . . . .230 B8
Hatkill La YO41 . . . . . . .169 B1
Hatterboard Dr YO12 . . .212 C6
Hatters YO23 . . . . .230 B3
Haugh La YO8 . . . . .202 F8

Haughton Com Sch DL1 . . .3 E7
Haughton Rd
  Darlington DL1 . . . . .3 D6
  York YO30 . . . . .228 C7
Hauling La YO23 . . . . . .191 C8
Hauxley Cl LS29 . . . . . .218 D5
Havelock Pl 17 YO21 . . .208 D7
Havelock St TS17 . . . . . . .6 B8
Haven The Selby YO8 . . .232 D5
  5 South Milford LS25 . . .195 F2
Haverah Ct YO30 . . . . . .224 F1
Havercroft Rd 15 YO14 .127 A8
Havernook La HG4 . . . . . .86 A3
Havers Hill YO11 . . . . . .100 A6
Haverthwaites Dr
  LS25 . . . . .188 F1
Havertop La WF6 . . . . . .200 C1
Havikil La HG5 . . . . .162 A5
Havikil Pk HG5 . . . . .162 A6
Havilland Rd TS17 . . . . . . .6 B6
Havre Pk 11 BB18 . . . . .171 E1
Haw Bank Ct BD23 . . . . .217 B5
Haw Gr BD23 . . . . .154 B3
Haw Hill View WF6 . . . .200 A2
Haw La BD23 . . . . .154 B3
Haw Pk 1 BD23 . . . . . . .217 E8
Hawber La BD20 . . . . . .174 C1
Hawdon Ave YO8 . . . . . .232 D5
Hawes Com Prim Sch
  DL8 . . . . .56 D4
Hawes Rd HG1 . . . . . . .220 B4
Hawes Visitor Ctr ★
  DL8 . . . . .56 D4
Hawke Garth 5 YO14 . .127 A8
Hawkridge Cl TS17 . . . . . .6 A3
Hawkshead Cl 3 YO24 . .230 B8
Hawkstone TS5 . . . . .7 C4
Hawkstone Cl TS14 . . . . .8 E6
Hawkswell La HG5 . . . . .40 E1
Hawkswood 1 DL2 . . . . .3 D1
Hawley St BB8 . . . . .186 B3
Hawse Rd YO8 . . . . .204 E8
Hawshaw Rd BD22 . . . . .186 E7
Hawsker cum Stainsacre CE
  VC Prim Sch YO22 . . . .33 A7
Hawsker Intake Rd
  YO22 . . . . .32 F5
Hawsker La
  Hawsker-cum-Stainsacre
    YO22 . . . . .13 F1
  Whitby YO22 . . . . .208 F6
Hawson St 9 YO11 . . . .100 B7
Hawthorn Ave
  2 Knaresborough HG5 . . .221 B7
  Knottingley WF11 . . . . . .201 D4
  Malton YO17 . . . . .215 D5
  Tadcaster LS24 . . . . . . .189 D5
Hawthorn Cl
  11 Addingham LS29 . . . .174 E4
  Hellifield BD23 . . . . .154 B4
  25 Leyburn DL8 . . . . . . .60 D5
  3 Pickering YO18 . . . . . .96 A6
  Stutton with Hazlewood
    LS24 . . . . .189 E5
Hawthorn Cres LS24 . . . . .7 C6
Hawthorn Croft 6 LS24 189 D5
Hawthorn Dr
  2 Topcliffe YO7 . . . . . . .89 B1
  Wilberfoss YO41 . . . . . . .185 E4
  Wistow YO8 . . . . .198 A5
Hawthorn Garth DN14 . .202 F4
Hawthorn Gr YO31 . . . . .228 E5
Hawthorn La YO18 . . . . . .96 A6
Hawthorn Pl YO32 . . . . .225 E4
Hawthorn Spinney
  YO32 . . . . .225 E3
Hawthorn St YO31 . . . . .228 E5
Hawthorn Terr YO32 . . .225 D4
Hawthorn Terr Cent 2
  YO32 . . . . .225 D3
Hawthorn Terr N
  YO32 . . . . .225 D4
Hawthorn Terr S
  YO32 . . . . .225 D3
Hawthorn Way YO14 . . .101 C1
Hawthorn Wlk 1 YO11 . .100 A7
Hawthorne Ave
  12 Haxby YO32 . . . . . . .166 E5
  10 Scotton DL9 . . . . . . .40 F2
Hawthorne Cl
  Burniston YO13 . . . . .75 D7
  10 Thorpe Willoughby
    YO8 . . . . .197 B2
Hawthorne Dr
  Barnoldswick BB18 . . . . .171 E2
  Guisborough TS14 . . . . . . .8 E6
Hawthorne Gr YO31 . . . .228 E5
Hawthorne Mews
  YO32 . . . . .167 A8
Hawthorns 2 YO19 . . . .197 F8
Hawthorns La BD23 . . . .133 B2
Hawthorns The
  20 Glusburn BD20 . . . . .187 E7
  10 Great Ayton TS9 . . . . .8 A2
Haxby Moor Rd
  Haxby YO32 . . . . .166 F7
  Towthorpe YO32 . . . . . .167 A7
Haxby Rd Clifton YO31 . .225 D1
  Middleton St George DL2 . . .4 C5
  New Earswick YO32 . . . .225 D6
  York YO31 . . . . .233 B4
Haxby Rd Prim Sch
  YO31 . . . . .228 D7
Hay Brow Cl YO13 . . . . . .75 C5
Hay Brow Cres YO13 . . . .75 C5
Hay La YO13 . . . . .75 C5
Hay-a-park La HG5 . . . .221 D7

Hayfield Ave LS23 . . . . .188 E8
Hayforth Cl YO30 . . . . .225 A2
Haygate La YO18 . . . . . . .95 F5
Haygill Nook BD23 . . . . .174 B5
Hayhills La BD20 . . . . . .174 B2
Hayton Wood View
  LS25 . . . . .194 F8
Haywain The LS29 . . . . .218 D3
Haywra Cres 6 HG1 . . . .219 E3
Haywra St HG1 . . . . . . .219 D3
Hazel Bank HG5 . . . . . .162 B6
Hazel Brow Farm ★
  DL11 . . . . .37 C4
Hazel Cl Pannal HG3 . . . .222 C3
  York YO32 . . . . .225 D2
Hazel Ct 11 Bedale DL8 . .63 B3
  York YO31 . . . . .228 E4
Hazel Dr HG3 . . . . .222 C3
Hazel Garth YO31 . . . . .229 B7
Hazel Gr
  Middlesbrough TS7 . . . . . .7 C6
  Pontefract WF8 . . . . . . .201 C1
  Sutton BD20 . . . . .187 E7
Hazel Gr Rd BD20 . . . . .187 E7
Hazel Hill YO12 . . . . .75 D3
Hazel Old La DN14 . . . .203 C2
Hazel Rd
  2 Boroughbridge YO51 . .141 B4
  2 Filey YO14 . . . . .101 A4
  Knottingley WF11 . . . . . .201 D3
Hazel Rise LS25 . . . . . . .200 B5
Hazelheads La HG5 . . . .221 C8
Hazelmere Ct YO32 . . . .225 E3
Hazelnut Gr YO30 . . . . .225 B2
Hazelwood Ave
  Garforth LS25 . . . . .194 D3
  York YO10 . . . . .229 D4
Hazing La DN14 . . . . . . .207 B6
Hazler La BD23 . . . . . . .157 D2
Headingley Cres 3 DL1 . . .3 F4
Headingley Rd 7 DN6 . .206 E2
Headland 30 YO32 . . . .166 E5
Headland La YO18 . . . . . .72 B4
Headlands La
  Howgrave DL8 . . . . .87 C2
  Knottingley WF11 . . . . . .201 C3
  Pontefract WF8 . . . . . . .201 B1
Headlands Prim Sch
  YO32 . . . . .225 D8
Headlands Rd YO62 . . . . .70 C2
Heads Bank DL8 . . . . . . .58 F3
Heads La BB18 . . . . . . .186 A4
Heads Rd Newton YO18 . .51 B4
  Pickering YO18 . . . . .71 F8
Headwell La LS24 . . . . .195 C2
Healaugh La YO26 . . . . .181 E4
Healaugh Priory ★
  LS24 . . . . .181 E1
Heald Brow BB18 . . . . .171 D2
Heald Dr WF10 . . . . . . .200 F4
Healdfield Rd WF10 . . . .201 A4
Healdwood Rd WF10 . . .200 F4
Healey Dr YO31 . . . . . . .228 F8
Healthfield Prim Sch
  DL1 . . . . .3 E5
Heath Cl 2 YO31 . . . . . .227 F2
Heath Cres BD20 . . . . . .173 C5
Heath Croft YO10 . . . . .231 F7
Heath Dr
  Boston Spa LS23 . . . . . .188 D8
  7 Low Bradley DL20 . . . .173 B3
Heath Gr HG2 . . . . .219 B1
Heath Moor Dr YO10 . . .231 F8
Heath Pk 27 LS29 . . . . .175 C2
Heath Ride YO12 . . . . . .167 B8
Heathcliff Gdns 5
  YO12 . . . . .212 C6
Heather Bank
  13 Stamford Bridge YO41 .168 D2
  York YO10 . . . . .229 D4
Heather Brow 16 BD23 . .172 B1
Heather Cl Selby YO8 . . .232 C3
  3 Whorlton DL6 . . . . . . .25 D1
  York YO30 . . . . .226 A4
Heather Croft 4 YO31 . .227 F2
Heather Ct LS29 . . . . . .218 B3
Heather Dr YO22 . . . . . .208 E3
Heather View BD23 . . . .217 B3
Heather Way 16 HG3 . . .161 B3
Heatherdene LS24 . . . . .189 E6
Heatherdene Rd 1 DL9 . .40 E4
Heathfield Pk DL2 . . . . . . .4 C5
Heathfield Rd 1 YO10 . .229 A3
Heathness Rd LS29 . . . .174 E5
Heathrow TS17 . . . . .6 C7
Heathrow Cl 13 DL2 . . . .4 C4
Heaths Ct HG4 . . . . . . .214 C4
Hebden Bank HG3 . . . . .138 F4
Hebden Rd BD23 . . . . . .134 E2
Hebdon Rise 2 YO26 . . .227 D4
Heber Dr BD23 . . . . .172 A5
Heber's Ghyll Dr 24
  LS29 . . . . .175 C2
Heber's Gr 21 LS25 . . . .175 C2
Hebron Rd TS9 . . . . .26 B7
Heck & Pollington Lake
  DN14 . . . . .207 E2
Heck Gill La HG3 . . . . . .160 A5
Heck La DN14 . . . . .207 C2
Heckler Cl 3 HG4 . . . . .214 C4
Heckler La HG4 . . . . . . .214 C4
Heddon Gr TS17 . . . . .6 A3
Hedley St TS14 . . . . .8 F7
Height La BD23 . . . . . . .174 C6

Height Lands La LS23 . .182 D6
Heights La BD20 . . . . . .174 A3
Helena St LS25 . . . . . . .200 C8
Helks Brow LA2 . . . . . . .128 C2
Hell Wath Gr HG4 . . . . .214 A2
Hell Wath La
  Littlethorpe HG4 . . . . . .214 A2
  Markingfield Hall HG4 . . .139 E6
Hellifield Com Prim Sch
  BD23 . . . . .154 B3
Hellifield Rd BD23 . . . . .155 A6
Hellifield Sta BD23 . . . . .154 B4
Helmsdale YO24 . . . . . .230 C6
Helmsley Castle ★
  YO62 . . . . .92 E6
Helmsley Com Prim Sch
  YO62 . . . . .92 F7
Helmsley Dr TS14 . . . . . . .8 F7
Helmsley Gr 16 YO32 . .166 D5
Helmsley Rd TS9 . . . . . . .26 C7
Helmsley Walled Gdn ★
  YO62 . . . . .92 E6
Helmsley Way DL7 . . . .210 C2
Helperby & Myton La
  YO61 . . . . .142 A7
Helperby La YO62 . . . . .141 C7
Helredale Gdns 7 YO22 .208 E4
Helredale Rd YO22 . . . . .208 E4
Helston Rd WF6 . . . . . . .200 A2
Helwath Rd YO13 . . . . . . .53 C5
Helwith Rd DL11 . . . . . . .38 C5
Hemingbrough CP Sch
  YO8 . . . . .198 F1
Hemingford Gdns TS15 . . .5 E2
Hemishor Dr LS26 . . . . .200 C8
Hemlington Hall Prim Sch
  TS8 . . . . .6 E5
Hemlington Hall Rd TS8 . .6 E5
Hemlington Lake & Recn Ctr
  TS8 . . . . .6 E5
Hemlington Rd TS8 . . . . .6 E5
Hemlock Ave YO31 . . . . .225 E1
Hempbridge Cl YO8 . . . .232 A5
Hempbridge Rd YO8 . . . .232 A5
Hempland Ave YO31 . . . .228 F6
Hempland Dr YO31 . . . . .229 A7
Hempland Jun Sch
  YO31 . . . . .229 B6
Hempland La YO31 . . . . .229 A7
Hempland Prim Sch
  YO31 . . . . .229 A6
Hemsby Rd WF10 . . . . . .200 E3
Henbusk La LA2 . . . . . . .130 A8
Hendon Garth YO30 . . . .225 A1
Henlow La YO60 . . . . . . .147 B4
Henrhyd Cl 26 TS17 . . . . .5 F4
Henrietta Cl DL10 . . . . .209 F8
Henrietta St YO22 . . . . .208 E7
Henry St BD23 . . . . .216 F3
Hensall CP Sch DN14 . . .203 C1
Hensall Sta DN14 . . . . .203 C1
Henshaws Coll HG1 . . . .220 B5
Henside La BD24 . . . . . .132 A5
Henside Rd BD24 . . . . . .132 A6
Henson Gr WF10 . . . . . .201 A4
Henson Rd DL1 . . . . .3 E5
Henwick Hall La YO8 . . .232 C1
Hepton Hill YO17 . . . . . .120 F2
Hepworth's La DN14 . . .204 C2
Herbert St 6 YO10 . . . . .228 E3
Herberts Way YO31 . . . .228 F7
Hercules St DL1 . . . . .3 E7
Herdborough Rd
  YO11 . . . . .100 A7
Herdsman Dr YO23 . . . .230 C3
Herdsman Rd 3 YO24 . .230 D8
Herdwick Cl 1 YO30 . . . .225 B1
Hereford Rd HG1 . . . . . .219 A2
Hergill La Baldersby HG4 . .88 C1
  Kirby Hill DL11 . . . . .19 F5
  Kirkby Fleetham with Fencote
    DL7 . . . . .63 C8
Herisson Cl 20 YO18 . . . .95 F7
Heritage Ctr The ★ TS12 . .9 D6
Herman Wlk YO24 . . . . .230 C8
Hermitage Cl DL10 . . . . .209 A7
Hermitage The ★ HG4 . . .86 C8
Hermitage Way YO22 . . . .32 A5
Heron Ave YO24 . . . . . . .230 C8
Heron Cl 1 Bedale DL8 . . .63 B3
  11 Thornton Dale YO18 . . .96 C5
Heron Ct 6 Filey YO14 . .101 A4
  6 Hunton DL9 . . . . .40 F2
Heron Dr DL1 . . . . .3 E5
Heron Gate TS14 . . . . . . .8 D6
Heron La YO12 . . . . .99 E6
Heron Rise YO32 . . . . . .225 F5
Heron Tree Cl DL8 . . . . . .60 D7
Heron Way YO17 . . . . . .215 D2
Herongate YO18 . . . . . . .95 F6
Herriot ★ YO7 . . . . .211 B3
Herriot Dr DL9 . . . . .41 A5
Herriot Way YO7 . . . . . .211 C4
Herriott Cl 4 YO11 . . . . .100 A7
Hertford Vale CE VC Prim
  Sch YO12 . . . . .99 D2
Hesketh Ave TS4 . . . . . . .7 A7
Hesketh Bank YO10 . . . .229 D3
Heslaker La BD23 . . . . . .216 C1
Hesledon Ave TS5 . . . . . .6 A6
Hesley La BD24 . . . . . . .153 A6
Heslin Cl 8 YO32 . . . . . .225 C8
Heslington Croft YO10 . .231 F7
Heslington Ct 2 YO10 . . .229 B1
Heslington Gdns 2 TS14 . .8 F7

Heslington La
Heslington YO10 ....229 A1
York YO10 ....228 E3
Heslington Rd YO10 .....228 E3
Hessay Pl **2** YO26 ....227 A3
Hetherton St YO30 ......233 A3
Hetton Garth **18** DL8 ....60 D5
Hewitson Rd DL1 ....3 E5
Hewitts La BD20 ....172 F2
Hewley Ave YO10 ....229 A4
Hewley Dr **9** YO13 ....99 A7
Heworth YO31 ....229 A6
Heworth CE Prim Sch
YO31 ....228 F6
Heworth Dr YO21 ....208 B6
Heworth Gn YO31 ....233 C4
Heworth Hall Dr YO31 ..228 F6
Heworth Mews YO31 ...228 E6
Heworth Pl YO31 ....228 F6
Heworth Rd YO31 ....228 F6
Heworth Village YO31 ..229 A6
Heyford Rd YO7 ....115 B1
Heygate Bank YO18 .....49 F3
Heygate La LS23 ......188 F6
Heyshaw Rd HG3 ......159 C8
Heythrop Dr
Guisborough TS14 ....8 F6
Middlesbrough TS5 ......6 D7
Heywood Rd HG2 ......219 C1
Hibernia St YO12 ......212 E5
Hicks La LS26 ....200 B6
Hickstead Ct **16** DL1 ....3 F6
Hidcote Gdns TS17 .....6 A4
High Back Side YO18 ...95 E8
High Bank
Ampleforth YO62 ....92 B2
Bradleys Both BD20 ...173 E3
5 Threshfield BD23 ...134 D2
High Bank Cl **7** LS29 ..174 F4
High Barmer YO13 .....75 B7
High Bentham Com Prim Sch
LA2 ....129 B8
High Bond End HG5 ....221 A7
High Bradley La BD20 .173 E4
High Catton Rd YO41 ..185 D8
High Church Wynd TS16 .5 D3
High Cleugh HG4 ......214 A4
High Conistcliffe CE Sch
DL2 ....2 C6
High Cragwell YO21 ....31 F7
High Crest **6** HG3 .....137 C4
High Croft **7** YO14 ....126 F8
High Croft Way **5** BD20 173 E1
High Ct HG5 ....221 A6
High Eggborough La
DN14 ....203 A1
High Fell Cl BD24 .....131 D1
High Field YO31 ....229 D4
High Fold BB18 ....186 A7
High Garth
Eastfield YO11 ....100 A4
Richmond DL10 ....209 B8
High Gill Rd TS7 ......7 E6
High Gn Catterick DL10 .41 D4
Hebden BD23 ....135 A2
High Gn Dr BD20 ......174 B1
High Hill Gr St **14** BD24 131 D2
High Hill La BD24 .....131 E2
High La Beadlam YO62 .93 C8
Birstwith HG3 ....160 C5
Cowling BD22 ....187 A4
Cropton YO18 ....71 C4
Dalby-cum-Skewsby
YO60 ....119 A2
Dalton DL11 ....19 D7
Fylingdales YO22 .....33 C5
Gillamoor YO62 ....70 A6
Grassington BD23 ....134 C3
Grinton DL11 ....37 D4
Hawes DL8 ....56 F4
Howsham YO60 ....147 B1
Kirby Sigston DL6 .....44 E1
Leake DL6 ....65 E6
Maltby TS15 ....6 C4
Muston YO14 ....100 F1
Myton-on-Swale YO61 142 B6
Newsham DL11 ....18 G7
Reeth, Fremington & Healaugh
DL11 ....37 F5
Spofforth with Stockeld
HG3 ....179 C4
Sutton upon Derwent
YO41 ....185 D3
Thirlby YO7 ....90 D6
Thornton Watlass DL8 ..62 C2
West Scrafton DL8 .....83 F6
West Witton DL8 ......59 D2
High Leir La YO7 ......67 D1
High Mdw
Gowdall DN14 ....204 A1
Selby YO8 ....232 B6
High Mill Dr **1** YO12 ...75 E5
High Mill La LS29 .....175 A5
High Mkt Pl **27** YO62 ...70 B1
High Moor Edge YO12 .212 A7
High Moor La
Boroughbridge HG5 ...141 A2
Brearton HG3 ....161 F8
Newton-on-Ouse YO30 165 C8
Scotton HG5 ....162 A5
High Moor Rd
North Rigton HG3 .....178 A5
Skelton YO30 ....140 F7
High Moor Way 11
YO11 ....100 A6

High Newbiggin St
YO31 ....233 B3
High Oaks YO31 ....229 B7
High Ousegate YO1 ....233 B2
High Peak TS14 ....8 F5
High Peter La HG3 ....140 A3
High Petergate YO1 ...233 B3
High Rd LA2 ....128 F5
High Riding Aske DL10 .20 D1
Richmond DL10 ....209 C8
High Rifts TS8 ....6 E5
High Riggs La YO18 ...96 C3
High Row
Bugthorpe YO41 ......169 D4
Caldwell DL11 ....1 C4
Darlington DL1 ....3 C5
Melsonby DL10 ....20 F7
6 Boroughbridge YO51 141 B5
Boston Spa LS23 .....188 E5
Bramham LS23 ....188 E5
Buckton/Bempton YO13 .97 D6
Burniston YO13 ....75 C8
Burton in Lonsdale LA6 102 F3
Carlton DN14 ....204 C2
Castleford WF10 ......200 E4
Cawood YO8 ....197 B8
Cottam YO25 ....150 E5
Cropton YO18 ....71 B4
Danby YO21 ....29 A6
Eaglescliffe TS15 ......5 D4
13 Eastfield YO11 .....100 A4
Gargrave BD23 ....155 D1
Glaisdale YO21 ....30 D4
Glusburn BD20 ......187 E6
Great Ayton TS9 ......7 F1
Great Broughton TS9 ..26 E4
Hampsthwaite HG3 ...160 F5
4 Helmsley YO62 ....92 F6
Heslerton YO17 ....123 F6
Hinderwell TS13 ......11 F7
Hovingham YO62 .....119 E6
Husthwaite YO61 .....117 B6
Ingleton LA6 ....103 D4
Kippax LS25 ....194 D1
Kirby Grindalythe YO17 149 D6
5 Knaresborough HG5 221 B5
Knottingley WF11 ....201 E5
Langtoft YO25 ....151 C8
Lastingham YO62 .....70 E5
9 Leyburn DL8 ....60 D5
Lingdale TS12 ....9 A8
Lockwood TS12 ....10 A5
Markington with Wallerthwaite
HG3 ....139 C4
Mickleby TS13 ....12 A4
Middlesbrough TS7 ....7 C8
Newton Mulgrave TS13 .11 E4
Normanton South WF6 200 A1
Northallerton DL7 ....210 D6
14 Norton DN6 ....206 E1
Old Byland & Scawton
YO62 ....92 A4
Oldstead YO7 ....91 E5
Pateley Bridge HG3 ...137 B4
Rawcliffe DN14 ....205 A1
Rillington YO17 ......122 F5
Scalby YO13 ....75 D5
6 Settle BD24 ....131 E2
Settrington YO17 .....122 F1
Sherburn YO17 ......124 D7
Skipton BD23 ....217 A4
Slingsby YO62 ....120 B5
Snainton YO13 ....98 A5
Snaith DN14 ....204 B1
South Milford LS25 ...195 E2
Spofforth HG3 ....179 E5
3 Staithes TS13 ......13 K2
Stillington YO61 ......144 B6
Stokesley TS9 ....26 C7
Swinton YO17 ....121 B4
Tadcaster LS24 ....189 E6
Thornton Dale YO18 ...96 E6
Thornton-le-Clay YO60 146 A4
Wharram YO17 ....149 A6
Whitby YO21 ....208 B3
Whixley YO26 ....164 A4
Whorlton DL6 ....45 D8
Wombleton YO62 .....93 E7
Wrelton YO18 ....71 C1
High St Agnesgate
HG4 ....214 C5
High Stakesby Rd
YO21 ....208 A6
High Stell YO21 ....4 C4
High Town Bank Rd
YO7 ....91 C5
High Trace DL6 ....210 E2
High Trees Ct LS25 ...195 F4
High View HG3 ....160 F8
High Wheatley LS29 ..218 E3
High Wlk YO12 ....212 E7
High Wood LS29 .....218 E3
Highbank Gr **1** HG2 ..220 D4
Highbury Ave TS5 ....6 F8
Highcliff Rd TS14 ....8 E4

Highcliffe Ct YO30 ....228 A6
Highcroft
Collingham LS22 .....188 A8
9 Grassington BD23 .134 C3
Highdale Ave **5** YO12 212 D8
Highdale Rd YO12 ....212 E7
Higher Hartley St 2
BD20 ....187 D7
Higher Lodge St 1
BD20 ....187 D7
Higher Rd BD20 ......152 F4
Higherlands Cl BD23 .155 D1
Highfield
Pollington DN14 .....207 F7
Scarborough YO12 ....212 E4
Highfield Ave WF8 ....201 D2
Highfield Cl YO25 ....126 A4
Highfield Cres YO8 ...198 B5
Highfield Ct YO8 .....232 B1
Highfield Dr
Allerton Bywater WF10 .200 C7
Garforth LS25 ....194 C3
Highfield Gn
Allerton Bywater WF10 200 C7
Sherburn in Elmet LS25 195 F3
Highfield Gr WF10 ...200 C7
Highfield La
Barwick in Elmet & Scholes
LS15 ....194 W3
Fangfoss YO41 ....169 B1
Gillamoor YO62 ....69 F5
Huddleston with Newthorpe
LS25 ....195 B2
Nawton YO62 ....69 C2
Scagglethorpe YO17 ..122 E2
Womersley DN6 ......206 D5
Highfield Pl **1** WF10 .200 D7
Highfield Prep Sch
HG1 ....219 B3
Highfield Rd
Aberford LS25 ....194 F8
29 Earby BB18 ....172 A1
Malton YO17 ....215 C5
Ripon HG4 ....214 B3
Whitby YO21 ....208 A7
Highfield Terr BD23 ..216 F3
Highfield View **3** YO8 198 B4
Highfield Villas LS25 .195 F3
Highfields La YO7 ....115 A1
Highgate Balne DN14 207 D6
Glusburn BD20 ......187 D8
Highgate Pk HG1 ....219 F3
Highgrove Cl YO30 ..224 E3
Highland Cl **9** WF8 ..201 C1
Highlands Ave **5** YO32 167 B7
Highlands Cl YO14 ...101 B1
Highmoor Cl YO24 ...230 D8
Highmoor Rd
Darlington DL1 ....3 F4
York YO24 ....230 D8
Highthorn Rd YO31 ..225 E2
Highthorne La YO61 .117 B5
Highway BD24 ....131 E3
Hilbeck Gr YO31 ....229 B6
Hilbra Ave YO32 ....225 D6
Hilda St **6** Selby YO8 232 C5
3 York YO8 ....228 E3
Hildenley Cl **6** YO12 .212 B5
Hilderthorpe YO7 .....7 C6
Hildewell **3** TS13 ....11 F7
Hildyard Cl TS9 ......26 C8
Hill Bank HG5 ....163 B7
Hill Cl DL11 ....38 B6
Hill Crest YO19 ......167 F1
Hill Crest Gdns YO24 227 F1
Hill End La BD22 ....186 F5
Hill Field YO8 ....232 B8
Hill Foot La HG3 ....222 B2
Hill House La DL2 ....4 C8
Hill La BB8 ....186 B4
Hill Rd WF10 ....200 F3
Hill Rise
Middleston St George DL2 4 D3
Skipton BD23 ....216 E5
Hill Rise Ave HG2 ...222 B8
Hill Rise Cl HG2 ....222 B8
Hill Side DL2 ....3 A3
Hill St
6 Barnoldswick BB18 171 E1
York YO24 ....227 E1
Hill The DL8 ....56 D4
Hill Top
24 Burley in Warfedale
LS29 ....176 C1
Castleford WF10 .....200 C4
Ilkley LS29 ....218 A2
Knottingley WF11 ....201 F2
Hill Top Ave HG1 ....219 D6
Hill Top Cl
Embsay BD23 ....217 C8
Harrogate HG1 ......219 D6
Stutton with Hazlewood
LS24 ....189 D4
Hill Top Cres HG1 ...219 D6
Hill Top Ct DL7 ......22 C3
Hill Top Dr HG1 .....219 D6
Hill Top Gr HG1 .....219 D6
Hill Top La Earby BB18 172 A1
Pannal HG3 ....222 A4
Hill Top Mount HG1 .219 D6
Hill Top Rd
Harrogate HG1 ......219 D6
4 Wistow YO8 ....197 D6
Hill Top Rise HG1 ...219 E6
Hill Top View HG3 ...159 F8
Hill Top Wlk HG1 ....219 D6
Hill View
Langthorpe YO51 ....141 A6

Hill View continued
Stillington YO61 ......144 C6
York YO31 ....229 C7
Hillam Comm La LS25 202 B7
Hillam H Cl **5** LS25 ..202 B7
Hillam Hall La **4** LS25 202 A7
Hillam Hall View 3
LS25 ....202 A7
Hillam La
Burton Salmon LS25 .201 F7
Hillam LS25 ....202 A7
Hillary Garth **9** YO26 227 E4
Hillbank Gr HG1 .....220 D4
Hillbank Rd HG1 ....220 D4
Hillbank View HG1 ..220 C4
Hillcrest
8 Monk Fryston LS25 202 A8
Tadcaster LS24 ......189 D5
Hillcrest Ave
Newby & Scalby YO12 75 E5
Poppleton YO26 .....224 A2
Silsden BD20 ....174 C1
Hillcrest Cl YO51 ....201 B3
Hillcrest Ct **2** LS24 .189 D5
Hillcrest Dr
Castleford WF10 .....201 B3
Loftus TS13 ....10 D8
Hillcrest Gdns YO51 141 A7
Hillcrest Gr **2** YO12 .75 E5
Hillcrest Mount WF10 201 B3
Hillgarth WF11 ......201 F2
Hillgarth Ct **4** YO41 185 B2
Hillhouse La DL2 .....4 C7
Hillingdon Rd TS4 ...7 B8
Hillocks La TS12 ....10 A5
Hills La BD23 ....155 E5
Hillsborough Terr 5
YO30 ....228 C7
Hillshaw Parkway
HG4 ....214 D5
Hillside Byram WF11 201 E4
Follifoot HG3 ....223 F4
3 Ingleby Arncliffe DL6 45 A7
Skipton BD23 ....217 B6
Hillside Cl
18 Addingham LS29 .174 F4
Bootham Stray YO30 225 B2
9 Monk Fryston LS25 202 A8
Threshfield BD23 ....134 B3
Hillside Cres BD23 ..217 C3
Hillside Dr BD23 ....134 B3
Hillside Gdns
Langtoft YO25 ....151 D5
Scarborough YO12 ...212 E1
Hillside Rd HG3 .....222 E3
Hillside Way YO17 ...150 B8
Hilltop Cres DL9 ....40 E4
Hilton Cl DL6 ....210 E8
Hilton Gn DL6 ....210 D8
Hilton Grange DL6 ..210 E8
Hilton La **7** HG5 ....221 A6
Hilton Rd TS9 ....6 F1
Hilton Sq DL6 ....210 E8
Hincks Hall La HG3 .139 C3
Hinderwell Com Prim Sch
YO12 ....212 D2
Hinderwell La
Hinderwell TS13 .....11 E8
Staithes TS13 ....13 K1
Hinderwell Pl YO12 .212 E2
Hinderwell Rd YO12 212 E1
Hindle Dr **39** YO14 ..101 B3
Hinsley La DN14 ....204 C2
Hinton Ave **1** YO24 .230 C8
Hinton Cl **9** WF8 ....201 C2
Hinton La WF11 .....201 C1
Hipswell CE Prim Sch
DL9 ....209 F1
Hipswell Rd DL9 ....209 E1
Hipswell Rd W DL9 .209 C1
Hird Ave **22** DL8 ....63 A2
Hird Rd TS15 ....5 D2
Hirds Yd **2** BD23 ....216 F3
Hirst Courtney & Temple
Hirst CP Sch YO8 ...203 E3
Hirst La HG3 ....160 E5
Hirst Rd YO8 ....204 A3
Hirst St WF10 ....200 C8
Hirstead Gdns YO12 212 B8
Hirstead Rd YO12 ...212 B8
Hob Cote La BD22 ..187 F1
Hob Moor Com Prim Sch
YO24 ....227 D2
Hob Moor Dr YO24 .227 E2
Hob Moor Jun Sch
YO24 ....227 E2
Hob Moor Oaks Sch
YO26 ....227 C6
Hobart Rd WF10 ....201 B5
Hobb Nook La LS21 .176 D4
Hobbs Cl DL9 ....209 C2
Hobgate YO24 ......227 D3
Hobmoor Terr YO24 227 F1
Hobson Cl YO23 ....230 B1
Hoctun Cl WF10 ....200 T3
Hodge La WF8 ......206 B3
Hodgson Fold LS29 .174 E5
Hodgson Hill YO13 ..54 B4
Hodgson La YO26 ...182 F8
Hodgson's La LS25 ..196 A5
Hogg La YO17 ....148 E6
Holbeck Ave
Middlesbrough TS5 ...6 E6
Scarborough YO11 ..213 B2
Holbeck Cl YO11 ...213 B2
Holbeck Hill YO11 ..213 B1
Holbeck Rd YO11 ...213 A2

Holbecks La YO51 ...141 F3
Holburns Croft **3** YO10 229 B1
Holden Gdns YO8 ...197 D2
Holderness Dr **7** DL3 3 A7
Hole House La BB7 ..152 B2
Hole La BD20 ....174 A2
Holes La WF11 ......201 E2
Holgate DL6 ....45 E8
Holgate Bank HG5 ..163 A8
Holgate Bridge Gdn 7
YO24 ....228 A3
Holgate Cl YO17 ....215 C5
Holgate Lodge Dr
YO26 ....227 E4
Holgate Rd YO24 ...233 A1
Holl Gate DL8 ....59 E3
Hollicarrs Cl YO19 ..192 A2
Hollies The YO8 ....198 C4
Hollin Gate LS21 ...176 E1
Hollin Hall Dr LS29 .175 C2
Hollin La LA2 ....129 F6
Hollin Top La YO21 .29 C7
Hollings The LS26 ..200 A6
Hollington St **9** BB8 186 A3
Hollingwood Gate 31
LS29 ....175 C2
Hollingwood Rise 32
LS29 ....175 C2
Hollingworth Cl 217 B3
Hollinhurst Brow LA2 128 F2
Hollins DL8 ....60 B3
Hollins Beck Cl LS25 200 D8
Hollins Cl HG3 ......161 A5
Hollins Cres HG1 ...219 C4
Hollins Gr WF10 ....200 C7
Hollins Hall HG3 ....161 A4
Hollins La Firby DL8 .63 B1
Hampsthwaite HG3 ..160 F5
Melmerby HG4 ......114 B8
Middleton Quernhow HG4 88 C1
Rosedale East Side YO18 49 D4
Hollins Mews HG1 ..219 C4
Hollins Rd
10 Barnoldswick BB18 171 D1
Harrogate HG1 ......219 C4
Hollis Cres YO32 ...167 B6
Hollow Gill Brow
BD24 ....153 C5
Hollow Moor La DL8 62 E7
Holly Bank Gr **3** YO24 227 F2
Holly Bank Rd YO24 227 F2
Holly Cl
Acaster Malbis YO23 191 C8
Full Sutton YO41 ....169 A2
Thirsk YO7 ....211 B2
Wrelton YO18 ....71 C1
Holly Ct **11** HG5 ....221 B6
Holly Garth **1** YO61 115 F1
Holly Garth Cl TS9 ..7 F1
Holly Gr WF10 ......200 C7
8 Thorpe Willoughby YO8 197 B2
Holly Hill DL10 .....209 C6
Holly Pk LS17 ......178 B3
Holly Rd **10** Bedale DL8 63 B3
Boston Spa LS23 ...188 D8
Holly Terr YO10 ....228 D1
Holly Tree Croft 2
YO19 ....184 F7
Holly Tree Ct
5 Hambleton YO8 ..196 F1
2 Whitby YO21 .....208 B6
Holly Tree Garth YO32 167 B3
Holly Tree La
Dunnington YO19 ...184 F7
Haxby YO32 ....225 D8
Holly Wlk YO12 ....212 D7
Hollybush Ave TS17 .6 B5
Hollybush Gn LS22 .188 B8
Hollygarth La DN14 202 D4
Hollyhurst Ave **1** TS4 6 F8
Hollyhurst Rd DL3 ..3 C6
Hollyrood Rd YO30 224 E3
Hollywalk Ave TS6 .7 E8
Hollywood YO13 ...232 B7
Holm Hill YO13 ....54 C2
Holm La LA2 ....130 E6
Holme Cl Earby BB18 186 A8
23 Sutton BD20 ....187 E7
Holme Cres BB8 ...186 A2
Holme Croft **1** BD23 134 C2
Holme Farm La LS23 188 A5
Holme Gn Rd YO23 190 F4
Holme Hill **2** YO11 .100 A6
Holme Hill La YO10 184 C4
Holme Ings LS29 ...175 B4
Holme La
Glusburn BD20 ......187 E7
Halton East BD23 ...174 B8
Newbiggin DL8 ......58 E1
Rudby TS9 ....25 E7
Selby YO8 ....232 D6
Holme St **12** BB8 ...186 A3
Holme The TS9 ....26 E4
Holme View LS29 ..218 A4
Holmebeck La HG4 .88 D1
Holmefield Cl **3** YO8 232 A1
Holmefield Cres HG4 214 C3
Holmefield Ct **2** YO8 232 A1
Holmefield La YO10 229 A1
Holmefield Rd
Glusburn BD20 ......187 E7
Ripon HG4 ....214 C3
Holmefields Rd TS6 .7 E8
Holmes Cres YO60 .146 C6
Holmes Dr **2** YO19 .192 A1
Holmes House ★ YO8 199 B3
Holmes Ind Est YO8 232 D6
Holmes The YO8 ...232 C6

Holmfield HG4 112 D7
Holmfield Cl WF8 201 C2
Holmfield Ct WF8 201 D2
Holmfield La WF8 201 C2
Holmstead Ave YO21 208 A5
Holmtree La HG4 113 B8
Holmwood Ave TS5 6 F8
Holnicote Cl 3 TS17 6 A3
Holray Pk DN14 204 C2
Holroyd Ave YO31 229 A5
Holtby Gr YO12 212 D5
Holtby La Holtby YO19 167 D1
Stockton-on-the-Forest YO32 226 F2
Holy Family RC High Sch DN14 204 C3
Holy Family RC Prim Sch DL3 3 B6
Holy Rood La LS25 201 C8
Holy Trinity CE Inf Sch HG4 214 B6
Holy Trinity CE Prim Sch HG4 214 B5
Holyrood Ave DL3 3 A5
Holyrood Cl TS17 6 B8
Holystone Dr TS17 6 A4
Holywell Gn TS16 5 E5
Holywell Halt Sta BD23 174 A8
Holywell La
Castleford WF10 201 A3
North Cowton DL7 22 C2
Home Farm Cl LA2 128 A6
Home Office Emergency Planning Coll YO61 143 D6
Homefield Cl YO23 230 A2
Homestead Cl
Eggborough DN14 203 A2
2 York YO32 225 F1
Homestead Garth 1 TS17 6 D6
Homestead Rd HG1 219 E2
Honey Pot 5 YO8 199 D7
Honey Pot Rd 2 DL10 41 C6
Honeypot La DL3 3 C7
Honeysuckle Cl
Romanby DL7 210 C1
Selby YO8 232 C2
Honister Gr TS5 6 D7
Honoldu Ct 29 TS17 5 F4
Hood La YO13 54 D2
Hoodstorth La HG3 158 F6
Hookstone Ave HG2 222 E7
Hookstone Chase HG2 220 D2
Hookstone Chase Com Prim Sch HG2 220 D2
Hookstone Cl HG2 220 C2
Hookstone Dr HG2 223 A8
Hookstone Garth HG3 159 E5
Hookstone Grange Ct 3 HG2 220 C2
Hookstone Grange Way 2 HG2 220 C2
Hookstone Oval 7 HG2 220 B1
Hookstone Pk HG2 220 D2
Hookstone Rd HG2 222 E7
Hookstone Way HG2 220 D2
Hookstone Wood Rd 9 HG2 220 B1
Hope St 30 Filey YO14 101 B3
Knaresborough HG5 221 B5
Scarborough YO12 213 A6
York YO10 233 C1
Hope Terr 7 YO21 208 D5
Hopetown La DL3 3 C6
Hopgrove La N YO32 226 C3
Hopgrove La S YO32 226 E3
Hopper Hill Rd YO11 99 F6
Hopper La LS21 159 C2
Hopperton St HG5 163 E4
Hopps's Rd 6 BD20 187 E8
Horn La BD20 174 B3
Hornbeam Cl YO30 225 B2
Hornbeam Cres HG2 222 F8
Hornbeam Pk
Harrogate HG2 222 F7
Knaresborough HG2 223 A6
Hornbeam Pk Ave HG2 222 F7
Hornbeam Pk Rd HG2 222 F7
Hornbeam Pk Sta HG2 222 F7
Hornbeam Sq N HG2 223 A7
Hornbeam Sq S HG2 223 A7
Hornbeam Sq W HG2 222 F7
Hornblower Cl 5 HG4 113 D2
Hornby Castle* DL8 62 C8
Hornby Cl 1 DL2 3 E1
Hornby Rd
Appleton Wiske DL6 24 A3
Roeburndale LA2 128 A2
Wray-with-Botton LA2 128 A6
Horndale Rd 5 YO14 101 B4
Horne Rd DL9 40 F4
Horner Ave YO61 144 A5
Horner Cl YO61 144 A5
Horner St YO30 228 B7
Horners Terr 13 YO22 208 E6
Hornsea Rd TS8 6 E5
Hornsey Garth 25 YO32 166 E5
Horse Bell Gate LA6 103 D4
Horse Course La YO17 122 E1
Horse Mill La HG3 139 D5
Horse Rd 12 YO22 208 E6
Horsefair 2 YO51 141 B5
Horseman Ave YO23 230 A3
Horseman Cl 2 YO23 230 A3
Horseman Dr YO23 230 A3
Horseman La YO23 230 A3
Horsemarket Rd YO17 215 B4
Horsemill Sq HG5 221 B5
Horseshoe Cave* BD24 132 A3
Horseshoe Cl DL9 40 F4
Horseshoe The YO24 230 E7
Horseway Gn YO18 49 D4
Horsfield Way YO19 184 F7
Horsman Ave YO10 233 C1
Horton-in-Ribblesdale CE VA Prim Sch BD24 105 D3
Horton-in-Ribbleside Sta BD24 105 C3
Hospital Fields Rd YO10 228 D1
Hospital La YO8 197 B4
Hospital Rd YO17 215 B4
Hospitium The* YO1 233 A3
Hostess La YO18 72 E4
Hotham Ave YO26 227 B2
Hothams Ct YO1 233 C2
Hothfield Jun Sch BD20 174 C1
Hothfield Terr BD23 216 F3
Houghton Ave WF11 201 D2
Houghton Banks 3 TS17 6 D6
Houndgate DL1 3 C5
Houndsway 6 YO24 230 B8
House of Correction Mus* HG4 214 D5
Hovingham CE VC Prim Sch YO62 119 E6
Hovingham Dr
6 Guisborough TS14 8 F7
Scarborough YO12 212 B4
Hovingham Hall* YO62 119 E6
How Hill Rd HG4 139 B6
How Stean Gorge* HG3 110 B4
Howard Ct DL10 41 F7
Howard Dr YO30 224 E2
Howard Link YO30 224 D2
Howard Rd
Catterick Garrison DL9 209 E1
Towthorpe YO32 167 B6
Howard St
3 Scarborough YO12 213 A7
York YO10 228 D2
Howden Dike TS15 5 E2
Howden La YO19 231 E1
Howden Rd
4 Barlby YO8 198 B4
Romanby DL7 210 B2
Silsden BD20 174 C1
Howdenshire Way DN14 205 F6
Howdlands La HG4 140 E7
Howe Ave DL10 41 E3
Howe Bank YO21 29 B7
Howe End YO62 70 B1
Howe Field Rd YO26 142 A2
Howe Hill Bank TS8 7 B2
Howe Hill Cl YO26 227 E4
Howe Hill La DL10 41 C6
Howe Hill Rd YO26 227 E4
Howe La YO41 170 A5
Howe Rd Malton YO17 122 A6
Norton YO17 215 E3
Howe St YO24 227 D3
Howes Rd 8 YO14 127 A8
Howgate DL8 57 F6
Howgill La
Barden BD23 157 E6
Rimington BB7 171 A1
Howhill Quarry Rd HG3 178 B7
Howhill Rd HG3 178 B8
Howker La YO61 116 F2
Howl Gate YO41 185 E8
Howlbeck Rd TS14 8 E7
Howldale La
Appleton-le-Moors YO62 70 F4
3 Beadlam YO62 93 D7
Howlgate La YO21 13 A1
Howsham Gates* YO60 146 F2
Howsham Hall Prep Sch YO60 146 F2
Howson La BD24 131 E4
Hoxton Rd YO12 212 F6
Hoylake Rd TS4 6 F8
Hoylake Way TS16 5 E4
Hubback Sq 5 DL3 3 A7
Hubert St 2 YO23 228 B1
Huby CE VC Prim Sch YO61 144 A4
Huby Ct
3 Guisborough TS14 8 F7
York YO10 228 E3
Huby Rd YO61 144 B3
Hudgin La Lockton YO18 72 E4
Wykeham YO13 98 D4
Hudson Cl
Malton YO17 215 C6
Stamford Bridge YO41 168 D2
2 Tadcaster LS24 189 E6
13 Wetherby LS22 180 C3
Hudson Cres 2 YO30 228 A7
Hudson St
Whitby YO21 208 D7
6 York YO30 228 C7
Hudson View 1 LS24 189 E6
Hudson Way LS24 189 E6
Hudswell La DL10 209 C5
Hugden Cl YO18 96 A6
Hugden Way YO17 215 F4
Huggate Dikes* YO42 170 F2
Huggate Hill YO17 170 E7
Hugh Field La YO8 199 A8
Hugh Field N La YO8 193 A1
Hugh St WF10 200 E4
Hull Rd Cliffe YO8 198 E2
Hemingbrough YO8 199 B1
Osbaldwick YO10 229 D3
York YO10 229 B3
Humber Dr 5 YO32 167 B6
Humber Rd TS17 6 B7
Hummersknott Ave DL3 3 A5
Hummersknott Sch & Language Coll DL3 3 A4
Humphrey Balk La YO7 114 D8
Humphrey Hill DL8 58 D1
Hundale Rd 5 TS15 25 C5
Hunday Field Rd YO51 141 E2
Hundens Day Hospl DL1 3 E5
Hundens La DL1 3 D6
Hungate
Bishop Monkton HG3 140 A5
Brompton YO13 98 C5
Pickering YO18 95 F6
York YO1 233 C2
Hungate Cl LS24 195 D8
Hungate Com Prim Sch 22 LS25 195 F4
Hungate Ct 11 YO14 126 F8
Hungate La YO14 126 F8
Hungate Rd LS25 195 F4
Hunger Hill LS29 218 C7
Hungerhill La YO62 93 F6
Hunmanby Prim Sch YO14 126 F8
Hunmanby Rd
Burton Fleming YO25 126 E3
Reighton YO14 127 C6
Hunmanby St YO14 100 F2
Hunmanby Sta YO14 127 A7
Hunt Ct YO31 233 C3
Hunt House Rd YO22 51 B6
Hunt St WF10 200 D4
Hunter St 8 YO21 208 D7
Hunters Cl
Dunnington YO19 184 E7
19 Easingwold YO61 143 C8
10 Haxby YO32 225 C8
4 Hurworth-on-Tees DL2 3 D1
Osgodby YO11 100 B7
Hunters Croft BD23 156 F1
Hunters Gn DL2 4 C3
Hunters Ride DL6 24 B3
Hunters Row 6 YO51 141 B4
Hunters Way
Norton YO17 215 D2
Selby YO8 232 B4
York YO24 230 F7
Hunters Wlk
Barlow YO8 204 D7
Kirk Deighton LS22 180 C4
Hunters Wood Way 21 YO19 184 F7
Huntington Mews YO31 228 D7
Huntington Prim Sch YO32 225 F4
Huntington Rd YO31 233 C4
Huntington Sec Sch YO32 225 E3
Huntington Sports Club YO32 226 A5
Hunton & Arrathorne Com Prim Sch DL8 61 F7
Hunton Rd DL8 40 E1
Huntriss Row YO11 213 A6
Huntsman's Wlk YO24 227 B1
Huntsmans La YO41 168 C2
Hurdle Cl YO17 215 E2
Hurgill Rd DL10 209 A7
Hurn Rd YO61 144 A4
Hurns La YO30 224 A7
Hurrell La YO18 96 E5
Hurricane Cl LS25 196 B4
Hurricane Way YO30 224 E3
Hurrs Rd 3 BD23 217 B4
Hurst Hill HG3 159 F7
Hurst's Yd YO1 233 C2
Hurstleigh Terr HG1 220 A3
Hurworth Comp Sch DL2 22 D8
Hurworth House Sch DL2 3 E1
Hurworth Prim Sch DL2 3 E1
Hurworth Rd
Hurworth DL2 3 F1
Hurworth-on-Tees DL2 22 D8
Neasham DL2 4 A1
Hussars Ct 6 YO12 75 F5
Husthwaite CE VC Sch YO61 117 B5
Husthwaite Rd
Coxwold YO61 117 D7
Easingwold YO61 117 B2
Hutchinson Dr DL6 210 E3
Hutchinson St 1 YO8 232 B6
Hutton Ave DL1 3 E7
Hutton Bank
3 Hutton Rudby TS15 25 D5
Ripon HG4 214 D7
Hutton Cl YO26 224 A2
Hutton Cross Rd YO13 98 E8
Hutton Gate HG2 222 D6
Hutton La
Guisborough TS14 8 E5
Hutton Conyers HG4 114 A4
Sharow HG4 214 E8
Hutton Rae La YO7 116 D7
Hutton Rudby Prim Sch TS15 25 C5
Hutton St YO26 182 A5
Hutton View Rd HG4 214 C7
Hutton Village Rd TS14 8 D5
Hutton's Mon* DL11 39 C6
Hutts La HG4 112 C7
Hyde Pk Rd
Harrogate HG1 219 E3
Knaresborough HG5 221 B8
Hydro Cl LS29 218 F3
Hydro Leisure Ctr The HG2 219 C5
Hyrst Gr YO31 228 E6

I

Ian St TS17 6 B8
I'anson Cl DL8 60 D6
I'anson Rd DL10 209 D7
Ibbetson Cl 16 HG4 86 C3
Iburndale La YO22 32 A6
Iddison Dr DL8 63 A2
Ikin Way YO32 225 F6
Ilkley Gr TS14 8 E5
Ilkley Gram Sch LS29 218 C3
Ilkley Hall Mews 5 LS29 218 B3
Ilkley Hall Pk 4 LS29 218 B3
Ilkley Pool & Lido LS29 218 B5
Ilkley Rd
Addingham LS29 175 A4
Ilkley LS29 176 C1
Ilkley Sch LS29 218 E5
Ilkley Sta LS29 218 B4
Ilkley Swimming Baths LS29 218 C5
Ilkley Toy Mus* LS29 219 B4
Ilton Bank HG4 85 E1
Ilton Garth YO30 225 A2
Imperial Ave TS17 6 B8
In Moor La HG3 109 F6
Ing Dene Ave 16 BB8 186 A3
Ing Dene Cl BD23 155 E3
Ingdale Howl YO62 92 C7
Ingdale La YO7 66 C3
Ingfield La BD24 131 D2
Ingham Cl YO22 32 A6
Ingleborough Ave YO10 229 B4
Ingleborough Cave* LA2 104 D2
Ingleborough Dr 4 BB18 171 D1
Ingleborough National Nature Reserve* LA6 104 D8
Ingleborough Pk Cl 3 LA6 103 D3
Ingleborough Pk Dr 2 LA6 103 D3
Inglebrook Sch WF8 201 B1
Ingleby Arncliffe CE VA Prim Sch DL6 45 A8
Ingleby Ave TS9 27 B6
Ingleby Dr LS24 189 E6
Ingleby Greenhow CE VC Prim Sch TS9 27 C5
Ingleby Manor* TS9 27 C4
Ingleby Mill Prim Sch TS17 6 A4
Ingleby Rd
Great & Little Broughton TS9 27 A5
Great Broughton TS9 26 E5
Ingleby Way TS17 6 B5
Ingleton Dr 16 YO61 143 D8
Ingleton Ind Est LA6 103 D3
Ingleton Mid Sch LA6 103 D3
Ingleton Prim Sch LA6 103 D3
Ingleton Wlk 3 YO31 229 A5
Ingman Lodge Rd BD24 78 F1
Ingramgate YO7 211 C3
Ingrish La YO23 182 C1
Ings Ave BD23 216 D3
Ings Cl 6 Pickering YO18 95 F6
5 Willerby YO12 99 D2
Ings Com Prim Sch BD23 216 D3
Ings Ct DN14 202 F4
Ings Dr
Low Bradley BD20 173 E3
Mickletown LS26 200 C6
Ings Field Rd YO26 142 A3
Ings La
Ainderby Quernhow YO7 88 D4
Beal DN14 202 D4
Bishop Monkton HG3 140 B5
Bishop Wilton YO42 169 D2
Bradleys Both BD20 173 E3
Brompton YO13 98 C4
Carlton DN14 204 E2
Cawood YO8 197 D8
Cononley BD20 173 D2
Cottingwith YO42 193 C5
Crakehall DL8 62 F5
Ebberston & Yedingham YO13 97 E4
Great Preston WF10 200 E6
Harome YO62 93 D4
Hensall DN14 203 D2
Husthwaite YO61 117 A6
Hutton Buscel YO13 99 A3
Ings La *continued*
Kellington DN14 202 F4
21 Kirkbymoorside YO62 70 B1
Kirkbymoorside YO62 94 B7
Lastingham YO62 70 F5
Lillings Ambo YO60 145 C2
Nether Poppleton YO26 224 B1
Pickering YO18 95 E4
Riccall YO19 197 E8
Roundhill Village TS15 5 D2
Skipton BD23 216 D2
Snape with Thorp DL8 87 B7
Stillington YO61 144 A6
Thorganby YO19 193 B5
Thorp Arch LS23 189 A8
Tollerton YO61 143 B2
Welburn YO62 94 A5
Wheldrake YO19 193 B7
Wighill LS24 189 D8
4 Willerby YO12 99 D2
Wistow YO8 198 A6
York YO10 229 A1
Ings Mere Ct WF11 201 C6
Ings Rd Cliffe YO8 198 D2
Dunsforths YO26 142 A3
Snaith DN14 204 C1
Thorganby YO19 193 B4
Ulleskelf LS24 190 C3
West Ayton YO13 99 B6
Wilberfoss YO41 185 E6
Ings Terr YO22 31 C4
Ings View 2 Bedale DL8 63 B3
Castleford WF10 201 A4
Mickletown LS26 200 C6
York YO30 224 D2
Ingsgarth YO18 95 F6
Ingthorne La LS25 195 F1
Ingthorns La LS25 195 F1
Ingthorpe La
Martons Both BD23 171 E7
Monk Fryston LS25 196 A1
Inhams La YO26 141 F2
Inholmes La
Tadcaster LS24 189 D6
Walton LS23 181 B2
Inman Gr HG5 221 B8
Inman Terr YO26 227 D4
Inman Wlk HG5 221 B8
Innisfree Cl HG2 220 B1
Innovation Cl YO10 229 B2
Innovation Way YO10 229 B2
Institute St 4 BD20 187 E7
Intake Ave YO30 228 C8
Intake La
Acaster Malbis YO23 191 C7
Beal WF11 202 D5
Carlton Miniott YO7 89 C4
Dunnington YO19 184 F7
Grassington BD23 134 E3
Habton YO17 121 E7
Heck DN14 207 C8
Tollerton YO61 143 B4
West Haddlesey YO8 202 F6
Intake The
3 Kippax LS25 194 D1
Osgodby YO11 100 B7
Intakefield Rd YO8 199 D7
Invicta Ct YO24 230 B8
Ireby Rd LA6 102 F3
Ireton St 3 YO12 212 E5
Iron Row LS29 176 C1
Irton Moor La YO12 212 A1
Irvine Way YO24 230 B7
Irwin Ave YO31 228 E6
Isabella Rd LS25 194 D5
Island Heritage* HG4 214 B8
Islebeck La YO7 115 F8
Iver Cl YO26 227 C5
Ivy Bank Ct 4 YO13 75 D5
Ivy Cl Follifoot HG3 223 F4
Marton YO51 141 D1
Ivy Cotts DL7 210 D4
Ivy Cres DL8 62 B4
Ivy Ct LS29 218 B3
Ivy House Cl 6 YO11 100 B6
Ivy House Gdns BD23 155 D1
Ivy La LS23 188 E8
Ivy Pl YO32 225 D3
Ivy Yd 16 YO22 208 E6

J

Jack Field La BD20 187 D6
Jack Hill La LS21 176 F6
Jack Hole YO61 142 F4
Jack La Crayke YO61 118 A1
Stillington YO61 144 C7
Wigglesworth BD23 153 C4
Jackson Cl YO11 100 B6
Jackson Dr TS9 26 C8
Jackson La YO41 185 E4
Jackson St
24 Glusburn BD20 187 E7
York YO31 233 C4
Jackson's La
Bradleys Both BD20 173 F3
Eastfield YO11 100 A8
Scarborough YO11 213 A1
Jackson's Wlk YO23 182 D3
Jacobi Cl YO30 228 A7
Jacques Gr BD20 174 C1
Jacques' La YO8 198 E4
Jaffa Rd DL9 209 E2
Jagger La DL10 20 E6

Jagoe Rd **8** BB18 ......172 A1
James Backhouse Pl
  YO24 ....227 E3
James Cl LS25 ....194 D4
James Ct DL10 ....209 F7
James La DL10 ....41 A2
James Nicholson Way
  YO30 ....225 A2
James Nicolson Link
  YO30 ....225 A2
James Pl **2** YO12 ....213 A6
James St
  Castleford WF10 ....200 E5
  20 Earby BB18 ......172 A1
  10 Glusburn BD20 ....187 E8
  Harrogate HG1 ....219 D2
  Scarborough YO12 .....213 A6
  Selby YO8 ....232 C6
  York YO10 ....228 E4
Jameson Cres YO12 ....212 B5
Jamesville Way YO7 ...115 B6
Jamieson Terr YO23 ...228 B1
Janesway LS25 ....194 C1
Janet's Foss★ BD23 ...133 B2
Jasmine Cl
  10 Snaith DN14 .....204 C1
  York YO32 ....225 D2
Jasper La HG3 ....179 A3
Jay Ave TS17 ....6 B4
Jaywick Cl YO32 .....167 B8
Jedburgh Dr DL3 ....2 F7
Jedwell Cl YO32 .....225 D5
Jeffry Bog Nature Reserve★
  YO60 ....147 C5
Jenkins Fold LA6 .....103 D3
Jennifer Gr **4** YO24 .227 D2
Jenny Field Dr HG3 ...219 B4
Jenny Frisk Rd TS12 ....9 E6
Jenny Gill Cres BD23 .217 B3
Jenny La DN14 ....207 B5
Jerry Carr Bank YO62 ..92 B1
Jerry Croft **2** BD23 .217 A4
Jerry La BD20 ....174 F1
Jersey Ct YO12 ....99 C7
Jervaulx Abbey★ HG4 ..85 D8
Jervaulx Dr HG5 .....221 D4
Jervaulx Rd DL7 ......64 A6
Jervis Ct YO41 ......185 C1
Jervis Rd YO24 ......230 E4
Jesmond Ct YO17 .....215 E3
Jesmond Gr **5** TS18 ...5 E7
Jesmond Rd
  Darlington DL1 ....3 F7
  Harrogate HG1 ....220 A3
Jew Leys La YO23 ....190 F3
Jewbury YO31 ....233 C3
Jewitt La LS22 ......188 B8
Jin Whin Ct WF10 ....200 B5
Jin-Whin Hill WF10 ...200 C4
Jobbing Cross YO61 ..116 C3
Jockey La
  Huntington YO32 .....225 D3
  5 Knaresborough HG5 .221 A6
Joffre Ave WF10 .....200 F3
John Breckon Rd YO21 .28 D5
John Dixon La DL1 .....3 F5
John of Gaunt's Castle★
  HG3 ....160 B1
John Smiths Brewery★
  LS24 ....189 C6
John St Darlington DL1 ..3 D6
  11 Earby BB18 ......172 A1
  35 Filey YO14 ......101 B3
  Great Ayton TS9 ....8 A2
  1 Harrogate HG1 .....219 D2
  Selby YO8 ....232 B6
  Whitby YO21 ....208 D7
  York YO31 ....228 E4
Johnson Cl
  Brompton on Swale DL10 .41 C7
  1 Thirsk YO7 ....211 C4
Johnson St YO8 ......232 B6
Johnson Way YO7 ....211 D2
Jolby La Cleasby DL10 ...2 E1
  Croft-on-Tees DL2 ....22 B8
  Newton Morrell DL10 ..21 F8
Jonah's La HG3 ......160 B1
Jonathan Garth **17** LS29 174 F4
Jorvik★ YO1 ....233 C2
Jorvik Cl YO26 ......227 C3
Joseph Rowntree Sec Sch
  YO32 ....225 E5
Jowett's La BD23 ....174 B4
Jowland Winn La YO8 .204 A4
Jubbergate YO1 .....233 B2
Jubilee Bank TS7 ......7 C8
Jubilee Cave★ BD24 ..131 F4
Jubilee Cl BD23 .....216 D3
Jubilee Croft BD23 ...153 F5
Jubilee Ct
  Richmond DL10 ......209 C4
  6 Tollerton YO61 ...143 B3
  Wigginton YO32 .....225 D8
Jubilee Rd
  Norton YO17 ....215 D4
  Wistow YO8 ....197 D6
Jubilee Terr YO26 ....227 F5
Judson Cl HG4 ......214 C4
Julia Ave YO32 ......226 B2
Junction Farm Prim Sch
  TS16 ....5 D5
Juniper Cl YO32 .....225 D3
Juniper Gr TS21 ......5 C8
Juniper Way **28** HG3 ..161 B3
Jura Dr DL1 ....3 E8

Jute Rd YO26 ....227 B5
Jutland Rd DL9 ......209 C2

K

Kader Ave TS5 ....6 D7
Kader Prim Sch TS5 ....6 D7
Kail La BD23 ....156 F8
Kangel Cl HG4 ......214 B3
Kareen Ave **3** YO12 ...99 E6
Kathryn Ave YO32 ....226 A2
Kay House La TS15 ....24 D5
Kaye Dr YO8 ....198 B4
Kays Bank YO61 .....117 C5
Kearby Cliff LS22 ....179 B1
Kearsley Cl TS16 ......5 E7
Kearsley Rd HG4 ....214 B7
Kearton DL11 ....37 D6
Keasden Rd LA2 .....130 A3
Keats Cl
  4 Pontefract WF8 ...201 B1
  York YO30 ....227 B1
Keats Wlk HG1 ......219 E2
Keble Cl YO23 ......231 B3
Keble Dr YO23 ......231 A2
Keble Garth LS25 ....194 E1
Keble Gdns YO23 ....231 B2
Keble Pk Cres YO23 ..231 A2
Keble Pk N YO23 ....231 B3
Keble Pk S YO23 ....231 A2
Keeper's Cl YO61 ....118 A1
Keepers Cliff YO25 ...150 A1
Keepers Gate **18** YO18 ..95 B5
Keepers Way **11** YO19 .184 F7
Keighley Rd
  Bradleys Both BD20 ...173 D3
  1 Colne BB8 ....186 A3
  Cowling BD22 ......187 B3
  2 Glusburn BD20 ....187 F7
  Ilkley LS29 ....218 A2
  Laneshaw Bridge BB8 .186 D3
  Skipton BD23 ......216 F2
  Trawden Forest BB8 ..186 B3
Keilder Rise TS8 ......6 E5
Keith Ave YO32 .....226 A4
Keith Rd TS4 ....6 E8
Kelbrook Prim Sch
  BB18 ....186 A7
Kelbrook Rd BB18 ...171 D1
Kelcbar Cl LS24 .....189 D6
Kelcbar Hill LS24 ...189 D6
Kelcbar Way LS24 ...189 D6
Kelcow Caves★ BD24 .131 D6
Keld Cl Melmerby HG4 .114 B6
  Pickering YO18 ....95 E7
  Scalby YO12 ....212 B8
Keld Head Orch **1** YO62 .70 B1
Keld Head Rd YO62 ...70 A1
Keld La
  Hutton-le-Hole YO62 ..70 C5
  Newton YO18 ....72 A5
  Thorpe Bassett YO17 .123 A3
Keld Runnels Rd YO13 .75 A4
Keldale **4** YO18 ....166 F5
Keldale Gdns HG4 ....214 F6
Keldgate Rd YO18 ....72 A3
Keldhead YO18 ......95 E8
Keldheads La DL8 ....59 F5
Kelfield Rd **9** YO19 .197 F8
Kell Bank HG4 ......85 E3
Kell Bank CE Prim Sch
  HG4 ....85 E3
Kell Beck **1** LS21 ..176 F1
Kell Syke La BD23 ...155 A6
Kellington La DN14 ..202 F2
Kellington Prim Sch
  DN14 ....202 F3
Kelvin Terr DL7 .....210 D4
Kemmel Cl DL9 ......40 E2
Kempton Cl **2** YO24 .227 B1
Kempton Ct **15** DL1 ...3 F7
Kendal Cl
  6 Dunnington YO19 ..184 F7
  Hellifield BD23 .....154 B3
Kendal Dr WF10 ....201 B4
Kendal Gdns YO26 ..181 D7
Kendal La YO26 .....181 D7
Kendal Rd
  Harrogate HG1 ......220 B3
  Long Preston BD23 ..154 A3
Kendalmans **4** BD24 .131 C5
Kendrew Cl **11** Bedale DL8 63 A2
  3 York YO32 ....225 F3
Kenilworth Ave HG2 ..222 D7
Kenilworth Dr **3** BB18 .172 A1
Kenlay Cl YO32 .....225 D4
Kennedy Dr **32** YO32 .166 E5
Kennels La LS14 ....188 A4
Kennet La LS25 .....194 D3
Kenneth Campbell Rd
  HG1 ....219 E2
Kennion Ct **2** HG2 ..220 B3
Kennion Rd HG2 ....220 B3
Kenrick Pl **5** YO26 ..227 B5
Kensal Rise YO10 ...228 C2
Kensington Ave
  Eston & South Bank TS6 .7 E8
  Thorner LS14 ......188 A3
Kensington Ct **1** YO24 .230 F4
Kensington Gdns DL1 ...3 B5
Kensington Rd YO30 ..224 D2
Kensington Sq **10** HG2 .219 C2
Kensington St YO23 ..228 B1
Kent Ave HG1 ....219 B3
Kent Cl HG4 ....214 A2
Kent Ct **7** DL9 ....209 C1
Kent Dr HG1 ....219 B3

Kent Rd Guisborough TS14 ..8 E5
  Harrogate HG1 ......219 B3
  Selby YO8 ....232 A6
Kent Rd N HG1 ......219 B3
Kent Rise HG1 ......219 A2
Kent St YO10 ......233 C1
Kentmere Dr YO30 ..224 F1
Kenton Cl **4** TS18 ...5 E8
Kerrside YO30 ......227 E8
Kershaw Ave WF10 ..201 A4
Kerver La YO19 .....184 F7
Kesteven Rd TS4 .....7 A7
Kestrel Dr **7** DL9 ..40 F2
Kestrel Mews **21** WF6 .200 A1
Kestrel View **2** YO12 ..99 E6
Kestrel Wood Way
  YO31 ....225 F2
Keswick Rd WF10 ...201 C5
Keswick Gr
  Darlington DL1 ....3 D4
  Middlesbrough TS5 ....6 D7
Keswick Way **5** YO32 .225 F5
Kettle End DL10 .....21 C7
Kettle Spring La HG3 .139 B1
Kettlebeck Brow LA2 .130 C5
Kettlesing Felliscliffe Com
  Prim Sch HG3 ......160 C4
Kettlestring La YO30 .225 A3
Kettlewell La LA2 ....57 A5
Kettlewell Prim Sch
  BD23 ....108 A3
Kew at Castle Howard★
  YO60 ....146 C8
Kex Gill Rd HG3 ....158 F2
Kexby Ave YO10 ....228 F3
Kexby Bridge★ YO41 .185 C6
Kexby Stray YO41 ..185 A5
Key La YO61 ....118 A1
Key Way YO19 ......231 F5
Keys Beck Rd YO18 ..71 B5
Keystone Ave **3** WF10 .200 F3
Khyber Pass YO21 ..208 D7
Kiddal La LS15 .....188 C2
Kidstones Bank DL8 ..81 E3
Kielder Dr DL1 ....3 D8
Kielder Oval HG2 ...220 D2
Kilburn Rd YO10 ...228 D2
Kildale Sta YO21 ....27 E8
Kildare Garth **5** YO62 .70 C1
Kildwick CE VC Prim Sch
  BD20 ....187 F8
Kilgram La HG4 ......85 E8
Kilham Rd YO25 ....151 D5
Killerby Dr **2** DL10 ..41 E4
Killerby La YO11 ....100 C5
Killin Rd DL1 ....3 E7
Killinghall CE Prim Sch
  HG3 ....161 C5
Kilmarnock Rd DL1 ...3 C5
Kiln Hill La
  Lawkland LA2 ......131 A6
  Silsden BD20 ......174 A3
Kiln La LA2 ....128 A6
Kilners Croft **11** LS29 .174 F4
Kilnsey Fold BD20 ...174 A1
Kilnsey Pk★ BD23 ..134 B6
Kilnwick Ct YO10 ...210 D3
Kilton La TS12 ......9 F7
Kilton Thorpe La TS13 .10 B8
Kimberley St LS29 ..218 C5
Kimberlows Wood Hill **3**
  YO10 ....229 C3
Kinbrace Dr YO24 ...230 B7
Kinderland★ YO12 ..213 B6
King Edward Ave
  WF10 ....200 C7
King Edward Rd HG4 .214 C3
King Edward St
  27 Glusburn BD20 ..187 E7
  Normanton South WF6 .200 A1
King Edward's Dr
  HG1 ....219 D5
King George Rd **1** HG4 214 C3
King Hill YO14 ......101 A2
King James Rd HG5 ..221 B5
King James's Sch
  HG5 ....221 B5
King Rudding Cl **6**
  YO19 ....198 A8
King Rudding La YO19 .198 B8
King St
  Castleford WF10 .....200 F3
  6 Cawood YO8 .....197 B8
  Muston YO14 ....100 F2
  Normanton South WF6 .200 A1
  Pateley Bridge HG3 ..137 B4
  Richmond DL10 .....209 C6
  Ripon HG4 ....214 C4
  Scarborough YO11 ...213 A6
  York YO1 ....233 B2
King's Cl **9** DL10 ...41 D5
King's Gate LA2 ....130 D3
King's Gdns YO7 ...211 B1
King's Manor Sch TS5 ..6 E7
King's Rd **6** HG1 ..219 D3
King's Sq YO1 .....233 C2
King's St **7** BD23 ..217 B4
King's Staith YO1 ..233 B2
Kingfisher Cl **7** YO12 ..99 F6
Kingfisher Ct
  22 Castleford WF10 .200 A1
  3 Scotton DL9 .....40 F2
Kingfisher Dr
  8 Bedale DL8 ....63 B3
  Guisborough TS14 ....8 E5
  14 Pickering YO18 ...95 F6
  Whitby YO22 ....208 E3

Kingfisher Reach
  17 Boroughbridge YO51 .141 B5
  5 Collingham LS22 ..180 A1
Kings Acre YO31 ....229 B6
Kings Arms Ct YO7 ..211 B3
Kings Ave **2** LS29 ..218 A4
Kings Cl **5** Barlby YO8 .198 B5
  19 Ilkley LS29 ......175 C2
Kings Ct YO1 ....233 B2
Kings Hall★ LS29 ...218 B4
Kings Keld Bank DL8 ..86 E5
Kings La YO13 ....97 D5
Kings Lea YO8 .....199 A8
Kings Mdws YO7 ....89 E3
Kings Mead HG2 ....219 A4
Kings Mill La **8** BD24 .131 D2
Kings Moor Rd YO32 .167 D2
Kings Rd Ilkley LS29 .218 A4
  Knaresborough HG5 ..221 C6
Kingsclere YO32 ....225 F1
Kingsland Terr **11** YO26 .227 F5
Kingsley Ave WF11 ..201 D3
Kingsley Cl HG1 ....220 C3
Kingsley Dr
  Castleford WF10 .....201 B3
  Harrogate HG1 ......220 A4
  2 Middleham DL8 ....60 E2
Kingsley Pk Mews **1**
  HG1 ....220 C3
Kingsley Pk Rd HG1 .220 C3
Kingsley Rd
  Harrogate HG1 ......220 B5
  Trawden Forest BB8 ..186 B3
Kingsthorpe YO24 ..227 D2
Kingston Ave YO24 ..214 C3
Kingston Cres YO8 ..196 E2
Kingston Dr
  24 Castleford WF6 ...200 B1
  Hambleton YO8 .....196 E1
  16 Normanton WF6 ..200 B1
  Norton YO17 ....215 E2
Kingston Garth **2** YO22 .33 C3
Kingston Gr **5** YO12 .212 B7
Kingstonia Gdns **3**
  HG4 ....214 C3
Kingsway
  Garforth LS25 ......194 B3
  Harrogate HG1 ......219 E3
  Pontefract WF8 .....201 B2
  Scalby YO12 ....212 C8
  6 Stamford Bridge YO41 .168 D2
  Weeton LS17 ....178 B2
Kingsway Dr
  Harrogate HG1 ......219 E2
  4 Ilkley LS29 ......218 A4
Kingsway Garth LS25 .194 B3
Kingsway N YO30 ...228 B2
Kingsway W YO24 ..227 D1
Kingswood Gr YO24 .227 D3
Kinloss Cl TS17 .....6 C7
Kinsey Cave★ BD24 .131 C1
Kintyre Dr TS17 .....6 B6
Kiplin Dr **14** DN6 ..206 E2
Kiplin Hall★ DL10 ...42 B4
Kipling Dr DL9 ......41 A5
Kipling Gr WF8 .....201 B2
Kippax Ash Tree Prim Sch
  LS25 ....194 D1
Kippax Greenfield Prim Sch
  LS25 ....194 D1
Kippax Leisure Ctr
  LS25 ....200 D8
Kippax N Jun & Inf Sch
  LS25 ....194 C2
Kir Cres YO24 ......227 C3
Kirby Hill CE Prim Sch
  YO51 ....141 B7
Kirby La
  Ebberston & Yedingham
  YO17 ....97 E1
  Sledmere YO25 .....150 A3
Kirby Misperton La
  YO17 ....121 C7
Kirby Misperton Rd
  YO17 ....95 F2
Kirk Balk YO17 .....169 E8
Kirk Balk La YO60 ..168 B7
Kirk Bank
  Conistone with Kilnsey
  BD23 ....134 B4
  Kirkby Malzeard HG4 .112 A5
Kirk Fenton Parochial CE VC
  Prim Sch LS24 .....196 B8
Kirk Gate
  Brompton YO13 .....98 C7
  Silpho YO13 ....74 E6
Kirk Hammerton CE Prim Sch
  YO26 ....164 C2
Kirk Hammerton La
  YO26 ....164 C3
Kirk Hills LS14 .....188 A3
Kirk Ings La YO7 ....66 B7
Kirk La
  Embsay with Eastby
  BD23 ....217 A4
  Tockwith YO26 .....181 C7
Kirk Rd Eaglescliffe TS15 ..5 F2
Kirk Smeaton CE VC Prim
  Sch WF8 ....206 B3
Kirk Syke La BD23 ..155 A5
Kirk View **1** YO26 ..227 C5
Kirkby & Great Broughton CE
  VA Prim Sch TS9 ....26 C6
Kirkby Ave Ripon HG4 .214 A6
  Selby YO8 ....232 B7
Kirkby Cl HG4 ......214 A6
Kirkby Dr HG4 .....214 A6

Kirkby Fleetham CE Prim Sch
  DL7 ....42 C1
Kirkby in Malhamdale United
  VA Prim Sch BD23 ..154 F8
Kirkby La
  Gillamoor YO62 ......70 A3
Kearby with Netherby
  HG3 ....179 B2
Kirkby TS9 ....26 D6
Kirkby Fleetham with Fencote
  DL7 ....42 C2
Sicklinghall LS22 ....179 D3
Kirkby Malzeard CE Prim Sch
  HG4 ....112 D5
Kirkby Overblow CE Prim Sch
  HG3 ....179 A4
Kirkby Rd
  North Stainley with Sleningford
  HG4 ....113 C4
  Ripon HG4 ....214 A6
  Selby YO8 ....232 B7
Kirkbymoorside Com Prim
  Sch YO62 ....70 A1
Kirkcaldy Fold WF6 ..200 B1
Kirkcroft YO32 .....225 C8
Kirkdale La YO62 ....93 F8
Kirkdale Rd YO10 ...229 D4
Kirkdale Way HG2 ..219 C1
Kirkfield La LS14 ....188 A3
Kirkfield Cres LS14 ..188 A3
Kirkfield La LS14 ....188 A3
Kirkfield Rd DL3 .....3 D8
Kirkgate
  Knaresborough HG5 ..221 A6
  7 Middleham DL8 ...60 E2
  12 Ripon HG4 ......214 C5
  Settle BD24 ....131 D2
  Sherburn in Elmet LS25 .195 E4
  Silsden BD20 ......174 C1
  Thirsk YO7 ....211 B3
Kirkgate La YO62 ....70 F4
Kirkham Augustinian Priory
  (rems of)★ YO60 ...146 F4
Kirkham Ave **1** YO31 .228 E8
Kirkham Bridge★
  YO60 ....146 F4
Kirkham Cl **6** YO21 .208 C6
Kirkham Ct **5** HG5 ..221 C4
Kirkham Gr HG1 ....219 F6
Kirkham Pl HG1 ....219 F6
Kirkham Rd
  Harrogate HG1 .....219 F6
  Middlesbrough TS7 ...7 D6
  Whitby YO21 ......208 C6
Kirkham View YO60 ..147 B4
Kirkhaw La WF11 ...201 D4
Kirkland Cl YO8 ....232 C4
Kirklands YO32 .....167 B6
Kirklands La YO41 ..169 C2
Kirklevington Prim Sch
  TS15 ....24 F8
Kirkstall Dr BB18 ...171 E2
Kirkstone Dr YO31 ..229 A6
Kirkstone Rd HG1 ..220 B4
Kirkwell YO23 .....231 A4
Kit La BD20 ....174 B3
Kitchen Dr YO8 ....232 B4
Kitchener Cl YO8 ...232 B5
Kitchener Rd
  Ripon HG4 ....113 D3
  Scotton DL9 ....40 E4
Kitchener St Selby YO8 .232 B6
  York YO31 ....228 D7
Kitemere Pl **2** YO24 .230 B8
Kitter La YO21 ......31 C8
Kitty Garth YO19 ...193 A7
Kitty Hill (Tumulus)★
  YO41 ....169 E3
Knapping Hill HG1 ..219 C5
Knapton Cl **1** YO30 .167 B6
Knapton La YO26 ...227 B4
Knapton Wold Rd
  YO17 ....123 C5
Knaresborough Ave TS7 ..7 D5
Knaresborough Castle★
  HG5 ....221 A5
Knaresborough House &
  Gdns★ HG5 ....221 A6
Knaresborough Mus★
  HG5 ....221 A5
Knaresborough Rd
  Bishop Monkton HG3 .140 B4
  Follifoot HG3 ......223 F5
  Harrogate HG2 .....219 F4
  Little Ribston LS22 ..180 A8
  Ripon HG4 ....214 C3
Knaresborough Sta
  HG5 ....221 A6
Knaresborough Swimming
  Pool HG5 ....221 B5
Knavesmire Cl YO23 ..93 C5
Knavesmire Cres
  YO23 ....228 B1
Knavesmire Prim Sch
  YO23 ....228 B1
Knavesmire Rd YO23 .228 A1
Knayton CE VC Prim Sch
  YO7 ....65 E3
Kneeton La DL10 ....21 C5
Knightsway LS25 ...194 B3
Knipe Point Dr **8** YO11 .100 B8
Knoll The
  3 Bramham LS23 ...188 E6
  York YO24 ....227 B2
Knolls Cl **11** YO11 ..100 B7
Knolls La YO62 ......67 F5
Knot La BB7 ....171 A5

Knott La
Easingwold YO61 ....143 C8
Steeton with Eastburn
BD20 ....187 F7
Knott Rd YO18 ....49 D5
Knottingley England La Jun &
Inf Sch WF11 ....201 A2
Knottingley High Sch
WF11 ....202 A2
Knottingley Rd WF8 ...201 D1
Knottingley Sta WF11 ..201 F2
Knotto Bottom Cl DL6 .210 F3
Knotto Bottom Way
DL6 ....210 F3
Knotts La BD23 ....152 E1
Knowle La
Ilton-cum-Pott HG4 ....85 D1
Kirby Knowle YO7 ....66 C2
Knowles Cl 5 TS15 ....24 E8
Knox Ave HG1 ....219 C5
Knox Chase HG1 ....219 C6
Knox Cl HG1 ....219 D6
Knox Dr HG1 ....219 C6
Knox Gdns HG1 ....219 C6
Knox Gr HG1 ....219 C6
Knox La Harrogate HG1 .219 D6
Scarborough YO11 ....213 B1
Knox Mill Bank HG3 ...219 B7
Knox Mill Cl HG3 .....219 B7
Knox Mill La HG3 .....219 B7
Knox Pk HG3 ....219 B7
Knox Rd HG1 ....219 C6
Knox Rise HG1 ....219 C6
Knox Way HG1 ....219 C6
Kyle Cl 3 YO61 ....143 C8
Kyle Way YO26 ....227 B8
Kyme Castle★ LS24 ..189 C7
Kyme St YO1 ....233 B1

L

La Bassee Rd DL9 .....209 D1
Laburnum Ave
Fylingdales YO22 ....33 C4
Thornaby TS17 ....6 B7
Laburnum Cl
5 Catterick Garrison DL9 209 B1
Rufforth YO23 ....182 C6
7 Snaith DN14 ....204 C1
3 Thorpe Willoughby YO8 197 B1
Laburnum Dr HG3 .....140 A5
Laburnum Garth 6
YO31 ....228 F8
Laburnum Gr
Harrogate HG1 ....219 C6
Richmond DL10 ....209 D8
Stillingfleet YO19 ......191 D4
Whitby YO21 ....208 B6
Laburnum Rd TS7 ......7 D8
Lacey Ave YO12 ....99 D7
Lachman Rd BB8 ......186 A2
Lack La YO62 ....93 C2
Lackon Bank HG3 .....160 D6
Lacy Gr LS22 ....180 C2
Ladgate La TS5 ....6 F6
Lady Anne Ct YO1 ....233 B1
Lady Balk La WF8 ....201 B1
Lady Edith's Ave YO12 .212 B6
Lady Edith's Cres
YO12 ....212 B6
Lady Edith's Dr YO12 .212 A6
Lady Edith's Pk YO12 .212 B7
Lady Elizabeth Hastings CE
Prim Sch LS23 ....180 F1
Lady Elizabeth Hastings CE
Sch LS23 ....180 A1
Lady Grace's Ride
YO12 ....212 A3
Lady Hamilton Gdns
YO24 ....227 E2
Lady Hartley Ct BB8 ..186 A3
Lady Hullocks Ct 12 TS9 .26 C7
Lady La HG3 ....222 A5
Lady Lumley's Sch
YO18 ....95 F7
Lady Mill Garth YO30 .228 B8
Lady Peckitts Yd YO1 .233 B2
Lady Rd YO30 ....228 B7
Lady Wortley Pl YO23 .231 B6
Ladycarr La YO61 ....143 B8
Ladysmith Ave YO21 .208 C7
Ladysmith Mews 13
YO32 ....167 A7
Ladysmith Rd DL9 .....40 C4
Ladywell La YO51 ....141 B5
Ladywell Rd YO51 ....141 B5
Lairs Cres YO13 ....98 A5
Lairs La YO13 ....98 A5
Lairum Rise LS23 .....188 E7
Laith Staid La LS25 ..195 D4
Laithbutts La LA2 ....130 A4
Lake View WF8 ....201 B2
Lakeber Ave LA2 .....129 A8
Lakeber Dr LA2 ......129 A8
Lakeside
Acaster Malbis YO23 ...191 C7
Darlington DL1 ....3 C4
Hunmanby Sands YO14 .101 A3
Lakeside Cl LS29 .....218 A5
Lakeside Ct 26 WF6 ..200 B1
Lakeside Gr 1 YO32 ..167 B8
Lakeside Mdws WF8 ..201 B2
Lakeside Prim Sch
YO30 ....224 F2
Lakeside Way YO17 ..215 D2
Laking La YO25 ......126 A3

Lamb Inn Rd 9 WF11 .202 A2
Lamb La TS17 ....6 A4
Lamb's La TS9 ....27 B4
Lambert Ct YO1 ......233 B1
Lambert Meml Hospl
YO7 ....211 B2
Lambert St
11 Skipton BD23 ......217 A3
2 Trawden BB8 ....186 B1
Lambeth St 8 BB8 ....186 A3
Lambourne Dr TS7 .....7 C6
Lambs La 12 YO18 .....95 F7
Lamel St YO10 ....229 A3
Lamplugh Cres YO23 .231 B3
Lanacar La DL8 ....56 A4
Lancar Cl 18 YO32 ...166 D5
Lancaster Cl 9 YO13 .75 D5
Lancaster Pk Rd HG2 .220 A3
Lancaster Rd
Harrogate HG2 ....219 C1
North Cowton DL7 ......22 C2
Lancaster St 6 YO11 .213 A6
Lancaster Way
Middlesbrough TS17 .....6 B6
17 Scalby YO13 ....75 D5
York YO30 ....225 A1
Lancers Ct 4 YO12 ..75 F5
Landalewood Rd YO30 .224 D1
Landau Cl YO30 ......227 F8
Landing La
Asselby DN14 ....205 D6
Barlby with Osgodby
YO8 ....232 F8
Haxby YO32 ....225 D1
Hemingbrough YO8 .....204 F8
Riccall YO19 ....197 D8
York YO26 ....227 E6
Landing Rd YO8 ......203 A7
Landings The 21 YO32 .166 F5
Lands La HG5 ....220 E7
Lane Ends La BD22 ...187 B3
Lane Foot Rd HG3 ....159 E8
Lane House La BB8 ...186 B1
Lane House Rd BD22 ..187 A6
Lane The
Gate Helmsley YO41 ...168 B2
Mickleby TS13 ....12 A4
Lanehead La DL11 .....18 H8
Lanehouse Rd TS17 ....6 B6
Laneshaw Bridge Prim Sch
BB8 ....186 B3
Lang Ave YO10 ......229 A4
Lang Gate YO13 ....74 E4
Lang Kirk Cl 2 BD20 .173 F1
Lang Rd
Bishopthorpe YO23 ....230 A3
York YO32 ....225 F6
Langbar Rd YO10 ....229 A6
Langbaurgh Cl TS9 ....8 A2
Langbaurgh Rd TS15 .25 C5
Langber End La LA6 ..154 A6
Langber La BD23 .....154 A6
Langberg Rd 19 YO21 .208 D6
Langbourne Rd YO21 .208 D6
Langburn La YO21 .....29 A7
Langburn's Bank YO21 .29 A7
Langcliffe Ave HG2 ..222 E8
Langcliffe Ave E HG2 .222 E8
Langcliffe Com Prim Sch
BD24 ....131 E4
Langcliffe Garth BD23 .108 B3
Langcliffe Rd BD24 ..131 D3
Langdale TS14 ....8 D6
Langdale Ave
3 Pontefract WF6 .....200 A2
York YO30 ....229 B6
Langdale Dr 2 WF6 ..200 A2
Langdale Gr YO8 .....232 B3
Langdale Mews 4 WF6 .200 A2
Langdale Rd 3 YO12 ..212 F7
Langdale Terr YO21 ..208 C7
Langdon Way TS16 ....5 D5
Langer Hill La HG3 ..160 B5
Langford Cl 21 LS29 .176 C1
Langford Ct 17 LS29 .176 C1
Langford La LS29 ....176 C1
Langford Mews 19 LS29 176 C1
Langford Rd LS29 ....176 C1
Langford Ride 30 LS29 176 C1
Langholm Cres DL3 ...3 C5
Langholme Dr YO26 ..227 C6
Langhorne Dr 2 DL11 .38 B6
Langley Ave TS17 .....5 D5
Langley Ct 1 YO32 ..225 F6
Langley Dr YO17 ....215 E1
Langleys Rd 6 DN6 ..206 E1
Langrickgate La YO42 .193 C5
Langsett Ave 7 YO14 .126 F7
Langsett Gr YO30 ...224 F3
Langstrothdale Rd
BD24 ....105 D7
Langthwaite La DL8 ..59 C3
Langtoft Prim Sch
YO25 ....151 C5
Langton Crossroads
YO17 ....148 B6
Langton Ct 1 YO17 ..167 A6
Langton La YO17 ....148 C8
Langton Prim Sch
YO17 ....147 F5
Langton Rd
Langton YO17 ....148 A7
Norton YO17 ....215 E2
Langwith Ave LS22 ..188 A8
Langwith Stray YO10 .184 C2
Lansdown Way 7 YO32 .166 F5
Lansdowne Rd TS15 ...5 E2

Lansdowne Terr 5
YO10 ....228 E3
Lanshaw Bank BD23 .175 A7
Lanshaw Croft YO30 .224 F1
Lantsbury Dr TS13 ...10 D8
Larch Gr 1 Filey YO14 .101 B4
Pannal HG3 ....222 E2
Larch Rd 6 YO7 ......89 A1
Larch Rise 4 YO7 ...117 D1
Larchfield YO31 .....229 C7
Larchfield Com TS8 ...6 F4
Larchfield Sports Ctr
DL3 ....3 C5
Larchfield St DL3 .....3 C5
Larkfield Cl
1 Copmanthorpe YO23 .230 A3
Harrogate HG2 ....222 A7
Larkfield Dr HG2 ....222 A7
Larkfield Rd
Harrogate HG2 ....222 A7
Selby YO8 ....232 A4
Larkfield Way HG2 ..222 A7
Larkhill Cl HG4 .....214 A6
Larkspur Gr 14 HG3 .161 B3
Larkspur Rd TS7 ......7 A6
Larpool Cres YO22 ..208 D3
Larpool Dr YO22 ....208 D3
Larpool La YO22 ....208 D4
Larpool La Ind Est
YO22 ....208 D5
Larun Beat The TS15 ..5 E2
Lascelles Ct DL6 ....210 E4
Lascelles Gr HG2 ...219 B1
Lascelles La
Malton YO17 ....215 E6
Northallerton DL6 .....210 E4
Lascelles Rd HG2 ...222 B8
Lasenby Cl YO32 ....225 D5
Lastingham Terr
YO10 ....228 D2
Latimer La TS14 ......8 E6
Latimer Rd DL1 ......3 E7
Lauderdale Dr TS14 ...8 F6
Laughton Ave YO12 .212 C5
Laundry La LA6 .....103 D3
Laundry Rd
4 Filey YO14 ....101 B3
3 Harrogate HG1 .....220 C4
Lauradale La BD23 ..134 D1
Laurel Ave TS4 ....7 A8
Laurel Cl Burniston YO13 .75 D8
Gateforth YO8 ....197 B1
Laurel Croft BD23 ...217 D8
Laurels Garth YO60 .145 C5
Laurels The 6 DL6 ..210 E2
Laurence Gr YO8 ....232 D3
Laurence Jackson Sch
TS14 ....8 F7
Lavender Ct 21 DL9 ..41 A5
Lavender Gr YO26 ...227 E5
Laveracks Ind Est
YO41 ....185 B3
Laverick Terr 7 YO8 .208 E6
Laverton Gdns HG3 .219 A4
Law La YO43 ....138 F1
Lawn Ave LS29 .....176 C1
Lawn La DN6 ....207 E3
Lawn Rd 35 LS29 ...176 C1
Lawnfield Dr HG3 ...140 B5
Lawnfield Rd HG3 ...140 B5
Lawns Cl YO32 ......29 E6
Lawns The HG2 .....222 C8
Lawnswood Dr YO30 .227 F8
Lawnway YO31 .....229 A7
Lawrence Cl YO12 ..212 A8
Lawrence Cres DL10 .209 E8
Lawrence Gr YO12 ..212 A8
Lawrence St YO10 ..228 E3
Lawsings Brow LA2 .130 B5
Lawson Ave 1 YO51 .141 B4
Lawson Rd YO24 ....230 F7
Lawsons Cl YO14 ...126 F7
Laycock Fields 11 BD22 .187 B6
Layerthorpe YO31 ...233 C3
Layfield Prim Sch
TS15 ....5 D2
Lazenby Dr 10 LS22 .180 B3
Lazenby Moor La HG5 .141 A4
Le Cateau Com Prim Sch
DL9 ....40 F4
Le Cateau Rd DL9 ...40 F4
Lea Croft LS23 ......188 E7
Lea La YO61 ....143 F4
Lea Way YO32 ......226 A4
Lead La Brompton DL6 ..43 F3
Nether Silton YO7 ......66 B7
Ripon HG4 ....214 B3
Westerdale YO21 ......28 E4
Lead Mill La YO1 ...233 C1
Leadhall Ave HG2 ...222 D6
Leadhall Cl HG2 ....222 D6
Leadhall Cres HG2 ..222 D6
Leadhall Dr HG2 ....222 D7
Leadhall Gdns HG2 .222 D6
Leadhall Gr HG2 ....222 D6
Leadhall La HG2 ....222 C6
Leadhall Rd HG2 ....222 C6
Leadhall View HG2 ..222 D6
Leadhall Way HG2 ..222 C5
Leading Post St 8
YO11 ....213 B6
Leadley Croft YO23 .230 A1
Leafield Rd DL3 ......3 D4
Leahope Ct TS17 .....6 C6
Leahurst Cl YO17 ...215 E2

Leake La YO7 ....65 F6
Leake St
Castleford WF10 ......200 F4
York YO10 ....228 E3
Lealholm Cres TS3 ....7 C8
Lealholm La YO21 ....30 C5
Lealholm Prim Sch
YO21 ....30 C6
Lealholm Sta YO21 ...30 B6
Leamington Rd LS29 .218 C5
Leamington Terr LS29 .218 C5
Learmans Way YO23 .230 C3
Learning La DN14 ...202 F1
Leas Head Rd YO22 ...32 B2
Leas La YO18 ....95 F5
Leas The
11 Brafferton YO61 ..115 F1
Darlington DL1 ....3 D8
8 Eastfield YO11 .....99 F7
Lease Rigg La YO22 ..31 A3
Leases La DL10 ......41 E2
Leases Rd DL10 ......63 C5
Leasmires Ave 10 YO61 .143 C8
Leat Cl YO17 ....215 D2
Leather Bank YO22 ..176 C1
Leathley La LS21 ....177 D1
Leavening Com Prim Sch
YO17 ....147 E2
Leazon Hill 1 YO7 ....6 D6
Leck St Peter's CE Prim Sch
LA6 ....102 A1
Leconfield Garth HG3 .223 F5
Ledbury Way TS14 ....8 E6
Ledesway 1 BD23 ...134 E3
Ledgate La LS25 ....201 E6
Ledston Ave DL6 ....194 D3
Ledston Mill La WF10 .200 F8
Ledston Hall★ WF10 .200 F8
Lee Ct DN14 ....207 A7
Lee View DN14 .....207 A7
Lee Way WF10 ......200 F3
Leech La DL8 ....41 E4
Leeds Barnsdale Rd
WF10 ....200 D3
Leeds La LS26 ......194 A3
Leeds Rd
Allerton Bywater WF10 .200 D7
Barwick in Elmet & Scholes
LS15 ....194 A7
Castleford WF10 ......200 E3
Collingham LS22 ......188 A8
Great Preston WF10 ..200 C7
Harrogate HG2 ....219 D1
Ilkley LS29 ....218 D5
Kippax LS25 ....194 C2
Mickletown LS26 ......200 A6
Pannal HG3 ....222 F3
Selby YO8 ....232 A4
Tadcaster LS24 ....189 D5
Leeman Rd YO26 ...233 A2
Leeming & Londonderry Com
Prim Sch DL7 ....63 D4
Leeming Bar Ind Est
DL7 ....63 C5
Leeming Bar Sta DL7 .63 C5
Leeming La
Brough with St Giles
DL10 ....41 D5
Burneston DL8 ....87 F8
4 Burton in Lonsdale LA6 102 F1
Catterick DL10 ....41 D4
Kirklington-cum-Upsland
YO7 ....88 A4
Langthorpe YO51 ......141 B6
Leeming DL7 ....63 C4
Melmerby HG4 ....114 D8
Theakston DL7 ....63 E1
Thornthwaite with Padside
HG3 ....159 D5
Leeming RAF Com Prim Sch
DL7 ....63 C3
Lees La DL7 ....210 B1
Leeside YO24 ....230 E8
Legion St LS25 .....195 F2
Legram La YO26 ....163 D8
Legram Rd YO26 ....163 D8
Leicester Cres LS29 .218 B5
Leicester Way
Aislaby TS16 ....5 D4
York YO1 ....233 C1
Leighton Cl YO12 ...99 E6
Leighton Croft 3 YO30 .224 F1
Leighton Rd 6 TS18 ..5 D8
Leisure Pk YO32 ....226 A2
Leith Rd DL3 ....3 A5
Leming Bar Sta DL7 .63 C5
Lendal YO1 ....233 B2
Lendales La YO18 ....95 E3
Lennerton La LS25 ..196 C3
Lennox Ave DL10 ...209 D7
Lennox Cl 2 YO14 ..127 A8
Lennox Pl HG3 .....113 D3
Leonard St 18 BB18 .171 D1
Leppington Dr YO12 .212 C4
Leppington La YO17 .147 D1
Lerecroft Rd YO24 ..230 D8
Lesley Ave YO10 ....231 E8
L'Espec St DL7 .....210 D3
Leven Bank Rd TS15 .25 D4
Leven Cl TS16 ....5 D4
Leven Ct TS9 ....8 A1
Leven Rd Eaglescliffe TS15 .5 E3
Stokesley TS9 ....26 B7
York YO10 ....230 D7
Leven Wynd 9 TS9 ...26 C7
Levendale 6 TS15 ....25 C5
Levendale Prim Sch
TS15 ....5 F3

Levens Cl HG3 ......161 B4
Levenside Great Ayton TS9 .7 F1
4 Hutton Rudby TS15 .25 D5
Stokesley TS9 ....26 C7
Levick Cres TS5 ......6 D8
Levisham St YO10 ...228 D2
Levisham Sta YO18 ...72 B5
Lewes Rd DL1 ....3 D4
Lewis Cl
1 Croft-on-Tees DL2 .22 C8
Northallerton DL6 .....210 F5
Lewis Rd DL6 ....210 F5
Lexden Ave TS5 ......6 D8
Leyburn Com Prim Sch
DL8 ....60 D5
Leyburn Gr 1 TS18 ...5 D8
Leyburn Old Globe Nature
Reserve★ DL8 ....60 B4
Leyburn Pl 8 YO14 .101 A3
Leyburn Rd Askrigg DL8 .57 F6
Darlington DL1 ....3 D7
Masham HG4 ....86 B4
Middleham DL8 ....60 E3
Scotton DL9 ....40 C4
Leyburn Sta DL8 .....60 D5
Leyes The YO10 ....229 C4
Leyfield Cl 1 YO32 .167 A7
Leyland Cl BB8 .....186 A2
Leyland Cres 3 HG1 .220 A3
Leyland Rd
Harrogate HG1 ....220 A3
York YO31 ....229 A5
Leys La
Boston Spa LS23 ......188 D8
Darrington WF11 ......206 A8
Glusburn BD20 ....187 B8
Knottingley WF11 .....201 F1
Little Smeaton WF8 ..206 B4
Leys Rd WF11 ......206 A7
Leysthorpe La YO62 ..93 B2
Liardet Rd 19 DL10 ..41 E4
Libanus Ct 16 TS17 ..5 F4
Library Sq YO1 .....233 B3
Lichfield Ct 6 YO23 .228 B1
Lichfield Gr HG3 ....219 A4
Lickley St HG4 .....214 D5
Lidget Croft BD20 ..173 E3
Lidget La HG5 ......163 B5
Lidget Rd BD20 ....173 E3
Lidgett Gr YO26 .....227 B6
Lidgett Gr Sch YO26 .227 B6
Lidgett La LS25 ....194 C3
Lidice Rd DN14 ....205 E2
Lidsty Hill YO62 ....70 E5
Lifeboat Mus★ YO21 .208 D7
Light Bank La BD20 .174 E2
Light La DL8 ....59 E5
Lightfoot's La YO12 .212 D3
Lightfoots Ave YO12 .212 D3
Lightfoots Cl YO12 .212 C3
Lightfoots Rd YO12 .212 D3
Lightmire La YO26 ..142 A1
Lightwater Valley Miniature
Rly★ HG4 ....113 C6
Lightwater Valley Theme
Pk★ HG4 ....113 C6
Lilac Ave
Appleton Roebuck YO23 .190 F5
Thornaby TS17 ....6 B7
York YO10 ....229 B3
Lilac Cl 7 LS29 .....175 A4
Lilac Gr Harrogate HG1 .219 E6
New Earswick YO32 ..225 D4
Lilac Rd TS7 ....7 D7
Lilac Wlk YO12 .....212 D7
Lilbourne Dr YO30 ..228 A8
Lile Cl DL10 ....209 C7
Lilla Cl YO8 ....208 A6
Lilling Ave 3 YO31 .228 E8
Lilling La YO60 .....145 E3
Lilling Low La YO60 .145 C2
Lilly Gate La HG3 ...162 A8
Limber Hill YO21 ....30 E4
Lime Ave YO31 .....228 F7
Lime Chase 10 YO62 .70 B1
Lime Cl 10 YO13 ...174 E4
Lime Gr Harrogate HG1 .219 F3
4 Whitby YO21 ......208 C6
Lime Kiln La LS22 ..180 B5
Lime La DL8 ....87 F2
Lime Rd Eaglescliffe TS16 .5 E3
Guisborough TS14 .....8 E7
Sinnington YO62 ......94 D8
Lime St HG1 ....219 F3
Lime Tree Ave
Boston Spa LS23 ......188 E8
8 Easingwold YO61 ..117 D1
Malton YO17 ....215 D6
York YO32 ....225 D3
Lime Tree Gr 8 YO8 .232 A6
Lime Tree Mews 15
YO19 ....184 F7
Lime Wlk HG4 ......214 B2
Limebar Bank Rd
YO51 ....141 D1
Limebar La YO51 ...141 C2
Limegarth 10 YO26 .165 F1
Limehouse La BD23 .216 E1
Limekiln Bank HG4 .113 C1
Limekiln Hill YO25 .150 B3
Limekiln La
Burton Leonard HG3 .140 A1
East Layton DL11 ......1 B1
8 Eastfield YO11 ....100 B6
Halton West BD23 ...154 A1

Limekiln La continued
North Stainley with Sleningford HG4 113 C5
Snape with Thorp HG4 86 D5
Limekiln Rd YO7 65 F5
Limes Ct YO31 228 F6
Limes The
Burniston YO13 75 C8
Helmsley YO62 92 F6
Stockton-on-the-Forest YO32 167 D2
Limestone Gr YO13 75 C8
Limestone La YO13 75 A5
Limestone Rd YO13 75 B7
Limestone Way YO13 75 C8
Limetree Cl 2 YO8 197 B1
Lime-tree Cres LS25 194 E1
Limetrees WF8 201 D2
Limpsey Gate La YO18 72 D6
Limpton Gate TS15 5 E2
Linacre Way DL1 3 D7
Lincoln Gr HG3 219 A5
Lincoln Rd 30 BB18 172 A1
Lincoln St YO26 227 F5
Lindale 2 YO24 230 C7
Linden Ave Darlington DL3 3 B5
Great Ayton TS9 7 F1
Linden Cl Great Ayton TS9 7 F2
4 Hutton Rudby TS15 25 C4
Sleights YO21 32 B7
York YO32 225 F5
Linden Cres
Great Ayton TS9 7 F1
5 Hutton Rudby TS15 25 C4
Middlesbrough TS7 7 B6
Linden Dr Hurworth DL2 3 D1
1 Hurworth-on-Tees DL2 22 D8
Linden Gdns DL10 209 D7
Linden Gr Great Ayton TS9 7 F1
Thornaby TS17 6 B8
1 York YO30 228 A8
Linden Rd 9 Earby BB18 172 A1
Great Ayton TS9 7 F1
Northallerton DL6 210 E4
Scalby YO12 212 A8
Linden Way
9 Thorpe Willoughby YO8 197 B2
Wetherby LS22 180 B4
Lindhead Sch YO13 75 C8
Lindhead Rd YO13 75 B8
Lindisfarne Rd TS3 7 C8
Lindley Rd YO30 224 F1
Lindley St Skipton BD23 216 F2
York YO24 227 F3
Lindley Wood Gr YO30 224 E3
Lindon Rd DL10 20 F1
Lindrick Cl
32 Castleford WF6 200 B1
3 Ripon HG4 214 B2
Lindrick Way HG3 219 A4
Lindsay Rd LS25 194 C3
Lindsey Ave YO26 227 D4
Linen Way 10 DL6 43 F3
Ling Croft LS23 188 D8
Ling Fields BD23 216 C4
Ling Gill National Nature Reserve* BD23 79 C1
Ling Hill YO12 212 B7
Ling La YO41 185 F6
Ling Trod YO17 123 D4
Lingcrag Gdns BD22 187 B6
Lingcroft Cl YO8 204 D4
Lingcroft La
Naburn YO19 231 E3
Tockwith LS22 181 A6
Lingdale Prim Sch TS12 9 F7
Lingdale Rd
Lockwood TS12 9 E7
Thornaby TS17 6 C7
Lingfield Ash TS8 7 A5
Lingfield Cl DL1 3 F5
Lingfield Cres YO24 227 F1
Lingfield Prim Sch TS7 7 B5
Lingfield Rd TS15 5 F3
Lingfield Way DL1 4 A5
Lingham La YO7 115 A3
Linghaw La LA2 129 C7
Lingholm Cres 9 YO11 99 F7
Lingholm La YO11 100 D4
Lingmoor La YO62 70 E3
Lingrow Cl 3 TS13 12 A7
Link Ave YO30 228 C8
Link Rd YO31 225 E2
Link Rd Ct YO19 229 D4
Link The
Copmanthorpe YO23 230 A3
Middlesbrough TS3 7 C8
Northallerton DL7 210 B2
Selby YO8 232 A4
York YO10 231 E8
Link Wlk 5 YO11 100 A6
Linkfoot La YO62 93 A6
Links Cl HG2 220 E3
Links Dr LA2 129 A8
Links Prim Sch The TS16 5 E5
Links The
7 North Featherstone WF7 200 E1
Tadcaster LS24 189 E5
Links Way HG2 220 E3
Linkway DN6 206 E2
Linnburn Mews 1 LS29 218 B3
Linnet Way YO24 230 C8
Linton Ave 9 LS22 180 B3
Linton Cl
Cloughton YO13 54 D1
19 Filey YO14 101 B3
Linton Com LS22 179 F1
Linton Ct 8 BD23 216 F3
Linton Falls 1 BD23 134 E2
Linton La LS22 180 B2
Linton Mdw 5 YO30 164 F7
Linton Mdws 7 LS22 180 B3
Linton on Ouse Prim Sch YO30 165 A7
Linton Pl 4 YO30 164 F7
Linton Rd
Collingham LS22 180 A1
Poppleton YO26 224 A1
Wetherby LS22 180 B3
Linton Rise 17 DL9 40 E4
Linton St 5 YO26 227 E5
Linton Woods YO30 165 A7
Linton Woods La YO30 165 A8
Linwith La DN14 204 C3
Linwood Ave TS9 26 C8
Lippersley La BD20 174 D3
Lisheen Ave WF10 200 F4
Lismore Pl YO12 212 E1
Lismore Rd YO12 212 E1
Lister Hill 5 BD20 187 E6
Lister St LS29 218 A4
Lister Way YO30 228 A7
Lisvane Ave YO12 212 D4
Litley Bank YO7 66 B5
Little Ave YO30 228 B8
Little Ayton La
Great Ayton TS9 8 A1
27 Roundhill Village TS17 5 F4
Little Beck Bank YO22 32 C4
Little Beck La YO22 32 B3
Little Beck Wood Nature Reserve* YO22 32 B3
Little Brook BD23 217 B4
Little Catterton La LS24 190 A7
Little Church La LS26 200 B5
Little Comm La DN14 207 C5
Little Croft HG3 139 C4
Little Crossing HG4 214 E2
Little Field La YO18 72 C5
Little Garth YO26 224 A2
Little Hallfield Rd YO31 228 E5
Little Harries La HG4 214 A7
Little Heck Comm La DN14 203 D1
Little Hutton La DL11 1 A4
Little Ings Cl LS24 196 C8
Little Ings La YO51 141 C5
Little King St 5 HG3 137 B4
Little La Brompton DL6 44 A3
12 Easingwold YO61 143 C8
Ellerton YO42 193 C1
11 Haxby YO32 166 E5
Ilkley LS29 218 C4
Little Smeaton DN6 206 D4
North Stainley with Sleningford HG4 113 C4
Little Mdws YO32 225 D8
Little Moor Cl YO13 54 C1
Little Moor La YO8 232 A8
Little Pasture 3 TS17 6 D5
Little Stonegate YO1 233 B3
Little Studley Cl HG4 214 C7
Little Studley Pk HG4 214 C8
Little Studley Rd HG4 214 C7
Little Westfield YO25 151 C3
Little Wood St YO17 215 E3
Littlebeck Dr DL1 3 E7
Littleboy Dr TS17 6 C8
Littledale YO18 95 F7
Littlefield Cl 5 YO26 165 F1
Littleside DL8 83 E7
Littlethorpe Cl
Harrogate HG3 219 A4
7 Strensall YO32 167 B8
Littlethorpe La HG4 214 D2
Littlethorpe Pk HG4 214 E3
Littlethorpe Potteries* HG4 140 A7
Littlethorpe Rd HG4 214 E3
Littondale Ave HG5 221 D6
Liverton La TS13 10 D6
Liverton Mill Bank TS12 10 B6
Liverton Rd TS13 10 D7
Livingstone Rd YO12 212 E6
Livingstone St YO26 227 F5
Lloyd Cl YO10 229 B1
Lob La YO41 168 D2
Lochrin Pl 2 YO26 227 B4
Lock Cl DN14 207 F6
Lock La
Castleford WF10 200 E5
Normanton WF6 200 A3
Lock La Sports Ctr WF10 200 F5
Lock Wlk DL10 41 E4
Locker La HG4 214 C4
Lockey Croft YO32 225 C8
Lockeys Terr 3 YO22 208 E6
Lockfield Dr BB18 171 E2
Lockgate Rd DN14 207 C4
Lockheed Cl TS18 5 F7
Lockton Cres TS17 6 A6
Lockton Ct LS24 196 B7
Lockton La YO18 72 E4
Lockton Rd YO21 208 A6
Lockwood Chase YO13 54 D1
Lockwood Prim Sch TS12 9 D7
Lockwood St YO31 233 C3
Lockyer Cl 4 YO30 228 A8
Locomotion Ct 5 TS16 5 D5
Loders Gn 5 YO11 99 F6
Lodge Cl 7 YO11 100 B6
Lodge Gdns
Gristhorpe YO14 100 E4
5 Snaith DN14 204 C1
Lodge La 5 Brompton DL6 43 F3
Danby YO21 29 D7
Gowdall DN14 203 F1
Newby with Mulwith HG4 140 E6
Wennington LA2 102 B1
Lodge Rd
Hutton-le-Hole YO62 70 C5
Lythe YO21 12 E3
Settle BD24 153 E8
Lodore Gr TS5 6 D7
Lofthouse La YO41 185 D7
Loftus Cl YO12 212 B4
Lombards Wynd DL10 209 C7
Londesborough Gr 5 YO8 197 B2
Londesborough Pk 10 YO12 99 D6
Londesborough Rd YO12 212 E4
Londesborough St 5 YO8 232 C5
London La DN6 207 D1
Long Acre Ct HG3 222 E2
Long Acre Wlk HG3 222 E2
Long Ashes Leisure Ctr BD23 134 B3
Long Band DL8 58 A8
Long Bank DL11 19 C6
Long Bank La BD23 153 E1
Long Barrow*
Thixendale YO17 170 A7
Willerby YO12 125 E7
Long Cl La YO10 233 C1
Long Crag View 1 HG3 161 B2
Long Cswy
Arkengarthdale DL11 16 C6
Halton East BD23 174 B8
Thirkleby High & Low with Osgodby YO7 90 D1
Long Cswy Rd
Danby YO21 29 E3
Hutton Buscel YO13 99 A4
Long Furrow YO32 225 C8
Long Gate BD22 187 D4
Long Gn 7 BB18 172 B1
Long Heads La LS25 195 F1
Long Hill End BD22 187 B5
Long Ing La BB18 171 E1
Long La
Barwick in Elmet LS15 194 C7
Borrowby YO7 65 E5
Brompton DL6 44 A6
Catton YO41 185 D6
Cawood YO8 197 A6
Cowling BD22 187 B7
East Ayton YO13 99 B7
Ellerton YO42 193 F1
Farndale East YO62 48 F4
Felliscliffe HG3 160 E3
Gayles DL11 19 E6
Heck DN14 207 D8
Heslington YO10 184 C3
Kirk Smeaton WF8 206 B1
Laneshaw Bridge BB8 186 B4
Lockwood TS12 10 B5
Normanby YO62 95 A4
Picton TS15 24 E6
Seamer YO12 99 E6
Slingsby YO62 120 D6
Tatham LA2 128 E7
Well DL8 87 C4
Long Level LA6 102 C8
Long Mann Hills Rd YO8 232 B4
Long Marston CE VC Prim Sch YO26 182 A6
Long Mdw 7 Colne BB8 186 A3
Skipton BD23 217 B5
Long Mdw Gate LS25 194 C2
Long Mdws
Garforth LS25 194 C3
6 Ilkley LS29 176 C1
Rillington YO17 122 F5
Long Newton La TS21 5 A6
Long Preston Endowed VA Prim Sch BD23 153 F5
Long Preston Sta BD23 153 F4
Long Rampart YO42 193 D3
Long Riddings LS29 174 F5
Long Ridge Dr YO26 224 A1
Long Ridge La YO26 224 A1
Long Royd Rd BB18 172 A1
Long St Asenby YO7 115 B6
Easingwold YO61 143 C8
Thirsk YO7 211 C3
Topcliffe YO7 115 C6
Long Stoop Standing Stone* HG3 160 A2
Long Stps 8 YO22 208 E6
Long Swales La HG4 112 D5
Long Trods 5 YO8 232 C6
Long Wlk
Knaresborough HG5 221 A6
Scarborough YO12 212 D7
Longacre WF10 200 E3
Longbank Rd TS7 7 D7
Longber La LA6 102 D4
Longbow Ave LS26 200 B6
Longcroft 2 YO32 166 E5
Longcroft Rd 1 LS29 218 E3
Longdale Ave 18 BD24 131 D2
Longdike La
Kippax LS25 200 E8
Thornton Steward HG4 61 E1
Longfield Comp Sch DL3 3 C8
Longfield Ct 21 BB18 171 D1
Longfield Rd DL3 3 C7
Longfield Terr YO30 233 A3
Longland La YO26 164 A3
Longlands Field Rd YO26 163 D8
Longlands La
Boroughbridge YO51 141 A3
Danby YO21 29 B6
Hetton BD23 155 F5
Sicklinghall LS22 179 E3
Thornton-le-Dale YO18 96 E5
Longlands Rd YO17 123 B3
Longmans Hill CP Sch YO8 232 C3
Longtons La BD23 152 F4
Longwestgate YO11 213 B6
Longwood Bank DL10 209 D5
Longwood Link 8 YO30 224 E3
Longwood Rd YO30 224 F3
Lonsdale Mdws LS23 188 E8
Lonsdale Pl 12 YO13 99 B8
Lonsdale Rd YO11 213 A3
Loos Rd DL9 40 F3
Loraine Cres DL1 3 C4
Lord Ave TS17 6 B5
Lord Deramore's Prim Sch YO10 229 C1
Lord Mayor's Wlk YO31 233 B3
Lord's Cl 23 BD24 131 D2
Lord's Cl Rd LA2 129 B3
Lord's La DL8 63 C2
Lords La
Ainderby Mires with Holtby DL8 41 F1
Hackforth DL8 62 E8
Upper Poppleton YO26 165 E2
Lords Moor La YO32 167 C7
Lordship La
16 Barlby YO8 198 A4
Wistow YO8 232 D8
Loriners Dr 7 YO23 230 B3
Loring Rd YO13 54 A7
Lorne St YO23 228 B1
Lorraine Ave 3 YO41 185 B2
Loscoe Cl WF6 200 C2
Loshpot La LS22 180 C5
Lothersdale Com Prim Sch BD20 186 F8
Lothersdale Rd BD20 187 B8
Lotherton La LS25 195 A7
Lotherton Way LS25 194 C4
Louisa St DL1 3 D5
Lousy Hill La YO22 32 C3
Louvain St 5 BB18 171 D2
Love La Brawby YO17 94 F1
Castleford WF10 200 E3
Easby DL10 209 E4
8 Leyburn DL8 60 D5
Nunthorpe YO10 231 C8
Whitby YO21 208 A7
York YO24 228 A2
Lovers' La DL7 64 F2
Low Bank
4 Embsay BD23 217 E8
Over Silton DL6 66 A8
Low Beck LS29 218 D5
Low Bentham Com Prim Sch LA2 128 F8
Low Bentham Rd LA2 128 F8
Low Catton Rd YO41 185 C8
Low Cl LS29 218 A5
Low Comm LS26 200 C4
Low Croft 6 YO32 167 A7
Low Demesne La LA6 103 D3
Low Demesne Cl 4 LA6 103 D3
Low Farm LS26 200 C8
Low Farm Cl
Bolton Percy YO23 190 D4
Thornton TS8 6 D4
Low Field La
Cold Kirby YO7 91 D7
Goldsborough HG5 163 A1
Marton cum Grafton YO51 141 E2
Staveley HG5 140 E1
Low Fields Dr YO24 227 C3
Low Fold BB18 186 A7
Low Garth YO22 32 A6
Low Garth Link 17 LS25 195 F4
Low Garth Rd LS25 195 F4
Low Gate DL8 57 F5
Low Gate La HG4 138 F7
Low Gn Catterick DL10 41 D4
Copmanthorpe YO23 230 B2
13 Knottingley WF11 202 A2
Menwith with Darley HG3 160 A6
Low Holland WF11 201 C6
Low Hospl Yd 6 YO22 208 E6
Low House La
Carlton Miniott YO7 89 C2
Dishforth YO7 115 B2
Low Hutton Pk YO60 147 C6
Low La Askrigg DL8 58 B4
Low La continued
Carperby-cum-Thoresby DL8 58 F4
Cononley BD20 173 C2
Cowling BD22 187 A8
Cropton YO18 71 B4
Dalby-cum-Skewsby YO60 119 B2
Dalton DL11 19 D7
Embsay with Eastby BD23 217 E8
Grassington BD23 134 E3
Grinton DL11 37 E5
Heslington YO10 229 D1
Howsham YO60 147 A1
Hutton-Sessay YO7 116 B7
Leck LA6 102 D7
Leyburn DL8 60 C4
Lythe YO21 12 D3
Maltby TS17 6 B3
Menwith with Darley HG3 159 F6
Mickleby TS13 12 A3
Middlesbrough TS5 6 E6
Muker DL11 36 C4
Newsham DL11 18 H7
Reeth, Fremington & Healaugh DL11 37 F5
Silsden BD20 174 B3
Spofforth with Stockeld HG3 179 C4
Stainburn LS21 177 F3
Sutton-under-Whitestonecliffe YO7 90 E6
Swinton YO17 121 C4
Thirkleby High & Low with Osgodby YO7 90 C1
West Rounton DL6 24 D3
Westow YO60 147 C4
Wigglesworth BD23 153 D3
Low Mdw YO8 232 C6
Low Mill* DL8 57 D5
Low Mill Cl YO10 229 D3
Low Mill Est HG4 214 E5
Low Mill La LS29 175 A4
Low Mill Rd HG4 214 D4
Low Moor Ave 3 YO10 231 F8
Low Moor La
Askham Richard YO23 182 D3
Brearton HG5 162 B7
East Harlsey DL6 44 C7
Fearby HG4 85 F3
Hessay YO26 182 C8
Rillington YO17 122 E6
Low Moor Rd YO18 71 F5
Low Moor S La YO17 122 D6
Low Moorgate YO17 122 F5
Low Ousegate YO1 233 B2
Low Peter La HG3 140 A3
Low Petergate YO1 233 B3
Low Pk Rd LS29 176 A3
Low Poppleton La YO26 227 B7
Low Rd Gainford DL2 1 C7
Gowdall DN14 204 A1
Irton YO12 75 B3
Kellington DN14 202 F4
Kirby Grindalythe YO17 149 F7
Newby & Scalby YO12 212 A6
Thirkleby High & Low with Osgodby YO7 116 E8
Low Skellgate HG4 214 C5
Low Sleights Rd LA6 104 B7
Low St Aiskew DL7 63 C6
Austwick LA2 130 E7
Burton in Lonsdale LA6 102 F3
Carlton DN14 204 C2
Husthwaite YO61 117 B6
Kirkby Fleetham with Fencote DL10 41 F2
Knottingley WF11 201 E4
Lastingham YO62 70 E5
Nunnington YO62 93 E2
Oswaldkirk YO62 92 F3
Ripon HG4 214 D5
22 Scalby YO13 75 D5
Sherburn in Elmet LS25 195 F4
Thornton-le-Clay YO60 146 A4
Low St Agnesgate HG4 214 D4
Low Stanghow Rd TS12 9 F6
Low Thorpe DL8 85 D8
Low Town Bank Rd YO61 91 B4
Low Tun Way YO62 69 A2
Low Wath Rd HG3 137 B4
Low Way 5 LS23 188 E5
Low Well Pk YO19 192 F7
Low Westfield Rd YO23 230 A1
Low Wood La
Glaisdale YO21 30 C6
Leyburn DL8 60 C4
Low Wood Rise LS29 218 F3
Lowcroft
9 Collingham LS22 188 A8
High Bentham LA2 129 B8
Lowcross Ave TS14 8 E5
Lowcross Dr TS9 26 E5
Lowdale Ave YO12 212 E8
Lowdale Ct 4 YO22 32 A6
Lower Clark St
2 Scarborough YO12 212 F6
13 Scarborough YO12 213 A7
Lower Constable Rd LS29 218 D3
Lower Croft St 39 BB18 172 A1

Lower Darnbrough St
  YO23 . . . . .233 B1
Lower Derwent Valley Nat
  Nature Reserve★
  YO42 . . . . .199 C8
Lower Flat Cliffs
  YO14 . . . . .101 C1
Lower Friargate YO1 . .233 B2
Lower Greenfoot 15
  BD24 . . . . .131 D2
Lower Mickletown
  LS26 . . . . .200 C6
Lower Oxford St
  WF10 . . . . .200 E4
Lower Pk Marina★
  BB18 . . . . .171 E1
Lower Priory St YO1 . .233 A1
Lower Sta Rd 3 WF6 . .200 A1
Lower Union St BD23 . .216 F3
Lower Wellington Rd
  LS29 . . . . .218 B4
Lower William St 3
  YO12 . . . . .212 F6
Lower York Ct HG1 . . .220 D6
Loweswater Rd 5 YO30 224 E1
Lowfield
  3 Eastfield YO11 . . . . .100 A6
  Hawes DL8 . . . . .56 C4
Lowfield Dr YO32 . . . .166 E5
Lowfield La
  Beamsley BD23 . . . . . .174 F7
  Kirkby Fleetham with Fencote
  DL7 . . . . .42 D2
  Langthorpe YO51 . . . . .141 A6
  Rufforth YO26 . . . . . . .227 A4
  Scrayingham YO41 . . . .169 A7
  Sharow HG4 . . . . .214 F6
  Snape with Thorp DL8 . . .87 A4
Lowfield Rd
  Barlby with Osgodby
  YO8 . . . . .198 B5
  Hillam LS25 . . . . .202 C8
  Malton YO17 . . . . .215 C6
Lowfield Sec Sch
  YO24 . . . . .227 D3
Lowfields 2 YO12 . . . . .99 D2
Lowfields Ave
  Ingleby Barwick TS17 . . . .6 A5
  Roundhill Village TS17 . . . .6 D5
Lowgate DN14 . . . . . . .207 D5
Lowgill La LA2 . . . . . . .128 F4
Lowick YO24 . . . . .230 C7
Lowkber La LA6 . . . . . .103 C5
Lowlands Dr DL7 . . . . . .63 C5
Lowmoor Rd YO8 . . . . .198 B6
Lown Hill YO24 . . . . . .227 C2
Lowna Rd YO62 . . . . . .70 B5
Lownorth Rd YO13 . . . . .53 C2
Lowskellgate 15 HG4 . .214 C5
Lowswater Rd WF11 . . .201 A1
Lowther Cres 3 LS26 . .194 A1
Lowther Ct YO31 . . . . .233 A1
Lowther Dr
  Garforth LS25 . . . . . . .194 C3
  Selby YO8 . . . . .232 E3
  2 Swillington LS26 . . .194 A1
Lowther St YO31 . . . . .233 A1
Lowther Terr YO24 . . . .228 A3
Loxley Cl YO30 . . . . . .224 F2
Loyne Pk LA6 . . . . .102 A4
Lucas Ave YO26 . . . . . .228 C8
Lucas Gr N YO26 . . . . .181 C7
Lucas Gr S YO26 . . . . .181 C7
Lucas Rd YO26 . . . . . . .181 C7
Luccombe Cl 7 TS17 . . . .6 A3
Lucerne Dr TS14 . . . . . . .8 E6
Lucia La TS14 . . . . .8 E6
Lucky La YO7 . . . . .89 E8
Lucombe Way YO32 . . .225 D4
Luddith Rd YO17 . . . . .148 D5
Ludlow Ave LS25 . . . . .194 D4
Lulsgate TS17 . . . . .6 C7
Lumb Gill La LS29 . . . .175 A3
Lumb La BD22 . . . . . . .187 A4
Lumb Mill Way BD23 . .157 E7
Lumby Hill LS25 . . . . . .202 A8
Lumby La
  Monk Fryston LS25 . . . .202 A8
  South Milford LS25 . . . .196 A1
Lumley Cl YO7 . . . . . . .211 D2
Lumley La Azerley HG4 .112 A5
  Kirkby Fleetham with Fencote ●
  DL7 . . . . .42 B1
Lumley Rd YO30 . . . . .228 B7
Lumley St WF10 . . . . . .200 D3
Lunar Pk★ YO11 . . . . .213 A5
Luncarr La HG4 . . . . . .114 B2
Lund Cl YO32 . . . . .225 C8
Lund Head La HG3 . . . .179 B2
Lund La Bubwith YO8 . .199 C6
  Cliffe YO8 . . . . .198 D4
  Hampsthwaite HG3 . . . .161 A5
Lund Rd YO62 . . . . .70 B7
Lund Sand La
  Easingwold YO61 . . . . .143 A8
  Raskelf YO61 . . . . .117 A1
Lund Sike La LS25 . . . .195 F2
Lund's Twr★ BD20 . . . .187 B3
Lundgreen La YO61 . . . .144 A3
Lundy Cl 10 YO30 . . . . .225 A1
Lunebeck Wlk TS17 . . . . .6 C5
Lunedale Ave
  Knaresborough HG5 . . . .221 C5
  Middlesbrough TS5 . . . . . .6 E8
Lunedale Rd DL3 . . . . . . .3 A6
Lunn La DN14 . . . . .202 D3
Lunnfields La WF11 . . . .201 E6

Lupton Bank HG3 . . . . .137 D3
Lupton Cl HG3 . . . . . . .137 D3
Lutton La YO17 . . . . . .123 F4
Luttons CP Sch YO17 . .150 B8
Lutyens The 22 LS29 . . .175 C2
Lycett Rd YO24 . . . . . .230 F6
Lych Gate 14 DL2 . . . . . . .3 E1
Lydford Rd 18 DL10 . . . .41 E4
Lydham Ct 2 YO24 . . . .230 C8
Lyell St YO12 . . . . .212 E6
Lynbrook Cl YO7 . . . . .211 B4
Lyndale LS25 . . . . .200 D8
Lyndale Gr YO10 . . . . .229 C3
Lyndale Gr 14 WF6 . . . .200 B1
Lynden Way YO24 . . . .227 D3
Lyndhurst Cl
  2 Norton DN6 . . . . . .206 F2
  9 Whitby YO21 . . . . . .208 D6
Lyndhurst Dr 1 DN6 . .206 F2
Lyndhurst Rise 3 DN6 .206 F2
Lyndon Ave
  Bramham LS23 . . . . . . .188 E6
  Garforth LS25 . . . . . . .194 C4
Lyndon Cl 1 LS23 . . . .188 E6
Lyndon Cres 4 LS23 . . .188 E6
Lyndon Rd LS23 . . . . . .188 E6
Lyndon Sq 2 LS23 . . . .188 E6
Lyndon Way LS23 . . . . .188 E6
Lynmouth Cl TS8 . . . . . . .6 E5
Lynndale Ave 6 BD20 . .187 F8
Lynton Ave LS23 . . . . .188 E8
Lynton Cl YO8 . . . . . . .232 B1
Lynton Gdns
  Brayton YO8 . . . . .232 B1
  Darlington DL1 . . . . .3 E5
  Harrogate HG1 . . . . . . .220 A3
Lynton Way DL6 . . . . . .210 D3
Lynwith Cl DN14 . . . . .204 C3
Lynwith Dr DN14 . . . . .204 C3
Lynwith Rd DN14 . . . . .204 C3
Lynwood Ave 3 YO23 . .230 A4
Lynwood Cl YO32 . . . . .167 A4
Lynwood View 4 YO23 .230 A4
Lynx La YO7 . . . . .115 B1
Lyon Rd BD20 . . . . .187 F7
Lyonette Rd DL1 . . . . . . .3 E7
Lyons Rd DL10 . . . . . . .209 C8
Lys Cres DL9 . . . . .209 C1
Lysander Cl YO30 . . . . .225 A3
Lytham Cl BD23 . . . . . .217 C3
Lytham Gdns BD23 . . . .217 C3
Lytham Rd DL1 . . . . .3 D5
Lythe Bank YO21 . . . . . .12 F4
  Sutton with Howgrave
  DL8 . . . . .87 F2
Lythe CE VC Prim Sch
  YO21 . . . . .12 E3
Lythe Fell Rd LA2 . . . . .129 B2
Lythe La LA2 . . . . .129 A3

M

MacArthurs Cl YO7 . . . .211 B2
MacDonell Cl 1 DL9 . .209 C1
MacKeridge La YO62 . . .48 F4
Mackie Dr TS14 . . . . .8 F7
MacKinnon Ave 1 WF6 200 B2
MacLagan Rd YO23 . . . .230 F4
Mafeking St HG1 . . . . . .219 F4
Magazine La YO8 . . . . .198 B3
Magazine Rd YO8 . . . . .198 B4
Magdalen's Cl HG4 . . . .214 D6
Magdalen's Rd HG4 . . . .214 D6
Magister Rd TS17 . . . . . .6 B7
Magnolia Gr YO32 . . . .225 D2
Magpie Garth YO12 . . . .99 E6
Maida Gr YO10 . . . . . . .228 D2
Maiden Bower (Motte &
  Bailey)★ YO7 . . . . . . .115 D5
Maiden Castle★ DL11 . .38 A5
Maiden Greve YO7 . . . .215 A4
Maidensgrave Henge★
  YO25 . . . . .126 F1
Maidstone Dr TS7 . . . . . .7 C5
Main Ave YO31 . . . . . . .228 F5
Main Rd Drax YO8 . . . .204 F5
  Gainford DL2 . . . . .1 D7
  Hambleton YO8 . . . . . .196 E1
  Hellifield BD23 . . . . . . .154 B3
  Stainforth BD24 . . . . . .131 E6
  Steeton with Eastburn
  BD20 . . . . .187 F1
  Weaverthorpe YO17 . . .124 E1
Main St Aberford LS25 .194 F8
  Addingham LS29 . . . . .174 F4
  Allerston YO18 . . . . . . .97 B5
  Alne YO61 . . . . .142 F4
  Amotherby YO17 . . . . .121 A4
  Appleton Roebuck YO23 190 F5
  Askham Bryan YO23 . . .182 F3
  Askrigg DL8 . . . . .57 E6
  Asselby DN14 . . . . . . .205 D7
  Austwick LA2 . . . . .130 E7
  Aysgarth DL8 . . . . .58 E3
  Barkston Ash LS24 . . . .195 E7
  Barwick in Elmet LS15 . .194 B8
  3 Beal DN14 . . . . . . .202 D4
  Bentham LA2 . . . . .128 E8
  Bilbrough YO23 . . . . . .182 C1
  Bilton-in-Ainsty with Bickerton
  LS22 . . . . .181 A5
  Bishop Monkton HG3 . .140 B5
  Bishopthorpe YO23 . . . .231 A4
  Boroughbridge YO51 . . .141 A3
  Brafferton YO61 . . . . . .141 F8
  Bubwith YO8 . . . . .199 C7
  Bugthorpe YO41 . . . . . .169 D4

Main St continued
  Burley in Wharfedale
  LS29 . . . . .176 C1
  Burton Salmon LS25 . . .201 F6
  Church Fenton LS24 . . .196 B7
  Cliffe YO8 . . . . .198 E2
  Cononley LS25 . . . . . . .173 D1
  Copmanthorpe YO23 . . .230 A2
  Cottingwith YO42 . . . . .193 C5
  Darley HG3 . . . . .160 A6
  Deighton YO19 . . . . . . .192 A7
  Earby BB18 . . . . .186 A4
  East Ayton/West Ayton
  YO13 . . . . .99 A7
  Eastfield YO11 . . . . . . .100 B6
  Ebberston & Yedingham
  YO13 . . . . .97 D5
  Ellerton YO42 . . . . .193 C1
  Elvington YO41 . . . . . . .185 C2
  Embsay BD23 . . . . .217 E8
  Escrick YO19 . . . . .192 A4
  Farnhill BD20 . . . . .173 E1
  Folkton YO11 . . . . .100 A4
  Follifoot HG3 . . . . .223 F5
  Ganton YO12 . . . . .125 A8
  Garforth LS25 . . . . .194 C3
  Gillamoor YO62 . . . . . . .70 A4
  Gilling East YO62 . . . . .118 F7
  Glusburn BD20 . . . . . . .187 E7
  Gowdall DN14 . . . . . . .204 A1
  13 Grassington BD23 . .134 E3
  Great Ouseburn YO26 . .164 B8
  Great Preston WF10 . . .200 D6
  Gristlthorp YO14 . . . . .100 E4
  Harome YO62 . . . . .93 C5
  Healaugh LS24 . . . . . . .181 F2
  Hebden BD23 . . . . .135 A1
  Heck DN14 . . . . .207 C8
  Helperby YO61 . . . . . . .142 A8
  Hemingbrough YO8 . . . .198 F1
  Hensall DN14 . . . . .203 D2
  Heslington YO10 . . . . . .229 B1
  Hessay YO26 . . . . .182 B8
  High Bentham LA2 . . . .129 A8
  Hovingham YO62 . . . . .119 E6
  Huby YO61 . . . . .144 A4
  Ingleton LA6 . . . . .103 D3
  Irton YO12 . . . . .99 C6
  Kelfield YO19 . . . . .191 D1
  Kellington DN14 . . . . . .202 F3
  Kirk Deighton LS22 . . . .180 B5
  Kirk Smeaton WF8 . . . .206 B3
  Kirkby Malham BD23 . . .154 F8
  Kirkby Malzeard HG4 . .112 C5
  Knapton YO26 . . . . . . .227 A5
  Langcliffe BD24 . . . . . .131 E4
  Ledston WF10 . . . . . . .200 F7
  Linton LS22 . . . . .180 A1
  Little Ouseburn YO26 . .164 A7
  Long Preston BD23 . . . .153 F5
  Low Bradley BD20 . . . .173 E3
  Menwith with Darley
  HG3 . . . . .160 A4
  Mickletown LS26 . . . . .200 B6
  Middleton YO18 . . . . . . .95 E8
  Monk Fryston LS25 . . . .201 F8
  1 Naburn YO19 . . . . . .191 D8
  Newton Kyme cum Toulston
  LS24 . . . . .189 C7
  North Duffield YO8 . . . .199 A8
  Nunthorpe YO10 . . . . . .231 D8
  Pannal HG3 . . . . .222 D3
  Pollington DN14 . . . . . .207 F6
  Poppleton YO26 . . . . . .165 F1
  Rathmell BD24 . . . . . . .153 C6
  Reighton YO14 . . . . . . .127 E5
  Riccall YO19 . . . . .198 A8
  Ryther cum Ossendyke
  LS24 . . . . .190 E2
  Saxton with Scarthingwell
  LS24 . . . . .195 D7
  Scholes LS15 . . . . .194 A7
  Scotton HG5 . . . . .162 A6
  Seamer YO12 . . . . .99 D6
  Sheriff Hutton YO60 . . .145 D5
  Shipton YO30 . . . . .165 F5
  Sicklinghall LS22 . . . . .179 D3
  Sinnington YO62 . . . . . .95 A8
  Stainforth BD24 . . . . . .131 E6
  Stamford Bridge YO41 . .168 D2
  Staveley HG5 . . . . .140 E1
  Stillington YO61 . . . . . .144 C6
  Threshfield BD23 . . . . .134 C2
  Thwing YO25 . . . . .126 B1
  Tollerton YO61 . . . . . . .143 A3
  Ulleskelf LS24 . . . . . . .190 C3
  Walton LS23 . . . . .181 A2
  Wath HG4 . . . . .114 A8
  Weeton LS17 . . . . .178 C1
  West Tanfield HG4 . . . . .87 A1
  Westow YO60 . . . . .147 B4
  Wheldrake YO19 . . . . . .192 F7
  Whittington LA6 . . . . . .102 A7
  Wilberfoss YO41 . . . . . .185 E5
  Wombleton YO62 . . . . . .93 E6
  Womersley DN6 . . . . . .206 C6
  Wray-with-Botton LA2 . .128 A6
Mains La YO60 . . . . . . .146 D5
Mains The DL3 . . . . . . .131 D3
Mainsfield Cl 1 BD24 . .131 D3
Mainsfield Rise 2
  BD24 . . . . .131 D3
Maison Dieu DL10 . . . .209 D7
Major St DL3 . . . . .3 D5
Malais La BD20 . . . . . . .187 D7
Malbys Gr YO23 . . . . . .230 B2
Malden Rd HG1 . . . . . .220 B3
Malham Gr YO31 . . . . . .229 B5

Malham Moor La
  BD23 . . . . .133 F4
Malham Rakes BD23 . . .133 A2
Malham Tarn★ BD24 . . .132 F6
Malham Tarn Field Ctr★
  BD24 . . . . .132 F6
Malham Tarn National Nature
  Reserve★ BD24 . . . . . .132 C5
Malham Visitor Ctr★
  BD23 . . . . .133 A1
Malham Way HG5 . . . . .221 D6
Malim Rd DL1 . . . . .3 F5
Mallard Cl 8 Filey YO14 .101 A4
  12 Pickering YO18 . . . . .95 F6
Mallard Rd 4 DL9 . . . . .40 F2
Mallard View YO17 . . . .215 D2
Mallard Way
  4 Eastfield YO12 . . . . .99 F6
  11 Haxby YO32 . . . . . .166 F5
Mallard Wlk 4 YO51 . . .141 B5
Mallinson Cl HG2 . . . . .222 D6
Mallinson Cres HG2 . . .222 D6
Mallinson Gate HG2 . . .222 D6
Mallinson Gr HG2 . . . . .222 D6
Mallinson Oval HG2 . . .222 D6
Mallinson Way HG2 . . .222 D6
Mallinson Hill Dr 5
  YO61 . . . . .117 D1
Mallorie Cl HG4 . . . . . .214 A5
Mallorie Ct HG4 . . . . . .214 B5
Mallorie Pk Dr HG4 . . .214 A4
Mallory Cl YO23 . . . . . .225 D4
Mallory Ct 17 DL1 . . . . . .3 F6
Mallowdale TS7 . . . . .7 C5
Malpas Dr DL7 . . . . . . .210 D4
Malpas Rd
  Brompton YO13 . . . . . . .98 C4
  Northallerton DL7 . . . . .210 D3
Malsis Prep Sch BD20 . .187 C7
Malt Dubs Cl LA6 . . . . .103 D3
Malt Kiln La YO23 . . . . .190 F5
Malt Kiln Terr LS24 . . . .189 D4
Malt Shoval Ct YO1 . . . .233 C2
Maltby Rd TS8 . . . . .6 C4
Malthouse La HG3 . . . . .222 D2
Maltings Bsns Ctr The
  YO17 . . . . .215 C3
Maltings Ct Alne YO61 . .142 F4
  6 Selby YO8 . . . . .232 C6
Maltings The
  8 Brafferton YO61 . . . .115 F1
  13 Pontefract WF8 . . . .201 B1
  Thirsk YO7 . . . . .211 B2
Maltkiln La
  Castleford WF10 . . . . . .200 F4
  Killinghall HG3 . . . . . . .161 C6
Maltings The LA6 . . . . .102 A7
Malton & Norton Hospl
  YO17 . . . . .215 B4
Malton Ave YO31 . . . . .228 E6
Malton Com Hospl
  YO17 . . . . .215 A5
Malton Com Prim Sch
  YO17 . . . . .215 D5
Malton Gate YO18 . . . . .96 D5
Malton La
  Allerston YO18 . . . . .97 B4
  Flaxton YO60 . . . . .146 A1
  Kirby Grindalythe YO17 .150 A8
Malton Mus★ YO17 . . . .215 C4
Malton Rd
  Hunmanby YO14 . . . . . .126 F8
  Huntington YO32 . . . . . .226 A1
  Leavening YO17 . . . . . .147 E2
  Pickering YO18 . . . . . . .95 F6
  Rillington YO17 . . . . . . .122 E4
  Scampston YO17 . . . . . .123 B7
  Slingsby YO62 . . . . . . .120 B5
  Swinton YO17 . . . . .121 C4
  York YO31 . . . . .228 F7
Malton St YO61 . . . . . . .117 D6
Malton St Marys RC Prim Sch
  YO17 . . . . .215 D5
Malton Sta★ YO17 . . . .215 C3
Malton Way YO30 . . . . .227 F8
Malvern Ave YO26 . . . .227 D5
Malvern Cl
  Huntington YO32 . . . . . .226 A5
  8 Hurworth-on-Tees DL2 . .3 E1
  Stokesley TS9 . . . . .26 C7
Malvern Cres
  Darlington DL3 . . . . .2 F7
  Scarborough YO12 . . . .212 D5
Malvern Dr
  Middlesbrough TS5 . . . . .6 E6
  Stokesley TS9 . . . . .26 C7
Malvern Rd WF11 . . . . .201 F2
Manchester St BB18 . . .171 D1
Mancroft YO32 . . . . . . .225 C8
Mandale Mill Prim Sch
  TS17 . . . . .6 B8
Mandale Rd TS5 . . . . . . .6 D8
Manfield CE Prim Sch
  DL2 . . . . .2 B4
Mangrill La LS14 . . . . . .188 C3
Manham Hill YO11 . . . . .99 F7
Mankin La HG4 . . . . . . .214 D1
Manley Cl YO32 . . . . . .225 D4
Manley Dr LS22 . . . . . .180 A3
Manley Gr LS29 . . . . . .218 D4
Manley Rd LS29 . . . . . .218 E4
Manley Rise LS29 . . . . .218 D3
Manor Ave YO12 . . . . . .212 D6
Manor Beeches The 3
  YO19 . . . . .184 E7

Low - Man 259

Manor CE Sec Sch
  YO26 . . . . .227 C7
Manor Chase YO26 . . . .181 F6
Manor Cl
  Burton in Lonsdale LA6 .102 F3
  5 Hemingbrough YO8 . .198 F1
  Ingleton LA6 . . . . .103 D3
  Kirk Smeaton WF8 . . . .206 B3
  13 Kirkbymoorside YO62 . .70 B1
  Low Worsall TS15 . . . . .24 B8
  6 North Duffield YO8 . .199 A7
  12 Norton DN6 . . . . . .206 E2
  5 Stokesley TS9 . . . . . .26 C7
  Topcliffe YO7 . . . . .115 C6
  Upper Poppleton YO26 .182 F8
  Wath HG4 . . . . .114 B7
  Whitby YO21 . . . . .208 B6
Manor Cres HG5 . . . . . .221 C6
Manor Croft YO42 . . . . .169 F1
Manor Ct
  6 Bubwith YO8 . . . . . .199 D7
  Fairburn WF11 . . . . . . .201 D7
  Follifoot HG3 . . . . .223 F5
  Kirkby Malzeard HG4 . .112 D5
  Knaresborough HG5 . . . .221 B5
  2 York YO32 . . . . .225 F6
Manor Dr
  2 Brafferton YO61 . . . .115 F1
  Camblesforth YO8 . . . . .204 C4
  4 Dunnington YO19 . . .184 E7
  Harrogate HG2 . . . . . . .222 C8
  Hilton TS15 . . . . .6 C2
  Kirby Hill YO51 . . . . . .141 A7
  Knaresborough HG5 . . . .221 C6
  5 North Duffield YO8 . .199 A7
  North Featherstone
  WF7 . . . . .200 E1
  Pickering YO18 . . . . . . .95 E7
  Scotton HG5 . . . . .162 A6
Manor Dr N YO26 . . . . .227 D4
Manor Dr S YO26 . . . . .227 D4
Manor Farm Cl
  1 Brayton YO8 . . . . . .232 A1
  Carlton DN14 . . . . .204 C2
  Copmanthorpe YO23 . . .230 A2
  Kellington DN14 . . . . . .202 F3
Manor Farm Ct YO8 . . .203 C4
Manor Farm Way TS8 . . .6 F5
Manor Fields DN14 . . . .205 B2
Manor Fold HG3 . . . . . .223 F5
Manor Garth
  Haxby YO32 . . . . .225 B8
  Kellington DN14 . . . . . .202 F3
  12 Kirklevington TS15 . .24 E8
  Ledsham LS25 . . . . . . .201 B8
  7 Norton DN6 . . . . . . .206 F2
  1 Riccall YO19 . . . . . .198 A8
  7 Spofforth HG3 . . . . .179 E6
Manor Garth Rd LS25 . .194 E1
Manor Gdns
  6 Hunmanby YO14 . . . .127 A8
  Killinghall HG3 . . . . . . .161 C5
  Kirkbymoorside YO62 . . .70 B1
  15 Knaresborough HG5 . .221 B6
  Scarborough YO12 . . . .212 E6
  Thorner LS14 . . . . .188 A3
Manor Gn
  Northallerton DL7 . . . . .210 C3
  Patrick Brompton DL8 . . .62 C6
Manor Gr Colburn DL9 . .40 F5
  Great Broughton TS9 . . .26 E5
Manor Heath YO23 . . . .230 A3
Manor House Art Gall &
  Mus★ LS29 . . . . .218 B4
Manor Inf Sch HG5 . . . .221 B6
Manor La
  Healaugh LS24 . . . . . . .181 E1
  Rawcliffe YO30 . . . . . . .224 D2
Manor Orchards HG5 . . .221 B6
Manor Pk
  Arkendale HG5 . . . . . . .163 A7
  Cowling BD22 . . . . . . .187 B6
  Ledston WF10 . . . . . . .200 F7
  Swinton WF10 . . . . . . .121 C4
Manor Pk Ave
  Great Preston WF10 . . .200 D7
  Pontefract WF8 . . . . . . .201 C2
Manor Pk Cl YO30 . . . .224 E2
Manor Pk Gr 2 YO30 . .224 E2
Manor Pk Rd YO30 . . . .224 E2
Manor Rd Beal DN14 . .202 C4
  Darlington DL3 . . . . .3 C4
  Easingwold YO61 . . . . .117 C1
  Fylingdales YO22 . . . . . .33 C4
  Harrogate HG2 . . . . . . .222 B8
  Hurworth-on-Tees DL2 . . .3 D1
  Killinghall HG3 . . . . . . .161 C5
  Knaresborough HG5 . . . .221 B6
  Scarborough YO12 . . . .212 E5
  Stutton with Hazlewood
  LS24 . . . . .189 D4
Manor Rise LS29 . . . . . .218 D4
Manor Vale La 28 YO62 . .70 B1
Manor View
  Castleford WF10 . . . . . .200 F3
  Oswaldkirk YO62 . . . . . .93 A1
  Rillington YO17 . . . . . . .122 F5
Manor View Rd YO11 . . .100 D5
Manor Way
  Glusburn BD20 . . . . . . .187 E6
  York YO30 . . . . .224 E2
Manor Wood TS8 . . . . . . .6 F6
Manorcroft WF6 . . . . . .200 A1
Manorfields 11 DL2 . . . . .3 E1
Manse Cres 28 LS29 . . .176 C1

Manse La HG5 . . . . . .221 D4
Manse Rd LS29 . . . . . . .176 C1
Manse Way BD20 . . . . .187 E7
Mansfield Ave TS17 . . . . . .6 B8
Mansfield Ct HG1 . . . . .219 C4
Mansfield Rd LS29 . . . .176 B1
Mansfield St YO31 . . . . .233 C4
Manston Ct 14 DL2 . . . . . .4 C4
Manston La LS15 . . . . . .194 A5
Manton Ave TS5 . . . . .6 D8
Maple Ave
  Bishopthorpe YO23 . . . . .231 A3
  Malton YO17 . . . . .215 D6
Maple Cl 5 Colburn DL9 . .40 F5
  Hambleton YO8 . . . . .197 B1
  2 South Milford LS25 . . .195 F2
Maple Croft YO61 . . . . .144 A5
Maple Ct
  Wheldrake YO19 . . . . . . .192 D8
  York YO10 . . . . .231 E6
Maple Dr YO12 . . . . . . .212 D7
Maple Garth HG4 . . . . . .114 B7
Maple Gr 12 Brayton YO8 .197 D1
  7 Linton-on-Ouse YO30 . .164 F7
  York YO10 . . . . .228 D5
Maple La YO61 . . . . . . .144 A5
Maple Rd DL10 . . . . . . .209 A8
Maple Tree Ave 10 YO8 .198 B4
Maple Wlk HG4 . . . . . . .214 B2
Maplehurst Ave YO31 . . .228 D7
Maplewood Paddock 2
  YO24 . . . . .227 C1
Mar Bank Balk HG5 . . . .163 A7
Marage Rd YO7 . . . . . . .211 B3
Marazion Dr DL3 . . . . .3 C8
Marbeck La HG5 . . . . . .140 F2
March Ave HG5 . . . . . . .221 A4
March St
  Normanton South WF6 . . .200 A1
  York YO31 . . . . .233 C4
Marchlyn Cres TS17 . . . . . .5 F4
Marderby La YO7 . . . . . . .90 C7
Maresfield Rd DL9 . . . . . .40 E3
Margaret Philipson Ct
  YO31 . . . . .233 C3
Margaret Rd HG2 . . . . . .219 B1
Margaret St YO10 . . . . . .233 C4
Margerison Cres LS29 . . .218 E3
Margerison Rd LS29 . . . .218 E3
Maria St 15 LS29 . . . . . .176 C1
Marias Ct 9 YO11 . . . . . .213 A6
Marigold Cl YO8 . . . . . . .232 C5
Marina Ave 3 DN14 . . . .204 B1
Marina Cres BD23 . . . . .216 D3
Marina Rd DL3 . . . . .3 D8
Marina Way HG4 . . . . . .214 A2
Marine Dr YO11 . . . . . . .213 C7
Marine Espl YO13 . . . . . . .54 A8
Marine Par 24 YO11 . . . .208 D7
Marine Villa Rd WF11 . . .201 F2
Mariner's Terr 16 YO14 . .101 B3
Marion Ave TS16 . . . . .5 D4
Marishes La
  Allerston YO17 . . . . .97 A2
  Thornton-le-Dale YO17 . . .96 E1
Marishes Low Rd
  YO17 . . . . .122 B8
Marjorie Waite Ct
  YO30 . . . . .228 B7
Mark House La BD23 . . . .155 C1
Mark La
  Fylingdales YO22 . . . . . . .33 C3
  Kirk Deighton LS22 . . . . .180 B5
Markenfield Hall ★
  HG4 . . . . .139 D6
Markenfield Rd HG3 . . . .219 B5
Market Cross Sh Ctr 13
  YO8 . . . . .232 C6
Market Flat La HG5 . . . . .162 C6
Market Hall YO11 . . . . . .213 B6
Market Hill 5 YO51 . . . . .141 B6
Market La 14 YO8 . . . . . .232 C5
Market Pl Askrigg DL8 . . .57 E5
  6 Bedale DL8 . . . . .63 A3
  2 Cawood YO8 . . . . .197 B8
  2 Easingwold YO61 . . . .143 C8
  Hawes DL8 . . . . .56 C4
  Helmsley YO62 . . . . .92 F6
  25 Kirkbymoorside YO62 . .70 B1
  3 Knaresborough HG5 . . .221 B6
  Malton YO17 . . . . .215 C4
  9 Masham HG4 . . . . .86 C3
  5 Middleham DL8 . . . . . .60 E2
  6 Normanton South WF6 . .200 A1
  Pickering YO18 . . . . .95 F7
  Richmond DL10 . . . . . . .209 C6
  11 Selby YO8 . . . . .232 C5
  10 Settle BD24 . . . . .131 D2
  9 Snaith DN14 . . . . .204 C1
  Thirsk YO7 . . . . .211 B3
  12 Wetherby LS22 . . . . . .180 C3
  11 Whitby YO22 . . . . . . .208 D7
Market Pl E 19 HG4 . . . .214 C5
Market Pl N 23 HG4 . . . .214 C5
Market Pl S 20 HG4 . . . .214 C5
Market Pl W 21 HG4 . . . .214 C5
Market Row DL7 . . . . . . .210 D4
Market Sq 18 DL8 . . . . . .209 C6
Market St Malton YO17 . .215 C4
  Normanton South WF6 . . .200 A1
  24 Scarborough YO11 . . .213 A6
  York YO1 . . . . .233 B2
Market Way 25 YO11 . . . .213 A6
Market Weighton Rd
  YO8 . . . . .198 B6

Markham Cres YO31 . . . .233 B4
Markham St YO31 . . . . . .233 B4
Markington CE Prim Sch
  HG3 . . . . .139 C3
Marl Hill La BD20 . . . . . .186 D8
Marlborough Ave
  3 Byram WF11 . . . . .201 F4
  Tadcaster LS24 . . . . .189 D5
  3 Whitby YO21 . . . . .208 B7
Marlborough Cl YO30 . . .224 D3
Marlborough Dr
  Darlington DL1 . . . . .3 C4
  Tadcaster LS24 . . . . .189 D5
Marlborough Gr
  Ilkley LS29 . . . . .218 D3
  Ripon HG4 . . . . .214 B6
  York YO10 . . . . .228 D2
Marlborough Rd HG1 . . . .219 E2
Marlborough Sq LS29 . . .218 C3
Marlborough St 11
  YO12 . . . . .213 A7
Marlborough Villas
  YO10 . . . . .228 D2
Marmiam Dr 2 YO32 . . . .167 D2
Marmion Ct HG4 . . . . .87 A1
Marmion Twr ★ HG4 . . . .87 A1
Marne Cl 1 DL9 . . . . .209 B1
Marne Rd DL9 . . . . .209 D1
Marquis St YO26 . . . . . . .227 D5
Marr The YO14 . . . . .100 F5
Marrick Priory (rems of) ★
  DL11 . . . . .38 E4
Marrick Rd TS18 . . . . .5 D8
Marridales DL8 . . . . .56 D4
Marriforth La HG4 . . . . . . .61 F2
Marrtree Bsns Pk
  WF10 . . . . .200 E3
Mars La TS13 . . . . .11 A4
Marsdens Pl 7 YO22 . . . .208 E6
Marsett La DL8 . . . . .57 B2
Marsh Croft WF11 . . . . . .201 E4
Marsh End WF11 . . . . . . .202 A3
Marsh La Asselby DN14 . .205 D7
  Barlow YO8 . . . . .204 B8
  Bolton Percy YO23 . . . . .190 D3
  Byram cum Sutton WF11 . .201 F4
  Cawood YO8 . . . . .197 D8
  Ingleby Greenhow TS9 . . . .27 B5
  Knottingley WF11 . . . . . .202 A2
  West Haddlesey WF8 . . . .202 F5
Marsh La Gdns DN14 . . . .202 A4
Marsh Rd WF10 . . . . .200 D3
Marshall Dr YO18 . . . . . . .96 A7
Marshall Mews 2
  WF10 . . . . .200 E4
Marshfield Rd 7 BD24 . . .131 D2
Marston Ave YO26 . . . . . .227 B3
Marston Bsns Pk
  YO26 . . . . .181 B7
Marston Cres YO26 . . . . .227 B3
Marston La
  Long Marston YO26 . . . . .182 A8
  Moor Monkton YO26 . . . .165 A1
Marston Moor Rd DL1 . . . . .3 C4
Marston Rd YO26 . . . . . .181 D7
Marston Way 3 LS22 . . . .180 B3
Marten Cl 2 YO30 . . . . . .228 A1
Martin Cheeseman Ct 3
  YO24 . . . . .230 C8
Martindale Rd DL1 . . . . . . .3 D7
Martinet Rd TS17 . . . . . . .6 A5
Martinet Rd TS17 . . . . . . .6 B7
Martinhoe Cl 4 TS17 . . . . .6 A3
Martins Ct YO26 . . . . . . .228 A5
Marton Abbey (Priory) ★
  YO61 . . . . .144 C8
Marton Ave TS4 . . . . .7 B8
Marton La YO21 . . . . . . .208 B6
Marton cum Grafton CE VA
  Prim Sch YO51 . . . . . . .141 D1
Marton La
  Arkendale HG5 . . . . .163 B8
  Wrelton YO18 . . . . .95 C7
Marton Manor Prim Sch
  TS7 . . . . .7 B6
Marton Moor Rd TS7 . . . . .7 D5
Marton Rd
  Coulby Newham TS4 . . . . . .7 B8
  Gargrave BD23 . . . . .172 C4
  Marton YO62 . . . . .94 F6
  Sinnington YO62 . . . . .95 A7
Marton St BD23 . . . . . . .216 D3
Marton Sta TS7 . . . . .7 C7
Martonside Way TS4 . . . . .7 A8
Marvell Rise HG2 . . . . . .219 E7
Marwood CE VA Sch TS9 . .7 F1
Marwood Dr TS9 . . . . .7 F1
Mary La YO26 . . . . .141 F3
Mary St 3 BD20 . . . . . . .173 F1
Marygate Barton DL10 . . .21 D7
  York YO30 . . . . .233 A3
Marygate La YO30 . . . . . .233 A3
Marykirk Rd TS17 . . . . . . .6 B6
Masefield Cl HG1 . . . . . .219 E7
Masham Bank HG4 . . . . . .85 D8
Masham CE VA Prim Sch
  HG4 . . . . .86 C3
Masham Cl HG2 . . . . . . .220 C1
Masham La DL8 . . . . .87 A4
Masham Rd Firby DL8 . . . .62 F1
  Harrogate HG2 . . . . .220 C1
  Snape with Thorp DL8 . . . .86 B8
Mask La YO41 . . . . .185 D4
Masongill Fell La LA6 . . .103 A6
Masonic La YO7 . . . . . . .211 B3
Maspin Moor Rd LS25 . . .202 C7

Massa Flatts Wood
  BD23 . . . . .216 E5
Massey St YO8 . . . . .232 C5
Master Rd TS17 . . . . .6 B7
Master's Gate YO18 . . . . .49 D4
Mastil Cl DL8 . . . . .62 D5
Mastil La DL8 . . . . .62 D5
Mastiles La BD23 . . . . . .134 A6
Matfen Ave TS7 . . . . .7 D6
Matthew La
  Bradleys Both BD20 . . . . .173 E3
  Green Hammerton YO26 . .164 C4
Mattison Way YO24 . . . . .227 E2
Maud La YO21 . . . . .177 A6
Maude Rd DL9 . . . . .209 A1
Maudon Ave YO10 . . . . . .96 A6
Maudon Gr YO17 . . . . . . .215 F4
Maufe Way 3 LS29 . . . . .218 B3
Maunby La YO7 . . . . .64 D1
Mawson Gr DL6 . . . . .65 B5
Mawson La HG4 . . . . . . .214 C4
Maxim Cl 5 DL9 . . . . .40 E4
Maxwell Rd LS29 . . . . . .218 D3
May Beck Farm Trail
  YO22 . . . . .32 D1
Mayfair Ave TS6 . . . . .7 D8
Mayfair Rd DL1 . . . . .3 D8
Mayfield Ave
  Ilkley LS29 . . . . .218 D4
  2 Scalby YO12 . . . . .75 E5
Mayfield Cl
  3 Glusburn BD20 . . . . . .187 E7
  Ilkley LS29 . . . . .218 D4
Mayfield Cres TS16 . . . . . .5 D5
Mayfield Dr
  5 Brayton YO8 . . . . .232 A1
  2 Seamer YO12 . . . . .99 D6
Mayfield Gdns LS29 . . . .218 D5
Mayfield Gr
  Harrogate HG1 . . . . .219 D3
  Knaresborough HG5 . . . . .221 C6
  York YO24 . . . . .230 E8
Mayfield Pl
  Harrogate HG1 . . . . .219 D3
  3 Whitby YO21 . . . . .208 C5
Mayfield Rd
  Brayton YO8 . . . . .232 A1
  Ilkley LS29 . . . . .218 C4
  Middlesbrough TS7 . . . . . . .7 D6
  Whitby YO21 . . . . .208 B5
Mayfield Terr HG1 . . . . . .219 D3
Maypole Gdns YO8 . . . . .197 B8
Maypole Gr 3 YO19 . . . .191 D8
Maypole Mews LS15 . . . .194 B8
Maythorn Rd YO31 . . . . .225 E2
Maythorpe YO23 . . . . . . .182 C6
Mayville Ave YO12 . . . . . .212 E6
Mcan Cl YO10 . . . . .229 D4
McArthur Designer Outlet
  YO19 . . . . .231 D4
McBean Stps ★ YO11 . . .213 A5
McDonald Rd HG4 . . . . . .113 D3
McMullen Rd DL1 . . . . . . .3 E6
Mead Cres TS17 . . . . .6 C8
Meadlands YO31 . . . . . . .229 B6
Meadow Ave 5 HG4 . . . .214 B2
Meadow Brook Chase 19
  WF6 . . . . .200 B1
Meadow Cl
  Cononley BD20 . . . . .173 D2
  7 Eastfield YO11 . . . . . .100 A6
  Hampsthwaite HG3 . . . . .160 F5
  Northallerton DL7 . . . . . .210 D2
  Thorpe Willoughby YO8 . .197 C2
Meadow Croft
  Brayton YO8 . . . . .232 A2
  Cononley BD20 . . . . .173 C2
Meadow Ct
  Rillington YO17 . . . . .122 F5
  Scruton DL7 . . . . .63 E7
  6 Willerby YO12 . . . . .99 D2
  3 York YO24 . . . . .230 E4
Meadow Dale Ct TS12 . . . .9 F7
Meadow Dr
  7 East Ayton/West Ayton
    YO13 . . . . .99 B8
  Harrogate HG1 . . . . .219 E7
  Scruton DL7 . . . . .63 E7
  Thorpe Willoughby YO8 . .197 B2
Meadow Garth
  2 Tadcaster LS24 . . . . . .189 F6
  Thirsk YO7 . . . . .211 B1
  Thorpe Willoughby YO8 . .197 C2
Meadow Gate HG1 . . . . . .219 E6
Meadow Gr 20 DL8 . . . . . .63 A2
Meadow La
  Cononley BD20 . . . . .173 C2
  2 Darley HG3 . . . . .160 A6
  3 Eastfield YO11 . . . . . .100 A6
  1 Haxby YO32 . . . . .225 D8
  Northallerton DL6 . . . . . .210 E6
  Snape DL8 . . . . .87 A4
Meadow Lea 21 BD20 . . .187 E7
Meadow Pl 5 YO8 . . . . . .232 B6
Meadow Rd
  Garforth LS25 . . . . .194 D4
  Knaresborough HG5 . . . . .221 B7
  2 Pickering YO18 . . . . . . .95 F7
Meadow Rise
  Harrogate HG1 . . . . .219 E7
  2 Skipton BD23 . . . . . . .217 B5
Meadow Springs Way 3
  YO61 . . . . .143 D8
Meadow Vale
  Green Hammerton YO26 . .164 C3
  2 Ripon HG4 . . . . .214 B2

Meadow View
  Barwick in Elmet & Scholes
    LS15 . . . . .194 B8
  Harrogate HG1 . . . . .219 E6
  Sherburn in Elmet LS25 . .195 F4
Meadow Way
  Barnoldswick BB18 . . . . .171 E2
  Harrogate HG1 . . . . .219 E7
  Heworth YO31 . . . . .228 F7
  Huntington YO32 . . . . . . .225 F4
  3 Tadcaster LS24 . . . . . .189 F6
Meadowbank Rd TS7 . . . . .7 D7
Meadowbeck Cl YO10 . . .229 B4
Meadowcroft
  Draughton BD23 . . . . . . .174 B7
  Harrogate HG1 . . . . .219 E6
Meadowcroft Dr HG3 . . .140 A5
Meadowfield
  Amotherby YO17 . . . . . . .121 A4
  8 Bedale DL8 . . . . .63 B3
  1 Bubwith YO8 . . . . .199 D7
  Lythe YO21 . . . . .13 A3
  8 Stokesley TS9 . . . . .26 C8
Meadowfield Dr
  6 Colburn DL9 . . . . .41 A5
  Darlington DL3 . . . . .3 A7
Meadowfields YO21 . . . . .208 C6
Meadowfields Cl 9
  YO61 . . . . .143 D8
Meadowfields Ct 17
  YO21 . . . . .208 D6
Meadowfields Dr
  YO31 . . . . .225 D2
Meadowings The TS15 . . . .5 D2
Meadowlands Cl 2 TS13 .11 A8
Meadows The
  Carlton DN14 . . . . .204 C3
  Castleford LS25 . . . . .200 C7
  Coulby Newham TS8 . . . . . .7 B5
  Hambleton YO8 . . . . .196 F1
  8 Middleton St George DL2 . .4 C4
  7 Monk Fryston LS25 . . .202 A8
  Riccall YO19 . . . . .197 F8
  Richmond DL10 . . . . . . .209 E7
  Scalby YO12 . . . . .212 B7
  2 Skelton YO30 . . . . . . .224 B5
  South Milford LS25 . . . . .195 F2
Meadowside Com Prim Sch
  HG5 . . . . .221 C6
Meads La YO12 . . . . .99 E5
Meads The 3 YO11 . . . . . .99 F6
Meadway YO8 . . . . .197 D2
Meadway Dr YO8 . . . . . .197 D2
Meagill La LS21 . . . . .159 E2
Meagill Rise LS21 . . . . . .176 E1
Meam Cl YO10 . . . . .229 D4
Meanee Rd 11 DL9 . . . . . .40 F2
Medbourne Gdns TS5 . . . .6 E7
Megson Pl YO7 . . . . .211 C4
Melander Cl YO26 . . . . . .227 C4
Melander Gdns 5 YO32 . .225 D7
Melbourne Dr YO7 . . . . . .90 E5
Melbourne Pl YO7 . . . . . .211 B2
Melbourne St YO10 . . . . .228 D2
Melcombe Ave 11 YO32 . .167 A7
Meldyke La TS8 . . . . .6 D5
Mellersh Rd 15 DL10 . . . .41 E4
Melling St Wilfred CE Prim
  Sch LA6 . . . . .102 A2
Melltown's Gn YO7 . . . . . .88 C6
Melmerby Gn La HG4 . . . .114 C5
Melmerby Gn Rd HG4 . . .114 B6
Melmerby Ind Est
  HG4 . . . . .114 B6
Melrose Cl 1 YO31 . . . . .229 A5
Melrose Cres
  Bishop Monkton HG3 . . . .140 A5
  Guisborough TS14 . . . . . . .9 A6
Melrose Dr 16 HG3 . . . . .176 C1
Melrose Rd HG3 . . . . . . .140 A5
Melrose St 4 YO12 . . . . .212 F6
Melrosegate YO31 . . . . . .228 F5
Melsonby Methodist Prim
  Sch DL10 . . . . .20 D1
Melton Ave YO30 . . . . . . .227 F8
Melton Dr
  Bishopthorpe YO23 . . . . .231 A3
  York YO30 . . . . .227 F8
Melville Gr 1 LS29 . . . . .218 E4
Melville Terr 52 YO14 . . .101 B3
Melwood Gr YO26 . . . . . .227 B5
Memorial Dr YO7 . . . . . . .7 B6
Mendip Cl 2 YO32 . . . . .225 F5
Menethorpe La YO17 . . . .147 D2
Menin Rd DL9 . . . . .209 B1
Menwith Hill Rd HG3 . . . .159 D1
Mercer Art Gall ★
  HG2 . . . . .219 C3
Mercer Dr YO26 . . . . . . .209 C1
Merchant Adventurers Hall ★
  YO1 . . . . .233 C2
Merchant Way YO23 . . . .230 B3
Merchant's Row 10
  YO11 . . . . .213 B6
Merchantgate YO1 . . . . . .233 C2
Merchants Ct YO31 . . . . .225 E2
Mercury Rd DL10 . . . . . .209 A8
Mere La YO11 . . . . .212 F1
Mere View Gdns YO12 . . . .99 F8
Merefield Way WF10 . . . .200 E2
Merewood Rd WF10 . . . .200 D3
Merioneth St 5 TS17 . . . . .5 F4
Merlin Covert 4 YO31 . . .225 F1
Merlinwood BD23 . . . . . .172 A4
Merrington Ave TS17 . . . . .6 D6
Merry Dale YO11 . . . . . . .100 A7
Merrybank La LS17 . . . . .178 A3

Merrybent Dr DL2 . . . . . . .2 F5
Merryfield HG2 . . . . .222 B7
Mesnes La DL8 . . . . .59 D3
Messines Rd LS29 . . . . . . .40 E3
Metcalfe La YO19 . . . . . .229 C5
Metcalfes Ct HG4 . . . . . .214 C6
Metes La YO12 . . . . .99 E5
Methley Inf Sch LS26 . . . .200 B5
Methley Jun Sch LS26 . . .200 B6
Methley La LS26 . . . . . . .200 A6
Methley Pk Hospl
  LS26 . . . . .200 A6
Methley Rd WF10 . . . . . .200 D4
Methodist Prim Sch
  DL11 . . . . .36 E5
Meuse Cl 4 DL9 . . . . . . .209 C1
Mewburn Rd DL3 . . . . .3 C8
Mewith La LA2 . . . . .129 B6
Mews The WF6 . . . . .200 A2
Meynell Rd DL3 . . . . .3 C7
Meyrick Ave LS22 . . . . . .180 D4
Michael Mount Rd
  YO11 . . . . .213 C1
Michael Syddall CE Aided
  Prim Sch DL10 . . . . .41 E5
Micklebury La HG4 . . . . . .86 A3
Mickleby La TS13 . . . . . . .11 F4
Mickledale La YO26 . . . . .163 D8
Micklefield CE Sch
  LS25 . . . . .195 A4
Micklefield Sta LS25 . . . .195 A3
Micklegate
  17 Pontefract WF8 . . . . .201 B1
  1 Selby YO8 . . . . .232 C5
  York YO1 . . . . .233 A2
Micklegate Bar Mus ★
  YO24 . . . . .233 A1
Micklethwaite View
  LS22 . . . . .180 C2
Mickletown Rd LS26 . . . .200 B6
Micklewaite Gr LS22 . . . .180 C2
Middle Bank Rd TS7 . . . . .7 D7
Middle Banks 24 YO32 . .166 E5
Middle Head Rd YO18 . . . .71 E8
Middle La Brayton YO8 . . .232 C1
  Brompton YO13 . . . . .98 C7
  Collingham LS22 . . . . . . .180 B1
  Hutton Buscel YO13 . . . . .74 F1
  Kettlewell with Starbotton
    BD23 . . . . .108 A3
  14 Knottingley WF11 . . . .202 A2
  Snainton YO13 . . . . .97 F4
Middle Moor La DL11 . . . .39 F5
Middle Oxford St
  WF10 . . . . .200 E4
Middle Rd TS17 . . . . .6 A5
Middle St Gayles DL11 . . .19 E6
  Swinton YO17 . . . . .121 B4
  Wilberfoss YO41 . . . . . . .185 F5
Middle Wlk YO12 . . . . . . .212 E7
Middlebrook Gdns
  YO8 . . . . .232 A2
Middlecave Cl YO17 . . . . .215 A4
Middlecave Dr YO17 . . . . .215 A4
Middlecave Rd YO17 . . . .215 A4
Middlecroft Dr YO32 . . . .167 A7
Middlecroft Gr 2 YO32 . .167 B7
Middlefield Cl
  19 Osgodby YO11 . . . . . .100 B7
  Weaverthorpe YO17 . . . . .124 E1
Middlefield La
  Kirk Smeaton WF8 . . . . . .206 A2
  Melmerby DL8 . . . . .84 A8
Middleham Ave YO31 . . . .228 E8
Middleham Castle ★
  DL8 . . . . .60 E2
Middleham CE Aided Prim
  Sch DL8 . . . . .60 E2
Middleham La DL8 . . . . . .60 E4
Middlesbrough Rd TS7 . . . .7 E6
Middlethorpe Dr
  YO24 . . . . .230 E7
Middlethorpe Gr YO24 . . .230 F7
Middleton Ave
  Ilkley LS29 . . . . .218 E5
  Thornaby TS17 . . . . .6 B6
Middleton Carr La
  YO18 . . . . .95 D7
Middleton Cl
  Egglescliffe TS16 . . . . . . .5 C5
  Settrington YO17 . . . . . . .122 D1
Middleton La
  Middleton YO18 . . . . .95 E8
  Middleton St George DL2 . . .4 C3
Middleton Rd
  Hutton Rudby TS15 . . . . . .25 D6
  Ilkley LS29 . . . . .218 A4
  Pickering YO18 . . . . .95 E7
  Sadberge DL2 . . . . .4 C7
  York YO24 . . . . .227 C2
Middleton St George Prim
  Sch DL2 . . . . .4 C4
Middleton Tyas CE Prim Sch
  DL10 . . . . .21 C5
Middleton Tyas La
  DL10 . . . . .21 B4
Middleway BD20 . . . . . . .174 C1
Middlewood Cl
  3 Fylingdales YO22 . . . . . .33 C3
  Rufforth YO23 . . . . .182 C6
Middlewood Cres 5
  YO22 . . . . .33 C3
Middlewood Garth 4
  YO22 . . . . .33 C3
Middlewood La YO22 . . . . .33 C3
Middycar Bank HG4 . . . . .138 F6
Midge Hall Cl 18 LS29 . . .176 C1

Midgeley Gate HG5 . . . . . . .162 F2
Midgeley La HG5 . . . . . .163 A3
Midgley Cl
　4 Embsay BD23 . . . . .217 C7
　21 Stamford Bridge YO41 .168 D2
Midgley Ct LS29 . . . . . . .176 C1
Midgley Rise 2 WF8 . . . . .201 B2
Midhope Way 15 YO14 . . .101 A3
Midland St YO26 . . . . . . .216 E3
Midway Ave YO26 . . . . . . .224 A1
Mightens' Bank DL8 . . . . .60 D4
Milbank Rd DL3 . . . . .3 B5
Milburn La YO7 . . . . .89 D3
Mildred Gr 5 YO24 . . . . . .227 C2
Mildred Sylvester Way
　WF6 . . . . .200 B1
Mile Hill Coldhill La
　LS25 . . . . .195 E5
Mile Planting DL10 . . . . . .209 F8
Milestone Ave YO23 . . . . .182 C6
Milford Mews 7 YO32 . . . .225 D7
Milford Rd LS25 . . . . .195 F3
Milford Way 8 YO32 . . . . .225 D7
Milking Hill YO61 . . . . . . .118 B4
Mill Balk DN14 . . . . .207 C8
Mill Bank
　Bishop Thornton HG3 . . . .138 F1
　Fylingdales YO22 . . . . .33 D2
　Lindrick with Studley
　　Royal & Fountains HG4 . .113 A3
　Norton YO17 . . . . .215 E3
Mill Bank Rd YO18 . . . . . . .72 C5
Mill Bridge BD23 . . . . . . .216 F4
Mill Brow LA2 . . . . .128 C2
Mill Brow Rd BB18 . . . . . .172 B1
Mill Chase Rd HG2 . . . . . .220 D5
Mill Cl
　Monk Fryston LS25 . . . . .202 A8
　Ravensworth DL11 . . . . . . .19 F6
　Settle BD24 . . . . .131 C2
　6 Spofforth HG3 . . . . . .179 E6
Mill Cotts YO17 . . . . .215 D4
Mill Croft
　Cowling BD22 . . . . .187 B6
　Richmond DL10 . . . . .209 A7
Mill Dam LS23 . . . . .188 F7
Mill Dam La WF8 . . . . . . .201 B2
Mill Dike La YO7 . . . . .116 F8
Mill Field La YO61 . . . . . . .91 B1
Mill Field Rd YO8 . . . . . . .203 B5
Mill Flats La DL8 . . . . .60 F3
Mill Garth 14 YO8 . . . . . . .198 F1
Mill Gate
　Gilling with Hartforth & Sedbury
　DL10 . . . . .20 E3
　Harrogate HG1 . . . . .219 C7
　Knayton with Brawith YO7 .65 F2
Mill Gn Way The YO22 . . . . .51 D8
Mill Hill Escrick YO19 . . . .192 B5
　16 Normanton South WF6 .200 A1
Mill Hill Cl 8 DL6 . . . . .43 F3
Mill Hill Com Prim Sch
　DL6 . . . . .210 E4
Mill Hill Cres DL6 . . . . . . .210 E3
Mill Hill Dr YO32 . . . . . . .225 F4
Mill Hill La
　Giggleswick BD24 . . . . . .131 C3
　Northallerton DL6 . . . . . .210 E3
Mill Hills La DL11 . . . . .38 E4
Mill House YO7 . . . . .65 D1
Mill La
　Acaster Malbis YO23 . . . .191 C8
　Ampleforth YO62 . . . . . . .118 C4
　Askham Richard YO23 . . .182 D2
　Askrigg DL8 . . . . .57 E6
　Aysgarth DL8 . . . . .58 E3
　Barlow YO8 . . . . .204 B7
　Bellerby DL8 . . . . .60 E8
　Bentham LA2 . . . . .128 F7
　3 Beverley HG3 . . . . . . .137 B4
　Boroughbridge YO51 . . . .141 B5
　Brayton YO8 . . . . .203 C8
　Buckton/Bempton YO13 . . .97 D5
　Burniston YO13 . . . . .75 C8
　Burton Leonard HG3 . . . .140 B2
　Carlton DN14 . . . . .204 D3
　Castleford WF10 . . . . . . .200 E5
　Cayton YO11 . . . . .100 C6
　Constable Burton DL8 . . . .61 C5
　Darlington DL1 . . . . .3 F6
　Earby BB18 . . . . .172 B1
　Easingwold YO61 . . . . . . .117 D1
　3 East Ayton/West Ayton
　YO13 . . . . .99 A7
　Eskdaleside cum Ugglebarnby
　YO22 . . . . .32 B6
　Exelby, Leeming & Newton
　DL7 . . . . .63 D3
　Facedy TS9 . . . . .25 F2
　Farndale East YO62 . . . . . .48 E4
　Gargrave BD23 . . . . .155 D1
　Great Ouseburn YO26 . . .164 C8
　Hambleton YO8 . . . . . . .196 F1
　Haxby YO32 . . . . .166 D5
　Hebden BD23 . . . . .135 A1
　2 Hemingbrough YO8 . . .198 F1
　Hessay YO23 . . . . .182 B7
　High Coniscliffe DL2 . . . . . .2 C6
　Kearby with Netherby
　LS22 . . . . .179 C2
　Kirk Hammerton YO26 . . .164 C2
　Knaresborough HG5 . . . .221 F8
　Langtoft YO25 . . . . .151 C7
　Leyburn DL8 . . . . .60 E4
　6 Linton-on-Ouse YO30 .164 F7
　Long Preston BD23 . . . . .153 F4
　Longnewton DL2 . . . . .4 F6
　Low Bradley BD20 . . . . . .173 E3

Mill La continued
　Mickletown LS26 . . . . . . .200 B6
　Middleton St George DL2 . . .4 D5
　Muston YO14 . . . . .101 A2
　Nether Silton YO7 . . . . . . .66 B6
　Newland YO8 . . . . .205 A3
　Northallerton DL7 . . . . . .210 C3
　Pannal HG3 . . . . .222 E2
　Pickering YO18 . . . . .95 F6
　Pontefract WF8 . . . . . . .201 C2
　Rawcliffe DN14 . . . . .204 F1
　Redmire DL8 . . . . .59 C5
　1 Riccall YO19 . . . . .192 A1
　Ryther cum Ossendyke
　LS24 . . . . .190 E1
　1 Scarborough YO12 . . . .212 E4
　Scruton DL7 . . . . .63 E5
　Sherburn in Elmet LS25 . .195 F2
　Skipton BD23 . . . . .216 F3
　Sledmere YO25 . . . . .149 F3
　Snape with Thorp DL8 . . . .87 B7
　South Milford LS25 . . . . .195 F2
　Spofforth with Stockeld
　HG3 . . . . .179 E6
　Stillington YO61 . . . . . . .144 C6
　Stutton with Hazlewood
　LS24 . . . . .189 E4
　Swinden BD23 . . . . .154 B1
　Thirkleby High & Low
　with Osgodby YO7 . . . . . .90 D2
　Thormanby YO61 . . . . . .116 E5
　Thrintoft DL7 . . . . .63 F8
　Whitwood WF10 . . . . . . .200 B2
　Wilberfoss YO41 . . . . . . .185 E6
　York YO31 . . . . .228 E6
　Youlton YO61 . . . . .142 F2
Mill La Ave YO60 . . . . . . .145 C5
Mill Mount YO24 . . . . . . .228 A3
Mill Mount Ct YO24 . . . . .228 A3
Mill Race The 4 DL2 . . . . . .22 C8
Mill Rd
　Burton Fleming YO25 . . . .126 D4
　Gillamoor YO62 . . . . .70 A5
　Goldsborough HG5 . . . . .221 F3
Mill Riggs TS9 . . . . .26 D7
Mill Rise DL6 . . . . .210 E2
Mill Row BD20 . . . . .187 F7
Mill St
　6 Barnoldswick BB18 . . . .171 D1
　Glusburn BD20 . . . . .187 F7
　Guisborough TS14 . . . . .8 F6
　Harome YO62 . . . . .93 C4
　Malton YO17 . . . . .215 E3
　Scarborough YO12 . . . . . .212 F5
　York YO1 . . . . .233 C1
Mill View
　5 Burley in Warfedale
　LS29 . . . . .176 C1
　Knottingley WF11 . . . . . .201 D2
Mill Wynd TS16 . . . . .5 E3
Millbank Ct YO7 . . . . .89 D4
Millbank La TS17 . . . . .6 B7
Millbeck Gn LS22 . . . . . . .188 A8
Millenium Rd BD20 . . . . . .173 D4
Millers Cl YO17 . . . . .215 D2
Millers Croft 2 YO23 . . . .230 B3
Millers La TS12 . . . . .9 F6
Millers Rd 2 YO7 . . . . . . .211 C3
Millfield YO51 . . . . .141 D2
Millfield Ave
　Northallerton DL6 . . . . . .210 E3
　York YO10 . . . . .228 F3
Millfield Cl
　Eaglescliffe TS16 . . . . .5 D4
　1 Leeming DL7 . . . . .63 D4
　Pickering YO18 . . . . .95 F6
　Wilberfoss YO41 . . . . . . .185 E5
Millfield Cres YO19 . . . . . .210 E3
Millfield Ct YO19 . . . . . . .192 F7
Millfield Dr YO8 . . . . .204 D4
Millfield Gdns YO26 . . . . .224 A2
Millfield Glade HG2 . . . . .220 D4
Millfield La
　Easingwold YO61 . . . . . . .117 C1
　Nether Poppleton YO26 . .227 B8
　Poppleton YO26 . . . . . . .224 A2
　York YO10 . . . . .229 A3
Millfield Rd
　17 Hemingbrough YO8 . . .198 F1
　Hemingbrough YO8 . . . . .204 F8
　York YO23 . . . . .228 B2
Millfield Rise YO61 . . . . . .117 C1
Millfield St 4 HG3 . . . . . . .137 B4
Millfields BD20 . . . . .174 B1
Millgarth Ct 7 LS22 . . . . .188 A8
Millgate 10 Masham HG4 . .86 C3
　Richmond DL10 . . . . .209 C6
　Selby YO8 . . . . .232 C6
　Thirsk YO7 . . . . .211 B3
Millgate House Gdn *
　DL10 . . . . .209 C6
Millgates YO26 . . . . .227 C6
Millholme Rise BD23 . . . .217 C8
Millings La YO51 . . . . .141 B7
Millrace Cl YO17 . . . . .215 D2
Millside YO17 . . . . .215 D2
Millthorpe Sec Sch
　YO23 . . . . .228 B2
Millway YO62 . . . . .92 C1
Milner La LS24 . . . . .195 D8
Milner Rd DL1 . . . . .3 D4
Milner St YO24 . . . . .227 D3
Milners La HG1 . . . . .219 F7
Milnthorpe Cl 6 LS23 . . . .188 E6
Milnthorpe Garth 7
　LS23 . . . . .188 E6
Milnthorpe Gdns 5
　LS23 . . . . .188 E6

Milnthorpe La LS23 . . . . . .188 E6
Milnthorpe Way LS23 . . . .188 E6
Milson Gr YO10 . . . . .229 A3
Milton Ave
　Malton YO17 . . . . .215 D5
　Scarborough YO12 . . . . . .212 E3
Milton Carr 8 YO30 . . . . .224 F1
Milton Cl HG1 . . . . .219 E7
Milton Gr 11 BB18 . . . . . .171 D2
Milton Rd Malton YO17 . . .215 C5
　Pannal HG3 . . . . .222 E3
　4 Skipton BD23 . . . . . . .217 A4
　York YO1 . . . . .228 F3
Minchin Cl 3 YO30 . . . . . .225 B1
Mine Mus * BB18 . . . . . . .172 A2
Minors Cres DL3 . . . . .3 A7
Minskip Rd HG5 . . . . .140 E3
Minster Ave YO31 . . . . . . .225 C8
Minster Cl
　3 Haxby YO32 . . . . .225 C8
　23 Ripon HG4 . . . . .214 C5
　York YO1 . . . . .233 B3
Minster Ct YO31 . . . . .233 B3
Minster Rd HG4 . . . . .214 C5
Minster Sch The YO1 . . . .233 B3
Minster View YO32 . . . . . .225 C8
Minster Wlk 12 DL2 . . . . . . .3 E1
Minster Yd YO1 . . . . .233 B3
Minsterley Dr TS5 . . . . .6 F7
Minter Cl 2 YO24 . . . . . . .227 B1
Mire Bank La DL8 . . . . .56 F4
Mire Ridge BB8 . . . . .186 A2
Mire Syke La HG5 . . . . . . .162 A5
Mires La Carthorpe DL8 . . . .87 D6
　Ulleskelf LS24 . . . . .190 B1
Mirkhill Rd YO8 . . . . .232 B6
Miry La YO15 . . . . .188 C1
Mistral Ct YO31 . . . . .228 E8
Mitchell Ave
　Aline YO61 . . . . .142 F4
　Catton YO41 . . . . .185 D8
　Settle BD24 . . . . .131 E1
Mitchell Way YO30 . . . . . .224 E3
Mitchel's La YO10 . . . . . . .231 F8
Miterdale 4 YO24 . . . . . . .230 C7
Mitford Cl 3 YO14 . . . . . .126 F8
Mitford Rd 2 YO14 . . . . . .126 F8
Mitford St 24 YO14 . . . . .101 B3
Mitton La BD20 . . . . .172 D1
Moat Field YO10 . . . . .229 C4
Moat Way YO8 . . . . .197 D1
Moatside Ct YO31 . . . . . . .233 B3
Mock Beggar Hall *
　BD23 . . . . .157 D7
Moins Ct YO10 . . . . .229 D4
Moiser Cl YO32 . . . . .225 D4
Mole End 15 YO18 . . . . . . .95 F6
Monarch Way YO26 . . . . . .227 D6
Monash Ave DL9 . . . . .209 C1
Monckton Dr WF10 . . . . . .201 B3
Monk Ave YO31 . . . . .228 F7
Monk Bar & Richard III Mus *
　YO31 . . . . .233 C3
Monk Bar Ct YO31 . . . . . .233 B3
Monk Fryston CE VC Prim
　Sch LS25 . . . . .202 A8
Monk Fryston Prim Sch
　LS25 . . . . .202 A8
Monk Gdns La YO62 . . . . . .93 A4
Monk Gn YO61 . . . . .142 F4
Monk Ing Rd HG3 . . . . . . .159 E8
Monk La YO8 . . . . .232 C7
Monk Pk Farm * YO7 . . . . .90 D4
Monk's Rd BD23 . . . . .107 D2
Monkbridge Ct YO31 . . . . .233 C4
Monket House Bank
　YO62 . . . . .48 C4
Monkgate YO31 . . . . .233 C3
Monkgate Cloisters
　YO31 . . . . .233 C3
Monkhill Ave WF8 . . . . . . .201 B1
Monkhill Dr WF8 . . . . .201 B1
Monkhill La WF8 . . . . .201 B2
Monkhill Mount WF8 . . . .201 B1
Monkholme La BD23 . . . . .134 C2
Monkroyd Ave BB18 . . . . .171 D1
Monks Cross Dr YO32 . . . .226 A3
Monks Cross Link
　YO32 . . . . .226 B4
Monks Cross Sh Pk
　YO32 . . . . .226 B3
Monkswell Pk HG5 . . . . . .221 D5
Monkton Rd 5 YO31 . . . . .225 F1
Monkton Rise 7 TS14 . . . . .8 F7
Monmouth Dr TS16 . . . . . . .5 E5
Monmouth St 5 BB8 . . . .186 A3
Mons Cl 3 DL9 . . . . .209 B1
Mons Rd DL9 . . . . .40 F4
Montage Studio Gall *
　YO21 . . . . .29 A7
Montague Cres LS25 . . . . .194 D4
Montague Rd YO23 . . . . . .231 A3
Montague St YO23 . . . . . .228 C1
Montague Wlk 6 YO26 . . .165 F1
Montagu's Harrier TS14 . . .8 D6
Montgomery Rd DL9 . . . . .209 C1
Montgomery St 3 . . . . . . .217 A3
Montpellier Ct 11 HG2 . . .219 C2
Montpellier Gdns 2
　HG1 . . . . .219 C2
Montpellier Hill HG2 . . . . .219 C2
Montpellier Mews 3
　HG1 . . . . .219 C2
Montpellier Par HG1 . . . .219 C2

Montpellier Rd 1 HG1 . . . .219 C2
Montpellier Sq 3 HG1 . . . .219 D2
Montpellier St 4 HG1 . . . .219 C2
Montrose St YO31 . . . . . . .228 D8
Moody Sty La 4 BD23 . . . .134 E3
Mook St YO60 . . . . .169 B8
Moons Acre 4 LS23 . . . . . .188 E7
Moor Ave 1 LS23 . . . . . . .188 E7
Moor Carr La YO8 . . . . . . .198 B5
Moor Cl Killinghall HG3 . . .219 A8
　10 Kirklevington TS15 . . . .24 E8
　Lockwood TS12 . . . . .10 A5
　Wheldrake YO19 . . . . . . .192 F8
Moor Cres BD23 . . . . .217 B4
Moor Croft 8 BD23 . . . . . .134 E3
Moor End La
　Crakehall DL8 . . . . .62 C3
　Sowerby YO7 . . . . .90 A2
Moor End Rd YO13 . . . . . . .53 D2
Moor Gn TS7 . . . . .7 D5
Moor Gr YO24 . . . . .230 E8
Moor Hill YO7 . . . . .147 E7
Moor House La YO61 . . . . .116 B1
Moor La
　Addingham LS29 . . . . . . .174 D5
　Aislaby YO21 . . . . .31 F7
　Aldfield HG4 . . . . .138 F8
　Arkendale HG5 . . . . .162 F8
　Arrathorne DL10 . . . . .41 A2
　Askwith LS21 . . . . .176 D4
　Bagby YO7 . . . . .90 C4
　6 Barlby YO8 . . . . .198 B5
　Bilbrough LS24 . . . . .182 B3
　Bilton-in-Ainsty with Bickerton
　YO26 . . . . .181 D5
　Bishopthorpe YO23 . . . . .230 E2
　Borrowby TS13 . . . . .11 C6
　Brawby YO17 . . . . .94 F2
　Brompton YO13 . . . . .74 B1
　Broughton YO17 . . . . . . .121 C4
　Burton Leonard HG3 . . . .140 B4
　Carthorpe DL8 . . . . .87 D4
　Catterton LS24 . . . . .190 A8
　Cleasby DL2 . . . . .2 F2
　Cliffe YO8 . . . . .198 F4
　Cloughton YO13 . . . . .54 C1
　Collingham LS23 . . . . . . .188 C8
　Coneythorpe & Clareton
　HG5 . . . . .163 B6
　Copmanthorpe YO23 . . . .230 A1
　Cropton YO18 . . . . .71 B6
　Crosby DL6 . . . . .65 C5
　Dalton DL11 . . . . .19 C6
　Dalton YO7 . . . . .116 B8
　Dishforth YO7 . . . . .114 F3
　Earswick YO32 . . . . .226 C8
　East Ayton/West Ayton
　YO13 . . . . .99 A3
　East Layton DL11 . . . . . . .20 B8
　Eastfield YO11 . . . . .100 A6
　Elslack BD23 . . . . .172 D3
　Embsay with Eastby
　BD23 . . . . .156 F1
　Full Sutton YO41 . . . . . . .168 F1
　Grassington BD23 . . . . . .134 E3
　Great Ouseburn YO26 . . .163 D7
　Great Ribston with Walshford
　LS22 . . . . .180 E8
　Halton East BD23 . . . . . .157 B1
　Haxby YO32 . . . . .166 D7
　Hunton DL8 . . . . .61 E8
　Hutton-le-Hole YO62 . . . . .70 C5
　Kearby with Netherby
　HG3 . . . . .179 B2
　Kelfield YO19 . . . . .191 E2
　Kirby Hill HG4 . . . . .140 F8
　Long Preston BD23 . . . . .153 F5
　Milby YO51 . . . . .141 C7
　Murton YO19 . . . . .229 F6
　Myton-on-Swale YO61 . . .142 B5
　Naburn YO19 . . . . .191 D8
　Nether Silton DL6 . . . . . . .66 C8
　Newsham DL11 . . . . .19 A7
　Newsham with Breckenbrough
　YO7 . . . . .65 A1
　Newton-on-Ouse YO30 . . .165 C7
　Rufforth YO23 . . . . .182 E6
　Ryther cum Ossendyke
　LS24 . . . . .196 B8
　Scalby YO12 . . . . .212 A8
　Settrington YO17 . . . . . . .122 C1
　Sherburn in Elmet LS25 . .195 F4
　Skelton YO30 . . . . .224 D6
　Snape with Thorp DL8 . . . .86 B6
　Steeton with Eastburn
　BD20 . . . . .187 F7
　Stillington YO61 . . . . . . .143 F6
　Strensall YO32 . . . . .167 B7
　Stutton with Hazlewood
　LS24 . . . . .189 D4
　Thirkleby High & Low with
　Osgodby YO7 . . . . .90 C1
　Thirsk YO7 . . . . .89 D3
　Tholthorpe YO61 . . . . . . .142 D6
　Thormanby YO61 . . . . . .116 E5
　Thornton Steward HG4 . . . .61 E2
　Thornton-le-Clay YO60 . . .145 F2
　Thorp Arch LS23 . . . . . . .180 E3
　Threshfield BD23 . . . . . . .134 B2
　Welburn YO62 . . . . .94 A5
　West Tanfield HG4 . . . . . .87 B2
　Weston LS21 . . . . .176 C2
　Wilstrop YO26 . . . . .181 D8
　Yafforth DL7 . . . . .43 B2
　York YO24 . . . . .230 C2
Moor La Trad Est
　LS25 . . . . .196 A3

Moor Lee La
　Eggborough DN14 . . . . . .207 B8
　Heck DN14 . . . . .203 B1
Moor Pk TS7 . . . . .7 D5
Moor Pk Cl
　2 Addingham LS29 . . . . .174 E4
　Pannal HG3 . . . . .178 A4
Moor Pk Cres 3 LS29 . . . .174 E4
Moor Pk Dr LS29 . . . . . . .174 E4
Moor Pk Gr 2 LS29 . . . . . .174 F4
Moor Pk Way 1 LS29 . . . .174 E4
Moor Rd Askrigg DL8 . . . . .57 E6
　Bishop Monkton HG3 . . . .139 F5
　Filey YO14 . . . . .101 B1
　Hunmanby YO14 . . . . . . .127 B7
　Ilkley LS29 . . . . .218 A1
　Knayton with Brawith YO7 .65 F2
　Leyburn DL8 . . . . .60 C5
　Marton cum Grafton
　YO51 . . . . .141 C2
　Melsonby DL10 . . . . .20 F6
　Muston YO14 . . . . .101 A2
　9 Sherburn in Elmet LS25 195 F4
　Stamford Bridge YO41 . . .168 D2
　Wykeham YO13 . . . . .74 B4
Moor Side LS23 . . . . .188 B8
Moor View 2 TS13 . . . . . . .11 F7
Moor Way YO22 . . . . .226 A4
Moorber La BD23 . . . . . . .171 F8
Moorberries TS15 . . . . .6 C2
Moorbridge Croft 6
　LS25 . . . . .196 A4
Moorcock La HG3 . . . . . . .159 F5
Moorcroft Rd YO24 . . . . . .230 D7
Moore Ave YO10 . . . . .229 B4
Moorfield Dr YO41 . . . . . .185 E6
Moorfield Rd LS29 . . . . . .218 F4
Moorfield Sch LS29 . . . . .218 C3
Moorfield Way YO41 . . . .185 E6
Moorfields
　Raskelf YO61 . . . . .116 F2
　3 Wistow YO8 . . . . .197 B6
Moorfields La YO62 . . . . . .93 E5
Moorfoot La BD20 . . . . . .173 D2
Moorgarth Ave 10 YO24 . .227 B1
Moorgate YO24 . . . . .227 D3
Moorgate Dr LS25 . . . . . .194 D1
Moorgate Rd LS25 . . . . . .194 D2
Moorhill La YO17 . . . . . . .147 E6
Moorhouse Cl 3 WF6 . . . .200 B2
Moorhouse La YO7 . . . . . . .89 E8
Moorland Ave
　6 Earby BB18 . . . . .172 B1
　Skipton BD23 . . . . .217 A4
Moorland Cl
　5 Embsay BD23 . . . . . . .217 E8
　Harrogate HG2 . . . . .220 D4
Moorland Garth 2
　YO32 . . . . .167 A7
Moorland Gdns YO23 . . . .230 A1
Moorland Rd
　Harrogate HG2 . . . . .220 D4
　Scarborough YO12 . . . . . .212 F7
　York YO10 . . . . .231 D8
Moorland Rise BD23 . . . . .217 E8
Moorland Terr BD23 . . . . .217 B4
Moorland View HG2 . . . . .220 D4
Moorlands Ilkley LS29 . . . .218 A2
　Skelton YO32 . . . . .166 B5
Moorlands Cl YO10 . . . . . .229 C4
Moorlands Fields
　YO10 . . . . .231 E8
Moorlands La
　Skelton YO30 . . . . .224 C6
　1 Tollerton YO61 . . . . . .143 B3
Moorlands Nature Reserve *
　YO32 . . . . .166 B5
Moorlands Pk YO21 . . . . . .29 A6
Moors Ctr The *
　Danby YO21 . . . . .29 D7
　Ilkley LS29 . . . . .218 A4
Moorsholm La TS13 . . . . . .10 C6
Moorside
　Melling-with-Wrayton
　LA6 . . . . .102 A2
　Scalby YO12 . . . . .212 A8
Moorside Ave HG4 . . . . . .214 B2
Moorside Cl LA6 . . . . .102 A2
Moorside Cty Jun & Inf Schs
　HG4 . . . . .214 B3
Moorside Dale 6 HG4 . . . .214 B2
Moorside La
　Addingham LS29 . . . . . . .175 A2
　Askwith LS21 . . . . .176 C4
Moorside Rd DL10 . . . . . .209 E8
Moorside View HG4 . . . . .214 C2
Moorview Rd
　Northallerton DL6 . . . . . .210 F5
　Skipton BD23 . . . . .217 B3
Moorview Way BD23 . . . . .217 B4
Morcar Rd YO41 . . . . .168 D1
Morehall Cl YO30 . . . . . . .224 F2
Morgan Dr TS14 . . . . .8 E6
Morgan St 4 YO12 . . . . . .212 F5
Morlais Ct 28 TS17 . . . . . . .5 F4
Morley Dr 10 YO13 . . . . . . .99 A7
Morley Gate DL11 . . . . . . .37 E5
Mornington Cres HG1 . . . .219 E4
Mornington Rd LS29 . . . . .218 C4
Mornington Terr HG1 . . . .219 E3
Morpeth Ave
　Coulby Newham TS4 . . . . . .7 A7
　Darlington DL1 . . . . .3 F7
Morpeth Gate DL8 . . . . . . .58 F1
Morrell Ct YO24 . . . . .230 B8

Morrell Way YO10 . . . . . . .229 A3
Morrets La YO8 . . . . .197 A1
Morris Fields 22 WF6 . . . . .200 B1
Morrison Rd TS14 . . . . .8 F7
Morritt Cl 3 YO31 . . . . . . .228 F8
Morton Carr La TS7 . . . . . .7 E6
Morton Cl YO8 . . . . .203 A4
Morton Rd DL1 . . . . .4 A5
Mosber La BD23 . . . . .172 C8
Moss Arc HG4 . . . . .214 C5
Moss End La BD22 . . . . . .186 F5
Moss Gn La
  Brayton YO8 . . . . .232 A2
  Hirst Courtney YO8 . . . . .203 F3
Moss Haven DN6 . . . . . . .207 D1
Moss Hill La HG4 . . . . . . .164 D5
Moss Rd DN6 . . . . .207 B1
Moss Side BB18 . . . . . . .171 E1
Moss St YO23 . . . . .233 A1
Moss Way TS18 . . . . .5 F7
Mossburn Dr YO62 . . . . . .119 E6
Mossdale Gr TS14 . . . . . .8 D6
Mossra La HG4 . . . . .85 F4
Mosswood Cres TS5 . . . . .6 D7
Mosswood La YO61 . . . . . .118 A1
Mossy La 56 C4
Mother Shipton's Cave &
Well * HG5 . . . . .221 A5
Moule Rise LS25 . . . . . . .194 E5
Moulton Hall * DL10 . . . . .21 D2
Moulton La DL7 . . . . .22 C3
Mounstrall La DL7 . . . . . .43 C1
Mount Ave YO8 . . . . .232 B3
Mount Bank DL6 . . . . . . .45 A5
Mount Cres YO17 . . . . . .215 B5
Mount Dr DL8 . . . . .60 D5
Mount Ephraim 6
  YO24 . . . . .228 A3
Mount Farm Cl YO22 . . . . .208 E3
Mount Gdns HG2 . . . . . . .222 E7
Mount Gr YO8 . . . . .232 B3
Mount Grace Priory *
DL6 . . . . .45 B5
Mount Leven Rd TS15 . . . .5 F3
Mount Par
  5 Harrogate HG1 . . . . . .219 D3
  York YO24 . . . . .228 A3
Mount Pk YO19 . . . . .198 A8
Mount Pk Ave YO12 . . . . .212 E5
Mount Pk Rd 7 YO12 . . . .212 E4
Mount Pleasant
  26 Addingham LS29 . . . . .174 F4
  High Bentham LA2 . . . . .129 A8
  Ilkley LS29 . . . . .218 C3
  Kippax LS25 . . . . .200 D8
  Newby & Scalby YO13 . . .75 C5
  Whitby YO22 . . . . .208 F5
Mount Pleasant Cl 9 DL2 .4 C4
Mount Pleasant E 2
YO22 . . . . .33 D4
Mount Pleasant Grange
TS18 . . . . .6 A8
Mount Pleasant N 1
YO22 . . . . .33 D4
Mount Pleasant Prim Sch
DL3 . . . . .3 A7
Mount Pleasant S 3
YO22 . . . . .33 D4
Mount Rd Malton YO17 . . .215 B4
  Northallerton DL6 . . . . . .210 F6
Mount Sch The YO24 . . . .228 A3
Mount Side Pk YO11 . . . . .212 E2
Mount Sq 26 YO8 . . . . . . .208 C7
Mount St HG2 . . . . .222 E7
Mount Terr YO24 . . . . . . .228 A3
Mount The
  Barwick in Elmet & Scholes
  LS15 . . . . .194 B7
  Castleford WF10 . . . . . . .201 B4
  Malton YO17 . . . . .215 B4
  Middlesbrough TS6 . . . . .7 E8
  Selby YO8 . . . . .232 B3
  8 Thornton Dale YO18 . . .96 D5
  York YO24 . . . . .233 A1
Mount Vale YO24 . . . . . . .228 A3
Mount Vale Dr YO24 . . . . .228 A3
Mount View
  Muston YO14 . . . . .101 A2
  Northallerton DL7 . . . . . .210 C6
Mount View Ave YO12 . . . .212 E3
Mount View Cl 4 YO12 . . .212 E3
Mount View Rd 9 YO11 100 B6
Mountside YO11 . . . . .212 F3
Mouseman Visitor Ctr *
YO61 . . . . .91 B2
Mowbray Castle (site of) *
HG4 . . . . .112 D5
Mowbray Cres
  17 Bedale DL8 . . . . .63 A2
  Hovingham YO62 . . . . . .119 E6
  Kirkby Malzeard HG4 . . . .112 D5
Mowbray Dr
  4 Hurworth-on-Tees DL2 . .3 E1
  York YO26 . . . . .227 C4
Mowbray Pl YO7 . . . . . . .211 B2
Mowbray Rd
  5 Catterick DL10 . . . . . .41 D5
  Northallerton DL6 . . . . . .210 E6
Mowbray Sch DL8 . . . . . .63 A2
Mowbray Sq HG1 . . . . . . .219 D3
Mowbray Terr
  Thirsk YO7 . . . . .211 B2
  West Tanfield HG4 . . . . . .87 A2
Mowden Inf Sch DL3 . . . . .3 A6
Mowthorp Rd YO12 . . . . . .75 A3

Mowthorpe La YO60 . . . . .145 F8
Mowthorpe Medieval
Village * YO17 . . . . . . .149 C6
Moxby La YO61 . . . . .144 D5
Moxby Priory * YO61 . . . . .144 A5
Muddy La LS22 . . . . .180 A1
Muff La TS8 . . . . .7 A3
Muirfield TS7 . . . . .7 D5
Muirfield Ave WF7 . . . . . .200 E1
Muirfield Rd TS16 . . . . . .5 E5
Muirfield Way 4 YO26 . . . .227 B5
Mulberry Ct YO32 . . . . . . .225 F6
Mulberry Dr 7 YO32 . . . . .166 E5
Mulberry Garth LS23 . . . . .188 F8
Mulgrave Castle *
YO21 . . . . .12 E2
Mulgrave Cres YO21 . . . . .208 B8
Mulgrave Dr 6 DL7 . . . . . .210 D2
Mulgrave Pl YO11 . . . . . . .213 D7
Mulgrave Rd YO21 . . . . . .208 A8
Mulgrave View YO22 . . . . .32 F7
Mullberry Gdns LS26 . . . . .200 A5
Mulwith Cl YO31 . . . . . . .229 A6
Mulwith La HG4 . . . . .140 E6
Muncaster Way YO22 . . . . .208 E3
Muncastergate YO31 . . . . .228 E7
Murchison Pl 8 YO12 . . . . .212 F6
Murchison St YO12 . . . . . .212 E6
Murray St 31 Filey YO14 . . .101 B3
  Scarborough YO12 . . . . . .212 F5
  York YO24 . . . . .227 F3
Murray Wlk DL3 . . . . .3 A5
Murrayfield Way 5 DL1 . . . .3 F6
YO31 . . . . .228 C7
Murton Bank YO62 . . . . . .67 E3
Murton Garth YO19 . . . . . .229 F6
Murton La YO19 . . . . .184 D7
Murton Way YO19 . . . . . . .229 E5
Mus of Victorian Whitby *
YO22 . . . . .208 D7
Muscoates La YO62 . . . . . .93 F3
Museum of Craven Life *
BD24 . . . . .131 E2
Museum St YO1 . . . . .233 B2
Musham Bank Rd YO11 . . .99 F7
Music in Miniature Ex *
YO22 . . . . .33 D3
Musterfield La HG4 . . . . . .113 B7
Muston Rd Filey YO14 . . . .101 A3
  Hunmanby YO14 . . . . . . .126 F8
Mutton Scalp Rd TS12 . . . .9 E7
My Love La HG3 . . . . .159 C5
Myer's Gn La HG3 . . . . . . .161 B5
Myers La DL7 . . . . .64 A8
Myra Bank La YO61 . . . . . .117 F3
Myron Rd TS17 . . . . .5 F5
Myrtle Ave
  Bishopthorpe YO23 . . . . .231 B3
  Selby YO8 . . . . .232 B3
Myrtle Gdns DL1 . . . . . . .3 D8
Myrtle Rd
  Eaglescliffe TS16 . . . . . . .5 E6
  3 Harrogate HG1 . . . . . .219 E3
Myrtle Sq 2 HG1 . . . . . . .219 E3
Myson Ave WF8 . . . . .201 C2
Myton La YO61 . . . . .142 C5
Myton Rd TS17 . . . . .6 A4

N

Nab View BD20 . . . . .174 C2
Nabs View YO12 . . . . .212 A8
Naburn CE Prim Sch
YO19 . . . . .191 D8
Naburn La
  Deighton YO19 . . . . .192 A7
  Fulford YO19 . . . . .231 D4
Naburn Pk Mews
YO19 . . . . .191 E8
Nairn Cl YO24 . . . . .230 C6
Nairnhead Cl TS8 . . . . . . .6 E5
Nalton Cl YO31 . . . . .230 A1
Nalton St YO8 . . . . .232 C5
Nanny Goat La
  Barwick in Elmet & Scholes
  LS25 . . . . .194 B4
  Hunton DL8 . . . . .61 F8
Nanny La LS24 . . . . .196 C7
Nansen St YO12 . . . . .212 E6
Nap Cote La HG3 . . . . . . .112 C4
Napier Cres YO12 . . . . . . .99 D7
Napier Rd HG4 . . . . .113 D3
Nares St YO12 . . . . .212 E6
Narrow La YO42 . . . . .193 D7
Narrowfield 8 YO22 . . . . . .32 A6
Nat La LS17 . . . . .178 A3
National Ctr for Early
Music * YO1 . . . . .233 C2
National Railway Mus *
YO26 . . . . .228 A4
Nattrass Wlk 7 DL8 . . . . . .63 B2
Navigation Rd YO1 . . . . . .233 C2
Navigation Sq BD23 . . . . .216 F4
Navigator Ct TS18 . . . . . .6 D8
Nawton Com Prim Sch
YO62 . . . . .93 D7
Nawton Rd YO62 . . . . . . .93 E7
Neasham Ct TS9 . . . . . . .26 C8
Neasham Hall DL2 . . . . . .4 B3
Neasham Rd
  Darlington DL1 . . . . .3 D4
  Low Dinsdale DL2 . . . . . .4 B3
Neile Cl DL7 . . . . .210 B4
Nell Bank Ctr * LS29 . . . . .218 D6
Nelson Rd LS29 . . . . .218 C4
Nelson St LS29 . . . . .218 B4

Nelson St
  7 Normanton South WF6 . .200 B2
  Scarborough YO12 . . . . . .212 F6
  Skipton BD23 . . . . .217 A3
  York YO31 . . . . .233 C4
Nelson's La YO24 . . . . . . .227 F1
Nesfield Cl
  17 Eastfield YO11 . . . . . .100 B6
  Harrogate HG1 . . . . .219 B5
Nesfield Rd LS29 . . . . . . .218 A5
Nesfield View 12 LS29 . . . .175 C2
Ness La
  Pickhill with Roxby YO7 . . .88 B6
  Tockwith YO26 . . . . .181 D3
Ness Rd 5 YO8 . . . . .232 D6
Nessgate YO1 . . . . .233 B2
Nestfield Cl WF8 . . . . . . .201 B2
Nestfield Ind Est DL1 . . . . .3 D6
Nether Way 20 YO11 . . . . .165 F1
Netherby Cl 6 YO22 . . . . . .32 A6
Netherby La
  Huttons Ambo YO60 . . . . .147 B6
  Sinnington YO62 . . . . . . .71 A1
Netherdale Cl LS22 . . . . . .180 D4
Netheredge Cl HG5 . . . . . .220 B5
Netheredge Dr HG5 . . . . . .220 B5
Netherfield Cl WF10 . . . . .200 C3
Netherfield La
  Thornton in Lonsdale
  LA6 . . . . .103 B4
  Ulleskelf LS24 . . . . .190 B3
  Westerdale YO21 . . . . . . .28 F6
  Wheldrake YO19 . . . . . . .192 C7
  Whixley YO26 . . . . .164 A4
Netherside Hall Sch
BD23 . . . . .134 C4
Netherwindings 18
YO32 . . . . .166 F5
Netherwoods 6 YO32 . . . . .167 B8
Nettledale Cl TS13 . . . . . .12 A7
Nettledale La YO13 . . . . . .97 F6
Nevern Cres TS17 . . . . . . .5 F4
Neville Cl DL2 . . . . .1 D8
Neville Cres BD23 . . . . . .155 D1
Neville Dr YO23 . . . . .231 A3
Neville Gr LS26 . . . . .194 A1
Neville Pits La DN14 . . . . .207 B4
Neville Rd Darlington DL3 . . .3 B5
  Gargrave BD23 . . . . . . .155 D1
Neville Row DL8 . . . . .87 D7
Neville St
  Normanton South WF6 . . .200 A1
  Skipton BD23 . . . . .217 A4
  York YO31 . . . . .233 C4
Neville Terr YO31 . . . . . . .233 C4
Neville Wlk DL10 . . . . . . .209 D7
Nevinson Gr YO10 . . . . . . .231 E8
Nevis Way YO24 . . . . .230 B7
Nevison Ave WF8 . . . . . . .201 C2
New Brook St LS29 . . . . . .218 B5
New Church Terr 12
YO8 . . . . .232 C5
New Cl La LA2 . . . . .130 C2
New Dales La YO8 . . . . . . .173 D4
New Earswick Prim Sch
YO32 . . . . .225 D3
New Earswick Sports Club
YO32 . . . . .225 D3
New Fen La YO8 . . . . .197 F6
New Forge Ct 17 YO32 . . . .166 F5
New Hall Rd WF8 . . . . . . .201 C2
New House Farm Malham
National Nature Reserve *
BD23 . . . . .133 D3
New House La BD23 . . . . .153 F5
New Ings La YO18 . . . . . . .96 E4
New Inn La
  Carthorpe DL8 . . . . .87 F6
  10 Easingwold YO61 . . . .143 C8
New La Aislaby YO18 . . . . .95 D4
  Beal DN14 . . . . .202 D3
  Bishopthorpe YO23 . . . . .231 A4
  Burton Salmon WF11 . . . .201 E6
  Green Hammerton YO26 . . .164 C3
  Hawes DL8 . . . . .56 E4
  Holgate YO24 . . . . .227 E3
  Huntington YO32 . . . . . . .225 F1
  Kildwick BD20 . . . . .173 F1
  Lillings Ambo YO60 . . . . .145 C3
  Little Ouseburn YO26 . . . .164 A8
  Long Marston YO23 . . . . .182 B3
  Neasham DL2 . . . . .4 A1
  Newland YO8 . . . . .205 A3
  Ravensworth DL11 . . . . . .20 A7
  Selby YO8 . . . . .232 C5
  Sherburn in Elmet LS25 . . .195 F3
  Sheriff Hutton YO60 . . . . .145 D5
  Stainburn LS21 . . . . . . .177 E4
  Strensall YO32 . . . . .167 B8
  West Tanfield DL8 . . . . . .87 C2
New Laithe Cl 5 BD20 . . . .217 B5
New Lennerton La
  LS25 . . . . .196 C3
New Mill La LS17 . . . . . . .188 F7
New Millgate YO8 . . . . . . .232 C6
New Parks Cres 8
YO12 . . . . .212 E8
New Pk Com Prim Sch
HG1 . . . . .219 C5
New Pk Rd 4 YO12 . . . . . .212 E4
New Pk Row HG1 . . . . . . .219 C5
New Potter Grange Rd
DN14 . . . . .205 E2
New Quay Rd YO21 . . . . . .208 D6
New Queen St 10 YO12 . . .213 A7
New Rd Allerston YO13 . . . .73 D6
  Allerton Mauleverer
  with Hopperton HG5 . . . .163 A4
  Appleton Roebuck YO23 . . .190 C5
  Appletreewick BD23 . . . . .157 E8
  Beningbrough YO30 . . . . .165 D5
  Birstwith HG3 . . . . .160 D6
  Bramham LS23 . . . . . . .188 C5
  Earby BB18 . . . . .172 A1

New Rd continued
  Fylingdales YO22 . . . . . . .33 D4
  Glaisdale YO21 . . . . .29 F3
  Guisborough TS14 . . . . . .8 F6
  Heck DN14 . . . . .203 D1
  Hessay YO26 . . . . .182 C8
  Hunmanby YO14 . . . . . . .126 F7
  Kirby Grindalythe YO17 . . .149 B6
  Kirby Hall YO26 . . . . . . .164 B8
  Kirkbymoorside YO62 . . . .70 B1
  Knottingley WF11 . . . . . .201 D3
  Ledsham LS25 . . . . .201 B8
  Lillings Ambo YO60 . . . . .145 D3
  Long Drax YO8 . . . . .204 E6
  Newsham DL11 . . . . .18 J8
  North Stainley with Sleningford
  HG4 . . . . .113 B8
  Norton DN6 . . . . .206 F2
  Raskelf YO61 . . . . .116 E3
  Reighton YO14 . . . . .127 E5
  Richmond DL10 . . . . . . .209 C6
  Rosedale East Side YO18 . .49 A7
  Scotton HG5 . . . . .162 A5
  24 Settle BD24 . . . . . . .131 D2
  Settrington YO17 . . . . . . .122 D1
  Spaunton YO62 . . . . .70 E5
  Stapleton WF8 . . . . .206 B5
  Terrington YO60 . . . . . . .119 E2
  Thornton in Lonsdale
  LA6 . . . . .103 B4
  Ulleskelf LS24 . . . . .190 B3
  Westerdale YO21 . . . . . . .28 F6
  Wheldrake YO19 . . . . . . .192 C7
  Whixley YO26 . . . . .164 A4
New Row
  15 Boroughbridge YO51 . .141 B5
  Eppleby DL11 . . . . .1 D4
  Trawden Forest BB8 . . . . .186 B2
New St Carleton BD23 . . . .173 B4
  Kippax LS25 . . . . .194 D1
  Langcliffe BD24 . . . . . . .131 E4
  Tadcaster LS24 . . . . . . .189 E6
  York YO1 . . . . .233 B2
New Sturton La LS25 . . . . .194 D4
New Way YO21 . . . . .29 C4
New Wlk Terr YO10 . . . . . .228 D2
Newall Ave LS21 . . . . . . .176 F1
Newall Carr Rd LS21 . . . . .176 F3
Newall Hall Pk 10 LS21 . . .177 A1
Newbiggin
  Malton YO17 . . . . .215 B5
  Richmond DL10 . . . . . . .209 B6
Newbiggin Cl TS16 . . . . . .5 C5
Newborough YO11 . . . . . . .213 A6
Newborough St YO30 . . . . .233 A4
Newbridge La BD23 . . . . . .174 B8
Newburgh Priory *
YO61 . . . . .117 E2
Newbury Ave YO24 . . . . . .227 D1
Newby Cl HG4 . . . . .214 D4
Newby Cres HG3 . . . . .219 A4
Newby Farm Cl 35 YO12 . .75 D5
Newby Farm Cres 36
YO12 . . . . .75 D5
Newby Farm Rd YO12 . . . .75 D5
Newby Hall & Gdns *
HG4 . . . . .140 C8
Newby Hall CE Prim Sch
HG4 . . . . .140 E7
Newby La DN14 . . . . .207 F8
Newby Pk * HG4 . . . . .140 D6
Newby St HG4 . . . . .214 D4
Newby Terr YO31 . . . . . . .228 D8
Newby & Scalby Prim Sch
YO12 . . . . .212 B8
Newcastle Farm Ct 4
WF11 . . . . .201 D6
Newchase Ct YO11 . . . . . .99 F6
Newcoln Rd YO12 . . . . . . .212 E1
Newcroft YO8 . . . . .232 B4
Newdale 3 YO32 . . . . .166 E5
Newfield Ave 6 WF6 . . . . .200 B1
Newfield Cl 3 WF6 . . . . . .200 B1
Newfield Cres
  Middlesbrough TS17 . . . . .6 C7
  Normanton South WF6 . . .200 B1
Newfield Ct 3 WF6 . . . . . .200 B1
Newfield La LS25 . . . . . . .201 B8
Newgate 2 Malton YO17 . . .215 C4
  York YO1 . . . . .233 B2
Newgate Bank YO62 . . . . .68 A4
Newgate Cl 36 TS17 . . . . .5 F4
Newgate Ct YO1 . . . . .233 B2
Newham Bridge Prim Sch
TS5 . . . . .6 F8
Newham Way TS8 . . . . . . .7 B5
Newhay La YO8 . . . . .198 E1
Newhold LS25 . . . . .194 D4
Newington Rd TS4 . . . . . .7 A8
Newkin DL8 . . . . .57 D5
Newlaithes Cres WF6 . . . . .200 B1
Newland Ave 1 HG2 . . . . . .220 A1
Newland Pk Cl YO10 . . . . .229 A3
Newland Pk Dr YO10 . . . . .228 F3
Newlands DL6 . . . . .210 F4
Newlands Ave
  Scarborough YO12 . . . . . .212 E8
  3 Whitby YO21 . . . . . . .208 C7
Newlands Ct YO11 . . . . . .211 D3
Newlands Dr
  2 Glusburn BD20 . . . . . .187 F8
  Ripon HG4 . . . . .214 B3
  York YO26 . . . . .227 B6
Newlands La
  Burniston YO13 . . . . .54 D1
  Upper Poppleton YO26 . . .182 E8
  Wintringham YO17 . . . . . .123 F3

Newlands Pk Ave
YO12 . . . . .212 D8
Newlands Pk Cres
YO12 . . . . .212 D8
Newlands Pk Dr YO12 .212 D8
Newlands Pk Gr 2
YO12 . . . . .212 D8
Newlands Pk Rd YO12 .212 D8
Newlands Rd
  Bishopthorpe YO23 . . . . .230 F4
  Darlington DL3 . . . . .3 B6
Newlands Sch TS4 . . . . . .6 F7
Newlyn Dr DL3 . . . . .3 C8
Newmarket St BD23 . . . . .217 A4
Newnham St HG2 . . . . . . .220 A3
Newnham Terr HG2 . . . . . .220 A3
Newport Ave YO8 . . . . . . .232 B4
Newport St 5 WF8 . . . . . .201 B1
Newroad End WF8 . . . . . .206 A6
Newsam Rd TS16 . . . . . . .5 D5
Newsham Hill DL11 . . . . . .18 J8
Newsham La
  Barugh (Great & Little)
  YO17 . . . . .95 A1
  Habton YO17 . . . . .121 A8
Newsham Rd YO7 . . . . . . .211 A3
Newsham Way DL7 . . . . . .210 B1
Newstead La HG4 . . . . . . .85 C7
Newsteads 12 DL8 . . . . . .63 B3
Newthorpe Rd 2 DN6 . . . .206 E2
Newton Cres 4 DL7 . . . . . .63 D4
Newton Dr TS17 . . . . .5 B6
Newton Gdns HG4 . . . . . .214 C4
Newton House Ct
YO61 . . . . .144 B3
Newton La
  Archdeacon Newton DL2 . .2 F8
  Ledsham WF10 . . . . .201 A6
  Newton Mulgrave TS13 . . .11 F6
Newton Pk YO30 . . . . . . .165 B7
Newton Rd
  Great Ayton TS9 . . . . . . .8 A2
  Tollerton YO61 . . . . .143 B3
Newton St YO21 . . . . .208 D6
Newton Terr YO1 . . . . . . .233 B1
Newton Way 15 BD23 . . . . .217 A4
Newtondale Cl HG5 . . . . . .221 D6
Newtondale Forest Dr
YO18 . . . . .72 B6
Newtondale Halt Sta
YO18 . . . . .51 D1
Nicholas Gdns YO10 . . . . .228 F3
Nicholas St YO10 . . . . . . .228 F3
Nichols Way LS22 . . . . . . .180 A3
Nicholson Ave HG4 . . . . . .113 D3
Nicklaus Dr TS16 . . . . . . .5 E5
Nickey Nackey La YO8 . . . .197 B8
Nicklaus Dr TS16 . . . . . . .5 E5
Nickstream La DL3 . . . . . .3 A7
Nidd Bank HG5 . . . . .220 F7
Nidd Cl YO26 . . . . .227 B8
Nidd Dr HG3 . . . . .160 E6
Nidd Gr YO24 . . . . .227 A2
Nidd La Birstwith HG3 . . . .160 E7
  Ripley HG3 . . . . .161 D7
Nidd Orch 4 HG3 . . . . . . .160 A6
Nidd Rise HG3 . . . . .160 E6
Nidd Viaduct * HG3 . . . . . .219 E6
Nidd Wlk 1 HG3 . . . . .137 B4
Nidderdale Dr HG5 . . . . . .221 D5
Nidderdale High Sch & Com
Coll HG3 . . . . .137 C4
Nidderdale Lodge
HG5 . . . . .221 E5
Nidderdale Lodge Pk
HG5 . . . . .221 E5
Nidderdale Mus *
HG3 . . . . .137 B5
Nidderdale Recn Ctr
HG3 . . . . .137 A5
Niddside HG3 . . . . .160 A6
Niffany Gdns 7 BD23 . . . . .216 D3
Nigel Gr 7 YO24 . . . . .227 F2
Nightingale Cl YO32 . . . . .225 E1
Nightingale Dr HG2 . . . . . .220 B3
Nightingale La 9 YO12 . . . .99 F6
Nile Rd LS29 . . . . .218 B4
Ninelands La LS25 . . . . . .194 C3
Ninelands Prim Sch
LS25 . . . . .194 C3
Ninelands Spur LS25 . . . . .194 C3
Ninevah La WF10 . . . . . . .200 C7
Ninth Ave YO31 . . . . .228 E5
Niso Terr YO11 . . . . .213 A6
No Man's Moor La DL8 . . . .61 E3
Noel's Ct DL10 . . . . .41 E5
Nolton Ct 35 TS17 . . . . . . .5 F4
Nook The Selby YO8 . . . . .232 D6
  South Milford LS25 . . . . .195 F2
Nookfield Cl YO22 . . . . . . .33 C4
Nooking The YO61 . . . . . .117 B6
Nora Ave HG5 . . . . .221 C6
Norby HG5 . . . . .221 B3
Norby Est YO7 . . . . .211 B3
Norby Front St YO7 . . . . . .211 B4
Norfolk Cl WF11 . . . . .201 D4
Norfolk Cres TS3 . . . . . . .7 C8
Norfolk Gdns YO26 . . . . . .181 C7
Norfolk Rd HG2 . . . . .222 C7
Norfolk St YO23 . . . . .228 C1
Norman Cl
  22 Pickering YO18 . . . . . .95 F7
  7 Thorpe Willoughby YO8 .197 B1
Norman Cres 11 YO14 . . . .101 B3
Norman Dr YO26 . . . . . . .227 C6
Norman Rd Aske DL10 . . . .20 D1
  Catterick Garrison DL9 . . .209 E1
  Richmond DL10 . . . . . . .209 C8
Norman Sq DL10 . . . . . . .209 D8

Norman St **5** YO10 ......229 A3
Normanby Prim Sch TS6 ..7 F8
Normanby Rd
 Middlesbrough TS7 ....7 D8
 Northallerton DL7 ....210 D2
Normanby Terr **18** YO21 208 D7
Normandy Cl **4** YO8 ..232 B6
Normanton Com Sch
 WF6 ....200 B2
Normanton Freeston High
 Sch WF6 ....200 A1
Normanton Ind Est
 WF6 ....200 B1
Normanton Public Baths
 WF6 ....200 A1
Normanton Sta WF6 ...200 A1
Normanton Town Mid Sch
 WF6 ....200 A1
Norseman Cl **7** YO19 .197 F8
Norseway **2** YO41 ....168 D1
North & S Cowton Com Prim
 Sch DL7 ....22 C3
North App LS24 ....189 A2
North Ave
 Castleford WF10 ....200 C4
 12 Glusburn BD20 ...187 E6
North Back La
 Stillington YO61 ....144 C6
 Terrington YO60 ....119 E1
North Baileygate WF8 201 B1
North Bay Rly★ YO12 ..212 E8
North Bglws HG4 ....214 D6
North Burton La YO14 .127 B4
North Cl **5** WF7 ......200 C1
North Cliff Ave YO12 ....75 D5
North Cliff Ctry Pk★
 YO14 ....101 C4
North Cotes Rd
 Hunmanby YO25 ....126 C5
 Wold Newton YO25 ....125 E5
North Cres LS25 ....195 F5
North Croft Gr Rd **1**
 LS29 ....218 A4
North Dr Kippax LS25 ..194 D2
 Sherburn in Elmet LS25 .195 F5
North Duffield CP Sch
 YO8 ....199 A8
North Eastern Terr
 YO24 ....230 E8
North End Bedale DL8 ..63 A4
 2 Hutton Rudby TS15 ..25 C5
 Osmotherley DL6 ....45 B4
North Field Ave YO23 .190 F5
North Field Cl YO23 ....190 F5
North Field La
 Askham Bryan YO23 ....182 F3
 Upper Poppleton YO26 .182 F7
North Field Way YO23 .190 F5
North Garth La YO60 ..145 D5
North Gr **2** LS22 .....180 C3
North Gr Ave **6** LS22 .180 C4
North Grange Ct YO30 .233 A4
North Hill Rd YO7 .....115 B6
North La
 Dringhouses YO24 .....230 E8
 Eastfield YO11 ....100 B6
 Gainford DL2 ....1 D8
 Great Timble LS21 .....176 E8
 Huntington YO32 ......225 F5
 Hutton Hang DL8 ....61 C4
 Wheldrake YO19 ....192 F7
North Leas Ave YO12 .212 D8
North Lodge Ave **2**
 HG1 ....219 C5
North Marine Rd
 YO12 ....212 F7
North Moor **7** YO32 .225 F5
North Moor Gdns
 YO32 ....225 F5
North Moor La YO61 ...118 C5
North Moor Rd
 Easingwold YO61 ......117 B2
 York YO32 ....225 F5
North Parade
 10 Burley in Warfedale
  LS29 ....176 C1
 Ilkley LS29 ....218 C4
 Skipton BD23 ....217 A2
 York YO30 ....233 A3
North Pk Dr HG1 ....219 C2
North Pk Rd HG1 ......219 C2
North Prom YO21 ......208 C7
North Rd Darlington DL1 ..3 D7
 5 Fairburn WF11 ....201 D6
 Glusburn BD20 ....187 E7
 Grosmont YO22 ....31 C4
 Hackforth DL8 ....62 E8
 3 Middleham DL8 ....60 E2
 Norton YO17 ....215 E3
 Ripon HG4 ....214 D6
 Stokesley TS9 ....26 C7
 Whitby YO21 ....208 D6
North Rd Prim Sch DL1 .3 D7
North Rd Sta DL1 ....3 D6
North Riding Rise DL7 ..65 B3
North Rigton CE Prim Sch
 LS17 ....178 C4
North Side TS15 ....25 C5
North St
 Addingham LS29 ....175 A4
 Barmby on the Marsh
  DN14 ....205 A7
 Barnoldswick BB18 ....171 D1
 Castleford WF10 ......201 B6
 Folkton YO11 ....100 A2
 Gargrave BD23 ....155 D1
 31 Glusburn BD20 ...187 E7
 Newby & Scalby YO13 ..75 C6

North St continued
 Ripon HG4 ....214 C6
 Scarborough YO11 .....213 A6
 Silsden BD20 ....174 C1
 Wetherby LS22 ....180 C3
 York YO1 ....233 B2
North St La **22** YO11 .213 A6
North Stainley CE Prim Sch
 HG4 ....113 C8
North Sweeming Ct
 LS25 ....196 B5
North Terr Gainford DL2 ..1 D7
 4 Scarborough YO11 .213 A6
 Whitby YO21 ....208 D7
North View
 Knottingley WF11 .....201 F2
 Little Ribston LS22 ....180 A3
North Yorkshire Moors Rly★
 YO18 ....95 F7
Northallerton Bsns Pk
 DL6 ....210 C7
Northallerton Coll
 DL6 ....210 E8
Northallerton Rd
 Brompton DL6 ....210 E7
 Dalton-on-Tees DL2 ....22 E6
 Leeming DL7 ....63 C4
 Thirsk YO7 ....211 A6
 Thornaby TS17 ....6 B7
Northallerton Rigg DL6 .43 D4
Northallerton Sta DL7 .210 C3
Northcarrs La YO61 ....144 A4
Northcliffe Dr **3** TS5 ..25 C5
Northcote Ave YO24 ...227 E3
Northcote Fold **3** LS22 .180 A1
Northcote Fold **3** LS22 180 A1
Northcroft YO31 ......166 F5
Northcroft Gr **11** LS29 .218 A4
Northern Backlight Theatre
 YO31 ....233 C4
Northfield **3** YO8 ...198 B5
Northfield Cl
 Stokesley TS9 ....26 C7
 Womersley DN6 ....206 C6
Northfield Ct LS24 ....196 B8
Northfield Dr
 Pontefract WF8 ....201 C1
 Stokesley TS9 ....26 C8
Northfield La
 Church Fenton LS24 ...196 B8
 Pockley YO62 ....69 B2
 3 Riccall YO19 ....191 F1
 South Milford LS25 ....195 E2
 Womersley DN6 ....206 C7
Northfield Mews **15**
 LS22 ....180 C2
Northfield Pl LS22 .....180 C3
Northfield Rd YO8 .....199 E8
Northfield Sch YO26 ...227 B5
Northfield Terr YO24 ..230 E8
Northfield Way YO15 ...75 D6
Northfields
 4 Hutton Rudby TS15 ...25 C5
 5 Strensall YO32 ....167 B8
Northfields Ave **4**
 BD24 ....131 D3
Northfields Cres **5**
 BD24 ....131 D3
Northfields La YO61 ...142 C6
Northgate Darlington DL1 .3 D5
 Guisborough TS14 ......8 F7
 Hunmanby YO14 ......126 F8
 Muston YO14 ....100 F1
 Pontefract WF8 ....201 B1
Northgate Cl **15** WF8 .201 B1
Northgate Jun Sch TS14 .8 F7
Northgate La
 1 Linton LS22 ....180 A1
 Warthill YO19 ....148 A3
Northgate Lodge **11**
 WF8 ....201 B1
Northgate Rise **2** LS22 180 A1
Northlands Ave **1** YO32 225 F7
Northleach Dr TS8 .....6 F5
Northminster Bsns Pk
 YO26 ....182 F7
Northstead Com Prim Sch
 YO12 ....212 D8
Northstead Flats
 YO12 ....212 D7
Northstead Manor Dr
 YO12 ....212 D7
Northumberland Ct **8**
 HG1 ....219 C5
Northumberland Rd
 TS17 ....6 B8
Northway Pickering YO18 .95 E7
 11 Scarborough YO12 .212 F6
 6 Whitby YO21 ....208 B7
Northwell Gate LS21 ..176 F1
Northwold Rd YO11 ...100 A7
Norton & Kirk Smeat
 WF8 ....206 C4
Norton Back La DL2 .....4 D8
Norton Cl HG4 ....114 A8
Norton Coll YO17 ......215 E2
Norton Com Prim Sch
 YO17 ....215 E3
Norton Comm La DN6 .206 F2
Norton Comm Rd
 DN6 ....207 A1
Norton Conyers★
 HG4 ....113 F7
Norton Cres DL2 ....4 C8
Norton Cty Jun & Inf Schs
 DN6 ....206 E2
Norton Gr Ind Est
 YO17 ....215 F4

Norton Mill La DN6 ....206 E2
Norton Priory DN6 ....206 E2
Norton Rd
 Norton YO17 ....215 C3
 Sadberge DL2 ....4 C7
Norton Twr★ BD23 ...156 B4
Norway Dr YO10 ......231 D8
Norwich Cl YO13 ....75 D6
Norwich Dr HG3 ....219 A5
Norwood Ave LS29 ....176 C1
Norwood Bottom Rd
 LS21 ....177 A5
Norwood Cl
 36 Burley in Warfedale
  LS29 ....176 C1
 2 Knaresborough HG5 .221 B7
Norwood Ct **1** HG5 ..221 B7
Norwood Gr HG3 ......219 B4
Norwood La
 Glusburn BD20 ....187 B8
 Pannal HG3 ....177 C2
Norwood Pl **8** YO12 ..212 F5
Norwood St
 Normanton WF6 ......200 B2
 Scarborough YO12 ....212 F5
Nossill La DL8 ....59 C3
Nosterfield Nature Reserve★
 HG4 ....87 B2
Nosterfield Rd HG4 ....87 B2
Notagreen Rd DL11 ....39 F6
Nought Bank Rd HG3 .137 B3
Nought Moor Rd HG3 .137 B3
Nova Scotia Way **4**
 YO19 ....198 A8
Nuffield Hospl HG2 ...219 C1
Nun Monkton Foundation
 Prim Sch YO26 ....165 A5
Nun's Cl YO10 ....209 B7
Nuneaton Dr TS8 ......6 E5
Nunmill St YO23 ......228 C2
Nunnery La
 Darlington DL3 ....3 A5
 York YO23 ....233 B1
Nunnington Cl TS17 ....6 B5
Nunnington Cres HG3 .219 A5
Nunnington Hall★
 YO62 ....93 F2
Nunnington Studios★
 YO62 ....93 E2
Nuns Gn La YO21 ......29 E3
Nunthorpe Ave YO23 ..228 C2
Nunthorpe Cres YO23 .228 B1
Nunthorpe Gdns TS7 ...7 D5
Nunthorpe Gr YO23 ...228 B2
Nunthorpe Prim Sch
 TS7 ....7 E6
Nunthorpe Rd YO23 ...233 A1
Nunthorpe Sta TS7 ....7 E6
Nurseries The
 3 Easingwold YO61 ..143 C8
 East Ayton YO13 ....99 C8
 10 Leyburn DL8 ......60 D5
 3 Whitby YO21 ......208 B6
Nursery Cl **19** YO26 ..198 F1
Nursery Ct YO26 ......224 A2
Nursery Dr YO24 ......227 E3
Nursery Gdns
 Thirsk YO7 ....211 C3
 York YO10 ....229 C3
Nursery La **4** LS29 ...175 A4
Nursery Rd YO26 ......224 A2
Nursery Way **8** LS23 .188 E7
Nutgill La Bentham LA2 .129 D8
 Ingleton LA2 ....103 D1
Nutwith La HG4 ....112 B8
Nydd Vale Rd HG1 .....219 D3
Nydd Vale Terr **10** HG1 .219 D3

O

Oak Ave
 Appleton Roebuck YO23 .190 E3
 Garforth LS25 ....194 C4
 Killinghall HG3 ....161 B2
Oak Beck Rd HG1 .....219 B5
Oak Beck Way HG1 ...219 B6
Oak Busk La YO60 ....145 F1
Oak Cl Filey YO14 ....101 B4
 9 Kirkbymoorside YO62 .70 B1
Oak Cres LS25 ....194 C4
Oak Dr Garforth LS25 .194 C4
 5 Thorpe Willoughby YO8 197 B1
 3 Topcliffe YO7 ....89 A1
Oak Field YO8 ....232 A1
Oak Field Ave YO22 ....51 D8
Oak Glade **6** YO31 ...225 F3
Oak Gr DL6 ....210 E6
Oak Hill TS8 ....7 B5
Oak La HG3 ....159 F8
Oak Rd Eaglescliffe TS16 ..5 E6
 Garforth LS25 ....194 C4
 Guisborough TS14 ......8 F7
 2 North Duffield YO8 .199 A7
 Ripon HG4 ....214 B2
 Scarborough YO12 ....212 D4
 Tockwith LS22 ....180 E7
 Whitby YO21 ....208 B6
Oak Ridge LS6 ....180 B3
Oak Rise **4** YO26 ....227 C3
Oak St **3** YO26 ......227 E5
Oak Terr HG2 ....219 C2
Oak Tree Cl
 2 Bedale DL8 ....63 A2
 Strensall YO32 ....167 B7
 Tees-side Airport DL2 ...4 E4
Oak Tree Ct
 Bubwith YO8 ....199 D7

Oak Tree Ct continued
 4 Wigginton YO32 ...225 D7
Oak Tree Dr DL8 ....62 F2
Oak Tree Gr YO32 ....225 D3
Oak Tree La YO32 ....225 C7
Oak Tree Rd **7** DL8 ...63 A2
Oak Tree Way YO32 ..168 F7
Oak Wood Rd LS22 ...180 B4
Oakbank HG1 ....219 C4
Oakburn Rd LS29 .....218 A3
Oakdale HG1 ....219 A3
Oakdale Ave HG1 .....219 B4
Oakdale Glen HG1 ....219 B3
Oakdale Manor HG1 ..161 B2
Oakdale Pl HG1 ....219 B4
Oakdale Rd YO30 .....224 F2
Oakdale Rise HG1 ....219 B4
Oakenshaw Dr TS5 .....6 E7
Oaker Bank HG1 ......161 B2
Oakfields DL10 ....21 D4
Oakhill Cres **3** YO32 .167 A6
Oakland Ave YO31 ....229 A7
Oakland Dr YO31 .....229 A7
Oakland Hills **28** WF6 .200 B1
Oaklands
 Camblesforth YO8 ....204 C5
 9 Great Ayton TS9 ....8 A2
 5 Ilkley LS29 ....218 A3
 5 Pickering YO18 .....96 A6
 6 Strensall YO32 ....167 B7
Oaklands Cres YO8 ...204 C5
Oaklands Rd TS6 ....7 F8
Oaklands Sec Sch
 YO24 ....227 C2
Oaklands Small Sch
 DN14 ....205 E4
Oaklands Sports Ctr
 YO24 ....227 C2
Oaklands The DL2 ....4 D3
Oaklands Way YO61 ..143 D8
Oakley Bank YO22 ....208 B2
Oakley Cl TS14 ....8 F5
Oakley Rd TS12 ....9 E7
Oakmont Cl **21** WF6 ..200 B1
Oakney Wood Dr YO8 .232 D1
Oakridge Com Prim Sch
 TS13 ....11 F7
Oakridge View **3** HG3 .161 B3
Oaks La LS23 ....188 E8
Oaks The
 Coulby Newham TS8 ...6 E5
 Dalton YO7 ....115 F7
 7 Masham HG4 ....86 C3
 Oak Tree DL2 ....4 E4
Oaksfield LS25 ....200 B5
Oaktree Ave DL9 ....40 E2
Oaktree Bank YO7 .....65 F3
Oaktree Dr DL7 ......210 C1
Oaktree Gr **5** TS18 ....5 D8
Oaktree Hill DL6 ....43 D6
Oaktree Junc DL2 ......4 E4
Oakville Rd YO12 .....212 E6
Oakville St YO31 .....228 D7
Oakwood Cl LS24 ....196 B7
Oakwood Pk DN14 ...207 F6
Oatlands Com Jun Sch
 HG2 ....222 F7
Oatlands Dr
 Harrogate HG2 ....222 F8
 11 Otley LS21 ....177 A1
Oatlands Gr **3** TS13 ..11 A8
Oatlands Inf Sch HG2 .222 E7
Occaney La HG3 ......162 D8
Occupation La LS24 ..188 E2
Occupation Rd TS6 .....7 F8
Ocean Rd YO21 ......208 C7
Ocean Terr YO14 .....100 F6
Ochrepit Hill YO42 ...170 A2
Oddie's La LA6 ....103 D5
Offerton Dr TS8 ....6 F5
Ogleforth YO31 ....233 B3
Okehampton Dr TS7 ...7 B6
Olav Rd DL10 ....209 C7
Old Barber HG1 ....219 D6
Old Boys Sch La **4** YO8 197 B8
Old Brewery Gdns **5**
 LS24 ....189 F6
Old Bridge Rise **3** LS29 218 A4
Old Chapel Cl **7** HG3 .161 B2
Old Church Gn YO26 .164 C2
Old Church La **9** HG3 .137 C4
Old Church Sch DL8 ...60 E2
Old Coach Rd HG3 ...137 F2
Old Coppice **14** YO32 .166 F5
Old Courthouse Mus★
 HG5 ....221 A5
Old Cricket Field La
 YO7 ....116 B6
Old Ct Cl YO17 ....215 D4
Old Dike Lands YO32 .225 C8
Old Farm Cl **5** YO18 ...95 F7
Old Farmyard The★
 HG3 ....161 C7
Old Favourites Wlk **8** DL3 3 A7
Old Garth Croft **3**
 WF11 ....201 D6
Old Gayle La DL8 ......56 D4
Old Great N Rd WF11 .201 E4
Old Hall Cl BD20 ......187 D7
Old Hall Croft BD23 ..155 D1
Old Hall La
 Gilling with Hartforth & Sedbury
  DL10 ....20 D3
 Kexby YO41 ....185 C5
Old Hall Rd BD20 .....187 D7
Old Hall Way BD20 ...187 D7

Old Hospl Compound **25**
 DL9 ....40 E3
Old House Gdns YO8 .203 A5
Old La Addingham LS29 .175 B8
 Broughton BD23 ....172 D5
 Cowling BD22 ....187 B3
 Earby BB18 ....172 A2
 Hambleton YO8 ....196 E1
 Hirst Courtney YO8 ...203 F3
 Horton in Ribblesdale
  BD24 ....105 A7
 Ilkley LS29 ....218 D3
 Kelbrook & Sough BB18 186 A6
 Long Marston YO26 ...182 A6
Old La Ct LS24 ....190 E7
Old London Rd LS25 ..189 D3
Old Malton Rd
 Malton YO17 ....215 D5
 7 Willerby YO12 ......99 D2
Old Maltongate YO17 .215 C4
Old Mill Cl **8** LS29 ...176 C1
Old Mill La LS23 ......188 F2
Old Mill Row **3** YO7 .211 C3
Old Mill View YO60 ...145 C5
Old Mill Wynd TS9 .....8 A1
Old Mkt Pl **6** HG4 ...214 C5
Old Moor La YO24 ....230 E7
Old Moor Rd LA2 .....128 B8
Old Oliver La BD24 ...152 F6
Old Orchard YO32 ...225 D8
Old Orchard The
 1 Easingwold YO61 ..143 C8
 Fulford YO10 ....231 E1
 Shipton YO30 ....165 F5
Old Pk La YO21 ....31 D6
Old Pk Mews HG4 ....214 B5
Old Quarry La LS25 ..195 E1
Old Raike BD23 ....152 F4
Old Rd
 Appleton Roebuck YO23 .190 E5
 Clapham LA2 ....130 C8
 Garsdale LA10 ....55 A6
 Ingleton LA6 ....103 E3
 Kirkby Overblow LS17 .178 E1
 Kirkbymoorside YO62 ..70 B1
 Thornton in Craven
  BD23 ....172 A3
Old Sawmill The BD24 153 B7
Old Sch Cl DL8 ....59 D3
Old Sch La YO8 ....198 B5
Old St The LS24 ......190 C8
Old Sta Rd **4** YO62 ..92 C1
Old Sta Way **20** DL8 .174 F4
Old Sta Yd★ YO62 .....92 F6
Old Stone Trough La
 BB18 ....186 A6
Old Stubble The **6** TS13 .11 K2
Old Sutton Rd YO7 ...211 B3
Old Trough Way HG1 .219 C6
Old Vicarage La **5**
 LS25 ....202 A8
Old Village The YO32 .225 F5
Old Wife's Way YO18 ..73 A8
Olde Mkt The TS16 .....5 D3
Oldfield Cl LS25 ......195 A4
Oldfield La
 Collingham LS22 ......180 C1
 Spaunton YO62 ....70 E4
 Sutton BD22 ....187 F1
Oldgate La LS25 ......195 D6
Oldham Cl TS12 ....9 E8
Oldham St TS12 ....9 D7
Oldman Ct YO24 .....230 C8
Oldstead Rd YO61 .....91 B3
Olicana Pk LS29 ......218 B5
Olive Gr HG1 ....220 B4
Olive Way HG1 ....220 B4
Olive Wlk HG1 ....220 B4
Oliver La YO17 ....121 C8
Oliver St **4** YO11 ....213 A4
Oliver's Cl **18** YO14 ..126 F8
Oliver's Mount Rd
 YO11 ....212 F2
Ollliver La DL10 ....20 F1
Ollliver Rd DL10 ......209 E4
Olympia Cres YO8 ....232 E6
Olympian Ct YO10 ...228 E4
Olympic Way DL10 ...209 B8
Omega St **7** HG1 ....219 C5
Onams La YO62 ....69 F4
One Acre Garth **2** YO8 196 E1
Onhams La YO60 .....146 E4
Opera House Casino★
 ....213 B6
Oran La DL10 ....41 E4
Orcaber La LA2 ....130 E6
Orchard Cl
 Appleton Roebuck YO23 .190 F5
 Barkston Ash LS24 ....195 E7
 Dalton-on-Tees DL2 ...22 D7
 1 Great Ayton TS9 ....8 A2
 6 Hartwith cum Winsley
  HG3 ....137 F1
 1 Knaresborough HG5 .221 B8
 3 Monk Fryston LS25 .202 A8
 9 Norton DN6 ....206 E2
 Selby YO8 ....232 A4
 Sharow HG4 ....214 F6
 6 South Milford LS25 .195 F2
 Wilberfoss YO41 ......185 E6
 York YO24 ....227 C1
Orchard Cotts **4** YO19 184 F7
Orchard Ct
 Bramham cum Oglethorpe
  LS23 ....188 F5

Orchard Ct continued
8 Knaresborough HG5 ..221 B5
Orchard Dr
Fairburn WF11 ....201 D7
Hambleton YO8 ....196 F2
Linton LS22 ....180 A2
Orchard Garth YO23 .230 B2
Orchard Gdns YO31 .225 E2
Orchard Gr
4 Brompton DL6 ....43 F3
1 Castleford WF10 ......200 D3
Orchard Head Cres
WF8 ....201 C2
Orchard Head Dr WF8 .201 C2
Orchard Head Jun & Inf Sch
WF8 ....201 C2
Orchard Head La WF8 201 C2
Orchard La
8 Addingham LS29 ......175 A4
Barkston Ash LS24 .....195 F6
Hebden BD23 ....135 A2
Ripley HG3 ....161 C1
Thirsk YO7 ....211 B1
Orchard Paddock 3
YO32 ....225 D8
Orchard Rd
Malton YO17 ....215 B4
Selby YO8 ....232 A4
3 Sleights YO22 ....32 A6
Upper Poppleton YO26 .224 A1
Orchard The
5 Ampleforth YO62 ......92 C1
Bishopthorpe YO25 ....231 A3
Burniston YO13 ....75 D8
Heslington YO10 ....229 A1
6 North Featherstone
WF7 ....200 E1
5 Roundhill Village TS17 ..6 C5
Sadberge DL2 ....4 C7
Scalby YO12 ....212 C7
Snainton YO13 ....98 A4
Thirsk YO7 ....211 C4
Tholthorpe YO61 ......142 D5
Orchard View
Markington with Wallerthwaite
HG3 ....139 E3
3 Skelton YO30 ....224 B5
Orchard Way
Hensall DN14 ....203 C2
Middlesbrough TS7 ....7 D8
Selby YO8 ....232 A4
1 Strensall YO32 ....167 B7
Thorpe Willoughby YO8 .197 B2
York YO24 ....227 E1
Orchards The
2 Beadlam YO62 ....93 D7
6 Brafferton YO61 .....115 F1
Leavening YO17 ....147 E1
Mickletown LS26 ....200 B5
Ripon HG4 ....214 C6
Westow YO60 ....147 B4
Orchid Ct 17 DL9 ....41 A5
Orchid Way 8 HG3 ....161 B3
Ordmerstones La YO8 ..96 C4
Ordnance La YO10 ....228 D1
Oriel Bank YO11 .....212 F3
Oriel Cl YO11 ....212 F3
Oriel Cres YO11 .....212 F3
Oriel Gr YO30 ....228 A8
Ormesby Bank TS7 .....7 D7
Ormesby Cres DL7 ....210 D2
Ormesby Prim Sch TS7 ..7 D8
Ormesby Rd TS7 ....7 C8
Orms Gill Gn La BD23 .154 D6
Orpington Rd TS3 ......7 C8
Orrin Cl YO24 ....230 C7
Osbaldwick La YO10 ..229 B4
Osbaldwick Link Rd
YO19 ....229 D4
Osbaldwick Prim Sch
YO10 ....229 C4
Osbaldwick Village
YO10 ....229 C4
Osborne Cl HG1 ......219 C4
Osborne Gdns HG1 ...219 D4
Osborne Pk YO12 ....212 D5
Osborne Rd HG1 .....219 D4
Osborne Terr 9 YO21 .208 D6
Osborne Wlk HG1 ....219 D4
Osbourne Dr 4 YO30 .224 E3
Osgodby Cl 9 YO11 ..100 B8
Osgodby Cres YO11 ..100 B7
Osgodby Gr 10 YO11 .100 B8
Osgodby Hall Rd YO11 .100 B7
Osgodby Hill YO11 ...100 B7
Osgodby La 12 YO11 .100 B8
Osgodby Way 11 YO11 .100 B8
Osgoodby Bank YO7 ...90 F3
Osmington Gdns 10
YO32 ....167 A2
Osmotherley Prim Sch
DL6 ....45 B4
Osprey Cl
4 Collingham LS22 ....180 A1
Guisborough TS14 ......8 D6
5 Scotton DL9 ....40 F2
4 York YO24 ....230 B8
Osprey Garth 4 YO12 .99 E6
Ostler's Cl YO23 ....230 C3
Ostman Rd YO26 .....227 C5
Oswaldene DL6 ....45 B4
Oswaldkirk Bank YO62 .93 A1
Oswestry Gn TS4 ....7 A7
Oswin Gr DL10 ....20 E4

Oswy Cotts YO21 ....208 D5
Oswy St 5 YO21 .....208 D5
Otley Rd
Harrogate HG2 ....222 B8
Killinghall HG3 ....161 B4
Pannal HG3 ....178 A7
Skipton BD23 ....217 B4
Stainburn HG3 ....177 F6
Otley St BD23 ....217 A4
Otter Dr 13 YO18 .....95 F6
Otter Way TS17 ....6 A5
Otterbeck Way 16 DL8 .63 B3
Otterwood Bank 6
YO24 ....227 B1
Otterwood La YO24 ..227 B1
Otterwood Paddock
YO41 ....168 C2
Oucher La HG3 ....140 B2
Oughtershaw Rd BD23 .80 C5
Oulston Rd YO61 .....117 D1
Our Ladys RC Prim Sch
YO24 ....227 E1
Ouse Acres YO26 ....227 D6
Ouse Bank YO8 ......232 E5
Ouse Lea YO30 ......228 A7
Ousebourn Ave YO26 .227 C6
Ousecliffe Gdns YO30 .228 A6
Ousegate YO8 ....232 D5
Ouston Cl LS24 .....189 F6
Ouston La LS24 .....189 F6
Out Gang La BD23 ...107 F1
Outgaits Cl 4 YO14 .126 F8
Outgaits La
Hunmanby YO14 ....127 A8
Muston YO14 ....100 F1
Outgang La
Osbaldwick YO19 ......229 D6
2 Pickering YO18 ....95 F6
Thornton-le-Dale YO18 .96 E6
Outgang Rd
Malton YO17 ....215 B5
Pickering YO18 ....96 A6
Scampston YO17 ....122 F7
Outgang The YO17 ...122 F4
Outgate Cnr DL6 ......23 F4
Outwood La LS24 ....190 C2
Oval The
Harrogate HG2 ....222 D8
Hurworth DL2 ....3 F1
Kellingley DN14 ....202 C3
Middlesbrough TS5 ......6 E6
Otley LS21 ....176 F1
3 Scarborough YO11 ...100 B8
Skipton BD23 ....217 B3
Over Nidd HG1 ....219 C6
Overburn Rd 8 BD20 .187 E6
Overdale YO11 ....100 A7
Overdale Cl YO24 ....230 D8
Overdale Com Prim Sch 7
YO11 ....100 A7
Overdale Ct BD23 ...217 A5
Overdale Grange 3
BD23 ....217 B5
Overdale Rd TS3 ......7 C8
Overgreen Cl YO13 ...75 D8
Overgreen La YO13 ...75 C8
Overgreen View YO13 .75 D8
Overscar Cl YO18 .....72 E3
Overton Rd YO30 ....165 F3
Ovington La DL11 ......1 A6
Ovington Terr YO23 ..228 B2
Owler Pk Rd LS29 ....175 C3
Owlwood Ct 7 YO19 .184 E7
Owlwood La 6 YO19 .184 E7
Owmen Field La YO62 .93 C5
Owston Ave 2 YO10 .229 A3
Owston Rd 1 YO14 ..126 F8
Ox Calder Cl 16 YO19 .184 E7
Ox Carr La YO32 .....167 B6
Ox Cl YO41 ....168 C2
Ox Cl La
Eldmire with Crakehill
YO7 ....115 E5
Myton-on-Swale YO61 .141 F5
North Deighton LS22 ..180 B7
Whixley YO13 ....163 F5
Ox Moor La
Cattal YO26 ....164 A1
Hunsingore LS22 ......180 E8
Oxcliff YO12 ....212 C8
Oxclose La Huby YO61 .144 B4
Hutton-le-Hole YO62 ...70 C4
Oxcroft 23 YO62 .....70 B1
Oxen La YO8 ....198 E3
Oxenby Pl 12 YO61 ..117 D1
Oxford Dr LS25 ....194 D1
Oxford Pl HG1 ....219 D2
Oxford St
Harrogate HG1 ....219 D2
6 Normanton South WF6 .200 B2
Scarborough YO12 .....212 F6
Skelton & Brotton TS12 ..9 D7
5 York YO24 ....228 A3
Oxford Terr 2 HG1 ...219 D1
Oxmoor La LS24 .....196 D7
Oxpasture Cl YO12 ...212 C4
Oxton Dr LS24 ......189 F6
Oxton La LS24 ....189 F6
Oyster Pk Jun Sch
WF10 ....201 B4

P

Packhorse Bridge ★
Dacre HG3 ....159 D6
Romanby DL7 ....210 B4

Pad Cote La BD22 ....187 A5
Padbury Ave 50 YO14 .101 B3
Padbury Cl 46 YO14 ..101 B3
Paddock Cl
Askham Richard YO23 .182 D3
Copmanthorpe YO23 ...230 A2
Norton YO17 ....215 D3
2 Pickering YO18 ....95 F6
Paddock Farm Wr Gdns ★
DL2 ....22 D4
Paddock Hill YO17 ...215 A4
Paddock House La
LS22 ....179 E1
Paddock Rise 13 YO61 .117 D1
Paddock The
14 Airmyn DN14 ......205 E4
Appleton Wiske DL6 ....24 B3
Burton Salmon LS25 ...201 F6
Catterick DL10 ....41 D4
Knaresborough HG5 ...221 C5
Melmerby HG4 ....114 B7
Middleton St George DL2 ..4 C3
Newby Wiske DL7 ....64 E2
8 Selby YO8 ....232 C6
Stokesley TS9 ....26 C8
9 Whitby YO21 ....208 D7
Wilberfoss YO41 ......185 E5
York YO26 ....227 C6
Paddock View WF10 ..201 A3
Paddock Way YO26 ...227 C6
Paddocks The HG3 ...223 F4
Page La YO62 ....93 E6
Pagnell Ave YO8 .....232 E4
Painsthorpe La YO41 .170 B5
Painter La YO8 ......196 E2
Palace Rd HG4 ....214 B7
Pale La Carleton BD23 .216 E1
Gateforth YO8 ....202 F7
Paley Gn La BD24 ...131 B2
Pallet Hill 10 DL10 ...41 D5
Palmer Gr YO8 ....232 A3
Palmer La YO1 ....233 C2
Palmes Cl YO19 .....191 E8
Palms Ct DL2 ....4 A5
Panman La YO19 .....184 F8
Pannal Ash Cl HG2 ..222 C8
Pannal Ash Cres HG2 .222 B7
Pannal Ash Dr HG2 ..222 B7
Pannal Ash Gr HG2 ..222 B7
Pannal Ash Rd HG2 ..222 B7
Pannal Ave HG3 .....222 E2
Pannal Bank HG3 ....222 E2
Pannal Cl 3 YO21 ...208 B5
Pannal Com Prim Sch
HG3 ....222 E3
Pannal Gn HG3 ......222 E3
Pannal Rd HG3 ......223 B4
Pannal Sta HG3 .....222 E2
Pannett Art Gall ★
YO11 ....208 C6
Pannett Way 8 YO21 .208 D6
Pannierman La YO7 ....7 D1
Panorama Cl 10 HG3 .137 C4
Panorama Dr LS29 ...175 C3
Panorama Wlk HG3 ..137 C4
Pant La LA2 ....130 C2
Parade Ct YO31 .....228 F6
Parade The
Harrogate HG1 ....219 C2
Whitby YO21 ....208 D7
Paradise YO11 ....213 B7
Paradise Cotts YO17 .170 F4
Paradise Field Est 2
YO61 ....143 D8
Paradise La Dalton YO7 .115 F8
Stutton with Hazlewood
LS24 ....189 A3
Paradise Rd YO7 .....67 A2
Paragon St YO10 ....233 C1
Parcevall Hall Gdns ★
BD23 ....157 E8
Parish Ghyll Dr LS29 .218 A3
Parish Ghyll La LS29 .218 A3
Parish Ghyll Rd LS29 .218 A3
Parish Ghyll Wlk LS29 .218 A3
Parison Ct WF10 ....200 A3
Park Ave Barlow YO8 .204 C7
Castleford WF10 ......200 F4
Glusburn BD20 ....187 E7
Great Preston WF10 ...200 B6
Harrogate HG2 ....219 C1
Hellifield BD23 ....154 B3
Kippax LS25 ....194 E1
Knaresborough HG5 ...221 B8
New Earswick YO32 ...225 D5
Normanton South WF6 .200 A1
Scarborough YO12 ....212 D4
Sherburn in Elmet LS25 .195 E4
Skipton BD23 ....216 F4
Swillington LS26 .....194 A1
Thornaby TS17 ....6 B8
Park Ave S HG2 .....222 D8
Park Bank YO21 ......29 E7
Park Chase
Harrogate HG1 ....219 C3
Hornby DL8 ....62 C8
Park Cl 6 Airmyn DN14 .205 E4
1 Easingwold YO61 ...143 D5
8 Knaresborough HG5 .221 B6
Skelton YO30 ....224 B4
Park Cres
6 Addingham LS29 ....175 A4
Castleford WF10 ......201 B4
Darlington DL1 ....3 D4
Embsay BD23 ....217 C7
Hellifield BD23 ....154 B3

Park Cres continued
York YO31 ....233 C4
Park Crest HG5 .....221 B6
Park Dale WF10 .....201 B5
Park Dr Campsall DN6 .206 E1
Glusburn BD20 ....187 E7
Harrogate HG2 ....222 D8
Knaresborough HG5 ...221 B6
13 Masham HG4 ....86 C3
Park Edge HG2 ......222 F8
Park End Prim Sch TS3 ..7 C8
Park Est YO32 ......225 D8
Park Gate
Knaresborough HG5 ...221 B8
Strensall YO32 ....167 B8
Park Gr
Knaresborough HG5 ...221 B8
Norton YO17 ....215 C3
Selby YO8 ....232 B3
Swillington LS26 .....200 A8
York YO31 ....233 C4
Park Gr Sch YO31 ...233 C4
Park Hill BB18 ......171 E1
Park House Gn
Harrogate HG1 ....219 C5
7 Spofforth HG3 ......179 E5
Park House La LA2 ..128 D5
Park Jun Sch WF10 ..200 F4
Park La Balne DN14 .207 C5
Barlow YO8 ....204 C7
Bishop Wilton YO42 ...169 F1
Borrowby YO7 ....65 E4
Buckden BD23 ....81 E2
Burn YO8 ....203 D7
Carleton BD23 ....173 A3
Cowling BD22 ....186 F5
Darlington DL1 ....3 D4
5 Easington TS13 .....11 A8
Glusburn BD20 ....187 E7
Great Preston WF10 ...200 E7
Guisborough TS14 ......8 E6
Kippax LS25 ....200 E8
Kirkbymoorside YO62 ..70 B1
Knaresborough HG5 ...221 C6
Ledsham LS25 ....201 B8
Luttons YO17 ....150 C8
Mickletown LS26 .....200 A5
5 Middleham DL8 .....60 E2
North Featherstone WF7 .200 F1
North Stainley with Sleningford
HG4 ....113 E5
Spofforth with Stockeld
HG3 ....179 D5
Tatham LA2 ....128 B3
West Tanfield HG4 ....113 A8
Wilberfoss YO41 ......185 E5
Womersley DN6 ....206 D6
York YO24 ....227 F3
Park La Cl YO42 .....169 F1
Park La Coll LS22 ...180 C3
Park La Inf Sch TS14 ..8 E5
Park Lands 4 HG5 ...179 E5
Park Lodge YO32 ....225 D4
Park Mount HG5 .....179 E5
Park Nook Rd YO8 ...196 F4
Park Par
Harrogate HG1 ....219 F2
Knaresborough HG5 ...221 B6
Park Pl Darlington DL1 ..3 D5
Hellifield BD23 ....154 B3
4 Knaresborough HG5 .221 B6
York YO31 ....233 C4
Park Rd Airmyn DN14 .205 E4
Asenby YO7 ....115 B6
Barlow YO8 ....204 C7
Castleford WF10 ......201 A3
Cowling BD22 ....187 B6
Glusburn BD20 ....187 E8
8 Harrogate HG2 .....219 D1
Norton-on-Derwent
YO17 ....215 C3
Pontefract WF8 ....201 A1
6 Scarborough YO12 ..212 E4
Spofforth HG3 ....179 E5
Park Rise 17 YO14 ..126 F8
Park Row
Knaresborough HG5 ...221 B5
Selby YO8 ....232 D5
Park Side Earby BB18 .186 A8
Follifoot HG3 ....223 E6
Park Sq
2 Knaresborough HG5 .221 B6
6 Ripon HG4 ....214 C4
Park St 16 Glusburn BD20 187 E8
1 Harrogate HG1 .....219 C5
Hovingham YO62 .....119 E6
Masham HG4 ....86 C3
Pickering YO18 ....95 F7
Ripon HG4 ....214 B5
Scarborough YO12 ....212 D4
Selby YO8 ....232 D5
1 Skipton BD23 ......216 F4
York YO24 ....233 A1
Park Terr
14 Knaresborough HG5 .221 B6
Whitby YO21 ....208 D6
York YO32 ....225 D5
Park The 14 YO13 ....75 D5
Park View
Castleford WF10 ......201 B3
Glaisdale YO21 ....30 D4
Harrogate HG1 ....219 D4
22 Leyburn DL8 ....60 D5
Middleton Tyas DL10 ...21 C4
Sherburn in Elmet LS25 .195 F4
Park View Dr BD23 ..134 B3

Park Way
Kirk Hammerton YO26 .164 C2
Knaresborough HG5 ...221 B8
Park Wood BD23 .....216 D5
Park Wood Cl BD23 ..216 E5
Park Wood Cres BD23 .216 D5
Park Wood Way BD23 .216 D5
Park Wynd DL10 .....209 C6
Parker Ave YO26 ....227 B2
Parker Dr 21 DL8 .....63 A2
Parker La YO26 .....164 C3
Parker St
Barnoldswick BB18 ...171 C2
15 Glusburn BD20 .....187 E8
Parkers Mount 20 YO62 .70 B1
Parkfield YO61 ......144 C6
Parkfield Ave TS5 .....6 E8
Parkfield Cl YO12 ...212 C4
Parkfield Gdns YO12 .212 D4
Parkfield La WF7 ....200 E1
Parkgate DL1 ....3 D5
Parkgate La DL10 .....41 B7
Parkin Ave YO8 .....232 E4
Parkinson App LS25 .194 C4
Parkinson's La LS21 .159 E2
Parkinson's Yd 5 DL10 .209 C6
Parkland Dr
Darlington DL3 ....3 A6
Tadcaster LS24 ....189 F6
Parkland Way YO32 ..225 D8
Parklands
Castleford WF10 ......200 F4
Ilkley LS29 ....218 A4
Parklands The
1 Ingleby Arncliffe DL6 ..45 A7
Scruton DL7 ....63 D7
Parkshill Ct DL10 ....20 F7
Parkside DL1 ....3 C4
Parkside Cl YO24 ....227 E3
Parkside Commercial Ctr
YO23 ....233 C1
Parkstone Pl TS16 .....5 E4
Parkway The YO12 ...212 B7
Parkways YO12 ......212 B7
Parkwood Dr 6 TS18 ..5 E8
Parliament Ave YO17 .215 E4
Parliament St
Harrogate HG1 ....219 C3
Norton YO17 ....215 E3
York YO1 ....233 B2
Parliament Terr 2 HG1 219 D2
Parlington Ct LS15 ..194 C8
Parlington Dr LS25 ..194 E8
Parlington La LS25 ..194 E7
Parlington Mdw LS15 .194 C7
Parlington Villas LS25 .194 E8
Parracombe Cl 6 TS17 ..6 A3
Parrock St 7 BB18 ..171 D1
Parsley Mews LS26 ..200 B6
Parson Back La DL6 ...25 B2
Parsonage Rd LS26 ..200 C6
Parsonage The 11 HG5 .221 A6
Parson's Cl YO8 .....208 A7
Parson's La
1 Addingham LS29 ....174 E1
Hutton Rudby DL6 .....25 A2
Parson's Wlk 11 DN14 .205 E4
Parsons Cl 10 DN14 ..205 E4
Parsons Cl La BD24 ..131 A2
Parsons La YO26 ....165 E1
Pasley Rd HG4 ......113 D3
Paston Wlk YO23 ....233 B1
Pasture Ave LS25 ....196 A4
Pasture Cl
Barnoldswick BB18 ...171 E2
4 Sherburn in Elmet
LS25 ....196 A4
Skelton YO30 ....224 B5
Skipton BD23 ....217 B5
2 Strensall YO32 .....167 B6
Wistow YO8 ....197 D6
Pasture Cres
Filey YO14 ....101 A4
3 Knaresborough HG5 .221 B7
Pasture Ct LS25 .....195 F4
Pasture Dr Bedale DL8 .63 A2
Castleford WF10 ......200 D3
Pasture Farm Cl YO10 .231 D6
Pasture Field La YO22 .32 C5
Pasture Fold 4 LS29 .176 C1
Pasture Hill YO17 ...169 E8
Pasture La
Ellerton YO42 ....193 C1
Helperby YO61 ....142 B8
Heworth YO31 ....229 B8
Hovingham YO62 .....119 E6
Kearby with Netherby
LS22 ....179 C5
Malton YO17 ....215 C5
Marton-le-Moor HG4 ..140 D8
2 Seamer YO12 ....99 D8
Pasture Rd
Embsay with Eastby
BD23 ....217 C8
Lockton YO18 ....73 A5
Pasture The 4 TS17 ..6 D5
Pasture View
Malton YO17 ....215 C6
Sherburn in Elmet LS25 .195 F4
Pasture Way
Castleford WF10 ......200 D3
Sherburn in Elmet LS25 .195 F4
Wistow YO8 ....197 D6
Pastures The
Carlton DN14 ....204 C3
Coulby Newham TS8 ....7 B5
16 Eastfield YO11 .....100 B6
Sherburn YO17 ....124 D7

Pastures The *continued*
4 York YO24 230 E8
Pateley Moor Cres DL2 3 E3
Pately Pl 1 YO26 227 D4
Paterson Cres DL6 210 E4
Patience La HG4 114 D3
Patrick Pool YO1 233 B2
Patterdale Dr YO30 224 E1
Patterham La DL8 59 D4
Pavement YO1 233 B2
Paver La YO1 233 C2
Pavilion Sq
7 Harrogate HG2 219 C1
11 Scarborough YO11 213 A5
Pavilion Terr 12 YO11 213 A5
Peacock's Cl DL7 63 E7
Peacocks Cl TS9 26 C8
Peak Alum Works★ YO13 53 F8
Peak Scar Rd YO62 67 C3
Pear Tree Acre LS23 180 F1
Pear Tree Ave
Long Drax YO8 204 F7
8 Poppleton YO26 165 F1
Pear Tree Cl
Skeeby DL10 20 F1
York YO32 225 F4
Pear Tree Gdns LS15 194 D7
Pear Tree Wlk YO17 215 B4
Pearl Rd TS17 6 B8
Pearl St HG1 220 C4
Pearson Garth YO13 99 A7
Pearson St WF6 200 A3
Peart La BD23 154 C8
Peartree Ct YO1 233 C3
Pease Ct
1 Eaglescliffe TS16 5 D5
Guisborough TS14 8 D5
4 Lingdale TS12 9 F7
Pease St Darlington DL1 3 E5
6 Lingdale TS12 9 F7
Peasey Hills Rd YO17 215 C5
Peasholm Ave YO12 212 F7
Peasholm Cres YO12 212 F7
Peasholm Dr YO12 212 E7
Peasholm Gap YO12 212 F8
Peasholm Gdns YO12 212 F7
Peasholm Rd YO12 212 F8
Peasholme Bridge YO12 212 E7
Peasholme Gn YO1 233 C2
Peasland La YO7 66 B5
Peaslands La YO18 96 D5
Peat La HG3 137 B3
Peatmoor La DL8 58 E5
Peckett's Holt HG1 219 D7
Peckett's Way HG1 219 D7
Peckfield HG4 214 C2
Peckfield Cl HG3 160 F5
Peckitt St YO1 233 B1
Peel Cl YO10 229 A1
Peel Gn BD23 154 B2
Peel Pl 11 LS29 176 C1
Peel St Thornaby TS17 6 B8
York YO1 233 C1
Peel Terr YO12 213 A7
Pefham La YO17 170 F4
Pegman Cl TS14 8 F7
Peirse Cl DL8 63 A2
Pelham Pl 15 YO32 167 A7
Pellentine Rd HG3 223 F4
Pemberton Cres TS4 7 A8
Pemberton Rd WF10 201 A6
Pembroke St
10 Skipton BD23 216 F3
York YO30 228 B7
Pembroke Way YO21 208 C5
Pembury Mews DL10 41 B6
Penberry Gdns 33 TS17 5 F4
Penders La TS15 5 E1
Penderyn Cres TS17 5 F4
Pendle St 4 BD23 216 D3
Pendleton Rd DL1 3 D7
Pendragon Castle★ CA17 14 A1
Penfold Ct BD23 154 B3
Penhill Ct DL7 210 C1
Penhowe La YO17 147 D4
Penistone Rd TS3 7 C8
Penley's Gr St YO31 233 C4
Penn La DL8 56 D4
Penn Rd DL10 209 B7
Pennine Way BD20 172 E2
Pennine Cl YO32 225 F4
Pennine View
Burneston DL8 87 E8
Northallerton DL7 210 B2
Pennine Way
11 Barnoldswick BB18 171 D1
Ingleby TS17 6 A4
Penniston La YO13 97 C4
Penny Gn BD24 131 D1
Penny La
1 Easingwold YO61 117 D1
Ripon HG4 214 C7
Penny La Ct YO1 233 C3
Penny Pot Gdns 4 HG3 161 B2
Penny Pot La HG3 160 D2
Penny Pot La or Rough Rd HG3 161 A2
Penny Royal Cl 7 HG3 161 B3
Pennycarr La YO61 143 D7
Pennyman Prim Sch TS3 7 D8
Pennypot La TS18 5 E7
Pennywort Gr 15 HG3 161 B3
Penrith Cres WF10 201 B5
Penrith Rd TS3 7 B8
Pentire Cl 11 YO30 225 A1
Pentland Dr YO32 225 E3
Penton Rd 20 YO11 100 B6
Penyghent Ave YO31 229 A5
Pen-y-ghent Way 5 BB18 171 D1
Penyghent Way TS17 6 A3
Peplow Cl LS25 201 F6
Peppercorn Cl 6 YO26 227 E4
Peppergarth The DL7 210 B3
Peppermint Dr 15 DL9 41 A5
Peppermint Way YO8 232 A5
Per Ardua Way 6 DL10 41 E4
Percy Cross Rigg YO21 9 A1
Percy Ct HG5 162 A6
Percy Dr 4 DN14 205 E4
Percy Rd Darlington DL3 3 C7
14 Hunmanby YO14 127 A8
Percy St YO31 233 B3
Percy's La YO1 233 C2
Perie Ave HG4 113 D3
Perry Ave TS17 6 B5
Peter Hill Dr YO30 228 A8
Peter La
Burton Leonard HG3 140 A2
York YO1 233 B2
Petercroft Cl 5 YO19 184 F7
Petercroft La YO19 184 F7
Peterhouse Cl DL1 3 D7
Petersbottom La LA2 129 B4
Petersway YO30 233 A4
Petre Ave YO8 232 E3
Petty Whin Cl 25 HG3 161 B3
Petyt Gr BD23 217 A4
Pew Tree Cl YO41 185 E6
Pheasant Dr 5 YO24 230 B8
Philadelphia Terr 2 YO23 228 B2
Philip La YO8 196 E2
Philip St 27 BB18 171 D1
Philippa's Dr HG2 222 D8
Philpin La LA6 104 C8
Phlashetts La DL8 87 A4
Phoenix Bvd YO26 228 A4
Phoenix Pk TS8 6 F6
Piave Rd DL9 40 D4
Picadilly Ct YO1 233 C2
Piccadilly YO1 233 C2
Pick Haven Garth DN14 202 F3
Pickard Cl BB18 171 E2
Pickard La BD20 174 C1
Pickering Castle★ YO18 95 F7
Pickering Com Inf Sch YO18 96 A7
Pickering Com Jun Sch 26 YO18 95 F7
Pickering Rd
East Ayton/West Ayton YO13 99 A7
Thornaby TS17 6 B8
Thornton-le-Dale YO18 96 C6
Pickering Sta YO18 95 F7
Pickeringmoor La YO7 64 C2
Pickhill CE Prim Sch YO7 88 C6
Picking Croft La HG3 161 B5
Pickrowfield La LS25 196 C6
Picks Ct YO7 211 B3
Pickwick Cl YO17 215 C5
Piece Croft 2 BD23 134 D2
Piece Fields 4 BD23 134 D2
Pier La 22 YO21 208 D7
Pier Rd YO21 208 D7
Piercy End YO62 70 B1
Pierremont Rd DL3 3 B6
Piggy La DL2 1 C7
Pighill Nook Rd LS25 202 C7
Pike Hills Mount YO23 230 A3
Pike La BD24 131 E4
Pike Rd 8 YO18 95 F6
Pikepurse La DL10 209 D8
Pilgrim St YO31 233 B4
Pill White La LS21 177 C3
Pilmoor Cl DL10 209 E8
Pilmoor Dr DL10 209 E8
Pindar Leisure Ctr YO11 100 A6
Pindar Rd YO11 100 A6
Pindar Sch YO11 100 A6
Pindars Way YO8 198 B4
Pinder Cl DL10 209 F8
Pinders Cres WF11 201 E3
Pinders Gn LS26 200 B4
Pinders Gn Ct LS26 200 B5
Pinders Gn Dr LS26 200 B5
Pinders Gn Fold LS26 200 B5
Pine Cl
Castleford WF10 200 F3
Skipton BD23 216 E4
Pine Croft HG4 112 F2
Pine Gr 1 DL6 210 E3
Pine Hill TS8 7 B5
Pine Rd Guisborough TS14 8 E7
Middlesbrough TS7 7 D8
Pine St HG1 219 E5
Pine Tree Ave YO17 122 F5
Pine Tree Cl YO8 197 B2
Pine Tree La 1 LS25 202 A7
Pine Wlk HG4 214 D2
Pinelands 4 YO32 225 D7
Pinelands Way YO10 229 C3
Pines Gdns 29 LS29 175 C2
Pines The LS17 178 B2
Pinetree Gr DL2 4 C4
Pinewood Ave YO14 101 B4
Pinewood Cl
5 Easington TS13 11 A8
2 Ilkley LS29 218 A3
5 Whitby YO21 208 C6
Pinewood Dr
Camblesforth YO8 204 D4
Scarborough YO12 212 D5
Pinewood Gate HG2 222 A7
Pinewood Gr
13 Bedale DL8 63 A2
6 York YO31 225 E2
Pinewood Hill 4 YO10 229 C3
Pinewood Rd TS7 7 C6
Pinewood Wlk 7 TS9 26 C8
Pinfold Ave LS25 195 F4
Pinfold Cl
Bilton-in-Ainsty with Bickerton LS22 181 B5
5 Riccall YO19 192 A1
3 Sherburn in Elmet LS25 195 F4
Pinfold Ct
Kirkby Malzeard HG4 112 D5
4 Sherburn in Elmet LS25 195 F4
4 York YO30 228 A7
Pinfold Dr DL6 210 E5
Pinfold Garth
Malton YO17 215 A4
6 Sherburn in Elmet LS25 195 F4
Pinfold Gn HG5 140 E1
Pinfold Hill YO8 197 D6
Pinfold La
Asselby DN14 205 F6
Kirk Smeaton WF8 206 B3
Mickletown LS26 200 C5
Moss DN6 207 D1
Norton DN6 206 E2
Norwood HG3 177 A8
Pollington DN14 207 F6
Pinfold Pl YO7 211 C3
Pinfold Rise LS25 194 F8
Pinfold The 5 BD23 216 F4
Pinfold View DN14 207 F6
Pinfold Way 5 LS25 195 F4
Pinhaw Rd BD23 217 A2
Pinnacle View BD22 187 A5
Pinsent Ct YO31 228 E8
Pioneer Way WF10 200 C2
Piper Hill 1 WF11 201 D6
Piper La Cowling BD22 187 B5
Thirsk YO7 211 C3
Piper Rd DL6 45 F6
Pipers Acre 4 YO18 95 F7
Pipers La YO26 141 F1
Pippin Rd YO17 215 B4
Pippin's App 17 WF6 200 A2
Pit Ings La YO7 115 F6
Pit La Ledston Luck LS25 194 F1
Micklefield LS25 195 A4
Mickletown LS26 200 B6
Pitman Rd YO17 215 C5
Place Hill DL11 38 B6
Plane Tree Way YO14 101 A4
Planetree La
Kirkby Fleetham with Fencote DL7 42 A1
Thornville YO26 164 A1
Plantation Ave HG3 222 A8
Plantation Cl HG2 222 A8
Plantation Dr
Barlby with Osgodby YO8 198 B5
York YO26 227 C6
Plantation Gr YO26 227 C6
Plantation Rd HG2 222 A8
Plantation Terr HG2 222 A8
Plantation The BD23 152 E3
Plantation Way 23 YO32 166 E5
Player Ct TS16 5 E5
Pleasance The 6 LS26 194 A1
Pleasant Row HG5 221 B8
Pleasant View 5 BB18 172 B1
Plews Way DL7 63 C5
Plompton Cl HG2 220 D1
Plompton Dr HG2 220 D2
Plompton Gr 3 HG2 220 D2
Plompton Rd HG3 223 F5
Plompton Way 1 HG2 220 D2
Plompton Wlk 2 HG2 220 D2
Plough Garth The DN14 202 F3
Ploughlands 1 YO32 225 C7
Ploughman's Cl YO23 230 C3
Ploughmans Ct 14 YO11 100 B7
Ploughmans' La YO32 225 C7
Plover Gdns 1 YO12 99 F6
Plum St YO17 215 D3
Plumer Ave YO31 229 A5
Plumer Rd DL9 209 B1
Plumpton La HG4 139 D8
Plumpton Pk HG2 220 D3
Plumpton Rocks★ HG5 179 D8
Pluntrain Dale La YO18 96 B7
Pocklington La YO42 169 F2
Pockthorpe La YO25 151 F2
Pocock Pl DL10 41 E4
Polam Hall Sch DL1 3 C4
Polam La DL1 3 C4
Polam Rd DL1 3 C4
Pole Rd BD22 187 F4
Pollard Cl YO32 225 E3
Pollard Gdns YO12 212 C4
Pollington Balne CE Prim Sch DN14 207 F6
Polperro Cl 21 WF6 200 A2
Pond Farm Cl TS13 11 F7
Pond Field Cl DL3 3 A4
Pond St 3 YO8 232 D6
Pond View DL6 65 F7
Pondfields Dr LS25 194 D1
Pontefract Castle★ WF8 201 C1
Pontefract Monkhill Sta WF8 201 B1
Pontefract Mus★ WF8 201 B1
Pontefract New Coll WF8 201 A1
Pontefract Pk Racecourse★ WF8 200 F2
Pontefract Rd
Castleford WF10 200 F4
Knottingley WF11 201 D2
Normanton South WF6 200 B2
Pool Ct 20 YO18 95 F6
Pool La YO26 164 E4
Poole La LS25 201 F6
Pope St WF6 200 B3
Poplar Ave
Castleford WF10 201 B4
6 Hutton Rudby TS15 25 D5
4 Kirkbymoorside YO62 70 B1
3 Wetherby LS22 180 C4
Poplar Cres
Harrogate HG1 219 F6
Northallerton DL7 210 C2
Poplar Dr WF6 200 A3
Poplar Gdns YO8 204 F5
Poplar Gn HG5 162 A6
Poplar Gr
Harrogate HG1 219 F6
York YO32 225 E3
Poplar Pl TS14 8 E7
Poplar Row 6 YO21 208 D7
Poplar St YO26 227 E5
Poplar View YO17 215 F4
Poplar Way HG1 219 F6
Poplars La YO17 123 A7
Poplars The
11 Brayton YO8 197 D1
2 Glusburn BD20 187 E6
Knottingley WF11 202 A1
Poppleton Hall Gdn YO26 224 A3
Poppleton Rd YO26 227 E4
Poppleton Rd Prim Sch YO26 227 E5
Poppleton Sta YO26 182 F8
Poppy Cl YO8 232 C2
Poppy Ct DL9 41 A5
Porch Farm Cl YO62 120 B5
Porch The DL10 21 D7
Pornic Ave YO13 75 D5
Porritt La YO12 99 D7
Portal Rd YO26 227 B6
Portholme Cres 7 YO8 232 C5
Portholme Ct YO8 232 C4
Portholme Dr YO8 232 C4
Portholme Rd YO8 232 C5
Portisham Pl 12 YO32 167 A7
Portland Cres HG1 219 D4
Portland St YO31 233 B4
Portland Way DL7 63 C5
Portman Rise TS14 8 F5
Post Office Row DN14 205 A1
Postern Cl YO23 233 B1
Postern La YO42 193 D6
Pot Bank HG3 178 A8
Potlands DL7 63 C4
Pott Bank HG4 85 A1
Pott Moor High Rd HG4 110 F8
Potter Cl YO13 99 B8
Potter Hill 1 YO18 95 F7
Potter La DL7 64 A5
Potter's Side La YO21 9 D1
Pottergate
Gilling East YO62 118 F7
14 Helmsley YO62 92 F6
Richmond DL10 209 C7
Potters Dr 4 YO23 230 B3
Potterton Cl LS15 194 C8
Potterton La
Barwick in Elmet LS15 194 C8
Barwick in Elmet & Scholes LS15 188 C1
Pottery La
Bishop Monkton HG4 140 A6
Knottingley WF11 201 E3
Littlethorpe HG4 214 E1
York YO31 228 E7
Pottery St WF10 200 D4
Potticar Bank YO62 119 D4
Pounteys Cl 4 DL2 4 C4
Powell St
Harrogate HG1 219 F4
Selby YO8 232 B6
Prail Cl 13 WF8 201 C1
Precentor's Ct YO31 233 B3
Preen Dr TS5 6 D8
Premier Rd TS7 7 D7
Premiere Pk 30 LS29 175 C2
Preseli Gr 31 TS17 5 F4
Preston Field Cross Rd YO13 74 E1
Preston Hall Mus★ TS18 5 F6
Preston La
Great Preston WF10 200 C7
Preston-on-Tees TS18 5 E7
Preston Prim Sch TS16 5 E6
Preston View LS26 194 A1
Preston Way TS9 26 C8
Prestwick Ct
15 Middleton St George DL2 4 C4
Rufforth YO26 227 B5
Pretoria St WF10 200 F4
Price's La YO23 233 B1
Priest Bank Rd 4 BD20 173 F1
Priest Cl YO14 126 F8
Priest Gill Bank DL11 19 F5
Priest La
Dunnington YO19 184 F5
Ripon HG4 214 D4
Priestcarr La YO26 163 D8
Primrose Ave
Hunmanby Sands YO14 101 B1
Swillington LS26 194 A1
Primrose Cl
Guisborough TS14 8 E6
13 Killinghall HG3 161 B3
Ripon HG4 214 C6
Primrose Ct 18 DL9 41 A5
Primrose Dene WF11 201 E4
Primrose Dr
Castleford WF10 201 D3
Filey YO14 101 B1
Ripon HG4 214 C6
Primrose Gr YO8 232 A6
Primrose Hill
9 Knottingley WF11 202 A3
2 Skipton BD23 216 F4
Primrose Hill Cl LS26 194 A1
Primrose Hill Dr
Great & Little Preston LS26 200 A8
15 Swillington LS26 194 A1
Primrose Hill Garth LS26 200 A8
Primrose Hill Gdns LS26 194 A1
Primrose Hill Gn LS26 200 A8
Primrose Hill Gr 16 LS26 194 A1
Primrose La LS23 188 E8
Primrose La Prim Sch 5 LS23 188 E8
Primrose Vale 1 WF11 202 A2
Primrose Valley Rd YO14 101 B1
Prince Henry Rd LS21 177 A1
Prince Henrys Gram Sch LS21 177 A1
Prince of Wales Terr YO11 213 A4
Prince Rupert Dr YO26 181 C7
Prince St WF10 200 C8
Princes Cres BD23 217 B4
Princes Dr BD23 217 A4
Princes Sq TS17 6 B6
Princes Villa Rd HG1 219 E2
Princess Ave HG5 221 C5
Princess Cl
Knaresborough HG5 221 C5
Ripon HG4 214 C6
Princess Ct 11 WF6 200 B1
Princess Dr
Knaresborough HG5 221 C5
West Haddlesey YO8 203 A5
York YO26 227 D6
Princess Gr 4 HG5 221 C5
Princess La 12 YO11 213 B6
Princess Mead HG5 163 A3
Princess Mount 3 HG5 221 C5
Princess Pl
1 Ripon HG4 214 C6
5 Whitby YO21 208 D6
Princess Rd
Darlington DL3 3 D8
Ilkley LS29 218 A3
Malton YO17 215 C4
Ripon HG4 214 C6
Strensall YO32 167 B7
Princess Royal La 4 YO11 212 F3
Princess Royal Pk 1 YO11 213 A3
Princess Royal Rd HG4 214 C3
Princess Royal Terr YO11 213 A3
Princess Royal Way HG3 222 E1
Princess Sq 11 YO11 213 B6
Princess St
Castleford WF10 200 F5
Normanton South WF6 200 A1
Scarborough YO11 213 B6
Princess Terr
Knaresborough HG5 221 C6
17 Scarborough YO11 213 B6
Prior Ave DL10 209 B7
Prior Pursglove Coll TS14 8 F7
Prior Wath Rd YO13 54 A5
Prior's La BD23 174 C8
Prior's Wlk YO26 227 D6
Priorpot Way YO17 215 F4
Priorwood Gdns TS17 6 A4
Priory Cl
Guisborough TS14 8 F7
Northallerton DL6 210 E5
Wilberfoss YO41 185 F6
Priory Dr YO21 208 A6
Priory La 1 DN14 204 C1
Priory Pk YO21 31 C4
Priory Pk Cl 3 LS25 202 A8
Priory Pk Gr 2 LS25 202 B8
Priory Pl YO11 100 B7
Priory Rd or Hall La DN6 206 E2

Priory St YO1 ....233 A1
Priory View 2 BD23 ....217 B5
Priory Villas DL10 ....209 D6
Priory Way
  Barnoldswick BB18 ......171 D1
  4 Ingleby Arncliffe DL6 ....45 A7
  1 Snaith DN14 ....204 B1
Priory Wood Way
  YO31 ....225 F2
Prison & Pol Mus★
  HG4 ....214 D5
Prissick Sports Ctr TS4 ..7 B8
Pritchett Rd TS3 ....7 C8
Promenade La HG1 ....219 C3
Promenade Sq HG1 ....219 C2
Prospect Ave
  Normanton South WF6 ....200 A2
  Sherburn in Elmet LS25 ..195 F4
Prospect Bank
  Bramham cum Oglethorpe
  LS23 ....188 F6
  Scarborough YO12 ....212 D6
Prospect Cl
  Camblesforth YO8 ....204 D5
  Harrogate HG2 ......220 C3
  Pollington DN14 ....207 F6
Prospect Cres
  13 Harrogate HG1 ....219 D2
  Scarborough YO12 ....212 D6
Prospect Ct 3 LS24 ....189 E6
Prospect Dr LS24 ....189 E6
Prospect Field 5 YO22 ..33 D4
Prospect Hill YO21 ....208 C5
Prospect Mount Rd
  YO12 ....212 C6
Prospect Pk YO12 ....212 D6
Prospect Pl
  Harrogate HG1 ......219 D2
  Northallerton DL6 ....210 F4
  28 Scarborough YO11 ..213 A6
  Skipton BD23 ....216 F4
  Thornton-le-Dale YO18 ..96 E6
  10 Whitby YO22 ......208 C6
  Wistow YO8 ....197 D6
Prospect Rd
  Harrogate HG2 ......220 C3
  9 Scarborough YO12 ..212 F6
Prospect St 14 BD20 ..187 E7
Prospect Terr
  Fulford YO31 ....231 D6
  15 Knaresborough HG5 ..221 A6
  1 Lingdale TS12 ......9 F7
  Micklefield LS25 ....195 A3
  York YO1 ....233 B1
Prospect View DL6 ....210 E4
Prospect Way
  5 Leeming DL7 ....63 D4
  Selby YO8 ....232 D4
Prospect Way Ind Est
  YO8 ....232 D4
Providence Gn 16 WF8 201 C2
Providence Pl
  13 Filey YO14 ......101 B3
  Mickletown LS26 ....200 D6
  15 Scarborough YO11 ..213 A6
  Skipton BD23 ....217 A4
Providence Terr HG1 ..219 D4
Pry Hills La
  Hartoft YO18 ....71 A8
  Rosedale East Side YO18 ..49 F2
Pudding Hill Rd DL11 ....1 B6
Pudding La YO13 ....97 F5
Pudding Pie Hill★
  YO7 ....211 D1
Pudsley Wlk DL1 ....3 D4
Pulleyn Cl 3 YO32 ....167 C8
Pulleyn Dr YO24 ......227 F1
Pump Hill 4 HG5 ......221 A6
Pump La
  Kirklevington TS15 ....24 F1
  4 Malton YO17 ......215 C6
Purey Cust Nuffield Hospl
  The YO1 ....233 B3
Pye Busk Cl LA2 ......129 B8
Pye La HG3 ....160 F8

Q
Quad Squad The★
  YO13 ....97 C6
Quaker Cl
  1 Reeth, Fremington &
    Healaugh DL11 ......38 B6
  Scarborough YO12 ....212 C5
Quaker Gn 1 YO24 ....230 C7
Quaker La DL6 ......210 D5
Quaker's La DL6 ....44 D7
Quakers La DL10 ....209 B7
Quant Mews YO10 ....229 B3
Quarry Ave 20 WF11 ..202 A2
Quarry Bank YO17 ....215 D5
Quarry Banks YO7 ....116 E7
Quarry Dr TS8 ....6 E5
Quarry Gate YO13 ....74 C1
Quarry Hill YO17 ......120 F4
Quarry Hill La LS22 ..180 B3
Quarry La
  Harrogate HG1 ......219 C6
  Osmotherley DL6 ......45 C5
  Pateley Bridge HG3 ..137 C4
Quarry Moor La HG4 ..214 C6
Quarry Mount YO12 ..212 E3
Quarry Oval HG1 ....219 C6

Quarry Rd
  Eaglescliffe TS18 ......5 F7
  Norton DN6 ....206 F2
  Richmond DL10 ....209 B7
  Ripon HG4 ....214 B2
Quay St YO11 ....213 B6
Quay The YO8 ......232 D6
Queen Anne's Ct 3 DL8 ..63 A2
Queen Anne's Dr 4 DL8 ..63 A2
Queen Annes Rd
  YO30 ....233 A3
Queen Dike★ YO17 ....170 B8
Queen Elizabeth Dr 10
  YO13 ....75 D5
Queen Elizabeth Way
  TS18 ....6 D6
Queen Elizabeth's Sixth Form
  Coll 1 DL3 ....5 C5
Queen Ethelburga's Coll
  YO26 ....164 C6
Queen Ethelburga's Dr 6
  HG3 ....161 B2
Queen Ethelburga's Par 8
  HG3 ....161 B2
Queen Margaret's Dr
  WF11 ....201 E4
Queen Margaret's Ind Est
  YO11 ....212 E2
Queen Margaret's Rd 6
  YO11 ....212 F3
Queen Margaret's Sch
  YO19 ....192 A5
Queen Margarets Ave 4
  WF11 ....201 E4
Queen Margarets Cl 3
  WF11 ....201 E4
Queen Marys Sch YO7 115 A7
Queen St
  10 Cowling BD22 ....187 B6
  Great Preston LS26 ..200 C7
  Normanton South WF6 ..200 A1
  18 Ripon HG4 ......214 C5
  Scarborough YO11 ....213 A6
  Skelton & Brotton TS12 ..9 D7
  York YO24 ....233 A2
Queen Victoria St
  YO23 ....228 B1
Queen's Cl 8 HG2 ....219 C1
Queen's Ct YO1 ......233 B2
Queen's Dr LS29 ....218 A3
Queen's Dr La LS29 ..218 A3
Queen's Gdns
  4 Ilkley LS29 ......218 A3
  Tadcaster LS24 ....189 E6
Queen's Par YO12 ....213 A7
Queen's Pk Dr WF10 ..201 A4
Queen's Rd
  Harrogate HG2 ......219 C1
  Ilkley LS29 ....218 A3
Queen's St 5 BD23 ....217 B4
Queen's Staith Rd
  YO1 ....233 B2
Queen's Terr
  3 Filey YO14 ......101 B3
  Scarborough YO12 ....213 A7
Queen's Way YO62 ......70 B1
Queens Ave DL9 ......40 E3
Queens Ct
  Malton YO17 ......215 D6
  Richmond DL10 ....209 C7
Queens Dr
  9 Stokesley TS9 ......26 C8
  Whitby YO22 ......208 B3
Queens Garth BD23 ..172 A3
Queens Gate HG1 ....219 E2
Queens Gdns YO7 ....211 C1
Queens Rd
  Knaresborough HG5 ..221 C6
  Richmond DL10 ....209 C7
Queens Staith Mews
  YO1 ....233 B1
Queensbury Ct 15 WF6 200 B1
Queensway WF8 ......201 C2
Queenswood Dr YO24 ..227 D2
Quentin Rd 19 DL9 ....40 E4
Quernmore Dr BB18 ..186 A7

R
Rabbit La YO17 ......215 F8
Raby La DL7 ....22 E3
Raby Pk LS22 ......180 B3
Raby Terr DL3 ....3 C5
Racca Ave 11 WF11 ..202 A2
Racca Gn WF11 ......202 A2
Race La Carlton YO8 ..204 B4
  Sessay YO61 ......116 C4
Racecourse Ct DL10 ..209 A8
Racecourse La DL7 ..210 D3
Racecourse Mews
  YO7 ....211 A2
Racecourse Rd
  East Ayton/West Ayton
  YO13 ....99 B8
  Irton YO12 ....212 A1
  Richmond DL10 ....209 B8
  York YO23 ....231 B8
Rachel La DL11 ....20 B5
Rag Robin Turn YO7 ..66 D6
Raghill La YO61 ....142 A8
Raglan St HG1 ......219 D2
Raglan Terr 3 YO21 ..208 D5
Raikes Ave BD23 ....216 F5
Raikes La BD23 ....156 A6
Raikes' La YO22 ......32 E3
Raikes Rd BD23 ....216 F5
Raikes The HG3 ....137 E3

Raikeswood Cres
  BD23 ....216 E5
Raikeswood Dr BD23 ..216 E5
Raikeswood Rd BD23 ..216 E5
Railer Bank HG4 ....112 E6
Railway Ave WF8 ....201 B1
Railway Cotts HG4 ....214 D1
Railway Rd
  Follifoot HG3 ......223 C7
  Ilkley LS29 ....218 B4
Railway St 16 Leyburn DL8 60 D5
  Norton YO17 ....215 C3
  Slingsby YO62 ......120 B5
Railway Terr
  Hurworth-on-Tees DL2 ..22 D8
  Ilkley LS29 ....218 C4
  5 Normanton South WF6 200 A1
  Thirsk YO7 ....211 B2
  York YO24 ....228 A4
Railway View
  Darlington DL1 ......3 D4
  Northallerton DL7 ....210 D3
  York YO23 ....230 E8
Raincliffe Ave
  29 Filey YO14 ......101 B3
  Scarborough YO12 ....212 C5
Raincliffe Cres YO12 ..212 C5
Raincliffe Gr YO12 ....212 C4
Raincliffe Sch YO12 ..212 B6
Raincliffe St 4 YO8 ..232 C5
Raindale Rd YO18 ....71 F6
Raines Dr 5 BD20 ....173 E3
Raines La BD23 ......134 D3
Raines Lea BD23 ....134 D3
Raines Mdws 6 BD23 134 D2
Raines Rd BD24 ....131 C1
Rainford Cl 7 YO10 ....99 D6
Rainhall Cres BB18 ..171 E1
Rainhall Rd BB18 ....171 D1
Rainham Cl TS17 ......6 B4
Rainsborough Way 3
  YO30 ....228 A4
Rainsburgh La YO25 ..126 A3
Raisdale Rd TS9 ......26 D1
Rake La YO21 ....30 D6
Rake The LA6 ......103 D4
Rakehill Rd LS15 ....194 B8
Raker Cl YO19 ......192 F7
Rakes BD23 ....134 C1
Rakes La BD23 ....171 B5
Raleigh St YO12 ....212 E6
Ralph Butterfield Prim Sch
  YO32 ....166 F5
Ralph Garth YO26 ....181 D7
Rampart The YO23 ..190 D4
Ramsay Cl YO11 ......233 C4
Ramsden Cl WF11 ....201 D4
Ramsden St LS25 ....200 C8
Ramsey Ave YO23 ....231 B3
Ramsey Gdns 38 TS17 ..5 F4
Ramsey St YO12 ....212 E6
Ramshaw Dr BD23 ....217 A1
Ramshill Rd YO11 ....213 A4
Randal La HG3 ......160 D4
Range Rd DL8 ......40 A2
Rankin's Well Rd 4
  BD23 ....217 B4
Rantreefold Rd LA2 ..128 F4
Rape Cl La YO11 ....118 E4
Rape La YO62 ....93 B7
Raper La YO61 ......117 B3
Raper View LS25 ....194 F8
Rarber Top La LA6 ..103 D2
Rarey Dr YO17 ......124 E1
Raskelf Rd
  7 Brafferton YO61 ..115 F1
  Easingwold YO61 ....117 B1
Ratcliffe Ct YO30 ....224 C5
Ratcliffe St YO30 ....228 B7
Rathmell La YO26 ....164 C2
Rathmell CE VA Prim Sch
  BD24 ....153 B7
Rattan Row YO25 ....151 C6
Ratten Row Hunton DL8 ..61 E7
  Seamer YO12 ....99 C5
Raven Cl 10 YO12 ....99 F6
Raven Gr YO26 ......227 C4
Raven Hall Rd YO13 ..53 F7
Ravens Cl Brow LA2 ..102 C1
Ravenscroft Way
  BB18 ....171 E2
Ravensdale Rd DL3 ....3 B4
Ravensthorpe Prep Sch
  DL3 ....3 B5
Ravensville 1 BD20 ..187 F7
Ravensworth Castle★
  DL11 ....20 A6
Ravensworth CE Prim Sch
  DL11 ....20 A6
Ravine Hill 17 YO14 ..101 B4
Ravine Rd YO14 ......101 B4
Ravine Top 7 YO14 ..101 B3
Raw Bank DL11 ......37 E8
Raw Gap HG5 ......221 A6
Raw La Fylingdales YO22 ..33 B4
  Kirkby Wharfe with
  North Milford LS24 ....190 A3
  Towton LS24 ....189 F3
Raw Pasture Bank
  YO22 ....33 B5
Raw Pasture La YO22 ..33 C7
Rawcliff Rd YO18 ......72 A5
Rawcliffe Ave YO30 ..227 F8
Rawcliffe Cl 5 YO30 ..224 E2
Rawcliffe Croft YO30 ..224 D2
Rawcliffe Dr YO30 ....227 F8
Rawcliffe in Snaith Prim Sch
  DN14 ....205 A1

Rawcliffe Inf Sch
  YO30 ....224 E1
Rawcliffe La YO30 ....224 F1
Rawcliffe Landing
  YO30 ....224 C3
Rawcliffe Rd DN14 ..205 A2
Rawcliffe Village
  YO30 ....224 E3
Rawcliffe Way YO30 ..224 E2
Rawdon Ave YO10 ....228 F4
Rawfield La WF11 ....201 D7
Rawlinson Rd DL9 ....209 D2
Rawson St YO12 ....219 E5
Ray Bridge La BD23 ..155 D1
Ray La HG4 ....114 B1
Raydale Cl 2 HG5 ....221 D5
Raygill La BD20 ......186 E8
Rayleigh Rd HG2 ....222 E8
Raylton Ave TS7 ......7 B5
Rayner St YO12 ....214 C5
Read Cl YO8 ....204 F5
Read Sch YO8 ......204 F5
Real Aeroplane Mus The★
  YO8 ....199 D5
Reas La YO51 ......141 D1
Reasty Hill YO13 ......53 E1
Reasty Rd YO13 ......53 D2
Recreation Rd
  17 Pickering YO18 ....95 F6
  2 Selby YO8 ......232 D6
Rectory Cl
  Bolton Percy YO23 ..190 D4
  Heslerton YO17 ....123 F6
Rectory Gdns YO23 ..228 B1
Rectory La
  Guisborough TS14 ....8 E6
  3 Hurworth-on-Tees DL2 ..22 C8
  Longnewton TS21 ....5 A7
  Nunnington YO62 ....93 E2
  Skipton BD23 ......217 A4
  Thornton-le-Dale YO18 ..96 E5
Red Bank Cl HG4 ....214 A3
Red Bank Dr HG4 ....214 A3
Red Bank Rd HG4 ....214 A3
Red Barnes Way DL1 ..3 E6
Red Brae Bank HG3 ..137 A3
Red Brow YO13 ......74 C5
Red Gate DL8 ......57 C6
Red Hall La TS15 ......6 A1
Red Hall Prim Sch DL1 ..3 F6
Red Hill La LS25 ....195 E1
Red Hills La HG3 ....140 B3
Red Hills Rd HG4 ....214 B7
Red La
  Green Hammerton YO26 ..164 C3
  4 Masham HG4 ......86 C3
Red Lion St BD23 ....216 F4
Red Rose Cl 3 DL3 ....3 A7
Red Scar Dr YO12 ....212 A4
Red Scar La
  Newby & Scalby YO12 ..75 C4
  Scalby YO12 ......212 A8
Red Twr★ YO1 ......228 E4
Red Way Brompton DL6 ..43 F6
  Danby YO21 ....29 E6
  Farndale East YO62 ....48 E4
  Nether Silton DL6 ....45 D1
Redburn Dr YO10 ....229 D4
Redcap La YO42 ....193 C5
Redcar Rd
  Guisborough TS14 ....8 F7
  Thornaby TS17 ......6 B7
Redcliff Cl 12 YO11 ..100 B7
Redcliffe Ct YO12 ....212 D7
Redcliffe Gdns YO12 ..212 C6
Redcliffe La YO11 ....100 C6
Redcliffe Rd YO12 ....212 D6
Redcoat Way 1 YO24 230 B8
Redeness St YO31 ....228 E5
Redfearn Mews HG2 ..222 D6
Redgrave Cl 4 YO31 ..228 E8
Redhill Ave WF10 ....201 A3
Redhill Cl HG1 ......219 D6
Redhill Dr WF10 ......201 A3
Redhill Field La YO23 182 D1
Redhill Inf Sch WF10 ..201 A3
Redhill La LS25 ....201 D8
Redhill Rd
  Castleford WF10 ....201 A4
  Harrogate HG1 ......219 C6
Redhill Wlk WF10 ....201 A3
Redhouse La YO8 ....204 F6
Redlish Rd HG3 ....136 E1
Redman Cl YO10 ....231 C8
Redmayne Sq YO7 ..167 B8
Redmire Sta DL8 ......59 C6
Redmires Cl YO30 ..225 A2
Redruth Dr 22 WF6 ..200 A2
Redshaw Cl 1 HG4 ..214 C4
Redshaw Gr 2 HG4 ..214 C4
Redthorn Dr YO31 ....225 F1
Redwood Dr 6 YO32 166 E5
Reebys La LA2 ......129 F5
Reedsham La BD22 ..186 F5
Reeth Com Prim Sch
  DL11 ....38 B6
Reeth Rd
  Middlesbrough TS5 ....6 E8
  Richmond DL10 ....209 A4
  2 Stockton-on-Tees TS18 ..5 E8
Reeval Cl 13 BB18 ..172 B1
Reeves The YO24 ....227 C1
Regency Ave TS6 ......7 E8
Regency Ct
  3 Ilkley LS29 ......218 A3
  Northallerton DL6 ....210 F3
Regency Mews
  Northallerton DL6 ....210 D4

Regency Mews continued
  2 York YO24 ......230 F8
Regency Pk TS17 ......6 B4
Regent Ave
  Harrogate HG1 ......219 E3
  Skipton BD23 ......217 B5
Regent Cres BD23 ..217 B5
Regent Dr BD23 ....217 B5
Regent Gr HG1 ......219 E4
Regent Mount 2 HG1 220 C4
Regent Par HG1 ....219 E3
Regent Pl HG1 ......220 C4
Regent Rd Ilkley LS29 ..218 A4
  Skipton BD23 ......217 B5
Regent St
  Castleford WF10 ....200 E4
  Harrogate HG1 ......219 E3
  Normanton WF6 ....200 B2
  1 Scarborough YO12 ..213 A6
  York YO10 ....228 E3
Regent Terr HG1 ....219 E3
Regents Ct 14 YO12 ..227 F5
Regimental Mus★
  YO1 ....233 B1
Reginald Gr YO23 ..228 C1
Reginald Terr YO4 ..232 B4
Reid St Prim Sch DL3 ..3 C6
Reid Terr TS14 ....8 F6
Reighton Ave YO30 ..227 F8
Reighton Dr 10 YO30 224 F1
Rein Ct LS25 ......194 F8
Reins HG5 ....163 A7
Reivaulx Dr TS5 ......6 F8
Renfield Gr WF6 ....200 B2
Renshaw Gdns 4 YO26 227 E4
Renton Cl HG3 ......140 B5
Reservoir La 7 YO11 ..100 B8
Residence La HG4 ..214 D5
Resolution Way YO21 208 B5
Retreat Hospl The
  YO10 ....228 F2
Reygate Gr YO23 ....230 B2
Reynard Crag La HG3 160 C6
Reynolds St 15 YO14 ..101 B3
Rhobell View 3 TS17 ..5 F4
Rhode's Hill La LS23 ..188 F6
Rhodes La LS23 ....188 D7
Rhodes St WF10 ....200 D4
Rhyddings Gdns LS29 218 D4
Rianbow La YO17 ....215 C6
Ribble Dr DL1 ....3 C3
Ribblehead Sta LA6 ..78 E1
Ribblehead Viaduct★
  LA6 ....78 D2
Ribston Rd
  Little Ribston LS22 ..180 A7
  Spofforth with Stockeld
  HG3 ....179 F6
Ribstone Gr YO31 ....229 B6
Riccal Dr
  25 Helmsley YO62 ....92 F6
  Huttons Ambo YO17 ..121 C1
Riccal Moor La YO62 ..93 E4
Riccall CP Sch YO19 ..191 F1
Riccall La YO19 ....191 D1
Rice Gate YO60 ......74 D8
Rice La Aldwark YO61 ..142 C2
  Flaxton YO60 ......145 F2
Richard Gossop Ct 41
  LS29 ....176 C1
Richard St YO8 ......232 B5
Richard Taylor CE Prim Sch
  HG1 ....219 E6
Richard Thorntons CE VA
  Prim Sch LA6 ......102 E3
Richardson Ct YO8 ..196 F1
Richardson St TS17 ..6 A7
Richardson St YO23 ..228 C2
Richmond Ave
  Harrogate HG2 ......222 C7
  Knottingley WF11 ....201 D3
Richmond Castle★
  DL10 ....209 C6
Richmond CE Prim Sch
  DL10 ....209 D7
Richmond Cl HG2 ....222 C7
Richmond Cl LS29 ..218 C3
Richmond Garth HG4 112 C5
Richmond Holt HG2 ..222 C7
Richmond Lower Sch
  DL10 ....209 C6
Richmond Methodist Prim
  Sch DL10 ....209 E7
Richmond Pl LS29 ..218 C3
Richmond Rd
  12 Barnoldswick BB18 ..171 D2
  Barton DL10 ......21 E6
  Brompton-on-Swale DL10 ..41 A6
  Croft-on-Tees DL10 ..21 F6
  Harrogate HG2 ......222 C7
  Hipswell DL9 ......209 D1
  Leyburn DL8 ....60 D5
  Skeeby DL10 ......20 F1
Richmond Rise DL7 ..210 C3
Richmond Sch DL10 ..209 D7
Richmond St YO31 ..228 E5
Richmond Swimming Pool
  DL10 ....209 D6
Richmondfield Ave
  LS15 ....194 C7
Richmondfield Cl
  LS15 ....194 C7
Richmondfield Cres
  LS15 ....194 C7
Richmondfield Cross
  LS15 ....194 C7
Richmondfield Dr
  LS15 ....194 B7

Richmondfield Garth
LS15 . . . . .194 C8
Richmondfield Gr
LS15 . . . . .194 C7
Richmondfield La
LS15 . . . . .194 C7
Richmondfield Mount
LS15 . . . . .194 C7
Richmondfield Way
LS15 . . . . .194 C7
Richmondshire Mus★
DL10 . . . . .209 C7
Richmondshire Sports Ctr
DL10 . . . . .209 C8
Ridding La DN14 . . . . .205 A1
Ridding Gate 5 LS21 . .176 F1
Ridding La DN14 . . . . .205 A1
Riddings Rd LS29 . . . .218 B3
Riders La YO60 . . . . . .146 F2
Ridge Gn YO13 . . . . . .75 D5
Ridge La Roxby TS13 . . . .11 A6
Silsden BD20 . . . . .174 B4
Sleights YO21 . . . . .32 B7
Staithes TS13 . . . . .13 H1
Ridge Rd LS25 . . . . . .200 C8
Ridge The
Coulby Newham TS8 . . . . . .7 A4
Linton LS22 . . . . .180 B2
Ridgedale Mount WF8 .201 B2
Ridgeway
Coulby Newham TS8 . . . . . .7 D5
Darlington DL3 . . . . .3 C8
10 Eastfield YO11 . . . . .99 F7
Skipton BD23 . . . . .216 E6
York YO26 . . . . .227 B3
Ridgeway The WF11 . . .201 F2
Riding Cl 4 BB18 . . . .171 E1
Ridings The
7 Boroughbridge YO51 . .141 B4
Norton YO17 . . . . .215 D2
Ridley Ave TS5 . . . . .6 E8
Ridleys Fold 14 LS29 . .174 F4
Ridsdale St DL1 . . . . . . .3 D5
Rievaulx Abbey★ YO62 . .92 B8
Rievaulx Bank YO62 . . .92 B8
Rievaulx Cl HG5 . . . . .221 C4
Rievaulx Ct 6 HG5 . . . .221 C4
Rievaulx Rd YO21 . . . .208 C6
Rievaulx Terr★ YO62 . .92 B7
Riffa La LS21 . . . . . . .177 E2
Rigg Bank HG4 . . . . . . .85 E3
Rigg The TS15 . . . . .5 E2
Rigg View YO22 . . . . . .32 F7
Riggs Rd YO17 . . . . . .121 F5
Riggs Spring 8 HG3 . . .137 F1
Rigton Hill LS17 . . . . .178 B4
Riley St 41 BB18 . . . . .172 A1
Rillington Com Prim Sch
YO17 . . . . .122 F5
Rimington Ave DL10 . .209 D6
Rimington Way YO11 . .100 B7
Ringing Keld Hill YO13 . .54 A3
Rings The TS17 . . . . .5 F5
Ringstone Rd
Bishopthorpe YO23 . . . .231 B5
York YO30 . . . . .224 F3
Ringstones La LA2 . . . .129 A4
Ringway LS25 . . . . . . .194 B3
Ringway Gr 11 DL2 . . . . .4 C4
Ringwood Rd DL9 . . . . .40 F3
Riparian Way BD20 . . .187 F8
Ripley Bank HG3 . . . . .137 C4
Ripley Castle★ HG3 . . .161 C7
Ripley Cl
11 Kirkbymoorside YO62 . .70 B1
Normanton South WF6 . .200 A1
Ripley Dr
Harrogate HG1 . . . . . . .219 C6
Normanton South WF6 . .200 A1
Ripley Endowed CE Prim Sch
HG3 . . . . .161 C7
Ripley Gr 3 YO32 . . . .166 E5
Ripley Rd
Knaresborough HG5 . . . .220 E8
Nidd HG3 . . . . .161 E6
Scotton HG5 . . . . .162 A5
Ripley Way HG1 . . . . . .219 C6
Ripley's Rd YO13 . . . . . .54 B1
Ripon & District Hospl
HG4 . . . . .214 B5
Ripon Bsns Pk HG4 . . .214 C4
Ripon By-pass HG4 . . .214 C2
Ripon Cath HG4 . . . . .214 C5
Ripon Cath CE Prim Sch
HG4 . . . . .214 D5
Ripon Cath Choir Sch
HG4 . . . . .214 A3
Ripon Coll HG4 . . . . . .214 A5
Ripon Courthouse★
HG4 . . . . .214 C5
Ripon Dr DL1 . . . . .3 D4
Ripon Gram Sch HG4 . .214 B4
Ripon Greystone Com Prim
Sch HG4 . . . . .214 C2
Ripon Horn The★
HG4 . . . . .214 C5
Ripon Leisure Ctr
HG4 . . . . .214 D3
Ripon Loop Nature Reserve★
HG4 . . . . .113 F4
Ripon Racecourse★
HG4 . . . . .214 F2
Ripon Rd
Harrogate HG3 . . . . . . .219 A7
Middlesbrough TS7 . . . . . .7 E6

Ripon Rd continued
Ripley HG3 . . . . .161 D8
South Stainley with Cayton
HG3 . . . . .139 E2
Ripon Swimming Baths
HG4 . . . . .214 B5
Ripon Way
Carlton Miniott YO7 . . . .89 C4
Harrogate HG1 . . . . . . .219 C5
Rise Carr Prim Sch DL3 . .3 C7
Rise The
Huttons Ambo YO60 . . . .147 C6
Knottingley WF11 . . . . .201 E4
Leavening YO17 . . . . . . .147 E1
Thornton Dale YO18 . . . . .96 D5
Whitby YO22 . . . . .208 E6
Riseber DL8 . . . . .60 C5
Risedale Com Coll
DL9 . . . . .209 F1
Risedale Rd DL9 . . . . . .209 B1
Risewood YO41 . . . . . .168 B3
Rishworth Gr YO22 . . .224 F2
Rivadale View LS29 . . .218 B3
Rivelin Way
10 Filey YO14 . . . . . . .101 A4
York YO30 . . . . .224 F2
Rivendell BD23 . . . . . .134 B3
River Cl 2 YO8 . . . . . .198 B5
River La
Brompton-on-Swale DL10 . .41 B6
Kilburn High & Low YO61 . .91 B2
West Haddlesey YO8 . . .203 A5
River Pl BD23 . . . . . . .155 D1
River Rd YO61 . . . . . . .91 C2
River St 1 Selby YO8 . .232 D6
Trawden BB8 . . . . .186 B3
York YO23 . . . . .233 B1
River View
1 Barlby YO8 . . . . . . .198 B5
Boston Spa LS23 . . . . . .188 F8
Ilkley LS29 . . . . .218 A3
Richmond DL10 . . . . . . .209 D6
River View Rd HG4 . . .214 C4
Riverdale 4 DN14 . . . .202 D4
Riverdale Gdns LS23 . .188 F8
Rivergarth DL1 . . . . .3 F7
Riversdale
17 Haxby YO32 . . . . . .166 F5
5 Settle BD24 . . . . . .131 D2
Riversdene TS9 . . . . . . .26 B7
Riverside Clapham LA2 .130 C8
Gargrave BD23 . . . . . . .155 D1
Rawcliffe DN14 . . . . . . .205 A2
28 Scalby YO13 . . . . . .75 D5
Riverside Ave LS21 . . .177 A1
Riverside Cl
1 Elvington YO41 . . . . .185 C2
Farnley LS21 . . . . .177 A1
West Haddlesey YO8 . . .203 A5
Riverside Com Prim Sch
LS24 . . . . .189 E6
Riverside Cres
5 Otley LS21 . . . . . . .177 A1
York YO32 . . . . .225 A4
Riverside Ct DN14 . . . .205 A2
Riverside Dr 3 LS21 . .177 A1
Riverside Gdns
2 Boroughbridge YO51 .141 B6
2 Elvington YO41 . . . . .185 C2
2 Poppleton YO26 . . . . .165 F1
Riverside Mews 6 YO7 .211 C3
Riverside Pk 4 LS21 . .177 A1
Riverside Rd DL10 . . . .209 C6
Riverside View YO17 . .215 B3
Riverside Way DL1 . . . . .3 E7
Riverside Wlk
Airton BD23 . . . . .155 A6
Ilkley LS29 . . . . .218 A5
1 Poppleton YO26 . . . . .165 F1
5 Strensall YO32 . . . . .167 A7
Riverslea TS9 . . . . .26 B7
Riversvale Dr 21 YO26 .165 F1
Riversway BD23 . . . . . .155 C1
Riverview Ind Est DL1 . .3 D6
Roach Grange Ave
LS25 . . . . .194 D2
Roall La DN14 . . . . . . .202 F4
Robert St
Harrogate HG1 . . . . . . .219 D1
Selby YO8 . . . . .232 C5
Robert Wilkinson Prim Sch
YO32 . . . . .167 A7
Roberts Cres HG1 . . . .219 D5
Roberts Sq HG1 . . . . . .219 D5
Robertson Rd
Colburn DL9 . . . . .40 F4
Ripon HG4 . . . . .113 D3
Robin Cl 6 WF8 . . . . . .201 B2
Robin Gr YO24 . . . . . . .227 F3
Robin Hood Cl YO21 . . .29 A6
Robin Hood Rd YO13 . . .53 F6
Robin Hood's Bay Mus★
YO22 . . . . .33 D4
Robin Hood's Bay Rd
YO22 . . . . .33 A3
Robin La Bentham LA2 .103 A1
High Bentham LA2 . . . . .129 A8
Huby YO61 . . . . .144 A4
Robinson St YO1 . . . . .233 C2
Robinson Dr
Harrogate HG2 . . . . . . .222 B6
York YO24 . . . . .227 D2
Robinson Rd 13 DL10 . . .41 E4
Robinson St WF10 . . . .200 D6
Robson Ave TS17 . . . . . .6 B5
Roche Ave
Harrogate HG1 . . . . . . .219 F6
York YO31 . . . . .228 E8

Rock Hill WF10 . . . . . .201 A3
Rock Terr WF10 . . . . . .201 A3
Rock View Terr BD23 . .217 D8
Rockingham Ave
YO31 . . . . .229 A5
Rockingham Cl YO17 . .215 D6
Rockingham Ct LS24 . .189 E2
Rockingham Dr YO12 . .212 B4
Rockland Gdns YO12 . .212 D5
Rockley Grange Gdn
LS25 . . . . .194 B3
Rocks La YO13 . . . . . . .75 D7
Rocks La YO13 . . . . . . .75 D7
Rockville Dr BD23 . . . .217 C8
Rockwell Ave DL1 . . . . . .3 E7
Rockwood Cl 1 BD23 . .216 E4
Rockwood Dr BD23 . . .216 E5
Rodney Terr 15 HG4 . . .86 C3
Roe La LS25 . . . . .202 C7
Roebuck La LS25 . . . . .176 F2
Roecliffe CE Prim Sch
YO51 . . . . .140 F4
Roecliffe La YO51 . . . .141 B5
Roedean Dr TS16 . . . . . .5 E4
Roger La TS8 . . . . .6 C4
Rogers Ct YO24 . . . . . .230 C8
Rogers Sq 1 HG1 . . . .219 D2
Roker Cl DL1 . . . . .3 F6
Roker Rd HG1 . . . . . . .219 E4
Roland Ct YO32 . . . . . .225 E3
Rolston Ave 3 YO31 . .225 E2
Roman Ave N 17 YO41 .168 D2
Roman Ave S 3 YO41 . .168 D1
Roman Camps★ YO30 .225 B2
Roman Cl
Newby & Scalby YO12 . .212 A7
4 Tadcaster LS24 . . . . .189 E6
Roman Cres DL9 . . . . .209 C1
Roman Fort of Olicana★
LS29 . . . . .218 B4
Roman Garth YO17 . . .215 C4
Roman Rd TS5 . . . . .6 E8
Roman Signal Sta★
YO21 . . . . .12 D6
Roman Town Mus★
YO51 . . . . .141 C5
Roman Way YO12 . . . .212 A7
Romanby Prim Sch
DL7 . . . . .210 B2
Romanby Rd DL7 . . . . .210 C3
Romans Cl YO19 . . . . .197 F8
Romany Rd 11 TS9 . . . . .8 A2
Rombalds Dr BD23 . . . .217 A4
Rombalds La LS29 . . . .218 B3
Rombalds View LS29 . .176 E1
Romille St 15 BD23 . . .217 A3
Romney Cl LS29 . . . . . .218 E8
Ronaldsway DL10 . . . . .209 F4
Ronaldshay Dr DL10 . .209 E8
Ronway Ave HG4 . . . . .214 B2
Rook St
25 Barnoldswick BB18 . .171 D1
Lothersdale BD20 . . . . .186 F8
Rookery Cl HG3 . . . . . .161 E1
Rookwood Ave LS25 . .200 C8
Rookwood Rd TS7 . . . . .7 D6
Roomer La HG4 . . . . . . .86 B1
Rope Wlk BD23 . . . . . .217 A4
Roper Ct LS21 . . . . . . .209 C7
Ropers Ct YO23 . . . . . .230 C3
Ropery La YO17 . . . . . .124 C1
Ropery The
15 Pickering YO18 . . . . .95 F7
Whitby YO21 . . . . .208 A6
Ropery Wlk YO7 . . . . . .215 C4
Ropewalk The YO31 . . .228 E5
Ropner Gdns DL2 . . . . . .4 C3
Rosamund Ave 21 YO18 .95 F7
Roscoe St YO12 . . . . . .212 F5
Rose & Crown Yd 20
YO21 . . . . .208 D6
Rose Ave
Sherburn in Elmet LS25 .195 F3
Whitby YO21 . . . . .208 B7
Rose Cres
Richmond DL10 . . . . . . .209 B7
Sherburn in Elmet LS25 .195 F3
Rose Ct LS25 . . . . .194 D4
Rose Hill Dr 13 TS9 . . . .26 C7
Rose Hill Way TS9 . . . . .26 C7
Rose La LS24 . . . . .196 A7
Rose Lea Cl 2 LS25 . . .202 A7
Rose St YO31 . . . . .228 C7
Rose Tree Gr YO32 . . . .225 D4
Rose Wood Prim Sch
TS8 . . . . .7 A4
Roseberry Ave
Great Ayton TS9 . . . . . . .8 A2
Stokesley TS9 . . . . .26 D8
Roseberry Cres TS9 . . . .8 A2
Roseberry Dr 8 TS9 . . . .8 A2
Roseberry Gn HG4 . . . .113 C7
Roseberry Gr YO30 . . .224 F3
Roseberry La
Guisborough TS9 . . . . . . .8 B3
Stillington YO61 . . . . . .144 B6
Roseberry Mount TS14 . .8 E6
Roseberry Prim Sch TS9 . .8 A2
Roseberry Rd TS9 . . . . . .8 A2
Roseberry Topping★
TS9 . . . . .8 C3
Rosebery Ave YO12 . . .212 E4
Rosebery St YO26 . . . .227 F6
Rosecomb Way 6
YO32 . . . . .225 D7
Rosecroft Sch TS13 . . . .10 D8
Rosecroft La TS13 . . . . .10 D7

Rosecroft Way YO30 . .227 E8
Rosecroft Way HG3 . . .222 D3
Rosedale Abbey Com Prim
Sch YO18 . . . . .49 E2
Rosedale Ave YO26 . . .227 C4
Rosedale Chy Bank
YO18 . . . . .49 E1
Rosedale Cl
Pannal HG3 . . . . .222 D3
3 Whitby YO21 . . . . . .208 C6
Rosedale Cres
Darlington DL3 . . . . .3 A6
Guisborough TS14 . . . . . .8 D6
Rosedale La
Hinderwell TS13 . . . . . . .11 F8
Staithes TS13 . . . . .13 L1
Rosedale St YO10 . . . .228 D2
Rosehill TS9 . . . . .8 A1
Rosehill Sq 11 HG5 . . .221 B5
Rosehurst Gr HG2 . . . .222 E2
Roseland Dr TS7 . . . . . . .7 C5
Rosemary Ct
20 Easingwold YO61 . . .143 C8
6 Tadcaster LS24 . . . . .189 E6
York YO1 . . . . .233 C2
Rosemary La 1 DL10 . .209 C6
Rosemary Pl YO1 . . . . .233 C2
Rosemary Row 5 LS24 .189 E6
Rosemoor Cl
Coulby Newham TS8 . . . . .7 B5
19 Hunmanby YO14 . . .126 F8
Rosemount Dr WF6 . . .200 C1
Rosemount Rd 2 YO21 .208 C5
Rosendale Ave YO17 . .215 F2
Rosevale Terr YO12 . . .212 E5
Roseville Ave
Harrogate HG1 . . . . . . .220 A3
Scarborough YO12 . . . .212 E6
Roseville Dr HG1 . . . . .220 A3
Roseville Rd HG1 . . . . .220 A3
Roseway HG1 . . . . .219 E5
Rosewood Cres HG1 . . .220 B3
Roseworth TS9 . . . . .26 C5
Rosley St BB8 . . . . . . .186 B3
Roslyn Rd HG2 . . . . . . .220 A2
Rossett Acre Prim Sch
HG2 . . . . .222 C6
Rossett Ave HG2 . . . . .222 C6
Rossett Beck HG2 . . . .222 C6
Rossett Cres HG2 . . . .222 D6
Rossett Dr HG2 . . . . . .222 C6
Rossett Garth HG2 . . .222 C5
Rossett Gdns HG2 . . . .222 C5
Rossett Gn La HG2 . . .222 C5
Rossett Holt Ave HG2 .222 C7
Rossett Holt Cl HG2 . .222 C8
Rossett Holt Dr HG2 . .222 C7
Rossett Holt Gr HG2 . .222 C7
Rossett Holt View
HG2 . . . . .222 C7
Rossett Pk Rd HG2 . . .222 D6
Rossett Sch HG2 . . . . .222 B6
Rossett Way HG2 . . . . .222 C6
Rossiter Dr WF11 . . . . .201 E2
Rosslyn Ct TS18 . . . . . . .5 F8
Rosslyn St 1 YO30 . . . .228 A6
Rossway DL1 . . . . .3 F8
Rostle Top Rd 10 BB18 .172 A1
Rotary Way HG4 . . . . . .214 D6
Roth Hill La YO19 . . . .192 E3
Rothbury Cl HG2 . . . . .220 D2
Rothbury Rd YO12 . . . .212 E5
Rothesay Gr TS7 . . . . . . .7 C5
Rotunda Mus★ YO11 . .213 A5
Rough Rd HG3 . . . . . . .161 A2
Roughaw Cl HG2 . . . . .216 F2
Roughaw Rd BD23 . . . .217 A2
Roughley Bank DL7 . . . .63 C5
Rougier St YO1 . . . . . . .233 A2
Round Hill Link YO30 . .224 F7
Roundell Rd BB18 . . . .171 E2
Roundhill Ave TS17 . . . . .5 F4
Roundhill Cl 5 DL2 . . . . .3 E1
Roundhill Jun Sch
WF11 . . . . .201 D3
Roundhill Rd DL2 . . . . . .3 E1
Routh Wlk 5 YO21 . . . .208 D7
Rowan Ave
3 Filey YO14 . . . . . . .101 A4
Malton YO17 . . . . .215 D6
York YO32 . . . . .225 D4
Rowan Cl
Gateforth YO8 . . . . . . .197 B1
Scarborough YO12 . . . .212 C6
Rowan Ct
8 Catterick DL10 . . . . .41 D5
Leyburn DL8 . . . . .60 D5
Rowan Dr 5 TS9 . . . . . .8 A2
Rowan Fields YO12 . . . .99 E7
Rowan Garth 22 BD20 .187 E7
Rowan La
16 Hellifield BD23 . . . .154 B3
Skirethorns BD23 . . . . .134 B3
Rowan Lea HG2 . . . . . .222 B7
Rowan Pl YO7 . . . . . . .225 D4
Rowan Sq 6 DL9 . . . . .209 B1
Rowans The YO7 . . . . .115 F7
Rowans Way DL7 . . . . .210 B4
Rowden La HG3 . . . . . .160 F5
Rowedale Cl 15 YO14 . .126 F8
Rowen Ave 6 YO61 . . .117 D1
Rowland Keld TS14 . . . . .8 E5
Rowland St 18 BD23 . . .217 A3
Rowlandhall La DN14 . .199 F2
Rowley Ct 2 YO32 . . . .225 F7
Rowley Dr LS29 . . . . . .218 E3
Rowmans The YO30 . . .224 C4
Rowntree Ave YO30 . . .228 C8

Roxburghe Dale WF7 . .200 C1
Roxby Ave TS14 . . . . .8 E5
Roxby Gdns
4 Eastfield YO12 . . . . .99 F7
5 Thornton Dale YO18 . .96 D5
Roxby La Roxby TS13 . .11 C7
Staithes TS13 . . . . .13 J1
Roxby Rd YO18 . . . . . . .96 D5
Roxby Terr 6 YO18 . . . .96 D5
Royal Albert Dr YO12 . .212 F8
Royal Ave YO11 . . . . . .212 F4
Royal Chase YO24 . . . .230 F8
Royal Cres
Harrogate HG2 . . . . . . .222 D8
12 Scarborough YO11 . .213 A4
Whitby YO21 . . . . .208 C7
Royal Cres La 8 YO11 . .212 F4
Royal George Dr TS16 . . .5 D5
Royal Hall★ HG1 . . . . .219 D3
Royal Par 8 HG1 . . . . .219 C2
Royal Pump House Mus★
HG2 . . . . .219 C2
Royd Cl 18 BD20 . . . . .187 E8
Royd The TS15 . . . . .5 D2
Royd's Rd YO8 . . . . . . .202 F6
Royds Ave WF10 . . . . . .201 B4
Ruby St 3 YO23 . . . . . .228 B1
Rudbeck Cl HG2 . . . . . .220 C1
Rudbeck Cres HG2 . . . .220 C1
Rudbeck Dr HG2 . . . . .220 C1
Rudby Bank TS15 . . . . . .25 D5
Rudby Lea TS15 . . . . . .25 D6
Rudcarr La YO19 . . . . .167 E1
Rudda Rd YO13 . . . . . . .53 D6
Rudding Dower HG3 . . .223 E7
Rudding La
Follifoot HG3 . . . . .223 C5
North Rigton HG3 . . . . .222 A1
Ruddings YO19 . . . . . . .193 A8
Ruddings Cl 9 YO32 . .225 C4
Ruddings La
Cowesby YO7 . . . . .66 C4
Crakehall DL8 . . . . .62 D4
Ellerton YO42 . . . . .193 E2
Ruddings Rd YO18 . . . . .72 B3
Ruddings The YO8 . . . .232 A4
Rudgate
Bilton-in-Ainsty with Bickerton
YO26 . . . . .181 B6
Newton Kyme cum Toulston
LS24 . . . . .189 B6
Walton LS23 . . . . .181 B1
Rudgate Gr YO26 . . . . .164 A4
Rudgate Pk LS23 . . . . .181 A2
Rudstone Gr LS25 . . . .195 F4
Ruebury La DL6 . . . . . . .45 B4
Rues La LS21 . . . . .176 C8
Ruff La YO61 . . . . .142 B5
Ruffa La YO18 . . . . .96 A6
Ruffhams Cl YO19 . . . .192 C5
Ruffin La YO17 . . . . . . .147 D5
Rufford Cl TS14 . . . . . . .8 E5
Rufforth Prim Sch
YO23 . . . . .182 C6
Rumford Way DL8 . . . . .60 D6
Rumple Croft 4 LS21 . .176 F1
Runnymede TS7 . . . . . . .7 D5
Runs Bank DL8 . . . . . . .60 D8
Runswick Ave
Middlesbrough TS5 . . . . . .6 E6
Whitby YO21 . . . . .208 B6
York YO26 . . . . .227 B4
Runswick La TS13 . . . . .11 F7
Rupert Rd LS29 . . . . . .218 A5
Rushmere TS8 . . . . .7 B5
Rusholme La YO8 . . . . .205 A5
Rushton Ave 21 BB18 . .172 A1
Rushwood Cl 6 YO32 . .166 F5
Ruskin Ave
Middlesbrough TS5 . . . . . .6 D7
6 Skipton BD23 . . . . .216 D3
Ruskin Cl DL2 . . . . .22 D7
Ruskin Dr WF10 . . . . . .201 A4
Russell Dixon Sq HG4 .214 B3
Russell Dr YO30 . . . . . .227 E8
Russell St
Harrogate HG2 . . . . . . .222 E7
Skipton BD23 . . . . .217 A3
York YO23 . . . . .228 B2
Russell Terr DL7 . . . . . . .63 D7
Russet Dr YO31 . . . . . .229 B5
Russet Gr YO12 . . . . . .212 C8
Russett Rd YO17 . . . . .215 B4
Ruston La YO13 . . . . . . .98 D7
Ruswarp Bank YO21 . . .208 B3
Ruswarp CE VC Prim Sch
YO21 . . . . .208 B3
Ruswarp Fields YO22 . .208 C3
Ruswarp La YO21 . . . . .208 B4
Ruswarp Pleasure Boats★
YO21 . . . . .208 B3
Ruswarp Sta YO22 . . . .208 C3
Rutland Cl
Copmanthorpe YO23 . . .230 A3
Harrogate HG1 . . . . . . .219 A2
Rutland Dr HG1 . . . . . .219 A2
Rutland Pl 4 YO62 . . . . .92 F7
Rutland Rd HG1 . . . . . .219 B2
Rutland St 38 YO14 . . .101 B3
Rutland Terr YO12 . . . .213 A7
Rutmoor Rd YO18 . . . . .71 E8
Rutson Hospl DL7 . . . .210 D5
Ryburn Cl YO30 . . . . . .224 F2
Rycroft Rd 3 YO12 . . . .75 E5

Rydal Ave
Middlesbrough TS5 . . . . .6 E8
York YO31 . . . . .229 A6
Rydal Cl 2 YO7 . . . . .89 C4
Rydal Cres 7 YO12 . . . . . .99 F7
Rydal Rd Darlington DL1 . . .3 E4
Harrogate HG1 . . . . .220 B3
Rydale Pal Sh Mall★
YO17 . . . . .215 C3
Ryder Cres 3 YO62 . . . . .70 B1
Ryder Sq YO17 . . . . . . .215 C4
Ryder's Wynd 3 DL10 . .209 C6
Rye Cl Haxby YO32 . . . . .225 C8
Huttons Ambo YO17 . . . . . .121 C1
Rye Hill Way TS8 . . . . . . .7 B4
Ryecroft 7 YO32 . . . . . .167 A6
Ryecroft Ave
10 Norton DN6 . . . . .206 E2
York YO24 . . . . .230 C7
Ryecroft Cl YO31 . . . . . .229 C8
Ryecroft Gdns DN14 . . .203 A2
Ryecroft Rd
Glusburn BD20 . . . . .187 D8
Norton DN6 . . . . .206 E1
Ryecroft Way 2 BD20 . .187 E8
Ryedale Cl
Helmsley YO62 . . . . .92 F7
Norton YO17 . . . . .215 F1
Pontefract WF6 . . . . .200 A3
Ulleskelf LS24 . . . . .190 B2
Ryedale Folk Mus★
YO62 . . . . .70 C5
Ryedale Leisure Ctr
YO18 . . . . .95 F7
Ryedale Pl LS29 . . . . . . .218 D3
Ryedale Pl WF6 . . . . . . .200 A3
Ryedale Sch YO62 . . . . .93 D7
Ryedale State Pk
YO17 . . . . .215 C3
Ryedale Swimming Pool
YO62 . . . . .93 D4
Ryedale View 2 YO62 . . .70 B1
Ryedale Way YO8 . . . . .232 C3
Ryefield Cl 12 YO11 . . . . .99 F7
Ryefield Rd 1 YO11 . . . .100 A6
Ryegate 13 YO24 . . . . . . .92 F6
Ryehill Cl YO32 . . . . . . .225 C8
Ryeland St 9 BD20 . . . . .187 E8
Ryelands Pk 1 TS13 . . . . .11 B4
Ryemoor Rd YO32 . . . . .225 C8
Rylatt Pl YO26 . . . . .227 B3
Rylstone Dr 1 BB18 . . . .171 D1
Rymer Way 4 YO7 . . . . .211 C3
Ryndle Cres YO12 . . . . .212 E8
Ryndle Wlk YO12 . . . . . .212 E8
Ryndleside YO12 . . . . . .212 E7
Ryngwoode Dr YO17 . . .215 C6
Ryton Old La YO17 . . . . .121 F6
Ryton Old Rd YO17 . . . .122 A5
Ryton Stile Rd YO17 . . .215 C7

S

Sackville Rd BD20 . . . . .174 C1
Sackville St
20 Barnoldswick BB18 . . .171 D1
Skipton BD23 . . . . .217 A3
Sacred Heart Prim Sch
LS29 . . . . .218 D4
Sacred Heart RC Prim Sch
DL7 . . . . .210 D2
Sadberge CE Sch DL2 . . .4 C8
Sadberge Ct YO10 . . . . .229 C3
Sadberge Rd DL2 . . . . . . .4 C5
Saddle Cl YO17 . . . . . . .215 D2
Saddlers Cl
1 Copmanthorpe YO23 . . .230 B3
Huntington YO32 . . . . .225 F2
Saddlers Croft 8 LS29 . .218 A4
Saddlers La WF11 . . . . . .201 E5
Saddlers Way YO26 . . . .182 A6
Sadler Dr TS7 . . . . .7 B6
Sadler Forster Way TS17 .6 B5
Sadlers YO61 . . . . .143 C6
Saffron Dr 6 DN14 . . . . .204 C1
Saffron Mdw 19 HG3 . . .161 B3
Sails Dr YO10 . . . . .229 B3
St Aelreds Cl YO31 . . . .228 C4
St Aelreds RC Prim Sch
YO31 . . . . .229 B5
St Agathas DL10 . . . . . .209 C7
St Aidan's Rd DL9 . . . . .209 D1
St Aidans CE High Sch
HG2 . . . . .219 F1
St Aidans Rd LS26 . . . . .200 B6
St Alkelda's Rd 1 DL8 . .60 E2
St Andrew Pl YO1 . . . . . .233 C2
St Andrew's Ave HG2 . . .220 A4
St Andrew's Cres HG2 . .220 A3
St Andrew's Gr 1 HG2 . .220 A3
St Andrew's Par 3 HG2 .220 A2
St Andrew's Pl 2 HG2 . .220 A4
St Andrew's Rd
Castleford WF10 . . . . .201 B5
4 Harrogate HG2 . . . . . . .220 B3
St Andrew's St 1 HG2 . .220 A3
St Andrew's Wlk HG2 . .220 A2
St Andrewgate YO1 . . . .233 C3
St Andrews Dr WF7 . . . .200 E1
St Andrews Gate HG4 . .112 D5
St Andrews Gr 2 DL7 . . .210 C4
St Andrews Mdws
HG4 . . . . .112 D5
St Andrews Rd YO21 . . .208 B5

St Ann Ct YO10 . . . . . . .228 E2
St Ann's Ct YO10 . . . . . .228 D2
St Ann's Staith 13 YO21 .208 D7
St Anne's Cres 3 DL10 . .41 E4
St Annes Gdns DL2 . . . . .4 C3
St Anthonys Ave 2 DL7 .210 E2
St Athan's Wlk HG2 . . . .222 C7
St Aubyn's Pl YO24 . . . .228 A4
St Augustine's Cath Sch
YO12 . . . . .212 C4
St Augustine's RC Prim Sch
Coulby Newham TS8 . . . . . .7 B5
2 Darlington DL3 . . . . .3 C5
St Barnabas' CE Prim Sch
YO26 . . . . .227 F5
St Barnabas St 13 YO26 .227 F5
St Bedes Ave 4 DL7 . . .210 D2
St Bedes RC Prim Sch
DL1 . . . . .3 D8
St Benedict Rd 3 YO23 .233 A1
St Benedict's Cath Prim Sch
LS25 . . . . .194 C4
St Benedicts RC Prim Sch
YO62 . . . . .92 C1
St Bernadette's RC Prim Sch
TS7 . . . . .7 D6
St Boltophs Cl 4 WF11 .202 A2
St Brides Ct 30 TS17 . . . .5 F4
St Bridget's Ct YO23 . . .228 C2
St Catherine's Rd HG2 .219 F1
St Catherines YO30 . . . .224 D6
St Catherines Cl YO30 . .224 C5
St Catherines Pl YO24 . .228 A3
St Chads Wharf YO23 . .231 C8
St Christopher Cl 3
DL7 . . . . .210 D2
St Christophers Dr 27
LS29 . . . . .174 F4
St Clare's RC Prim Sch
TS5 . . . . .6 D6
St Clares Abbey DL3 . . . .3 B5
St Clement's Gr YO23 . .228 C2
St Clement's Rd HG2 . . .220 A2
St Clements Rd S
HG2 . . . . .220 A2
St Cuthbert Dr DL7 . . . .210 B3
St Cuthbert's Ave 4 DL7 .41 A5
St Cuthbert's Gn DL10 . .21 D8
St Cuthberts CE Sch
HG3 . . . . .137 B4
St Cuthberts Wlk TS13 . .10 D8
St David's RC Tech Coll
TS5 . . . . .6 E7
St David's View 9 DN14 .205 E4
St Davids Gr 34 TS17 . . . .5 F4
St Davids Rd LS21 . . . . .176 F1
St Denys' Rd YO1 . . . . . .233 C2
St Edmunds YO41 . . . . . .168 D2
St Edmunds Cl 1 DL10 . .41 C6
St Edward's Cl YO24 . . .230 F8
St Edwin's Cl DL2 . . . . . .2 C6
St Edwards Com Prim Sch 3
LS23 . . . . .188 E8
St Edwards Cl 2 WF11 . .201 F4
St Francis Xavier Sch
DL10 . . . . .209 E8
St Gabriels RC Prim Sch TS7 . .7 D8
St George's Ave HG2 . . .222 D7
St George's Gate DL2 . . .4 B5
St George's Pl YO24 . . .227 F2
St George's RC Prim Sch
YO10 . . . . .228 D2
St George's Rd HG2 . . . .222 D7
St George's Wlk HG2 . . .222 D6
St George's Gr 3 DL7 . .210 E2
St Georges RC Prim Sch
YO11 . . . . .100 A7
St Georges Terr TS13 . . .10 D8
St Giles' Cl 1 DL9 . . . . .41 A5
St Giles Cl YO7 . . . . .211 C3
St Giles Ct YO31 . . . . . .233 B4
St Giles Rd YO30 . . . . . .224 B5
St Giles Way YO23 . . . .230 A2
St Gregory's Cl DL8 . . . .62 E4
St Gregory's Mews
YO1 . . . . .233 A2
St Hedda's RC Prim Sch
YO21 . . . . .31 A4
St Helena 11 YO51 . . . .141 B5
St Helen's Dr LS25 . . . . .194 F4
St Helen's La
Borrowby YO7 . . . . .65 E4
Reighton YO14 . . . . .127 C6
St Helen's Rd
Harrogate HG2 . . . . .223 A8
5 York YO24 . . . . .230 E8
St Helen's Rise YO19 . . .193 A7
St Helen's Sq
26 Scarborough YO11 . . .213 A6
York YO1 . . . . .233 B2
St Helen's Way LS29 . . .218 D4
St Helens Cl DL7 . . . . . . .64 A7
St Helens Dr DL7 . . . . . .64 A7
St Helens Wlk TS13 . . . .10 D8
St Hilary Cl DL10 . . . . . .209 B7
St Hilda's Bsns Ctr
YO22 . . . . .208 E6
St Hilda's Cres YO17 . . .124 C8
St Hilda's Gdns YO17 . .208 C7
St Hilda's RC Prim Sch
YO21 . . . . .208 D5
St Hilda's Rd HG2 . . . . .219 D1
St Hilda's St YO17 . . . . .124 D7
St Hilda's Terr YO21 . . .208 D6
St Hilda's Wlk 6 YO62 . .92 C1
St Hildas Ampleforth CE VC
Sch YO62 . . . . .92 C1
St Hildas Mews YO10 . .229 B4

St Hildas Rd 5 DL7 . . . .210 D2
St Ians Croft 32 LS29 . . .174 F4
St Ives Cl 3 WF8 . . . . . .201 B2
St Ives Cres WF10 . . . . .201 B3
St James' Bsns Pk
HG5 . . . . .221 E4
St James CE Prim Sch
LS22 . . . . .180 C3
St James Chapel Flats
DL10 . . . . .209 B6
St James Cl
Melsonby DL10 . . . . .20 F7
York YO31 . . . . .224 E3
St James Ct
Rawcliffe DN14 . . . . .205 A1
Skipton BD23 . . . . .217 B4
St James' Dr HG2 . . . . . .222 E8
St James Dr DL7 . . . . . . .210 D2
St James Gn 9 YO7 . . . .211 C3
St James' Mdw 16 YO51 .141 B5
St James Mount YO24 . .228 A2
St James Pl 5 YO24 . . . .227 D1
St James' Rd LS29 . . . . .218 A3
St James Rd
Northallerton DL7 . . . . . . .210 B2
Scarborough YO12 . . . . . .212 E4
St James Terr YO8 . . . . .232 C5
St James' St 7 LS22 . . .180 C3
St John Fisher Cath High Sch
HG2 . . . . .223 A8
St John Mews YO8 . . . . .232 B4
St John of God Hospl
DL10 . . . . .41 F7
St John St
Harrogate HG1 . . . . .219 D2
York YO31 . . . . .233 B3
St John the Baptist RC Aided
Prim Sch WF6 . . . . .200 B1
St John's Ave
42 Filey YO14 . . . . .101 B3
Milby YO51 . . . . .141 B7
Scarborough YO12 . . . . . .212 E5
St John's Cl
Aberford LS25 . . . . .188 F1
Bishop Monkton HG3 . . . .140 B5
St John's Cres
Bishop Monkton HG3 . . . .140 A5
Harrogate HG1 . . . . .219 D5
3 Leeming DL7 . . . . .63 D4
York YO31 . . . . .233 C4
St John's Dr
Harrogate HG1 . . . . .219 D6
North Rigton LS17 . . . . . . .178 B4
St John's Garth LS25 . . .194 F8
St John's Gr HG1 . . . . . .219 C5
St John's Rd
Bishop Monkton HG3 . . . .140 A5
Clifford LS23 . . . . .188 E7
Harrogate HG1 . . . . .219 D5
Ilkley LS29 . . . . .218 E4
2 Leeming DL7 . . . . .63 D4
Scarborough YO12 . . . . . .212 E5
Scotton HG5 . . . . .162 A6
9 Stamford Bridge YO41 .168 D2
St John's St BD20 . . . . . .173 C1
St John's View LS23 . . . .188 E8
St John's Way
Bishop Monkton HG3 . . . .140 A5
Harrogate HG1 . . . . .219 D6
St John's Wlk
Harrogate HG1 . . . . .219 D6
Milby YO51 . . . . .141 B7
St Johns Ave 25 LS29 . .174 F4
St Johns Cath Sch for the
Deaf 7 LS23 . . . . .188 E8
St Johns CE Prim Sch
DL1 . . . . .3 E4
St Johns Cl
Northallerton DL6 . . . . . . .210 E2
Sharow HG4 . . . . .214 F7
St Johns Ct
Skipton BD23 . . . . .217 A4
Ulleskelf LS24 . . . . .190 C3
St Johns Pk DL11 . . . . . . .2 A1
St Johns Rd DL9 . . . . . . .209 F1
St Joseph's Cl 2 YO12 . .212 C8
St Joseph's Cl LS25 . . . .194 C3
St Joseph's St LS24 . . . .189 E6
St Josephs Cath Prim Sch
Harrogate HG1 . . . . .219 C5
14 Tadcaster LS24 . . . . . .189 E6
Wetherby LS22 . . . . .180 C3
St Josephs RC Prim Sch
Castleford WF10 . . . . .200 F4
Loftus TS13 . . . . .10 D8
27 Pickering YO18 . . . . . .95 F7
St Josephs RC Sch
BB18 . . . . .171 D2
St Lawrences CE Prim Sch
YO10 . . . . .228 E3
St Leonard's Cl
1 Harrogate HG2 . . . . . . .220 B1
8 Malton YO17 . . . . .215 C4
St Leonard's Cres
YO12 . . . . .212 D8
St Leonard's Oval
HG2 . . . . .220 A1
St Leonard's Pl YO30 . . .233 B3
St Leonard's Rd HG2 . . .220 A2
St Leonards Ave YO8 . . .198 B4
St Leonards Cl 30 LS29 .174 F4
St Leonards Rd TS14 . . . .8 E4
St Luke's Cl
6 Boston Spa LS23 . . . . .188 E7
Harrogate HG1 . . . . .219 D4
St Luke's Cres YO12 . . .212 C6
St Luke's Gr YO30 . . . . .228 B2
St Luke's Mount HG1 . . .219 D4

St Lukes Cl DL7 . . . . . . .22 C2
St Lukes Hospl TS4 . . . . .7 A8
St Margaret's Ave
LS26 . . . . .200 B6
St Margaret's Cl 3 HG5 .221 A6
St Margaret's Garth 2
HG5 . . . . .221 A6
St Margaret's Gdns 1
HG5 . . . . .221 A6
St Margaret's Rd
Knaresborough HG5 . . . . .221 A6
Mickletown LS26 . . . . .200 B6
St Margaret's Terr
6 Ilkley LS29 . . . . .218 B3
York YO1 . . . . .228 E4
St Margarets Cl DL2 . . . .4 C3
St Mark's Ave HG2 . . . . .222 D7
St Mark's Cl 1 YO12 . . .212 C8
St Mark's Gr YO30 . . . . .224 E2
St Martin's La YO1 . . . . .233 A2
St Martin's Pl 10 YO11 .213 A4
St Martin's Rd 9 YO11 .213 A4
St Martin's Sch YO12 . . .93 D8
St Martins Ave 2 LS21 .176 F1
St Martins CE VA Prim Sch
YO11 . . . . .213 C1
St Martins Cl 18 DL9 . . .40 E4
St Martins Way 11 TS15 .24 E8
St Mary's App YO8 . . . .196 F1
St Mary's Ave
Barnoldswick BB18 . . . . . .171 E2
Harrogate HG2 . . . . .219 C2
12 Hemingbrough YO8 . .198 F1
14 Swillington LS26 . . . . .194 A1
Thirsk YO7 . . . . .211 C4
St Mary's CE Prim Sch
6 Boston Spa LS23 . . . . .188 E8
Longnewton TS21 . . . . .5 A7
St Mary's Cl
Barton DL10 . . . . .21 D7
15 Haxby YO32 . . . . . . .166 E5
Ilkley LS29 . . . . .218 C4
South Cowton DL7 . . . . . . .22 E2
Strensall YO32 . . . . .167 A7
Thirsk YO7 . . . . .211 C4
St Mary's Coll YO11 . . . .6 F7
St Mary's Cres YO22 . . .208 E6
St Mary's Ct
Allerton Bywater LS26 . . . .200 D6
York YO24 . . . . .233 A1
St Mary's Dr YO7 . . . . . .211 C4
St Mary's Gdns BD23 . . .173 B4
St Mary's Gr YO10 . . . . .229 C4
St Mary's La YO30 . . . . .233 A3
St Mary's Mus★ YO1 . . .233 B2
St Mary's RC Prim Sch
Malton YO17 . . . . .215 D5
Selby YO8 . . . . .232 B2
St Mary's St 5 YO8 . . . .213 B6
St Mary's Terr YO30 . . .233 A4
St Mary's Way YO7 . . . .211 C4
St Mary's Wlk
Harrogate HG1 . . . . .219 C1
Micklefield LS25 . . . . .194 F4
Middlesbrough TS5 . . . . . . .6 E8
Scarborough YO11 . . . . . .213 A7
Thirsk YO7 . . . . .211 C4
St Marys Cath TS8 . . . . . .7 B5
St Marys Cath Prim Sch
YO23 . . . . .182 D3
St Marys CE Prim Sch
DL10 . . . . .209 E7
St Marys Cl
Cottingwith YO42 . . . . . . .193 C5
14 Stokesley TS9 . . . . . . .26 C7
St Marys Ct YO7 . . . . . . .90 C3
St Marys Gate HG4 . . . .214 D5
St Marys Hospl YO12 . . .212 F6
St Marys RC Prim Sch
HG5 . . . . .221 A7
St Marys Terr YO30 . . . .233 A3
St Matthew's Cl
20 Leyburn DL8 . . . . .60 D5
4 Naburn YO19 . . . . . . .191 D8
St Maurice's Rd YO31 . .233 C3
St Michael St 6 YO7 . . .215 C4
St Michael's La YO11 . . .213 C1
St Michael's Mead
HG4 . . . . .138 E6
St Michaels Ct 1 DL7 . .210 D2
St Michaels Gn 15 WF6 .200 A1
St Michaels Way 29
LS29 . . . . .174 F4
St Monica Hospl YO61 . .143 C8
St Monicas Ct 4 YO61 . .143 D8
St Monicas Garth 17
YO61 . . . . .143 D8
St Nicholas Ave YO19 . .231 D4
St Nicholas CE Prim Sch
HG4 . . . . .87 A1
St Nicholas Cl
Copmanthorpe YO23 . . . .230 A3
Richmond DL10 . . . . .209 F8
St Nicholas Cliff 5
YO11 . . . . .213 A5
St Nicholas Cres
YO23 . . . . .230 A3
St Nicholas Croft
YO23 . . . . .182 E3
St Nicholas Dr DL10 . . .209 F7
St Nicholas Fields Nature
Reserve★ YO10 . . . . . .228 F4
St Nicholas Gdns TS15 . .5 F2
St Nicholas Pl 1 YO10 . .228 F3

St Nicholas Rd
Copmanthorpe YO23 . . . .230 A3
Harrogate HG2 . . . . .220 B2
Ilkley LS29 . . . . .218 A5
St Nicholas St
Norton YO17 . . . . .215 D3
Scarborough YO11 . . . . . .213 A6
St Nicholas Way 22
YO32 . . . . .166 E5
St Nicholas Wlk HG2 . . .220 B2
St Olave's Cl HG4 . . . . . .214 A3
St Olave's Rd YO30 . . . .233 A4
St Olave's Sch YO30 . . .233 A3
St Oswald's CE Prim Sch
YO10 . . . . .231 E7
St Oswald's Cl
Catton YO41 . . . . .185 F6
Oswaldkirk YO62 . . . . .93 A1
St Oswald's Rd YO10 . . .231 D8
14 Catterick Garrison DL9 .40 E4
Sowerby YO7 . . . . .89 F3
St Oswalds Ct
6 Filey YO14 . . . . .101 B3
York YO10 . . . . .231 E7
St Oswalds Rd 13 DL9 . .40 E4
St Patrick's Way HG2 . . .220 B2
St Patricks RC Comp Sch
TS17 . . . . .6 C7
St Paul's CE Prim Sch
YO24 . . . . .228 A3
St Paul's Cl DL10 . . . . . .41 B6
St Paul's Dr DL10 . . . . . .41 B6
St Paul's Gr LS29 . . . . . .218 D4
St Paul's Sq TS17 . . . . . .6 B8
St Paul's Sq YO24 . . . . .228 A3
St Paul's Terr
Darlington DL3 . . . . .3 C7
York YO24 . . . . .228 A4
St Paulinas RC VA Prim Sch
TS14 . . . . .8 D6
St Paulinus Dr YO7 . . . .210 B3
St Pauls Cl 4 DL7 . . . . .210 E2
St Pauls Ct 3 WF8 . . . . .201 C2
St Pauls Mews YO24 . . .228 A3
St Pauls Rise YO12 . . . .174 F4
St Peter & St Paul RC Prim
Sch DL8 . . . . .60 D5
St Peter St YO17 . . . . . .215 D3
St Peter's Brafferton CE VA
Prim Sch YO61 . . . . . . .115 F1
St Peter's Cath Prim Sch
YO12 . . . . .212 D8
St Peter's Cl 2 DL9 . . . .41 A5
St Peter's Cres YO12 . . .215 D3
St Peter's Ct YO22 . . . . .208 F4
St Peter's Garth LS14 . . .188 A3
St Peter's Gr YO30 . . . . .233 A4
St Peter's Rd Drax YO8 . .204 F5
Whitby YO22 . . . . .208 F4
St Peter's Sch YO30 . . . .233 A4
St Peter's Sq 7 HG2 . . .219 C2
St Peters CE Prim Sch
HG2 . . . . .219 D1
St Peters Cl YO26 . . . . .227 A5
St Peters Ct
31 Addingham LS29 . . . .174 F4
York YO30 . . . . .233 A4
St Philip's Gr YO30 . . . .228 A8
St Philip's Way 33 LS29 .176 C1
St Princes Sq 14 HG1 . .219 D2
St Princes St 12 HG1 . .219 D2
St Richards Rd 3 LS21 .176 F1
St Robert's Cave★
HG5 . . . . .221 C4
St Robert's Gdns HG5 . .221 B4
St Robert's RC Prim Sch
HG1 . . . . .219 F4
St Robert's Rd HG5 . . . .221 B4
St Roberts Mews 4
HG1 . . . . .219 D1
St Ronan's Cl 3 HG2 . . .220 A1
St Ronan's Rd 2 HG2 . .220 A1
St Sampsons Sq YO1 . . .233 B2
St Saviour's Pl YO1 . . . .233 C2
St Saviourgate YO1 . . . .233 C2
St Sepulchre St 7
YO11 . . . . .213 B6
St Simon's Chapel (rems
of)★ DL8 . . . . .84 A7
St Stephen's Cl BD23 . . .216 F4
St Stephen's Rd YO24 . .227 C2
St Stephen's Sq YO24 . .227 C2
St Stephens Cath Prim Sch
18 BD23 . . . . .216 F4
St Stephens Gdns 1
DL7 . . . . .210 E2
St Stephens Mews
YO30 . . . . .225 A2
St Swithin's Wlk YO26 . .227 E4
St Teresa's RC Prim Sch
DL1 . . . . .3 C4
St Thomas' Pl YO31 . . . .233 B4
St Thomas St YO11 . . . .213 A6
St Thomas's Cl 2 YO10 .229 C4
St Thomas's Way
YO26 . . . . .164 C3
St Trinians Cl DL10 . . . .209 F8
St Trinians Dr DL10 . . . .209 F8
St Wilfred Dr DL7 . . . . . .210 B3
St Wilfred's Gdns★
HG4 . . . . .214 C6
St Wilfred's RC Prim Sch
YO31 . . . . .233 C3
St Wilfrid's Cath High Sch
WF7 . . . . .200 E1
St Wilfrid's Cl 7 YO32 . .167 B6
St Wilfrid's Cres 9 YO8 .197 D1

St Wilfrid's Ct YO31 ....233 C3
St Wilfrid's Gdns HG4 ....214 C6
St Wilfrid's Pl 2 HG4 ....214 C5
St Wilfrid's Rd
  1 Ripon HG4 ....214 C5
  8 Strensall YO32 .....167 E6
St Wilfrids RC Prim Sch
  HG4 ....214 B5
St Williams Coll YO31 ....233 B3
St Winifred's Ave HG2 ....219 F1
St Winifred's Cl HG2 .....219 F1
St Winifred's Rd HG2 .....219 F1
St Wulstan Cl YO31 ......228 E7
Saithes Seaton Cty Prim Sch
  TS13 ....13 K2
Salents La
  Birdsall YO17 ....148 C4
  Duggleby YO17 ....149 B6
Salerno Cl 6 DL9 ....209 C1
Salisbury Cl 15 WF6 .....200 A2
Salisbury Dr 9 HG1 .....161 B3
Salisbury Rd YO26 ....227 F5
Salisbury St
  Scarborough YO12 .....212 E3
  Skipton BD23 ....216 E5
Salisbury Terr YO26 .....227 F5
Sallow Heath 16 HG3 .....161 B3
Salmon La DL8 ....87 B6
Salmond Rd 5 YO24 .....227 B1
Salt Pan Well Stps 11
  YO22 ....208 E6
Salt Pans Rd YO13 ....54 C2
Saltburn Rd TS17 ....6 B8
Salter Rd YO11 ....99 F6
Salterforth La BB18 .....171 E1
Salterforth Rd BB18 .....172 A1
Saltergate Bank HG3 ......72 F8
Saltergate Com Jun & Inf Sch
  HG3 ....219 A5
Saltergate Dr HG3 ....161 B3
Saltergill La TS15 ....24 C8
Saltergill Sch TS15 ....5 D1
Salters Ave DL1 ....3 E6
Salters La DL1 ....3 F4
Salters La DL1 ....3 D8
Salters La S DL1 ....3 E7
Saltersgill Ave TS4 ....6 F8
Saltersgill Cl 3 TS4 ......6 F8
Salton La YO62 ....94 B1
Salutation Rd DL3 ....3 A4
Sam La YO61 ....142 D8
Samuel Smith Old Brewery*
  LS24 ....189 E6
San Carlos Cl 1 DL9 .....40 E3
Sand Hutton CE VC Prim Sch
  YO41 ....168 B5
Sand Hutton Ct YO41 .....168 B5
Sand La
  Barlby with Osgodby
    YO8 ....198 B4
  Bubwith YO8 ....199 D5
  Heslerton YO17 ......123 F7
  Huby YO61 ....144 A5
  Oldstead YO61 ....91 D4
  Sherburn YO17 ....124 D7
  South Milford LS25 ...195 F2
  Stillington YO61 ......144 A6
  Wistow YO8 ....197 E6
Sandacre Ct YO26 ....227 C5
Sandbeck DL10 ....209 C5
Sandbeck Ind Est
  LS22 ....180 C4
Sandbeck La LS22 ....180 D4
Sandbeck Way LS22 .....180 C4
Sandcroft Cl 4 YO24 ....230 D8
Sandcroft Rd YO24 ......230 D8
Sanders Way DL10 ....41 E4
Sanderson Ave WF6 .....200 A1
Sanderson Rd DL2 ....3 F1
Sandfield La YO7 ....88 D4
Sandfield Terr 4 LS24 ..189 F6
Sandgate 14 YO22 ....208 D7
Sandgate Dr LS25 ....194 D1
Sandgate La LS25 ....194 E2
Sandgate Rise LS25 .....194 E1
Sandgate Terr LS25 .....194 E1
Sandhill Bank YO21 ......9 C1
Sandhill Cl
  Harrogate HG1 ....219 E6
  Pontefract WF8 ......201 B2
Sandhill Dr HG1 ....219 F6
Sandhill La 17 Bedale DL8 .63 B3
  Brayton YO8 ....197 D2
  Sutton upon Derwent
    YO41 ....185 E2
Sandhill Rise WF8 ......201 B2
Sandhill Way HG1 ....219 F6
Sandholme 2 YO32 ......166 F5
Sandholme Cl
  14 Easingwold YO61 ..143 D8
  22 Settle BD24 ....131 D2
Sandholmes La YO7 ....89 E3
Sandhurst Gdns 4
  YO12 ....212 B7
Sandhutton La YO7 ....89 B4
Sandiacres 5 YO8 ....197 D1
Sandmartin Ct YO24 .....230 D8
Sandmoor Cl 5 YO21 ....208 B5
Sandown Cl Bagby YO7 ...90 B3
  York YO24 ....227 E2
Sandpiper Cl
  6 Eastfield YO12 ......99 E6
  1 Filey YO14 ....101 A4
Sandpit La YO62 ....69 B1
Sandriggs DL3 ....3 B7
Sandringham Cl YO32 ...225 D7
Sandringham Rd
  Byram cum Sutton WF11 .201 E4

Sandringham Rd continued
  Lockwood TS12 ....9 F6
  Middlesbrough TS3 .....7 B8
  6 Ripon HG4 ....214 C3
  6 Wetherby LS22 .....180 C3
Sandringham St
  4 Scarborough YO12 ..212 F7
  York YO10 ....228 D2
Sandrock Rd 3 WF8 ....201 C1
Sands Cl YO14 ....127 D7
Sands La
  Hunmanby YO14 ......127 A8
  Rillington YO17 ....122 F5
Sands Rd YO14 ....127 B7
Sandsend Rd
  Newholm-cum-Dunsley
    YO21 ....13 A3
  Whitby YO21 ....208 A8
Sandside
  Scarborough YO11 ....213 B6
  Whitby YO21 ....208 D7
Sandsprunt La YO13 ......97 E6
Sandstock Rd YO31 .....229 B7
Sandwath La LS24 ......196 A8
Sandway Ave 12 YO8 ...197 B1
Sandway Cl 11 YO8 ....197 B1
Sandway Dr
  1 Camblesforth YO8 ..204 C4
  1 Thorpe Willoughby YO8 197 B1
Sandwith La YO8 ....204 B4
Sandwood Pk TS14 ....8 D5
Sandy Bank
  Farnham HG5 ....162 D7
  Northallerton DL6 ....210 F3
  Romanby DL6 ....65 A7
Sandy Flatts La TS5 ......6 F6
Sandy Gap YO32 ....225 C7
Sandy Gate HG3 ....159 A6
Sandy La Aline YO61 ....143 A4
  Dalton YO7 ....116 A8
  5 Embsay BD23 ......217 C7
  Harton YO60 ....168 B8
  16 Haxby YO32 ......166 E5
  High & Low Bishopside
    HG3 ....137 D3
  Humberton YO61 .....141 D8
  North Duffield YO8 ...198 F8
  Ripon HG4 ....214 B2
  Scampston YO17 .....123 B5
  Stockton on the Forest
    YO32 ....167 E4
Sandy La Bsns Ctr
  BD23 ....216 E3
Sandy Leas La TS21 .....5 A8
Sandy Rise YO8 ....232 C3
Sandybed Cres YO12 ...212 C4
Sandybed La
  Scarborough YO12 ....212 C4
  Wykeham YO13 ....98 F6
Sandyforth La BD22 ....186 E5
Sandyland 22 YO32 ....166 E5
Sandyridge YO26 ....224 A3
Sarah's Croft BD23 ....155 A1
Sargeant Ave YO23 ....230 F4
Saunters Way WF6 .....200 A3
Savile Rd
  Castleford WF10 .....200 E4
  Mickletown LS26 .....200 B6
Saville Gr YO30 ....228 A8
Saville St YO17 ....215 C4
Saw Wells La LS24 ....195 F6
Sawley Cl BD23 ....217 C7
Sawley Moor La HG4 ...138 C6
Sawley St 1 BD23 .....216 D3
Sawmill La YO62 ....92 F6
Sawyer's Cres YO23 ...230 C2
Sawyers Garth 9 LS24 .175 A4
Sawyers Wlk 9 YO19 ..184 F7
Saxford Way 8 YO12 ..166 D5
Saxon Cl Shipton YO30 .165 F5
  6 Thorpe Willoughby YO8 197 B1
Saxon Dr YO17 ....122 F5
Saxon Pl YO31 ....228 E7
Saxon Rd
  Catterick Garrison DL9 .209 C1
  Ripon HG4 ....214 D5
  Stamford Bridge YO41 .168 D2
  Whitby YO21 ....208 B7
Saxon Vale YO30 ......165 F5
Saxonfield TS8 ....7 A6
Saxton CE VC Prim Sch
  LS24 ....195 D7
Saxton Ct LS24 ....195 D8
Saxton La LS24 ....195 E8
Saxty Way YO7 ....211 A1
Scabbate Gate BD23 ...108 B3
Scackleton Bank
  YO62 ....119 C4
Scackleton La YO62 ...119 C3
Scafell Cl 4 YO30 ....224 E1
Scagglethorpe La
  YO17 ....122 C4
Scaife Gdns YO31 .....228 D7
Scaife Shay La YO7 ....116 A7
Scaife St YO31 ....228 C7
Scalby Ave YO12 ....212 C8
Scalby Beck Rd 27 YO13 .75 D5
Scalby Mills Rd YO12 ...75 F5
Scalby Sch YO12 ......212 B8
Scaldhill La YO51 ......141 C7
Scale Hill LS21 ....177 D2
Scale The BD23 ....157 D3
Scallow Bank La DL8 ....59 B6
Scalm La
  Hambleton YO8 ....196 F2
  Selby YO8 ....197 A4

Scampston Hall*
  YO17 ....123 A6
Scampton Cl TS17 ......6 A6
Scar Field 9 BD23 .....134 E2
Scar Hos DL11 ....35 F5
Scar Rd BD23 ....171 E6
Scar St BD23 ....134 E2
Scarah Bank HG3 ......161 B8
Scarbeck Bank DL11 ....19 D7
Scarborough Art Gall*
  YO11 ....213 A5
Scarborough Bsns Pk
  YO11 ....99 F6
Scarborough Castle*
  YO11 ....213 C7
Scarborough Coll
  YO11 ....213 A2
Scarborough General Hospl
  YO12 ....212 B6
Scarborough Indoor Pool*
  YO12 ....212 E8
Scarborough Rd
  Gristhorpe YO14 .....101 A4
  Heslerton YO17 ......123 F7
  Langtoft YO25 ....151 C2
  Norton YO17 ....215 F4
  Norton-on-Derwent
    YO17 ....122 A3
  Seamer YO12 ....99 D6
  Stainton Dale YO13 ...53 F8
Scarborough Sixth Form Coll
  YO12 ....212 C4
Scarborough Sports Ctr
  YO11 ....213 A2
Scarborough Sta
  YO11 ....212 F5
Scarborough Terr
  YO30 ....233 B4
Scarcroft Hill YO24 ....228 B2
Scarcroft La YO23 .....233 A1
Scarcroft Prim Sch
  YO23 ....233 A1
Scarcroft Rd YO24 ....233 A1
Scarcroft View YO23 ..233 A1
Scardale Cres YO12 ...212 E8
Scardale Ct YO8 ......232 A2
Scarer's La YO60 ......142 B2
Scargill Rd HG1 ....219 B3
Scarlet Balk La YO17 ..122 C1
Scarth Cl 3 TS12 ......9 F7
Scarth Nick
  Preston-under-Scar DL8 .59 E6
  Whorlton DL6 ....45 D6
Scarthingwell Cres
  LS24 ....195 D8
Scarthingwell La LS24 .195 E8
Scate Moor La YO26 ..163 F3
Scawling End Rd YO61 ..91 C3
Scawthorpe Cl WF8 ....201 C1
Scawton Ave 1 YO31 ..225 E2
Scholars Gate TS14 .....8 E5
Scholars Pk DL3 ....3 B5
Scholes La DL6 ....187 F1
Scholes Pk Ave 3 YO12 .75 D5
Scholes Pk Cliff 1 YO12 .75 F5
Scholes Pk Dr 2 YO12 ..75 F5
Scholes Pk Rd YO12 ....75 E5
Scholes Rd WF10 .....201 B5
Scholla La DL6 ....210 F5
Scholla View DL6 .....210 F5
School Cl Huby YO61 ..144 A4
  Selby YO8 ....232 B3
  16 Stamford Bridge YO41 168 D2
School Croft WF11 ....201 E4
School Fields BB18 ....172 A2
School Garth YO7 ......89 E3
School Hill
  Bainbridge DL8 ....57 D5
  8 Settle BD24 ....131 E2
School House Dr YO12 .99 D6
School La
  Addingham LS29 .....174 F5
  Askham Richard YO23 .182 D3
  Bellerby DL8 ....60 D7
  Bishopthorpe YO23 ..231 A4
  Burton Fleming YO25 .126 E3
  Collingham LS22 .....188 A8
  Copmanthorpe YO23 .230 A2
  Dacre HG3 ....159 D9
  Earby BB7 ....172 A1
  Easington BB7 ......152 B3
  Eppleby DL11 ....1 D4
  Great Ayton TS9 ......8 A1
  Heslington YO10 ....229 B1
  Laneshaw Bridge BB8 .186 C3
  Lawkland LA2 ....130 D3
  Lotherton cum Aberford
    LS25 ....194 F8
  Malton YO17 ....215 C4
  4 Nawton YO62 ......93 D7
  Newton-le-Willows DL8 .62 B4
  Osmotherley DL6 .....45 B4
  23 Poppleton YO26 ..165 F1
  South Milford LS25 ...195 F2
  8 Spofforth HG3 ....179 E6
  Thornton-le-Beans DL6 .65 B5
  Walton LS23 ....180 F2
  Wray-with-Botton LA2 .128 A6
  York YO10 ....231 E7
School Rd
  Hemingbrough YO8 ..198 F1
  Wetherby LS22 ......180 C3
School St
  Castleford WF10 .....200 F5
  2 Earby BB18 ....186 A7

School St continued
  York YO24 ....227 D3
Schoolgate LS15 ......194 C8
Score Ray La YO26 .....164 A5
Scoreby La YO41 ......168 B1
Scoresby Terr 2 YO21 .208 D5
Scoska Wood National
  Nature Reserve*
  BD23 ....107 B3
Scosthrop La BD23 ....154 E6
Scotch Cnr
  Middleton Tyas DL10 ..21 B4
  Oldstead YO61 ....91 C4
Scotch George La
  YO60 ....168 A8
Scotpit La DL6 ....43 E4
Scots Dike Terr DL10 ..209 D6
Scots Dyke Cl DL10 ....20 F7
Scott Cl
  35 Glusburn BD20 ...187 E7
  13 Swillington LS26 ..194 A1
Scott Moncrieff Rd
  YO32 ....167 B6
Scott Rd YO8 ....232 C6
Scott St YO23 ....228 C2
Scotton Bank DL8 ......40 D2
Scotton Ct HG5 ....162 A6
Scotton Dr HG5 ....220 C8
Scotton Gdns 8 DL9 ...40 E3
Scotton Gr
  Knaresborough HG5 ..220 C8
  Scotton HG5 ....162 A5
Scotton Lingerfield Com
  Prim Sch HG5 ....162 B7
Scotton Moor HG5 ....220 C8
Scotton Pk DL9 ....40 E3
Scotton Rd DL9 ....40 E3
Scriftain La LS22 ......180 C5
Scriven Gr 8 YO32 ....166 F5
Scriven Rd HG5 ....221 A7
Scroggs La DL8 ....86 E7
Scrogs La DL8 ....59 B6
Scrope Ave 4 YO31 ...225 E2
Scugdale Rd DL6 ....45 E8
Scurragh House La
  DL10 ....21 C2
Scurragh La DL10 ......21 B2
Sea App YO14 ....100 F6
Sea Cliff Cres YO11 ...213 B2
Sea Cliff Rd YO11 .....213 B2
Sea Life & Marine
  Sanctuary* YO12 ....75 F5
Sea View YO14 ....101 C1
Sea View Cl
  5 Scarborough YO11 .100 B8
  Whitby YO21 ....208 A6
Sea View Cres YO11 ...100 B8
Sea View Dr 13 YO11 ..100 B8
Sea View Gdns 6 YO11 .100 B8
Sea View Gr 4 YO11 ..100 B8
Seafield Ave 1 YO11 ..100 B7
Seafire Cl YO30 ....225 A3
Seagram Cres DL10 ...209 C8
Seakel La YO23 ....182 C2
Seal Bank BD23 ....81 D1
Seamer & Irton Com Prim
  Sch YO12 ....99 D6
Seamer Moor Hill
  YO12 ....212 B1
Seamer Moor La YO12 .212 B1
Seamer Rd
  East Ayton YO13 ......99 B7
  Eastfield YO12 ....99 F8
  Hilton TS15 ....6 C2
  Maltby TS8 ....6 E3
  Scarborough YO12 ...212 E3
  Thornton TS8 ....6 D4
Seamer Rd Cnr YO12 ..212 E4
Seamer Rd Ret Pk
  YO12 ....212 E1
Seamer St 2 YO12 ....212 E3
Seamer Sta YO11 ......99 F6
Seaton Cl YO10 ....229 C4
Seaton Cres TS13 ......13 K2
Seaton Garth TS13 .....13 K2
Seave Cl La YO26 .....164 D2
Seavegate 4 YO13 ....99 B8
Seavegate Cl 3 YO13 ..99 B8
Seaview Ave 5 YO12 ..75 E5
Second Ave
  Menwith with Darley
    HG3 ....160 A4
  9 Pickering YO18 .....95 F7
  Wetherby LS22 ......180 C3
  York YO31 ....228 F6
Second Comm La YO8 .197 C4
Sedber La 5 BD23 ....134 E2
Sedbergh Dr LS29 ....218 B3
Sedbergh Pk LS29 ....218 B3
Sedbusk La DL8 ....56 D6
Sedge Rise LS24 ......189 D5
Sedgefield Rd TS5 .....6 E6
Sedley Cl HG1 ....219 E7
Seed Hill LA6 ....103 D4
Sefton Ave YO31 .....228 F6
Sefton Dr LS29 ....218 B3
Sefton Way TS15 ......5 D2
Seg La YO8 ....204 F3
Seggans Rd YO26 .....142 A1
Segrave Rd DL9 ....40 E4
Segrave Wlk 10 YO26 .227 E4
Selbourne 8 BB18 ....172 B1
Selby Abbey YO8 .....232 D4
Selby Abbey CE Prim Sch
  YO8 ....232 C5
Selby Bsns Pk YO8 ...232 D1
Selby Coll Selby YO8 .232 F3

Selby Coll continued
  Selby YO8 ....232 C5
Selby CP Sch YO8 ....232 B4
Selby Cres DL3 ....3 A7
Selby High Sch YO8 ..232 B4
Selby Ironworks Bsns Ctr
  YO8 ....232 D5
Selby Rd
  Eggborough DN14 ...202 F1
  Fulford YO19 ....231 E6
  Garforth LS25 ......194 B3
  Ledston LS25 ....195 A2
  Riccall YO19 ....198 A8
  Snaith DN14 ....204 C1
  Swillington LS15 ....194 A3
  Wistow YO8 ....197 D6
  Womersley DN14 ....207 A4
Selby Rly Sports Club
  YO8 ....232 D3
Selby Sta YO8 ....232 D5
Seldon Rd YO26 ......227 E5
Self Gdns YO62 ....70 F3
Selley Pk Dr YO12 ....212 B4
Selside Shaw BD24 ...105 A7
Selstone Cres 7 YO22 .32 A6
Semer Wr Nature Reserve*
  DL8 ....57 B1
Senhouse Rd DL1 ......3 F5
Seph Way YO17 ....215 D4
Sergeant Bank HG4 ...86 B8
Sessay CE VC Prim Sch
  YO7 ....116 C5
Sessions House Yd 10
  WF8 ....201 B1
Settle CE VC Prim Sch
  BD24 ....131 E2
Settle Coll BD24 ......131 D3
Settle Mid Sch BD24 ..131 D3
Settle Rd BD23 ....155 A6
Settle Sta BD24 ......131 D2
Settle Swimming Pool
  BD24 ....131 D3
Settrington All Saint's CE
  Prim Sch YO17 .....122 D1
Settrington Rd YO12 ..212 B6
Seven St YO17 ....121 C1
Seven Wells YO17 ....121 A4
Seventh Ave YO31 ....228 F5
Severfield Cl YO7 ....211 D2
Severn Dr
  Garforth LS25 ......194 D3
  Guisborough TS14 ....8 E6
Severn Gn YO26 ......227 C8
Severn Way DL1 ....3 D3
Severus Ave YO26 ....227 D4
Severus St YO24 .....227 D4
Sewell's Cave* LA2 ..131 A5
Sexhow La TS9 ....25 F4
Seymour Cres TS16 ....5 D4
Seymour Gr
  Eaglescliffe TS16 .....5 D4
  York YO31 ....228 F6
Shackleton Cl YO21 ..208 C5
Shady La BD20 ....173 C2
Shaftesbury Ave DN14 .202 C3
Shaker Stile Rd YO18 ..96 B7
Shakespeare Ave 2
  DN6 ....206 E1
Shakespeare Cl 3 DL10 .41 C7
Shakespeare Cres
  WF10 ....201 B3
Shallowdale Gr 1 YO10 .229 C3
Shambles YO1 ....233 B2
Shambles La YO7 .....114 B5
Shambles The 2 YO17 .215 B4
Shandon Pk TS8 ....7 B5
Shandy Hall* YO61 ...117 D8
Shannon Cl 26 LS29 ..175 C2
Shannon Lea DL4 ......3 A4
Sharow CE Prim Sch
  HG4 ....214 F7
Sharow La HG4 ....214 E6
Sharp Hill La YO8 ....204 F6
Sharpe Howe* YO11 .126 A8
Sharphaw Ave BD23 ..217 A2
Sharphaw View BD23 .155 D1
Shaw Ave WF6 ....200 B1
Shaw Barn La LS22 ...180 B3
Shaw Cl WF6 ....200 B1
Shaw Cres YO61 .....144 A5
Shaw Dr YO62 ....70 B1
Shaw La Farnham HG5 .162 C7
  Fenwick DN6 ....207 D2
  North Rigton HG3 ...178 B6
  Spofforth with Stockeld
    HG3 ....179 D7
Shaw Rise WF6 ......200 B1
Shawclose La YO62 ....67 E4
Shawcroft Ct DL10 ...209 E8
Shawl Terr 11 DL8 .....60 D5
Shaws La
  Barwick in Elmet & Scholes
    LS15 ....194 B7
  Hawes DL8 ....56 A4
Shaw's Terr YO24 ....233 A1
Sheep Rake La YO25 .151 E4
Sheep St 11 BD23 ....216 F4
Sheepcote La HG3 ...159 F5
Sheepcote La YO14 ..127 A8
Sheepfoot Hill YO17 ..215 D4
Sheepwalk La
  Castleford WF10 ....201 B3
  Kirby Grindalythe YO17 150 B7
Sheepwash Bank YO7 .66 D5
Sheepwash La DN14 ..207 A7

Sheldrake Cl 9 YO14 101 A4
Sheldrake Rd WF10 200 E3
Shelley Cl YO11 100 B6
Shelley Ct HG1 219 E7
Shelley Dr WF11 201 D2
Shelley Gr YO30 224 F1
Shelley Rd TS4 6 F8
Shelton Ave 2 YO13 99 B8
Shepherd Ct TS12 9 E7
Shepherd Gate LA2 130 F5
Shepherd Hill DL6 45 D8
Shepherd's Rd YO62 70 B4
Shepherdfields La
YO60 146 E5
Shepherdies The HG4 113 C8
Shepherds Dr 13 YO11 100 B7
Sherbrooke Cl 18 YO62 70 B1
Sherburn CE VC Prim Sch
YO17 124 D7
Sherburn Enterprise Pk
LS25 196 B4
Sherburn High Sch
LS25 195 F3
Sherburn in Elmet Sta
LS25 196 A4
Sherburn Rd YO8 232 A8
Sherburn St 1 YO8 197 B8
Sherburn Willows Nature
Reserve* LS25 195 E3
Sheridan Rd BB8 186 B3
Sheriff Hutton Castle (rems
of)* YO60 145 D5
Sheriff Hutton Prim Sch
YO60 145 C5
Sherriff Hutton House*
YO60 145 D4
Sherringham Dr YO24 230 D8
Sherwood Brow BD24 131 D7
Sherwood Cl
Hunton DL8 61 E7
13 Norton DN6 206 E1
Sherwood Dr HG2 220 D2
Sherwood Gr
Huntington YO32 225 F1
York YO26 227 B6
Sherwood Rd TS17 6 B6
Sherwood St 5 YO12 212 F5
Shetland Cl TS5 6 E6
Shilton Garth Cl 3
YO32 225 F7
Shipton Low Rd YO30 165 E5
Shipton Rd
Clifton YO30 227 F8
Rawcliffe YO30 224 D2
York YO30 228 A7
Shipton St 3 YO30 228 B7
Shipton St Inf Sch
YO30 228 B7
Shipyard Ind Est YO8 232 E5
Shipyard Rd YO8 232 E5
Shirbutt La YO26 182 C8
Shire Cl 18 YO11 100 B7
Shire Croft 17 YO11 100 B7
Shire Fold YO11 100 B6
Shire Garth DL6 24 B1
Shire Gr YO17 95 D2
Shire Rd YO7 211 B4
Shires Croft BD23 217 E8
Shires La BD23 217 D8
Shirley Ave Ripon HG4 214 B4
York YO26 227 C6
Shoebridge Ave BD20 187 F7
Shop Hill YO22 33 B4
Shop La Cowling BD22 187 A6
Danby YO21 29 B3
Middleton YO18 95 D8
Short Cl TS18 5 F7
Short La
Farndale East YO62 48 F4
West Haddlesey YO8 202 F6
Short Lee La BD23 216 F6
Short Rd YO7 115 B2
Shortacre La YO42 193 E2
Shortbank Cl BD23 217 B3
Shortbank Rd BD23 217 B3
Shorthorn La 1 DL3 3 A7
Shortsill La HG5 163 B5
Shotel Cl YO30 227 F8
Showfield Cl LS25 195 F4
Showfield Dr 17 YO61 143 C8
Showfield La YO17 215 C6
Shrubberies The YO8 198 E2
Shute Rd DL9 209 E1
Shutt La DL8 56 E6
Shuttleworth St 36
BB18 172 A1
Shuttocks Fold LS25 194 D2
Sicklinghall Com Prim Sch
LS22 179 D3
Sicklinghall Rd LS22 179 F3
Side Gate YO12 99 D1
Sidegate La BD20 186 F8
Sidgwick Ct 7 BD23 217 A3
Siding La YO8 198 B5
Sidings La YO61 143 B4
Sidings The
12 Bridgehouse Gate HG3 137 B4
Settle BD24 131 D2
Skipton BD23 216 E3
Sidmouth Cl TS8 7 D6
Sidmouth Sq 9 DL9 40 E4
Signals Ct 7 YO12 75 F5
Sigston Castle* DL6 44 D2
Sike La YO7 115 B6
Sikelands La DL11 38 F4
Silicar La HG4 88 B1
Sills La YO30 165 B6
Silly La LA2 129 A2
Silsden Rd
Addingham LS29 174 D4
Low Bradley BD20 173 E3
Silver Garth DL10 21 C7
Silver Hill DL7 22 C2
Silver Mdws DL10 21 D7
Silver St Askrigg DL8 57 E5
Barton DL10 21 C7
Fairburn WF11 201 D6
Hackforth DL8 62 E8
4 Knaresborough HG5 221 B5
Masham HG4 86 C3
Reeth, Fremington & Healaugh
DL11 38 B6
3 Riccall YO19 198 A8
8 Scarborough YO11 213 A6
Thirsk YO7 211 C1
Whitby YO21 208 D7
Whitley DN14 207 A7
York YO1 233 B2
Silverdale Cl 5 HG3 160 A6
Silverdale Ct YO24 230 D7
Silverdale Rd BD24 131 F8
Silverfields Rd HG1 220 A3
Silverton Rd TS14 8 F5
Silverwood Ave 5
YO14 101 A3
Sim Balk La YO24 230 E5
Simbach Cl BD23 217 B3
Simon Howe
Ganton YO12 125 A5
Sherburn YO12 124 F6
Simpson Ave 6 YO14 126 F8
Simpson Cl BB18 171 E2
Simpson's La Jun & Inf Sch
WF11 201 E2
Simpson's Yd 3 YO8 232 C6
Simpsons La WF11 201 E2
Sinclair Ct YO12 212 E5
Sinderby La YO7 88 B4
Sinks La DL8 62 C4
Sinnington Cl TS14 8 F6
Sinnington Cliff Rd
YO62 95 A8
Sinnington Com Prim Sch
YO62 94 F8
Sinnington Rd TS17 6 B6
Sir Douglas Pk TS17 6 A7
Sir John's La LS25 195 E4
Sirocco Ct YO31 228 D8
Sissy Bank DL8 59 D6
Sitwell Gr YO26 227 C5
Sitwell St YO12 212 E5
Siward St YO10 229 A3
Siward's Way YO10 229 A2
Siwards How* YO10 229 B1
Sixth Ave YO31 228 E5
Skates La YO61 144 B3
Sked Dale YO17 124 E6
Skeeby Cl 3 TS18 5 D8
Skegmer La YO60 145 F4
Skelda Rise LS29 218 B3
Skelder Rd YO21 31 E8
Skeldergate YO1 233 B2
Skelf St LS24 190 C1
Skelgate La DL11 38 B6
Skellbank HG4 214 B4
Skellbank Cl HG4 214 B4
Skelldale Cl HG4 214 E4
Skelldale View HG4 214 E4
Skellfield Terr HG4 214 D4
Skellgarth HG4 214 C5
Skellgill La DL8 57 C6
Skelton Ct 3 YO30 228 A6
Skelton Ellers TS14 9 A8
Skelton La
Givendale HG4 140 C8
Marske DL11 39 B7
Skelton YO32 224 D8
Skelton Prim Sch
YO30 224 C5
Skelton Rd
Skelton YO51 140 E6
Thornaby TS17 6 B8
Skelton Windmill*
YO51 140 F8
Skerne Pk Prim Sch DL1 3 C4
Skerningham Ave 9 DL3 3 A7
Skeugh Head La DL11 35 E6
Skeugh La YO61 144 D6
Skewsby Gr YO31 225 F1
Skibeden BD23 217 E6
Skibeden Ct 4 BD23 217 B5
Skiddaw YO24 230 C7
Skiddaw Ct TS7 7 C6
Skinner La 14 WF8 201 B1
Skinner St YO21 208 D7
Skiplam Cl 4 YO12 212 B5
Skiplam Rd YO62 69 D2
Skipper La YO25 125 E3
Skipton Castle*
BD23 217 A5
Skipton Cres HG1 219 D5
Skipton Girl's High Sch
BD23 216 E5
Skipton Hospl BD23 216 E3
Skipton Little Theatre*
BD23 216 F3
Skipton Old Rd BB8 186 A3
Skipton Parish Church Sch
BD23 217 A3
Skipton Rd
Addingham LS29 174 E5
Barnoldswick BB18 171 E2
Bradleys Both BD20 173 D4
Skipton Rd *continued*
Colne BB8 186 A2
Cononley BD20 173 C2
Earby BB18 172 A2
Embsay with Eastby
BD23 217 C7
Farnhill BD20 187 E8
Felliscliffe HG3 160 E3
Fewston LS21 159 D2
Gargrave BD23 155 D1
Glusburn BD20 187 F8
Harrogate HG3 219 A5
Hellifield BD23 154 B3
Ilkley LS29 218 A4
Silsden BD20 174 B1
Skipton BD23 217 B6
Skipton St HG1 219 D4
Skipton Sta BD23 216 E3
Skipwith Comm Nature
Reserve* YO8 198 E8
Skipwith Rd YO19 192 B6
Skirt Bank YO7 66 C7
Skottowe Cres TS9 7 F2
Skottowe Dr TS9 7 F2
Skuff Rd BD23 157 B8
Skurkhill La YO62 92 E7
Skyreholme Bank
BD23 157 F7
Skyreholme La BD23 157 E7
Slack La HG3 160 B4
Slackgap La CA17 14 A8
Sladeburn Dr 2 DL6 210 E3
Slaidburn Rd LA2 129 B4
Slate Hill YO21 29 D4
Slates La LS29 218 B7
Slayde The TS15 5 E2
Sled Gates YO22 33 B3
Sled La DL10 41 F4
Sledgate YO17 122 F5
Sledgate Garth YO17 122 F5
Sledmere CE VC Prim Sch
YO25 150 B3
Sledmere House*
YO25 150 B3
Sledmere Rd YO25 151 B6
Sleegill DL10 209 B6
Sleigh La YO60 120 A1
Sleightholme Dale Rd
YO62 69 D5
Sleightholme Moor Rd
DL11 16 D7
Sleights CE VC Prim Sch
YO22 32 A6
Sleights La
Acklam YO17 169 E7
Amotherby YO17 121 A6
Birstwith HG3 160 C4
Rainton with Newby YO7 114 E5
Sleights Rd YO62 69 D6
Sleights Sta YO22 32 A7
Sleights The LS17 178 A2
Slessor Rd
8 Catterick DL10 41 E4
York YO24 227 B1
Slice La LS24 190 A6
Slim Rd DL9 209 C2
Slingsby Ave HG5 221 A7
Slingsby Bank YO62 120 C4
Slingsby Castle (rems of)*
YO62 120 B5
Slingsby Com Prim Sch
YO62 120 B5
Slingsby Cres HG1 219 F4
Slingsby Garth 19 YO62 70 B1
Slingsby Gdns DL7 210 B3
Slingsby Gr YO24 230 E8
Slingsby Wlk HG2 219 F1
Slip Inn Bank DL11 19 E6
Slippery Ford La
BD22 187 E3
Smales' St YO1 233 B1
Smary La YO19 184 D7
Smawthorne Ave
WF10 200 E4
Smawthorne Gr WF10 200 E4
Smawthorne Henry Moore
Prim Sch WF10 200 E3
Smawthorne La WF10 200 E4
Smay La YO22 33 D5
Smearbottoms La
BD23 133 C3
Smeathorns Rd TS12 9 F4
Smeatley's La DN6 206 C4
Smeaton Gr
5 Swillington LS26 194 A1
York YO26 227 C5
Smeaton Rd YO41 185 D7
Smiddy Hill
19 Pickering YO18 95 F6
Walton LS23 181 A2
Smiddyfields 5 YO22 32 A6
Smirthwaite View 14
WF6 200 A1
Smith Cl YO10 231 F8
Smith La HG4 114 A4
Smith St 19 BB18 171 D1
Smith's La Egton YO22 30 E3
Flaxton YO60 145 D1
Smithfield Cl 7 HG4 214 B2
Smithfield Rd DL1 3 D4
Smithgutter La DL10 21 C4
Smithie Cl YO32 225 D5
Smithson Ave WF10 201 B3
Smithson Cl DL10 21 D2
Smithson Ct YO17 215 B5
Smithson Gr 4 YO51 141 B4
Smithson's La HG3 177 A8
Smithsons Ct HG4 214 C5
Smithy Croft Rd BD23 155 D1
Smithy La Denton LS29 176 A4
Scotton HG5 162 A6
Thornton in Lonsdale
LA6 103 A4
Ulleskelf LS24 190 C2
Smuts Rd DL9 209 D1
Smythy La YO25 125 D4
Snainton CE VC Prim Sch
YO13 98 A5
Snainton La YO13 97 F7
Snaith Rd
Pollington DN14 207 F7
Rawcliffe DN14 205 A1
Snaith Sta DN14 204 C1
Snaizeholme Rd DL8 55 E1
Snape Castle* DL8 87 A7
Snape Com Prim Sch
DL8 87 A7
Snape Hill YO62 93 E7
Snargate Hill YO61 118 E3
Sneaton La YO22 208 B1
Sneaton Thorpe La
YO22 32 E5
Sneck Gate La TS8 7 B2
Sneck Yate Bank YO7 67 A2
Snipe Cl 5 YO14 101 A4
Snipe La Hurworth DL2 3 C3
Loftus TS13 11 A6
Snowden Carr Rd
LS21 176 E5
Snowden Cl 4 HG4 214 B2
Snowdon Cl YO23 182 D3
Snowdon Gr 4 TS17 5 F4
Snowfield Ind Est
YO17 215 C6
Snowfield La YO61 142 F5
Snydale Ave WF6 200 B1
Snydale Cl WF6 200 B1
Snydale Ct 10 WF6 200 B1
Snydale Gr WF6 200 B1
Snydale Rd WF6 200 A1
Sober Hall Ave TS17 6 A4
Socarrs La YO62 119 F7
Sockburn La DL2 23 B8
Somerset Cl 6 YO30 224 E3
Somerset Rd
2 Harrogate HG2 219 C1
York YO31 228 D8
Somerset Terr YO11 213 A5
Somme Barracks DL9 40 F3
Sommerset Pastures
YO61 116 F2
Sopwith Cl TS18 5 F8
Sorrel Gr 29 HG3 161 B3
Sorrell Gr TS14 8 D6
Sough La BB18 186 A8
Sour La BD23 216 B6
Sourby La LS21 176 D7
Soursikes Field Rd
YO51 141 D5
South App
Aberford LS25 188 F1
Bramham cum Oglethorpe
LS23 188 C5
Stutton with Hazlewood
LS24 189 A2
South Ave
Castleford WF10 200 C4
20 Scalby YO13 75 D5
South Back La
Stillington YO61 144 C6
Terrington YO60 119 E1
Tollerton YO61 143 B2
South Baileygate WF8 201 C1
South Bank Ave YO23 228 B1
South Beech Ave HG2 220 C3
South Cleveland Hospl
TS4 7 B8
South Cliff Dr YO14 101 B1
South Craven Sch 36
BD20 187 E7
South Cres Ripon HG4 214 C4
Thirsk YO7 211 B2
South Cres Ave 54 YO14 101 B3
South Cres Cl 51 YO14 101 B3
South Cres Rd YO14 101 B3
South Dowber La YO7 211 D4
South Down Rd 3 YO32 225 F5
South Dr HG2 222 E8
South Duffield Rd
YO8 198 C4
South End Bedale DL8 63 A3
Burniston YO13 75 D7
Osmotherley DL6 45 B3
South End Ave 6 DL8 63 A3
South End Cl YO13 75 D7
South End La DN14 207 B4
South Espl YO1 233 B1
South Field La YO26 181 B6
South Gate 18 YO62 92 F6
South Grange Rd HG4 214 B2
South Hawksworth St 7
LS29 218 B4
South House Pavement
Nature Reserve*
BD24 104 F8
South Ings La YO62 70 F3
South Kilvington CE VC Prim
Sch YO7 211 B4
South La
Bishop Wilton YO42 169 F1
Cawood YO8 197 B7
Thornton Dale YO18 96 D6
South Milford Com Prim Sch
9 LS25 195 F2
South Milford Sta
LS25 195 F2
South Moor La
Garriston DL8 61 A7
Sowerby YO7 89 F3
South Otterington CE VC
Prim Sch DL7 64 F2
South Parade
Hurworth-on-Tees DL2 22 C8
Ilkley LS29 218 A4
Northallerton DL7 210 D3
Norton YO17 215 E3
8 Selby YO8 232 C5
York YO24 233 A1
South Pk Ave TS6 7 E8
South Pk La LS22 180 A8
South Pk Rd HG1 219 E1
South Ridge LS25 194 D1
South Ruddings La
YO19 192 F7
South Side TS15 25 C5
South St
Barmby on the Marsh
DN14 205 A7
Burton Fleming YO25 126 E2
Scalby YO13 75 D5
7 Scarborough YO11 213 A4
South Terr YO7 211 B2
South Town La TS13 10 E8
South Vale DL6 210 E2
South View
Burniston YO13 75 D7
Castleford WF10 201 B5
2 Egglescliffe TS16 5 D4
3 Glusburn BD20 173 E1
Healaugh LS24 182 A2
Hunton DL8 61 E7
Ilkley LS29 218 B3
19 Leyburn DL8 60 D5
Northallerton DL6 210 F6
Ripon HG4 214 D2
2 Rudby TS15 25 D5
6 Whitby YO21 208 D5
South View Terr BD20 174 B1
South Wood La 11 BD23 134 E3
Southdean Dr TS8 6 F6
Southdene 48 YO14 101 B3
Southend Ave DL3 3 C4
Southend Gdns 8 YO21 208 C6
Southerscales Nature
Reserve* LA6 104 C7
Southey St 1 BD23 217 A3
Southfield YO17 122 D3
Southfield Ave HG4 214 B2
Southfield Cl
6 Hurworth-on-Tees DL2 3 E1
Rufforth YO23 182 D6
Southfield Cres 2
YO24 230 E8
Southfield La
23 Addingham LS29 174 F4
Kellington DN14 202 E2
Southfield Rd
28 Addingham LS29 174 F4
Burley in Warfedale
LS29 176 C1
Littlethorpe HG4 214 B2
Southfield Terr
22 Addingham LS29 174 F4
7 Skipton BD23 216 F3
Southfields Rd YO32 167 B7
Southgate
Eastfield YO12 99 E6
Pickering YO18 95 F7
Ripon HG4 214 C4
Southgate Ave HG4 214 C4
Southgate Cl 7 HG4 214 C4
Southlands
4 Haxby YO32 166 E5
19 Helmsley YO62 92 F6
16 Hemingbrough YO8 198 F1
2 High & Low Bishopside
HG3 137 B4
Southlands Ave 5
YO21 208 C7
Southlands Cl
Escrick YO19 192 B6
8 South Milford LS25 195 F2
Southlands Gr YO12 212 B7
Southlands Rd YO23 228 B2
Southlea YO17 122 F5
Southmoor La WF11 202 B1
Southmoor Rd YO19 192 F5
Southolme Cl 22 YO51 141 B5
Southolme Dr 7 YO30 224 F1
Southolme Wlk 23 YO51 141 B5
Southville Terr HG1 219 B5
Southway
Harrogate HG2 222 C8
Ilkley LS29 218 D3
Southwold 7 YO11 100 B7
Southwold Cl 5 YO11 100 B7
Southwold Rise 6
YO11 100 B7
Southwood TS8 7 B4
Southwood Rd YO41 193 C8
Sovereign Gdns 2 WF6 200 A1
Sovereign Pk HG1 219 B2
Sowarth Field 21 BD24 131 D2
Sowerby Cres TS9 26 B7
Sowerby Prim Sch
YO7 211 B1
Sowerby Rd Thirsk YO7 211 B2
York YO26 227 D4
Sowerby Terr YO7 211 B2
Sowerby Way TS16 5 D5
Sowgate La WF8 201 D2
Spa Complex The*
YO11 213 B4
Spa La Harrogate HG2 220 C3

Spa La continued
Middleton YO18 . . . .**95** B6
Spa Mews HG2 . . . . . .**220** D3
Spa Pk Maze★ HG4 . . .**214** B5
Spa Rd Gainford DL2 . . . . .**1** C7
Harrogate HG2 . . . .**220** C3
Spa St HG2 . . . .**220** C3
Spa Terr 🔟 HG2 . . . . . .**220** C3
Spa YO11 . . . .**213** A4
Spalding Ave YO30 . . . .**228** B7
Sparrington La YO61 . . .**144** B5
Sparrow Hall Dr DL1 . . . .**3** E8
Spartal La LS25 . . . . . .**200** F8
Spaunton Bank YO62 . . .**70** E5
Spaunton La YO62 . . . . .**70** E4
Spawd Bone La WF11 . . .**201** F2
Speculation St YO1 . . . .**228** E4
Speedwell Rd WF10 . . .**200** C3
Speeton Ave TS5 . . . .**6** F7
Spellow Cres HG5 . . . . .**140** E1
Spellow Gr HG5 . . . .**140** E1
Spen Brow LA2 . . . .**128** E6
Spen Comon La LS24 . . .**188** F3
Spen La YO1 . . . .**233** C3
Spence Ct 🔺 TS9 . . . .**8** A2
Spenceley Pl DL11 . . . . . .**2** A2
Spencer Cl 🔺 BD20 . . . .**187** F8
Spencer St
🔺 Glusburn BD20 . . . . .**187** E7
🔺 York YO23 . . . .**233** B1
Spencer Wlk BD23 . . . .**217** C3
Spencer's Holt HG1 . . . .**219** D7
Spencer's Way HG1 . . . .**219** D7
Speng La YO26 . . . .**182** B4
Spennithorne CE Prim Sch
DL8 . . . .**60** B1
Spey Bank YO24 . . . . . .**230** C6
Spiker's Hill La YO13 . . . .**74** F2
Spindle Cl YO24 . . . . . .**230** C8
Spindle Mill BD23 . . . . .**216** F4
Spink La WF8 . . . .**201** B1
Spinksburn La HG3 . . . .**159** F1
Spinner La HG3 . . . .**161** A8
Spinners Ct BD23 . . . . .**216** F4
Spinney The
Darlington DL3 . . . .**3** B4
Draughton BD23 . . . . . .**174** B7
🔺 Easingwold YO61 . . . .**143** C8
Knaresborough HG5 . . . .**221** C6
🔺 Scarborough YO12 . . .**212** B5
Tees-side Airport DL2 . . . .**4** D4
York YO24 . . . .**230** F7
Spinniker Dr 🔺 YO11 . . .**208** C5
Spital Bridge YO22 . . . .**208** E5
Spital Field Ct 🔺 YO17 . .**215** C4
Spital Rd YO12 . . . .**99** E3
Spital St YO12 . . . .**215** B4
Spital The TS15 . . . .**5** D3
Spitalcroft HG5 . . . .**221** B4
Spitalfields TS15 . . . .**5** D3
Spitfire Ct DL10 . . . .**41** F6
Spitfire Way LS25 . . . . .**196** B4
Spitlands La HG5 . . . . . .**163** B7
Spittal Hardwick La
WF10 . . . .**201** B3
Spittlerush La DN6 . . . .**206** D2
Spofforth Castle★
HG3 . . . .**179** D6
Spofforth CE Contolled Prim
Sch HG3 . . . .**179** E5
Spofforth Hill LS22 . . . .**180** B3
Spofforth La
Follifoot HG3 . . . .**223** F4
North Deighton LS22 . . .**180** A6
Spofforth Rd HG3 . . . . .**223** F4
Spofforth La LS22 . . . . .**180** A7
Spout La LA2 . . . .**102** B2
Spreight La Stps YO11 . .**213** B4
Spring Bank YO12 . . . . .**212** E3
Spring Bank Cl HG4 . . . .**214** C7
Spring Bank Mdw
HG4 . . . .**214** C7
Spring Bank Rd HG4 . . .**214** C7
Spring Cl
Garforth LS25 . . . .**194** D4
Middlesbrough TS18 . . . . .**6** B8
🔢 Sleights YO22 . . . .**32** A6
Spring Ct HG3 . . . .**160** E6
Spring Gdns 🔟 YO11 . . .**100** B6
Spring Gr
Harrogate HG1 . . . .**219** C3
Laneshaw Bridge BB8 . . .**186** A3
Spring Hall Garth
YO17 . . . .**215** A3
Spring Hill
Stonegrave YO62 . . . .**93** C6
Welbury DL6 . . . .**24** B1
Whitby YO21 . . . .**208** D6
Spring Hill Sch HG4 . . .**113** E4
Spring Hill Terr 🔟
YO21 . . . .**208** D6
Spring La Birdforth YO7 . .**116** F8
Kirkby Overblow HG3 . . .**179** A2
Long Marston YO26 . . . .**182** A5
Pannal HG3 . . . .**222** C3
Wetherby LS22 . . . .**180** E3
York YO10 . . . .**229** A1
Spring Mount HG1 . . . . .**219** C3
Spring Rise BD23 . . . . .**174** B7
Spring St 🔺 YO61 . . . . .**143** C8
Spring Terr DL7 . . . .**210** C4
Spring Vale YO21 . . . . .**208** C6
Spring Way TS18 . . . .**5** F8
Spring Wlk YO8 . . . .**232** A1
Springbank
Marton cum Grafton
YO51 . . . .**141** E2
Swillington LS25 . . . . . .**194** B3

Springbank Ave YO19 . .**184** E7
Springfield
Bentham LA2 . . . .**129** B8
Clifford LS23 . . . .**188** E7
🔺 Scarborough YO11 . . .**213** B6
Skeeby DL10 . . . .**21** A1
Stokesley TS9 . . . .**26** C7
Springfield Ave
🔺 Earby BB18 . . . .**172** B1
Harrogate HG1 . . . .**219** C3
Ilkley LS29 . . . .**218** C4
🔟 Pontefract WF8 . . . . .**201** C1
Springfield Cl
Barlby with Osgodby
YO8 . . . .**198** B5
🔢 Boroughbridge YO51 .**141** B5
Heworth YO31 . . . .**229** C7
🔺 Leyburn DL8 . . . .**60** D5
🔢 Pateley Bridge HG3 . .**137** C4
Ripon HG4 . . . .**214** B7
Thirsk YO7 . . . .**211** B4
Springfield Cres
Bentham LA2 . . . .**129** B8
🔺 Kirk Smeaton WF8 . . .**206** C3
Springfield Ct
🔢 Grassington BD23 . . .**134** E2
Sherburn in Elmet LS25 . .**195** F5
Springfield Dr
🔢 Barlby YO8 . . . .**198** B5
🔢 Boroughbridge YO51 .**141** B5
Springfield Garth
YO17 . . . .**215** D3
Springfield Gdns 🔢 TS9 .**26** C7
Springfield Gr
🔢 Boroughbridge YO51 .**141** B5
Kirklevington TS15 . . . . . .**5** F1
Springfield La
🔢 Kirkbymoorside YO62 . .**70** C1
Tockwith YO26 . . . .**181** C7
Springfield Mews
HG1 . . . .**219** C3
Springfield Mount
LS29 . . . .**174** F5
Springfield Pl LS25 . . . .**194** B3
Springfield Prim Sch
DL1 . . . .**3** E7
Springfield Rd
🔢 Boroughbridge YO51 .**141** B5
Darlington DL1 . . . .**3** E7
🔢 Grassington BD23 . . .**134** E2
🔺 Poppleton YO26 . . . . .**165** F1
Sherburn in Elmet LS25 . .**195** F5
Springfield Rise 🔢
YO26 . . . .**164** A8
Springfield Terr YO17 . .**124** D7
Springfield Way
🔺 Pateley Bridge HG3 . .**137** C4
York YO31 . . . .**229** B7
Springfields
🔢 Knottingley WF11 . . . .**202** A2
🔺 Skipton BD23 . . . .**217** B4
Springfields Ave 🔢
WF11 . . . .**202** A2
Springhead Specl Sch
YO12 . . . .**212** E2
Springhill Cl YO12 . . . . .**212** E4
Springhill Ct 🔢 LS24 . . .**189** E6
Springhill La YO12 . . . . .**212** D3
Springhill Rd YO12 . . . . .**212** E4
Springmead Dr BD23 . . .**194** C3
Springmount 🔢 BB18 . . .**172** B1
Springs La
Ellerton-on-Swale DL10 . . .**41** F4
Ilkley LS29 . . . .**218** C4
Walton LS23 . . . .**180** F3
Whashton DL11 . . . .**20** B4
Springs Leisure Ctr TS17 .**6** B8
Springs Terr LS29 . . . . .**218** B4
Springs The 🔺 DL8 . . . . .**60** E2
Springwater Sch HG2 . .**220** D4
Springwell Ave 🔢 LS26 .**194** A1
Springwell Cl 🔢 BD22 . .**187** B6
Springwell Gdns 🔢
DL7 . . . .**210** D4
Springwell La DL7 . . . . .**210** D4
Springwell Rd 🔟 LS26 . .**194** A1
Springwell Terr E 🔢
DL7 . . . .**210** D4
Springwell Terr W 🔢
DL7 . . . .**210** D4
Springwood YO32 . . . . .**225** D7
Spruce Cl YO32 . . . .**225** D2
Spruce Gill Ave 🔺 DL8 . .**63** B3
Spruce Gill Dr 🔺 DL8 . . .**63** B3
Spruisty Rd HG1 . . . . . .**219** C4
Spurr Ct YO24 . . . .**230** C8
Spurriergate YO1 . . . . .**233** B2
Square The
Boston Spa LS23 . . . . . .**188** F8
Castleford WF10 . . . . . .**201** B4
Ingleton LA6 . . . .**103** C4
Kippax LS25 . . . .**194** D1
Knottingley WF11 . . . . . .**201** E3
Leeming DL7 . . . .**63** F3
🔺 Tadcaster LS24 . . . . . .**189** F6
Stable Rd YO8 . . . .**204** D7
Stabler Cl 🔢 YO32 . . . . .**166** D5
Stablers Wlk
Earswick YO32 . . . .**225** D4
🔢 Pontefract WF6 . . . . .**200** A2
Stables La LS23 . . . . . .**188** F8
Stackhouse La
Giggleswick BD24 . . . . . .**131** D4
Lawkland BD24 . . . .**130** F2
Stags Way DL10 . . . .**41** F7
Stainburn Ave WF10 . . .**201** A3
Stainburn La LS21 . . . . .**177** E2
Staindale TS14 . . . .**8** D6

Staindale Cl YO30 . . . . .**224** E2
Staindrop Dr TS5 . . . .**6** F7
Staindrop Rd DL3 . . . .**3** A6
Stained Glass Ctr★
. . . .**100** C5
Stainforth Gdns TS17 . . . .**6** B5
Stainforth La BD24 . . . .**131** D5
Stainforth Rd BD24 . . . .**131** E4
Stainsacre La
Hawsker-cum-Stainsacre
YO22 . . . .**32** F6
Whitby YO22 . . . .**208** F3
Stainsby Rd TS5 . . . .**6** D8
Stainton Rd TS9 . . . .**6** F1
Stainton Way
Coulby Newham TS8 . . . . .**7** A5
Stainton & Thornton TS8 . . .**6** E5
Staintondale Shire Horse
Farm★ **54** C5
Staithe St 🔺 YO8 . . . . . .**199** D7
Staithes Cl 🔺 YO26 . . . .**227** B4
Staithes La TS13 . . . .**13** K2
Stake Rd DL8 . . . .**57** C1
Stakesby Com Prim Sch
YO21 . . . .**208** B6
Stakesby Rd YO21 . . . . .**208** B6
Stakesby Vale YO21 . . . .**208** C6
Stakesby Vale Ct
YO21 . . . .**208** B6
Stamford Bridge Inf Sch
YO41 . . . .**168** D2
Stamford Bridge Rd
YO19 . . . .**184** E7
Stamford Bridge W
YO41 . . . .**168** C2
Stamford St E 🔟 YO26 . .**227** F5
Stamford St W 🔢 YO26 .**227** F5
Stammergate YO7 . . . . .**211** C3
Stammergate La YO21 . .**180** A1
Stamp Hill Cl 🔺 LS29 . . .**174** E4
Stan Valley 🔢 WF8 . . . .**206** C3
Standard Ct DL7 . . . . . .**210** B6
Standard Way DL6 . . . . .**210** B6
Standard Way Ind Est
DL6 . . . .**210** C6
Standridge Clough La
BB18 . . . .**172** B1
Standroyd Dr BB8 . . . . .**186** A3
Standroyd Rd BB8 . . . . .**186** A3
Stang La
Arkengarthdale DL11 . . . .**17** E3
Farnham HG5 . . . .**162** C7
Hope DL11 . . . .**18** A8
Stang Top
Arkengarthdale DL11 . . . .**17** A6
Hope DL11 . . . .**18** A6
Stanghow Rd TS12 . . . . . .**9** F8
Stangs La BD23 . . . .**157** D6
Stanhope Dr HG2 . . . . . .**220** B2
Stanhope Gr TS5 . . . .**6** E8
Stanhope Rd N DL3 . . . . .**3** C5
Staniland Dr YO8 . . . . . .**232** A5
Stanley Ave YO32 . . . . .**225** D7
Stanley Cl
🔺 Catterick Garrison DL9 . .**40** E3
🔢 Eastfield YO11 . . . . . .**100** B6
Stanley Gr Aske DL10 . . . .**20** D1
Great Ayton TS9 . . . .**7** F1
Richmond DL10 . . . .**209** D8
Stanley St
Castleford WF10 . . . . . .**200** F4
🔺 Scarborough YO12 . . .**213** A7
York YO31 . . . .**233** C4
Stansfield Brow BD20 . .**187** A8
Stansfield Dr WF10 . . . .**201** B4
Stansfield Rd WF10 . . . .**201** A4
Stanstead Way TS17 . . . . .**6** C7
Stansted Gr DL2 . . . .**4** D4
Stanyforth Cres YO26 . .**164** C2
Stape Rd YO18 . . . .**71** F7
Stapleton Bank DL2 . . . . .**3** A2
Stapleton Cl
🔢 Bedale DL8 . . . .**63** B2
🔢 Seamer YO12 . . . .**99** D6
Stapley La DL8 . . . .**87** F4
Star Carr La YO12 . . . . . .**99** E4
Starbeck Cl 🔺 YO21 . . . .**208** B5
Starbeck Com Prim Sch
HG2 . . . .**220** D4
Starbeck Sta HG2 . . . . .**220** C4
Starbeck Swimming Baths
HG2 . . . .**220** D3
Starfits La
Fadmoor YO62 . . . .**69** F3
Welburn YO62 . . . .**94** A8
Stark Bank Rd HG4 . . . . .**85** C7
Starkey Cres YO31 . . . . .**229** A5
Starkey La 🔺 BD20 . . . .**173** F1
Starmire BD22 . . . .**187** A6
Starra Field La YO26 . . .**163** F5
Station Ave
🔺 Filey YO14 . . . .**101** B3
Harrogate HG1 . . . .**219** C4
New Earswick YO32 . . . .**225** D3
Whitby YO21 . . . .**208** B7
York YO1 . . . .**233** A2
Station Bridge HG1 . . . .**219** D2
Station Cl Dacre HG3 . . .**159** F8
🔢 East Ayton/West Ayton
YO13 . . . .**99** A7
Hambleton YO8 . . . .**196** F2
Sharow HG4 . . . .**214** D7
Station Dr HG4 . . . .**214** D7
Station Fields LS25 . . . .**194** C4
Station Gr 🔢 YO26 . . . .**227** F5
Station La
Barmby on the Marsh
DN14 . . . .**205** B7

Station La continued
Burton Leonard HG3 . . . .**139** F3
Cliffe YO8 . . . .**198** D3
Cloughton YO13 . . . .**54** D1
Gristhorpe YO14 . . . . . .**100** E4
Morton-on-Swale DL7 . . . .**64** A7
Shipton YO30 . . . .**165** E5
Station Par HG1 . . . . . .**219** D2
Station Plaza★ LS29 . . .**218** B3
Station Rd
Ampleforth YO62 . . . .**92** C1
Beadlam YO62 . . . .**93** D7
Brompton DL6 . . . .**43** F4
Brompton-on-Swale DL10 . .**41** B6
Burley in Warfedale
LS29 . . . .**176** C1
Carlton DN14 . . . .**204** C3
Castleford WF10 . . . . . .**200** E4
Cayton YO11 . . . .**100** B5
Church Fenton LS24 . . . .**196** B7
Clapham LA2 . . . .**130** C7
Copmanthorpe YO23 . . . .**230** B2
Danby YO21 . . . .**29** A7
Fylingdales YO22 . . . .**33** C4
Gainford DL2 . . . .**1** C8
Gilling East YO62 . . . . . .**118** F8
Glusburn BD20 . . . .**187** E8
Goldsborough HG5 . . . . .**163** A3
Great Ayton TS9 . . . .**8** A1
Great Preston WF10 . . . .**200** E6
Hambleton YO8 . . . .**196** F1
Haxby YO32 . . . .**166** F5
Hellifield BD23 . . . .**154** B4
Helmsley YO62 . . . .**92** F6
Hensall DN14 . . . .**203** C1
Heslerton YO17 . . . .**97** D1
High Bentham LA2 . . . . .**129** A8
Hinderwell TS13 . . . .**11** F7
Horton in Ribblesdale
BD24 . . . .**105** C3
Ilkley LS29 . . . .**218** B4
Kildale YO21 . . . .**27** E8
Kippax LS25 . . . .**200** C8
Kirk Hammerton YO26 . .**164** D2
🔢 Knaresborough HG5 . .**221** A6
Long Preston BD23 . . . .**153** F4
Menwith with Darley
HG3 . . . .**160** A6
Mickletown LS26 . . . . . .**200** A6
Middleton St George DL2 . .**4** C5
Normanton WF6 . . . . . .**200** A2
Norton DN6 . . . .**206** F2
Nunnington YO62 . . . . . .**93** E2
Pannal HG3 . . . .**222** E2
🔢 Poppleton YO26 . . . . .**165** F1
Rawcliffe DN14 . . . .**205** A1
Riccall YO19 . . . .**198** A8
Richmond DL10 . . . .**209** C7
Scalby YO13 . . . .**75** D5
Scruton DL7 . . . .**63** E6
Selby YO8 . . . .**232** D5
Settle BD24 . . . .**131** C2
Sleights YO22 . . . .**32** A6
Snainton YO13 . . . .**97** F4
South Otterington DL7 . . .**64** F2
Sowerby YO7 . . . .**211** A2
Stainton Dale YO13 . . . . .**54** A8
Stokesley TS9 . . . .**26** C7
Tadcaster LS24 . . . .**189** D6
Thirsk YO7 . . . .**89** D4
Threshfield BD23 . . . . . .**134** D2
Tollerton YO61 . . . .**143** B3
Wharram YO17 . . . .**148** F4
Whixley YO26 . . . .**164** A3
Wistow YO8 . . . .**197** C6
Womersley DN6 . . . .**206** D5
York YO1 . . . .**233** A2
Station Rise YO1 . . . . . .**233** A2
Station Sq
🔺 Strensall YO32 . . . . . .**167** B7
🔺 Whitby YO21 . . . .**208** D6
Station Terr
🔺 Boroughbridge YO51 . .**141** B6
Great Preston WF10 . . . .**200** E6
Station View
Cliffe YO8 . . . .**198** D3
🔢 Harrogate HG1 . . . . . .**220** C4
Seamer YO12 . . . .**99** E7
🔢 Skipton BD23 . . . .**216** D3
Station Way YO17 . . . . .**215** C3
Staupes Rd HG3 . . . . . .**160** B4
Staveley Com Prim Sch
HG5 . . . .**140** E1
Staveley Nature Reserve★
HG5 . . . .**140** E2
Staxton Carr La YO12 . . . .**99** D3
Staxton Hill YO12 . . . . .**125** C8
Staynor Ave YO8 . . . . . .**232** E3
Stead La LS14 . . . .**188** A3
Stean La HG3 . . . .**110** A4
Steelmoor La YO60 . . . .**146** C2
Steeple Cl 🔺 YO12 . . . . .**166** D5
Steeton La LS24 . . . . . .**190** D7
Steeton Way LS25 . . . . .**195** F2
Steincroft Rd 🔺 LS25 . . .**195** F2
Stella Gdns WF8 . . . . . .**201** C1
Stelling Rd DL11 . . . .**38** E7
Stephen Bank DL11 . . . .**18** H8
Stephen Joseph Theatre★
YO11 . . . .**212** F5
Stephen's Wlk YO8 . . . .**232** B1
Stephenson Cl
Knaresborough HG5 . . . .**221** B4
York YO31 . . . .**225** E1
Stephenson Rd 🔢 DL10 . .**41** C2
Stephenson Way
YO26 . . . .**227** F5
Stephenson's La YO26 . .**164** A2

Stephensons Way
LS29 . . . .**218** C4
Stephenwath La YO41 . .**169** C5
Stepin Turn YO62 . . . . . .**49** B1
Stepney Ave YO12 . . . . .**212** C4
Stepney Cl YO12 . . . . . .**212** C5
Stepney Dr YO12 . . . . . .**212** C5
Stepney Gr YO12 . . . . . .**212** C5
Stepney Hill YO12 . . . . .**212** B3
Stepney Rd YO12 . . . . . .**212** D4
Stepney Rise YO12 . . . . .**212** D5
Sterling Pk YO30 . . . . . .**225** A3
Sterne Ave YO31 . . . . . .**229** A5
Sterne Way YO61 . . . . . .**144** C3
Steven Way HG4 . . . . . .**214** B6
Stevenson Pl HG5 . . . . .**220** F5
Steward Cl YO8 . . . .**197** D1
Stewart La YO19 . . . . . .**191** C4
Stillington Prim Sch
YO61 . . . .**144** C7
Stillington Rd
Easingwold YO61 . . . . . .**143** D8
Huby YO61 . . . .**144** A4
Stinton La
Boroughbridge YO51 . . . .**141** C4
Helperby YO61 . . . .**142** A8
Stirling Gr YO10 . . . . . .**231** F8
Stirling Rd
Burley in Warfedale
LS29 . . . .**176** B1
York YO30 . . . .**224** F3
Stirling Way TS17 . . . .**6** B6
Stirrup Cl Norton YO17 . .**215** C3
York YO24 . . . .**230** B8
Stirton La BD23 . . . .**216** C5
Stirtonber BD23 . . . .**216** E5
Stittenham Hill YO60 . . . .**5** B1
Stobarts La TS15 . . . .**5** B1
Stock Stile La 🔺 HG3 . . .**160** D5
Stockdale Cl 🔢 HG5 . . . .**221** B5
Stockdale Ct DL6 . . . . . .**210** F3
Stockdale Rd BD24 . . . .**131** C2
Stockdale Wlk HG5 . . . .**221** B5
Stockeld Rd LS29 . . . . . .**218** A4
Stockeld Way LS29 . . . . .**218** A5
Stockfield La YO51 . . . .**141** D2
Stockfield Pk House★
LS22 . . . .**179** F4
Stockhill Cl 🔢 YO19 . . . .**184** E7
Stockholm Cl 🔟 YO10 . .**231** D8
Stocking Hill TS9 . . . . . .**25** E2
Stocking La
Hambleton YO8 . . . .**196** E1
Hillam LS25 . . . .**202** B7
Knottingley WF11 . . . . . .**202** B2
Lotherton cum Aberford
LS25 . . . .**195** A7
Stockinger La LS29 . . . .**174** F4
Stockings La YO62 . . . . . .**92** F2
Stocks La 🔟 HG3 . . . . . .**160** A6
Stockshill YO12 . . . .**99** D6
Stockshott La BD20 . . . .**173** C2
Stockton Hall YO32 . . . .**167** D3
Stockton La
Heworth YO32 . . . .**226** D1
York YO31 . . . .**229** A7
Stockton on the Forest Prim
Sch YO32 . . . .**167** D3
Stockton Rd
Darlington DL1 . . . .**3** F7
Sadberge DL2 . . . .**4** C7
South Kilvington YO7 . . .**211** B6
Stockwell Ave
Ingleby TS17 . . . .**6** B5
Knaresborough HG5 . . . .**221** B7
Stockwell Cres 🔢 HG5 . .**221** B7
Stockwell Ct 🔢 HG5 . . . .**221** B6
Stockwell Dr HG5 . . . . . .**221** B7
Stockwell Gr HG5 . . . . . .**221** B7
Stockwell La HG5 . . . . . .**221** B6
Stockwell Pl HG5 . . . . . .**221** B7
Stockwell Rd HG5 . . . . . .**221** B7
Stockwell View HG5 . . . .**221** B7
Stockwith La YO8 . . . . . .**204** A4
Stokelake Rd 🔢 HG1 . . .**219** E3
Stokesley Com Prim Sch
TS9 . . . .**26** C7
Stokesley Ind Pk TS9 . . . .**26** D6
Stokesley Leisure Ctr
TS9 . . . .**26** D7
Stokesley Rd
Brompton DL6 . . . .**44** A3
Coulby Newham TS7 . . . . .**7** B7
Guisborough TS14 . . . . . .**8** C6
Middlesbrough TS7 . . . . . .**7** B6
Northallerton DL6 . . . . .**210** E7
Stokesley Sch TS9 . . . . . .**26** D7
Stone Bramble 🔢 HG3 . .**161** B3
Stone Bridge Dr YO41 . .**185** F5
Stone Ct 🔺 YO13 . . . .**75** D5
Stone Dale YO42 . . . . . .**170** D3
Stone Garth 🔢 YO62 . . . .**92** F6
Stone Gate YO26 . . . . . .**164** A4
Stone Head La BD22 . . . .**186** E6
Stone Man La DL11 . . . . .**19** C5
Stone Quarry Rd YO13 . . .**75** C8
Stone Riggs YO32 . . . . . .**167** D2
Stone Rings Cl HG2 . . . .**222** E5
Stone Rings Grange
HG2 . . . .**222** E5
Stone Rings La HG2 . . . .**222** E5
Stone Stoup Hill TS9 . . . .**27** C5
Stonebeck Ave HG1 . . . .**219** B4

Stonebeck Gate La
YO21 . . . . .29 D4
Stonebow The
Thornton-le-Beans DL6 . . . .65 B5
York YO1 . . . . .233 C2
Stonebridge Cres 2 TS17 .6 C6
Stonebridgegate HG4 .214 D5
Stonecrop Ave 5 HG4 .161 B3
Stonecrop Dr 1 HG3 .161 B3
Stonecross Rd YO21 . . .208 A6
Stoned Horse La
YO26 . . . . .164 C4
Stonefall Ave HG2 . . . .220 C3
Stonefall Dr HG2 . . . . .220 B2
Stonefall Mews HG2 . .220 C3
Stonefall Pl 2 HG2 . . .220 B2
Stonefield Ave YO61 . .143 C8
Stonefield Garth 9
YO61 . . . . .143 C8
Stonefield La 4 YO61 .143 C8
Stonegate
Hunmanby YO14 . . . . . . .126 F8
York YO1 . . . . .233 B3
Stonehaven Way DL1 . . .3 F8
Stonelands Ct 2 YO30 .225 A1
Stoneleigh Gate YO26 .164 B3
Stonepit Balk YO17 . . .149 C5
Stonepit Hill YO17 . . . .149 C4
Stonepit La
Birdsall YO17 . . . . .148 D1
Gristhorpe YO14 . . . . . . .100 E5
Stones Ct YO24 . . . . . .227 E2
Stonesdale Cl 3 HG5 .221 D5
Stonesdale La DL11 . . . .35 E8
Stonethwaite 5 YO24 .230 C7
Stoney Bank Rd BB18 .172 B1
Stoney Haggs Rd YO12 .99 E7
Stoneyborough Cl
YO7 . . . . .211 C4
Stoneybrough La YO7 .211 C4
Stony Cross YO62 . . . . .93 E7
Stony Ct YO13 . . . . .75 D5
Stony La
East Harlsey DL6 . . . . . . .44 F5
Scalby YO13 . . . . .75 D5
Stonygate Bank DL11 . .20 A5
Stooperdale Ave DL3 . . .3 B7
Stoopes Hill 8 BB18 . .172 B1
Storey Cl YO62 . . . . . . .92 F6
Storiths La BD23 . . . . .175 A8
Storking La YO41 . . . . .185 F6
Storr La YO13 . . . . .74 E5
Storth Gill La BD24 . . .131 A1
Stourton Rd LS29 . . . . .175 C3
Stow Ct YO32 . . . . .225 E3
Stps The LS22 . . . . . . .180 C2
Strafford Rd 14 DL10 . . .41 E4
Straight La
Addingham LS29 . . . . . . .174 E3
Aldwark YO61 . . . . .142 C3
Burton Leonard HG3 . . . . .140 A3
Holtby YO19 . . . . .184 F8
Middleham DL8 . . . . .60 F2
Straights The DL8 . . . . .58 C4
Strait La
Copt Hewick HG4 . . . . . . .114 B2
Danby YO21 . . . . .29 C6
Hurworth DL2 . . . . .3 F1
Stainton & Thornton TS8 . . .6 D5
Weeton LS17 . . . . .178 B2
Well DL8 . . . . .87 A3
Straits La YO13 . . . . . . .99 A3
Stranglands La WF11 .201 C3
Stratford Way YO32 . . .225 E3
Strathmore Dr 9 TS15 . .24 E8
Strathmore Rd LS29 . . .218 E4
Straw Gate DL2 . . . . . . .3 A2
Strawberry Fileds Prim Sch
LS25 . . . . .194 C3
Strawberry Ct YO12 . . .212 D4
Strawberry Dale HG1 .219 D3
Strawberry Dale Ave 3
HG1 . . . . .219 D3
Strawberry Dale Sq 1
HG1 . . . . .219 D3
Strawberry Dale Terr 2
HG1 . . . . .219 D3
Strawgate Gr DL2 . . . . . .3 A3
Stray Garth YO31 . . . . .228 F7
Stray Rd
Harrogate HG2 . . . . .222 D4
York YO31 . . . . .229 B6
Stray Rein HG2 . . . . . . .219 E1
Stray The Darlington DL1 . .3 E5
Henderskelfe YO60 . . . . . .146 D8
Longnewton TS21 . . . . .5 A7
Stray Wlk HG2 . . . . . . .222 D4
Straylands Gr YO31 . . .228 F8
Street 1 LS23 . . . . .189 A4
Street 2
Thorp Arch LS23 . . . . . . .181 A1
Walton LS23 . . . . .189 A8
Street 3 LS23 . . . . .181 A1
Street 5 LS23 . . . . .181 A1
Street 6 LS23 . . . . .181 A2
Street 7 LS23 . . . . .181 B1
Street 8 LS23 . . . . .181 B1
Street Head La BD22 . .187 F1
Street La Bewerley HG3 .137 A8
Bubwith YO8 . . . . .199 F5
Colton LS24 . . . . .190 D7
Glaisdale YO21 . . . . .29 C1
Middleton YO18 . . . . .95 E7
Pickhill with Roxby YO7 . . .88 B6

Street The 8 LS29 . . .174 E4
Strensall Comm Nature
Reserve★ YO60 . . . . . . .167 D8
Strensall Dr 11 YO12 . . .75 F5
Strensall Pk YO32 . . . .167 A5
Strensall Rd
Earswick YO32 . . . . .226 A7
York YO32 . . . . .225 F6
Stretton Cl WF7 . . . . . .200 D1
Strickland Rd 13 YO14 .127 A8
Strikes La BD20 . . . . . .187 F6
Stripe La
Hartwith cum Winsley
HG3 . . . . .160 B8
Skelton YO30 . . . . .224 B5
Stripe The 6 TS9 . . . . . .26 C7
Stuart Ave DL10 . . . . . .209 C8
Stuart Cl
4 Scarborough YO11 . . .100 B7
1 Strensall YO32 . . . . . .167 C8
Stuart Gr
Eggborough DN14 . . . . . .203 A2
1 Pontefract WF6 . . . . .200 A2
9 Thorpe Willoughby YO8 .197 B1
Stuart Rd YO24 . . . . . .227 D1
Stuart St
10 Barnoldswick BB18 . .171 E1
Pontefract WF8 . . . . .201 B1
Stubbing La BD23 . . . . .81 B1
Stubbing Nook La DL8 . .62 B2
Stubbs La
Cridling Stubbs WF11 . . . .206 A8
Norton DN6 . . . . .206 E2
Stainton Dale YO13 . . . . . .53 F5
Stubbs Rd DN6 . . . . . . .206 D3
Stubden Gr YO30 . . . . .224 F2
Stubham Rise LS29 . . .218 A5
Stud Fold Bank HG3 . . .110 B3
Studford Ring★ YO62 . .92 C2
Studley La HG4 . . . . . . .113 C1
Studley Rd
Harrogate HG1 . . . . .219 D3
Ripon HG4 . . . . .214 A4
Studley Roger HG4 . . . . . .113 C1
Studley Terr 15 YO22 .208 E6
Stump Cross Caverns★
HG3 . . . . .136 A2
Stumpcross Ct 14 WF8 .201 C2
Stumpcross La WF8 . . .201 C2
Stumpcross Mdws
WF8 . . . . .201 D1
Stumpcross Way 15
WF8 . . . . .201 C2
Stumps La HG3 . . . . . . .160 A5
Stunstead Rd BB8 . . . . .186 A1
Sturdee Gr YO31 . . . . . .228 D7
Sturdy House La
Marske DL11 . . . . .19 E2
Whashton DL11 . . . . .20 A4
Sturton Grange La
LS25 . . . . .194 D4
Sturton La LS25 . . . . . .194 D4
Stuteville Cl 4 YO62 . . .70 C1
Stutton Rd LS24 . . . . . .189 D4
Stygate La DN6 . . . . . . .206 E1
Sudforth La DN14 . . . . .202 C3
Suffield Hill YO13 . . . . .75 A5
Sugar Hill 9 LS29 . . . .174 F4
Sugar Loaf Ct 13 TS17 . .5 F4
Summer Hill Rd LS26 . .200 B6
Summerbridge Com Prim
Sch HG3 . . . . .138 A1
Summerfield BD23 . . . .172 A3
Summerfield Cl 1
WF11 . . . . .201 F4
Summerfield Dr WF11 .201 F4
Summerfield La YO22 . . .33 A7
Summerfield Rd YO24 .230 C7
Sun La LS29 . . . . .176 C1
Sun Lounge Theatre
YO14 . . . . .101 B3
Sun St Cononley BD20 . .173 C1
4 Cowling BD22 . . . . . .187 B6
Thornaby TS17 . . . . .6 A8
Sunderland Rd BD20 . . .173 E3
Sundew Heath 24 HG3 .161 B3
Sunmoor Dr BD23 . . . . .217 A4
Sunningdale LS25 . . . . .194 F4
Sunningdale Cl 1 YO26 .227 B5
Sunningdale Dr TS16 . . .5 E5
Sunningdale Gr 1
YO21 . . . . .208 B5
Sunningdales 27 WF6 .200 B1
Sunny Bank 3 WF11 . . .202 A2
Sunny Bank Rd 6 BD20 187 E7
Sunnybank Rd LS25 . . .195 A3
Sunnycrest Ave DL10 . .209 D8
Sunnydale 3 YO32 . . . .225 D7
Sunnyfield TS9 . . . . .7 C5
Sunnyside TS8 . . . . .7 D5
Sunnyside Prim Sch TS8 .7 A6
Sunset Dr LS29 . . . . . . .218 D5
Sunset Terr LS29 . . . . .218 E5
Sunstar Gr TS7 . . . . .7 B6
Sur Gate
Harwood Dale YO13 . . . . . .53 F1
Suffield-cum-Everley
YO13 . . . . .74 F8
Surrey Way YO30 . . . . .227 F8
Surtees St Darlington DL3 . .3 C6
York YO30 . . . . .228 B7
Sussex Cl Bedale DL8 . . .63 A2
York YO10 . . . . .229 C2
Sussex Ct 10 DL9 . . . . .209 C1
Sussex Rd YO10 . . . . . .229 C2
Sussex St Bedale DL8 . . .63 A2
14 Scarborough YO11 . . .213 A6

Sussex Way 14 YO32 . .167 A7
Sutcliffe Ct 6 YO21 . . .208 B6
Sutcliffe Gall★ YO21 .208 D7
Sutherland Rd YO18 . . . .71 C6
Sutherland St YO23 . . .228 B1
Sutor Cl YO23 . . . . .230 B3
Sutton Ave 7 DL9 . . . . .41 A5
Sutton Bank YO7 . . . . . .91 A5
Sutton Bank Visitor Ctr★
YO7 . . . . .91 B6
Sutton Bridge★ YO41 .185 C2
Sutton Ct 5 YO7 . . . . . .211 C3
Sutton Dr DL7 . . . . .210 C2
Sutton Grange Cl HG3 .219 B4
Sutton in Craven CE VC Prim
Sch 39 BD20 . . . . .187 F7
Sutton in Craven Com Prim
Sch 38 BD20 . . . . .187 F7
Sutton La Byram WF11 .201 E4
Byram cum Sutton
WF11 . . . . .202 A4
Ellington High & Low HG4 . .86 A5
Fearby HG4 . . . . .85 F4
Steeton with Eastburn
BD20 . . . . .187 F7
Sutton Pk★ YO61 . . . . .114 C3
Sutton Rd YO7 . . . . .211 E3
Sutton St YO7 . . . . .211 C3
Sutton upon Derwent CE VC
Prim Sch YO41 . . . . . .185 C2
Sutton Way
Middlesbrough TS4 . . . . . . .6 F8
York YO30 . . . . .228 B8
Sutton-on-the-Forest CE
Prim Sch YO61 . . . . . .144 C3
Sutton-under-
Whitestonecliffe
CE VC Prim Sch YO7 . . .90 E5
Swadford St BD23 . . . . .216 F4
Swain Ct DL6 . . . . .210 D5
Swainby & Potto CE Prim Sch
DL6 . . . . .45 D8
Swainby Abbey★ DL8 . .88 B8
Swainby Ellers DL6 . . . .25 D1
Swainby La DL8 . . . . . . .87 F7
Swainsea Dr 3 YO18 . . .95 F7
Swainsea La YO18 . . . . .95 F8
Swainstead Raike
BD24 . . . . .153 B8
Swainston Ct TS5 . . . . . .6 E7
Swale App 25 WF6 . . . .200 B1
Swale Ave YO24 . . . . . .230 E8
Swale Hall La DL11 . . . .38 B5
Swale La Catterick DL10 .41 E5
Pickhill with Roxby YO7 . . .88 C7
Swale Pasture La DL10 .41 E5
Swale View YO7 . . . . . . .41 A5
Swaledale Ave DL3 . . . . .3 B6
Swaledale Folk Mus★
DL11 . . . . .38 C6
Swaledale Rd 22 DL9 . . .40 E4
Swalegate DL10 . . . . . .209 C8
Swallow Cl TS14 . . . . . . .8 D6
Swallows The 3 YO32 .167 B8
Swan Cl YO19 . . . . .192 A7
Swan Farm Ct YO19 . . .192 A7
Swan Hill Rd YO11 . . . .213 A6
Swan La YO7 . . . . .65 F2
Swan Rd HG1 . . . . .219 C2
Swan St BD23 . . . . .173 B4
Swan Syke Dr 8 DN6 . .206 F2
Swang Rd YO13 . . . . . . .75 A6
Swanhills La YO13 . . . . .98 F3
Swanland Rd YO62 . . . . .92 F7
Swann St YO23 . . . . . . .233 A1
Swarcliffe Rd HG1 . . . . .220 B4
Swartha La BD20 . . . . . .174 D2
Swarthlands La YO13 . . .75 D7
Sweeming La LS25 . . . . .196 C5
Sweet Bits La HG5 . . . . .221 C8
Sweet Briar HG5 . . . . . .219 A4
Sweetbecks Cl 12 YO11 .100 A6
Swillington La LS26 . . . .194 A2
Swillington Prim Sch
LS26 . . . . .194 A1
Swinburn Ct 4 HG4 . . . .86 C3
Swinburn Rd 11 HG4 . . .86 C3
Swinburne Cl HG1 . . . . .219 E7
Swinburne Rd TS16 . . . .5 E6
Swincliffe La HG3 . . . . .160 D5
Swindale La TS12 . . . . . .9 F5
Swindon La HG3 . . . . . .178 E4
Swinegate YO1 . . . . . . .233 B2
Swinegate Ct E YO1 . . .233 B3
Swineherd La YO62 . . . .70 C1
Swinneybeck Bank
HG4 . . . . .85 E5
Swinsty Ct YO30 . . . . . .224 F1
Swinton Cl HG2 . . . . . . .222 B8
Swinton La YO17 . . . . . .121 B3
Swinton Rd HG4 . . . . . . .86 C3
Swinton Terr HG4 . . . . . .86 C3
Swire Way DL10 . . . . . . .20 F7
Swires La BD23 . . . . . . .173 C3
Swordfish Way LS25 . . .196 B4
Sycamore Ave
4 Catton YO7 . . . . .89 A1
Filey YO14 . . . . .101 A4
Kippax LS25 . . . . .194 C1
Knottingley WF11 . . . . . . .201 E1
Malton YO17 . . . . .215 D5
Richmond DL10 . . . . .209 A8
York YO32 . . . . .225 D4
Sycamore Cl
Bishop Monkton HG3 . . . .140 A5
Clint HG3 . . . . .160 F8
1 Haxby YO32 . . . . .225 D7
3 Hurworth-on-Tees DL2 . .3 E1

Sycamore Cl *continued*
Selby YO8 . . . . .232 A4
Skelton YO30 . . . . .224 C5
Slingsby YO62 . . . . .120 B5
Spennithorne DL8 . . . . . . .60 F4
Sycamore Ct
2 Catterick DL10 . . . . . .41 D5
Hellifield BD23 . . . . .154 B3
2 Pontefract WF8 . . . . .201 C1
Sycamore Dr
11 Addingham LS29 . . . .175 A4
9 Bedale DL8 . . . . .63 A2
Harrogate HG2 . . . . .220 C3
Norton-le-Clay YO7 . . . . . .115 B1
Sycamore Gr
Sherburn YO17 . . . . .124 E7
Steeton with Eastburn
BD20 . . . . .187 F7
Sycamore La DL7 . . . . . .63 D4
Sycamore Pl
New Earswick YO32 . . . . .225 D4
York YO30 . . . . .233 A3
Sycamore Rd
Barlby with Osgodby
YO8 . . . . .198 B5
Ripon HG4 . . . . .214 B2
Sycamore Terr YO30 . . .233 A3
Sycamore View 17 YO26 .165 F1
Sycamore Way 16 BB18 .171 D1
Sydall's Way 1 DL10 . . .41 E4
Sydney Ave E DL6 . . . . .210 E4
Sydney St 5 YO12 . . . .212 F7
Sykehead La YO62 . . . . .93 D6
Sykes Barrel 3 BD24 . .131 D3
Sykes Gr HG1 . . . . .219 C5
Sykes La YO61 . . . . . . .143 B3

T

Tabard Hamlet 5 DN14 .202 F2
Tabard Rd 6 DN14 . . . .202 F2
Tabards The 7 DN14 . . .202 F2
Tadcaster E Com Prim Sch 6
LS24 . . . . .189 F6
Tadcaster Gram Sch
LS24 . . . . .189 B5
Tadcaster Leisure Ctr
LS24 . . . . .189 E6
Tadcaster Rd YO24 . . . .227 F1
Tadcaster Rd Dringhouses
YO23 . . . . .230 E5
Tadcaster Sports & Leisure
Ctr LS24 . . . . .189 E6
Talbenny Gr 32 TS17 . . .5 F4
Talbot Ct YO22 . . . . . . .208 E5
Talbot St WF6 . . . . .200 A1
Talisman Cl 9 TS16 . . . .5 D5
Tally Hill YO61 . . . . . . .144 A4
Talybont Gr 19 TS17 . . .5 F4
Tameside TS9 . . . . .26 C8
Tamworth Rd 9 YO30 . .225 A1
Tanfield Dr 1 LS29 . . . .176 C1
Tanfield La HG4 . . . . . . .114 A8
Tang Hall La YO31 . . . . .229 A5
Tang Hall Prim Sch
YO31 . . . . .228 F5
Tang Rd HG3 . . . . .160 D4
Tanner Row YO1 . . . . . .233 A2
Tanner's Moat YO1 . . . .233 A2
Tannery Ct 10 HG5 . . . .221 B5
Tannery La DL7 . . . . . . .210 D5
Tanpit La
Easingwold YO61 . . . . . . .143 C8
Walden Stubbs DN6 . . . . .206 E3
Tanshelf Sta WF8 . . . . .201 A1
Tansy Cl 2 HG3 . . . . . .161 B3
Tansy Rd 3 HG3 . . . . . .161 B3
Tanton Rd TS9 . . . . .7 B1
Tarbard Ave 14 HG4 . . .113 D2
Tarbert Cres 2 YO24 . .230 B7
Tarn Ct LS29 . . . . .218 C4
Tarn Moor Cres BD23 . .216 E6
Tarr Stps TS17 . . . . .6 A3
Tasmania Sq TS7 . . . . . .7 C6
Tate Cl YO8 . . . . .197 D6
Tate Hill YO22 . . . . .208 D7
Tate Rd DL10 . . . . .209 C8
Tatefield Pl 1 LS25 . . . .194 D1
Tatham Fells Sch LA2 . .128 F3
Tatton Cl YO30 . . . . . . .225 A1
Taurus Cl YO23 . . . . . . .233 A1
Taylor Gr LS26 . . . . . . .200 C6
Taylor Hill YO18 . . . . . . .71 F4
Taylor La LS15 . . . . .194 A7
Taylor St 8 BB18 . . . . .171 D1
Taylorsons Terr 2
YO22 . . . . .208 E6
Teal Cl Castleford WF10 .200 E3
2 Filey YO14 . . . . .101 A4
Teal Dr YO24 . . . . .230 C8
Teal La YO18 . . . . .95 F7
Teal Rd DL1 . . . . .3 E5
Tebay Cl YO7 . . . . .211 C2
Tebay St YO7 . . . . .7 D8
Tedder Ave TS17 . . . . . . .6 B6
Tedder Prim Sch TS17 . . .6 B6
Tedder Rd YO24 . . . . . .227 B1
Tedworth Cl TS14 . . . . . .8 F5
Tees Bank Ave TS18 . . . .5 E6
Tees Cottage Pumping Sta &
Mus★ DL3 . . . . .2 F4
Tees Grange Ave DL3 . . .3 A5
Tees View Gainford DL2 . .1 D7
Hurworth DL2 . . . . .3 C1
Hurworth-on-Tees DL2 . . . .22 C8
Teesdale Ave DL3 . . . . . .3 A4

Teesdale Rd DL9 . . . . . .40 E4
Teesgate TS17 . . . . .6 C8
Teeside Tertiary Coll
TS4 . . . . .7 B8
Teesside High Sch TS16 . .5 E5
Teesside Ind Est TS17 . . .6 C5
Teeswater Dr 12 DL3 . . .3 A7
Teesway DL2 . . . . .4 A1
Telford Cl WF10 . . . . . .200 D4
Telford Terr 1 YO24 . . .228 B2
Templar Cl DN14 . . . . . .202 F1
Templar Gdns LS22 . . . .180 C4
Templar Way YO30 . . . .232 C2
Temple Ave YO10 . . . . .229 B4
Temple Bank DL8 . . . . . .59 A3
Temple Ct DL10 . . . . . .209 B6
Temple Garth YO23 . . . .230 C1
Temple La
Burton cum Walden DL8 . . .82 D3
Copmanthorpe YO23 . . . . .230 C1
Temple Manor★ YO8 .203 D4
Temple Rd YO23 . . . . . .230 F4
Temple Sq DL10 . . . . . .209 B6
Temple St WF10 . . . . . .200 F4
Templeford Half Acres Jun &
Inf Sch WF10 . . . . .200 E4
Templemead YO31 . . . . .228 E8
Tems Side 3 BD24 . . . .131 D2
Tems St 2 BD24 . . . . . .131 D2
Ten Thorn La YO26 . . . .227 A4
Tennant St YO8 . . . . . . .232 B6
Tennent Rd YO24 . . . . .227 B2
Tennis Ct La YO61 . . . .143 A3
Tennyson Ave
1 Campsall DN6 . . . . . .206 E1
Harrogate HG1 . . . . .219 E7
Scarborough YO12 . . . . . .212 F7
York YO30 . . . . .228 C7
Tennyson Way 3 WF8 .201 B1
Tenter Fields YO7 . . . . . .88 D1
Tenter Hill LS23 . . . . . .188 D5
Tentergate Ave 4 HG5 .221 A7
Tentergate Cl 3 HG5 . . .221 A7
Tentergate Gdns 2
HG5 . . . . .221 A7
Tentergate La HG5 . . . .221 A7
Tentergate Rd 5 HG5 . .221 A7
Tenters Cl WF11 . . . . . .201 E3
Tern Pk 6 LS22 . . . . . . .180 A1
Terrington Bank YO60 .119 C2
Terrington CE VA Prim Sch
YO60 . . . . .119 E1
Terrington Cl 1 YO32 . .167 B8
Terrington Hall Sch
YO60 . . . . .119 F1
Terrington S Bank
YO60 . . . . .119 D1
Terrington View YO60 .145 C5
Terror Twr★ YO11 . . . . .213 B6
Terry Ave YO1 . . . . .233 B1
Terry St YO23 . . . . .228 C1
Tetherings La YO13 . . . .98 F5
Tewit Well Ave HG2 . . . .222 D8
Tewit Well Rd HG2 . . . . .222 F4
Thackadale La YO17 . . .121 A1
Thackeray Gr TS5 . . . . . .6 F8
Thacking La LA6 . . . . . .103 D4
Thames Ave
Guisborough TS14 . . . . . . .8 E6
Thornaby TS17 . . . . .6 B7
Thanet Rd YO24 . . . . . .227 D1
Thanets Ct 9 BD23 . . . .216 F3
Thatch Cl YO8 . . . . .232 C4
Thatchers Croft YO23 . .230 C3
Theakston Hargill DL8 . .87 E8
Theakston La DL10 . . . .209 C5
Theresa Cl YO31 . . . . . .225 F1
Thickrash Brow LA2 . . .129 A7
Thief La Barlow YO8 . . .232 F1
York YO10 . . . . .228 F3
Thiefgate La YO61 . . . . .86 C3
Thiefhole La DL7 . . . . . .65 B3
Third Ave
10 Wetherby LS22 . . . .180 C3
York YO31 . . . . .228 F5
Thirkleby Way YO10 . . .229 C4
Thirlby Way 8 TS14 . . . .8 F7
Thirlmere Cl 3 YO7 . . . .89 C4
Thirlmere Dr YO31 . . . .229 A6
Thirlway Dr HG4 . . . . . .214 B2
Thirsk Bank
Angram Grange YO61 . . . .117 B8
Thornton-le-Moor DL7 . . . .65 B3
Thirsk Bsns Pk YO7 . . .211 B2
Thirsk Com Prim Sch
YO7 . . . . .211 C4
Thirsk Ind Pk YO7 . . . . .211 D2
Thirsk Mus★ YO7 . . . . .211 B3
Thirsk Racecourse★
YO7 . . . . .211 A3
Thirsk Rd
Eaglescliffe TS15 . . . . .5 E2
Easingwold YO61 . . . . . . .117 B1
Kirkby TS9 . . . . .26 C6
Romanby DL6 . . . . .210 F1
Thirsk Sch & Sixth Form Coll
YO7 . . . . .211 B4
Thirsk Sta YO7 . . . . .89 D4
Thirsk Swimming Pool
YO7 . . . . .211 C2
Thirty Acre La HG5 . . . .163 A6
Thirwall Dr TS17 . . . . . . .6 A4
Thistle Cl
Northallerton DL7 . . . . . . .210 D1
Selby YO8 . . . . .232 C2
Thistle Hill HG5 . . . . . . .221 B3
Thistle Rise TS8 . . . . . . .6 F6
Thistlebar Rd YO51 . . . .141 D2

Thomas Chippendale Prim Sch LS21 ...176 F1
Thomas Gill Rd **7** HG3 .137 F1
Thomas St **6** Selby YO8 .232 D6
2 York YO10 ...228 E3
Thomason Cl YO22 ...31 C1
Thomason Foss (Waterfall)★ YO22 ...31 C1
Thompson Cl
9 Barlby YO8 ...198 B4
29 Scalby YO12 ...75 D5
Thompson Dr **2** YO32 ..167 B8
Thompson Pl **6** YO26 ..227 E5
Thompson St E DL1 ...3 D7
Thompson St W DL3 ...3 C5
Thoresby La DL8 ...59 B5
Thoresby Rd YO24 ...227 B1
Thorington Gdns TS17 ...6 B4
Thorn Nook YO31 ...228 F8
Thorn Tree Ave **4** YO14 101 B4
Thorn Wath La YO62 ...48 E4
Thornaby Com Sch TS17 .6 B7
Thornaby Rd TS17 ...6 B7
Thornaby Swimming Baths TS17 ...6 A4
Thornaby Village Prim Sch TS17 ...6 B7
Thornborough Cres **4** DL8 ...60 D5
Thornbrough Rd DL6 .210 E3
Thornburgh Rd **6** YO11 ..99 F6
Thorncroft **8** YO19 ..184 F7
Thorndale St BD23 ...154 B3
Thornden Bldgs YO8 .232 D5
Thorndikes La HG5 ...141 D3
Thorne Cl **18** WF6 ...200 B1
Thorner CE Prim Sch LS14 ...188 A3
Thorner Gr BD20 ...174 C2
Thorner La LS23 ...188 B5
Thorner Rd LS23 ...188 B4
Thornfield Ave
Dishforth YO7 ...115 A4
5 York YO31 ...228 F8
Thornfield Bsns Pk DL7 ...210 B6
Thornfield Dr **7** DL8 ...225 E2
Thornfield Gr TS5 ...6 E8
Thornfield Rd DL8 ...87 C3
Thornhill
6 Eastfield YO11 ..100 A6
Northallerton DL6 ...209 B6
Richmond DL10 ...209 B6
Thornhill Rd WF10 ...200 F3
Thornhills **19** YO32 ...166 F5
Thornlands **9** YO61 ...117 D1
Thornley Ave DL7 ...210 D3
Thorns La YO51 ...140 F4
Thornthwaite Brow HG3 ...159 E5
Thornton Cl
15 Easingwold YO61 ..143 D8
Stainton & Thornton TS8 ..6 D4
Thornton Dale CE VC Prim Sch YO18 ...96 C5
Thornton La Dent LA10 ..78 A4
Marishes YO17 ...96 B1
Thornton in Lonsdale LA6 ...103 C4
Thornton-on-the-Hill YO61 ...117 D4
Thornton Moor Cl YO30 ...224 F2
Thornton Rd
Coulby Newham TS8 ...6 D4
Pickering YO18 ...96 A6
Thornton St
14 Burley in Warfedale LS29 ...176 C1
Darlington DL3 ...3 C5
3 Skipton BD23 ...216 D3
Thornton Vale TS8 ...6 E4
Thornton Watlass CE Prim Sch HG4 ...86 D8
Thornton-in-Craven Com Prim Sch BD23 ...172 A3
Thorntree Gdns DL2 ...4 C4
Thorntree Gr YO30 ...225 B2
Thorntree La DN14 ...207 C6
Thorntree Rd
Northallerton DL6 ...210 F6
Thornaby TS17 ...6 B7
Thornview Rd DL3 ...154 B3
Thornwood Ave TS17 ...6 A5
Thornwood Covert **1** YO24 ...227 C1
Thorny Hill La YO51 ...141 E2
Thorny La YO42 ...169 F2
Thorp Arch Pk LS23 ...180 F1
Thorp Arch Trad Est LS23 ...189 A8
Thorp Perrow Arboretum & Falconry Ctr★ DL8 ..87 A4
Thorpe Bassett La YO17 ...122 E1
Thorpe Chase HG4 ...214 E3
Thorpe Gn Bank **1** YO22 33 C3
Thorpe Gn La YO26 ...164 B7
Thorpe La
Ampleforth YO62 ...118 B8
Cawood YO8 ...197 B8
Cracoe BD23 ...156 C2
Fylingdales YO22 ...33 C4
Thorpe BD23 ...156 D8
Thorpe Prebend House - Heritage Ctr★ HG4 ..214 E5
Thorpe Rd HG4 ...86 C2
Thorpe St YO23 ...228 B2

Thorpe Willoughby CP Sch YO8 ...197 B2
Threapland BD23 ...156 C7
Three Lakes Ind Est YO8 ...232 D2
Three Lakes Ret Pk YO8 ...232 D3
Three Tuns Wynd **7** TS9 .26 C7
Threshfield Prim Sch BD23 ...134 D2
Thrintoft La DL7 ...64 A7
Thrintoft Moor La DL7 ..64 A8
Thrope La HG3 ...110 C4
Throstle Farm Sch WF11 ...201 F1
Throstle Nest Cl LS21 ..176 E1
Throstle Nest Dr HG2 .222 D6
Throxenby Gr **3** YO12 .212 B7
Throxenby La YO12 ...212 B7
Thruscross La HG3 ...159 B5
Thrussendale Rd YO17 ...169 E8
Thunderhead Ridge WF10 ...200 F3
Thurland Castle★ LA6 .102 B3
Thurston Rd DL6 ...210 C7
Thwaite Holme La DL8 ..57 F5
Thwaite La LA2 ...128 E5
Thwaites Ave LS29 ...218 C4
Thwaites La
Markington with Wallerthwaite HG3 ...139 D5
Nether Silton YO7 ...66 C7
Thirkleby High & Low with Osgodby YO7 ...90 E1
Thweng Way TS14 ...8 E5
Thwing Rd YO25 ...126 E2
Tib Garth LS22 ...180 A2
Tibby Butts **26** YO13 ...75 D5
Tickergate La DL7 ...63 A8
Tile Cl BD23 ...217 B3
Tillman Cl **6** BD24 ..131 D2
Tilmire Cl **2** YO10 ..231 F8
Timble Gr HG1 ...219 B5
Timmys La DL2 ...3 F1
Tindall St YO12 ...212 F5
Tinker La YO23 ...182 D6
Tinkers' La HG3 ...139 A1
Tinkingfield La LS22 ..181 A5
Tinkler La Milby YO51 .141 C6
Winsley HG3 ...160 E8
Tinkler's La WF11 ...202 D6
Tinley Garth YO62 ...70 B1
Tinley Gdns **3** YO62 ...70 B1
Tintagel Ct WF6 ...200 A2
Tiplady Cl **18** YO61 ..143 C8
Tippaty La WF11 ...202 A4
Tirril Way TS7 ...7 C5
Tithe Barn Fold LS15 ..194 B8
Tithe Barn Rd **2** WF11 .202 A2
Tithe Barn Way DN14 .202 F3
Tithe Cl YO24 ...227 B1
Tithe La WF4 ...114 F1
Tivoli Pl LS29 ...218 C3
Toadham La DN14 ...207 C5
Toby Ct YO32 ...167 A7
Toc La YO51 ...97 C5
Tockwith CE VC Prim Sch YO26 ...181 C7
Tockwith La YO26 ...181 D5
Tockwith Rd
Long Marston YO26 ...181 F6
Tockwith LS22 ...180 F7
Tod Holes La BD23 ...153 B4
Todd La DL7 ...63 B8
Todds Ct **8** YO7 ...211 C3
Todley Hall Rd BD22 ..187 F3
Todmanhaw La BD23 ..153 E3
Trafford Ct **19** DL1 ...3 C6
Toft Gn YO1 ...233 A2
Toft Ings La YO61 ...143 B8
Tofta Rd YO13 ...54 A5
Tofting La YO17 ...148 B5
Tofts Cl TS15 ...24 B8
Tofts Fort The★ DL11 ....1 D2
Tofts La Danby YO21 ...29 B5
Follifoot HG3 ...223 F4
Humberton YO61 ...141 F4
Pickering YO18 ...95 F3
Tholthorpe YO61 ...142 D6
Welbury DL6 ...24 B1
Tofts Rd YO18 ...95 F3
Toll Bar Cl **3** YO8 ...196 E1
Toll Bar Rd WF10 ...200 C4
Toll Bar Way LS24 ...189 F7
Tollergate YO11 ...213 A7
Tollerton Rd YO30 ...165 B7
Tollesby La TS7 ...7 B6
Tollesby Rd TS5 ...6 F8
Tom Cat La
Bilton-in-Ainsty with Bickerton LS22 ...181 A5
Birdsall YO17 ...148 B4
Tom Dando Cl WF6 ...200 C1
Tom Hall Ct **12** DL8 ...63 A2
Tom La Cowling BD22 ..186 E7
Dunsforths YO26 ...141 F3
Tom Smith's Cross YO62 ...92 B4
Tomahawk Trail WF10 .200 F3
Tomgill Bank DL8 ...58 E2
Tomlinson Way LS25 ..195 E4
Top Fold WF11 ...201 D6
Top House Farm Mews **2** WF11 ...201 D6
Top La Colne BB8 ...186 B3
Copmanthorpe YO23 ...230 B3
Norwood LS21 ...177 A6

Top Stone Cl LS25 ...201 F6
Topcliff Ct YO8 ...232 B7
Topcliffe CE VC Prim Sch YO7 ...115 C7
Topcliffe Rd
Sowerby YO7 ...89 C3
Thirsk YO7 ...211 B1
Thornaby TS17 ...6 C7
Toremill Cl YO32 ...225 D4
Torrance Dr DL1 ...3 F8
Torridon Pl YO24 ...230 B7
Torrs Rd HG1 ...220 A3
Tostig Ave YO26 ...227 C5
Tostig Cl **14** YO41 ..168 D2
Toulston La LS23 ...188 F5
Tout Hill YO60 ...146 E5
Tow Scar Rd LA6 ...103 C5
Tow Top La BD23 ...173 A1
Tower Cres LS24 ...189 D6
Tower Croft **7** YO61 ..117 D1
Tower Pl YO1 ...233 B1
Tower Rd Darlington DL3 ...3 B8
Ripon HG4 ...214 C6
Tower St
Harrogate HG1 ...219 D1
10 Richmond DL10 ...209 C6
York YO1 ...233 B1
Tower St Castle W **4** DL10 ...209 C6
Tower The★ YO18 ...139 B6
Tower View DN14 ...204 C2
Towers Paddock WF10 ...201 A4
Town End YO7 ...211 B2
Town End Ave DN14 ...204 C3
Town End Cl
16 Glusburn BD20 ...187 E7
9 Pickering YO18 ...96 A6
Town End Gdns **3** YO32 ...166 D5
Town Farm Cl **16** YO62 ..70 B1
Town Gn Dr TS9 ...26 E5
Town Head Ave **1** BD24 ...131 E2
Town Head Way **14** BD24 ...131 D2
Town Hill LS23 ...188 E5
Town St
Bishop Thornton HG3 ...138 F1
Brandsby-cum-Stearsby YO61 ...118 D3
Malton YO17 ...215 E6
Nidd HG3 ...161 E7
Scampston YO17 ...123 A6
Settrington YO17 ...123 A6
Townclose View LS25 ..200 C8
Townend LS25 ...164 A8
Townend Pl **5** BD20 ..187 E7
Townend Rd YO42 ...193 D1
Townend St YO31 ...233 B4
Townhead **2** BD24 ...131 E2
Townhead Fold **12** LS29 .174 F4
Townhead La LA2 ...130 E8
Towthorpe Moor La YO32 ...167 C5
Towthorpe Rd YO32 ..166 F5
Towton Ave **9** YO24 ..227 F5
Trafalgar Ct **10** HG1 ..219 D1
Trafalgar Rd
11 Harrogate HG1 ...219 D1
Ilkley LS29 ...218 B4
Scarborough YO12 ...212 F7
Trafalgar Sq YO12 ...212 F7
Trafalgar St YO23 ...228 B1
Trafalgar St W YO12 ...212 F7
Trafalgar Terr YO12 ...212 F7
Trafford Rd **4** DN6 ...206 E2
Train La **14** YO18 ...95 F7
Tranby Ave YO10 ...229 D4
Tranmire Cl YO7 ...211 D4
Tranmore La DN14 ...203 B3
Trans Wlk LS24 ...190 B1
Tranter Rd TS4 ...6 F8
Trapping Hill HG3 ...110 C4
Trattles Hill YO13 ...54 F2
Travellers Garth YO17 .121 C1
Trawden Forest Prim Sch **4** BB8 ...186 A1
Trawden Rd BB8 ...186 A3
Treasurer's House★ YO31 ...233 B3
Trecastell **25** TS17 ...5 F4
Treesdale Rd **1** HG2 ..219 C1
Trefoil Cl TS14 ...8 D6
Trefoil Dr **4** HG3 ...161 B3
Trefoil Wood TS7 ...7 B7
Trencar La YO61 ...91 A2
Trenchard Ave TS17 ...6 B6
Trenchard St **8** YO7 ...89 B1
Trenfield Ct YO24 ...227 F3
Trenholme Cl **7** TS17 ...5 D6
Trenholme La TS15 ...25 B3
Trent Ave
Garforth LS25 ...194 D3
Pontefract WF6 ...200 A2
4 York YO32 ...225 F6
Trent Way YO24 ...230 D7
Trentholme Dr **2** YO24 .228 A2
Trevine Gdns TS17 ...5 F4
Trevino Ct TS16 ...5 E5
Trevithick Cl **7** TS16 ...5 D5
Trevor Gr **8** YO24 ...227 F2
Tribune Way YO30 ...225 B2
Trimdon Ave TS5 ...6 D6

Trinity Church Sq **9** DL10 ...209 C6
Trinity Cl **1** YO11 ...212 F3
Trinity Gdns **2** YO11 .212 F3
Trinity La Ripon HG4 ...214 B5
York YO1 ...233 A2
Trinity Mews DL3 ...3 C5
Trinity Pk YO8 ...232 B7
Trinity Rd Darlington DL3 ...3 C5
Harrogate HG2 ...219 D1
Scarborough YO11 ...212 F3
Trinket La LA2 ...128 B6
Trip Garth LS22 ...180 A1
Trip La Collingham LS22 .180 A1
Sicklinghall LS22 ...179 F1
Triplins La HG4 ...113 B6
Tristram Ave DL3 ...3 C7
Troon Cl **2** YO26 ...227 B5
Trousdale Hill YO60 ...147 A7
Troutbeck **7** YO24 ...230 C7
Troutbeck Cl **11** YO18 ..95 F6
Troutsdale Ave YO30 ..224 E2
Trumfleet La DN6 ...207 D1
Trundles La **7** WF11 ..202 A2
Truro Cres **8** HG3 ...161 B3
Truro Dr **19** WF6 ...200 A2
Truro Rd **7** HG3 ...161 B3
Truro Wlk **28** HG3 ...200 A2
Trust Fold LS25 ...201 E6
Tubwell Rd DL1 ...3 C5
Tucker Cl **10** YO8 ...197 B1
Tudor Cl **10** YO8 ...197 B1
Tudor Rd
Richmond DL10 ...209 D7
York YO24 ...227 C2
Tudor Way YO32 ...167 C8
Tufton Pl BD23 ...216 F3
Tuke Ave YO10 ...229 B4
Tumbledown Cl **5** DL9 .40 E4
Tune St **9** YO8 ...198 B4
Tunstall Rd
Catterick DL10 ...41 D4
Harrogate HG2 ...220 B3
Turbary La YO32 ...226 E6
Turbary Rd LA6 ...103 B7
Turfy Hill DL8 ...56 C4
Turker Cl DL6 ...210 E5
Turker La DL6 ...210 F6
Turkey La Baldersby YO7 .88 D1
Catton YO7 ...114 F8
Turks Head Ct YO1 ...233 C3
Turnberry Ave TS16 ...5 E4
Turnberry Dr YO26 ...227 B4
Turnberry Way TS8 ...7 C5
Turner Cl DL9 ...209 C2
Turner Cres **6** LS21 ..177 A1
Turner La LS29 ...174 E4
Turner St **13** BB18 ...171 E1
Turner's Croft YO10 ...229 A1
Turners Sq **9** YO8 ...232 C5
Turnham La YO8 ...198 C2
Turnhead Cres YO8 ...198 B5
Turnhead Ct YO8 ...198 B6
Turnmire Rd **1** YO7 ...230 E8
Turnpike La LS22 ...181 B5
Turnpike Rd LS24 ...189 F7
Turnshaw Rd BD22 ...187 F1
Turpin Ct YO1 ...233 C1
Turpin La LS25 ...196 A2
Turton Rd TS15 ...5 D2
Turver's La WF11 ...202 A3
Tuscany Way WF6 ...200 A3
Tuthill **13** YO11 ...213 B6
Tutin Rd DL7 ...63 C5
Tweed Ave TS17 ...6 B6
Twelve Acre Bank DL8 ...40 E1
Twin Pike Way **14** YO32 .166 E5
Twine Wlk **7** LA6 ...102 F3
Twizzie Gill View **6** TS13 ...11 A8
Two Laws Rd BB8 ...187 B1
Tyler Cl WF6 ...200 C1
Tyn Garth YO19 ...191 D8
Tyne Cres DL1 ...3 D3
Typhoon Cl DL10 ...41 F6
Tyseley Gr **4** BB18 ...172 A1
Tyson Pl HG2 ...220 B2

U

Uldale Cl **5** HG5 ...221 D5
Uldale Dr TS16 ...5 E4
Ulla Gn LS24 ...190 B2
Ulleskelf Sta LS24 ...190 B2
Ullswater YO24 ...230 D7
Ullswater Ave TS5 ...6 E8
Ullswater Dr LS22 ...180 A3
Ullswater Rise **5** LS22 .180 B3
Ulnaby La DL2 ...2 C7
Under Cliffe **17** YO19 ..95 F7
Undercliffe Rise LS29 ..218 E2
Undercroft **7** YO19 ...184 F7
Underlands La HG4 ...114 C2
Underwit Rd YO8 ...204 C4
Union House BD23 ...217 A3
Union La YO8 ...232 C4
Union St **28** Filey YO14 ..101 B3
Harrogate HG1 ...219 D3
2 Knaresborough HG5 .221 A5
12 Scarborough YO11 .213 A6
Union Terr
5 Skipton BD23 ...216 F3
York YO31 ...233 B4
Unity Cl HG1 ...219 D5
Unity Gr HG1 ...219 D5
Unity St **1** BB18 ...186 A7

University Coll of Scarborough YO12 ...213 B1
University of York
Heslington YO10 ...228 F1
York YO10 ...233 A3
University Rd YO10 ...228 F2
Upgang La YO21 ...208 B7
Upgarth Cl **2** TS13 ...12 A7
Uplands BD23 ...217 B5
Uplands Ave **8** YO13 ...99 B8
Uplands Rd DL3 ...3 B5
Uplands The YO12 ...212 A7
Upper Carr La YO18 ...96 A4
Upper Dunsforth Carrs Nature Reserve★ YO26 ...142 A1
Upper Gn La TS18 ...6 A7
Upper Hanover St **6** YO26 ...227 F5
Upper Newborough St **1** YO30 ...228 C7
Upper Nidderdale High Sch HG3 ...137 B4
Upper Poppleton Jun Sch YO26 ...165 F1
Upper Price St YO23 ...233 A1
Upper Sackville St **5** BD23 ...217 A3
Upper St Paul's Terr YO24 ...228 A4
Upper Union St BD23 ..216 F3
Upper Wharfedale Mus★ BD23 ...134 E2
Upper Wharfedale Folk Mus★ BD23 ...134 E2
Upper Wharfedale Sch BD23 ...134 D2
Uppercommon La DN14 ...202 F3
Uppercroft **4** YO32 ...225 C8
Uppergate LA6 ...103 C4
Upsall Dr DL3 ...3 C4
Upsall La
South Kilvington YO7 ...211 C7
Thornborough YO7 ...90 A8
Upsall YO7 ...66 B1
Upsall Rd YO7 ...66 B1
Upwell Rd DL7 ...210 D4
Ure Bank HG4 ...214 D7
Ure Bank Maltings HG4 ...214 D8
Ure Bank Terr HG4 ...214 C7
Ure Bank Top HG4 ...214 D7
Uredale Glass★ HG4 ...86 C3
Urlay Nook Rd TS16 ...5 C5
Usher La YO32 ...166 F6
Usk Ct **21** TS17 ...5 F4

V

Vale Ave WF11 ...201 E2
Vale Cres
Bishop Wilton YO42 ...169 F2
Knottingley WF11 ...201 E2
Vale Crest WF11 ...201 E2
Vale Ct HG5 ...221 A6
Vale Sch WF11 ...201 E2
Vale The
10 Collingham LS22 ...188 A8
Middlesbrough TS5 ...6 F8
Skelton YO30 ...224 B5
Vale View HG4 ...114 B2
Valient Way TS17 ...6 B8
Valley Bride Rd **16** YO11 213 F5
Valley Bridge Par YO11 ...213 A5
Valley Dr
Barnoldswick BB18 ...171 E2
Eaglescliffe TS15 ...5 E3
Great Preston LS26 ...200 C8
Harrogate HG2 ...219 C1
Ilkley LS29 ...218 D4
Valley Gdn TS16 ...5 D4
Valley Gdns★ HG2 ...219 C2
Valley Mount HG2 ...219 C2
Valley Rd
Barnoldswick BB18 ...171 E1
3 Darley HG3 ...160 A6
32 Earby BB18 ...172 A1
Harrogate HG2 ...219 C2
Ilkley LS29 ...218 D5
Kippax LS25 ...194 C2
Northallerton DL6 ...210 F3
Scarborough YO12 ...212 E4
Whitby YO21 ...208 A8
Valley Ridge LS25 ...194 C2
Valley St N DL1 ...3 D5
Valley View
3 Ampleforth YO62 ...92 C1
Clint HG3 ...160 F8
Danby YO21 ...29 C6
3 Glusburn BD20 ...187 E8
Wheldrake YO19 ...192 F7
Valuation La **1** YO51 ..141 B5
Van Mildert Way TS18 ...5 F8
Vanbrugh Dr YO10 ...229 C3
Vanbrugh Way YO10 ...229 A2
Vane Ct TS21 ...4 F7
Vane Terr DL3 ...3 B6
Vasey Cl **5** DL8 ...63 B2
Vaughan Rd **10** DN6 ..206 E1
Vavasour Ct YO23 ...230 B2
Vaynor Dr **17** TS17 ...5 F4
Venables Rd TS14 ...8 E7

Vernon Cl YO23 ....**231** A3
Vernon Gr 4 YO12 ....**212** D8
Vernon Pl 3 YO11 ....**213** A5
Vernon Rd
  Harrogate HG2 ....**222** E7
  2 Scarborough YO11 ...**213** A5
  Trawden Forest BB8 ...**186** B3
  York YO30 ....**224** E2
Vesper Dr YO24 ....**227** B3
Vesper Wlk YO32 ......**225** F6
Vicar Hill La YO7 ....**116** D8
Vicarage Cl
  2 Bubwith YO8 ....**199** D7
  12 Hunmanby YO14 ....**126** F8
  Seamer YO12 ....**99** D6
Vicarage Gdns 1 YO10 .**229** D6
Vicarage La
  Bishop Wilton YO42 ...**169** A1
  Bramham LS23 ....**188** E5
  10 Knaresborough HG5 .**221** B5
  Naburn YO19 ....**191** E8
  Sherburn YO17 ....**124** D8
Vicarage Rd
  Barnoldswick BB18 ....**171** E2
  16 Catterick Garrison DL9 ..**40** E4
  3 Kelbrook & Sough
  BB18 ....**186** A7
Vicar's La YO61 ......**144** C6
Vicars Cl YO23 ....**230** D1
Vicars Croft DL6 .....**210** E5
Vicars Terr WF10 .....**200** D6
Vickers Cl TS18 ....**5** F7
Vickers Rd 2 DL9 .....**40** E4
Vickers St 1 WF10 ....**200** E4
Victor St YO1 ....**233** B1
Victoria Ave
  10 Filey YO14 ....**101** B3
  Harrogate HG1 ....**219** D2
  Ilkley LS29 ....**175** C2
  Knaresborough HG5 ...**221** B8
  Ripon HG4 ....**214** D5
  Thirsk YO7 ....**211** B2
Victoria Cave ★ BD24 ..**131** F4
Victoria Cl
  Great Preston WF10 ...**200** E6
  Ilkley LS29 ....**218** A4
Victoria Ct 15 YO26 ...**227** F5
Victoria Dr 9 LS29 ....**175** C2
Victoria Emb DL1 ....**3** C4
Victoria Farm Cl YO23 .**182** C6
Victoria Gdns 17 LS29 .**175** C2
Victoria Gr
  5 Ilkley LS29 ....**175** C2
  Ripon HG4 ....**214** C5
Victoria Par 13 YO11 ..**212** F5
Victoria Pk 1 YO12 ...**212** F7
Victoria Pk Ave 2 YO12 **212** F7
Victoria Pk Mount
  YO12 ....**212** F7
Victoria Pl 3 YO21 ....**208** D6
Victoria Rd
  1 Barnoldswick BB18 ..**171** A1
  28 Burley in Wharfedale
  LS29 ....**176** C1
  Cowling BD22 ....**187** B6
  Darlington DL1 ....**3** C5
  Earby BB18 ....**172** A1
  Glusburn BD20 ......**187** E7
  Harrogate HG2 ....**219** C1
  10 Ilkley LS29 ....**175** C2
  1 Malton YO17 ......**215** B4
  Richmond DL10 ......**209** B7
  Scarborough YO11 ....**212** F5
  Thornaby TS17 ....**6** B8
Victoria Sh Ctr HG1 ...**219** D2
Victoria Sq BD23 .....**216** F4
Victoria St
  24 Earby BB18 ....**172** A1
  Glusburn BD20 ......**187** E7
  Great Preston WF10 ..**200** E6
  Pontefract WF8 ......**201** B2
  Scarborough YO12 ....**212** F6
  Settle BD24 ....**131** C2
  10 Skipton BD23 .....**216** F4
  1 York YO23 ....**233** B1
Victoria Terr
  1 Harrogate HG1 .....**220** C4
  Northallerton DL7 ....**210** D4
  3 Skipton BD23 .....**216** F4
Victoria Way 2 YO32 ..**225** F8
Victoria Works Ind Est
  BD20 ....**187** F8
Victory Rd LS29 ......**218** B4
Viewley Hill Ave TS8 ...**6** F5
Viewley Hill Prim Sch
  TS8 ....**6** F5
Viking Cl 20 YO41 ....**168** D2
Viking Dr 5 YO19 ....**197** F8
Viking Rd
  Stamford Bridge YO41 .**168** D2
  York YO26 ....**227** C5
Vikings Ct 6 DL6 .....**43** F3
Villa Cl YO8 ....**198** F1
Villa Ct YO26 ....**227** B7
Villa Fields 4 DN14 ..**204** C1
Villa Gr 2 YO31 .....**228** E6
Village Farm Ct 7
  DN14 ....**202** D4
Village Fold DL7 .....**42** B1
Village Garth 1 YO61 .**166** E5
Village Paddock TS18 ...**5** E8
Village Rd TS15 ....**24** B8
Village St YO30 ......**224** E3
Village The
  Boston Spa LS23 .....**180** F1

Village The continued
  Haxby YO32 ....**166** E5
  Skelton YO30 ....**224** B5
  Stockton on the Forest
  YO32 ....**167** D3
  Strensall YO32 ......**167** B7
  York YO10 ....**229** C4
Village Wy DL7 ....**42** B1
Villiers Ct 8 YO62 ....**92** F6
Vimy Rd DL9 ....**40** E3
Vincent St 9 YO12 ....**213** A7
Vincent Way YO24 .....**230** C8
Vine Cl TS14 ....**8** F6
Vine Farm Cl YO26 ....**164** A4
Vine Gdns YO8 ....**199** D7
Vine Gr YO17 ....**215** E4
Vine St Darlington DL3 ...**3** B6
  Norton YO17 ....**215** E4
  6 Scarborough YO12 ..**212** F6
  York YO23 ....**228** C2
Vinstra Cl DL10 ....**209** D8
Virginia Gdns TS5 ......**6** E6
Vivars Way YO8 ....**232** D5
Vivers Pl 1 YO62 ......**70** C1
Vivis La YO8 ....**95** F6
Volta St YO8 ....**232** E4
Vulcan Way TS17 ....**6** B6
Vyner St Ripon HG4 ....**214** D4
  York YO31 ....**228** C7

W

Waddington St 37 BB18 **172** A1
Wade House La YO8 ....**204** F4
Waggoners Dr 3 YO23 .**230** B3
Wain Cl
  15 Eastfield YO11 ....**100** B7
  South Milford LS25 ...**195** E2
Wain Gap LS25 ....**195** F2
Wain's Gr YO24 ......**230** D2
Wain's La YO12 ....**99** D2
Wain's Rd YO24 ......**230** D8
Waincroft 8 YO32 ....**167** A6
Waindyke Way WF6 ....**200** B1
Wainers Cl 5 YO23 ...**230** B3
Wainfleet Rd HG1 ....**219** D6
Waingates La YO51 ...**140** F4
Wainman's Cl BD22 ...**187** B6
Wainstones Cl TS9 ......**7** F1
Wainstones Dr TS9 .....**7** F1
Waite La YO13 ....**53** F2
Waithwith Rd DL9 ....**209** B1
Waitlands La DL11 .....**20** A7
Wakefield Coll WF10 ..**200** D3
Wakefield Rd
  Garforth LS25 ....**194** B3
  10 Normanton South WF6 **200** A1
  Swillington LS26 .....**194** A2
Wakeman Rd HG4 .....**214** C3
Walburn Head DL11 ....**39** D3
Walden Stubbs Rd
  DN6 ....**206** E2
Wales St DL3 ....**3** C7
Walker Cl BD20 ......**187** D1
Walker Dr YO24 ......**230** C8
Walker La
  Menwith with Darley
  HG3 ....**160** A6
  Wheldrake YO19 .....**192** F7
Walker St YO21 ......**208** D6
Walker Terr HG3 ......**223** F8
Walker's La BD20 ....**184** B4
Walkers Fold HG5 ....**221** B5
Walkers Row TS14 ......**8** F7
Walkerville Ave 22 DL9 ..**41** A4
Walkerville Ind Est DL9 **41** B5
Walkington La YO30 ..**165** B3
Walled Gdn The ★
  YO17 ....**123** A6
Wallgates La YO17 ....**215** D4
Walmgate YO1 ....**233** C2
Walmsley Gdns YO12 ..**212** C5
Walney Rd YO31 ......**229** A5
Walnut Cl
  Saxton with Scarthingwell
  LS24 ....**195** D8
  York YO10 ....**229** A1
Walnut Gn YO17 ......**215** E3
Walnut Gr HG1 ....**219** E6
Walpole St YO31 .....**228** D7
Walton Ave
  Gargrave BD23 ......**155** C1
  Middlesbrough TS5 .....**6** E6
  Pannal HG3 ....**222** F2
Walton Chase LS23 ...**180** F2
Walton Cl
  Gargrave BD23 ......**172** C8
  Huby YO61 ....**144** A4
Walton La HG3 ....**222** F2
Walton Pk HG3 ......**222** F2
Walton Pl Pannal HG3 .**222** E2
  York YO26 ....**227** B3
Walton Rd
  Walton LS23 ....**181** A2
  Wetherby LS22 ......**180** E2
Walton St
  5 Cowling BD22 .....**187** B6
  Skipton BD23 ....**216** F1
Walworth Ave HG2 ....**220** B3
Walworth St N 4 YO26 **227** F5
Walworth St S 9 YO26 **227** F5
Wand Hill TS12 ....**9** E8
Wand La DN14 ....**203** C4
Wandale La YO17 ......**95** A2
Wandales Cl YO17 ....**215** F3
Wandales Ct YO13 .....**75** D8
Wandales Dr YO13 .....**75** D8

Wandales La YO60 ....**146** B6
Wandales Rd YO13 .....**75** D8
Wandell Balk YO61 ...**144** B6
Wandels La YO21 ......**29** B6
Wandesford Gr DL9 ...**209** F1
Wandhill 31 YO62 ....**166** E5
Wandhill Gdns TS12 ....**9** E8
Wandhill La YO7 ....**66** D1
Wandle The YO26 ....**227** A2
Wapping La YO62 ......**94** C7
War Dike La YO13 .....**54** B6
War Field La LS22 ....**180** F6
Warbler Cl TS17 ....**6** A5
Ward Ct YO23 ....**233** B1
Ward St BD23 ....**217** A4
Wardale Ave TS5 ....**6** E6
Wardrop Rd DL9 .....**209** C1
Wareham Rd YO11 .....**99** F6
Warehill La YO11 .....**143** C2
Warlbeck 23 LS29 ....**175** C2
Warley Wise La BB8 ..**186** B6
Warren Ave WF11 ....**201** E4
Warren La
  Bramham cum Oglethorpe
  LS24 ....**189** A5
  Brearton HG3 ....**162** A8
  Kirkby Malzeard HG4 ..**112** D4
Warren Pl HG1 ....**219** D5
Warrener La DL10 .....**20** C6
Warth La LA6 ....**103** C3
Warthill CE VC Prim Sch
  YO19 ....**167** F2
Warwick Cl YO60 .....**145** D5
Warwick Cres HG2 ....**222** E8
Warwick Dr 2 BB18 ..**172** A1
Warwick Pl 2 YO62 ...**92** F7
Warwick St YO31 .....**228** D7
Wasdale Cl 2 YO30 ..**224** E1
Wash Beck La YO62 ...**93** F6
Washbeck Cl YO12 ....**212** E4
Washbrook Dr DL3 .....**3** C8
Washburn 18 YO14 ...**101** A3
Washburn Cotts LS21 ..**159** F1
Washburn Courts HG3 .**159** F1
Washburn Dr 4 BD20 ..**187** E8
Washfold La DL8 ......**60** B6
Washford Cl TS17 ......**6** A3
Washington Ave DL2 ....**4** D4
Washington Cl HG4 ...**214** C2
Wass Bank Rd YO61 ...**91** F2
Wass Way TS16 ....**5** D5
Waste La YO62 ....**48** F2
Watchet Rd 11 DL9 ....**40** E4
Water Bag Bank 8 HG5 **221** A6
Water End YO26 ......**227** E5
Water Gap YO18 ......**97** B5
Water Garth DN14 ....**202** F4
Water Hill La YO8 ....**232** B6
Water Houses BD24 ...**132** E6
Water La
  Camblesforth YO8 ....**204** D5
  8 Clifton YO30 .....**225** A1
  Dalton YO7 ....**115** E2
  Dunnington YO19 ....**184** F7
  Eggborough DN14 ....**203** A2
  Exelby, Leeming & Newton
  DL7 ....**63** D4
  Hemingbrough YO8 ...**198** F1
  Huttons Ambo YO60 ..**147** C6
  Kirby Grindalythe YO17 .**149** B6
  Kirby Underdale YO41 .**170** A3
  Kirk Smeaton WF8 ...**206** C3
  Knaresborough HG5 ..**221** C8
  Loftus TS13 ....**10** E8
  North Stainley with Sleningford
  HG4 ....**113** C6
  7 Pontefract WF8 ...**201** C1
  Selby YO8 ....**232** C6
  South Stainley with Cayton
  HG3 ....**139** D2
  Thorpe Bassett YO17 .**123** A3
  Welburn YO60 ......**146** E7
  Whitby YO21 ....**208** B3
  York YO30 ....**228** A7
Water Skellgate HG4 ..**214** C5
Water Slack La YO26 ..**164** C4
Water St Earby BB18 ..**172** A1
  Gargrave BD23 ......**155** D1
  Malton YO17 ....**215** C4
  Skipton BD23 ....**216** F4
Water St Com Prim Sch 15
  BD23 ....**216** F4
Water Way Garth
  DN14 ....**207** F6
Waterdale Pk YO31 ...**225** D4
Waterfall Fold 1 WF8 .**201** C2
Waterfalls Wlk ★ LA6 .**103** D6
Watergate
  Mickletown LS26 .....**200** A5
  7 Pontefract WF8 ...**201** B1
Watergate Rd HG3 ....**139** A4
Waterhouse La 29 YO11 **213** A6
Waterings 19 YO32 ...**166** D5
Waterloo
  Grosmont YO22 ......**31** C4
  12 Richmond DL10 ...**209** C6
Waterloo Cl WF10 ....**200** C3
Waterloo Rd BB18 ....**186** A7
Waterloo St
  Harrogate HG1 ......**219** E4
  2 Richmond DL10 ...**209** C6
Waterman Ct 3 YO24 .**227** B1
Watermill Cl HG4 .....**113** C7
Watermill Croft HG4 ..**113** C7
Watermill La HG4 .....**113** C7
Waters End DL2 ....**1** D7
Waters La DL10 ....**20** E3

Watershed Mill Bsns Ctr
  BD24 ....**131** D3
Watershed Mill Visitor Ctr ★
  BD24 ....**131** D3
Waterside
  3 Boroughbridge YO51 **141** B6
  Knaresborough HG5 ..**221** A5
  4 Ripon HG4 ....**214** C4
  Skipton BD23 ....**216** F2
  7 Thirsk YO7 ....**211** C3
Watersmeet Cl 5 TS17 ..**6** A4
Watersole La LS22 ....**180** D2
Waterstead Cres 1
  YO21 ....**208** D5
Waterstead La YO21 ..**208** D5
Watery La Airton BD23 .**155** A5
  Giggleswick BD24 ....**131** C1
  Snape with Thorp DL8 ..**86** F7
Wath La Catton YO41 ..**185** C8
  Copgrove HG3 ....**140** D1
  High & Low Bishopside
  HG3 ....**137** B6
  Humberton YO61 ....**141** B8
  Ulleskelf LS24 ......**190** B2
Wath Rd HG3 ....**137** B5
Wathcote Cl DL10 ....**209** F8
Wathcote Pl DL10 ....**209** F8
Wathgill Camp DL11 ..**39** C3
Watlass La DL8 ....**86** D7
Watlass Moor La HG4 ..**86** D7
Watling Cl DL11 ....**19** E6
Watling Rd WF10 ....**201** C5
Watson Cl 9 YO14 ....**127** A8
Watson St
  4 Normanton South WF6 **200** A1
  York YO24 ....**228** A3
Watson Terr 2 YO24 ..**228** A3
Watson's Houses 7
  BD23 ....**216** F4
Watson's La
  Newton Kyme cum Toulston
  LS24 ....**189** A4
  Norwood HG3 ....**177** B8
  Reighton YO14 ......**127** D6
Wattle Syke LS22 ....**180** B3
Wattlers Cl YO23 .....**230** C3
Wattlesyke LS22 .....**188** C8
Wavell Com Inf & Jun Sch
  DL9 ....**209** D1
Wavell Rd DL9 ....**209** D1
Wavell St YO8 ....**232** A6
Waveney Gr YO30 ....**228** B8
Waver La DN14 ......**204** C2
Waverley Cl HG4 ....**214** C2
Waverley Cres HG2 ..**222** E8
Waverley St YO31 ...**233** C3
Waydale Cl YO62 ....**70** A2
Wayfaring Cl YO17 ..**215** F2
Wayne Tarbard Cl 12
  HG4 ....**113** D2
Waynefleet Gr 3 YO10 **229** A3
Wayside Ave HG2 ....**220** B1
Wayside Cl 4 HG2 ...**220** B1
Wayside Cres HG2 ...**220** A1
Wayside Gr HG2 .....**220** A1
Wayside Ltd LS17 ....**178** B2
Wayside The DL2 ......**3** E1
Wayside Wlk 5 HG2 ..**220** B1
Weaponness Dr YO11 .**213** A2
Weaponness La
  Eastfield YO11 ....**99** F8
  Scarborough YO11 ...**212** F1
Weaponness Pk YO11 .**213** A2
Weaponness Valley Cl 5
  YO11 ....**212** F3
Weaponness Valley Rd
  YO11 ....**212** E3
Weardale TS14 ....**8** D5
Weardale Rd 20 DL9 ..**40** E4
Weary Bank TS15 .....**25** B8
Weavers Cl YO23 ....**230** B3
Weavers Ct
  3 Stokesley TS9 .....**26** C7
  Trawden BB8 ....**186** A1
Weavers Gn DL7 .....**210** C3
Weavers Pk YO23 ....**230** B3
Weaverthorpe CE VC Prim
  Sch YO17 ....**124** E2
Webster Pl 1 WF6 ...**200** A1
Weddall Cl YO24 .....**227** F1
Wedderburn Ave HG2 .**220** D2
Wedderburn Cl HG2 ..**220** C3
Wedderburn Cty Inf Sch
  HG2 ....**220** B2
Wedderburn Dr HG2 ..**220** B2
Wedderburn Lodge 2
  HG2 ....**220** B1
Wedderburn Rd HG2 ..**220** B1
Weedling Gate LS24 ..**189** D4
Weeland Cl 16 WF11 ..**202** A2
Weeland Rd Beal DN14 .**202** E3
  Hensall DN14 ....**203** E2
Weeton La LS17 ......**178** D1
Weeton Sta LS17 .....**178** B2
Weets View BB18 ....**171** E2
Welbeck Ave DL1 .....**3** E7
Welborn Cl YO10 ....**229** A4
Welborn Ct YO10 .....**99** F2
Welburn Dr 12 YO10 ..**99** D6
Welburn Com Prim Sch
  YO60 ....**146** D6
Welburn Gr TS7 ....**7** D7
Welburn Hall Sch YO62 **94** E7
Welburn La YO60 ....**147** A8
Welbury Cl 2 BB18 ..**172** B1
Welfare Ave LS15 ....**194** C8
Welford Rd 36 YO14 ..**101** B3
Welham Hill YO17 ....**147** E7

Welham Rd YO17 .....**215** D3
Well Bank DL8 ....**87** A4
Well Cl
  Great & Little Preston
  LS25 ....**200** C8
  3 Whitby YO21 .....**208** D7
Well Cl Terr 4 YO21 ..**208** D7
Well La Kippax LS25 ..**194** D1
  Redmire DL8 ....**59** C5
  Seamer TS9 ....**6** F2
  Snape with Thorp DL8 ..**87** A6
  South Milford LS25 ..**195** F2
  Yearsley YO61 ......**118** C5
Welland Dr LS25 .....**194** D3
Welland Rise YO26 ...**227** D5
Wellbrook Cl TS17 .....**6** B4
Wellesley Cl YO30 ...**225** A2
Wellesleys Mews
  DL10 ....**209** B7
Wellfield Cl HG2 .....**222** B6
Wellfield La 13 LS29 .**176** C1
Wellhouse St 5 BB18 .**171** E1
Wellington Ct 9 HG2 .**219** C2
Wellington Gdns 4 LS29 **223** A4
Wellington Lodge Llamas ★
  YO13 ....**54** B5
Wellington Mews 9
  HG4 ....**214** C5
Wellington Pl DL10 ...**209** B7
Wellington Rd
  Ilkley LS29 ....**218** A4
  2 Whitby YO21 .....**208** D6
Wellington Row YO1 ..**233** A2
Wellington Sq 6 HG2 .**219** C2
Wellington St
  1 Knaresborough HG5 .**221** B5
  10 Ripon HG4 ....**214** C5
  12 Skipton BD23 ....**217** A3
  York YO10 ....**228** E3
Wellington Terr YO21 .**208** D7
Wellington Way 4 DL10 **41** C7
Wellingtonia Dr 5 DN6 **206** E1
Wells Cl YO8 ....**232** A5
Wells La Barton DL10 ..**21** D7
  Kellington DN14 .....**202** E3
  Malton YO17 ....**215** C4
Wells Mews LS29 ....**218** B3
Wells Prom LS29 .....**218** B4
Wells Rd LS29 ....**218** B3
Wells Wlk 13 YO18 ....**95** F7
Wells Wlk The LS29 ..**218** B4
Wellspring Cl TS17 .....**6** D7
Welton Ave YO26 ....**227** C6
Welton Ct YO21 .....**208** D7
Welwyn Dr YO10 .....**231** E8
Wemyss Rd 11 HG4 ..**113** D2
Wendel Ave LS15 ....**194** B8
Wendy Ave HG4 .....**214** B3
Wenham Rd YO24 ....**230** C8
Wenlock Dr YO19 ....**192** B6
Wenlock Terr YO10 ..**228** D1
Wenning Ave LA2 ....**129** A7
Wenning Bank LA2 ...**130** A6
Wennington Hall Sch
  LA2 ....**102** B1
Wennington Rd LA2 ..**128** A6
Wennington Sta LA2 .**128** B8
Wensley Gr HG2 .....**222** D7
Wensley Rd
  Harrogate HG2 ......**222** D7
  15 Leyburn DL8 .....**60** D5
  Northallerton DL7 ...**210** B2
Wensleydale Ave 2
  BD23 ....**217** B4
Wensleydale Creamery ★
  DL8 ....**56** C4
Wensleydale Dr YO10 .**229** D4
Wensleydale Pottery ★
  DL8 ....**56** D4
Wensleydale Rd DL9 ..**40** E4
Wensleydale Sch The
  DL8 ....**60** D5
Wentcliffe Dr BB18 ..**172** A1
Wentdale 1 WF8 .....**206** C3
Wentworth Ave YO61 .**116** F5
Wentworth Cl
  Camblesforth YO8 ...**204** D4
  Harrogate HG2 ......**220** D4
  Kellington DN14 ....**203** A2
Wentworth Cres
  Harrogate HG2 ......**220** D3
  2 Whitby YO21 .....**208** B5
Wentworth Dr HG2 ...**220** D4
Wentworth Gate LS22 .**180** A3
Wentworth Rd YO24 ..**228** B2
Wentworth St YO17 ..**215** B5
Wentworth Way
  Eaglescliffe TS16 .....**5** E4
  5 Hunmanby YO14 ..**126** F8
  York YO10 ....**228** F2
Werkdyke The YO1 ...**233** C3
Werner Ct 4 WF10 ...**200** F3
Wescoe Hill La LS17 .**178** B1
Wesley Pl YO1 ....**233** C2
Wesley Rd YO22 ......**33** C4
Wesley Sq 2 TS13 ...**13** K2
Wesson Cl 6 DL9 ....**40** E4
West Acres 2 WF11 ..**201** E4
West Acres Cl 7 YO13 ..**99** A7
West Auckland Rd DL3 ..**3** A7
West Ave
  Boston Spa LS23 ....**180** E1
  Burton Fleming YO25 .**126** E3
  5 Easingwold YO61 ..**143** D8
  Filey YO14 ....**101** B3
  19 Scalby YO13 .....**75** D5
West Bank
  Scarborough YO12 ...**212** E4

West Bank *continued*
York YO24 227 E3
West Bank Rd BD23 216 E4
West Barnby La YO21 12 B3
West Beck Way TS8 7 B6
West Burton CE Prim Sch DL8 58 F1
West Cam Rd BD23 79 E6
West Cl Carthorpe DL8 87 E6
Normanton WF6 200 A1
Swinton YO17 121 B4
West Cl Rd 13 BB18 171 D2
West Cliff Ave 5 YO21 208 B7
West Cliff Prim Sch YO21 208 C7
West Cliffe Cnr 9 HG2 219 C1
West Cliffe Gr HG2 219 B1
West Cliffe Mews 5 HG2 219 C1
West Cliffe Mount HG2 219 B1
West Cliffe Terr HG2 219 B1
West Craven High Tech Coll BB18 171 E1
West Craven Swimming Pool BB18 171 E1
West Croft
19 Addingham LS29 174 F4
6 Glusburn BD20 187 E6
West Ct 8 YO19 197 F8
West Dale LS23 180 E1
West Dene BD20 174 B2
West Dike Rd YO18 71 F5
West Edge Rd WF8 206 A3
West End
Boston Spa LS23 180 E1
Guisborough TS14 8 E6
Hurworth-on-Tees DL2 3 E1
Hutton Rudby TS15 25 C5
Kirkbymoorside YO62 70 B1
Muston YO14 100 F2
Osmotherley DL6 45 B4
Pollington DN14 207 F6
Rawcliffe DN14 205 A2
Sheriff Hutton YO60 145 C5
Stokesley TS9 26 C7
Strensall YO32 167 A7
West End App LS24 190 B3
West End Ave
Appleton Roebuck YO23 190 F5
Harrogate HG2 222 D8
Richmond DL10 209 A7
West End Cl
North Duffield YO8 199 A8
9 Strensall YO32 167 B7
West End Ct 5 YO11 100 B6
West End Gdns
Egglescliffe TS16 5 D4
Pollington DN14 207 F6
West End Rd DN6 206 E2
West End View 4 YO11 100 B6
West End Way TS18 5 F8
West Field La
Arkendale HG5 163 A8
East Witton Town DL8 60 F1
Upper Poppleton YO26 165 E1
West Field Rd 2 BB18 171 D2
West Fields YO62 70 B1
West Garforth Jun Sch LS25 194 C3
West Garth
Cayton YO11 100 B6
Sherburn YO17 124 D8
Ulleskelf LS24 190 B3
West Garth Gdns 23 YO11 100 B6
West Gate
Thornton-le-Dale YO18 96 C5
Wetherby LS22 180 B3
Wykeham YO13 98 D6
West Gr
Bishop Thornton HG3 139 A2
Swinton YO17 121 B4
West Gr Rd HG1 219 D4
West Hall La LS29 175 A5
West Heslerton CE VC Prim Sch YO17 123 F6
West Ing La BD23 171 A5
West Ings Cl 4 WF11 202 A3
West Ings Cres 5 WF11 202 A3
West Ings Ct 1 WF11 202 A3
West Ings La 2 WF11 202 A3
West Ings Mews 6 WF11 202 A3
West Ings Way 3 WF11 202 A3
West La
Appleton Wiske DL6 24 A3
Askwith LS21 176 C3
Azerley HG4 112 F3
Bewerley HG3 136 E4
Boston Spa LS23 180 E1
Burn YO8 203 C6
Burniston YO13 54 C1
Burton Fleming YO25 126 E3
Caldwell DL11 1 B4
Cononley BD20 173 C2
Dalton-on-Tees DL2 22 D6
Danby YO21 29 C8
East Layton DL11 20 A8
Embsay BD23 217 D8
Hampsthwaite HG3 161 A4
Hornby DL6 23 F4
Littlethorpe HG4 214 A2
2 Low Bradley BD20 173 E3
Melsonby DL10 20 E7
Mickleby TS13 12 A4
Nether Silton YO7 66 B7
West La *continued*
North Deighton LS22 179 F6
Snainton YO13 97 F5
Stillington YO61 143 F7
Sutton BD20 187 E6
Sykehouse DN14 207 F2
Whixley YO26 163 F5
West Lea Ave HG2 222 B7
West Lodge Gdns YO17 215 A4
West Lund 17 YO62 70 B1
West Lund La YO62 94 B8
West Mead WF10 201 A4
West Moor La DL8 61 E4
West Moor Rd
Darlington DL2 3 E3
Raskelf YO61 116 E2
West Mount LS24 189 E5
West Oaks Sch 4 LS23 188 E8
West Par Rd 11 YO12 212 F5
West Parade LS29 218 C4
West Pasture
Kirkbymoorside YO62 70 B1
7 Pickering YO18 95 F6
West Pier YO11 213 B6
West Pk
Harrogate HG2 219 D1
Selby YO8 232 A4
West Pk Ave YO12 212 C8
West Pk Cres YO12 212 C7
West Pk Hospl DL3 3 A7
West Pk Rd 13 YO13 75 D5
West Rd Carleton BD23 173 A4
12 Filey YO14 101 B3
Melsonby DL10 20 F7
West Row DL2 4 C7
West Sandgate Terr 19 YO11 213 B6
West Side Rd YO13 53 A1
West Sq 7 YO11 212 F5
West St
Castleford WF10 200 E4
Eaglescliffe TS15 5 D4
Gargrave BD23 155 D1
Gayles DL11 19 E6
Harrogate HG1 219 C5
Ilkley LS29 218 B4
Muston YO14 100 F2
Normanton South WF6 200 A1
Scarborough YO11 213 A4
Swinton YO17 121 B4
West Terr
Richmond DL10 209 B7
Scarborough YO11 212 F4
15 Whitby YO21 208 D7
West Thorpe YO24 230 D8
West Vale 37 YO14 101 B3
West View
Carleton BD23 173 B4
Darlington DL3 3 A5
Draughton BD23 174 B7
Ilkley LS29 218 B3
Kippax LS25 194 D1
Micklefield LS25 195 A3
North Deighton LS22 180 A6
Ripon HG4 214 D2
Sherburn in Elmet LS25 195 E3
West View Ave 25 LS29 176 C1
West View Rd 26 LS29 176 C1
West View Terr
Eaglescliffe TS16 5 D4
16 Knaresborough HG5 221 A6
West Villa YO61 144 A4
West Way YO61 118 A1
West Wood La YO23 182 E4
Westacres 5 DL2 4 C4
Westbeck Gdns TS5 6 F8
Westborough 1 YO11 213 A5
Westbourne Ave
Harrogate HG2 222 D8
Whitby YO21 208 A6
Westbourne Cl YO21 208 A6
Westbourne Cres LS25 194 B3
Westbourne Gdns YO8 232 C4
Westbourne Gr
8 Pickering YO18 95 F7
3 Ripon HG4 214 C5
11 Scarborough YO11 213 A4
Selby YO8 232 C4
Whitby YO21 208 A6
Westbourne Pk YO12 212 E4
Westbourne Rd
Scarborough YO11 212 F3
Selby YO8 232 C4
Whitby YO21 208 A6
Westbourne Terr
Selby YO8 232 C4
Thirsk YO7 211 A2
Westbury St TS17 6 B8
Westcroft La YO8 196 E1
Westdene HG2 222 B7
Westend La DN14 207 B6
Westerdale 4 YO18 95 F6
Westerdale Ct 2 YO30 228 A6
Western Ave WF8 201 C1
Western Ct 15 WF8 201 C1
Western Gales Way 33 WF6 200 B1
Western Prim Sch HG2 219 C1
Western Rd BD23 217 B3
Western Terr YO32 225 D3
Western Way 1 YO18 95 E7
Westerns La HG3 139 C4
Westfield YO8 232 B4
Westfield Ave
Castleford WF10 200 E2
Castleford LS25 200 D7
3 Eggborough DN14 202 F2
Rawcliffe DN14 205 A1
6 Scalby YO12 75 E5
Selby YO8 232 B4
Westfield Cl
2 Eggborough DN14 202 F2
21 Haxby YO32 166 E5
South Milford LS25 195 E2
Westfield Cres 12 LS24 189 E6
Westfield Ct
Copmanthorpe YO23 230 A2
1 South Milford LS25 195 F2
Westfield Dr
Hurworth-on-Tees DL2 3 E1
York YO10 231 D8
Westfield Gn YO26 181 C7
Westfield Gr
Allerton Bywater WF10 200 D7
4 Eggborough DN14 202 F2
12 Haxby YO32 166 D5
Westfield La
Exelby, Leeming & Newton DL8 63 C2
Kippax LS25 194 C1
Ledsham LS25 195 C1
Lockton YO18 72 E4
Normanby YO62 94 F4
Norton WF8 206 C2
South Milford LS25 195 F2
Thirsk YO7 211 A3
Thoralby DL8 58 D1
Thorganby YO19 193 A5
Thornton-le-Dale YO18 96 C5
Wigginton YO32 166 D5
Westfield Pl
19 Haxby YO32 166 E5
York YO24 227 A1
Westfield Prim Com Sch YO24 227 B2
Westfield Rd
1 Eggborough DN14 202 F2
20 Haxby YO32 166 E5
3 North Duffield YO8 199 A7
Rawcliffe DN14 205 A1
Selby YO8 232 B4
2 Stokesley TS9 26 C7
Tockwith YO26 181 C7
Westfield Sq 8 LS24 189 E6
Westfield Terr
2 Great Preston WF10 200 D7
Tadcaster LS24 189 E6
9 Thornton Dale YO18 96 D5
Westfield Way YO17 215 F4
Westfields
Castleford WF10 200 E3
Richmond DL10 209 A7
Scorton DL10 41 E7
Westfields Ct DL10 209 B7
Westfold YO17 215 E6
Westgarth
Collingham LS22 180 A2
Northallerton DL7 210 D4
Westgate
22 Barnoldswick BB18 171 D1
Egglescliffe TS15 5 D3
Guisborough TS14 8 F6
Malton YO17 215 E6
Pickering YO18 95 E7
Rillington YO17 122 F5
Ripon HG4 214 C5
Tadcaster LS24 189 E6
Thirsk YO7 211 B2
Westgate Carr Rd YO18 95 D5
Westgate La
Malton YO17 215 D6
Thornton in Lonsdale LA6 103 C5
Westgate Rd DL3 3 B7
Westholme 10 TS15 25 C5
Westholme Bank DL8 58 F2
Westholme Cres 2 HG4 86 C3
Westholme Ct 3 HG4 86 C3
Westholme Dr YO30 224 E1
Westholme Rd 1 HG4 86 C3
Westland Cl 3 BD20 187 F7
Westlands
Bilton-in-Ainsty with Bickerton YO26 181 D5
6 Kirklevington TS15 24 E8
Pickering YO18 96 A7
Stokesley TS9 26 B7
Westlands Ave 1 YO21 208 C7
Westlands Gr YO31 228 F7
Westlands La YO7 211 A4
Westlands Rd DL3 3 B6
Westlands Way TS18 5 F8
Westminster Bsns Ctr YO26 227 C8
Westminster Cl HG3 222 C3
Westminster Cres HG3 222 D2
Westminster Dr HG3 222 D3
Westminster Gate HG3 222 C3
Westminster Gr HG3 222 D3
Westminster Pl YO26 224 B1
Westminster Rd
Pannal HG3 222 C3
York YO30 228 A6
Westminster Rise HG3 222 D2
Westmoreland St
Darlington DL3 3 C7
1 Harrogate HG1 219 E3
Westmoreland St *continued*
19 Skipton BD23 217 A3
Westmount Cl HG4 214 B6
Weston Cres 7 LS21 176 F1
Weston Dr LS21 176 E1
Weston La LS21 176 F1
Weston Moor Rd LS21 176 E4
Weston Pk View LS21 176 E1
Weston Rd LS29 218 B4
Weston Ridge LS21 176 F1
Westover Rd YO12 212 F4
Westpit La YO32 167 A7
Westridge Cres 1 DL9 40 F5
Westside Cl YO17 215 B4
Westside Rd
Bransdale YO62 48 B5
Fadmoor YO62 69 E7
Westview Cl
3 Low Bradley BD20 173 E3
York YO26 227 B7
Westville Ave LS29 218 A4
Westville Cl 6 LS29 218 A4
Westville House Prep Sch LS29 218 D7
Westville Oval HG1 219 C6
Westville Rd LS29 218 A4
Westway Eastfield YO11 99 F7
Harrogate HG2 222 B8
Westwood
Carleton BD23 173 B4
Scarborough YO11 212 F5
Westwood Cl 2 YO11 212 F4
Westwood Dr LS29 218 A2
Westwood Gdns 3 YO11 212 F4
Westwood La
Ampleforth YO62 92 A2
West Tanfield HG4 86 E1
Westwood Mews
Carleton BD23 173 B4
12 Dunnington YO19 184 F7
Westwood Rd
Ripon HG4 214 A2
Scarborough YO11 212 F4
Westwood Terr YO23 228 B1
Westwood Way LS23 188 E8
Wetherby Bsns Ctr LS22 180 B3
Wetherby Bsns Pk LS22 180 C3
Wetherby High Sch LS22 180 C3
Wetherby La LS22 180 D7
Wetherby Leisure Ctr LS22 180 C2
Wetherby Racecourse★ LS22 180 E3
Wetherby Rd
8 Boroughbridge YO51 141 B4
Bramham cum Oglethorpe LS23 188 E6
Harrogate HG2 220 B1
Kirk Deighton LS22 180 B5
Knaresborough HG5 221 D4
Sicklinghall LS22 179 E3
Tadcaster LS24 189 D6
Walton LS23 180 F2
Wetherby LS22 180 B2
York YO26 227 B3
Wethercote La YO7 67 C1
Wetlands La DL11 18 G7
Weydale Ave YO12 212 E8
Weymouth Ave TS8 7 A7
Weymouth Rd 1 HG1 219 E4
Whaddon Chase TS14 8 F6
Whaites La YO7 115 C5
Whales La DN14 202 E3
Wham La BD24 130 F1
Wharfe Dr YO24 230 D8
Wharfe Gr 8 LS22 180 B3
Wharfe La
Grassington BD23 134 D3
Kearby with Netherby LS22 179 B1
Wharfe Pk 2 LS29 175 A4
Wharfe View
Grassington BD23 134 D3
Kirkby Overblow HG3 179 A4
Wharfe View Rd LS29 218 B4
Wharfedale YO14 101 A3
Wharfedale Ave HG2 222 A7
Wharfedale Cl 1 BD23 217 B4
Wharfedale Cres
Harrogate HG2 222 B7
Tadcaster LS24 189 E6
Wharfedale Dr
Ilkley LS29 218 C4
Normanton WF6 200 A3
Wharfedale General Hospl LS21 176 F1
Wharfedale Pl HG2 222 A7
Wharfedale View 6 LS29 174 F4
Wharfeside Ave BD23 134 D3
Wharfeside La LS29 218 C5
Wharncliffe Pl 14 YO14 101 A3
Wharnscliffe Dr YO30 224 F2
Wharram Quarry Nature Reserve★ YO17 148 F4
Wharton Ave YO30 228 B7
Wharton Rd 8 YO41 168 D2
Whartons Prim Sch The LS21 177 A2
Whartons The LS21 177 A1
Whashton Rd Aske DL10 20 C1
Richmond DL10 209 C8
Wheatcroft 6 YO32 167 A6
Wheatcroft Ave YO11 213 B1
Wheatcroft Com Prim Sch YO11 213 B1
Wheatdale Rd LS24 190 B2
Wheatear La TS17 6 A5
Wheatfield La YO32 225 C8
Wheatlands
Great Ayton TS9 8 A2
Ilkley LS29 218 C4
Wheatlands Ave 8 BD20 187 E8
Wheatlands Dr 4 TS13 11 A8
Wheatlands Gr
Harrogate HG2 222 E8
York YO26 227 C6
Wheatlands La
7 Glusburn BD20 187 E8
Roecliffe YO51 140 E4
Wheatlands Rd HG2 222 E7
Wheatlands Rd E HG2 222 E8
Wheatlands Way HG2 222 F8
Wheatley Ave
Ilkley LS29 218 E3
Normanton South WF6 200 A1
Wheatley Dr YO32 225 C8
Wheatley Gdns 2 LS29 218 E3
Wheatley Gr LS29 218 E3
Wheatley La 3 LS29 218 E3
Wheatley Rd LS29 218 C3
Wheatley Rise LS29 218 E3
Wheeldale Cres TS17 6 B7
Wheeldale Rd YO18 51 A4
Wheeldrake Cl 1 TS14 8 F7
Wheelgate YO17 215 C4
Wheelgate Sq 7 YO17 215 C4
Wheelhouse Sq YO12 212 F6
Wheelhouse The 4 YO30 224 B5
Wheels La YO8 204 F3
Wheelwright Cl
Copmanthorpe YO23 230 B2
Sutton upon Derwent YO41 185 C1
Wheelwrights Courts BD23 154 B3
Wheldale La WF10 201 B5
Wheldon Rd WF10 201 A5
Wheldrake CE Prim Sch YO19 193 A8
Wheldrake Ings Nature Reserve★ YO19 193 C7
Wheldrake La
Deighton YO19 184 B1
Escrick YO19 192 B5
Whenby Gr YO31 225 F1
Whenby La YO60 145 C6
Whernside TS7 7 C5
Whernside Ave YO31 229 A5
Whessoe Rd DL3 3 C8
Whin Bank YO12 212 D5
Whin Cl
3 Strensall YO32 167 B6
York YO24 230 F7
Whin Garth YO24 230 F6
Whin Gn YO22 32 A6
Whin Hill YO17 147 E1
Whin La
South Milford LS25 195 D2
Warlaby DL7 64 C5
Whin Rd YO24 230 F6
Whinbeck Ave WF6 200 B1
Whinbush Way DL1 3 F8
Whinchat Tail TS14 8 D6
Whincup Ave HG5 221 B6
Whincup Cl 6 HG5 221 B6
Whincup Gr 7 HG5 221 B6
Whinfield 34 LS29 175 C2
Whinfield Ct BD23 216 F3
Whinfield Rd DL1 3 E7
Whinfield Rd Jun & Inf Sch DL1 3 F7
Whinfields The 1 HG3 138 A1
Whingroves TS17 6 C8
Whinmoor Hill YO7 66 C2
Whinney La HG3 222 A5
Whinney Mire La LA2 103 E1
Whinny Bank YO61 117 C8
Whinny Gill Rd BD23 217 B3
Whinny Hagg La YO8 197 A2
Whinny Hill DL9 40 E3
Whinny La YO60 168 A7
Whinnythwaite La YO26 181 C8
Whins La
Spofforth with Stockeld HG3 179 E4
Thorp Arch LS23 180 F1
Whins The YO12 212 A7
Whinstone Prim Sch TS17 6 A5
Whinstone View 13 TS9 8 A2
Whinwath La DL8 87 F4
Whipley Bank HG3 161 A8
Whipley La HG3 161 A7
Whip-ma-whop-ma-gate YO1 233 C2
Whipperdale Bank
Leyburn DL8 60 A8
Redmire DL8 38 F1
Whistler Cl YO23 230 C3
Whistler Dr WF10 200 F2
Whiston Dr 18 YO14 101 B3
Whit Moor Rd HG3 158 F5
Whitby Ave
Guisborough TS14 8 F6
York YO31 229 A7

Whitby Benedictine Abbey
(rems of)★ YO22 ....208 E7
Whitby Bsns Pk YO22 ....32 F8
Whitby Com Coll
YO21 ....208 C5
Whitby Dr YO31 ....229 A7
Whitby Gate YO18 ....96 D6
Whitby Hospl YO21 .....208 D6
Whitby Jet Heritage Ctr★
YO22 ....208 E7
Whitby Leisure Ctr
YO21 ....208 C7
Whitby Mus & Art Gall★
YO21 ....208 C6
Whitby Pavilion & Theatre
YO21 ....208 C8
Whitby Rd
Guisborough TS14 ....9 A7
Pickering YO18 ....96 B8
Staithes YO13 ....13 K2
Whitby Sta YO21 ......208 D6
Whitby Way DL3 ....3 A7
Whitcliffe Ave HG4 .....214 B4
Whitcliffe Cres HG4 ....214 B3
Whitcliffe Dr HG4 ......214 B3
Whitcliffe Gr HG4 ......214 B3
Whitcliffe Grange
DL10 ....209 A7
Whitcliffe La
Littlethorpe HG4 ......139 D8
Ripon HG4 ....214 A2
Whitcliffe Pl DL10 .....209 A7
Whitcliffe Terr DL10 ...209 A7
White Bridge Rd YO21 .208 B8
White Canons Ct ４
DL10 ....209 E8
White Canons Wlk ３
DL10 ....209 E8
White Cross Rd YO31 ..228 D6
White Cross Way
YO41 ....169 A2
White Friars Cl DL10 ..209 E8
White Friars Gdns ６
DL10 ....209 E8
White Friars Wlk ５
DL10 ....209 E8
White Gate
Hesleton YO17 ....123 B4
Sherburn YO17 ....124 C6
White Gate Hill YO11 ...100 B2
White Hart Cres ４ DL1 ..3 F6
White Hill La BD20 ....172 E1
White Hills Croft
BD23 ....216 E6
White Hills La BD23 ....216 E6
White Horse Cl ６ YO32 225 F5
White Horse Fold
WF10 ....200 F7
White Horse La ９ YO21 ..99 D6
White Horse Mews ３
HG3 ....179 E5
White Horse of Kilburn★
YO61 ....91 B4
White House Croft TS21 .5 A7
White House Dale
YO24 ....227 F1
White House Dr YO24 ..227 F1
White House Gdns ４
YO24 ....228 A2
White House Gr １
YO41 ....185 E6
White House Rise
YO24 ....227 F1
White House Wynd
DL6 ....24 D2
White La BD22 ....187 F1
White Lands DL10 ......209 E7
White Lee Ave BB8 .....186 B1
White Ley Rd DN6 .....206 C1
White Leys Cl BB18 ....171 F1
White Leys Rd YO21 ...208 A7
White Lilac Cl DL10 ...209 E7
White Lodge YO8 ......232 B4
White Pastures DL10 ..209 E7
White Point Ave １
YO21 ....208 B7
White Point Ct YO21 ..208 B8
White Point Rd YO21 ..208 B8
White Rose Ave ３
YO32 ....225 D3
White Rose Candles★
DL8 ....60 C5
White Rose Cl
Huby YO61 ....144 A5
８ Linton-on-Ouse YO30 .164 F7
Nether Poppleton YO26 .224 C1
White Rose Cres DL10 .209 E7
White Rose Gr ５ YO32 .225 D3
White Rose Way
Nether Poppleton YO26 .227 C8
Thirsk YO7 ....211 D4
White Scar Cave★
LA6 ....104 A4
White Sprunt Hill
YO17 ....125 A1
White St YO8 ....232 B6
White Wall La HG3 ....160 D4
White Way YO13 ....99 A7
White Way Heads YO18 .51 F4
Whitebridge Dr DL1 .....3 D8
Whitecarr La YO62 ......95 A5
Whitecliffe Cres LS26 ..194 A1
Whitecliffe Dr ２ LS26 .194 A1
Whitecliffe Rise LS26 ..194 A1
Whitecote La LS25 ....195 D2

Whitecross Gdns
YO31 ....228 D7
Whitecross Hill DL8 .....87 F3
Whitefield Bglws
DN14 ....206 F8
Whitefield La DN14 ....202 E1
Whitefields Dr DL10 ...209 E7
Whitefields Gate １
DL10 ....209 E8
Whitefields Wlk ２
DL10 ....209 E8
Whitefriars Ct ９ BD24 .131 D2
Whitegate ７ TS13 .....13 K2
Whitegate La HG4 ......114 F1
Whitehall Landing
YO22 ....208 D5
Whitehead Hill 18 YO11 .213 B6
Whitehill Rd BD22 .....187 E3
Whitehouse Ave LS26 ..200 B8
Whitehouse Cres
LS26 ....200 B8
Whitehouse Dr LS26 ..200 B8
Whitehouse La
Great & Little Preston
LS26 ....200 B8
Swillington LS26 ......194 B2
Whitelass Cl YO7 ......211 B4
Whitemoor La YO8 ....198 C6
Whiteoak Ave YO61 ...143 C8
Whitepits La LA2 ......129 A5
Whiterose Dr YO41 ....168 D2
Whiterow Rd DL8 ......82 F7
Whitestone Ct YO7 ....211 D3
Whitestone Dr YO31 ...225 E2
Whitethorn Cl YO31 ...225 E2
Whitewall YO17 ....215 D1
Whitewall Cnr Hill
YO17 ....147 E8
Whiteway Head HG5 ..221 A4
Whitewood Ctr WF10 ..200 D3
Whitfield Ave YO18 .....96 A6
Whitkirk Rd 17 YO14 .101 B3
Whitley & Eggborough CP
Sch DN14 ....202 F1
Whitley Bridge Sta
DN14 ....202 F1
Whitley Cl YO30 ......225 A1
Whitley Pl WF10 ......200 E6
Whitley Rd
Elvington YO41 ....185 A3
Norton-le-Clay YO7 ...115 B1
Thornaby TS17 ....6 B6
Whitley Thorpe La
DN14 ....206 F7
Whitsundale Cl ４ HG5 .221 D5
Whittle St ６ YO7 ......89 B1
Whitton Croft Rd ９
LS29 ....218 B4
Whitton Pl YO10 ......229 C4
Whitwell Dr HG4 ......114 B8
Whitwell Rd YO60 ....146 E5
Whitwood Comm La
WF10 ....200 C3
Whitwood La WF10 ...200 C3
Whixley Field La YO26 .164 B4
Whixley La YO26 ......163 E2
Whorlton Castle (rems of)★
DL6 ....25 D1
Whorlton La DL6 ....45 E8
Whyett Bank YO21 .....28 F6
Wickets The
８ Hutton Rudby TS15 ..25 C5
Middlesbrough TS7 ......7 B6
Widdale Rd HG5 ......221 D5
Widdowfield St DL3 .....3 C6
Wide Howe La YO7 ...114 E8
Wide La YO14 ....127 E5
Widgeon Cl ４ YO14 ..101 A4
Wigby Cl HG3 ....140 A2
Wigginton Prim Sch
YO32 ....166 D5
Wigginton Rd YO31 ...233 B4
Wigginton Terr YO31 ..228 C8
Wighill Garth LS24 ...189 E6
Wighill La LS24 ....181 F3
Wighill St 25 BD20 ....187 E1
Wilberforce Ave YO30 .228 B7
Wilberfoss CE VC Prim Sch
YO41 ....185 E6
Wilcock La BD20 .....173 F2
Wild Rd DL1 ....4 A4
Wildair Cl ２ DL8 ....3 A7
Wilfreds Gr ８ YO8 ...198 B4
Wilfreds Rd ５ YO8 ...198 B4
Wilken Cres TS14 ......8 F7
Wilkinson Ct HG4 .....214 B6
Wilkinson St TS12 ......9 E7
Wilkinson Way
６ Otley LS21 ....176 F1
５ Strensall YO32 .....167 A7
Wilkinsons Ct 22 YO61 .143 C8
Willance Gr DL10 .....209 A7
Willans Gr YO26 ......227 E4
Willaston Cres HG2 ...220 A2
Willaston Rd １ HG1 ..220 A3
Willerby Carr La YO12 ..99 C3
Willgutter La BD22 ...187 F1
William Crossthwaite
TS17 ....6 B4
William Jacques Dr
YO8 ....198 C4
William Plows Ave
YO10 ....228 E2
William Rd YO8 ....198 B4
William St 18 BB18 ...172 A1
William's Hill Ring & Bailey★
DL8 ....60 E2

Williamson Cl 14 HG4 .214 C5
Williamson Dr ８ HG4 .214 C5
Williamson Gdns HG4 .214 A4
Willis St TS15 ....25 C5
Willis St YO10 ....228 E3
Willitoft Rd YO8 ......199 F6
Willoughby Way YO8 .230 B8
Willow Ave
Catterick Garrison DL9 .209 B1
Clifford LS23 ....188 E7
Willow Bank
14 Brayton YO8 ....197 D1
York YO32 ....225 E4
Willow Bank Dr １ WF8 201 C1
Willow Beck Rd DL6 ..210 D6
Willow Bridge La YO7 .115 F8
Willow Brook Cl YO17 .215 F4
Willow Chase The TS21 ..4 F7
Willow Cl
20 Burley in Warfedale
LS29 ....176 C1
５ Filey YO14 ....101 B4
Willow Cres
Clifford LS23 ....188 E7
Richmond DL10 ......209 D8
Willow Ct Kexby YO41 .168 C2
２ North Featherstone
WF7 ....200 E1
６ Pickering YO18 .....95 F6
Willow Dr ６ Bedale DL8 .63 B3
Eston & South Bank TS6 ..7 E8
１ North Duffield YO8 ..199 A7
Willow Garth
Ferrensby HG5 ....162 F7
Scalby YO12 ....212 A7
10 Thornton Dale YO18 ..96 D5
Willow Garth Ave
BD20 ....187 E8
Willow Garth La DN6 ..207 A1
Willow Glade
５ Boston Spa LS23 ...188 E7
York YO32 ....225 F3
Willow Gr
８ Boston Spa LS23 ...188 E7
Earswick YO32 ....226 A4
Harrogate HG1 ......219 E5
York YO31 ....228 F7
Willow La
Boston Spa LS23 ....188 E7
North Featherstone
WF7 ....200 E1
Willow La E ４ WF7 ...200 E1
Willow Pk Rd YO41 ...185 F5
Willow Rd
９ Campsall DN6 .....206 E1
Darlington DL3 ....3 B6
10 Knottingley WF11 ..202 A3
Northallerton DL7 ....210 D2
Willow Rise
５ Kirkbymoorside YO62 .70 B1
Tadcaster LS24 ......189 D5
Thorpe Willoughby YO8 197 B1
Willow Tree Gdns ９
LS29 ....176 C1
Willow View
１ Catterick DL10 .....41 D5
Cliffe YO8 ....198 E3
Willow Way ４ BD20 ..187 E6
Willow Wlk １ HG4 ...214 B2
Willowbank TS8 ....7 A5
Willowbridge Cl ８
WF10 ....200 D3
Willowbridge La
WF10 ....200 C3
Willowbridge Rd WF8 206 C2
Willowbridge Way
WF10 ....200 C3
Willowdene La WF8 ..201 B2
Willowgarth TS9 ....25 C5
Willowgate 24 YO18 ...95 F7
Willows Ave TS8 ....6 C4
Willows The
１ Hambleton YO8 ....196 E1
Middlesbrough TS7 ....7 C6
８ Strensall YO32 .....167 B7
Willy Howe★ YO25 ...126 C3
Willymath Cl YO13 .....75 D7
Wilmot Rd LS29 ......218 C4
Wilson St
Castleford WF10 .....200 E4
Guisborough TS14 ......8 F6
Lockwood TS12 ....9 F7
16 Pontefract WF8 ....201 B1
Sutton BD20 ....187 F7
Wilson's Gr ５ YO13 ...99 A7
Wilsthorpe Gr １ YO10 .231 F8
Wilstrop Farm Rd
YO23 ....230 A2
Wilton Carr La YO18 ...97 C3
Wilton Ings La YO18 ...97 A4
Wilton La TS14 ....8 F7
Wilton Rd LS29 ....218 A3
Wilton Rise YO24 .....227 F3
Wimbledon Cl ２ DL1 ..3 F6
Wimpole Cl ６ YO30 ..225 A1
Winchester Ave ３
YO26 ....227 E4
Winchester Gr １ YO26 .227 E4
Winchester Way DL1 ...3 F8
Windermere YO24 ....230 D7
Windermere Dr WF11 .201 F1
Windgate Hill La YO18 .197 B6
Windle La BD20 ......173 D1
Windleston Dr TS3 ......7 B8
Windmill Gdns YO8 ..232 B2
Windmill Gr LS24 ....189 D5
Windmill La
Norton DN6 ....206 D1

Windmill La continued
York YO10 ....229 B2
Windmill Mdw 13 DN6 .206 E2
Windmill Mdws YO41 .185 E6
Windmill Rd LS23 ....188 F6
Windmill Rise
Aberford LS25 ....194 F7
Tadcaster LS24 ......189 D5
York YO26 ....227 E3
Windrose Cl WF6 .....200 A2
Windross Sq 11 YO61 .143 C8
Windsor Ave
Richmond DL10 .....209 D8
Skipton BD23 ....217 A4
Windsor Cl 17 WF6 ...200 B1
Windsor Cres
Middlesbrough TS7 ....7 D6
７ Whitby YO21 ......208 D6
Windsor Dr
２ Haxby YO32 ....166 D5
Lockwood TS12 ....9 F7
Windsor Garth YO24 .227 D1
Windsor La HG5 ......221 B5
Windsor Pl BB18 .....171 E2
Windsor Rd
24 Catterick Garrison DL9 .40 E4
４ Harrogate HG2 ....220 A1
Ripon HG4 ....214 C3
Thornaby TS17 ....6 B7
Windsor St １ YO23 ..228 B1
Windsor Terr YO21 ...208 D6
Windy Hill LA2 ....129 B8
Winewall La BB8 .....186 B2
Winewall Rd 11 BB8 ..186 A5
Winksley Banks Rd
HG4 ....112 E2
Winksley Gr HG3 ....219 A4
Winn La YO7 ....115 C6
Winnow La LS23 .....188 D8
Winscar Gr ９ YO30 ..224 E3
Winston Ave BD20 ...187 E8
Winston Ct
Northallerton DL6 ...210 E6
Norton YO17 ....215 E3
Winter Gap La BD20 .186 D8
Winter Gn 21 HG3 ...161 B3
Winterburn La BD23 .155 D5
Winterscale Ct TO1 ..228 D2
Winterscale St YO10 .228 D2
Winthropp Cl YO17 ..215 C5
Winton Rd DL6 ....210 E6
Wise House La YO17 .215 F7
Wisker La YO32 ......226 C7
Wisp Hill 12 BD23 ...134 E3
Wistow Parochial CE VC Prim
Sch YO8 ....197 D6
Wistow Rd YO8 ......232 A8
Wistowgate YO8 .....197 B8
Witch La YO25 ....127 D2
Witham Dr YO32 ....226 A6
Withington Rd ６ YO62 .92 F7
Witton Cres DL3 ....3 A7
Witton Steeps DL8 ...59 E2
Wizards Workshop★
YO21 ....208 C8
Wobeck La HG4 ......114 B7
Woburn Cl YO33 .....167 B8
Woburn Way WF6 ....200 B1
Wold Newton Foundation
Sch YO25 ....126 A4
Wold Newton Rd
YO25 ....126 E3
Wold Rd YO17 ....149 E8
Wold St YO17 ....215 D3
Wold View YO14 .....100 F3
Wold View Gr ５ YO12 ..99 E6
Woldcroft YO41 .....185 C2
Wolds Way Lavender★
YO17 ....123 B5
Woldview Rd YO41 ..185 F5
Wolfe Ave YO31 .....228 F5
Wolsey Ave YO8 .....197 B8
Wolsey Cl 11 LS25 ...195 F4
Wolsey Croft LS25 ..195 F4
Wolsey Dr YO23 .....231 A3
Wolsey Gdns 12 LS25 .195 F4
Wolsey St YO10 .....228 E3
Wolsingham Dr TS5 ..6 E7
Wolsley St YO10 .....229 C3
Wolviston Ave YO10 .229 C3
Womersley CE VC Jun & Inf
Sch DN6 ....206 C6
Womersley Pk Gdns
DN6 ....206 D5
Womersley Rd WF11 .202 A2
Wood Acre Cl BD23 ..134 C3
Wood Aven Cl 35 HG3 .161 B3
Wood Cl
Bradleys Both BD20 .173 D3
Skipton BD23 ....216 E5
７ Strensall YO32 ....167 A7
14 Thorpe Willoughby
YO8 ....197 B1
Wood End La DL8 ...59 D5
Wood End Mus★
YO11 ....213 A5
Wood Gate YO13 ......74 A1
Wood Gn WF10 ......200 C3
Wood Hill Cl YO51 ..141 D7
Wood La
Acaster Selby YO23 ..191 B2
Austwick LA2 ....131 A8
Birkin WF11 ....202 D6
Gainford DL2 ....1 D7
10 Grassington BD23 .134 E2
Great Preston LS26 ..200 C7
Low Conicliffe & Merrybent
DL2 ....2 E4

Wood La continued
Spennithorne DL8 ......61 A3
Thorp Arch LS23 .....180 F2
13 Thorpe Willoughby
YO8 ....197 B1
Threshfield BD23 ....134 B3
Whitwood WF10 .....200 C3
Wood Lea １ WF11 ...201 E4
Wood Pk Cl TS9 ......220 B1
Wood Row LS26 .....200 A6
Wood St
Castleford WF10 ....200 E4
Norton YO17 ....215 D3
York YO31 ....228 E6
Wood View
Airmyn DN14 ....205 E3
Embsay BD23 ....217 C7
Harrogate HG1 ......219 C3
Wood View Ave WF10 .200 D4
Wood Way YO32 ....226 A4
Woodall Ave YO12 ..212 F7
Woodall Ct ５ YO8 ..197 D6
Wood's Cl YO13 ......75 C8
Wood's Gr YO13 .....75 C8
Woodbine Cl 12 TS9 ...8 A2
Woodbine Terr ９ HG1 .219 D3
Woodbridge Ave LS25 .194 C4
Woodburn Dr ３ DL8 ...60 D5
Woodcock Cl
Eston & South Bank TS6 ..7 F8
９ Haxby YO32 ....166 F5
Woodcock Dr ８ DL9 ..40 F2
Woodcrest Rd DL3 .....3 B4
Wooden Hill La DL7 ..210 B2
Woodend WF10 ......200 C7
Woodend Cres WF10 ..200 C4
Woodfield Ave HG1 ..219 E4
Woodfield Cl HG1 ....219 E4
Woodfield Com Prim Sch
HG1 ....219 F5
Woodfield Dr
Harrogate HG1 ......219 E4
６ Low Bradley BD20 .173 E4
Woodfield Gdns ５ HG1 219 E4
Woodfield Gr HG1 ...219 E4
Woodfield Pl ６ HG1 ..219 E4
Woodfield Rd HG1 ...219 E4
Woodfield Sq HG1 ...219 E4
Woodfield View HG1 .219 E4
Woodfield Wlk HG1 ..219 E4
Woodford Pl １ YO24 .227 D1
Woodgate YO12 .....212 C4
Woodhall Dr HG1 ....219 E4
Woodhall Gr
Harrogate HG1 ......219 E4
Mickleton LS26 .....200 B6
４ Stockton-on-Tees TS18 ..5 D8
Woodhall Hall
Hemingbrough YO8 ..199 B3
Womersley DN6 .....206 E4
Woodhead Field La
YO62 ....70 A4
Woodhill View ３ LS22 .180 C3
Woodhouse Gr ４ YO31 .229 A5
Woodhouse La BD23 .157 B7
Woodhouse Rd
Guisborough TS14 ....8 E6
Thorganby YO19 ....193 A3
Woodland Ave YO12 .212 D6
Woodland Chase
YO30 ....225 B1
Woodland Cl YO12 ..212 D6
Woodland Cres ８ LS26 194 A1
Woodland Dr DL7 .....63 F3
Woodland Gr YO12 ..212 C6
Woodland Pl
New Earswick YO32 ..225 E4
Scarborough YO12 ..212 C6
Woodland Ravine
YO12 ....212 D6
Woodland Rd DL3 .....3 B6
Woodland Rise YO12 .212 D6
Woodland St ８ BD20 .187 B6
Woodland Terr DL3 ....3 B6
Woodland View ５ YO7 .89 A1
Woodland Way
８ Airmyn DN14 .....205 E4
Longnewton TS21 ....4 F7
York YO32 ....225 E4
Woodlands
Escrick YO19 ....192 B5
Ilkley LS29 ....218 D4
Woodlands Ave
Harrogate HG2 ......220 B1
Haxby YO32 ....225 C8
Norton YO17 ....215 E2
Rillington YO17 .....122 F5
Tadcaster LS24 .....189 D5
Woodlands Cl
15 Barlby with Osgodby
YO8 ....198 B4
Goldsborough HG5 ..163 A3
Harrogate HG2 .....220 C2
15 Ilkley LS29 ....175 C2
Sherburn in Elmet LS25 .195 F2
Woodlands Com Jun Sch
HG2 ....220 B2
Woodlands Cres HG2 .220 C2
Woodlands Croft
LS25 ....200 D8
Woodlands Ct
13 Barlby with Osgodby
YO8 ....198 B4
３ Harrogate HG2 ...220 B1
Woodlands Dr
14 Barlby with Osgodby
YO8 ....198 B4

Woodlands Dr *continued*
Egglescliffe TS15 . . . . .5 E3
Garforth LS25 . . . . .194 D3
Harrogate HG2 . . . . . . .220 C1
Middlesbrough TS6 . . . . .7 F8
Scarborough YO12 . . . .212 B5
Skipton BD23 . . . . .216 E5
Woodlands Gdns DL2 . . .4 C5
Woodlands Gn 8 HG2 . .220 B1
Woodlands Gr
Harrogate HG2 . . . . . . .220 C2
8 Ilkley LS29 . . . . .175 C2
Kippax LS25 . . . . .200 E8
Rillington YO17 . . . . . . .122 F5
York YO31 . . . . .229 A7
Woodlands La LS25 . . .202 B7
Woodlands Rd
Harrogate HG2 . . . . . . .220 C2
Rillington YO17 . . . . . . .122 F5
Woodlands Rise
1 Harrogate HG2 . . . . . .220 C2
14 Ilkley LS29 . . . . . . .175 C2
Norton DN6 . . . . .206 E1
Woodlands Sch The
YO12 . . . . .212 B5
Woodlands The TS7 . . .7 D5
Woodlands View
11 Barlby with Osgodby
YO8 . . . . .198 B4
Kippax LS25 . . . . .200 E8
3 Tadcaster LS24 . . . . .189 D5
2 Thornton Dale YO18 . . .96 D5
Woodlands Way
Hurworth DL2 . . . . .3 D1
7 Hurworth-on-Tees DL2 . .22 D8
Woodlands Wlk
Harrogate HG2 . . . . . . .220 C2
Scarborough YO12 . . . .212 D6
Skipton BD23 . . . . .216 E5
Stokesley TS9 . . . . .26 C8
Woodlea Ave YO26 . . .227 C4
Woodlea Bank YO26 . .227 D4
Woodlea Cres YO26 . .227 C4
Woodlea Gr YO26 . . . .227 D5
Woodleigh Ave LS25 . .194 C4
Woodleigh Cl 2 YO32 .167 A6
Woodleigh Sch YO17 . . .148 B4
Woodley Gr TS7 . . . . . . .7 D7
Woodman La LA6 . . . .102 B6
Woodman Terr BD23 . .216 F4
Woodmanwray La
HG3 . . . . .159 C8
Woodpark Ave HG5 . . .221 A7
Woodpark Dr HG5 . . . .221 A7
Woodpecker Rd 12
LS29 . . . . .176 C1
Woodrow Ave TS7 . . . . .7 B6
Woodrow Cres LS26 . .200 A6
Woodroyd Gdns LS29 . .218 F3
Woodruff Cl 27 HG3 . . .161 B3
Woodrush TS8 . . . . .7 B4
Woods Ct HG2 . . . . . . .222 C6
Woods La YO26 . . . . . .142 B2
Woods Pl LS29 . . . . . . .218 C4
Woodside
Castleford WF10 . . . . . .201 B4
Harrogate HG1 . . . . . . .219 E2
Hutton Rudby TS15 . . . . .25 C6
5 Leyburn DL8 . . . . .60 D5
Woodside Ave YO31 . . .229 A6
Woodside Cl 3 YO61 . .117 D1
Woodside Gr
Allerton Bywater WF10 . .200 C7
3 Stockton-on-Tees TS18 . . .5 E8
Woodside La BD20 . . . .173 C2

Woodside Rd
Ganton YO12 . . . . .125 A8
Silsden BD20 . . . . .174 B1
Woodside St WF10 . . .200 C7
Woodsmill Quay YO1 . .233 B2
Woodstock Cl DL6 . . . .210 B6
Woodstock Way YO7 . .211 D3
Woodthorpe Prim Sch
YO24 . . . . .230 C7
Woodvale TS8 . . . . .7 B5
Woodvale Rd DL3 . . . . . .3 B4
Woodview Cl DN14 . . . .207 A7
Woodville Ave
Middlesbrough TS4 . . . . . .6 F8
3 Scalby YO12 . . . . . . .212 D8
Woodville Terr YO8 . . .232 E3
Woolcotts Cl 1 TS17 . . .6 A3
Wooldale Dr YO14 . . . .101 B4
Wooler St YO12 . . . . . .212 E5
Woolmoor Cl YO7 . . . .211 D4
Woolnough Ave YO10 . .229 B3
Woolpots La YO61 . . . .117 B4
Woolsington Dr DL2 . . . .4 C4
Worcester Dr YO31 . . .229 B5
Wordsworth App 2
WF8 . . . . .201 B1
Wordsworth Ave 4
DN6 . . . . .206 E1
Wordsworth Cl YO13 . . .75 C5
Wordsworth Cres
Harrogate HG2 . . . . . . .222 C8
York YO24 . . . . .230 D7
Wordsworth Dr WF11 . .201 D3
Workhouse Mus of Poor
Law ★ HG4 . . . . .214 C6
Worsall Rd TS15 . . . . . . .5 D2
Worsall Toll Bar TS15 . . .24 B7
Worsendale Rd YO42 . .169 F2
Worsley Cl TS16 . . . . . . .5 E7
Worsley Cres TS7 . . . . . .7 B5
Worsley Ct YO17 . . . . . .215 A3
Woundales La
Knayton with Brawith YO7 . .65 F4
Upsall YO7 . . . . .66 A2
Wrangham Dr 1 YO14 . .127 A8
Wray with Botton Endowed
Sch LA2 . . . . .128 A6
Wray's Ave YO31 . . . . .225 E1
Wrea Head Cl 2 YO13 . . .75 D5
Wrea La 1 YO12 . . . . . .212 F6
Wreaks La HG4 . . . . . .111 E6
Wreaks Rd
Birstwith HG3 . . . . .160 E6
Harrogate HG1 . . . . . . .220 B3
Wrelton Cliff Rd YO18 . . .95 B8
Wrelton Hall Gdns
YO18 . . . . .71 C1
Wren Croft 5 WF8 . . . .201 B4
Wren Hall La YO8 . . . .204 E6
Wren La 2 YO8 . . . . . .232 D6
Wrenbeck Ave 1 LS21 . .177 A1
Wrenbeck Cl 2 LS21 . . .177 A1
Wrenbeck Dr LS21 . . . .177 A1
Wressle Sta YO8 . . . . .199 D2
Wrexham Rd LS29 . . . .176 B1
Wreyfield Dr YO12 . . . .212 C7
Wright St 30 BD20 . . . .187 E7
Wrights La WF11 . . . . .206 B8
Wycar 1 DL8 . . . . .63 A2
Wycliffe Ave
Northallerton DL7 . . . . . .210 C2
York YO10 . . . . .229 B3
Wycliffe Rd DL7 . . . . . . .22 E1
Wycoller Ctry Pk ★
BB8 . . . . .186 D2

Wydale La YO13 . . . . . . .98 B6
Wydale Rd YO10 . . . . .229 D4
Wydale Rise YO13 . . . . .98 A5
Wydra La HG3 . . . . . . .159 F1
Wykeham Abbey ★
YO13 . . . . .98 E5
Wykeham Ave TS14 . . . .8 E5
Wykeham Carr Rd
YO13 . . . . .98 E3
Wykeham CE VC Prim Sch
YO13 . . . . .98 E6
Wykeham Dale YO62 . . .93 B8
Wykeham La YO13 . . . . .98 E7
Wykeham Rd YO17 . . . .122 A5
Wykeham St YO12 . . . .212 E5
Wykeham Way TS8 . . . . .7 A6
Wylam Ave DL1 . . . . .3 D7
Wynam La YO41 . . . . . .185 C1
Wynbrook Ct YO13 . . . . .75 C5
Wynd The 3 Bedale DL8 . .63 A3
Hawes DL8 . . . . .56 D4
Hutton Rudby TS15 . . . . .25 D5
Skeeby DL10 . . . . .20 F1
Wytherstone Gdn ★
YO62 . . . . .69 B1
Wyvil Cres LS29 . . . . . .218 E4
Wyvil Rd LS29 . . . . .218 E5
Wyville Gr DL8 . . . . .61 E7

X

Xscape ★ WF10 . . . . . . .200 F2

Y

Yafforth Rd DL7 . . . . . .210 B6
Yall Flat La YO21 . . . . . .29 B6
Yan Brow YO62 . . . . . . .70 C3
Yarborough Cl DL10 . . . .41 B2
Yarburgh Cl 4 DN14 . . .204 B1
Yarburgh Gr 2 YO26 . . .227 E5
Yarburgh Way YO10 . . .229 C3
Yarde Ave DL10 . . . . . . .41 E4
Yarker Bank La DL8 . . . .60 C6
Yarlside La BD23 . . . . .171 B4
Yarm Back La TS18 . . . . .5 D8
Yarm La TS9 . . . . .7 D1
Yarm Prim Sch TS15 . . . . .5 E2
Yarm Rd Darlington DL1 . . .3 E5
Egglescliffe TS16 . . . . . . .5 E5
Hilton TS15 . . . . .6 C2
Middleton St George DL2 . . .4 C4
Yarm Rd Ind Est DL1 . . . .3 F5
Yarm Sta TS15 . . . . .5 E2
Yarrow Dr HG3 . . . . . . .161 B3
Yatts Rd YO18 . . . . .96 A8
Yaud Sike La YO18 . . . . .95 E5
Yeadon Wlk 12 DL2 . . . . .4 C4
Yealand Ave BD24 . . . .131 D3
Yearby Cl TS5 . . . . .6 D7
Yearsley Cres YO31 . . .228 D7
Yearsley Gr Prim Sch
YO32 . . . . .225 F1
Yearsley Moor Bank
YO62 . . . . .118 B7
Yearsley Swimming Pool
YO31 . . . . .228 D8
Yederick Rd YO13 . . . . .98 B8
Yedingham Priory (site of) ★
YO17 . . . . .97 D2

Yedmandale Rd
2 East Ayton/West Ayton
YO13 . . . . .99 A7
Hutton Buscel YO13 . . . . .98 F7
Yeomans Mount 11 HG3 137 B4
Yew Tree Cl
Acaster Malbis YO23 . . . .191 C8
Harrogate HG2 . . . . . . .222 C4
8 Low Bradley BD20 . . .173 E3
Rufforth YO23 . . . . .182 C6
Selby YO8 . . . . .232 C6
13 Sleights YO22 . . . . . .32 A6
Yew Tree Gdns HG2 . . .222 B5
Yew Tree La HG2 . . . . .222 C5
Yew Tree Mews YO19 . .229 C5
Yew Tree Pk DN14 . . . .207 A7
Yew Tree Wlk HG2 . . . .222 B6
Yew Wlk The TS21 . . . . .4 F7
Yewbank Cl 3 LS29 . . .218 A4
Yewbank Terr LS29 . . . .218 A4
Yewcroft LS29 . . . . .218 A4
Yewdale Rd HG2 . . . . . .220 A1
Yiewsley Dr DL3 . . . . . . .3 A5
YMCA Leisure Ctr
YO11 . . . . .213 A6
YMCA Theatre & L Ctr ★
YO11 . . . . .213 A7
Yoadwath Bank YO62 . . .70 C3
Yoredale Ave
Darlington DL3 . . . . .3 B6
17 Leyburn DL8 . . . . . . .60 D5
York Abbey ★ YO30 . . . .233 A3
York Art Gall ★ YO30 . . .233 B3
York Barbican Leisure Ctr
YO10 . . . . .233 C1
York Bridge Rd YO61 . .143 B2
York Castle Mus ★
YO1 . . . . .233 C1
York City Football Club
YO30 . . . . .233 A4
York Cl 2 HG5 . . . . . . .221 C5
York Coll YO30 . . . . . . .230 E6
York District Hospl
YO30 . . . . .233 B4
York Dungeon ★ YO1 . . .233 B2
York Garth 1 HG5 . . . . .221 C5
York Ind Pk YO17 . . . . . .121 C1
York La Flaxton YO60 . . .167 E8
Knaresborough HG5 . . . .221 B5
York Minster ★ YO1 . . . .233 B3
York Model Rly ★
YO24 . . . . .233 A2
York Pl Harrogate HG2 . .219 E1
Knaresborough HG5 . . . .221 B5
Scarborough YO11 . . . . .213 A5
York Racecourse (The
Knavesmire) ★ YO24 . .228 A4
York Rd Bagby YO7 . . . .211 D2
Barlby YO8 . . . . .198 B5
Bilbrough YO23 . . . . . . .182 B2
Bilton-in-Ainsty with Bickerton
LS22 . . . . .181 A4
Boroughbridge YO51 . . .141 B5
37 Burley in Warfedale
LS22 . . . . .176 C1
Cliffe YO8 . . . . .198 E3
Colburn DL9 . . . . .40 F4
Cottam YO25 . . . . .151 B2
Dunnington YO19 . . . . . .184 D6
Easingwold YO61 . . . . . .143 C7
Flaxby HG5 . . . . .163 B5
Green Hammerton YO26 . .164 B3
Harrogate HG1 . . . . . . .219 C2
Haxby YO32 . . . . .225 D7
Kilham YO25 . . . . .151 F3

York Rd *continued*
Kirk Hammerton YO26 . . .164 C3
Knaresborough HG5 . . . .221 D5
Leavening YO17 . . . . . . .147 E2
Long Marston YO26 . . . .182 A6
Malton YO17 . . . . .215 A3
Middlesbrough TS7 . . . . . .7 D6
Naburn YO19 . . . . .191 D8
North Duffield YO8 . . . . .199 A8
Riccall YO19 . . . . .192 A1
Sledmere YO25 . . . . . . .150 E1
Sowerby YO7 . . . . .211 E1
Stillingfleet YO19 . . . . . .191 D4
Strensall YO32 . . . . .167 A6
Sutton-on-the-Forest
YO61 . . . . .144 C2
Tadcaster LS24 . . . . . . .189 F6
Wetherby LS22 . . . . . . .180 C3
York YO26 . . . . .227 C3
York Rd Ind Est LS22 . . . .180 C3
York Rise BD23 . . . . . . .154 B3
York St
Barnoldswick BB18 . . . . .171 D1
Castleford WF10 . . . . . .200 E4
Crathorne TS15 . . . . .24 E6
5 Dunnington YO19 . . . .184 E7
12 Glusburn BD20 . . . . .187 E8
1 Selby YO8 . . . . .232 C5
York St John, Coll of the Univ
of Leeds YO10 . . . . . . .229 B3
York Sta YO24 . . . . . . .233 A2
York Steiner Sch
YO10 . . . . .228 D1
York View DL10 . . . . . . .209 E8
York Villas WF6 . . . . . . .200 A1
Yorkdale Ct 4 YO8 . . . .196 F1
Yorkdale Dr 3 YO8 . . . .196 F1
Yorkersgate YO17 . . . . .215 B4
Yorkshire Air Mus ★
YO41 . . . . .184 F3
Yorkshire Carriage Mus ★
DL8 . . . . .58 F3
Yorkshire Coast Coll of F & H
Ed YO12 . . . . .212 B6
Yorkshire Dales Falconry &
Wildlife Conservation Ctr ★
LA2 . . . . .131 A5
Yorkshire Dales National Pk
Ctr ★ BD24 . . . . .131 D3
Yorkshire Lavender ★
YO60 . . . . .119 E1
Yorkshire Mus ★ YO30 . .233 A3
Yorkshire Mus of Farming ★
YO19 . . . . .184 D7
Young Bank La YO62 . . .70 C2
Young's Ct LS25 . . . . . .194 F7
Young's Dr 3 HG3 . . . . .161 B2
Youngs Way 10 DL10 . . . .41 E4
Ypres Rd DL9 . . . . .209 C1
Yule La YO26 . . . . .164 C3

Z

Zetland Dr DL10 . . . . . .209 F8
Zetland St DL6 . . . . . . .210 D4

PHILIP'S MAPS
the Gold Standard for drivers

◆ **Philip's street atlases cover every county in England, Wales, Northern Ireland and much of Scotland**

◆ Every named street is shown, including alleys, lanes and walkways

◆ Thousands of additional features marked: stations, public buildings, car parks, places of interest

◆ Route-planning maps to get you close to your destination

◆ Postcodes on the maps and in the index

◆ Widely used by the emergency services, transport companies and local authorities

BEST BUY •BEST BUY• **Auto EXPRESS** •BEST BUY• BEST BUY

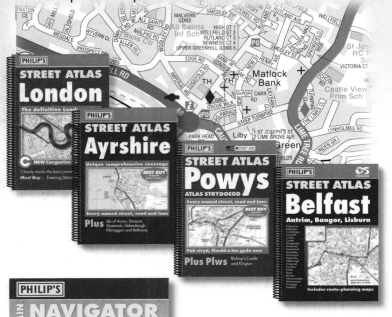

PHILIP'S
STREET ATLAS
London
The definitive Lond...
C NEW Congestion...
'Clearly marks the best journe...
Must Buy ... Evening Stand...

PHILIP'S
STREET ATLAS
Ayrshire
Unique comprehensive coverage
BEST BUY
Plus Isle of Arran, Dunoon, Greenock, Helensburgh, Kilcreggan and Rothesay
Every named street, road and lane

PHILIP'S
STREET ATLAS
Powys
ATLAS STRYDOEDD
Every named street, road and lane
BEST BUY
Pob stryd, ffordd a lôn gyda enw
Plus Plws Bishop's Castle and Kington

PHILIP'S
STREET ATLAS
Belfast
Antrim, Bangor, Lisburn
Includes route-planning maps

PHILIP'S
NAVIGATOR BRITAIN
NAVIGATOR Britain
New speed camera sites, now with speed limits
30
Major roads named as well as numbered
Thousands of farms, houses, tracks and footpaths
'The ultimate in UK mapping'
The Sunday Times

For national mapping, choose
Philip's Navigator Britain
the most detailed road atlas available of England, Wales and Scotland. Hailed by Auto Express as 'the ultimate road atlas', the atlas shows every road and lane in Britain.

Street atlases currently available

England
Bedfordshire and Luton
Berkshire
Birmingham and West Midlands
Bristol and Bath
Buckinghamshire and Milton Keynes
Cambridgeshire and Peterborough
Cheshire
Cornwall
Cumbria
Derbyshire
Devon
Dorset
County Durham and Teesside
Essex
North Essex
South Essex
Gloucestershire and Bristol
Hampshire
North Hampshire
South Hampshire
Herefordshire Monmouthshire
Hertfordshire
Isle of Wight
Kent
East Kent
West Kent
Lancashire
Leicestershire and Rutland
Lincolnshire
Liverpool and Merseyside
London
Greater Manchester
Norfolk
Northamptonshire
Northumberland
Nottinghamshire
Oxfordshire
Shropshire
Somerset
Staffordshire
Suffolk

Surrey
East Sussex
West Sussex
Tyne and Wear
Warwickshire and Coventry
Wiltshire and Swindon
Worcestershire
East Yorkshire Northern Lincolnshire
North Yorkshire
South Yorkshire
West Yorkshire

Wales
Anglesey, Conwy and Gwynedd
Cardiff, Swansea and The Valleys
Carmarthenshire, Pembrokeshire and Swansea
Ceredigion and South Gwynedd
Denbighshire, Flintshire, Wrexham
Herefordshire Monmouthshire
Powys

Scotland
Aberdeenshire
Ayrshire
Dumfries and Galloway
Edinburgh and East Central Scotland
Fife and Tayside
Glasgow and West Central Scotland
Inverness and Moray
Lanarkshire
Scottish Borders

Northern Ireland
County Antrim and County Londonderry
County Armagh and County Down
Belfast
County Tyrone and County Fermanagh